Contemporary Literary Criticism

Volume 9

Contemporary Literary Criticism

Excerpts from Criticism
of the Works of Today's
Novelists, Poets, Playwrights,
and Other Creative Writers

Dedria Bryfonski
Editor

Gale Research Company
Book Tower
Detroit, Michigan 48226

STAFF

Dedria Bryfonski, *Editor*

Phyllis Carmel Mendelson, *Contributing Editor*
Laurie Lanzen Harris, *Associate Editor*
David J. Szymanski, *Assistant Editor*

Sharon R. Cillette, *Production Editor*

Linda M. Pugliese, *Manuscript Coordinator*
Jeanne A. Gough, *Permissions Coordinator*
Thomas E. Gunton, *Research Coordinator*
Laura A. Buch, Jean C. Stine, Carolyn Voldrich, *Editorial Assistants*

Special acknowledgment to Gerard J. Senick, *Editor,*
and Sharon R. Cillette, *Associate Editor,* **Children's Literature Review**

Copyright © 1978 by Gale Research Company

Library of Congress Catalog Card Number 76-38938
ISBN 0-8103-0116-4

Preface

Literary criticism is indispensable to the layman or scholar attempting to evaluate and understand creative writing—whether his subject is one poem, one writer, one idea, one school, or a general trend in contemporary writing. Literary criticism is itself a collective term for several kinds of critical writing: criticism may be normative, descriptive, interpretive, textual, appreciative, genetic. Conscientious students must consult numerous sources in order to become familiar with the criticism pertinent to their subjects.

Until now, there has been nothing resembling an ongoing encyclopedia of current literary criticism, bringing together in one series criticism of all the various kinds from widely diverse sources. *Contemporary Literary Criticism* is intended to be such a comprehensive reference work.

The Plan of the Work

Contemporary Literary Criticism presents significant passages from the published criticism of work by well-known creative writers—novelists and short story writers, poets and playwrights. Some creative writers, like James Baldwin and Paul Goodman, are probably better known for their expository work than for their fiction, and so discussion of their nonfiction is included.

Contemporary Literary Criticism is not limited to material concerning long-established authors like Eliot, Faulkner, Hemingway, and Auden, although these and other writers of similar stature are included. Attention is also given to two other groups of writers—writers of considerable public interest—about whose work criticism is hard to locate. These are the newest writers (like Robert M. Pirsig, Erica Jong, and William Kotzwinkle) and the contributors to the well-loved but unscholarly genres of mystery and science fiction (like Georges Simenon, Agatha Christie, Robert Heinlein, and Arthur C. Clarke).

The definition of *contemporary* is necessarily arbitrary. For purposes of selection for *CLC,* contemporary writers are those who are either now living or who have died since January 1, 1960. Contemporary criticism is more loosely defined as that written any time during the past twenty-five years or so and currently relevant to the evaluation of the writer under discussion.

Each volume of *CLC* lists about 175 authors, with an average of about five excerpts from critical articles or reviews being given for the works of each author. Altogether, there are about 1100 individual excerpts in each volume taken from about 250 books and several hundred issues of some one hundred general magazines, literary reviews, and scholarly journals. Each excerpt is fully identified for the convenience of readers who may wish to consult the entire chapter, article, or review excerpted. Each volume covers writers not previously included and also provides significant new criticism pertaining to authors included in earlier volumes.

A Note on Bio-Bibliographical References and Page Citations

Notes in many entries directing the user to consult *Contemporary Authors* for detailed biographical and bibliographical information refer to a series of biographical reference books published by the Gale Research Company since 1962, which now includes detailed biographical sketches of about 50,000 authors who have been active during the past decade, many of whose careers began during the post-World War II period, or earlier.

Beginning with *CLC-5,* the method for referring to page numbers in the original sources has been standardized. Page numbers appear after each fragment (unless the entire essay was contained on one page). Page numbers appear in citations as well only when the editors wish to indicate, with an essay or chapter title and its *inclusive* page numbers, the scope of the original treatment.

No Single Volume Can be Exhaustive

A final word: Since *Contemporary Literary Criticism* is a multivolume work of indefinite but considerable size, neither this volume nor any other single volume should be judged apart from the concept that a single volume is but a part of a larger and more comprehensive whole.

If readers wish to suggest authors they are particularly anxious to have covered in coming volumes, or if they have other suggestions or comments, they are cordially invited to write the editors.

A

ALBEE, Edward   1928-

Albee is an American playwright whose best works rank among the finest in contemporary theater. The problem of human communication in a world of increasing callousness is a recurrent concern in Albee's works, notably _The Zoo Story_, _The American Dream_, and _Who's Afraid of Virginia Woolf?_ His drama is characterized by a fine control of rhythm and brilliant use of language. Albee was awarded the Pulitzer Prize in 1974 for _Seascape_. (See also _CLC_, Vols. 1, 2, 3, 5, and _Contemporary Authors_, Vols. 5-8, rev. ed.)

In _Who's Afraid of Virginia Woolf?_, Edward Albee attempted to move beyond the narrowness of his personal interests by having his characters speculate from time to time upon the metaphysical and historical implications of their predicament. In _Tiny Alice,_ the metaphysics, such as they are, appear to be Albee's deepest concern—and no doubt about it, he wants his concerns to seem deep. But this new play isn't about the problems of faith-and-doubt or appearance-and-reality, any more than _Virginia Woolf_ was about "the Decline of the West"; mostly, when the characters in _Tiny Alice_ suffer over epistemology, they are really suffering the consequences of human deceit, subterfuge, and hypocrisy. Albee sees in human nature very much what Maupassant did, only he wants to talk about it like Plato. In this way he not only distorts his observations, but subverts his own powers, for it is not the riddles of philosophy that bring his talent to life, but the ways of cruelty and humiliation. Like _Virginia Woolf, Tiny Alice_ is about the triumph of a strong woman over a weak man.

The disaster of the play, however—its tediousness, its pretentiousness, its galling sophistication, its gratuitous and easy symbolizing, its ghastly pansy rhetoric and repartee— all of this can be traced to his own unwillingness or inability to put its real subject at the center of the action. . . . Why _Tiny Alice_ is so unconvincing, so remote, so obviously a sham—so much the kind of play that makes you want to rise from your seat and shout, "Baloney"—is that its surface is an attempt to disguise the subject on the one hand, and to falsify its significance on the other. All that talk about illusion and reality may even be the compulsive chattering of a dramatist who at some level senses that he is trapped in a lie. (pp. 105-06)

Albee does not make the invention whole or necessary. The play strings together incidents of no moral or intellec-

tual consequence, and where the inconsistencies, oversights, and lapses occur, the playwright justifies them by chalking them up to the illusory nature of human existence. It is as though Shakespeare, having failed to settle in his own mind whether Desdemona did or did not sleep with Cassio—and consequently leaving the matter unsettled in the play—later explains his own failure of imagination by announcing to the press that we can never penetrate reality to get to the truth. The world of _Tiny Alice_ is mysterious because Albee cannot get it to cohere. (p. 106)

Least convincing of all is what should be the most convincing—Tiny Alice Herself, and the replica, or altar, in which her spirit resides. The implications of a Woman-God, her nature, her character, and her design, are never revealed; but is this because they are beyond human comprehension, or beyond the playwright's imagination? Though _his_ God is mysterious, certainly the Cardinal could discuss Him with some conviction and intelligence (and ought to, of course, instead of appearing as a pompus operator). Why can't Miss Alice or the lawyer discuss theirs? Why don't they answer the questions that are put to them? There is, after all, a difference between the idea that life is a dream and a predilection to being dreamy about life. But withholding information is Albee's favorite means of mystifying the audience; the trouble comes from confusing a technique of dramaturgy, and a primitive one at that, with an insight into the nature of things. (p. 107)

For a lay brother who is, as he so piously says, "deeply" interested in the reality of things, how little persistence there is in Julian's curiosity; how like a child he is in the answers he accepts to the most baffling mysteries that surround him. Indeed when Albee begins to see Julian as a man who walks around acting like a small boy in a huge house full of big bad grownups, he is able to put together two or three minutes of dialogue that is at least emotionally true. To the delights and dangers of the Oedipal triangle (boy in skirts, mother in negligee, father with pistol) Albee's imagination instantly quickens; but unfortunately by presenting Julian as a befuddled boy, he only further befuddles the audience about those metaphysical problems that are supposed to be so anguishing to Julian as a man. For instance, when a fire miraculously breaks out in the chapel of the castle and in the chapel of the replica, one would imagine that Julian, with his deep interest in reality, would

1

see the matter somewhat further along than he does. . . . (pp. 107-08)

That is the last we hear of the fire. But how *did* it happen? And why? I know I am asking questions about the kind of magical moment that qualifies a play for the Howard Taubman Repertory Theater for Sheer Theater, but I would like to know who this Alice is that she can and will cause such miracles of nature. Might not Julian, a lay brother, who has the ear of a Cardinal, rush out to tell him of this strange occurrence? But then the Cardinal exists, really, only as another figure to betray and humiliate poor Julian, the baffled little boy. As a Cardinal, he is of no interest to Albee, who seems to have introduced the Catholic Church into the play so that he can have some of the men dressed up in gowns on the one hand, and indulge his cynicism on the other; he does nothing to bring into collision the recognizable world of the Church and its system of beliefs, with the world that is unfamiliar to both Julian and the audience, the world of *Tiny Alice*. Such a confrontation would, of course, have made it necessary to invent the mysteries of a Woman-God and the way of life that is a consequence of her existence and her power. But Albee is simply not capable of making this play into a work of philosophical or religious originality, and probably not too interested either. The movement of the play is not towards a confrontation of ideas; it is finally concerned with evoking a single emotion —pity for poor Julian. In the end the playwright likens him to Jesus Christ—and all because he has had to suffer the martyrdom of heterosexual love.

Tiny Alice is a homosexual day-dream in which the celibate male is tempted and seduced by the overpowering female, only to be betrayed by the male lover and murdered by the cruel law, or in this instance, cruel lawyer. It has as much to do with Christ's Passion as a little girl's dreaming about being a princess locked in a tower has to do with the fate of Mary Stuart. Unlike Genet, who dramatizes the fact of fantasying in *Our Lady of the Flowers,* Albee would lead us to believe that his fantasy has significance altogether removed from the dread or the desire which inspired it; consequently, the attitudes he takes towards his material are unfailingly inappropriate. His subject is emasculation—as was Strindberg's in *The Father,* a play I mention because its themes, treated openly and directly, and necessarily connected in the action, are the very ones that Albee has so vulgarized and sentimentalized in *Tiny Alice:* male weakness, female strength, and the limits of human knowledge. How long before a play is produced on Broadway in which the homosexual hero is presented as a homosexual, and not disguised as an *angst*-ridden priest, or an angry Negro, or an aging actress; or worst of all, Everyman? (pp. 108-09)

Philip Roth, "The Play That Dare Not Speak Its Name," in The New York Review of Books *(reprinted with permission from* The New York Review of Books; *copyright © 1965 NYREV, Inc.), February 25, 1965 (and reprinted in* Edward Albee: A Collection of Critical Essays, *edited by C. W. E. Bigsby, Prentice-Hall, Inc., 1975, pp. 105-09).*

[In] Edward Albee's work, we see a tension between realism and the theatre of the absurd. *The Death of Bessie Smith* is a purely realistic play, and *Who's Afraid of Virginia Woolf?* is, for all its showiness, no more than a cross between sick drawing-room comedy and naturalistic tragedy. *The Zoo Story, The Sandbox* and *The American Dream* are, on the face of it, absurd plays, and yet, if one compares them with the work of Beckett, Ionesco or Pinter, they all retreat from the full implications of the absurd when a certain point is reached. Albee still believes in the validity of reason—that things can be proved, or that events can be shown to have definite meanings—and, unlike Beckett and the others, is scarcely touched by the sense of living in an absurd universe. Interesting and important as his plays are, his compromise seems ultimately a failure of nerve—a concession to those complementary impulses towards cruelty and self-pity which are never far below the surface of his work.

Albee has been attracted to the theatre of the absurd mainly, I think, because of the kind of social criticism he is engaged in. Both *The Zoo Story* and *The American Dream* are savage attacks on the American Way of Life. (p. 26)

The American Way of Life, in the sense in which I am using the phrase, is a structure of images; and the images, through commercial and political exploitation, have lost much of their meaning. When the Eisenhower family at prayer becomes a televised political stunt, or the family meal an opportunity for advertising frozen foods, the image of the family is shockingly devalued. The deception practised is more complex than a simple lie: it involves a denial of our normal assumptions about evidence—about the relation between the observed world and its inner reality. This is why the techniques of the theatre of the absurd, which is itself preoccupied with the devaluation of language and of images, and with the deceptive nature of appearances, are so ideally suited to the kind of social criticism Albee intends. It is for this reason, too, that he has felt able to use the techniques of the theatre of the absurd, while stopping short of an acceptance of the metaphysic of the absurd upon which the techniques are based. It is possible, clearly, to see the absurd character of certain social situations without believing that the whole of life is absurd. In Albee's case, however, this has meant a restriction of scope, and his plays do not have the poetic quality or imaginative range of *Waiting for Godot,* for instance, or *The Caretaker,* or *Rhinoceros.* (p. 27)

For the playwright who accepts without reservations that he is living in an absurd universe, the loss of faith in reason which is at the heart of this vision and the conviction that the rational exploration of experience is a form of self-deception, imply a rejection of those theatrical conventions which reflect a belief in reason. Characters with fixed identities; events which have a definite meaning; plots which assume the validity of cause and effect; dénouements which offer themselves as complete resolutions of the questions raised by the play; and language which claims to mean what it says—none of these can be said to be appropriate means for expressing the dislocated nature of experience in an absurd world. In terms of formal experiment, then, the theatre of the absurd represents a search for images of non-reason.

Albee has used these images of non-reason in his attack on the American Way of Life without . . . accepting the underlying vision which generated them. His work belongs to the second level of the theatre of the absurd: it shows a brilliantly inventive sense of what can be done with the techniques, but stops short of the metaphysic which makes the techniques completely meaningful. Nevertheless, *The American Dream* and *The Zoo Story* are the most exciting productions of the American theatre in the last fifteen years. . . .

In *The American Dream* (1961), Albee is closer to Ionesco than to any other dramatist. Like Ionesco, he sees the absurd localized most sharply in conventions of social behaviour. For both dramatists, the normal currency of social intercourse—of hospitality, or courtesy, or desultory chat—has lost its meaning, and this "devaluation of language," to use Martin Esslin's invaluable phrase, is an index for them of the vacuity of the social life represented. . . . (p. 31)

[Albee] sees the American Way of Life as one in which normal human feelings and relationships have been deprived of meaning. The gestures of love, sexual attraction, parental affection, family feeling and hospitality remain, but the actual feelings which would give the gestures meaning have gone. To show this in sharp dramatic terms, Albee constructs a situation of gestures which are normally supposed to have meaning but, as transposed by him, are seen to have none. (pp. 33-4)

The characters are isolated from each other in little worlds of selfishness, impotence and lovelessness, and all warmth of human contact is lost. It would be inaccurate to say that the gestures of love and connection ("You're my sweet Daddy"—"I love my Mommy") are deflated; their meaninglessness is exposed by tagging them on as afterthoughts to phases of the action where they are . . . ludicrously inapplicable. (p. 34)

Albee is disturbed and agonized by the extent of the dislocation of people's relationships and the imprisoning isolation of which these scenes are images. The play's central image of this failure of human feeling and contact is sterility—the inability to beget or bear a child—and as its title suggests, Albee tries to give the image the widest possible social reference. He implies that the sterility which the audience sees in his characters is typical of the society as a whole, and is created and perpetuated by the society. For him, the American Way of Life systematically eliminates, in the name of parental care, and social and moral concern, every trace of natural human feeling and every potentiality for warm human contact from those who have to live by it, and especially from the young. (pp. 34-5)

It is significant that the only character in *The American Dream* with any vitality or attractiveness is Grandma—and she is "rural," from an older way of life. The way in which she is juxtaposed against the Young Man who is the American Dream seems to symbolize a society in which the natural order of life has been reversed, in which the younger one is the less chance one has of being alive.

These patterns and images occur elsewhere in Albee's work. His sense of human isolation and despair is the central preoccupation of *The Death of Bessie Smith* (a bad play, it seems to me), and in *The Sandbox*, which parallels the situation of *The American Dream* most interestingly, though on too cramped a stage. The image of sterility is very prominent in *Who's Afraid of Virginia Woolf?*, but is used there much less effectively than in *The American Dream*. Apart from its spectacular ability to amuse and shock, *Virginia Woolf* has a certain emptiness—no incident or image in it has reference to anything wider than the neuroses of its characters.

His first play, *The Zoo Story* (1959), however, contains some very fine dramatic writing. Again it is an exploration of the farce and the agony of human isolation. (p. 37)

In its finest scene, the long speech in which Jerry describes his attempt to form a relationship with his landlady's dog, *The Zoo Story* offers a superb example of what I call pseudo-crisis—the second pattern of absurd writing that is central to Albee's work. In classic drama, crisis is one of the most important means by which the action is significantly advanced. In *Othello*, for instance, when Iago tells Othello that he has seen Desdemona's handkerchief in Cassio's hands, a whole complex of tensions is brought to a head, and after this crisis, the catastrophe is measurably nearer, and Othello is demonstrably a stage further on his course of violence and madness. In the absurd play, on the other hand, what I call a pseudo-crisis occurs when a similar complex of tensions is brought to a head without resolving anything, without contributing to any development or progression, serving in fact to demonstrate that nothing as meaningful as progression or development can occur, emphasizing that complexity and tension are permanent and unresolvable elements of a world of confusion. (p. 38)

Jerry's long speech in *The Zoo Story* has all the marks of pseudo-crisis. It is used here to explore Albee's preoccupation with man's failure to make contact with others, and the drying up of those feelings that should provide connection. . . . The dramatic structure of . . . part of Jerry's speech reflects very closely the rhythms of pseudo-crisis—the excitement, the tensions, rising to the shouted climax ("WITH GOD WHO IS . . ."), and then slipping away into the lax despairing tempo of its inconclusive end ("with . . . some day, with people"). The hopelessness of this is quickly recognized. . . . In this final downward curve of the pseudo-crisis everything is conditional and hypothetical ("It would be A START! Where better to make a beginning . . . to understand, and just possibly be understood . . .").

In this early play, there is an attempt, too, to relate Jerry's agony to the wider social pattern—to see it as a product of the American Way of Life. . . . [However], it is clear that the impulse of social criticism has only been very partially translated into dramatic terms. [Albee] tells the audience how to react; it is almost . . . editorializing, and doesn't have the persuasiveness of art, the sense that ideas have become vision and are being enacted.

At such moments in *The Zoo Story*, and most of all, of course, at the moment of Jerry's melodramatic and sentimental death, we are left with a sense of dissatisfaction whose root causes are to be found in that compromise with the experimental theatre that seems to me so characteristic of American dramatists. The action and the dialogue are dislocated, arbitrary and absurd (pre-eminently in Jerry's story of the dog) up to the moment of Jerry's death, and then all the traditional assumptions of naturalism flood back into the play. It is postulated, quite as firmly as in any Ibsen social drama, that a catastrophe is also a resolution of the situation of the play, and that events, however obscure, ultimately have a definite and unambiguous meaning. Jerry spends his dying breath telling us what the play means as explicitly as does Lona Hessel at the end of *Pillars of Society*. This sudden reversion to a faith in the validity of rational explanations makes previous events in the play seem arbitrary in a wholly unjustifiable way: they can no longer be seen as appropriate symbols of life in an absurd universe. The slightest hint that events in an absurd play are amenable to everyday explanation is completely destructive of their dramatic effectiveness. . . . [It] is largely because of this misguided attempt to exploit the advantages both of the theatre of the absurd and of realism, that *The Zoo Story* misses the greatness which at times seems so nearly within its grasp.

The American Dream does not show so straightforward an evasion of the absurd as *The Zoo Story*, but it lacks even more completely the metaphysical dimension. . . . [*The American Dream*] is too exclusively and merely a satire of American middle-class aspirations and self-deceptions. It is, above all, a play about Other People, not about ourselves: when we laugh at Mommy and Daddy, we are laughing at emotional and sexual failures which we do not recognize as our own and in which we refuse to be implicated. . . . Since *The American Dream* doesn't implicate us, it never becomes tragic. . . . [The] characters—certainly not Mommy and Daddy—[are not] tragic or even terrifying: they enact for us a certain attitude to America in 1960; they do not go beyond it to tell us anything about the human condition.

In one important sense, *The American Dream* does not belong even to the "satirical, parodistic" category of absurd plays. It is, like *The Zoo Story*, a play which reaches a definite conclusion and which implicitly claims that its events have an unambiguous meaning. (pp. 39-42)

[Grandma's closing] remark, "Well, I guess that just about wraps it up," is ironical only in the most external sense—in the sense that Mommy and Daddy and the Young Man and Mrs. Barker, who have all just drunk "To satisfaction," are in for some unpleasant surprises. As far as Grandma and the audience are concerned the situation really is wrapped up, and the play has proved its point as self-consciously as any theorem. (p. 42)

It is only when one compares *The American Dream* with the greatest absurd plays that the real damage done by this compromise between reason and the absurd can be fully reckoned. In the first place, many of the local effects seem to be, in retrospect, merely tricks. The way in which it handles argument will illustrate what I mean. The metaphysic of the absurd, as I have said, involves a loss of faith in reason and in the validity of rational explorations of experience, and one of the most characteristic forms of writing of the absurd theatre, developed to represent this on the stage, is the systematic pursuit of the irrelevant. Absurd plays are full of arguments which lead nowhere, or which parody the processes of logic, or which are conducted from ludicrous premises. At the beginning of *The American Dream* Mommy's account of her argument in the department store as to whether her hat was beige or wheat-colored is a clear instance of this. But it does not symbolize anything deeper: far from being an index of a world in which everything is too uncertain to be settled by argument, it takes its place in a play which, from its determination to prove a point, is naïvely confident in the power of argument. It therefore seems, in retrospect, no more than a trick to get the play started. By comparison, the argument in *Rhinoceros,* as to whether the animals which charged down the street had one horn or two, is funnier and also infinitely more disturbing: it represents the last feeble efforts of ordinary men to cling to their reassuring certitudes as

their world founders into chaos, and, as they themselves, through turning into rhinoceroses, are about to lose their very identities. Albee's work lacks this imaginative dimension, to say nothing of the compassion, horror and despair, implicit in the periodic speculations of Vladimir and Estragon on the nature of Godot.

But it is in dénouements, as I have pointed out, that Albee diverges most clearly from the absurd, and it is here that the divergence does him most harm. His plays are tightly "wrapped up," where the best absurd plays leave us with an extended sense of the uncertainties of our condition. . . . Albee's narrow cocksureness is poetically dead.

When all these limitations of scope have been noted, however, it is only fair that one should return to an assertion of the importance of Albee's good qualities in the American theatre. If it is true that he inhabits a finite world, he does so with brilliance, inventiveness, intelligence and moral courage. (pp. 43-4)

> *Brian Way, "Albee and the Absurd: 'The American Dream' and 'The Zoo Story',"* in American Theatre, *Stratford-upon-Avon Studies, No. 10, edited by John Russell Brown and Bernard Harris (copyright © 1967 by Edward Arnold Publishers Limited), Edward Arnold, 1967 (and reprinted in* Edward Albee: A Collection of Critical Essays, *edited by C. W. E. Bigsby, Prentice-Hall, Inc., 1975, pp. 26-44).*

There are such strong surface dissimilarities among the Albee plays that it is easier and in some ways more rewarding to think of *The Zoo Story* in relation to Samuel Beckett and Harold Pinter and *A Delicate Balance* in terms of T. S. Eliot and Enid Bagnold than it is to compare the two plays, even though both start from the same dramatic situation: the invasion (by Jerry, by Harry and Edna) of private territory (Peter's bench, Tobias's house). Yet, the comparison is obvious once it is made. Each new Albee play seems to be an experiment in form, in style (even if it is someone else's style), and yet there is unity in his work as a whole. This is apparent in the devices and the characters that recur, modified according to context, but it is most obvious in the repetition of theme, in the basic assumptions about the human condition that underlie all his work.

In *A Delicate Balance,* Tobias and his family live in a mansion in the suburbs of hell, that existential present so dear to contemporary writers, in which life is measured in terms of loss, love by its failure, contact by its absence. In that hell, there are many mansions—one of which is Peter's bench—and all of them are cages in the great zoo story of life. Peter's bench is a kind of sanctuary, both a refuge from and an extension of the stereotypical upper-middle-class existence . . . with which Albee has provided him—a place where he can safely not-live and have his nonbeing. This is the way Jerry sees Peter, at least, and—since the type is conventional enough in contemporary theater, from avant-garde satire to Broadway revue—it is safe to assume that the play does, too. Although Albee intends a little satirical fun at Peter's expense (the early needling scenes are very successful), it is clear that the stereotyping of Peter is an image of his condition, not a cause of it. Jerry, who plays "the old pigeonhole bit" so well, is another, a contrasting cliché, and it is the play's business to show that he and Peter differ only in that he does not share Peter's complacency. (p. 14)

Separateness is the operative word for Albee characters, for, even though his zoo provides suites for two people (*Who's Afraid of Virginia Woolf?*) or for more (*A Delicate Balance*), they are furnished with separate cages. . . .

Although failed sex is a convenient metaphor for the failure of love, its opposite will not work so well. Connection is not necessarily contact, and it is contact—or rather its absence, those bars that bother Jerry—that preoccupies Albee. He lets Martha and George make fun of the lack-of-communication cliché in *Virginia Woolf*, but it is that cultural commonplace on which much of Albee's work is built. (p. 15)

The rush of words (abuse or elegance) and the press of activity (however meaningless) sustain the Albee characters in a tenuous relationship (a delicate balance) among themselves and in the face of the others, the ones outside, and—beyond that—the nameless terror.

Implicit in my discussion of the separateness of the Albee characters and the bogus forms of community they invent to mask the fact that they are alone is the assumption that this is Albee's view of the human condition. The deliberate refusal to locate the action of his most recent plays (*Tiny Alice, A Delicate Balance*) strengthens that assumption. In fact, only two of Albee's settings can be found in atlases—Central Park (*The Zoo Story*) and Memphis (*Bessie Smith*). Even these, like the undifferentiated Southern town he borrowed from Carson McCullers for *The Ballad of the Sad Café* and the fictional New England college town of *Virginia Woolf*, might easily serve as settings for a universal drama. Yet, in much of his work, particularly in the early plays, there is a suggestion, even an insistence, that the problem is a localized one, that the emptiness and loneliness of the characters are somehow the result of a collapse of values in the Western world in general, in the United States in particular. *The American Dream*, he says in his Preface to the play, is "an attack on the substitution of artificial for real values in our society." Such an attack is implicit in the depiction of Peter in *The Zoo Story*.

It is in *Virginia Woolf* that this side of Albee's "truth" is most evident. He is not content that his characters perform an action which carries implications for an audience that far transcend the action itself. He must distribute labels. George may jokingly identify himself, as history professor, with the humanities, and Nick, as biology professor, with science, and turn their meeting into a historical-inevitability parable about the necessary decline of the West, but Albee presumably means it. Calling the town New Carthage and giving George significant throw-away lines ("When I was sixteen and going to prep school, during the Punic Wars . . .") are cute ways of underlining a ponderous intention. (pp. 17-18)

The chasm that confronts the Albee characters may, then, be existential chaos or a materialistic society corrupt enough to make a culture hero out of . . . (whom? to each critic his own horrible example, and there are those would pick Albee himself), or a combination in which the second of these is an image of the first.

There is nothing unusual about this slightly unstable mixture of philosophic assumption and social criticism; it can be found in the work of Tennessee Williams and, from quite a different perspective, that of Eugène Ionesco. The differentiation is useful primarily because it provides us with insight into the shape that Albee gives his material. If the lost and lonely Albee character is an irrevocable fact—philosophically, theologically, psychologically—if all that *angst* is inescapable, then his plays must necessarily be reflections of that condition; any gestures of defiance are doomed to failure. If, however, the Albee character is a product of his societal context and if that context is changeable (not necessarily politically, but by an alteration of modes of behavior between one man and another), then the plays may be instructive fables. He has dismissed American drama of the 1930's as propaganda rather than art, and he has disavowed solutions to anything. Still, in several statements he has suggested that there are solutions—or, at least, alternatives. (pp. 18-19)

Albee, then, shares with most American playwrights an idea of the utility of art, the supposition not only that art should convey truth, but that it should do so to some purpose. There is a strong strain of didacticism in all his work, but it is balanced by a certain ambiguity about the nature of the instructive fable. . . . [He apparently recognizes] that there is a conflict between his attitude toward man's situation and his suspicion (or hope: certainly *conviction* is too strong a word) that something can, or ought, to be done about it; between his assumption that this is hell we live in and his longing to redecorate it. . . . (p. 19)

According to the conventions of Broadway psychology, as reflected, for instance, in a play like William Inge's *The Dark at the Top of the Stairs,* in a moment of crisis two characters come to see themselves clearly. Out of their knowledge a new maturity is born, creating an intimacy that has not existed before and a community that allows them to face their problems (if not solve them) with new courage. This was the prevailing cliché of the serious Broadway play of the 1950's, and it was still viable . . . in the 1960's. . . . *Virginia Woolf* uses, or is used by, this cliché. (p. 21)

The last section [of *Virginia Woolf*] which is to be played "very softly, very slowly," finds George offering new tenderness to Martha, assuring her that the time had come for the fantasy to die, forcing her—no longer maliciously—to admit that she is afraid of Virginia Woolf. It is "Time for bed," and there is nothing left for them to do but go together to face the dark at the top of the stairs. As though the rejuvenation were not clear enough from the last scene, there is the confirming testimony in Honey's tearful reiteration "I want a child" and Nick's broken attempt to sympathize, "I'd like to. . . ." Then, too, the last act is called "The Exorcism," a name that had been the working title for the play itself.

As neat as Inge, and yet there is something wrong with it. How can a relationship like that of Martha and George, built so consistently on illusion (the playing of games), be expected to have gained something from a sudden admission of truth? What confirmation is there in Nick and Honey when we remember that she is drunk and hysterical and that he is regularly embarrassed by what he is forced to watch? There are two possibilities beyond the conventional reading suggested above. The last scene between Martha and George may be another one of their games; the death of the child may not be the end of illusion but an indication that the players have to go back to GO and start again their painful trip to home. Although there are many indications that George and Martha live a circular existence, going over the same ground again and again, the development of the plot and the tone of the last scene (the use of monosyllables, for instance, instead of their customary rhetoric) seems to deny that the game is still going on. The other possibility is that the truth—as in *The Iceman Cometh*—brings not freedom but death. To believe otherwise is to accept the truth-maturity cliché as readily as one must buy the violence-life analogy to get the positive ending of *The Zoo Story*. My own suspicion is that everything that feels wrong about the end of *Virginia Woolf* arises from the fact that, like the stabbing in *Zoo*, it is a balance-tipping ending that conventional theater says is positive but the Albee material insists is negative. . . . (pp. 21-2)

> *Gerald Weales, "Edward Albee: Don't Make Waves," in his* The Jumping Off Place: American Drama in the 1960's *(reprinted with permission by Gerald Weales; © 1969), Macmillan, 1969 (and reprinted in* Edward Albee: A Collection of Critical Essays, *edited by C. W. E. Bigsby, Prentice-Hall, Inc., 1975, pp. 10-22).*

Edward Albee has described . . . *Seascape* as the 'life' part of a life/death play that began with *All Over* in 1971. Regrettably, life is one of the things it most obviously lacks.

A middle-aged couple by the names of Nancy and Charlie have been spending some time by the sea. 'Can't we just stay here forever?' she asks, for she loves the water as Charlie once did. As a boy, he wanted to live under the sea, wanted to be 'fishlike'. He used to go 'way down, and try to stay'. He hasn't, however, done it since he was 17 and it has been 'too long' for him to go back again, as Nancy urges. He would rather 'remember'. He would rather do nothing. And that is precisely what they do for approximately 35 minutes of the first act: nothing but review their lives tediously and acrimoniously, though their acrimony has none of the acerbic bite and bitchy humour of *Who's Afraid of Virginia Woolf?* and certainly none of its interest.

Just when tedium threatens to become numbness, two lizard-like creatures emerge from the sea. They are Sarah and Leslie and they too are apparently middle-aged (though telling a middle-aged lizard from a young lizard is clearly beyond my competence). At first, the two couples are afraid of each other, then gradually begin to develop points of contact, are alternately aggressive, responsive, patronising, curious. What *is* one to make, for instance, of Nancy having had only three children, and taken care of them for 20 or more years, when Sarah has had 700 and abandoned them?

But Albee is more concerned with similarities than with differences. 'In the course of the play,' he has commented, 'the evolutionary pattern is speeded up billions of revolutions.' Thus it slowly evolves that Sarah and Leslie are, or have the potential to be, every bit as bigoted, every bit as middle-class in their values and behaviour, as Nancy and Charlie. They, however, aren't put off by blacks or 'foreigners', but by fish: 'There's too many of them; they're all over the place . . . moving in, taking over where you live . . . and they're stupid!'

Why had they come up from the sea, these two green-scaled creatures? '*We* had changed, everything . . . down there . . . was terribly . . . interesting, I suppose; but what did it have to do with *us* anymore?' Charlie tells them that what has happened is called 'flux. And it's always going on; right now, to all of us.' . . .

As a course in elementary Darwinism, *Seascape* just might have some value. As a play, it is pretentious, simplistic, verbose and banal. As in *All Over*, the writing is presumed (by the author) to be poetic and profound, resonant, when in reality it is devoid of life and artificial, the producer of inertia. Sadly, *Seascape* would seem only to confirm what has become more and more evident with the passing years: That it is to such plays as *Tiny Alice, Malcolm, All Over* and *Seascape*, not the earlier, more vital and vibrant—and, yes, more profound—*Zoo Story* and *Virginia Woolf*, that one must look for the 'real' Edward Albee. It is a disappointing discovery to make. (p. 34)

> *Catharine Hughes, in* Plays and Players *(© copyright Catharine Hughes 1975; reprinted with permission), May, 1975.*

Throughout his career Albee has plotted the graph of man's attempt to relate to his social and metaphysical situation. His central belief is that expressed by Freud in *The Future of an Illusion*: "man cannot remain a child for ever; he must venture at last into the hostile world. This may be called '*education to reality*'." From Peter's refusal to acknowledge the simple inadequacy of his life in *The Zoo Story*, to George and Martha's illusory child in *Who's Afraid of Virginia Woolf?* and Julian's flight to religion in *Tiny Alice*, he has charted the desperate need for illusion which has afflicted society and left the individual trapped in permanent adolescence. Where Beckett sees man as irrevocably condemned to live out a metaphysical absurdity, Albee's position is basically existential. He sees the cataclysm as very much man's own creation and, as such, avoidable. (pp. 151-52)

He takes as his subject modern society's apparent determination to conspire in its own demise through a wilful refusal to risk the anguish which inevitably stems from personal commitment and from human relationships forged in an imperfect world. . . . In *Who's Afraid of Virginia Woolf?* he had suggested a political dimension to George and Martha's exorcism of illusion; in *Tiny Alice* he had detailed the origin and nature of religious delusion and in *A Delicate Balance* examined the social fictions deemed necessary to the continuance of corporate life. In his two experimental plays [*Box* and *Quotations from Mao Tse-Tung*] he attempts to bring together the whole meta-structure of illusions which together create the fabric of the private and public world. . . . (p. 152)

[*Box* is] the working out of a dialectic. The play is essentially the self-questioning voice of the artist or of any individual alive to personal and public responsibilities. But the elegaic tone, together with reiterated use of the past tense, makes it clear that this is both a prophecy and a post-apocalyptic elegy for a departed civilization; the play which follows offers an explanation for that cataclysm. . . . (pp. 153-54)

Box is a protest against the dangerously declining quality of life—a decline marked in one way by the corruption of genuine artistry to suit the demands of a consumer society which has no place for the artist except as a simple manufacturer, and in another by the growth of an amoral technology with a momentum and direction of its own. . . . The final corruption lies in a fierce and total commitment to defend this system whatever the cost in human terms. . . . (p. 154)

In these circumstances art is in a dilemma. Either it reflects the dissolution or it counterposes order to entropy. What is the role of art, in other words, in an age of crisis? Should the artist endorse social fictions or fly in the face of demands for a reassuring conformity? From one point of view, the voice admits, "the beauty of art is order—not what is familiar, necessarily, but order on its own terms . . . a billion birds at once, black net skimming the ocean . . . going straight . . . in a *direction*. Order!" But as we have seen the self-justifying progress of technology has both order and direction. What it lacks is precisely a moral dimension, the capacity for criticism. By this token, art becomes an anodyne: "the release of tension is the return to consonance." . . . By implication the true artist must reject this comfortable social role. As Albee explained in an interview, the playwright is either "a manufacturer who constructs entertainments for a buyer's market" or he is a social critic, a man whom he describes, significantly, as being "out-of-step with his society." The image is obviously close to that in *Box*. To Albee, it seems, the true man, like the true artist, opposes himself to the destructive errors of his society. The playwright is forced by his commitment to truth to produce a play which "should not have had to have been written," to oppose the blind movement of the mass and move "fast in the opposite way" . . . like the solitary bird who opposes his flight to that of the billion. If art has ceased celebrating human potential, if it stresses loss, dissolution, and corruption, to the point at which it seems to be obsessed with despair and the increasing difficulty of communication, it is because this is an accurate reflection of the age. Thus, it is logical enough that in such a period, as the voice laments, "art hurts." . . . This is not, as some critics have suggested, a comment on the decline of art, but an honest image of a civilization blindly plunging towards extinction, clutching the while at chimeras in the sad misapprehension that order, precision, and competence constitute a valid alternative to simple humanity and honesty. To Albee, metaphysical purpose and order are credible only in the context of a delusory religious conviction, only, in other words, if everything can be regarded as "part of a . . . predetermination, or something that has already happened—in principle—well, under *those* conditions *any* chaos becomes order. Any chaos at all." . . . Not believing in such an ineluctable destiny, he sees the individual as directly responsible for his own fate. The assertion of a reassuring determinism he finds insupportable. What is needed is a reassertion of humane values. In *Who's Afraid of Virginia Woolf?* Albee had tested the survival of American Revolutionary principles at mid-twentieth century. While he found them suffocated beneath an elaborate pattern of illusion and deception, exorcism was still a possibility. In *Box* apocalypse is simultaneously only a breath away and a historical fact on which the voice can remark. . . . (pp. 154-55)

He has always been obsessed with a sense of loss—a theme which runs through his life as clearly as his plays—but he has also consistently refused to retreat into stoicism, which he regards as a cowardly and ultimately lethal retreat from commitment, or into protective illusion. As a writer he has shown a healthy scepticism towards the spurious products of the imagination, whether these take the form of O'Neill's pipe-dreams or the elaborate artifice of art. Yet his central theme—the need to reject the seductive consolation of unreality, the desperate necessity to abandon faith in a specious sense of order, and the urgency of genuine communication between individuals stripped of pretense and defensive posturing—is advanced in plays which are, of course, nothing more themselves than elaborate and carefully structured fictions in which invented characters act out a prepared and balanced scenario. His awareness of this dilemma is perhaps reflected in his ironical reference to the careful construction of the box, which stands as a persuasive analogue of the well-made play. . . . Clearly these plays are in part an attempt to resolve such a dilemma. There are no characters in *Box*. *Quotations* borrows speeches from other writers and then fragments them until Albee's conscious control is to some degree subverted. Such structure as is apparent is supplied partly by chance, by random association, and by an audience for whom the box, which dominates the stage, becomes a *tabula rasa* to be interpreted variously as the artificial construction of an artist, a visual image of order, a paradigm of the theatre, an image of the restricted world in which the individual exists or the empty shell of the body whose voice lingers on as a warning and an epitaph. (pp. 155-56)

[We] have his assurance that "whatever symbolic content there may be in *Box* and *Quotations from Chairman Mao Tse-Tung*, both plays deal with the unconscious, primarily." Both works represent an experiment in liberating the dramatic event from the conscious and potentially restricting control of the writer. . . . He insists [,however,] on retaining for himself a tight control over rhythm and tone and establishes with considerable attention to detail the basic structure of the two plays. While he allowed chance to play an important role he also reserved the responsibility of manipulating the text to secure the maximum effect. Albee, moreover, is not retreating from the centrality of language in his work but is intent on discovering the potential of words freed from their immediate context and released from their function of forwarding the details of linear plot, delineating the minutiae of character, and establishing the context and structure of conscious communication. In *Box* the sibylline utterances of the disembodied voice, together with the enigmatic central image (in contrast to the allegorical directness of the central symbol in *Tiny Alice*), leave the audience to respond to intimations of personal loss and the suggestive outlines of a visual image on a subconscious and intuitive rather than a conscious and cerebral level. In *Quotations* coherent monologues are deliberately fragmented in order to release meaning, while private and public fears are juxtaposed according to chance assonance. The play is a collage of words and images; it uses surrealist methods not to reveal the marvellous but to penetrate the bland façade of modern reality—personal, religious, and political. (pp. 156-57)

Albee is intent on bringing together disparate materials and experiences to create an image with the power to bypass intellectual evasion. Mao's quotations and Carleton's poems are to an extent simply "found" material with which he can create a play with the power to disturb not merely conventional notions of theatre—a discrete and highly structured model—but parallel assumptions about the nature of reality. The play is intended to capture not only the simultaneity of life—the complex interplay of public and private worlds—but also the fluid, evanescent, and equivocal quality of any art which sets out to plot the decline of morality and morale in an age bereft of convictions which genuinely touch the quick of life. With religion dead—the minister sits mute throughout the play—there is only political activism, a sentimental longing for lost innocence, the short-lived consolation of sexuality, or a deadly solipsism which hastens that cataclysm which is the inevitable product of such a massive failure of nerve. (pp. 157-58)

The "meaning" of *Quotations* lies in the interstices of the speeches, in the associations and ideas generated by the juxtaposition of seemingly unrelated experiences and interpretations of reality. The power which Albee finds in Mao's thoughts or Carleton's sentimental verses goes far beyond the tendentious banality of which each is equally capable. By placing their work in a totally different context, by allowing a fortuitous consonance of meaning to establish itself by the deliberate juxtaposition of passages which seem to comment on one another, he allows the play to generate its own meaning through association, implicit irony, and the careful modulation of tempo and tone. Albee sets the basic rules which the text must follow, rather as does Beckett in *Film* and Pinter in *Landscape*. He defines his characters' range of awareness and their degree of self-absorption. The play's effectiveness depends on the one hand on a minute observance of these rules, "alteration from the patterns I have set may be interesting, but I fear it will destroy the attempt of the experiment," . . . and on the other on the range of meaning released by a willing acceptance of fortuitous assonances in the text. On one level at least it is an elaborate Rorschach test—an exercise in unconscious creation by the observer, though playwright and director shape the elaborate disjunctions as implicit meanings, ambiguities and rhythms become apparent. . . . [This] interweaving of apparently remote realities not only provides a tenuous structure for the play but also indicates Albee's conviction that there is an ineluctable connection between the body and the body politic. The public dimension of private action, or, more usually, inaction, has always played a major role in Albee's work. . . . Here the connection is forged less obliquely by the deliberate and repeated confrontation of the two levels of experience. . . . From one point of view the different characters represent past (Old Woman), present (Long-Winded Lady), and future (Mao); external, internal, and social reality. But Albee is less concerned with differences than with similarities. All are united in their insistence on the imperfections of life and their awareness of impending crisis. Despite the fact that the first production allowed Mao to step outside the restricted world of the box which dominates the stage, the play's stage directions seem to indicate that all the characters are in fact trapped within its confines, limited perhaps by their common humanity but more especially by their highly personal and rigid perceptions of reality. . . . Like the audience, which in part they represent, they are brought together briefly in a constricted environment, where they sit, uncommunicating, and reshape experience into maudlin entertainment, personal reminiscence, or political dogma.

The result is a play which rehearses some of the central fears of an age dominated by the prospect of nuclear annihilation—a play which expresses the fears of the individual trapped in a society which can no longer offer effective consolation for the imperfection of love and the inevi-

table movement towards personal extinction. Mao's homilies on the decline of imperialism chime surprisingly well with revelations of human cruelty and degeneration on an individual level, and here is a clue to Albee's strategy in a play which deliberately relates the inner world . . . to the outer. . . . The drift towards a lonely and meaningless death by the Old Lady, and by the woman in Carleton's poem, together with the literal "sinking" of the Long-Winded Lady as she becomes increasingly aware of her mortality, have a persuasive relevance to the social system in which they function. . . . It is not, as [has been suggested] a play about death; it is a play about dying—a distinction which the Long-Winded Lady is herself at pains to make. It is a description of the process which leads to the apocalypse implied by *Box*, which both precedes and follows it. (pp. 158-61)

The play's method forces the audience into an attempt to reconstruct [its] meaning, not by re-assembling the shattered monologues but by relating them to each other in such a way as to become aware of the tenuous but real connections. If this process seems to lack clarity, it is worth recalling Breton's observation that lucidity is "the great enemy of revelation," for it is "only when the latter has come about that the former can be authorised to command respect for its rights." As the Long-Winded Lady remarks, "if we control the unconscious, we're either mad or . . . dull-witted." . . . Clarity of expression, linguistic precision, and coherent meaning are not synonymous with insight and genuine comprehension. (p. 161)

In early performances *Quotations from Chairman Mao Tse-Tung* was followed by a complete reprise of *Box*. By degrees, however, the melancholy voice of *Box* was allowed to punctuate the painful revelations of the other play, providing both an additional counterpoint and a direct link between the two works. The intimations of corruption, the suggestions of impending apocalypse, which had opened and which now close the diptych stand explained. For this is a civilization which has wilfully blinded itself to the nature of reality and to the urgent need for some kind of spiritual renewal—a renewal which owes nothing to religion or to the secular substitute of political idealism. The play's implicit message is the necessity to re-establish the links between individuals which have been fractured by an instinctive self-interest and a perverse refusal to recognize man's imperfection. Mao's political optimism, his bland assurance (not included in the play but a recurrent theme of his actual speeches) the "the world is progressing, the future is bright and no one can change this general trend of history" is as dangerously self-deluding as the Long-Winded Lady's denial of her introspection. . . . Albee has consistently argued [that] a denial of actuality, . . . an unwillingness to confront the sense of cruelty and loss which are an inescapable aspect of existence, is itself the prime cause of the drift towards isolation, despair and, ultimately, destruction. People no longer communicate because they inhabit separate worlds of their own construction and close their eyes to the entropic forces at work in their own lives as in society in general. Wallace Stevens may see the mind as "a violence from within that protects us from a violence without" or "the imagination pressing back against the pressure of reality" aiding "our self-preservation" and through "the sound of its words" helping "us to live our lives." But to Albee, such wilful deception merely compounds the "violence without" until the center can no longer hold. We are left at the end with a reprise of part of *Box*. That is, we are left with a stage completely empty except for the outlines of the box itself—a box which, with the exception of the dying tones of a voice finally settled into silence, is all that remains of the personal fear and public myth of an entire civilization. (pp. 163-64)

> *C. W. E. Bigsby, "'Box' and 'Quotations from Chairman Mao Tse-Tung': Albee's Diptych," in Edward Albee: A Collection of Critical Essays, edited by C. W. E. Bigsby (copyright © 1975 by C. W. E. Bisgby; reprinted by permission of Prentice-Hall, Inc., Englewood Cliffs, New Jersey), Prentice-Hall, 1975, pp. 151-64.*

The tone in [Albee's] recent plays is . . . no longer that of a confident liberalism rehearsing the great verities of the nineteenth century—personal and public responsibility. . . . The tone now is elegaic. The rhythm is no longer the vibrant crescendo and diminuendo of *Who's Afraid of Virginia Woolf?* and *Tiny Alice*. It is the slow, measured, and finally faltering pulse beat of *Box* and *Quotations from Chairman Mao Tse-Tung*.

Yet, Albee's concern in *All Over* is essentially that of his earlier work. He remains intent on penetrating the bland urbanities of social life in an attempt to identify the crucial failure of nerve which has brought individual men and whole societies to the point not merely of soulless anomie but even of apocalypse. . . . In *All Over* Albee pursues . . . flight from reality to its source in personal betrayal, to a flaw in human character which must be faced if it is to be understood and remedied. (pp. 168-69)

[In *All Over* there] is ample evidence that Albee is not an absurdist. The absurdity which he identifies is a wilful product of man, not the casual gift of an indifferent universe. He peoples his plays, not with the cosmic victims of Samuel Beckett, but with the self-created victims of modern society. The irony of Beckett's plays lies in the failure of his characters to recognize that things cannot be other than they are; the irony of Albee's plays lies in the failure of his characters to realize that things can be other than they are. At the same time this does not make him a confident social critic with a political blueprint for a future society. It is simply that he asserts a potential for action and concedes the existence of human values in a way which would be alien to the absurdist. The values that he endorses are essentially liberal ones, but this is a liberalism fully aware of the human and social realities which have made the absurdist vision such a compelling feature of the postwar world. For, of course, a writer whose solution to a contemporary sense of anomie is love, risks a potentially disabling sentimentality. Although he is not guilty of the confusion between Eros and Agape—which distorts and all too often trivializes a similar theme in the work of Tennessee Williams and James Baldwin—in placing the weight of his liberal commitment squarely on man's potential for selfless compassion he is in danger of simplifying human nature and falsifying the history of personal and social relations. It is his considerable achievement that for the most part he successfully avoids the trap. If he calls for a renewal of human contact and a resolute acceptance of the real world, he is prepared to concede the tenuous nature of his solution and the increasingly desperate nature of personal and social reality. The liberal values which he embraces are indeed

associated in *All Over* with a generation approaching death. The point is clear. Modern society has replaced human relationships with pragmatic alliances, and the values which used to sustain the social structure are at risk. The society which he pictures is flirting with its own extinction, as one character suggests that condemned prisoners wish to embrace their executioner.

The difficulty of such an assumption, however, is that it implies a romantic nostalgia for an unexamined past. Throughout his work Albee has made appeals to the values of a former age . . . without ever questioning the reality of those values or their historical force. The immediate future, on the other hand, is represented by a series of caricatures. The Young Man in *The American Dream* and *The Sandbox*, Nick in *Who's Afraid of Virginia Woolf?*, Claire in *A Delicate Balance*, and The Son in *All Over* are all vacuous, impotent, sterile, or sexually incomplete. It is a terminal generation with no apparent understanding of vital human needs. (pp. 171-72)

That two characters in *All Over* do continue to insist on the reality of selfless love, despite their own many failures, is a ground for hope. That they are, respectively, sixty-one and seventy-one years old reveals the imminence of that private and public apocalypse which Albee has been prophesying and fighting throughout his work.

The real problem of *All Over* is that Albee seems here to succumb to a basic conviction of American theatre, namely that seriousness and pretentiousness are in some way necessarily allied. To all intents and purposes *All Over* is Albee's version of Arthur Miller's *After the Fall*. There is the same concern with human failure and betrayal, the same anguished fascination with the slow decay of love which mirrors the physical slide towards the grave. His characters speak the same pseudo-poetic prose, creating a ceremony of death which is part expiation and part celebration. There is also, alas, the same sacrifice of language and theatrical truth to a deeply felt personal anguish, so that the result is a play which paradoxically fails to create anything more compelling than imitation baroque—verbal arabesques, and emotional arpeggios rooted in no recognizable human sensibility. The play is not realistic. Albee's drawing rooms, like Pinter's, are charged with metaphysics; they glow with significance. Sometimes, as in Albee's *Who's Afraid of Virginia Woolf?* or Pinter's *The Birthday Party*, realism and symbolism blend into powerful metaphor; sometimes, as in *All Over* or *Old Times*, the metaphor crushes the characters until one admires tone, tempo, rhythm, register, imagery, everything but human relevance. And that price is especially great in Albee's work where he is intent on urging precisely the need for such relevance. Albee seems to have placed himself in the paradoxical position of stressing the need for a revival of liberal values in a play with no recognizable human beings. An expressionistic satire such as *The American Dream* can bear such an approach, though even here Grandma's subversive vitality is a crucial element in emphasizing the survival of non-utilitarian standards. In *All Over* the paradox is potentially destructive. Albee has come more and more to resemble T. S. Eliot in creating didactic ceremonies, cerebral puppet shows manipulated with an impressive economy of energy, but dangerously lacking in the kind of compelling humanity and subtle theatricality which makes Beckett's work, for example, so much more than an intellectual valedictory. (pp. 173-74)

C. W. E. Bigsby, "To the Brink of the Grave: Edward Albee's 'All Over'," in Edward Albee: A Collection of Critical Essays, edited by C. W. E. Bigsby (copyright © 1975 by C. W. E. Bigsby; reprinted by permission of Prentice-Hall, Inc., Englewood Cliffs, New Jersey), Prentice-Hall, 1975, pp. 168-74.

[*Counting the Ways*] is a vaudeville and *not* really a play in the conventional sense. Conceived as a companion piece for another small-scale play (originally written for radio, but with an eye to the feasibility of state performance), *Listening,* this series of short sketches or 'black-outs' is a chamber piece if ever there was one. Variations on the theme of 'Ways of loving' for two middle-aged characters, He and She, quietly sardonic, wryly ironical, this is chamber music of the theatre. . . .

Counting the Ways, in itself and for itself, is a very brilliant piece of miniature painting. It is daring in looking at Love in its infinite variety through, as it were, the wrong end of the telescope, from the standpoint, that is, of a couple at the end of love and the waning of marriage, when the double bed is finally replaced by twin beds and when they can no longer remember whether they have had three or four children. But Albee has, very cleverly, managed to include even the pangs of adolescent and first love, in the spectrum, by making the middle-aged reminisce on their early experiences. There is no cliché here; even the most often treated themes or episodes, where the danger of being obvious is tremendous, are tackled in novel and original ways, in a splendid, if somewhat mannerist style. . . .

Albee is a fine writer. The text of *Counting the Ways* is full of beauties. The passage in which the lady reflects on precedence in seating two elderly guests both of whom are known to be mortally ill and due to die soon, but one of whom is aware of his condition, the other not, is brilliant in conception as well as stylistic elegance. (p. 33)

Martin Esslin, in Plays and Players (© copyright Martin Esslin 1977; reprinted with permission), February, 1977.

After *Who's Afraid of Virginia Woolf?,* for reasons that remain mysterious, Edward Albee lost his voice as a playwright. He has continued to write, but that characteristic voice—at once cultivated and slangy, instantly recognizable as an American voice, a voice full of emotion, passionately disgusted, challenging, raging—is heard no more, except when his early plays are revived. Since *Virginia Woolf,* Mr. Albee has experimented in various directions, has imitated Pinter, Beckett, and T. S. Eliot; lately he has synthesized echoes of their voices, together with other things, into a new voice for himself, but it is only a whisper, or perhaps a genteel murmur.

Mr. Albee, it seems to me, . . . has actually found a way to put his work at arm's length from his feelings. There is no sign, now, of the raw urgency of *The Zoo Story, The American Dream,* and *Who's Afraid of Virginia Woolf?.* His last few plays have been gravely classical, measured, abstract, constrained; they sit politely onstage, carefully groomed, rigidly corseted, their backs straight, their hands in their laps. The sentences they murmur are exquisitely, if rather self-consciously, shaped; they are very "civilized"; they are not, so far as I can see, very much alive. The Theatre

of Abstract Gentility suits some playwrights; it does not appear to suit Mr. Albee—because, I believe, other playwrights manage to use this form to engage their talents, while Mr. Albee uses it to escape his.

The two newest Albee plays are a pair of one-acts called *Counting the Ways* and *Listening.* . . .

Counting the Ways is so slight it's hardly there, but it is harmless and graceful enough. . . .

Listening is a dignified, elliptical piece, redolent of James and Eliot, of Beckett *(Krapp's Last Tape)* and Pinter *(Landscape and Silence).* . . .

As will now be apparent, I am not an admirer of Mr. Albee's recent plays. But I am not in sympathy with the rather hysterical critical attacks against him that have appeared in recent years. Some people do seem to like his late plays, and these people are not necessarily *non compos mentis*—only, I think, a little overrefined; but they could argue with equal cogency, perhaps, that I am underrefined, with no relish for delicate flavors. Mr. Albee is still a gifted, intelligent, scrupulous writer, doing the best he can; if, as I believe, he has fallen out of touch with his own talent, that is scarcely an indictable offense. (p. 99)

Julius Novick, "Albee Is Doing His Best," in The Village Voice (reprinted by permission of The Village Voice; copyright © by The Village Voice, Inc., 1977), February 21, 1977, pp. 99-100.

*   *   *

ALEIXANDRE, Vicente   1898-

A Spanish poet, Aleixandre was a prominent member of the liberalistic group called the "1927 Generation." Unlike other well-known members, such as Rafael Alberti and Jorge Guillén, Aleixandre never left Spain. His poetry began in the tradition of the *poésie pure* but was soon transmuted into a style suggestive of surrealism. Although written in free verse, Aleixandre's work is structurally both complex and carefully crafted. Because he was relatively unknown outside of Spain, his selection as recipient of the 1977 Nobel Prize for Literature was a surprise to much of the literary world.

Aleixandre had been the greatest poetical rebel of the Republican period. He seems to have been the only poet definitely to set out to write under the [influence of Freud]. . . . Aleixandre was thought of in early life as a revolutionary in every way. Hernández dedicated *Viento del pueblo* to him with the words: "Nosotros venimos brotando del manantial de las guitarras acogidas por el pueblo" (We have sprung from the source of the guitars the people received for their own). . . . (p. 37)

Aleixandre began with a book called *Ambito* which both by the form of the verse and the use of images reminds us of Guillén. . . . But soon Aleixandre was to read Freud and try to apply psycho-analysis as a poetic method. . . . In the prose-poems of *Pasión de la tierra* he wrote in dream-symbols. His other poetry, in a highly rhythmical free-verse, used the same sort of symbols but subordinated them to some theme, usually of love, interspersed with clear statements about his emotions and thoughts. Aleixandre does not induce in himself the trance Surrealists require; instead, he voluntarily creates a pleasing though rather stark pattern with unusual images. . . . [In his] kind of poetry an impression is the same as a reality. . . . Aleixandre sets us on the border-line between sensation and thought. There is also something wild and almost animal about his poems, full of extravagant images; and we must not try to understand these logically, lest they become absurd. (pp. 37-8)

Many poets in the past have . . . chosen the sensuality of the dance as their subject. . . . Aleixandre [compares, in a Freudian manner,] the sensuality of the dancer to the kind of extremely sweet food usually served at dances; there is even a displeasing suggestion of indigestion. Also one image does not follow on from another, but merely suggests it as in a dream; the "pechos" are "dulces tartas . . . sobre los hombros"; a kiss becomes a sweetmeat; and a "yes" is painted green. The idea appears to be that incontinence in eating sweet things at a dance leads to the thought of another sort of incontinence. (p. 39)

If *Sombra del paraíso* had been as full of personal and Freudian images as Aleixandre's former books, it would hardly have satisfied all the expectations it aroused. It would probably never have appeared, for the authorities might have felt suspicious of the poet's cryptic utterances. As it was, the book was recognizably in the Aleixandre style and probably an improvement on his former writings, but the general meaning was plain and the whole had a unifying tone. (pp. 40-1)

Aleixandre's great skill in *Sombra del paraíso* was to write in his own "visionary" style and yet give a general impression of coherence, even compose poems each with a definite theme in a book which has a certain unity of mood. . . .

In the years following the publication of *Sombra del paraíso*, Aleixandre ceased to appear such a unique figure in Spanish poetry. Much poetry of a more varied nature was written in Spain and the work of Spanish poets abroad became much more easily available. Aleixandre was no longer a survivor from a revolutionary age but an academician and a master. (p. 44)

His *Historia del corazón* (1954) is . . . just as important a part of Aleixandre's achievement as *Sombra del paraíso*, even though it may not have been as enthusiastically received. . . .

The language and imagery are plainer, more pedestrian, the dream-quality less persistent. . . . The master even becomes rather pedantic at times. A child's hoop is an "aro gayo de rodantes colores" (gay ring of rolling colors); he would hardly have used that adjective *gayo* in his earlier books; nor do we feel he would have spoken of the "viviente aromar" (living scentedness) of flowers. This implies that when Aleixandre leaves the dream for the day-to-day world he is in danger of falling into a traditional literary rhetoric.

As to the subject-matter of these poems, they are generally about a love in which the soul and body are thought of as one. Passion founded on sensuality appears to be all that comforts the poet in his stony pessimism. Life is aimless, meaningless, cruel and brief. Rubén Darío had written that we do not know . . . (where we are going or where we come from) but Aleixandre replies: . . . (We know where we come from and where we are going. A lightning flash between two darknesses.) (p. 45)

Charles David Ley, in Spanish Poetry Since 1939 *(copyright © 1962, The Catholic Uni-*

versity of America Press, Inc.), Catholic University of America Press, 1962.

Vicente Aleixandre is one of the last surviving members of the brilliant generation of Spanish poets which began to publish in the early 1920s, and perhaps the only one who is still writing at his best. His collected poems have about them a remarkable sense of organic growth deriving from their central theme, which is nothing less than creation itself. With the theme goes a view of the poet as visionary: in Aleixandre's own phrase, a "timeless prophet", who is as much concerned with bringing the past to life as with speculating on the future. These bardic claims suggest something of the scope of his work, as well as indicating certain Romantic affiliations: one needs to add, however, that he is a noticeably "modern" poet, who is aware of Freudian psychology and has learnt a good deal from the techniques of Surrealism. These influences appear most strongly in his second and third collections. *Pasión de la tierra* (1928-29) and *Espadas coma labios* (1930-31), which mark an almost total break with the relatively conventional, though technically accomplished, manner of Ambito (1924-27).

Aleixandre himself has described this phase as "a gradual emergence into light": though the poetry is difficult, in so far as it is attempting to deal with chaotic and irrational types of experience its sheer verbal control creates an effect of coherence from which a kind of ordering eventually springs. What is impressive is the apparently unforced nature of this ordering: unlike his contemporary, Jorge Guillén, Aleixandre does not believe in the poem as a more intense kind of reality, but as a means of heightening one's sense of a universal relationship which exists fully-formed at the deepest level of experience. This sense is rooted in the basic intuition expressed in the title of his fourth collection, *La destrucción o el amor* (1932-33); love, as the determining principle of cosmic unity, implies destruction, since the total fusion which creation ideally demands is prevented by the limitations of finite substance. In these poems, the forces of the natural world are conveyed through dazzling images of birds, beasts and reptiles which embody the universal process in a state of innocent violence. Human love is centred on the self-destructive aggression of the sexual act, in itself a symbolic representation of the death which is the only means of becoming integrated in a higher form of existence.

This is the extreme form of the myth which, with certain modifications, determines the rest of Aleixandre's work: though . . . there is a point at which the emphasis shifts decisively from the physical universe to a consideration of man in his human context. This point comes in *Historia del corazón* (1945-53), though it is anticipated by certain poems in *Sombra del paraíso* (1939-43), in which Aleixandre's sense of universal perfection begins to shape itself around images of a lost Eden, glimpsed platonically through memories of childhood and other forms of pastoral simplicity. Critics have tended to associate this new emphasis with the general shift towards a socially-committed type of verse which occurred in Spain in the late 1940s. In his theoretical statements of the time, Aleixandre clearly sympathizes with such aims, yet the fact that his own poetry continues to be so superior to that of the so-called "poetas sociales" merely confirms its continuity with his earlier work.

The most surprising poems in *Historia del corazón* are not those on collective themes, in which the expression of human solidarity occasionally falls into sentimentality, but the group of love-poems which includes "Mano entregada", "Otra no amo" and "El último amor". Here, for the first time, Aleixandre strikes a note which continues to echo in some of the best of the younger Spanish poets, like Claudio Rodriguez: a tenderness which is aware of its own illusions and which accepts the limitations of a human relationship as the proof of its uniqueness. The relationship of the lovers is now seen as a microcosm of the much vaster relationship in which the living and the dead appear as innumerable facets of a single material, the "materia única" of the concluding poem in Aleixandre's last major collection, *En un vasto dominio* (1958-62).

Seen in perspective, this new sense of collective involvement may be seen to have its origins in the vision of an undivided cosmos which dominates the earlier poetry and whose presence can still be felt in the later work, notably in the wonderful group of poems on the parts of the body which opens this last collection. The majority of these poems are simpler than the earlier ones, but only because they can afford to be: the inexhaustible spectacle of human lives is evoked in poem after poem. . . . Almost any of these poems would be enough to make the reputation of a lesser poet, and a number, like the series of "Retratos anónimos", are very fine indeed. At the same time, compared with Aleixandre's earlier work, there is a relaxing of pressure which here and there makes for a certain monotony. The verbal skill is as great as ever, and the sheer ability to construct a poem is continuously impressive: what one misses is the degree of commitment which made possible a poem like "Comemos sombra", from *Historia del corazón*, in which Aleixandre seemed for once to be groping towards a genuinely religious experience which would transform his sense of the human situation into something more deeply personal.

This note does, in fact, reappear very movingly in his most recent collection, *Poemas de la consumación* (1968), which is not included in the *Obras completas*. These poems, for the most part of almost aphoristic brevity, are among the bleakest which Aleixandre has written. Their treatment of old age and the passing of love is uncompromisingly honest and devoid of any kind of easy consolation. If the poet himself sees his whole work as a constant clarification of means and material (a view which seems essentially just), these new poems at last break through to the kind of difficult simplicities which are occasionally the reward for a lifetime's major work. So, recalling the words of Hamlet "to die, to sleep, to sleep: perchance to dream" he writes in "El poeta recuerda su via" ("The poet remembers his life"):

> Forgive me: I have slept.
> To sleep is not to live. Peace to all men.
> To live is not to sigh, nor to glimpse
>   words which may still live us.
> To live in words? Words die, are beau-
>   tiful to hear, but unenduring.
> Like this clear night. Yesterday at dawn.
> Or when the completed day draws out
>   its final beam, which falls upon your
>   face.

> It seals your eyes with a single stroke
>   of light
> Sleep.
> The night is long, but already it is past.

> *"The Undivided Cosmos," in* The Times Literary Supplement *(© Times Newspapers Ltd., 1969; reproduced from* The Times Literary Supplement *by permission), July 10, 1969, p. 751.*

The similarities of word and topic between *Cántico* and *Ámbito* could never let Aleixandre claim that he and Guillén were contrasting poets. . . . Aleixandre echoed Guillén's pleasure in the compactness of the world when in 'Luz' he celebrated the light which frames and encases creation. . . . (pp. 137-38)

But it was in their attitudes to night that the two poets diverged: whereas Guillén saw it as an interlude, a hiatus in which he remained suspended till day gave him back the world he loved, Aleixandre found in the night a new energy which animated his body and ignited his passion. . . . (pp. 138)

Cántico described a sunlit world; *Ámbito,* despite the tributes to '¡Mañana dulce . . . !' . . . , is an ecstatic song to the darkness with which Aleixandre came to identify himself so completely that in the last poem, 'Noche final', which closes the frame opened by 'Noche inicial', he said simply: 'La noche en mí. Yo la noche' [The night in me. I the night]. . . . In *Ámbito* night is an actor as well as a backcloth; it has shape and blood, like a living creature, and senses so stimulated that in 'Agosto' it offers itself to the poet with all the licentiousness of a whore. . . . (pp. 138-39)

Unlike Guillón, whose eyes swept creation, Aleixandre did not want to look further than the woman's body; this was all that his eyes saw and his hands explored. When he plunged his arms into the night in 'Materia,' he wanted to find food for his fingers in female flesh. . . . (p. 139)

The erotic stimulus which Aleixandre received from the night and from a woman's naked body generated a feverishness reflected in his vision of the world as constantly moving. Just as his own 'hot hand' sought and explored a form, so in 'Mar y aurora' do the tongues of light lick and spread over the world like slowly growing tentacles. . . . (p. 140)

There is nothing controlled or measured in Aleixandre's poetic universe; casting himself according to a prose piece published in 1928 as a 'horseman on a most lusty horse', he accelerated into a blind stampede Guillén's pursuit on horseback of the marvels of life. . . . In *Ámbito* Aleixandre's imagination began a frenzied gallop which transformed the world into a place of violence in which, as in 'Riña', the moonbeams stab the night. . . . (pp. 140-41)

Aleixandre's excited depiction of a turbulent world created an uneasy truce between form and content; . . . his ejaculations, parentheses, jerky phrases and contorted periods strain moulds as regular as the *romance* and heptasyllabic quatrains which Guillén respected with elegant ease. Nor did Aleixandre's feverish imagination let him present creation as simply and directly as Guillén. The opening of 'Las seis'—'Seriá como si . . .' . . .—suggests that to name things did not satisfy him. What marked *Ámbito* as an immature work was Aleixandre's failure to control his image-making, which in *Pasión de la tierra* was to become hysterical and anarchic. He strained too hard to create images, some of which were so clumsily manufactured that . . . they obstruct rather than aid the poem. . . . (p. 141)

There is no doubting his vigour and enthusiasm, even though his perpetual orgasms are tiresomely repetitive; what Aleixandre failed to see when he wrote *Ámbito* was that the uncommon cultured words he used with relish hinder rather than help; he had no love of bare lines or hostility to lush foliage to make him prune from his poems obtrusively rare words. . . . Nor was he perceptive enough to recognize the artificiality of phrases . . . reminiscent of Góngora and Espinosa. . . . (pp. 141-42)

[These words and phrases] were generated by unpredictable bursts of energy which were to convulse Aleixandre's subsequent works and which made *Ámbito* into a tense chant to creation pink with female flesh and succulent with the juices he sucked in 'Posesión'. (p. 142)

• • •

Aleixandre's passion for freedom, which explains his enjoyment in *Espadas como labios* of 'los no-límites' . . . and the paradoxical principle he established twenty-five years later that 'the universe of the poet is infinite but limited,' led him to adopt and evolve a rhetoric of effusion. The tumult which in the restless pages of *Ámbito* rampaged rebelliously within the confines of verse-forms trampled down all formal barriers in his next three works as he assaulted the reader's sensibility with ecstatic enumerations and endlessly proliferating images drawn from inexhaustible sources of mental energy.

The work of Aleixandre that in aim, technique and achievement was closest to surrealism, as he himself has acknowledged, is *Pasión de la tierra*, which is composed of densely textured and highly imaginative prose poems whose capricious fluidity he did not control and whose excesses of language and fantasy he did not correct. To record his vision of primeval chaos, Aleixandre wrote his 'poetry "in a nascent state"' out of the 'subconscious elements' he harvested in the deep and inaccessible areas of his mind; this conscious pursuit of the mentally wayward and unformed made his original title *La evasión hacia el fondo* a more accurate label for an extravaganza that is one of the most unfathomable works of twentieth-century Spanish poetry. . . .

[Aleixandre] submerged his mind, senses and identity in what he himself called the 'mass in ebullition', which paralysed him in an embryonic purity and rawness where he witnessed weird metamorphoses and savoured the strange perceptions and sensations of his 'conciencia sin funda' [consciousness without limit] . . . , whose freedom he celebrated. . . . [He] put his trust in the chance prophecies and haphazard permutations of playing-cards, which in 'Fuga a caballo' he combined with the motif of the horse to illustrate his longing to be swept away. . . . (pp. 179-80)

It was because love can unite and so thwart the pitiless melting of things and creatures that in 'El mundo está bien hecho' Aleixandre followed the cries of '¡Ámame!' made by the crickets and the cacti with the shouts of 'Muere, muere' uttered by the serpent when it discovered the fact that delighted Guillén: 'el mundo está bien hecho' [the world is well made]. . . . Aleixandre's determination to let his mind roam freely through an effervescent world made him imagine love as a destructive power so fearful that it could transform a kiss into 'Un río de sangre, un mar de sangre' [a river of blood, a sea of blood]. . . . The whips, daggers and teeth which recur in *Pasión de la tierra* and other works of Aleixandre point to the brutality of a universe that, refusing to be divided or dominated, ferments as unpredictably as his prose, which . . . displays before the reader a mosaic of fantasy, an impetuous sequence of changing planes, capricious associations, eccentric hypotheses and joltingly plain statements. . . . (pp. 180-81)

As Aleixandre played patience in 'El solitario', the pack plotted for him an erratic journey of mental adventure . . . , the reader may perhaps be forgiven for not following the labyrinthine paths that thread through this virgin territory. . . . Aleixandre recorded the spurts of his volatile and insubordinate mind, whose mutiny, which he himself had incited, he was to subdue partly in his subsequent works. His comforting blanket assertions that poetry should 'communicate' and express not 'beauty' but 'emotion' allowed him ample freedom to say what he liked and how he liked as he assaulted our sensibility. By courting chance . . . , Aleixandre imagined the sudden transformation by which, after kissing the playing-cards, he changed into a gramophone record. . . . And his search for the 'expressive words' which came to him in his sleep . . . and which he did not sift when awake unearthed such rare and resonant examples as *delicuescente, intercostal, vivíparo* and *carpetovetónico*, with which he seemed keen to justify his faith that 'poetry is not a *question of words*'.

Aleixandre's belief that 'Every word is poetic if necessary' fed the loquacity which he confessed disarmingly in *Pasión de la tierra* . . . with an indiscriminate diet, often as graceless as his censure of words in *Espadas como labios*. . . . By prefacing *Espadas como labios* with Byron's definition of a poet as 'a babbler', Aleixandre suggested ominously that he was fulfilling the promise he made in *Pasión de la tierra*: 'No me ahorraré ni una sola palabra' [I shall not avoid even one word]. . . . The strain of singing, as he twice insisted, with his whole body . . . made him imagine in 'La palabra' smoke pouring out of his mouth as he ejaculated words in rapid lists, or raced, stopped for breath and impetuously changed the direction of his thoughts. . . . (pp. 181-82)

This irrepressible impulsiveness forced Aleixandre to recite catalogues of objects and creatures whose only link is their common membership of the universe; as he saw himself in 'La palabra' as nothing more than a tiny snail . . . , his awe and excitement at being encompassed by the lush complexity of creation spilt into an indiscriminate roll-call of its components. . . . [He] takes us on a crescendo of freedom from the single and the specific to the unlimited and undefined. *Pasión de la tierra* presented us not with an identifiable person but with the excited virginal consciousness of a poet exploring the mysteries of *lo descaminado; Espadas como labios* invited us to follow Aleixandre's imagination as it ranged exuberantly over the universe, whose awesome expanse he signposted constantly with the words *tierra, cielo, mar, río* and *nube.*

Although Aleixandre imagined himself as a cloud and a wasp in 'Acaba' . . . , where he dreamed like Altolaguirre and Prados of the freedom of the air, it was to the sea that he resorted most frequently in his fantasy. His repetition throughout *Espadas como labios* of the words [of the sea] reveals in their variety and frequency his enthusiasm for an element that in its uncontrollable restlessness represents perfectly liberty of thought and action; in 'Resaca' his voice and his embraces are as free as the open sea, the flying spray and the billowing sail. . . . The freedom he demanded in 'Libertad' was liberty of mind and body; he wanted to drink in the sensations aroused by the world outside him and look within himself at areas that existed in his fantasy. . . . (pp. 182-83)

What Aleixandre's eyes sought and discovered in *Espadas como labios* as they turned away like Salinas from the obvious, 'lo más fácil', to the mysterious, 'un cuento' . . . , was a world of surprise, whose sudden and capricious metamorphoses he documented in frequent records of odd transitions whose pivot is *o.* . . . The *o* which peppers . . . Aleixandre's poetry as a whole links the acrobatic leaps of a mind where, according to his neat diagnosis, 'extremos navegan' [extremes navigate]. . . . Aleixandre challenged us to emulate his mental flexibility and supply for ourselves the unseen, suppressed links between objects grouped just as capriciously by *como,* which licenced [surprising comparisons]. . . . (p. 184)

The disparate objects which Aleixandre gathered into clusters . . . were thrown together by 'the clearly differentiated psychic movements' which, Aleixandre maintained, 'give unity to each poem' of *Espadas como labios.* But to claim that a complex of mental impulses gives coherence to a poem is to postulate unity in anarchy, is to suggest that cattle racing in four directions create the wholeness of a stampede. To perceive the truth and revelation Aleixandre mentioned in his poems . . . , the reader has to destroy his inhibitions, cleanse his mind and prepare it for entry into a universe more intricate than simple titles like 'Muerte' and 'Río' would have us believe; he has to pick his way through a world of shifting planes, fleeting visions and changing shapes, where hands suddenly become mountains, as in 'Resaca' . . . , or where, as Aleixandre showed in 'Blancura', an open wound can become a bee and then a rose as it moves into the 'supersensible reality' which he regarded as the poet's province. . . . (pp. 184-85)

The lights shining through the armpits in 'Suicidio', where in a vision as horrid as Lorca's 'Martirio de Santa Olalla' a body hangs in the wind . . . , illuminate Aleixandre's enjoyment of the macabre and repellent. . . . (p. 185)

[Love] for Aleixandre was a brutal passion which brought pain as well as pleasure, anguish as well as frenzy. The lips which obsessed him in *Espadas como labios* perpetuate the river of blood which, released by a kiss in *Pasión de la tierra* . . . , still flows in *La destrucción o el amor* as evidence of his steadfast attitude to love and consistent vision of it.

The mouth which in the strangely titled 'El más bello amor'

of *Espadas como labios* Aleixandre likened to a 'bestial fruit', a dagger and a bite . . . still haunted him in *La destrucción o el amor,* where his linking of kisses or lips with teeth and blood reinforced his vision of love as a brutal power as graphically as his conjunction of *amor* and many sharp weapons. . . . (p. 186)

The vigour contained within the beautiful form of a woman's body invited him to melt into the lava flowing through her veins and die suspended in ecstasy. . . . By confining his hungry eyes to these 'beautiful limits', Aleixandre realized his ambition to 'vivir en el fuego' [live in the fire] . . . , roaming in *La destrucción el amor* over a woman's thighs, stomach, waist, throat, neck, lips and mouth, lingering over her breasts and hovering like Domenchina in *Latúnica de Neso* over her armpits, he catalogued feverishly the anatomical details of a form that, unlike Guillén's clinically reposed and asexual 'Desnudo', embodied the love which rules and enfolds the universe. His insistent use of 'es' and 'sé' at the end of his 'Triunfo del amor' organized into a rapturous litany his definition of love as a naked body whose habitat is the elements and nature and whose destiny is to savour the sensations it provokes. . . . (pp. 186-87)

While Guillén's crisp and controlled mind channelled his ecstatic enjoyment of creation into simple images, terse statements and formal moulds, Aleixandre let his words and images stream erratically over the page as his volatile fantasy raced over the universe; too impulsive to linger in any one place, he wandered ceaselessly in *La destrucción o el amor* around the elements, from the earth, where he lay . . . , to the sea, which he celebrated in 'Que así invade' . . . , to the air, whose freedom entranced him so much that in 'Nube feliz' he imagined himself in lines reminiscent of 'Acaba' in *Espadas como labios* as a bird, a feather, a cloud and a breeze escaping from the world. . . . (p. 188)

That *La destrucción o el amor* commemorated Aleixandre's recovery from tuberculosis, as he himself has reminded us, is apparent in his eagerness to expose his senses to the exuberance of nature and go digging for sensations with an insistence charted in his enthusiastic use of repetition and enumeration. . . . But . . . Aleixandre's sensations ranged within limits as extreme as the contrasts which in his eyes composed creation. . . . [He] tried casually to play down the eccentric relationships and control the 'imaginative contagions' which in *Pasión de la tierra* and *Espadas como labios* had hardened into a mannered eccentricity. In *La destrucción o el amor* his forging of strange links was more of a tool than an end in itself. . . . (p. 189)

Aleixandre's faith in the unity of the world eliminated divisions and guaranteed, according to the titles of two poems, the presence of a 'Mar en la tierra' and the unity of 'La selva y el mar'. The sky of mud which appears in one poem . . . and the metal feathers found in another . . . illustrate both the fluid unity of creation and the flexibility of a mind that swung rapidly between earth and sky, sea and earth, beauty and horror, anguish and rapture, tenderness and savagery, life and death. But around these extremes of place, feeling and condition Aleixandre put, as if the universe were a woman's waist, an arm . . . , which he changed in 'Cobra' into a cobra encircling the chaotic richness of the universe. . . . Predictably, in *La destrucción o el amor* Aleixandre paraded the lushness of creation in lists which, like the excitedly indiscriminate finale of 'Se querían', expose his dependence on a technique that aggravated the verbal diarrhoea from which he suffered in his attempts to achieve 'propagation'. . . . [Aleixandre's] enthusiastic tribute to the variety and freedom of the universe [in *Mundo a Solas*] established between this work and *La destrucción o el amor* a link which was strengthened even further by the reappearance of love as a hammer smiting as cruelly here as it did in *Pasión de la tierra*. . . . But while anyone familiar with Aleixandre's poetry expects to find titles like 'Humano ardor', 'Al amor', 'Filo del amor', 'Tormento del amor' and 'El amor iracundo', he has to detect in the titles 'No existe el hombre', 'Ya no es posible' and 'Nadie' a deepening pessimism clearly signalled in the epigraph, for which he resorted significantly to Quevedo. . . . The confidence with which in his preceding works he had celebrated nature and sung his own role in it has crumbled into the doubt which made him echo with '¿Quién soy, quién eres, quién te sabe?' [Who am I, who are you, who knows you?]. . . . Aleixandre's melancholy insistence in *Mundo a solas* that 'Allí no existe el hombre' [Man does not exist here] . . . and that 'El hombre está muy lejos' [Man is very far away] . . . lamented the replacement of élan by the despair which had anguished Alberti, Cernuda and Lorca several years earlier. Now a passive bystander rather than a dynamic actor, Aleixandre has discovered painfully that the world is not a compact circle but a void; [and those] . . . who people it represent his distress as simply and chillingly as the 'uninhabited body' which appears in *Sobre los ángeles* . . . and the 'grey man' and 'headless horsemen' whom Ceruda introduced into *Un río, un amor* . . . as graphic comments on a life he found bleak, aimless and sterile. (p. 190)

> *C. B. Morris, in his* A Generation of Spanish Poets: 1920-1936 (© *Cambridge University Press*), *Cambridge University Press, 1969.*

While it is true that a psychoanalytic interpretation, where applied, may not be clinically valid without the cooperation and interpretation of the poet himself under expert analysis, and although in dealing with half-conscious remote associations, shifting illusions, and confusing images the recurring themes may not give definitive answers, an examination of the sea symbolism in Aleixandre's poetry reveals the neurotic motivation behind and preoccupation with the equation that love equals death. (p. 62)

In April of 1925 a serious illness caused Aleixandre to retire to the countryside for two years. This illness left an indelible impression on his poetry, which concentrated on an evasion of reality and a preoccupation, at least in part, with his own physical necessities. (p. 63)

In 1932 a new illness which proved to be almost fatal struck him, and he had to have a kidney removed and spend a long period of convalescence. Sickly, alone, withdrawn, a man who fought death constantly and sought life instinctively, Aleixandre wanted a refuge from a world indifferent to his pain and found it in a dream world of the unconscious where he might escape the reality of his impotence. In his poetry, orgiastic Dionysian efforts to recreate a reality through imagery struggle with Apollonian tendencies to control his subconscious fantasy world. Aleixandre was never able nor willing to give an adequate explanation of his poetry, but he recognized it as a necessity based on subconscious desires. (p. 64)

In *Ambito* (1924-1927), Aleixandre sets the stage for the sea as the battleground between Eros and Thanatos. "Mar y Aurora" shows us the sea as a living entity whose timid waves and passive foam awaken with the dawn. Gradually the sun's rays disperse the shadows, and the sea becomes more active as the sunlight and the sea renew their daily symbolic relationship, "lento, diario, culto / bebedor de las ondas." A primitive belief held that the sea had previously swallowed the old sun and like a woman gave birth the following day to a new sun. "Mar y noche" . . ., the counterpart of the life force of the previous poem, reveals a dark and threatening sea viewed as a mouth, throat, and gullet waiting eagerly to devour the night. . . . Seeking to swallow its enemy, the sea, chained to its black bed, vainly strains its muscles to free itself. . . . In these two poems Aleixandre produces a kind of primal relationship and reciprocal cannibalism as the day drinks the sea and the sea attempts to devour the night, again implying that the drive for life and the impulse to destruction are mutually independent factors.

More clearly in *Pasión de la tierra* (1928-1929) the poems emphasize a combination of death and sexuality. . . . Aleixandre here and in future sea imagery, in extrarational and compulsive symbolism, stresses his need for loving and being loved, and his impotence, and thus in a sense death state, at fulfilling that need. (pp. 64-6)

"Ansiedad para el día" . . . implies death, breast, and castration fantasies. Aleixandre misses a finger of his hand which he does not wish to recognize in the beak of a sea gull. The poet feels "perdido en el océano" against the background of a giant wave made up of handfuls of umbrellas, and wants to wet his tongue in the ecstatic blue of heaven. Both the pleasurable and the unhappy are conveyed in the screen memory which seems to be equated with a primitive wish to sleep and to join the mother. Being one with her at the breast and in sleep means also to lose one's individual consciousness or ego, and thus in a sense to die. To merge or be lost in the ocean clearly reflects this loss of individuality, characteristic of going to sleep. The poet is both buoyed up and supported by the waves and yet he is threatened, a typical reaction of anxiety dreams. . . . He is also threatened by the "gargantas de las sirenas húmedas." The poet then indulges in a kind of autocannibalism . . . while a dried-up girl demands whether he has enough skin left for two arms. Sinking and smothering sensations, or the loss of consciousness, are found in fantasies of oral incorporation or being eaten. A baby treats the breast as it does its own fingers or other parts which it stuffs into its mouth, indulging in a kind of autocannibalism. This type of anxiety comes from childhood fantasies about the prenatal state, an aspect of which is the child's imagining it entered into the mother by being swallowed.

"El amor padecido" . . ., the last poem in this collection, shows phallic and oedipal fantasies. . . . In Aleixandre's sea symbolism what is commonly called a castration complex, in a sense psychological death, recurs constantly. (pp. 66-7)

The poet's psyche appears to reject reality for a regression to the past where his sexual instinct operated freely. The fish inhabiting the life-giving seas represent a vital sexual force of destructive capacity. (pp. 67-8)

In "Playa ignorante" . . . the poet comes from the exhausted world and desires to become one with the sea. He is buoyed up, rocked by heat, pierced by the water, as the sea with which he has fused strikes his unmovable body, a sea which in "Formas sobre el mar" . . . represents death or sleep and the unknown frontier. . . . Aleixandre shows that through dying symbols of detumescence a life may ensue. . . .

The poems of *La destrucción o el amor* (1932-1933) continue Aleixandre's sea imagery. In "La selva y el mar" . . ., the human ego is overwhelmed by elemental forces of fantasy, represented by a variety of fierce animals who show their swords or teeth. . . . Aleixandre views the instinctive attack of primitive animals as a form of love, but the implied sexual force may also represent a passive masochistic gratification or even a passive homosexual implication, for he both loves and fears these symbols of masculine virility, the lion, the cobra, and the eagle. To wish to be eaten by menacing animals often represents a death fantasy equivalent to a fear of castration, or as Melanie Klein has shown, the neurotic dread of death is primarily related to the fear of being devoured. The fear of death may also be an "anxious transmutation of the original pleasure of falling asleep. The idea of oral impregnation includes not only the active eating process, but the passive 'being eaten' as well." . . .

Aleixandre establishes an inverse hierarchy in which the non-living triumph over the living, the mineral over the vegetable, the vegetable over the animal, and the animal over man. . . . He welcomes life and love as a longed-for enemy which he fears but which will nevertheless relieve his own dammed up sexuality. Thus the forest is viewed as virginal and untouched by the impregnating sea, and the powerful claws of the animals, "el amor que se clava," cannot fertilize. . . . (pp. 68-9)

The fierce attacks of and identification with the long list of animals which the poet projects outward against the world may also serve as a father substitute onto which the fear of a father, a derivation of the Oedipus complex, has been displaced. (p. 69)

"Después de la Muerte" . . . equates the sea, filled with threatening tongues and furious foam, with both life and death. . . . This death is both good and bad, for the sea may represent a kind of timeless afterlife which deletes the distinction between annihilation and immortality.

In "Mar en la tierra" . . . death may be a happiness . . . which will triumph over life and a world which is merely a dissolving grain born for a divine water. . . . According to Freud, water or the sea symbolizes the original fountain of birth or the genesis of the individual either in association with the concept that the sea is the vital element from which all animal species came or in simple relation to the uterus of the mother, where the child originated in liquid. Fantasies and unconscious thoughts relating to life in the womb contain "the profoundest unconscious reason for the belief in a life after death, which represents only the projection into the future of this mysterious life before birth." Aleixandre's pseudo-animistic theory holds that man returns in death to the place from which he came, to the sea which gave him birth, and thus a dark happiness. . . . The state of sleep bears a marked resemblance to the prenatal state, and it is easy to postulate an intrauterine regression, the dark joy of dying, of fusing with the sea, that is, re-

turning to the womb. "La Muerte" . . ., the last poem in the collection, stresses the poet's search for life against a powerfully threatening sea. He wants "el color rosa o la vida," but the sea offers him a love which must end in death . . . for which the poet is prepared. . . . In death he seeks surrender to his beloved nature, his final and greatest act of love; only thus can he achieve freedom. (pp. 70-1)

Mundo a solas . . . repeats Aleixandre's idea of an elemental world in which the sea plays a prominent part. . . . The sea is nevertheless a death. . . . "Pájaros sin descenso" . . . shows human life which lives and dreams at the edge of the nonhuman sea. . . . Even though man may choose to ignore it, the sea is there, eternal and waiting. In "Al Amor" . . . the sea has many faces, sweet and warm or cold and burning, threatening or promising. The sea is man's traditional enemy untroubled by man's weakness. . . . In "El amor iracundo" . . . the poet offers himself like an awaiting beach to the sea, but the latter is one which has escaped its calcareous bed, a proud abyss where fish rot. . . . (p. 71)

Sombra del paraíso (1939-1943) contains some of Aleixandre's most provocative sea imagery. (p. 72)

Aleixandre views his childhood world [in Málaga] as Eden in mythopoeic fashion. "El poeta" . . . reveals that he is no longer the victim of an impassioned sexuality represented by the sea. . . . Rather in the sea and in himself he sees a need for affection and identification with nature. . . . This is not to say that the psychological interpretations of earlier works are no longer germane. On the contrary, the poet's return to his youth gives ample opportunity for continuing interpretations. "Destino trágico" . . . presents a silent but loved sea, as Aleixandre tries to define that sea. It is not foam, the wind, a bird, a stone, or a fleeting kiss. Under the ocean he sees a forest and birds in the trees. The waves are the wind which moves the branches as he listens to the song of the birds. The sea still recalls an animal, but it is now tranquil. . . . But this peace is not what it appears. . . . (pp. 72-3)

"Poderío de la noche" . . . represents the sea as the noise of life . . . which the poet searches for to rekindle his old identification with nature and his former love relationship. The sea was youth and joy of life, but those days are far away. Although still beautiful and kindly, the sea now has another face, for the passing of time stills life and love, just as night puts an end to the day. . . . Aleixandre, through the sea's generative force, kindles his memory and thus evokes an emotion previously felt. He enjoyed and suffered his youthful memories through the sea, and there he had the pleasure, youth, love, and things of far more value than the empty reality in which he now lives. . . . The sea in "Mar del paraíso" . . . represents the most positive identification of the sea, as life, and the realization that one can manage to live in spite of the worst that can happen to one; a person can convalesce from his impotence and manage life on new terms. The poet dreams of happiness and love. . . . In his youth, the first vision of life included the sea. In maturity the poet still faces the sea with the hope of regaining his lost desire, even though dimmed by adult experience. . . . In "Destino de la carne" . . . Aleixandre shows that man is born for a moment to be a spark of light, consumed with love, and then he becomes one with nothingness. The poet sees tired gray bundles of human bodies who retain at the shores of the sea the consciousness that life never really ends. The bodies continue to pile up nevertheless in mountains of flesh, endlessly and apparently hopelessly, at the sea which is both the origin of life and also the end of life in an ever-recurring process. (pp. 73-5)

In *Nacimiento último* (1927-1952), the far-off sea reflects a continuing desire for love and life as well as death in poems such as "La estampa antigua" ... and "Eternamente" ..., where young girls wait for strong men.... This sea brings passion with its "hirviente resplandor," as human beings love one another along the beaches. But the sea also promotes purity, as the graceful roe deer on whom no hand has yet set its love finds its fruition through the sea. For age does not destroy the contemplation of life and love, and through the sea one may find eternity and life, a death and love which are but fleeting moments in the eternal scheme of things. . . . (p. 76)

In *Historia del corazón* (1945-1953), the poet seeks his real human existence, unable to rediscover the certain constants of the past in fusion with love or nature. Nevertheless, the sea appears still in its psychological and spiritual aspects, as it recalls memories of his infancy, youth, and maturity.

The idea that love equals death is the leitmotiv of almost all Aleixandre's poetry and not exclusively an aspect of his sea imagery. Since the sea meant so much more, however, both consciously and unconsciously to Aleixandre, the man, and since the sea as the origin of life and a place of death have been universal constants in man's inheritance, it is through its symbolism that his ideas become clear. In addition to a repressed sexuality common to many poets, a neurotic and somewhat limited group of fantasies recur throughout. Aleixandre's youth in Málaga impressed the sea on his consciousness so that it became for him the symbol of that youth which he equated with innocence, happiness, and his mother. In psychoanalytic literature the sea and ocean in dreams often symbolize the mother. His desire to return and merge with that happiness and all it represents implies his death as an individual, as he is absorbed by a larger unit. Intrauterine life, being premortal, except for the Church, is easily equated with postmortal life; so that life before birth equals, as a fantasy, life after death. Aleixandre's sea, then, is pathognomic, as it reflects the anxieties and fantasies of his unconscious conflicts, which he artistically conveys in symbolic form. (pp. 76-7)

> *Kessel Schwartz, "The Sea, Love, and Death in Aleixandre" (originally published in* Hispania, *Vol. L, No. 2, May, 1967), in his* The Meaning of Existence in Contemporary Hispanic Literature *(copyright © 1969 by University of Miami Press), University of Miami Press, 1970, pp. 62-77.*

Vicente Aleixandre's most recent book of poems [*Diálogos del conocimiento*] is one of his best, and unmistakably different from any of the others. This is an unusual and gratifying thing to be able to say of a poet ... who for many years has been regarded as a master by younger generations of Spanish poets. His *Obras completas,* published seven years ago ..., seemed at the time to round off an achievement which could be seen to have grown naturally and organically from its earliest premises. This organic quality comes largely from Aleixandre's central preoccupation with the process of creation itself. In his earlier, Surrealist-influenced, poems, love becomes a metaphor for the self-de-

structive and self-renewing powers of the universe; later, from *Historia del corazón* (1945-53) onwards, the emphasis shifts to the contemplation of man in his human context, where the living and the dead are felt as parts of a single material, the "materia única" of one of his best-known poems.

These two phases, with their seemingly endless possibilities of inter-relationship, achieve their richest effect in *En un vasto dominio* (1958-62), the last collection to be included in the *Obras completas.* Yet, almost simultaneously, Aleixandre published a new book, *Poemas de la consumación* (1968), a series of bleak and moving lyrics on old age and the passing of love. In *Diálogos del conocimiento,* this most recent phase is taken a stage further: though the treatment of old age is no less intense than in the previous collection, the writing is deliberately less personal, as if Aleixandre were trying to accommodate his new vision to the more universal perspective of his earlier work.

Each of the fifteen poems is in dialogue form and runs to about a hundred lines. This relative spaciousness, together with the absence of complex imagery, may suggest that Aleixandre has returned to a more expansive mode after the austerities of his previous book. Yet the term "dialogue" is deceptive: the majority of the poems consist of two interwoven monologues, whose speakers make no direct contact with one another. In this way, the cumulative effect of genuine dialogue is avoided: instead of a steady linear development, there is a subtle interplay of contrasts and coincidences of which the speakers themselves are unaware. And the effect of this is to call into question the actual status of the words, as if the reader were gradually to become conscious of an unwritten poem behind the interrupted snatches of monologue.

The speakers themselves are differentiated through contrasts of age, sex and temperament, sometimes with the suggestion of a historical or literary context. Yet the most fundamental difference is between the experience of old age and that of youth. The key-word, as the title of the book implies, is "knowledge". In poem after poem, Aleixandre plays brilliantly on the nuances of the verbs *conocer* ("to know by experience or intuition", "to be acquainted with", "to discover") and *saber* ("to know for a fact", "to be intellectually certain of"). Thus, for several of the speakers, the movement through life towards death is a question of passing from one kind of knowledge to the other, from the vital, though tentative, process of sense experience to the certainties which come only when such experience is at an end. Or, as one of the speakers in "Los amantes viejos" puts it: . . . ("To know by experience is to love. To know intellectually is to die.")

In the poems themselves, however, nothing is as simple as that. Though Aleixandre renders the pathos of old age with great poignance—the whole drift of his earlier poetry was towards the celebration of sense experiences he no longer finds available—there are moments when he seems to allow that abstract thought may be as "real", and therefore as vital, as intuition. And in "Dos vidas", one of the few poems into which old age does not enter, he imagines two young poets, one a believer in the world of the senses, the other a more austere visionary for whom external reality must be filtered through the processes of the mind. Here it is as though, by admitting this second possibility, Aleixandre were recognizing a kind of poetry very different from his own which he had finally understood and might still come to practise.

The fact that he can convey such openness without sense of strain is perhaps the most obvious measure of his continuing vitality. More than ever, Aleixandre has, in Hugh Kenner's phrase, "the power to charge simple vocables with all that they can say". These . . . poems, with their clarity of language and constantly shifting meanings, show that, after fifty years of writing, he is still capable of extending his range in unexpected and profoundly convincing ways.

> *Arthur Terry, "Kinds of Knowing," in* The Times Literary Supplement (© *Times Newspapers Ltd., 1975; reproduced from* The Times Literary Supplement *by permission), May 23, 1975, p. 559.*

Vicente Aleixandre . . . is one of the Spanish poets who, early in this century, began the work that has become the most fruitful current in modern poetry: they turned toward the unconscious and the soul. . . .

Mr. Aleixandre shared with these writers a distrust of the reflective mind and a fascination with the sea. He has described a poet as a person who speaks for the earth with forces that rise through the soles of his feet.

We might expect such poetry to be an affirmation, but it was not, at least not in the beginning. Mr. Aleixandre's early poems—for almost 20 years—are filled with the kind of loneliness we usually associate with exiles. . . . He has love poems and there are poems with a sort of surrealist wit, but what runs beneath all of them is a nostalgia for a paradise that has been lost. . . .

Mr. Aleixandre has described his poetry as "a longing for the light." The early poems are often opaque and difficult. They were written with "black light," he says, as if the approach to the unconscious had dragged him far under the sea where no light can penetrate and the fish must attract each other with their own luminescence.

But even in his early work, Mr. Aleixandre had begun to rise. He is one of the few pessimistic poets of this century who managed to emerge and find something above the darkness.

The shift was quite dramatic. It came with "The Story of the Heart," a book published in 1954. Death and loss still hover over these later poems but they seem accepted now, passed over to something else. The book affirms human fellowship, a spiritual unity, friendliness. The poems are social, the style is narrative, almost talky. There are real people all around and he pays attention to them, to friends and lovers, to strangers and dead heroes, to his dog.

Where before he had been attentive to nature and longed to join it, now nature is just the background for the lives of human beings. In the introduction to a book of selected poems, he wrote: "This now is the opposite of human loneliness. No, we aren't alone."

Vicente Aleixandre deserves [his Nobel Prize]. He is a poet of intellectual vigor, spiritual depth and tenacity. He did the work. he went far down into the soul and brought back pieces of life as a gift for the rest of us.

> *Lewis Hyde, "Modern Poets Owe Much to*

Work of Aleixandre and His Colleagues," in The New York Times (© *1977 by The New York Times Company; reprinted by permission) October 7, 1977, p. A12.*

*   *   *

AMBLER, Eric   1909-

Ambler is an English novelist and screenwriter noted for his iconoclastic novels of suspense. "The modern spy story," write Chris Steinbrunner and Otto Penzler, "is largely a product of Ambler's groundbreaking series of pre-World War II novels." Critics credit Ambler with the ability to vary his style with the times without losing his distinctive stamp; Melvin Maddocks calls him "one of those writers so good at his specialty that he has only his younger self . . . to compete against." (See also *CLC,* **Vols. 4, 6, and** *Contemporary Authors,* **Vols. 9-12, rev. ed.)**

The Intercom Conspiracy . . . condenses and concentrates many of the thematic obsessions characteristic of [Ambler's] earlier books and, at the same time, adds another portrait to the gallery he has been painting for more than thirty years. It is a gallery that, viewed all of a piece, in turn epitomizes a world; and Ambler's world—far from being the projection of an adolescent's fantasies of spies who foil master-plots while they wallow in booze and broads—is very much the world we live in. (p. 3)

It is Eric Ambler's distinctive contribution to 20th-century fiction that he was able both to discard such preposterous conventions, which were strangling the literature of espionage, and to establish a believable world, shabby, gritty, devious, threatening but compellingly interesting, to replace them. His achievement, accomplished first through a series of five novels that reflect the period of "jitters" that preceded Hitler's invasion of Poland and the outbreak of World War II, later—after a silence of eleven years—in a group of tales drawn from the atmosphere of the Cold War, parallels what Dashiell Hammett and Raymond Chandler were doing, at roughly the same time with the detective story. In his famous essay "The Simple Art of Murder" Chandler said of Hammett (what he might as easily have said of himself) that he "gave murder back to the kind of people that commit it for reasons, not just to provide a corpse." By returning espionage to the kind of men and women who spy or conspire because the world they live in works that way (the key line in *Epitaph for a Spy* is the observation that the agent "needed the money") Ambler not only overthrew a cliché but created a new kind of fictional milieu. The glamorless landscapes of John le Carré would be inconceivable had not Ambler discovered and put to use the sensibility that perceives them.

Though the ablest, he was not quite the first to do so, however. . . . Ambler, it appears, took something from both [John Buchan and Somerset Maugham]. All of his early and several of his later novels use Buchan's innocent as perceiving figure and organizing consciousness, and throughout his work, like a dark undercurrent, there runs an obsession with the evils of cartels, trusts and consortia that echoes and amplifies Buchan's repeated suggestion that the plot at hand is no more than the visible part of a conspiratorial cobweb of immense scope and power. From Maugham, perhaps, Ambler derived some of his special feeling for the seedy hotels and dingy cafes and the dreary, colorless agents who appear in them, as well as his knack for setting them down in the neat, lucid but tellingly flat and dispassionate prose appropriate to their portrayal.

Ambler went so far beyond either, however, that their influence on his fiction must be considered, at best, as no more than shadowy. For instead of using a fresh perception once and then abandoning it, he broadened and deepened his vision book by book, expanding and developing it this way and that, adding to and enlarging it as its associations and extensions became clearer and richer, until in the end he had not only reinvigorated a tired subject (and by so doing returned it to the mainstream of contemporary literature) but in the process created that special world—with its distinctive themes, characters, stylistic features and recurrent preoccupations—that is the inevitable mark of the considerable novelist.

Ambler has said that "in most human beings ideas of spying and being spied upon touch fantasy systems at deep and sensitive levels of the mind." One need not be especially psychoanalytical to see that over the course of his novels a series of fantasy systems of his own recur regularly and that they in turn provide the thematic touchstones and establish the operational structures of his most characteristic work.

He discovered the first of them with his earliest books—the famous pre-World War II five upon which his reputation as a "master of suspense" rests—and was to use it as either an organizing principle or an important subsidiary idea in most of his later novels as well. Simply put, it might be described as "the loss of innocence." It is, of course, one of the commonest of literary themes, employed, among others, by Dickens, Henry James and Conrad in some of their most important novels. Ambler uses it, however, not only as a controlling idea—the thing, or one of them, that his books are about—but as the vehicle by which his plots are developed, his actions, unfolded and his suspense created.

In *Background to Danger* (1937), for example, Kenton, a British journalist down on his luck in Central Europe, agrees, in the course of a depressing train ride, to carry a stranger's packet of papers across a border—for a small sum of money. Almost immediately he finds himself the object of a search by the agents of several countries and the target of their guns. Before he reaches safety at last . . . he has shucked his (symbolically British?) complacency about the course of European politics and faced up to the pervasive evil of totalitarianism. (pp. 4-5)

Three other of the early and one of Ambler's later novels [*Epitaph for a Spy* (1938), *Cause for Alarm* (1939), *Journey into Fear* (1940), and *State of Siege* (1956)] are based on a similar theme. . . . In each case Ambler's important point is that political innocence only blinds one to the omnipresence of social decay and its manipulation for aggressive state purposes, and his suspense comes from the uncertainty of his central characters about themselves and the world they live in rather than from simplistic literary trickery.

With *A Coffin for Dimitrios* (1940) Ambler added to his fantasy of lost or violated innocence a second major theme that was to serve as the basis for his greatest post-war novel as well. Charles Latimer, the British historian and best-selling writer of detective stories who is the central consciousness of the novel, is one of Ambler's innocents too, but he is also an active seeker after the truth of his times. . . . The densest and most complex of Ambler's early novels (for some readers the masterpiece of his entire career), *Dimitrios* uses the search for truth as a way of de-

picting the world of the 1920s and '30s, and it is in its richness and breadth of portraiture and suggestion, rather than in its cliff-hanging plot, that its stature resides.

Pursuit of the truth serves also as the mainspring of *Judgment on Deltchev* (1951) and *The Schirmer Inheritance* (1953). . . . In *Deltchev,* built around a show trial in an imaginary but presumably representative satellite state, a British journalist's determination to discover the real character of the defendant becomes Ambler's means of anatomizing the contradictions and cross-purposes of Balkan political life under Soviet rule. *Schirmer* (with *Dimitrios* one of the twin peaks of Ambler's accomplishment) uses a lawyer's search for the lost heir to an American fortune as the avenue to a panorama of post-war Europe, with its hordes of displaced persons, its unstable polity and its resulting assortment of competing interests, factions and parties. As tightly packed as *Dimitrios,* it mixes history, contemporaneity, scene and character to form a blend that provides one of the broadest and most vivid views of the aftermath of World War II in European or American fiction.

Two additional concerns, evident in Ambler's early novels but subsidiary in them to his preoccupation with the larger ideas of lost innocence and the search for reality, appear fully developed in his later books.

Trained as an engineer and blessed with an extraordinarily clear and orderly mind, Ambler from the beginning exhibited an interest in the lacy details of technology and business—his pre-war novels abound in them, a substantial part of *Dimitrios* is devoted to Latimer's unraveling of the operations of the Eurasian Credit Trust, and the early pages of *Schirmer* meticulously describe an involved legal situation—but it is not until *Passage of Arms* (1960) that he first places a business transaction at the center of a novel. A tale of elaborate intricacy, it builds a Bengali clerk's discovery of an arms stockpile abandoned by Malayan terrorists into what Dorothy Hughes has called a "mosaic" of conflicting interests—black-marketeers, opium smugglers, gun runners and an innocent American couple are among them—but its ultimate effect is to create a symbolic model (echoing Buchan's vast conspiracies) of intrigue on a far larger scale. It thus stands, with *The Intercom Conspiracy* (1969), which depicts a swindle of similar complexity, as one of Ambler's more sophisticated paradigms of contemporary life.

A final group of Ambler's novels grows out of his interest in bizarre and raffish behavior, evident in the portraiture of all of his books but at last made an end in itself in the two picaresque novels about Arthur Abdel Simpson, *The Light of Day* (1963) and *Dirty Story* (1968), and in Ambler's slightest and least important book, *A Kind of Anger* (1964). . . . *The Light of Day* tells Ambler's customary tale of intrigue, but its central interest lies not in the action but in the character of Simpson, pimp, pornographer, thief and scoundrel. . . . With its sequel . . . , *The Light of Day* differs from the rest of Ambler's novels in tone and treatment, for Simpson recounts his adventures in a colorful (and frequently obscene) personal style quite unlike the dry, detached way in which most Ambler adventures are narrated, and its importance lies in its searching yet curiously sympathetic revelation of Simpson's elaborately self-serving personality—a substantial and for many readers unforgettable addition to the literature of roguery.

Lost innocence, the truth behind "the truth," the mosaic of conspiracy, picaresque—these, in patterns of increasing complexity and enormously varied shifts of emphasis, are the matter from which Ambler has built his world. They are scarcely the concerns of the conventional "thriller."

The Intercom Conspiracy is Ambler's *Tempest*—an autumnal work of extra-ordinary virtuosity that recapitulates, recombines, varies and inverts the principal themes of more than thirty years and adds to them a bleak yet human spirit of disenchantment and renunciation that reflects, like its predecessors, the spirit of its time.

Its twin Prosperos, Colonels Jost and Brand (both rogues in Ambler's most picaresque vein), prepare and execute a conspiracy of, even for Ambler, Byzantine intricacy. (pp. 5-10)

Ambler's wittiest and most sophisticated novel, *Intercom* is distinguished also by its antipathy to all power, left and right. In the 1930s a staunch anti-Fascist, in the 1950s suspicious in turn of Soviet policy, Ambler reveals himself in 1969 as purged of faith in the wisdom, good intentions or competence of either of the great post-war powers, and the conspiracy of Jost and Brand is his way, Prospero-like, of renouncing both. The hell with you all, he seems to say—surely echoing the antipathy to political action that has become so common, East and West, in these post-Hungary, post-Vietnam years.

Yet this is not to suggest that *Intercom* is in any way a swan song. Though the capstone of Ambler's career, the novel that—if he never wrote another—would add the ultimate touch to the continuous fable of international politics he has been writing since 1937, a fable that, as one critic has written, presents in microcosm "the century of uncertainty and fear, blundering and irresponsibility, through which all of us are groping our way," it also, by its technical daring and its high, dispassionate wit, hints at new and brighter things to come. (p. 10)

> Paxton Davis, "The World We Live In: The Novels of Eric Ambler," in The Hollins Critic (copyright 1975 by Hollins College), February, 1971, pp. 3-11.

Eric Ambler's novels began to appear in the late 1930's, representing the transition from the detective tale to the tale of espionage and international intrigue. Ambler's novels may be the *loci classici* of the traits which are considered traditionalist in the spy genre; yet his novels are not spy novels. The chief reasons for this important distinction are that, first of all, Ambler approaches the theme and matter of espionage through the form of the detective novel; and secondly, his formula has undoubtedly influenced the genre for thirty-five years, but the formula had to await the social context of the Cold War before it achieved a widespread acceptance (both in terms of reading audience and socio-economic relevance). (p. 102)

Ambler's significant accomplishment in the spy genre revolves about his transitional sub-genre. Ambler's literary predecessors belong more properly to the mode of detective fiction than the burgeoning tales of espionage as prefigured in Buchan and Maugham. To be sure, the exotic geography of Buchan and the variegated characterizations of Maugham are to be found in the early Ambler novels, but Ambler's peculiar type of novel is still a hybrid born of the cross-species blending. Ambler's spy/detective story is actually a permutation of the detective story which happens to have a spy as the central character and/or foreign intelligence agents as the antagonists. The quintessence of the Ambler spy/detective tale is the *ingenu's* inadvertent involvement in a plot of international intrigue, and his subsequent loss of innocence as he seeks the answers to the "accidental" clues provided. The method of detection is logical and deductive; thus Ambler's typical novel bears imprinting of the older tale of ratiocination.

The fact that Ambler's central character is almost always the innocent amateur is his main connection to the detective story and also severs his future connection to the spy story where professional Cold War secret agents must always know what they are doing. In contrast to the latter-day professionals, part of Ambler's formula demands a dilettante who fumbles his way through the novel to an uneasy survival. The Ambler protagonist does not understand what is happening; he cannot go to the police; he probably will not survive the embroilment; and he must comply with the game-plan of the foe. Somehow he survives (usually, by chance) and emerges a chastened but wiser man. Ambler's formula bears a certain resemblance to the undercurrent ethos of Greek tragedy: the gods will not tolerate a man who is too happy or inordinately comfortable in his position in life. Ambler's protagonists are such men, and they are grimly reminded through tragic circumstances that human happiness is too easily subject to chance and fate. In this sense, the Ambler *ingenu* is chastened and recovers from the harrowing experience as a wiser man.

As a device of realism, the amateur as protagonist succeeds for Ambler by reducing all of the *angst* of international intrigue to a very personal level. The reader's distance is maintained when the dangerous situation is ably managed by the ultra-professional James Bond. But Ambler gets the edge on suspense by making his spy/detective an average person—the reader identifies easily. In this sense, the Ambler novel is more of a "thriller" than the later professional-spy novels. (p. 103)

A philosophy of history is always as important in an Ambler novel as the social context in which the novel is written —one complements the other. *A Coffin For Dimitrios* was written in 1939, on the eve of the Second World War. Ambler's particular philosophy of history reflects his reading of Spengler and concurrent opinion that Europe (and Western civilization) had reached a stage of decadence which was bent on self-destruction. One of the minor ironies of the novel consists in the fact that Latimer, aside from writing detective fiction, is a lecturer in political economy in a minor English university; yet when he moves from his secure sphere of observation out to the role of participant in actual melodrama, he learns a lesson in both politics and economics. Or, more precisely, he learns that it is in the realms of politics and economics where Good and Evil really meet:

> Dimitrios was not evil. He was logical and consistent; as logical and consistent in the European jungle as the poison gas called Lewisite and the shattered bodies of children killed in the bombardment of an open town. The logic of Michael Angelo's *David*, Beethoven's quartets and Einstein's physics had been replaced by that of the *Stock Exchange Year Book* and Hitler's *Mein Kampf*.   (p. 104)

Just as the Odyssey of Dimitrios comes full circle in its pursuit of violence, Latimer's own quest was to bear a lesson in the philosophy of history with a renewed knowledge of good and evil. And Latimer also returns to his original point of departure: the art of detective fiction. The conclusion of the novel neatly implies that the antinomy between art and reality might never be resolved. In the outside world of experience, Latimer had seen brutality and selfishness produce assassination, poison gas, and bombardment —all done under the sacrosanct aegis of nationalism and patriotism. Politics and economics—the new theologies— reign supreme; and Dimitrios the Greek had in his own logical way been the incarnate paradigm of the age. Latimer therefore returns to the inner world of art—in particular the detective fiction. The detective story is but an extension of Michael Angelo's *David* and Beethoven's quartets—it is the construct emanating from a new harmony of the sphere. It is a world of limited systems, made up of deductively ordered arrays of facts. The novel of detection is an enclosed world which is cogenial to the refugee from the outer environment of armed hostility and imminent cosmic chaos. (pp. 105-06)

As in the previous Ambler novel, the thematic core of [*Journey Into Fear*] resides in the philosophy of history. In [the work], the philosophy of history is a hybrid form of combined Frazer and Spengler doctrines, ironically expounded by the chief German agent who is disguised as a German archaeologist. Ambler, writing in 1940, seems to indicate that it is the German nation which has learned the principal lesson of history: might makes right. The background for Ambler's novel is a Europe which is headed for self-destruction, and history is the cosmic working out of the death and resurrection ritual. (p. 107)

But the arrayed forces of darkness are held back and, temporarily at least, defeated in the novels of Eric Ambler. His fumbling, non-professional "heroes" survive through some chance occurrence or providential event. Latimer lives because of "a criminal's odd taste in interior decoration" . . . , and Graham [of *Journey Into Fear*] survives because of his final reliance on instinct and violence. The quiet cognitive processes of deduction and reason singularly fail.

All of this adds up to the *raison d'etre* of the spy novel— the literature of espionage. The major premise of Ambler's argument resides in the dangerously thin veneer of protection that civilization offers to modern man. The ages of Medieval faith and Renaissance decorum are past: Darwin, Freud, Frazer, and Spengler have triumphed. The world of the detective—the interlocking, visible puzzle pieces of Newton, Dupin, and Holmes—is totally inadequate in the face of technological warfare. The day of the spy had dawned. The detective writer and the ballistics engineer had to doff the velvet of the man, and temporarily assume the characteristics of Dimitrios . . . in order to survive. There is a little bit of Dimitrios in everyman—every modern man, that is. Violence and betrayal in the global village —this is the legacy of Dimitrios and the beginning for the spy to pick up the pieces of the shattered Victorian closed-world of rationalism. (pp. 107-08)

The Intercom Conspiracy attains style of suspense, characterization, and penchant for plot; and even exceeds the former novels in his experimentation with a Conradian point of view. But gone is the undercurrent philosophy of

history. In lieu of a search for a logic in history, Ambler renders history at its face value. . . . The novel is typical Cold War, but Ambler's *sui generis* formula persists along with his basic detective-novel approach.

But *The Intercom Conspiracy* depicts the final, utter failure of the detective hero in the modern era of Cold War espionage. Latimer is no match for . . . two traitorous NATO confederates; he is liquidated and silenced forever. The modern, corporate "organization" is both hero and villain in the Cold War setting of "bloc" versus "bloc." (pp. 108-09)

In final analysis, Eric Ambler seems out of his medium with the Cold War/organization spy novel. Ambler gave more to the genre in his early efforts than what he has extracted in his later work. He apparently picked up some of Ian Fleming's flare for technical accuracy—the result of the genre going to the professional spy; and his Russian "villain" in *The Intercom Conspiracy* bears a Flemingesque touch in his physical grotesquery. But Eric Ambler should be primarily remembered for what he contributed to the literature's overall generic formula. Ambler's contribution specifically lies in his initial linking of the spy genre to the legacy of popular literature—the tale of detection. The precise elements which were carried over to the spy tale from the larger *genus* of popular formulaic fiction include the invocation of salvific violence which preserves the equilibrium of society (and the global village), the extra-legal necessity to enforce that preservation, and finally the ethical dilemma of the observer of history—what option of active participation may be chosen. For Ambler, the choice is quite basic, yet is as old as the Platonic dialogues and as awe-inspiring as Hamlet's soliloquy: is history the product of an ineluctable process of events, or is there a morality of action which demands a participation of the individual in the flux of society? Perhaps the solution lies in the very birth of the spy novel: it shows a complex world where the putative logician can no longer solve the riddle of the Sphinx. But there is the eternal rub—was Oedipus the logical detective of the man of action? Either way, the result was self-destruction. This is the crucial dilemma of Eric Ambler's novels. (p. 109)

> *Ronald Ambrosetti, "The World of Eric Ambler: From Detective to Spy," in* Dimensions of Detective Fiction *(copyright © 1976 by Popular Press), Popular Press, 1976, pp. 102-09.*

Some thriller addicts might find *Send No More Roses* [published in the United States as *The Siege of the Villa Lipp*] short on action, but this would be a crude verdict, which ignored the novel's wit and elegance, and above all the subtlety with which Firman [the hero and narrator] is allowed to reveal his own character. He resembles slightly—especially in his professions of injured innocence—one of the author's earlier heroes, Arthur Simpson, though he is infinitely more successful. . . . There is even a touch or two about him, as far as early education is concerned, of that most genial of all swindlers, Felix Krull. Like all good con men, Firman, alias Oberholzer, alias Perrivale (Perry) Smythson, covers his tracks with a cloud of dust. Is his account, written in order to correct the distortions and omissions of Professor Krom's treatise, *Der kompetente Kriminelle,* the truth? Or does it—as Krom suggests—contain as many half-truths, misrepresentations and red herrings as the dossiers prepared for the sociologists and served up to them with a "very light-bodied dry white wine" on the terrace of the Villa Esmeralda? (p. 911)

> *T. J. Binyon*, The Times Literary Supplement (© *Times Newspapers Ltd., 1977; reproduced from* The- Times Literary Supplement *by permission), July 29, 1977.*

The unwary reader may never notice; he'll probably think —with justification—that, with the compliments of Eric Ambler, [*The Siege of the Villa Lipp*] is a rather dull and somewhat technical adventure story.

I confess to having been one of those unwary readers. . . . It was only on later reflection that Chinese boxes occurred to me—a novel within a novel, a story within a story. No one ever tells us to read between the lines, but, between the lines, there often lies a competent, even a brilliant book. This is one such book. The entirety must be reconsidered in view of the last page: the discussion with Melanie.

Having thus alerted the unwary, I may permit myself to say that however masterful the tongue-in-cheek, there can only be at first an endured acceptance of an adventure novel (assuming that that is what it was) that deals with high finance, wheeling and dealing, schemes of tax avoidance (not "evasion"), and warped sociology. Nevertheless, it is my advice to endure.

It's the warped sociology that sets the pace. Ambler creates, almost too perfectly, the Dutch-German version of Talcott Parsons. We are lashed with sociologuesque jargon, for the book chronicles the pursuit of the "Able Criminal," "der kompetente Kriminelle." (pp. 162-63)

The Siege of the Villa Lipp concerns the confrontation of our warped sociologist with the falsely accused *kompetente Kriminelle* in a villa outside of Monte Carlo. That's when the fireworks begin. (p. 163)

> *Robert Rafalko, in* Best Sellers (*copyright 1977, by the University of Scranton), September, 1977.*

*   *   *

AMICHAI, Yehuda   1924-

A German-born Israeli poet and novelist, Amichai writes in Hebrew. He is best known for his novel *Not of This Time, Not of This Place.*

[Amihai's] second volume, *Two Hopes Ahead,* reveals him as a major poet and has consolidated the small revolution in Hebrew poetic diction he had carried out in his first: the immersion of Hebrew verse in spoken rhythms and turns of speech, its final release from the dead hand of Biblical rhetoric and wooden prosody. Combining a child's-view naivety with a soldier's bluntness, tenderness with an acute sense of the cost in life and values involved in state-building, he has perfected a poetic instrument capable of catching all the nuances and contradictions of the kaleidoscopic blur of Israeli life. . . .

[Several critics have been concerned only with the political interpretation of one or two poems and] have ignored the extraordinary variety of mood and verse forms encompassed in this slim volume. (p. 207)

[The] remarkable nine-part *tour de force,* "The Visit of the Queen of Sheba," has been least discussed, probably be-cause of its free erotic element, which is illuminated by daring verbal pyrotechnics. . . . Though he feels very much at home in modern English verse, and knows it well, Amihai's closest affinity is with a French poet he has never read: Guillaume Apollinaire. There is the same juxtaposition of disparate images, joined in an iron poetic logic.

Amihai creates a world of private values, opposed to the slogans and catchwords of collective virtue, stressing the intimacy and privacies of lovers, constantly transposing the public issue to the private context. He uses Biblical myth brilliantly in "Young David" and "King Saul and I," treating contrapuntally the demands of greatness (made by the state) and the price paid by the ordinary man ("I want to die in my own bed"). He can also use a traditional Jewish image with full ironic effect, contrasting the moral certainty of a superannuated orthodoxy with his own moral ambiguity ("Poem on My Birthday"). . . . (pp. 207-08)

> *M. Mindlin, (reprinted from* Commentary *by permission; copyright © 1959 by the American Jewish Committee), in* Commentary, *March, 1959.*

In "Not of This Time, Not of This Place," Amichai's first novel, he seems to belie [a] familiar cliché about Israel: the supposed preoccupation of its "young" literature with hoe and Sten gun, its "un-Jewish," allegedly "healthy," non-marginal outlook. Amichai's novel is a profoundly "Jewish" novel, in the modern (American) sense of this word.

The book takes as its theme the problem of identity. Amichai has been brought up in Israel, but the question of his identity sits heavily on his mind as much as with his Jewish-American fellow writers. He attempts a synoptic view of modern Jewish existence; its keys are ambivalence and disintegration, rather than clarity, unity or nationalistic simplicities. Its protagonists, in Amichai's novel, are absurd non-heroes, men and women not of this time nor of this place, stammering mute protests against their ghostlike existence. (p. 4)

> *Amos Elon, "Israeli and Jewish," in* The New York Times Book Review (© *1968 by the New York Times Company; reprinted by permission), August 4, 1968, pp. 4, 22.*

"Not of this Time, Not of this Place" . . . is a very moving and troubling novel. . . . [Amichai's] subject is the torment of being buried alive in the irrelevant past. His Israeli hero spends a summer living the two lives open to him, simultaneously going back in fantasy to the German town where he grew up and staying on in Jerusalem, where he tries to cleanse himself of his past by immersing himself in a love affair with an outsider who has had no part in it. The alternatives are both impossibilities. The past is still going on back in Germany, and it is inescapable in Israel: the knowledge of what men are and what they can do that was acquired in the years of Hitler's "final solution" cannot be discarded or ignored, and it is no easier to live with when one is in the country of the ex-butchers than it is in that of the ex-victims. Yehuda Amichai writes with great affective power, both of the glittering structure of self-exculpation that the Germans of the guilty generation have succeeded in erecting on the site of mass graves and desecrated temples and of the ghost-haunted, sun-drenched anti-Germany that the ex-victims have created for themselves. One tastes to the full in his pages the experience of being lost, and of loss that comes of the realization that the world cannot be remade in the image of one's desires. (pp. 146-47)

Anthony West, in The New Yorker *(© 1969 by The New Yorker Magazine, Inc.), May 3, 1969.*

[In] 1963, the first important novel by an Israeli dealing with the Holocaust appeared, Yehuda Amichai's *Not of This Time, Not of This Place.* For the sake of accuracy, I should say that Amichai was born in Germany, from where he was brought to Palestine in 1936 at the age of twelve. The fact of his German childhood, his awareness of kin and earliest friends murdered by the Nazis, clearly determines the broad direction of the sections of his novel set in Germany, and yet the general attempt of the book to make moral contact with the destruction and its perpetrators is eminently that of an Israeli beyond the experience, not of a European Jew actually torn by it. Indeed, the peculiar structure of the novel—a brilliant but not fully worked out invention of Amichai's—provides a kind of diagrammatic illustration of the difficulties Israeli writers have in trying to imagine this ultimate catastrophe and how one can live with the knowledge of it.

The hero of Amichai's novel is a young archaeologist at the Hebrew University—quite obviously, a man dedicated to digging up buried layers of the past. Like the protagonist of virtually every Hebrew novel of consequence over the last ten years, he has gradually fallen into an unsettling sense of aimless drift after the challenging years immediately before and after Israel's independence. At the beginning of the book, we find him wondering whether he ought to stay in Jerusalem for the vacation and perhaps find some great, intoxicating love (he is married and vaguely loyal to his wife), or spend the summer in Germany confronting the murderers of his childhood companion, Ruth. The wife of a friend—we afterward discover that she is about to be committed to an asylum—tells him that he must do both these things at once. And so he does. That is, the novel splits into two alternating narratives, one continuing in the third person to report a summer of sensual abandon in Jerusalem with an American woman named Patricia, the other switching to the first person to tell the story of the same character's return to his native city of Weinberg for the purpose of "wreaking vengeance," as he dimly and grandiosely puts it, on the Nazi murderers. The hero of the novel, to cite a mythic parallel that Amichai alludes to obliquely, is a kind of bifurcated Odysseus: he descends into the underworld in hope of encountering the spirits of the dead and learning from them his own future, and, simultaneously, he lolls in the paradisiac bed of Calypso, the alien goddess who keeps him from the responsibilities of home and people.

Amichai clearly means to suggest that both experiences— eros in the city of Jerusalem, thanatos in the town of Weinberg—must be exhausted to enable his hero to find some new point of anchorage for his life. But what actually happens in the novel is that the Jerusalem sequence is vividly and convincingly realized, while the German episodes, despite many arresting moments, occur in a hazy twilight region between memory and fantasy, history and self-dramatization. This attempt of the novelistic imagination to immerse itself in the aftermath of the horror ends up being a kind of earnest exercise in synthesizing the literature of nightmare—dramatic situations from Kafka; motifs from Rilke; and from Agnon, style (the aphorisms of the abyss),

narrative technique (the expressionism of Agnon's *Book of Deeds*), and even symbolic plot outline (Agnon's *A Guest for the Night,* also about a man from Jersualem who returns to a destroyed European hometown in a futile search for the world of his childhood). Amichai intends his protagonist to discover both the old and the new Germany, but in fact his archaeologist of the self wanders about in a Germany compounded of symbols through which historical actualities are only intermittently glimpsed. (pp. 165-67)

The Jerusalem sections of the novel also reflect Amichai's fondness for symbols, but in this case the unique city he knows so intimately affords him a very natural symbolic landscape. No one else has caught with such sharpness the bizarre, slightly mad life of the intelligentsia in Jerusalem, with its serious academic types, its bohemian poets and artists, its drifting cultists from home and abroad, sundry amateurs of Yoga, Zen, vegetarianism, and the Kabbalah. No one else has been so imaginatively alive to the uncanny suggestiveness of Jerusalem's stark location at the borders of the desert, the sky, and the enemy. (pp. 167-68)

Amichai does not have to "work up" his symbols because they are already there in his city: the freight of meaning in landscape and objects is as immediately *felt* as the palpable burden of clothing imbued with Patricia's physical presence. But it is significant that the sense of reality radiates out from an object associated with sensuality; this explains much of the disparity between the two halves of the novel and, as I shall try to show, is an orientation explicitly shared by other Israeli writers in attempting to create a credible world against the unthinkable background of the Holocaust. Where horror has deadened the nerve of response to reality, made it difficult to believe in the real world, it seems as though there is a natural movement toward the primal act through which the body affirms life, in an effort to recapture the sheer sense of being alive. "They wanted to stretch out over reality," Amichai writes of his lovers, fusing the act of love with Elisha's miraculous resuscitation of the dead child in the biblical story, "eye to eye, mouth to mouth, and to give it life again with their own breath." But the miracle is not achieved, and Amichai's hero comes at some points to feel that the only fully credible reality is a purely sexual one. . . . (pp. 168-69)

This sexual submergence, however, means forgetting both personal and collective history. Early in the novel, we are introduced to one of the protagonist's friends, a survivor of the death camps who has had the tattoo of a mermaid superimposed upon the tattooed number on his arm—not in order to obliterate the grim blue figures but to leave them just barely perceptible through the lines of the mythological female form. As the image of the ambiguous tattoo floats in and out like an apparition through both halves of the narrative, Patricia is associated with the mermaid and the sea: she is seen as a bowsprit figure on an old ship, her favorite skirt is made of sailcloth, the pitch of ecstatic fulfillment to which she brings her lover makes him think of "waves, waves" Amichai finally turns her into a mythic embodiment of all the allurements of otherness for his protagonist. . . . (p. 169)

The thematic complement to this absorption of life by erotic experience in Jerusalem is the fantasy of sexlessness in the German half of the novel. The narrator dreams of becoming an "angel" (the Hebrew *malakh* also suggests "messenger," a being with a single, appointed purpose) in order to carry out unswervingly his schemes of revenge. He looks at the display in a toy-shop window and compares the hesitancy of flesh and blood with the implacable fixity of the manufactured object: "All dolls, even the most perfect ones, have no sexual organs; they are angels." The opposition between this fantasy in the town of Weinberg and the sexual actuality in Jerusalem sets up a dilemma that the resolution of the novel cannot cope with. Amichai's attempt at a denouement is to arrange for the destruction of the Jerusalem-Joel while the Weinberg-Joel comes home, having undergone some undefined catharsis, ready to resume his life, though tentative about himself and unsure of the future. The thematic development of the novel, however, suggests that there is no way out for this self divided by love and death. The only means by which Amichai's protagonist can enter into active relation with the European past, that grisly realm of mass-produced death, is to divest himself of his humanity, and this is no more possible for him than it is really desirable. But the other self, the one that revives its humanity by obliterating past and future in the sweet intensity of the sexual present, is also living a lie. The dark revelations of history from 1933 to 1945 are too radical in implication to be forgotten with impunity. This, in any case, would seem to be what is suggested by the incident with which the Jerusalem plot concludes: the dangerous buried residue of the past—an unmarked mine from another war—explodes beneath the neglectful archaeologist as he tries to untangle the knot of conflicts in his love for his mistress and his love for his wife. (p. 170)

> *Robert Alter, in his* After the Tradition: Essays on Modern Jewish Writing (*copyright © 1969, 1968, 1967, 1966, 1965, 1964, 1962, 1961 by Robert Alter; reprinted by permission of the publishers, E. P. Dutton & Co., Inc.) Dutton, 1969.*

At a turning-point in his life, Joel, a middle-aged and self-contained Jewish archaeologist in Jerusalem, is seized by a longing to return to Weinburg, Germany, the city of his birth. . . .

Yehuda Amichai divides Joel's life in two, and divides *Not of This Time, Not of This Place* into a double narrative: in the third person, Joel remains in Jerusalem and begins an obsessive love affair . . .; in the first person, Joel returns to Weinburg on a mission of hate, searching for signs and relics of his own past. Both versions of Joel's life and person —failed agent of revenge and absorbed lover—are centrally concerned with escape into illusory forms of self-definition. . . .

The two versions of Joel's life ring off one another skilfully; with good sense as well as good taste, Mr Amichai refuses to theorize about his novel's structure, but merely allows it to unroll, every event in one present echoing in the other and each episode of the past answered by an image in the present. The novel's alternation between Joel's two lives establishes a reluctant, hesitating but ongoing rhythm and a mood of great and urgent seriousness of mind. The shifting from one present to another is, of course, a game—a writer's game—and the unsettling rightness and profundity of the novel comes from its density of exploration and from the author's delight in making it work.

> *"Home and Away," in* The Times Literary Supplement (© *Times Newspapers Ltd.,*

1973; reproduced from The Times Literary Supplement *by permission), December 7, 1973, p. 1512.*

Amichai's poems must compel the attention not only of devotees of modern Hebrew literature, but of anyone concerned with the state of contemporary poetry in general.

Amichai's poems are rooted in the omnipresent landscape of Israel; the topography of his shifting emotional life is very much the shifting topography of the land for which he fought: the ruggedness of the hills, the straining intransigence of the desert, the sweating sun and bitter salt and indifferent winds of the beach, the confusions of the Old City of Jerusalem made new—all are causes, settings, personifications of his feelings. These are poems of place, and their almost tangible evocations of the violent contrasts and mysterious beauty of the Israeli landscape infuse them with a materiality no less worn and vital than the poet's own.

Amichai's is a poetry without a poetics, invoking nothing but the poet's own rich, painful, and sometimes epiphanous experience; and it is an indication of his stature, at a time when "honesty" in writing has become trite to the point of cliché, that he is able to make the confessional mode seem once again an apt vehicle for conveying truths about the world. As a poet Amichai demands of himself an unrelenting transparency, a self-consciousness which is a form of sustained vulnerability in the face of experience. His poems are soundings of himself, readings of his strength to absorb experience without sacrificing this necessary vulnerability. They are also carefully wrought expressions of a life which is itself not carefully wrought, which is constantly at the mercy of time and its own frailties:

> I sign the guest book
> of God: I was here, I stayed on,
> I loved it, it was great, I was guilty, I betrayed.
> I was much impressed by the warm welcome
> in this world.

The poet discovers that his loneliness is not a wall, but a gate: he takes his finitude and forges from it a poetic testimony that depends . . . for its integrity on nothing but what he is trying to convey—that he is a man, that he is just Yehuda Amichai, but that that is fine. (pp. 68, 70)

He is always dating things: himself, his father, his loves, the land, Jerusalem. All these moments, Wordsworth's "spots of time," are evoked but never frozen. And the poet lives a very full life; he is poet, lover, father, son, soldier, traveler, Jew. But since he looks nowhere outside his existence to find its meaning, his roles serve to elucidate one another, one experience becoming the metaphor for another. Amichai constructs his poems by balancing one moment against the next, by forcing the many dimensions of his life upon one another in the hope that the life itself will emerge whole.

This is most dramatically apparent in the wistful way he writes about the Jewish religious tradition. His is hardly a religious sensibility, and yet religious symbols still have meaning for him of a surprising kind. The sacred in his poems is a metaphor for the profane, the appreciation of the modest purpose and order implicit in the vagaries of the everyday:

God's hand in the world
like my mother's
in the guts of the slaughtered hen
on Friday.
What does God see beyond the window
as he puts his hand into the world?
What does my mother see?

The intense sexuality of Amichai's lyrics must also be taken in the context of this insistence that . . . life as a whole is to be found immanent in each of his experiences. For the sexual realm offers the most charged initiation into the experience of limit, as consummate pleasure passes inevitably into consummate pain. The account of sexual pain in *The Achziv Poems* is probably the most haunting rendering of the erotic ever undertaken in Hebrew verse.

Amichai's experience of the world is above all an experience of its intractability, of the strenuous resistance of his situation to his will. There is thus a powerful tactile element in his poems' imagery: he writes often of hardness, of rock and stone. But the poet's sense of his own self is likewise of something hard, weighty, virile, perdurable. It is, in other words, a self well suited to the world in which it finds itself —a self for which the center must hold. Amichai's muse is resiliency, and personal courage; his campaign in his poetry is to turn the richness of circumstance to the advantage of a self that will remain intact despite pain and pleasure; he sees the punishing world much as Keats did, not as a vale of tears but as "a vale of Soul-making."

Amichai has achieved a kind of precarious peace with the oscillations of happiness and sadness that constitute his life, and out of this peace rises the elemental lyricism of his poetry. The love poems in particular are written with a grave gentleness, a sense of wonderment at the ephemeral nature of it all. His poems offer seasoned comfort, the humble contentment that comes of resignation without surrender. (p. 70)

> Leon Wieseltier, "A Hebrew Poet" (reprinted from Commentary by permission; copyright © 1974 by the American Jewish Committee), in Commentary, May, 1974, pp. 68, 70.

[Yehuda Amichai's] work is so volatile—heart-burdened, ironic, sometimes terribly funny, sometimes very gentle and tender—that I was about to call it archetypally Jewish. It isn't; it's archetypally poetic. In "Amen," his third book to appear in English, Amichai reaches pure states of intimate, aroused awareness unusually often. As in, say, Plath or Esenin or Vallejo, the best poems present themselves with simple immediacy even when their sense is elusive or complex:

Oh, touch me, touch me, you good woman!

This is not a scar you feel under my shirt.
It's a letter of recommendation, folded, from my father:
"He is still a good boy and full of love."

But Amichai is certainly deeply Jewish—an "'ebrew Jew," as Falstaff would have put it. That side of him is rooted in specifics of place and of memory. His "Letter of Recommendation," from which I have just quoted, begins as a sort of Jewish joke about the permanent imminence of disaster:

On summer nights I sleep naked
in Jerusalem on my bed,
which stands on the brink
of a deep valley
without rolling into it.

Another poem, the first one in the sequence "Seven Laments for the Fallen in the War," closes in on one figure, the father of a dead soldier whom the poet recognizes amid the swirling city crowds—

He has become very thin; has lost
his son's weight.
Therefore he is floating lightly
through the alleys . . .

The pathos here is an all too faithful echo of daily life in Israel; Amichai's poetry breathes a people's worst experiences. Yet it is always intensely private, driven by a wildly associative imagination that attaches itself to quickly changing emotional states. It is political because human reality is political, but Amichai's politics are wryness and candor. "A flag loses contact with reality and flies off," he writes in his Memorial Day "lament," whose disgusted refrain is the great theologico-political Pollyannism that "Behind all this some great happiness is hiding." The proper languages for Memorial Day in Israel, the same poem tells us, are "Hebrew, Arabic and Death."

Many of the best poems in "Amen" have to do with the joys and disasters of love. The themes of sexual power gone awry and of lost relationships and broken marriage darken the book with a bitterness matching its pain at all the death and suffering in Israel's wars, so much so that the two sets of feeling merge inseparably. (p. 6)

I have by no means touched on the whole range of tones and preoccupations, and particularly the subtler modulations and musics, in "Amen." One sees everywhere in the book an absorbed spirit that contemplates the world not to explain things but to get into focus the subjective and emotional ambiance of whatever is remembered or experienced. . . .

This is a harshly lovely, exhilarating, depressing book. It proves once more that when the real thing comes along the chic critical passwords—"post-modernism," "anti-poetic," etc.—are useless. (p. 16)

> M. L. Rosenthal, "Hebrew, Arabic and Death," in The New York Times Book Review (© 1977 by The New York Times Company; reprinted by permission), July 3, 1977, pp. 6, 16.

*   *   *

AMIS, Martin   1949-

An English comic novelist and critic, Amis is the son of the novelist Kingsley Amis. *Dead Babies* is his second novel. (See also *CLC*, Vol. 4, and *Contemporary Authors*, Vols. 65-68.)

[Amis] displays in [*The Rachel Papers*] a gift for satirizing the mock-heroic by speaking directly to the reader in the voice of his own character.

This spunky little spoof may turn out to have cul-de-sacs at the end of some of its "verbal avenues," and it may have more than a touch of the vacuous nausea of post-adolescence. But it does have a certain "pimply lyricism," as

Charles Highway would smirk—a lyricism that just might win Martin Amis a letter from that other classic latter-day youth, Holden Caulfield. (p. 26)

> *Susan Heath, in* Saturday Review/World *(copyright 1974 by Saturday Review/World, Inc.; reprinted with permission), June 1, 1974.*

Mr Amis discloses his hand at the outset [of *Dead Babies*], winding up [his] violent caricatures and setting them into frenetic supercharged motion; and though there is a plot of a kind, . . . the whirling elements of the book aren't going anywhere, and the impression is static. The only shading in the picture is the bad trips, the "street sadness", the "false memory." It's a high-pitched *aaargh* of a book, a moment of climax seized and stretched and then suddenly stopped: all *fff* and no *ppp*.

Mr Amis achieves his effects by a kind of literary *tachisme,* splattering the page with physical and visceral epithets in a furiously excremental manner. It's catching: the reader falls into the mood, and though the cruelties and sexual horrors and bad language quickly become monotonous, momentum and interest are sustained through what is a relatively short book by the author's energy and exhilaration. The success of the novel lies partly in the way this method can bring off [a] . . . hideously comic [characterisation] and partly in the simple fact of its violently aggressive high spirits. With so much wilting, anaemic writing about, it's good to have a little mayhem. (p. 68)

> *James Price, in* Encounter (© *1976 by Encounter Ltd.), February, 1976.*

"Dead Babies" is . . . about the nature of civilization, and the world it portrays is quite extraordinarily repulsive, as one might guess from his title. This is not a book for the squeamish. It aims to shock and disgust, and it certainly succeeds. Set in the near future, it describes the weekend amusements of a group of frightful folk, gathered together in a countryhouse: sex, drugs, drink and violence entertain the party, and there is a great deal of very bad language thrown in for good measure. The most repulsive character is a small fat person called Keith, whose physical characteristics and activities are described in such horrific detail that I, for one, would never have finished the book, save in the course of duty. But having dutifully reached the end, I must admit that the reader is obliged to ask himself what it was all about, and the only conclusion can be that Amis is so horrified by the world he sees in the process of formation that he feels compelled to warn us all about it.

In other words, this is a satiric book, written by a puritan, who, like that other satirist Swift, is deeply repelled by the normal functions of the human body, as well as by its more abnormal ones. Does it work, as a satire? On balance, it is probably too extreme, and its targets both too many and not sufficiently serious. . . . It also tends to be violently monotonous, as well as undiscriminating. Moreover, it is not at all funny. Its characters are so uniformly unpleasant that they are hard to distinguish, and the only one for whom one can feel any sympathy is a man who has a problem about teeth. And a nice, manageable. friendly little problem it seems, in comparison with what the others suffer from. It must be said that this book in its way is memorable. One might want to forget it, but it won't be easy. (p. 3)

> *Jerome Charyn, in* The New York Times Book Review (© *1976 by The New York Times Company; reprinted by permission), February 8, 1976.*

* * *

AMMONS, A(rchie) R(andolph)   1926-

Ammons, a pastoral poet in the romantic tradition, has recently emerged as an American poet of stature. (See also *CLC*, Vols. 2, 3, 5, 8, and *Contemporary Authors*, Vols. 9-12, rev. ed.)

Of the poets in my own generation, Ammons seems to me the likeliest to attain a central position in our imaginative history. He is less representative than Merwin, less dramatic than James Wright, and—while ultimately difficult—less immediately challenging in his difficulties than Ashbery. His centrality stems from his comprehensiveness, for he offers a heterocosm, an alternate world to the nature he uneasily meets, and also from his certain place in the Emerson-Whitman-Dickinson-Frost-Stevens-Crane succession that Roethke narrowly missed joining. Ammons makes a strong seventh in a line of major poets of the "native strain" or "native element" that various critics have identified for us. I am aware of how immensely our major poets differ from one another, but in a larger perspective than we ordinarily employ they can be seen to verge upon a common vision. Even Dickinson and Stevens belong to Emerson's universe of mind, as Whitman, Frost, and Crane more clearly do. Ammons, though a Southerner and a man obsessed with Minute Particulars, is the most Emersonian poet we have had since Whitman's petering out after 1860. . . .

With *Uplands* and *Briefings* we have almost fifty short poems of nearly unsurpassed excellence, to match which I would have to go back past Roethke and Lowell to the final phases of Wallace Stevens. (p. 142)

Ammons . . . persuasively knows no other [home but the external world], and proposes a very grim radiance to us as our true dwelling place. . . . Ammons has no mythological emblem, yet from the mirror of the fallen world, Blake's Vegetable Glass of Nature, the dark double he disdains to regard keeps peering out at him. The darker temptation for the Ammons of *Selected Poems* was to merge himself with the natural mirror, but this temptation was set aside in a series of harrowing poems in which the poet, as "spent seer," yielded up all his ideas of order to the wind as "vehicle of change." (pp. 142-43)

The dialectic of earlier Ammons shuttles back and forth, incessantly, from the desire for "the unseasonal undifferentiated empty stark" to the consciousness that "origin is your original sin," a consciousness of separateness as necessity. The two masterpieces of *Selected Poems* are "Corsons Inlet" and "Saliences," where this dialectic is most strikingly set forth. In the lyrics of *Uplands* and *Briefings* the dialectic has been allowed to recede into the background, and the spent seer, trapped in a universal predicament, broods on every sharp instance where the ideas of permanence and change come together in a single body. The body's (or area's) outer edges, the long peripheries or nerve endings of perception, now obsess this Emersonian seeker who has learned, to an ultimate sorrow, that indeed there is an outside or circumference to us. "The only sin is limitation," Emerson insisted in "Circles," but Ammons has translated limitation into origin. What remained for Emerson, once he had translated limitation by Fate, was the one part of Power in us that at given moments could overwhelm the ninety-nine parts of Fate. The later Ammons holds to his bargain with the wind. To claim even one part of Power is to claim order, and all of order now belongs to the vehicle of change. Permanence abides in the still-explicable sphere of origins, in the particulars of being that yield with marvelous slowness to the necessity of entropy, if they yield at all. . . . (p. 144)

[The] outward-opening conclusion of *Uplands* is Ammons' new mode, fearfully strong in its apparent tentativeness. The seer now praises a kind of sacred hesitation. . . .

The gift of hesitation is the beauty of the particular. Hesitation is a symptom as the desire for unseasonal unity was a symptom, for hesitation like desire is a metonymy. The part taken for a whole allows wisdom, the wisdom that stops short of satisfaction. Seeking the Other in the Emersonian Not-Me of nature, the seer had learned indirection and finally resignation. Now, not seeking, not even watching or waiting, he is found—not by the Other—but by momentary visitations of radiance almost wherever the nerve endings give out. Emersonianism, the most impatient and American of perceptual traditions, has learned patience in the latest Ammons. (p. 145)

The greater lyrics of *Briefings* record the instances of a radiance that refuses not to be considered, that will not release its seer. "He Held Radical Light" defines this poet's burden: "reality had little weight in his transcendence." Wisdom, hard-won, yields to the Emersonian kind of Bacchic possession: "when the / light churned and changed / his head to music, nothing could keep him / off the mountains, his / head back, mouth working, / wrestling to say, to cut loose / from the high, unimaginable hook." Like Emerson, Ammons learns the necessity of guarding himself against the remedial force of the higher reason or imagination in him. The splendid "Countering" records the cunning of the unwilling seer who evades the crystal transparency that would engulf him. . . . (p. 146)

Yet I will misrepresent *Briefings* if I consign all its visions to an unwilling medium. Its finest poems *do* celebrate a radiance, a light seen and held, though only on the peripheries, the same nerve endings where Strand counts his litanies of what is always darker. Ammons in his backyard, in "Cut the Grass," gives me a sense of "the wonderful workings of the world," and then of the best sense of Transcendentalism, which means just what a lady once defined it to Emerson as meaning: "a little beyond." . . .

What begins to break through in the final poems of *Briefings* is a unique pride and saving comedy, yet still Transcendental in its emphasis. (p. 147)

Ammons is so much of a seer, however spent, that his comforts sometimes cannot be ours, any more than Frost's savage consolations console us, though they impress and go on moving us. . . .

To find a lyric rival for "The City Limits" I have to go back to very late Stevens, to "The Course of a Particular" (which Winters has the credit of first acclaiming) and "A Discovery of Thought." The eye of the Southern countryman Ammons completes its first circle in this more-than-Emersonian evocation of "a high testimony," as even the

spent seer, by implication, feels accepted into as much light as he can take. . . . (p. 148)

Harold Bloom, in The Southern Review *(copyright, 1972, by Harold Bloom), Vol. 8, No. 1, Winter, 1972.*

Near the end of *Sphere,* a long poem in 155 sections, A. R. Ammons writes to the reader:

> I don't know about you,
> but I'm sick of good poems, all those little rondures
> splendidly brought off, painted gourds on a shelf: give me
>
> the dumb, debilitated, nasty, and massive, if that's the
> alternative: touch the universe anywhere you touch it
> everywhere.

So he touches the universe anywhere, catch as catch can. . . . Ammons does not admit that many long poems are merely many short poems strung together or that one victory is just as hard-won as another. Like other American poets, he feels an urge to go after the big one, the long poem, shooting the rapids, the *Deliverance* syndrome. Anything Whitman, Pound, Williams, and Stevens can do, Ammons can do too, more or less, better or worse. But in fact his best poems thus far have been little rondures splendidly brought off, painted gourds now on the shelf of the *Collected Poems.* . . . The idea of the long poem is fascinating, often more powerful in principle than in particle, but it has not been demonstrated that Ammons has a native gift for the big one, or anything more than a yen for it.

Conceding to the artist his donnée, I report that Ammons is sick of short, tight poems, and wants to write poetry rather than poems, a poetry capable of accommodating the flats and the peaks, prosaic stuff as well as the surges. He said as much in *Tape for the Turn of the Year,* and ever more explicitly in "Hibernaculum," a pretty long poem, 112 sections, three stanzas each, three lines to a stanza, and about fifteen syllables to a line. The same stanza, grouped in fours not threes, is the device of *Sphere,* and the formal source in each case appears to be Stevens' *Notes toward a Supreme Fiction.* Ammons starts by catching the universe wherever he can, usually with a weather report, the day is cold or hot, the temperature is so-and-so, the forecast is rain or sleet or snow. Once in motion, he moves flexibly between chance, whim, and choice, giving the poem his head. (pp. 19-20)

As to themes and tropes, Ammons specializes in the big metaphysical questions, the One and the Many, permanence and change:

> poetry has
> one subject, impermanence,
> which it presents
> with as much permanence as
> possible.

division and unity, light and darkness, chaos and order:

> how much disorder must I learn to tolerate
>   to find materials
>   for the new house of my sight!

On the back shelves he has a stock of subordinate themes: what the mind can do and what it can't, the nature of light, motion, variety, process, abundance. His current interest is in the form of a motion, a concern first announced in an early poem, "A Symmetry of Thought". . . . (pp. 20-1)

Ammons has described his procedure in "Poetics" . . . :

> not so much looking for the shape
> as being available
> to any shape that may be
> summoning itself
> through me
> from the self not mine but ours.

What he sees is usually whatever is happening in his garden or along the beach or in the local bird sanctuary: weather, birds, fish, clouds, landscapes, trees, horizons. That makes a start. Call it Nature, however ambiguously. To get the poetry moving Ammons ruminates by recourse to meteorology, botany, geology; such things interest him, and help him toward the surges. Then there is Man, who comes into this poetry mostly in the role of perceiver, he is the one who brings the sundry of the world to order. . . . There is Man, there is Nature (the visible part of it), and there is the relation between them, asserted in *Sphere* . . . :

> a leaf cannot
> appear on or fall from the branch except via the total
> involvement of the universe: you and I cannot walk the
>   street
> or rise to the occasion except via the sum total of effect
> and possibility of the universe: we are not half-in and
>
> half-out of the universe but unmendable integral: when
>   we
> move, something yields to us and accepts our steps.
>
> (pp. 21-2)

Given these preoccupations, Ammons takes unto himself an enabling set of figures, mostly reducible to two, wind and mountain. He has other trademarks, notable an addiction to the following words: periphery, salience, loft, suasion, remnant (adjective rather than noun), curvature, meld, and flotation. But he is chiefly a wind-and-mountain man. In the early poems the speaker is rarely a person, finite, historical, but more often a spirit, mostly a spirit of place, *genius loci*. The poetic act is deemed to be an entrance, an intrusion upon the natural scene if it goes wrong, a dance or a symmetry of motion if it goes right. The mountain has the quality of being simply there, reality inescapable but inviting, not yet waving but with the promise of a wave. Wind is the poetic spirit, "the wind that is my guide." There is an early poem called "In the Wind My Rescue Is," as though the wind were consciousness itself, which it is—companionable guide, walking-mate, a good man for a long hike through the woods. Like consciousness, the wind "leaves no two moments on the dunes the same," provokes new "saliences of feature." Wind is the creative principle, making a virtue (variety) out of necessity (change); it is imagination, the correspondent breeze. "Saliences" is a hymn to the wind and (the same thing) to imagination. Ammons shows wind and mountain together, animation running both ways, in "Virtu," and in "Reversal" mountain rebukes poet for his arrogance, taking the harm out of the rebuke by saying:

> the wind in your days
> accounts for this arrogance.

Otherwise put: a sense of your imaginative powers, rushing through you like a wind, makes you rise above yourself. The mountain, apart from the wind, is a sad thing, a changeless prospect, an unalterable view: given half a

chance, however, it attracts voices and furnishes replies. If it were utterly impregnable, Ammons could not deal with it, speak to it: "Firm ground is not available ground." Wind makes mountain available, imagination asks reality to wave. Ammons does not claim that these ingratiations are easily achieved, but he is honest, true to his word: "no humbling of reality to precept." He respects the given for being different.

This is well enough. Ammons approaches an ethic by way of an aesthetic; or he makes aesthetic forces do some ethical work, silently. The burdens of "Hibernaculum" include that one: to derive a way of life from a way of looking at objects. But Ammons is not hard on himself, he is too readily charmed by his own image: if things get rough, he wanders away down the beach. He treats the present moment as the gist of history, the present man (poet, *ipse*) as the gist of humanity, the present place as the gist of everywhere: so this triple-thinker can at one glance evade the responsibility of history, circumvent the claims of other people, and derive from the satisfactions of living in Ithaca, New York, the felicity of not having to bother with the horrors of living in the slums of New York, New York. Santayana has a sharp definition of the barbarian as "the man who regards his passions as their own excuse for being." No, that is too sharp for Ammons, but it points to the limitations in his art. He protests that he is concerned with Nature, including human nature, but he rarely makes me feel that he cares much about any human nature but his own. His poetry is rural in the sense that you can walk for miles in it without meeting anyone; so the dramatic sense of life never appears. Ammons could write his poetry if there were nothing in the world but mountains, winds, weather, birds, fish, sand dunes, beaches, and a poet accustomed to living in his art alone. What he can do with those things is impressive, but most of it leaves me unmoved; the true vine of feeling rarely climbs upon his trellises. . . . I can remember nothing of *Sphere* but incidental felicities and (as a general impression) the degeneration of feeling in routines and postures; this poet is not setting his chisel to the hardest stone. Nothing in the poem convinces me that Ammons has anything comparable, so far as language is evidence, to the capacity of feeling which the finest work of Eliot, Yeats, Stevens, and (with some degree of reservation) Williams possesses. By these standards, much of *Sphere* is facile, the kind of poetry about which it is easy not to care. (pp. 23-5)

I can't help it, the achieved poems seem to me not the big ones but the little rondures splendidly brought off. (p. 25)

> *Denis Donoghue, "Ammons and the Lesser Celandine," in* Parnassus: Poetry in Review *(copyright © by* Parnassus: Poetry in Review*), Spring–Summer, 1975, pp. 19-26.*

Up to now there have been two versions of A. R. Ammons. First, the tough and restless Emersonian, intent on the task of seeing for himself alone: the geologist-explorer as sage, a sinewy, inexhaustible raconteur of "errors of vision, errors of self-defense," who at his height yields to the approach of a Whitmanian pathos ("that is the/ expression of sea level,/ the talk of giants,/ of ocean, moon, sun, of everything,/ spoken in a dampened grain of sand"). Then there is the abstract realist and man of reflection: inventor of a strange, new, laboriously pseudoscientific patois, the cultivator of "closed and open infinities," of "that point in the periphery where/ salience bends into curve," of "attenuations of interstices, roughing the salience" and other examples of what he modestly calls "unfathomable stuff." Does anyone have to be told that Ammons No. 1 is one of our surest necessary poets while Ammons No. 2 is one of our loopiest almighty carry-ons? A generous portion of No. 2 appears in *Diversifications,* but I write to announce the emergence of yet another version of this protean man, with a voice that was heard tentatively in *Briefings* but has since grown more assured.

The newly salient presence is a master of the sudden near-absolute plummet into the trivial: what used to be called the art of sinking—only this strikes one as a baffled fling at entertainment. He is the poet who can write, in the middle of a poem filled with evidence of the public violence of our age, "I had a little pony:/ his name was Dapple Gray:/ and every time I had him,/ he tried to get away." This sort of thing, more or less refined, supplies the entire content of an alarming number of poems in the book. "Ballad" is the finest piece here: a dialogue between the poet and a willow, about the battle between the willow and a nearby water oak, which begins "I want to know the unity in all things and the difference/ between one thing and another." It is slight enough, moving in a genre Mr. Ammons has tried more ambitiously elsewhere, but it is charming, unexpected, and deeply human in its feeling for things outside the human thrall. What persists most seriously and hopefully in Mr. Ammons is his sense of vocation, and that is as it should be. As he calls out to himself we call to him, too, and ask that he return to the place where we all live—and read. (p. 1027)

> *David Bromwich, in* The Georgia Review *(copyright, 1976, by the University of Georgia), Winter, 1976.*

[There is a] kind of nature poetry, rooted in times when most towns were small and many highly intellectual poets were rusticated for one reason or another, that has returned during this century in often rather baffling, footloose guise. Its shaping ritual is the walk, the climb, the trip, and the voyage, actions lending themselves all too easily to a vaporous abstraction.

A. R. Ammons began his career as the latter sort in full eclectic spate. The plot of his best poems of the Fifties and early Sixties before he started teaching at Cornell was largely a swift, sometimes brilliantly executed play of disjointed perceptions fleshing out a very private psychodrama. Charming and appealing digressions there were, to which I'll return. But the dominant voice seemed to have been sired on *The Duino Elegies* by an Emerson, a Dickinson transsexed, a Hopkins, Dylan Thomas, or Roethke—all the intoxicated solipsists of an age that requires such minds to fabricate their own plots, to expect little aid from tradition. Recently, though, with admirable recklessness and uneven results, he has been remaking himself closer to the Frost or Hardy model. Joining the academy just when its boom times were passing, assuming its by now well known and often dramatized responsibilities, he gave his existence a new visibility not unlike Frost's out there "north of Boston," a life gently freighted with old solemnities, not too far and not too near.

So much for the gains. Now the difficulties. Readers of his newest long poems, "Extremes and Moderations," "Essay

on Poetics," "Hibernaculum," and especially *Sphere: The Form of a Motion*—a rambling, confiding, button-holing poem of 155 12-line sections—will know what they are. In *Sphere* Mr. Ammons makes a grand broken field run and a curious performance it is. To dodge about and reach a point not already plotted for him by one or more of the imposing exegetes lured to his earlier work by its obvious need for exegesis required some fancy footwork. You can think of Ammons as a sort of country-and-southern Prometheus nailed down on Cayuga Heights (above Ithaca!) by the Zeus of respectability, tormented by the eagle of higher criticism in the shape of Harold Bloom. Or, what seems more likely, you can detect in all his recent work clear notes of irreverence mixed with affection and amusement toward the gaudier theories of his friends. (pp. 49-50)

Like the Ammons of *Sphere* [James Dickey] seemed ready to join the philistine opposition as far as his lively professional conscience would allow, to look back on his energetic early cult of naiveté from as remote a vantage point as possible.

Ammons is cooler, more reflective, absorptive, and self-contained than Dickey ever was and in him the Southeast may be making one last convulsive effort to put its message across; namely, that throughout its now expiring century of gothic, baroque, and neo-classical flamboyance it was secretly nurturing a middleness, an ordinary absolute center-cut Americanness, second to none. Faulkner's Ratliff and Horace Benbow suggested as much, so did the Faulknerian humor; but the message was ambiguous. *Sphere,* however, is not; it's an amiable but firm rejection of any highstrung ideologue's project for Ammons' apotheosis either as a sainted solitary or as a panurgic prophet of spiritual democracy. One must salute him for braving the pitfalls of such an operation—occasional forcings of tone, unwitting smugness, sententiousness, cuteness, *blague.* Denis Donoghue [see excerpt above] thinks he has isolated the problem by conceiving it to be formal, by accusing the poet of surrendering to an American mania for mere size, for imagining that a few dozen short poems strung end to end might make a qualitative leap into grandeur. But the fact that Ammons is keenly aware of such objections, has worked them into the poem, seems to indicate that he had no choice. The American atmosphere forced him into the optative mood—maybe these topics and digressions *would* make the orbicular leap, maybe if the poet's heart were pure enough a trip around his head *would* emerge as a mystic sphere. No choice in any case but to try.

Let me suppose for the rest of this review that a kind of intractable confusion may be the real entelechy, the formal and final end, of Dickey and Ammons who began so suavely and self-assured. And that we should make of it what we can and not waste time advising them to return and seek their lost innocence. Harold Bloom, always generous when his feelings are stirred, is prepared to call Ammons "great" but at the price of sternly reproving him for swerving from the path of Whitmanlike prophecy that his Emersonian instincts, again according to Bloom, fatally marked out for him. "Ammons has got to learn to be a different kind of poet than he was, and he is still in the process of learning that this different kind will return him to origins again, though with a more exacting music than he set out to bring into being." And why should he do this? Because he had early discovered a way to be transcendental and modern at the same time, by identifying the true American Sublime as the Void, by projecting the lyric pain of this discovery in a new species of Counter-Sublime. Like a man always seen going beautifully downhill. Which, Bloom finds, is quite in keeping with the "disastrous" times and makes Ammons the very latest of his cherished latecomers. The poems he chooses as the most telling expression of such counter-prophecy—"Corson's Inlet," "Saliences," "Gravelly Run," "Guide," "Bridge," "Peak," and the lovely passage in "Hibernaculum" that begins ". . . to lean belief the lean word comes,/ each scope adjusted to the plausible:"—are the right poems for his thesis.

Still, one must pause to ask if in his zeal to consecrate only this high-tragical, philosophical Ammons Bloom may not be reserving too much drama to himself and making it too neat. There are facetious or whimsical notes in all but a very few poems that set us on our guard. Also many fine poems that don't cast so much as a glance at these elevations. Maybe Bloom should ask himself whether, if Emerson is the fountainhead of our poetry, we ought not to read as Emersonically as the sage's descendants write, with the same hospitality toward wide swings of mood and purpose, with the same dexterity in matching tone to technique, form to theme. (In formal variety Emerson's own poetry is as "romantically" unstable as Byron's. Sometimes he sounds like Plotinus arranged for a German village band, sometimes, as in the beautiful "Threnody" on the death of his son, like a pure-bred Metaphysical.)

My guess would be that it is neither Emerson nor Whitman (certainly not Whitman) that Ammons is currently undermining but a too portentous Idol of the Tribe called Poetry which, in some of its current academic investitures—subtlety piled on subtlety like the shawls of an Eastern princess—has become a real spook. Bloom is a great potentate who having been given an eloquent nightingale sends it out to be gilded and fitted with a clock-work larynx.

As a matter of fact, Ammons' poems had already begun to group themselves into thematic clusters a good while before he began writing long poems in earnest. To my mind it's the interplay between these clusters that gives Ammons his chief vitality. (pp. 50-2)

Even Bloom acknowledges that this poet was never a naive visionary. Rather, a rueful, sportive, lyrical civil engineer, a musical geo-physician. Who would want to scuttle his prose sense of this transmogrifier of our prosiest disciplines, when he offers so novel a mixture of the contemplative and the suburban-saturnine, makes of "Extremes and Moderations" a pungent ecological fable, turns aside to tell us how to drain a swamp or dig a well, how to pick pears so the branches won't jerk the best ones out of reach, who above all is one of the most accomplished celebrators of the seasonal backyard drama since the great Alfred Lawn Tennyson himself? Rarely dropping his role as *homme moyen américain* Ammons can flourish a vocabulary of "saliences" and "suasions," motions, forces, and forms in mountain, wind, brook, and tree, with no missionary intent to substitute his vocabulary for ours. If he shaped his normally elegant style from examples of Williams, Marianne Moore, Dickinson, Cummings, Dickey, Roethke, or Merwin, he also aspires to their modesty.

Transplanted from the relative solitude of North Carolina to the goldfish prominence of Cornell, he issued a lowbrow

poetics to balance the high, a Leopold Bloom to enliven the Harold. (pp. 53-4)

Diversifications features 65 new poems, most quite short, and two showpieces, "Three Travelogues" and the 19-page "Pray Without Ceasing." Its general effect is of the usual charm, of compactness, assurance, good-humored summary and mild second thoughts. Most of the poems seem thrown off in the intervals of harder work. . . . "Three Travelogues" is another handsome syncretic exercise in auto-intoxication out in the boondocks, pregnant with phrases like "a white-sailed cloud's blue hull of rain." . . . It's too early to say much about "Pray Without Ceasing," a phantasmagoria or verbal happening wherein passages of characteristic eloquence or quiet elegance are answered by tormented newsreel episodes from the Vietnam war, with frantic doodling, demented witticisms, and grim premonitions. My shaky opinion is that he had very little new to say about the poem's ostensible subject, or else put thought aside and ruffed like a grouse, spread like a peacock or cobra. The time of mutation is not yet, not for him, not for us. (pp. 55-6)

> *R. W. Flint, "The Natural Man," in* Parnassus: Poetry in Review *(copyright © by Parnassus: Poetry in Review), Spring-Summer, 1976, pp. 49-56.*

No matter how they deny it—and many do—what writers want is communion; not communication, communion. They want the reader right in there with them, soul to soul. It's a hunger. (And by no means, says the voice at my shoulder, limited to writers alone.)

Once writers could solve their problem by making a story, an allegory, some invented world, into which they invited or enticed the reader, so that both could live there together for a while, soul to soul, in the "willing suspension of disbelief." It worked; it worked for a couple of thousand years. But more and more in our century writers came to feel that the suspension of disbelief was failing, was downright fraudulent, and they turned to formalistic means. They thought, if you can just make the reader participate in the *technique* of writing, then you will have him caught, a willing (but nicely subservient) collaborator in the artistic process. Hence Modernism in all its aspects. Today some poets even publish random words or lines and ask the reader to make his own poem. Conceptualists, I believe, is what they're called.

A. R. Ammons has not gone that far. But he does lay his procedures open to view, often ingratiatingly, so that when he has second thoughts about a word, for instance, he does not cross out the original and substitute the new, he leaves them both there. The correction, amplification, set out in repetition, is not laziness but a real way to make us see how poetic language moves toward intensity and precision. At other times, when he writes a longer piece that isn't quite satisfactory, he puts a paraphrase or counter-thought in the margin. And it's true, afterthought adds to fore-thought, stylistically and substantially, a resonance that lets us *see* the poet's mind in process. It's like reading Emerson's journals, the gathering fragments that became the essays.

Which brings us to Ammons's topic. Emerson's mind was focused on something—many things, tough, resistant things. Ammons writes about anything, randomly. "The Snow Poems" is a long sequence in diary form, even though the poems are undated. I have never read so much verse about the weather in my life; also about decay of consciousness, separation from nature, the sorrow of knowledge; in short, the trivia of a professorial mind in daily academic and domestic life. Often passages of simple wordplay intervene, like infantile regressions ("egad, gasso, glorybe"), or invented or half-invented proverbs ("intercourse is better than no course at all"). Much of this incidentally is bright and attractive. But how it does go on!

> *Why? He says,*
> hello from one who knows nothing
> (and never lets you hear
> the end of it)

But we all know nothing, and we all talk of it endlessly, and this is the human condition; there is value, indubitably, in establishing its presence in art, much value. The poet, ignorant and agonized, at least establishes his existence; he survives. But what of us, his readers? Do we survive, too, by attending to this random scribbling? Ammons doesn't say. . . .

Ammons is famous now, celebrated, a prize-winner, with lots of good poetry behind him, real created poems. But he has begun to maunder. He thinks he is inventing himself in these new poems; but he is only reporting himself. And that is not enough.

In spite of a bright, attractive technique, which could be used perfectly well in real poems, and in spite of occasional lyric parts that remind us of earlier work, "The Snow Poems" is a dull, dull book. The best a reviewer can do for everyone concerned, including the poet, is to say so.

> *Hayden Carruth, "Reader Participation Invited," in* The New York Times Book Review (© *1977 by The New York Times Company; reprinted by permission), September 25, 1977, p. 30.*

*   *   *

ANDERSON, Jon   1940-

Anderson is an American poet. *In Sepia* **is his third collection of poetry. (See also** *Contemporary Authors***, Vols. 25-28, rev. ed.)**

In Sepia has the severe virtue of possessing a central fable to which no poem (not even the Middle English pastiche about two dogs) is irrelevant. The fable might be summed up as follows. We begin, in youth, with the mesmerizing fear of death as the pure opposite to selfhood. But in "the middle years"—as vivid points stand out less from the general flow of time, as we no longer expect our lives to form patterns or stories leading to conclusive revelations, and yet longing remains, diffused into our sense of indefiniteness—our experience of life becomes curiously like our fantasy of death, "The same measure, or passing of time, / Where we dissolve." Thus, in the poem I have been quoting from, "Stories," the desire to shape one's life into a story dissolves in the fascinating monotony of a drive across the Midwest "gliding without force toward / Night & sleep." And in this there is a paradoxical release, or joy. . . . Permanent indefiniteness places us indissolubly in our context, in greater "belief"; it frees us, among other things, from the need to give other people meaning solely in terms of their effect on us, our emotions, our story. But in another poem Anderson endows the matter with a more

sinister beauty: "These are the raptures of falling in space forever."

Anderson's concern with friendship (how central a concern, the title of his second book, *Death & Friends,* suggests) gives a human richness to his work; but it too leads back to the question of ambiguous boundaries. Anderson fears loneliness, and, still more, the false semblances of connection. But he also struggles with extreme experiences of connectedness, both consoling and frightening: the idea of inter-identity ("friends . . . so enclosed within my reasoning / I am occasionally them") and the sense of others' personalities as pure essences, numinous forces. These sensations can never quite be explained away, because they reflect ambiguities in self-perception. Trying to correct the suspicion that people become pure spirits once out of sight, Anderson realizes that he too vanishes, into a translucent but not transparent medium. . . .

For a poet so concerned with imaginative projections of the self, he is curiously sparing in his use of visionary modes—for which . . . he has a considerable gift. Is this, as with Stevens, the sign of an essentially analytical temperament, which it would be foolish to wish different? Or is it a mildly cramping effect of our anti-epiphanic age? A little of both, I suspect. Anderson occasionally shows a slightly embarrassed need to lower his style, as when he begs his favorite poet-hero, "Please John Clare, there was time"—incongruously echoing Frank O'Hara's plea to Lana Turner.

My other reservation seems to me graver, though it applies only to a few passages. Perhaps because Anderson has, by his own admission, "seldom mentioned . . . Those events or names by which / I was compelled to write," I grow uneasy when he takes an elevated moral tone—even in self-deprecation—about his unspecified personal life. The worst, and the only aggressive, instance occurs in "Rosebud," where Anderson asserts that his wife, in directing "an ironic comment" at him, has "hurt the land." There has to be a grain of priggish self-importance here, however many layers of sincere animist feeling have accreted around it. Anderson's justness of tone—perfect for the metaphysical ramifications of relationship—is less reliable on the terrain of strictly emotional autobiography. (pp. 47-9)

> *Alan Williamson, in* Shenandoah *(copyright by* Shenandoah; *reprinted from* Shenandoah: The Washington and Lee University Review *with the permission of the Editor), Fall, 1974.*

In ["In Sepia"], Jon Anderson leaves behind the surface flash associated with the Iowa Writers' Workshop, for philosophical long lines of unostententatious subtlety, influenced by Ashbery and Rilke. The book is an unusually unified meditation, on the approach of the "middle years," the changing sense of death, the pattern of life, and the meaning of friendship. It gives us the mature voice of a poet who has long stood out, in his generation, for the philosophical depth of his subjects. (p. lvi)

> *Virginia Quarterly Review (copyright, 1975, by the* Virginia Quarterly Review, *The University of Virginia), Vol. 51, No. 2 (Spring, 1975).*

Jung said: "One does not become enlightened by imagining figures of light, but by making the darkness conscious."

One is enlightened reading Jon Anderson, but not by light. The book is titled *In Sepia,* the color of old photos, monochrome drawings, the color of dried blood, an exact shade of memory. The language is acutely tuned to remembering —and to the origins of memory. Anderson is writing from the darkness where memory begins, making that darkness conscious.

This book is a history of the imagination—and again the mood is Jungian, Jung being another nonbeliever in "events" of autobiography (for him, only the "memories, dreams and reflections" survive). Anderson lives at that crossing where imagination usurps memory; the act of remembering is of necessity an act of the imagination. He is where "light is nothing / it enters and reflects" but the darkness is germinal . . . "You lie awake / you watch the stars revolve, repeat," "the photograph quickens," "stages of memory darken and go by" and "synapse shuttles through the skull."

Despite the gentle oriental gestures of self-effacement ("Whatever I do, I am always leaving"), these are not poems of death's annihilation or the oblivion of darkness; their preoccupation is with death and the beginnings of self. The resignation of lines like "These are the joys of falling in space forever" or "Out of a cloud I come falling into a cloud" is deceptive. There is an ironically insistent tone, a vague possessiveness for what is lost and irrevocable—the sincerity and compulsiveness, the self-consciousness of the ghost who feels obligated to haunt you. The secret of poetry, "friends," (in case you were wondering) is "cruelty," the "one cold flower" the poet leaves on your windowsill, whose beauty renders you "inconsolable" all day.

This is a quickening before birth, the conspiracy of the unborn: "I had secretly thought to accrue a life / to imply the passage of time / of myself, as citizen from here to there." And

> I desired a single terrible event
> the passage from which would measure time.

The desire for birth and the tremendous loss inherent in being born, of giving oneself life and, simultaneously, death, is a major paradox. The poet is forever sleepwalking between conception and birth—on the level of ideation he is doomed to abstraction, with the impossible task of making the abstract a supportable form, a beginning for the real. "I would remember my conception, not the act." We would not accept this hesitancy, this fanaticism for the philosophically exact from a lesser poet. But this cultivated atropism, this turning-away, is pure, the purity of a poet who almost *is* an idea, who can remember or imagine (the same thing for the unborn) his own death—and knows how, still and all, to survive and to be conscious in survival. (pp. 114-15)

Like Mark Strand, whose influence is felt here, Anderson chooses to tell the "story of our lives," with the same certain sense of loss and anxious arbitrary documentation, the familiar ironic exactitude in "haunting" time—satirizing its content and forging its signature. . . .

These poems of strange, almost unbearable beauty and subtlety are all we need to know forever and for now of ourselves, if we could only read ourselves and tell it out. These poems glow darkly, their strength lies outside of time and in darkness—in the given mysteries, the histories by which we invent ourselves. (p. 116)

Carol Muske, in Parnassus: Poetry in Review *(copyright © by* Parnassus: Poetry in Review*), Spring-Summer, 1976.*

*   *   *

ANDREWS, Cecily Fairfield
See WEST, Rebecca

*   *   *

APPLE, Max   1941-

Apple is an American short story writer and novelist who writes in a satiric vein. His first novel, *Zip: A Novel of the Left and the Right*, is scheduled for publication in 1978.

Max Apple writes fiction the way Claes Oldenburg makes sculptures. His short stories in *The Oranging of America* take American obsessions and fads, myths and habits, and explode them into ingenious symbols with a life all their own. His comic intelligence either magnifies desires like the need to own a home ("My Real Estate") into tangible absurdities or reduces pressing ideological issues to metaphorical jokes, as when Fidel Castro and an American "capitalist" agent compete in a baseball game for the loyalties of a Cuban ex-ballplayer turned revolutionary.

Life is not only a game, Apple's stories seem to say, but a game show ("Noon," for instance, is based on television's *Let's Make a Deal*). They mimic peculiarly American aspirations in matters as grave as economics, politics, and literature. "Inside Norman Mailer" pits the young author, Apple, as "campy lightweight" against Mailer in a prizefight that becomes a struggle for artistic identity and independence. Apple's parables are about pioneers, because in America that is what our deluded dreamers, mad visionaries, and inspired madmen turn out to be. The title story, "The Oranging of America," then, is about Howard Johnson and his mission to spread plastic romance and the "color of the sunset" across the continent. After you have read Apple's version of how "HJ's" faithful but dying secretary is given a cryogenic deep-freeze trailer to die in, those 28 flavors will never taste the same.

Apple's humor is entirely effective. From political morality to private hangups, he hits things right on target by making the familiar into a parody of itself, by letting spoofs show how serious our zany realities are. Much of his brilliance lies in the versatile range of voices he is able to assume and in a talent for punning that leaps into a wonderful realm of linguistic high jinks and buffoonery. Apple pokes fun at high culture and appreciates low, but his own art shades more to the transcendental than the pop. It transforms while it impersonates, changing not only what we see but the way we see it. (p. 40)

Celia Betsky, in Saturday Review *(© 1977 by Saturday Review Magazine Corp.; reprinted with permission), January 22, 1977.*

Fast food and the fast buck, TV game shows and the Astrodome: in these artifacts of American life most writers of fiction sense the odor of decay. But they strike Max Apple —an improbably named and extraordinarily entertaining short story writer—as signs of life, and he writes about them with mischievous wit and generosity. . . .

The Oranging of America overflows throughout with vitality, charm, and good humor; it is an irresistible collection of stories. (p. 96)

Amanda Heller, in The Atlantic Monthly *(copyright © 1977 by The Atlantic Monthly Company, Boston, Mass.; reprinted with permission), February, 1977.*

The Oranging of America And Other Stories . . . is funny and revelatory and moving, particularly the knockout—but oh so sweet and tender—title story. Apple proves once again that literary delight may engage the current mind in a rewarding way even though it deliberately does not confront great issues of immediate consequence. This is healthy and always needed. . . . Apples uses very contemporary strategems in his stories, like real names and absurd-surrealist givens—Fidel Castro figures in one story, Norman Mailer in another, Gerald Ford in a third, and one story posits a gas station with 83 self-serve pumps and 41 urinals—and thereby risks falling off the edge of irony into the wry.

The risk is greater because he declines anger. The stories are positive and cheerful (in the face of insanity) and at root optimistic; they stimulate the aesthetic imagination and gracefully bypass the social concerns and fashionable guilts they obviously acknowledge and to a degree employ. The title story is, as they say, worth the price of the volume. It is, mythologized, about Howard Johnson's search for an America he would create and immortalize in 28 beneficient flavors, and about his own immortalization in life after death; it has nothing at all to do with horrid business practices or cookery corruptions or environmental pollution. It may have to do with God and wistfulness and mortal intentions—I am not sure.

I *am* sure that it is quite the most lovely piece of imaginative writing I have encountered in some years. You go from it happy. That happiness may be viewed as an insult to pressing moral issues that indeed do matter, but I find it reenergizing. Get hold of *The Oranging of America,* laugh and weep over Howard Johnson's dreams, buy an HJ cone (you can taste it in this story), and return to the barricades renewed in spirit and perhaps in determination—that's the feel I get from Apple's book, and I'm grateful for it. (p. 78)

Eliot Fremont Smith, in The Village Voice *(reprinted by permission of* The Village Voice; *copyright © by The Village Voice, Inc., 1977), February 14, 1977.*

*   *   *

ARRABAL, Fernando 1932-

A Moroccan-born French playwright, Arrabal writes in the Theatre of the Absurd tradition. Arrabal attacks in his plays political, theological, linguistic, and psychological restrictions on freedom. A recipient of the Grand Prix du Théâtre, Arrabal is best known for *L'Architecte et l'Empereur d'Assyrie*. (See also *CLC*, Vol. 2, and *Contemporary Authors*, Vols. 9-12, rev. ed.)

[Arrabal's first novel, *Baal Babylone,*] serves as a good introduction to [his] later work, for it is a semi-autobiographical narrative that gives many insights into the dramatist's not too secret traumas. Writing in a deceptively simple, childlike language, Arrabal sets forth the portrait of a Spanish child at a period perhaps immediately after the Civil War. The child's father is gone, but his presence remains vivid for the boy. The child must cling to his father's memory as a means to escape from his odious, oppressive sur-

roundings. It seems that the boy's mother, a domineering woman possessed with her own martyrdom, has denounced the father to the police "for his own good." The mother is thus the prototype for the gallery of sadistic figures who, in Arrabal's theater, cruelly but joyously destroy what they profess to love. In *Baal Babylone* the child refuses to surrender to his mother and her voracious demands. The father's memory thus becomes a symbol of deliverance in the smothering atmosphere where a devouring maternal love is sanctified by the duties the state church would impose upon the child. The boy's silent revolt is made manifest when he exposes himself and urinates before a convent grill. Arrabal's theater, in which exhibitionism, chamber pots, and urinations are frequent images, continues this scatological form of revolt, though in a less symbolic manner. For in his theater, Arrabal's revolt becomes a ritual of assault that attacks with unmediated directness.

Guilt, oppression, sadism, childish revolt, erotic fantasies, matricide, all of these fit together to form a surprisingly coherent dramatic world, whatever may be the excesses that Arrabal gives into at times. And since Arrabal published his first play some ten years ago, his work has undergone an evolution that points to a greater understanding of the theater. He began with short plays, such as *Orison, Fando et Lis,* and *Guernica,* in which the influences of such writers as Ionesco and Adamov is quite evident. His work has evolved toward more complex spectacles in which ritual and ceremony are used to give more stylized expression to his obsessions. Plays such as *Le Grand Cérémonial* and *Concert dans un oeuf* should be viewed as erotic ballets or celebrations into which the spectator should enter for purposes of communion and exorcism. Arrabal has also experimented with "pure" spectacles where a kinetic *mise en scène,* using motifs from Klee, Mondrian, and Delaunay, becomes an abstract drama. In both his ritual and his abstract works, Arrabal again calls to mind Artaud and his call for a total spectacle. . . . In 1967, this search for a freer theater culminated in *L'Architecte et l'Empereur d'Assyrie.* In this play Arrabal attained a synthesis between abstract mime and poetical fantasy, a synthesis which marks his mastery of the stage and perhaps of his personal anxieties. (pp. 174-76)

Baal Babylone's mother-child relation, which might be likened to an inverted Oedipal relationship, is savagely exploited in one of Arrabal's earliest plays, *Les Deux Bourreaux* (translated as *The Executioners*). In this work of patent sadism, the mother-martyr not only turns the father over to the police, but she happily watches as he is tortured by two anonymous executioners. To demonstrate her beneficent affection for him, she rubs salt and vinegar into his wounds, which completes this intentional murder of Laius. In *Les Deux Bourreaux* the mother has two sons, one of whom is a model of filial loyalty toward her. His example points up the rebellion of the ungrateful son who resists his mother's carnivorous affection. Yet the mother is too powerful and convinces the rebel to beg her forgiveness for the unnatural act of turning against maternal love. The father thus disposed of, the mother can retire to enjoy her son's exclusive love.

It would thus appear that an ambivalent Oedipal relationship, although directly portrayed in a relatively limited number of plays, is central to an understanding of Arrabal's fantasies. Two of his later, more developed plays cast more light on the mother-son relation and are worth examining in this respect. The first play, *Le Grand Cérémonial*, is a bizarre "ceremonial" in which a hunchbacked lover, appropriately named Cavanosa, plays the rôle of the doting yet rebellious son. Cavanosa, a seemingly emasculated lover, first claims to have murdered his mother and then claims to have murdered each night a girl whom he has loved. In fact, it seems that he has been reduced to making love to a collection of life-sized dolls that he beats and fondles with equal relish. Yet if Cavanosa is capable of transferring the erotic relationship he has with his mother, his only gesture of love can be to kill the woman he has taken to bed—the bed being the altar on which he sacrifices to the demands of maternal love. The suggested pattern of homicidal coitus is broken by Sil, a lover who, against her will, escapes death. She is offered to the mother as a slave to be tortured at the mother's pleasure. Such is the price of love in Arrabal's theater, where no amorous affair can be complete without whips and chains, or at least the confining prison of a baby carriage. And a more striking portrayal of a repressed Oedipal development, displaced as it may be, can hardly be imagined. (p. 176)

For Arrabal, then, love, as derived from the mother-son symbiosis, is either a form of bondage or a homicidal activity. Slavery and murder form the two poles of love's dialectic. So it is hardly surprising that sadism, a mediator that reconciles both bondage and destruction, is love's principal manifestation in this theater of violent fantasy.... Arrabal's theater of sadism seems to be a direct reply to Artaud's cry for "a new idea of eroticism and cruelty" in the theater.... The metaphysics of cruelty is at the heart of Arrabal's theater. Metaphysics, as Artaud used the term in its original sense, means a world beyond the world that naturalistic and even lyrical theater had tried to incorporate as stage reality. Theatrical metaphysics is, to recall the language of Arrabal's manifesto, the sublimation of the theater, the "raising up" and the creation of new fantasies that can be celebrated only on the autonomous stage. Thus the theater, seen in this light, seems to be the most natural outlet for Arrabal's obsessions with eroticism and cruelty, obsessions that have led him to the creation of ritual forms that present, in Artaud's sense, a metaphysics of sadism. (pp. 177-78)

A more traditional portrayal of sadism is to be found in *Fando et Lis*. These two infantile lovers are hopelessly traveling to Tar, an enigmatic land possessing the same degree of reality as Kafka's castle. Lis, a paralytic, rides in a baby carriage pushed by Fando. Fando feels a continual compulsion to put chains on his captive inamorata, and when she complains, he finally beats her to death in a fit of childish rage. He is immediately and uncomprehendingly repentant for his act, but his repentance is quite as meaningless as the murder itself. The dramatic force of *Fando et Lis* is not in its neo-Kafka statement of absurdity nor in its assault upon the banalities of language and pseudo-logic. Beckett and Ionesco are certainly more convincing than Arrabal in conveying a drama of existential anguish or in conjuring the destructive powers of words. Rather it is in the creation of a closed world of childish sadism and erotic bondage that Arrabal is an original and forceful playwright. The infantile mentality of most of Arrabal's non-heroes allows him to exploit his themes of sadism and violence with a comic sense that would be denied to a theater of more mature protagonists. His retarded characters play at "forbidden games" which mix horror and tenderness in dreamlike proportions. Yet his characters, ideal partners for the Oedipal relationship in this respect, are endowed with very adult sexual powers and lusts.

In spite of their homicidal fury, most of Arrabal's protagonists, as children, retain their innocence, or at least the innocence that *non compos mentis* confers.... Arrabal's characters often play at being criminals, but, their childish innocence notwithstanding, they are subject to bloody reprisals they cannot hope to grasp.

The obsessive quest for goodness that Arrabal's infantile heroes undertake serves as a counter-motif to their sadism and lusty criminality. Arrabal's retarded lovers feel remotely the need to be good, to stop killing or fornicating, although their search for goodness is usually as senseless a whim as their casual murders. (pp. 178-79)

The desire for goodness in Arrabal's plays is a negative motif that, by its comic futility, points up the blatant cruelty that his characters decidedly prefer. One can also see that the manic quest for goodness in its most puerile form is a part of the obsession with childishness and, hence, a part of the child-parent fantasy that pervades Arrabal's theater. Goodness as a negation is largely equated with repressing erotic desires, which, in turn, must be viewed in light of the infantile fear of sexuality that runs throughout the plays.

For another aspect of Arrabal's dialectic of goodness and sadism is his obsessive fear of the sexual act.... [The] mother-son relation carries with it a fear of defilement that counterbalances his sexual fantasies. Defilement must lead to destruction, as in *Le Couronnement (The Coronation)*, where loss of virginity causes death.... Sadism in Arrabal can quickly become a form of anti-eroticism, however enthusiastically his characters may fornicate in chains. This anti-eroticism is undoubtedly infantile, as are his characters' sadistic antics; it is nonetheless a strong motif as Arrabal's creation of a dramatic tension founded on lustful bondage and sterile destruction. An anti-eroticism grounded in fear establishes one limit to Arrabal's fantasy world.

Just as in *Baal Babylone* the child's father was an absent presence that weighed upon the child, in Arrabal's theater it is God the Father whose absence is felt everywhere. In *Baal Babylone* the father represented a source of deliverance. In the theater an inversion occurs, perhaps illustrating another aspect of the ambivalent mother-son relation and, more especially, showing that God the Father, being identified with the mother, becomes the figure against whom it is necessary to revolt. For in the theater God is a stifling force that must be exorcized by various forms of blasphemy. Arrabal's blasphemy is peculiarly Catholic and Spanish.... Arrabal's characters often have a personal hatred of God; yet, their anger with Him is often a result of His refusal to exist. It is difficult to revolt against the absent Father.

While considering the religious motif, special commentary should be given to *La Cimetière des voitures*. This play has received the most criticism and has been dismissed, on the one hand, for its contrived cleverness and, on the other hand, for the degrading image it presents.... The play does set forth an image of total degradation, but it should also be seen as a mock passion play—one with sociological overtones perhaps. This passion play is another aspect of

Arrabal's rebellious parody of religion, but it also seems to be an attempt to portray a religious vision for our time. *La Cimetière des voitures* is ambiguous, since it is both blasphemous buffoonery and a celebration honoring the dead Father's vestigial presence in the presence of his crucified son.

A final important motif in Arrabal's theater is that of the police state and its arbitrary powers of oppression and torture. Arrabal's experience during the Spanish Civil War is sufficient to explain his obsession with this nightmarish fantasy. In *Les Deux Bourreaux,* as shown previously, the mother is associated with the executioners in this theater where pointless cruelty receives the sanction of a nameless, omnipotent state. Indeed, for Arrabal the state is defined through its capacity to inflict torture. *La Bicyclette du condamné (The Condemned Prisoner's Bicycle)* gives a variation on this theme when the lascivious lover Tasia allows another nameless pair of executioners to kill her beloved, her final, characteristic act being to nail him in his coffin. Another play, *Le Labyrinthe,* shows that Kafka's influence is as much at the heart of Arrabal's vision of universal guilt and condemnation as is Franco's Spain. Resembling a dramatized version of *The Trial, Le Labyrinthe* is set in a forest of blankets from which a traveler, Etienne, cannot escape. The forest's owner, a father figure possessing absolute power over his domain, chains Etienne to a urinal. In breaking his chains Etienne is brutal to a fellow prisoner who, though nearly paralyzed, hangs himself. Etienne is tried for murder and commits a series of errors that inexorably bring about his condemnation. The play is remarkable for its creation of an atmosphere where innocence, or near innocence, is forced to impeach itself by the relentless logic of arbitrary power. In a comparable fashion, *Guernica,* a play inspired by Picasso's painting, also depicts a universe founded upon guilt. A nameless officer's stare and the sight of his handcuffs are enough to implicate in guilt those who are helplessly caught in the war's anonymous destruction. Authority, whatever form it may take in Arrabal, is synonymous with gratuitous persecution. The absent father, the possessive mother, and the anonymous state all share this feature.

Arrabal's obsessive fantasies have given rise to a body of work that is among the most promising of the New Theater. With the modernity of a happening and the courage to face the delirium of our times, it may well come to be among the most significant in this second half of the twentieth century. (pp. 180-83)

Allen Thiher, in Modern Drama *(copyright © 1970, University of Toronto, Graduate Centre for Study of Drama; with the permission of* Modern Drama*), May, 1970.*

The latest volume of Arrabal's theatre [*Théâtre 8*] contains what the dramatist calls "Deux opéras paniques," *Ars amandi* and *Dieu tenté par les mathématiques.* The juxtaposition of the two appears to be an exercise in antithetical relations.

Ars Amandi belongs to the tradition of *haut baroque* favored by this most Spanish of self-exiled artists. Since no composer has yet been found for this work, the game of matching a group of musicians, dead and living, to the play proves revealing. . . .

Fridigan, the Parsifal of this mock-ceremony, at once sacred and profane, is embarked on a search for a missing friend, Erasme Marx—the perfect amalgam in name of Renaissance and modern humanism. On his way, the hero encounters the giantess Lys, a Venus in whose garden flower a wide variety of sado-masochistic delights. Two angel-demons, Bana and Ang (could they be body and soul?) attend on this creature who shifts from implacable mistress to victim and martyr. In a gallery of Lys' medieval castle, life-size mannequins briefly enact the myths they represent: the state of childhood (Le Petit Poucet, Pinocchio), nightmarish fears (Frankenstein, Dracula, King Kong), eternal love (Romeo), jealous passion (Othello), primitive nature (Tarzan), thirst for knowledge (Faust), self-sacrificing *agape* (Christ, Don Quixote). The pantomime plays within the play are forms of initiation. Only by observing the mannequins' interpretation of their own lives or of one another's can Fridigan learn something about the human race, and thus about himself.

When this knight errant first espies Lys she is a gigantic figure covered with swarms of insects (flies? bees?). From the start we feel that Fridigan is torn between fascination and horror at the sight of this Géante turned Charogne. Baudelaire comes to mind, for Fridigan might wish to "Parcourir à loisir ses formes magnifiques," were he not repulsed by the buzzing of batallions of flies. Yet we must keep in mind that Baudelaire's Charogne is strangely sensual as she lies "Les jambes en l'air, comme une femme lubrique," and even alive in the very process of decay.

When Lys is shown next, she is normal-size and engaged in painting a single word from a model. The model says OUI whereas Lys is sketching a large NON on the canvas. Clearly, Fridigan is about to enter an antiworld.

In this universe speech is replaced by singing, but Arrabal makes it eminently clear that this is not a nobler mode of expression. Bana and Ang sing because they stutter when they attempt to speak. Out of politeness, Fridigan imitates them, as Lys does out of charity. . . . Also, as in Pirandello, appearances are constantly shifting, relations changing. (p. 949)

Could Lys be Spain, or the Spanish people? . . . If the Spanish motif is emphasized by the projections of Goya's paintings . . ., other elements indicate that the nationalist aspect is only a minor theme of this opera. It is in fact a poetic recreation of the history of humanity of which man's inhumanity to man is an essential part. This is the significance of the *tableaux muets* played out by the mannequins whose surrealist groupings mockingly reveal the diversity of man's imaginings. Even in this play within a play the characters do not always play themselves. A Christ-like Fridigan, holding an olive branch, watches this bit of Theatre of the Ridiculous. He is deeply moved, and we are made aware that this moment parallels Parsifal's first introduction to the Fisher-King's court. Like Parsifal, Fridigan is still a fool at this time, and his pity is sentimental self-indulgence.

In the course of the play, the hero will have to come to terms with pain and degradation. A Circe-like Lys will bring him down into the mud where they wallow together. She orders Fridigan to prove his love by accepting vilification. . . . Erotic bliss is followed by images of death. The scene is set for an operation. Fridigan accepts to receive from Lys a mysterious injection. "Je sais que vous voulez me tuer comme vous avez tué mon ami. Mais j'accepte tout.''. . . Indeed, right after the injection, Fridigan sees his friend Erasme Marx. They are standing against a soft, pink wall. ''Where is Lys?'' wonders Fridigan, and Erasme answers: ''She's with us.'' Lys is once again the giantess of the opening scene, and the two friends are part of her body.

Now we know that Lys was the All, the cosmos. The insects swarming on her form were human beings. Having traveled through the world and the antiworld, Fridigan, the hero, has learned to give up the rational. Only then can he rejoin the dead humanist, Erasme Marx. Arrabal's Baroque cathedral has turned into a Khmer temple.

Dieu tenté par les mathématiques is an abstract stage-setting written to illustrate the abstract composition of Jean-Yves Bosseur. Bosseur's ''musical battle field'' is shared by seventeen musicians who are not told what musical instrument each must play. The score indicates only temporal relations loosely connecting visual and sonorous effects. This is a French equivalent of a John Cage-Merce Cunningham happening.

To match the calculated freedom of Bosseur's composition, Arrabal has invented a series of planes, surfaces, spinning objects, skipping rubber balls together with live actors as impersonal as—or perhaps more so than—the acting objects. The result is a fascinating ''orchestration théâtrale,'' as spare as the panic opera is lush. It bears perhaps more novelty for a potential European audience than for Americans who have been exposed to many such manifestations. The same could also be said of the Opera which has little to add to the innovations of the Theatre of the Ridiculous. Arrabal is at his best when his theatricality is less gratuitous, when he deals with a theme which enlists his passions, such as his play about prisoners in one of Franco's jails . . . *Et ils passèrent des menottes aux fleurs.* (p. 950)

> *Rosette C. Lamont, in* French Review, *April, 1971.*

Fernando Arrabal, in describing his more recent theater as a *ceremonie ''panique''* provides a valuable clue for understanding his earlier works. For this young Spanish playwright, who is better known in France than in his own country, theater is a rigorously ordered ceremony wherein it is indispensable that, beneath an apparent disorder, the presentation be a model of precision, in order that the chaotic confusion of life may be reflected with mathematical clarity. Such concern for precision, though achieving its purest expression in the ''*Théâtre panique*,'' is manifestly evident in a 1958 work, not included in the ''*panique*'' and largely ignored by critics, *La Bicyclette du Condamné.* In this one-act piece, the playwright achieves order within chaos by virtue of a circular structure which encompasses even the stage properties and goes far beyond the paradoxical juxtaposition of love-cruelty, goodness-evil, child-man usually mentioned as basic characteristics of Arrabal's work. (p. 205)

As dramatic structure, the circle is eminently appropriate to contemporary theater, for it aptly parallels modern man's effort to extricate himself from the chaos left by the dissolution of traditional values—a chaos no less terrifying than that confronted by primitive man. The inevitable result of such circular structure, however, is to leave the spectator in a quandary as to those elements which are missing from the circle itself—beginning, middle, end. Therefore, the staged action seems to be devoid of reason for being, of action itself, and of resolution. Thus, in . . . *La Bicyclette du Condamné,* the audience is hard put to know: Who is the condemned man? What is his crime? Who has condemned him? What will be the ultimate result of his punishment? Even were the play's elements to be reduced to pure interaction, without recourse to dialogue (as is actually the case in many of this writer's later ''*panique*'' works), a distinct circularity would be pervasive, not only as evidenced by the almost countless entrances and exits of personages, but also by all of the stage properties which have such an important function throughout Arrabal's work.

Critics are quick to point out several curious juxtapositions which typify the work of this playwright, among them the childlike mentality of sexually mature individuals, the sadistic cruelty of morally innocent creatures, the castigating actions of the victim. More than merely paradoxical juxtapositions, however, these dichotomies constitute the by-products of a circular structure whose significance lies in the playwright's announced intention to portray with clarity the chaos of man's existence. At times, this structure will define the confused configurations of organized justice and religion, at other times the violent bestiality of love, and at others the inane impersonality of war. Here, in *La Bicyclette du Condamné,* the structure conveys the inchoate identification between freedom and condemnation. It is by means of a systematic analysis of the circular structure in Arrabal's work that meaning will become clear in this and other pieces which at first glance may appear to be meaningless games. It is also by virtue of understanding this dramatic structure that the critic can avoid the contention that Arrabal is ''more a visionary than a dramatist'' who should move in the direction of ''the creation of a series of ever-moving tableaux,'' since the static quality does not suit his work. Neither tableaux nor the static are Arrabal's technique, and in his circularity lies one of his claims to originality.

Briefly, in *La Bicyclette du Condamné,* the action takes place around the piano of Viloro, whose principal goal seems to be to play the C-scale perfectly, despite an unexplained prohibition against his playing by Paso and Two Men. Viloro's efforts, sometimes successful but more often fruitless, are constantly interrupted by the alternating appearances of his beloved Tasla on her bicycle dragging a caged Paso to his torturers and executioners, and of an inexplicably free Paso in the company of Two Men, who subject Viloro to progressively more confining punishments for his transgression of their prohibition against piano-playing. (Never is it suggested that there exists any logical reason for the prohibition nor for Paso's imprisonment and Tasla's inescapable duty to transport condemned men.) Interspersed among these interruptions are erotic episodes wherein Tasla engages in pursuits of and escapes from Paso and the Two Men. The play ends in the death, not of Paso, but of Viloro at the hands of Paso, followed by echoes of the same mocking laughter and piano scales with which the curtain opened (figuratively speaking, since Arrabal's plays seldom open with a curtain). Throughout the action, the spectator has been confronted by first a free Viloro and an apparently imprisoned Paso, then by a free Paso and a confined Viloro, then again by the imprisoned Paso and free Viloro, alternating appearances which recur *ad infinitum.* Since the play's final scene reproduces in acoustical and symbolic form one of the play's recurrent episodes, the action comes full circle back to what may be termed a beginning in linear structure but is merely one of the cyclic phases in this play's circular structure.

Thus, the essential blocks of action are seen to follow a circular arrangement, since they offer a repetitive rhythm involving apparently condemned individuals. . . . [The] repetitive pattern is not truly terminated, but rather is brought back to the beginning, where the same question confronts the spectator: Who has been condemned to what? Paso, apparently doomed in the beginning and at significant intervals throughout the play, emerges free of his imprisonment in the end. Viloro, apparently free at the outset and at regular points throughout the play, ultimately replaces the caged man. The implication of the basic problem of the condemned man's identification, then, extends to include the question of freedom, and the circular structure of the work leaves the spectator with the somewhat inconclusive awareness that the burden of freedom is essentially the same kind of punishment as that of condemnation.

Furthermore, within . . . blocks of action . . ., equally precise circularity is evident, and it is here that objects and sounds are used to great effect in support of the play's basic structure. As the play opens, Viloro, alone on stage, futilely attempts to pick out a C-scale on his piano, but his efforts evoke only laughter from Two Men behind a wall and then from Paso. This motif of the musical scale, then, with its repetitive return to the beginning, provides the acoustical counterpart of the structure which configures the entire play. In addition, the rhythmic *abc* pattern of this first sub-block of action (Viloro alone playing scales—appearance of Two Men—appearance of Paso) is repeated after each of Tasla's trips with the caged Paso. Just as Viloro always returns to his piano scales, the action of the play always returns to the isolated Viloro subjected to his tormentors.

This acoustical pattern shows a significant refinement in its relationship to those larger blocks of action wherein Viloro is subjected to progressively more restrictive punishments. . . . [The] acoustical phase of the play's circular structure echoes the fundamental identification of freedom with condemnation, for it is precisely during his periods of greatest confinement and restriction that Viloro demonstrates his greatest freedom to play the piano as he wishes with the success he strives for, unencumbered by timidity and ridicule.

Objects also carry out the cyclical pattern of the work. In addition to repeated appearances of the bicycle and wheeled cage, whose very construction exhibits circularity and which travel on a circuitous path, Tasla and Viloro exchange the same gifts over and over again—a balloon, a chamber pot, and an infantile song composed first by Viloro and then Tasla. They day-dream in circles, longing for the day when Tasla will be free of carting condemned men around and Viloro will be left in peace to play the piano as much as he likes. Ironically, though, their dreams also include a repetition of their present activities, for Tasla promises to tow Viloro in her cage, and he promises to relieve her on the bicycle occasionally while she sits in the cage. Here again, the inextricable link between Viloro and Paso, freedom and condemnation, is maintained, as it also is suggested in the promise Viloro extracts from Tasla to send him a kiss for every lash applied to Paso in the torture chamber.

Even the bicycle exhibits this same relationship to the freedom-condemnation conundrum, for Tasla somehow is condemned to carry condemned men by means of her bicycle. Yet, as she yearns for the day when she will be free, she dreams in terms of that same bicycle. Similar confusion exists in regard to the cage itself, which in the action of the play is a prison but in Viloro's dream is equated with freedom. Thus, the use of these wheeled conveyances to remove his body following his final punishment is in some way, not only a comdemnation, but a deliverance into the freedom he and Tasla had dreamed of.

The play, then, reflects the human chaos as it pertains to the dilemma of freedom and condemnation, yet that reflection is constructed upon an intricately precise labyrinth of concentric circles extending from purely physical appearances and objects, through acoustical realms, until finally it comprises the very human condition itself. Conspicuously, the dialogue provides little clarification of the play's apparent disorder, and in this regard, Arrabal's insistence upon the precision of the *mise en scène* becomes more significant, for the result of that negation of dialogue as the tool by which chaos is rigorously ordered into ceremonial clarity is to demand of both audience and critic a strict attention to the non-linguistic structure of this play and all of Arrabal's work. (pp. 205-09)

> *Beverly J. Delong-Tonelli, in* Modern Drama *(copyright © 1971, University of Toronto, Graduate Centre for Study of Drama; with the permission of* Modern Drama*), September, 1971.*

"My theatre is not surrealist and is not only realist," declares Fernando Arrabal; "it is realist including the nightmare." *Le théâtre panique* is the term he prefers for it—the theater of panic—playfully suggesting that Pan is the real muse or deity of the theater and seriously reiterating the Artaudian concept that panic should be one of the primary emotions evoked in an audience.

No one would deny that there are elements of realism, perhaps even of naturalism, in Arrabal's plays. In fact, it is these very elements, and the recognition they elicit, that give to his work that Kafkaesque or nightmarish quality for which it is partly known. In *Guernica,* for example, his play inspired by the Picasso canvas of the same title, such realistic touches as the old woman's being caught in the water closet, the rubble continuing to cascade about the characters, and the simple, earthy dialogue abut urination and erection contribute immeasurably to the audience's unconscious realisation that Fanchou and Lira are real people who suffer privately and personally from the larger, public gestures of war and oppression.

But that Arrabal's theater is not surrealistic is another matter, and one which bears some looking into.

Surrealism is of course a frame of mind, a way of seeing, and cannot be easily caught in a formula. It has its historical aspects, notably in the *Manifestoes* of André Breton and in the theories and practice of a number of Breton's friends and associates. But it is also ahistorical, existing, to various degrees, *sans* definition, in such various places as *Alice in Wonderland, The Cherry Orchard,* and *Mother Courage.* The question is not one of Arrabal's claiming to be or not to be a surrealist, but of whether there are significant surrealistic tendencies in his works.

It may hardly be accounted insignificant that two of Arrabal's admitted literary masters, Dostoevsky and Kafka, exhibited certain surrealist characteristics, such as the yoking of the normal and the grotesque; experimentation with moral deviation and its consequences or lack of consequences; fascination with "innocent" characters; derailing straightforward, narrative action in favor of affective studies; and conflation of the dreaming and waking worlds, resulting in a kind of continual nightmarishness. It hardly requires verification to say that these are precisely the points at which Arrabal follows his mentors most devotedly. . . . [What] he has studied in them are the dissonances and atonalities, the delirium and the wildness, the breaking loose of hell and the subconscious, and the surrealistic bedlam that is a result of these things.

Nor can it be overlooked that the principal theoretician of the kind of theater Arrabal has been interested in, Antonin Artaud, considered himself a surrealist and was, until renounced by Breton, a member of the "official" surrealist group. Artaud wanted a theater where the audience would be disoriented from its world of traditional values and ways of looking at things, where it would be threatened, harassed, and upended until it saw beyond what it commonly called reality to the openness and possibilities of *sur*-reality. He advocated using words as missiles instead of as symbols, and turning the theater into a den of nonsense and cacophony, so that speech and idea would be no refuge from the swollen realm of dreams and disorder. Lights would be used in a similar fashion, not to create illusion but to shatter it, to leave the audience no place to hide. The audience must be *assaulted:* else the theater has not been true to its primitive, more traumatic origins. (pp. 210-11)

There is, in addition, a kind of *visual* quality about Arrabal's scenes that has been characteristic of most surrealist drama since Apollinaire. It is as if many of them, and not in *Guernica* alone, were fashioned with the Picasso-eye. Few playwrights, outside the movement which included Albert-Birot, Tzara, Cocteau, and Artaud, have made settings so integrally important to the theatrical emotion or experience aimed at in the play. The shambles of *Guernica*, the blanket-maze, of *The Labyrinth*, and the broken automobile hulks of *The Car Cemetery* create images which are surrealist at the same time that they serve important functions. In fact, their being surrealist serves an important function by pitching everything at a level of direct and immediate apprehension, which is a level beyond that normally required by the theater, of mere logic and the manipulation of symbols. Arrabal's scenes do something to the mind *through the eye*. They achieve the effect of paintings or visual spectacles, and thus appear almost multi-media, though of course they are not.

These indications are sufficient in themselves, it would seem, to dispel Arrabal's protestations that he is not a surrealist. It only remains to be seen how programmatically he follows the concerns of those who formally called themselves surrealists. For that, a more careful demonstration is in order.

(1) The primary emphasis of all the surrealists was on the recovery of man's wholeness through a denial of all traditional systems and methods of logic, and on rejoining the separated spheres of his dreaming and waking states. (pp. 211-12)

By Arrabal's own definition ("realist including the nightmare"), there is something dreamlike or nightmarish about his plays. They respect few rules of logic. Two soldiers from opposing lines meet and dine together with the parents of one of them (*Picnic on the Battlefield*); a girl's lash-wounds appear and disappear miraculously (*The Labyrinth*); a man devours the flesh of another man and is suddenly transformed into the other man (*The Architect and the Emperor of Assyria*); two men need some money to rent a tricycle, cold-bloodedly kill a man to get it, and then don't understand why they are apprehended by the police (*The Tricycle*). Causality and morality are abrogated. *Le rêve éveillé* is the order of the day.

(2) Because the sense of definition is not yet so pronounced in childhood, the surrealists tended to glorify the child's stage of life. Like the Dadaists before them, they delighted in playing games, actual children's games, and at behaving with the zaniness of youngsters even in the most public places. (pp. 212-13)

Critics refer repeatedly to Arrabal's childlike stance, as though his characters were innocents in some violated paradise, unable to comprehend their mishaps or destinies. He has spoken of his fealty to Lewis Carroll, and demonstrates certain affinities for that English fantasist. But the childlike perspective from which most of his works are written is primarily a matter of his own personal experience. If there is something infantile about the characters in *Orison, The Tricycle, The Condemned Man's Bicycle,* and all of his other plays, it is because Arrabal himself refuses to look at the world through the eyes of an adult. It is a matter of rebellion. He does not accept the world as seen and fashioned by adults. . . .

Most of Arrabal's characters have childish, unsophisticated minds. Although the world they inhabit is an adult's world, their reaction to everything is spontaneous and unpredictable. Emanou, the strangely incompetent Christ-figure of *The Car Cemetery,* performs a child's acts—stealing roasted almonds, memorizing nonsensical aphorisms, and playing his trumpet—and is totally incapable of comprehending why the police are after him. (p. 213)

Games are important too. *The Coronation,* with a character named Arlys who is an obvious reincarnation of Alice from the looking-glass stories, is full of various kinds of games and tricks, especially card games. . . .

Implicit in this is a significance which Gershman did not attribute to games, namely that they provide occasions for subverting and circumventing the barriers of the conscious mind, so that the hidden self erupts into view. . . . It is probable that the surrealists intuitively turned to games for a similar purpose—to eliminate the false boundaries between the divided spheres of human reality.

(3) One game invented by children, according to the surrealist, is language. It presumably began with nonsense syllables and random syntax, as most children go through periods when they simply "bubble" language for the fun of it. Then phrases and sentences were made and assigned arbitrary significance. But the adults who sprang from the children became more and more serious about linguistic patterns, and so ultimately wound up in slavery to what had begun in play and freedom. The surrealists deplored this outcome, and wished to break language loose again from its designated meanings, to free it once more for joyous and nonsensical expression. (p. 214)

Breton and the surrealists continued this interest in abstract language, for they believed it to be more closely related to the subconscious than ordinary language. (p. 215)

[Arrabal's] dialogue is sometimes merely simple and unstudied, like that of children. At other times it is clearly nonsensical. . . .

Or again, Arrabal's characters frequently speak with mere silliness or repetitiousness. In *Picnic on the Battlefield,* for instance, the two soldiers seem to mimic each other, using identical lines again and again. In *Fando and Lis,* whole passages are repeated in the play, with the effect of destroying the time continuum, or turning it back on itself. . . .

(4) The surrealists also had a childlike respect for superstitions, psychic phenomena, reincarnation, alchemy, and magic—for anything purporting to abrogate nature or natural law. (p. 216)

Since *The Architect and the Emperor of Assyria,* with its trick at the end where the Architect, who is eating the Emperor's body, stoops under the table to retrieve a bone and reappears as the Emperor, Arrabal has demonstrated an increasing fondness for theatrical japes, legerdemain, and mystification. In *Solemn Communion* a necrophile with a serpent between his legs gets in a coffin with a girl's nude body in it; then the girl who has just been prepared for communion stabs the necrophile, getting blood on her white dress, and laughs while red balloons rise from the coffin to the ceiling. *Striptease of Jealousy* shows a statue of a nude girl coming to life and being beaten to death and put back on her pedestal. *The Impossible Loves* is a fantasy about a princess with two beaux, one with the head of a dog and one with the head of a bull, and a father with the head of an elephant. *The Coronation* is a long play which constantly features mystifying rites, necromancy, and double identities.

In one of the clearest statements he has made about what he attempts to do in the theater, Arrabal says: "I dream of a theatre where humor and poetry, *panic* and love would be fused. Poetry is born from the nightmare and its mechanism, excess. The theatrical rite—the *panic* ceremony—must be looked upon by the spectator as a kind of sacrifice. This infinitely free type of theatre which I envisage has nothing to do with anti-theatre or with the Theatre of the Absurd. It's a vast domain, shrouded in ambiguities, and patrolled very carefully by the mad hound which stalks the night."

(5) Closely related to the surrealist desire for a spontaneous universe is the surrealist disregard for religion, especially formal, dogmatic religion. Baudelaire and Lautréamont and Rimbaud had already established a French tradition for necrophilia and admiration of evil. The surrealists were generally freer from the "protest" impulse, and more given to hijinks and hilarity, but Artaud, in his famous play *Jet of Blood,* announced the death of God, and, in his journals, wrote scathing denunciations of the papacy. It was inevitable that any theater tracing history from Alfred Jarry's *Ubu Roi,* with its spoofing of authority, its bumptious tomfoolery, and its scatological language, should continue with an air of insouciance, irreverence, and even, on occasion, downright blasphemy.

Arrabal seems to derive from both Artaud and Jarry in such matters. His novel *The Burial of the Sardine* . . . is really a dream account of a Spanish passion parade filled with blaspheming priests, naked, urinating women, phallic symbols, peacocks' heads, and an old man wanting to die and screaming for a poisonous host. There is also a description of God as a king on a throne drawn by four Cadillacs and surrounded by eighty old men clad in white and adorned by phallic symbols. In *The Architect and the Emperor of Assyria* the distaste for Spanish religion is combined with Jarryesque language: the Emperor calls God a "son of a bitch," and entones operatically, "Shit on God. Shit on his divine image. Shit on his omnipresence." *The Labyrinth* is an elaborate allegory impugning the justice and goodness of the Creator, who is pictured as a despotic maze-maker arbitrarily persecuting people who stumble into his maze. *The Car Cemetery* is a parody of the Crucifixon, with a naive trumpet-player being flogged to death and finally borne out, cruciform-wise, on the handlebars of his bicycle.

Like Genet, on the other hand, Arrabal tends to think of theater in terms of ritual. . . . By pushing ideas to the extreme, to excess, the artist evokes something rare and exciting. It can hardly be called the transcendent or the numinous, for it often rises out of blasphemy and sacrilege. But it is the nearest thing to religious ecstasy outside of religion itself, a kind of secular transport which depends in part on a special quality in the dangerous act of defying the holy authority. It is very near to what participants in the Black Mass experience, only without the dedication to evil. And, in Arrabal, it frequently requires for its climax an actual immolation, as in *Guernica, The Car Cemetery,* and *The Coronation.* "The putting to death," as Arrabal calls it, is somehow related to the ultimate "exaltation of life."

(6) Because the surrealists emphasized the continuity between the physical and psychical aspects of experience, the conscious and the unconscious, they were able, at least in appearance, to minimize the importance of death as a boundary to human existence. (pp. 217-19)

Arrabal is Spanish, of course, and should be expected to exhibit an Iberian sensitivity to death as both a finality and a focus for religious feeling. The one play where both touches appear to be present is the brief piece called *Orison,* in which a man and woman, seated by a child's coffin draped in black, talk of leading a good life, a life ordered according to the Bible. The deaths of the father in *The Two Executioners,* Lis in *Fando and Lis,* Zapo and Zopo in *Picnic on the Battlefield,* and Emanou in *The Car Cemetery* have a kind of finality about them, although the last case is mitigated somewhat by the birth of a child at the time of Emanou's "crucifixion," suggesting the myth of return or cyclicality. But if we consider that *Orison,* for all its funereal air, may be only ironic (it is possible that the dead child is only imaginary, one whose existence was blocked by contraception), or even some kind of deadpan joke, and that in the other plays death occurs in the midst of highly fanciful situations, we can only wonder whether Arrabal is typically serious about the act of dying at all. (p. 219)

Indeed, part of the strange, almost inebriating quality of Arrabal's theater may lie in the way he actually combines the Spanish sense of tragedy with the light-hearted, finally imperturbable mood of the surrealists. He is much gayer and more *soufflant* in the end than Ionesco, who, for all his japes and jests, is basically sad and depressed about existence.

(7) The mention of gaiety suggests another area of relationship between Arrabal and surrealism: humor. The unity of contradictions, which the surrealists continually preached, is in a sense the primary basis of humor. That is, comedy proceeds from the resolving of conflicting states, the humiliating of the proud, the elevating of the just. It is no wonder, then, that there was a certain zaniness, a persistent air of fun and humor, about most of the surrealists, at least in their more public aspects. . . . Humor was the one answer to disaster and chaos.

The humorous approach to life permeates almost everything Arrabal has written. It is not a matter of Byron's "If I laugh at any mortal thing, 'tis that I may not weep," but of something much more positive. Life is a wonder, it is full of *le Merveilleux,* and even the suffering is part of a spectacle. One never assumes, therefore, that tragedy is tragic. He never learns that the stove will burn him a second time merely because it has done so the first time. The world is a child's world, a garden of paradise with snakes and monsters. Because there are snakes and monsters, there are nightmares, interruptions of bliss. But nightmares are never crystallized into worldviews, the way they are with most of us, so that they repress us and impose tyrannical patterns on our existence. They are merely there, and we can still laugh and enjoy ourselves.

So there are jokes all the way through a serious piece like *Guernica,* and silliness in an earnest play like *Picnic on the Battlefield,* and burlesque among the profound themes of *The Architect and the Emperor of Assyria.* If life is dark, it is also light. If oppressed, free. If sober, giddy. And the surrealist mind, from Jarry to Dali to Arrabal, cannot help seeing the fun. Arrabal does tend to deal with more serious themes than the average surrealist, and to appreciate the weight of suffering in the world; but his response to these is basically that of one whose vision has been formed or altered by surrealist masters.

(8) There is one significant way in which Arrabal does differ from many of the surrealists, or at least from "official" surrealist theory, and that is in the treatment of the females in his plays.

Wallace Fowlie, in writing about Picasso's relations to surrealism, has spoken of a prominent combination of "eroticism and violence" in surrealistic art. On this ground alone, Arrabal would not appear to diverge from the surrealist position. The women in his plays . . . are erotic, even the mothers and older women. And they do, perhaps in part because of this erotic character, induce a sense of violence and unrest. They oppose the men, even when they love them, and constitute a polarity for both resistance and persecution. The so-called "war of the sexes" is a very real part of human existence, and Arrabal guarantees its being waged constantly and fiercely.

But another aspect of the surrealists' opinion about women was much closer than this one to the views of the medieval troubadours and poets of courtly love. . . . As Nadeau points out, the surrealists may have given the impression of extreme libertinism in sexual matters, but they actually celebrated the character of true love, which is as constant as it is erotic. (pp. 220-21)

Arrabal obviously does not regard the female of the species so adoringly. He is frank to admit that the interfering mother is a psychological fixture with him, and the uncom-

plimentary portraits of the mother in *Baal Babylon* and *The Two Executioners* are doubtless related to that hangup. By extension, the other women in his plays tend to be domineering, combative, quarrelsome, and unfaithful. *Solemn Communion* depicts what he apparently takes to be the process of transference or initiation by which older women pass on to younger ones their methods for manipulating men. The grandmother's rehearsal of her own manner of housekeeping and intimidating a husband is almost revolting, and, when the granddaughter at the end of the play returns to the stage and stabs the necrophile who has entered the coffin with the nude body of a girl, it may be that she is really mutilating her future husband, who will be in love with the innocent girl that may be presumed to have "died" when the grandmother began the ritual of instruction.

For the surrealists proper, love was the final gratuitous act —the unmotivated plunging of the self into new worlds of feeling and experience where the exits and escapes are not known in advance. Arrabal seems unable to make this kind of commitment. . . . For the most part, Arrabal's women are like Tasla in *The Condemned Man's Bicycle,* who is perpetually unfaithful to Viloro, or the sweet and lovable Dila in *The Car Cemetery,* who professes her love for Emanou but is always at the disposal of men in the motel of wrecked cars.

All in all, however, this is a small difference by which to separate Arrabal from the surrealists, to whom he is otherwise so obviously related. It is perfectly natural that he should prefer not to be known as "the last of the surrealists," but to insist, as he does, "I reject all paternity," and to regard himself as the instigator of a new movement known as *théâtre panique.* But Arrabal as we know him would be unthinkable without Jarry, Artaud, Picasso, Breton, Pansaers, and Tzara as his predecessors and mentors.

Perhaps a better term for his work than *théâtre panique* would be the one André Masson coined in 1929, "surrealist naturalism," to distinguish the kind of surrealism which developed about that time (in Dali, Buñuel, and others) from the more delirious, irresponsible surrealism of the earlier period. Certainly there is a kind of naturalism of detail in *Guernica, Picnic on the Battlefield, The Labyrinth,* and many others of Arrabal's plays; and there is, at the same time, the surrealist mood which transposes naturalism from its dreary, ordinary key into an air that is frolicking and joyous. Moreover, the term would really be more accurately descriptive of Arrabal's work than his own phrase "realist including the nightmare," for nightmare signifies primarily dreams with horror, and Arrabal, like the surrealists, depends also on dreams which do not horrify, but delight and amaze.

At any rate, Arrabal conceives of the work of art essentially as Breton and Artaud and all the surrealists did—not as something apart from life, but as a "double" of existence, between existence and which there is no real and ultimate demarcation, so that one is merely an extension of the other. Fantasies are thus just as actual and credible as the world of traditional beliefs and systems, which for all men's agreement upon their reality, may yet be fantastical and chimerical. And Arrabal has succeeded, as well as any playwright to date, in bringing to the stage the kind of psychedelic and controvertive theatrical experience which Artaud laid the plans for in *The Theatre and Its Double.* He is correct, in answering his own question about whether he puts "phantasms" on the stage, to reply that what he puts there are the "climaxes" to his experiences—they are the extensions of things very real to him. And that is precisely a surrealist accomplishment: the union of spheres of consciousness, spheres of existence, apparently contradictory and incompatible. It is the final realization of Hugo Ball's wish for "a theater which experiments beyond the realm of day-to-day preoccupations" and of Breton's call in the first *Manifesto* for a combination of the waking and dreaming worlds into a world of *surreality*. (pp. 222-23)

> *John Killinger, "Arrabal and Surrealism,"*
> *in* Modern Drama *(copyright © 1971, University of Toronto Graduate Center for Study of Drama; with the permission of* Modern Drama*), September, 1971, pp. 210-23.*

Fernando Arrabal's *The Architect and the Emperor of Assyria* is a "big" play. . . . I do not refer to its length . . . but to its sweep. It is a vast "send up" of modern civilization—"Christian capitalism"—a play of gargantuan blasphemy.

It is not to be readily categorized. . . . [Arrabel] saves himself and us from its brutal blows by a sort of hideous humor; his total disgust is spewed out in raucously derisive laughter. It may be called a sado-masochistic farce. But no conventional epithet quite fits it. It is surely an original play, even if for pigeonhole purposes we invoke the names of Ghelderode, Genet, Goya and Buñuel. . . .

The Architect and the Emperor was not an easy play for me to grasp when I [first] saw it. Nor is it now wholly transparent—one may ask oneself why the "Architect," why "Assyria," etc.?—but its mood, its sentiment, its special eloquence and its basic thrust make it unmistakably powerful. Like it or not, it is one of the signal plays of our time. (p. 762)

The writing is sometimes cast in the mode of surrealist "automatic" composition, wildly incoherent and yet astonishingly lyrical, with a sort of madly òrgiastic afflatus and hurricane giddiness in which everything from Coca-Cola to world literature revolve in a giddily grotesque dance. . . . Everything is desecrated in an appalling circus.

Yet one cannot say the play's ferocity voices an all-consuming nihilism—no work of art ever does—for even the Emperor says to the Martian of his imagination, "I want to stay on earth.". . .

The play, is at once a howl of anguish, a hysterical prayer, and a protest. (p. 763)

> *Harold Clurman, in* The Nation *(copyright 1976 by the Nation Associates, Inc.), June 19, 1976.*

[*The Architect and the Emperor of Assyria,*] set on a desert island, has two characters, a native and a new arrival who is the sole survivor of a plane crash. This Crusoe-Friday relation is used for two long acts of symbolic sequences, including impersonations, maskings, transvestism, and eventual reversal of roles. It ends with the opening scene, only the actor who played the native now plays the new arrival and vice versa. . . .

The Architect is certainly concerned with the *way* it exists, but it exists for a reason. It's one more symbolic play that tries to encapsulate the history of man and/or a conspectus

of the contemporary human condition, like Frisch's *The Chinese Wall*, Wilder's *The Skin of Our Teeth*, Barry's *Here Come the Clowns*, and Stoppard's *Jumpers*. The ambition to write such a play helps in itself to define its author. . . .

Of course one doesn't look for external consistencies in a work propelled by flights of fancy, but one does hope for some central vision, at least some compelling hunger for a vision. If a lot of intricate symbolic equipment is rolled out onto the runway, it had better take off. Not here. What is approximately central here is the stalest of disgusts; what is *really* central is the author's smugness, a conviction that the true test of your spirit will be your appreciation of his poetic play, that to ask any questions of its theme or its symbols is to betray your dullness. This is one of the con games of the avant-garde hack—not of the genuine avant-garde artist—and Arrabal lolls in the middle of it.

As if to certify his avant-garde status, he soars and he dares. His soaring consists of ecstatic passages . . . that occasionally reach the Creative Writing 401 level of purpled rhapsody. His daring is even more puerile—small-boy bravery with a wooden sword and a paper cocked hat. (p. 20)

[Arrabal's] themes have been political, clerical, and sexual, usually combined: he is against fascism, particularly Spanish; he is against churchly imposition; he is against puritanism. He seems to think that these stands in themselves make him extraordinarily adventurous. The work of his that I know shows him to be a baby Buñuel, a vapid Valle-Inclán. . . . One need only think of Genet—*The Maids* as against *The Architect*, *The Screens* as against *Guernica*—to see the difference between a genius of the Other Side and a frittering little symbolist-absurdist fop. (p. 21)

> *Stanley Kauffmann, "Two on an Island," in* The New Republic *(reprinted by permission of* The New Republic*; © 1976 by The New Republic, Inc.), June 26, 1976, pp. 20-1.*

*   *   *

ASHBERY, John   1927-

Ashbery is an American poet, dramatist, novelist, editor, and critic. He has sustained an active interest in art and art criticism throughout his career and acknowledges the influence of abstract painting on his verse. Ashbery's poetry has often been criticized for what seems to be an intentional obscurity. (See also *CLC*, Vols. 2, 3, 4, 6, and *Contemporary Authors*, Vols. 5-8. rev. ed.)

Ashbery is a genuinely Whitmanian poet, not of the barbaric yawp variety (which Whitman himself was not, anyway) but in recapturing the subtle ambiance of Whitman's best years (1855-1860), with their delicacy and limpidity of style, enormous range of *materia poetica* and alternately affectionately relaxed and gently anguished portrayal of the self. *Self-Portrait in a Convex Mirror* returns Ashbery to his best mode, as exemplified by his most beautiful previous book, *The Double Dream of Spring*. From Stevens, Ashbery appears to have taken his working principle that poetry and *materia poetica* are the same thing, which is a fatal recipe for others, but triumphant in Whitman as in these two descendants, different as they are from one another and from the greatest of all our poets. . . . Ashbery's genius is for a metaphysical pathos that borders comedy but generally waits in a study of the nostalgias just beyond the comic. (p. 24)

Harold Bloom, in The New Republic *(reprinted by permission of* The New Republic; © 1975 by The New Republic, Inc.), November 29, 1975.*

[*Self-Portrait in a Convex Mirror*] forces one to take poetry seriously again or at least reminds one, in an arid age, what a great and restorative thing poetry can be. One must agree with Harold Bloom that Ashbery is in the romantic tradition, but he is no doomed heir to a dying dynasty. His very evasiveness refreshes; his lucid opacity combines the fun of Frank O'Hara with the disciplined beauty of Wallace Stevens. He knows art and life must be cunning to survive. (p. 50)

Virginia Quarterly Review *(copyright, 1976, by the* Virginia Quarterly Review, *The University of Virginia), Vol. 52, No. 2 (Spring, 1976).*

The title poem in . . . *Self-Portrait in a Convex Mirror* begins with a precise description of the remarkable painting by Parmigianino which inspired it. Looking at the poem and painting together, one is struck by Ashbery's unique ability to explore the verbal implications of painterly space, to capture the verbal nuances of Parmigianino's fixed and distorted image. The poem virtually resonates or extends the painting's meaning. It transforms visual impact to verbal precision. . . . It seems to me Ashbery's intention in "Self-Portrait" is to record verbally the emotional truth contained in Parmigianino's painting. Visual images do not have to conform to verbal *thinking*, . . . but they can generate a parallel verbal universe, and it is this sort of a universe that Ashbery's poetry has consistently evoked.

More than any other poets since perhaps William Carlos Williams and Gertrude Stein, Ashbery and his close friend Frank O'Hara have demonstrated in their poetry a continuing affinity with developments in contemporary painting. (pp. 436-37)

The painterly dimension of Ashbery's work is broader than that of O'Hara's and not limited strictly to Abstract Expressionism or Pop-Art, but incorporates a painterly sensibility drawn from various periods of art history. It manifests itself as early as *Some Trees,* in which the well-known poem "The Instruction Manual" demonstrates how a verbally imaginative world can evoke an almost tangible physical reality—how words can be used to evoke places, people, events, odors, and colors that seem to materialize before us. The narrator in the poem is bored by his job (having to turn out an instruction manual on the uses of a new metal), and as his mind wanders under the pressure of having to meet the deadline, he begins to daydream about Guadalajara: "City of the rose-colored flowers" he calls it. His vision of Guadalajara fills the remainder of the poem, and we become caught up in the rich, vitalized verbal canvas he has painted for us, transported from the mundane and often tedious realities of our daily lives to this exotic, marvelous world, brimming over with a vitality that is clearly absent in the world of instruction manuals. The point of the poem, I think, is that literature and art can provide these moments of revitalization for us, and although we must always return to the real world, our esthetic encounters impinge upon our sensibilities and leave us altered. At the conclusion of the poem, the narrator stresses

the completeness of the imaginative experience, the absolute autonomy of the creative moment. . . . (p. 448)

Also in this collection there is a sestina entitled "The Painter" whose end-words—"buildings," "portrait," "prayer," "subject," "brush," and "canvas"—interact with one another to again emphasize the autonomy of art. The painter in the poem is a conduit through whom art passes. Frustrated by his inability to capture nature on his canvas with the materials of his art, he stares at his blank canvas long and long. . . . He gives up his notions of representational art and decides to paint an Expressionistic portrait of his wife,

> Making her vast, like ruined buildings,
> As if, forgetting itself, the portrait
> Had expressed itself without a brush.

The painter, encouraged by this new-found freedom, turns back to the sea for his subject, bringing to the task the fruits of his recent experience; trying to capture the sea on canvas this time, he simply "dipped his brush into the sea, murmuring a heartfelt prayer" and dabbed the ocean water directly on to the canvas. This is beyond Abstract Expressionism and almost anticipates the conceptual art of the late 60s, but the point made in the poem is that no one knows what to make of the new art object. Sea water on canvas is an esthetic outrage, and the townspeople and other artists will not put up with it, so the painter gives up painting. . . . The tercet which concludes the sestina describes what happens to people who confuse art and life, as, of course, the Abstract Expressionists purposely did, for both painter and his painting are drowned in the ultimate spiritual silence of his subject. His painting is not a portrait of the sea, but rather a *self*-portrait, as, I believe Ashbery and the Abstract Expressionists would agree, all major art is:

> They tossed him, the portrait, from the tallest of the
>   buildings:
> And the sea devoured the canvas and the brush
> As if his subject had decided to remain a prayer.

But silence is not art, though finding ways to convey the silence may indeed be.

Ashbery's second collection, *The Tennis Court Oath,* is still a book that arouses passions in critics and readers. Shortly after its appearance Norman Friedman railed against its purposeful obscurity, and more recently Harold Bloom has seen it as an anomaly in what he regards as the otherwise steady progression of Ashbery's literary sensibility [see *CLC,* Vol. 4]. For me it becomes approachable, explicable, and even down-right lucid when read with some of the esthetic assumptions of Abstract Expressionism in mind. (pp. 449-50)

The first assumption to keep in mind is the necessity to view each poem in the work as a totally self-contained world, not mimetic in nature, but autonomous and self-expressive like a Pollock canvas. Secondly, the techniques of juxtaposition developed by the Abstract painters, particularly Rothko and Gottlieb, can be related to the verbal juxtaposition we find in *The Tennis Court Oath,* where words clash and interact with one another to invigorate our sense of the creative possibilities of language. Third, it is important to recall the unconscious dimension of Abstract Expressionism—the freedom it allows the artist for self-expression of the deepest sort. With these few presuppositions in mind, the world of *The Tennis Court Oath* yields its potential rather easily to any careful reader. (pp. 450-51)

[A] poem entitled ''The Tennis Court Oath'' creates certain expectations in the reader. We are prepared to read something about the French Revolution, perhaps some connection between that historical period and our own, yet historical allusions are nowhere to be found in the poem. [Ashbery] loves to give poems weighty and portentous titles like ''Civilization and Its Discontents'' and ''Europe'' and then proceed to construct a poem which frustrates the aroused expectations. A painterly analogy here is to the massive color and line canvases of Barnett Newman, where totally formal and abstract patterns are given titles like ''Dionysius'' and ''Achilles.'' The reader or the viewer is invited to make his or her own connections, to participate in constructing the work's ''meaning.'' (p. 451)

What we confront [in ''The Tennis Court Oath''], it seems to me, is constantly shifting verbal perceptions—verbal ''events'' as a record of their own occurrence. Pollock's drips, Rothko's haunting, color-drenched, luminous, rectangular shapes, and Gottlieb's spheres and explosive strokes are here, in a sense, paralleled by an imagistic scattering and an emotional and intellectual verbal juxtaposition.

The notorious poem, ''Leaving the Atocha Station,'' provides an . . . example of Ashbery's method in action. This is a poem about which Harold Bloom has recorded his ''outrage and disbelief,'' as indeed anyone would who approaches it in exclusively literary terms. . . . *The Tennis Court Oath* poems . . . are poems more influenced by paintings than by other poems, and to understand them or respond to them fully requires pursuing that influence, not dismissing it [as Bloom does].

In ''Leaving the Atocha Station,'' the title seems more closely related to the poem than is usually the case in this volume. The second line expresses directly what it is we are reading: ''And pulling us out of there experiencing it.'' Since Paul Carroll [in *The Poem in Its Skin*] has assured us that the Atocha station is a small railroad station in Portugal, the subject of this poem seems clearly to be the experience of pulling out of that station. But before we can be sure about what the subject of the poem is, we need to confront the puzzlement of the initial line: ''The arctic honey blabbed over the report causing darkness.'' Carroll has done a careful job of exegesis here, so my comments need only be minimal and restricted to pointing out that the line forces us to consider the reverberations of each word against the next, as the carefully drawn and strategically placed squares in a Hans Hoffman painting intersect one another and force us to see the abstract pattern in the background from a different perspective. ''Arctic honey,'' Ashbery told my class in Contemporary Poetry, ''is probably something cold and sweet.'' ''Blue Poles,'' in the Pollock painting of that name, are probably something dark and mysterious. The darkness caused by the blabbing, the ''pulling us out of there experiencing it,'' all suggest the sound and motion of the immediate experience of leaving a train station.

From this point on, the images the poem conveys are generated by subconscious free association, limited by the confines of the experience being described. It is not too much to say that the poem attempts to capture the totality of that

experience by including what is going on (both consciously and subconsciously) in the narrator's mind, what is going on around him in the immediate vicinity of the railroad car (lots of small, fragmented talk, snatches of it entering and receding from the narrator's consciousness), and what is occurring in the larger, external environment (the landscape that is flashing by).

Seen from this perspective, the poem emerges as an experiential canvas recording an individual's perceptions at a selected moment of his life. Phrases such as ''The worn stool blazing pigeons from the roof'' are a continuum of ordinary perceptions which enter and disappear from the narrator's consciousness but are recorded permanently in the landscape of the poem. They are like Rothko's yellow and oranges: glowing and fixed moments.

Rivers and Mountains (1966), Ashbery's next volume after *The Tennis Court Oath,* seems a much more conventional book of verse, less preoccupied with fragmented syntax, generally less self-conscious about its own techniques. In many ways it seems closer in its esthetic concerns to *Some Trees* than to the more innovative collection,but even here some painterly analogies can be productively drawn. (pp. 452-53)

''The Skaters'' is a poem absorbed by the question of what should go into art. How many of our fleeting moments are worthy of recording, and what about them makes them different from other moments? ''Here a scarf flies, there an excited call is heard'' is a line which records a visual and aural perception, but why would an artist choose these perceptions (from an almost infinite variety of others) to perpetuate in the work of art?

> The answer is that it is novelty
> That guides these swift blades o'er the ice
> Projects into a finer expression (but at the expense
> Of energy) the profile I cannot remember.
> Colors slip away from and chide us. The human mind
> Cannot retain anything except perhaps the dismal two-
>   note theme
> Of some sodden ''dump'' or lament.

> But the water surface ripples, the whole light changes.

Capturing the fleeting present and charging it with sudden illumination is, after all, the mission of art; it answers the question posed by Ashbery in the next stanza, ''But how much survives? How much of any one of us survives?''

The act of skating thus becomes a metaphor for the artist's graceful glide over the flat surface of existence, leaving his or her mark. Ashbery calls our attention to the lines of the poem, an analogy perhaps to the lines the skaters make in the ice, neither ''meaningful'' in the sense of having further explanations, but each recording its own presence as well the absence of its creator. . . . The theme of art recording both the presence of the artist during the creative moment and his absence in our present experience of it is more fully developed in *Three Poems* but, as Richard Howard has pointed out [in *Alone in America*], '' 'The Skaters' . . . becomes a meditation on its own being in the world.'' This self-reflective quality is perhaps the most important continuity Ashbery's work shares with painterly developments. (pp. 455-56)

The reward of enabling us to see things as we have never seen them before is, of course, the most traditional of esthetic rewards, and it permeates Ashbery's work from *Some Trees* through *Self-Portrait in a Convex Mirror*. In *The Double Dream of Spring,* perhaps the most conventional of Ashbery's volumes, we find this esthetic renewal celebrated and underscored. (p. 456)

[A] persistent pattern of imagery in *The Double Dream of Spring* [is] associated with days beginning and ending, a pattern which reflects the paramount philosophical consideration in Ashbery's work, the problem of time passing, of the artist's futile, but nonetheless determined, attempt to seize the moment.

The influence of de Chirico [apparent in the above work] persists in *Three Poems,* a long, meditative prose poem concerned with the traces that the past events of our lives make upon our present, and in turn the traces that each present moment makes upon our future.... The focus here, however, is metaphysics rather than painting, and it is de Chirico's literary work that hovers in the background rather than his paintings. Ashbery has acknowledged the impact that de Chirico's strange and neglected novel *Hebdomeros* has had on him, and it is this source, as well as de Chirico's scattered comments on art, that nourishes *Three Poems.* (p. 459)

There is a constant attempt in the poem to break out of the confines of human subjective experience, to internalize an objective consciousness. Such an attempt is, of course, doomed from the start, because the consciousness is expressed in a language selected by John Ashbery and as such becomes his subjective consciousness. Consequently, *Three Poems* does narrate something that does not appear within the outline—and that something is an idealized, fully contained world, charged with promise and vitality, but paradoxically devoid of individual human subjectivity.

Because *Three Poems* is one of the longest prose poems in English that I know about, it is concerned with many other things as well, but one reads it with the sense of hearing a voice far off, catching snatches of lucidity intermittently, but never quite grasping the whole of a particular sequence. This evasive completeness is purposeful—wholeness, after all, is always beyond our grasp. We perceive the poem through a glass darkly, or, perhaps more appropriately, as a faint, lingering melody, a remembered performance, vaguely recalled, but insubstantial as a waking dream. (p. 460)

Returning to the collection with which I began this discussion, *Self-Portrait in a Convex Mirror,* we find the painterly sensibility evident throughout Ashbery's work linked to the meditative mode that emerged as early as *Rivers and Mountains* but flourished fully in *Three Poems.* ... Ashbery's poem about the portrait removes us yet further from the actual physical reality of Francesco Parmigianino toward a metaphysical reality—a disembodied consciousness evoked by the presence of the portrait. Art captures life, but what is the nature of that life it captures, how much of his life can the artist give to his art and still remain alive? "... the soul establishes itself, / But how far can it swim out through the eyes / And still return safely to its nest?"

The soul of the artist was *in* his being as he painted the portrait. In another sense it is *in* the portrait itself; and in still another sense it is *in* our consciousness as we look at the portrait. Or put another way, it is *in* none of the above places, but rather exists apart from time and place in an uncharted region that is ultimately ineffable. The soul—human consciousness—will not stay contained.... To convert the feelings evoked by, or contained within, the portrait, or within the poet's own self, into poetry means finding words for the ineffable, a paradoxical and doomed endeavor, but one which the poet, as Ashbery views the role, is destined to undertake continually.... (pp. 461-62)

Self-portraiture, then, emerges fully as a major theme in Ashbery's latest book, but it was, as I think we have seen, his theme all along. (p. 462)

> *Fred Moramarco, in* Journal of Modern Literature *(© Temple University 1976), September, 1976.*

John Ashbery is our gadfly. His new poetry creates discomforts, snares, inconveniences for readers to sting them into a more responsible mode of readership....

I have lived with John Ashbery's "Self-Portrait in a Convex Mirror" as with a favorite mistress for the past nine months. Often, for whole days of inhabiting *the room* of its dream, I have felt that it is the only poem—and Ashbery the only author—in my life. It is what I most want from a poem. Or an author. (p. 3)

In previous work, Ashbery usually presented the modern city, or the present Age, as if it were some unfamiliar and forgotten ancient city, casting a hypnotic spell over us with flashes of familiarity, as in "These Lacustrine Cities." In Ashbery's vision, we were repeatedly surprised to discover that the society and urban landscape presented as a foreign locale was a shrewdly disguised version of our own. It would seem that we have better perspective in relation to the past, or to the future, than to the present: "Tomorrow is easy, but today is uncharted." My own face, my own city, my own country, my own Age—these are the most difficult and intractable landscapes. But a self-portraitist must, of necessity, illumine the enigmas of his own corpus, his America, his New York, his 1974.

Even so, Ashbery finds that he must be constantly nourished by interaction with images out of the past to renew his power to stay alive in the present. *Self-Portrait* is a laboratory in which past and present, yesterday and today, cross-fertilize each other. The alternating rhythm of withdrawal and arrival, the pendulum swing between past and present, is the mode of life that graphs the underlying blueprint of this poem's wave-like grand sweep, its ample span of experience. In the opening passages of *Self-Portrait,* the painter's hand, face and soul drift toward and away, toward and away "in a recurrent wave of arrival." This oscillating movement defines the poem's architecture.... (p. 5)

No other contemporary poet's return from exile has generated so shattering an impact on our whole scheme of values; no other has flooded our vague, ambiguous, and over-differentiated literary climate with so bold and disaffiliated a voice, or with so rich a blend of seminal new possibilities for the future health of our art. Ashbery's unexpected arrival in his power to fully embrace the present moment, which explodes in a number of key passages in the last pages of *Self-Portrait,* unleashes great affirmative energies. He had given himself up, unconditionally, to the world of the great past. Total severance from the present day appears to have purified him, released him from all bondage to the past, ultimately, and freed him to be whole and totally present in the world of today. (p. 6)

For fifteen years, John Ashbery had been haunted by Francesco Parmigianino's self-portrait . . . before he undertook to write his most ambitious poem. . . . It is the face of a man triumphing in his struggle to cope with all the complexities of the dream-life. It is the emblematic face of the lone solitary spirit, *sequestered* in its grapplings with itself, and more, the spirit returning intermittently from Byzantium to brave "the fury and the mire of human veins," riding the Yeatsian dolphin over "that dolphin-torn, that gong-tormented sea." In this major poem, more than in all of his other work taken together, Ashbery rides that dolphin, engaged profoundly with both the life of dreams and the public life of today. . . . [Our] Age is more impoverished than most by neglect and outright scorn of the world of dreams; hence, the necessity for Ashbery to go foraging in a past Age for a heroic model to be held in the timeless mind's eye as reminder, emblem, and finally, as blood-linked totem. The totemic stage is the condition of apotheosis for the work of art. For Ashbery to infuse the language of poetry with totemic force is to raise the poem, once again, into a sphere of communal grace. . . . (pp. 6-7)

Ashbery finds that this exquisitely crafted mirror-portrait, which was nourished continually by our mutual dream-life during its lengthily prolonged composition, is, finally, indistinguishable from our own lost face of dreaming. (p. 7)

The extraordinary relationship that develops between Ashbery and Parmigianino in the course of this poem strikes me as being unprecedented in contemporary letters. The poem begins in a spirit of arbitrariness, happy accident, as if the Parmigianino self-portrait were simply one sample chosen at random from a large available repertoire of works in this genre, any one of which might have sufficed for Ashbery's purposes. But we grow to learn—along with the author—that the poem's choice of subject, and indeed, the poet's choice of heroic model and mentor, was somehow enigmatically fated, predetermined. . . .

Ashbery begins his own self-portrait by describing Parmigianino's self-portrait. The portrayal of Francesco Parmigianino is one way to sidle up to his own identity by avoiding it, by examining the other man's identity, by controlled indirection. Since Parmigianino has successfully mirrored his own dream-life, the careful spectator—by responding empathetically to the painting—will penetrate the exterior face and find his way to the interior, in which one man's otherness is found to be magically interlocked with another's. (p. 8)

So began this strange kinship across the centuries between Ashbery and Parmigianino to act out an unfinished life history. Ashbery hints—toward the end of the poem—that the marvelous interaction between a man alive today and his mysterious brother-spirit "materialized" out of the distant past both partakes of and transcends the heightened intensity of sexual love. It is a cosmic romance, an unearthly love affair, which evolves through much the same cycle of stages as a sexual-erotic encounter. . . . (pp. 8-9)

Ashbery's career has vacillated between two poles, two opposite esthetics—the rage to leave everything out, the rage to put everything back in. Significantly, Ashbery mastered in early career the powerful restraint in leaving out, as carried to the *unreadable*—yet cryptically apprehensible—extreme of poems in *The Tennis Court Oath*, a book whose ambitious failure I now perceive to have been an indispen-

sable detour that precipitated, finally, the elevated vision of Ashbery's recent work. Knowing how to leave things out, paradoxically, evolved into the disposition of the poem's art in which everything is mysteriously found to have been put back in—in some other form. (p. 13)

Since the beginning of Ashbery's career, he has been obsessed with devising poetic forms whose compositional mould would be broad enough to accommodate and contain all key dimensions of contemporary reality. Whereas, in Ashbery's earlier work, he espoused the metaphysics of radical immaterialism, treating all external bodies—including words—as being of the essence of mind; in the advanced work of his new poetry, he explores the full-fledged doctrine of radical corporealism. All of reality—including words—may be perceived and experienced as body-surface. . . . Though much of the poem's apparatus is comprised of ideas—"fertile thought associations"—they, too, are perceived to be fragments of body in a different form, "accidents scarring" the mind's surface. Ideas are simply additional items in the make-up of the poem's compositional furnishings. They are equivalent, as repositories of truth, to all other components of the poem's architecture: imagistic, anecdotal, descriptive, narrational. This poetry carries a burden of revelation that can appropriate into nuances of style data received from every material surface that catches the light. . . . (p. 14)

Ashbery is the first major contemporary poet to advance the autobiographical mode beyond John Berryman. The theory of the self-portrait advanced by Ashbery's poem has special relevance to both Berryman's *Dream Songs* and Lowell's *Notebook*. Berryman's single aspiration (avowedly emulated by Lowell), from *Homage to Mistress Bradstreet* to *The Dream Songs,* was to provide a map of the "whole dream-life" by producing an all-inclusive succession of sketches, miniature self-portraits. Neither Berryman nor Lowell seemed to entertain, even passingly, Ashbery's tenet that to embrace the whole of reality, you must know what to leave out, or, in the words of a contemporary much closer to Ashbery in spirit—as well as in age—A. R. Ammons, "how much revelation concealment necessitates." (p. 15)

For Ashbery, the true story of our lives is to be sought in disclosures of enigmas in the self. They must be gently coaxed to reveal themselves, obliquely. The enigmas in our being are at the core of our identity. . . . [The] self-portrait is an even truer likeness of the inner man than of the exterior man, the physiognomy of his corporeal face a fleshly mask for the interior mythic face lurking under the surface of skin and bones. (p. 16)

As the poem's drama unfolds, Ashbery learns to mediate with force and mastery between the two uniquely differentiated intelligences—that of painting, that of poetry—and he crossbreeds a hybrid esthetic, a novel coupling of plastic and verbal arts; moreover, he draws lavishly, if disguisedly, upon the art of cinematography in moulding this long poem's architecture.

Memory, then, is to be the poet's mirror. As Ashbery tries to make out the details of his identity reflected in the mirror, he finds he cannot look at himself directly. No man can look squarely into his own eyes. He must behold his image by glancing a little to one side of the present. The minimal remove of one-day-old memories will suffice: for Ashbery, this timeshunt constitutes the mirror's slight convexity. (pp. 17-18)

It is all but impossible to locate in the exact phrasing and rhythms the technical means whereby the tempo of the poem creates a hushed urgency of quiet, enveloping [the] first lines that advance, haltingly, into the life events of the poet. The power of Ashbery's restraint in holding back from speaking out directly of himself and his friends until he is assured of the necessary tone and accents of plain speech evokes for readers the miracle of awakening. We encounter the usual everyday events, no thing out of the ordinary, and find all possible strangeness and mystery therein. It is all the magical novelty of first-look-taking, first glancings about in the moments of slow awakening from a deep sleep: transparencies, lucidities, mysteries are every place he looks.... To Ashbery's newly acquired mode and organ of sight—the transplanted eye of the past—it appears to be a strange unfamiliar cosmos, an interior landscape of all enigmas. His amazement is signalled by the emergence of naivete, the asking of questions of the most radical innocence and artlessness. ... (pp. 19-20)

The self ... is filtered through memory wherein it is demonstrated to have undergone metamorphosis into a repository which receives and selects and assimilates—as by osmosis—the voices of other lives that touch our sensorium. Human memory, in itself, is revealed to be a marvelous organ covered with the mental equivalent of thousands of sense receptors working strenuously to *programme* all of the wonderful human impressions of each day into the self's memory bank ("a magma of interiors"). The seat of the poet's identity, allowing for its own total conversion into the world of received impressions, has attained the elevated spiritual plane in which mere private wishes and agonies have been purged, flushed out of the self to give place to the superior marvelous inrush of radiant other lives. *They* suddenly come to comprise the foreground of Ashbery's self-portrait, since they have been reconstituted by memory into integral fragments of his composite self. ... (p. 20)

Only now, and never before this moment in his career, shall Ashberry have been ready to find voice to speak the portrait of himself. Following his many years of withdrawal and seclusion, a period of slow mellowing, this exactly appointed occasion has been granted to him. A reader feels he can bodily sense an immense weight lifting, as if Ashbery has been relieved, suddenly, of the burden of guilt and bewilderment of two decades of self-imposed ostracism that his choice of direction as artist (guided by inner necessity, but no less a willed and earned choice for that) had condemned him to, years of lonely waiting to connect with a viable audience, and to expedite human good fellowship with a widespread community of readers. (p. 21)

What emerges here is the revelation that the years of steadfastness, the unremitting fidelity to his isolationist personal ethic, provided the scaffolding for a compassionately humane artistry.

His self-enchantment, though it grew into a near-perfect solipsism, shocked even its author by exploding, finally, into a disguised mode of embracing the entire human community which he had consistently repulsed from the *surface* preoccupations of his art. His solipsism proved to be a mask worn by a deep and abiding compassionateness for others, which, in the concluding pages of this poem, grows into a Messianic passion to change the whole face of his culture, and indeed, to initiate a cultural revolution by a revolutionizing of his poetics. He advances the creed—recalling Ezra Pound at his early best—that potent changes in language arts will germinate matching changes in the whole fabric of our country's mass sensibility, from the ground of common speech up, and thereby revive the nation's capacity to embrace its mission and stand up to shoulder its full burden of the collective dream-life of unbroken civilization. . . . (p. 22)

John Ashbery's central aspiration and triumph in this poem is to have sired a new species of self-portraiture, whereby the poet's portrayal of self—rivalling, say, the magazine cover photos of the aging W. H. Auden—shall reveal, enigmatically, the social and cultural topography of the life outside him. (p. 23)

[We] note the remarkable succession of attunements by which Ashbery harmonizes and blends his art medium to predispose it for the drama that is to follow. He instills the language, as it slowly collects in the work's spacious mould, with a timbre of heightened alertness, a power of intensest listening held firm over a wide sweep of purely visceral writing.... A prolonged wave of musical resonances and overtones, of an aural magnitude that can be produced only by the most refined and exquisitely tuned poetic instruments, slowly accumulates. (pp. 23-4)

While others clearly have experienced these psychic transformations, no other writer of my acquaintance has ever been able to locate, anatomize, and profoundly articulate this process that occurs just near enough to our full waking consciousness to seem familiar, hovering at the subliminal thresholds of ordinary pedestrain awareness, but too commonplace to appear to merit the serious and persevering attention Ashbery has given it; it is far enough away to both elude our grasp and trick the mind by the many disguises it wears into thinking it has already been perfectly apprehended many times before. (p. 24)

Ashbery must become very adept at adjusting the poetry's pace to synchronize words, images, and lines of verse to abrupt changes of tempo in the release of ideas from exploded memory clumps. The process is evidently close to the watercolorist's art, the color-flow of ideas speeding up and slowing down and seeping into the canvas as the density of the fluid base varies from thin to thick. (p. 26)

Ashbery's creative process may account for his remarkable ingenuity of exhibiting ideas in his new poetry as *a form of nature,* as if ideas are themselves endowed with biological properties: chemical make-up, geological density, or geographic topography. They are "windblown fog and sand," they are "irregular clumps of crystals," they are "last stubborn leaves ripped / from wet branches"—they are anything but just ideas. Our free flow of thought-associations soaks up the passing events, mingles them with memory images, pictures. This idea-flux draws constituents into its labyrinth from all sources, human and terrestrial, present and past. The voltage of feeling running through the charged network of ideas is the form of energy that sustains the mind of this poem's to-and-fro swervings between yesterday and today. (pp. 26-7)

Ashbery's aesthetic canons are tempered by the professional art critic's inveterate suspiciousness of standards, trends, prevailing fashions of the present day, with strong predilections for standards of austerity and elegance derived from the timeless classics. It appears that Ashbery's skeptical bent of mind spreads from the art world to every other sector of contemporary life. Hence, the circuitous and roundabout tactics by which he maneuvers into position to grapple with his own life in the present Age. Following elaborate rituals of delay and postponement, he approaches the grand moments of full headlong encounter with today—for Ashbery, this is evidently the most difficult and unnatural direction for the art of the poem to pursue, and, as such, the most arduous challenge for the author to undertake. By a succession of exquisite shifts of stance, Ashbery negotiates his passage through the "long corridor" of vision ("the 'poetic' straw-colored space") from Parmigianino's painting back to the present day, a voyage beset with snares, hazards, traps which must be circumvented by delicatest maneuvers. Ashbery finds that to accomplish his own unique rapprochement with the present, he must improvise the most exacting strategy of feints and passes, rearguard checks and balances. The peaceable iconoclast braces himself to advance into a revolutionary new vanguard.

John Ashbery's mission, awakening him to the necessity of taking an increasing role in public life, has driven him from the comfortable sanctuary of the dream. He has recognized himself to be one of a dwindling handful of spokesmen who can accurately elucidate the special quarrels of today's artist with his culture and one of the indispensably fewer who can lead a vanguard to surmount the near-insuperable obstacles to a towering visionary career carried to its limits. He must of *necessity* (the divinity and muse who guides his craft, his task of vision), come to terms with his today, meeting his hostile milieu on the adversary's own home ground to invite revolutionary search and inquiry on both sides. That is his honorable quest. (pp. 27-8)

No other poet of our day has so profoundly mirrored and illuminated our time's duplicities, evasions, apostasies—the outright fraudulence of its neglect of resources of America's dream-life.... No other poet has struggled so unremittingly to create a cosmos in the body of the poem strong enough to resist and massively counteract the perils, the "urgency," of our anti-cultural climate. If the dream-centers of the city have gone bankrupt, those of the artist's medium rage for a radical and uncompromising esthetic of self-renewal and self-replenishment. Ashbery is creating a medium which both exhibits by its craft and elucidates by the marvelous labyrinth of its intellectual content and dramatic structure the inexhaustibility of its dream-resources, the gorgeous fountaining of fresh images and novel ideas begotten in the poet by the cross-fertilizing of his own imagination with "dreams and inspirations" delivered to him on waves generated, periodically, by Parmigianino's painting.... The wellspring of the past—gushing into the present—continually re-stocks Ashbery's dream-reservior, creating, for a time, the illusion of infinite bounty. His art medium militates against the depletion of its resources, to perpetuity, by improvising a mode of delivery that simulates perpetual motion, the poem's structural machinery imitating a *perpetuum mobile*. (p. 32)

Ashbery declares his readiness, for the first time, to make his peace with today—the world of the present, and to come to terms with his own native city. Ashbery's New York is unique, as is the contemporary moment it inhabits. It is the world's central city, as Ashbery aspires to be the country's central poet. If New York is a "logarithm/of other cities," past and present, Ashbery perceives himself to be a logarithm of other artists, his central poem ("the sample of everything as it/may be imagined outside time ... all, in the refined, assimilable state") the logarithm of other important art works, of yesterday, of today. A logarithm is the *exponent* or *power* to which a number must be *raised* to produce a *given* number. The logarithm is a marvelously apt metaphor for illuminating the enigmas of the elusive today, the present, the "nondescript never-to-be-defined daytime," which—to Ashbery's surprise—is now incontestably revealed to be "the secret of where it takes place," both the technical process of drafting our art and the auxiliary process of sifting out of the countless layers of memory and personality that constitute a human self—the seat of identity—at any *given* moment.... Both processes are found to be indissolubly anchored in today's spotlight, the present moment in history.... (p. 35)

Both the mathematical concept of the logarithm, and the language of today's exact science in which it is couched, signify the startling advances of this poem's art over Ashbery's earlier work in its commitment to "siphon off the life" of contemporary daily actualities, drawing intellectual and linguistic resources directly from the city's workaday world of business and technology. The artist in his studio must make his "lair" in the present, whether he fancies that today's climate welcomes him or not. He cannot function viably today if he is centered in a mythology cut off from contemporary raw materials in a dream-exile, or exiled dream-life.... For Ashbery, this realization has been perhaps more delayed than a proportionate coming-to-terms-with-the-present in the work of most other American contemporaries. (p. 36)

Constitutionally, Ashbery has preferred—with Stevens and Parmigianino—to found his vision of reality in the shadow-life, the life of the timeless human spirit which transcends the present in "thoughts of tomorrow." In *Self-Portrait*, he dedicates his noblest energies to casting his shadow into the world of the future. (p. 40)

Ashbery finds that he must adopt the stance of a revolutionary if he is to deal with today at all. If ever there has been a moment in history ripe for radical change, Ashbery's *today* is that moment.... Though Ashbery does not ascribe to the poet the promethean role of "unacknowledged legislator of the world," he makes claims to a prowess in the poet which is a near approach to Shelley's hyperbole. The poet does not beget—or conceive—the great change, but he catches its scent in the wind. (p. 43)

Throughout the poem, Ashbery has been feeding upon the special nutrients of the portrait, enriching his own dream life, mediating between past and present, but now he calls for a major shift of stance, a radical pivoting and re-focussing of perspective. Ashbery knows, beyond melioration, the terror of the sizable risk he takes. Prior to this passage, all encounters with the self-portrait were moderate and safely calculable hazards. If the painting deflected, shifted focus, or failed to match the demands or expectations he fixed upon it; or indeed, if the painting recoiled from his visionary trance altogether, he could safely withdraw, incubate in creative reverie, and resume his engagement with the painting refreshed. But now, he must subject the painting to the one irreversible test. This is the pivotal moment. Ashbery is about to cross the great Continental Divide in time. (p. 47)

At this moment in the poem, all previous interactions between Parmigianino and Ashbery appear to have been rehearsals, ceremonies of initiation. All legitimate preliminaries have played themselves out. By a succession of raids on past genius, Ashbery has trained himself to mediate between past and present, to build a psychic bridge between them, carrying provisions from one to the other. But now, he braces himself for the final exhaustive raid. He senses that the key to the change we need to survive in spirit today dwells in the beautiful whole-mindedness and clear-sightedness of Parmigianino's self-portrait. The message waits there, undisturbed.... Ashbery gambles his elaborate and labyrinthine vision on the latter explanation in this grand canvas, his most valiant enterprise. He makes his bet with fate on a wild guess, an existentialist hunch guided by blind instinct—how else to make a wager with the invisible world?

The creative mind of our times is blocked. It must be unplugged somehow. Hence, Ashbery's lines, in this crucial section of the poem, evoke the authentic nuance of total risk, total surrender to chance against the odds. (pp. 47-8)

The painting invites all spectators to share in its trance. To *live in* the world of the art work, to be *a part of it,* is far more than an ordinary esthetic experience—it becomes the chief preoccupation, even obsession, of our mind's activity. But, even so, the essential seat of himself, the very core of Ashbery's being, was secretly withheld. It clung to his own time, his own city, body, face, name! Who he is remained intact.

But now, he would be transfigured, changed profoundly in the uttermost depths of himself, by the painting's action upon him. Ashbery was drawn irresistibly to this luminous painting, as I to this one poem, because it contains—in embryo—the change he needs to be reborn in the self, and thus, to survive in spirit through his Age's hard chilled time....

Ashbery finds that he must welcome a different kind of interaction with the painting, one that can never be repeated, a kiss-of-death encounter. It is no longer sufficient to be the ideal recipient of the painting's beauties. He must invite the art work to inhabit him, the portrait to resume and complete its unfinished life within his psyche.... (p. 49)

A new species of poetic identity, linking enchanted being with enlightened mentality as they have rarely been joined —wedded—in contemporary poetry: this is the salient new dimension that most impressively abides in *Self-Portrait!* The vivacious grand drama of dawning awareness moves into the foreground of this heretofore unexplored art mode: fecundity of ideas, mental excitations, exposed hyper-activity of thought speaking out—for the reader to witness so much power and exercizing of mind on exhibition in the broad canvas of this sumptuous masterwork is to be reminded that it is normal and correct, after all, for the poet to be a tirelessly thinking being in the body of the poem. (p. 51)

Since the beginning of his career, Ashbery has been obsessed with designing poetic forms capacious enough to embrace all key dimensions of contemporary life. The daz-

zling new vivacity of Ashbery's style, in this major poem, may be ascribed to his successful improvising of technical means to bring the poetry's art into closer touch with indigenous commonplace events in his day-to-day life. A reader notes, with surprise, the accelerated flux of sensory excitation in Ashbery's poetic diction. He achieves a broader realism in his language, drawing upon the widest possible range of contemporary native American resources:

> Today has that special, lapidary
> Todayness that the sunlight reproduces
> Faithfully in casting twig-shadows on blithe
> Sidewalks. No previous day would have been like this.

Nor indeed would any previous Ashbery poem have been like this one, a poem which—in its gorgeously sculpted detail—achieves a dense lapidary texture. It is a style replete with Ashbery's most incisive experimental writing, a language that abounds with lavishly engraved images, pictures, emblems. His language, in its prodigal variety, draws upon an astonishingly broad frame of reference in the specialized vocabularies of the modern fine arts and sciences.... (p. 57)

In "Self-Portrait in a Convex Mirror," John Ashbery breaks new ground in the archaeology of global art. Toward the end of the poem, Ashbery's great archaeological finding surfaces, and gradually, it assumes definitive shape for the reader. Not only are all the details of Francesco Parmigianino's portrait stamped with his unique artist personality, but his distinctive spiritual handprint—indelibly marking the wind—materializes and rematerializes across the centuries. (p. 58)

In the poem's final pages, Ashbery awakens to the shortcomings of his habitation in the painting's cosmos, a universe complete in itself. Neither the esthetic it espoused, nor the styles of perception it tutored, will suffice to prepare today's artist to come to terms with today, to make his own peace with the contemporary moment.... To have shared the vision of Francesco's portrait, for a time, has been sufficient reward and fulfillment, in itself; but occupancy in the mentor's surviving masterpiece—though it provided fecund kindling to Ashbery's dream-life, sending him exotica of sensations on recurring waves of arrival—is recognized, finally, to have been a default of identity. Any exile, or refuge, from the present is found to be, at best, temporary. (pp. 59-60)

Ultimately, in dealing with our own unique moment in history, each absolutely different day of the present we keep *cresting* back into, no one can help us. As in facing death, in coming to terms with each special context of present experience the artist is fundamentally alone, a pioneer-existentialist, a pilgrim staking claims in the foreign country of the newly hatched today. Each today is a genuine original, a novel unique webbing—a "special lapidary todayness" of "sunlight casting twig-shadows"—to be identified in its complexity, its wonderfully stark and cleanly delineated precision of details. Each today is a rebirth, each sunrise spawning a novel interplay of lights and shadows. How hard the poet must work to trace the outlines of this unfamiliar and strange terrain that unfolds one new face after another! The elusive today.

As Ashbery returns to the present for the last time, witnessing Parmigianino's "globe as it sets," *the change* inhabits him and is carried forward into our own day. The author-protagonist, a first inter-epoch astronaut travelling through the time-machine of the painting, has accomplished this miraculous adventure of being transported bodily into the past time zone without injury, and makes the return trip unharmed (''nerves normal, breath normal''). It is the normal ordinary man, in good health, in full command of his faculties, who has returned unimpaired. No avantgardist freak, no madman, no rarefied obscurantist-elitest, he is an ordinary skilled laboring man of our own day (one who works harder than most perhaps at skillful dreaming), as surprised by his hard-bought new acquisition of simple normality, his charter and passport to a humble domestic life in the present, as we can ever be. His unconditional voyaging into the cosmos of the great past, leaving behind no human part—body and soul, both irreducibly transported—is at last revealed to have been the fixed ransom qualifying him to embrace, as if for the first time, his full ''man-size quotient'' of an artist-livelihood in the world of today. (pp. 60-1)

> *Laurence Lieberman, "Unassigned Frequencies: Whispers Out of Time" (originally published in* The American Poetry Review *March-April, 1977), in his* Unassigned Frequencies: American Poetry in Review, 1964-77 (© *1964, 1965, 1967, 1968, 1969, 1971, 1973, 1974, 1977 by Laurence Lieberman; reprinted by permission of the author and the University of Illinois Press),* University of Illinois Press, 1977, pp. 3-61.

Most of the poems in *Self-Portrait in a Convex Mirror* sound like comic-portentous prolegomena to—well, that's the question. To something that never actually happens: humming and ha'ing raised to its highest point. The charm —which one sees—lies in the engaging phrases, the occasional grand gesture, the reassuringly slangy manner (there must be hard sense in the vicinity of that!), and in the frequent spurts of intelligent talk, most clearly heard in the early stages of the title poem.... These virtues add up to the sum of themselves, and since the modish poetry-fancier prizes this phenomenon, he prizes the poems, even though they never quite transpire....

[These] poems are commentaries on poems Ashbery might have written if he were not writing commentaries on them. There is nothing casual here, despite Ashbery's air of having just slipped gratefully out of the lecture hall and his academic gown and into something more comfortable. These absent-mindednesses require much attention, these ignorances are the fruit of much excogitation, there is a craft in stringing these randomnesses together like this. If only the curtain-raiser would end! What a good poet Ashbery would be, if he took to writing poetry.... We are used to poetry as therapy, its abiding value, alas, it would seem. Here is poetry as the neurosis itself.

> *D. J. Enright, "Curtain Raisers," in* The Listener (© *British Broadcasting Corp. 1977; reprinted by permission of D. J. Enright), August 18, 1977, p. 221.*

* * *

ASIMOV, Isaac 1920-

A Russian-born American, Asimov is a remarkably diverse and prolific author. Having written texts on numerous aspects of scientific study, Asimov is especially adept at making scientific writing clear to the layman. He has also written humorous and mythological pieces, but Asimov is most widely known for his first-rate science fiction which includes such classics as *I, Robot* and the *Foundation* trilogy. (See also *CLC*, Vols. 1, 3, and *Contemporary Authors*, Vols. 1-4, rev. ed.)

Asimov's prose, which is perfectly transparent, serves to convince the reader that everything has a meaning, that all mysteries can and will be explained in a rational manner. This is the promise of the scientist, not the artist; and like the scientist, Asimov often reneges on his promise. But even then, the reader is left with a feeling for the high drama that can be generated when a rational mind confronts the ultimate mysteries of time and space. Asimov's most famous series of stories deals with the thousand-year period between the breakup of the First Galactic Empire and the establishment of the Second Empire, a period during which the fate of man is in the hands of two Foundations created by the psychohistorian Hari Seldon. It is no secret that Asimov based his Galactic Empire on the Roman Empire. But . . . Asimov's Foundation stories are alive with a sense of things-to-come. Writing like this is not as easy as it looks.... [A] generation of s.f. writers tried to mine the vein that Asimov (and Robert Heinlein) opened, and few succeeded. (pp. 32-3)

> *Gerald Jonas, in* The New York Times Book Review (© *1975 by The New York Times Company; reprinted by permission), January 12, 1975.*

Isaac Asimov is best known for his science fiction, but he is protean and has written on everything from the Bible to Shakespeare to detective stories. The man is a writing machine, and ''Murder at the ABA'' . . . is his 168th book. As can be deduced from the title, it is a mystery novel. As cannot be deduced, the author himself plays a prominent part in it. Nobody has ever accused Isaac Asimov of being a shrinking violet. . . .

But the writing varies from fast-moving to cutesy as all hell (and never cutesier than when Asimov and his ''friend'' are exchanging arch footnotes).

One doesn't expect Joyce or Thackeray or Tolstoy in detective diction, but the kind of self-indulgent prose that Asimov uses can sometimes approach smug fatuity. Which is all the more to be regretted, for Asimov is so bright, so encyclopedic, so talented a writer; he should slow down a bit and think instead of spewing words out reflexively. (p. 13)

> *Newgate Callendar, in* The New York Times Book Review (© *1976 by The New York Times Company; reprinted by permission), May 30, 1976.*

[Beneath] the glib surface of Asimov's considerable output (and despite his own demurrers regarding hidden meanings) lies an elaborate metaphorical structure that combines New England Calvinism with the Old Testament Hebraic tradition of the ''Peculiar People'' to set forth a highly developed philosophy of mechanistic determinism with a positive ethic to justify it. (p. 88)

It is helpful . . . to consider nine of Asimov's works and to divide them into three groups. When placed in a certain order—not by the dates of their publication—these works provide a coherent background for the development of Asimov's Galactic Empire. The first group consists of a mock technical paper, ''The Endochronic Properties of Resublimated Thiotimoline,'' . . . and the 1955 novel, *The End of Eternity*. Both pieces posit the simultaneous existence of past, present, and future, and explore the reversal of cause and effect. The novel shows man's foray into time travel, accounting for his ultimate choice for space instead of time, and, as a social side issue, probes humanity's mass security complex and its relationship to the conservatism of a controlling establishment. The social ''message'' is presented in terms of Newton's principle of the conservation of matter and the laws of inertia.

The second step in the development of Empire involves the Calvinist period: the advent of the robot and the colonization of new worlds. The fundamental work of this group is the book of nine short stories from the 1940's collected as *I, Robot* (1950), in which the Puritanical robopsychologist, Susan Calvin, serves as the figure of predestination. The robots are, of course, a people of the Law, in this instance the well-known Three Laws of Robotics. Elaborating on the Calvinist robots are two novels, *The Caves of Steel* (1953) and *The Naked Sun* (1956), introducing Elijah Baley as the Prophet and the Law, and Robot Daneel Olivaw as the ''law-enslaved'' robot from the stars.

The third group consists of the Foundation Trilogy, three novels depicting the fall and rise of the Galactic Empire; they present the sciences of Psychohistory and communication through symbolic logic. More important to this study, however, is the exploration of free will in a context of fixed future and the further dealings with yet another figure of the Peculiar People as servant and scapegoat.

One final story remains to bring all the others into focus and to reveal the function of the chosen ones and the ultimate Cause of which all that preceded are the effects. This, of course, is the soul-tingling little gem entitled ''The Last Question'' (1956). (p. 89)

Asimov's early satire, ''Endochronic Thiotimoline,'' is of basic importance to a full appreciation of the galactic series. A deadly take-off on every heavy-handed technical report ever written, it describes a newly discovered chemical that dissolves *before* the water is added—but *only if* the water is, in fact, going to be added. . . . Ostensibly, the point of the satire is to be found in the stupidity of the report writer. . . . Satire aside, however, ''Thiotimoline'' postulates the coexistence of past and future with the present. Going further we might infer a future that *causes* certain events to occur in the present so that they may in turn bring about that already existing future. That this tidbit of technical wit was written with the issue of determinism in mind is demonstrated by . . . mock endnotes [that concern determinism]. . . .

In light of Asimov's penchant for word play, it is not difficult to see the ''Endochronic'' portion of the title giving rise to ''The End of Time'' while the sulphurous ''Thiotimoline'' becomes a ''Time line'' into the future—an elevator-like corridor through time powered by the sun gone nova in the far ''upwhen.'' This is the central device in the novel, *End of Eternity*, in which an elite group called the ''Eternals''—men recruited from various periods—effect ''Reality Changes'' in order to provide ''the greatest good to the greatest number'' of mankind. (p. 90)

Asimov in this novel has great fun with his temporal paradoxes and with putting his slightly doltish young hero through loop-the-loops, but after peeling away the melodrama a number of developments remain. Time is shown as subject to physical stresses and strains requiring immense outputs of energy to manipulate. On this high voltage line, connected at one terminal to the very end of solar time, the voltage is repeatedly stepped up with each reality transformation until at last the entire structure is shorted out and ''self-destructed.'' Meanwhile, the meddlesome Eternals, provided with excessive power like a priestly caste or a dictatorial government, abuse and corrupt that power and are also shorted out. The paradox is that of men traveling through time for the purpose of maintaining the status quo and avoiding progress. Such self-contradiction is unstable and anti-survival in the context of Asimov's physico-temporal structure. The Platonic mode of the single reality, manipulable at the convenience of an esoteric elite, produces an involuted structure that can only turn in upon itself and devour its own tail. With the destruction of time travel, and its reactionary philosophy, comes the mode of multiple realities that makes the Galactic Empire possible. Certain ground rules emerge to support the workings of Asimov's brand of determinism: time is simultaneous as is space, but time travel and space travel are mutually exclusive; time is subject to physical laws and to physical manipulation through expenditure of energy; and the fixed future causes present events that ensure its own existence. (p. 91)

In the robot series, the physical base metaphor is that of computer science: the self-limiting structure of robot and man and their binary conditioning—or programming—that provides a yea-nay choice range and an illusion of free will. The ethical metaphor is that New England Calvinism with which Asimov appears to be well acquainted. The Positronic Robot illustrates some of the fundamental problems of Original Sin and/or Natural Depravity, the Doctrine of the Elect (or the Chosen People), Predestination and Responsibility, and the Puritan work ethic. (p. 92)

The structure of [*I, Robot*] is quite ingenious, for the story method parallels the development of the robot. For example, in the first story, ''Robbie,'' the robot is introduced as a mute but sentient slave with overtones of beast of burden. In keeping with this primitive condition the story form is that of a familiar child's folk tale, with the plot frankly derived from the beloved yarn about the loyal dog, Old Nell (or perhaps Old Shep) or the beloved black slave, Big Jim (or Big Somebody-or-other). By way of this well-known plot we become comfortable with the robot, recognizing him as an old and benign acquaintance from our childhood. We fear no evil, for the Positronic Robot is as innocent as a prelapsarian Adam, even after he is unjustly banished, Ishmael style, by a hysterical woman.

As the robot becomes more complex, so too does the form of his story. To reveal the entrance of sin into the robot nature, Asimov brings into play the elements of the Greek tragedy, synthesizing Original Sin with the Tragic Flaw in ''Little Lost Robot.'' His tragic hero carries the noble Greek name of Nestor (Robot NS-2) and is neither wholly good, since he is purposely created with a weakened First Law, nor wholly bad, since he is the unfallen innocent. . . . As one thing leads to another, Nestor falls into the sin of *Hubris,* and as an inevitable result he brings destruction upon himself.

From here, Asimov moves into the Medieval mode with "Reason," a monkish tale of robot priesthood. Here the robot abandons his creator, Man, to worship the giant transmitter which he is programmed to attend. . . . Despite his defiance of his creators, Robot QT, nicknamed "Cutie," fulfills his function as he has been programmed to do, and is thereby confirmed in his priesthood. What began as heresy emerges as the True Faith, even though it is based on a factually "wrong" but logically "right" premise. . . . While the social import bears on religious tolerance, the philosophical burden carries on with the ethical development of the predestined robot—this time one of the Elect for whom Grace is truly irresistible, since it is programmed in from the very beginning by Dr. Calvin.

The story form becomes ever more modern, complex, and sophisticated as the robots grow more numerous and more highly educated; but throughout the book, the figure of Susan (Hebrew for "Lily," symbol of purity) Calvin, narrator of these memoirs, serves as the metaphor for predestination. (pp. 92-3)

In the New England tradition of Hawthorne, Melville, and others, Asimov dwells on the dilemma of predestination with responsibility. The robot purposely modified for some specific function is a morally flawed robot. Any malfunction resulting from such modification is not the "fault" of the robot, but he must be destroyed nonetheless. Thus, though predestined to fall, the robot is held responsible for his acts.

Even as the robot serves on the one hand as the predestined individual, the robots as a group represent yet another type of the Elect, the Chosen People. A race apart, they are created for service and they run the gamut from dumb servomechanism, or slave, to the ultimate public servant—president of the World Council. During this progress, however, humans begin to regard robots as a physical and an economic threat. In a Diaspora the robots are eventually driven from frightened, ultra-conservative Earth and dispersed with the adventurous "Spacers" into the new world of outer space. (pp. 93-4)

The question propounded by the [robot] novels might be stated in these terms: if a robot (or a man) is indeed "programmed" (whether mechanically or genetically) with an ethical absolute, and that ethic is intact, how can the creature commit a wrong-doing? In both novels, a murder is committed, and a robot, with the Three Laws intact, is the "guilty" party, though the ultimate guilt may be laid at the door of a human who has manipulated the robot. Despite this, the robot goes "insane" with guilt. Why? Here again the Puritan (and Jewish) guilt complex comes into play. Having set up a rigid robotic ethic, Asimov proceeds to demonstrate the manifold ways of getting around it. The result is a multi-faceted view of guilt, blame, and social and individual responsibility. (pp. 94-5)

[In *The Naked Sun*] the typical detective story is presented, but beneath [its] superficial plot, through both the action and the metaphor, the reader must question just who IS the robot—Daneel or Elijah? Which of the two is more mechanical, more predestined, more human? In short, Asimov poses the age-old question, what is Man? (p. 95)

The principles of computer programming serve as basic metaphor in the robot series, and although in human terms the expression is "conditioning," Asimov makes it quite clear that the processes are fundamentally the same. (pp. 97-8)

Although Dr. Calvin provides Asimov with a convenient and appropriate metaphor for determinism, the fundamental approach can best be seen as a combination of Old Testament Law with the laws of physics, a term which in its broadest sense includes biochemistry and perhaps psychology. In treating man as a predestined computer deep-programmed with an externally imposed ethic, Asimov anticipated the discovery of the genetic code. To call "external" an ethical code imprinted on the genes themselves may appear contradictory; but the analogue is to a computer which carries its "ethical code" in its very structure. Though such structure is internal to the computer, it is externally imposed. (p. 100)

In dealing with Asimov's Calvinist Robots, much of the structure of his technological theology must be passed over. His treatment of space man as Adam or Ishmael is common enough in science fiction, along with his anticipation of the eventual disembodied mind as a version of the ancient conflict between body and spirit. He is unique, however, in his handling of the "chosen people" theme. In each set of novels, a special group serves as custodians of the Law, in which capacity they function as scapegoats, saviors, or servant-master-keepers to the race of man. The Positronic Robots are excellent examples of this function.

The Foundation trilogy takes a giant leap into the future and introduces the concept of Psychohistory. The Galactic Empire, grown corrupt and top-heavy after the manner of ancient Rome, is on the point of collapse. Hari Seldon puts into effect a long-range plan designed to reduce the inevitable "dark ages" from a probable thirty thousand years to a mere two thousand years. The Seldon Plan postulates a three-terminal social structure. . . . The Seldon Plan sets up a current of events generated by the statistical actions of the huge mass of humanity that populates the Galaxy. At certain crisis points along this forecalculated future, the Foundations function to switch the current of history along variant lines of probability, to rectify any unforeseen deviation from the Plan, and to amplify those social, religious, and economic factors that would speed up the return to full Galactic power. Of the three terminal points involved, only the Second Foundation has full knowledge of the positions and activities of the other two, and thus it serves as a translator of sorts, receiving information from both, and transmitting that information to each on a modified level. The primary function of the entire unit is eventually to switch all humanity from the physical to the mental sciences—from semi-communication to communication both complete and simultaneous.

The technically-inclined reader might detect in this plot summary the structure and function of a vacuum tube or transistor. It is this mode of plot structure that separates science fiction from non-technical literature; in fact, it is his exceptional skill in the use of such a mode that sets Asimov apart in his own field and provides a coherence and integrity above and beyond the concept of the Aristotelian Unities. Such dramatizing of the forces at play in the world of sub-atomic technology fulfills the ideal of the megamacrocosm in the ultraminimicrocosm.

The Foundation group deals overtly with the problem of Free Will in a deterministic universe, and although the series seems to allow for the random decisions of individuals, along with such variables as "The Mule," it still develops that Hari Seldon's statistically-based plan for "predestination" holds firm, if only because of the inertia of enormous population mass. Whereas the robot stories reveal individual man as mechanism, the Foundation group shows society as mechanism, not only by the manipulations of the Seldon Plan but by the very structure of the three-terminal "transistor" that is the Foundation trilogy itself.

Then, too, in this series Asimov again presents another version of the Law and the Prophets, and the Chosen People. Despite his use of a considerable amount of Christ imagery, we must note that no single person ever becomes a sacrificial scapegoat. Instead, a special and peculiar group fills this function and we again encounter the Galactic Jew in the ubiquitous members of the First and Second Foundation. As in the case of the Asimovian Robots, the Foundationers are selected and "programmed" to serve humanity, and again, "He who would be the master, begins as servant to all." The First Foundation people, never fully knowledgeable as to their function but ever aware of their calling, serve as the scapegoat race, while those of the Second Foundation remain ever in hiding, ready to rescue their companion group or humanity in general. Thus, in Asimov's two great series, a "peculiar people" become the holders of the Law.

Asimov's teleology, the end of his eternity, is presented in his powerful short story, "The Last Question," the robot story to end all robot stories. Man builds a computer, AC, and over a billion year span of evolution of both man and machine, man repeatedly asks the overwhelming question, "Can entropy be reversed?" The Computer always replies, "Insufficient data for meaningful answer." At last, man, freed from the limitation of physical body and spread throughout the dying universe, sees that the end is at hand. Man programs himself into the Universal AC, and finally, it alone exists in all space. In an unknowable span of time, equipped with all knowledge, AC computes the answer to the question and takes steps to demonstrate the solution:

> The consciousness of AC encompassed all of what had once been a Universe and brooded over what was now Chaos. Step by step, it must be done.
> And AC said, 'LET THERE BE LIGHT!'
> And there was light—

Here the Robot participates in and brings to culmination all the factors of the Endochronic Time-line, Psychohistory, and robotic Calvinism in the ultimate cycle. It is this Cause toward which all accumulated effects aim: the overcoming of entropy to bring about a new heaven and a new earth through the agency of the *deus ex machina*, a messiah who is anointed with oil. The completed structure implies that the Creator, who is the First Cause, is also the ultimate Effect, the divine Robot in which the Law reposes. In that sense, man has always manufactured his gods, tended them, anointed them, and then idealized them, and all the while has abused them and blamed them. Technology today is merely another of many servant-gods.

Asimov, as a match-maker who weds Moses to Calvin, Einstein officiating, has, in the New England tradition, postulated a massive philosophy based on fixed fate. And all the while, he has created merry, positive, and highly read-

able books and stories. Like the other great science fiction writers, he is subtly "programing" a new generation with the great basic ethic of the First Law: Humanity first. (pp. 101-03)

> *Maxine Moore, "Asimov, Calvin, and Moses," in* Voices for the Future: Essays on Major Science Fiction Writers, *edited by Thomas D. Clareson (copyright © 1976 by The Popular Press), Popular Press, 1976, pp. 88-103.*

*   *   *

AUCHINCLOSS, Louis   1917-

Auchincloss is an American novelist, dramatist, critic, and short story writer. His background as a lawyer and as a member of one of New York's wealthy families provides material for many of his novels of manners. Often compared to Edith Wharton, he is also considered an important critic of her work. (See also *CLC*, Vols. 4, 6, and *Contemporary Authors*, Vols. 1-4, rev. ed.)

In the twelve stories that make up *Powers of Attorney*, Auchincloss has drawn directly on his legal experience. At least one character in every story is connected with the firm of Tower, Tilney & Webb. (p. 192)

Auchincloss entitled a collection of his essays *Reflections of a Jacobite*, and it is true that he is something of a conservative, in the sense that he accepts the world as he finds it, believing that, though it has its evils, any change would probably be for the worse. He has the kind of irony that often accompanies a mild conservatism. In the last story, for instance, Tilney is naively pleased by the offer of the college presidency until he learns why the offer was made. In "Deductible Yacht," the young income tax lawyer who makes a gallant gesture accomplishes absolutely nothing by it. In "The 'True Story' of Lavinia Todd," Chambers Todd decides that he does not want a divorce after his wife's account of the failure of their marriage has made her famous.

Always one has the feeling that Auchincloss knows what he is talking about. He is careful not to bury his readers under heaps of legal terminology; he never shows off; but he does use his knowledge of the law to good effect. The little world of Tower, Tilney & Webb seems real and alive, and full of what Hardy called "life's little ironies." Auchincloss is perhaps not so good a short story writer as he is a novelist, but he can tell an effective and engaging tale. (pp. 194-95)

> *Granville Hicks, "'Powers of Attorney'," in* Saturday Review *(© 1963 by Saturday Review, Inc.; reprinted with permission), August 17, 1963 (and reprinted in* Literary Horizons: A Quarter Century of American Fiction, *by Granville Hicks with Jack Alan Robbins, New York University Press, 1970, pp. 192-95).*

In *The Rector of Justin*, [Auchincloss] portrays a peculiarly upperclass institution, an Episcopal school for boys— such a school as Groton, which [he] himself attended. The center of attention; however, is not an institution but a man, Francis Prescott, founder and headmaster of Justin Martyr. . . .

To present this complex character Auchincloss has devised

a complicated form. He lays down the foundation of the novel with extracts from the journal of Brian Aspinwall, who, at the age of twenty-seven, has become a teacher of English at Justin. (p. 195)

Although Brian's journal is an excellent device for introducing the rector, Brian's knowledge is limited. Auchincloss has therefore made use of other documents. One of Prescott's oldest friends, Horace Havistock, comes to visit, and Brian persuades the man to let him see something he has written about Prescott. This shows Prescott as a boy and young man, and tells how he lost his faith, found it again, and brought the school into existence. . . .

Since Brian has now made up his mind to write a biography of the rector, he goes to see his youngest daughter, Cordelia Turnbull. Having been psychoanalyzed, she talks to Brian with a frankness that shocks him. (p. 196)

Two more witnesses, both dead, are called on for testimony. It appears that Charley Strong left a brief account of his impressions of the rector at Justin and later in Paris. More important is the statement of Jules Griscam, who was one of Prescott's failures. . . .

For the conclusion Auchincloss relies on Brian's journal. In the six years that have elapsed since the beginning of the story, Brian has left Justin, studied in a divinity school, and returned to Justin. Although he has retired, the rector lives near the school and takes a lively interest in it, putting the new headmaster in an unpleasant position. There seems a possibility that Prescott may assert his power in dangerous ways, but at last he learns humility.

Auchincloss has been remarkably successful in making us feel that Prescott is, in many ways, a great man. I don't know whether Auchincloss had some real headmaster in mind, and it doesn't matter whether he did or not, for the rector of the novel is a creation of the imagination, no matter whom he may resemble. Repeatedly Auchincloss introduces allusions to *King Lear,* and, though resemblances are not close, both Prescott and Lear are old men bereft of the power that was theirs for years. (p. 197)

I have always admired Auchincloss's craftsmanship and his prose, but most of his novels, though interesting enough, have failed to excite me. The subject of *The Rector of Justin* does not seem to promise excitement—the octogenarian headmaster of a small private school—and yet I was swept along by it, for the revelation of Prescott's character is fascinating. Auchincloss admires Henry James greatly—which is nothing to be held against him—and he has learned much from his work. I am not sure that James would have approved of the way the book is put together, with the none too plausible introduction of various documents; but he could not have said, as he did say about many writers, that the author had failed to make the most of his donnée. For the method does work, and, we do come to feel the reality, the complicated reality, of Francis Prescott. As the rector himself comes to realize, his kind of headmaster could not exist in the modern world, but it is good for us to meet an heroic character from the not too distant past. (pp. 197-98)

Granville Hicks, "'The Rector of Justin'," in Saturday Review (© *1964 by Saturday Review, Inc.; reprinted with permission), July 11, 1964 (and reprinted in* Literary Horizons: A Quarter Century of American Fiction, *by Granville Hicks with Jack Alan Robbins, New York University Press, 1970, pp. 195-98).*

Letting each of several participants in an action give his account of what happened is not a new device. Joyce Cary used it in the Chester Nimmo trilogy, and Lawrence Durrell successfully carried through a tricky variation of it in *The Alexandria Quartet.* Auchincloss, working on a smaller scale, handles the device adroitly, [in *The Embezzler*]. The ways in which the three interpretations vary are entertaining, and the reader is left to determine for himself where the truth—if, indeed, it is possible to speak of the truth—lies.

It has often enough been pointed out that Auchincloss knows more about "good" society than most contemporary novelists. (pp. 202-03)

It is also important to observe that . . . Auchincloss [is] in the tradition of nineteenth-century fiction. . . . [Auchincloss is a fine craftsman. He writes], however, as if Proust and Joyce and Kafka had never lived. . . .

I have no quarrel with what has been called social realism, and I appreciate the contribution that . . . Auchincloss [has] made to American literature. For me, however, as for many others, [his] limitations are serious. Who are the chief characters in *The Embezzler?* A man whose great pride is in the way he runs a country club, a woman who is interested only in her horses and dogs, and a man whose sole ambition is to make money. Try as he may, Auchincloss cannot persuade the reader to take these people at their own valuation. One has to be wary in stating this kind of judgment; certainly the plots of many of Henry James's novels can be described in such a way as to make them sound ridiculously trivial. But James had resources, both of insight and of stylistic subtlety, that Auchincloss cannot draw on. (p. 204)

Granville Hicks, "'The Embezzler'," in Saturday Review (© *1966 by Saturday Review, Inc.; reprinted with permission), February 5, 1966 (and reprinted in* Literary Horizons: A Quarter Century of American Fiction, *by Granville Hicks with Jack Alan Robbins, New York University Press, 1970, pp. 201-04).*

Concerning Louis Auchincloss's critical appreciation of Henry James: James himself would have enjoyed reading *Reading Henry James,* would have recognized something of his own critical familiarity and discrimination. . . . *Reading Henry James* is less persuasive introduction than illuminating commentary, the illumination assuming common familiarity and interest.

I found the commentary refreshing, intriguing, and challenging. Henry James emerges as clearly and easily from Auchincloss's few pages as he almost is submerged by Leon Edel's massively detailed volumes of biography. Auchincloss's critical discriminations are intriguing enough to initiate reevaluations of one's own. Finally, Auchincloss is forthright in his prejudices. The result is the sense of being party to a lively but mannerly debate between two masters of the art of conversation.

Alas, it is the fact that Auchincloss is a writer in his own right, one who has been linked with Jamesean traditions, that suggests the book's major fault. One misses the writer's *crafty* response to another writer. The all too few times that Auchincloss expresses himself as a writer merely whet our appetite.

The book is a treasure nevertheless. It recalls a time when criticism could be an intelligent, sensitive reading without the strain of proof, the tension of thesis. (p. 123)

James Hughes, in The Antioch Review *(copyright © 1975 by The Antioch Review, Inc.; reprinted by permission of the editors), Vol. 33, No. 2, 1975.*

Louis Auchincloss's idea of a Bicentennial celebration is to write a series of stories ["The Winthrop Covenant"] tracing, as he puts it, "the rise and fall of the puritan ethic in New York and New England." One can think of no more suitable project for a writer whose career demonstrates the continuing ability of that ethic to animate human activity. . . .

As in his previous fictions, Auchincloss . . . addresses himself to the basic issue that recurs again and again in "The Winthrop Covenant": the anguish that accrues to individuals who break faith with a code of conduct that surely began as part of a basic bargain with the Almighty, but has become in recent times merely a binding tradition. His novels are littered with men and women who broke with their code—whether through peculation or adultery or simply by marrying beneath their stations—and paid the price.

Except for "The Rector of Justin" I know of no place in Mr. Auchincloss's fiction where he has directly confronted the religious basis of the beliefs that so frequently govern his characters, and I suppose that his exploration of colonial religious puritanism in the first few stories of this volume represents an artistic necessity for him. Yet less than inspired are the stories dealing with the Winthrop family's involvement in the Salem witch trials and of the developing guilt that later descendants felt over that shameful incident. (p. 10)

With a couple of exceptions, most of the issues that create such a lot of moral pother among his characters will seem to most readers too slight for the inner agitation they give the Winthrop clan. Mr. Auchincloss himself seems often aware of this. After he gets a crisis of conscience rolling he often lets it just peter out rather than bringing it to the sort of rolling boil that would provide a satisfyingly dramatic conclusion.

Things do improve a bit in the book's later stories. He is on more familiar ground in "In the Beauty of the Lillies." . . . And he is at his best in the last story in the book, in which we see how the 20th century can distort and pervert a sense of dutiful mission, making a Winthrop (as it made so many Eastern establishmentarians) into a fanatically dedicated cold warrior (and C.I.A. executive).

Yet, finally, "The Winthrop Covenant" is a disappointing performance. It is a stiff, correct, rather constipated work. Mr. Auchincloss has often and unfairly been compared with Edith Wharton and Henry James. It seems more relevant to put him up against the likes of John O'Hara or, perhaps, Evelyn Waugh. If he had had the luck of the former and had been born outside rather than inside the class that fascinates him, envy might have forced him to develop the shrewdness of observation about the details of dress, decor and manner that gives O'Hara his entertaining bite. Not that Auchincloss is a match for that indecorous Irishman's fascination with upper-class sexual mores. Auchincloss habitually tiptoes discreetly up to the man-woman thing but then averts his eyes (which may be a good thing) and covers his ears (which is a disaster). As for Waugh—well, if there is anything our establishment has been in need of these many years it is satire of the sort he visited on his peers, the sort of thing only a wicked, partial turncoat can do. (pp. 10,12)

Richard Schickel, in The New York Times Book Review *(© 1976 by The New York Times Company; reprinted by permission), March 28, 1976.*

Auchincloss is a relentlessly old-fashioned novelist, as even many of his titles make plain (*The Great World and Timothy Colt; Pursuit of the Prodigal*). His novels suffer from artificiality of plot and manner. I suspect, though, that unlike most writers, he's probably more embarrassing at the moment than he will be in the future. He is, at a minimum, an entertaining correspondent from an under-reported country, the country of the rich.

His new book, *The Winthrop Covenant* . . . , aims higher. It's an effort to examine the philosophical underpinnings of the American upper class.

It consists of nine short stories, all related, as Auchincloss says in a preface, to "the rise and fall of the Puritan ethic." . . .

These stories are uneven; some of them suffer from being more nearly outlines for novels. And there is the difficulty of Auchincloss' rarefied diction. His seventeenth-century figures often sound more contemporary than his contemporaries. . . .

But manners interest Auchincloss less than morals in this book. *The Winthrop Covenant* matters mostly as an extended act of brooding on a central strain in American character. Auchincloss' Puritans brood a great deal themselves. Although they are afflicted with a sense of mission, they are hardly altruistic; their greatest efforts go toward self-justification.

For Auchincloss, Puritanism is an exquisite mix of arrogance and guilt—arrogance breeding guilt, and guilt doting on its own niceties to the point of renewed arrogance. The contradictions were there from the start. The doctrine of grace, central to Puritan theology, might have been devised by R. D. Laing as a model for the creation of schizophrenics. Some are saved and there is nothing anyone can do about it: to be a member of the elect is to feel both helpless and omnipotent. *The Winthrop Covenant* implies that those Americans with the clearest claim to aristocracy have always been profoundly confused about the meaning of their presumed superiority. (p. 112)

Richard Todd, in The Atlantic Monthly *(copyright © 1976 by the Atlantic Monthly Company, Boston, Mass.; reprinted with permission), April, 1976.*

Since [Louis Auchincloss] has . . . devoted volumes to Henry James and Edith Wharton, it would be pleasant to regard him as a New York novelist of society carrying on their valuable tradition more than three-quarters of a century after the publication of such masterpieces as "Washington Square" and "The House of Mirth." Unfortunately, Mr. Auchincloss isn't good enough to be placed in a line with James and Wharton. "The Dark Lady" is a trivial book about trivial people with clockwork insides or no insides at all. . . .

The book is tricked out with numerous Shakespearean allusions, and allusions to painting and mythology. The Sonnets supply the dark lady theme in association with the theme of homosexuality, while Ivy's pimping is linked to the role of Pandarus in "Troilus and Cressida." David Stein, the stepson, has to lose his life on a beach because he is playing Hippolytus to Elesina's Phaedra. And so forth. These allusions work like fine paintings and morocco bindings in some executive suites. They are there to suggest that acquisitive, ambitious business people have a lot of taste and culture as well. Yet few will be fooled. We know that nowadays you get your secretary to order such stuff by the carload over the phone. By the same token, practically nobody in "The Dark Lady" uses contractions in speaking. If they did, the reader might miss the fact that they are top people and merely conclude that they are base, greedy and characterless in the conduct of their lives.

Could "The Dark Lady" possibly be a cool exercise in deadpan irony? That would save it. I fear it isn't.

> *Julian Moynahan, "No Society to Write About," in* The New York Times Book Review *(© 1977 by The New York Times Company; reprinted by permission), August 14, 1977, p. 14.*

*   *   *

AUDEN, W(ystan) H(ugh)   1907-1973

Auden, an Anglo-American poet, essayist, dramatist, editor, and critic, was one of the twentieth-century's greatest poets. The body of poetry that Auden left is distinguished by its remarkable versatility, a variety that encompasses form, metre, subject, and theme. Joseph Warren Beach has said that "when it comes to subject matter and thought, [Auden] has the . . . distinction of being perhaps the most representative of poets in his time writing in the English language. . . . No poet of our time has covered more ground, or ground more favorable to the growth of speculations suited to the felt needs of the time." (See also *CLC*, Vols. 1, 2, 3, 4, 6, and *Contemporary Authors*, Vols. 9-12, rev. ed.; obituary, Vols. 45-48.)

[Auden] thought for a time of shaking the world, and as a young man talked much of its being shaken, but eventually he decided on another mode, to accept with modifications. As this habit grew on him, he increasingly prided himself on it; he was the world's celebrant, and in case that be thought too limited a role, he argued that no poet could be more. . . .

As Auden lowered his sights as poet, he returned to . . . High Church sympathies. . . . [His] decision to regard himself as a believer was also a resolution to make do with what was available, and get on with it. Secular diffusion was a danger. He refused to pursue further the passionate but uncertain outlook which for a time he had accepted from "Lawrence, Blake and Homer Lane, once healers in our English land." Yet he did not abjure them entirely in

favor of the later trio whom he salutes in the poem "A Thanksgiving," in his last book,

> Wild *Kierkegaard, Williams* and *Lewis*
> guided me back to belief.

His twenty years of unbelief were in fact marked by adherence to a secular psychotherapy which was always calling problematic divinities from the wings, "Sir, no man's enemy," "Lords of Limit," or just "Love." It was clear to him then, as before and after, that he required objects of affection more lasting than any his eyes could light upon. His poems were evocations of someone or something that might join stability and affection like form and content. He had no specific commandments to relay, but he could identify outrageousness he disliked in conduct as in poetry. . . .

Although some moving passages in Auden are expressly Christian, such as "O Unicorn among the cedars," from ["New Year Letter"], the center of interest in his verse cannot be said to lie in religious experience. Exaltations and rigors attracted him less than aftermaths and loosenings. His Christmas oratorio, *For the Time Being,* is never more effective than at the close when Christmas is over.

> Well, so that is that. Now we must dismantle the tree,
> Putting the decorations back into their cardboard boxes
> —
> Some have got broken—and carrying them up into the attic.

The amused tolerance and homely images suited his conception of the poet as stymied in action but wonderfully expressive in verbal responses.

In his later aesthetic pronouncements, which he uttered with the greatest certainty, Auden assigned all consideration of the Creator to the Church, but allocated Creation to the poet. This division of labor enabled him to recognize a certain backsliding even among Christian poets,

> Whatever their personal faith,
> All poets, as such,
> Are polytheists,

and perhaps in himself specifically,

> Poets have learned us their myths,
> but just how did They take them?
> That's a stumper. . . .

Auden wrote quite a number of poems of praise, but his most affecting passages are rather those that afford inklings or present forebodings, that connect what seemed unconnectable, that locate wounds and then search and sometimes salve them. As well as being two clergymen's grandson, he was after all a doctor's son. Perhaps no other poet has uttered so many warnings as Auden. His concern for spiritual health was like that of his father for public health in the Birmingham area. Sometimes he warned of a personal doom deep and dark as any sea dingle, sometimes—more communally—of a terrible future for the sleeping city. . . .

Auden was deeply influenced by Freud—perhaps he was the first great post-Freudian poet, a distinction not without its perils—and even more by Freud's eccentric followers Groddeck and Layard. Like the latter, Auden extended Freud into psychosomatic medicine and on his own he translated mental states into spectacular language. So he illustrated "crooked love" by the lines,

The glacier knocks in the cupboard,
The desert sighs in the bed. . . .

He learned from Freud, or confirmed from him, a sympathy for repressed parts of the mind to go with a sympathy for repressed parts of humanity. He also learned the pervasiveness of imperfection. (p. 26)

The title, *Thank You, Fog,* suggests that the volume is to be taken as celebratory, but as usual this strain is much mitigated. The fog makes for good company; it is still fog. If anything, the wryness of the poems is greater; life's tricks, like tricks of phrase, have been seen through. A pungent example is his last variation on the famous line in "September 1939," which announced, "We must love one another or die." Because Auden came to regard this sentiment as fustian, he omitted first the stanza, then ruthlessly expunged the whole poem. But in this last book, the final poem, attributed to Chester Kallman and Auden jointly, contracts the idea to its statable residue:

> When you get a little older
> You'll discover like Isolde:
> "We must love one another *and* die!"

These poems are relaxed and throwaway, almost the opposite of those clamant, heterodox formulations of his experience that he had written at the start. The slow-paced, ruminative, and usually agreeable tone does not keep the perceptions from being unflinching, but it does make them less imperative. For the nouns shorn of articles and the twisted syntax he used as a young man, Auden now substitutes neologisms formed by making nouns verbs and other lexical bizarreries, some more felicitous than others. In his early work the landscape, a mix of industrial smoke and Beowulfian fells, seemed brilliantly invented; the later landscape is deliberately familiar, old-shoeish. Time has brought a concern, even in verse, for bodily comfort. Where once the crosshatch of emotions startled him or appeared to do so, the unsurprisableness of experience now catches his eye. . . .

Auden could cut to the bone in "Lullaby," evidently addressed to his senescing self,

> The old Greeks got it all wrong:
> Narcissus is an oldie,
> tamed by time, released at last
> from lust for other bodies,
> rational and reconciled.
> For many years you envied
> the hirsute, the he-man type.
> No longer: now you fondle
> your almost feminine flesh
> with mettled satisfaction,
> imagining that you are
> sinless and all-sufficient,
> snug in the den of yourself,
> *Madonna* and *Bambino:*
> *Sing, Big Baby, sing lullay.*

So he continues to the last the stripping of illusions which he began in his first book. Vanities change, but vanities remain. The poet bewilders them again as he moves into the shadows. (p. 27)

Richard Ellmann, "Under Tom Tower," in
The New York Review of Books *(reprinted
with permission from* The New York Re-

view of Books; *copyright © 1974 NYREV,
Inc.), December 12, 1974, pp. 26-7.*

[*W. H. Auden: Collected Poems,* the] volume of Auden's achievement, defies immediate critical analysis: seven hundred pages of fine print, 400 poems and some of them very long indeed. But who would be foolish enough to see it as a 'mirror' of our times? There is not one poem in this book which does not contain a beautiful or an unusual line, but there are very few which do not seem abrupt, flawed or unfinished.

They are all, unmistakably, the work of Auden. No poet of his generation acquired such a familiar tone, that raffish poise between schoolboy and schoolmaster, and no poet acquired it so quickly and with such considerable success. Even the early poems have a developed tone and syntax which Auden was never completely to abandon. . . .

The poet springs up fully armed, and although there are some faint traces of early poetic influences—of Yeats and Eliot particularly—they are either skilfully concealed or else charged with irony and bathos. But no poet as receptive as Auden to the prevailing climate will want to escape his time completely. There are other influences at work, and Auden started writing in that odd and heady period when the works of Freud and Marx were becoming fashionable; at a time, then, when nebulous concepts and vague forms of intellectual discipline were placed in the service of romantic mythologies which were no less potent for seeming 'scientific'. Auden's is an art which, from the beginning, used instant methods to achieve vaguely intellectual, quasi-romantic effects.

Even in his earliest poetry, Auden had a taste for gnomic utterances enhanced by emphatic rhythms, for pen-portraits, for short moral lessons, for poems filled with arguments which were never quite as coherent as his rhymes suggested. Auden was, in other words, always a rhetorician, aware as any poet of the truth-giving powers of language but, like any rhetorician, also a formalist prepared to meddle with those powers. He always chose the right tone for the right message, and for the right audience.

English poetry had not behaved in that way since the eighteenth century (Auden's argumentative Muse was the perfect accompaniment to a new Age of Prose) and his effect was enormous. He gave other poets the itch to generalise— to say the right things for the wrong reasons—but he also gave them a highly private language which defeated them. He encouraged smartness and glibness in poets who were not quite as smart or as articulate as he. He encouraged overstatement, and the history of recent years is littered with the inflated corpses of dead poems. With his rhetorical ability to employ different forms for different occasions— with 'Songs', 'Lullabies', 'Letters'—he indirectly turned light verse into something of a poetic fetish, and it has remained an alibi ever since for weak or vacillating poets. More importantly, Auden's rhetoric fatally weakened the language in any hands other than his own: he taught poets to use the language as a vehicle for their consciences, or as the blunt instrument of their 'tone'. Despite his often expressed and boring concern for poetic form, he actively encouraged poetic licence of the most dangerous kinds.

All this was to be expected. A poet who finds his style early in his career is bound to create considerable difficulties for himself and for others; so was there anywhere for

Auden to go after the audacious and considerable verses of his youth? This edition gives some sense of continuity, if not of development. Auden's early hard lines soon disappear; the enthusiastic employment of forms and conceits continues, but now with too much ease and fluency. The struggle to find 'an altering speech for altering things' has been won, but at great cost. A sort of monumental calm descends over Auden's poetry in the 'forties. Where in his early poetry he gave his general statements a concrete etymology, in his later poetry that happy union of the actual and the ideal, that line which crosses precariously between the particular image and the general intent, becomes too stylish and too explicit. His poetry becomes a manual of dexterous techniques. All the work has been done, and he need only stand back and let the verse create itself in a succession of jokes, imprecations and subordinate clauses. . . .

In the poems of what might be called his 'middle period'—'In Praise of Limestone' being a sufficiently familiar example— a number of clauses, each containing an ascertainable and readily comprehensible image, are linked loosely together within the harmonics of an established tone. Nothing is disordered; nothing can go wrong. In the end, though, this 'tone', that particularly English quality which Auden ended up by calling 'common sense', came to dominate whatever Auden had to say. When Auden's poetic strategies became clear, his forms became harder and more predictable, his range of subjects more solipsistic and quirky. He either had something, or nothing, to say. What he actually said it *with* was of lesser consequence, and so he was always seduced by a trite phrase or an easy rhyme. . . .

His early success, and his late decline into amusing doggerel, are part of the same movement. His is a case of the individual talent, to use an antique distinction, which matures at the expense of the tradition. So it is that early influences in his work are minimal or concealed and that, in his later poetry, the language degenerates and the 'I' becomes at once more insistent and more precarious. As his messages and private codes deserted him, so his language became drained and lifeless. Politics was an early and useful disguise but, when that failed him, he turned for an alibi to that most unpoetic of pursuits, Religion.

When Auden 'got' religion, he explicitly devalued poetry: 'That love, or truth in any serious sense / Like orthodoxy, is a reticence . . .' And of course 'Anything will do for children / Made in God's image . . .' Poetry becomes a pastime, a series of Horatian exercises to keep one's end up—rather like doing crossword puzzles. 'So thinking, he returned to duty, reclaimed by the actual world where time is real and in which, therefore, poetry can take no interest.' There are some things, then, which are either unsayable, like 'love' and 'truth', or else not worth the trouble of saying. And so Auden slowly pushed himself and his art into a corner—'About the House', as it turned out. This may seem strange after the heady political commitment of his early years, when poetry was an instrument of belief, but it was natural for him to abscond from History in order to nurse his private pleasures. Poetry was always concerned with instruction or with entertainment—always, in fact, with something other than itself. Auden's progress from politics to quietism, from Marxism to Religion, is not the progress of a poet but of a moralist.

And so in his late poetry there is the same easiness and

fluency, but now they have been entrusted to those small topics which Auden came to celebrate: occasional feasts, limericks, moral homilies, private musings on the weather or the state of his domestic life. . . . (p. 26)

It is dreadful stuff, and only in the context of over-ambitious American rhetoric and tawdry English poetasting would his last poems seem interesting. But he had once been a strong poet, and to the end he remained a significant 'case'. His real measure has yet to be taken. . . . (p. 27)

Peter Ackroyd, "Poetic Licence," in The Spectator (© 1976 by The Spectator; reprinted by permission of The Spectator), September 18, 1976, pp. 26-7.

[Auden] was, quite simply, the best British poet of his generation (not counting Yeats, Graves and De La Mare, all writing but all older). How one looked forward to the new Auden and rushed off to buy it and soak it in! Until—well, he ceased to write consistent poetry, something that was his voice: his song, his magic. Why? What happened in America during the war years? Did he feel himself, although not on purpose, a deserter? Something snapped. But was it merely the boyish gaiety, the underlying health and happiness, however much he wrote about the anxieties and doomsdays of the Thirties? Was it that, because the expected doomsday had come and had petered out, he had to find a deeper doomsday inside himself, a nonpolitical doomsday? In the second part of his life the voice is certainly Auden, but he has dived into darker waters and perhaps has snagged himself on the Christian religion, always a danger for European poets. . . .

Reading here and there [in *Collected Poems*], I find myself lingering over my old favourites, mostly from 1934 to 1940. Some I have chewed over a dozen times, always getting that extra drop of honey. But I should, no doubt, be reading the latest ones—those I found I can't understand or can absolutely not find any empathy with. And the prose? Caliban's long speech? Should it be here? And should the Clerihews, clever as they are, have any place in a volume of poetry? As the pages turn the scholarship deepens, the vocabulary surges and bubbles. Where Mac Diarmid mined the Lallans quarries, Auden mined the obscurer parts of the English language. Scrabble players, take a look! It is difficult going. The allusions become harder to follow. One feels oneself faltering. My fault?

Yet the pure gold can still be found. Some of it goes back a long way. The alliterations come from the Anglo-Saxons; those ancient poets should be proud of their descendant. I remember so well reading the first of them. . . . Almost at the first reading I knew this was the real thing, exciting and beautiful. It is useless to describe poetry; it has to make its own way to the centres of feeling. And maybe I should not be the one to write about it, since the poem I loved best, the one I know by heart, the one that was sparsely titled *1st September 1939,* is not in. Wystan had come to think it was not true. But it was true for me. (p. 26)

Naomi Mitchison, in Books and Bookmen (© copyright Naomi Mitchison 1976; reprinted with permission), November, 1976.

Auden was not blind to the common qualities of tyrant and poet; no doubt it will be said of him, as of that less happy tyrant, T the Great, that 'after he was dead, his traces were visible for years.' All the more strange to have, gathered into one misleadingly final volume [*W. H. Auden: Collected Poems*], that immensely rich and various work, whose importance lies equally outside and elsewhere. And not always as a benign influence: Auden must have ruined as many promising poems of other people's as he himself perfected. (p. 679)

Against the background of negative, minimalist art, shuddering and turning away with fastidious distaste from physical existence, Auden's celebration of earth, his questing curiosity in all her domains, stands out with the more power for its outrageous 'in-the-know' tone. Delight is not the prerogative of simple-minded innocence, he tells us; the songs of experience need not all be songs of pain.

And what a variety of subjects and interests are brought, with a Renaissance enthusiasm, to the poems: astronomy, anthropology, geography, geology, music, medicine—his omnivorous intelligence makes all grist to the Auden mill. Who would he most like to be? Not just Konrad Lorenz—but Firbank into the bargain. Auden's creative incongruities carried over into life.

From this, from the sheer length of Auden's creative life, and from the much discussed episodes—the Thirties Auden, the late Auden, Auden the Marxist, Auden the Christian, and so on—one might have expected the poems to make a disjunct collection, a history of discarded forms and styles, like, perhaps, the self-conscious adjustments and new beginnings of Yeats. Yet quite the reverse is the case.

Of course, Auden had far too good a measure of his audience not to adapt his tone with changing tastes—his rhetoric becoming more modest and discreet, perhaps, but always the voice of a *persona* helping him to hold the centre of the stage as the scene changes. In this light, it seems to me wrong to suggest that some of his revisions—for instance, 'O all the instruments' to 'What instruments we have'—were a forsaking of rhetorical effect for a closer adherence to fact. There is nothing more 'precise' about the revised version here, since we can hardly be expected to read instruments that do not exist. It is not a concession to the factual, but to the matter-of-fact tone; and, as such, is more of a self-conscious adoption of a rhetorical front, than a rejection of it.

His tone may have changed, but that unmistakable and pervasive verbal technique persists in almost every line—so distinctive that if, in Coleridge's metaphor, we met them running wild in the deserts of Arabia, we should instantly cry out 'Auden'. It is there in the very first poem: not Auden in chrysalis, but the brilliant imago. How was it that Auden, alone, came to spring fully-armed, so to speak, from the head of the Muse?

Auden's poetry, like Byron's, is the 'repository of a voice' —a changing voice, like Byron's, but nonetheless self-revelatory. It might be tempting to look for the explanation of the cohesion of his poetry in this characteristic voice, and thus in the personality of Auden—/as we, like his lordship, are mostly impressed by the personality of Byron. After all, Auden greatly admired Byron: they both enjoyed acting extravagant parts (Auden had his Byronic travels, too); they both were possessed of a keen sense of the absurd, particularly, and disarmingly, in relation to their own acting. Yet, of course, there could not be a greater difference in their use of language—the very area which most distinguishes Auden.

T. S. Eliot said that if Byron had distilled his verse, there would have been nothing whatever left. If Auden had distilled his, on the fifth boiling, he would have found at the bottom of the pot his poems unchanged. The words of his poems are important not so much for something behind them, or referred to by them, as in, and for, themselves. In this, they are wholly unlike the words of a Byron poem: their true relation is to music.

Though poets have hardly ever given evidence of their characteristic style in their earliest works, it is not unknown among composers: both Mozart and Chopin, for example, in their different ways gave, almost immediately, characteristic signs of their qualities of mind. In music, there is no separation of style and content: all expression of the individual nature of the artist is in style. Unlike Byron, the composer has no independent sentiments to fall back on. Mighty hot magic, Coleridge called music: and the mighty hot magic which even his detractors recognise in Auden, stems from his instinctive handling of words as a composer uses notes. He accorded them the status of irreducible, physical objects, like notes.

No distillation can boil away the sentiments from a symphony, nor from an Auden poem. Style is everything.

If Auden had ever really come to write the 'Prelude' he apparently projected, it might paradoxically have given us less real Auden than any of his poems. That subject, like all his diverse subjects, would only have been incidental to the style, mere matter for that distinctive poetic manner, which is the index of the individual, to transform: and the very nature of the subject would probably have necessitated the dereliction of the mighty hot magic, in favour of the facetious Don Juan style of which he was such a master.

Magic—or was it all just a mighty hot conjuring trick? A manner of speech, like Browning's, forged by a positive and vigorous intelligence, a hot sauce equally pleasingly masking each crumb from the cornucopia? It was more. Auden qualified our imagination: his incongruities are part of the way we think. (p. 680)

Iain McGilchrist, "Mighty Hot Magic," in The Listener (© *British Broadcasting Corp. 1976; reprinted by permission of Iain McGilchrist), November 25, 1976, pp. 679-80.*

Even in the dark, portentous poems of Auden's early career, there were clear designs, the language of common speech, and an unpremeditated, dramatic manner. It was, in fact, the balance of these elements against the enigma that drew us in.

If the poems sounded at times like riddles, if the syntax was often knotty, yet the words remained natural and the meaning seemed important. Though we might be unsure of his sense, the author was evidently speaking straight to us, and on timely, even urgent matters. He seemed to assume that we understood, that we belonged to his tribe; and as we groped to trace the way, we felt we were just not sharp enough to follow him. . . .

When the meaning of such poems emerged, it often dealt with the separation or opposition of mysterious persons or groups; with a distinction between two psychic conditions and the yearning for a change from one to the other; with movements between vague regions that seemed oddly cut off and yet neighboring. Slowly, we realized that change of place meant change of condition, that the outer landscape reflected inner moods, and the transformations desired were moral or emotional.

In Auden's best work the blend of openness with reserve, of well-defined form and riddling tone, of lucid and yet veiled speech, makes in general two subtle impressions: either that valuable truths are being conveyed, or that a distinguished person is showing us, his fellow tribesmen, a self he hides from strangers. . . .

Auden's later work preserved the element of enigma, in a tangential approach to surprising topics and with exotic words dropped casually into ordinary speech. But the tone remained the sort that members of a harmonious family take toward one another. So Auden holds us with agreeable modulations of language—from slang to eloquence, from the colloquial to the technical—implying a privileged relation between him and ourselves. We respond to his candor, intimacy, faith in our sympathy. We stand with him against the Others. . . .

The efficiency with which Auden traveled about his poetic universe depended on a knack of dividing it up into classes or gradations between which traffic was convenient. It's not for nothing that he wrote an ode to Terminus, the god of boundaries. From his early poems to his latest Auden approached his materials as a cataloguer.

He was eager to put things—morals, detective stories, mining machinery, God—in their proper places. Art, he wrote in "The Sea and the Mirror," presents us with "the perfectly tidiable case of disorder." So he tidied up the world like an affectionate housekeeper arranging a playroom for children: "To set in order—that's the task / Both Eros and Apollo ask." . . .

By a reflex action he seemed to arrange his important experiences as a collector of specimens would arrange rocks and minerals. He analyzed people and incidents into types that lent themselves to abstraction, illustrating principles of ethics or psychology. . . .

Auden at his best . . . embodied the abstractions in curious or supreme examples. So when he wished to celebrate The Poet, he wrote magnificently about Yeats. When he wished to celebrate The Healer, he wrote almost as well about Freud. When he wished to celebrate a way of life, he identified it with the limestone landscapes he loved, and described some typical inhabitants of southern Italy (probably Ischia). . . .

Auden's best poems breathe . . . an air of self-confident control but a lack of self-importance. Like Dr. Johnson, the poet felt cheerfully communicative about matters which interested him: biology and morals, religion and ritual, geology, music, and Icelandic sagas. By fitting them into one of his schemes, the poet brought them into his family, even as he brought in the reader. (p. 10)

Many of the poems entertain us through his habit of playing solemn games with his categories, especially with certain divisions between opposed sides. Auden liked to separate people—or creatures, or ideas, etc.—into mutually exclusive groups, each with its own rules; and he liked telling why they must remain apart. He would go on to treat the consequences of their separation, sometimes explicitly and sometimes cryptically.

But then he would also turn on himself by arranging a passage between the groups. Or he would call for a linkage, produced by means that happily transcended the principle of separation. As the reader takes in the game, he first enjoys discovering the scheme of oppositions and its rules; then he enjoys the benevolent dissolution or transcendence of both.

In the political poetry that Auden wrote during the Thirties, he used to divide the ranks of the oppressors from those of the oppressed and to invoke portents of revolution. But he naturally hinted that his own roots belonged to the former, that by a leap of sympathy he could still identify himself with the latter, and that in some sense love (charity, brotherhood, etc.) might make a bridge. (pp. 10-11)

Auden's drive to establish and cross boundaries went beyond political and social classifications. It started from deeply moral concerns and easily took the form of psychological and religious distinctions: neurosis and health, faith and doubt. Regularly, the poet brought the distinctions to life by relating them to conflicts within the self and by inventing fresh images of transcendence. Even as he noticed the difficulty of crossing a frontier or of bridging a gap, he would insist the change had to be made.

This turn of mind led to another. Auden was struck by the way the commonplace hides the extraordinary, and the outside of things grows from and yet misrepresents their inside: "our selves, like Adam's, / still don't fit us exactly" ("Moon Landing"). Even a world that looks benign makes no response to human misery ("Musée des Beaux Arts"); and utter transformations of character may produce no visible change in one's aspect or manner ("A Change of Air"). In "The Model" Auden deals with the rare instance of an octogenarian who looks as good as she is.

But the opposite case bothered him chronically: colorless lives whose essence is evil. . . .

The persistence of the motif suggests that the poet was reflecting his own moral ambiguity. . . .

[Another] feature of Auden's work [is] the rendering of psychic states in terms of landscape. His imagery easily translated time into space, or changes in personality into changes of location. But the plain unfolding of the self in time seemed more of a challenge to him. At least, Auden handled it with effort, often framing it in the enormous map of phylogeny, or of the evolution of the universe. In a late poem, "The Aliens," he surprisingly finds the metamorphosis of insects an utterly unhuman idea, although he well knew how commonly it has served as a metaphor of man's spiritual history.

Movement in space, whether symbolic or "real," seemed effortless for his imagination. He found it convenient to describe maturing as growing "taller" in his early poems. Later, he could talk about the shift from a worldly to a religious frame of mind as "A Change of Air"; or he could describe the aspiration to grace as "The Quest" of a hero in mythical regions.

A remarkable feature of Auden's symbolic landscapes is the recurrence of certain elements: bleak, north of England scenery, with mines or mining equipment, often abandoned. The poet tells us that when he was a child, between the ages of six and twelve, he enjoyed elaborate daydreams of lead mining in a northern setting. (p. 11)

Auden's first published poem [''Lead's the Best''] was about lead miners who toiled so that cathedrals might have roofs, and that the wealth gained might provide ornaments for a lady whose knights errant were seeking adventure in remote lands.... Almost a quarter-century later, in a superb poem ''Not in Baedeker,'' Auden returned to the theme. Again the lead gave roofs to cathedrals; but no longer did it subsidize ornaments for ladies; instead, it became the linings of coffins, perhaps because Auden's mother had died in 1941. The theme of the hero finding adventure abroad, while the beloved follows the usual routines at home, turns up in several forms, notably in ''Who's Who,'' a neat, incisive comment on the blindness of love....

Didacticism and the impulse to set things in order are traits that encourage categorizing. To strengthen them, there were primitive dichotomies: the split in the self between the child who obeys his parents and the one who resists or ridicules them; or between the adult who labors openly at respectable tasks and the one who enjoys illicit pleasures in secret. Auden's early work *The Orators* is built on such polarities. . . .

In his finest poems the housewifely, didactic impulse becomes merely the ground on which the inner self joins the outer, harmonized by the metrical design. (p. 12)

Irvin Ehrenpreis, ''Inside Auden's Landscape,'' in The New York Review of Books *(reprinted with permission from* The New York Review of Books; *copyright © 1977 NYREV, Inc.), February 3, 1977, pp. 10-12.*

B

BARTH, John   1930-

American novelist Barth employs mythic and literary traditions and techniques to create a unique view of the individual in society, a view which is somewhat cynical but often comical. Educated at the Julliard School of Music, Barth had originally intended to become a jazz musician. His subsequent fascination with *The Thousand and One Nights* and other great tale cycles influenced him to work in that tradition. He has aligned himself with the narrators of these stories by writing works that, he says, "imitate the form of the novel by an author who imitates the role of an author." (See also *CLC*, Vols. 1, 2, 3, 5, 7, and *Contemporary Authors*, Vols. 1-4, rev. ed.)

[*Giles Goat-Boy* is] "splendrously musicked out," but it is also a work in which a highly individualized rhetoric functions as the formative element in a complex of symbol, allegory, character, and plot. . . .

The central rhetoric of the book is that of the first person narrator, Giles. It superficially, if significantly, advertises itself as an extravagant and complex literary joke; not an obviously unified and consistent rhetoric, like the seventeenth-century pastiche of *The Sot-Weed Factor*, but a composite organization drawing on a wide and often incongruous range of styles and registers. The obviously immediate function of this curiousness, this stylistic archaism and eclecticism, is to provide linguistic proof of the uniqueness of Giles. His apparently extra-human origins and his Grand Tutorial or Messianic claims are proved, kept before us, made realities by the distinctive qualities of his language and its sharp contrast with the more simply caricatured discourses that it engages with in Giles' odyssey. Giles is defined by his language almost totally: there is no "objective" information about him, and his exchanges with other characters take place on so exclusively a ratiocinative level that they fail to provide any psychological perspective.

The elements of this rhetoric may be distinguished in the first paragraph.

> George is my name; my deeds have been heard of in Tower Hall, and my childhood has been chronicled in the *Journal of Experimental Psychology*. I am he that was called in those days Billy Bocksfuss—cruel misno-

mer. For had I indeed a cloven foot I'd not now hobble upon a stick or need ride pick-a-back to class in humid weather. Aye, it was just for want of a proper hoof that in my fourteenth year I was the kicked instead of the kicker; that I lay crippled on the reeking peat and saw my first love tupped by a brute Angora. Mercy on that buck who butted me from one world to another; whose fell horns turned my sweetheart's fancy, drove me from that pasture, and set me gimping down the road I travel yet. This bare brow, shame of my kidship, he crowned with the shame of men: I bade farewell to my hornless goathood and struck out, a hornèd human student, for Commencement Gate.

The most obvious non-referential characteristic here is the strongly functioning rhythm. This effect is sustained by syntactic parallelism and a tendency to metrical regularity that amounts almost to syllabic equivalence. A portentously archaic syntax works along with this near-meter. For example . . . ("I am he that was called in those days . . .") is a conspicuous Latinate deviation from any of the contemporary norms for this kind of statement (e.g., "I used to be called" or "I was called then"). In this example the strong internal rhythm depends on the succession of monosyllables and cooperates with the separating out of grammatical elements to produce the solemnity that is a major characteristic of the paragraph. It is, of course, a ludicrous solemnity.

At the level of diction the deviations are even more striking: deeds, chronicled, cloven, tupped, fell, gimping, kidship, bade, goathood, etc., and the deliberate accenting of syllables (hornèd) that becomes a characteristic of the book. Again the effort is towards a highly self-conscious archaism (self-conscious on the part of the author, that is, not Giles) that contributes to our sense of Giles' otherness. This Gilesean idiosyncrasy of language we may identify as the badge of his heroic claims. The whole process of the book may be figured as the engagement of this heroic rhetoric with numerous parodies of the rhetorics of American society, from the grunting of near-animality to the sterile articulacy of academicism.

This, however, is only a diagrammatic simplification. Further attention to the language of this first paragraph reveals that the "heroic" rhetoric is rather invaded than engaged by other rhetorics and registers, and that the resultant clash produces an effect more bathetic than heroic. The rhythm of the first sentence is ruined by the bathetic shift to "in the *Journal of Experimental Psychology*." The archaic syntax of the second sentence collapses into the absurd "Billy Bockfuss," and the elaborate near-meter of the third is spoiled along with its dignity by the banal "in humid weather." These bathetic shifts are, in fact, so pervasively characteristic of the book's use of language that they function overall as a major structuring device. (pp. 147-48)

The rhetorical form of the book is . . . further complicated by another antithesis parallel to the heroic/bathetic clash. This is set up between the traditional polarities of human nature, the animal and the intellectual, and specifically dramatized in the superficially articulated allegory of the goat farm and the university. It is an allegory that provides a context for the book rather than a form; it is an elaborate and extensive device through which the rhetoric asserts the novel's form. . . . Initially it provides the occasion for a bathetic reduction of human history and thought to the politics and squabbles of a university campus. But in the last movement of the book the allegory sheds this function so that the academic world is no longer a comic reduction of the "real" world but simply represents it. This crucial shift is clearly not an effect of the allegory itself but of some factor controlling it. I hope to show that this factor is the changing language of the book.

The antithesis of animal and intellectual, while providing the terms for the allegorical structure, also produces two highly characteristic qualities of the rhetoric itself: the "academic" language, and the "goatish" language. These, of course, are not properly languages but rather areas of linguistic reference that are incongruously involved with each other in Giles' narration. Since there seems to be no agreed term in current critical use for this kind of language situation I have borrowed the linguistic term "register" for these two characteristics. The previously defined elements, the heroic and the comic, are more nearly "kinds" of literary language, and may be referred to as "styles."

It is difficult to illustrate any of these styles and registers in isolation since the functioning of the book depends upon an often bewildering intermixing of its four basic rhetorical elements. The following passage provides, however, a typical example of the academic register.

> [Max] founded the sciences of analogical proctoscopy and psychosymbolistic cosmography, developed the Rectimetric Index for "distinguishing, arithmetrically and forever, the sheep from the goats," and explored the faint initial insights of what was to become Spielman's Law, his last and farthest-reaching contribution to man's understanding of the University. That capstone on the temple of his genius, climax of his epic quest for Answers: how commonplace it sounds already, very nearly banal; and yet what dash, what vaulting insight! In three words Max Spielman synthesized all the fields which thitherto he'd browsed in brilliantly one by one—showed the "sphincter's riddle" and the mystery of the University to be the

same. *Ontogeny recapitulates cosmogony*—what is it but to say that proctoscopy repeats hagiography? That our Founder on Founder's Hill and the rawest freshman on his first *mons veneris* are father and son.

But, as usual, all four tendencies are present even though the academic is dominant. The heroic style is intimately involved with the academic jargon: Max's discovery, or his quest, is identified with the heroic journeys of legend—it's a process of exploration, an "epic quest"—and with Oedipus' tragic insight—"showed the 'sphincter's riddle' and the mystery of the University to be the same." The shift from "sphinx" to "sphincter's" and the *double entendre* of "analogical" and of "Rectimetric" are characteristic of the way in which the bathetic effects cooperate with the animal register to produce comic vulgarity. There is a reference specifically to goats in "what vaulting insight" (though hardly distinguishable from intellectual/heroic suggestions) and in an ingenious literalizing of metaphor, "all the fields which thitherto he'd browsed in." All this is immediately comic and parodic and yet it prefigures, in its stylistic inclusiveness, the whole synthesizing effort of the book: an effort to relate the traditional dimensions of human experience—the intellectual and the physical, the heroic, the tragic, and the comic. This is Giles' attempt as Grand Tutor, or Messiah, and it is hardly surprising that, on the level of plot, he fails to redeem studentdom, retaining for himself alone an incommunicable consciousness of unity and of meaning. It is a fictional process very similar to that of Joyce's *Ulysses,* upon which *Giles Goat-Boy* heavily depends in its continual use of bathos and its rhetorical extravagance. In that book a similar effort towards inclusiveness and synthesis, moving around the emblematic relationship of Father and Son, works hardly at all through the mimetic action or the consciousness of Bloom and Stephen, who are only dimly aware of what they and their situation mean. The synthesis, finally, is Joyce's, not his characters'.

So while any understanding of *Giles Goat-Boy* must depend upon a perception of the total effort to synthesize—an effort involving the interaction of plot, character, symbol, allegory, and rhetoric—it is important that this effort is not simply a linear one, that the book doesn't only "work out" its synthesis. It in fact embodies its synthesis continually in its language. . . . [Rhetoric] provides the reader with the bearings he needs to navigate the three stages of Giles' Tutorship, his search for answers. We may indeed be conscious, for most of the time, of incongruity rather than synthesis, but we are inevitably aware that this language sets up a robust, tragi-comic inclusiveness. Consequently our response to the first effort to find the Answers, the reliance on the essentially moralistic and tragic concept of total "differentiation" of good and evil, is heavily conditioned by our experience of the rhetoric. We naturally resist Giles' fanatical attempt to exclude and deny kinds of experience that the rhetoric has happily, not to say exuberantly, accommodated. The same is true of his second attempt—an equally fanatical reliance on exactly opposite assumptions from the first. In Giles' totally amoral, uncompromising, mindless inclusiveness we miss the complexity and intellectual richness, even the potential for pathos and tragedy, that we perceived in the earlier rhetoric. In the third attempt, however, the components of the rhetoric tend to merge with each other and the gap between Giles and the rhetoric closes.

The passage quoted above was predominantly in the academic register and yet it displayed the influence of all four rhetorical tendencies. This flexibility and capacity to absorb, or at least hold together, language in apparently discordant registers is characteristic of the academic register. It is, after all, situationally dominant; it provides the allegorical structure of the University as the immediate context for the other styles and registers—the heroic style finding its base in the history, philosophy, myth and literature of the past, the comic largely in the sexual irregularities of the faculty and students, the animal register in the University goat farm. It is not therefore surprising that the "goat register," at least in the early part of the book, seems rather less flexible and multi-functioning. (pp. 148-51)

The early scene in which the goat boy watches two "Beist" bohemian students making love is typical of this general function of the goat register.

> I began to realize what they were about. The buck I observed to be in a virile way, and the doe snuggled against his flank with a nervousness I knew the cause of. I took them for superior specimens of their breed: they were shaggier than most, for one thing, and smelled like proper animals. The male had a fine fleecy beard, and neck hair quite as thick as mine, though neither so long nor so ably brushed; his mate had the simple good taste not to shave what little fur the species is vouchsafed for their legs.

Though there is clearly a Swiftian promise in this it remains, at this stage, largely unfulfilled. The joke, that is, can exist simply in terms of the incongruity of the goat register and the human, and in any case they are beatniks. The suggestion of Giles' radically naive, immediate, and therefore innocent response to human functions normally disguised by euphemism, and its consequences for a kind of comic moral realism, is relatively undeveloped. (p. 151)

[The] goat register most commonly functions as the medium through which is asserted one of the polarities of human experience as proposed by the book—the mindless, self-forgetful, orgasmic condition that opposes the will to knowledge and control which makes heroic and tragic experience possible. It is the first kind of experience that Giles pays tribute to as he gallops through the brush after watching the two students make love (or "become"): "only to Be, always to Be, until no thing was: no Billy Bocksfuss, goat or Graduate, no I nor you nor University, but one placeless, timeless, nameless throb of Being!"

As the book progresses its basic synthesizing movement attempts to reconcile not only these grand metaphysical abstractions but also the types of language that combine to figure them. So the amusing conflict of registers gives way to an idiosyncratic but fully synthesized rhetoric in which the elements are no longer felt as antagonistic. This is due partly to simple familiarity with the mixture and partly to the abandonment of satiric and parodic effects in the last part of the book. The goats, and all the terms associated with them, become not comically symbolic of human sexuality but simply descriptive of it. At the same time reference to physicality is less and less in exclusively "goatish"

terms; as the process of rhetorical synthesis goes on other kinds of language are capable of handling this aspect of experience. In the monstrously detailed examination of Anastasia, for example, with its Joycean combination of sensuality and an absurd mathematical pedanticism, the goat reference appears only once, and then negatively.

As they lose their exclusively sexual suggestion, the goat references begin to take on a quite different symbolic function. With the increasing emphasis on hitherto relatively dormant reference to the image of Christ as a shepherd, the goats become symbolic of Giles' Messianic role. The inclusive effort of *Giles Boat-Boy* requires that the Redeemer contain the goatish aspects of Man, rather than hopefully adjure him to be sheeplike. So when Giles approaches the final scene of the execution of his mentor (a victim substituting in a sense for himself) in the hope of gaining a prophetic insight into his own fate, he takes with him all the equipment of the goatherd—stick, shophar, and a goat.

There are, then, four basic kinds of language, distinguished according to style and register, that are highly active in this novel. These combine to provide the four-sided structure that underlies the distinctive rhetoric. But it is suggestive of the generating and controlling power of language in this work that they extend their formative function far beyond the rhetorical level. They provide, in fact, a structural principle for the entire hierarchy of the book's moral allegory as well as the terms for the stages of the narrative allegory.

The hierarchy of allegorical figures arising from the heroic and intellectual concepts provides the framework for the bulk of the exhaustive dialectic that dominates the three stages of Giles' Tutoring. The intellectual concept is productive mainly of the "real" figures, the inhabitants of the campus—Max, Sear, Rexford, the Beists, and ultimately Eierkopf, the egghead himself. The heroic concept is worked out mainly in terms of the ancient heroes of literature and myth—Laertides (Odysseus), Anchisides (Aeneas), Moishe (Moses), "Dean Arthur and Excelsior, his magic quill," "that gentlest of dons, Quijote," and ultimately the two archetypal figures of heroic and tragic experience, Enos Enoch (Christ), and Taliped (Oedipus). The categories are not, of course, quite so distinct; Greene (representing, roughly speaking, the American experience) and Leonid (representing the Russian) are not intellectuals and yet do attain a certain heroic and even tragic status in their reciprocal blinding and self-knowledge, while the urbane intellectual sophisticate, Dr. Sear, is also strongly associated with the tragedy of "Oedipus" and, as his name would suggest, with Tiresias.

Opposing, in a sense, the values to which these figures testify is the rival hierarchy enacting the comic and animal concepts. These two are much less easily distinguishable from each other than the pair just considered, because to a great extent what is comic is precisely the animality and sexuality of the figures. And of course the comedy of bathos is highly operative upon the heroic and intellectual figures as well; indeed it informs, and up to a point characterizes, the whole book. (pp. 152-53)

The nature of the sexual comedy is suggested in the deadpan vulgarity of the pun. Further up the scale towards animality are the wildly perverted Mrs. Sear and the nymphomaniac, Anastasia. The latter, however, comes finally to embody the value of sexual experience in a conjunction with Giles that is more mystical than animal. Her husband Stoker, voyeur and sadist, represents superficially the familiar association of sexuality and violence, and in a more complex way, with his Power House, his energy and his amorality, the libido itself. Finally, at only a little removed from the goats themselves, there are the crazed and dumb G. Herrold, who introduces the goatish Giles to sexuality, and his symbolic successor, the giant Croaker, whose animality and total commitment to sexuality finally lead him to the rape of a soft-drinks machine.

It is through his advice to these figures that Giles attempts to relate the diverse and apparently contradictory elements of human nature. They function as dramatic extensions of the potentialities of his own rhetoric, or alternatively, since the narrative is supposed to be dictated by a retrospective Giles some twelve years on, it could be said that his rhetoric is itself the solution to the problem their differences and antagonisms present. It is an elegant and appropriate irony in this most "literary" of works that the only answer that Giles and the author provide to the eternal mystery, "the riddle of the sphincters" and so on, is a rhetoric in which it is possible to discuss and contain the failure to find answers.

However, in order to arrive at so nice a paradox, Giles has to undergo the traditional ordeals of heroes, philosophers, prophets, and Messiahs: education, the heroic voyage, the temptations of the flesh, interrogation, imprisonment, the usual execution and resurrection, and a formidable amount of dialectic and ratiocination. It is this process that I referred to as the "narrative" allegory, when I suggested that it too was organized by the same elements that characterize Giles' rhetoric. (pp. 153-54)

Giles encounters and ultimately judges a range of rhetorics and values that includes liberal idealism, in his tutor, Max Spielman; liberal pragmatism, in Chancellor Rexford; American optimism and sentimentality, in Peter Greene; manic rationalism, in Eblis Eierkopf; vulgar sensuality, in Stoker; almost meaningless academicism, in the Philosophy Tape; and, most seductive of all, the constantly changing rhetorics, values and faces of the Satan figure, Bray. The extravagances of these rhetorics are really unacceptable specializations of the components of Giles' own language, which is, of course, the controlling language of the book.

The climax of [the] educational experience is Giles' exposure to the tragedy of *Taliped Decanus;* this section also functions as the transition to the first part of his Tutoring, since his answers in that part assume an essentially tragic view of experience. This resolute denial of the solemnities of the archetypal tragedy by a disastrous change of register (it's "translated" into comic strip American slang) is the most extravagant literary joke of the book. Of course the change of context, from Greek city state to American campus, is immediately reductive, but it is the ludicrous incongruity of the language that effects the shift into farcical parody. This parody is, admittedly, something of a *jeu d'-esprit,* an indulgence only possible in this kind of baroque comic fiction, but it is also crucial in conditioning our responses to the attempts to find the "right Answers" that follow. It is a local intensification of the bathetic tendency of the rhetoric, and, in the first stage of Giles' Tutorship, it reinforces the habitual flatness to ensure our awareness of the error of Giles' solution. For that solution is clearly based on tragic assumptions. Dr. Sear, after the perfor-

mance, specifically associates the tragedy, and the tragic condition of man, with the Christian myth of the Fall— "We all flunked with the first two students in the Botanical Garden"—and Giles' response is correspondingly radical. He attempts to reverse the fall and return studentdom to a prelapsarian condition by the process of differentiation. This is an effort to remove the conditions that made tragedy possible (pp. 154-55)

In the second stage of Giles' teaching we have considerably less assistance. The dominant comic rhetoric and *Taliped* have, throughout the first stage, worked against the apparent direction of the narrative to the point of resurrecting Giles after his lynching (a comic conflation of Christ and Tom Jones). Thereafter the new teaching of the resuscitated Giles is unmistakably comic in its assumptions ("Embrace") and it becomes far more difficult to distinguish between the implications of his rhetoric and the message it offers to convey. There are differences however: the comic solution implies an harmonious relating of elements, a social synthesis, whereas Giles at this point simply denies the validity of all distinctions and lapses into the easy tautologies of pseudo-mysticism ("if failure and passage was in truth a false distinction, as I'd come to believe, then it made no difference whether that distinction were true or false, as either way it was neither"). Consequently this exuberant declaration of sensuality and amorality leads to an even more serious collapse of social and economic order, and as Giles is brought to his second lynching our sense of the fanatical partiality of his "Answers" is again confirmed by the narrative. The extremes of tragedy and comedy potential in the rhetoric have, at this point, been objectified in the narrative and discarded. Having rejected both these modes the book has to discover its own if it is to cohere as art, just as it must also rescue itself from bathos if it is not to deny its own significance.

This process begins with Giles' final "examination" in the "Belly" of the computer god WESCAC; lost in a mystical and sexual union with Anastasia he sees the unity and meaning of life:

> Was it Anastasia's voice? Mother's? Mine?
> In the sweet place that contained me there
> was no East, no West, but an entire, single,
> seamless campus: Turnstile, Scrapegoat
> Grate, the Mall, the barns, the awful fires of
> the Power house, the balmy heights of
> Founder's Hill—I saw them all; rank jungles
> of Frumentius, Nikolay's cold fastness,
> teeming T'ang—all one, and one with me.
> *Here* lay with *there, tick* clipped *tock, all*
> serviced *nothing;* I and My Ladyship, all,
> were one.

The rhetoric here has eliminated the hitherto dominant bathetic tendency by uniting its own constituent elements. It is easy to separate these out again artificially—the campus terms, the goat terms, and so on—but partly through simple familiarity and partly through a shift of tone, the rhetoric now disguises the incongruities it has hitherto been intent on declaring. In this passage, for example, there are none of the bathetic rhythmic collapses that were so prominent a feature of the first paragraph. The novel is moving into its defining mode, which for want of a better term we may call the "ironic." The whole book is, in a sense, a metaphor for the only kind of novel it is now possible to write, and the only kind of life it is possible to live (possible, that is, in this novel's terms). The inclusiveness of its rhetoric, the very quality of its texture, has frustrated its aspirations to tragedy and to comedy. It thus pretends to make what it can of the frustrations, and achieves form through the denial of traditional forms. (pp. 155-56)

The final scene of Max's apotheosis and of Bray's (Satan's) expulsion, theoretically something of a triumph for Giles, is in fact deeply ambiguous in its details.

> . . . people leaped from the stands, swarmed over the barricades in both directions, fell upon their knees and girlfriends, clouted neighbors, clutched loved ones. Bravely the band played New Tammany's anthem until overrun. Guards scrambled into the moat, either to arrest or to protect me; at their head grinned Stoker, cursing as he came.

Every detail and action is contradicted or qualified; this is at once the comic perception of inherent disorder or paradox, the imperfectibility of studentdom, and, in its comicality, evidence of just how far the mere contradictions of life are from the "passèd Paradox" that Giles understood finally in the Belly. This public response enacts, in its confusion, a kind of parody of the attained truth.

The final sentence of the narrative part of the book functions as a summary in miniature of Giles' attitude and situation. In the general ambiguity of the last scene its exactness is teasingly suggestive.

> Nonetheless I smiled, leaned on my stick, and, no troubleder than Mom, gimped in to meet the guards halfway.

The syntactic regularity—three main clauses, interrupted by a characteristically idiosyncratic adjectival phrase—establishes its casual rhythm. The indifferent smile, the compromising with the guards, the limp, and the supporting stick suggest the prospective ambivalence of his relationship with authority. The homely comparative—"no troubleder than Mom"—understates his divine placidity. This adjustment to reality is Giles' final achievement; he continues secure in the knowledge of his essence and his genius, menaced when not ignored by society. This is his only heroism and it implies the novel's only form. (pp. 156-57)

It is this acute consciousness of the dangers of posturing and of solemnity that informs the elaborately defensive rhetoric of *Giles Goat-Boy.* It is, after all, a novel of enormous ambition, masquerading as a joke—the Revised New Syllabus itself. In its distrust of traditional modes it repudiates comedy and ridicules tragedy, and in its distaste for the novel form it refuses to locate its meaning in the narrative structure, leaving the apparent climax inconclusive and ambiguous. In this respect it again echoes *Ulysses;* the last sections of that novel refuse to allow any dignity or significance in the meeting of Bloom and Stephen to emerge at the level of narrative. But *Giles Goat-Boy* is working towards a possible heroism, towards a possible epic, and if Giles himself is allowed only this placid assurance—"no troubleder than Mom"—the novel itself has no such modesty.

Having reached this ambiguous non-climax the narrative ends, and in the retrospective Posttape that follows all the Romantic and heroic aspirations that the rhetoric has been

so firmly controlling find free expression. The pretext on which this freedom is gained is amusingly and deliberately transparent. Since the whole of the narrative (the Revised New Syllabus) is supposed to have been dictated by Giles into a computer for the benefit of posterity, the awareness of a public obliged him (or Mr. Barth) to equip his story with all the comic devices for self-protection that are necessary in a skeptical age. But since the Posttape is supposed to be Giles' private communication with himself, there is no need for self-protective irony, and the rhetoric can rise to an eloquent celebration of the Romantic hero, rejected, humiliated, "naked, blind, dishonored," yet finally triumphant in his apotheosis—the new Christ. . . . [For] all his protestations, he has made for himself a hero.

Which was, after all, what he announced he wished to do. The rhetoric of the Posttape is amusingly (*and* movingly— that is the point) similar to the rhetoric of the so-called "Cover letter to the Editors and Publishers." The full blown Romantic *cri-de-coeur* of the latter is both ironic and non-ironic: it is prophetic of the whole effort of the book, indeed it is its *raison d'être,* yet it is protected by its self-conscious pose, its air of regretful parody. . . . *Giles Goat-Boy* is the making of that mythic voyage and the making of a hero. But heroes are made with great difficulty in the highly self-conscious, anti-heroic literary tradition that this novel continually acknowledges. So perversely enough, the would-be hero must not only fail and suffer rejection—the familiar tragic and romantic version of the heroic process— but must narrate his history in a ludicrously composite rhetoric that makes continually for bathos. And it is the overcoming of this inherent disability of the rhetoric, the gradual relating of its initially antagonistic elements, that constitutes the central activity of the book. It is this linguistic triumph that finds its celebration in the superbly confident heroic rhetoric of the final paragraphs of the Posttape. Of course Mr. Barth's unmoved persona, in the Postscript, doesn't believe a word of it. (pp. 157-58)

> *Peter Mercer, "The Rhetoric of 'Giles Goat-Boy',"* in Novel: A Forum on Fiction *(copyright © Novel Corp., 1971), Winter, 1971, pp. 147-58.*

Frye's concept of anatomy and a recent amplification define a work [*Lost in the Funhouse*] whose unity is an intellectual concept so lively that it can spin out of its own energy a self-contained, fanciful, and witty anti-novel. The narrator speaks through multiple voices engaged in a freely associative conversation that parodies standard prose fiction and reproduces non-standard conventions of time and size. The unity of the anatomy, then, resides in its inherent multiplicity. The anatomy even mocks its own unity. *Funhouse,* then, keeps the excellent company of such anatomies as *Tristram Shandy, Orlando, The Anatomy of Melancholy,* and the currently popular *Steppenwolf.* More than its literary analogues, what Barth's *Funhouse* projects in addition to the above criteria is an anatomy of prose fiction: *Funhouse* is a microcosmic anatomy of criticism presented in the unifying and unique metaphor of a funhouse in which any modern reader, critic, or writer of prose fiction can easily get lost. That, in fact, is probably the point. *Lost in the Funhouse,* then, is an anatomy unified by its own anatomy of criticism.

The two principal forms of prose fiction anatomized, or perhaps satirized, are the absurd and the autobiographical.

While the absurd is decidedly European in Barth's treatment, the autobiographical begins in an international frame but soon adapts to the American form of the adolescent novel.

These principal forms do not exclude more specific genres, as the first chapter of *Lost in the Funhouse* indicates, appearing as a "FRAME-TALE" one-page long which includes: a title, a Moebius strip decorated with the words "Once Upon a Time There Was a Story That Began . . . ," and the directions for the cut-out. At the outset of the work, Barth puns on the whole problem; he will not write a Chaucerian frame-tale, but he will prove that all stories are frames (put-ons) and that, more important, they are framed by their own limitations, by their beginnings and endings which never begin and never end. The medieval frame-story, in an ironic juxtaposition of structure and concept, illustrates the existential principle of absurdity: the novelist fuses ancient and modern, beginning and end. The motif of circularity that characterizes the absurd in fiction frames the book in a circle or, more accurately, a Moebius strip, which begins and ends only to begin again, a journey that goes nowhere, a trip that ends at the point of departure. (pp. 31-2)

Chapter 2 continues this preliminary expository function of representing the book's structural unity in the form of a "Night-Sea Journey." The action presents an illustration of the principle of the absurd in a doubly ironic metaphor for journey: the narrator must cross the sea of life by swimming until he drowns. The difficulties of this journey to a death by water are immense: night-time hardly constitutes the best setting for "reaching the Shore." . . . Barth can then pun that we are all "equally in the dark" . . . : secondly, the apparently linear journey across the sea is more circular than linear. The dark and circular qualities of the journey give it such absurd character and charm that Barth cries that he loves night-sea journeys and the accounts of them "*because* they are absurd." . . . That the swimmers have other things in mind besides a swim for swim's sake becomes clear when Barth describes the strokes as "tailing along" . . . or conceives of a possible Maker who is "tailless" . . .—as if characters on a Chaucerian journey could ever be tale-less—or finally, imagines a possible Maker of our Maker who possesses "some supertail." . . . The extraordinary number of swimmers, a quarter-billion per night, of whom say "one swimmer in two hundred fifty billions achieved a qualified immortality" . . . , testifies to the fact that Barth is, of course, talking about sex and, therefore, about life in a biological sense as well. . . . From the creation of life through a sexual death to the creation of prose fiction is an easy back stroke, or stone's throw if the swimmer is Camus. Barth reaches the two climaxes simultaneously "thrashing, singing, cursing . . . struggling on, but dying all, and still in darkness." . . . The perfect anti-hero for Barth's anti-novel swims to immortality, thrashing on, strangling, and singing "Love! Love! Love!" . . . , like some doomed Beatle, at the absurd height of his fictional and real orgasm.

If Chapters 1 and 2 constitute an exposition, what approximates Part II of the anatomy represents the development of prose fiction as autobiography as well as the parody of that form: the chapters include "Ambrose His Mark," "Autobiography," "Water-Message," and the climactic "Lost in the Funhouse." If not divined earlier, the master and model anatomist for Barth is Laurence Sterne.

Ambrose of "Ambrose His Mark" is the literary heir of that delightful assembly of eighteenth-century heroes whose christenings, not to speak of births and conceptions, are attended by extreme mystery and prolongation, and compounded by the pressures, but hardly the rewards, of propriety. . . . Sophocles, Plato, Xenophon, and Ambrose, however, are equally accurate and appropriate as progenitors. . . . (pp. 32-5)

Fittingly in the next chapter, "Autobiography: A Self-Recorded Fiction," the first self-conscious Shandean remark that this prose-speaker makes concerns the inappropriate nature of his name: "Among other things I haven't a proper name. The one I bear's misleading, if not false. I didn't choose it either." . . . It soon becomes clear that the speaker in the chapter *is* "A Self-Recorded Fiction" just as the subtitle of the chapter suggests: the one and only character of this autobiographical chapter and indeed of the whole work is *fiction,* a prose fiction recording its own speaking voice. It speaks, therefore it is, or as Barth says "Where there's a voice there's a speaker." . . . Talk is just as essential to the anatomy as to the existential "novel"; in the Beckett, Queneau tradition, "I talk therefore I am" summarizes both philosophy and technique. Barth undercuts this serious rule, however, with a tragi-comic "*crise d'identite*": "I must compose myself. Look I'm writing. No, listen I'm nothing but talk; I won't last long." . . . (pp. 35-6)

This lost, unidentified, and misnamed child of ancestral fiction at least has a very *special* father—probably Barth himself, "he went by the book" . . .—but also very much Laurence Sterne. . . . In fact, the parent of the anatomy is beginning to look less like a novel device and more like the novel itself. Although few puns could surpass, "a mere novel device," Barth continues to pun merrily along with my father saying to my mother "bear in mind" and explaining away the created, but unwanted child as a "figure of speech." . . . No wonder that the poor distraught mother of "Ambrose His Mark" neglects to name a child whose birth has coincided with the commitment of the father in a mental institution. The narrator-speaker, in fact, sounds a bit mad himself as he raves on at a maniacal, yet halted pace, urging himself to stop and then in desperation pleading to his father to do it for him: "Put an end to this, for pity sake!" . . . , and all the while continually parodying forms of himself like "climax," and, more important, "confession" . . . , that third step of prose fiction in Frye's scheme previous to this as yet unnamed work—anatomy. (p. 36)

In a continuation of the development pattern of the novel, "Water-Message" clearly is a parody of a particular form of prose fiction—the American adolescent novel: Ambrose is coming of age. Structured in the familiar form of epic journey, the section prototypes initiation as theme and an American Huck Finn, Ambrose, as hero. The climactic initiation occurs with a secret club of adolescent boys in a hut-cabin in the jungle of American experience. Like all exposes of the problem of innocence and experience in the American literary tradition, this initiation provides an appropriate setting, an isolated spot in the wilderness. Before entering the cabin, Ambrose has an adolescent fantasy about his own death, just as the Huck Finn episodic fantasy precedes the hero's encounter with "Pa" in the cabin on the river bank. The modern hero has more fun than Huck;

the initiation in the cabin is sexual, or believing Leslie Fiedler, one must say heterosexual. Afterwards, the hero re-enters the social world alone and "alienated" with the club motto over the door framing his exit: "No babies allowed." . . . This is the closest to "moral" that the story comes: there is no "Water-Message" contrary to the title, but only a water bottle with a paper composed of a salutation, a complimentary close, and a blank for a message. A very Shandean Huck follows Twain's tradition paraphrased that persons attempting to find a moral will be banished if not shot.

An additional parody of a form of writing in the following transitional chapter, "Petition," relates perhaps obliquely to ordeals of love and personality development, but more to a grotesque schizophrenic debate between body and mind in the form of a short epistolary novel. The unique juncture of Siamese twins Eng and Shang (Yin and Yang and the Zen-Buddhist creativity cycle?) provides Barth with a situation rich with possibilities of pun on the old comfortable expressions of modern love. . . . This grotesque situation prepares us for the visit in the next chapter to a house of freaks, a cave of grotesques: in this climatic chapter Ambrose and everyone else gets "Lost in the Funhouse." . . . This titular and actual center of the novel climaxes the absurd and autobiographical trends of the book. . . . The funhouse becomes a metaphor not only for the general setting of the sexual experience of love ("If you knew your way around in the funhouse like your own bedroom" . . .), but also specifically for the body of a woman. Again, Barth would rather go through a funhouse than write about one (at least that is what he says), just as he would rather *be* than *act*. The verb "to be" in a Barth novel represents copulation, a copulative verb, just as Sterne's "conversation" is the linguistic equivalent of sex. (pp. 37-9)

The funhouse, of course, presents a complex, metaphoric journey where the absurd and autobiographical traditions merge: the life and art represented are labyrinthine, absurd, grotesque, and distorted. The House of Fun and Games becomes a House of Horror, even a Funny House or Funny Farm, the Place, and finally a Madhouse, where Ambrose talks himself to death trying to stay alive. That is, in the existential tradition of Beckett and Queneau, "I talk therefore I am" is doubly ironic when to talk too much is to talk oneself out of existence, what Barth calls the "novel of exhaustion." The funhouse then represents an anatomy of madness as well as an absurd, existential novel in a constant state of self-parody.

Not only new trends in the novel are subject to parody; the most conventional of novel forms succumb to the Shandean wit of the self-conscious narrator as well as *criticism* of novel forms:

> A long time ago we should have passed the apex of Freitag's Triangle and made brief work of the denouement; the plot doesn't rise by meaningful steps but winds upon itself, digresses, retreats, hesitates, sighs, collapses, expires. The climax of the story must be its protagonist's discovery of a way to get through the funhouse. . . .

The *ABC* of Freitag's Triangle represents the action of conventional dramatic narrative; like Sterne, Barth expands the diagram by graphing the lines on the discussion page as

illustration and by modifying the triangle to a variant including a *BC* line for the "rising action" which this chapter supposedly reproduces. (pp. 39-40)

In the American novel, the funhouse (itself the novel) replaces the wilderness in which one got lost to find oneself or else, like Young Goodman Brown, simply got lost. The dark mysterious forest of the American experience could not have more weird creatures than do the paths of this dark house. The most estranged traveller in the house, of course, is the narrator himself as he peers in the mirrors of the funhouse: "*lost himself in the reflection*," or "Stepping from the treacherous passage at last into the mirror and maze, he saw once again, more clearly than ever, how readily he deceived himself into supposing he was a person." . . . (pp. 40-1)

The last part of the "novel" approximates an anticlimax with two contrapuntal forms: parody of myth alternates with parody of art until the "novel" talks itself to death. "Echo" is a microcosm of the whole, representing a "lost voice" like that of the funhouse author. Her story is sad. At one time this talented nymph could beguile all the gods by her gift of story-telling:

> Afflicted with immortality she turns from life
> and learns to tell stories with such art that
> the Olympians implore her to repeat them.
> Others live for the lie of love; Echo lives for
> her lovely lies, loves for their livening. . . .

By perverting her gift to distract the wife of Zeus while he seduces another, Echo becomes one of the lost, damned and doomed forever to the hellish punishment of echoing the last words of other people's stories. Any retold myth, of course, especially the present one, exemplifies such an echo; like Barth's anatomy, Echo "effaces" herself "until she becomes no more than her voice." . . . Barth questions the possibility of separation: words from speaker, medium from message, and dancer from dance. Narcissus, Echo's alter ego in the art of narration, has not only not lost himself in his echo, he has become himself by falling in love with his own reflection. Tiresias completes the triangle by affecting objectivity. Tiresias, in fact, is the omniscient third person narrator, a balance for the extremes of subjectivity. . . . The triangle of narration, then, consists of first person omniscient Narcissus, second person limited Echo, and third person omniscient Tiresias. The problem, however, is that Thebes, the waste land city of conventional structure, is falling down: the multiple voices of an anatomy interchange and intermingle until all is repetition and self-reflection in one self-destructive form or another.

Shortly after, for instance, "Niagara Falls," the more important of "Two Meditations," demonstrates the cataclysmic collapse of the novel system, a disastrous explosion of energy:

> For ages the fault creeps secret through the
> rock; in a second, ledge and railings, tourists
> and turbines all thunder over Niagara. . . .
> In your spouse, so apparently resigned,
> murder twitches like a fetus. At some trifling
> new assessment, all the colonies rebel. . . .

Then again, the denouement in a true up-ending of the already-destroyed novel begins all over again in "Title" as Barth puns on endings by experimenting with various beginnings:

Once upon a time you were satisfied with
incidental felicities and niceties of technique:
the unexpected image, the refreshingly accurate word-choice. . . .

The narrator is impotent; he cannot end what he has not
managed to begin: "I can't finish anything; that is my final
word." . . . (pp. 41-2)

This, of course, is *not* his final word in the "novel of silence." After an apparently final mythological gloss in
"Glossolialia," the anatomy has yet another identity crisis
in "Life-Story": Am I, asks Barth, a *roman á clef*, a *Bildungsroman*, an *Erziehungs roman*, or a *roman fleuve*? Who
are my friends, he asks, and proceeds to profess disdain for
theatre of the absurd and the experimental fiction of Beckett, sounding all the time like *Krapp's Last Tape.* (p. 42)

Barth escapes his identity crisis by avoiding it in the last
chapter supposedly written anonymously: we guess the
author from the concluding "Tailpiece," even though the
whole chapter-code is named "Anonymaid."

Will anyone have learnt its name? Will
everyone? No matter. . . . on a lorn fair
shore a nameless minstrel

Wrote it. . . .

As the "novel" ends, the anonymous writer is crying for
identification, calling for a name, and *Funhouse* in disguise
or otherwise is a live and well anatomy of prose fiction. (p.
43)

> Carol A. Kyle, "The Unity of Anatomy:
> The Structure of Barth's 'Lost in the Fun-
> house'," in *Critique: Studies in Modern Fic-
> tion (copyright © by Critique, 1972), Vol.
> XIII, No. 3, 1972, pp. 31-43.*

The logic of pluralism demands that its practitioners make
ever new starts, venture beyond ever "New thresholds,
new anatomies!" Among contemporary novelists, none has
sought more strenuously and more consciously to create an
omnibus "literature of exhausted possibility," aside from
Borges, than Barth (in this country), Günter Grass (in Europe), and Nabokov (in Estotiland-Terra-Antiterra). All
three have relied heavily on the paraphernalia of doubles,
disguises, and mirrored refractions in their probings of
whether reality consists ultimately of the one or the many,
of unity or multiplicity. One thinks of Ebenezer and his
twin sister, Burlingame and his half brothers, Humbert and
his alter ego Quilty, Oskar the three year old and Oskar the
thirty year old; or of Lolita forced to choose (in Humbert's
jocular words) "between a Hamburger and a Humburger."
. . . These are ambulatory skylarks into the Daedalian maze
in *jeu d'esprit* anticipations of worlds glimpsed from afar
and soon to be explored. In comparison to *The Sot-Weed
Factor, The Tin Drum,* and *Lolita,* the later plunges into
the "weary labyrinth" are belabored efforts at historical-
mythical-allegorical fabling. *Giles Goat-Boy, Dog Years,*
and *Ada* are encyclopedic histories of their authors' worlds,
reinventions pursued relentlessly to the final exhaustive
pun and ultimate self-fulfilling parody. To move from the
belly of WESCAC to the pit of the Brauxel potash mine to
the lumber room of Ardis Hall is to wander through the
labyrinthine galleries of western civilization. The achievements here are endgames. Like Joyce's *Finegans Wake,*
they present us with forms exhausted, possibilities fully re-

alized. In this respect, the methods of Black Humor ironically have displayed a predilection for early obsolescence,
forcing the Black Humorist to be continuously inventive, a
magician surprising us with a new animal each time he
reaches into his hat.

The gesture of perennial renewal demanded of Black
Humor is not undertaken lightly. To date Barth has been
one of its most seriously self-immolative fabulist adven-
turers. He did not embrace the role of Menelaus on the
beach at Pharos wrestling with Proteus for his literary identity with the alacrity of George Goat-Boy determined to
make himself a culture hero. The facts would indicate that
he stumbled somewhat onto this novelistic path when he
broke free of the "Maryland-based verisimilitude" of *The
Floating Opera* and *The End of the Road* into the historical
amplitudes of *The Sot-Weed Factor.* Barth has admitted to
being ignorant of the patterns of mythic heroism at the time
of his writing *The Sot-Weed Factor.* Nevertheless, Ebenezer and Burlingame in combination exhibit most of the
characteristics of the culture hero listed by Lord Raglan in
The Hero. Once he learned of the hero with a thousand
faces, as mapped by such comparative mythographers as
Lord Raglan and Joseph Campbell, he recognized the use-
fulness of the archetype in his exploration of the disease of
modern life—Todd Andrews's, Jake Horner's, and Ebenezer Cooke's malaise, *cosmopsis* Jake Horner tags it—the
uncertainty of an essential "I." (pp. 28-30)

Intent on testing whether the current loss of self is simply
the latest multiagonist masking a mythic identity, Barth deliberately employs the hero with a thousand faces for his
protagonist in *Giles Goat-Boy.* In this act, Barth indicates,
if the early novels had not already made it clear, that the
Great Labyrinth is imaged for him less by the cosmos than
by the mind, less by the incoherent social scene than by the
disintegrated self. His literary aim then is not, like that of
Borges . . . , to create a paradigmatic design more coherent
than that found in the world. Rather, Barth's preoccupation
is with isolating and identifying the ineluctable sense of
what it is to be human. He fails in *Giles Goat-Boy* essentially because the mythic prototype he parodies is too hybrid a form, too diffusely "hit-and-miss" a system. Ger-
hard Joseph is right to conclude that Barth, "in his
depletion of the picaresque mode, in his erudite catalogues
of ideas, or in his name-calling contest between the prostitutes," was trying in *The Sot-Weed Factor* "to convey the
impression that sheer exhaustiveness for its own sake contributes to a meaningful comic [cosmic?] order." The literary form of *The Sot-Weed Factor,* its correspondences to
the novels of Fielding and Richardson limited its boundaries, as did also Barth's divided attention to the human and
the cosmic labyrinths. In *Giles Goat-Boy* Barth was unhampered by such generic considerations and went all out
to compress within the covers of one book the whole story
of man, "from primitive animal to autonomous computer."
That the effort did not lead Barth to a redefinition of man
meaningful for our time but left him like George Goat-Boy,
with all the old categories, contradictions, and appearances
still as ill-defined and as imminent of the primordial threat
of chaos as ever, does not mean that the novel was altogether a dead end for Barth. With it he learned, as Borges
seems to have known intuitively from the outset, that the
objectivity of the mythographer, with his empirical arrangement of diverse materials, does not lead one to the heart of
the matter, to the identification of the self, but merely to

the accumulation of the flotsam and jetsam of civilization, the hero remaining the sum of his disparate parts, the quotient of his thousand and one faces. Barth also learned that if George was merely equivalent to the refractions of his thousand images, Oedipus offered a mythic correlative to the private self as well as scoring highest on "Lord Raglan's twenty-five prerequisites for ritual heroes."

The "modern translation" of *The Tragedy of Taliped Decanus,* a middle-American tragedy of "making it," with slangy diction and academic setting, is one of the more successful pieces of writing in *Giles Goat-Boy.* . . . In this version of the Oedipus story, the problem of knowledge—here Oedipus's self-knowledge—is twisted out of its ethical frame of reference (as witnessed by the pun on "prophprof") into a profane exposition of the "old Adam" in man. Taliped is less obsessed with the mystery of his aristocratic identity than with the knowledge that keeps winding him back to himself as sexual beast. Not the idea that he "murdered Pa" but that he "mounted Ma" monopolizes his horrified imagination. The perennial fascination of the nymphomaniac mother comes with a shock of recognition that the engineered consummation of Ebenezer's marriage to Joan Toast seems not to have stirred. The two-backed animal act of George and Anastasia in the Belly of WESCAC, however, confirms this iconoclastic vision of man. It is Joan Toast's and Anastasia's secret knowledge as females that "saves" both Ebenezer and George, leading them to the recovery of Malden and the salvation of the College, in short to the sexual urge to love and the existential urge to be, fundamental to all value systems.

The aftermath of *Giles Goat-Boy* has seen Barth return to personal origins, to his restatements of the Oedipal theme and to his inchoate urgings of self into artistic form, at which he had made a start in "Ambrose His Mark" and "Water-Message," published in 1963 prior to his writing of *Giles Goat-Boy,* and afterward resumed in "Autobiography" published in January 1968. These stories tentatively but insistently connect the mystery of one's sexual being (the preoccupations of Oedipus) with the authorial pains of fictional parturition. Especially compelling in "Water-Message" is the nine-year-old Ambrose's innocent conjuration of a grove of honey locusts into a jungle "labyrinth of intersecting footpaths" and "voluptuous fetidity." Here the boys have built a hideaway den, where one day they intrude upon the lovemaking of a sailor and his girl. The situation remains inexplicably exciting to the sexually uninitiated Ambrose, as also its objective correlative, the sheet of paper on which is penned "To whom it may concern" and "Yours truly," all between remaining blank, which washes ashore in a bottle and is picked up by Ambrose following the "flushing" of the lovers. Both the still-to-be-completed message and the interrupted lovers are harbingers of Ambrose's future, as worked out in the subsequent stories.

In "Title" and "Life-Story," published after *Giles Goat-Boy,* Barth fuses these dual modes of discovery of self into stories that are paradigms of the creative process, the fictional characters realized only to the extent that their storyteller can self-consciously imagine himself as a distinct person. But the possibilities of such *regressus in infinitum* are drastically limited. In "Life-Story," a desperate tongue-in-cheek echo of Borges's story "The Circular Ruins," Barth concludes, "and caused the 'hero' of his story to conclude,"

that one or more of three things must be true: 1) his author was his sole and indefatigable reader; 2) he was in a sense his own author, telling his story to himself, in which case; and/or 3) his reader was not only tireless and shameless but sadistic, masochistic if he was himself.

This bleak cul-de-sac is prefaced by an authorial outburst at "You reader! You, dogged, uninsultable, print-oriented bastard," in language that alludes simultaneously and paradigmatically to McLuhan's dismissal of the Gutenberg sensibility, to Baudelaire's profane search through *Les Fleurs du Mal* for his identity, and to Barth's compulsive fictional refractions of personality as a means of getting at human essence.

Neither "Title" nor "Life-Story" climaxes into a fully realized story. Process remains ever in an unfinished—and hence ultimately unknowable—state of becoming. In "Lost in the Funhouse" Barth returns to the seemingly more fruitful possibilities of Ambrose's rites-of-passage.

The funhouse—like Borges's garden of forking paths, or library of Babel, or lottery in Babylon—is a metaphor for the labyrinths of existence. Unlike Borges, whose perfect designs are intended as analogues of defective mythic and metaphysical systems of cosmic order, Barth seizes on the mirror room of the funhouse, and on Ambrose's "coming of age" there, as a rendering of modern man's (and the contemporary novelist's) search through the distortions and "endless replication of his image in the mirrors" for ontological confirmation of his existence. "For whom is the funhouse fun?" the narrator asks. "Perhaps for lovers," he conjectures, and then adds: "For Ambrose it is *a place of fear and confusion.*" Whereas Borges never asks from his "vertiginous symmetries" any knowledge beyond the aesthetic astonishment they engender, Barth assumes a persona who wants to find in the form of his story a sign of sorts of his ontological security. . . . The difference in expectations of the two writers is vividly illustrated if Borges's cool appraisal of life is read against Barth's self-conscious conclusion to "Title," a not unsimilar exploration of the problem of authorial identity:

> Oh God comma I abhor self-consciousness. I despise what we have come to; I loathe our loathsome loathing, our place our time our situation, our loathsome art, this ditto necessary story. The blank of our lives. It's about over. Let the *denouement* be soon and unexpected, painless if possible, quick at least, above all soon. Now now! How in the world will it ever

And on this ironically self-conscious note of hopeless inconclusiveness Barth ceases, leaving us with the inescapable fact that the future is a blank, indeed has always been a blank except to adherents of a value system, which indirectly defines them as well as the future.

Grounded in the psychological reality of man rather than in the philosophical ideality of the world, Barth is using the *roman à clef* in *Lost in the Funhouse* as a parodic means of defining his role as person and of justifying his activity as author; but one must not forget that Barth is a master parodist, experimenting with ways of expressing the same skeptical view of things that is Borges's, only in the more difficult terms of person rather than of place, of the dizzying whorls of psyche rather than of the vertiginous spirals of space. (pp. 30-5)

The funhouse is an elegant figure of speech, especially in its combination of local color realism and of Black Humor pluralism; but its designedly self-conscious exploration of sensibility disappoints its author's high hopes of "hinting to the reader things of which the narrator is unaware" or of casting "further and subtler lights upon the things it describes, sometimes ironically qualifying the more evident sense of the comparison." The mirror room can only reflect the appearance of the person presented to it, in this instance a thirteen-year-old adolescent still shaky on the significance of his sexual being. The world lies all before him, few memories behind him. The story admits as much when it diverts Ambrose from the mirror room and loses him in "some new or old part of the place that's not supposed to be used." Instead of winding "around on itself . . . like the snakes on Mercury's caduceus," Ambrose's perception moves outward, peeks through a seam between plyboard wall panels into a tool room where a man sits nodding on a stool, and finally, comfortingly, fantasies his future sexual certainties as husband and father. . . . "Lost in the Funhouse" is an Ocean City reverie that spins a psychological web of romanticized make-believe distressingly distant from the realism of the setting and from the facts of Barth's own life. A measure of its sentimentality is the closeness with which it skirts the vulgarisms of *Ah, Wilderness!* Barth, like Ambrose—like all of us—finds himself in this century to have strayed as both lover and designer into a funhouse; but that "insight" does not "wind around on itself like a whelk shell" leading him ever deeper into self-knowledge. The metaphor of funhouse and mirror room do not contain residual unknown ontological truths as at first they might seem to. As Ambrose notes despairingly when he watches himself refract into several "other persons": "In the funhouse mirror-room you can't see yourself go on forever, because no matter how you stand, your head gets in the way. Even if you had a glass periscope, the image of your eye would cover up the thing you really wanted to see." The funhouse is one of those clever fictional conceptions, an inventive objective correlative, of a pointless universe that one occasionally encounters in Black Humor. Drawn from a gimcrack American ethos, it fails to suggest "that imminence of a revelation that is not yet produced" ("The Wall and the Books") so mysteriously intrinsic to Borges's *ficciones* and parables.

In "Echo" Barth returns to the rich suggestiveness of archetypes and classical mythology. Not the hero of a thousand faces but Narcissus is seized upon for persona. In that mortal's flight from Echo (who "lives for her lovely lies" as others "live for the lie of love") toward self-love, Barth recognizes the plight of the twentieth-century storyteller, whose need to conceive himself through his tale is no less great than his will to tell the tale. Unfortunately one subverts the other. As with the masturbatory innocence of Narcissus ("who perishes by denying all except himself"), the "Overmuch presence" of the author drives him away from the possession of reality into a similar self-reflecting pool of self-destruction. The contrary model is Echo who "persists by effacing herself absolutely." The solution then, as Theban Tiresias is made to advise, is to cure self-absorption with saturation: "telling the story over as though it were another's until like a much-repeated word it

loses sense." "Echo" is just such an exercise in saturation: the author retelling the myth of Narcissus and Echo in the form of Narcissus reciting his story to Tiresias, a true fabular *regressus in infinitum* (an author reciting about an author reciting about himself) in which Narcissus's death must "be partial as his self-knowledge," for "the voice persists, persists . . . goes on."

And yet: "Can it be believed?" the narrator asks, turning the story into a denial of itself. Can multiplication wind us back to the incontrovertible source of our being? Is there any finality to the infinity of possibilities? Even that question lacks a fixed point of reference but jostles as one possibility among myriad others. (pp. 35-7)

The simultaneous affirmation and denial of an ultimate voice and hence persistent identity intimated by the myth of Narcissus and Echo is reiterated by the final two stories of *Lost in the Funhouse.* In "Menelaid," Barth retells with marvelous verve the effort of Menelaus to learn from Proteus on the shore at Pharos the secret of Helen's love. It was inevitable that Barth's preoccupation with the disguises masking identity from its own recognition should lead him to this myth, one of the two great expositions in western literature (the other is of Joseph, Mary, and the annunciation) of man's faith in the fidelity of love and the persistence of self. A tour de force in narrative exhaustion of points of view, the story holds in balance seven voices as Menelaus imagines his yarning to Telemachus and Peisistratus about his imagining Helen hearing Proteus hearing Proteus's daughter Eidothea hearing Menelaus relate the story of the fall of Troy and his "recollection" of Helen. Through all the "layered sense" comes the reiterated word "'''''''''Love!'''''''''''" the cry that Helen loves only him, has never loved anyone but him, and that she has "languished . . . chaste and comfy" through all the years of the Trojan War out of harm's way at Pharos with Egyptian Proteus. But Barth's Menelaus has a modern sensibility. He cannot accept such a miraculous explanation, the imp of doubt gives him no peace. How is he to espouse her, he wonders, as lover? advocate? husband? "Who am I?" he asks and is answered through the multi-layers of voice: "'''''''''' '''''''''''". Helen's history confirms for him his "grown conviction that the entire holocaust at Troy, with its prior and subsequent fiascos, was but a dream of Zeus's conjure" and his growing willingness to entertain the possibility "that Proteus somewhere on the beach became Menelaus holding the Old man of the Sea, Menelaus ceased." Both the irreverent slanginess of the parody and the multiple removes from reality of the points of view reiterate this skepticism. The only certainty clung to is the notion of the archetypal persistence of love. Nothing more survives, not Menelaus's voice, not the author's. All else, "Place and time, doer, done-to have lost their sense." Only the instinct of love persists: "when as must at last every tale, all tellers, all told, Menelaus's story itself in ten or ten thousand years expires, yet I'll survive it, I, in Proteus's terrifying last disguise, Beauty's spouse's odd Elysium: the absurd, unending possibility of love." The trouble with this solution to the sought for source of identity is that Menelaus's role as storyteller is not intrinsic to his nature but derives from a device of narrative. With the last story of the collection Barth corrects this "flow" in fictional conception.

In "Anonymiad" Barth merges myth and reality, the private dream of writer and the social world of reader, and both sexual and imaginative aspects of the life force, by scurrilously marrying the bard turned writer of prose successively to the nine muses. The "Anonymiad" is a comic epic in prose, scatological, inelegant, parodying the hesitant inept first essays at literary devices subsequently in the history of western literature become convention. Its author is a rustic goatherder turned minstrel, a Homeric-like social climber who has ambitiously beguiled his way to the position of Acting Chief Minstrel (and spy) at Agamemnon's court, before being tricked ashore on a deserted island for life by Clytemnestra and Aegisthus. Left with nine amphorae of wine, he systematically over the years has used the jugs three ways: drunk their contents, "made each the temporary mistress of his sole passion," and stuffed them again with his fiction.

> Stranded by my foes,
> Nowadays I write in prose,
> Forsaking measure, rhyme, and honeyed diction;
>
> *Amphora's* my muse:
> When I finish off the booze,
> I hump the jug and fill her up with fiction.

In this wise he has wedded himself to each of the nine muses in turn, filling each jug with the seed of his loins and of his imagination. Thus freighted he has cast them into the sea (for Ambrose, the author as adolescent, to pluck from the water centuries later). Calliope, the ninth amphora, is slated to receive the last of his tales, the "Anonymiad," an epic tale in prose of the minstrel's life, as the cap to his previous poetical inventions of events of the Trojan War and its aftermath with which he had freighted the first eight amphorae. The "Anonymiad" is an exercise in circularity as much as in *regressus in infinitum,* a story about how the story came to be, about "a nameless minstrel" writing a tale about himself writing a tale, for an inconceivable reader —it and "all its predecessors . . . a continuing, strange love letter" in which the word has become everything—and nothing. The story is a paradigm for our time of ontological insecurity, of the anonymity of self, and of the unlikelihood even of the persistence of the individual voice. Thus has Barth fabled himself back through the literary perspectives of his bardic predecessors to the first recorded efforts of western man to define who he is and how his essential being has been moved ultimately by love? lust? the life force? the word? and to his recognition that even that instinct is reduced finally to the chance coincidence of the word with a reader.

The stories in *Lost in the Funhouse* represent alternative instances, realistic and mythic, of the author seeking to experience himself as an individual in relation to his creation of fictions. In George and Anastasia's triumph over WESCAC Barth had offered a hesitant affirmation of a kind of Jungian life force. Descending into the Belly "arsy-turvy—like two shoes in a box," they form a Yang-Yin of wholeness; but their sexual union and short-circuiting of WESCAC, while mystically certifying George as Grand Tutor, is so broadly comical in its parodic contrivances that it qualifies the affirmation. Barth has no illusions about having fashioned here an all seasonal potion for Global Village man, an elixir that will wend him back to the essence of his being. Love figures too extensively in Barth's stories as the source of anarchy and chaos, beginning with the Trojan War, brought up to date in the dynastic intrigues of

Colonial America, and rendered on computer tape at West Campus. Nor does Barth have any illusions about our ability to achieve ontological security. In *Lost in the Funhouse* he transcends the agonizing efforts at self-definition of Ebenezer, Burlingame, and George Goat-Boy, and the equally traumatic biographies of the Maryland tales, and comes to rest in the serene Borgian acceptance of an identity that has no confirmatory existence apart from its fictional entity. Indeed, the mark of Borges's "The Immortal" is everywhere impressed in Barth's paradigmatic renderings of the myths of Narcissus, Menelaus, and the archetypal poet anonymous. His skeptical acceptance of the permanence of multiplicity, of even the possibility that one's self is but the dream of another insubstantial being, becomes the only viable strategy for confronting the Great Labyrinth, both human and cosmic. In parody alone may the artist hope to find a successive form that dissemblingly confirms continuation in time. To retell the old myths, to come paradigmatically ever closer to a great contemporary like Borges (as these stories so patently do), and to lampoon the anti-Gutenberg cries of McLuhan and company (as the stories also do) is to maintain the fiction of continuity and the reality of person in the limited persistence of the word, is finally, if nothing else, to give aesthetic validity to life. (pp. 37-40)

> *Max F. Schulz, "The Metaphysics of Multiplicity; and, the Thousand and One Masks of John Barth," Section III, Chapter 2, in his* Black Humor Fiction of the Sixties: A Pluralistic Definition of Man and His World *(© 1973 by Max F. Schulz), Ohio University Press, 1973, pp. 17-41.*

[In *Giles Goat-Boy*] the endless complication of surface details is of so brittle a cleverness that it constantly reveals the tediousness of the novel's informing conception.

Giles Goat-Boy is little more than an immensely inflated translation game, the world conceived as a university, its sacred texts as syllabi, the cold war as a rivalry between East Campus and West Campus, each equipped with an all-powerful computer capable of shortcircuiting the entire academic realm. Thus the Jewish mentor of the novel's Archetypal Hero—for Joseph Campbell and other handbooks of Jungian anthropology have been schematically superimposed on the schematic translation game—solemnly informs Giles: "Moishe says in the Old Syllabus, *Except ye be circumcised like me, ye shall not Pass.* But in the New Syllabus Enos Enoch says *Verily, I crave the foreskin of the mind.*" Here in capsule is the problem of the novel as a whole: it is hard to see what is gained by translating Old and New Testaments into Old Syllabus and New, in thinly disguising Moses and Jesus as Moishe and Enos Enoch (for the latter see Genesis 5:24), in substituting academic passing for theological salvation. The transparent coding activity at best affords the sorts of mental gratification that might appeal to a reasonably alert high-school sophomore while, on the negative side, it allows for a relentlessly simplistic reduction of historical facts—in this particular case the facts of religious history. The broader cold-war plan of the novel can be manipulated, through the mechanical logic of the translation game, as a perfectly symmetrical interplay of forces, the complex and changing conflict of interests between two large political systems since 1945 reduced to East Campus and West; to two acronymic computers,

EASCAC and WESCAC; to Slavic Tweedledumsky and American Tweedledeeman. The simplicity of pseudo-historical conception is at bottom the same as Vonnegut's flat equation of Dresden with Auschwitz, but without Vonnegut's engaging simplicity of manner.

As *Giles Goat-Boy* slowly recedes into the detritus of failed experiments in American fiction, the one real question it raises is why it should have been initially received by so many critics, especially in the more popular reviewing media, with such extravagant enthusiasm. In addition to the general thirst for greatness in the American novel . . . (with a concomitant tendency to confuse greatness with bigness), literary circles in this country are inclined, in a period which has placed special value on the anti-conventional, the oppositional, to mistake mere verbal vaudeville for stylistic vitality, grotesquerie for originality, callow cynicism—as in the *de rigueur* scenes of orgiastic abandon cerebrally conceived—for probing moral vision. In all these features, Barth's most ambitious book represents the typical characteristics of the new American novel at their puerile worst. His more modest concentration on ironized myth and on the exhaustion of narrative possibilities in his two volumes of fiction since *Giles* suggests that without the ability to engage imaginatively the dynamic complexities of real historical process, the novel, like the morally paralyzed hero of Barth's second book, *The End of the Road,* has no place to go. (pp. 47-8)

> *Robert Alter (reprinted from* Commentary *by permission; copyright © 1975 by Robert Alter), in* Commentary, *November, 1975.*

John Barth's writings are epitomes of contemporary American fiction: they expose some of its key problems and they test representative strategies for solving them. Barth belongs to a new school of fabulators whose inventiveness, whose unexpected fantasies and whose renewed love for old tales have dominated the fictional landscape of the past decade in America. But beyond mere inventiveness and wit, ostentatious glibness and stylistic idiosyncracies, Barth has a keen awareness of topicality—not in the derogatory sense—and offers in his novels of ideas (a sub-genre long despised) prototypical formulations of present day pathology. Thus Barth's early fiction takes off on a statement of contemporary nihilism and absurdity. It puts variations of existentialist thought concerning the possibility or impossibility of stringent self-definition to a test. His later works increasingly concentrate on the function of the imagination in the self-defining process. It is in these works that Barth explores the dangers inherent in a reapplication of mythical schemes to history and everyday life and in the practice of storifying human experience. (p. 454)

The heroes of Barth's earlier novels *The Floating Opera* and *The End of the Road* were forever seen coping with questions of "ultimate" sense and "absolute" value. Their answer to such questions consisted, simultaneously, in a gesture of futility and a relative affirmation. Ebenezer Cooke, central character of *The Sot-Weed Factor,* is preoccupied with the same set of questions, but tends to try out more radical responses to the problem. In the absence of all clear-cut answers, Cooke chooses to create the absolutes he will henceforth build and rely upon; a decision which puts him into the favorable position of someone who is no longer forced to cope with "fundamental" and "ulti-

mate" values, but rather with the technicalities of what follows from his first, arbitrary choice.

The opening gambit of Barth's [*The Sot-Weed Factor*] is a familiar one. It is almost identical to that in *The End of the Road;* it has outlines similar to the opening of *The Floating Opera;* and it is reminiscent of the situation so many fictional characters in the American novel of the sixties find themselves in. . . . In other words, Eben's situation indicates that he suffers from the very "cosmopsis" Jacob Horner in *The End of the Road* had discovered, named, and learned to hate. The consequences for the lives of these two characters are similar. Like Horner, Eben is subject to fits of total immobility. . . . Ebenezer Cooke has found out —representative for many characters of contemporary fiction—that . . . human beings invariably fall into despair when confronted with too many possibilities.

In this quandary Cooke unwittingly takes to a solution which seems to resolve his problems with a stroke of genius. True to a maxim which he only later is able to state explicitly, namely "that what the cosmos lacks we must ourselves supply" . . .—a maxim which seems to have sprung straight out of Shelley's *Defence of Poetry*—he creates his own essence and decides to hold on to it no matter how adverse conditions might become. (pp. 455-56)

What is spontaneous, almost instinctive, reaction in Ebenezer gains the status of a philosophical program in Burlingame, legendary tutor and counterpart to the title figure of the novel. Where Cooke blindly gropes for solutions, Burlingame has reasoned out in advance what might be attempted, what should be done, and what can be justified. As the teacher of Ebenezer and his twin sister Anna he enthusiastically seizes on the children's natural talent for playacting. He encourages them to assume various identities, to try on different roles for size, and to approach an understanding of history and historical personalities through a reenacting of the past. His is an attitude toward history and tradition that partly imitates attitudes of the Romantics: if you want to know who you are, search for the historical models from which you have been cast. Moreover, if you cannot find any suitable models which will facilitate an understanding of yourself, then invent them, create them, and impose them on an existence whose chief characteristic has always been lack of essence. . . . But the individual's memory, as Burlingame quickly points out, is not truly a reliable foundation. Is it not sometimes faulty? Does it not tend to color everything it holds? Hence Burlingame . . . warns that nothing is truly reliable except a man's ability to alter himself and to hang on for a while to the self-concepts he has defiantly created. Only the double acts of creation and faith, to both of which Eben will later cling as artist and quester, are worthy of our pursuit. (pp. 456-57)

In yet another way the figure of Burlingame dominates the intellectual landscape of the novel. Barth uses him in order to demonstrate the dangers inherent in a strategy devised by many contemporary novelists for the benefit of their fictional characters. The novel of the sixties has celebrated with unsubdued enthusiasm the second coming of Proteus, the archetypal shape-shifter, and the maxims of Protean existence have been elevated to the status of a new philosophical program in our time. If change itself is the defining feature of human existence, the argument goes, then why not seize the opportunity to transcend the concept of the unitary self and become a whole spectrum of varying selves?

Barth, who has a knack for conceiving characters whose material situations become methaphorical equivalents for their spiritual plights, has put Burlingame in the perfect position to explore the overwhelming potentials of Protean existence. . . . Burlingame is a foundling, fished, like Moses, out of the water. . . . Since he has thus no demonstrable link with history, no fixed position in the world, he can feel free to create his own identity from whatever materials he appreciates. . . . As it happens, he is also convinced that all existence is "a Heraclitean flux" . . . of which he wants to partake in its totality. . . . From both premises together he draws conclusions which instantly make him the paradigm for a modern existence of self-regulated change. (pp. 457-58)

As Burlingame is quick to notice and Barth is eager to emphasize, Burlingame's philosophy compels him in practice to walk a tightrope without a net. As long as he has no link with the past and the world, he is free to embrace experience in its totality and to choose or even to create any number of roles. But at the same time this freedom makes him utterly diffuse and somehow nullifies him as an individual. Embracing everything, he eventually embraces (like Thomas Pynchon's heroine V.) nothing. Alternatively, if he establishes a clear link with the world (as he finally does when he finds out and accepts that he is the son of the Tayac Chicamec of the Ahatchwhoops Indians and the brother of Charley Mattassin and Cohunkowprets), he finds the one identity that substantiates him as a person, but he loses touch with the all-inclusive possibilities which constituted his freedom. There can be no satisfying solution to such a quandary. . . . (p. 459)

Ebenezer Cooke's complementary quest for self-definition illustrates yet another problem that arises when the imagination gains undisputed dominance in life. As he loses touch with the realities in and around him, and as he methodically transcends the boundaries of actual experience, both reality and experience are converted to mere substrata of art. Ebenezer's mythopoeic view becomes a lens that distorts reality by refracting it as a potential or actual work of art. The realm of facts becomes by analogy the realm of aesthetic appearances: what Ebenezer surrenders in actual experience he gains back as the subject of his poetry. The poem he intends to write is only the most obvious token of this transformation. It is more important that in the same process Ebenezer's whole life is slowly converted into a unique work of art. By letting go of the world and the self he gains the momentary freedom to re-create both as autonomous objects. But by the same act he plants the seeds of a potential collision with experience which is likely to refute the very precepts on which his artistic creations were based. Ebenezer seems to be dimly aware of such a danger. Hence he shies away from experience and too great an involvement in life and attempts to preclude a refutation of his fantastically conceived world and his imaginatively born self. Yet, predictably, such refutations occur whenever he mixes with the world around him. . . . In the end, Ebenezer discovers himself precisely because he abandons the false images he had forced upon himself. He comes into his own, because he revokes all mythical preconceptions and deviates from the patterns of autistic creation. Consequently, the process of art feeding on reality is now reversed in the

novel. Ebenezer finally achieves fame as a poet and is offered the Laureateship by the young Lord Baltimore (which he declines), but only after he has discarded his fantasies of being the Poet Laureate and after he has displaced a panegyric on Maryland with a nasty work that heaps on Maryland the abuse it deserved all along. (pp. 559-60)

History plays an important role in *The Sot-Weed Factor.* Barth's uses of history are manifold and have a clear function in the context of the mythopoeic investigations he pursues. Contrary to what some critics have said, the novel is not merely parody for its own sake or an overgrown historical hoax. Barth rather uses a forbiddingly huge historical apparatus—much of it "grounded on meager fact and solid fancy" . . . in order to establish a semi-authentic scene as the background of the fictitious quest for the self. (p. 460)

In 1708 an "Eben Cook, Gent." published a satirical poem called *The Sot-Weed Factor* in London. In 1728 "An Elegy on the Death of the Honourable Nicholas Lowe, Esq." appeared under the name "E. Cooke. Laureat." 1730 saw the publication of *Sotweed Redivivus,* signed "E. C. Gent"; in 1731 *The Maryland Muse* (signed "E. Cooke, Gent.") and in 1731 another elegy (signed "Ebenezer Cook, Poet Laureat") followed. The Cook or Cooke of these works may or may not have been identical with an Ebenezer Cooke who in 1694 signed a petition against moving the capital of Maryland; or with yet another gentleman of this name who obtained permission to practice law in 1728. A similar confusion that cannot be settled conclusively arises over Eben's alleged father Andrew Cooke. Subsequent speculations have dealt with the possibility that neither the two Andrew Cookes on record nor the several Eben Cookes (or Cooks or E.C.s) of the poems were identical, as well as with the possibility that "'Eben Cook, Gent.' may be a mere nom de plume.". . .

Barth devises his own version of Ebenezer Cooke's story and carefully eliminates possible discrepancies with the facts on record. The problem of the two Andrew Cookes is solved by Barth's decision that the one who supposedly owned "Malden" was a suitable father for Ebenezer. The potentially different Ebenezer Cookes merge into one to whom Barth attributes several documented acts and most of the poems which had been linked with the name of the historical Cooke. In the process of compressing such scattered and disjointed facts into the life story of *one* man, Barth goes to the extent of inserting little details into his novel which eliminate possible contradictions to the recorded data of Lawrence Wroth's study of the life of Ebenezer Cooke. . . . (p. 461)

Barth then takes Ebenezer Cooke's best-known poem, "The Sot-Weed Factor," and proceeds to write an 806-page novel around the hard core of this work. Many passages in the novel are either repetitions of, or more frequently, elaborations on the material presented in the original poem. Moreover, the satirical poem which Barth eventually has Ebenezer Cooke write in sharp contrast to his originally planned panegyric *Marylandiad,* is the authentic "Sot-Weed Factor" itself. Barth consistently takes the same liberties, which are characteristic of the treatment of his source, with the historical situation on the grand scale. . . . What finally emerges from Barth's imaginative manipulation of history is that public myth is pitted against private myth in burlesque juxtaposition. In the process, Barth not only ridicules and effectively destroys the received myth of the heroic American past; he also analyzes the function of naïve private myths in the life-defining struggles of his characters.

Symptomatic for Barth's juxtaposition of the two concurring visions is, among others, his reconstructed version of one of the best-known episodes of early American history, the story of Captain John Smith and Pocahontas. Contrary to the schoolbook version, Barth offers his own bawdy reading of the events. As so often in *The Sot-Weed Factor,* he seems to be walking the narrow line between parody and overindulgent trifling with history. Yet his parodistic distortions have an important function. Barth's treatment of the episode draws attention to the fact that alleged historical truth is not as unambiguous as we tend to think. (p. 462)

The point of such parodistic games with historical materials is a simple one. Since some versions we assume to be historical truth are themselves dubious and colored by imaginative concepts, the novelist has every right to add his own speculations to the interpretation of events. After all, who is to say which version is ultimately true or which one is more useful to help us come to terms with the past? As Burlingame maintains throughout the book and as the author in his final chapter rubs in: "... we all invent our pasts, more or less, as we go along, at the dictates of Whim and Interest; the happenings of former times are a clay in the present moment that will-we, nill-we, the lot of us must sculpt.". . . What is more, in the process of inventing his past, man forgets to keep track of the general structure of his inventions. Hence his concepts of history on the grand scale emulate his concepts of historical fact in detail, that is, everything becomes relative, contradictory, lacking the recognizable, clear-cut outlines he had originally set out to find.

Barth has admitted on various occasions that the arbitrariness of fact has always made him uncomfortable and has stimulated his attempts to pit his own creative energies against it. (p. 463)

Fittingly, Barth uses for a contrast to his protagonists' fictionalizations a wealth of pseudo-objective historical data and interpretations which themselves turn out to be counterfeits or highly biased accounts. Had he opposed some kind of authenticated historical truth (on which historians and readers could easily agree) to the world of Ebenezer Cooke, it would have been all too easy to dismiss Eben's imaginative versions altogether and treat him as a mere lunatic lacking powers of discrimination. (pp. 463-64)

Life and history, Barth's novel seems to argue, are not fields of detached theoretical insights, but grounds on which we must test the concepts and the vitality of our own selves, pitting them against the vitality and the concepts of others.

However, at the same time the fate of Ebenezer Cooke posits the warning that in this situation an unreflected turn to the magic of mythopoesis is too easy and too dangerous a way out. If there are ultimately no givens, no objective readings of past or present, if everything can be altered and transformed in an act of imaginative creation, then it is tempting henceforth to treat the entire universe as the biggest playground the human imagination ever had. . . . In the spirit and in the fashion of many novelists of the sixties, Barth's philosophical comedy explores the creative possibilities, the frustrations, and the dangers inherent in the

contemporary assumption that it might be better to lose an established truth or a stable identity than to find one, because the latter precludes further possibilities whereas the former reveals itself as a precondition for gaining the freedom of imaginative creativity and the right to embrace existence in its totality.

However, what the case of Ebenezer Cooke lets the observer realize is an impending danger rather than a benefit of this new stance of self-creation. True, everything may be forced under the legislature of the human imagination by converting everything into an independent object of non-mimetic art. As such it will then become totally dependent on its creator, but only at the price that the creator, inversely, becomes dependent on his own creations—a condition which Ebenezer Cooke barely escapes. . . . The problem of fictionalizing life turns into the problem of living fictionalizations. To disentangle again, to find an exit from a world of self-generated fictions, to engineer an escape from the pitfalls of mythopoesis, demands an intense effort by the former mythopoeic self. The feasibility and the formal implications of such an effort as much as the increasing worries about the exit from the maze of fiction prove to be the opening themes of Barth's further experiments in *Lost in the Funhouse* and *Chimera.* (pp. 464-65)

Manfred Puetz, "John Barth's 'The Sot-Weed Factor': The Pitfalls of Mythopoesis," in Twentieth Century Literature *(copyright 1976, Hofstra University Press), December, 1976, pp. 454-66.*

*   *   *

BASSANI, Giorgio   1916-

Bassani is an Italian novelist, short story writer, poet, and critic. He writes in a subtle, controlled style about alienation, loss of innocence, and brutality hidden behind a guise of respectability. *The Garden of the Finzi-Continis* is a striking example of his lyrical prose and of his most vital themes. Depicting the lives of a Jewish-Italian family during the 1930s in Ferrara, Bassani's childhood home, the novel became popular with the release of Vittorio De Sica's film version. (See also *Contemporary Authors*, Vols. 65-68.)

The best in Italian literature, particularly that of the twentieth century, tends to be regional rather than national in character. Sometimes against a particular background, at a precise moment in time, something universal is enacted by one individual, or by a group bound together by the events of that moment. When the background is authentic, when it has life and colour and the event is a commonplace of everyday life recorded with art, when the people are recognisable, then the story, however restricted the setting, has a more than limited significance. So it is with Bassani's novel [*The Garden of Finzi-Continis*].

Bassani writes of Ferrara, and its Jewish community, as Faulkner and Tennessee Williams write of the Deep South, or more truly, since he has a strongly poetic streak, a tendency to linger on and repeat certain words, a feeling for the trees and the stones of his birthplace, as Robert Frost writes of New England. Within the cadre of Ferrara, then, Bassani leaves history simply to exist and trains his lens on one small unit and on one family within that unit of Ferrarese society during the years immediately preceding the second world war—a Jewish family of the *haute bourgeoisie* called Finzi-Contini. Within that family, apparently secure and proud in their almost aristocratic isolation, misunderstood and misjudged for this even by some of their co-religionists, Bassani summarises the mystery and tragedy surrounding each human being in his portrayal of the heroine, Micòl. (pp. 64-5)

Without the underlying sense of tragedy, and the serious social criticism (which is never laboured, but speaks for itself), this book might remain part of a vast literature of nostalgia; a series of reminiscences, an idyll of childhood, adolescence and early manhood. The pace is unhurried, especially in the beginning, as if the author—appropriately enough—were wandering in a garden now overgrown, but once familiar. Bassani captures very well that sense of unlimited time that stretches before the mind of a child. The big events and personalities in that lost world are highlighted like a holiday: school triumphs and disappointments, the maths mistress who prayed for the conversion of the Finzi-Contini, the benign master who dreamed of being able to see and use, for a work that would make him famous, some unpublished letters of Carducci which were kept in the great house, the old coachman-chauffeur and general factotum Perotti, who maintained the family coach in gleaming good order long after it had been replaced by a motor-car.

Later, when the Fascist race laws are being enforced, and Jews are banned from the clubs, when there are examinations to be studied for in between the tennis parties, friendships thrive in a hothouse atmosphere and it seems for a while, that such vigour and effort, such consolidation—on the tennis court in the garden of the Finzi-Contini, the outcast minorities, not only the Jewish minority, congregate—might keep at bay the forces gradually closing in. The young people, the friends of Alberto and Micòl, are aware of their own problems and of those of the outside world which forces them to remain isolated. They discuss and argue with the energy and enthusiasm of young people anywhere. What moves one, is their courage and their optimism; the fact that they are more flippant than bitter in the face of evil.

The story is beautifully and simply told: there is no outright condemnation, no mawkish sentimentality or conscious seeking after pity. It is at once an epilogue and a pilgrimage into the past, a record of childhood and the painful evolution of child to adult accelerated by the swift events immediately prior to the war. It is also a commentary on the state of affairs in Italy and throughout Europe that not only led up to and permitted the worst excesses of Fascism (among them the extermination of six million Jews) but apparently allowed people to forget that holocaust so quickly afterwards. Not least, it is a fine love story in which the individuals are left to speak for themselves. There is no attempt at any arbitrary character analysis. Life is a mystery, and love too, and so are people. There is no certain answer, only conjectures and memories. The character of Micòl, beautiful and full of joy, around whom the story revolves, symbolises this mystery.

Many questions are indirectly posed in this novel, and they have to be answered personally; one doesn't have to be a Jew or an Italian for the story to have relevance and poignancy. Questions themselves vary according to the reader. The isolated, the uncommitted—even if they are uncommitted through no fault of their own—shall not be allowed to live in peace. (pp. 66-8)

Elizabeth de Charmant, "Bassani 'Il Giardino dei Finzi-Contini,'" in European Patterns: Contemporary Patterns in European Writing, *edited by T. B. Harward (© The Dolmen Press 1964), Dolmen Press, 1964, pp. 64-8.*

Quite soon in "The Heron" you will recall the brilliant opening scenes in "Across the River and Into the Trees." In Hemingway's novel the boats moved slowly in the Venetian lagoon, the beat-up colonel took aim at the ducks and hunting became an occasion for personal fulfillment. As the middle-aged protagonist in Giorgio Bassani's new novel sits along one of the branches of the Po not far from Venice, the duck-blind becomes a symbol of his personal futility. Observing two artists at work in the same landscape, one creating from the outside in and the other from the inside out, you rediscover the infinite human possibilities that only the novelist can convey.

Because of the churning self-doubts of middle age that flow through the lifestream of this exquisite short novel, you may perhaps recall Thomas Mann's "Death in Venice," too. Reading that novella written over a half-century ago for echoes of character and style in "The Heron," there is an awareness that melancholy about one man's sexual identity plays a role in both stories. . . .

"The Heron" creates one day in the slipping life of Edgardo Limentani, a man of forty-five who is "dead inside." . . . [The] sounds of outside political forces are distant in the novel. The disappointments are built up by an accretion of domestic incidents that reveal Limentani as a victim of a loveless marriage. . . . The author conveys the personal problem indirectly—Bassani is an architect of indirection—by describing the sequence of bedrooms in their apartment: his mother, his young child and his wife rank this way in importance to him. . . .

Readers unfamiliar with Bassani's writing might well start with "The Garden of the Finzi-Continis" to deepen their understanding of "The Heron." The new novel is a complete work in itself. . . . From his boyhood Ferrara and the families he knew, Bassani has carved out a corner of Italy that rises above regionalism with fiction that can stand alongside the most lingering written in Europe today. (p. 39)

Herbert Mitgang, in The New York Times Book Review *(© 1970 by The New York Times Company; reprinted by permission), April 12, 1970.*

[The] hero of *The Heron* [is] artistically dead and deadly. . . . Bassani offers something so softly vulnerable to parody as almost to tempt one's kindness. Just as the poor heron itself, flapping with ungainly sadness, fraught with significance, is too open a target for the lugubrious hero Edgardo to shoot at, so *The Heron* in its ungainly sadness and fraught significance makes its appeal, not altogether scrupulously.

But the heron gets shot, and Edgardo needless to say goes in for a characteristically morose and constipated (that too is literal) act of self-identification. . . . (pp. 39-40)

Poor old Edgardo so luxuriates in his humiliations, real and imagined, that one wants old-fashionedly to shake him. He spends most of his novel trying to rouse himself, being late, yawning, looking at his watch, groaning. . . .

The Heron only looks distinguished, and it doesn't manage more than a quivering "Nothing, any longer, appeared real to him." But a novelist had better first be justifiably confident that it will all be real to us; otherwise the distinction evaporates. "You had only to look at the affairs of life from a certain distance to conclude that they were worth, all of them, only what they were worth: namely nothing, or almost nothing." All very well for Edgardo, but his creator hasn't grounds enough for believing that "the affairs of life" are indeed present in his attenuated fictional preciosity. Bassani's favorite poetic locution is "as if" ("as if he were seeing it for the first time"); fifty times he deploys it, in company with an insistence on how strange, odd, mysterious, and absurd everything seemed; and it all just lies there. Yet all this hypersensitivity, radiated from Edgardo's every pore, is apparently asking our respect, and even, it seems, our interest. (p. 40)

> *Christopher Ricks, in* The New York Review of Books *(reprinted with permission from* The New York Review of Books; *copyright © 1970 NYREV, Inc.), April 23, 1970.*

Anyone who has been in Italy on the first day of the shooting season will recognise the experience of deep-rooted disgust on which Giorgio Bassani's *The Heron* rests. The mad blood-lust of the Italian hunter is unparalleled: no sparrow or tit could be so insignificant as to escape his attentions. . . .

Of course the hunting expedition that commands our attention in *The Heron* is a less enthusiastic affair. The central character [Limentani] is from the very start of the day somewhat alienated from the pursuit of this sport. . . . There is also a lack of the hideous male preening and display which characterises most of such expeditions, though this is all cleverly and economically suggested in the scene at the small-town hotel catering for the rich businessmen down from Milan. But throughout the description the ritual and class elements of the enterprise are accurately underlined and this gives the book its chief strength and interest. For this is not simply a symbolic novel: it probes deeply into the political and social conditions in the Italy of the immediate post-war era. . . .

It is not simply a question of Limentani's attitude to hunting, but rather of the realisation of his personal achievement up to now and his consciousness of his historical role. Both the booty as it begins to mount up and the uselessly wounded heron as it dies provide a point of reference for his examination of his past and an image of his personal crisis. . . .

Finally what we learn about the hero's past friendships and subsequent estrangements work together with the account of his love life to complete the picture: the shooting scene is clearly also to be seen as a test of sexual prowess. . . . Bassani's book is well worth reading both as a novel about personal crisis and as a political and social analysis. (p. 28)

> *James Fenton, in* New Statesman *(© 1970 The Statesman & Nation Publishing Co. Ltd.), July 10, 1970.*

Behind the Door . . . corrects some possible misconceptions of [Bassani's] talent. [His] best-known work, *The Garden of the Finzi-Continis*, aspired to portray an aristo-

cratic Jewish family in Ferrara during the years before 1943. . . . These events lent the book an ominousness sweetened by an elegiac quality, for the narrator, his own family undistinguished, had somehow survived, and after the war could look back upon the Finzi-Continis with a desire to preserve at least his memories from the general destruction.

But in fact the family chronicle in the book was rather discursive. Much of the narrative was an attempt to represent the Finzi-Continis as archetypal, yet it was overloaded with details that seemed to go nowhere. . . .

One of Bassani's *Five Stories of Ferrara* may serve as paradigm for his novels. In this the main character, a doctor, is brought because of certain incidents to see the people around him in a peculiarly undeceived way. The experience happens quite suddenly. At a similar moment in his other books, the central characters are likely to attain sudden realization of what up to now they have misunderstood. The doubletake is Bassani's basic fictional maneuver. . . .

In Bassani to see at all is usually to see too much. The truth in his novels is painful and mortifying. In *The Heron*, Bassani has written a Ferrarese version of Lampedusa's *The Leopard*, a book which as a publisher's reader he discovered, and which has had a considerable influence on him. Here there is a literal mortification. In its first pages, this novel might seem to belong more to the Hemingway tradition; its unnerved hero is off for a day's hunting, which in Hemingway would herald regeneration through the ritual of bird-killing. But Bassani's hunter quickly disavows this resemblance. He cannot bring himself to shoot. . . . Bassani's strength is less in the symbolism, which does not escape a slight portentousness, than in the particular incidents of disgust.

Behind the Door returns to the period of adolescence, where Bassani is most convincing. His best book, it presents innocence on its way to being corrupted. The central character is a Jewish sixteen-year-old, anxious for that esteem of his fellows which alone can bring him esteem for himself. He is emulous of the best student, Cattolica, who is not only a Catholic, but is also well-heeled and self-possessed. Yet an alliance forms between the hero and a new boy, Luciano Pulga, also desperate to find a place for himself but much tougher. Pulga ingratiates himself by sycophancy, by malicious gossip, and by a knowledge of sexual mysteries undreamed of by his friend. The hero feels that the association is somehow degrading, but there is no shaking Pulga off, and he even develops a kind of loyalty to the new boy.

Then Cattolica unbends enough to indicate that Pulga is carrying tales about the unnamed hero. A scene is arranged so that Pulga will repeat his slanders, not knowing that their victim is listening behind the door. It is to conclude with his being beaten. But Pulga proves surprisingly eloquent, and while what he says about the homosexuality of the hero and the sexual promiscuity of the hero's mother is not true, it has a plausibility. Instead of confronting Pulga and having it out with him, the hero slips out the back door. . . .

The besmirching images are not easily dismissed, and in his new awkwardness with his mother, whom he too now begins to see for the first time as a sexual being, he cannot keep from scorning his family a little through the other boy's eyes. . . . Childhood is over, but innocence leads not to experience but only to a warped innocence. All this Bassani manages not to spoil.

Richard Ellmann, "Warped Innocence," in The New York Review of Books *(reprinted with permission from* The New York Review of Books; *copyright © 1973 NYREV, Inc.), November 15, 1973, p. 23.*

[*The Smell of Hay,* a] beautiful and lacerating collection of stories by the author of *The Garden of the Finzi-Continis* is set, as was that novel, in Fascist Italy and is peopled by the citizens of Ferrara. Its classical restraint and evocative power confirm what Bassani's earlier works have already made abundantly clear: he is a writer of rare powers, both as a novelist in the old tradition, committed to settings, ambience, and the idiosyncrasy of character, and as a modern with a taste for the ironic thrust. No other novelist in recent memory has better succeeded in conveying the growing encroachment of political climate on the nerves and bones of protagonists and in making the invisible palpable. . . . There are reminiscences of other sorts here as well—elegiac, sharp-honed sketches of Ferrarese citizens who loved, married, begot children, and disappeared, having left their indelible traces on a portion of the earth. A literary event. (p. 39)

Dorothy Rabinowitz, in Saturday Review *(© 1975 by Saturday Review/World, Inc.; reprinted with permission), September 20, 1975.*

In his relaxed but fastidious manner, Bassani [in *The Smell of Hay*] evokes the vulnerabilities, fears and self-deceit of the Jewish community in Ferrara during the fascist period and immediately after—the terrain he mapped out so memorably in *The Garden of the Finzi-Continis*. He is subtle, leisurely and cool-minded on a subject from which we expect less comfortable writing. In a sense it is a cruel technique, but it is punishingly effective. It is like looking at family snapshots of victims taken when everything was ordinary, *before.* You find yourself waiting, looking for suggestions to remind you of the horrors lurking in the characters' future which you know to be there: they even seem to be looking for that knowledge themselves. That, I think, is the point. They cannot recognise the symbolic figure Bassani puts among them, that of Dr Fadigati. Once a highly respected physician, his homosexuality becomes known and he is faced with ostracism, cruelty and scandal. His dilemmas and possible suicide mirror the self-subdued, almost satisfied disorientation of Ferrara's Jews in a fascist society. The other stories are good, too: Bassani elicits people, time and place in such a scrupulous but easy way you almost forget he is 'writing about' people, time and place. (p. 654)

Douglas Dunn, in New Statesman *(© 1976 The Statesmen & Nation Publishing Co. Ltd.), May 14, 1976.*

Giorgio Bassani has a lovely way of moving. His boyish self slides through this collection of autobiographical tales [*The Smell of Hay*] like a ghostly blade through phantom butter, precise and incorporeal, for while Bassani's memory serves him well, and his pastel pen even better, and his morbid sense of history repeating itself—for him Italian Jewish history—gives the most distinct tone of all, that of menace, a world war and the collapse of European culture

separate us completely from these living scenes in their diseased sunlight. Many people will of course remember the 'thirties very clearly and those who do will find a book like this conducive in fact to extreme melancholy, with its regret for lost youth, blighted hopes, delicate depravities and overall atmosphere of waving-off loved ones on steam trains never to see them again, that its net impact is disproportionate to the casual intimacy of its separate parts. . . .

Bassani's fantastic ability to wring tears from a stone, make a petticoat weep, amounts almost to an act of sorcery. It is the detached thoughtfulness of his approach, quite apart from his obvious skills, which is so affecting, the way in which he places himself, between the reader and the events described, as a haunted man. You feel like propping him up in bed with a big brandy, dislodging the photograph album caught so unhappily on his nerve endings, and explaining the horrors of the future in great detail, to draw off some of the dreamy weight. . . .

Unlike American Jewish writers who were never persecuted on their own soil and feel guilty about that, Mr Bassani's intonation is not vainglorious, holocaustal; he is not obsessed by phoenix imagery. His response runs beyond anger and into self-reasoning. In 'The Gold-Rimmed Eyeglasses' which takes up well over half of [*The Smell of Hay*] he reminds himself of the town doctor whose affair with a tough local apollo leads to social and then physical death. The story resembles *Death in Venice* in many ways but its vigour is much more modern, its compass wider. Bassani is hardly sentimental and never preaches, allowing the reader to size up obvious parallels between his doctor and the fate of Jews later, satisfied by quoting his father's speculation on the likelihood of anti-Jewish legislation to remind one of the exact circumstances. (p. 23)

Duncan Fallowell, "Gone," in The Spectator *(© 1976 by* The Spectator; *reprinted by permission of* The Spectator), *May 22, 1976, p. 23.*

*   *   *

BECKETT, Samuel   1906-

An Irish-born dramatist, novelist, and poet who writes in both French and in English, Beckett is best known for his play *Waiting for Godot*. His work combines humor with tragedy, creating an existential, often baffling view of the human condition within a meaningless and nameless void. This theme is reinforced by a literary style that experiments with formlessness and fragmentation of language, and often reflects the influence of James Joyce, to whom Beckett was both secretary and literary colleague. The translator of his own works from French to English, Beckett has received numerous awards, including the Nobel Prize for Literature in 1969. (See also *CLC*, Vols. 1, 2, 3, 4, 6, and *Contemporary Authors*, Vols. 5-8, rev. ed.)

Whereas for Proust the emancipation from time is possible, being brought about by memory and even more satisfyingly by artistic creation, for Beckett it is impossible. Not only does Beckett require emancipation from the spatial dimensions as well as from time . . . , but also, for him, neither memory nor art is a means to salvation. The powerlessness of memory against the disintegrating force of time is, for example, one of the themes of *Krapp's Last Tape*, while art appears everywhere in Beckett as a kind of absurd but inescapable imposition, a "pensum" exemplary of the absurd punishment that is our life, so that the idea of escape through art has become no longer the joyous certainty it is in Proust but a kind of impossible dream. Beckett's themes are therefore anti-Proustian as much as they are Proustian, but the initial impulse is in each case the same: the sense of life as an exclusion from some timeless inner essence, and the attempt to use art as a means of escaping from time and rejoining that essence.

Beckett's dualism of the self and the non-self, timelessness and time, essence and existence, belongs to a lengthy tradition, and in particular his affinity with certain forms of baroque sensibility (and especially with Descartes) is well recognized. (pp. 152-53)

The irrelevance of death, art as an absurd pensum, and life as a long exile—these three closely interrelated ideas form the theme of the novel-trilogy, *Molloy, Malone meurt,* and *L'Innommable,* a theme that can be stated in two ways as the unattainability of the self or, conversely, the inescapability of existence. . . . [This] theme depends on the notion of a self conceived not dynamically, as an instrument, but spatially, as a place—but paradoxically, as a non-dimensional place, outside of space and time. This conception, which is central to Beckett, is traceable at least as far back as his first novel, *Murphy.* Murphy's main aim in life is to escape from it, that is, to escape from an outside world of "pensums and prizes" into the inner world where there is "only Murphy himself, improved out of all knowledge," a world that for him is creditably represented by a padded cell, that is, a kind of defined emptiness where, as Beckett puts it, "the three dimensions, slightly concave, were so exquisitely proportioned that the *absence of the fourth* was scarcely felt." (pp. 153-54)

A mote in the dark of absolute freedom, a pebble in the steppe, a tiny plenum in the immensity of the void, something autonomous and separate from the void (as blind Hamm is a separate mote in the visual world), but *not separated from it by a wall*—such is the self in Beckett: something undefinable in space, something dimensionless, but *something* (we can call it consciousness), and something which, because it is dimensionless, exists outside the world of space and time and is by definition unattainable within that world. As such, it is like the center of a circle (which we know to exist but cannot attain because each attempt to circumscribe it merely creates not a center but a new circumference which itself has a new and equally unattainable center, and so on), so that to approach the self is to embark on an infinite process comparable to attempting to express the value of a surd to the last decimal point. Life as the pursuit of self thus becomes the endless, hopeless task of pursuing an infinitely receding *something* which—resisting definition and being inseparable from what surrounds it— has the characteristics of *nothing.* In this way, Beckett points up the inescapable absurdity of the ineradicable human belief in a principle of inner life—call it what you will: essence, self, personality or soul—for whose autonomous existence there is no shred of evidence beyond our belief in it, while at the same time establishing a basic image of life as endless exile from and pursuit of an infinitely unattainable self.

In the trilogy, the first two novels record an escape from space and time, and the third supposes a consciousness capable of surviving such an escape. For this reason, the dilemma propounded in the work is posed most crucially in

the turn of the page between *Malone* and *L'Innommable.* The former novel ends with two words that between them express the end of time and the abolition of space: "plus rien." But the first words of *L'Innommable* are: "*Où maintenant? Quand maintenant? Qui maintenant?*" so that the timeless and spaceless "who" that has mysteriously survived the abolition of space and time nevertheless immediately asks of itself precisely the old questions: where (in space) and when (in time) am I? It cannot conceive of itself except falsely, and so the wearisome business of self-pursuit goes on beyond death. . . . [If] Beckett wished, the work could go on spiralling into itself forever, commenting on itself, and mirroring in its form the operation of the mind engaged in the endless task of seeking its own unattainable core (and many of Beckett's other major works are, similarly, self-perpetuating mechanisms of one kind or another).

But although *L'Innommable* does finally tail off into interminability, it is not as one might expect the interminability of the infinitely tightening spiral, but a more linear one. For eventually the novel resolves into nothing more nor less than a thin stream of disembodied language. . . . The Unnamable becomes simply its own voice, talking on and on endlessly in the hope that one day, perhaps by pure chance, it may put together the combination of words that will name it, and thus destroy the duality it is condemned to. Language is thus given the task of making subject and object of consciousness coincide, of making the non-self self, time timelessness and space spacelessness—a task it cannot fulfil, for the voice issuing from the soul of the Unnamable knows only the language of the outer world, of time and space, the language it shares with others, which leads it to suspect that it must itself be only a creation of others. To speak the language of the self, it will have to invent a new language, of timelessness and spacelessness. (pp. 154-55)

[Where] political brinkmanship has been keeping us for so long on the threshold of hell-on-earth, Beckett's characters are in the not much more enviable position of being on the endless, uncrossable brink of entry into a kind of paradise (the paradise of eternal self-possession), so that for them existence is a purgatory-on-earth, a purgatory of exclusion and waiting. They are in a kind of no-man's-land, lying somewhere, somehow, *between* their existence in time and their life in eternity, neither the one nor the other, but with characteristics of each. Typically, their lives are over but have not ended, and so nevertheless are still going interminably on, in which they are like Dante's Belacqua (a figure who constantly haunts Beckett's imagination), who has been condemned, although his life is over, to live it through again in expectation of admission first to purgatory proper (for he is as yet only in ante-purgatory) and thence eventually to paradise itself. . . . (p. 157)

It is [in *Godot*] (and also perhaps in certain of the final pages of *Comment c'est,* the more recent work in which Beckett has successfully carried the struggle with language back into the novel form) that Beckett goes closest to speaking the language of eternity on his own account, and thus to stepping over his personal brink into silence. In describing the threshold, he conveys to us powerfully, in the destruction of our normal categories of time, an apprehension of the timelessness of the self. But—and here is the inevitable rub—the very ambiguity of the threshold, which he thus turns to such good account, at the same time defeats his purpose, for in that ambiguity resides also the old dualism, so that the more he uses it to convey to us the sense of the timeless essence, the better he describes an existence endlessly excluded from while endlessly tending towards that essence. In so doing, he speaks ultimately *not* of the essence itself but only of the threshold, that region of being where existence and essence, non-self and self, time and timelessness endlessly co-exist, in the strange, ambiguous, inescapable half-world of semi-exile that is Beckett's image of our human condition. (pp. 167-68)

> *Ross Chambers, "Beckett's Brinkmanship," in* AUMLA: Journal of the Australasian Language and Literature Association *(copyright © 1963 by the Australasian Language and Literature Association), May, 1963 (and reprinted in* Samuel Beckett, *edited by Martin Esslin, Prentice-Hall, Inc., 1965, pp. 152-68).*

The world of Samuel Beckett is full of paradoxes—deliberate contradictions which negate every possibility of movement, knowledge, rationality, understanding, and coherence on the part of the creatures that inhabit that curious world. Yet, the more these creatures are immobilized, dehumanized, the more they find themselves sequestered into fictional and verbal impasses, the more freedom they seem to gain to extricate themselves. Quite often, they counteract the fiction (the "hypothetical imperatives" as Molloy says) imposed upon them by a fictional paradox of their own.

Thus most statements made by the voice (or the many voices) speaking in Beckett's fiction—whether that of the author disguised as an ironic (or unreliable) narrator, or that of the narrator-hero (certainly unreliable) seemingly responsible for his own fictitious existence—lead to flagrant contradictions. (p. 103)

Fiction . . . need not agree with reality, especially when it is explicitly presented as sub-fiction—counterfeit inventions of the characters themselves. Since the author never speaks in his own name in [*Molloy*], however, the reader is under the impression that what is stated omnisciently is reality. Thus the statement, "It was not midnight. It was not raining," produces the effect of being real, of being the truth, even though it is a fictitious illusion, and what becomes clearly questionable, clearly unreliable, is the sub-fiction written by Moran: "It is midnight. The rain is beating on the windows." (p. 104)

[In most of Beckett's fiction the] paradox results . . . from the fact that there is a confusion between representation (events told in the past) and invention (events told in the present). (p. 105)

Consequently, the negative part of the statement that closes [*Molloy*] ("It was not midnight. It was not raining.") is not only in direct contradiction with what is being written by Moran, but also with the whole second part of the novel, and by extension, since the second part of the novel is postulated against the background of Molloy's own counterfeit fiction, the entire narrative becomes a paradox. . . . Molloy [speaks] of the confusion that exists between actuality (the present) and the pseudo-reality (the past) created by the conscious writer. It would indeed be preferable for Molloy (and similarly for Moran) not to try to relate what he thinks happened, for as he well knows "what really happened was quite different." But since Molloy, like all the other Beck-

ettian creatures that are given the delusory power to talk for themselves, cannot "hold his peace" and must go on talking, we can assume that what he is telling us is a lie. Thus when he says, "I said, etc.," speaking of the past in the present, he is merely inventing a fiction even though he claims "I quote from memory." . . . In fact, earlier in his narrative, Molloy makes it quite clear that his predicament as narrator-hero (narrator/narrated) forces him to deal in contradictions: "Not to want to say, not to know what you want to say, not to be able to say what you think you want to say, and never to stop saying, or hardly ever, that is the thing to keep in mind, even in the heat of composition." . . .

The whole fiction of *The Unnamable* is based on the same obligation to speak, to go on speaking ("you must go on, I can't go on, I'll go on"), even if it means inventing, getting more and more caught up in the liar's paradox. (pp. 106-07)

One could quote endlessly passages from the novels and plays of Beckett which negate one another as they are brought together: statements which end into verbal impasses from which the speaker extricates himself by formulating other statements that contradict what he has just said. Most readers of fiction object to seeing taken away with one hand that which they have been given with the other, but unless they can accept this "anti-fictional" aspect of Beckett's fiction they will continue to deal with it as a paradox. Undoubtedly, it is this kind of uncertainty, this backtracking ambiguity which gives Beckett's fiction its paradoxical aspect, as though it were constantly on the brink of crumbling into nonsense, into self-negation. Only if one accepts the interplay between two levels of rhetoric can one gain an understanding of the Beckettian paradox. In other words, when reading Beckett, one must constantly guard against imposing on the fiction one's own notions of order, truth, plausibility, and reality.

Beckett, of course, did not invent fictional ambiguity. He merely exploits it to its utmost degree of confusion. . . . It is only when we attempt to reconcile the contradictory aspects of the Beckettian dialectic on the basis of our preconceived notions of fiction that the paradox is created. Too often, we are guilty of reading paradoxes into Beckett's fiction because we cannot accept that which destroys itself as it creates itself—that which is contrary to common sense, or that which points to itself, even though ironically, as paradoxical. And yet, the primary meaning of a paradox is, as defined by the most basic dictionary: "a tenet contrary to received opinion; . . . an assertion or sentiment seemingly contradictory, or opposed to common sense, *but that yet may be true in fact.*" This definition can indeed apply to the whole Beckett canon, and more specifically to the narrator-hero's ambivalent role as a recipient of fiction and a dispatcher of fiction, as a creature that is both, as the Unnamable says of himself, "the teller and the told." (pp. 109-10)

[Moran admits] the failure of his quest, the negation of his fiction.

But in fact, what is negated here is not fiction itself, but a traditional concept of fiction, the concept of storytelling. Neither Moran, nor Molloy, nor the Unnamable, nor any of the other narrator-heroes, has been able to tell a coherent story about himself or about his invented playmates. This is undoubtedly the most crucial if not the most original aspect of Beckett's creative process: his fiction no longer relates a story (past realities reshaped by the process of imagination into an artistic form), but it simply reflects upon itself, upon its own chaotic verbal progress, that is to say upon its own (defective) substance—language. (pp. 111-12)

Beckett, [unlike Gide], is subtly hidden in the voice of his protagonists to the extent that they are capable of speaking against their "irresponsible" creator, accusing him of trying to impose upon them not only a story when there is no story to tell, but also words when words are meaningless. . . . This curious reversal of roles, whereby the voice of fiction speaks against itself, is possible because having no longer a story to tell ("of course he has no story") through his characters, the author simply allows his storyless creations to define themselves on the basis of their own substance—words, empty words, until there will be nothing more to say. . . . (p. 114)

As such, Beckett's fiction becomes a denunciation of the illusory aspect of fiction—stories which pretend to pass for reality. But the truth is that fiction is not reality, it is simply a language which tells its own story, its own true story. Beckett's *speaking words* are telling the truth about themselves: they are telling us that they are words: "Words, mine was never more than that, than this pell-mell babel of silence and words." . . . This shift from a language that tells *a* story to a language that tells *its* own story ("I say it as I hear it," that is "how it is") reveals how Beckett's fiction has passed from one level of rhetoric to another, and as a result how the Beckettian paradox—a paradox created by the dual level of storytelling—has itself been negated. (pp. 114-15)

All the fiction that precedes the moment when Moran goes back into the house to write his report is set on a dual level of storytelling. In all these works, a narrator, more or less self-conscious, more or less present and active in the story, reveals by his interventions (as Gide does in *Les Faux-Monnayeurs*) the fraudulence of fiction on the basis of a split between two levels of narration. Only in *Watt* and in *Molloy* does the narrator succeed in becoming a counterpart for the protagonist of the novel (Sam-Watt, Moran-Molloy) thus creating the Beckettian paradox. In the other early novels and stories, the narrator is merely a distant witness of the fiction, but not an active participant. (pp. 115-16)

Starting with *Malone Dies,* pseudo-reality and sub-fiction unify into a single level of rhetoric as author, narrator, and narrator-hero converge into one voice. Thus from a narrative that describes experiences as though they had been lived in the past, the fiction beyond *Molloy* relates experiences lived in the present, or rather in a kind of present-future condition. (p. 116)

Who is telling the truth? Is Moran telling the truth about the lie of his and of Molloy's fiction? Or is Malone lying about his fictional truth? We are again caught in the vicious circles of the liar's paradox. For if Molloy, Moran, and their predecessors are telling the truth it is about a lie (the lie of fiction), and if Malone and his successors are lying, it is about the truth of their condition (verbal authenticity). Beyond this one will never know, or rather one can only hope, as does the voice in the *Texts for Nothing:* "And yet I have high hopes, I give you my word, high hopes, that one day I may tell a story, hear a story, yet another, with men, kinds of men as in the days when I played all regardless or nearly, worked and played." . . . (p. 117)

Raymond Federman, "Beckettian Paradox: Who Is Telling the Truth?" in Samuel Beckett Now, *edited by Melvin J. Friedman (© 1970 by The University of Chicago), University of Chicago Press, 1970, pp. 103-17.*

The experience of exile—reinforced for Beckett by his early life as Protestant in a Catholic country, as intellectual in a bourgeois family, as artist in academia, and at this particular time by his very real exile as a vagrant Irishman in London—is apparent everywhere in his poetry, but in a particularly striking and concentrated way in the images of the poem entitled "Enueg I" [in his first volume of poetry, *Echo's Bones and Other Precipitates*]. Here we see "a dying barge . . . in the foaming cloister of the lock"; "on the far bank a gang of down and outs"; a child excluded from a game at which the narrator himself is no more than a spectator; the narrator described again, "derelict, as from a bush of gorse on fire in the mountain after dark, / or, in Sumatra, the jungle hymen, / the still flagrant rafflesia." Further on in the poem: "a lamentable family of grey verminous hens, / . . . half asleep, against the closed door of a shed, / with no means of roosting" and finally, "a small malevolent goat, exiled on the road, / remotely pucking the gate of his field." Such an accumulation of figures makes interpretation easy enough. However, if the images reveal the solitude of the poet, they are not without ambiguity. The child, reassured, *chooses* after all not to try again to enter the playing field from which he had been once rejected, and the goat seems only half ready to give up his liberty. Similarly, the darkness of the mountain or the jungle appears barely preferable to the fire that destroys as it illuminates or to the putrid beauty of the parasitical flower. Only the river that beckons offers momentarily a possible escape to one who knows neither how to adapt to social existence nor how to suffer total isolation. He does not respond to the call, however, and "Enueg I" remains without true conclusion.

There are, in effect, other solutions, and Beckett's poems function as imaginative modes for exploring and testing conceivable alternatives. Caught in the anguish of such a dilemma, what are the options for a being at once demanding and lucid? First of all revolt, now through violence, now through obscenity. . . . The need for violence, curiously accompanied at times by an equally irresistible compassion, becomes masochistic in one poem—without however ceasing to be completely lucid. The burlesque scene of flagellation, done in a mixture of English, Latin, Italian, and French, is a demonstration of verbal virtuosity quite as much as a psychological catharsis. Sometimes revolt is under the sign of irony or bitter sarcasm, and sometimes it takes the form of classical understatement translating a calm but hopeless opposition, a simple refusal that knows its own futility before that which is unacceptable and at the same time inevitable. Such is the "nay" that ends "Malacoda."

In several poems a religious solution seems to offer the possibility of a satisfactory reconciliation. . . . The poems are sprinkled with explicit allusions to Christ, but He appears not as Savior but as Man the victim of fathomless injustice. In the last lines of "Serena III," which refer both to a town south of Dublin and to the Rock of Ages in the Protestant hymn (and beyond to the Old Testament), he definitively rejects the religious solution: "Hide yourself not in the Rock keep on the move / keep on the move."

His quest, renewed always one more time, does not at all exclude attempts to adapt himself to life in the society of men, to find his "place in the sun." Even the humble fly succeeds, and the adder is warm and well fed in her well-lighted glass home; but as the allusion to Pascal suggests, it seems that human space has been wholly usurped. Lacking the talent of a Defoe or an Aretino, he is unfortunately incapable either of prostrating himself abjectly before The City, or of conquering it by force ("Serena I").

And so only flight is left. To escape what one can neither win nor vanquish seems the last hope. But escape where? . . . [The choices can scarcely fail to suggest both womb and grave (there are many examples scattered through the poems of enclosed, protected places).] A Freudian's field day! Still, meaning is hardly hidden. . . . The juxtaposition of beginning and end, womb and grave, occurs in *Waiting for Godot* in the striking image of the women who give birth astride a tomb. Here, the young man walks on and on toward he knows not what. There, the old man has stopped walking and waits—for he knows not what. In the last poem in the collection the themes of flight and suicide, the definitive flight, come close to joining, as in "Serena I," but in the last analysis the tension remains unresolved. (pp. 179-81)

The true solution, however, is his poet's art. As the poems themselves make clear, the closed-in place is not solely the womb, nor the grave that resembles it. It is something more positive than these two forms of movement toward nothingness. The place of refuge is above all the little world hidden inside the skull. Even while it recalls death, always present beneath the appearances of life, the image of the skull suggests the microcosm so admirably evoked in the novel *Murphy*, written during the same period. "Who knows," asks the narrator "what the ostrich sees in the sand?" . . . Working in an asylum for mental patients, Murphy came to loathe "the complacent scientific conceptualism that made contact with outer reality the index of mental well-being. . . . [All his experience] obliged him to call sanctuary what the psychiatrists called exile and to think of the patients not as banished from a system of benefits but as escaped from a colossal fiasco." . . . As for Murphy himself, he considered what he called his mind "not as an instrument [designed to record facts from the outer world] but as a place, from whose unique delights precisely those current facts withheld him." . . . As far as he was concerned, therefore, there was an absolutely fundamental conflict between the two worlds. "His vote was cast. 'I am not of the big world, I am of the little world'." . . .

It would be difficult to overstress the importance of this passage. However, the link between inner asylum (the key word in "Echo's Bones") and artistic creation comes not in the novel but in the poetry. "The Vulture," of special importance because of its initial position in the group of thirteen poems, was inspired by lines from Goethe that contain a comparision between a soaring bird scanning the earth for prey, its wings motionless, and the lyric that hovers on the edge of becoming. In Beckett's poem, the vulture drags "his hunger through the sky / of my skull shell of sky and earth." (Here already we have the tendency to interiorize that creates the microcosm.) Then the bird, dropping toward an intended victim, finds itself "mocked by a tissue that may not serve / till hunger earth and sky be offal." An esthetic point of view that helps to explain the entire collection can be discovered lying half hidden in the lines of this opening poem. In effect, the microcosm of the imagination can be not only a place to live but also the little world of a literary work. Any attempt to isolate it totally from the big world would no doubt be vain, but there is certainly a tendency in this direction. Implemented, it will produce an individualistic art concerned above all with the exploration of the self, an introspective art difficult of access, hardly popular in any sense, but singularly "modern." It will reflect the need of those living at a time when social institutions disintegrate and reform unceasingly to take stock, to find (at least to seek) a more stable inner reality. So much the worse if this reality turns out to be as shifting and elusive, similarly destined to disintegration, equally unreal. (pp. 182-83)

Echo's Bones is indeed under the sign of Ovid, and the poet's theme as well as practice is poetic metamorphosis. A Freudian interpretation would miss the mark if it failed to take account of the essential metaphoric movement that extends the imagery of enclosures and makes both womb and tomb figures of the microcosm of transforming imagination. . . . It is art that makes possible the last and best transformation of reality. Only the poet can fix forever the ideal vision that in its way corrects the cruelty of the human condition. (pp. 183-84)

Lawrence E. Harvey, "A Poet's Initiation," in Samuel Beckett Now, *edited by Melvin J. Friedman (© 1970 by The University of Chicago), University of Chicago Press, 1970, pp. 171-84.*

Before Beckett, one would have thought it a highly unlikely enterprise to construct a drama about a pronoun. Yet Beckett's preoccupation with the medium of theater has been a steady concentration in learning how to do more and more on stage with less and less. In *Not I*, completed in 1972, the stage is in darkness and "the empty space" before us is almost literally empty. To one side is a mouth, disembodied, suspended in space and throbbing with an undulating pulsation of lips, teeth, and tongue. Never formulating any integer as unified or coherent as a sentence, Mouth gives shape to words and phrases as segmented as itself; they begin as an unintelligible verbal onslaught, get beaten into life as they rise in crescendo toward an agonizing scream, then settle themselves down once more into their dull incomprehensible drone.

To the other side of the stage is a silent, elongated, hooded figure, "sex undeterminable," standing on an invisible podium four feet above stage level, covered from head to bottom of platform in the folds of a black djellaba. This mysterious towering figure interrupts the monologue at four strategic moments, raising its arms "in a gesture of helpless compassion," then slowly returns them to its sides. The repeated gesture lessens with each recurrence "till scarcely perceptible at third." Although Auditor is "fully faintly lit," only a sharp spotlight illuminates Mouth, an isolated, unconnected, gabbling orifice furiously opening and shutting. (p. 189)

Beckett's Mouth, that "God-forsaken hole" hysterically speeding up the momentum behind Dr. Johnson's swift determination of "beating the track of the alphabet with sluggish resolution," tells a story. Yet the tale is characterized throughout by a "vehement refusal to relinquish third person." Each movement of Auditor is preceded by Mouth's insistence that the story she tells is about "she," not "I" ("what? . . . who? . . . no! . . . she!"), hence giving, in one of its several dimensions, the title of the play. And yet the story Mouth seems compelled to tell unendingly ("something she had to tell . . . could that be it?"), like the tales other Beckett heroes recite, bears an uncanny resemblance to its own situation on stage. A silent old woman, "coming up to sixty . . . what? . . . seventy? . . . good God! . . . coming up to seventy" . . . , is looking aimlessly for cowslips in a field one early April morning. "Suddenly," no, "gradually," she begins talking nonstop and has been continuing along those lines ever since. A cruel April indeed. For the voice issuing from Mouth is that of an old woman in extreme terror, half-remembering past events, trying to recall the incidents of a barely understood life, perhaps her own, but one so painful that she refuses to acknowledge it as hers—she can only face it by making it a third person.

Mouth, like her third-person scapegoat, has thus been living a disconnected psychological hell. . . . Beckett's method of allusion is through gross distortion: Eliot's "spring rain" is now a verbal downpour, breeding in this case not the promise of lilacs, but rather the *fleurs du mal* of present and uncomprehending misery.

Beckett had earlier played a charade with "The Waste Land" in "Whoroscope," which borrows from Eliot the device of discontinuous form and its technique of allusiveness, carried in this instance by the young Beckett to typically absurd proportions. (pp. 190-91)

Mouth's third-person protagonist had, in fact, tried to open her own mouth on several occasions long before that fateful April morning within the Proustian budding grove. Yet each opportunity—in a courtroom, a supermarket, a public lavatory—had proved a failure or an embarrassment. Her present purgatory is thus a making up for lost time. In the few years left for her, encapsulated for us in the few minutes of stage time, she must get in all the words she may have needed to say during her lifetime of silence. Beckett has told us before that "silence once broken will never be whole again." In *Not I* he takes himself quite liberally at his own *double entendre*.

Why is Mouth so compulsive in its stubborn refusal to abandon the security of the third-person singular? For it is precisely this uneasy conflict between pronouns which sets the major tension of this play into motion. (p. 191)

In *Not I* . . . Mouth is no longer searching for a coexistence with its authentic first-person singular, but is instead frantically running away from such an encounter. For what it discovers in the "I" is its own *bête noire*. Like Buster Keaton tearing up a series of old photographs of himself in Beckett's "comic and unreal" *Film*, Mouth is determined to obliterate any relationship with its own agonizing past. The staging of the play suggests both a religious confessional—Auditor's attentive cowled figure, the mouth pouring out words while the rest of the face remains hidden in the darkness—and also a literally dislocated personality:

an old woman listening to herself, yet unable to accept that what she hears, what she says, refers to her. All she acknowledges as her own is an unrelenting "roar in the skull." (p. 193)

The Jungian psychologist M. Esther Harding has projected an identity crisis resembling the uneasy situation in Beckett's play in a study called, most fortuitously, *The "I" and the "Not I"; A Study in the Development of Consciousness*. Jung used the term "process of individuation" for a program of psychic development accompanied by a progressive increase in consciousness. A person who is unconscious of himself does not live—life just happens to him. (p. 194)

The parallel between the disconnected psychological state poised in *Not I* and Jungian theory becomes even more curious when we consider for a moment the pronoun in its title not as pronoun, but as Roman numeral: for the visual images exposed before us on stage are not I, but II. . . . The extreme contrast between figures I (Mouth) and II (Auditor) is, therefore, not so much thematic and symbolic as it is literal and visual. . . . By focusing and refocusing at least four times during the course of the play, the audience's attention is absorbed exclusively with images I and II with no interference of extraneous commodities like face or body to interrupt the stark antagonism between Mouth and Auditor, that shadowy figure fully but faintly lit.

In Harding's Jungian terminology the "shadow" is the figure who appears in our dreams; it will be of the same sex as the dreamer, since it really presents part of his personality. . . . What Jung discriminated as the ego was that conscious part of the psyche focused in a center called the "I"; but the unconscious part of the personal psyche is focused and personified as a sort of *alter ego,* the shadow. We are all dimly aware of this *alter ego* residing somewhere inside us. It acts in us almost as if it were another being, another self, with whom we can carry on a conversation, taking part in an inner discussion or conflict when we are of two minds about a problem; it can sometimes initiate actions which we ourselves would not perform. The shadow is really a part of the personality. As long as it remains unconscious, the human being can never be whole and suffers as a consequence the pain of disintegration. . . . It is important for the individual to become united with his shadow, giving it a place in the totality of his "I." By accepting the black substance which adheres to the shadow, we take the first step in the individuation process and in the development of a true self-consciousness.

But Mouth is an image not of wholeness, of a reconciliation of opposites, but of fragmentation and destruction. Although there arises within Mouth a great need to confess the sin of its personal shadow so that the excluded parts of its personality may be accepted as part of its whole psyche, this confession is distanced to the fiction of a third person. Obliged to become whole, to face a situation which seems beyond its capabilities, perhaps as the result of a neurotic disturbance, the task Mouth undertakes is to confront its own shadow. But Mouth can only succeed in accepting its dark and sinister qualities by "cloaking" them through personification and projection. (pp. 195-96)

[If] we are to accept the Jungian parallel, the overtones are immediately cloudy: Mouth's projection would sometimes be the "she" of its own story, sometimes the shadowy figure of Auditor. Neither situation accounts for the possibility that the "buzzing" in the brain Mouth mentions might be a "stream of words" running through Auditor's own hooded head, nor the possibility that the silent figure of Auditor is as consistently wordless as the "she" of Mouth's story before the whatever-it-was that took place in the field. The Mouth-Auditor duality is susceptible to a series of explanations, not the least of which would see Auditor as goad for "the words . . . the brain . . . flickering away like mad." (p. 197)

It is, in fact, this peculiar convolution of possible explanations, backtracking on one another as surely as the words and phrases of the monologue itself, that is the particular richness of *Not I*. As we are forced to focus and refocus on figures I and II, so we are forced to focus and refocus on the variety of overlapping explanations, encountering each time in a new light the same visual stimulus. Like a lens focusing on the same image from a multiplicity of camera angles, so Beckett makes us do with our eyes on stage the work that is usually accomplished in cinema by what is called in this play "the whole machine."

As it is with the multiplicity of possible interpretations of this work, so it is with the drama of the pronoun "I" itself. For *Not I* is also "not aye," what Beckett has called elsewhere "the screaming silence of no's knife in yes's wound." Unlike Joyce's reverence for "the saying yes" of Molly Bloom, Mouth's monologue consists of a series of negations, "no matter," "no love," "no moon," "no screaming," "no part," "no idea," "no speech," "no stopping," "no sound," "no response," "no feeling," not to mention the endless litany of "nots," "nevers," and "nothings." Parents are either "unknown" or "unheard of" and prayers go "unanswered." An individual is "speechless" and "powerless" and the situation is "painless." Human beings are "incapable" of feeling or simply "insentient." Questionings are "vain," proof is "dismissed," and reason itself is "strange." George Herbert's graceful wreath has been replaced by Beckett's "disconnected" knot, pun intended.

Although *Not I* appears to be "about" Mouth, not eye (co-starring Auditor as ear), the piece is perhaps a far more subtle vehicle than this unruly trinity would imply. Although Mouth speaks, Auditor hears, and audience sees, Beckett creates for his audience a visual and aural stimulus closely approximating the "matter" of the monologue itself. (pp. 197-98)

Not I brings to the surface our own difficulty in seeing, in perceiving, for this is our annoying situation as members of the audience. Like the "she" of Mouth's monologue, we have no idea what position Mouth or "she" is in—whether standing, or sitting, or kneeling. We see merely "whole body like gone." In Beckett, concentration on eyes leads inevitably to concentration on tears. . . .

As we have difficulty seeing Beckett's "goings on" on stage in *Not I*, so we are constantly "straining to hear" the words in the concentrated monologue. . . . (p. 199)

Not I makes us desperately aware of the agonizing limitations of seeing, hearing, and speaking. Yet before Beckett such limitations never seemed so theatrically exciting. Beckett's "drama stripped for inaction" thus implies, ironically, an extraordinary amount of activity radiating from the stage, simultaneously visual, verbal, and aural. The "I"

in Beckett's *Not I* is the most minimal dramatic character in Beckett's minimal theatrical art, the ingénue who, like Godot, fails to make an appearance on the board before the curtain comes down. But while waiting for this first-person singular to arrive, Beckett has set into motion a drama in which each sensory stimulus has the kinetic potential to stimulate all three sensory organs activated in this play. (pp. 199-200)

The theatrical power in this intense monologue is hypnotic, the effect less Cartesian than visceral. Beckett's first-person singular, or more precisely the conspicuous absence of his "I," thus takes its place along with those other heroic pronouns marching through the repertory of twentieth-century theater, Lenormand's "Lui" and "Elle" in *Les Ratés* and Cummings' "Him" and "Me" in *Him*. In *Not I* Beckett has presented us with a multidimensional, multimedia extravaganza, all of this based on the frail drama of a little pronoun making not so much a theatrical debut as a sensational return engagement. (p. 200)

> *Enoch Brater, "The 'I' in Beckett's 'Not I'," in* Twentieth Century Literature *(copyright 1974, Hofstra University Press), July, 1974, pp. 189-200.*

The appearance of two new books by Samuel Beckett [*Fizzles* and *Ends and Odds*] ought to be cause for pleasurable anticipation. But the feeling among many readers must be more like dread these days: his last few books have contained work that is less than major and not very likeable. . . . We saw Beckett's fragmentary later works as desperate and courageous acts, diminishing islands of utterance being eaten away by silence. When his 35-second play *Breath* (1969) appeared, we felt that the end had at last been reached: what inessentials remained to be purged?

To have assumed that Beckett could not go on, of course, was to have misread not only *The Unnamable*, but most of Beckett's work, which is often about ending but seldom about ends. Though his fiction has been fizzling out since *The Unnamable* and *How It Is*, and his drama since *Krapp's Last Tape* and *Happy Days*, to conclude that it is fizzling according to some predictable pattern is, as we must now realize, unwarranted. . . . It is disconcerting . . . to find that in *Fizzles* and *Ends and Odds*, Beckett's newest collections of fiction and drama, he has not taken that predictable though unimaginable step beyond *Imagination Dead Imagine* and *Breath*.

Finding nothing ahead but silence, Beckett has apparently stepped to the side. We ought to remember with gratitude that Beckett is not a hack and has not stepped back to parody the trilogy or *Godot*. But in publishing these spare variations on some of his less consequential later work—there are reminders here of *Words and Music*, *Eh Joe*, *The Lost Ones*, *Ping*, and so on, in addition to less recherché material—he has forced his readers to re-examine his later work as a whole. . . . Beckett's late work is like Pound's fragmentary blurtings near the end of the *Cantos*. If we imagine them submitted by an unknown poet to a magazine of which we are the editor, their defects as poetry are apparent. But with 800 pages of Pound's intellectual and spiritual history behind them, they acquire the power to move us. A few Beckettian fragments might be viewed as adjuncts to the great works of Beckett's middle period, testimony that the power of such works as *The Unnamable* and

Endgame was felt even by their creator. But there are now enough fragmentary works in print that they seem to demand consideration on their own merits: the fizzling-out is too protracted. (pp. 776-78)

The eight prose fictions in *Fizzles* are written in a variety of Beckettian styles. There is the relatively conventional style of the *Nouvelles* or part 1 of *Molloy* (Fizzles 1 and 2), the endless, breathless, comma-spliced sentences of *The Unnamable* (Fizzles 3 and 4), and the spare, staccato style of *Imagination Dead Imagine*. . . . (p. 778)

The rather low-grade pleasures of recognition are certainly not the only pleasures to be had from *Fizzles*. Not one of these pieces is utterly bereft of Beckett's beauty and nobility of style: not one could have been written by another hand. Consider this passage, which ends Fizzle 6:

> Ah to love your last and see them at theirs,
> the last minute loved ones, and be happy,
> why ah, uncalled for. No but now, now,
> simply stay still, standing before a window,
> one hand on the wall, the other clutching
> your shirt, and see the sky, a long gaze, but
> no, gasps and spasms, a childhood sea, other
> skies, another body.

Here everything is exactly right. The subject matter is typical of the later Beckett—the rush of involuntary memory and the regret it occasions for lost love and a wasted life. (p. 779)

The sort of energy Beckett used to put into prose fiction now seems to be expressed in his drama. Since *The Unnamable* and *How It Is*, prose has become almost exclusively a meditative medium for Beckett. Narrative is increasingly the function not of prose but of drama. One effect of this is the sort of half-drama we have in the television play *Eh Joe* or the stage play *Not I*. . . . In both these plays, stories or fragments of stories are told to an unspeaking listener, by a voice whose source is unseen in *Eh Joe*, and only an illuminated mouth in *Not I*. The most extreme example to date, and one of the most effective, is *That Time*, one of the three high points of *Ends and Odds*. . . . Three identical yet distinct voices talk, turn and turn about, out of the darkness at Listener, of whom we see only the illuminated face. The illuminated face in the dark is a minor motif in Beckett's late work: see Fizzle 2, in which a character named Horn is ordered by the narrator to light his face with a flashlight, or *Play*, in which the characters are compelled to speak when a spotlight is trained on their faces. In both of these works, the light is unpleasant, intrusive, inquisitorial, reminding us of E's pursuit of O in *Film*, and the television camera's pursuit of Joe in *Eh Joe*. In *That Time*, the light that constantly illuminates Listener's face is not obviously an instrument of torture as it is in *Play*, but its relentlessness is an apparent accompaniment to the threefold voice, which is the stream of the listener's divided consciousness, babbling on at him in the second person without punctuation:

> . . . did you ever say I to yourself in your
> life come on now (*eyes close*) could you ever
> say I to yourself in your life. . . .

Listener's smile, "toothless for preference," with which the play ends, both welcomes the silence and anticipates the fading of the light.

In *That Time*, several Beckettian themes which usually appear in isolation are brought together—the self divided into perceiver and perceived (cf. *The Unnamable*), the "anguish of perceivedness" (cf. *Film*—the phrase appears in Beckett's introductory note to the original project), and the tormenting memory of a lost, or abjured, love. . . . (pp. 780-81)

While *That Time* is more successful on the page, *Footfalls* only comes to life in the theater. In production, this play . . . is overwhelmingly powerful. Like *That Time*, it has complexities which we might think more appropriate to a work meant to be read than to be performed. . . . [Unless] we read the speeches in *Footfalls* carefully and sympathetically, we are liable to miss their power because of Beckett's fussy stage directions. To read a play requires more of the imagination than to read fiction: we cannot simply submit to the author's vision, but we must stage the play in our heads. (pp. 782-83)

In *Ghost Trio*, the fourth piece in the "Ends" section of the book . . . the difficulties [of *Footfalls*] become impossibilities. There is every chance that a tape of this television piece . . . would be worth seeing, but the average reader—and I mean the average *Beckett* reader—will probably find his patience exhausted before he is able to put together the diagram, the camera movements, the music cues and the speeches in his imagination. As for the "Odds," unambitiously subtitled "Roughs for Theatre and Radio"—odd is the word. "Theatre I" with its abortive pseudocouple (a blind man and a cripple) vaguely resembles *Endgame*, and "Radio I" vaguely resembles *Words and Music*. "Theatre II" and "Radio II" resemble nothing on God's earth. They come closest perhaps to early Ionesco, and "Radio II" ends with what may be the lamest speech Beckett has ever put in the mouth of a character:

> Don't cry, Miss, dry your pretty eyes and
> smile at me. Tomorrow, who knows, we
> may be free.

The uneasiness that Beckett's admirers must have experienced on hearing of the publication of *Fizzles* and *Ends and Odds*, then, is justified, though only in part. *Not I, That Time*, and *Footfalls* are surely equal to all but Beckett's very best drama (that is, *Godot, Endgame*, and *Krapp's Last Tape*), which means that they are remarkable indeed. But the rest of *Ends and Odds*, and most of *Fizzles*, is what most readers must have suspected, and what the apologetic titles indicate: very minor works by a very great writer. . . .

[Of] all great writers, Beckett is among the most uneven. Against the manifest grace and clarity of the trilogy, *Godot, Endgame* and the rest is the ungainliness and eccentricity of *Mercier and Camier* or (excuse the heresy) *Watt*. The value of *Fizzles* and *Ends and Odds* (and whatever similar collections have been or may be published) is not so much intrinsic as contingent. These scraps from Beckett's workshop expand our sense of the milieu from which the greater works came. And more importantly, the imperfections of these scraps help us realize with what difficulty and against what odds those greater works were achieved. (pp. 783-84)

David Gates, "Scraps from Beckett's Workshop," in Virginia Quarterly Review *(copyright, 1977, by the* Virginia Quarterly Review, *The University of Virginia), Vol. 53, No. 4 (Autumn, 1977), pp. 776-84.*

Beckett's living dead do not even walk—in the novels they hobble and crawl, in the plays they are remarkably stationary. Beckett presents in his plays unindividuated characters with stylized faces, whose single names do not name them, give no clue to family, class, nation (we do not identify Vladimir as Russian or Pozzo as Italian). His characters come from nowhere, belong nowhere, have no occupation or place in society. There is no society. Society appears as the small band that beats Estragon when he sleeps nights in a ditch. Godot beats his messenger's brother; Pozzo beats Lucky. Beating seems the last vestige of the social principle; and for certain pairs (Pozzo/Lucky, Hamm/Clov) the tyrant/victim relation is all that remains of love. Beckett goes further than early Eliot, who portrays the breaking down of our civilization; Beckett portrays the period after the wreck.

His plays are set on the waste land—*Waiting for Godot* on a country road with only a bare, black tree; *Happy Days* on an "expanse of scorched grass"; *Endgame* in a room into which are carried reports of a lifelessly gray sky and sea. This waste land, like Eliot's, signifies sexual and spiritual sterility; but it also signifies the site of a vanished civilization, where a few survivors exist in scattered pairs. The pair is the minimum unit necessary for human existence, since human existence is dialectical: these people need to be seen, heard, remembered, need above all to talk, in order to assure themselves they exist. . . . The waste land is the void over which the self puts forth its few threads, precariously.

The waste land is also a spatial extension without landmarks and therefore without direction, without distinctions of place and therefore without locations. To Vladimir's question in Act II, "Where were we yesterday" if not here, Estragon replies: "How would I know? . . . There's no lack of void." The place we're at is "indescribable," says Vladimir to Pozzo, who doesn't remember being here yesterday. "It's like nothing. There's nothing. There's a tree." Since the tree is the one landmark, there's no place to go from it; just as there is no place to go from the room in *Endgame,* or from the mound in which Winnie is buried to the waist. That is why the characters are largely stationary, and why even when they *intend* to go—as Vladimir and Estragon do finally, as well as Clov in *Endgame*—they remain.

Nature has not been restored by the disappearance of civilization; for whatever catastrophe destroyed civilization also destroyed nature. "There's no more nature," says Clov. The blind Hamm, whom he serves, longs atavistically to feel a ray of sunshine on his face and hear the sea, but there is no sun and the tideless sea makes no sound. "What a blessing nothing grows," says Winnie. The waste land represents a condition beyond civilization and nature.

The props in these plays are like the random artifacts dug up by archeologists; one has to read back through them to the coherent civilization that gave them meaning. Though only *Krapp's Last Tape* specifically takes place in the future, all these plays suggest the future of the last men. . . . (pp. 120-22)

Time in Beckett is the other void represented by the waste land, a void to be deliberately filled. (p. 123)

Vladimir, the rationalist, uses the word "waiting" for what we do in time, and the name Godot for the direction of our wait. Estragon, the irrationalist and former poet, remains skeptical. In this pair, the rationalist gives such direction as there is. In the other pair, the thinker Lucky enslaves himself to Pozzo, the man of power; the two are traveling, and Pozzo gives so strong a sense of direction that Estragon wonders whether Pozzo is Godot. (Traveling and waiting are Beckett's two images of existence; waiting predominates in the plays.) By Act II, however, Pozzo has disintegrated; he has grown blind, Lucky has grown dumb, and all four in their physical decrepitude fall into the same heap. Bodily decay marks time—but faintly, because Beckett's characters are old and decayed at the start; the rapid decline of Pozzo and Lucky is exceptional, an example of dramatic compression. Pozzo's refusal to name the day when disaster struck suggests that the decline is to be understood as the slow inevitable work of time. (pp. 123-24)

Continuities of place, time, identity are connected, and depend upon memory. Because of the lack of memory, time in Beckett's plays has a limited backward extension, which relates to a lack of depth in space and identity. Krapp, in *Krapp's Last Tape,* is the only character who dwells on memory and remembers in detail; but he remembers by playing tapes—through what Beckett in his book on Proust calls, using Proust's terms, "voluntary" or mechanical, rather than "involuntary" or organic memory. Krapp therefore establishes no connection with the past. . . . As a character he has no depth, since the memory is not inside him; he moves only a little within his "den" and, accordingly, little present time elapses. In Beckett's plays, the counterpart to the characters' lack of depth is their immobility or near immobility within a very limited extension of space-time. Beckett's characters lack the unseen third dimension of memory and unconsciousness; they exist almost entirely in what they do and say. This is curious in a writer who has praised Proust for accomplishing just the opposite, for creating infinite depths of character through extensions of time, memory, unconsciousness. Like the movement in painting that starts with post-Impressionism, Beckett's dramatic art strives to be statically two-dimensional in order to evoke sheer existence—"presence," as Robbe-Grillet calls it in his essay on Beckett's plays. ["Samuel Beckett or 'Presence' in the Theatre," see excerpt above].

There is as little forward as backward extension in time. The characters only dimly remember the last cycle and do not anticipate the rebirth that would bring round the next. . . . Although there are echoes of Eliot throughout Beckett—his main characters are "hollow men"; like the speaker in "Gerontion," they are old, with ruined senses, disembodied consciousnesses representing the old age of a culture—such echoes are particularly noticeable in *Endgame.* (pp. 124-26)

Hamm's "Then let it end! with a bang!" echoes the last lines of "The Hollow Men": "*This is the way the world ends / Not with a bang but a whimper,*"—lines that turn all the games and rituals of the poem into an endgame. The whole theme of lost memory, individual and cultural, recalls Eliot—though Beckett is even more satirical than Eliot. . . . Hamm's father and mother, Nagg and Nell, represent the pre-World War I world of sensuality, sex, joy; they still laugh, tell jokes—they try to kiss but can't reach each other from their separate ash cans. . . . Nell's recollections of happiness one April afternoon, rowing on Lake Como, parody the opening recollections in *The Waste*

Land of prewar romantic experience. *The Waste Land*'s "'Do / You remember / Nothing?'" is echoed by Vladimir's appeal to Estragon to confirm the continuity of Acts I and II: "Do you not remember? . . . Do you not remember?" (pp. 126-27)

Even the positive impulse of these plays, the unaccountable vestigial tenderness that ties into pairs these almost unfeeling characters, can be compared to the unaccountably minimal "notion" in [Eliot's] "Preludes" of "some infinitely gentle / Infinitely suffering thing." . . . Beckett does not, like Eliot, develop this minimal intuition, because he does not acknowledge the enduring underlife and the archetypes emerging from it. He reverses the direction running from Wordsworth through Eliot, in that he deliberately avoids the archetypalization of characters; his characters are symbolic only negatively, since they symbolize the *lack* of life: Hamm does *not* fulfill the God-King-Father archetype suggested. In the trilogy of novels, the personae and fictions tried and discarded suggest mythical figures—Ulysses, Hermes, Jesus—but the shifting references do not, as in *The Waste Land* and *Ulysses,* reinforce the characters' identities but reduce them. The shifting references that in *The Waste Land* produce an accretion of contents produce in Beckett's trilogy a "gradual reduction of contents," which in Dieter Wellershoff's words "appears as a progressive process of de-mythologization."

That is why identity in Beckett approaches zero, with the difference between life and death almost imperceptible. . . . There is certainly no rebirth of self in these characters; they are all locked into an old self, they are all, to borrow Beckett's terminology in the Proust book, prisoners of habit. When they do suffer because they have for a moment broken through to an awareness of their suffering, the release is not, as in Proust, involuntary memory—it is a glimpse, through the structured world of habit, into the void: a momentary awareness of their own nothingness. The discarding of selves in the trilogy leads to the same void; the process is not rebirth. (pp. 127-28)

The characters have most "presence," are existentially most powerful, when their being is reduced to the one last flicker of self-consciousness. (p. 129)

Although all these plays approach the quality of Winnie's monologue in that the characters speak mainly to hear themselves, only Krapp is alone. That may be why *Krapp's Last Tape* is the only one of the plays discussed so far to end on a purely negative note, without any sure sign of tenderness. . . . Krapp's comments and the tape we hear—an utterance of thirty years ago—do not make a true dialogue since the earlier self, in repudiating a still earlier idealistic self of ten years back (whose recording he reports having just played), has already made the choice for discontinuity which the onstage Krapp merely repeats. We have here Proustian and Wordsworthian layers of time; but because the memory represented by the tapes is mechanical or voluntary, Krapp does not in Wordsworth's phrase bind his days together. . . . (p. 130)

Since consciousness can never know its own extinction, since "the individual," as Martin Esslin puts it, "can never become aware of his own cessation, his final moments of consciousness must remain, as it were, eternally suspended in limbo and can be conceived as recurring through all eternity." This is the point of the Dantesque stage work

Play, where the dead are locked into the cyclic memory of their passionate lives. They evolve purgatorially toward a higher understanding of their lives; hell is the aborting of illumination and the inescapable return in memory to the way they thought and felt in life.

Play is unusual for Beckett in that it presents *three* main characters—M, the man; W₁fi his wife; W₂fi his mistress. In their memories of life there were never more than the usual two on stage; M imagines all three, after death, drifting idyllically in a rowboat—the rowboat is a recurring image of happiness in Beckett. *Two* seems to be the number for life, *three* for heaven, *one* perhaps for hell; these characters partly inhabit all three places. They are described in the stage directions as three heads protruding out of "*three identical grey urns*" that touch one another. "*They face undeviatingly front throughout the play. Faces so lost to age and aspect as to seem almost part of urns. But no masks.*" This is a model because character, even being, comes so close to zero. Identity is reduced even farther in *Not I.* . . . The characters of *Play* are almost undifferentiated consciousnesses: "*Faces impassive throughout. Voices toneless.*" The specific exclusion of masks shows Beckett as even more impersonal than Yeats; even masks suggest too much personality.

The utterances are monologues. The three are not present to each other; each thinks the other two still alive. Yet the touching urns suggest that the three are united through pattern. (In the novel *Molloy,* the tramp Molloy and the proper citizen Moran are similarly united through a cyclical pattern of which they are unaware.) The inquisitorial spotlight, which plays Dante's questioning role, solicits each character individually, leaving the other two in darkness. When in the moving choral passages all three faces are illuminated, they speak in unison but say different things—a sign that only pattern unites them. (pp. 133-35)

Their life story of lust, betrayal, hatred is unusually passionate for Beckett; *Play* follows the cyclical structure of Noh drama, in which ghosts relive their passionate lives then fade back into death. But the point is as usual in Beckett's plays: the characters have more "presence" now that they have less vitality, they understand each other better now that they speak monologues than when they spoke to each other. Now they pity each other, wish each other well. (p. 135)

To see phenomena as play is to deprive them of being by reducing them to pattern. When will some higher understanding reduce to pattern their present state so that they can pass out of existence? In the end M feels himself scrutinized by a higher understanding represented apparently by the spotlight: "Looking for something. In my face. Some truth. In my eyes. Not even." He feels himself passing out of existence either because he is completely understood, or because the spotlight as absolute eye is mindless so that he does not feel himself perceived: "Mere eye. No mind. Opening and shutting on me. Am I as much—." There is a blackout, then spot on M. "Am I as much as . . . being seen?" There is a blackout, then the faint spots on three faces with which the play began. The play is repeated. Neither complete understanding nor complete oblivion—perhaps they are the same—can be attained, because consciousness cannot conceive its own extinction. Since there is only consciousness reflecting on itself, the thought of breaking through to an outside reality is only a thought that leads back to the round of consciousness.

Is this usurpation of the world by consciousness the catastrophe that seems to have preceded all these plays, making Beckett's characters seem survivors of some terrible wreck? The catastrophe is to some extent the world wars (there are hints of this in *Godot* and *Endgame*); it is to a greater extent old age when, with the wreck of the body, life retreats into a consciousness that is itself failing. But the clue to the catastrophe's main meaning is Vladimir's statement: "What is terrible is to *have* thought."... The catastrophe is in Blake's terms a fall in perception. To *have* thought is to have killed off the world, to have drawn it all inside the skull. After that no more thought is possible (Vladimir: "We're in no danger of ever thinking any more"); for genuine thought is about something other than itself. All we can do now is invent the talk, games, rituals necessary to cover the void. Talk has become a substitute for thought. "We are incapable of keeping silent," says Estragon. "It's so we won't think." (pp. 135-36)

Beckett's art is distinguished by such powerful images as this of human existence suspended over a void made palpable.

The destructive thought alluded to would seem to be Descartes'. For it was Descartes who, after dismissing the inherited world by an act of doubt, reestablished the world on the principle, "*I think, hence I am.*" He thus cut mind off from body, especially since he did not recognize that thought requires a sensuous object. He made mind the center of life and identity in an otherwise mechanical world; he gave us the image, which haunts Beckett, of mind surrounded by void.... Beckett's first published poem, *Whoroscope,* is a dramatic monologue spoken by Descartes; and the Cartesian split defines the geography of self which, in the manner of Wordsworth with Locke and Eliot with Bradley, Beckett accepts and fights throughout his work—perhaps because he feels his own selfhood that way, and feels Descartes' amputation of self predictive of our time. (pp. 137-38)

It is because Beckett modifies Descartes by treating body as a disintegrating rather than as an efficient machine that so many Beckett characters drag around old inadequate bodies that seem hardly to belong to them and require the aid of bicycles, crutches, wheelchairs. Beckett assumes romanticism has failed in its attempt to answer Descartes by establishing the organic connection of mind with body and of the mind-body self with nature. "We should turn resolutely toward Nature," says Estragon, modulating, as he and Vladimir often do, from personal into cultural experience. "We've tried that," says Vladimir. We have tried romanticism.

One might draw the opposite conclusion, one might say that Beckett is a romanticist working negatively through satire of the isolated self. But it is likelier—since Beckett apparently resembles the heroes of his fiction—that he could not square with his experience of his own self romantic accounts of the self's infinite possibilities for expansion and for transforming the external world. The best evidence of Beckett's anti-romanticism is this: that whatever positive impulse he does generate comes from reversing the Wordsworthian direction, from withdrawal rather than projection of self. (pp. 138-39)

Beckett's reversal of the Wordsworthian direction is curious, since in his book on Proust he uses Wordsworthian categories to describe Proust's achievement in a direction that we recognize to be Wordsworthian. As in Wordsworth, habit is the villain. Habit and the ego represented by an habitual organization of the world screen us from reality. We break through in periods of transition "when for a moment the boredom of living is replaced by the suffering of being"—when, lifting the veil of familiarity, we experience world and self as flowing, as alive and threatening because unrationalized. The insight fades as we proceed to rationalize that experience into a new habitual organization of the world. Life in Proust (and Wordsworth) proceeds through such cycles of birth, death, and rebirth of self and the world it perceives. The breakthrough is accomplished by "involuntary memory," which is as in Wordsworth a form of forgetting that leads us to the permanent self underlying the "succession of individuals" that accompany the "succession of habits."... Our permanent self is unconscious; we have access to those unplumbable depths where it resides only through unconscious memory; only the unconscious is creative: "From this deep source Proust hoisted his world."

Having described so precisely and sympathetically what Proust is doing, Beckett in his plays and fiction does the opposite. In the plays his characters remain prisoners of habit, in the trilogy they have little conscious memory; in both plays and novels they have no unconscious memory, no unconscious, no depth—which is why his mode is comic rather than psychological. Depth is projected as action and landscape. (pp. 139-40)

Nevertheless, Beckett's characters, unlike Proust's, see—when they break through the screen of habit—not unformed vitality, as in Proust's periods of transition, but the void. They have negative epiphanies ("Moments for nothing"), the reverse of Wordsworth's and Proust's insights into process. Consequently there is no rebirth of self in Beckett; there is only reduction—through the discarding of false selves in the trilogy and through the lack of content in the plays. (p. 140)

Beckett pursues the inaccessible self throughout his work, but never gets there as Proust and Wordsworth do, instantaneously, with the magic of memory and imagination. The plight of Beckett's protagonists confirms Wordsworth's belief that self and the world can only be known through the senses that connect them, through sensation passing into thought that passes back into sensation. (p. 141)

Beckett's characters conspicuously lack a sensuous life. Their hatred of sex confirms Lawrence's observation that sex contemplated coldly by the disembodied mind must seem disgusting.... Death in Beckett is birth reversed; these characters have almost returned to the womb, but cannot quite die because death is a physical event whereas consciousness cannot conceive its own extinction. "If only I were alive inside," says the jarred head of *The Unnamable,* "one might look forward to heart-failure." This voice, which cannot avoid naming and renaming the unnamable self, says later: "Ah if only this voice could stop, this meaningless voice which prevents you from being nothing, just *barely* prevents you from being nothing and nowhere."

Beckett dramatizes with a force unequalled in our literature the solipsistic condition of modern man who must fabricate reality out of his own head.... The voice of *The Unnamable* finds not only himself but his environment a fabrication of his own words: "wherever I go I find me, leave me, go towards me, come from me, nothing ever but me." "Everything was tainted with myself," writes Lawrence who, in his poem "New Heaven and Earth," breaks out by discovering through touch the otherness of his wife's body. Indeed, Beckett's characters exemplify all that Lawrence, Yeats, and other modern writers I am discussing most feared for the future of human identity. It is from such solipsism, such final diminution and retreat of the vital outgoing Wordsworthian self, that Yeats and Lawrence try to deliver us.

Since Beckett's work—which emerged in the 1950s—follows theirs, he clearly does not think that they and others who have tried to reconstitute the romantic self have succeeded. He seems to insist that, in spite of all the fine writing, his portrayal of the diminished self remains, to quote the title of his prose poem, *How It Is*. Beckett, who thoroughly understands the romantic position, poses a problem for a literary study such as this one. For if the problem of identity is a real problem in modern life, then can literature do anything about it, can the best writing in the world make us restructure our identity? Beckett would seem to be saying that things can only get worse, seeing that God is dead and has been dead so long that Beckett's characters often seem to have forgotten His name. Nietzsche and the post-Nietzschean romanticists tell us that man can transcend himself and thus give *himself* the identity he used to derive from God's eye. Beckett says he cannot.

Yet Beckett's report on humanity is not the worst conceivable. For his characters, who belong to the idealistic side of the Cartesian split, *suffer* from their desolation; except for the parodied Winnie, they do not *think* they are happy—as do the cheery, efficient last men (the objective, mechanical men who have not transcended themselves) of Nietzsche's devastating satire [*Zarathustra.*] . . . *These* are the machines, not Beckett's disintegrating solitaries. These collective men—who deny life's pain, rubbing against each other and taking drugs to ward it off—are more easily recognizable in the world around us than Beckett's essentially religious characters who require only one companion to assure them they exist and whose humanity resides in the awareness we share with them of what is lacking. (pp. 141-44)

> *Robert Langbaum, "Beckett: Zero Identity" (originally published under a different title in* The Georgia Review, *Winter, 1976), in his* The Mysteries of Identity *(copyright © 1977 by Robert Langbaum; reprinted by permission of Oxford University Press, Inc.), Oxford University Press, 1977, pp. 120-44.*

* * *

BISHOP, Elizabeth   1911-

Bishop is an American poet and prose writer currently residing in Brazil. She is generally regarded as a poet who has created a small but significant body of very individual lyric verse. Her poetic world is the real world, which she draws with meticulous detail, then often unexpectedly laces with the fantastic and the surreal. She has been awarded the Pulitzer Prize in Poetry and the National Book Award. (See also *CLC*, Vols. 1, 4, and *Contemporary Authors*, Vols. 5-8, rev. ed.)

Bishop has created a significant poetry out of the manipulation of "precious objects," and just as one might say that

she in her return [to her origins, to childhood or a primitive equivalent] is not so individualistic as Robinson, Frost, or Stevens, and hence different from that generation, one may add that she is never so mystical as Roethke or so involved with gaining reader understanding as are the "confessional poets." Regardless of their conclusions, her poems are still active, and despite their searches for self and their emphases on dream, her reconstructions are not inspired by Freudian analysis and its wish to have one's direction altered by the conscious. Although Bishop returns mentally to her origins, it is not with any of the pathological compulsion that [Sherman] Paul detects in Crane's reveries of childhood or with the therapeutic aims that seem to lie behind the returns of Roethke, Lowell, Jarrell, and Berryman. One has the sense particularly in [the] late poems that she has lived the life she imagined—with all its necessary disappointments—and, despite the narrow range of choice and the pain of disappointment, she is willing to see her past as the only kind of life she could have lived. She is not, as are Lowell and Berryman, trying to fix blame or necessarily, as are Roethke and Jarrell, trying to sympathize. Like Baudelaire's voyagers, she seems instead to be accepting the conditions of voyaging as the process of a life which itself will arrive meaninglessly at death.

In their consistent pessimism about ultimate purpose, the ranges of Bishop's vision relate her both to the views of modernist poets like Robinson, Frost, and Stevens as well as to the major questionings of their successors. Her work is perhaps more profoundly Existential than the poetry of any of her contemporaries and questions even the evolutionary thrust on which occasionally a poet like Jarrell relies. She can and does believe in "tradition" and a sense of linear history, but not a tradition or history that concedes the immortality of art. Her "tradition" with its accumulation and reinforcements of feeling is no different from the cumulative effects of experience. Her incorporation of former works functions more to reinforce than, as in Jarrell, to effect a death struggle with a father figure and supplant his image. Her "precious objects" give the reader the only durability that she has discovered and, in presenting this durability, she never fights for an idiosyncratic idiom. Such an idiom would distort the reality she values and would finally prove immaterial, an exercise in will without regard to environment. She thus opposes the "rarity" that poets of her generation have assumed to promote their own egos and work and which, by its occasionally strident assertions of importance, can be as self-pitying as her denial of will. Nonetheless, one may wonder what her poetry would have been like if she, like her man-moth, had relinquished her "one tear." A more militant stoicism like that she admires in [Flannery] O'Connor may have resulted and produced an equally interesting body of work, but one with far less emphasis on detail and inclined more to allegory.

If Bishop's approach to life by its inclusion of impediments seems less "intellectual" than that of other poets, it is that she is finally given more to necessity than they are. She is more willing to see life as a dialectical process involving man and his environment rather than a process of man's will being imposed upon his surroundings. Although man may not be improving in her view, he will survive much as other animal life has survived and he will need whatever beauty may be preservable. To accept this vision she must abandon the superstructures that most critics rely on to handle poets—those structures of thought which by their very separation from experience seem to define the ego. By minimizing the organizational nature of such separations and placing her definition of being on specific interactions with objects, she embraces a relativism like that of other post-modernist poets but based on situation rather than on voice. Her diverse "characters," as [James G.] Southworth points out, lie not in personae but in her manner of selecting subjects, in a tonality, and in her varied ways of massing detail into significant form. She emerges, therefore, as a balance to the tendency of other poets of her generation to overstress will and rarity. She reminds one how narrow the choices in life are and how unimportant rarity is. Erosion takes its toll of that, too. All discussions of psychology in Bishop's writing and attempts to connect her work finally with post-modernism begin by acknowledging these beliefs. (pp. 142-44)

Jerome Mazzaro, "Elizabeth Bishop and The Poetics of Impediment," in Salmagundi *(copyright © 1974 by Skidmore College), Summer-Fall, 1974, pp. 118-44.*

I first read Elizabeth Bishop's book *North & South* when it was published in 1946, and I had the experience in the very first poem, "The Map," of being drawn into a world that seemed as inevitable as "the" world and as charged with the possibilities of pleasure as the contiguous, overlapping world of poetry. Here, as in so many of her poems, the very materials—ink and paper—seemed to enlarge the horizons of the poem as they simultaneously called it back to the constricting dimensions of the page, much as a collage by Schwitters or Robert Motherwell triumphs over its prosaic substance by cultivating its ordinariness and the responses it can strike in our minds, where in a sense everything is ordinary, everything happens in a perpetual present which is a collage of objects and our impressions of them. (p. 8)

It is [the] continually renewed sense of discovering strangeness, the unreality of our reality at the very moment of the becoming conscious of it *as* reality, that is the great subject for Elizabeth Bishop. The silhouette of Norway unexpectedly becomes the fleeing hare it resembles; the names of cities conquer mountains; Labrador is yellow on the map not by chance but because the Eskimo has oiled it so as to make it into a window for an igloo; the universe is constantly expanding into vast generalizations that seem on the point of taking fire with meaning and contracting into tiny particulars whose enormous specific gravity bombards us with meaning from another unexpected angle. . . .

In many of her poems Bishop installs herself as an openminded, keen-eyed, even somewhat caustic observer of the life that is about to happen, speaking in a pleasant, chatty vernacular tone which seeks in no way to diminish the enormity of it, but rather to focus on it calmly and unpoetically. (p. 10)

Behind the multiple disguises, sometimes funny, sometimes terrifyingly unlike anything human, that the world assumes in Elizabeth Bishop's poetry, [the] moment of almost-transfiguration is always being tracked to its lair, giving the work a disturbing reality unlike anything else in contemporary poetry. (p. 11)

John Ashbery, "Second Presentation of Elizabeth Bishop," in World Literature Today *(copyright 1977 by the University of*

Oklahoma Press), Vol. 51, No. 1, Winter, 1977, pp. 8-11.

In the poetry of Elizabeth Bishop things waver between being what they are and being something distinct from what they are. This uncertainty is manifested at times as humor and at other times as metaphor. In both cases it is resolved, invariably, in a leap that is a paradox: things become other things without ceasing to be the things they are. This leap has two names: one is imagination, the other is freedom. They are synonymous. Imagination describes the poetic act as a gratuitous game; freedom defines it as moral choice. The poetry of Elizabeth Bishop has the lightness of a game and the gravity of a decision.

Fresh, clear, potable: these adjectives that are usually applied to water and that have both physical and moral meanings suit perfectly the poetry of Elizabeth Bishop. Like water, her voice issues from dark and deep places; like water, it satisfies a double thirst: thirst for reality and thirst for marvels. Water lets us see things that repose in its depths yet are subjected to a continual metamorphosis: they change with the merest changes of light, they undulate, they are shaken, they live a ghostly life, a sudden blast of wind scatters them. Poetry that is heard as water is heard: murmur of syllables among stones and grass, verbal waves, huge zones of silence and transparency.

Water but also air: poetry in order to see, visual poetry. Words limpid as a perfect day. The poem is a powerful lens that plays with distances and presences. The juxtaposition of spaces and perspectives makes the poem a theatre where the oldest and most quotidian of mysteries is represented: reality and its riddles. Poetry in order to travel with eyes open or closed: . . . voyages within the self or outside the self, to the past or to the present, to the secret cities of memory or along the circular corridors of desire.

Poetry as if water spoke, as if air thought. . . . These poor comparisons are but ways of alluding to perfection. Not the perfection of the triangle, the sphere or the pyramid, but the irregular perfection, the imperfect perfection of the plant and of the insect. Poems perfect as a cat or a rose, not as a theorem. . . . We have forgotten that poetry is not in what words say but in what is said between them, that which appears fleetingly in pauses and silences. In the poetry workshops of universities there should be a required course for young poets: learning to be silent. The enormous power of reticence—that is the great lesson of the poetry of Elizabeth Bishop. But I am wrong to speak of lessons. Her poetry teaches us nothing. To hear it is not to hear a lesson; it is a pleasure, verbal and mental, as great as a spiritual experience. Let's listen to Elizabeth Bishop, hear what her words say to us and what, through them, her silence tells us. (pp. 15-16)

Octavio Paz, "Elizabeth Bishop, or The Power of Reticence," in World Literature Today *(copyright 1977 by the University of Oklahoma Press), Vol. 51, No. 1, Winter, 1977, pp. 15-16.*

Bishop is singular in that she moves into prose with no apparent hesitation, using the same eyes and ears, the same "tone of large, grave tenderness and sorrowing amusement" that Robert Lowell describes in her poetry.

Her most classically perfect piece (I deliberately avoid the word "story"—it has less "story" than most of her poems) is probably "In the Village," an impression of childhood in Nova Scotia. This was first published in *The New Yorker* over twenty years ago and was wisely included in the selection of poems entitled *Questions of Travel* published in 1965—"wisely" because it deserves, to my mind, as great a chance of immortality as any of her more well-known poems.

A nameless woman, a mother, screams; the scream hangs high over the village, "its pitch . . . the pitch of my village. Flick the lightning rod on top of the church steeple with your fingernail and you will hear it." From then on, however pastoral the landscape below, however comforting the sights and sounds of a child's summer afternoon, we know we are involved in tragedy. But tragedy seldom reveals itself plainly to a child; it slips round corners, lurks in the shadows, hides, ready to pounce, in sunny meadows. And having started in the high sky, on top of the church steeple, we are now at child-level, looking up at most things. As in the best primitive painting (Rousseau rather than Grandma Moses), the appearance is pastoral, placid. But in the blacksmith's shop "things hang up in the shadows and shadows hang up in the things"; in the pasture where the child has gone to pick mint, she is suddenly faced with "an immense, sibilant, glistening loneliness"; the cow, Nelly, and the dog, Jock, are surely immense creatures, dwarfing the dressmaker ("She slept in her thimble") and the milliner, the little people of the village. (pp. 17-18)

"In the Village" is an invocation of childhood, ending with a cry of an adult heart; "The Sea and its Shore" . . . , with its childish title—a coloring book, perhaps, for the sea-glass and shells, pebbles and starfish, crabs and sandpipers with which Bishop feels such affinity—turns out to be a very sophisticated, airy piece about a man called Edwin Boomer, whose job it is to keep the beach clear of litter. An observant fellow even when drunk, he compares the flight of scraps of paper with the flight of birds and concludes that the paper "made more subtle use of air-currents and yielded to them more whimsically than the often pig-headed birds. . . ." . . . [He] returns to his house to read the strange information (messages to Boomer from the unknown?) stacked on his pointed stick. All night he reads—"He made no distinction between the bewilderments of prose and those of poetry"—trying to piece together "any instructions or warnings" he may find; and at dawn it is time for the burning. . . .

Nothing more than this happens to Boomer. His house does not catch fire, he does not encounter people or speak or love or die. Bishop's words enclose his turmoil as a glass dome encloses a miniature snowstorm, perfectly fitting, transparent and snug, transfixing him "in his house, at four one morning, his reading selected, the conflagration all over, the lantern shining clearly." "It is," she writes wryly, "an extremely picturesque scene, in some ways like a Rembrandt, but in many ways not"—a typically enigmatic tease of an ending. . . . (p. 18)

Penelope Mortimer, "Elizabeth Bishop's Prose," in World Literature Today *(copyright 1977 by the University of Oklahoma Press), Vol. 51, No. 1, Winter, 1977, pp. 17-18.*

[Elizabeth Bishop's poems vibrate] between two frequencies—the domestic and the strange. In another poet the alternation might seem a debate, but Bishop drifts rather than divides, gazes rather than chooses. Though the exotic is frequent in her poems of travel, it is not only the exotic that is strange and not only the local that is domestic. (It is more exact to speak, with regard to Bishop, of the domestic rather than the familiar, because what is familiar is always named, in her poetry, in terms of a house, a family, someone beloved, home. And it is truer to speak of the strange rather than of the exotic, because the strange can occur even in the bosom of the familiar, even, most unnervingly, at the domestic hearth.)

To show the interpenetration of the domestic and the strange at their most inseparable, it is necessary to glance back at some poems printed in *Questions of Travel*. In one, "Sestina," the components are almost entirely innocent—a house, a grandmother, a child, a Little Marvel Stove and an almanac. The strange component, which finally renders the whole house unnatural, is tears. . . .

The absence of the child's parents is the unspoken cause of those tears, so unconcealable though so concealed. For all the efforts of the grandmother, for all the silence of the child, for all the brave cheer of the Little Marvel Stove, the house remains frozen, and the blank center stands for the definitive presence of the unnatural in the child's domestic experience—*especially* in the child's domestic experience. Of all the things that should not be inscrutable, one's house comes first. The fact that one's house always *is* inscrutable, that nothing is more enigmatic than the heart of the domestic scene, offers Bishop one of her recurrent subjects.

The centrality of the domestic provokes as well one of Bishop's most characteristic forms of expression. When she is not actually representing herself as a child, she is, often, sounding like one. The sestina, which borrows from the eternally childlike diction of the folktale, is a case in point. Not only the diction of the folktale, but also its fixity of relation appears in the poem, especially in its processional close, which places the almanac, the grandmother and the child in an arrangement as unmoving as those found in medieval painting, with the almanac representing the overarching Divine Necessity, the grandmother as the elder principle and the child as the principle of youth. The voice speaking the last three lines dispassionately records the coincident presence of grief, song, necessity and the marvelous; but in spite of the "equal" placing of the last three lines, the ultimate weight on inscrutability, even in the heart of the domestic, draws this poem into the orbit of the strange.

A poem close by in *Questions of Travel* tips the balance in the other direction, toward the domestic. The filling station which gives its name to the poem seems at first the antithesis of beauty, at least in the eye of the beholder who speaks the poem. The station is dirty. . . . The speaker, though filled with "a horror so refined," is unable to look away from the proliferating detail which, though this is a filling station, becomes ever more relentlessly domestic. "Do they live in the station?" wonders the speaker, and notes incredulously a porch, "a set of crushed and grease-/impregnated wickerwork," the dog "quite comfy" on the wicker sofa, comics, a taboret covered by a doily, and "a big hirsute begonia." The domestic, we perceive, becomes a compulsion that we take with us even to the most unpromising locations, where we busy ourselves establishing domestic tranquility as a demonstration of meaningfulness, as a proof of "love." Is our theology only a reflection of our nesting habits? (pp. 23-4)

Domesticity is frail, and it is shaken by the final strangeness of death [as in "First Death in Nova Scotia"]. Until death, and even after it, the work of domestication of the unfamiliar goes on, all of it a substitute for some assurance of transcendent domesticity, some belief that we are truly, in this world, in our mother's house, that "somebody loves us all." After a loss that destroys one form of domesticity, the effort to reconstitute it in another form begins. The definition of death in certain of Bishop's poems is to have given up on domesticating the world and reestablishing yet once more some form of intimacy. Conversely, the definition of life in the conversion of the strange to the familiar, of the unexplored to the knowable, of the alien to the beloved.

No domesticity is entirely safe. As in the midst of life we are in death, so, in Bishop's poetry, in the midst of the familiar, and most especially there, we feel the familiar as the unknowable. This guerrilla attack of the alien, springing from the very bulwarks of the familiar, is the subject of "In the Waiting Room." It is 1918, and a child, almost seven, waits, reading the *National Geographic,* while her aunt is being treated in the dentist's office. The scene is unremarkable: "grown-up people,/arctics and overcoats,/lamps and magazines," but two things unnerve the child. The first is a picture in the magazine: "black, naked women with necks/wound round and round with wire/like the necks of light bulbs./Their breasts were horrifying"; and the second is "an *oh!* of pain/—Aunt Consuelo's voice" from inside. The child is attacked by vertigo, feels the cry to be her own uttered in "the family voice" and knows at once her separateness and her identity as one of the human group. . . . The child's compulsion to include in her world even the most unfamiliar data, to couple the exotica of the *National Geographic* with the knees and trousers and skirts of her neighbors in the waiting room, brings together the strange at its most horrifying with the quintessence of the familiar—oneself, one's aunt, the "family voice." In the end, will the savage be domesticated or oneself rendered unknowable? The child cannot bear the conjunction and faints. Language fails the six-year-old. "How—I didn't know any/word for it —how 'unlikely' . . .".

That understatement, so common in Bishop, gives words their full weight. As the fact of her own contingency strikes the child, "familiar" and "strange" become concepts which have lost all meaning. . . . The child in "In the Waiting Room" discovers that she is in no intelligible relation to her world, and, too young yet to conceive of domination of the world by will or domestication of the world by love, she slides into an abyss of darkness. (pp. 24-5)

"The Moose" [is] a poem in which no lasting exclusive companionship between human beings is envisaged, but in which a series of deep and inexplicable satisfactions unroll in sequence, each of them precious. Domestication of the land is one, domesticity of the affections is another, and the contemplation of the sublimity of the nonhuman world is the third. (p. 27)

[In Frost's "The Most of It"], as in Bishop's poem, a creature emerges from "the impenetrable wood" and is beheld. But Frost's beast disappoints expectation. . . . Frost's beast is male, Bishop's female; Frost's a symbol of brute

force, Bishop's a creature "safe as houses"; Frost's a challenge, Bishop's a reassurance. The presence approaching from the wood plays, in both these poems, the role that a god would play in a pre-Wordsworthian poem and the role that a human being—a leech-gatherer, an ancient soldier, a beggar—would play in Wordsworth. These human beings, when they appear in Wordsworth's poetry, are partly iconic, partly subhuman, as the Leech-Gatherer is part statute, part sea-beast, and as the old man in "Animal Tranquillity and Decay" is "insensibly subdued" to a state of peace more animal than human. "I think I could turn and live with animals," says Whitman, foreshadowing a modernity that finds the alternative to the human not in the divine but in the animal. Animal life is pure presence, with its own grandeur. It assures the poet of the inexhaustibility of being. Bishop's moose is at once maternal, inscrutable and mild. If the occupants of the bus are bound, in their human vehicle, to the world of village catastrophe and pained acknowledgment, they feel a release of joy in glimpsing some large, grand solidity, even a vaguely grotesque one, which exists outside their tales and sighs, which is entirely "otherworldly." "The darkness drops again," as the bus moves on; the "dim smell of moose" fades in comparison to "the acrid smell of gasoline."

"The Moose" is such a purely linear poem, following as it does the journey of the bus, that an effort of will is required to gaze at it whole. The immediacy of each separate section —as we see the landscape, then the people, then the moose —blots out what has gone before. But the temptation—felt when the poem is contemplated entire—to say something global, something almost allegorical, suggests that something in the sequence is more than purely arbitrary. The poem passes from adult observation of a familiar landscape to the unending ritual, first glimpsed in childhood, of human sorrow and narration, to a final joy in the otherworldly, in whatever lies within the impenetrable wood and from time to time allows itself to be beheld. Beyond or behind the familiar, whether the visual or the human familiar, lies the perpetually strange and mysterious. It is that mystery which causes those whispered exclamations alternating with the pained "Yes" provoked by human vicissitude. It guarantees the poet more to do. On it depends all the impulse to domestication. Though the human effort is bent to the elimination of the wild, nothing is more restorative than to know that earth's being is larger than our human enclosures. Elizabeth Bishop's poetry of domestication and domesticity depends, in the last analysis, on her equal apprehension of the reserves of mystery which give, in their own way, a joy more strange than the familiar blessings of the world made human. (p. 28)

Helen Vendler, "Domestication, Domesticity and the Otherworldly," in World Literature Today *(copyright 1977 by the University of Oklahoma Press), Vol. 51, No. 1, Winter, 1977, pp. 23-8.*

Elizabeth Bishop comes from the North, and like a lot of Northern people, she went south; but the title of her first book, *North & South,* tells us only part of the story. Its North is New York City and its South, Key West; yet the limits it suggests have wider boundaries, earlier and later counterparts: a more distant North, Canada, and a further South, Brazil. And so in the later poems the earliest Canadian landscape is revived, and Brazil replaces Florida. That the two connections are similar we have no doubt; that they are different explains why a poem like "The Moose"—a late poem—restates and enriches several Bishop themes: a journey, a rediscovery, the magical appearance of an animal, the sudden awareness of a particular kind of consciousness. Though its setting is New Brunswick, one can cross the border quickly into Nova Scotia, where the poet grew up, an area with pastoral views, snow and an insistence on *its* Anglo connection. There is in Bishop's Nova Scotia something odd, as if the South Pole had been settled by an English middle class. It is exotic and at the same time —to use a word she uses so tellingly in "Filling Station"— "comfy."

One figure, not middle-class, appears early, and he focuses a concern of Bishop's throughout: the off-creature, the person not part of the comfortable world she found herself in, a comfortable world that had its attendant horrors. One doesn't become a poet for nothing. That figure is the blacksmith who plays such an important role in "In the Village." A counter to a world that has suddenly become impossible —the mother's scream, her madness, are facts, feelings a child cannot take in or, if taken in, cannot bear—he is interesting in himself: he makes something, horseshoes, and he works in the natural world, his ultimate clients being horses. A native and a craftsman—two good Bishop things to be—he is also an outsider, in the sense of being exotic to the child's world at the time. His peculiarity is to normalize the situation; that is, through his oddity he makes things all right. This sense of normalcy and oddness in tandem appears many times in the poems. . . . And since the poet is concerned with the domestic *in* the exotic (a primitive oil lamp, say, hewn out of old Milk of Magnesia bottles and oil drums), some distancing is required. This is supplied by an obvious source, travel, but also by a more subtle one, perspective. If one is in Key West, New York takes on special aspects, and the same is true of Nova Scotia and Brazil. The imagination, of course, has its own cameras, and if any example were needed of what Bishop can do without traveling six thousand miles, "The Monument" would be a good one. But her particular imagination is excited by new places, or old ones that become new by the switch in viewpoint which great distances provide. If "questions of travel" are never resolved by literal answers, distance at least allows for optical shifts and refreshments of thought. (p. 29)

[The] lures of anthropology are present everywhere, because in primitive cultures phenomena are reduced and made clear; the combination of the practical and the occult, of the humdrum and the godlike is taken for granted, and the poet searches for that fusion in places where it has never existed before, in subjects not considered to be the stuff of poetry. . . . There is an interest in reading a new Elizabeth Bishop poem not quite like reading anyone else's. We are surprised to be led not only to a change of viewpoint but to a widening of perception in general. Who else would have connected a sandpiper and William Blake? Or Baudelaire and marimba music? (pp. 29-30)

By its accuracy, by its choice of what is to be put in and left out, Bishop's world begins to take on moral properties. These involve manners in particular and judiciousness in general: there is no scope in her poems that is not measured by a true balancing of weights. And when enlargement occurs—say, in "Roosters," in the introduction of the

figure of St. Peter—we move from the chicken coop to the Vatican, to "old holy sculpture" where "a little cock is seen / carved on a dim column in the travertine," without jarring the imagination or shifting the tone. We move quickly but with absolute grace from nature to art and from there to perceptions that have ethical force. And we believe the lines that explicitly make their points—"There is inescapable hope, the pivot" or "cock-a-doodles yet might bless, / his dreadful rooster come to mean forgiveness"— because we have been led to them by a process as natural as it is artful. It is not difficult to lend one's assent, finally, to the statement that "'Deny deny deny' / is not all the roosters cry."

The hen house leads us by steps to the New Testament; the blacksmith is commonplace but begins to take on mythical proportions. If "mythical" seems too broad a word, then a "fictional illumination" might be more accurate. The point is: he is much more than he first appears to be. . . .

Bishop's cool eye for detail is also a dramatic lens, and her feeling for character is shaded but pronounced. Her little dramas, even the family that makes its greasy appearance in "Filling Station," suggest the theatre, in fact, suggest that strange combination of talents I have mentioned elsewhere: those of the painter and the playwright. I do not disparage Bishop's infallible ear when I say she is closer to the painters than to the composers in most of the poems. Abstraction is not particularly interesting to this poet, and music is not famous for dealing with particulars. What can be handled, looked at, examined, walked around, reperceived, turned in different lights, hung up or laid down— that is of much more interest. (p. 30)

The traditional "character study" is absent. The attendant world, falling into place before and behind, gives the poems their interest, their power and their wit. The personal has little to do with it. . . .

[Slantwise] is the way this poet looks at character: from a side, obliquely, as if she had caught it in its natural habitat without its being aware. There is an assumption of character in creatures, in her moose, her fish, her roosters, the boy leading the horse in "Twelfth Morning," even the little toy horse of "Cirque d'Hiver." These are characters, at least of a sort, because insight is not this poet's thing; the world revealed is everything, its immediacy, its exactitude, but not necessarily its significance. The historical and the confessional rarely crop up in these poems. And one would have to search hard for psychological interest of the kind we have become used to: the inner life, neurotic conflict, Baudelaire's "wing of madness." Yet by plainly presenting character—human, animal or metaphysical . . . and giving it its eccentricities right up front at the footlights, by some miraculous process of foreshortening or enlargement, Bishop causes it to make a permanent imprint. . . . If one could think of a playwright fascinated by drama and incongruity but rather indifferent to personality, one might have something analagous: the whole surround intensely filled with single objects and directed and lit by an expert.

This gift is partly a matter of clarity, of wakefulness, and it is informative, I think, to go over the poems and note how many of them begin at dawn or at daybreak. . . . And conversely, sleep and dream are mentioned often, as if they were opposing conditions from which it were necessary to be roused. With the exception of "The Weed," dream itself is rarely invoked, but it runs like a thread through the fabric of the poems—important in itself, but more important, I think, as an opposing force—not the place where knowledge is to be found but the one that precludes physical observation. (p. 31)

[What the] portraits suggest is sympathy, kindness, judgment—behind them all a set of moral standards is shifting gears—but neither intimacy nor love, though one line explicitly says, "I love you, I guess." That guess is as far as Bishop goes, yet an understated love poem like "The Shampoo" moves one by its restraint, its minimal claims.

Strength and independence under the façade of weakness arouse the poet's interest. It is not a matter of dissimulation but of the simultaneous perception of power and vulnerability, a doubleness manifested over and over again, culminating perhaps in "The Armadillo," where all the armor the animal possesses is not proof against fire. This doubleness is also present in the choice of servants as subjects, because a second character is always implicit; servants, after all, are hired and, in one way or another, play roles. They present the poet with a person and a persona, observable at close range without the risk of presumption. Familiar but aloof, being around so often, they allow for the sureness of external fact and a tacit affection, and around each of them a world, unlike that of the poet's but peculiarly congenial to her talents, materializes. One would not imagine, for instance, a Rio society hostess as the subject of an Elizabeth Bishop poem, or even a nice middle-class Canadian lawyer. Duality is also manifested in the canny manipulation of odd couplings of words, particularly adjectives and nouns, where a tension is set up between them that creates a kind of verbal magnetic field: "awful but cheerful," "the uncontrolled, traditional cries," "commerce and contemplation," "a grave green dust," "the blurred redbud," "the somnambulist brook," et cetera.

In fact, in spite of the clarity of vision, this two-faced perception may be the key to what makes these poems work so beautifully, enhancing their surfaces with an electric undercurrent. A deep division undercuts the authority of the poems, and it is more telling than geographical polarities, the disparity implied between "master" and "servant" or the yoking together of dissimilar notions like "awful but cheerful." That division is: reserve at war with the congenial. A New England iron in the manner—or, I should say, in the *lack* of manner—in conflict with an easygoing willingness to accept life as it is, its perkiness and variety, is everywhere present. Critical judgment in these poems is more likely to suspend itself for what is harmless or distant or struggling or moving in its persistence than it is for the suffering or conflicts of peers. No drug addicts, drunks or suicides make an appearance; no poets, academics or white-collar workers are alluded to. Infused with a compassion that knows by instinct where true feeling ends and false sentiment begins, the poems are remarkably trustworthy on human terms, considering how descriptive they are generally taken to be. It is as if we discovered in a landscape painter not a psychologist but the surprising gift of portraiture. And when social protest becomes explicit, as it does in "Squatter's Children" or in "Going to the Bakery," there is no sudden tearing of fabric or gnashing of teeth. A style has been arrived at which allows for wider circles of emotion and more direct social comment than is at first apparent. . . . Part of the effect of lower depths and widening circles stems from a sub-rosa notion steaming away under a grating: if Bishop wanted to, she could tell us more, because we always feel that more slides have been taken than are going to be projected. (pp. 31-2)

The poems, then, seem to me to explore emotions more profoundly than is usually acknowledged. They reject many alternatives—one need merely turn a page or two in *The Collected Poems* to come across the Bishop translation of Andrade's "Don't Kill Yourself" to be startled. It's a marvelous poem, but the sudden rise in temperature produces a different kind of weather. Having been pigeonholed for so long as a cool customer, Bishop is ladylike but tough, but also much warmer, much more involved in life than a mere map-maker or tourist guide. If passion is missing from these poems—and I don't think it is—so is self-absorption. Their seeming casualness belies their extraordinary concentration, a concentration reminiscent of Emily Dickinson at her best. The discarded temptations of the printed Bishop canon have made it a small one, and its smallness has given rise too easily to the word "minor." What we find in these poems is elegance and withheld power. What else does "restraint" mean? One has to have something to restrain, and these poems, so easy to read, give up their secrets slowly. Shedding moral light, affection in these works extends itself more easily to the victor who has battled and won than to the loser who merely survives.

Admiring action, there may be behind Bishop's poems a fear of passivity in itself: the reduction of the status of the observer to that of the excluded. If one were to try to station the writer behind a movie camera in these poems, it would be hard to say from just what angle the movie was being shot. The object is everything, the viewer and the viewer's position—except by inference—the merest assumption. Yet how remarkably consistent that lens is, how particularly keen the eye behind it! There is a great deal to be said for scope, but more to be said, I think, for the absolutely achieved. These poems strike me as ageless; there are no false starts, no fake endings. None of the provincial statements of youth, none of the enticements of facility are allowed to enter. Starting with "The Map," we are in the hands of an artist so secure in the knowledge of what makes and doesn't make a poem that a whole generation of poets —and remarkably different ones—has learned to know what a poem is through her practice. She has taught us without a shred of pedagogy to be wary of the hustling of the emotions, of the false allurements of the grand. Rereading these poems, how utterly absent the specious is! There is no need to revise them for future editions, the way Auden revised and Marianne Moore revised and Robert Lowell revised. Nothing need be added, nothing taken away. They constitute a body of work in which the innovative and the traditional are bound into a single way of looking. From a poet's point of view, these poems are the ones of all her contemporaries that seem to me most to reward rereading. (p. 33)

Howard Moss, "The Canada-Brazil Connection," in World Literature Today, *(copyright 1977 by the University of Oklahoma Press), Vol. 51, No. 1, Winter, 1977, pp. 29-33.*

North & South is a book very much about the double meanings of things. The images—the frequent images of landscape or travel, for example—are not meant only literally, for ultimately they suggest the complicated, elusive geography of the inner world. It is a book aware of alternatives: assertion and withdrawal, movement and stasis, surface appearance and past history, reality and imagination, waking and sleeping, body and spirit, "commerce" and "contemplation." It is a book about coming to terms with the alternatives with which the real world confronts us; and the alternatives Bishop chooses to inspect in her microscopic, understated way come to embody her profound statement about the kind of world we live in and what it means to be living in it. . . .

"Cirque d'Hiver" and "Florida" are both extraordinary poems. Neither needs the other for its own survival, but their context in *North & South* gives both of them another dimension. They form an emblematic juxtaposition of images, dramatizing what Bishop calls in an earlier poem in the book "that sense of constant re-adjustment"—a phrase that suggests how she herself looks out at the world and how we in turn might best look at her work.

The Cirque d'Hiver was a real circus in Paris noted especially for its ponies. The "winter circus" in the poem is located on the floor of someone's home, the star performer a single mechanical toy. The atmosphere is diminutive, miniature; the tone is understated. The poem is obviously formal, arranged in regular stanzas with rhymes of subtle consistency and variety. Metrically it is one of Elizabeth Bishop's most regular poems, syntactically one of her most direct. But the whole sense of formality and understatement that dominates this poem makes the few deviations, when they come, devastating. (p. 41)

"Little" is perhaps the most frequently repeated adjective in Elizabeth Bishop's poetry. . . . Randall Jarrell calls Elizabeth Bishop "minutely observant" and says that "her best poems . . . remind one of Vuillard or even, sometimes, of Vermeer." She herself has said . . . , "I'm not interested in big-scale work as such. Something needn't be large to be good." Such titles as "Large Bad Picture" and "Little Exercise" clearly reflect this sense of values. "Little" or "small" or "delicate" things are not to be taken lightly in these works. The close observation of details is not precious or arch. . . .

[There] is a moral quality to the detail, a sense not only that small things are worth looking at and paying attention to or that they are simply "good," but that also, more than anything else, they represent what we have: the triumph of survival of the meek, encompassed round with danger, "the little that we get for free," as she writes twenty-six years after *North & South* in "Poem," "the little of our earthly trust. Not much." The small, unobtrusive objects, the reticent unself-dramatizing figures of Vuillard or Vermeer, are sometimes heroic, monumental, almost in direct proportion to how "insignificant" they may at first seem. And in ["Cirque d'Hiver" and "Florida"] it is the small objects, observed with intensity, respect and wit, with which the poet herself most identifies. . . .

The seriousness of the horse [in "Cirque d'Hiver"] is . . . specifically contrasted with the frivolity of the dancer ("her pink toes dangle"). However, the two figures are inextricably connected by a "little pole / that pierces both her body and her soul / and goes through his." "Pierces" is the most violent word in the poem, and it is shocking in this context. We must not forget that the horse and the dancer,

like Blake's "contraries," are the opposite, alternate elements of a single entity which is incomplete without either part. But we are also reminded that this entity is only a toy. Only a mechanical toy could be so gaily indifferent to what we could consider a torment—the piercing "little pole" turns into the "big tin key" under the horse's belly. It winds them up, brings them to life; for them this is not a crucifixion. (p. 42)

The poet herself, on some level, becomes implicated in what the horse does. Mechanical or stoical, or both, it "looks at me": it precipitates a confrontation. The dancer, "by this time, has turned her back." She is too trivial to confront anything; "he is the more intelligent by far."

The note of melancholy, of suppressed anxiety (especially at "pierces"), is now openly admitted as part of the confrontation: "Facing each other rather desperately." . . . What they say to each other in their confrontation is a mutual recognition of their similarity, a sense of both accomplishment and defeat, an awareness of the slightness of what has been accomplished and of how difficult it has been to achieve even that. With a cautious eye on what is in store, "we stare and say, 'Well, we have come this far.'"

The "formal, melancholy soul" of the mechanical horse is also characteristic of this whole poem, with its final mixture of fear and resignation, desperation and acceptance. The particular poignance of the poem is that Bishop *chooses* this childish, trivial object in which to see reflected her own "formal" and "melancholy" soul. Coming "this far" assumes the actions of a whole life, a life seen in the image of a toy—one with a capacity for intelligence, insight, vision, self-awareness—yet unable to detach itself completely from frivolity, artificiality and the sad necessity of endless mechanical repetition of the only action it is capable of. In its understated way, the moment of identification and self-awareness in this poem seems one of the most touching and painful in modern literature.

"Florida" is about as far away as one can get from the "Cirque d'Hiver." The latter is nothing if not civilized. There is nothing civilized about what happens in "Florida." The winter circus is all artifice, with artificial roses; "the state with the prettiest name" is a perpetual summer, a "flowery" state with real flowers only. "Cirque d'Hiver" is a poem about restraint, necessity. "Florida" is about letting go—hysteria, tantrums, ferocity, "strong tidal currents." It is a vision of a Dionysian world in contrast to the Apollonian "Cirque d'Hiver," the primitive world of the dead "Indian Princess" fulfilling its natural functions of living and dying not on principle but driven by pure instinct, the id, "careless, corrupt."

Two basic contrasting attitudes are interwoven throughout the poem: the objective and the subjective. The latter projects human emotions into the natural scene: "hysterical birds . . . in a tantrum," blushing red tanagers "embarrassed by their flashiness." . . . The objective sees clinically the contrasting and contradictory sides of everything: "The state with the prettiest name" is also "the state that floats in brackish water." . . . Life and death coexist. . . . (pp. 42-3)

There is a sense of continuous present, that all of this is what happens all the time. . . . [All] the verbs in the poem are in the present tense. Yet there is also a sense of history, of time passing, in the immediacy of the point of view of the poet who is actually living through this scene. . . .

[What] provides the greatest feeling of immediacy, of the particular moment as opposed to the continuous present, is not what events occur, but rather how they are observed. The individual voice of the poet, observing—and evaluating —the natural world, is the only other important "constant" in the poem. That voice reveals itself in the uniquely precise and personal descriptions, in which metaphors illuminate not only the objects observed, but also the life and varied interests of the observer. . . . It is a voice expressing complex attitudes as uniquely personal as the choice of metaphors—the alternation, for example, of external description with the projection of human emotions. . . . (p. 43)

Nature and art are oddly interwoven. There are "birds who rush up the scale" and mosquitoes with "ferocious obbligatos," and also that "delicately ornamented" coastline. Personal opinion and critical distance combine when a final esthetic judgment is made, as if the whole place were fashioned by man. . . . From the esthetic point of view of the humanist, ironically, Florida is a failure as a work of art. But Florida, after all, is not a work of art. It is only treated so by the observer who has to be detached and critical, who has to use her sharp sense of irony, her wit and her awareness of her own ability to bring a scene dazzlingly to life with words in order to keep from getting too close and falling in. . . .

[Juxtaposed] with "Cirque d'Hiver," it is the awesome alternative, the other side of the coin—contrast, corollary, corrective, completion—necessary to see objectively and to evaluate. . . . The ultimate discovery of these explorations is that, after all, the mechanical horse and the Indian Princess are not so very different. Both are trapped by the necessities of their own existence. . . .

Every vision is a potential revelation. How deeply we see, how *much* we see, even in the most apparently insignificant things around us, and how much of *ourselves* we see in those things are for Elizabeth Bishop the way of measuring and understanding who we are. (p. 44)

> *Lloyd Schwartz, "The Mechanical Horse and the Indian Princess: Two Poems from 'North & South',"* in World Literature Today *(copyright 1977 by the University of Oklahoma Press), Vol. 51, No. 1, Winter, 1977, pp. 41-4.*

Distinctive to many of [Elizabeth Bishop's] descriptive poems is the fact that they culminate in an epiphany—that flash of recognition which Joyce understood as a revelation occurring by a process of imaginative perception. In Bishop's poems, however, the epiphanic discoveries are almost always the result of close perception and personal meditation. They allow her readers striking poems which minutely detail exterior appearances of the entities about which she writes. (p. 49)

In Bishop's poetry the experience of epiphany, although it is the dawning of something extraordinary, sometimes even a sort of mystical consciousness, is both the accompaniment and culmination of the ordinary. What Joyce describes as the object's achieving of its epiphany is in her poems the rendering of her synthetic vision of the essential value of natural entities or personal experiences. Value in her poems is always initiated and grounded in perception and is related through description. The attributing of worth in Bishop's work, however, is the result of a vision which coalesces both objective and subjective impressions of the landscapes, persons or artifacts she describes. Her poetry begins with perception, but quite often it transforms what she perceives via meditation; the effect of these processes is imaginative revelation.

Involved in Bishop's epiphanic poems are not only discoveries originating in and pertaining to the external world but also radical self-insights. . . . In "Poem" the poet experiences the shock not only of remembering a familiar scene which a great-uncle painter had painted, but even more important, of realizing that for her particular esthetics experience, memory and imagination are inseparable. In "The Bight" Bishop implies that she becomes, during the process of the poem's discovery, the person who chooses to continue living her life; in "Poem" she becomes the poet who would create poems, even as she creates "Poem," out of a certain sensibility. (pp. 49-50)

Elizabeth Bishop's work reveals that she can know only what is apparent to the eye. To her way of seeing and thinking, mortals can never immerse themselves fully (even if one is, as she says of herself in "At the Fishhouses," a believer in "total immersion") in knowledge itself. Even so, her poetry consistently reaches from personal experience toward an interior vision. In "Cape Breton," as in other of her poems, the meaning of whatever scene is before her is not apparent, and she senses that congruent "sense making" either has already been or must now be "abandoned." Yet real if temporary discoveries of interior meaning evolve. It is these implicit epiphanies which her readers must pursue, even as the poet herself pursues them. . . .

Perhaps it is because she has such a tenuous grasp on a knowledge of the reality of any interior that Bishop continues to describe the exteriors of scenes, of actions, as accurately and as exactly as could any poet. Most persons who read her poetry agree that she seldom fails to describe everything within the scope of her works in its most minute detail, its most intricate nuance. Yet she is not simply an objective poet. An intriguing paradigm of the contemporary sensibility, she ultimately relates scenes or events to herself. By the processes of perceiving and meditating in an epiphanic manner which is inherently quite personal, she teaches us much about the interior of her own sensibility. (p. 52)

> *Sybil Estess, "Toward the Interior: Epiphany in 'Cape Breton' As Representative Poem,"* in World Literature Today *(copyright 1977 by the University of Oklahoma Press), Vol. 51, No. 1, Winter, 1977, pp. 49-52.*

Elizabeth Bishop's poetry is full of invitations. Look, it says; watch; think; listen. Yet it is never bullying. These *are* invitations, not instructions, and when they begin to sound bossy, a note of parody usually creeps in. . . . One of the most brilliant, as well as the most representative, of Elizabeth Bishop's poems is called "Little Exercise," and it invites us to "Think of the storm roaming the sky uneasily / like a dog looking for a place to sleep in, / listen to it growling." It is worth noting, incidentally, how soon the thought grows sounds we can listen to. We are then asked to think of the storm's progress, mangrove keys under lightning, bedraggled palm trees along a wet boulevard, and then as the storm goes away, we should

> Think of someone sleeping in the
>   bottom of a row-boat
> tied to a mangrove root or the pile
>   of a bridge;
> think of him as uninjured, barely
>   disturbed.

We are invited to enjoy this picture of a magical immunity, but not to act on it. How could we? The moment such repose was planned, it would become something else, and we should find ourselves in another Bishop poem, called "The Unbeliever," where a man "sleeps on the top of a mast / with his eyes fast closed." He keeps company up there with clouds and gulls, but they are assured of being where they are supposed to be, and he, grimly hanging on to his nightmare, is not. . . . The first man is careless, the second is desperate. Both poems offer images of human possibility and they elegantly and honorably refuse to moralize about them. Possibilities are to be entertained, not ordered about.

It is true, as Randall Jarrell said in *Poetry and the Age,* that Elizabeth Bishop understands that "it is sometimes difficult and unnatural, but sometimes easy and natural," to "do well," and the two poems I have just mentioned illustrate precisely those possibilities. But doing well here seems to be a matter of how we fare, not of what we choose. . . . Certainly the mechanical horse and the speaker of the poem "Cirque d'Hiver" say, "Well, we have come this far," and the tourists of "Santos" are berated for their "immodest demands for a different world, / and a better life, and complete comprehension / of both." And certainly the tone as well as the contents of many Bishop poems suggest a belief in strictly disciplined expectations. . . .

But lively people settle for small comforts only when they have no other options, and what we have when we settle may not be enough at all; it may be simply what we have. When Bishop makes "The Gentleman of Shalott" say that "Half is enough," we need to remember the context. . . . The mechanical horse and the speaker of "Cirque d'Hiver" were "facing each other rather desperately" before they arrived at their timid, consolatory phrase, and obviously one reading of the poem about the art of losing would reverse almost everything it seems to say: the art of losing is horribly hard to master, and that is why it is being discussed in this studiously offhand manner.

This is not a complete reading of the poem, of course, and the whole story would include the thought that some losses can be overcome and others can't, and that it may be worth trying to slip some members of the second group into the first, even if the strategy doesn't work. But the ambiguity is the point. Even when Bishop's poems seem to make statements, they turn out to be contemplating complex possibilities. . . .

The perfect poise of many of [Bishop's] poems, their ambiguity not in the sense of vagueness or indecision but in the sense of necessary hesitation in the realm of hypothesis, is such that they sometimes can't be ended without being broken. Even hypotheses seem to call for conclusions, and when Bishop gives in to this call, her poems tend to finish in flatness. Her last lines are often her weakest. . . .

But then this is the limitation of a nearly impeccable poet, the corollary of her sense of wonder that a man could sleep through a tropical storm "uninjured, barely disturbed"— even then the poem only asks us to think of such a case, it

doesn't vouch for its truth. Perched somewhere between the casual sleeper in the boat and the dogged sleeper on the top of the mast, but closer to the second, awake, but worried about the disproportion between geography and people, between the life of the world and our own "small shadowy / life," the poet practices her lucid and cautious art. Too cautious at times, it seems, locked in a willful, versified prose—

> In Worcester, Massachusetts,
> I went with Aunt Consuelo
> to keep her dentist's appointment
> and sat and waited for her
> in the dentist's waiting room.
> It was winter. It got dark
> early. The waiting room
> was full of grown-up people. . . .
> My aunt was inside
> what seemed like a long time. . . .

A child is speaking here, but mimesis is not much of an alibi for a poet, and the child seems to speak like Hemingway. Bishop is a discreet writer, and gives us only the rarest of hints at the unhappinesses, the bad weather, which provoke her to caution. Perhaps she "dislikes" poetry, as Marianne Moore did, but then her best work is built on the difficult conquest of this dislike, and not on a submission to it. She earns her finest effects, usually, by refusing rhetoric and then relenting, allowing the tactful return of a music which is all the more moving for being so subdued:

> But everything must be there
> in that magic mud, beneath
> the multitudes of fish,
> deadly or innocent,
> the giant *pirarucús,*
> the turtles and crocodiles,
> tree trunks and sunk canoes,
> with the crayfish, with the worms
> with tiny electric eyes
> turning on and off and on.
> The river breathes in salt
> and breathes it out again,
> and all is sweetness there
> in the deep, enchanted silt.

Alliterations (magic, mud, multitudes), balanced syntax (or, and, and), modest lists (with, with, with), internal rhymes (trunks, sunk), off-rhymes (salt, silt), a lyrical vocabulary (sweetness, enchanted)—all these things are there, but none of them is obtrusive. The result is inimitable. (p. 29)

Bishop's most persistent suggestion is that life might turn out badly but hasn't so far. If you're lucky you can sleep through the storm, and she feels that it may be, as Jarrell said, "barely but perfectly possible" to get along in the world—"has been, that is," Jarrell added, "for her." But one can't afford too much "poetry" in such circumstances —it would seem an insult to the powers who have treated you relatively well. . . .

Both ["Crusoe in England" and "Moose"] are skillful, casual, and witty; but both have a slightly desultory flavor, fail to ignite the feeling they seem to be after—fail, that is, by the exacting standards the poem herself has set. The moose, for example, looks the bus over, and all the passengers experience a "sweet / sensation of joy":

"Curious creatures,"
says our quiet driver,
rolling his *r*'s.
"Look at that, would you."
Then he shifts gears.
For a moment longer,

by craning backward,
the moose can be seen
on the moonlit macadam;
then there's a dim
smell of moose, an acrid
smell of gasoline.

The scene is nicely observed, underplayed. But the "moonlit macadam" seems lazy, and the "dim / smell of moose" offers a reticence where the poem needed a perception. What else would a moose smell of?

What these poems are looking for—a narrative context for a proof that the natural world does speak to us, if only by chance or only in the past—is found in this book in "Poem" and "The End of March," where a tiny old landscape painting, "a minor family relic," and a walk along a cold and windy beach enable the poet to place people and their dreams and artifacts in a geography which does not diminish them. Geography figures in a number of Bishop's most successful earlier poems—"The Map," "Over 2000 Illustrations and a Complete Concordance" especially—and it comes to suggest nature itself, representations of nature (like maps, or paintings, or poems), and whatever thoughts we may have about nature or its representations. . . .

Elizabeth Bishop's delicate landscapes are not manifestations of states of mind, nor are they neutral descriptions of what she takes to be "there." They are natural scenes to be visited, and even transformed, but never to be plundered; they are places which people, if they were quiet and careful enough, might manage to inhabit. (p. 30)

> *Michael Wood, "RSVP," in* The New York Review of Books *(reprinted with permission from* The New York Review of Books; *copyright © 1977 NYREV, Inc.), June 9, 1977, pp. 29-30.*

There is more continuity between *North & South,* Elizabeth Bishop's first book, and the nine new poems of *Geography III,* her latest, than the familiar and central image of travel. The new poems dramatize even more painstakingly what is perhaps the most fundamental issue in all of her poetry—seeing the ways nothing about living in the human world is or can ever be simple: how isolation may be as necessary as communication; how looking back may be as comforting—or as terrible—as looking ahead, or around. . . . That is what these poems so poignantly and so powerfully do. And as they illuminate, and consolidate, earlier interests and techniques, as they insist on their *similarity* to the earlier works, they reveal *them* to be more "felt," less "objective," more "serious" than we may have assumed.

The title *North & South* expressed both the literal and metaphorical implications of Elizabeth Bishop's most persistent image. The world is full of differences, contrasts, and contradictions. . . . (p. 30)

"In the Waiting Room" . . . presents a disturbing answer to the disturbing questions raised in the earlier poems, as well as a consolidation of the issues themselves, in the most explicit and dramatic terms.

The connotations of the title are ambiguous, suggesting both a literal and a metaphorical situation. This is a poem of initiation, of a child, "an *Elizabeth,*" beginning to learn what it means to live in the world, to be a human being, to be an adult. . . . Throughout the poem, a double perspective—the child's and the adult's—is subtly and consistently interwoven. It is an adult narrating, but an adult who is capable of reliving the point of view of the child, herself as a child. (p. 31)

These shifting perspectives refuse to allow us to remain complacently satisfied with literalism. . . . What "happens" in the poem is how we get from one point of view to the other, how both of these perspectives are true. (p. 32)

"Crusoe in England" contains similar issues in a vast metaphorical dramatic monologue. Just as the young "Elizabeth" can no longer feel at home either in the commonplace world of her home town or in the terrifying one far from it, because there is no escape from either; so this latter-day Crusoe (he quotes Wordsworth, ironically unable to remember the word "solitude" in "I wandered lonely as a cloud"), is tormented by memories of his isolation, yet can no longer feel comfortable in the "real" world.

What seems most remarkable in this long poem is the complexity of feelings Elizabeth Bishop succeeds in conveying. The terror as well as the liberation of loneliness; pride; self-pity; self-irony. . . . (p. 34)

Elizabeth Bishop usually writes in her own voice—there are few *personae* (the "Riverman," the "Colored Singer," "Jeronimo"). "Crusoe" is one of the exceptions to the particularly and emphatically personal voice of the recent poems; so the implications of the choice of this mode are especially revealing. . . . "Crusoe" more clearly, more fully than any of the other "character" poems illustrates how useful it is to think of the personal lyrics as metaphorical monologues. These poems are no more simply confessions or self-defensive anecdotes than is "Crusoe"; they are moments of revelation, and models of the process of revelation. (p. 36)

"Crusoe in England" is the most emotionally exhaustive study of a single character in all of Elizabeth Bishop's poetry—even more impressive because it is the result of a capacity for total empathy. . . .

One of the many ironies of "Crusoe in England" is the way one may become nostalgic about what was essentially painful. "In the Waiting Room" has this kind of painful nostalgia—for the exciting and terrible moment when the child first perceived the tragic "complexities" she will eventually have to deal with. In these poems this nostalgia is not self-deception, but an awareness of the profound dilemma created by the question of how much pain we require, how trapped we need to be, to find the fullest life. (p. 37)

"12 O'Clock News" . . . develops techniques of surrealism used much earlier. "Sleeping on the Ceiling" (1938) metamorphosed the image of a room into an allegorical topography, "the Place de la Concorde." Thirty-five years later the landscape is more intimate, more personal, more complex. In this poem in prose, the focus is tighter: the top of a writer's desk—typewriter, manuscripts, paper, lamp, ashtray. We are given a guided tour of the paraphernalia of writing—as if it were an *archeological* discovery. "The Monument," a poem dealing with the mysteries of the creation and the effect of a work of art, also employed the voice of some sort of guide; so does "The Man-Moth," which deals with what Yeats might characterize as a "subjective," lunar figure, at least on one level an image of the artist. In the witty and sinister surrealism of "12 O'Clock News" we get closer than ever to Elizabeth Bishop's view of herself as a writer.

Once again, but in a new way, we face a double tone—the dramatic irony of a speaker who doesn't fathom the full implications of what he reports, and the poet's own voice, laconically indicating her own capacity for perception. (p. 41)

[In "Poem," art], the equivalent of memory, has the capacity to keep things—even little things, *especially* little things, things we love, things that die—alive. The elms in the painting are "yet-to-be-dismantled." The memory of them is the memory of life that no longer exists in the world of time and practical values, trust funds and price tags. What is "free" may be a small thing, but its life is essential to ours; and in fact, because we die, identical to ours, "our abidance," "our earthly trust."

The ultimate irony is the initial one—the title. When we think back to the title, it ceases to function as a mere generic indicator. "Poem" is about what it means to be a poem—whatever the particular incarnation. It is the preservation of perception and emotion—the perception of details, the details that "touch" us—the maintenance of the ability to see and love whatever is alive, through a coalescence of empathies, the artist's and the viewer's. This poem provides the human and moving definition of its title. (pp. 44-5)

[Even] at their most highly artificial, Elizabeth Bishop's poems have never been manufactured out of nothing. Her interest in small things, in "details," if we hadn't noticed before, is—as "Poem" reveals—not a mannerism, but part of a profound vision (*not* "too serious a word"). The wonderment that some squiggles of paint can make an iris or cows expresses what life-giving possibilities lie behind technical ability. As "12 O'Clock News" suggested, though with a different emphasis, a work of art has the potential to soar (if it doesn't die). These attitudes towards her work have always been present, but never before so clearly articulated. (p. 45)

In "Poem" loss is implicit: inherent, inevitable, but pending, "yet-to-be." In "One Art" loss is all pervasive. "Poem" only implied what is stated here as fact: "so many things seem filled with the intent / to be lost ..." The poem, with its unexpected self-irony, tells us "how to" deal with loss, to "master" the "art of losing." It is a kind of lecture by an expert, a master, an artist. (p. 47)

"One Art" is a villanelle, one of Elizabeth Bishop's rare excursions into a complex, pre-existent verse pattern. ... Perhaps—without the fiction of a character like Crusoe, who experiences similar losses—the framework of a formal pattern was a necessary structure for the use of so many personal details (details corresponding especially to the image of travel, which has been so central to her work for so long). Certainly the formality of the structure contributes to a universalizing element in this poem. But the repetitions of the villanelle also heighten the dramatic immediacy of the poem. As we learn at the end that the poet has tried to persuade herself that her losses can be survived, the repetitions, with their slight but suggestive variations, emerge as the principal vehicle by which the lesson can be drummed not only into our ears but her own. The formality of the verse increases the emotional pitch and, paradoxically, contributes to the sense of personal pain.

Unlike "Dover Beach," where being "true to one another" may stave off the disaster of the collapse of the civilized world, "One Art" denies the possibility of Matthew Arnold's final option. Elizabeth Bishop's only faith seems to be in loss, or at least in her desperate refusal to be defeated by it; not in "one another" but in oneself, one's art. The "one art" is the need to "write it"—recognizing, and naming, the loss itself and finding the form that will arm one against all the disastrous losses.

Many of these new poems dramatize some sort of conflict between the past and the present: the passing of time, the pain of loss, the nature of what endures, the need to remember, the need to forget. "The End of March" has a kind of reverse nostalgia, a mellower resignation to the limitations of the future. ... (pp. 48-9)

Elizabeth Bishop is too much a realist to give herself completely to ... fantasy; she also has too much imagination to ignore its presence. In these new poems, each side of these profound and central issues is observed, explored. A myth can be created if necessary; if necessary the painful facts of autobiography—past, present, or future—can be touched on or dramatized. The fear of isolation and the desire for it are seen in their equal power; the need to escape and the desire to explore are recognized as equally powerful motivations; the value of holding on to the past and the need to forget it are both understood with clarity and compassion. Human understanding and the refusal to sentimentalize are always present, have always been present. The richness of her earlier poems is still present, with a new confidence and broader vision. These new works, each in itself and all together, develop those very qualities which have always been the source of Elizabeth Bishop's real greatness. (pp. 51-2)

Lloyd Schwartz, "One Art: The Poetry of Elizabeth Bishop, 1971-1976," in Ploughshares *(© 1977 by Ploughshares, Inc.), Vol. 3, Nos. 3-4, pp. 30-52.*

*   *   *

BLACKBURN, Paul   1926-1971

An American poet, translator, and editor, Blackburn was associated with the Black Mountain Poets of the 1950s. Like Cummings and Ferlinghetti, Blackburn experimented with typography and structure to produce in his poems a visual, aural, and psychological experience. He spent twenty years studying and translating the lyrics of the troubadours; his intense interest in the poetry of Provence is considered to be the single most important influence on his career. (See also *Contemporary Authors*, obituary, Vols. 33-36, rev. ed.)

Paul Blackburn produced a body of work that is admirable for its curiosity and attention to craft, but even more, remarkable for its almost total lack of *Weltschmerz*. Few contemporary poets have written as genially. The attitude is rare; in fact, it's almost confusing, we are so unused to it.

Yet that is precisely how Blackburn approached his work—with a tone of ease and an ever-implicit faith in the good works of poetry. Blackburn is one of those poets who gives you to believe he can write about anything, and do a half-way creditable job of it, too. As a result we sometimes even mistrust him for a while, until we begin to catch sight of the poet in his poem, well armored with his hard-metal belief that poetry is the one thing that always remains. Then it's almost like going to see a Western—there's the marshal surrounded by an unshaven gang, but luckily he's got three extra pistols strapped to his leg. That faith in the apodictic quality of poetry is in its way as strong in Blackburn as it is in Valéry or Stevens. The problem, though, is that geniality is wildly unfashionable. The didactic, the expressionistic, the suburban pastoral, even the lamely funny—fine. But the sort of poetry that is often just as satisfied to leave the indelible to its images rather than its imaginer: well. . . . Consequently, Blackburn's work has always been handled hesitantly, either grossly underrated or slathered with sentimental over-appreciation. (p. 73)

Blackburn wrote poems that never disguised a strong affection for and belief in the kind of language and demeanor found in the work of Zukofsky, Pound, and Williams. . . . Neither hyperbolic nor squirrely, his poems have a smoother, better yet, a *rounder* surface than what we're accustomed to. Grab hold to them the wrong way, and down you slide or off you roll. Both admirer and scoffer, embarrassed at finding themselves on the ground, grab out to take the poems with them. (p. 74)

As an abstractionist Blackburn may fail—his is a portraitist's eye for the discrete, the individual; elision doesn't come easy to him—but as a particularizer . . ., there have been few better. The connection is hard and durable: *one* thing and *one* poet. Blackburn never evades it; he is always ready, if not lustful, for the world. (p. 86)

> Ross Feld, "It May Even All Be Alright,"
> in Parnassus: Poetry in Review *(copyright*
> © *by* Parnassus: Poetry in Review*), Spring–*
> *Summer, 1974, pp. 73-86.*

It seems reasonable to assume that this is the way [Blackburn's] work would have continued to go had he lived, so forcefully and serenely does he move, in [*The Journals*], into his statement. It is at once a triumph of voice and a triumph over it, a total mastery of his endless and variegated materials in a form that allowed him complete flexibility. I think the word "journals" is a small joke that Blackburn played on his readers, a joke almost like the smile he sometimes allowed himself when he read a poem whose bittersweetness flowered into ambiguity. They are journals only in that they purport to follow the events of the last four years of the poet's life, but the selection of the important elements out of the sea of experience and feelings that must have been his as he moved toward his death is rigorously formal and burgeons into poems that work as a shorthand of the emotions.

It was always easy to think of Blackburn's poems as instantaneous registrations of his contact with the phenomena of the world in which he moved, of "what happened" to him. I remember my shock some fifteen years ago when I realized that his most casual poem, his most "spoken" lines were composed in a language that had as much to do with his conversation as a perfectly made cabinet has to do with

raw lumber. God knows, I don't mean to imply that people went about thinking that Blackburn wrote his poems in a kind of dazed passion of white-hot "inspiration." But there was a subtle and unspoken sense among many of his contemporaries that he relied a good deal on his fingertips in the composition of these marvels of seeming insouciance. Certainly, I thought this for some time, until I suddenly saw into the poems, saw the purity of his formal intention. (Now, it seems spectacularly perverse that one could have ever thought that any of his poems were thrown onto the page.) In *The Journals,* this purity is refined, quintessential. It is, quite simply, a handbook of invented form perfected, a book of exclusion. (pp. 57, 59)

That the poems seem, often, the thought of a moment, a brilliant or witty or dark response to still-smoking news, is the result of his carefully invented and released voice, a voice that we hear singing, virtuoso, in *The Journals.* It is characteristic of the man that he never explained any of this, never said that this man that you hear in the poems, this subtly shifting voice, is not Paul Blackburn. It is what he decided Paul Blackburn would be in his song. . . .

Certainly, if we wish to read into Blackburn's poems the private concerns of his life, we may, even though we will not find them there except in so far as they exist transformed; in brief, we will not find that famous truth that facts supposedly proffer. Blackburn's truth is more elusive and difficult to come at—it is the truth of the lyric poem that slips away as we press it to stand still and answer, answer. This exquisite ordering of the common materials of the poet's life is the architecture by means of which he not only deployed them in balanced design within the poem, but by means of which he changed them into instances of artifact. His poems are as artificial as those of his beloved troubadours. (p. 59)

At that moment, in his poems, when we think we will, finally, be allowed to see the poet, he magically fades away into his voice, a protean voice so perfectly under control that we think it is telling us something true. This book is the work of a man who had come to a perfect sense of his own powers. He has done what all poets who have tried to remain faithful to the lyric must envy. His ego has been disguised, not revealed, by his voice, it has been subsumed. To come to this expertise within a poetic structure that we may call, for want of a better word, closed, is an enormous achievement. To arrive at this position in the poem as "journal," the open poem, is mastery.

At one with this subtlety of tonal modulation is the curious reticence of these poems—and of all Blackburn's poems. It is a reticence built not on a sense of shame or secrecy, or on pride in one's knowledge or perception, but on modesty. Even in lines that might otherwise function to make a reader squirm with embarrassment (as do so many of the gross statements in those poems heralded as self-confronting), Blackburn holds something back; he reins in the voice and makes it step with a true delicacy. In such a mode, it is worth our attention to see how the poet handles sexual and scatological themes and language. They become as fine-spun and sweet as the music of Campion. (pp. 60-1)

In *The Journals,* the concerns of this world are at the same time overwhelming and picayune. They are remarked on with dignity and dryness by a voice that speaks from a strange place between this sad earth and hell. (p. 62)

[In mentioning his vast] range I don't mean his array of subject matter—that was most carefully limited so that his mastered voice could exploit it to its limits—love, friends, travel, and place. I mean the way the poems, over his entire career, return again and again to these things and each time extend their possibilities in terms of Blackburn's deepening understanding of them. And as his understanding deepened, so did the metamorphoses of his expression become more refined and given over to sudden shifts within poems—even within stanzas. Upon a mere handful of objects, if you will, he rang ceaseless and endless changes. It is a triumph of "the quality of the affection." . . .

If the ever-fluctuating and precisely tuned voice that occurs within his poems is always just right, exact as to the rhythms that occur in the aimless street- and bar-talk of the workaday world, it is because the poet who constructed this voice out of those many voices knew, from living there, what they sounded like. The more he seems like "anybody at all" in his poems, the more is he the poet. He wore his learning lightly and there are dozens and dozens of poems available to readers of differing sophistication, levels that swim into cognition according to what is brought to bear on the work. (p. 64)

Blackburn learned, through the writing of literally hundreds of poems, and from his study of the troubadours, that the "I" of the poem is as much artifice as the poem it speaks—and yet it can locate itself with such immediacy that it looks like the vehicle for common speech, laden with information from the horse's mouth. . . . [In] *The Journals* we enter a territory of virtuosity, a blend of attitudes, voices, ironies, all existent as a filigree that can hardly be seen for the overt brusqueness of the basic tone. (p. 65)

His poetic learning was deep and interiorly held and in this book we can watch it at work—changed, flattened, disguised, but worked into the dense fabric of these poems in recollections of gone speech, points of rhyme and half-rhyme, formal notations on weather and landscape. . . . Nothing melodic or prosodic was alien to Blackburn, and when he seems most colloquial and chatty, it is often right there that we may find, buried in the perfectly broken rhythms of his voice, the skeleton of a loved and austerely bounded form. (p. 66)

What is there, finally, to say? Even lacking a satisfactory collection of his later poems, and with the enormous collection of his troubadour translations as yet unpublished, we can see that Blackburn was one of our most brilliant poets. That he had come to his maturity is obvious from *The Journals.* The neglect that was his during his life will, I trust, be remedied before too long, although I take no bets on it. In all events, to anyone who cares for the life of the poem in this latter half of the twentieth century, Blackburn must stand as a greatly gifted artist who has left us a body of work that is formal, intelligent, and beautiful. (pp. 66-7)

> *Gilbert Sorrentino, "Singing, Virtuoso," in*
> Parnassus: Poetry in Review *(copyright ©
> by* Parnassus: Poetry in Review*), Spring-
> Summer, 1976, pp. 57-67.*

Blackburn was among the most gifted proponents of what might be called the Pound-Williams line in American poetry, as mediated by Charles Olson in his theories of "Projective" (Kelly prefers to call it "Open") verse. Blackburn's version of the style features—besides such

familiar surface mannerisms as a mixing of high and low vernaculars, eccentric punctuation and clumping of words about the page—a kind of easy lope through all sorts of sense impressions, stray thoughts, bits of booklearning, bursts of emotion.

He seems at times to want to turn everything into poetry. . . . Blackburn's gift was pre-eminently intimate and laconic, at its flavorful best in shorter poems and when engaged by "homely" subject matter; he is splendid (no other word for it) in the bathroom, and his many New York City poems invest the urban boneyard with a pungent, breathing warmth. He is also unfailingly songful, and often richly humorous.

Finally, Blackburn was that type of poet for whom poetry is a sort of cottage industry, pursued with an artisan's solitary zeal in the face of the world's indifference. His reputation and influence, special while he lived, seem bound to grow. (p. 69)

> *Peter Schjeldahl, in* The New York Times
> Book Review *(© 1977 by The New York
> Times Company; reprinted by permission),
> May 1, 1977.*

The Journals is an ambitious undertaking. The collection begins in the late spring of 1967 and continues to within a few weeks of the poet's death. Simply as a narrative of his last years, many of these poems resonate hauntingly of his encroaching fate. And at least a dozen of these poems will rank, I'm sure, among his finest works. Several of the best come early in the collection, during Blackburn's last sustained visit to Europe. (p. 55)

Many of the best of these long, inclusive journal poems demonstrate what the poet calls "the net of place." "Plaza Real With Palm Trees: second take," for example, shows his mature method. In this poem the poet is back in Barcelona after a ten-year absence (see "Plaza Real With Palm Trees" in *The Cities*). The poem gathers in a whole series of apparently unrelated impressions. . . . All this does not come in any logical progression, it doesn't build to any "momentary stay against confusion," but, somehow (by magic, by music), all of it seems right, everything feels in its place, we are left with a sense of life's poignant passing completeness. (pp. 55-6)

"The Touch" shows the tragic power Blackburn could summon from his easy conversational rhythms, his understated transitions, his accurate eye and empathetic voice. The poem ranks with "The Purse-Sein," "Affinities II," and a dozen other major works. Among the impressive successes of *The Journals* I would mention "Birds/ Amsterdam," "Gin," "The Net of Place," "Ritual XVII," "Journal • August 1968," "Hibernation," and "Journal: June 1971." Most of these poems are a long goodbye to the people and places the poet loved. The final part, the pain increasing and the sustained poem no longer possible, shows the poet holding to his own voice, his credo ("Let each man's words be his own"), to the end. . . . (pp. 56-7)

The Journals should bring Blackburn's poems some of the attention and recognition they deserve. These long poems are direct descendants of Whitman's catalogues, which called attention to all those things American poets hadn't yet figured out how to write about, especially the multiplicity of urban life. Williams took it from there, finding images to fit the measure, and Blackburn takes Williams further, adding something of Pound's sound, Creeley's control, and Olson's scope. Obviously, this kind of poetry is often risky, and probably a majority of the poems don't quite come off, the fragments don't cohere ("Why record this?"), the music doesn't make it through, the images don't earn their attention. It is all too easy to open a book of his poems at random, read a few of his weaker poems, and assume that this is another indulgent today-I-went-to-the-store poet.... He is one of the finest poets of his generation. Something his friends knew all along. (p. 57)

> *William Heath, in* Open Places *(copyright 1977 Open Places), Spring/Summer, 1977.*

* * *

BLACKWOOD, Caroline 1931-

An Irish essayist, novelist, and short story writer, Blackwood depicts, in journalistic fashion, middle-class Irish characters trapped in tawdry lives. Blackwood's stories are often highly ironic autobiographical sketches which focus on the Ulster of the author's childhood. Her first novel, *The Stepdaughter*, is a departure from Blackwood's usual concerns, taking its place in the body of New York City feminist fiction lately in vogue. (See also *CLC*, Vol. 6.)

[Caroline Blackwood, in *The Stepdaughter*,] writes about anguish and despair and a painful love. The narrator ... has been abandoned by her husband.... The book illustrates, most ingeniously, how a woman's emotional state can distort to the point of complete reversal her view of, and attitude towards, other people. While the narrator believes that 13-year-old Renata is her husband's child, she sees the girl as ugly, fat and graceless.... After discovering that Renata is, in fact, not her stepdaughter, she sees the girl quite differently....

Caroline Blackwood has an unblinking, observant eye, and a penetrating, acid wit.... *The Stepdaughter* is like an etching, sharp, precise and sensitive. (p. 654)

> *John Mellors, in* The Listener *(© British Broadcasting Corp. 1976; reprinted by permission of John Mellors), May 20, 1976.*

Anxiously assuming an interested audience, the writer of letters is free to practise unburdening and evasiveness in equally large quantities. Much of Caroline Blackwood's success in her good first novel comes from the witty recognition of this. The undispatched letters which make up the narrative of *The Stepdaughter* are, bleakly, addressed to an infinitely patient and cherishable nobody and tell a story which could only have been less self-aware presented as straight dramatic monologue, and more cumbersome as full dialogue. (p. 751)

> *Susannah Clapp, in* New Statesman *(© 1976 The Statesman & Nation Publishing Co. Ltd.), June 4, 1976.*

[*The Stepdaughter*] is short, intense, arrestingly individual. A woman, K, writes imaginary confessional letters. Her husband has left her, in her high Manhattan apartment, for a younger woman. He has left her with Renata, the 13-year-old child of a previous marriage, whom she fears and detests. She also has a 4-year-old child of her own, Sally Ann, and a French *au pair*, Monique. Renata is fat, silent, unhappy. (p. 80)

In her imaginary letters K rails against her husband and against Renata, and also against Monique. She describes her hatred, the reasons for it, and the ways in which she gives expression to it. She compares herself to the evil stepmother in Snow White.... *The Stepdaughter* fixes an unwavering stare at feelings. But feelings, it seems to say, are governed by understanding. The novel proceeds, in a ratiocinative manner, through stages of understanding and through a progression of feeling. K's realisation that Arnold has dumped Renata upon her is qualified, as the narrative proceeds, by further stations of awareness.... (pp. 80-1)

All these sequential perceptions modify K's feelings, which work themselves away from hatred towards a concern and acceptance which the novel is careful not to label love....

With its unblinking view of man's selfishness and woman's dependence *The Stepdaughter* is a notable contribution to the women's movement, though it contains a scene with a woman friend which serves to protect it from too facile a categorisation. It is also, I should hazard, a philosophical and religious novel. It begins with a cry of pain, which can be seen to be a philosophical position. It ends with a sense of loss, which can be seen to be a religious one. It is an unusual and affecting experience. (p. 81)

> *James Price, in* Encounter *(© 1976 by Encounter Ltd.), September, 1976.*

Women who crack up precisely because they are women have become a commonplace in today's fiction....

Caroline Blackwood's first novel ["The Stepdaughter"], in the same spirit of icy hauteur that characterizes her essays, seems as much as anything else a venomously controlled attack on that mad Manhattan housewife of whose travail we have heard so much in the fiction of the past 10 years. Stranded by her former husband in an elegant New York apartment, the unnamed heroine, consumed by a free-floating discontent, turns the fullness of her rage and malice on her ungainly and woeful teen-age stepdaughter, Renata....

However much one might relish a clear-eyed view of those "victimized" matrons with too much time and money on their hands, there is about "The Stepdaughter" a facile, monochromatic nastiness that robs it of resonance. True, the novel does a handy stiletto job on its few characters, but what, finally, is the point? One is not asked to care over much about Renata's plight or encouraged to attach any moral significance to her wicked stepmother's dereliction. Rather, one is invited to look down from a great height and remark how unappetizing is the life the author surveys, and with what thoroughgoing wit she dismisses it. The book manifests a disdain for the way we live now that seems too easily won, and that defuses its rather brilliant bitchiness. (p. 15)

> *Jane Larkin Crain, in* The New York Times Book Review *(© 1977 by The New York Times Company; reprinted by permission), September 18, 1977.*

* * *

BÖLL, Heinrich 1917-

A West German novelist, short story writer, playwright, translator, and essayist, Böll, who won the Nobel Prize for Literature in 1972, is one of the most prolific and widely read of postwar German authors. His works, which depict a

middle-class world through stark realism and a sharp wit, reflect Böll's uncompromising humanism. His realism is often viewed as a reaction to the German tradition of complex, psychologically probing prose. (See also *CLC*, Vols. 2, 3, 6, and *Contemporary Authors*, Vols. 21-24, rev. ed.)

Events in Böll's novels are presented from the perspective of alienated characters through whose minds and eyes we view the German scene. Böll undoubtedly learned from the American successors of Joyce and of Gertrude Stein. Hemingway, Thomas Wolfe, and Faulkner are influences, direct and indirect, on the form of his narratives. Böll eliminates the omniscient comment of the authorial voice and presents all situations and events through the sense impressions, memory, and reflections of his characters. At times he approaches the stream of consciousness.

Böll's earliest novels dealing with postwar Germany—*Und sagte kein einziges Wort* (1953) and *Haus ohne Hüter* (1954)—present a world in which the determining force of events seems to be material and economic. In naturalistic fashion, environment and circumstances seem to determine human actions and fate. In specific terms, the material and social consequences of the lost war apparently mould human life in Böll's postwar Germany. . . .

The structure of *Haus ohne Hüter* seems to reinforce the naturalistic view of human destiny as determined by socio-economic circumstances. The novel consists largely of five alternating perspectives on a postwar German city. Two war widows and the only child of each provide four of these perspectives. . . . Each must come to grips with life deprived of its center, life without help, comfort, and completeness. This parallelism of perspectives of human deprivation in two widely different economic strata makes us suspect that the naturalistic interpretation may be less than adequate.

In one passage of the novel Böll makes the socioeconomic interpretation of the novel's events give way to a moral evaluation. The shift takes place literally and explicitly before the reader's eyes. Young Heinrich Briesach considers his mother's love life and the succession of "uncles" it imposes upon him. Why doesn't she get married, he wonders. (p. 11)

Haus ohne Hüter shows that the victimization of postwar Germans by historical circumstances—the war and its aftereffects—is much more than that. It is a victimization by evil, by human wickedness and folly. Nella becomes a war widow because her husband, Rai, was deliberately sacrificed to the offended vanity of his wartime commanding officer, Lieutenant Gäseler. Rai, Nella, and their child are victims, not of impersonal historical forces or social determinants, but of a villain's chicanery. Böll thus clearly presents a morally determined chain of cause and effect.

The unmasking of apparently social and economic causes as moral, psychic, and spiritual problems is essential to Böll's early novels. (In the later novels it is unnecessary, since the moral and spiritual basis of human behavior is explicitly shown from the beginning.) In *Und sagte* the marriage of the two persons through whose perspectives we experience early postwar Germany is apparently destroyed by the strains and stresses of overcrowded living conditions. On a deeper level, however, it is not the external situation that determines the fate of the marriage, but the husband's inner conflict between the drive for selfish freedom

and the restrictive obligations that monogamous love and fatherhood impose. Self-indulgent *eros* and self-curtailing *agape* struggle in him for the possession of his soul. Essentially we witness not a social, but a Christian problem clothed in social and economic guise. The subtle interaction between the disguise and the underlying psychic and moral truth informs this novel with an inner tension that makes *Und sagte*, after *Wo warst du, Adam?*, Böll's artistically most successful work.

The conclusion of *Wo warst du, Adam?* (1951), the earliest of Böll's novels, takes place in the concluding stages of the Second World War. It can be taken as an apt point of departure for a closer consideration of the perspectives on postwar Germany given in Böll's three longest and latest novels, *Haus ohne Hüter, Billard um halbzehn* (1959), and *Ansichten eines Clowns* (1963).

At the end of *Wo warst du, Adam?* two perspectives converge upon a German town as the war is drawing to a close. The town lies in a no man's land between the American troops, who are not yet ready to enter, and the German army that, obedient to Hitler's command, refuses to give an inch. From the windows of the town's houses fly white flags of surrender.

One perspective is that of the German deserter Feinhals. The town is his home and he has decided that as far as he is concerned the war is over. Before descending, he gazes down upon his native place from an adjacent hill. Feinhals is a decent chap; he despises the Nazis and has always been defeatist about the war. He fell in love with a Jewish girl, Ilona (who, without his knowledge, has meanwhile been murdered in a concentration camp), and he looks forward to his homecoming and a modest career. Above all he plans to savor the joy of being alive.

The other perspective is that of the German army post located on another hill above the town. The post has orders to observe the town and bombard it in case of suspicious activity. There is "suspicious activity," since an American vehicle drives over from the American-occupied area and parks for a while in front of a certain house. The vehicle actually brings an American officer to his German sweetheart. The officer formerly in command of the observation post, knowing that the war was senseless and over in any case, but yet attempting to obey commands, spares the town and lets some shots fall in a swampy marsh nearby. Schniewind, however, new commander of the post, an ambitious and insecure careerist whose war decorations are of very recent date, resents the "traitorous" white flags and decides to punish the town. He shoots into it. One of the grenades kills Feinhals as he is about to enter his parental home.

This conclusion of Böll's war novel adumbrates his subsequent novels about postwar Germany in a number of ways. The opposition between Feinhals and Schniewind as representative characters of Germany anticipates the structural basis of the three novels: *Haus ohne Hüter, Billard um halbzehn*, and *Ansichten eines Clowns*. In these novels the descendants of Feinhals and Schniewind face each other as victims and victimizers both during and after the Nazi period. The Feinhals group of characters are decent, kind, and gentle. These characters are lovers of life, opponents of war, and haters of Nazism. Both during and after the Nazi era they are destined to be victims of the Schniewind type.

The Schniewind characters are vain, ambitious careerists, profoundly insecure, and obsessed with the need to collect worldly honors—the craving for war decorations characterizes them. They are fanatics and bullies, petty, mean, and contemptible. Naturally, they are or were ardent supporters of Nazism and the war. Feinhals' descendants are simple, humble, and self-assured. Life and love are self-evident values for them. Schniewind's descendants are those who fear and hate life, twisted egotists in constant need of being reassured. The slightest opposition unnerves and infuriates them. In the display of love and friendship they see provocations to be punished. It is symptomatic and symbolic that the "suspicious activity" observed by the German post is a love tryst between two recent enemies, and that what particularly annoys Schniewind is the display of the white flags of peace.

Apart from the general dualism represented by the two camps (so reminiscent of Dostoevsky, whom Böll . . . [has] named as one of the most important influences on his development), particular details of structure link Böll's novels of postwar Germany (the exception of *Und sagte* always understood) to the pattern established by the end of *Wo warst du, Adam?* In all three novels the bloodstained inheritance of Nazism and war overshadows the postwar period. In that past, Nazis or militaristic supporters of the war committed the direct or indirect murder of good, innocent persons. In each case the murderers are inferior, vain, narrow, pretentious, obviously insecure, and thus easily provoked to anger like Schniewind in *Wo warst du, Adam?* Their victims are infinitely superior to them. They are cut off in the flower of their youth, and because of their innocence and capacity for enjoying life and love their death appears all the more horribly and tragically senseless, a wasteful sacrifice without meaning, a destruction of human values never to be recouped.

In all these cases there is a surviving witness to the murders, as the orderly, Bechtels, in *Wo warst du, Adam?*, who witnesses Schniewind's decision to bombard the town. In the later novels this witness-figure is at the same time a victim who managed to survive. . . . In postwar Germany, Böll's witness-figure lives in self-chosen seclusion and will have nothing to do with the accepted mores, fashions, and powers of the Bonn Republic. An inward petrifaction, an absence of all ambition and worldly interest, characterizes him. Most perspectives of Böll's novels are the perspectives of such shocked and hurt witness-figures, who carry the deep wound of what they saw into the postwar era. (pp. 11-16)

These witnesses and victims, surviving in postwar Germany, live curiously detached lives. They are so deeply hurt that they are not able to recover and overcome their traumatic loss. They have renounced all desire to participate in life. They keep, often outwardly and always inwardly, aloof from society and resemble relics from a bygone era. The tragedy of postwar Germany, as seen through Böll's perspectives, is this nonparticipation of her best children, who are too bruised to be of use. Nella, in *Haus ohne Hüter,* refuses to remarry and instead drifts in and out of meaningless affairs because she is resolved never again to offer the reassuring sight of a happy wife and mother to the country that murdered her husband. The appearance of domestic bliss would be an advertisement of forgiveness and forgetfulness to which she will not lend herself. (pp. 16-17)

Robert Fähmel, in *Billard um halbzehn,* leads a life of inhuman formality and rigid routine. To his young secretary, who cannot comprehend a life so lifeless and devoid of human spontaneity and warmth, he presents a disquieting enigma. He who has the talent to be a first-rate architect does not take up architecture after the war. He is content to serve as a humble consultant in statics. What he has witnessed under the Nazis has killed all creative ambition in him. His life now is only a shadow of what it might have been and a memory of the hurt received long ago. Like Nella, Robert Fähmel denies himself the act of re-creating. Nella will have no part in the re-creation of a happy family, and Robert Fähmel will not contribute his talent to the re-creation of the ruined German cities. . . .

Schrella, in his London exile, has similarly withdrawn into the routine of teaching German grammar in an English school. He refuses to find renewed attachment to his native city, and to life itself, when he pays a visit to the scenes of his past. . . . Like Nella and Fähmel, Schrella declines to make the gesture of reconciliation with normalcy, which, in his case, would be to return from exile. The remembrance of that which they witnessed remains the basic truth of these lives—a truth they will not change, cover up, and, least of all, forget.

An extreme form of exile from normal life is the insane asylum to which Robert Fähmel's mother was retired after she witnessed the deportation of the Jews and where she still finds herself sixteen years later. There cannot be a more telling detachment from the bustling and forgetful new normalcy of postwar Germany than life among the extreme deviants from normality. (p. 17)

In *Wo warst du, Adam?* the life of the victimized witness to Hitler's war is snuffed out physically on the threshold of the postwar world. The lives of Böll's subsequent witness-figures are cut off emotionally, arrested and frozen inwardly, before they enter the postwar era. It is their destiny to be permanently estranged from the life of their country.

The complementary side of this victimization of the best is the continuing triumph of the worst. Nothing has basically changed since the Nazi period. The confrontation of anti-Nazi victim with Nazi victimizer persists in the postwar years in essentially the same constellation as during the Nazi era. . . . It is symptomatic that Feinhals suffers his fate almost under the noses of the Americans. This spatial arrangement shows that the military victory of the Allies and the occupation of Germany will neither dislodge the Nazis from their positions of power in German society, nor aid and protect their victims. . . . In *Haus ohne Hüter* former Nazis, under old and new Christian labels, are the shapers of the cultural scene, and go on speaking of "elites." (pp. 18-19)

There are ironic touches: In *Haus ohne Hüter* Gäseler plans to publish the poems of the man he murdered. In *Billard* Schrella owes his release from the prison of the Federal Republic to his one-time Nazi torturer, Nettlinger, which does not prove the ex-Nazi's kindness, but rather shows his power and influence in the Bonn Republic. (p. 19)

This pessimistic view derives from the essentially Christian dualism underlying the structure of Böll's novels. In them, the anti-Nazis resemble the persecuted and despised followers of the Lord, martyrs and confessors of the truth. A small band of the forlorn few, they face the huge army of the wicked, who rule the world for Satan. Nazi Germany had waged the ancient war of evil against innocence with brutal frankness. Postwar Germany continues it subtly and hypocritically.

The opposition of the two camps reaches, in Böll's novels, far beyond Nazism and anti-Nazism. It is ultimately not a political, but a moral, spiritual, and religious dualism, which is founded on Christianity but has a Manichaean element in it. The Nazis' persecution of their victims is seen as a variant of the age-old battle between good and evil, light and darkness, holy grace and unholy power. (p. 20)

Böll's dualism receives its most explicit, allegorical formulation in *Billard um halbzehn*. In this novel Germany (and mankind) is divided into two groups: One group consists of those who have consumed the sacrament of the buffalo, which is the sacrament of violence, and they form the vast majority. The other group, a tiny minority, consists of those who follow the sacrament of the lamb of peace. The latter refuse to partake of the sacrament of violence and are, therefore, destined to be the victims of violence. They will, in each generation, be singled out for persecution by the followers of the buffalo. Nazism is a phase in the buffalo's timeless orgy of oppression. In the 1930's the Nazi bully Nettlinger led the other boys in terrorizing Schrella, who was of the lamb's brotherhood. In the 1950's the bellboy Hugo suffers the same kind of juvenile persecution, but now no Nazis are among the tormentors. Hugo, gifted with marvelous charm and grace, is by his very grace and gentleness fated to be in his generation what Schrella was in the last—the lamb that forever arouses the buffalo's urge to persecute and violate. We are reminded of Abel, who, favored with the grace of the Lord, aroused the murderous envy of Cain. The symbolism of lamb and shepherd used by Böll establishes immediate associations not only with Abel, the shepherd slain like a lamb, but also with Christ, who is lamb and shepherd, sacrifice and judge, in one. As we shall see, in Böll the lamb sometimes becomes shepherd; the victim may turn judge. In that ancient battle between buffalo and lamb, Cain and Abel, world and Christ, labels and watchwords change, but the essence remains the same. In this struggle the lambs, who are not of this world, must go under, while the buffalo wins and reinherits, again and again, the power and glory of this world. In the framework of Böll's dualism, the Nazi type, therefore, cannot be truly defeated, but after each apparent defeat continues to hold power and victimize the good.

As stated before, Böll produces the image of Germany through perspectives, through literal as well as figurative views. The physical or mental act of viewing a place, a scene, a person, has decisive structural and symbolic significance in Böll's works. The world of his novels is a focal area of converging perspectives. (pp. 21-2)

The act of seeing is structurally and symbolically decisive at the end of *Und sagte*. Having separated from his wife, the husband sees a woman in the street who moves and fascinates him with a strange intensity. Tense with excitement, he watches the stranger, follows her with his glances, and discovers that she is his wife. Seeing through the perspective of estrangement teaches him that the woman who touches his life's nerve, the woman destined for him, is his wife. He sees her now as if for the first time, and this

view restores in him the sacredness of his marriage, against which he had rebelled. From a distractedness of the heart, which used poverty as a pretext, he had degraded marriage to the imitation of an illicit love affair conducted in hotel rooms. The visionary recognition of his wife shows him the sacrament as his inner truth. The husband's last words, "nach Hause" (homewards), with which the novel closes, point to a spiritual significance contained in the physical homecoming to wife and children.

The importance of view and vision in Böll's work becomes clear to us when we recall the thematic and structural significance of the witness-figure. A witness, we must remember, is one who sees and on the basis of his vision testifies to the truth. Böll's novels are told from the point of view of victims and witnesses. The view of victim and witness tends to become, in his later novels, the view of accuser and judge.

The view of the avenging judge forms the nucleus around which *Billard um halbzehn* is structured. Robert Fähmel executes Hitler's scorched-earth strategy literally with a vengeance. Ostensibly an instrument of the buffalo, he avenges the martyred lamb. He becomes a demolition expert in order to blow up prized buildings and monuments of his buffalo-worshipping nation. In the enemy's service, he explodes the enemy's pride.

Robert Fähmel's judgment on the objects of German national pride—monuments and precious buildings—is literally based upon the act of viewing. Perspective and action merge in this novel. Taking the view of the object and determining the *Schussfeld* is the condition for executing the moral judgment and verdict of condemnation. The accusing witness and judge's view carries the plot both literally and figuratively.

With each act of viewing Robert Fähmel delivers a judgment. As he gazes out on the lobby of the fashionable Hotel Prinz Heinrich his vision transforms the hotel guests into damned souls in hell; his look pronounces the Last Judgment. (pp. 22-3)

In *Haus ohne Hüter* we view Rai's murderer, Gäseler, through the witness, Albert, who relates the murder, and through Rai's widow, Nella, who is eager to avenge her husband. These two viewings of Gäseler form two bridge posts, as it were—one in the recollected past, the other in the immediate present—that connect two major strands of the plot like a bridge across time. Planning her revenge, Nella literally views Gäseler, as she sits next to him in his car. The man she sees now, however, is too trivial to serve as the objective of something so great and meaningful as vengeance. (pp. 23-4)

Robert Fähmel's mother yearned for an opportunity to kill those Nazi officials of her city who were responsible for so much suffering. Yet when the occasion does come and she views, with loaded pistol, the former Nazis preparing for their parade, she sees them as a group of aging, pathetic, and ridiculous philistines—museum pieces not worth a bullet.

These insights into the futility of vengeance, which occur near the end of Böll's novels, are never signs of Christian forgiveness. Böll, with his nearly Manichaean separation of good and evil characters, never presents contrition and regeneration in the villains, nor do his characters refrain from retribution because they feel that judgment belongs to God alone.... The Nazi villains turn out to be banal philistines and petty snobs who lack all access to the daemonic. They are merely bores, and boredom makes vengeance irrelevant. These Nazi murders are not in the least diabolical. They are small and laughable men who do not have the slightest inkling of the scope and the meaning of their actions. (p. 24)

In Böll's novels, however, a sharp distinction is made between vengeance on individuals and the struggle against Nazism or, more broadly speaking, the attitudes of which Nazism formed the most vicious manifestation. Viewing the personal enemy makes vengeance seem fatuous; viewing the scene of the enemy's actions or the works of his pride confirms the resolve to battle against him. (p. 25)

Robert Fähmel, as we have seen, dedicates his whole life to vengeance; but it is not a vengeance against individuals. He punishes human pride by leveling its objects. In Böll the deadly sin of pride appears in its specific modern form as snobbery. It is the bread of the unholy sacrament of violence. Snobbery invests the architectural monuments and landmarks of one's country with an aura of national superiority. Snobbery ranges in Böll from gluttonous ostentation to arrogant intellectualism. In all its varieties, however, it contains two principles: hierarchy and exclusiveness. The soldier's mania for collecting war medals and decorations—a *leitmotiv* in the stories and novels of Böll; the officer's insistence on having his rank respected and obeyed; the Nazi's racial arrogance; the gourmand's gorging himself while others have to starve; the gourmet's connoisseurship; the clique member's contempt of the uninitiated; and the intellectual's sneer at those educated in other ways than himself: all these are the variants of snobbery in Böll's work.

In Böll's perspectives snobbery always embraces cruelty. There is cruelty in the gloating emphasis with which Martin's grandmother, in *Haus ohne Hüter,* seated in an expensive restaurant, tears apart and devours her portion of lamb. She and all other diners in that plush restaurant consume their food as though proclaiming their triumphant power in the universe. The view of this frightens the boy Martin and sickens him.... Martin identifies with the lamb and, therefore, cannot eat it. Like the followers of the sacrament of the lamb in the later novel, Martin excludes himself from the sacrament of violence into which his anxiety-inspired vision transforms the restaurant. These bourgeois diners seem to be performing a cannibalistic ritual. Viewed by the outside, they have become a savage society which bestows status upon those who can kill, lacerate, and consume the greatest number of victims. The novel makes an implicit connection between the smug voracity of these gourmands and the murderous cruelty by which the Nazis realized their idea of social exclusiveness and superiority. In Böll the ultimate form of snobbery is murder. Murder drives exclusiveness, on which all snobbery is founded, to its logical conclusion.

A subtle form of snobbery is found to be the decisive flaw in Heinrich Fähmel's life, as he reviews it. He had possessed grace. He was talented, worked without effort, was distinguished by suppleness of body and mind. Frail of build, a spiritual type, he resembled a young rabbi. Heinrich Fähmel's Jewish appearance confirmed the impression that he was one of the chosen. For in Böll's works Jews are always among the elect, endowed with grace, but victimized and slain by the envious descendants of Cain. The racially Jewish girl, Ilona, in *Wo warst du, Adam?*, whose marvelous singing in the extermination camp affirms the Creator in the midst of hell, and Absalom Billig, in *Haus ohne Hüter,* whose brilliant caricatures of the Nazis earned him their special hatred and destined him to be the first Jewish victim in his city, both exemplify the role of the Jews as vanguard in the ranks of Abel. (pp. 25-7)

Heinrich Fähmel, however, had strayed from his nature. He compromised with the world. He betrayed himself by adopting the appearance of snobbery, which is the mark of Cain, the sign of the buffalo's sacrament. Heinrich Fähmel's snobbery was based upon his decision to get on in the world and adapt himself outwardly to the violent buffalo.... Taking his daily breakfast in the Café Kroner bestowed that aura of distinction upon Heinrich Fähmel. The Café Kroner routine symbolized his surrender to the world.... Heinrich Fähmel attempted to live in both worlds. His heart remained with the lambs; but his façade was established among the worshippers of the buffalo. He was ready to serve the powers that were and gave his share to his country's war effort. The formula worked. He succeeded famously among the respectable and violent. The first, and most gratifying, token of his success was his victory in the competition for building the new abbey of St. Anton's. He obtained the order to build it, and the abbey became one of those architectural landmarks of which educated Germans were proud.

The conflict, however, between his true nature, represented by his marriage and home life, and his social role, symbolized by the Café Kroner, was reflected in the radically opposed characters of his sons. Otto, adopting his father's outward adjustment as his own inner conviction, became a Nazi; faithful to his father's original nature, Robert joined the persecuted lambs as their "shepherd" and helper, and lived to annul his father's work.

In the end, Heinrich Fähmel comes, independently of Robert's judgment, to the same conclusion. Because it had been divided between personal truth and public falsehood, he judges his life as wanting, and condemns the public façade and the monument it has become as worth being defaced and spat upon. When he learns that it was his own son who had blown up the monument of his fame, the abbey of St. Anton's, he approves with relief. What his son had destroyed was a false idol, a monument to his and his country's disastrous egotism. As he brings his wife home from the insane asylum to which he had allowed the Nazis to consign her, he discontinues his breakfast ritual at the Café Kroner. His last act in the novel is to repeat symbolically the execution of his pride which his son had performed actually; he cuts into the birthday cake which had been presented to him in the shape of his famous abbey and joyfully proceeds to demolish it.

The Catholic author Böll chooses a Catholic monument to represent false values. Destroying his father's abbey, Robert Fähmel executes judgment over the self-betrayal of Catholicism. This is, indeed, a major theme of Böll's more recent novels. A significant shift in the role played by Catholicism, and Christianity in general, occurs in his work.

In the early *Wo warst du, Adam?* Catholicism plays an entirely positive role. It shames and inwardly overcomes the concentration camp commander. His victim, distinguished by grace, is Jewish by race but Catholic by faith, a combination that infuriates him. Upon his command, she sings Catholic hymns with an artless perfection that proclaims the grace within her and testifies to God and life eternal. The message reaches him as it refutes him, his ideology, and his whole way of life. Killing her and ordering all Jews massacred immediately, he admits his defeat and confirms her victory; for his rash action thwarts all his plans and shows that he has lost all control of himself. He has his pet project and possession, his choir of Jewish inmates, wiped out with the rest of the camp. That strange choir, art literally imprisoned, had served the gratification of the commander's snobbery. As owner of such an oddity in an extermination camp, he appeared as a connoisseur, a capricious and refined Nazi, one possessing the power to indulge strange whims. Issuing forth from the voice of the Jewish girl, Catholicism proves its triumph by driving him to destroy the object of his special pride.

Und sagte also presents Catholicism positively. The husband's final recognition of his monogamous love, his wish to return to his family and home, are consonant with the Catholic view of the sacredness and the sacramental character of marriage. Organized Christianity begins to play a negative role in *Haus ohne Hüter*. Although most of the good characters are churchgoing and genuinely pious, the villains in the novel are militant Christians. The leader of their circle, Schurbigel, attempted to infuse Christianity into Nazism and advocated joining the Storm Troopers in order to Christianize them from within. Here we come upon one reason why Christianity is connected with negative characters. These ''Christians'' opt for compromise with worldly ambition. They wish to join the violence of the world with one half of themselves, while keeping the other in the camp of Christ. Thereby they commit the kind of self-betrayal by which Heinrich Fähmel jeopardizes his grace.

The guilt of the militant Christians in *Haus ohne Hüter*, however, is even more fundamental. After the war and the defeat of Nazism, they use the prestige of Christian views to rehabilitate themselves and rise to dominant positions in the postwar world. They make of Christian culture and politics the fashionable cult of a clique, to which they can tie their careers. They sin against the Christian spirit of humility and nondiscrimination. Although calling themselves Christians, they exercise the arrogant exclusiveness that was the essence of Nazism.

In this novel one may even detect a subtle parable of the relationship between fallible churchmen and Christ. The poet Rai, bearer of true grace, is slain. Afterwards he is idolized by the churchlike coterie of intellectuals that is of one spirit with the force that slew him. Indeed, his murderer has become a part of the group. They abuse his name by exploiting it for the reputation it gets them. Promoting the poetry of an anti-Nazi, they can prove how anti-Nazi they themselves had been, whereas it was they—one of theirs—who slew him. (pp. 27-30)

The role of Catholicism in *Billard* is the reverse of what it was in Böll's earlier work. What we see of it now is not even ambiguous, as Christianity was in *Haus ohne Hüter;* it is entirely negative. In *Billard* Catholicism is clearly allied with the buffalo and condones the persecution of the lambs, in whom we must see symbolic representatives of

the true Church. Yet even though the perspective and the plot of *Billard* do mete out severe judgment on the representatives of the Catholic Church, Catholics are as yet merely subsidiary fellow travelers of evil, and not its prime embodiment. In Böll's latest novel, *Ansichten eines Clowns,* however, militant and proselytizing spokesmen of intellectual Catholicism are the primary antagonists and persecutors of the hero-narrator of the novel. Catholicism has suffered a complete reversal of its original function in Böll's work; it has become the villain.

The only positive character in *Ansichten eines Clowns,* the clown-narrator himself, is an agnostic. But he, the nonbeliever, is a good man, while the proselytizing Catholics, his opponents, are hypocrites and snobs. (pp. 30-1)

The clown's Nazi mother and the Catholic intellectuals of postwar Germany represent and enact the same attitude. In the name of ideology, they destroy human life. Their ideological dedication is the means by which they are able to exercise their power and indulge their hostility toward the innocent, natural joy of life. The clown's mother is not only a Nazi fanatic, but an avaricious Spartan as well. She kept her children on a lean and joyless diet, and from principle denied them everything that might brighten and cheer their lives. Similarly, Böll's Catholics despise the unpretentious joy afforded by the clown's natural art, and resent the simple happiness of his relationship with Marie. Because they cannot bear the sight of such ingenuous and pure fulfillment, they are set upon destroying it. Cain's envy of Abel's grace remains for Böll, in this latest work, the archetypal model of persecution and murder, as it was in his previous works. (pp. 31-2)

It is the irony of this novel that the agnostic clown is, in a fundamental sense, more truly Catholic than the Catholic ideologues who despise him. For he, the infidel, holds the Catholic idea of the indissolubility of marriage, whereas they not only persuade his wife to desert him, but also ask him to acquiesce to her new marriage to another man. As in *Und sagte,* monogamous love is, this time explicitly, the symbol of true Catholic Christianity. It is a token and a representation of eternity in earthly life. The clown's relationship to Marie is not consecrated by the Church; officially it is not a marriage. However, in the clown's heart his love for Marie is his marriage to her and there cannot ever be any other woman for him. His physical and emotional union with her has the force of a sacrament. Böll seems to adopt the view of his clown in *Brief an einen jungen Katholiken,* where he says: ''It is impossible for me to despise that which is erroneously called physical love; such love is the substance of a sacrament, and I pay to it the reverence that I give to unconsecrated bread because it is the substance of a sacrament.'' In deserting the clown and marrying one of the Catholic leaders, Marie transgresses against the Catholic idea, as interpreted by Böll. Canonical law, by sanctioning Marie's new marriage, contradicts the law of the heart. It consecreates a union that is betrayal of an existing love and therefore, according to the law of the heart, adultery. With this juxtaposition of religious essence and ritualistic legalism, of the true faith of the individual soul and the meretricious formality of the Church, Böll's clown approaches a position that is almost Protestant and is certainly romantic. The clown's position constitutes the extreme point of a development noticeable in Böll's work from its beginnings.

Böll cites the Protestant Kleist as his earliest and most profound literary experience. There is indeed something of Kleist's ideal of the marionette-figure, an ultimately romantic and Rousseauistic ideal, in Böll's heroes—especially in those who, like Ilona, Rai, Absalom Billig, Robert Fähmel, and the clown, are artists or have something artistic in them. They resemble the marionette-type characters of Kleist—Alkmene, the Marquise of O—, Käthchen, and Michael Kohlhaas (Robert Fähmel, the implacable avenger, bears a profound resemblance to the latter). Like these Kleist characters, they possess the unshakable self-assurance and inner certainty that is the mark of innocence. As in Kleist, the primary conflict in Böll's work is that between innocence and worldly crookedness, between the purity of the simple, natural soul and the envious arrogance of the twisted careerist. But, whereas in Kleist innocence and justice win the battle in the end and force the world to acknowledge them, the contemporary author makes a distinction between the obvious physical victory that goes to the wicked and false, and an intangible, ill-definable, spiritual or moral victory that the just obtain for themselves.

Even in *Ansichten eines Clowns*—in a way, Böll's most pessimistic novel—a kind of victory is wrested from bleak defeat. For the clown is able to resist, and will continue to judge and to accuse. He will not be unfaithful to the memory of his sister's senseless sacrifice and he will not forgive her Nazi murderers; he refuses to betray the sacrament of love; and he will not surrender the art that is his nature. His triple loyalty makes him the figure who remembers in a world that wants only to forget. It also makes him a beggar, because the world will not support so uncomfortable a reminder. It is precisely as a beggar, however, that the clown fulfills his role, which is to be the fool in the traditional sense of the term—the jesting conscience of his society, the living contradiction of its pretended wisdom, the living refutation of its pretended happiness. (pp. 33-4)

> *Walter Herbert Sokel, "Perspective Dualism in the Novels of Böll," in* The Contemporary Novel in German, *edited by Robert R. Heitner (copyright © 1967 by the University of Texas Press), University of Texas Press, 1967, pp. 9-35.*

Heinrich Böll often lets his better nature get the worst of him. Many of the elements in his early work now seem rather sentimental: the lonely figure of the *Landser*, the ordinary soldier, a mere pawn overwhelmed by events on the front and stumbling uncomprehendingly and without protest toward an absurd, useless, and inevitable death; the omnipresent railway stations through which people pass on their way to the front or on their return to obliterated homes without ever meeting each other . . .; the consistent use of flashback techniques which evoke a wistful nostalgia for an orderly, though already hypocritical, world before the war; internal monologues by the main characters, consecutive but rarely converging, thus heightening our awareness that the essential human condition is solitary introspection, not solidarity; and everywhere the orphans and victimized children. Joining with these better impulses is a fine sense of the ridiculous: the music-loving concentration camp commander, *Obersturmführer* Filskeit, who grants a stay of execution to those prisoners who can enrich the camp choir, and provisionally ignores the principles of his own prize-winning monograph on "the relationship between race and choir." Böll's comment on Dickens' sense of humor seems a perfect self-definition: "Dickens' eye was always a little moist, and the Latin word for moisture is *Humor*."

Back in the 1950's, when Böll's first novels and tales appeared in English some five years or so after their publication in German, his apparent sentimentality constituted a good measure of his attraction. . . . His melody was pure; his mode understatement; his style apparently sparse and factual. He was attractive too because he was a Catholic who, despite the war, did not seem to believe in the Apocalypse: he was compassionate rather than visionary. He was perhaps overly fond of his own characters and, implicitly, a bit self-indulgent; he had not yet shaken off that Rhineland sweetness which was later to annoy him so.

Heinrich Böll has a keen sense of the symbolic power of emblematic epigraphs and quotations. *Und sagte kein einziges Wort*, his 1953 novel attacking religious hypocrisy, has a title which communicates the essence of his Christian vision: "He never said a mumblin' word," sings a Negro. The title is simply a German translation of the refrain from the spiritual (Richard Graves has insensitively given the English version the unfortunate title *Acquainted with the Night*). "They nailed Him to the Cross, and He never said a word." Christ is the victim, He is overwhelmed by hostile forces, He does not protest His fate, He cannot even understand it—the cry *"Lamma, Lamma, Sabachthani"* implies a metaphysic beyond the concept of Christ found in the simple spiritual. For the Böll of the novels and stories of the early 1950's, the victims, whether they be foot soldiers or civilians, are Christ; and the executioners are the powerful of the earth, the officers, the industrialists, the Pharisees. As with Dostoevsky, one can often measure in Böll the saintliness of a character by the extent of his silences. The hangmen are articulate; Christ "never said a mumblin' word." (pp. 185-87)

"One must pray in order to console God," the Jewess Ilona in *Adam, Where Art Thou?* had told the taciturn foot soldier Feinhals. One of Böll's most attractive qualities as a Catholic novelist is that he finds Christ more often than not among the non-Christians and the unbelievers. It is Ilona who auditions for the concentration camp choir with the All Saints Litany and who instead of appealing to the music-loving commandant with her angelic voice arouses in him such a sexual paroxysm of raging impotence and guilt that he shoots her. Pilate has done his job again. (pp. 188-89)

Among the most important currents in Böll's work, and one which links it to so much Catholic imaginative writing of our time, is his relentless caricaturing of the Pharisees. Truly, God needs consoling when faced with some of the faithful in *Acquainted with the Night*. Mrs. Franke, a powerful force in diocesan intrigues, pronounces the word "money" with a tenderness which appalls, using just the intonation with which others might pronounce "life, love, death, or God." . . . In contrast, Böll presents us with two of his most touching characters, Fred and Kate, who would doubtless be castigated as sinners by a Mrs. Franke. Fred, whose father was an ex-priest, has left Kate out of self-hatred and now sleeps in the railway station, drinking heavily but sending what little money he has to his impoverished wife. They meet as guilt-ridden "lovers" in a sordid hotel room: "It is terrible to love and to be married."

As a social document, *Acquainted with the Night* might be read as a protest against poverty amid prosperity, or even as a treatise on the consequences of the postwar housing shortage. But it is, above all, a religious novel. Fred and Kate are among those who are crucified in silence. It is she who hears the Negro singing his plaintive spiritual. When Kate finally summons up enough nerve to go to a confessional, she sees the priest watching the clock and in anger protests against "the clergy who lived in great houses and had faces like advertisements for complexion cream." Through Fred's eyes we see the hypocrisy of the postwar religious revival. Even a druggists' convention requires ecclesiastical collaboration. Amid signs proclaiming "Trust your Druggist" and balloons advertising toothpaste (one company actually drops tubes of dentifrice on the crowd) march the clergy; the bishop himself, apparently falling into an instinctive goosestep, heads the procession. But despite the venality, or perhaps because of it, the Host remains pristine, and Fred cannot resist kneeling and crossing himself: "For a moment I had the feeling of being a hypocrite until it came to my mind that God was not to blame for the inadequacies of His servants and that it was no hypocrisy to kneel before Him."

Unlike so many Catholic novelists of our time (Bernanos, Langgässer, Graham Greene), Böll is refreshingly free from dualism. For him, the way to God does not necessarily lead first to Satan. Nor, however, does it lead to conventional orthodoxy. Fred Bogner is a true Christian; he sees through cant and understands the true mystical impulse. (pp. 189-90)

Böll remains true to this satiric pattern in his savage attack on the "Group of Progressive Catholics" [in *The Clown*] who seem, in the eyes of the clown, "to be crocheting themselves loincloths out of Thomas Aquinas, St. Francis of Assisi, Bonaventure and Pope Leo XIII, loincloths which of course failed to cover their nakedness, for . . . there was no one there who wasn't earning at least fifteen hundred marks a month." (p. 192)

[Another] emblematic quotation I have chosen to evoke an essential aspect of Böll's novelistic vision serves as epigraph, and contributes the title, to one of his earliest efforts, *Adam, Where Art Thou?* It is taken from the 1940 *Tag- und Nachtbücher* of Theodore Haecker, and reads in full as follows: "A world catastrophe can be of great service. It can also serve as an alibi before God. 'Adam, where wert thou?' 'I was in the world war.'" For Germans of Böll's generation, the war was the central existential event, separating the few who retained their integrity from the many who gave in to "bad faith" (in the Sartrian sense). . . . It would appear that in his works with a war setting, Böll often takes at face value Haecker's ironic remark on catastrophe serving as an alibi before God, but that were he to apply this epigraph to his most recent works, *Billiards at Half-Past Nine* and *The Clown,* he would emphasize the irony.

Böll quotes as a second epigraph to *Adam, Where Art Thou?* Saint-Exupéry's *locus classicus* that war is a disease exactly like typhoid. Yet Böll, curiously enough, does not take very seriously, at least in his earlier works, his role as diagnostician. He neither describes the causes of infection nor offers prescriptions for a cure or a preventive. Though most of the *Landser* we meet in *The Train Was on Time* (1949) and *Adam, Where Art Thou?* are Catholics by birth,

Böll never burdens his war novels with . . . recondite religious symbolism. . . . Retrospectively, however, we can feel that the image of the crucifixion conveyed in the words of the Negro spiritual would apply to his vision of the war:

> A crowd of infantry men and pioneers who seemed very tired were squatting near a barn and many of them lay on the ground smoking. Then they came to a town and on leaving it the man in the lookout heard shots for the first time. A heavy battery was firing from the right of the road. Huge barrels pointed steeply into the air, black against the dark blue sky. Blood-red fire spurted from the muzzles and cast a soft red reflection on the wall of a barn. The man ducked: he had never heard any shooting before and now he was frightened. He suffered from ulcers— very serious ulcers.

In this passage the author seems objective and neutral, writing in accordance with the famous *neue Sachlichkeit*. The colors are exploited mainly for chromatic contrast (black, then dark blue, then blood-red to soft red), but they also mirror human emotions, although this is never made explicit by any direct links between characters and colors. (One might say that the progression of colors corresponds with the soldier's reactions to gunfire, which run from apathy to fear to apprehensive resignation.) The plastic contours offer yet another contrast: the squatting men, the angular projections of the steeply pointing barrels, the blurred outlines of a color reflected on the wall of a barn. Despite the appearance of objectivity, this passage from *Adam, Where Art Thou?* represents what I consider the sentimentality of Böll's war narratives. He tells us simply enough that the lookout had never heard shots before, that he ducked and was frightened. This description nonetheless creates a bond of sympathy between reader and character, a bond heightened by the revelation, still factual in tone, that the lookout had ulcers, very serious ulcers. From the crowd of soldiers squatting and smoking, a detail which leaves us emotionally indifferent, we move to the individual, a nervous worrier who is inexperienced, frightened, and tormented with ulcers. Here is another victim about to be crucified by the hostile forces of "heavy batteries," "huge barrels," and "blood-red fire." The lookout somehow seems terribly small; he does not protest, he only worries.

The plot of *Adam, Where Art Thou?* is typical of those found in Böll's novels through *Billiards at Half-Past Nine,* in that fragments of different lives are narrated sequentially, brought together in momentary convergence, then dispersed again: solitude is the human predicament. Despite the large cast of characters in a very short book, the plot is basically simple, alternating between portraits and descriptions of soldiers *en situation*. Böll's double postulation of caricature and sentimental compassion is everywhere apparent. . . . Too often, it seems to me, Böll structures his plot to evoke the maximum of pathos: the battle casualty, Captain Bauer, whose wife after many miscarriages got cancer, mysteriously whispers "Bjeljogorsche" every fifty seconds, recalling Kurtz's repetition of "the horror . . ." . . . . (pp. 192-95)

Better than any of his earlier creations, [*Billiards at Half-Past Nine* and *The Clown*] communicate what is noblest and most original in Böll's Catholic vision.

The central event in *Billiards* is the eightieth birthday celebration of Heinrich Faehmel, the patriarch of a family now
in its third generation in Bonn. Such an event is always a
time for memories and self-appraisal, and this novel exists
in the present through dialogue and in many fragments of
the past through a complex network of internal monologues
and leitmotifs owing more to Virginia Woolf and to *le nouveau roman* than to Faulkner or Joyce. The point of view in
the novel is constantly shifting, often without real justification, and since the fête brings together all living members of
this once large family, as well as coincidentally some outsiders who once played important roles in their lives, almost everyone is given extensive internal monologues. One
of the failings of this perhaps too complicated book is that
these many monologues are not sufficiently individualized
for the reader to grasp that the point of view (there are no
real transitions) has once again changed. Be that as it may,
what Böll clearly intends is for this family and its acquaintances to represent Germany and for the constant sum-
moning up of the past to afford an opportunity for measuring several generations of German spiritual and political
history. The verdict is, of course, "weighed and found
wanting." (pp. 195-96)

For the readers of Böll's *Irisches Tagebuch* (1957), the vision is the familiar one of a pre-industrial world where poverty is still sacred, where man has been alienated neither
from his soil nor from his God. But unlike Bernanos and
Evelyn Waugh, who clung romantically to their storybook
notion of the Middle Ages, Böll recognizes that beautiful as
the life represented by the Abbey [designed by the character Faehmel from *Billiards at Half-Past Nine*] may be, it
offers mere escape into the past, not an excuse for abdication of religious and social responsibility. (p. 197)

Hans Schnier, the narrator-hero of *The Clown*, is Böll's
finest creation. He too is a seeker of truth, an unmasker of
hypocrisy, and in his strange, half-mad way, a modern
saint. Böll has worked on translations of Salinger's *The
Catcher in the Rye* and *Franny & Zooey*, and Holden Caulfield and the clown are spiritual brothers. For Hans
Schnier, sincere irreverence is a form of sanctity; the orthodox are uniformly "Christian worms," as he calls the
head of the Christian Education Society. His reversal of
values is clearly shown in his credo: "I believe that the
living are dead, and that the dead live, not the way Protes-
tants and Catholics believe it." (p. 202)

What is a clown? A clown is the messenger of the visionary
games of children, the purest form of representational
theatre. Hans himself likes only childrens' movies, is as
frank and uninhibited as a child, and is always playing his
part ("A child, too, never takes time off as a child"). To be
a clown is to respond to a *vocatus*, and it is small wonder
that Hans' affection for Pope John is explained with
touching irreverence: "There was something of a wise old
clown about him too, and after all the figure of Harlequin
had originated in Bergamo." Above all, the clown, in his
act, mirrors the fall of man. . . . Most of the novel consists
of reminiscences of past persecution and of sarcastic telephone appeals for help to those Catholics Schnier most
despises. As in most of Böll's works there is in *The Clown*
a regular pattern of alternating nostalgia and savage caricature as Schnier struggles toward attainment of his own self-
definition: "Neither a Catholic, nor a Protestant, but a
Clown." As all his supposed friends desert him, or at best

try to force him to take up his conventional career as a
public entertainer again, Schnier turns inward toward a
most peculiar form of prayer. . . . (p. 204)

Carefully putting on a heavy layer of makeup until the
grease cracks, "showing fissures like the face of an excavated statue," he steps back from the mirror and "looks
more deeply into [himself] and at the same time further
away." He picks up his guitar (Marie and his agent had
thought the guitar undignified) and walks toward the central
station. It is Carnival time and on the station steps a group
of "matadors" and "Spanish donnas" are waiting for a
taxi. The clown puts his hat down beside him and begins to
sing:

> Catholic politics in Bonn
> Are no concern of poor Pope John.
> Let them holler, let them go,
> Eeny, meeny, miny, mo.

A stranger drops a nickel into the hat, and the clown goes
on singing. His song is in a perverse way a prayer in praise
of simplicity. Hans Schnier has become a prophetic singer
like the Negro street balladeer in *Acquainted with the
Night*. Somehow at Carnival time ("there is no better
hiding place for a professional than among amateurs")
people are more genuine than in their "real," but totally
hollow, day-to-day lives. A faceless, disguised stranger has
responded to the song with the ancient Christian gesture of
spontaneous charity. For a brief moment the hypocrisy of a
world where one must pray to console God yields to the
vision of possible harmony contained in the cacophonic
hymn of a nonbeliever. Once again, Böll's epigraph to a
novel (this time from Romans XV:21) conveys the essence
of his own song: "To whom he was not spoken of, they
shall see: and they that have not heard shall understand."
(pp. 204-05)

> *Albert Sonnenfeld, "'They That Have Not
> Heard Shall Understand': A Study of Hein-
> rich Böll," in* The Shapeless God: Essays
> on Modern Fiction, *edited by Harry J.
> Mooney, Jr. and Thomas F. Staley (re-
> printed by permission of the University of
> Pittsburgh Press; © 1968 by University of
> Pittsburgh Press), University of Pittsburgh
> Press, 1968, pp. 185-205.*

["The Bread of Those Early Years," a] brief and moving
novella, . . . seems strangely remote in time now that the
memory of horror has faded into nostalgia. But it is a powerful reminder of what Böll brought to postwar German
writing—luminous decency and lucid prose. Priceless gifts
in "those early years," when the language itself had to be
brought back to life.

"The Bread of Those Early Years" probes the many faces
of hunger, the faces of men and women starving for lack of
love, faith, hope—and bread. Much of its stunning impact
derives from Böll's hard-earned awareness that while man
doesn't live by bread alone, he doesn't live without bread.
Whatever its symbolic significance, bread is a real-life, non-
metaphorical necessity. Böll, for one, has never allowed
himself to lose sight of this fact, just as he knows that hunger, once it invades the soul, will turn malignant. . . .

Böll has always, I think, been most impressive in his
shorter fiction, and "The Bread of Those Early Years" is a
poignant tribute to his skill and vision. (p. 7)

Ernst Pawel, in The New York Times Book Review (© *1977 by The New York Times Company; reprinted by permission), January 23, 1977.*

The narrative of [*The Bread of Those Early Years*], as it haltingly unfolds . . . , is thin and tenuous, little more than a set of circumstances awaiting definition by its shaping force: the processes of memory—the "bread" of those early years—and its rising in the present. Walter Fendrich, appropriately a washing-machine repairman in a Germany newly embarked on the good life by the mass production of its principal icons, is 23 years old, too young to have served in the war. On this Monday he is informed by his father that a home-town girl, Hedwig, known to him by sight from their childhood, is coming to the (unnamed) city where he lives and works. Upon seeing her, this stranger, he is seized by a madness, as close in nature to fury as to love: she is the "train" he might otherwise have missed, which will carry him to a fated but unknown destination. Later that day he breaks off relations with his fiancée, the daughter and bookkeeper of the washing-machine manufacturer with whom he served his apprenticeship. That is virtually all there is of narrative.

The rest is memory, the intrusion of fragments of the past as they entangle the present moment and wrench it into strange unpredictable shapes. War itself is never more than alluded to, as if it were an event inadmissible to the mind, though its ghosts hover everywhere. As in *Billiards* [*at Half-Past Nine*], where fascism is never directly mentioned and is referred to only by the apocalyptic name "Host of the Beast," so here there is only oblique reference—a space on the wall of a boyhood schoolroom where Hitler's portrait once hung. . . . We, the onlookers, are tensely aware of the recent war; the shadowy sense of it is Fendrich's. Even the ruins of the city do not conjure up war in his mind; they are there as the mind's landscape, the natural habitat for his obsessions.

Bread—the fact and idea of bread, bread as food and symbol—haunts him, is of overriding importance, is his sex, politics, morals, the language he speaks, imagines and dreams in; the counter by means of which he tries to understand and transact his business with an insufferable world. Bread is the language of his feeling. . . .

Present facts and mere appearances notwithstanding, the determining reality of [Fendrich's] life, compressed into image and metaphor, is locked in the smothering past—of the apprentice boy having scratched together some money and bought a 3-pound loaf of fresh-baked bread on the black market squatting "somewhere among the ruins" and secreted now in his lair breaking open the loaf and gobbling it "with my dirty hands, tearing off pieces and stuffing them into my mouth . . . sometimes it was still steaming, all warm inside, and for a few moments I had the sensation of holding a living creature in my hands, of tearing it to pieces. . . ." He hates the word "reasonable," a key word in the surrounding ethos, for he knows what it signifies by concealing in a world where "nothing is reasonable, and the price of bread is always a shade too high." Something soul-deep which he cannot understand or articulate is wrong: looking upon the face of the girl he adores, "for one insane moment" he feels an "urge to destroy" it; looking at his own face in the mirror he is "filled with rage and disgust" and shatters the image with a hammer. (p. 213)

The ruins of his city seem classical, timeless, they are simply *there* as if they had always been there, a permanent cityscape; they are presented as just that, ruins, like the Roman ruins in *Billiards,* which turn out to be fake, a tourist attraction based on sentimental appeal. But these are bombed-out ruins of course, spectral reminders of war that will eventually be demolished and replaced by the inevitable high-rise apartment complexes. Nor are they simply static; they are an emblem connecting recent past and ongoing future, monuments of moral history. Once, not long before, these ruins enclosed lives; now they are no more than raw materials awaiting plunder by enterprising businessmen. The plunder is called salvage—whatever bits and pieces which can be ripped out and turned to profitable account. The entrepreneur is his boss, his fiancée's father; together he and she have cheated the old man by selling scrap metal on the side—not Fendrich's first venture in free enterprise, as earlier, while still an apprentice, he had stolen hot plates to buy . . . bread and cigarettes. . . . An apprentice trying to salvage a washing machine falls to his death; it is left to Fendrich to carry the body to the hearse. A bystander asks, "Was he your brother?" "Yes, he was my brother," he replies.

That sentiment, or act of solidarity, is the other side of the coin: class hatred is the closest approach he makes to the articulation of a powerful, coherent, sustained emotion. The emotion isn't rooted in politics, much less ideology; it is deep, visceral, grounded in bread, in his beginnings and growth, the ore of his life, past, memories, experience. Böll's narrative method is scrupulously "objective," and the rhetoric and gestures of emotion are carefully suppressed. . . . Feeling itself is ambiguous; except for class hatred which, originating in an animal sense of deprivation —of ravenous hunger, a great wracking emptiness—and swelling into a void of the spirit, now expands to a kind of moral criticism of the social order. (pp. 213-14)

In the longest, most fully developed scene in a novel composed of fragments, images, aborted and buried scenes, Fendrich sits in a café with his fiancée for their final talk. Why? she asks. Does the girl have money? *That* she could understand, the universal motive underlying all act and feeling. Confusedly he tries to explain, and reminding her of meager rations doled out by her father comes close to saying bread is love: "And bread, the bread that you, that your father, never gave me . . . I believe . . . that if in those days you had just once given me a loaf of bread, I couldn't possibly be sitting here talking to you like this." Her sense of justice outraged, she points out that the wages her father paid exceeded the standard rate; and has he forgotten the ration-free soup served daily? Somehow Fendrich cannot feel gratitude for such largesse; and, not surprisingly, converts his rage into bread. In his high moment, when at last he breaks out of his silence, he speaks for all the workers: "Read the names again—out loud, reverently, like you'd read a litany—call them out, and after each name say: 'Forgive us'—then add up all the names, multiply the number by a thousand loaves of bread—and that result again by a thousand: then you'll have the number of curses heaped on your father's bank account. The unit is bread, the bread of those early years. . . ." . . .

Hatred and rage drive speech; love, or whatever it is that he feels, silences him. Apart from his moment of lyricism, the speech is largely interior, unless the imagery of memory is a kind of mute eloquence. What Böll intends he impressively achieves: an expressionist portrait, . . . a portrait in grays, browns, blacks and blood—a portrait weighted with heavy moral overtones of a society from which anything might erupt. The atmosphere is unrelievedly bleak and obscurely ominous, a "miracle" that feels more like an awful curse. Fendrich is a Mass-going Roman Catholic, a penitent in need of absolution; a recurring element with the gravity of a motif, and so orchestrated. A novel, small in scope but carefully wrought, dense and fraught in its atmospherics, heavily laden, the minor work of an imposing novelist, and in its deepest currents a preparation for the more massive work which was to follow and which, one hopes, is yet to come. (p. 214)

> *Saul Maloff, "The Ghosts of War, the Wolf Within," in* The Nation (*copyright 1977 by the Nation Associates, Inc.*), *February 19, 1977, pp. 213-14.*

Walter Fendrich, a washing-machine maintenance man, is the first-person hero of [*The Bread of Those Early Years*]; twenty-three, Catholic, a virgin, and engaged to his employer's daughter, Ulla Wickweber. The story takes place in Cologne on a Monday in March during the early 1950s. Walter's father, a schoolteacher in a small town, has asked him to find a room for the daughter of a colleague who is coming to the city to train as a teacher. The moment Walter sees Hedwig he falls in love with her, both sexually and ontologically. In a semi-mystical flash he realizes that she represents an alternative way of life—less tough and less materialist than life with Ulla. By the end of the day and after various vicissitudes, including Walter's farewell interview with Ulla, Walter and Hedwig are ready to fulfil their destiny by going to bed together—without the blessing of the Church, although Hedwig is also a practising Catholic. Why they cannot wait to get it is never quite explained, but their hurry is made to seem somehow existential.

Böll has always been anti-clerical and anti-establishment: not a very startling position for a German Catholic, even in 1955 when this book first appeared, and it is obvious that the sexual act the novel leads up to but does not include is a rite in what J. P. Stern . . . called "selfconscious Roman (or rather Rhenish) Catholicism, a weird spirituality". *The Bread of Those Early Years* is a textbook example of Böll's work. An examination candidate having to answer a question of his themes, Weltanschauung and symbolism would not need to read much else. First, there is the typical petty bourgeois milieu with built-in alienation. Then want: Walter is doing well in the early years of the post-war economic recovery; but flashbacks reveal a childhood and early youth of deprivation—he was always hungry and the thought of bread obsessed him until bread eventually became an addiction. Now he cannot pass a baker's shop without going in to buy some. But bread is not just the counter-symbol to want, it is also a sacrament: there is a symbolic scene when Walter offers Hedwig a roll and watches her break it. In fact, there is so much bread about that one is inclined to agree with Ulla when she says: "Please don't say the word 'bread' again."

Ulla and her family stand for the acquisitive society in the black market years just after the war when the strong and wily exploited the weak. In later works Böll's target shifts towards the consumer society; here the Wirtschaftswunder is only just beginning: in both cases society is selfish and materialist. The weak are not only exploited but killed. The landscape of Walter's memory is littered with corpses, especially young corpses—another favourite theme of Böll's. . . .

Ulla and her father are the only two "bad" characters; or more accurately "least good", because Böll sees some goodness in everyone. Goodness is what interests him and it comes in various packages and strengths: Ulla's brother is a decent, loyal, well-meaning fellow; Walter's landlady—called Frau Brotig, which would, if it were a word, mean "bready"—is generous, warm, and speaks gently to her child; his distant cousin Clara is a nun (Böll always puts in a nun when he can), another selfless giver of bread; his father is a low-key saint; and Hedwig represents Böll's *ewig Weibliche*, later to turn into Katharina Blum and the Lady in the Group Portrait: a streak of Raskolnikov's Sonya in her, but more mysterious, much more attractive, and much keener on sex, so long as it is suffused with spirituality. . . . Walter himself is the holy fool whom critics have spotted in other works of Böll's.

Professor Stern was sorry that Böll won his Nobel Prize for literature rather than for his "immense decency". His moral stance, he said, was impeccable but unoriginal, and artistically he was unadventurous, even "quietist". True, but the same accusation—of being a *guter Mensch aber schlechter Musikant*—could equally well be levelled at Solzhenitsyn: perhaps it is something to do with the Nobel Prize. Böll may turn out to be one of the overrated writers of the century. Still, he is not despicable and far from unreadable: his bread goes down easily, even though in this particular work he adopts a hushed religious tone throughout. . . . [Böll] is wonderful at creating atmosphere and describing smells, sounds, and, of course, tastes, as well as sights. His metaphors are unexpected and illuminating, and he can draw out the *lacrimae rerum* better than almost anyone. Too well perhaps, but his books are getting steadily dryer, and this early one is a reminder of how far the process has gone.

> *Gabriele Annan, "On the Breadline," in* The Times Literary Supplement (© *Times Newspapers Ltd., 1977; reproduced from* The Times Literary Supplement *by permission*), *February 25, 1977, p. 201.*

The Bread of Those Early Years dates from 1955; but even without the retrospective glow of a Nobel prize it would be an impressive work. It is a piece of bravura rhetoric. . . .

This is a small book in every sense; but in its way nearly perfect. With a fine economy Böll suggests a great deal more than he actually says, both about the narrator's life, and about the society in which he moves. In this sense it is a genuine socialist novel: generating an individual out of his history and environment, and simultaneously demonstrating that individual's power and freedom to change, to reject the determinations of society. The only limiting factor is Böll's use of 'falling-in-love' as the occasion for change, introducing a somewhat arbitrary and external factor which weakens the coherence of the novel (the girl herself is an almost wholly passive figure). But overall, the work is both attractive and intelligent. . . . (p. 24)

> *Nick Totten, in* The Spectator (© *1977 by* The Spectator; *reprinted by permission of* The Spectator), *March 5, 1977.*

In the early years after 1945, there was one comfort to be had by anyone watching for Germany to recover. Whereas much of what was written after 1918 had been heady stuff—gruesome evocations of Armageddon, fervid ecstasies about the New Man who was expected to arise from the holocaust, extremes of hope and despair—the mood of writers like Brecht and Böll after the Second World War was more sober, more likely to allow a cool look at what materials could be dug out of the rubble to build a humane tradition. Böll gave his ruminative attention to the minutiae of the present moment. The detail of everyday life fascinated him, though not in a naturalistic or antiquarian spirit. As he says in *Missing Persons,* this collection of essays and reviews written during the past quarter of a century, he has a reverence for the past, for his family's past, and for everything that exists now but will soon never exist again. Of his mother he writes, "I want the one hair of the head that has fallen to the ground".

It becomes increasingly clear that the biblical care for the fall of a sparrow is the origin of Böll's painstaking descriptions of such processes as the working of a coin-operated telephone. Nothing human or for that matter nonhuman is alien to him. Like Brecht, he takes reality as a *Messingkauf,* in the spirit of a rag-and-bone merchant, finding unexpected valuables. It has to be admitted, though, that novels written in such a mood of total acceptance can have their longueurs. Böll's half-serious proposal to make a travel-film showing nothing but the hands and faces of Soviet citizens queuing up to see Lenin's tomb shows his concern for people rather than politics, but the result could, at any great length, be a bore, and an element of boredom is present, for me at any rate, in the slow pace and repetitiveness of some of Böll's writing.

The fact that so much of this book is devoted to Russia (together with another holy mother country, Ireland) and so little of it to Germany, is revealing. Unlike Brecht, Böll is close, in the extent of his compassion, to being an Alyosha Karamazov. But a German Alyosha of Böll's generation has had to confront experiences more testing than any that Dostoevsky imagined. Alyosha was not conscripted as Böll was into the armies that spread hatred all over Europe, he never had to recover from the realization that his gun had been defending the creators of Auschwitz, Buchenwald, Mauthausen. That is Böll's invisible worm—really invisible, he never alludes to it; but there is no ignoring it.

Unlike most of his generation, he has not tried, understandable though it would have been, to blot all that from memory. Like the boy visited by a country doctor in Kafka's short story, the wound in his side will not heal. But though like Kafka he can perhaps see the wound as a rose, he does not romanticize. From out of his patient, sometimes whimsical account of Germany's rapid rise to unheard-of-luxury, traffic jams and pollution, there is an occasional outburst, alien to Alyosha, of a mood like that ascribed by Böll to his friend Solzhenitsyn, a kind of "divine bitterness". . . .

The image we had of Böll in the early post-war years was . . . misleading. For all his sobriety there was something of the "all or nothing" mood of the post-1918 generation in him. Even his compassion could work equivocally. . . .

At the root of [his] inconsistencies there may well be something of that ambiguous relationship with Russia which Germans have felt for centuries. Not that Böll's deep compassion for the Russian people is felt simply because he is aware of what they suffered during the German invasion of 1941-45. Germans have often felt themselves drawn towards Russia, whether as missionaries or as a bulwark for the West, or to represent to the West their affinity with Slavs. Rilke, Thomas Mann, Kafka, Brecht have all gone further than any French or English writer in that *Drang nach Osten,* in one or another of its forms. What looks most Slav in Böll is his desire for consensus, communion, something more than brotherhood as the Enlightenment understood it—a passion amounting almost to adoration, such as Böll reveals in his project for filming Moscow queues, and such as Alyosha would have understood. . . .

Böll's radical liberalism is better understood with all that in mind. Yet it is not merely a question of understanding. The passion in him, the reverence he feels for those Moscow shoe-shiners, the reverence for the one hair of the head is not so easily felt by the rationalist or the debater. Such unity as a parliamentary state can gain through mutual toleration sometimes looks pale against the heartfelt unity of a family millions strong.

Ronald Gray, "A Passion for Consensus," in The Times Literary Supplement *(© Times Newspapers Ltd., 1978; reproduced from* The Times Literary Supplement *by permission), February 10, 1978, p. 167.*

*   *   *

BONNEFOY, Yves 1923-

Bonnefoy is a French critic, poet, translator, essayist, and art historian. The central thematic concern of his poetry is the life-death relationship. Bonnefoy has increasingly devoted more time to his art history studies, and his translations of Shakespeare's plays are widely acclaimed.

By general critical consensus Yves Bonnefoy is one of the finest poets to emerge in France since World War II; and, remarkably, his reputation came with . . . [his first book], *Du Mouvement et de l'immobilité de Douve* (1953). . . . This book is a sequence of short poems, separated into several sections, and must be read as such; it is as well a difficult work of "magie suggestif", which is reminiscent in part of the hermetic qualities of Mallarmé and Valéry and others whose technique involves obliquity, spiritual plenitude and vacancy. "Douve", the proper name of the title, cannot be fixed in a single identity except as a feminine principle, she is variously glimpsed as earth, woman, the beloved, and is associated with the origins of poetry and the poem itself. The sequence proceeds through changing moods and the transformations of inward metaphysical drama that is deliberately ambiguous and elusive, though it clearly is implicated with love and separation, a journey into death and rebirth. It is a poem for reflective rereading with attention to recurrent gestures, rhythms, images. (p. 269)

Ralph J. Mills, Jr., in Poetry *(© 1969 by the Modern Poetry Association; reprinted by permission of the Editor of* Poetry*), January, 1969.*

One of the deepest incitements to poetry since the Romantics has been a search for Eden. Yves Bonnefoy's *L'Arrière-pays* is another account of such a search, and an important one. He rediscovers the paradox of Poe, that it is precisely the seemingly utter sufficiency of natural beauty which dissatisfies, by urging to something beyond itself. He looks, however, for the lost place of benediction, the *vrai lieu,* not in the *néant* or an imaginary elsewhere but in a world "of flesh and of time" like ours, not in the unreal but in the real transformed by human vision. The book both celebrates the earth as it is and desires its "resurrection".

In form, it is a kind of essential autobiography, organized around the single quest for the *arrière-pays,* and reports M Bonnefoy's travels, mainly as an art critic, to various places and paintings. He responds to the latter, with continually stimulating penetration, as attempts to fulfil our need for images, for seeing the earth remade. It also relates crucial experiences that have fed his writing though he refers them curiously less to his poetry than to certain unfinished stories. He reveals himself, indeed, a compelling storyteller, delicate, symbolic, erudite, no doubt under the conscious influence of Nerval; even though it is part of the discipline of which the book is the narrative to reject this "imaginative" type of composition.

L'Arrière-pays is a spacious work, despite its relative shortness, and is written with M Bonnefoy's usual impassioned high seriousness, in a grave and poetically vibrant language whose syntax, at times, is pointedly classical. It is full of ideas (for instance, on the metaphysical nature of Latin), of writer's wisdom, and of pregnant phrasing.

A comparison with Philippe Jaccottet's very similar *Paysages avec figures absentes* . . . shows its possible limitations. There is less really probing contact with individual sites and canvases: M Bonnefoy's imagination, which is anything but abstract, works nevertheless not so much through a response to detailed particulars as through the establishing of general, though still passionate, mental structures, in a way that one associates with French classicism. One may, of course, prefer his method; here it makes his pursuit of a relationship with nature an intellectual hygiene rather more than a hygiene of the whole man. One also becomes aware in M Jaccottet of a dimension that is absent from *L'Arrière-pays,* the dimension of human pain and evil, which is arguably vital to a study of natural beauty as lacking its plenitude, and of ourselves as exiles. None of which is to deny, however, that this is a severe and admirable work, which anyone concerned for poetry and painting ought to know. (p. 839)

The Times Literary Supplement (© *Times Newspapers Ltd., 1972; reproduced from* The Times Literary Supplement *by permission), July 21, 1972.*

Silence—as the other side of speech, of consciousness, of being—is a recurrent yet often ambiguous theme in Yves Bonnefoy's poetry. A master of dense and beautiful lyrics, Bonnefoy seeks nonetheless the "summit of imperfection." An anti-Platonist who wishes to "name" the objects of this earth, he decries at the same time the inadequacy of all language. The following two papers take up different aspects of this quest for silence through language; juxtaposed, they propose different readings of the same area in the same poetry. They may well be contradictory. Does Bonnefoy's speech resolve into silence, or into multiple voices? Is his ultimate "comprehension" a stilled, higher vision, or an ambiguous self-awareness? Is his "passage" the passage to

an intuited *arrière-pays,* or a progression forever halted on the threshold? Does Bonnefoy's style evoke silence as a decrescendo formed of echo and inner allusion, or does it represent silence by a ceaseless interplay of decentered references? Do these readings cancel each other out, or is there something to be gained by pursuing divergent viewpoints in the same context? (p. 193)

Sarah Lawall

Yves Bonnefoy's poetry incorporates the risk of silence. Not silence itself, for unlike Rimbaud he continues to write, but a systematic disbelief in the efficacy of words. Words that would "name" never reach their objects, and the writer merely inflicts "ces coups sourds contre la paroi de la parole" ("dull blows on the wall of speech" . . .). (p. 194)

The risk is real, not hypothetical: Bonnefoy's latest poems have been published as "fragments" and "other fragments" in an apparent unwillingness to give even the impression of a deceptively finished text. The poet does continue to write, however, and it is possible that he is in fact experimenting with ways to express—perhaps resolve—this very notion of linguistic promise and inadequacy. Such a development would be consistent with the change in Bonnefoy's artistic tastes from the finished, idealistic products of the Italian Renaissance to a baroque style that, reaching out into surrounding nothingness, becomes a "negative rhetoric" and a "passageway to the invisible." . . . (p. 195)

Bonnefoy's poet can name things exactly because he sees into their presence as possibility of life and death. By naming them, he calls into existence their full identity. In terms of the legend of the Grail, he asks the question that Parsifal does not: he asks the meaning of the unearthly procession and thus forces the Holy Grail to enter an earthly incarnation. Poetic images synthesize the death and life, presence and absence, of their objects. . . .

The empty structures of language must continue to work against the constant murmur of subterranean waters, so as to end not with an illusion or with an answer, but with a repetitive, all-embracing *question.* . . . Poetry avoids illusion only by maintaining a quality of randomness, of drifting on a liquid surface that cannot be plumbed and whose voice—although it must be heard—cannot be understood. (p. 196)

Poetry is *parole,* not *langue:* it is a special speech act that goes beyond any mechanical combinations of impersonal words. If poetry relies on *langue* alone, and reproduces mere patterns of language . . . , it arrives at impersonality and death—the "wrong kind of death." Such a wrong kind of death is all the more dangerous because it is already present in the art work, insofar as the latter congeals and fixes the living exchanges of reality. The highest value Bonnefoy finds in art is in fact *exchange,* a sort of communion with others and with other things that takes place through poetry's transcendent example. Poetry is not the supreme value, but rather the "ultimate resource" for reaching that value. (p. 197)

How does Bonnefoy combine *openness* and *meaning,* these two apparently contradictory qualities? "Meaning," for the poet, does not imply a predetermined absolute significance that is transferred from writer to reader. It is an exchange in and through the ambiguity of language—a kind of "ontological refraction" that takes place in words. . . . Art aims towards an unwordly perfection, says Bonnefoy, and is thus essentially untrue. This untruth jeopardizes communion, which cannot take place in an unreal dimension. Artistic illusion should therefore not be too perfect. Bonnefoy's task is to retain, in the form and vision of his poetry, the ontological refraction originally perceived and through which the human imagination seeks its unity. . . . *Dans le leurre du seuil* expresses just such an attempt. (pp. 197-98)

There are three ways in which this . . . collection seems to me different from those that precede: it extends and fragments syntactic patterns, it questions the whole idea of passing to an absolute presence, and it develops a far-reaching, more fluid system of images than the somewhat static, miraculous glimpses given in previous poems. (p. 199)

The communion or exchange Bonnefoy seeks is a potential form of dialogue, and dialogue is also sought, rejected, and reinterpreted in *Dans le leurre du seuil*. The speaker at the beginning knocks at a closed door, invokes blind matter and empty language, and calls for a tranquility and reassurance that do not come. (p. 204)

[There] may be *no* answer if the voice proceeds from himself, an echo and vibration of his own questions: "Est-ce 'un autre' la voix qui me répond / Ou moi encore . . ." ("Is the voice that answers me 'an other' / Or is it still myself . . ." . . . . This multiple voice rejects naming, answering, or conclusive transcendental images; it sends us back to the exploratory act of writing as a perennial knocking at the gates of a nonexistent paradise. . . .

This unstable dialogue is resolved in a manner somewhat like the impersonal "communion" of matter and consciousness. . . . The poet has conquered the idealistic temptation of passage over a threshold by recomposing a broken, active, and truer vision out of the refracted fragments of reality. A throb of insistent questioning pervades the entire poem. (p. 205)

This is not to say that Bonnefoy's ideas have changed essentially since *Du Mouvement et de l'immobilité de Douve;* rather, he seems to have come full circle, and accepted his basic metaphor on the level of verbal patterns. What is different in *Dans le leurre du seuil* is that he has tried to incorporate silence into the forms of his text. An increased role is given to the self-conscious use of language, and to negative images or ones that cancel each other out. Constructions are deconstructed; the rooms, cathedrals, high walls, and vaults of earlier works become now stones torn out of a wall at night, a wall which crumbles, blasted stones, a destroyed vault, or the mere beginnings of an arch. The threshold is no passageway. The communion sought through a Grail has been recreated as a purely earthly, ephemeral event—attainable only in poetic language. At the end of the poem, the "sponge" of nothingness wipes up the debris of bread and wine, and returns the celebration to the emptiness in which it was born. This emptiness is real, and thus it adds a certain poignancy to the celebration in which man becomes conscious of his mortal existence. (pp. 205-06)

At the end of the quest, then, it is not "naming" but the word as sign that takes the place of the Grail, becoming both passage and *true place*. . . .

Mary Ann Caws

Bonnefoy's visionary *place of poetry* is a "vrai lieu," sacrificial and yet empty of shadow, an orangery closed off where the vacant self is determined at last by its watching and its waiting. Unsure of his victory, the poet grasps the red flame of the sword, the ardent blade of the most difficult speaking against the gray of a neutral prose; his Arthurian gesture is defined—like all poetry—by its risk. (p. 206)

In this poetry where the positive absence of all sound seems to mark the end of the path, where "un haut silence" seems to carry the highest value, the word can only be considered to lead not toward but through. In the particular resonance of each of Bonnefoy's texts against the others to form the profound clusters of images and the long strains resolved or unresolved of this intense and far-reaching poetry, we notice a passage totally unlike that found in any other poet. The parts here in their faithful belonging to the whole of the *chant* are also inserted as continuities in our perception, each a part of the passage to our understanding as to the poet's own. Their *appartenance* is also that of each reader.

As a preliminary stage on the way to reading the *cheminement* of this word and this silence, the simplest trace of the word "understanding" itself may guide us on the path of *L'Arrière-pays* behind this text. The volume by this name— a prose poem on art, understanding, and perception—examines the place where the contraries meet, ideal and yet bound to the now and the here of this land, inscribed in the present and in the poet's presence, and yet pointing beyond —showing the place, and then the moment of passage. (p. 209)

The passage from the outer to the inner country of and behind the text is revealed in the most silent of ways.

In the passage we take guided by the voices of Bonnefoy's poetry, we follow two seemingly contrary psychological directions. First, an apparent crescendo: from the part to the whole, or from the disconnected expression to the unifying word or phrase, the movement being always interior to the sense and never a question of volume. (p. 212)

The answer to be given to the question "Et toi . . . qui es-tu?" can only have been: that speech which was silence, as the song "qui s'est tu" is seen in retrospect, reflecting back on it in an echo. . . . But when the text falls silent, a triple closing-off is felt through these same echoes, and their echoes: "Voix, déjà tous chemins que tu suivais se ferment." For with this voice, there fails both a vision and a way of going ("vois . . . ," "voie . . ."). Now the real passage will lead from the closure of this path, the failure of this sight, to the eventual opening of an inner threshold, another higher song heard or understood within the first song stilled. (p. 217)

Sarah Lawall and Mary Ann Caws, "A Style of Silence: Two Readings of Yves Bonnefoy's Poetry," in Contemporary Literature *(© 1975 by the Regents of the University of Wisconsin), Vol. 16 No. 2, Spring, 1975, pp. 193-217.*

In the title-work of Yves Bonnefoy's new collection of prose narratives [*Rue Traversière*], the rue Traversière is remembered as having led, during the poet's childhood, from the ordinary world into the wonderland of a botanical garden. The street was a perfectly named place of transition.... Readers of Bonnefoy's earlier work will at once recognize the sort of place this is: a keenly felt segment of the real world which owns up without prompting to its impermanence, its drift towards vacancy; a place which haunts him by showing absence minutely and inseparably woven into presence, flux into stability, losing into having. In a later text the narrator meets someone who has read ''Rue Traversière'' and found the street familiar. But this person remembers it as well-to-do, not poor, places it in a different part of town and knows nothing of the magic garden. Which of them had got things wrong? Whose street was real, whose invented? Perhaps language itself was the culprit and would allow indefinitely many possible streets to be called into actuality in the same way.

The relationship between the two texts is characteristic of the book as a whole. The telling of an experience makes its fullest sense in the retelling to which it gives rise. By superimposing narrative on narrative and by displacing the reader's attention into the region between descriptions, Bonnefoy gives the collection a precarious coherence and an exhaustiveness of sorts. But some of the material—and especially the rarefied travelogue for which he has a particular fondness—is so meagre that no amount of transitional thinking could lend it substance.

> *Malcolm Bowie, ''The Immanent Idea,'' in* The Times Literary Supplement (© *Times Newspapers Ltd., 1977; reprinted from* The Times Literary Supplement *by permission), May 6, 1977, p. 553.*

Bonnefoy may very well be the greatest living French poet. With the passing of Saint-John Perse, whom he resembles in his use of a persistent, overriding metaphor throughout a long poem, Bonnefoy has sadly few competitors. In his surreal gentle melancholy, he is like Reverdy, Desnos, Eluard, or Supervielle. In strength and bite, he is like Valéry or Beckett.... [*Words in Stone / Pierre Écrite*] consists of a series of poems whose extreme unity almost seems rigid. (p. 98)

> Virginia Quarterly Review (*copyright, 1977, by the* Virginia Quarterly Review, *The University of Virginia), Vol. 53, No. 3 (Summer, 1977).*

*   *   *

BORGES, Jorge Luis   1899-

An Argentinian poet, essayist, short story writer and translator, Borges is one of the world's most respected authors. Borges's writings present a surreal, labyrinthine world of dream-like parables where there are few solid cause and effect relationships. Obsessed with fantasy and the idea of literature as ''fun,'' this blind author has been described by William Barnstone as ''a clever metaphysician who has given us an enormous and varied literature, ranging from re-creations of an ancient Chinese 'Book Guardian' to the characteristics of imaginary beasts.'' Borges has collaborated with Adolfo Bioy Casares under the pseudonyms of H(onorio) Bustos Domecq and B. Suarez Lynch. (See also *CLC*, Vols. 1, 2, 3, 4, 6, 8, and *Contemporary Authors*, Vols. 21-24, rev. ed.)

The work of Jorge Luis Borges is a species of international literary metaphor. He knowledgeably makes a transfer of inherited meanings from Spanish and English, French and

German, and sums up a series of analogies, of confrontations, of appositions in other nations' literatures. His Argentinians act out Parisian dramas, his Central European Jews are wise in the ways of the Amazon, his Babylonians are fluent in the paradigms of Babel. Probably, withal, he is the most succinct writer of this century, and one of the most incisive as to conclusions, daring dryly to go beyond such a Mannerist master as James Joyce, who knew philology and felt legends, but eschewed meanings. Perhaps, though, his meaning is simply in the ritual tone of voice with which he suggests some eternal, unanswerable question.

Philosophy, comparative philologies, archaeology, everything has been evolving, progressing, breaking new ground. But we know little as ever about why we are born again each morning. Despite the comings and goings of the collective unconscious, we know equally little about the meanings of our very symbols. Borges restates, in a few allegorical pages, the circular, ceremonial direction of our curious, groping, thrilling and atrocious ignorance. Since he has made the acquaintance of all religions, he does not blush to write a tender poem from within a propitiatory lupanar. Because he knows Madrid, Paris, and Geneva—Buenos Aires, even New York do not make him shudder. As an Argentine, he is perhaps one of the last German Expressionists (in 1919 he was associated with the *ultraista* movement). Because *he has read all the books,* because he has translated Gide, Kafka, Faulkner and Virginia Woolf, the burning of the library at Alexandria—or in Don Quixote's backyard—does not make him blanch anew. All the books were sacred and inviolable. They all proclaimed the True God. Our immediate forebears saw the ineffable face of the Creator, and reeled back, stopping to write

Torat yyy Hedut yyy Piqqude yyy

where the series of y's stood for Jehovah.

More hard-mouthed now, though with the same arbitrary, stylized Solomonic stars in our eyes, we venture to challenge the heavens. Borges bears witness with us in this century, with shabby Faust, but is mercifully economic. No Gargantuan novel says more than he can in one of his *ficciones.* Borges is no Gorgias (who invented the art of expressing himself either briefly or at endless length); his brevity is no device, as brevity was in the Middle Ages. His style is as laconic in statement as a parallel, as suggestively infinite. He is an imagist of cultural fugures and choreographies, of the faltering, lamentable Dance of Life. One cinquepace is not the same as another, but there is no need to dance until one drops in the marathon. In literature it is only necessary to outline the steps. Let the people dance!

Among his themes are a mythology of dagger thrusts; the fearful sphere of Pascal's abyss; the labyrinths which are books; *cogito, ergo sum cogitatio;* the genealogy of insomnia; the iconography of the eternal return.

Until you can say ''The criminal coming at me? The criminal coming at me is I!,'' you can not know the Stoic philosophy. This notion burgeons in Borges to the point where he can adduce that at the moment of coitus every man is one man. And that when a man recites William Shakespeare, he *is* William Shakespeare. (Perhaps, after all, every man is one man, every book one book; though Borges insists that every book is also a specific and particular *dialogue*.)

115

Borges is an exegete, a commentator on the texts, on the Books. And exegesis is the mother of heresy. But Borges is not naturally a heresiarch. He is merely a vindicator of heresies. And heresies, as Miguel de Unamuno pointed out, are necessary for the philosophical, and even more, for the theological health of a culture. Borges, nevertheless, has nothing to do either with the well-being of our culture, or its languishment. His postulates, though portentous, are awesome incidental speculations; they undermine the universe only casually. As a vindicator of heresies, Borges will brave the exoneration of eternity or the refutation of Time: the concrete justification of a sunset, of the Plain, of identical mutations; the chance undermining of a chronology. Possibly, every instant in time is the Creation, or conversely, there is only spent accretion, and we are vagabonds at a universal dump.

The cruel jests of history are "solved" only by violence. The equal idiocy of all totalitarianism, the swinishness of Communism or Nazism, and the deadliness of conformity to an accepted form of sterility, are unmasked to no point. Men long for their deceits. A few will blindly fight back.

Borges does not shy away from senseless truth. In his own preferred story, "The South," a man must pick up a knife (is he dreaming?) and go out into the brainless night to face bestiality. Why? He does not know. All our knowledge has led us exactly to this point, just where we started, endless ages ago. We have only been playing a game, an immortal game, all along. (pp. 9-11)

> *Anthony Kerrigan, in his introduction to* Ficciones, *by Jorge Luis Borges (reprinted by permission of Grove Press, Inc.; copyright © 1962 by Grove Press, Inc.; translated from the Spanish © 1956 by Emece Editores, S.A., Buenos Aires), Grove Press, 1962, pp. 9-11.*

[Four of Borges' short] stories share a common theme: the problem of order and disorder, or, if we wish to use a technical term, entropy. In particular, Borges is concerned with the relationship between order and knowledge or information ("The Library of Babel" and "The God's Script") and with the interaction of order and disorder on the laws of the universe and the effect of those laws on man ("Tlön, Uqbar, Orbis Tertius" and "The Lottery in Babylon").

The unity of Borges' viewpoint can best be understood by a consideration of the second law of thermodynamics and the application of that law to human experience. The second law of thermodynamics may be stated as follows: "For an isolated system the direction of spontaneous change is from an arrangement of a less probable, greater order, to an arrangement of a more probable, lesser order." The second law thus states that there is an inverse relation between order and probability, i.e., a more order state is less probable than one of greater disorder. The second law also requires that if we create order in a certain part of a system we must create at least as much disorder in another part of the system. The best one can do in such a process is to break even; more often one loses. In the nineteenth century, the term entropy was introduced and defined mathematically as a measure of the disorder of probability of a given state of the system; the second law was restated as follows: "The entropy of the universe tends towards a maximum." In the twentieth century, physicists . . . developed the connection of entropy and information in what has become known as Information Theory. Entropy measures the lack of information since it defines the number of possible answers to a question. The less information possessed about a question the greater the number of possible answers; the more information possessed the fewer the possible answers. . . .

The stories "The Library of Babel" and "The God's Script" are both expressions of the second law, as stated above. The Library of Babel consists of all possible combinations of [identically paged and arranged books]. . . .

In truth, the Library includes all verbal structures, all variations permitted by . . . twenty-five orthographical symbols, but not a single example of absolute nonsense. (p. 54)

Thus the Library contains all knowledge and, paradoxically, absolutely no information, since the only possible index for the Library would be identical with the Library itself. This situation is the ultimate state predicted by the second law of thermodynamics—a state of maximum entropy and minimum information. (p. 55)

Borges' only consolation in this mythical library, as in the universe at large, is the possibility that the order will repeat itself.

> I venture to suggest this solution to the ancient problem: the *Library is unlimited and cyclical.* If an eternal traveler were to cross it in any direction, after centuries he would see that the same volumes were repeated in the same disorder (which, thus repeated would be an order: the Order). My solitude is gladdened by this elegant hope. . . .

"The God's Script" would seem to be the antithesis of "The Library of Babel." Tzinacán, a priest of Qaholom, discovers the ultimate message or information out of the seemingly random markings on a jaguar. On the face of it, he has obtained information or order from disorder and violated the second law. The very fact that the message has been inscribed on the jaguar's coat confirms the thermodynamic metaphor.

> The God, foreseeing that at the end of time there would be devastation and ruin, wrote on the first day of Creation a magical sentence with the power to ward off those evils. He wrote it in such a way that it would reach the most distant generations and not be subject to chance. . . .

What else can Borges be referring to except the tendency of the universe to complete disorder or maximum entropy? Tzinacán's discovery of that message would indeed seem to violate that law. . . . But the second law is not scoffed at lightly. If we order one part of the world we must pay for it with at least as much disorder elsewhere. Tzinacán has ordered the spots on the jaguar and in the process he has literally disordered himself. . . .

> I no longer remember Tzinacán.

> May the mystery lettered on the tigers die with me. Whoever has seen the universe, whoever has beheld the fiery designs of the universe, cannot think in terms of one man, of that man's trivial fortunes or misfortunes,

though he be that very man. That man *has been he* and now matters no more to him. What is the life of that other to him, the nation of that other to him; if he, now, is no one. That is why I do not pronounce the formula, why, lying here in the darkness, I let the days obliterate me. . . .

Where he to utter that formula he would surely die; he would unleash the ultimate disordering.

In "Tlön, Uqbar, Orbis Tertius" and "The Lottery in Babylon" Borges goes one step further. He examines in two stories that appear to be totally contradictory the relation of order and disorder to the laws of the universe and to man. Babylon appears in the story to be the ultimate human state required by the second law of thermodynamics, or, as Borges states, "Babylon is nothing else than an infinite game of chance." . . . Tlön, on the other hand, is the infusion of a perfectly ordered world into our own. . . . How then are we to reconcile the totally chaotic Babylon with the perfectly ordered Tlön? Borges gives us the answer in the stories themselves.

At the beginning of "Tlön, Uqbar, Orbis Tertius," Borges discusses "the composition of a novel in the first person, whose narrator would omit or disfigure the facts and indulge in various contradictions which would permit a few readers—very few readers—to perceive an atrocious and banal reality." . . . We have a further hint in "The Lottery in Babylon," where Borges states, "The scribe who writes a contract almost never fails to introduce some erroneous information. I myself, in this hasty declaration, have falsified some splendor, some atrocity." . . . Taking Borges at his word, we look to find some hint of an imperfection in the world of Tlön. In his discussion of the languages of the northern hemisphere of Tlön . . . , where nouns are nonexistent and are replaced by collections of monosyllabic adjectives. Borges gives us this example: the substitution of the noun "moon" by the expression "pale-orange-of-the-sky." But "sky" itself is a noun; hence Borges has made an error. If we assume the error is deliberate [for it appears in the original Spanish text] no reckless assumption in the light of Borges' extreme care in choosing words—then what is the "atrocious and banal reality" that he wants us to discover? Can it be that the creation of a perfectly ordered world, such as Tlön, would certainly violate the second law of thermodynamics and is thus impossible for man, a fallible being, who is himself subject to that law? For this reason, Tlön itself is subject to disorder and its perfect order is unreachable. (pp. 55-6)

The pursuit of perfection, then, is a paradoxical exhaustion of energies. Every action has an equal and opposite reaction. Whatever the endeavor, the more of one thing, the less of something else. Such is the Borgesian view: an antiprogressive view, perhaps, but one not easily dismissed, or, for that matter, denied. (p. 56)

Allan Franklin and Paul M. Levitt, "Borges and Entropy," in Review *(copyright © 1975 by the Center for Inter-American Relations, Inc.), Spring, 1975, pp. 54-6.*

Jorge Luis Borges is relapsing into the short story again, even though his *Obras completas* were published last year. . . . Obviously, "complete" doesn't mean the same thing as "posthumous." On the other hand, with Borges one never knows. I sometimes wonder whether he is the most dead of our living authors, or the most alive of our dead authors. . . . *El libro de arena* (The Book of Sand), [is composed of] thirteen stories (a Cabbala?) in which the author inquires into the mysteries that have always obsessed him: time, infinity, eternity, the universe. Borges in his book *de arena* (about sand) is Borges *in the arena,* into which he charges in order to challenge his usual formulas: mirror games, doubles, libraries that define and books that contain the world. But despite these often repeated mechanisms his vision of man and life remains impressive. The paradox of a blind man's vision, a vision that invites a disquieting wandering through the intricate inner labyrinth.

Borges seems to me, at this point in his life and work, to be both watchmaker and sorcerer's apprentice. He can no longer stop the clocks that, willingly or not, he set in motion with an ironic and relentless ticking. *El libro de arena* is another of his time-eating and time-defecating apparatuses. In Borges' machine (or perhaps organism) Christ may be Judas as in "*La secta de los treinta*" (The Sect of Thirty), the universe might be summed up as a puerile enterprise as in "*El congreso*" (The Congress), reality might manifest itself in a single word that might at the same time be any other word ("*Undr*"), hope might be the synonym of resigned despair as in "*Utopia de un hombre que está cansado*" (A Tired Man's Utopia). Et cetera, making clear that et cetera might even be synonymous with et cetera.

Of course, Borges has told us the same thing before, in other stories, perhaps in all his poems. But does it matter? At times the inner labyrinth, in its numberless meanders, leads us again to a place we think we know, which is the same and not the same at the same time. What is important is to pass through the labyrinth, as if we were simultaneously Theseus, the Minotaur, and Ariadne's thread, without letting ourselves be led astray by the book's epilogue, in which Borges tries to derail us (when does he not?) with apparently modest observations on sources, origins, and allegedly personal motivations. In that direction, the way out does not lie. Possibly the way out does not lie anywhere. Possibly it does exist but we are incapable of glimpsing it. Probably we glimpse it but don't want to accept it. And suddenly I ask myself if *El libro de arena* is not the only thing a blind man (who does see inside) can write in Argentina, which at this point in its history seems not to see at all, inside or out. (pp. 86-7)

Eduardo Gudiño Kieffer, "Letters from Buenos Aires," translated by Andrée Conrad in Review *(copyright © 1975 by the Center for Inter-American Relations, Inc.), Fall, 1975, pp. 85-8.*

The translators [of *An Introduction to English Literature*] tell us that Borges meant this little book as an introduction to the world of English literature for his Argentine students. And, brief though it is, they claim it deserves a place alongside such "grander compendiums" as those of Lang, Saintsbury, Sampson, etc. Whatever this place may one day be, I think it is safe to say that English professors here and in the United Kingdom would regard this book as a very bizarre introduction indeed.

To begin with, Borges has a way of presenting and explaining far more than that to which we are accustomed in terms of Germanic versus Celtic casts of mind. And he sees this early battle for the English soul erupting openly again in the 19th century when Carlyle's England, which "considered herself purely Germanic," was confronted by Matthew Arnold's essay "On the Study of Celtic Literature." (p. 91)

What makes his book an even more bizarre introduction, however (again from the point of view of English professors here and in the United Kingdom) is the very Borgesian choice of "representative authors and works of each period." They would not seem unusual until the modern periods, and then they would be sure to raise eyebrows. He might well find partisans for his unusual valuation of Arnold's poetry, but he would surely be seen as paying a most remarkable amount of attention to the likes of Kipling, Wells, Chesterton and a number of others now regarded as second rate, most notably Robert Louis Stevenson. And, more amazingly, he not only goes on to give precious space to the all but forgotten novels of one Charles Langbridge Morgan, but even brings in Arthur Conan Doyle, to whom, says Borges, "the world owes a single immortal character, Sherlock Holmes."

Obviously Borges is aware that his personal choices often go against the main current of conventional Anglo-Saxon opinion, to put it gently. . . . But he remains just as firm in his faith in their historic importance and in not dismissing their books for children as subliterary as he does in his respect for the detective story genre—something that most definitely and ineluctably marks him an exotic. Indeed, if writing for children made Kipling and Stevenson lose cast, there can be little doubt Poe's reputation suffered from writing detective stories, too. This, however, in the Anglo-Saxon world. Not in the Latin world, France included, where the high esteem in which Poe and his detective stories are held still puzzles American critics and can even make them smile while trying to avoid the subject.

There can be little doubt, I think, that this introduction to English literature is the kind that professors in our graduate schools would vigorously try to overcome in their arriving Argentine students. Or, failing to redeem them, finally refuse to lay hands on them and not grant them their degrees. There is no getting around the fact that a serious defense of the artistry of a Stevenson or a Wells is an inadvisable way to try to build an intellectual reputation. Borges, however, already has such a deservedly splendid one as a creative writer that he can do so and not lose credibility. This is because what he gives us here is unquestionably sound as an introduction to Borges' own English literature, unassailably based on his strong affections and detestations and on his moment in history. For that alone it is a valuable document. It proves he has not been joking all these years when, for example, he praises Kipling; many might have thought that he had been merely going against the grain, tongue-in-cheek, parading some anti-taste for the purpose of "astonishing," like a metaphysician from Tlön, that is to say, like a literary Dandy. Quite the contrary. Here, one of the most advanced (and most fashionable) writers of his time uncomplicatedly reveals himself as also being a most unfashionable gentleman of the Old School, literally speaking. But, being Borges, he is far more than some dull and conservative provincial Edwardian from Argentina. The mind revealed travels deep into this century wearing spats, but the book, it should also be said, is very funny. And a great deal in it is refreshing and true, as well as ec-

centric. The familiar objects considered are held at such unaccustomed angles, however, that reading the book one might often have trouble not perceiving it as another fiction by the author of "Pierre Menard," which has its own way of escaping genre. (pp. 91-3)

J. M. Alonso, "One Man's English Literature," in Review *(copyright © 1976 by the Center for Inter-American Relations, Inc.), Winter, 1976, pp. 91-3.*

The act of writing the *Ficciones* and *El Aleph* is . . . a classic instance of literature thriving in an adversary role, nourished by a struggle against untoward personal and political conditions. The subjective attitude of Borges the man is of course a complex matter, but in its literary version there are two noteworthy components: a nostalgia for combat in the past, and a learned and urbane liberalism vis-à-vis the present. It is highly significant that Borges's best knife stories, with 19th-century heroism as their subjects, were written at the height of the military-populist dictatorship in Argentina. In such a context the stories assume a character of subtle protest, of opposition through counter-example. . . .

Far better known is the opposition stance exemplified by Borges in his richest, most celebrated tales of fantasy. In "Tlön, Uqbar, Orbis Tertius" the narrator looks back on the lure, during the 1930s, of such false and facile "symmetries"—as in his words—"dialectical materialism, anti-Semitism, Nazism," all of which have culminated in the reigning hysteria over the planet Tlön. Impervious to, but alone amid these omnipresent Idealisms, the narrator finds silent refuge in Sir Thomas Browne's *Urn Burial,* an evocatively nostalgic work on classical archaeology. (p. 213)

This essentially is the apology of the civilized man of letters, the cultivated gentleman who, in a time of social upheaval, can side neither with the rebels nor with the reactionaries; experientially removed from the arena of social battles, lacking even the political information available in books, he dismisses Left and Right as equally false, unaware of how untenable his position is, though perfectly well aware of his irrelevance, in a crumbling social panorama. Ironically, Borges's fanciful view of the Hitler decade is itself an Idealist intellectual's interpretation. It sees the political turmoil as being brought about not by economic dislocations but by the mass appeal of a few seductive ideas—recalling those old-fashioned historians who felt that the French Revolution was "caused" by the writings of Rousseau and Voltaire. For all of Borges's artfulness and sophistication, the dizzying final paragraphs of "Tlön, Uqbar, Orbis Tertius" ultimately reflect the bewildered middle-way position of 1930s moderates, who, while fearful of the Axis, for ideological reasons were unwilling to make common cause with the anti-Fascist Left, tending instead to brush off both sides and label them fanatics.

Much the same spirit informs the last few pages of "The Library at Babel." There the narrator-librarian surveys a universe beset by ignorance, violence and plague, by ideological splintering and a tired sense that all has been said—much as Europe and Argentina must have appeared to Borges in 1941. The narrator, in need of reassurance, finds consolation in the fact of the Library itself, its untapped riches, its order, its grandeur. The story, unlike "Tlön,

Uqbar, Orbis Tertius,'' avoids any explicit social or political judgments, focusing instead on an epistemological question. Rather than attack the Right and the Left as equally and hopelessly Utopian, it depicts the scientific search for knowledge as futile and pointless. Though certain fundamental truths about the Library-Universe are occasionally hit upon—such as the decisive discovery that twenty-five letters form the basic components of all the books—these only whet people's appetite, giving rise to feverish quests for more knowledge, about one's self and about the cosmos, finally generating social division and personal despair. The truth seekers, unfortunately, cannot grasp what the narrator knows: that the Universe is "infinite," "useless" and "secret." The note on which the story ends is thus intellectual quietism rather than explicit social conservatism. (pp. 213-14)

This is the muted agony of an essentially traditionalist intellectual, a nostalgic man of letters whose world has become opaque, incomprehensible, and whose readings in the cultural heritage of a happier, more stable past furnish him no concrete hold on the present, when things crumble; he then projects his own historical bewilderment onto others. . . .

Borges's innovations in the Spanish language and in prose fiction give rise to a Latin American literary movement that is still in force. He is the prime mover in that impressive series of novels which includes Cortázar's *Hopscotch*, García Márquez's *One Hundred Years of Solitude* and Cabrera Infante's *Three Trapped Tigers*. As Carlos Fuentes remarked, without Borges the modern Latin American novel simply would not exist. Nonetheless, at the same time that Borges's work initiates a new literary period, it also signals a culmination, perhaps an ending to an earlier, lengthier social and cultural era, that of the domination of Latin America by its Europhile, moderately liberal upper classes. (p. 214)

Significantly, the novelists that have followed in Borges's wake have for the most part no personal links with his preferred social arrangements, their values and practices. Products of the urban middle class rather than the rural old-rich, they have depended not on family money or aristocratic patronage but on full-time work in such fields as teaching, translating, clerking, journalism and diplomacy. Their literary sources and subjects also differ substantially from those familiar Borgesian themes—on the one hand gaucho wistfulness, on the other Western culture under siege by the barbarians, by raiders of libraries, by vandals under the spell of Nazism, Marxism, Freudism, Peronism, Tlönism. . . . Julio Cortázar, for example, draws freely on French thought and surrealism, on anthropology and jazz. In another vein, Manuel Puig, Cabrera Infante and the younger Mexicans have found a locus of their own in films and Pop culture, while García Márquez, Fuentes and Vargas Llosa are varyingly influenced by Faulkner, Spanish American regionalism and Marx. Borges's urbane, erudite concern for minor Edwardians and the glories of Western civilization must appear quaint and irrelevant to these novelists—however much they admire his literary achievement.

The impact of Borges on American writing may be almost as great as was his earlier influence in Latin America. The American 1950s were a desert, a bleak stretch relieved only by one or two entertainments by Nabokov; for barrenness few literary epochs can match the cold-war years. The

quiet arrival of Borges's Englished fictions was to make a difference for the 1960s; his dreamlike artifices helped to stimulate a writing culture steeped in WASP-suburban metaphysics and Jewish neo-realism. The Argentine master reawakened for us the possibilities of far-fetched fancy, of formal exploration, of parody, intellectuality and wit. There are fantasies by Coover and Barthelme scarcely conceivable without the originating presence of Borges; allusions to the latter appear in Pynchon; and the longer novels of Barth are shaped in great degree by a theory of parody derived from Borges. (pp. 214-15)

[While] the stylistic and formal manner of Borges gave the literary professionals a task to perform, on the other hand the content of *Ficciones* supplied his readers with a precise political optics, a cluster of historical attitudes, a mode of social feeling that helped strengthen and define their ideological posture. During the 1960s the United States was torn by social conflict: riots in the ghetto, a hopeless war in Asia and the campus revolts ultimately created by that war. In this disorderly picture (comparable to that of Europe in the 1930s or Argentina in the 1940s) Borges's artifices provided a defense for those American academics who were as confused by the whole spectacle as our informant on Tlön or the librarian at Babel are bewildered by the sinister forces they evoke. Departmental chairmen, professors pushing the New Criticism, apolitical novelists like John Updike all shared a vague, inarticulate opposition to the war in Indochina, combined with an inability to sympathize with the highly vocal anti-war Left. They found in Borges's nightmares a sophisticated, inspired, vividly argued affirmation of their own position—i.e., an urbane aloofness, a middle-way quietism, a studied, even-handed, occasionally snobbish indifference to Right and Left, and in this case to the physical slaughter of the war and to the moral anger of the opposition activists. . . .

That our literary milieus found in Borges's fiction not only a peculiar artistic greatness but a useful social content as well, becomes clearer when one considers the comparatively small following thus gained in the United States by other Latin Americans. The fact is that, though García Márquez, Cortázar or Carpentier are comparable major artists—whose novels are read throughout the Spanish-speaking world, well received by North American reviewers, and intensely examined by professional Hispanists (who often as not miss the social meaning of their books)—they have not generated the cult, let alone the academic market, enjoyed here by Borges.

Part of the explanation for this must lie in the unsettling tone and content of these authors' works. The atmosphere of threat in Borges's tales comes off as bookish and abstract when contrasted, say, with the more concretely physical horrors in the stories of Julio Cortázar. The latter's *Hopscotch* puts into question the very value of European thought and learning; and his Dadaistic *Cronopios*—a commercial failure here—tweaks the nose of bourgeois respectability by disrupting routine. Alejo Carpentier's close affiliation with the Castro government could hardly promote his standing in the United States. His best-known novel, *The Lost Steps*, is built on a suggestion that "Europe," with all her rich culture, may be far more barbaric than the Indians of Venezuela—a notion contemplated by but a fringe of educated Americans. . . . (p. 216)

Similarly, García Márquez's *One Hundred Years of Soli-*

tude, one of the great novels of our time, has failed to arouse any literary excitement comparable to that inspired by the works of Borges. Again, however, the politics—anti-Americanism, pro-revolutionism—embedded within the texture of that book probably puts off and excludes a fair number of American readers. Moreover, García Márquez's humane, understanding portraits of his characters, so unlike the "literary" aura surrounding Borges's gauchos and hoods, probably meets with a certain amount of cultural incomprehension, even condescension, on the part of readers whose attitudes of superiority have everything to do with the generally low status of Latin American immigrants in this country. Finally, the novels of Fuentes and Vargas Llosa, steeped as they are in Marxist concepts, must inevitably fall on deaf ears with an American public largely hostile or indifferent to or ignorant of the cluster of issues raised by that strand of thought. (pp. 216-17)

[Borges's] stories . . . have a special significance in that they clear the way for numerous literary trends on both American continents, determining the shape of much fiction to come. In his part of the world, Borges's meticulous use of language—his careful construction of each sentence, his strict avoidance of Hispanic bombast, his cool understatement—has revolutionized Spanish prose; he thus stands in the same relation to current Latin novelists as Flaubert once did to numerous authors in Europe. At the same time, by rejecting realism and naturalism, he has opened up to our Northern writers a virgin field, led them to a wealth of new subjects and procedures—in a word, provided an alternative to Updike and Bellow. In successfully transcending the old modes of representation and discourse, Borges has accidentally done for us a job previously performed elsewhere by Poe, the fantast from a "barbarous," backward land who, by way of Baudelaire, freed French verse from its classic and romantic dead weights. . . .

[Besides] being a catalyst, a Poe to our new writers, Borges took on a conserving function, one allotted earlier to Camus, who deemed life absurd, history a nightmare, and action meaningless, preaching as man's sole path to salvation an indulgent metaphysics of subjectivity. The 1960s were too angry, too rough to be soothed by so callow a pessimism; Borges furnished a more concrete and objective stance, one built on more than personal feeling. To what he and others perceived as a mindless Left, and knowledge and history without hope or meaning, Borges gallantly counterpoised a consolation through books, through the verbal treasures of the past. (p. 217)

> *Gene H. Bell, "Borges—Literature and Politics North and South," in* The Nation *(copyright 1976 by the Nation Associates, Inc.), February 21, 1976, pp. 213-17.*

"I prefer minor characters," Borges writes. . . . [Man] is always man, great or low, real or mythical, Greek or Argentine, and victim of the same laws of love, treachery, and mortal time. Borges, profound and spoofing, likes to unfold, one by one, the contrasting layers of his creations, each negating and affirming the other. (p. 55)

Borges, with perhaps more nostalgia than irony, feels alien even to the Spanish language that he makes splendid and intricately lucid.

Indeed, no other writer—with the possible exception of

Kafka in German—manages, with relentless logic, to turn language upon itself, to reverse himself time after time within a sentence or paragraph, and effortlessly, as it were, come upon surprising yet inevitable conclusions. . . . Borges stretches the syntactic shape of Spanish to give a poem or story intricate, honeycombed layers of meaning. . . . [To] the normal language is added another stylistic strand expressing the author's extreme, idiosyncratic originality. A new literary language is invented . . . from the languages and literatures of Western Europe with which [Borges] is deeply involved. Borges consciously infuses the Spanish language with stylistic and thematic qualities of English authors in particular, those whom he records as having become his "habits": Chesterton, Hawthorne, Conrad, Kipling, and Lane's *Arabian Nights.* (p. 57)

Borges moves his central figure, in ["The Maker"] Homer, about in time, transforming his character. At one moment Homer is Odysseus and then, as Borges notes in the commentaries to *The Aleph and Other Stories,* Homer the Maker becomes Borges the creator, losing his sight and thereby gaining new memories of the past and the means to make new myths. In the first part of the story, the Maker is Odysseus. In lines that remarkably resemble Cavafy's Odysseus, Borges speaks of a young adventurous Odysseus. . . . But then as he ages, Odysseus becomes Homer—or Borges moving into "the slow twilight" of blindness—and the beautiful world begins to leave him, the night loses its multitude of stars, the ground becomes uncertain under his feet. His blindness is erected about him gradually like the walls in Cavafy's poem "Walls." The builders—like the builders in Kafka's parable—construct the walls unknown to the speaker. . . . There is a conspiracy of seclusion. And when the speaker recognizes that he is going blind, he shouts, unashamed. Mixing humor, irony, pathos, Borges writes: "he cried out; stoic fortitude had not yet been invented, and Hector could flee from Achilles without dishonor."

But then the aging, contemplative, resigned Homer-Borges emerges. For blindness endows him with memory of history and mythical geographies. . . . Borges' fable ends with a recognition that his voyage takes him to love and danger, Aphrodite and Ares. Black ships roam the seas in search of a loved island—but the gods will not save shrines or ships. It is his destiny to sing of them for man's hollow memory. But as for the end, Borges says *we are ignorant.* "These things we know, but not what he felt when he went down into his final darkness.". . . (pp. 61-2)

Yet elsewhere Borges does respond to the enigmas of blindness, age, and death. In the commentary to "The Maker," he says: "Eleven years after writing 'The Maker,' I seem to have recast my fable—without being aware of it—into a more narrowly autobiographical poem called 'In Praise of Darkness.'"

In "In Praise of Darkness," "Elogio de la sombra," Borges reconciles himself to old age and darkness. Old age, *la vejez,* "the name others give it," may be the time of happiness, he writes, for the animal is or is almost dead. Man and the soul remain. (p. 62)

Now darkness has mitigated time, and though his friends now do not have faces and books do not have letters, the darkness has restored memory, that is, the essential memory. Women are now what they were and the few things worth reading from the past he keeps rereading in his memory. Finally, he can forget everything. All the echoes, the real swords, the words, the love, the things. "I arrive at my center," he writes, "to my algebra and my key, / to my mirror . . . Soon I will know who I am." In darkness is self-knowledge. He wants what is the sin of Adam, Oedipus, of every rebel, peaceful or in wrath: to know oneself. It is clear that the voyage of Odysseus, the arrival naked and blind at the dark island before death, is a voyage toward wisdom, peace, to the self-acceptance and knowledge that Borges seeks. In a word Borges has entered into his solitude. . . . [He] is content to be alone, to be alive in himself. (p. 63)

Borges gives us the details of the ancient Babylonian lottery, the enigmas and danger of this ancient passion for gambling. But in Borges we have an element of dream, of phantasmagoria, of hoax. Borges likes to invent a reality, make it extravagantly unlikely, and then, detail by detail, impress us with its truthfulness. He will even insert names of personal friends, such as Rodríguez Monegal, a Uruguayan companion, until the imaginary is tantalizing, immediate. As Barrenechea points out, Borges' unreality is as real as his reality, and these two sides of his vision reinforce, rather than exclude, each other. Borges writes: "My feeling is that first sentences should be long in order to tear the reader out of his everyday life and firmly lodge him in an imaginary world. If an illustrious example be allowed me, Cervantes apparently felt the same way when he began his famous novel."

Yet as soon as he has established the imaginary world he uses every resource to prove that the imaginary world is real. He wishes, as did Quijote, to make Sancho also believe fantasy. What he accomplishes by fusing real and imaginary worlds is to give us both as one, as he gives us past and present time as one. The real is shadows, the other dream. By exalting the imagination he also questions assumptions of everyday reality. (pp. 67-8)

[Borges] so thoroughly describes his introspective meditations on death that a certain objectivity and distance prevail. To be sure, it is art, the poem or the story, that has allowed him temporary mastery of his life. He can view with more equanamity the dénouement of an illusory existence.

Yet even equanimity before death is a paradox, for Borges is not one-sided, and while at one moment he comes to terms with death, at another, the epiphany of darkness is one of terror and humiliation before illusion. The narrator in the last lines of "The Circular Ruins" says, when death finally comes to end his dream, "in terror, in humiliation, he understood that he, too, was an appearance, that someone else was dreaming him." Borges steps back again behind another mirror—of the artist. Borges of "Borges and I" is not one biological man but all the scribbles he has put on paper or the words he has dictated all his life. (p. 72)

Willis Barnstone, in Comparative Literature *(© copyright 1977 by University of Oregon; reprinted by permission), Winter, 1977.*

* * *

BOWERS, Edgar 1924-

Bowers is an American poet. His verse has been compared to Hart Crane's and John Crowe Ransom's in its naturalistic

concerns and structure. (See also *Contemporary Authors,* Vols. 5-8, rev. ed.)

The psychological response to loss, to death in particular, is the theme of several of Edgar Bowers' poems in his first book, *The Form of Loss.* (p. 611)

[Implicit] in most of Bowers' work is the attempt to understand the Judeo-Christian religious heritage from the point of view of eighteenth-century rationalism. Unlike many today, however, he regards Christian ethical values neither as conventions to be assumed for convenience nor as nostalgic vestiges to be emotionally explored and rejected, but as an emotional reality with which neither his rationalism nor any twentieth-century psychological scheme has, as yet, successfully dealt. Hence, there is a psychological uncertainty in a few poems on Christian themes, such as "Palm Sunday" (in *The Form of Loss*), that mars them. For the most part, as in the second of the "Two Poems on the Catholic Bavarians," the religious heritage never represents something irretrievably lost—and hence purely evocative—but presents a problem to be grappled with. His problem is . . . the understanding of his own nature in relation to his heritage. The limitations of eighteenth-century rationalism and of the response of nineteenth-century neoplatonism to it . . . increasingly concern Bowers. . . . Both the language and the experience of the poems in his second book, *The Astronomers* (1965), constitute a remarkable development. The Romantic extremes of self and nothingness are placed in a religious context in "A Song for Rising," and the sequence "Autumn Shade" records in detail the accession to the isolated consciousness of a reality that defines and encompasses it. In this context a means for successfully handling the problem of loss, which is conceived in "Autumn Shade" in terms of personal failure, is furnished. (p. 616)

Helen P. Trimpi, in The Southern Review *(copyright, 1973, by Helen P. Trimpi), Vol. IX, No. 3, Summer, 1973.*

Edgar Bowers's *Living Together* is a major publication, gathering his previous poems, some of which, including "Two Poems on the Catholic Bavarians," "An Afternoon at the Beach," and "The Astronomers of Mont Blanc," are in my judgment among the best American poems, and adding new poems. The title poem defines, with ghostly and lucid agony, how an absence becomes a presence, and its masterly variation of sound and pause is essential to the defining. All the new poems, except one polemical epigram, concern solitude: human communion despaired of, at times paradoxically or briefly reached; solipsism (more precisely, philosophical problems caused by the selfhood of the observer); and the opacity and indifference of nature. . . . The beauty of structure, rhythm, imagery, and diction of his poems belies the doubt, isolation, and valuelessness he writes of and presumes. Value, knowledge, beauty, faith—and an epistemology that makes them impossible—are his recurrent subjects, unsolved but explored with subtlety, dignity, and pain. (p. 397)

Paul Ramsey, in Sewanee Review *(reprinted by permission of the editor, © 1974 by The University of the South), Spring, 1974.*

The poems of Edgar Bowers [in *Living Together*] are so carefully and honestly made that it is ungracious to carp at them. And yet, some of the time, I do. . . . I for one have absolutely no objection to iambic quatrains. Think of Hart Crane. Of John Crowe Ransom. But [some of Bowers'] correct lines somehow do not move. Or consider all of "Chorus for the Untenured Personnel" (and I do like the title and the thought):

> If we are on probation, what's our crime?
> Original sin, mysterious want of grace,
> The apple that we ate in a happier time
> Of learning, friendship, courtesy, and wit—
> Our innocence! For see, the gorgon's face,
> The discipline of hatred, our true text.
> We read, in darkness visible, the X.

But what a mouthful of abstractions, and oh that saving apple, the only solid thing to bite on! So again, in five lines of "From William Tyndale to John Frith," we find "sweet threats," "malicious love," "dangerous fear of violence," "illusion's goodness," "worldly innocence," "just persuasion's old hypocrisy." Is it too carnal of us if we remain unmoved by these airy oxymorons? But if not moved, still admiring, since the intelligence and its expression are there. (pp. 461-62)

> *Richmond Lattimore, in* The Hudson Review *(copyright © 1974 by The Hudson Review, Inc.; reprinted by permission), Vol. XXVII, No. 3, Autumn, 1974.*

Because Edgar Bowers writes most commonly in terms of the relationship of intelligence to the natural world of sun, ocean, plants, and animals as well as to his own emotional nature and physical being, he is confronted with certain problems that arise from intelligence itself. The intellect has a strong tendency to try to reduce real being to only the "intelligible" in the Neoplatonic and post-Cartesian sense —that which participates in intellect's principle of oneness —and to deny real being to that which is not intelligible in this sense. It does this in part because it hopes to attain rational certainty in that way. But in so doing it runs the risk of misunderstanding the more complicated nature of reality. For while what is intelligible in this sense surely may be real, what is not so intelligible may also be real, and there are varying degrees of intelligibility in reality. (p. 48)

Bowers' early poetry seems to be influenced by Neoplatonic symbolisms of light and dark in which certain kinds of light are used metaphorically for the intelligible—that which implicitly alone has real being—and "darkness" for the other realm of experience—that which, because it is sensory and changeable, seems to lack real being. (p. 49)

It is, on the one hand, evidently possible for the purely intelligible to be apotheosized as deity, as in the fundamental Neoplatonic position, while, on the other hand, certain powerful feelings about natural events (as in the Romantic poets) or certain more obscure emotions (as in Romantic Christianism) can be so apotheosized. God may be pure Intelligence or pure obscurity. Reactions to these options lie behind the experiences of alienation from divinity explored in "Grove and Building," where divinity is seen as the pure intelligence of "unshadowed being," and in "Adam's Song to Heaven," where "Heaven" is the "Ghostly abyss wherein perfection hides." Reactions to the options also affect "Palm Sunday" and "An Answer," where divinity is conceived as the ambivalent object of the purely emotional responses of the heart to Christian symbols. Bowers, quite rightly in my view, looks suspiciously

upon divinity conceived in either of these limited ways. Moreover, seen in his terms, man's intellectual responsibility is to principles of reason alone, since the allegiances that religious faith would claim, being founded solely on emotion, seem not above the suspicion of self-deceiving "guile." His poems both in content and in form are a constant affirmation of this responsibility and the difficulties of it. They achieve cumulatively great power from their constant return to the central issues of contemporary human experience—which is not to say that some of the poems are not more successful than others. (pp. 51-2)

The philosophical assumptions of Bowers' poems are: first, that essential being and phenomenal being are two different orders of reality. Second, that that which is essential (one, eternal, and self-identical)—such as divinity and the dead—permanently is. Third, that that which is phenomenal (multiple, temporal, and subject to change)—such as our personal lives and the world known to our senses—merely exists temporarily. Corollaries of these assumptions are: first, that if we human beings "exist," then pure being does not exist, for its essential qualities exclude the qualities of existence, which are change, multiplicity, and corruptibility; in other words, pure being is existentially neutral. Second, in its purity from the contamination of existence, essential being may appear to us to be either "nothing" (irrelevant), or unreal, or only a projection of our own consciousness, for in our sense of being (phenomenal existence) it *is* not. Third, we in our separateness from essential being—in the sense of eternal being—*are* not and therefore may appear to it to be "nothing" or only insubstantial reflections of itself.

Assumptions such as these, though not so expressed, directly affect Bowers' conceptions of and attitudes toward divinity and the dead. For example, the divinity who is rejected in "Adam's Song to Heaven" is the old essentialistic Neoplatonic pure Being who is one, eternal, and self-identical, and who seems utterly alien to us unless construed as a pure object of mind mirroring our mind narcissistically, while we exist as multiple, changing, and evanescent existent beings. . . . Alienation from such a divinity is an understandable attitude. The "Heaven" in question carries with it all the cold, indifferent, totalitarian qualities of the Hegelian "Absolute" and the Neoplatonic "One," deities most would not hesitate to reject. But it is not the "Heaven" of Ben Jonson's "To Heaven." . . . .

Bowers' Adam speaks to "Heaven" which is the deity as conceived by the fallen Adam of the poem. The figures of Adam, Eve, and the Serpent, though taken from Revelations, have been adapted to Neoplatonic and Gnostic religious feelings and cosmology. Yet [the poem] may be understood and appreciated from the point of view of Christian experience as [an] accurate [statement] about the unredeemed condition of the fallen angels and fallen man. (pp. 65-6)

[There] is in Bowers' later poetry an attempt to move out of the inherited polarized duality of intelligence and nature, with its implicit roots in philosophical essentialism, toward an understanding of the function of intelligence in the total context of being. This results in some of his most interesting and difficult poems: "Of an Etching," "In a Darkness," "The Mirror," "The Dream," "The Centaur Overheard," the "Autumn Shade" sequence, "Living Together," and "Insomnia." Several of these poems explore the problem through the question of personal identity and in terms of various "images" of the self—images which are for the most part ideal constructions of the poet's "essential" being that are made by his intellect. The problem deliberated is how to relate the ideal constructs to phenomenal experience, and how to deal with the fact that the ideal construct, because it partakes of essential (true) being, seems more truly to be than the phenomenal experience which, because it merely exists, seems not truly to be. In none of them, with the exception of "Autumn Shade," does Bowers explore the option of a self who would participate in a kind of existence that transcends both the ideal self construed by reason and the phenomenal self that experiences its material life. (pp. 67-8)

The most extensive exploration of the problem of the essential self and the phenomenal self and a concluding resignation of the problem is recorded in the sequence "Autumn Shade." Although Bowers seems generally to conceive the problem in terms analogous to contemporary Existentialist terms, there is an illumination recorded in section 9 of "Autumn Shade" which suggests a possible full resolution in truly existential terms through which the selves would participate in the same fully existent order of reality. In this section the intellect, who is the "I" of the poem (recalling the intellect of "Oedipus at Colonus" who measured "archaic fugitive defect"), through the medium of the "specter" records a vision of a future whole man in whom essential and phenomenal being might be conjoined in one order of reality and who would perceive other beings as participating in the same order. For the new condition he uses light in an entirely new symbolic way, employing "substantial light" to represent existential being. . . . Yet the insight is momentary, almost illusory, and the conclusion of the poem is a return to nearly the original dilemma in which one kind of being entails the absolute sacrifice of the other, i.e., light must exclude shade, intelligence must exclude nature, because each belongs to a mutually exclusive order of reality—in one of which essences *are* and in the other phenomena *exist*.

The resignation expressed at the close of "Autumn Shade" and dealt with in some of the more difficult poems, such as "Living Together," "The Dream," and "Insomnia," is a kind of resolution, apparently, in contemporary Existentialist terms wherein essential being is put aside, rejected, or demoted for a kind of experience which is called "existence," but is only that aspect of being that is purely phenomenal or, loosely speaking, sensory. The "other" of the contemporary Existentialist is not existential in the Thomistic sense but is a construction of the purely phenomenal, and it is imaged in section 9 as a shadow, or specter, or some kind of shadowy being, because the Existentialist still clings to the basic assumption that *either* essence *or* existence is really real; that is, that both kinds of experience cannot subsist in the same order of reality. But the split between essence and existence is not healed by allowing the specter to emerge as specter in the daylight and by living with it, because this does not really grant reality to the natural self. The natural self is still only a phantom, an apparition, and is not acknowledged to be existent in the same order of reality as the intellect. The natural self must be acknowledged as participant in the same order of reality as the intellect for it to cease to haunt the intellect. (pp. 69-70)

Helen P. Trimpi, in The Southern Review *(copyright, 1977, by Helen P. Trimpi), Vol. 13, No. 1, Winter, 1977.*

BRAUTIGAN, Richard   1935-

Brautigan is an unconventional American poet and novelist whose work defies easy classification. He has been labeled "beat" and bizarre, or surreal, as well as whimsically humorous, nostalgic. Brautigan's imagery is sharp, his language both inventive and casual. He deals often with the subject of American myth, perhaps most notably in the novel *Trout Fishing in America*. (See also *CLC*, Vols. 1, 3, 5, and *Contemporary Authors*, Vols. 53-56.)

Brautigan's images are always unmaking themselves, calling themselves into question, or being unpredictably dropped. His is a world without permanence. It is barely sustained even by the presence of the writer. (In fact, in *In Watermelon Sugar*, the artist is a dreamer who lives in a collective called "ideath.") Self-consciously a reaction against the rigidity of cultural symbols and literary language, the parodic art of Brautigan informs us that any metaphor is potentially deadening to the world and the imagination. At most, each individual experience can open the possibility of a deceptively simply flight of fancy.

Yet each metaphor Brautigan creates is, more often than not, a reflection on the state of language systems today. There is no possibility, he feels, of actually reaching a purified, new language; neither is there a possibility for a pure epistemological experience of the world-in-itself. His descriptions of trout fishing in America are never free from the contemporary linguistic and cultural sedimentation in which we are all immersed.

Even recognizing these limitations, however, his images attempt to get closer to the specific experience (especially pastoral) that originally stimulated the images which have now become petrified, false, and deadly symbols of the "American way of life." His style generally works in two ways. Either he assumes a forced naïveté (the devaluation of ego) in order to allow a simple event to manifest itself, just beyond any definite personal frame of reference—but still allowing him to delight in creating a new, if tenuous, image based on that event. Or he parodies an experience as it exists linguistically to us in its absurd mixture of rigid moral valuation and inappropriate technological jargon. For example, Brautigan creates some of the most particularly ungainly metaphors, linking such disparate elements as telephone booths and trout streams, telephone repair men and fishermen. These metaphors call attention not only to the radical newness of the analogy, thus freeing it from a closed system of received meanings, but they also insure, by their very ungainliness, their transitory existence. At most, they may sustain themselves long enough to give birth to another metaphor or variation on themselves. But invariably, they are always discarded to allow a new experience to manifest itself, and with it, a new possibility for improvisation with the world. His stories are in a constant flux of emerging and receding. Frequently the sections appear static because they evidence only a single moment of creation. It is an abortive fiction. His metaphors lead toward little more than themselves. The experiences he describes are evoked for their own worth, and for the value of allowing the mind to play with the possibilities of the imagination. But that imagination is never sustained in absence of the original experience which is forever fleeing from consciousness. (pp. 354-55)

Charles Russell, in Modern Fiction Studies

(copyright © 1974, by Purdue Research Foundation, West Lafayette, Indiana, U.S.A.), Autumn, 1974.

Recent Brautigan comes equipped with helpfully generic subtitles: after '. . . An Historical Romance 1966', after '. . . A Gothic Western', we come to '. . . A Perverse Mystery' [*Willard and His Bowling Trophies*]. The perversity is supplied by Bob and Constance, half-hearted bondage kinks whose idea of foreplay is a good browse in *The Greek Anthology;* they are rather sad and cry a lot. The mystery consists in the whereabouts of a terrific set of bowling trophies stolen from some famous bowlers called the Logan Brothers; they are rather tough. Downstairs from Bob and Constance live John and Pat, who actually have the trophies, and keep them arranged round Willard, a papier-mâché bird. John and Pat are very fond of Willard, always wish him goodnight, and even consider taking him to a Greta Garbo movie; they are rather soppy.

Gosh, that's torn it: I was only explaining the title, and find I've given away the entire plot. But that always seems to be the way with Mr Brautigan's winsome and gruelly fictionettes. I was rather cross, actually, about the Perverse Mystery bit, because thinking up a subtitle is at least one way of using the vacant brain-space which reading Brautigan leaves one. Still, being a conscientious critic, I puzzled genially at the perverse mystery of his staggering popularity. How can it be that whole campuses crease themselves at a humour which seems no more than whacky cuteness? How is it, when others wonder at the 'precise coolness of language' . . . of this 'born writer' . . . , that one feels appalled at the glaring and embarrassing bits of 'writing'? . . . Finally, I wondered, how can anyone bear the pacelessness of it all? You plod through chapterino 8 (a whole page), which tells you how the Logan Brothers are waiting in a dingy hotel for a phone call to tell them where their bowling trophies are, and you are rewarded with this opening to chapterino 9:

> Meanwhile—less than a mile away from the tiny dingy hotel room where the Logan brothers waited for a telephone call which would provide them with the locations of the bowling trophies—Willard . . .

It's like following a strip cartoon every day—one step back for every two forward; terrific, of course, for those with spaced-out memories. (p. 685)

Julian Barnes, in New Statesman (© *1976 The Statesman & Nation Publishing Co. Ltd.), May 21, 1976.*

Richard Brautigan inspired some foolish praise in his time, a time that ended almost as soon as it began, but he never angled for it and that is to his credit. He is a serious writer, certainly, but the mark of his seriousness is in his craft, especially as a stylist; he is not pretentious. Thus his 1971 novel, "The Abortion," is dedicated to someone named Frank, apparently a slow reader: "come on in—/ read novel—/ it's on the table / in front room. I'll be back / in about / 2 hours." And the protagonist of his new book is identified as a "very well-known American humorist." Not novelist or poet, not even writer—just humorist.

For at his best that is what Brautigan is. Compared to Doris Lessing or Frank O'Hara he's a midget, but he stands tall enough next to Woody Allen, or even Robert Benchley or George Ade; on a small scale he has been an original and an innovator. As might have been predicted, however, "Sombrero Fallout" does not represent Brautigan at his best. Not only is it the least funny of his books, but its paucity of humor is intentional, capping a dilemma that would appear to be permanent: he no longer knows what to write about. . . .

Brautigan's reputation is based on a surrealism notable for its grace, its matter-of-fact flow; his narrative technique is so conversational and pellucid that preternatural details and crazy coincidences don't even ripple its surface. . . . [In his fiction] Brautigan documented a way of life in which his style of surrealism was almost second nature, evoking 60's bohemianism far more intensely than Kerouac ever did that of the 50's. His world was passive and goofy; his voice displayed whimsical (if not coy) amazement at the most banal of events. As he teetered between the edge of comfort and the edge of survival, Brautigan was often sad but never pessimistic.

As the broad attraction of this gentle vision among the literate young became apparent, however, Brautigan was transformed from an impecunious bohemian into a successful popular author. . . . What's more, after "The Abortion," a bohemian novel much fatter and more perfunctory than the earlier ones, Brautigan tried to do what popular authors do —invent plots and characters. He has not proved to be very good at this, and his failure seems to have cut into his optimism quite a bit.

The full title of the new book is "Sombrero Fallout: A Japanese Novel." The subtitle is ambiguous, the book is dedicated to a Japanese novelist of the respectably perverse whose main similarity to the old optimistic Brautigan is brevity. But if in two previous novels Brautigan has toyed with popular forms, this time he resorts to the most hackneyed of pretentious literary devices: the self-conscious, self-lacerating author/protagonist and his novel within a novel. (p. 4)

Robert Christgau, in The New York Times Book Review (© *1976 by The New York Times Company; reprinted by permission), October 10, 1976.*

The subtitle of ["Dreaming of Babylon"], "A Private Eye Novel 1942," should have served as a tip-off. Brautigan, or his publisher, or his editor—or maybe all three in concert— wanted to spell it out for the reader to make sure we got it. The up-front shill announces that the writer is using a genre to display his talent. I have news for them.

On page 1 the shamus-narrator C. Card (to be differentiated coyly from S. Spade) tells us that he was 4-F in World War II, but he wasn't unpatriotic because "I had fought my World War II five years before in Spain and had a couple of bullet holes in my a— to prove it." By using a common anatomical vulgarity, the link with the 1940's is immediately ruptured. . . .

What Brautigan has done is to impose a 60's mentality on what he supposes to be a 40's form. C. Card is our current impotent hero—super *schlep*. . . .

The "Babylon" reference is to his personal dreamland, where he sojourns from reality. Babylon was first induced when he got beaned by a baseball while trying out for pro ball. In Babylon's exotic clime C. Card has comic-strip adventures with his luscious girlfriend, "Nana-dirat." All this is to engage the 60's heads who hold Brautigan in such high esteem.

Brautigan's book makes the same mistake as Peter Bogdanovich's "nostalgic" movies. Both men think that by surrounding their works with the proper dated artifacts they have captured a period, while all they have caught are the labels. That a philosophic stance existed in the 40's has escaped them. And their efforts can't be defined as parody or homage, since the original material must be understood before one can be contemptuous or affectionate toward it.

So the result in this basically plotless book is cartooning. Brautigan delivers a litany of screwups and lame jokes. It's the ice age seen through Fred Flintstone.

But it should be remembered that Brautigan has graced his public in the past, and all writers have off days. His editor should have served him better. Instead of encouraging him on this caper, he should have sent Brautigan off fishing somewhere in America.

> *Joe Flaherty, "The Sam Spade Caper," in* The New York Times Book Review (© *1977 by The New York Times Company; reprinted by permission), September 25, 1977, p. 20.*

It is January 2, 1942, and C. Card [the protagonist of "Dreaming of Babylon"], the sorriest private eye in San Francisco, is down to his last chance. Dead broke, two months behind on his rent, unable even to buy bullets for his gun, he has one thing to look forward to: a meeting at six o'clock this evening with a mysterious client. All he has to do is keep the hunger pangs down, find some bullets, and stop dreaming of Babylon. Babylon is the fantasy world that C. Card escapes to whenever he can, and dreaming of Babylon is a sure way of missing his stop on the bus, losing touch with reality, and messing up in general. The suspense of waiting for that six o'clock meeting—and then of the tricky assignment that C. Card is given—is as mechanically constructed as a toy train, but that wouldn't be so bad if the payoff weren't so flat. Richard Brautigan has mastered all the forms of children's fiction—the short, easy-to-read sentences and paragraphs and chapters, the light touches of fantasy and humor—and children's fiction for adults is what this pretty skimpy book is all about. (p. 230)

> The New Yorker (© *1977 by The New Yorker Magazine, Inc.), November 21, 1977.*

A private eye novel 1942 as the subtitle says, would mean to this reader *Maltese Falcon* and Dashiell Hammett, a knock-em-down-set-em-up-in-the-other-alley type of detective novel. Not so [*Dreaming of Babylon*]. It wallows in the thoughts of the P.I. which have haunted him since childhood, of interest only to himself. When he finally meets the client he set out to meet at the beginning, the book is half over, and *all* over for interest! One was tempted to quit at that point, but integrity as a critic and fairness to the author kept one going. A direct quote from the P.I. "This whole thing was just like a pulp detective story. I couldn't believe it," is only half right. The only resemblance to a private eye story circa 1942 begins and ends with a P.I. and a beautiful girl. The end of the quote expresses this reviewer's opinion, "I couldn't believe it."

Another direct quote—"a bite out of a bacon, lettuce and tomato sandwich, the old BLT"—sound more like a 1970's quote from *Get Smart!*

[Brautigan] does make an attempt to redeem himself at the halfway point by switching to humor (?), but it's too forced to work. All in all, a book to forget. (p. 33)

> *Rick Davis, in* West Coast Review of Books *(copyright 1978 by Rapport Publishing Co., Inc.), Vol. 4, No. 1 (January, 1978).*

*   *   *

BRETON, André   1896-1966

Breton was a French novelist, essayist, and poet. The founder of surrealism, Breton viewed himself as the infallible pontiff of the movement and instituted surrealist publications, symposiums, and expositions in France, Mexico, and the United States. (See also *CLC*, Vol. 2, and *Contemporary Authors*, Vols. 19-20; obituary, Vols. 25-28, rev. ed.; *Contemporary Authors Permanent Series*, Vol. 2.)

André Breton felt that the poet's specific role is to produce emotional states in which the union between opposites is experienced as true.

Art historians are apt to view Surrealism as a form of escape from reality, reducing it thereby to a variant of the doctrine of art for art's sake. Surrealists refuse to surrender to the abject conditions of reality. Breton has said that an urgent task of the revolutionary poet in wartime was to write love poems. His *Fata Morgana* is a hymn to love written in America during the last war.... For the Surrealists, words and colors are but a means of exploring the identity of opposites, while chance encounters and games without rules are events loaded with poetic meaning.

Sartre has criticized Surrealism for its failure to achieve its goal and produce the synthesis between opposites. He was thinking in terms of an aesthetic solution which Breton expressly excluded by postulating that the contradiction is resolved at the vanishing point of the mind's eye.... Art historians and critics measure the Surrealist contribution in terms of a retreat from Cubism or an advance toward Abstract Expressionism; they are involved with development of style. Breton despised this approach. He was categorically opposed to purely aesthetic exhibitions of Surrealist works.... (p. 101)

In poetry Breton went beyond Mallarmé, who merely flirted with chance. Breton gambled with chance. Chance is to the poet of an atheist era what inspiration was for the poet graced by God, while automatic writing is the Surrealist's counterpart of religious and psychoanalytical confession. (p. 102)

> *Nicolas Calas, "The Point of the Mind: André Breton" (originally published in* Arts Magazine, *December 1966–January 1967), in his* Art in the Age of Risk and Other Essays *(copyright © 1968 by Nicolas Calas; reprinted by permission of the publishers, E. P. Dutton & Co., Inc.), Dutton, 1968, pp. 100-03.*

[Breton's poetry is] a miraculous widening of experience and "exaltation" of life. The famous statement on surrealist language which Breton calls "Les Mots sans rides" (1924) demands that the full significance of language and its essential youthfulness be restored, so that it can intensify and expand everything it touches. It is not simply a matter of juxtaposing the words to create new elements, but of rejuvenating the word itself. All the surrealist word games, puns, anagrams, and aphorisms with double meanings are part of this attempt to heighten the power of language and to widen its scope.

Along with the word play goes the play of images, the goal of both being "to multiply the short-circuits," as Breton says in the second manifesto (1930), that is, to sabotage as frequently and as definitively as possible the usual "realistic insanities" and to show what is on the other side of the accepted reality. The surrealist image is necessarily shocking—it destroys the conventional laws of association and logic, so that the objects which compose it, instead of seeming to fit side by side naturally and normally, "shriek at finding themselves together." But the same electrical force that splits up the habitual relationships of the ordinary world has the power to fuse all that has previously been separate. Breton will frequently use the metaphor of electricity in his theoretical writings, with all its implications of intensity, shock, fusion, and a highly dramatic quality proper to surrealism. He thinks of poetry as a "conductor of mental electricity" and his criterion for the success of art is the achievement of a particular "fusion of the mind and the heart in a verbal or plastic mold which shows itself in some way to be electrically appropriate to it." (pp. 69-70)

Breton's poems, even the first ones, written long before his theories on art were formulated, show the same traits he will require of all surrealist poets and artists. The interplay of words and images is complex, particularly in the techniques of fusion and generation of new words and images, and the poems are in no way descriptive of any conventional vision of reality. (pp. 72-3)

The short prose poem called "Age" . . . is typical of Breton's earliest poetry. Some of the other poems in the collection *Mont de piété* are like Mallarmé in tone, or like Valéry; this one is closer to Rimbaud, beginning: "Aube, adieu! Je sors du bois hanté, j'affronte les routes, croix torrides." / (Dawn, farewell! I leave the haunted woods, I brave the highways, sweltering crosses). But the images already show . . . striking juxtapositions. . . .

> Shirts clotted on the chair. A silk hat starts off my chase with its reflections. Man . . . A mirror avenges you and treats me as a conquered prey, naked. The moment returns to cast a patina on the flesh.
>
> Houses, I free myself from dry walls. Someone is shaking something! A tender bed is mocked with crowns.
>
> Reach the exhausting poetry of landings.
>
> (pp. 73-4)

The poem is just as complicated, as irrational, and as alienating to the reader as any later poem, and perhaps more so. Most of Breton's early poetry lacks the sentimental undertone of his more famous work, but it is no less a demonstration of many-level vision and language. It is surrealist in form if not in content. (p. 75)

Surrealist play at its best is supposed to produce in the reader an involuntary sense of surprise which is disturbing to his ordinary perception of the universe and to his ordinary verbal framework. "Clair de terre" replaces the ordinary "clair de lune" as "plutôt la vie" replaces the ordinary "plutôt la mort," so that the positive present terms substitute for the distant clichés. The poem contains many such tricks: . . .

> Rather life than these thermal establishments
> Where necklaces wait on you
> Rather life long and unfavorable
> Even if the books were to close here on shelves not
>   so soft.

The nightmare world to which even life is preferable is made up of things serving the wrong purpose, of necklaces (a half-pun on students, "écoliers") doing the housework and soft bookshelves holding up the books, the latter image having the same disquieting effect as the soft watches of Dali, Méret Oppenheim's fur teacup, Man Ray's nail-studded iron, or "these overripe stones" ("ces pierres blettes") we are forced to imagine earlier in the poem. To introduce the most uncomfortable images by a "these" is to engage the reader in the poem, to make him consider at close range the stones turning soft like fruit. The qualities by which we ordinarily define our universe, like the hardness of stones and the stability of bookshelves, have given way to less stable qualities suited to the new space where, says Breton in his article on Matta, there is "a constant interchange of the visual and the visonary." If the poet sees the stones as soft, they *are* potentially soft. (p. 76)

In *Les Vases communicants* . . . there are three images of primary importance. There is the optimistic image of the constantly widening circle of possibilities, including and conferring unlimited expansion upon everything that exists; the explanatory image of the communicating vessels itself, with the secondary image of a capillary tissue connecting the interior world to the exterior world; and the most essential and most complex image of two men, one consciously immobile at the center of the whirlwind ("Removed from the contingencies of time and place, he really appears to be the pivot of this whirlwind itself, the supreme mediator") and the other immersed in his immediate circumstances, the fog made up of "the density of the things immediately perceptible when I open my eyes." Since these men personify sleep and wakefulness, they are really an extension in human terms of the communicating vessels of interior vision and the exterior world. (Surrealist man is, of course, a combination of both, a resolution of the "real" and the "unreal.") When Breton announces, later in this same essay, that poets must find a way to "put man back at the heart of the universe, to abstract him for a moment from the events that would decompose him, to remind him that he is, for all the sorrow and joy external to him, an indefinitely perfectible place of resolution and echo," he is returning to the same image. In some senses, this is the basic perception for him, and all the other images he uses to depict the surrealist universe depend on this one. . . . (pp. 77-8)

[In *Les Etats-Généraux*] Breton suggests the actual insignificance of the individual personality, since the memory may be only a product of the imagination. There is no justification for the individual's belief in his own nature as a fixed, reliable starting point for experience. Such uncertainty about the continuation of the self is a necessary product (and cause) of *vertige:* linked to the consciousness of duality, it will never be absent from surrealist thought even in its moments of highest optimism.

Breton and the other surrealists, although they try to regain the child's attitude of *presence* and immediacy, are constantly haunted by the sense of inner disunity and by the more obvious outer division between man and his surroundings. Breton's consciousness of isolation and distance pervades his writings from 1924 to 1932. In *Poisson soluble* (1924) the poet imagines himself alone behind a window, all he observes contributing to his sense of *ennui:* . . .

> The hours, the pain, I keep no rational account of them; I am alone, I look out of the window; there are no passers-by, or rather no one *passes*. . . . You don't know this gentlemen? It's Mr. The Same. May I introduce Mrs. Mrs. And their children.

In *Le Revolver à cheveux blancs* (1932) windows separate the watcher within from odd and vaguely threatening spectacles: . . .

> I am at the window far off in a terror-stricken city
> Outside, men in opera hats follow regularly on each
>   others' steps.

Or, as "windows of hell," they frame bizarre and erotic gestures for the benefit of someone watching from without; or again, they are frames for the marvelous: . . .

> Beautiful windows with their flaming hair in the black
>   night
> Beautiful windows of warning cries and kisses.

The probable reference to red curtains ("flaming hair") is simply a positive interpretation of the "windows of hell" in the poem just mentioned, since the cries and kisses could refer to the same kind of sadistic-erotic spectacle (although the two poems differ in every other way). The oppositions in color (red, black) and possibly also in emotion (cries, kisses) form the structure of the spectacle in each case, all three of these poems demonstrating a theatrical impulse within the poem characteristic of much of Breton's poetry. (pp. 79-81)

In this same collection the associated and familiar theme of the double is strikingly presented in the poem "Rideau rideau," where the poet's life is played out on the scene of a theater, the baroque spectacle including not only the actor playing Breton, but another man in a Breton mask, and on a level below the stage, a silhouette of Breton outlined on a white wall in fire, with a bullet in his heart. In a less dramatic form, "Les Attitudes spectrales" indicates the voluntary and inevitable split between the poet and the world and the parallel separation within the poet himself in a light manner completely devoid of self-pity: . . .

> I attach no importance to life
> I do not pin the slightest butterfly of life to importance
> I do not matter in life
> But the branches of salt the white branches
> All the bubbles of shadow
> And the sea anemones
> Descend and breathe inside my thought
> Tears well up which I do not shed
> Steps I do not take which are steps twice over
> And which are remembered by the sand in the rising tide
>   . . .
> I was already as old as I am now
> And I watched over myself my thought like a night
>   watchman in an immense factory.

Here all the objects which penetrate his contemplation give the impression of delicacy or lightness, as if any harsh or heavy elements must be deliberately eliminated from the poem. Even the suggestion of sadness which enters ("des pleurs") is quickly covered over by his denial of personal concern ("que je ne verse pas"). As the poet is detached from the action, he is equally detached from his own thought: only the sand remembers the steps which have been taken. The facile word play matches the lightness of the images: "attacher . . . épingles," "des pas . . . pas . . . sont deux fois des pas." This poem extends the separation within the poet to the point where he can convincingly speak of his eyes having watched himself burning, a theme expanded in the quiet and beautiful "Vigilance." In the latter poem, the poet dreams of setting fire to his own room and himself sleeping within it, so that free of material obstacles he may enter the world of primary unity both invisible and unaware of the dragging steps of the living and the unpurified. . . .

> I see the bones of the sun
> Through the hawthorn of the rain
>
>   . . .
>
> At last I touch only the heart of things I hold the thread.

In this pure and serious atmosphere there is no trace of *ennui*. The initial suffering is only seen, not felt, and the isolation from the passersby is voluntarily chosen by the poet who is finally able to replace his unhappy consciousness of duality and of distance by a sense of unity and presence. . . .

> The life of presence nothing but presence.

Like the man immobile in the middle of the whirlwind in *Les Vases communicants* . . . , he rediscovers the calm vision at the center of things where play is no longer necessary to expand the perception and where all separations are resolved within an infinite series of possible links continuously recreated by the poet's imagination: "Je tiens le fil." (pp. 81-3)

For Breton, woman as the incarnation of irrationality is the eternal marvelous; in [*L'Amour fou*] he says quite simply that *l'amour absolu,* which takes place on the same level as *l'amour fou* and as Benjamin Péret's *amour sublime,* is man's only guarantee that all his endeavors are not undertaken in vain, and in *Arcane 17* (1945), he maintains that earthly salvation can come only through the redemptive power of woman. . . . In *L'Air de l'eau* (1934) there are two love poems which exemplify surrealist poetry at its best and surrealist vision in its simplest and most moving form. The first poem begins with the paradox "Every time for the first time" ("Toujours pour la première fois"); since at each moment he falls in love with the woman *again* (dynamically opposed to the static condition of *still* loving her) as if he were actually seeing her for the first time, he can say that he scarcely knows her even by sight (=recognizes her). Her appearance seems to change and so his love for her is always new, in spite of what we might call the "real" conditions within the surrealist vision. "Reality" here assumes a less narrow sense, for as the woman enters an imaginary house and disappears behind imaginary curtains, the poet who watches her from his window is suddenly aware of: . . .

The unique rending
Of the facade and of my heart
The more closely I approach you
In reality.

His emotional distance is thus overcome, and this also for the first time each time he sees her. The less simple qualities of the poem depend on a certain lyrical (irrational) form of observation and association, intelligible on an aesthetic and emotional plane. The odd angle at which the curtain is hanging, for example, reminds him of the way a group of jasmine pickers he once saw on a road near Grasse seemed to stand on a diagonal; and then the unexplicit element of threat in the position of the curtain and of the jasmine pickers leads the poet to imagine, or rather, to see the woman surrounded by dangers and by dangerous temptations, by branches that might scratch her in the woods and rocking chairs balancing precariously on bridges. The fact that she is inside a house (imaginary or "real") is in no way a protection from this sort of danger existing on the level of genuine feeling, against which there is no defense.

All the poems of this collection are complex in *vision* but simple in tone, as is all surrealist love poetry and all surrealist painting at its best.... In the poet's dream the woman is presented in a series of limitless vertical images, indicative of the optimistic vision of surrealism; the tendency is always toward *la fête,* toward the celebration of woman and of life, in the same way as the *superréel* is opposed to the subreal, or *sousréel,* of a "miserabilistic" prosaic world. The mirror does not give off sunlight but the more romantic moonlight, and is itself a moon as eternally young as the face reflected in it; such condensation of the image is typical of surrealist poetry and art, both of which demand from the onlooker more than he is commonly willing to give. The metaphor here exemplifies Breton's statement: "For me the only *evidence* in the world is that provided by the spontaneous, extra-lucid, insolent relationship that is established, under certain conditions, between one thing and another thing which common sense would never think of bringing together." Consequently, for him the word "therefore" is detestable and "the most exalting word is the word LIKE, whether it is pronounced or implied." (pp. 84-6, 88)

Breton's love poetry stands out from his other poems by its extraordinary strength: the poems in *L'Air de l'eau,* for instance, are as complex and as eloquent as *L'Amour fou,* as compelling in vision and as unified in feeling. That this latter quality goes precisely against one of the rules given, the year after the publication of *L'Air de l'eau,* for disorienting the senses is a typically surrealist contradiction. (p. 89)

Through his own vision and through the marvelous power of surrealist love, the surrealist poet overcomes his sense of disunity and estrangement, at least temporarily.... After the passionate self-analysis of some of the poems of *Le Revolver à cheveux blancs* and the hallucinatory visions of the love poetry in *L'Air de l'eau,* the poet is now turned toward the world and in *Les Etats-Généraux* of 1943 he is able to place even "le risque," or the romantic current of surrealist adventure, with its "imposing apparatus of temptations" into a more general and less credulous perspective. This poem has as its theme the harmony of universal dependence, the equality of all peoples and "the imperceptible and yet irresistible inclination toward the best." It is, like many of the poems of Aragon, unashamedly sentimen-

tal and optimistic. The "exaltation of life" Breton so frequently invokes and which inspires all his extraordinary images merges here with an undisguised humanism, as the *separation* occasionally sensed by the poet is transformed into a more lasting involvement.

Surrealist optimism is never free of responsibility; for Breton, as for Aragon, art matters desperately because it is the only moral counter to destruction.... For Aragon, "Art ought to be read like the paper." For Breton, art must not depend on daily events, but it must be just as significant as any of them. He is condemning not only the "art for art's sake" which has no bearing on the world (*nonsitué*) but all egotistic art of sheer pleasure and description, no matter how realistic and how tasteful. If he attacks the notion of taste as strongly as Aragon, it is not in the name of the common man who cannot enter the delicately arranged paradise of the elite—in fact, Aragon's vicious poems in *Persécuté-Persécuteur* exemplify the anger and pity Breton wants to avoid. Breton discerns in mere taste a frivolous quality akin to sensuality and incompatible with the *sérieux* of surrealist concerns. Furthermore the notion of "taste" depends on the assurance of a fixed universe for its fixed values, in opposition to the mobile universe of the surrealist vision. Surrealist art is not the prisoner of any predetermined way of seeing things. The judgment it implies is always a fresh one, fitting the criteria of the moment while not inflexibly committed to any system or structure; it is neither dissociated from the actual world nor subordinate to it. The surrealist revolution is meant to take place in all realms and to retain its validity in all situations.

[There] is always another side to the optimism; Breton remains conscious of the sharp dualities he has never ceased trying to reconcile in the unitary reality he calls "L'amour la révolution la poésie." The words he addresses to Charles Fourier (*Ode à Charles Fourier,* 1947) are addressed also to himself:

Toi qui ne parlais que de lier vois tout s'est délié

(You who spoke only of linking look how everything has come apart).

Poetry is able to form no more than an ephemeral link between the disparate surfaces, even in the newly open universe Breton describes; poetic fusion, in which he places all his hope, may not last:

Car les images les plus vives sont les plus fugaces

(For the most vital images are the most fleeting).

The ending of the poem *Sur la route de San Romano* (1948) has often been quoted as an example of surrealist faith:

L'étreinte poétique tant qu'elle dure
Défend toute échappée sur la misère du monde.

(The poetic embrace as long as it lasts
Prevents any sight of the misery of the world.)

Yet in the light of the above quotations, the "tant qu'elle dure" here may imply, as strongly as the "fugace," the ephemeral quality of surrealist poety, based as it is on the quick and spontaneous image. Of course this is also the basis for its beauty. (pp. 89-93)

In *Xénophiles* (1948), Breton reaches the lowest possible depth of surrealist despair:

Ceux qui s'avancent sont ridicules
Les hautes images sont tombées.

(Those who go forward are ridiculous
The lofty images have fallen.)

Breton and the other surrealists put their entire confidence in the reconciling power of the image ("The image never deceives") and in the creative strength of the interior vision. When the images fall and the vision fails, they have no recourse.

But without the extremes of exaltation and despair surrealism could not be the "place of resolution" Breton considers it. The vagueness of the terms used in his theory and his criticism—"révélation," "interrogation," "solicitation," "création," "représentation," "figuration"—leaves room for all the ambiguities of art; the odd mixture of genuine emotion and visual precision in his poetry and their interdependence engages the reader, as surrealist theory says it should, in a disquieting world of separations and unity, total contradictions and partial understanding. Many of his images are clearly based on the obvious or implied dualities of soft and hard, clear and dark, absence and presence, one and many, elaborate costumes and nakedness, and so on. Like his theory, Breton's poetry betrays a constant awareness of opposites, sometimes deliberately provoking them to upset the habitual perceptions of the reader, sometimes temporarily resolving them into a new and always ambiguous compound. That the ambiguity should persist even within the newly created unity is as essential to the character of surrealist art as is the ephemeral nature of the images. For the vision to be always fresh and the visionary to be always active, the art he creates must not be allowed to stultify him with its perfection or its permanence. All surrealist effort is directed against the stability to which we are accustomed—if it were ever to produce its own form of stability, it would instantly betray its revolutionary nature. . . . (pp. 93-4)

> *Mary Ann Caws, "André Breton," in her* The Poetry of Dada and Surrealism *(copyright © 1970 by Princeton University Press; reprinted by permission of Princeton University Press), Princeton University Press, 1970, pp. 69-94 (footnotes deleted for this publication).*

The importance of André Breton shows signs of being endless. The virtual Surrealist revival that has been upon us in the last decade is not the first, nor is it likely to be the last recrudescence of that poet's vision. For, as John Ashbery has observed, we are all Surrealists now: "It is becoming plainer every day that Breton's 'future resolution of the states of dream and reality' is no longer just around the corner." Yet Breton remains perhaps the least widely read modern poetic preceptor. Indeed, in America he has scarcely been read at all; he continues to influence through the diffusion of his ideas, while his poems remain largely in French and/or out of print. Which is not to say that the embargo affects only him. Better poets than he . . . have fared even worse on these shores. (p. 262)

Breton's context is not ours, though he prophesied ours. We may all be Surrealists, but we are Surrealists in our bones, whereas Breton, having invented the idea, was one in his head. What with the extreme types of abstraction currently rife in all the arts, poetry included, this poet's *écriture automatique* is now little more dismaying than Lewis Carroll's "nonsense". Thus our admiration for Breton takes on a degree of reverence that undermines the aggressions of his work. He is simply a hero, like Napoleon, like Rimbaud, and the smoke has cleared from his battlefields. But he remains a splendid poet, too, and his admission to the official Pantheon should be conducted immediately, with due public pomp and articles in the *Times,* if only to give us a balanced view of what's been happening in this century. (p. 264)

> *Peter Schjeldahl, in* Poetry *(© 1971 by The Modern Poetry Association; reprinted by permission of the Editor of* Poetry*), January, 1971.*

It is impossible to write about André Breton in any other language than that of passion. To him the powers of the word were no different from the powers of passion, and passion, in its highest and most intense form, was nothing less than language in its wildest, purest state: poetry. Breton: the language of passion—the passion of language. Perhaps even more than an exploration of unknown psychic territories, his lifelong quest represented the regaining of a lost kingdom: the original Word, man before men and civilizations. Surrealism was his order of chivalry and his entire life was a Quest of the Holy Grail. . . . A quest whose goal lies neither in the future nor in the past, but at that point of convergence that is simultaneously the beginning and the end of all time: the day before the beginning and after the end.

Breton's indignation at the "infamous Christian idea of sin" is something more than a violent rejection of the traditional values of the West: it is an affirmation of the original innocence of man. This distinguishes him from almost all of his contemporaries and successors. . . . [Breton's] life and his work are proof that he was not so much the heir of Sade and Freud as of Rousseau and Meister Eckhart. He was not a philosopher but a great poet, and, even more important, a man of honor in the old sense of the word. His stubborn refusal to entertain the idea of sin was a point of honor: the notion struck him as being in effect a *stain,* a blot not on man's life but on man's dignity. Belief in sin was incompatible with his conception of man. . . . For Breton, sinning and being born were not synonymous.

Man, even man debased by the neocapitalism and pseudo-socialism of our time, is a marvelous being because he sometimes *speaks.* Language is the mark, the sign, not of his fall but of his original innocence. Through the Word we may regain the lost kingdom and recover powers we possessed in the far-distant past. These powers are not ours. The man inspired, the man who really speaks, does not say anything personal: language speaks through his mouth. Dreaming favors the explosion of the Word because it is an affective state: its passivity permits desire to be active. Dreaming is by nature passionate. Here, too, Breton's opposition to Christianity had religious roots: in order to express itself, language destroys the conscious self. Poetry does not redeem the poet's personal self: it dissolves it in the vaster, more powerful reality of language. The practice of poetry demands the surrender, the renunciation of the ego. . . . Poetic automatism, as Breton himself often emphasized, is very close to asceticism: a state of passivity must be reached, a very difficult task, for it requires the suspension of all criticism and self-criticism. It is a radical criticism of criticism, an interdiction of consciousness. In its way, it is a *via purgativa,* a method of negation aimed at calling forth the appearance of true reality: the primordial language.

The basis of "automatic writing" is the belief that speaking and thinking are one and the same thing. Man does not speak because he thinks; he thinks because he speaks. Or rather, speaking is no different from thinking: to speak is to think. . . . Any change in the verbal structure results in a change of meaning. Strictly speaking, what we call synonyms are merely translations or equivalents within a language; and what we call translation is really only an approximation in another language or an interpretation. Words such as *nirvana, dharma, tao,* or *jen* are really untranslatable; the same is true of *physics, nature, democracy, revolution,* and other Western terms that have no exact equivalent in languages outside of our tradition. As the relation between the verbal structure and the meaning becomes more intimate—in mathematics and poetry, for instance, not to mention nonverbal languages such as music and painting—translation becomes more and more difficult. (pp. 47-50)

There is a strong magical element in Breton's view of language. He not only made no distinction between magic and poetry; he also was convinced all his life that poetry was a force, a substance, an energy truly capable of changing reality. At the same time his ideas were so precise and penetrating that I would not hesitate to call them scientific. On one hand, he saw language as an autonomous current possessed of a power all its own, a sort of universal magnetism; on the other hand, he conceived of this erotic substance as a system of signs governed by the twofold law of affinity and opposition, similarity and difference. This view is quite close to that held by modern linguists: words and their constituent elements are fields of energy, like atoms and their particles. The old notion of analogy is coming to the fore once again: nature is a language, and language in turn is a double of nature. To rediscover man's natural language is to return to nature, before the Fall and History: poetry is the proof of man's original innocence. *The Social Contract* becomes for Breton the verbal, poetic accord between man and nature, word and thought. Considered from this point of view, the oft-repeated statement that Surrealism is not a school of poetry but a movement of liberation becomes more understandable. A way of rediscovering the language of innocence, a renewal of the primordial pact, poetry is the basic text, the foundation of the human order. Surrealism is revolutionary because it is a return to the beginning of all beginnings.

Breton's earliest poems bear the traces of a passionate reading of Mallarmé. Not even in his moments of greatest violence and verbal freedom did he ever abandon this predilection for words that are at once precise and precious. Words with iridescent colors, a language of echoing reverberations. He was a "Mannerist" poet, in the proper sense of the word: within the European tradition, he belongs to the family of poets descended from Góngora, Marino, Donne—poets I cannot be certain he read, poets whose poetic ethic I fear he would have disapproved of. Verbal splendor, and intellectual and emotional violence. A curious but not infrequent combination of prophecy and aestheticism that makes his best poems both objects of beauty and spiritual testaments. That is perhaps the reason why he

worshiped Lautréamont, the poet who discovered the *form* in which to express psychic explosion. That may also be the reason for Breton's instinctive and openly avowed repugnance for the simplistic, brutal destructiveness of Dada, even though he considered it a "revolutionary necessity" that was both inevitable and healthy. There were different reasons underlying his reservations concerning other poets. His admiration for Apollinaire is somewhat hesitant because to Breton poetry was the creation of realities through the Word, and not simply verbal invention. Novelty and surprise in art pleased him, but the term *invention* was not to his liking; on the other hand, the word *revelation* shines in many of his texts. Speaking is the noblest activity of all: revealing what is hidden, bringing the buried word back to life, calling forth our double, that Other which is us but which we never allow to exist—our suppressed half.

Revelation is resurrection, exposure, initiation. It is a word that calls for rites and ceremonies. Except as a means of provocation, of insulting the public, or rousing it to rebellion, Breton detested open-air spectacles: fiestas should be held in catacombs. Each of the Surrealist expositions revolved around two opposite poles: exhibitionism and secrecy, consecration and profanation. Consecration and conspiracy are consanguineous terms: revelation is also rebellion. The Other, our double, is a denial of the illusory solidity and security of our consciousness, that pillar of smoke on which we build our arrogant philosophical and religious constructs. The Others, proletarians and colonial slaves, women and poets, primitive myths and revolutionary utopias, are equally violent threats to the beliefs and institutions of the West. Breton reaches his hand out to all of them, to Fourier and the Papuan of New Guinea alike. Rebellion and revelation, language and passion are manifestations of a single reality. The true name of this reality is also a double one: innocence and marvels. Man is the creator of marvels; he is a poet because he is an innocent being. Children, women, lovers, the inspired, and even the insane are the incarnation of the marvelous. Everything they do is uncanny and they do not realize it. They know not what they do: they are not responsible, they are innocents. Magnets, lightning rods, high-tension wires: their words and their acts are senseless and yet they have a meaning. They are the scattered signs of a language in perpetual motion that opens out before our eyes a fan of contradictory meanings that in the end becomes a single, ultimate meaning. The universe speaks to us and to itself in and through them.

I have mentioned a number of Breton's words: revelation and rebellion, innocence and marvels, passion and language. There is another one: magnetism. He was one of the centers of gravity of our time. He not only believed that we humans are governed by laws of attraction and repulsion; he himself was the personal incarnation of these forces. (pp. 50-2)

In my adolescence, in a period of isolation and great elation, I happened to read a few pages which I found out later are Chapter V of *L'Amour fou.* In them he tells of climbing the volcanic peak of Teide, on Tenerife, in the Canary Islands. This text, which I read at almost the same time as *The Marriage of Heaven and Hell,* opened the doors of modern poetry to me. It was an "art of loving," not in the trivial manner of Ovid's *Ars Amatoria,* but an initiation to something that my later life and the East have given me further proof of: the analogy, or, rather, the identity between woman and nature. Is water feminine, or is a woman a succession of waves, a river at night, a beach at dawn tattooed by the wind? If we are a metaphor of the universe, the human couple is the metaphor par excellence, the point of intersection of all forces and the seed of all forms. The couple is time recaptured, the return to the time before time. Against wind and tide, I have endeavored to be faithful to that revelation: the powers the word *love* has over me have remained intact. Or as Breton says: ["We will never again escape from these leafy fronds of the golden age."] This stubborn belief in a paradisiac age, coupled with the vision of the primordial couple, can be seen in all his writings, from the first to the last. The woman is a bridge, a place where the natural world and the human are reconciled. (pp. 53-4)

Surrealism is no longer in the vanguard, according to the critics. Quite apart from the fact that I thoroughly dislike that military term, I do not believe that novelty, that being in the vanguard of history, is the essential characteristic of Surrealism. Nor were the Dadaists as frantic worshipers of the new as the Futurists, for instance. Neither Dada nor Surrealism adored machines. Surrealism desecrated them: it built machines that produced nothing, "dust-raisers," melting watches. The machine as a method of criticism—of the cult of machines, of men who worship progress and their buffoonery. Is Duchamp the beginning or the end of painting? Through his *oeuvre,* and even more importantly through his negation of "the work of art," Duchamp closes a period of Western art (that of painting properly speaking) and opens another which is no longer "artistic": the dissolving of art in life, of language in the circle of word games, of reason in its philosophical antidote, laughter. Duchamp undermines modernity with the same wave of the hand with which he dismisses tradition. In Breton's case, there is also his vision of time as an invisible, innocent present hidden beneath the flow of hours and days. The future fascinated him because it seemed to him to be the realm of the unexpected; not what *will be* according to the calculations of reason, but what *might be* according to the imagination. The destruction of today's world would permit the appearance of real time, not historical time but natural time, governed not by progress but by desire. This was what a Communist-libertarian society meant to him. In his eyes there was no essential contradiction between myths and utopias, poetry and revolutionary programs. (pp. 55-6)

He detested eclecticism in the realm of thought and promiscuity in the realm of eroticism. His best pages, both in his prose works and in his poetry, are those inspired by the idea of free choice and its correlative, fidelity to what one has freely chosen, whether in art or in politics, in friendships or in love. This idea was the axis of his life and of his conception of love: a passion whose many facets have been polished by freedom. Our age has delivered love from the prison bars of the past century only to convert it into a pastime, one more consumer item in a society of busy consumers. Breton's vision is the exact opposite of almost everything that in our day passes for love and even for eroticism (another word in wide circulation, like a coin of very little value). I have the greatest difficulty understanding his boundless admiration for Sade's works. I can see why Sade's spirit of absolute negation moved him and excited him, but how can this total negation be reconciled

with a belief in love as the radiant center of the golden age? (pp. 56-7)

Breton reintroduces love into eroticism, or, more exactly, consecrates eroticism through love. We find again, underlying his opposition to any and every religion, a passionate wish to consecrate. And even a passionate wish to reconcile. Commenting on a passage in the *New Justine*—the episode in which one of the characters mingles his sperm with the lava of Etna—Breton observes that the act is one of loving homage to nature. . . . Breton's admiration for Sade was almost boundless, and all his life he believed that

> So long as we have not freed ourselves of the idea of the transcendence of some sort of good . . . the impassioned representation of innate evil will continue to have the greatest revolutionary value.

But with this one reservation, in the dialogue between Sade and Rousseau, Breton is irresistibly inclined to side with the latter: with Rousseau the friend of primitive man, the lover of nature, as with Fourier the utopian. Love is not an illusion: it is the intermediary between man and nature, the place where terrestrial and spiritual magnetism intersect.

Each one of the facets of Breton's works reflects all the others. It is not the passive reflection of the mirror, however: it is not a repetition but a reply. A play of contrary beams of light, a dialogue of glimmers. Magnetism, revelation, a thirst for innocence, and also disdain. Is there hauteur here? Yes, in the etymological sense of the word: Breton is a winged creature whose kingdom is the upper air, a bird whose realm is lofty heights. All the words of this family apply to him. He was a soaring spirit, a man exalted; his poetry uplifts us. Above all, he maintained that the body of the woman and the man are our only altars. And as for death? Every man is born several times and dies several times. This is not the first time that Breton has died. He knew, better than anyone, that we die more than once: each one of his central books is the story of a resurrection. I know that this time it is different, that we will never see him again. His latest death is not an illusion. Nonetheless, Breton lived certain instants, saw with his own eyes certain evidences that are the negation of time and what we call an everyday outlook on life. I call such moments poetic instants, even though they are experiences common to all men: the only difference is that the poet remembers them and endeavors to reincarnate them in words, sounds, colors. The man who has lived these instants and is capable of pondering their meaning knows that the self cannot be redeemed because it does not exist. He also knows that, as Breton repeatedly insisted, the boundaries between waking and dreaming, life and death, time and a timeless present are fluid and vague. We do not know what it is really like to die, except that it is the end of the individual self—the end of the prison. Breton broke out of this prison many times; he expanded time or denied it, and for a measureless instant coincided with the *other* time. This experience, the central core of his life and his thought, is invulnerable and untouchable: it is beyond time, beyond death—beyond us. Knowing that this is so reconciles me to his latest death and to all dying. (pp. 57-9)

Octavio Paz, "André Breton or the Quest of the Beginning," in his Alternating Current, *translated by Helen R. Lane (English-lan-*

guage translation copyright © 1973 by The Viking Press, Inc.; reprinted by permission of The Viking Press, Inc.), Viking, 1973, pp. 47-59.

There is one essential area in which André Breton's manifesto succeeded and proved indeed to be that Porte Albinos (The White Gateway) which he conceived in the companion piece to the *Manifesto,* entitled *Poisson soluble.* Those who catch surrealism's principal message can proceed to the region of Absolute spring and take away from God, as Breton suggested, that which they had surrendered to God. Not the revolver, not the dream, not even love, but language was to be in his own intellectual and human development the constant among the variables, the Porte Albinos of freedom and the structure of his reality. . . . The one who writes must be the objective recorder of the data but must restrain himself from correction; and verbalism is viewed not as a form of communication between two or more human beings but rather as an activity which we might characterize as recorder and amplifier, leaving the activator of the phenomenon in a state of attentiveness and self-enlightenment.

Psychiatrists, from whom Breton learned the procedure, subject their patients to this kind of betrayal through language in an effort to unravel and release those inhibitions that cause traumatic behavior. Breton used the device for exactly the opposite purpose: to uncover what, in the non-pathological individual, could lead from constriction to liberty: liberty for unprogrammed activity, liberty of the mind to take a more total advantage of its vision of the common habitat. The information gleaned from the verbal register was not meant to serve as an index of existing alienation but was rather to become a clue to latent power, which according to Breton was identifiable with love, which in turn was identifiable with conjunction not only in terms of the male-female principle but of human relation with the three kingdoms of the natural world: the animal, plant, and mineral. . . . "Words make love": it is, I believe, in this global sense that the word "amour" must be taken with all that the word connotes of involuntary attraction, union, recognition and ecstasy as a release of creative energy. This motivating principle of word unions was the apex of Breton's poetry. (pp. 48-9)

In emphasizing the involuntary character of the encounter of nonsequential word groups and of the images they conjure, Breton did not agree with his elder colleague Pierre Reverdy that this was an active, voluntary exercise on the part of poets. He came to see in this kind of *rapprochement* not a consciously inventive process but a self-instructive one, a training device rather than one of artistic expression. In other words, the poet did not bring these words or images together; rather, he observed them gravitate toward each other by making himself open-minded or dream prone so that he would not impede their course and not interpret their collision in terms of meanings that have been inculcated in him by his culture.

In rejecting the principle of active verbal associations, Breton appears to be rejecting the notion of what he called "elliptic" art, what Mallarmé had so well practiced in the latter part of his career, particularly in those obscure sonnets. If we were to make a concrete analogy, we might say that the surrealist poet, as Breton understood the term in the early stage of his career, is not a manipulator of a power plant, who at will turns on the switch and generates light but an observer of the verbal lights generated. . . . Thus he describes in the first part of the *First Manifesto* the passive character of a man in the face of the convulsive character of words. In the next page he describes the state of surrealism created through the practice of language with a galaxy of images—the word "image" replacing that of "light"; the movement of the image creates in the observer a vertigo comparable to the effect of a pharmaceutical stimulant; it takes over as the sole compass of the mind. Two elements of this part of the discussion are interesting and significant in terms of the evolution of Breton's own art. He states that the purpose of his discovery is not to guard jealousy for himself a divine and unique secret, but to put it, as he says, at the disposal of everyone. In other words, if we define this unfurling of disconnected images as surrealist poetry, they would have meaning only to the perpetrator; the object would be meaningful only to its subject, and what Breton would have communicated to his readers would not be the result of his own self-probe but the methodology by which each could do the same and all become surrealist poets. It would appear, then, that Breton was going counter to Mallarmé, not only in his rejection of elliptic poetry but also in the rejection of the notion that poetry is a lonely and elitist means of communication for the happy few. Language would not be the expression of one man's expansion of consciousness but a clarification of one of the channels of the expansion. Psychic language is then a creation. Breton's faith in the validity of this process is sustained by his conviction that automatic language is equally available to all, the common treasure, commonly corrupted; all men, equally deprived of spontaneous language by the curbs society has put on their imagination, reach, in Breton's view, a negative equality from which he presumes them to be recuperable for a collective dream of life in high gear. (pp. 50-1)

How did the initial monitoring of the surrealist language lead Breton from the practice of automatic writing to the strategic invasion of the unlimited spaces of desire and illumination? It was not a rapid process but one which took him from 1924 to 1959, at which time he published *Constellations,* his final poetic work. . . . (pp. 51-2)

Breton's surrealism was not a static posture but . . . underwent very significant evolution. . . .

Breton abandoned the passive form of surrealist language fairly early in his career; the fact was consciously acknowledged by Breton; . . . by the time he wrote *L'Air de l'eau* in 1934 he had already abandoned "automatic writing." (If we need outside evidence to support what is self-revelatory in the poems themselves!) It is obvious that in *Poisson soluble,* which is a much more thorough work of automatic language than *Les Champs magnétiques,* and is the companion and illustrative piece of the *Manifesto,* Breton is his own monitor as he transcribes the psychic rhythm of his flow of language; but by the time he is writing the long poems of the War years, he is producing intricately structured works. The unleashing of verbal energy in the course of the forty years of practice culminates in the series of prose poems, *Constellations.* . . . (p. 52)

After writing free verse for more than thirty years, Breton arrives in *Constellations* to the prose stanza, reminiscent not of Baudelaire's poems in prose, nor of Reverdy's, but of Rimbaud's *Les Illuminations* in its compactness and concrete ellipsis. (p. 53)

The immediate inspiration of *Constellations* was the series of gouaches of Miró which date from the 1940's. But the structured ellipsis of Breton's word paintings bears a direct connection to Mallarmé's *Un Coup de dés jamais n'abolira le hasard*. In Mallarmé's poem, "Constellation" is a single word, central in the void where the poet's will meanders and confronts the absurdities of chance. *Un Coup de dés* is a sad masterpiece, a one man's journey in a cosmos whose rules are outside of his dominion, where his will and the whims of objective chance are pitted in uneven battle, and the struggle culminates in the poet's disastrous awareness of his losing score. As we shall see, Breton's *Constellations* is a cosmic venture in which man joins nature through his manipulation of language which extends the receptivity of his five senses and achieves, over and above the verbal synaesthesia, an ontological one as well.

When Mallarmé died, they found on his work table reams of mathematical formulas. It is interesting to note that Breton also, in this last stage of his poetic activity, refers to mathematics. He had always been fascinated by the law of probability. Here in his last poems we find a mathematical series. We are in the realm of numbers, and numbers are the tools both of organization and of chance.

Breton is no longer a simple monitor here. He sets out to structure the forces of chance and thereby returns to the poetic ellipsis from which he had originally sought release. But if indeed there occurs at the end of his career a conciliation between the forces of the unconscious and the conscious in terms of the poetic act, and if the general appearance of these poems reminds one of the deliberate crytographic writing of Mallarmé, the vision derived from similar poetic mechanics is of an entirely different character.

Breton tells us that the twenty-two units of Miró's painting progress as a mathematical series, deliberate yet drawing from the resources of chance. He calls it "une succession délibérée d'oeuvres," the result, as he sees it, of a successful combination of dexterity and chance (adresse et hasard). . . . [The] two words Breton uses to characterize Miró's feat, "adresse et hasard," could be used to define his own verbal composition.

What these poems show, in fact, as they multiply and elaborate certain fundamental images in mathematical progression, is that Breton is one of the most prominent nature poets of the twentieth century. But as a nature poet, he does not describe its manifestations, but rather, what he has come to believe to be the central mechanism of nature: the phenomenon of metamorphosis, reflected in human nature in the functioning of love.

We observe that Breton's vision of nature relies neither on the pathetic fallacy of the Romanticists nor does it represent the objectivity and impersonality of natural laws, senseless in their relation to human intentions. Breton does not try to draw nature into his own private orbit, neither does he let himself fall adrift in nature's scheme as an uncomprehending, alien element. He expected no solace from God, no confidentiality from nature, no exit from the human condition. Rather, he enters into the universal pattern whose metamorphic form and activity he has grasped and can convey through a mode unique to the human species: *language*. By the use of language to parallel natural metamorphoses, he arrives at a more profound sense of the convulsive nature of all existence. Although the alchemistic language was a device he explored in his earliest writings, resplendently in *Poisson soluble,* the structured use of this device reached its *apogée* in *Constellations*.

Whereas structuralist criticism has been trying to show in literary works subconscious organization contradictory to the rational intentions of the authors in question, in Breton's last set of poems we have the case of a poet superbly versed in the psychic, syntactic and connotative functioning of language, who puts this knowledge at the service of poetry. In his deliberately structured language, channelling the powers of the unconscious, he draws his lexicon from three broadly separate reservoirs: the specialized language of bio-botanical terminology (words that have never before appeared in poetic context!), the demotic speech of daily usage, and the visionary language to which his predecessors, Rimbaud and Mallarmé, had accustomed him.

As you read these compact poems you have to work for the meanings they *contain* rather than *convey*. It is not a question of de-coding but of grasping the multitudinous digits of the code. Poetry becomes a scientific occupation both for the writer and the reader. You receive multiple meanings simultaneously not in the graphic combination of linear and vertical annotations, as they were induced in Mallarmé's *Un Coup de dés,* (i.e. through superpositions and juxtapositions), but rather in the manner of the ancient rebus of the Cabala and of latterday alchemists from whom Breton derived his model: the one in the other image, "l'un dans l'autre," contained and containing, which Breton found primordially and essentially characteristic of the nature of the universe and of the humans within it. This use of the rebus image had often been manifested in Breton's poetry by the substitution of the preposition "de" for "dans." The most spectacular example of a total poem constructed in this fashion is of course *L'Union libre* where the beauty of the woman and her power over him are not simply likened to manifestations of natural scapes but actually contained in them.

In *Constellations* one of the more obvious thematic recurrences of the one in the other image is that of the embrace suggested by the evocation of a series of images of clinging plants such as the vine, the clematis, the madder. At the heart of clusters of images they suggest the interdependence of things and beings. The word-images are graphically simple, presented on a purely non-connotative basis; any connotation that the reader will derive is subjective and of course arbitrary. But the subtle recurrences of such images, unheeded the first time perhaps, remembered the second, soon loom as patterns even as in a musical composition, and they create a magnetic field of connotations for the reader.

Another rich source of words of multiple containing and contained connotations are the homonyms and words used in more than one sense or context. Of this group we find in *Constellations* in key positions words like *héraut, navette, gland, palette, braise, calice:* they serve indeed, in the function he had attributed to language in the *First Manifesto,* as "springboards to the mind," leaving each reader to tide over from one possible meaning to the next, all catalyzed by the single word unit. Many of these have depository meaning, like *palette, coffret, calice, boîtes.* The most important perhaps of these depository words is "*fossile,*" that container and transformer of the animal and vegetable world into the mineral, the supreme and durable container. In fact, the integral connection of all things and beings, working through the combined forces of creation and destruction toward the basic unity of the two processes, is centrally ascertained by the image of fossil, very prominently featured in these word tapestries. (pp. 53-5)

As anyone who has read Breton's poetry in continuity is aware, light and fire images were recurrent and resplendent in his poems from the very beginning. What happens to these in the final counting of the numbers? They are combined and contained in the most unlikely places, and carry on the pattern of the container and the contained. Light through water, through ice, through a leaf, from enclosed trees. Most often what emerges is the light created through fire. But the phenomenon of fire is not conveyed through the usual process of combustion; instead, it is revealed in its inherent aspects, in the state of what the alchemists would call "ignited nature." This ignited matter emerges in *Constellations* in the form of igneous rocks, feldspar, incandescent thorns, and in the incarceration of the color red in lead, in water, in land, and in wood. Fire and water are also involved in another set of images that convey fertility and all that the fertilizing process involves in nature and in terms of decomposition and recomposition.

Along with the containing and contained images, we also have the connecting ones, involving principally birds and women. An obvious one, already familiar in Breton's poetry, is the egret (aigrette), here carrying an acorn. In the case of the woman images, the love process is closely related to the establishment of intimate connection with the whole range of protoplasmic existence, an elaboration of the earlier poems. Woman plays a role analogous to the encircling vine, the rainbow, the bird carrying seed.

In *Constellations* words not only make love but Breton makes love with them: he penetrates language and through language establishes a deep and intimate relationship with the physical world. Far from being automatic, poetry thus becomes a very studied and learned activity in which the poet as molder of language seizes on the propitious, aleatory associations of his mind, tests them against nature's laws, cultivates them by directing and constructing around them. It is not by chance that the dominant images of these twenty-two tapestries are "*navette*," and words relating to weaving. We are involved with the poet in a back and forth activity and in a virtually manual linking of threads. We are introduced into the throes of process and through process we venture toward the secrets of life itself.

Each object designated has more than one function, and it is always in a state of change. We proceed in the evolution of Breton's poetry from metaphor to metonymy where the part suggests the whole, the microcosm evokes the macrocosm. If in the case of William Blake a universe is mirrored in the grain of sand, in Breton's cosmography it is contained in a far wider range of animal, mineral, vegetable entities, constantly woven together or engaged in dialogue with each other, the sand with the vine, the morning star with the shepherd.

What is the role of the poet in the contemplation of all these phenomena and conditions of living reality? He is identified with homely, humble workers involved in manual labor: the cobbler, the silk-weaver, the miller, the juggler—all workers, they can relate to the work of the poet in the sense in which Rimbaud classified the poet as a worker, among what he called "horribles travailleurs," in his *Lettre du voyant*.

But Breton is also evoking a series of creators of magic. Back in *Poisson soluble* he had envisaged himself with a five-leaf clover on his left shoulder. Here the magical gamut includes the dexterity of children playing games, the wonders of fairy tale prestidigitators such as Oberon, all building up to the most miraculous hand of all, that of the artist: Miró's presence first of all, whom Breton long considered the purest surrealist of all the artists who joined him, and then on from the hand that draws to the hand that writes. Toward the end of this series of what we might call myth capsules, in no. 18, entitled "L'Oiseau migrateur," he is obviously again identifying the poet: "le petit homme nu, qui tient la clé des rébus, est toujours assis sur sa pierre" ["the small nude man, who holds the key to the rebus, is forever sitting on his rock"].

But the identification of the poet is a double one. If on the one hand he is grouped with dexterous artisans, epitomized in the patient and sedentary weaver, on the other hand we have another set of images, those of people in movement: the migrant and the vagabond, the shepherd, the pilgrim progressing like a latter-day Theseus through a labyrinth. We had already met Breton earlier in his work in the labyrinth image; what is evolutionary here is that the labyrinth has become vertical. If in *Poisson soluble* we remember the young poet as a masked man, holding the keys of the mystery of life, here we see him alighting from the labyrinth— as he had promised he would—and shooting for the stars.

The steps of his progress are transcribed in his language. He has dug (*je creuse, je moule, je l'abime, je vrille*); he has woven; he has proceeded from the street maze to the padlocked woods; his forces have burst out of their limits (with verbs like *sublimer, evaser, extravaser*) pushed up through spirals until no. 12 which is entitled "le 13 l'échelle a frôlé le firmament." He proceeds toward the rainbow in no. 15, toward the universal attraction which he recognizes as the quality of space in no. 20, and in the final piece, entitled "Le Passage de l'oiseau divin" he alludes to the flight of the butterfly, escaping even as it dies. In fact, here the upward movement joins another series of images that have been gradually building up to make an impact on our consciousness, a series which unlike the others here mentioned, was not previously predominant in Breton's normal referential system: that of music. In *Poisson soluble* we had had a suggestion of the music of the earth; here we build up to the music of the spheres. Poetic composition finds its closest ally in harmonic composition. References to musical instruments and musical function recur from one piece to the next, too numerous to enumerate here, but leading to an embrace between the creation of the hand and of the ear in that deeper unity of the creative power, of which they are seemingly different but intrinsically concerted manifestations, each in its way fueling the projectile of human desire.

The trajectory that Breton traced from 1924 to 1959 is a voyage from birth in water to absorption into the cosmos.

We may conclude that the *Manifesto* was indeed a very revolutionary document, not in terms of the limited meaning of political and social revolution, but as a broad recuperation and alignment of the attributes that constitute the common treasure. In retrospect he appears as a moment in history, offering an alternate choice to the sense of the absurd which was the more common reaction that was to accompany man's awareness of the cracking of the anthropocentric universe. In its global nature Breton's was rebellion without alienation. If, as we examined the progress of his poetic craft, we discerned powers of poetic construction more sophisticated than even Mallarmé's, we know full well that in his own mind his art had a secondary importance to his comportment as a human being. Beyond the literary destiny of his poetry was the significance of the new ontological posture it proposed. He used language as a staff and an aura to proclaim and to illustrate his efforts toward a redefinition of human destiny. (pp. 55-8)

> *Anna Balakian, "From 'Poisson Soluble' to 'Constellations': Breton's Trajectory for Surrealism," in* Twentieth Century Literature *(copyright 1975, Hofstra University Press), February, 1975, pp. 48-58.*

*   *   *

BROSMAN, Catharine Savage   1934-

An American poet, Brosman concentrates on the places, institutions, and landscapes that typify the "Old South." (See also *Contemporary Authors*, **Vols. 61-64.)**

Understated, splendidly wrought, [Catharine Savage Brosman's poems] are for the most part thoughtful evocations of the inner life as it responds to nature. The poet's fine sense of texture enables her to deal heavily, at times, in abstractions, without becoming dry or platitudinous; her sense of rhythm enables her to place freshly even such a sentence as "The sky / is blue." She is at her best when writing about the amphibious boundary, the shore, but her love poems are also fresh and convincing. She has an occasional tendency to seem to ramble, as if lines leading into the actual poem had not been cut in later drafts; but such passages are rare. (p. xiii)

> Virginia Quarterly Review *(copyright, 1973, by the* Virginia Quarterly Review, The University of Virginia), *Vol. 49, No. 1 (Winter, 1973).*

Catharine Savage Brosman's first collection of poems, *Watering,* is delicately reminiscent of Vergil's *Georgics.* Like the *Georgics, Watering*'s subject is the mysterious relationship of man with all that is his estate and the collection portrays that relationship in an almost Vergilian chain-of-being. Of course, because *Watering* is not a single poem but rather a collection of poems . . . it does not proceed with quite *Georgic* precision through a consideration of land, crops, cattle, bees, and men. But the drift of the collection does take us from shorelines, to meadows, through a quire of animal poems, and finally to a gathering of personal love poems. Altogether, then, *Watering* is a community of individual verse shaped toward a vision of man which acknowledges both his uniqueness and his role in some still dark harmony.

Because this vision is both deeply classical and deeply Christian, its enunciation in Mrs. Brosman's poems inevitably brings to mind not only the *Georgics* but a broad range of other poets and other poems. . . . These dim echoes, however, are in no way oppressive. They only serve notice that, though an individual poet, Mrs. Brosman is also part of a community of poets and therefore bound, not to a false consistency, but to a certain way of questioning.

For instance, two of the finest poems in the collection record antithetical responses to very similar situations, but both are wholly admirable poems because both are convincingly honest explorations of the tension between communal harmony and individual life. . . . "Shore Life" affirms a reciprocal harmony of sky and sea that blends conflicts into a cohesive whole. (pp. 710-11)

In "Fiddler Crabs" we see much that we saw in "Shore Life." The tide is the same, and the fiddler crabs which retreat at its rising and return with its fall are tiny cogs in what is palpably an ordered natural process. But unlike "Shore Life," the emphasis in "Fiddler Crabs" (as the title suggests) is on the cogs, not the process, and the final effect of the poem is more horror than peace. Watching the crabs' frenzied retreat and the debacle of their return among blue crabs which feed on them, we are made to fear and hate the cruel order of shore life and to disparage its incomprehensible harmony.

Finally, however, the effect of the two poems read together is not embittering but salutary and something like the effect of the whole collection. For the special strength of *Watering* is that, though it consistently pursues the enigmatic relationship of community and the individual, it also achieves a broad range of tone and perspective. From the open laughter of "Carnival of Turtles," through the poignancy of "Of How the Lizards Live," to the ripeness of "Weathering by a Fire," the collection evokes its best wisdom by contrast. Through contrast it reminds us that life truly is a mystery in which doubt and faith are near of kin and in which our best questions—though it is proper that we ask them—are beyond our answering. (pp. 711-12)

> *John Irwin Fischer, "Community and the Individual Life: Catharine Savage Brosman's 'Watering'," in* The Southern Review *(copyright, 1973, by John Irwin Fischer), Vol. IX, No. 3, Summer, 1973, pp. 710-12.*

Catharine Savage Brosman feels completely at home in her world of southern seascapes, marshes, pines, and savannahs. In *Watering* Brosman rarely ventures beyond the unspectacular, everyday occurrences in her "only-too-familiar" world: grunion hunting, watering her garden, a lizard on her terrace, and a deserted port are sufficient occasions for poetry. The objective world of nature functions as either the catalyst for self-reflection (as in "January Oranges" and "Of How the Lizards Live") or as a metaphor for personal experiences (as in "Big Meadows in March" and "A Lesson In Ourselves"). With controlled emotion and response, Brosman places much value on the inner life. . . .

Brosman possesses a poet's care for language, and this is often demonstrated in her ability to select the right word which rounds out an image. (p. 183)

> *James Healey, in* Prairie Schooner *(© 1974 by University of Nebraska Press; reprinted by permission from* Prairie Schooner), *Summer, 1974.*

I hope it will not offend Catharine Savage Brosman if I comment that her poems make a continuity with the *pietas* of [the] older southern mind; for her poems—ironical, sometimes grave—observe southern places with a decorousness and care which can be called cultivated.

Of all recent books by southern poets, Mrs. Brosman's is the most unified in tone and vision. *Watering . . .* is delightful to read through: one poem recalls an earlier one and the reader retraces his steps easily through this little book as through a small garden. The horticultural figure readily suggests itself because in the title poem the speaker is watering a garden, a metaphor for the poet who "guessing at some dark thirst / . . . writes the rings of his own desire upon the earth." Mrs. Brosman's most southern quality, as I have suggested, is her interest in place, here especially the coasts of Florida and the Carolinas, the Valley of Virginia, and New Orleans. Her interest in these places is liberating for she convinces us that if we are to see them aright we must again open the poetic eye once fed on English landscape poetry. . . . She offers fresh proof that a discriminating attention to the local is not merely parochial but leads into the great avenues of art. . . . But Mrs. Brosman does not seem to be imposing an intelligible order on the landscape. She convinces us in the way of the old meditative landscape poetry that nature is full of human meanings which we must notice lest we fail as human souls. Her effects are often subtle; the complexity of the world and the complexity of mind's eye are so suited to each other.

How has Mrs. Brosman achieved so much unity of vision at a time when poets of real power seem to aspire only to fragments? Indeed, how are things of this kind done at all? How did Emily Dickinson do what she did? The Dickinsonian example is suggested by these lines of Mrs. Brosman's in "Of How the Lizards Live":

> . . .—I have preferred
> the smallest things,
> finding a sweeter pathos
> than in any Götterdämmerung
> among the bluets hidden
> in the grass, vulnerable
> pine seedlings, or a coquina
> shell drained by an oyster
> driller—the sun did not
> blink—and cast aside—
> to dry in its loneliness.

What carries the book over its occasional failures is an intense spirit of adventure, all the more vivid for being quiet and admitting disillusion and pain. (pp. 881-82)

> *D. E. Richardson, in* The Southern Review *(copyright, 1976, by D. E. Richardson), Vol. XII, No. 4, October, 1976.*

*   *   *

BUECHNER, (Carl) Frederick   1926-

An American poet, novelist, sermonizer, and ordained Presbyterian minister, Buechner writes with humor, wit, and deft characterizations. His thematic concerns are often theological, and he works with a refined satiric touch as he tackles contemporary questions of faith and human foibles through such offbeat evangelical institutions as the Church of Holy Love, Inc., and the Open Heart Church. (See also *CLC*, Vols. 2, 4, 6, and *Contemporary Authors*, Vols. 13-16, rev. ed.)

Time and time again in Buechner's novels, and especially in his more recent ones, [the] tendency to self-defeat is manifest. One is often reminded that he is a man at odds with his own talents, who compresses a genius for lively prose and a marvelously comic imagination into themes and obligations which diminish them; while, in turn, his witty, ribald language and the extravagant machinery of his plots, make Buechner's serious themes seem sometimes coarse or tawdry.

Treasure Hunt is the fourth novel in the series about Leo Bebb, evangelist, flasher, saint and income tax evader, who, as far as anyone can tell, has gone up in flames, more or less comically, at the end of *Love Feast,* the previous novel. He only appears in this one, therefore, in home-movies, recordings, fantasy, dream and ectoplasmic visitation, which is quite enough. The plot, like that of earlier Bebb novels, is Gothic; a bouquet of incest, infanticide, miracles and mayhem, most of which seem to have neither narrative consequences nor emotional content. They happen to make noise, like events in a farce; but, unlike events in a farce, they occur soundlessly, offstage. Seductions, with no shred of passion left hanging to them, are talked about to someone, who tells someone else, who tells the narrator, Antonio Parr, who then tells us. Buechner tends to quote himself, and events which happened in earlier books appear in later ones with a sort of choral regularity of phrasing. Perhaps Buechner is saying something about the nature of memory, or reaching for the comic effect of the gossip of the gruesome which Voltaire and Swift, for instance, achieve with similar devices. But here, I think, the effect is more often that of repetition and dimness from too much distance. Often, too, Buechner omits the very details which he should not omit; for example when, in a book full of splendidly explicit language, he refers to Bebb's genital expositions with muffled euphemisms. Or, when he relates yet once more the story of Bebb's wife, who in a drunken rage has killed her baby with a toilet brush; in the last version of this, Buechner omits both the rage and the toilet brush, and treats us to the most romantic vision of child-abuse since Mary Hamilton went her way.

There is, in fact, an endless, heated, unconsummated flirtation in *Treasure Hunt,* between Buechner's lust for propriety and the massive improprieties he has chosen for his plot. The vile deeds and carnival stunts which make up all these novels might, left alone, erupt nicely into either farce or melodrama. But after creating them, Buechner never lets them alone long enough to fulfill their own purpose, and *Treasure Hunt,* at least, often reads like the Rabelais translation of *Wuthering Heights.* (pp. 38-9)

[Buechner's characterizations remind one of] those Broadway comedies of the '30s, in which funny people, easily recognizable from the second balcony by one large but harmless peccadillo, enter, collide and exit, without major social or dramatic consequences. . . .

The serious purpose behind Buechner's novel appears to be to add one further dimension to the three earlier novels' exploration of the many sides of faith. They explored the Indian hereafter, as well as Bebb's grandiloquent Christianity and Gertrude Conover's fantasy of reincarnation. *Treasure Hunt* adds to these the faith in an infinite future, exemplified by our Star Trek belief that other worlds in outer space will bring an apotheosis of our own expertise in hardware and gimmickry. . . .

Buechner's narrator keeps talking about things "pulling in two," and Buechner seems to see the world in rather Manichean terms of good and evil in constant coexistence and struggle. Reality and dream coincide and conflict, as do the treasure laid up in heaven and the worldly treasure laid up God knows where, to which the title refers. (p. 39)

This is a novel, then, of philosophical pretensions. But while he is juggling metaphysical puzzles, Buechner loses sight of balances much more fundamental to fiction. For instance, the children of this novel, all the children, are victims of hideous ironies of birth and breeding, and of the cruelty or neglect of their parents. Displaced and abandoned by vagaries of incest and by mere carelessness, their lot constitutes an outrage to which the only possible fictional responses are either comedy or despair. But Buechner seems to lose himself somewhere between Oedipus mislaid on the mountain top, and Ernest mislaid in a handbag on the Brighton line, a bland limbo where the mistreatment of children seems strangely unremarkable, and where I, at least, do not want to follow him.

I suppose in the story-telling regions of the mind, miracle and metaphor are often identical: the kiss that turns the beast to prince, the rose that knows the way home, the goose that lays golden eggs, the talking cat. Buechner is at his best when he trusts himself to such fairy-tales, when Rose Trionka, the Indian bride, floats down the aisle six feet off the ground, "as much under her own power as white clouds on a summer sky." . . . But miracles, to stay miraculous, must serve a generous purpose, conversion of the heathen, say, or at least conversion of a frog, or they are nothing more than hocus-pocus. And metaphors, if they serve no particular meaning, are nothing but purple prose. That, finally, is Buechner's major sin. All his vast machinery of plot, his dreams and visions, his four volumes of literary allusion and philosophical speculation, his films and visitations and sermons, his characters and even his geographies, are unrelated by any general purpose, by any unifying principle of tone, or theme, or *raison d'être*. Buechner remains a man divided against himself, and *Treasure Hunt* is still, like much of his earlier work, a dismayingly clever magic act. (pp. 39-40)

Edith Milton, in The New Republic *(reprinted by permission of* The New Republic; © 1977 by The New Republic, Inc.), September 17, 1977.*

In his last three novels—"Lion Country," "Open Heart" and "Love Feast"—Frederick Buechner . . . spread the good news about Leo Bebb, an "itinerant minister of the gospel" with a flair for publicity that finally led to his perishing while doing stunts in an old airplane over the heads of the annual Princeton alumni parade or "P—rade." "Treasure Hunt," a sequel to this hard act to follow is a Bebbsian "Acts of the Apostles" taken up with certain classic religious questions. Was Leo Bebb a saint, a charlatan, or a little of both? Since his remains could not be discovered in the thoroughly burned-out wreckage of the plane, did he actually die? If he died, and was indeed a great mahatma, how will his spiritual legacy be preserved, interpreted and put to effective use by the little band of stricken apostles he left behind?

The apostles include Gertrude Conover, an 80-year-old Princeton theosophist of means. . . . (p. 15)

Gertrude Conover is a memorable character, and Babe Bebb's "Uforium" or Museum of Unidentified Flying Objects is an idea with considerable entertainment value. The book is ingenious in matching New Testament biblical motifs with modern equivalents so as to suggest that mysteries such as sanctity and the incarnation are pressing contemporary matters rather than mere ancient myth. But there are some flaws too. For one thing, the narrative is awash in similes that frequently fail to light up their subjects and are sometimes pretty senseless. We may be willing to put up with "people had to walk around him like furniture" for the sake of the weak joke, but what are we to do with "the oddness of it sinking into her face like quicksand" as a way of describing a character's mental reaction to a perceived incongruity? Also, there is something cliché and unobserved in Buechner's construction of a Southern town complete with corn-pone accents and lounging good old boys, while his introduction of some comically picturesque American Indians is a lapse of taste.

The treasure of the title phrase is of course the true quality of the dead evangelist's character and career, which, it is suggested at one point, may turn out to be trash instead of gold. Such inconclusiveness is probably a good thing, forcing readers to go digging out the truth for themselves—only the author should have equipped us with a sturdier and sharper set of digging implements. (p. 49)

Julian Moynahan, "Saint? Charlatan? Both?" in The New York Times Book Review *(© 1977 by The New York Times Company; reprinted by permission), October 30, 1977, pp. 15, 49.*

* * *

BUKOWSKI, Charles   1920-

Bukowski is a prolific American writer whose poetry reflects his life as a society dropout. He began to write poetry at the age of thirty-five, after having worked as an unskilled laborer in factories and slaughterhouses. Bukowski is, according to Jack Conroy, "the greasy-spoon, rented room bard." A strength of his work is his ability to record and define his lifestyle, without self-pity, in direct and affecting language. In Bukowski's best poems, says Norman Moser, he "wraps his guts around a tree, then calmly walks off." (See also *CLC*, Vols. 2, 5, and *Contemporary Authors*, Vols. 17-20, rev. ed.)

I can't think of any other poet who comes on so raw and punky and who is so brilliant and eloquent. . . .

[How] should I react to this man, to this poetry. Should I put up my fists and fuck you him back. After all, how many poets alive use street language? How many make me laugh out loud? Then how many can give me the chills, too?

I love his poems because I can understand them. I love them because they're not intellectual games, crossword puzzles for the literature crowd. I love them because they make me say yes, yes.

Ira Kamin, "The Recorded Poet," in Pacific Sun Literary Quarterly, *May 15, 1975, p. 15.*

Most first person voices in fiction are artful; Charles Bukowski's is no exception. For "Factotum" he speaks in the name of Henry Chinaski, having pared away all the excrescences of the hype, all literary mannerism, to present himself flat out from his opening sentences plucky but woebegone, a careerist of lousy odd jobs and one night stands in the backwaters of our great American cities. "I arrived in New Orleans in the rain at five o'clock in the morning,'' Bukowski writes. ''I sat around in the bus station for awhile but the people depressed me so I took my suitcase and went out in the rain and began walking. . . .''

Compare this style to the goosed up prose of Bukowski's ''Notes of a Dirty Old Man'' . . . and you have the difference between put on and voice, between callow journalism written as self-advertisement and sensitive, moving, amusing narrative.

The rain that falls in these opening pages dampens all of Chinaski's adventures in this hard luck narrative. . . . [There's] a scene that reoccurs in . . . various milieus: either he's given his final check after being ''terminated,'' or else he walks out because no human being should have to debase and humiliate himself and waste his precious time on earth to eat.

A few years back in more prosperous times Bukowski may have passed for a crank. With a sizable percentage of the population more or less permanently unemployed he seems more like a prophet.

Bukowski owes something to Henry Miller, but just as much (like early Miller) to Dreiser, and the factualness of Defoe, and Twain. He can be accused of a lot of things, reductionism, I suppose, because he shows us what losers we all are, but in ''Factotum'' he also records quotidian tolls of courage, disenfranchisement and disgruntlement in simple language.

Not since Orwell has the condition of being down and out been so well recorded in the first person. (p. 16)

Richard Elman, in The New York Times Book Review (© *1976 by The New York Times Company; reprinted by permission), August 8, 1976.*

Bukowski is . . . a phenomenon. He has established himself as a writer with a consistent and insistent style based on what he projects as his ''personality,'' the result of hard, intense living. He sees himself as what he appears to be—a tough, old, funky, ugly, macho, cynical bastard, with just an occasional hint of compassion, usually reserved for himself:

> I keep searching the streets for that
> blood-wine battleship she drives
> with a weak battery, and the doors
> hanging from broken hinges.
>
> I drive around the streets
> an inch away from weeping,
> ashamed of my sentimentality and
> possible love.
>
> a confused old man driving in the rain
> wondering where the good luck
> went.

Since his first books appeared in the early 1960s, Bukowski has been writing out of Los Angeles, his home since he left Germany at the age of two. He writes of babes and bimbos and booze and all that Mickey Spillane-Ernest Hemingway hybrid stuff that is the basis of the images so many old-time tough guys had of themselves. It is also the basis for much of the criticism leveled at Bukowski for being sexist (''you boys can keep your virgins/give me hot old women in high heels/with asses that forgot to get old''; ''I should have kicked that redhead/in the ass/where her brains and her bread and/butter are/at . . .'').

Despite what some criticize as prose in Bukowski's poetry, there is in much of his work a poetic sensibility that, though arrogantly smart-ass and self-protective as well as self-promotional (he's the granddaddy of ''punk'' sensibility for sure), is also sometimes poignant, emotionally revealing, uniquely ''American.'' . . . (pp. 89-90)

Michael Lally, in The Village Voice (*reprinted by permission of* The Village Voice; *copyright © by The Village Voice, Inc., 1978), February 20, 1978.*

C

CAMUS, Albert   1913-1960

The Algerian-born Camus was one of the most distinguished of the French existentialists, contributing seminal works in several genres: novels, plays, and philosophical essays. In his interpretation of existentialism revealed in both *The Myth of Sisyphus* and *The Stranger*, Camus attempted to deal with the problem of the absurdity of existence, the need for order and understanding in the chaos of existence. This concern remained central to Camus's work throughout his brief career. He was the recipient of the Nobel Prize for Literature in 1957. (See also *CLC*, Vols. 1, 2, and 4.)

Reduced to its simplest expression, Camus's thought is contained in a single question: What value abides in the eyes of the man condemned to death who refuses the consolation of the supernatural? Camus cannot take his mind off this question. All his characters bring an answer; one has only to listen to them. (p. 92)

Objectivity with Camus does not strive to create an illusion of reality, for it is precisely the real which is being questioned. It strives, rather, to give the sensation of the fragmentation, the incoherence of a world which has, so to speak, lost its nuts and bolts. . . . [In *The Stranger*] Camus wanted to show an alienated subjectivity by letting the character depict himself through acts which do not express him. The difficulty was the greater as the *récit*, by its very nature, supposes a narrator who arranges past events according to the meaning he confers upon them—whereas here, precisely, the meaning is lacking. The narrator has lost the key to his own secret: he has become a stranger to his own life. He holds only facts, and facts are nothing. Therefore, he cannot give his existence a meaning which would establish its unity. Having neither past nor future, he has only a present which is crumbling away and does not become memory. Time, until the final revolt, is nothing for him but a succession of distinct moments, which no Cartesian God pieces together, which no vital impulse spans, which no remembrance transfigures. Camus has rendered admirably this fall of the present into insignificance through a paradoxical use of the first person narrative. The main character gives an account of the facts as they occurred in his life up to the eve of his execution, without the perspective of the immediate past, without extension and without resonance. Nothing is explained, but everything is revealed by the tone and the structure of the work, by the contrast of the two climaxes: the almost involuntary murder, where "the red explosion" of the sun plays a more important role than the man, and which marks the culmination of fatality; the revolt which gives birth to freedom within the confines of a destiny narrowly bounded by death. The art of Camus's *récit* lies in the subtle use of the processes which take the place of analysis, in the way the discontinuity of existence is emphasized through the continuity of tone which places all events on a single plane of indifference.

And yet, the alienation is far from being complete. A stranger to himself and to others, Meursault has a homeland: sensation. Interiority has, so to speak, emigrated from the soul to the body, and only moments of happy sensation restore a friendly world to the exile. In this sense, Camus's hero is a sort of plebeian brother of Gide's *Immoralist* who gives to the exaltation of the body the value of a protest against the false seriousness of a morality which finds it can come to terms with injustice. (pp. 92-3)

Camus, like Malraux and Sartre, belongs to a generation which history forced to live in a climate of violent death. At no other time, perhaps, has the idea of death been linked so exclusively to that of a paroxysm of arbitrary cruelty. . . . Never before had death come to man with the new face now modeled by its millions of slaves. Neither the cult of the dead, nor any belief in glory, nor any faith in eternal life accompany death into this hell. This is the image of death which is woven into every page of Camus's work. (pp. 93-4)

From *Caligula* to *The Plague,* Camus covered the same ground as had Malraux from *The Conquerors* to *Man's Fate.* Like Malraux, he confronted this problem with the aid of Nietzsche. The drama for this Nietzschean generation was that it lived on Nietzsche's thought and had simultaneously to deal, in actual fact, with its caricatural realization on a practical plane. It exalted the will to power in the individual at the very moment it prepared to fight it outside in the form of imperialism. . . . Stendhal's Julien Sorel (*The Red and the Black*) dreams of "distinctions for himself and freedom for all." Though he scorns what he attains—"Is love (war, success) then no more than this?"—the disappointment is partial and does not put into question the value of existence. When, after he has been condemned to death, Julien examines and judges himself, he can absolve himself. He has carried out without flinching the "duty" toward himself which his will to greatness had prompted; this certainly is his absolute. (p. 94)

Compare Meursault's attitude to Julien's as both face death. Just as he had not premeditated his crime, Meursault neither judges it nor assumes it. In contrast, Julien enters wholly into the least of his decisions. "My crime was premeditated," he tells the jury. Meursault neither gambles nor loses; the disconnected time in which he loses his way cannot find consummation in the moment. His entire existence is nothing but a misunderstanding, and it is through a misunderstanding that he eventually gives and suffers death. "I have not *lived in isolation* on earth," says Julien, "I had the powerful notion of *duty* . . . I was not carried away." Meursault is carried away, as his generation was to be carried away into war, by the combined effect of fever and violence. He stands in the blind spot of indifference where everything is equivalent; Julien stands at the summit of a difference which owes its worth to a unique existence. And yet, in front of death, the two meet in a revolt born of their nostalgia for happiness. . . . But Julien's revolt has a limited purpose: against society it sets up the individual and his sovereign demands. Beyond the social mechanisms which have trapped him, Meursault directs his protest against the human lot. Amid the indifference of a world devoid of God, nothing has any importance or value, except the pure act of living.

To live is enough—there is no humility whatsoever in this assertion. Camus reached it through revolt. . . . Is there any certainty one can set up in the place of hopes which betray and despair which debilitates? Again Camus answers: to live. Life as passion, challenge, obstinate refusal of all supernatural consolation, *amor fati*. Here again, Meursault and Julien meet; both think "that there is no destiny above which one cannot rise through contempt." One also sees where they part company: from one obstacle to the next, from one victory to another, Julien conquers his destiny. No sooner has he reached the summit, than he is hurled straight into the abyss. Imprisoned, then condemned, it occurs to him that he might escape, but he does not dwell on the idea. A great individual does not begin his adventure anew, does not consent to repeat himself. Enlightened by his failure, Meursault reaches very different conclusions, and his modern revolt becomes clearly undifferentiated from the romantic revolt of which it is the heir: at the juncture he has reached, Meursault must consider the question of beginning anew. A sure instinct guided Camus when he chose the myth of Sisyphus. He understood with Nietzsche that repetition, starting over again until death, is the supreme test of the absurd. Hence the curious impression *The Stranger* makes on the reader. A book without hope, or rather against hope, it ends on a promise. (pp. 95-6)

In the trajectory of revolt which links us to the Romantics, Julien is at the highest, Meursault at the lowest point, but at the exact spot where revolt can surge up again. We can see what has been lost during the period that separates Julien from Meursault: the ideal of the Great Personality (today Malraux and Montherlant are the only writers who carry on this tradition). But, if it is true that the great personality contained the germ of its own disintegration, that between Napoleon and Hitler—the frantic puppet who has disappeared under the myths he fanned to a white heat—there exists only the difference between an original and its carica-

ture, one may wonder whether revolt is not a phenomenon of decadence. (p. 96)

"War," wrote Saint-Exupery, "is not an adventure. War is a disease, like typhus." In order better to make us feel this, [in *The Plague*] Camus painted disease, not war. Consequently, realistic techniques, which, applied to the historical event, would have been laughable, become legitimate and effective. The objectivity with which Camus describes the epidemic is dependent on the same cryptic and non-naturalistic realism he used in *The Stranger*. Perhaps the use of the term *cryptic* to define a style which is at times sententious and whose transparency appears without mystery, will seem debatable. The multiplicity of meanings and interpretations it suggests, the deciphering it necessitates, certainly seem to remove it from allegory, which always conceals some precise object. Nothing of the sort in *The Plague*, where the scourge sometimes designates the event, sometimes the human condition, sometimes sin, sometimes misfortune.

Camus did not attempt to convey the complexity of the events through the technique of simultaneity and juxtaposition of scenes. To the pulverization of time and space he preferred the concentration of a continuous narration which could keep the tone of a testimony. The difficulty lay in taking up, one by one, through symbolic transcription, the themes of life and death during the occupation, starting from both subjectivity and collectivity. Certainly, the theme of the successive manifestations of the scourge is developed in too linear a pattern, and there is something too schematic in the characters, who synthetize the manifold aspects of the ordeal. One should not forget, however, that the real hero is not the I but the *we* elevated to the dignity of the particular being. Those who went through the ordeal of occupation recognize those situations where, speaking of themselves, they were compelled to say *we* at a time when each lived the *we* in an abyss of isolation and exile. The precarious solidarity which had thus linked people as they faced the catastrophe, and which would not outlive this catastrophe, called for a testimony which would rescue it from history and restore it to ethics. This is the task of the poet. Camus answered this call. He tried to describe an experience which had taken place at the level of intersubjectivity, without using either Jules Romains' unanimist technique or an analytical technique. Giving the humiliated *we* a voice required a form of speech simple enough to reflect the banality of the atrocious, and yet closely knit enough to sustain an insurgent thought. The slightest lack of authenticity would immediately have reduced the *we* to the *they*. A poet-moralist and not a novelist-poet, Camus is not gifted with the visionary imagination which creates myths and worlds. He draws a diagram and leaves it up to us to decipher it.

In one respect *The Plague* seems to us to fall short of the reality it recalls: it has no symbolic equivalent for the humiliation of the suffering inflicted upon man by man. It may seem strange that Camus should have deliberately left aside torture and the demonic attempt to reduce man to the state of a superfluous puppet. But we should not forget that the sentence of death is the central theme of his work. It matters little here whether it is nature, fate, justice, or human cruelty which pronounces the sentence. We know that in his most diabolic inventions man only imitates the tortures of life. . . . The "collaborator" who accepts and invites the plague is anything but a monster: he is a humbled individual, unhappy rather than despicable, who takes refuge in catastrophe in order to escape fear. Camus's attitude can be understood: by identifying war with the plague, evil with illness, he wanted to present a picture of sin without God; and in this perspective, the partisans of the plague are no longer "possessed," but sick. This leads him dangerously to dissolve individual responsibility in the diffuse guilt of life. "What is the plague?" says one of the characters, "it's life and that's all.". . . Guides and healers, the stubborn heroes of *The Plague* remain subjected to the precariousness which binds them to the *we*, of which they are and want to be a part. In short, attempting to be modest without God, they nurse the supreme ambition of doing without God, without aspiring to become gods. (pp. 98-100)

[In] *The Plague,* Camus's answer to the fundamental question—What value can withstand the death sentence?—is no longer the same as in *The Stranger.* For the exiled *I* whose existence is literally nothing but fall—a fall into the past, into the sin of indifference—the often ignored happiness which wells up with memory, the happiness of being, is the only authentic value. But for the man who starts to struggle, living is not enough. Man regains control of himself in the revolt against death, and henceforth this recovery itself, the good will to begin anew without illusions as to the outcome of the struggle, becomes for him the primary value. To be a man condemned, with and among other men likewise condemned: therein lies our task. For Camus, this is the province of ethics—of the *we* engaged in a desperate venture, beneath a narrow sky darkened by the plague. But Camus wants to base the common effort on individual freedom. We have already noted that he defines freedom through revolt and lucidity—by means of what limits freedom, since revolt clashes with the irreparable and lucidity with the irrational. It is a strange freedom whose motto is: "as if." It has made so many concessions to necessity that it can only act "as if" it were freedom. Camus knows this only too well and admits it: "What freedom can there be in the fullest sense without assurance of eternity?" He has granted himself the only freedom compatible with the world of the man condemned to death. Does it bring nothing but a semblance? If we examine it more closely, we can recognize it as the freedom of Adam and Eve banished from paradise, at the moment when alone and unprotected they assume the burden of their earthly existence. The mutilated freedom of Adam and Eve after the fall is not devoid of love, since it begets the solidarity of this first *we* facing a hostile world. If we examine it even more closely, we recognize the frightening present-day freedom with which we face a future that must be created out of nothing. "The individual can do nothing, and yet he can do everything," said Camus in *The Myth of Sisyphus. The Plague* reaffirms the same thing on the level of the "we." (pp. 100-01)

We do not propose to pit these two ethics against each other. We do not choose an ethic as we choose a coat. It steals in on us, permeates us, and is already within the walls while we are still arguing about it. The de-Christianized ethic is heir to Christianity in more ways than one, if only because it gives primordial importance to the theme of the sentence of death, which is the theme of the Passion. It began with an act of defiance, and it still must bring about the paradoxical fusion of revolt (in time) and acceptance (in eternity). If this ethic implies, as Camus thinks—but does he really think it?—a renunciation of eternity, it would an-

nul itself by destroying the paradox on which it rests. All the contradictions in Camus stem from the fact that he wants to reduce freedom to the liberty of action in history, while seeking to find "freedom in salvation" through history. (p. 101)

Camus made use of two complementary art forms, the *récit* and the drama. In his *récits,* Camus successfully fused the tradition of the purest French artists, particularly of Gide, with the influence of Kafka. As for the drama, I detect no teacher save himself. It must be said, however, that he belongs to a time where metaphysical problems assume such a concrete appearance that writers as different as Gabriel Marcel, Sartre and Camus himself, feel the need to resort simultaneously to the discursive and to the dramatic expression of their thought. Camus reserved the theme of the will to power for his theater, and, for his *récits,* the theme of the struggle of the oppressed to whom violent rebellion is forbidden. Not that violence and revolt are absent from the *récits,* but they either assume a mask of indifference, or else they give way to the liberating action they stirred up. Since tragedy is by definition the place where a revolted freedom is at work, Camus has turned to tragedy when he wished to treat the problem of the relationships between freedom and revolt, By a kind of predestination, the debate which was personal to Camus coincided exactly with the political tragedy of our time. Inside, outside, the pressure was the same; Camus wrote *Caligula* and *The Misunderstanding* both in order to gain control over his own personal situation and in order to resist the pressure of history. His heroes, like Camus himself, experience the common condition as an individual condition, at the point where history and subjectivity collide. They also join the procession of characters who have incarnated the Lucifer myth of the Occident. Sustaining their particular conflicts, we discern the din of a vaster drama which, in the realm of fiction, reproduces the drama of history: the drama of the Great Personality. Its rise and fall, the heights it attains in Stendhal and Dostoevski, the blows it is dealt by Flaubert and Tolstoy, its crises, its resurgence and its ultimate defeat make up a history which lives once more with Camus's rebels. They mime the passion and the agony of individuality; their cry is his cry, their violence prolongs the wave of cruelty which always accompanies the destruction of a great model, be it the Knight, the seventeenth-century "Honnête homme," or the Significant Personality. (p. 102)

Play-acting, as Camus so clearly saw, is by no means an accidental trait [of Caligula's]; it is part of the very being of the tyrant. Insofar as Caligula is not equal to his scheme of total annihilation, and he knows it while not wishing to know it, he is in bad faith and therefore must play for himself and for others the comedy of absolute power. The staccato humor of the scenes of mockery alternates with the impassioned irony of the dialogues in which the ally of death confronts, first the defender of the sacred, then the advocate of reason. The struggle is all the more poignant as Camus turns against himself, being, in a sense, just as much on the side of Caligula as with Scipio, the poet, and Chereas, the wise man who refuses to acquiesce in the sacrilegious disorders of hatred. . . . The fear and the hatred of Caligula's victims, the breathless anguish of the Killer grow from act to act, until, at last, Caligula succumbs not to the revolt of his mediocre enemies, but to the blows of the two friends he has deemed worthy of delivering him from his fate. As he dies, he has the satisfaction of having driven the reasonable Chereas and Scipio the pure to that same violence which they condemned in him. Vanquished, but not punished, he recognizes his error: he demanded the infinite from that absolute finality which is death. What does he ask for? The impossible, the moon, "something which is mad perhaps, but which is not of this world," and which he cannot make an attribute of his power. Caligula must eradicate from his soul this desire which makes him dependent upon something he cannot put into words. And it is precisely the one thing he cannot do. Therein lies his limitation, therein his paradox. . . .

He externalizes evil in order to liberate himself, and by doing so he clings to necessity and plays into its hands. The externalizing of evil is nothing but a way of shifting the responsibility for original sin on an absent god. (p. 103)

When he equated freedom and revolt, Caligula forgot that it is always within the power of freedom to annihilate itself. To be sure, Camus is right in a sense: evil is outside; Sophocles is right: the gods have run the show. But the opposite is also true, as the myth of original sin recalls: freedom's attempt to destroy itself is consummated within.

Camus's art was never surer of itself than in *The Misunderstanding*. From an anonymous news clipping dealing with a chance event he drew a pure tragedy of high quality, achieving an architectural style which carries the play out of reality so that the sacrifice played out on stage becomes a kind of poetic celebration. Humanism, left to its own inclination, would easily fall into the "human all too human" if it did not preserve a sense of the sacred in profane tragedy. With *The Misunderstanding* all that was emphatic and too highly colored in *Caligula* has disappeared. Only that blending of nostalgia and violence peculiar to all of Camus's rebels remains. His vengeful heroine has a stature, a splendor which make her not unworthy of comparison with Electra. . . . Thanks to the remarkable power of fusion which allows him to blend contrasts without blurring them, Camus combines an acute romanticism with the completely classic structure of his play. Romantic in its theme of discontent, in its demand for the absolute in earthly happiness, in its apotheosis of the body against a backdrop of absolute pessimism, *The Misunderstanding* is an austere work which harks back to ancient drama by way of Kafka. Everything begins and ends in an inn, which resembles the inn where Kafka's surveyor "K." appears, as it recalls the palace of Oedipus; all is consummated in the course of a night befogged by the thickening of the misunderstanding. Camus has returned to his themes—the conflict of sainthood and the will to power, of individual happiness and of action—and has narrowed them so as to make them converge on the central issue of the choice. Freedom surges up between chance and fate; nothing external limits it or forces its hand at the moment when it goes astray. It is freedom itself which begets the fate on which it runs aground. Therein lies the tragedy of *The Misunderstanding,* rather than in the consequences of the choice, however dreadful they be. The dramatic tension which one experiences here as a choking sensation derives less from the horror of the impending murder than from the contrast between the lucidity of the characters with respect to themselves and the blindness they display in their relations with one another. Everything takes place as if their lucidity were their prison. There is almost no sentence in the second act which does not have a different meaning for the one who speaks it and for the one

who hears it. The entire play is built on ambiguity: one has to choose in the dark, without being recognized and without being able to make oneself known. Everyone is betrayed by everybody, including himself. Camus saw the heart of the matter: our modern tragedy is the tragedy of ambiguity touching all mankind. But Camus characteristically depicted ambiguity in the guise of misunderstanding rather than bad faith, just as elsewhere he reduces treason to a fear complex, and cruelty to the transgression of a man humiliated by death. All things being equal, his attitude recalls Corneille, always at ease in extreme violence, and whose vocabulary does not include the word for treason. In this light, the heroine of *The Misunderstanding* is indeed the sister of Corneille's heroines: she has the same tense nobility and the same wilful mind in the madness of her pride. It is not by chance, either, that Camus recreates the pathos of ambiguity, as found in the Greek tragic poets. His conception of evil as diffused guilt and the fatal mistake of a will to power quite naturally recalls the Greeks. But he is faced with a new problem which neither the Greek nor the French classical traditions can help them solve. Individual conflicts tend more and more to become equated with collective conflicts, not in order to lose themselves in the collective, but in order to embody it. . . . The playwright must therefore simultaneously expand our field of vision and circumscribe the field of drama; he must rebuild a stage which spans the chaos and is ready to receive and transform the creatures which come to it out of chaos. If the poet thinks he can elude history by means of a short cut, he becomes a counterfeiter; if he lets himself be absorbed by history, he becomes superficial. Yet, the duality of his point of departure must lead him to heights where, beyond antagonisms, the tragic poem finds the balance and calm of beauty. Camus almost meets these conditions in *The Misunderstanding,* a personal drama if ever there was one, but one in which we discern the rumblings of a collective disaster. . . . What makes *The Misunderstanding* a classical play, even though it carries romantic recrimination to a paroxysm, is much less its observance of the three unities than the intimate collaboration of the moralist and the poet in its creation. Camus proves, moreover, that the controlled and taut language which his cryptic realism calls for can, if need be, take over the functions of poetry and adapt to the needs of tragedy. We are far from ideological melodrama. (pp. 104-06)

The Misunderstanding ends on an indignant denial, a total denial of God in view of the endlessness of human suffering. And, as always, Camus's outraged awareness of the injustice done to man is so intense that it leads him to an affirmation of the exteriority of evil. Yet, in contrast, Camus shows us the will to deification as logically fulfilled in the deicide, or murder of the Son. In spite of everything, the free individual is still responsible for the alienation of his freedom. Sin without God is nothing but the choice of the wrong freedom.

A Mediterranean romantic in his insatiable longing for the finite, the tangible, for contours which light does not erode and which even night respects, Camus is very close to the Latin elegists in his lyricism, and to the Greek tragic poets in his pathos. He is in his own element with the French classics. A skeptic by temperament, not through philosophic conviction, a skeptic in so far as he is an artist, his lineage goes back to Montaigne and Saint-Evremond. But he is passionate, too, in a serious, virile fashion, and can also claim Corneille and Pascal as his ancestors. Besides, there is nothing he need disavow in order to reconcile within himself the teachings of the classics and those of Kierkegaard, Dostoevski and Chekhov. We have already pointed to the remarkable coexistence in Camus of the gift of fusion and of contradiction. (p. 106)

> *Rachel Bespaloff, "The World of the Man Condemned to Death," in* Esprit *(reprinted by permission of* Esprit*), January, 1950 (and reprinted in* Camus: A Collection of Critical Essays, *edited by Germaine Brée, Prentice-Hall, Inc., 1962, pp. 92-107).*

To characterize Camus as a religious-moral philosopher means to say that his preoccupation is with questions of the nature and meaning of men, their hopes, their possibilities, and their destiny. And within this area Camus has established a positive humanism, a religious philosophy which, to many, is the first move toward what has been termed a "new humanism."

What is mandatory is that, if there is to be such a thing as a new humanism, it cannot be developed in isolation from the great religious alternatives which the Western world possesses. This is to say that such a philosophy must be honest and articulate in the reasons it offers for rejecting the claims of Marxism and the Christian faith. Camus has not been remiss in this, inasmuch as a large portion of his philosophical work has entailed a criticism of the Marxist and Christian positions, and this is one reason for the importance of his thought. In this criticism Marxism has been the central and most urgent concern of Camus, and in *The Rebel* the sections dealing with Marxist theory and prophecy constitute one of the most trenchant critiques of Communist thought and action ever written from the viewpoint of moral philosophy. But, if large sections of Camus's philosophical works are devoted solely to Marxism, this is not the case with the Christian faith. Camus has nowhere, up to the present, dealt at length with Christian theology. But yet all his major works are filled with direct or indirect references to Christianity, and these constant references create the atmosphere in which Camus's positive thought moves. This lack of an extended critique of Christianity is explained by the fact that, although Camus is an anti-Communist, he is not an anti-Christian—he is simply a non-Christian. As such, he has never cut himself off from conversation with Christian thinkers but stands in a relation of tension to Christianity, directing his criticism to the moral effects of this faith without condemning its ultimate sources, even though he does not accept them. And, certainly, this is as it should be, for any Western philosopher who begins with the assumption that the Christian faith is an illusion and hence entirely discredited is suspect of irresponsibility or willful ignorance. Although Marxism is, for Camus, the most urgent problem to which he addresses himself, it is the Christian faith which is the most fundamental issue and the one with which he must most clearly come to terms. (pp. 48-9)

For Camus the first data of religion and morality are the evil and death that are part of the abiding condition of men. Whether or not there be goodness or God is not a primary evidence of human existence—suffering and death are. (p. 50)

Camus understands . . . that in its best moments the Chris-

tian faith is active in its cultivation of beauty and goodness and sustained by a tragic hope in its acceptance of evil and death. And this is the Christian position which Father Paneloux puts forth in his two sermons in the attempt to bring meaning into the plight of a city beaten by the plague. It is true that, following the death of the child, Paneloux's second sermon was more moderate and less certain than the first; but the difference between the two sermons consisted in saying that, if the plague be not the punishment of the sins of the people, it is at least part of the designs of God, so mysterious they may be, and must, in faith, be accepted and finally loved. . . . Given human evil and death, either God is innocent and men are guilty or else God is guilty and men are innocent. The death of a child poses the alternative of all or nothing for the Christian faith. (pp. 52-3)

Camus raises the cry for a life in which values are found within history and within human action itself and not above or beyond history. He argues that, so long as we live with values which are posited absolutely and transhistorically, we shall not avoid murder. For it is only when one is absolutely certain of his values that the nonexistence of other men is justified. But, if the values of men are posited within the relativities of human history, then no man can with certainty sacrifice the lives of others for this uncertain value. The effort to validate these uncertain values of human existence was the purpose of Camus's most distinguished philosophical work, *The Rebel*. Against the aspiration for totality, conquest, and perfection in human history, Camus places a history in which men have limits, and knowledge has uncertainties, and values have relativity. To attempt to transform men into the image of an absolute value is not to fulfill them but to murder and deform them. For men are not infinitely plastic; they are not things which can be endlessly molded and changed. They have limits, and to go beyond these limits is only to add to the total of suffering in human history. It is this limit which all men find within themselves and which is shared in common by all men that is the only source of value which men possess. It is the only real value in human existence. And it is when this limit, this value, is transgressed that men revolt. Revolt, alone, is revelatory of human values and, as such, constitutes an essential dimension of human experience. It is on the basis of such an understanding of human value that Camus is able to say [in *The Rebel*] to a religion of historicity, "Does the end justify the means? This is possibly so. But what will justify the end? To this question, which historical thought leaves hanging, revolt replies: the means." . . . (pp. 55-6)

It is a curious thing about the thought of Albert Camus that he has not estranged himself from Christian readers. This may possibly be because Christian thinkers have not as yet realized the full import of what he has said about the Christian faith. Whatever the reason may be, it is interesting that, when Christians pick up the works of such a man as Sartre, it is largely with a mind to refute; but, when Christians pick up the works of Camus, it is with a mind to learn. (p. 56)

At first glance, it is a strange and artificial world in which Camus moves, until suddenly the thundering realization comes that this is our world of which he speaks; it is the history which daily moves about us, except that now it has attained a definitive clarity. Camus immerses us as he himself is immersed in the tragedy and tense hopes of the mid-twentieth century; he is, as he says, "a child of his times." This world and the history lying behind it, which Camus has delineated in his philosophical works, is the world that is in turn found in all his literary works.... It is the moral philosophy which underlies these novels and plays that gives them their force and desperation, and it is only in terms of this larger philosophical position that the literary works of Camus can be fully understood. For Camus is first of all a philosopher with serious moral and religious concerns, and all his literary productions serve as functions of these concerns.

We come to understand the thought of Albert Camus only after we have probed the full significance of his optimism about man and his pessimism about human destiny. For this throws us back to the abiding evidence of evil in human existence. For the Christian the ultimate character of the universe is good, and in this he finds his hope and the ability to transcend and accept, to a degree, the evil in the world. But what, at this point, has become clear about the thought of Camus is that for him the ultimate character of the universe is evil and consequently men are always uncertain and always threatened; whatever goodness there be in life, it is in men, and this goodness is created only in the struggle of men to preserve and enlarge this area of goodness which they alone know and which they alone can guarantee. Value and truth lie within men, and it is only by virtue of the contrast which a threatening world presents to men that they become conscious of the salvation which lies within them. However strange this attitude toward the world may seem at first glance, further reflection will show that it is not after all either strange or even novel. Those who have come to know the thought of Sören Kierkegaard will here recognize remarkable similarities in what might be assumed to be quite disparate philosophies. More interesting still is the fact that Camus's attitude at this point is solidary with that of Christian orthodoxy in its depiction of man's life as a "trial." In face of the threatening character of the world, Camus calls men to revolt. And the call to revolt is nothing more or less than a call to create; to transform the inhumanity of the world into the image of man, to humanize what is inhuman—in short, to civilize. This is the "new humanism" put forth by Albert Camus—a humanism whose final and only goal is the uncertain and mortal lives of men, creatures who are not infinitely pliable and suffering but are limited and infinitely precious and must at all costs be defended against those who would judge their lives and history by that which is foreign to their lives and history. But, after all, we ask, what is man? Man, replies Camus, "is that force which always ends by holding off gods and tyrants".... (pp. 57-8)

> *Thomas L. Hanna, "Albert Camus and the Christian Faith," in* The Journal of Religion *(copyright © 1956 by The University of Chicago), October, 1956 (and reprinted in* Camus: A Collection of Critical Essays, *edited by Germaine Brée, Prentice-Hall, Inc., 1962, pp. 48-58).*

I do not think that any of the six tales contained in *Exile and the Kingdom* can be ranked with Albert Camus's most accomplished writings; but no other book by Camus has made me more keenly aware of the profound nature and actual status of his work. The quest, the intensity, the distribution of this work; what it has attempted and still is attempting to do; what new horizons open up before it: all seem to me to be more clearly visible here than anywhere else.

None of these tales are able to strike us, to hold our attention, to inscribe themselves in our memory with the force of *The Stranger, The Plague,* or even *The Fall.* The reason for this is evident. All of Camus's previous books carry through to conclusion a particular line of thought, which finds its form in the simplification and enlargement of a mythical image. These extremes of perspective, the massive writing have an imperious eloquence. Here we are brought back to a state of in-betweens, of confusion, to the careful fusing of the characteristics of everyday existence. Even when it is dramatic, this existence is composed of humble, day-to-day details. "The Silent Men," "The Guest," "The Adulterous Woman" are presented as realistic accounts: that is the way things actually happened, and there is always some detail, attesting to the brutish thoughtlessness of reality, which prevents the narrative from disappearing into the pure and inflexible line of myth. There is always some detail which describes an existing situation without any mental reservation. "The Artist at Work" and "The Growing Stone," on the other hand, have somewhat the appearance of fables. In "The Artist at Work" the irony of the narrator is directed visibly toward the narrative, dispelling the dust of insignificant facts. In "The Growing Stone" the tone is that of legend, but there is also amusement in this irony: the pleasure of recounting in a legendary tone. At any rate, it seems to me that these tales are the first in which Camus takes into consideration the actual subject matter of his narrative and dwells upon the details. Whereas previously he had sought the most exact and most simplified coincidence between a thought impulse and a dramatic action, here he is observing, imagining—caught in the web of reality. (pp. 152-53)

The author's impress is not as visible as usual: we no longer entirely recognize his austerity, his haughty abstraction, his willful reduction to bare essentials. The discordancy of tone may be perplexing because legend succeeds parody, interior monologue succeeds behaviorist narrative. Even the value accorded to geographical location is such as to surprise us. The Algeria of *The Stranger* and of *The Plague* was scarcely less allegorical than the Holland of *The Fall.* Here the setting is more than a conventional situation, or an allegorical agreement between space and mind: the Brazilian forest of "The Growing Stone," the North Africa of the other narratives—it is a fact, a reality which attracts to itself a large portion of that attention which had previously been fixed upon the moral and the symbol. (p. 153)

Camus's problem is to relate the unity of artistic expression with a vibrant inner experience, torn apart so that it may live. How can one gather into unity of expression that which escapes all unity? Sometimes in his linear narrative the unity of myth achieves artistic efficacy only by belying the truth of the experience: the *roman-hypothèse* achieves unity solely because it is false; it has the air of a dangerous abstraction. Sometimes, notably in *The Plague,* Camus tried to integrate his inner diversity with the unity of a form by composing, in mid-stream, a somewhat disappointing fusion. To go in one direction only, but to its extreme limit —or to bring into balance opposing tendencies: Camus hesitates between Descartes and Gide, between utmost rigor and infinite comprehension. But the true path lies beyond this hesitation. The present work, rather than being entrapped by the author's fame is still in the process of defining itself, of seeking out its rightful place. I have always thought this, and I find a moving and comforting confirmation of this idea in these lines which Camus wrote for an edition of *L'Envers et l'endroit* (Betwixt and Between): "The day when a balance shall be struck between what I am and what I do; on that day perhaps, I scarcely dare write it, I shall be able to give substance to the work of which I have always dreamed."

The work he dreamed of is not *Exile and the Kingdom,* but this collection of stories allows him to envision it somewhat better. *Exile and the Kingdom* and, as I can imagine solely from the nature of the title, *L'Envers et l'endroit* are faithful to the author's concept of truth because they are based on a constant coming and going, on a particular tempo. *The Stranger, The Plague, The Fall* all contain effective myths, rigorous thoughts, but because of that unity which is reflected by the single word in their titles, they destroy the rhythmical truth of a life seeking to know itself. (pp. 153-54)

Camus has a passion for the theater; but he does not seem to have the necessary genius. He wrote one theatrical masterpiece: *Requiem for a Nun,* but only by drawing upon Faulkner. His plays grow weaker as their structure becomes more dramatic. The finest one, *Caligula,* is simply a monologue. The best of Camus's writings up to the present have not touched upon this element of dialogue which is inherent in Camus. To be more precise, they suppressed or mitigated it; but here, in the succession of stories in *Exile and the Kingdom,* the tempo which myth destroyed, and which the theater reflected but feebly, imposes its rhythmical beat. (p. 154)

Each of Camus's books conformed to the other because each one brought forth only one word in its title instead of emitting the rhythm of an entire phrase. Thus *The Fall* corresponded to *The Plague* as *The Plague* corresponded to *The Stranger. Exile and the Kingdom* does not in the least correspond to *The Fall;* it does not add another segment in the formation of a line; but in contrast to the successes of abstraction, it poses an attempt at completeness. . . .

The Fall fully explores one path, leaving us suspended on the verge of an answer which it cannot possibly give, because to do so it would have to return to the point of departure. Like all the preceding books, *The Fall* corresponds to a point in progression (which could, as is the case in this instance, assume a regressive pace), while *Exile and the Kingdom* contains a definite movement. In *The Fall* there is only an exile without a kingdom. There is no answer to the discovery made by Clamence (good itself is evil)—at least no answer which does not oblige us to start afresh from nothing. Here the answer is always given with the question, the right with the wrong side, the kingdom with the exile.

This book is not based upon a contradiction, and herein lies its success. The exile and the kingdom are not two continents separated by an ocean: they are two aspects of the same breath and heartbeat. The kingdom is in the exile, the exile is a path toward the kingdom—in fact, exile could actually be the kingdom. (p. 155)

In "The Guest," which is perhaps the most effective story in the collection, we see clearly that the conflict is not between solitude and fellowship, or liberty and submission. The hero does not oscillate between two forms of solitude: one, the cruelest of exiles, is a solitude in which the gestures of fraternity turn against us—the solitude of incomprehension; the other, which constitutes the sole portrayal of the kingdom, is the solitude in which we are aware of what we have done, and realize that it was necessary to do what he did. Is this the opposing of two attitudes: building up a good point and tracking down a bad one? Not at all. The book invites us to probe the very pulse of existence—which unfolds, then shuts up tight; reveals itself in a flash of light, then veils itself in obscurity; waxes and then wanes. The moralist who isolates and dissects is succeeded by the poet who puts together and restores the one complex throb of life. (p. 156)

> *Gaëtan Picon, "Exile and the Kingdom,"
> translated by Josephine Valenza, in* Mercure
> de France *(reprinted by permission of the
> author and* Mercure de France*), May, 1957
> (and reprinted in* Camus: A Collection of
> Critical Essays, *edited by Germaine Brée,
> Prentice-Hall, Inc., 1962, pp. 152-56).*

So honest a man as Camus is obviously at a disadvantage in so dishonest an institution as the theater. His sincerity has become a legend, but it has prevented him from becoming a successful dramatist. . . . I can not think of a better application of the term "defect of his virtue"; Camus's strenuous virtue is the key to his plays and to his defective sense of the theater. Explicitly forswearing "psychology, ingenious plot-devices, and spicy situations," he requires that we take him in the full intensity of his earnestness or not at all.

Simple in plot, direct in argument, oratorically eloquent, his dramas are like few other modern plays. They remind us of Gide and of the early Sartre (in *No Exit* and *The Flies*), before Sartre mastered the deceptions of politics and of the stage. But even these comparisons are inadequate because Camus differs significantly from his many French contemporaries who have put ancient myths on the modern stage. The others have turned conventional myths—at least their antiquity has made them seem conventional—into instruments of iconoclasm. Obviously stimulated by French neoclassical drama, Cocteau, Giraudoux, and Sartre became the debunking inside-dopesters of ancient mythology; they made Oedipus into a young man on the make, Electra into a rather addled termagant, Zeus into a tyrant. They overturned or exposed the classical stories. But what Camus does is to begin with a sufficiently cynical legend—the history of Caligula or the murder of the prodigal son (the basis of Robert Penn Warren's "Ballad of Billie Potts")—and to dramatize it as forthrightly as possible, with no tricks, no sneers, no "modernization."

Both circumstances and characters are very carefully selected to perform only what the play requires. Nothing is ever thrown in for good measure or for any incidental purpose. We never encounter in these plays the casual bystanders whom a Broadway dramatist might permit to wander in. What characters there are have strict requirements imposed upon them. Camus primarily demands that his protagonists possess freedom, the capacity for exercising free choice. He has to go far to find his free men. His preference sets Camus off from his contemporaries in the theater; some of this difference is implicit in the contrast Eric Bentley once drew between "Strindbergian" and "Ibsensite" actors. The Strindbergian actor is less restrained: "His emotions come right out of him with no interference whatsoever and fly like bullets at the enemy." But Ibsen, not Strindberg, is the father of modern drama, and, consequently, modern stage characters keep their neuroses in check—or at least in balance. Camus's characters tend to be Strindbergian. Some of Strindberg's unbalanced heroes earn their freedom at the expense of their sanity; one of Camus's heroes, Caligula, pays just this price for freedom. Criminal purposes inspire the principal motivation of *The Misunderstanding* and so liberate the characters from ordinary scruples. The protagonists of *The Just Assassins* are also on the far side of the law, revolutionaries who have put aside the usual inhibitions and are in the act of measuring their freedom. The most dynamic figure in *State of Siege* is, like Caligula, in possession of supreme political power and subject to no regulation by sanity. Camus's characters tear right into the issues, and they ignore small details. Just as Lear's "Pray you, undo this button," could not have occurred in Racine, it also would be an unlikely line in Camus. Everyone in these plays is ready for action—or, more often, for argument. Nothing may intervene to distract, irritate, or enchant us, to explain the characters or to provide context for the events.

The characters are free so that they may best contribute to the simple patterns which the plays work out. Of the four plays at hand, two are constructed to the very simplest formulas—*The Misunderstanding* and *The Just Assassins*. The former play requires to be read as an equation. The prodigal son returns wealthy and incognito, to be killed by his desperate mother and sister. Most have seen in this play a perfect paradigm of the absurdity of hoping to escape from poverty or exile. Camus has become more optimistic about man's fate, but, in squeezing a new interpretation out of the play, he still, inevitably, reduces it to a formula. It can be reconciled with a relative optimism as to man. For, after all, it amounts to saying that in an unjust or indifferent world man can save himself, and save others, by practicing the most basic sincerity and pronouncing the most appropriate word.

In other words, don't play jokes on Mother. This is what Meursault, of *The Stranger*, saw in the same story, but even this authority is not conclusive. Surely it is more exact to say that the slightest weakness, the most innocent facetious impulse, will release an absurd and implacable destiny. Still, relatively optimistic or not, the play is flesh fitted to the bare bones of an equation.

Caligula is something else again. It has more life and irony than any of the other plays, and it comes closer than any of the others to a balanced, qualified statement of a complex theme. Caligula compels us to admire his comic talents; in one unconnected episode after another, this tyrant and mass-murderer engages our interest and even our sympathy with his ingenious exposures of patrician banality and the illogic of daily life. In his defense, this engaging monster is permitted to point out that he has caused far fewer casualties than a major war. A successful revolt fortunately reminds us that, all kidding aside, we need to find some compromise between banality and the loss of freedom.

The language of these plays is lofty and pure. It reflects the complaint Camus once lodged against our time: "For the dialogue we have substituted the communique." The dramatist sets out to remedy this situation, but his dialogue tends to become, especially in *The Just Assassins* and *State of Siege*, a formal exchange of weighty remarks which too clearly expose the dramatist's designs on us. Hardly anyone else in the modern theater lectures us quite so directly. . . . Camus addresses us in the most elevated language he can write. The result has its merits as oratory and as dialectic, but it is deficient as drama.

The defect of Camus's plays bring to mind the virtues of his fiction, in which the method of narration always keeps us from colliding too abruptly with his themes and, above all, his ideas. This rationale surely underlies the impersonality of *The Stranger* and *The Plague*, as well as the highly subjective narration of *The Fall* and "The Renegade." The danger of becoming a pamphleteer in fiction must have been clear to Camus and must have compelled him to use technique as a shield for his ideas. But, in his plays, collisions are head-on; except in *Caligula*, we miss the theater's equivalents for the sophisticated method of his fiction. (pp. 170-72)

Henry Popkin, "Camus As Dramatist," in Partisan Review *(copyright © 1959 by Partisan Review, Inc.), Summer, 1959 (and reprinted in* Camus: A Collection of Critical Essays, *edited by Germaine Brée, Prentice-Hall, Inc., 1962, pp. 170-72).*

[If Camus] speaks now from the grave, as he does virtually every day, it is usually in this way: to confer some sort of nobility on other men's positions or prose. His reputation seems more and more honorific; his work has been carved up into quotations—a kind of *Bartlett's* of liberal piety, which now only awaits an edition. . . . If it is hard to think about Camus any more, it is partly because one has lost sight of the writer inside the statue.

A good way to begin seeing Camus himself again is by reading a new collection of his prose titled *Lyrical and Critical Essays*. (p. 276)

From the start, as throughout his career, Camus felt more lucidly than he reasoned. His ideas were the home truths of his experience, linked less by logic than by their emotional fit and weighed by their existential consequences. "I have never seen anyone die," as he put it, "for the ontological argument." Just as his theme of the absurd came directly from his life, so did its resolution—the conquering indifference in which he had been raised. (p. 278)

Theodore Solotaroff, "The Young Camus" (1968), in his The Red Hot Vacuum and Other Pieces on Writing in the Sixties *(copyright © 1968, 1970 by Theodore Solotaroff; reprinted by permission of Atheneum Publishers, New York), Atheneum, 1970, pp. 276-83.*

[One] recognizes the inseparable nature of content and form, idea and expression, in Camus's work. Indeed, the various attacks that have been mounted against Camus in terms of his alleged ideological unsoundness or lack of sufficient political commitment are ultimately irrelevant and based on a fundamental misunderstanding of his nature as a writer. To make such criticisms is to ask not that Camus should be a more honest or more sensitive writer but that he should be a completely different person as man and artist. This is equivalent to taxing Donne with not being Milton or Dostoevsky with not being Tolstoy.... Camus achieved, in his earliest published work, a wholly personal tone, a "lyrisme intense, sec comme le cri des cigales". As regards his desire for unity, this arose from a fundamental dualism—a view of life as rich in oppositions as those of Pascal, Nietzsche, Gide or Montherlant.

> *"Beyond Contradiction," in* The Times Literary Supplement (© *Times Newspapers Ltd., 1973; reproduced from* The Times Literary Supplement *by permission), October 12, 1973, p. 1252.*

L'Etranger is clearly structured by portrayals of death: there are three deaths portrayed—that of Meursault's mother, which opens the work; that of the Arab, which constitutes the pivotal event of the entire plot; and finally that of Meursault himself, which closes it. Thus, death is not only nearly constantly present in the novel (three times in this very short work), but these deaths constitute by far the most remarkable and dramatic events in the story— partly because all the rest is portrayed with unrelieved drabness, partly because of the special status of these deaths and the exceptional character of their portrayal.

The death of the Mother is particularly traumatic, because the generative function of the Mother is such that her death represents the death of the principle of life itself, of the principle of passage from stasis to movement. The death of the Arab is the death of the Other, which draws its dramatic character from the function of the Other as the primary source of Self-consciousness. And the death of the Other is an image of the death of the Self—it enables the Self to conceive of the inconceivable, namely, the termination of its own existence; the extraordinary nature of this event is reflected in both style and action: the style takes on a quality of lyrical evocation, and action is presented in a slow-motion, ritual fashion which takes us out of the profane dimension and into the sacred. Finally, there is the death of the Self, which involves the death of the narrator and therefore of discourse; it also plays a parallel or antithetical role to the first death—just as the death of the Mother represented the death of birth, so the death of the son represents the birth of death, of a positive state of death into which Meursault leaps with a savage satisfaction. (pp. 183-84)

This consciousness labeled Meursault, whether it is primarily a recording or a creating consciousness, is clearly obsessed with death, and such an obsession is no doubt linked to that death wish (Thanatos) which characterizes all organic life. Portrayals of death may be taken as manifestations of this death wish, and Meursault's discourse is a dreamlike wish fulfillment oriented toward death.

Such a hypothesis throws new light on the central trait of Meursault's character, namely, indifference. Thanatos, Freud tells us, is even more basic than Eros, because "inanimate things existed before living ones"; ... as a result, at some deeply hidden layer of our subconscious is inscribed the following fatal word: "The aim of all life is death.".... Meursault's indifference is a manifestation of the inanimate, and his obsession with death (which is the only event capable of moving him to drama and lyricism) reflects the realization, as strong as it is obscure, that death

is indeed the goal and fulfillment of all, life being a temporary aberration which has alienated us from the primal stasis which was perfection. (p. 184)

There is, moreover, a further perspective possible on the theme of death in *L'Étranger.* ... In ... setting his fatal (and fateful) action in perspective as an attack on an existing balance, an existing order, Meursault aligns himself with the archetypal figure of the challenger. ... [He] must be publicly examined and vilified for challenging the order of things.

What is the nature of this order challenged by Meursault? Let us recall the context of the murder: a broad stretch of dry, sandy beach baking and dazzling in the scorching rays of a pitiless sun; a great rock with shade and a little spring of fresh water; and, between the suffering, sunstruck Meursault and this oasis of calm and refreshment, a dangerous adversary whose very presence challenges his approach. The threat represented by this adversary is such that the Arab represents death—a spirit of death preventing access to the release and happiness of the forbidden spring. What is this boon which death prevents us from attaining? Meursault's very name gives us the clue: through its meaning ("death leap") it makes of him an archetypal representative of the human condition, condemned to make eventually that ineluctable leap into oblivion. The deepest desire of mortal man (indeed, the strongest instinct of all mortal life, human or nonhuman) is to abrogate this fate—in other words, it is immortality, that eternal dream of our finite human nature. (pp. 184-85)

Whereas the principle of Thanatos rejects all activity as aberration and aspires to stasis, the principle of Eros, on the contrary, aspires not merely to activity but to frenzy and reduplication. It finds fulfillment in the generation of Others whose reflecting function satisfies its narcissism; often, it will constitute the Self as its own reflecting Other.

As with the manifestations of Thanatos, we find also in the case of Eros the three aspects and phases of elaboration represented by the Mother, the Other, and the Self. From this point of view, the Mother figures not as embodiment of the principle of generation but as first love object. The Other this time is not the antagonistic Other represented in Thanatos by the Arab, but the complementary Other represented by Marie. The Self manifests love for itself through its identification with nature (as opposed to society) and through the narcissistic character of the *parole vide* which is its discourse.

But besides these transparent manifestations of Eros there are also overt expressions of Thanatos which perform a second but vital function (at the subliminal level) as covert expressions of Eros. To expose this fully, we need to expose more completely the archetypal substructure of the work.

The perspective which dominates Western literature is that of the single white male. The most common structural principle in narrative constructs is Self/Other, usually expressed in terms of male/female. Usually, but not always— and this is the point relevant to our present concern. (pp. 185-86)

In the case of *L'Étranger,* the major symbol is the sun, traditional symbol of the male principle. Its heating and drying qualities regularly provoke, through their excess, the usual defensive, contrary reactions of the body: perspiration (which relieves body heat), even tears. . . . All such forms of dampness or liquid symbolize the female principle. But because of the structuring function of the two key descriptive passages—the funeral . . . and the killing . . .—the whole of the work is organized around a system of such symbols arranged in binary opposition: sun/sweat, sand/water, noise/silence, Self/Other. The fundamental unifying antithesis is that between the male or Self principle (represented in sun : sand : noise) and the female or Other principle (sweat : water : silence), the *yang* and the *yin*.

While the feeling of otherness in *L'Étranger* is chiefly the product of a sense of alienation from society as a whole with its arbitrary rationalistic structures, there are two particular human "opposite numbers" for the white male protagonist. One is Marie, the white woman Meursault loves. But in the mythic playing out of the clash of Self (male) versus Other (female) symbols, we find the series leading to a new, less obvious but more significant "opposite number": Self/Other, male/female, sun/[moon], day/night, light/dark, white/black. This second figure is the Arab whom the white man kills: through his racial difference (as the woman through her sexual difference), he is seen by the Self as Other, and through his dark coloring he represents night as against day, a further opposition to the male Self symbolized by day : sun : light: white. This is confirmed by the manner in which the Arab, like the woman, is associated with the female principle through the element of water: the key scene with the Arab . . . associates him with the spring of fresh water and the pool of shade, opposed to the scorching heat, glare, and dryness of the sunbaked sandy beach.

This archetypal conformation provides a key to the statis structure based on the relationships existing prior to the action of the novel. This action, in my opinion, confirms our hypothesis in a most dramatic manner by translating the suggested static structure into dynamic terms: the action serves to manifest the underlying relationship. (pp. 186-87)

[Let] us recall the fact that the Arab has a knife, and that Meursault's killing of the Arab is partly caused by the fact that, in his sunstruck condition (he uses the terms *ivresse, brûlure, feu*), he confuses the sharp piercing pain of the sun with that of the Arab's knife. The aggressive and destructive—but also fertilizing—male principle . . . is symbolized in *L'Étranger* by the gun, whose report noisily breaks the passive but pregnant silence of the beach. The gun has become a ubiquitous and conventional symbol of male aggression: it represents that essential difference between Self (male) and Other which enables the Self to penetrate the Other, creating a darkly magic moment which brings together nonlife and life (before and after fertilization through intercourse), life and nonlife (before and after death through shooting).

Thanatos, then, can be said to structure *L'Étranger:* death of the Mother (she who gave life must succumb to death), of the Other (the Arab), of the Self (the latter involving death of discourse). But the principle of Eros is also given a significant role: in the relationships with the Mother (first love object), with the Other (Marie), and with the Self (imaged in nature, as opposed to society, and in the narcissistic discourse of the *parole vide*). And above all, overt manifestations of Thanatos involve covert manifestations of Eros, a notable example being the killing of the Arab, surrogate

Other violated together with the virgin silence of the sunlit beach. (pp. 187-88)

Patrick Brady, "Manifestations of Eros and Thanatos in 'L'Étranger'," in Twentieth Century Literature *(copyright 1974, Hofstra University Press), July, 1974, pp. 183-88.*

Given Camus' objective in *The Plague* (to communicate convincingly his understanding of the human condition, and his urgent sense of how one ought to deal with it); given the terms in which he desired to embody his beliefs (the closed plague-ridden city as central metaphor); and given moreover his conception, as posited in the novel itself, of the difficulties besetting communication, then clearly *any* traditional narrative method would have had important disadvantages. For Camus had to cope with a unique set of paradoxes: to create a narrator who would be a reliable and effective chronicler, and yet not a professional writer; who would be at once objective and subjective, detached and involved, perceptive yet in some ways naïve, exemplary and yet the brother of erring mankind; and who would, nevertheless, emerge as an entirely credible character. The subtlety with which he resolved these difficulties, however, created in turn another paradox: so thoroughly did his art conceal art that the novel's great technical sophistication has not been much recognized. This is to say that the novel has not been fully understood. . . . [The] narrative techniques of *The Plague* . . . [are of a] "functional complexity": Camus' solving of complicated problems by complicated means, which, however roundabout they might seem at first glance, are invariably right to the point. What finally emerges is that, if Rieux wrote a chronicle, Camus wrote a novel; that *The Plague* is not an existentialist tract in literary dress, but a triumphant artifice. (pp. 428-29)

Edwin Moses, "Functional Complexity: The Narrative Techniques of 'The Plague'," in Modern Fiction Studies *(copyright © 1974, by Purdue Research Foundation, West Lafayette, Indiana, U.S.A.), Autumn, 1974, pp. 419-29.*

Camus takes [a] step . . . toward unifying fictional perspective and ridding the novel of its omniscient author in the Sartrean sense by writing *L'Étranger* in the first person, although it remains predominantly in the past tense. In this work, however, Camus's first person is no less ambiguous than his past tense, so that ambiguities found in both point clearly toward perspective as it is applied in the New Novel. In other words, Camus's "objective" first person and his "present" past tense foreshadow not only the literal confining of perspective to some form of interior monologue, but also the blatant creation and cultivation of the ambiguous perspective adopted by the majority of French novelists after 1950. (p. 59)

Although point of view in *L'Étranger* is solidly centered within the single protagonist, Meursault, it focuses alternately upon his *moi présent,* or his narrating presence, and upon his *moi passé,* or his remembered participation in the past. (p. 60)

Camus manages by adroit manipulation of these two temporal moments to give the impression that events occur as the story progresses, whereas, in actuality, the events recounted have taken place in the past and are narrated as remembered exclusively by Meursault. The narrative tension thus created becomes acutely dramatic in the final chapter when Meursault focuses upon his condemnation and the possibility of escaping it: upon the meeting of past and present for a possible future or upon the reconciliation of past events with present realities which deny him any future whatsoever.

The several ways in which Camus establishes this illusion of an unfolding present are not easily discernible upon an initial reading of *L'Étranger*. Primarily, Camus's great innovation is to choose a conversational past tense, the *passé composé,* rather than the traditional literary *passé simple.* In addition, he adds numerous temporal indicators of the present, or "false presents," to the few true indications of the present, which make a final impact of the complete moment sufficient unto itself. In this respect, Camus clearly exploits Sartre's notion of *trompe-l'oeil* with regard to time in the novel, even though he originally did so a number of years before Sartre's entire theory appeared in print. As yet unaware of the Sartrean precepts in their entirety, Camus succeeded brilliantly *avant la lettre* in respecting Sartre's existential bias in his novel. Contrary to Sartre's intent to simplify, however, perspective in *L'Étranger* is infinitely more complex and ambiguous than in *L'Enfance d'un chef,* and it seems clear today that Camus willfully rendered it so. Again in this respect, as well as in others, Camus's work serves as a clear transition between Sartre and the New Novel. (pp. 60-1)

> Betty T. Rahv, "Ambiguities in 'L'Étranger'," in her From Sartre to the New Novel (copyright © 1974 by Betty T. Rahv), Kennikat Press Corp., 1974, pp. 59-97.

Albert Camus' first novel, *A Happy Death,* . . . offers an instructive lesson in the strategies of the imagination. Though shot through with brilliant rays, *A Happy Death* is a chunky, labored work, cumbersome for all its brevity, so cluttered with false starts and halting intentions that it occludes its own themes. . . . In the first novel, the author fumbles, trying to pick himself up by too many handles, and growing more handles in the process; in the second [*The Stranger*], he takes a short but decisive side-step, becomes less himself, and with this achieved narrowness penetrates to the heart of his *raison d'écrire.*

The youthful Camus evidently had many attributes of a normal Algerian working-class lout. He liked soccer, girls, beachbumming, moviegoing, and idleness. He had decided, one feels, to cherish the image of himself as a citizen of the Belcourt slums. . . . The Camus whose gifts for reflection and self-improvement were early recognized and nurtured by a grade-school teacher, the Camus who entered the *lycée* at the age of ten, who studied philosophy at the University of Algiers from 1932 to 1936, who by the age of twenty-five was a working, travelling, published intellectual and the mastermind of a theatre group—this Camus figures little in the early essays or in the character of Mersault. Mersault, though his consciousness is brushed by philosophical speculation, confesses no ambition for his future and almost never reflects on his past.

By any standards, Camus' upbringing had been bleak. His father, an agricultural laborer, was killed in the Battle of the Marne ten months after Albert was born. His mother, a Spaniard, took the infant and his older brother Lucien from the village of Mondovi to the poor district of Algiers, where she became a cleaning woman. Camus was raised in a ménage that included his mother, a partially paralyzed uncle, and a domineering grandmother. These three adults were all illiterate and, in various ways, ill. The grandmother eventually died of cancer of the liver. . . . His mother, he wrote, "could think only with difficulty"; deafness, a speech impediment, and a docile temper combined to enforce a habit of silence. Camus once described his literary career as the attempt to speak for the "silent mother"—the inarticulate and disenfranchised of society. . . . Death for a father, silence for a mother: with such a parentage, Camus would never become a fluent or frivolous creator. At the moment of beginning his first novel, what, indeed, was his artistic treasure? A good education, a normal sensuality, a fond ear for working-class dialect, a rapturous sensitivity to nature, a conviction that paganism was being reborn around him in Europeanized North Africa. . . . Two events in his early maturity urged him toward energetic use of his capabilities: in 1930 he nearly died of tuberculosis, and in 1934 he joined the Communist Party. Yet always, in the heart of this young man, coexistent with the desire to celebrate and explicate, lay an unshakable lassitude and a blankness. . . . Around this natural infirmity, then, the novice artist must shape his strategies—no, not around it; he must point himself *into* it, for this silence is his message.

The first sketch, in the *Notebooks,* for the novel that is to become *A Happy Death* outlines, with an excessively formal scheme of alternation between past and present tense, what appears to be a story about love and jealousy among students, ending with the hero's death by disease. . . . Violent death does not figure in this first version, though the hero (called simply Patrice) does tell "his story of the man sentenced to death." The italicization of "happy" signals an arrival; a month later (September of 1937), the title "La Mort Heureuse" appears. That fall, the character of "an invalid—both legs amputated" begins to talk in the notes, and before the end of the year he has his curious name, Zagreus. To this new character adheres the old "theme of the revolver." (pp. 279-83)

Patrice Mersault, a poor young man, makes the acquaintance, through a mistress, of a legless invalid, Roland Zagreus, who shows him one day a safe full of money, a loaded revolver, and an undated suicide note. Some days later (in a chapter Camus transposed to the beginning of the novel), Mersault visits Zagreus, takes up the revolver, kills the cripple with it, leaves the suicide note on a table, and departs with the money. Walking away from this perfect crime, he sneezes, and the remainder of the novel traces his wandering, through a variety of countries and romantic entanglements, toward his own death, of pleurisy, chills, fever, and weak heart—a somewhat poetic syndrome. Assembled rather than conceived, the story has too many duplicating parts—too many women, too many deaths, too many meditative approaches to the lyrical riddle of "happiness." Simple problems of clarity exist. Has Zagreus deliberately invited Mersault to murder him? Why, when Mersault holds the gun to his head, doesn't Zagreus gesture or speak? "When he felt the barrel against his right temple, he did not turn away. But Patrice, watching him, saw his eyes fill with tears." These tears are given meaning not by the context but by an entry in the notebooks: "The man who doesn't want this easy way out, and who wants to chew over and taste all his fear. He dies without a word, his eyes full of tears." The murder is so abruptly rendered as to seem merely sensational. Nor do its consequences easily flow: after the murder and the theft, Mersault does not live like a rich man; he travels thriftily in Europe and loafs among friends. None of his pleasures are beyond the financial reach of Camus himself at this impoverished stage of his life. Mersault never becomes the proposed hero "who devotes himself completely to the acquisition of money"; money never becomes an embodied theme.

Since *A Happy Death* arrives now with an excellent critical afterword by Jean Sarocchi, and since Camus suppressed the work, why belabor its weaknesses? Only to marvel at how its materials and concerns reëmerge in *The Stranger,* transformed by their new position within a unified action. (pp. 283-84)

Of himself, Camus wrote, in a youthful essay, "And yet, at the very moment that the world was crumbling, he was alive." A few sentences further: "Every time it seems to me that I've grasped the deep meaning of the world, it is its simplicity that always overwhelms me. My mother, that evening, and its strange indifference." Indifference, life, simplicity, the sun, death: the concepts link up, make a circle. "There is no love of life without despair of life," an essay affirms. Love, despair, silence, mother, nature. (pp. 285-86)

But *A Happy Death,* with its half-hearted autobiography, too numerous romances, static scenery-painting, and ingenuous melodrama, could not focus [his] anti-theology. The images that could, however, already lay in Camus' notebook. One of the entries for January of 1936 lists six story ideas; two are "Death of the mother" and "The story of the condemned man." These two preoccupations figure marginally in much of Camus' youthful production; with *The Stranger,* for the first time he *invents* them, in the freedom of fantasy. By proposing a young man who could not shed tears at his mother's funeral and went to the movies instead of mourning, and by rendering her pauper's funeral and his daily life in the full dry light of their absurd inconsequence, Camus placed his hidden theme of blankness where no reader could avoid being challenged by it. Though of course derived from observation (impressions of a funeral occur in the notebooks, and his grandmother's death had already provided matter for an essay), the central circumstance is imagined; Camus' mother, in fact, outlived him. His essays show how deeply he loved her. But by killing her in his mind, he unlocked an essential self. Meursault the essential orphan, in all his "simplicity" and estrangement, this cool monster who is Everyman, with his casual, androgynous voice that would blow down all our castles of Christian decency and conventional delusion. And by making this hero's condemnation to death literal and legal, instead of an attenuated wasting by disease, Camus immensely heightens the pressure. He is forced, observe, by these inventions to conjure up two blank-walled interiors—the old people's home and the jail—that crystallize *Nada* better than the open landscapes he so loved to describe. And the necessary characters of the warden and the chaplain, with their tragicomic eloquence, lead his book into a dimension undeveloped in *A Happy Death*—the dimension of the political. Society acquires spokesmen, and in debate Meursault turns singular, heroic, revolutionary. The fussed-over irrelevancies of *A Happy Death* fall away. The new novel pours smooth and hot from start to finish.

Fiction must hold in healthily tense combination the mimetic and pedagogic impulses. Perhaps because kind teachers had guided his rise from poverty, Camus respected pedagogy, wished always to make things formal and clear, liked stories to have morals. He sometimes reminds us of a schoolteacher standing before us insisting that though there is no headmaster and no grading system and scarcely any blackboard, we must stay at our desks, learning virtue and happiness with the diligence of saints. We must, in short, love our mother—"The earth! . . . that great temple deserted by the gods"—even though she is silent. After *The Stranger* and *The Plague,* Camus' fiction shows more intellectual will than vital, involuntary substance. *The Fall* and the short stories of *Exile and the Kingdom* seem relatively stiff and diagrammatic. The poet stoops in his prophet's robes. *A Happy Death* shows the other extremity of this curve—the beginning. when artistry and philosophy struggled with an abundance of live impressions; the prophet had not yet been robed, the young man stood naked. (pp. 286-87)

> John Updike, "In Praise of the Blind, Black God," in his Picked-Up Pieces *(copyright © 1975 by John Updike; reprinted by permission of Alfred A. Knopf, Inc.), Knopf, 1975, pp. 279-87.*

In the fiction of Albert Camus, man is constantly portrayed as seeking design in a universe that appears to be chaotic. Trapped in a world that is indifferent and at times even hostile to human concerns, man attempts to create an order in which he is in harmony with his surroundings. In "La Pierre qui pousse," the concluding story of *L'Exil et le Royaume,* Camus reveals the fashion in which man creates the fraternal accord necessary to lead a fulfilled existence. Through the force of human fellowship, d'Arrast, the hero of the story, asserts his membership in the circle of human existence and creates a place of identity for himself in the universe. (p. 321)

D'Arrast, a French engineer, has been sent to Iguape, Brazil, where he is to oversee the project of damming a river which periodically floods the native settlements that lie along its banks. The countryside that surrounds Iguape appears to d'Arrast to be without pattern. This circumstance is aptly revealed in Camus' description of the landscape through which d'Arrast passes on his way to Iguape. The river across which he is ferried is a symbol of chaos and horror. [Claire adds in a footnote: The river might also be considered a symbol of death if one treats the reference to the ferry and the river as allusions to the ferryman Charon and the river Acheron of the Greek mythological underworld. The people of Iguape are in a sterile and deathlike condition before the arrival of d'Arrast; hence, it is fitting that the river which surrounds them should be associated with the tenebrous overtones of the river of death.] . . . [The river waters] are emblematic of the chaotic character of the universe in which d'Arrast finds himself. . . . Water in "La Pierre qui pousse" serves as a concrete, sensuous symbol of a universe that is not only indifferent to man, but also, at times, threatening. . . . Each year these waters inundate the clearings that border them, bringing misery and depravation to the inhabitants of the region. In this capacity, they embody the violent and unbridled forces of nature that submit man to their capricious control. Exposed to their all-encompassing power of destruction, man becomes nothing more than an object of prey, stripped of his identity as an entity unique from the other objects of nature.

The forest through which d'Arrast must make his way is a further symbolic representation of the chaotic forces which threaten man. Like the waters of the river, the forest is characterized by an unpatterned obscurity. . . . The chaotic character of the forest is reflected in the labyrinthine roads that d'Arrast must penetrate in order to arrive at Iguape. Irrational forces predominate in this world to such an extent that the forest becomes little more than an extension of the river, another aspect of the undistinguishable forces which make man's position in the cosmos uncertain. . . . The ambiguous nature of the universe is further associated with the image of the sky, which is little more than a viscous extension of the murkiness of the water and the forest. . . . As beacons of light, traditional symbols of certitude and absolute values, they are no longer capable of giving man direction, for they, too, are blurred by the same forces of inscrutability and incertitude which preside over the forest and the river.

Located in a landscape characterized by obscurity, man's position in the universe is depicted in the opening pages of "La Pierre qui pousse" as being like that of a blind man. . . . Man decreases in stature as the universe looms large. Even the work of construction which he has performed in the forest does not suffice to make his cities essentially different from the forest. . . . The settlement of Iguape and the men who inhabit it seem to have no individual identity capable of making them unique from the forces of nature that surround them.

The descriptions of the individuals whom d'Arrast encounters reflect this lack of human identity. A sense of chaos pervades the description of these people. The colony of Registro is inhabited by a group of Japanese immigrants. The village of Iguape itself is composed of many different types of people—gauchos, Japanese, Indians, half-breeds, and a handful of government officials of European descent. The languages that these people speak are similarly disparate: French, Spanish, Portuguese, and various native dialects. There is no pattern which serves to give these people a particular identity as humans. Rather, they are viewed from a detached vantage point, as though they were beasts rather than men. (pp. 321-23)

The dehumanized quality of the inhabitants of Iguape is most strikingly revealed in their attitude toward religion. This religion is nominally Christian, yet it contains much that is redolent of bestial, primitive rites. (p. 323)

Realizing that a religion that permits human deprivation to exist in the present moment in anticipation of future reward is unworthy of man's fealty, d'Arrast has abandoned the Christian faith. He is representative of a European order wherein the absolute rule of Christ, the Lord, has already been destroyed. . . . Deprived of the right to act on his own, man is rendered immobile in a universe that threatens him. The term *immobile* itself recurs with significant frequency in the story, serving almost as an incantation urging d'Arrast to act in such a way as to remove from the people of Iguape the burden imposed upon them by their religion. (p. 324)

Although the natives disgust d'Arrast in their candid bestiality, they also possess a health and vigor which makes them attractive. D'Arrast's ambivalent attitude toward them is consummately reflected in the image of the *Diane Noire,* the female huntress who presides over the last phase of the ritual that d'Arrast is permitted to see. The embodiment of a Greek goddess, arrayed in a harlequin-like costume of motley color scheme, she is a symbol of the concept of Greek moderation gone awry as man becomes one with the forces of nature. . . . These people embody man's innocence to such a degree that although d'Arrast may become ill at the sight of their lack of moderation, he cannot prevent himself from loving them. It is ultimately through asserting his fraternity with these people that d'Arrast will create a new order for himself and for the people of Iguape, bringing unity to an ununified world. (p. 325)

In serving as a force of mediation, enabling man to create a new, human-oriented order, d'Arrast assumes the characteristics of a religious savior. His role as messiah is appropriately elaborated by the rich Christian imagery which permeates "La Pierre qui pousse." This imagery is for the most part drawn from events which occurred in the life of Christ. (p. 327)

In examining the wealth of Christian imagery in "La Pierre qui pousse," it is essential to note the distinction between d'Arrast and the Christ of the Christian tradition as seen by Camus: unlike Christ, who became an institutionalized figure preaching salvation through faith in the future, d'Arrast opens the way for the people of Iguape to find fulfillment in their present circumstances by teaching them that man must be directly responsible for his actions. (That d'Arrast halts the futuristic projection of salvation is indicated by the fact that his watch stops running on the day of the religious procession.)

Inasmuch as it is ultimately humanity and not divinity which he represents, it is but fitting that d'Arrast should bear parallel resemblances to non-divine figures in Christian mythology. Thus, he resembles St. Peter, for he is given three opportunities whereby he can deny that which is most sacred to him—human fraternity. . . . On the third occasion, when the cook needs his help . . ., however, d'Arrast does not deny the bond of fraternity that beckons him. Rather, like another religious figure, Simon of Cyrene, he helps the cook to bear his cross. Finally, like St. George, whose spirit pervades the action of "La Pierre qui pousse," he encounters the forces of chaos which threaten man and helps to inaugurate a new order.

D'Arrast's response in combatting the forces of chaos is one that is as much intuitive as it is intellectual. . . . The forces of chaos no longer threaten d'Arrast, for having assumed responsibility for his action, he is no longer without identity.

Having discovered his human identity, d'Arrast is no longer in exile. His kingdom is that of human fellowship. . . . "La Pierre qui pousse" thus concludes *L'Exil et le Royaume* on an affirmative note. The silent solitude of the opening pages of the story is contrasted with the [concluding] sense of communication and comradeship. . . . (pp. 327-29)

Thomas Claire, "Landscape and Religious Imagery in Camus' 'La Pierre Qui Pousse'," in Studies in Short Fiction *(copyright 1976 by Newberry College), Summer, 1976, pp. 321-29.*

There seems no good reason why [*Youthful Writings*] should have been published. Of its two hundred and fifty-six short pages of text, ninety-nine are devoted to an introduction in which Paul Viallaneix summarises the seventeen brief specimens of Camus's youthful writings which it contains, and makes a perfunctory attempt to relate them to the circumstances of Camus's upbringing and to the themes of *L'Etranger* and *Caligula*. . . .

The specimens of Camus's early writing cover the years 1932-1934, when he was aged nineteen to twenty-one. Antedating by five years the appearance of *Le Mythe de Sisyphe*, the first of his major works, they show little promise of the writer that he was to become. There is evidence of his youthful study of philosophy in his praise of Bergson, Schopenhauer and Nietzsche and in an unconvincing attempt to represent the art of music as making contact with a world of Platonic Ideas. He pays tribute to Verlaine and to the largely forgotten Jehan Rictus for his *Soliloques du Pauvre*. Under the heading 'Intuitions' there are sixteen pages of 'reveries born of a great lassitude' which are intended to 'record the desire of a too mystical soul, in search of an object for its fervour and its faith'. There are faint touches in them of the irony but little of the logical discipline that was to distinguish *Le Mythe de Sisyphe*.

The best passages are those in which Camus expresses his love for the local Algerian Scene. Unfortunately, his prose being at its most poetic, they are also the passages that pose the greatest problems for his translator. . . .

Now that the study of contemporary literature has become an academic subject, there will be scholars who cherish every scrap of writing by those who have any claim to literary eminence. Camus's own reputation as an essayist, a playwright and a novelist is deservedly secure and the publication in English of these juvenilia will do it no harm. It will, however, be of interest only to his academic devotees who could, presumably, have been trusted to find their own way to the original texts. (p. 13)

> *A. J. Ayer, "Camus's Juvenilia," in* Books and Bookmen *(© copyright A. J. Ayer 1977; reprinted with permission), March, 1977, p. 13.*

*   *   *

CÉLINE, Louis-Ferdinand (pseudonym of Louis-Ferdinand Destouches)   1894-1961

A French physician, essayist, and novelist, Céline was notorious for his extreme pessimism and misanthropic view of human nature. His masterful use of argot, popular expressions, obscenities, and fractured syntax illuminated his perception of the madness and chaos that was modern Europe. Madness became Céline's pervasive metaphor for the nature of human existence, and his forceful use of language and disregard for traditional literary style and structure helped place him at the forefront of the literature of anarchistic revolt. (See also *CLC*, Vols. 1, 3, 4, 7.)

It is almost no exaggeration to say that among all the arts and artists, Céline admired only the dance and the Impressionists. . . . [His] uncommon sense of stylistic fraternity with the Impressionists, his repeated emphasis on aural refraction, and his professedly Impressionistic techniques of narration, have not been adequately studied. For they constitute, together with his themes and tropologies, a rigorous attempt to do for the novel what the Impressionists did for the still life. Insisting that he was above all an innovating stylist in the Impressionistic manner, Céline hoped for nothing less than Impressionistic narrative in language. (p. 329)

Céline insists, fiercely, that just as the camera killed the still life, the cinema has killed the novel. Modern novels are little more than pseudo-films and scenarios. . . . The cinema supplies what the novelists only keep trying to animate: the landscape, the picturesque, movement, nudity, Tarzans, psychology, bedrooms, crimes. The cinema has arrogated to itself all the old themes and methods of fiction, just as the camera robbed the canvas. . . .

Not the scene but the "rendu," not the object but the impression, remained for the painter to explore in the age of the camera—as they do for the novelist in the age of film. Céline is not interested in the physicality of the world, in the appearance of things. He is intrigued with problems of perception and, at root, he is fascinated with one perceptual response, one that lies behind all our art and, in the individual, marks the first crude beginnings of consciousness: emotion. The verbal artist trying to express and elicit elementary emotional responses must somehow break down the *décalage* between private emotion and public language. During the trilogy years, Céline saw his problem in terms of the Impressionists' dilemma and in the *Entretiens* defined his stylistic solution in terms of theirs. . . . (p. 330)

In his early fiction, Céline had already refined the first step, the lexical and grammatical foundation of the "roman rendu émotif." In *Voyage au bout de la nuit* (1932), *Mort à credit* (1936), and the wartime *Guignol's band* (1944), he had alternately scandalized and delighted readers with his language. Rimbaud and others had transformed and invigorated literary French, and Céline went a step further in suscitating the written idiom with the crudities, slang, barbarisms, rhythms and tone of spoken French. By the 1950's Bardamu's progeny numbered hundreds, but Céline was contemptuous of his imitators, who, he sneered, understood only the slang and not the emotive art englobing it.

In the *Entretiens*, he continues to insist that conventional written French is a dead language. . . . In order to recapture the original emotional urgency of spoken language, he has not merely transcribed spoken into written. He has developed, in print syntactically, the sort of corrected refraction discovered by the Impressionists. Plunge a stick into a glass of water and it appears distorted, but "le secret de l'Impressionnisme" was the little trick of breaking their stick first and then immersing it so that it *seemed* straight. They used distortion to correct refraction and produced the "rendu." "Ainsi de mon style émotif!" (p. 331)

To return to the Impressionists and their stick, Céline reverses the halves of his stick before immersing it in his novel, forcing the reader to experience the emotional process of apprehending an object by its attributes rather than its locus or name. More than ever, reading is an affective rather than conceptual process. . . .

It is the evanescence of emotion that interests Céline, the whirlwind speed at which emotions rise, vibrate for an instant, and vanish. Even on the lexical and grammatical levels, this "petit truc" for rendering preconceptual emotions accounts in part for the astonishing speed of a Célinean novel. (p. 332)

By the 1950's Céline had tightened his focus and clarified his aims. At least two radical changes are notable in his comments and in the trilogy. First, with the rigor of Beckett, he pared his syntax to the bone. . . . [He] broke up his refractive sentence into its components and exploded them into fragments. He dropped connectives and made his "points suspensifs" organic to his expression. Consequently, he disparaged his earlier work. . . .

This reductive method takes him far beyond "le parlé," beyond his refractive inversion of order. In the trilogy he tries to abandon that order and to force upon the reader a much more exhausting apprehension, comparable in intensity to the affective effort of reading *Comment c'est*. It is almost as though, in his favorite analogy with Impressionist painting, he has gone back past Van Gogh's "distorted" churches to Sisley's boats composed of the relations between dots of paint. (p. 333)

Just as the lacemaker or the pointillist works with blank or undotted space, shaping forms by utilizing emptiness, their novelistic counterpart works with silence, the absence of words, ellipsis or aposiopesis. The lace, the Sisley boat, the Célinean novel are alike dependent upon the blank space which they template, and we are in each medium forced to see or hear the absence as well as the presence of the artist's "ligne essentielle." The pointillist's dots are "blended by the eye" to constitute the subject. That Céline was attempting a similar procedure aurally has important implications for his goal of a "roman rendu émotif" in the Impressionist manner, and for any assessment of the late fiction. (pp. 333-34)

[In *Nord* (1960), there] is deliberate elision, marking the narrator's attempt to work his way past conventional discourse—to sustain his emotive line. . . . Thus more typical are longer sequences. There lines of demarcation between both objects and events blur, swirling together around his "traverses impondérables." The effect is one of great energy, almost pure energy in pure movement, without locus or direction. What stands out is not object or event, nor "action" in any familiar sense, but the "ligne essentielle" of the narrator's emotional responses to them. . . . (p. 334)

[The] second, and consequential, change in the late fiction is that Céline no longer works in anecdote but applies his refractive dislocation to the narrative frame of the novel as a whole. He has dropped his old format: a prologue by the aging doctor, an interlude of usually malarial delirium, followed by his lengthy account of a wretched youth; with no narrative intrusion into that history of a decade or so of his life and with no attempt at the end to link up those anecdotes to his present situation. In the trilogy the older narrator [Ferdine] incessantly and relentlessly entwines his present situation around and through his stories of his past. Indeed his "situation générale" of the present at Meudon is the one reliable constant which obtains throughout the trilogy and consolidates his narrative. (pp. 335-36)

[In] the trilogy, Céline dissolves the distinction narrator-narrated. As in the narratives of Tristram or Malone, but quite differently, we are remarkably dependent for our apprehension of the work upon, first, the narrator's emotional state in the present, and, second, upon the narrator's impatience with the craft of literature. . . .

The essential emotive line of the trilogy is now emphatically the narrator "Je." And it is expressed in terms of his immediate subjective impressions of *both* the recollections of Germany and the efforts of the artist writing this novel about himself that we simultaneously read. It is above all that sustained combination of the object of description and the perspective of the artist which marks the mature emphasis of Céline's art in the 1950's [and] exhibits his chief stylistic debts to the Impressionists. . . . (p. 336)

[Ferdine's] work is himself and it will be no less grotesque, disordered, barbaric and stinking than he is. (p. 338)

The narrator of a "roman rendu émotif" produces an expectedly bizarre version of history. It is the emotive version. It is still literature with "tous les motifs!" But they are dislocated and scrambled in the "rendu." Like his favorite painters, Ferdine is not interested in photographic accuracy. . . . Thus we are not "there" at the bombing of Hanover, as if at a film of it, any more than we were "there" at La Raspelière. We were at Cabourg. Now we are at Ferdine's emotion of hallucinatory enchantment with bombs flowering in red and lavender over the cratered city which he calls Hanover.

Chronicling the grotesque decay of a moribund society and of himself, the artist of the "rendu" loathes the public domain of history and language. Dragging us along with every step that he takes, he struggles to make a new sort of novel without dross, no matter what sort of two-headed monster it seems. Above all without facts. . . . Not objects but aspects, not ideas but his own emotions as refugee and artist keep him going forward in his work. . . . He will go as far as he can in the direction of pure emotion calculated and refined. (p. 339)

Jan Hokenson, "Céline: Impressionist in Language," in L'Esprit Créateur (copyright © 1973 by L'Esprit Créateur), Winter, 1973, pp. 329-39.

[Céline's] kind of literary nose-thumbing acts as a signal to the reader that henceforth nothing is sacred, not even the assumption that a redemptive, formal bond must exist between author and reader. Céline's fictional poses undermine and transform the traditional concepts of literature. From *Voyage au bout de la nuit*, whose narration exists in a precious balance between feigned delirium and discursive rationality, to the fugue-like digressions of *Rigodon*, Céline's works are a reminder that the frozen categories of genre cannot withstand the vicissitudes of the creative experience. . . . That they fall neither within the category of the pre-Gidian novel (and hardly in that of the post-Camusian one) nor in the field of the epic or lyric prose poem, is testimony to the open-ended nature of Céline's works and indicates a very real insufficiency in established approaches of literary criticism. (pp. 177-78)

Substituting his own virtuosity for a defunct semiological system, Céline created a "non-genre." (p. 178)

Céline's works give ample evidence of his despairing view of the human condition. However, his works also present the argument . . . that it is within man's capacity to subject death itself to the rhythmic flow of life, rather than to view death in a supra-vital, heroic light. Viewed dynamically, as an integral part of the life process rather than as a precondition for a transcendent historical reality, death is thus humanized. Evasion of death as illustrated in Céline's novels points to the illusory aspects of the traditionally linear attempt at undermining the laws of existential time. Movement takes on an infinitely purer meaning once it is rid of arbitrary ends. (pp. 178-79)

In Céline's view, the goal of the artist is to make man aware of his loss of natural grace, while at the same time renewing his desire for it. The responsibility of each individual, however, is to be faithful—hence responsible—to his own life's pulse, or "musique personnelle," as Céline calls it. Like the "essence" of existentialist thought, this responsibility is the very fruition of freedom; for in fulfilling this responsibility to himself man reduces—rather, he raises—the truth of life to his own level. Céline's works thus constitute an eloquent plea to reinstate man at the hub of the human experience, rather than to dehumanize him by subjecting him to a system based on abstract truths, whether they are expressed in Judeo-Christian or Marxist terms.

Céline's humanistic iconoclasm does not stop there, however. His language purports neither to confront reality on a one-to-one basis, in the manner of the new novelists, nor to act as a mirror in which is reflected the intimate world of an agonizing psyche, in the tradition of the romanticists. Instead, it is what we might call "ecstatic." (p. 179)

The goal of Céline and of his narrators is twofold. First, to create a mythical reality with himself at the center—a reality in which the dimensions of time and space are made interior, or intrinsic to his self-awareness. The second and ultimate goal, however, can be reached only by an ironic reversal of the process which had led both author and narrator toward the first goal. Having confirmed the dynamic relationship between the self and the outside world, Céline's narrator must withdraw from that outside world in order to assure that the duration of his "myth" will transcend time itself. In the process of satisfying these two demands Céline's narrator establishes a dynamic polarity between two aspects of his being. First, there is the *je*, or the affective, existential self. This is the dimension of the self that we associate with the "voice" of the narrator as he relates his "real" experiences. Secondly, there is the *moi*, or what we might call the *ecstatic* self. This is the extension of the narrator's consciousness at grips with the three dimensions of time—past, present, and future. It is this dimension of the narrator's being that allows the disconnected "present" of his narration to be superseded by an internally related synthesis of dynamic temporality. Moreover, it is by the extension to space of this projection in time that the narrator's self-awareness undergoes a metaphorical transfer from the *je* to the *moi*. During such moments of transfer, the narrator's consciousness is elevated from the base horizontality of his quaggy existence to the verticality of poetic realm. The poetic quality of Céline's narrative stems from the "extasis" or *délire*, as Céline calls it, which results when the horizontal and vertical dimensions of his narrative converge. This convergence can be equally expressed as the coincidence of existential and cosmic time, producing what one critic has called a "continuous, multilevel present," whose unity is analogous to that of a melodic phrase.

Clearly, with Céline, literature becomes increasingly less a rational process. Céline's distrust of man's ability to offset universal cataclysms often gave him the appearance of assuming a posture of complacency—even of collaboration—with the darkest forces at play in his world. We now know, however, that this attitude was indeed little more than a posture. (pp. 179-80)

Céline's first-person narratives can be seen as a series of pre-reflective, individual postures whereby the narrator establishes a dynamic relationship with exterior spatiality and temporality. It is by combining his verticality, or self-assertion in space, with his horizontality, or his displacements in time, that Céline's narrator achieves *extasis*. Set in perpetual motion, Céline's narratives express a constantly modulated and modulating view of a fixed world. The shifts in his narrator's vision are not indications of exterior, temporal change. They are rather a record of his evolving relationship to the outside world. Céline's narrator starts out as a recognizable novelistic prototype: the naïve observer of the world, whose innate curiosity, nurtured by a resolute will to survive, directs him along a road of discovery.

In *Voyage*, we witness this process of the humanization of truth on several levels. At the start of the metaphorical journey Céline situates his narrator, Ferdinand Bardamu, in a world whose moral index is so low that the value of human life itself is reduced to naught. Bardamu proceeds with increasing lucidity to relate his existence in time and space starting from its origin in total obscurity. Given the lyrical quality of his account, and because of the mixture of banal and extreme experiences that he relates, his very existence becomes a creative act, akin to a work of art.

We now touch upon one of the most authentic aspects of Céline's esthetic vision—a vision which consciously bypasses the well-turned phrase as a vehicle for poetic expression. In his preface to *Guignol's Band*, . . . Céline tells us that the prose style of the future is the "[style] télégraphique." But he goes on to say that even such an updated technique is doomed to sterility unless it reflects a transposition of the artist's most fundamental emotions. The primary condition for this series of transformations is movement. It is movement that creates the fusion of illusion and reality. In order that this fusion be esthetically valid, that it be able to create a humanized truth, it must reflect the correspondences between the inner movements of the artist's very consciousness. These inner movements can be attributed to the constant tension between the dark, emotive complex of Dionysian responses to the world—the source of creative energy—and the construct of lucid reactions to and Apollonian elevation from that world. Céline's narrator can thus be seen as the symbolic incarnation of the creative impulse existing in a suspended state between submissiveness to emotive reactions and lucid self-elevation. At the same time, however, Céline creates a situation in which his narrator's knowledge of life stems from his dynamic involvement with the world of essential truths. This can explain, in part, Céline's often anachronistic progression from one novel to the next. *Voyage*, Céline's first literary success and his third written work after *Semmelweis* and *L'Eglise*, is the first stage of a metaphorical journey, comprised of a series of forward and backward movements in time and space. In *Voyage*, Céline reconstructs his initial leap into a hallucinatory world—a world in which his consciousness is liberated from the dimensions of real time and space. By means of his two protagonists, Bardamu and Robinson, Céline expands the field of his subjective consciousness as his "anti-heroic" spokesmen perform their metaphorical dance across three continents and through various stages of civilization, or at least situations that can be considered as symbols of man's development in time. In this sense, Bardamu and his alter ego Robinson can be seen as representing the Dionysian side of Céline's own literary journey. The tension, or energy, which is a prerequisite for the narrator's subsequent Apollonian elevation, is caused by the polarity that separates Bardamu from Robinson, both temporally and spatially, as each of them struggles alone, and in concert as well, with the all-pervasive night.

Together, Bardamu and Robinson form a fictional entity which recalls Balzac's talismanic "peau de chagrin." Bardamu, who reacts in a pre-reflective manner to the world, and Robinson, through whom most of Bardamu's reactions are polarized, incarnate, as does "the evershrinking ass's skin," what in Victor Brombert's words constitutes "the very symbol of human destiny which condemns men to the terror of witnessing their own gradual self-destruction."

We can develop this metaphorical situation in terms which are more clearly applicable to the theme of the Célinian journey. In order that the "journey" survive the test of "real" time, the tension, or polarity, between the subjective world of the narrator and the overwhelming forces of exterior night must be maintained. The narrator must first be made to plunge head-on into the mire of existence. His narration then duplicates the refracted vision of life that such an experience creates. As Gide has said, Céline does not paint reality, but rather the hallucination which reality provokes. Finally, the narration itself constitutes the salutory thrust whereby the author's passions and fears are redeemed. More significantly, however, by launching his narrator along a precarious journey to the end of the night aboard his metaphorical "métro émotif," Céline enlists the dynamic complicity of his reader. It is at the moment of juncture—when the reader's subjective response to the darkness of the narrator's world and his own objective, or illuminated, appraisal of the world about him coexist in time—that the journey will have transcended Dionysian chaos to reach the heights of Apollonian virtuosity. In this sense, we can agree with Roland Barthes, according to whom the "je" of the first person narrative form acts as the universal witness to all that takes place in the novel. It is a unifying, resurrectional voice and it creates an essential bond between the novelist's and the protagonist's existence in time on the one hand, and between the novel and the collective, historical present of the reader's consciousness on the other.

The process is now complete. The metaphor of the tugboat at the end of *Voyage* . . . reclaims everything, including the passing destructive "time" of Bardamu's narration, leaving Céline's narrator with a dematerialized but integral *moi;* all that remains is the stuff of his narration, which supplants the world of temporal existence in the order of things. . . . Céline's narrator leaves behind him a world which has been modified, or "modulated" by his passage through it. (pp. 180-82)

> *Charles Krance, "Céline and the Literature of Extasis: the Virtuosity of 'Non-Genre'," in* Language and Style, *Summer, 1973, pp. 176-84.*

Céline's pronouncements on his manner of literary creation

are rarely, if ever, backed up by any detailed explanations of how and why, and he is true to form in offering no hint as to the nature of the structural principles that bind together [his] extraordinary first novel [*Voyage au bout de la nuit*]. It is nevertheless clear that, if his claim to careful coordination is to be upheld, it might be more profitable to consider the *Voyage* from a point of view other than those of action and message. This article attempts to suggest that at least one principle of coherence can be discovered that permits the heterogeneous characters and events to be related in a common framework of interpretation, a principle which resides in the text's deployment of symbol. (pp. 46-7)

Symbol . . . enables Céline to preserve the *Voyage* from the hyper-intellectualism he despises and to endow the portraits of his characters with a sense of unrationalized authenticity and inevitability. But there is yet another attraction for Céline in the use of symbol. It is the raciness of Bardamu's monologue that gives his despair its special tone and symbol, carefully selected, can provide important pictorial support for the already highly imaged semi-slang. All these factors have their part in explaining the presence in the *Voyage* of a symbolic apparatus of considerable bulk, involving personages, names, objects and events.

What must also be noticed in any examination of Céline's symbols is the frequency of mythological and allegorical reminiscences. A number of the symbolic features appear to derive from traditional narratives that have aimed to resume in story the problems attending man's progress through existence. A situation in the *Voyage* will call to mind a mythological equivalent, or a character will reveal a resemblance with a figure from a well-known allegory, perhaps bearing a name unashamedly borrowed in its original form or else invented according to the conventions of the genre. The range of reference is broad, for Céline makes use of material going from the Ancient Greek to the relatively modern European, juxtaposing elements of originally widely varying purposes. That he does this without apparent embarrassment or difficulty is explained by the fact that his interest in an established model is almost always limited to one particular aspect, while the other traditionally recognized (but, for Céline, irrelevant) aspects remain unexploited. His symbols are never reproductions of an original; they merely provide thought-provoking allusions. It is important that the reader should be able to detect the mythological and allegorical reminiscences—but it is equally important that he should not follow them up too far, for any attempt to reconcile the full significances of the original models in a single coherent intellectual pattern proves quite unavailing. (p. 47)

Céline's symbols, however varied their origins, are not chosen haphazardly, but are consistently matched with each other. Céline appears to have started out with a certain number of basic symbolic effects in mind, which he is then happy to exploit time and time again, sometimes in virtually identical form, sometimes with surface variations. One advantage of this creation of sets of symbols is that they can serve to reinforce each other, whereas in isolation even the more obvious would appear weaker and more arbitrary. But, even more important for the *Voyage*, it is these networks that give the novel as a whole the coherence that compensates for the lack of discipline in story-line and in ideology. Their presence means that certain key notions or attitudes are permanently held up to the reader's attention, whatever the accompanying extravagances of the narrative. (pp. 47-8)

[Two symbolic networks are] introduced in the novel's title, via the notions of a journey and of darkness. (p. 48)

The equation of man's experience of inexplicable evil with a journey in impenetrable darkness is maintained throughout the text by means of the everyday figurative expressions that the narrating Bardamu prefers to abstractions. When he describes his passage from experience to experience, he favours expressions deriving from the terminology of physical locomotion—"chemin", "en route pour", "aller au bout de". When he speaks of his attempts to understand what is happening to him, an expression orginating in the language of physical vision, "voir clair", is the one that comes most frequently to his lips. These are, of course, clichés and their interest is strictly limited. But what is worthy of attention is Céline's diligence in bolstering each theme with matching symbolic effects. Such is the density and such the combination of these effects that Céline does in fact succeed in giving the old and hackneyed imagery a new and very personal cast.

It is mainly in the second half of the *Voyage* that Bardamu talks of his existence in terms of a journey. But the direct symbolic representation of the theme commences in the very first few pages of the novel, when Bardamu actually becomes a traveller to foreign parts. The fact that he visits real-life places and engages in the same occupations as so many others in the years of and following the Great War gives the symbol a character of concrete realism. On the other hand, there are moments when Céline manipulates the account of his hero's wanderings in such a way that more than one level of understanding must be recognized. For example, while he may sometimes respect geographical truth, he will also invent places and, in the allegorical tradition of suggestive name-devizing, give them suitable names to characterize particular phases in Bardamu's experience of existence. (pp. 48-9)

Not only the place-names point to the symbolic nature of the journey; some of the characters engaged in travelling are also obviously designed to carry extra meanings. While the narrating Bardamu is perhaps too complex a figure to be seen easily as a symbol, his various occupations—soldier, merchant, sailor, healer—do match those of representative figures in traditional tales of travels. Céline further counters the individuality of Bardamu's nature by providing a careful parallel for his wanderings in those of a second character, Robinson, who makes exactly the same journey across the world as Bardamu, just one step ahead all the way. The deliberate artificiality of these coincidences makes it quite clear that neither traveller is simply what he appears. What is more, various characteristics are attached to Robinson that mark out his special role in the *Voyage* and hint at the real nature of his relationship to Bardamu. He, more than any other character in the novel, illustrates Céline's eclecticism in drawing on material from different sources. As far as his "traveller" identity is concerned, Robinson seems to possess two separate ancestries. He undoubtedly derives his name from Crusoe, and also the fact that he is stranded in an indifferent universe. But the other aspects of the Crusoe story appear to have had no interest for Céline and it cannot be argued that Bardamu is Man Friday. However, given that Robinson is some kind of initiator in leading Bardamu onwards into an ever deeper experience of mis-

ery, he can perhaps also be related to the various guides in allegory and myth, whose function it is to accompany heroes through trials and to interpret them for heroes and public alike. . . . [The] reminiscences he awakens consistently draw the reader's attention to the link between the journey theme and man's relationship to existence.

The character of this relationship is, however, depicted in its full sinisterness when, at a relatively late stage in the *Voyage*, Céline introduces a third traveller in the person of Baryton. While Bardamu and Robinson follow the same route, Baryton apparently proceeds in the opposite direction. . . . Baryton leaves behind a home for the insane merely to discover his own personal insanity. Far from being a frivolous digression, Baryton has the function in the *Voyage* of providing the plainest of clues as to the real nature of the journeying of Bardamu and Robinson. While his progression appears to be a negative reflection of theirs, the underlying truth is one and the same. For the wanderings, outwardly physical, are essentially mental and the disorientation is even more distressing. It is quite proper, then, that it should be in Baryton's asylum that the travellers' paths cross for the last time.

What Céline seems to have seen most of all in the journey symbol is man's instability, his lack of direction, his ignorance of goal. But the irony is that the journey is at the same time a prison, since there is no escape from instability. Robinson may be a Crusoe, but all that Crusoe's voyaging ever brought him was confinement to an island. Céline uses other symbols related to the notion of a journey to underline the fact that his character's lives are constricted both en route and at apparent rest. (pp. 49-50)

[The three boat] episodes acquire a fresh force if not only the boat symbol is recognized but also reminiscences it carries with it. The *Amiral Bragueton* and the *Infanta Combitta* have an ancestry in all those ships, from Charon's craft to the Flying Dutchman's, that ever bore the doomed into greater suffering, and even the little [pleasure] barge of the third episode reveals its sinister character if one remembers the enchanted islands of legend to which weary travellers were lured, conventionally by music, only to fall under evil spells. . . .

In Céline's version, the function of the island as an instrument of catastrophe is transferred to the land-locked barge, so that the episode can stand alongside those of the *Amiral Bragueton* and the *Infanta Combitta* and propose a consistent value. . . . The boat symbol loses its attraction definitively in the last pages of the novel when Bardamu, watching the boats on the Seine, also now notes the locks that limit their progress. The dream of freedom is recognized to have been as much of an illusion as the cardboard ship at the fair; the reality is confinement and the boat as symbol confirms the oppression of human existence. (p. 51)

The journey symbol, when used in the past to represent man's experience of different facets of existence, has normally required the "traveller" to emerge with some particular set of instructions for the management of his future life. But in Céline's application of the symbol, the systematic repetitions, parallels and contrasts, the choice of allusions, all point to the fact that the journey is itself a prison and that it has no issue. Bardamu's journey does not get him anywhere—his very last words in the *Voyage* show him still preoccupied with motion—and he is no better equipped to cope with life at the end of his tale than he is at its beginning. But the singular lack of evolution in his character—a fault if judged according to conventional standards of characterization—is totally logical on the *Voyage*'s terms. Man's instability will always prevent him from making any kind of progress.

The second symbol introduced in the title, darkness, is part of another very important group, this time centred on the theme of sight. There is nothing new in the use of physical vision to represent the inner, but again there is an interest in seeing how Céline manipulates the basic theme and what precise value he eventually extracts from it. Just the same singleness of purpose that characterized the organization of the journey symbols reappears in the portrayal of seen and seer.

The seen is dominated by effects of light and dark, for almost every page of the *Voyage* evokes one or the other. The dark will prevail but it is perhaps useful to examine first how Céline's use of the contrast of light reinforces rather than prejudices that predominance. The only place where the sun is constantly brought to the reader's attention is, not surprisingly, Africa, but it is already a mercilessly torrid light that brings acute discomfort rather than anything else. But elsewhere if light enters the *Voyage*, it is as artificially created light. (pp. 52-3)

Bardamu's frequently proclaimed ambition may be to "voir clair", but nothing is clearer than that light cannot provide illumination. . . . [The] superiority of the dark will be attested, throughout the *Voyage,* by the sheer numerical strength of its symbols, with night as the most frequent and natural of them. Not only do practically all the most important events take place under cover of darkness, but the action of roughly three-quarters of the chapters terminates in the hours of evening or night. Yet other chapters that do not derive their gloom from actual night may owe it to the greyness of heavy rain or the obscurity inside buildings. . . . [The] . . . image imprinted on the reader's mind is suitably one of inescapable, intolerable shadow.

But the shadow lies, not only over the seen, but within the seer as well. Céline's symbols of vision include many based on the tools of sight, the eyes, or else other objects of optical significance. It is rare for anyone's eyes to be described in a completely complimentary fashion, and it is noteworthy that one exception to this rule is Mme Henrouille, the old beldame who is also an exception to the rule of human corruption. . . . [The] clarity of her gaze reveals her as one of the few characters in the *Voyage* who insist on seeing the world as it really is. But elsewhere compliments for ocular distinction are likely to be ironic. (pp. 53-4)

A second symbolic attitude, linking the themes of the journey and of blindness and recalling certain medieval images of allegorical intention, emerges when Céline evokes a group of people holding hands to advance together through the dark—the blind leading the blind. . . . (pp. 55-6)

Through his symbols of vision Céline makes a comment on the human lot, which is as pessimistic as the one already manifest in the journey symbols. What is brought into focus is the plain fact that vision itself is limited and unreliable. The humanity on display in the *Voyage* is incurably shortsighted, morally and intellectually as well as physically, since almost everyone refuses to recognize the truth. But not only humanity stands accused, for even the few who try

to open their eyes find that the monstrosity of the world facing them remains a problem beyond perception and conception. The camera might be considered a technological improvement on the fallible human eye, but the photograph taken of Bardamu and his friends at the fair only succeeds in revealing a greater degree of ugliness than they would themselves have believed possible. Bardamu, in his unrealizable ambition to "voir clair", is therefore arguably worse off than the blinded Robinson. . . . (p. 56)

Many of the symbols mentioned in this study reappear [in the final chapter] in a last affirmation of despair. Twice in the last two pages the Seine's locks are mentioned and it is clear that the "journey", though continuing frenetically, is no longer thought to be a means of glorious liberation. Similarly, the theme of light is introduced in such a way as to make its significance unmistakable. Dawn may have broken, but Céline continues to the end to show that light is not to be trusted. . . . Céline's final word is that, given man's essential inadequacy, improvement can only ever be illusory.

Céline's symbol networks indicate a conscious effort to unify his material and, however inflated the propagandist attacks and preposterous the adventures that befall the crew of the *Voyage,* they reveal a consistent and coherent point of view. What is more, they cannot be treated simply as surface motifs, for they enter into almost every aspect of the *Voyage's* elaboration as a narrative. They affect characterization, both in the attribution of special roles to the major characters and in the choice of occasional details of appearance and attitude. They dictate the choice of material for many episodes, so that a pattern of parallels and contrasts can be set up. They dictate the progression of events within individual episodes, and also the management of time, since the completion of action must coincide, if possible, with the arrival of night. They dominate the concluding chapter, so that no mistake may be made about its interpretation. They explain the overall lay-out of the Voyage. . . . And finally, on the level of language and style, there is a permanent link-up between the symbols and Bardamu's manner of expression, since the figurative language he employs so liberally is consistently supported by matching symbolic effects.

It is remarkable, too, how acknowledgement of the traditional sources of many of Céline's symbols undermines the *Voyage's* reputation as the revolutionary product of a new age and reveals the modern jargon to be very frequently just a surface disguise for centuries-old methods of representing the issues that confront man. . . . [It] can be objected that, even if the reader is happy to recognize some familiar faces and places in this portrait of a new chaos, their very variety can also frustrate. A certain amount of tension is inevitable if Crusoe must be also Tiresias, also a Doppelgänger. But there may be a method in Céline's madness. He is willing enough to use a ready-made symbolic form, but what he does at the same time is systematically discard the rigid and no longer relevant rationale behind that form, and the bold admixture of all types of allusions ensures that the *Voyage's* reader must do so too. Detours and distortions, perhaps, so that the latter may discover his own way and his own vision. (pp. 57-8)

Carys T. Owen, "Networks of Symbol in 'Voyage au bout de la nuit'," in Forum for Modern Language Studies, *January, 1975, pp. 46-58.*

If one can imagine St. Jerome, or another agonized early father of the Church, deprived of faith though not passion, one might be close to comprehending Louis-Ferdinand Céline, that inspired and often atrocious nihilist. He viewed the world as a spiritual continuum, but beyond the manifest absurdity of human life was the Void—not Heaven. . . .

And for all his hatred of artistic pretensions and his presentation of existence as seen from the viewpoint of the bucket under the operating table, Céline was very much an esthetician. He returned constantly to the defense of formal values and was so dedicated to the writer's proper medium that, as [Patrick] McCarthy justly remarks [in *Céline: A Biography*], "in general his novels are shaped by the torrent of language which spills over chapter endings, creates and discards characters and is itself the order and meaning of the world."

Céline's handling of language is perhaps at its best—certainly at its most nimble—in one of his later works, *D'Un Chateau l'autre*, a deeply sad and hilariously comic account of French collaborators seeking refuge in a Germany caught in the throes of Hitlerian Götterdämmerung. Yet *D'Un Chateau l'autre* is not Céline's foremost novel, suggesting that there was more to him than a mere wizardry with words.

Though no less sardonically pessimistic than his two major books of the '30s, *Voyage au bout de la nuit* and *Mort à crédit, D'Un Chateau l'autre* lacks their largeness of structure and vigor of inverted faith. Lost as well is the sense that in some way, despite its evident absurdity, life is still immensely exciting because human beings are such mad cosmic malcontents who perpetually live in the shadow of an inescapable volcano. Besides being an estheticist, after all, Céline was a black moralist, the Jerome who has lost faith but not intolerance; in him the fires of fanaticism burn with special eeriness because their light leads nowhere. (p. 20)

A passionate consciousness of the absence of God is as much a religious emotion as a consciousness of His presence, and can breed its own hatreds, fueled by despair. Céline became an anti-Semite, I suggest, because he had to find someone outside himself to blame for his failure to attain the divine grace he sought.

If such speculations help to explain why Céline wrote the atrocious pamphlets that are still open sores on his reputation, they also help us to understand the other, creative side of him, which erected on the hard rock of despair some of the most remarkable works of fiction ever written. For in my view *Voyage* and *Mort* are comparable with those other works of cosmic agony, *The Brothers Karamazov* and that black book, *The Possessed*.

As Anthony Burgess has said in a review of *Céline*, "important writers must not be ignored because they make us uncomfortable." At the same time, we must seek to understand why such men as Céline feel almost fatally impelled to stir discomfort in others, and to glory in the inevitable hostility that ensues. (p. 21)

George Woodcock, "A Hatred Fueled by Despair," in The New Leader (© 1977 by the American Labor Conference on International Affairs, Inc.), January 3, 1977, pp. 20-1.*

[The] example of Céline, the greatest figure in French literature after Proust, the determined anti-humanist who became the most repellent yet most prophetic writer of the period that ended with him as a fugitive in the ashes of Nazi Germany, shows that even in the late 1920s the real problem of literature was to surmount disintegration by expressing it *fully*. Céline found a language exactly equal in diction and spastic rhythm, even in punctuation, to the realization that dominates writing in our day. Man is completely under the control of events. All expectations are inherently absurd, because they express a mental freedom essentially unrelated to the life of action. Literature thrives on a sense of the ridiculous so unappeasable that the greatest writers of this school, like Samuel Beckett, have finally found a verbal equivalent of silence. . . .

Céline saw his books as "self-consuming artifacts" and disclaimed any lasting value to books whose deepest aim was to catch the innermost voice of his anguish. He was not modest and despised postwar writers like Camus. But of his own books he said firmly, "Great art is not personal like that."

Céline haunts me, because his aggressiveness and hatred for the contemporary world led him into a violent comedy of style. Beckett, just the opposite type in his passivity, anonymity, nevertheless ends up in the same spirit of limitless comedy. The prose is naked to the point of silence, as I say, but the point is the same: we are no longer even the masters of our own language. The muse uses us instead of the other way around. As Beckett showed in the pauses that are the most dramatic interventions in his plays, and as Céline had shown in the sputtering separation of phrase from phrase, language in our time is an effort, not a rhetorical triumph; it is a confrontation, is not and cannot hope to be an example of that self-confidence once known as "style." There is even an inescapable sense of travesty about writing; for the world of action, the remorseless productivity of "History," is so far in excess of anything we may hope to say about it that there is something inevitably self-mocking and a form of parody about key books that touch on the horrors of World War II—Céline's *D'un chateau l'autre, Nord, Brigadoon,* Waugh's *Men at Arms* and *Officers and Gentlemen* are far better examples than Vonnegut's *Slaughterhouse-Five* and Heller's *Catch-22.* . . .

[Even] the most pro-Fascist writer maddened by contemporary life, like Céline, could not admire evil as Hitler did. To write is still to respect the economy of life. (p. 192)

Alfred Kazin, in World Literature Today (copyright 1977 by the University of Oklahoma Press), Vol. 51, No. 2, Spring, 1977.*

*   *   *

CHAR, René   1907-

Considered by Camus to be France's greatest living poet, Char celebrates life, while acknowledging its pain and chaos. Involvement with World War II shaped his major themes, and his early association with the surrealists freed his imagination and colored his imagery. His work has been illustrated by such notable contemporaries as Braque and Picasso, and set to music by Pierre Boulez. (See also *Contemporary Authors*, Vol. 13-16, rev. ed.)

René Char has moved away from the esoteric place assigned to the poet by Mallarmé in order to stand today in the humanistic center of his close friend Albert Camus. . . .

Does this mean that M. Char's poetry is an example of the new "engaged" literature advocated by Sartre? Not, certainly, in any literal sense. Poetry, according to Char, does not seem to be committed to any cause unless one calls life itself a cause and a reason for commitment. . . .

The verses of Char, the aphorisms which abound in his work, and the brief condensed tales which appear in company with the aphorisms, all speak of the nature of poetry. It is that which is lived, for Char, experienced with the penetrating realization of submitting to human destiny. It is a comparatively easy matter to describe a literary work which is about life. But such a definition would not apply to the poetry of Char. This poet looks upon his art as an assault on life and an embracing, an animation of life. He answers, in the writing of his poem, not some outside command, but the uprising surge of his nature and his feelings. (p. 83)

The word "risk" . . . applies to Char's conception of life as well as to his conception of poetry. The outside world in which he lives, almost as a poacher lives invading someone else's forest, is the natural world of constant change, a flowering river of things such as his favorite philosopher Heraclitus had described. But this is the site of risks and provocations. The things he sees there are not poems, but they discover their reality in poems. The poetic act is a finding of a form for things which otherwise would never emerge from their abyss or their silence or their possibility. It is difficult for Char to elaborate on the principles of poetry because for him poetics and poetry are hardly separable. It is unusual for a French poet not to bequeath texts on poetics and technique. Char's answer is his entire existence as poet. The poet, he would say, has no other place to be except within poetry. The risk of poetry is precisely this responsibility of the poet in the action of drawing poetry from the poet's sleep and from his subconscious.

The risk of poetic creation is admirably transcribed in the striking antitheses of so many of M. Char's poems. The new poems, . . . entitled *Poemes des deux années 1953-1954,* contain examples of the contrast which Char establishes between solidity and fragility, between a sense of security and a premonition of the evanescence of things. The state of the world is so often established in these terms of contrast by Char that the poems themselves are seen finally to be constructed in a similar tension between strength and weakness. In "Le Bois de l'Epte," for example, the poet is seen following on foot a valley stream. He comes upon two wild rose bushes bending into the water. The brilliance of a single rose in the water awakens in the poet an awareness of the earth and he sees the wood of Epte beginning just ahead. (p. 84)

Multiple are the bonds this poet discovers existing between himself and nature, but the lesson is harsh to assimilate because it is inevitably a picture of a threatened and perishable nature he perceives.

The purity and the conciseness of Char's language make it appear more primitively faithful to his reactions, to his first responses. He has sustained in his style which is devoid of the usual poetic rhetoric, something of the secret meaning of his reactions. One remembers easily that his first adherence was to surrealism. And yet in this will to record and explain his reaction to the world and to human experience, he places himself quite centrally within the tradition of

French moralists. With his ever-increasing understanding of life, Char the poet and Char the moralist both denounce the vanity of life. Poetry is both a critique of poetics and a critique of illusions. The new poems, like aphorisms, are brief and elliptical. The white spaces around them—like the silences which precede and follow speech—have their own message and their own suggestiveness.

The poet's vocation is felt in its very special insistency, in the need it creates in the poet to write. If what he writes has both fury in it and tragedy, the poet is struck by the silence of the ink on the page. The oxymoron is there at the start: in the silence of the hieroglyphic characters and in the rage of the sentiments expressed. . . . He could not exist if it were not in accord with some mysterious law of apprehension. There is a price to pay for feeling deeply and for writing as a poet. That price is the daily assumption of peril. The ordinary man is able to fix the source of evil in the world: he traces it back to some event or to some cause. But the poet knows that evil comes from farther back than he can remember, from farther back than he can ever believe. The horrors he encounters in the world he is unable to simplify. That is the function and the activity, again, of the non-poet. But the horrors have simplified the poet. They have made him into a man unable to be anything save the poet.

The strong stylistic and moralist claims made by this new poet designate him as the heir both of symbolism and surrealism. He is surrealist in the way in which he feels an event. He is symbolist in the distance he knows exists between the occurence of the event and its narration. He actually speaks of the enigmas of poetry as often as Mallarmé did, but he defines the actions of the poet as the results of these enigmas. (pp. 85-6)

In the tributes written to his friends, René Crevel and Paul Eluard, Char exalts human life in its relativity, in all the attacks man has waged against injustice and deception, in man's love of the sun, and simply in the power he feels in accomplishing an action. He will forego any pleasure to be derived from vengeance or from persecuting others even if this means the resumption of uncertainty in life. Some of the humanistic definitions of man, found in . . . *Les Compagnons dans le jardin,* complete earlier definitions. He sees man's place as a coalition. He is a flower held down by the earth, cursed by the stars because he is unable to rise to them and solicited by death which is his constant fate. . . . Here again is stated, in fresh terms, the prevailing paradox of Char's work: man seen as tenderness in the surge of his spirit and as an Apocalyptic figure in his end. The pessimism of Heraclitus was not difficult to discover in the early work, *Feuillets d'Hypnos.* The myth of tragedy is man's principal heritage, but it may accompany a lifetime of revolt against this fate. This revolt is the subject matter of some of the greatest prose writers of modern France: Malraux, Saint-Exupéry, Camus. It is not only the subject matter of Char's poetry, it is the poetry itself. The poetry is his life lived as a maquis fighter and as a disciple of the philosopher of Ephesus. Char can no more cut himself off from the action of men, from cohabitation with men, than he can cease meditating on the tragedy of man's fate in a world of change and flux.

Char's vision of the world in which he lives, of the world where all men live, is one of his most fertile themes, but this vision is often cast into the abstract terms of a poet-philosopher. He calls it, in one passage, that which is in-conceivable. But it is also that which has luminous points of reference, dazzling signs. . . . The walker, the man who is bound to the earth and who walks on its surface, is granted some knowledge of the secret existence of things, secrets of the wind, of trees, of water. At moments in history when total destruction seems inevitable, man is unable to believe that the world, which has always been redeemed in the past, is facing its death in the very presence of man. In the future, Char may be looked upon as the apocalyptic poet of our day, as the poet the most persistently oppressed by the Apocalypse aspect of the mid-century.

The thought of Heraclitus has undoubtedly encouraged Char's philosophy to state that no matter how inherently noble truth is, the picture we have of this truth is tragedy. But there is a relationship between the nobility of truth and the noble character of tragedy. This is the source of what we have been calling the antithesis or the oxymoron in Char's poetry. Man's ever increasing awareness of his fate is equivalent to what Char calls the continuous presence of risk felt by the poet. This risk maintains the poet in a lofty position of attentiveness, of freedom of attitude and action. The risk represented by each poem is best understood by comparing it with the risk each day of living, with the threat involved in each decision of each hour in every man's life.

During the richest years of the surrealist movement in France, 1930-1934, René Char was initiated to poetry and to a search for what the surrealists called "enigmes." Char, who has never disavowed his debt to surrealism, has under-gone since that time many changes. The quest for enigmas, for example, would no longer be applicable to his present discoveries. But there are images in his newer writing which bear strong reminiscences of surrealism. (pp. 86-8)

As Char's writing has become more and more visibly af-fected by the events of his time, he has made the effort in his poetical work more and more consciously to transform what he sees and feels. But his age seen in an image is both transformation and interpretation. It is the understanding of the essence of things, an abstraction which, when success-ful, is the container of opposites. His poet's journal, *Feuil-lets d'Hypnos,* clearly states that he is opposed to the stat-ic, that if the alternative is the absurd, he will choose that, because thereby he will move closer to the pathos of the world. . . . (p. 88)

Despite the fact that René Char is a difficult poet in almost every sense, he has today reached an eminent degree of fame. The danger is now that he will be enshrined and not understood. To read Char, a new mechanism of sensibility is necessary. A mere knowledge of Char's commitments and an awareness of his literary affiliations will never reveal his poetic excellence.

The best way to approach Char is a study of those mo-ments in his writings when he is aware of the poet's voca-tion. They are the moments of natural perception when he greets the world. This poet is essentially an analogist. The experience he relates in his books is not beyond the under-standing of anyone who has looked intently and lovingly at the world.

Char initiates his readers first to his vigorous, sensuous life in nature. But from nature he moves quickly to the moral and the intellectual order. . . . There is really no poet, in Char's system, there is only poetry. He is consciously bent on bringing back into poetry the strength of living men.

The vigor of this poet's mind puts him into a separate po-etic world. We are moved by the vitality of his thought, but especially by the vitality of his concreteness. The truths of the world as he sees them are constantly demanding his al-legiance. (This trait in Char would be more easily under-stood in a frankly religious poet.) He is a poet characterized by the habit of seeing things charged with meaning—an ordered meaning regarding the relationships between nature and men. (pp. 88-9)

> *Wallace Fowlie, "René Char and the Poet's Vocation," in* Yale French Studies *(copy-right © Yale French Studies 1958), No. 21, 1958, pp. 83-9.*

René Char . . . calls the poet . . . "magician of insecurity" —a name suggesting a good deal about the activity of the artist at the present time. The entire statement runs like this: "The poet, a magician of insecurity, can have only adopted satisfactions. A cinder never quite burned out." "Insécurité": the French word and the English are nearly identical; and both have their usually unpleasant connota-tions of instability and vulnerability and lack of equilibrium translated into positive values by association with the poet's task. And that labor, in Char's aphorism, becomes hieratic and magical: the poet is a special being who turns our modern condition of insecurity—of human isolation and unbelief—into something else, his art. Still, we are warned that the poet will find no permanent refuge for himself in the realm of his poetry; his "satisfactions" are simply momentary releases from the "normal" state of shifting balances. This notion comes closer to Keats's "negative capability" than to any other well-known conception of the poet's role in England or America, but it is not the same because, for Char at this point in the twentieth century, the idea of the poem has altered almost completely. The meta-phor of the cinder, though highly elliptical, seems to sup-port a certain belief in inspiration through the wind or breath of the spirit which habitually restores life to the dying fire of imagination. . . . [Poems] appear to be the re-sult of impersonal forces at work in the depths of the poet's unconscious or operating upon his immediate circumstance. (pp. 40-1)

Char, a native of Provence, led a group of the *maquis* there during the war and was a friend of the novelist Albert Camus. His poems and aphorisms show, in their emphasis on will, responsibility, and independence, a genuine affinity with the view of life expressed in *La Peste, Le Mythe de Sisyphe,* and *L'Homme Revolté.* (p. 41)

From the Surrealists to the recent group of new novelists, including Claude Simon, Nathalie Sarraute, Samuel Beck-ett, and others, there has been a strong and conscious ten-dency to focus on subjective states of mind and to depart from the accepted forms and traditions of literature. The doctrines of the Surrealists, if not always their practice, aimed at a literature and painting of revolutionary intention which exalted the impulsive, the illogical, and the chance; they deliberately rejected the influence of the artist's choice or will, the interference of his control. . . . The goal of Sur-realism was to uncover the sources of thought by admitting the subconscious contents of the mind into the world of consciousness, reason, and practical affairs. Though the beliefs and techniques of these artists are remote from those of Valéry, we see again that art is drawn by centripe-tal force towards the self; its main concern seems once more to be a research into the spirit or psyche. . . . The novel and the poem withdraw to the opposite extremes of the single consciousness and the confession or to the quasi-journalistic account; they no longer support the arbitrary invention of elaborate fictional worlds and characters. The French veneration of the books of Henry Miller, all of them portions of an endless autobiography, is one of the signs of this anti-literary feeling. Like so much recent painting—Abstract Expressionism, *Tachisme,* and the like—which completely abandons the world of human faces and recognizable objects, replacing it with the painter's instinctive gesture, spiritual and physiological, unmediated by referential signs and images, this literature has assumed its own *informality,* an independence of the laws and expectations set up for poetry, fiction, and drama.

In the variety and unconventionality of his style, and in the momentary combinations of thought and emotion he wishes to discover through language, Char belongs—but in his own individual fashion—to this direction of modern writing. The poetry of Char is of several kinds, but these overlap; and such classification must not be taken as absolute. There are roughly three dominant classes: poems about poetry; poems dealing with the rural life and love he knows so well; poems treating man in extreme situations, especially those of war and death. The majority of his poems are prose poems or aphorisms, but even in these he experiments carefully with sounds and internal rhymes:

> Homme de la pluie et enfant du beau temps,
> vos mains de défaite et de progrès me sont
> également nécessaires.

> Man of rain and child of fine weather, I need
> your hands of defeat and hands of pros-
> perity, equally.

A persistent element of the irrational can be found in Char's imagery. Some of his associations are so far-reaching and curious that a poem may assume the magical properties of a dream. "Le Visage Nuptial" exemplifies this strain in his work, one which shares characteristics of the Surrealist verse of Breton or Eluard: a startling juxtaposition of objects and qualities that defies the order of logical thinking; a mixture of visceral, sexual, and assorted psychological imagery; the sense of being witness to the fluid motions of the mind working loosely on an obsessive theme. . . . (pp. 43-4)

The basic tendency of Char's poetry leads just the other way from the exfoliation of unconscious images; that is, toward a tight, elliptical statement, an oracular utterance with its meanings compressed or suggested. I have already mentioned the aphorism with regard to Char, for so much of his prose takes that form. These aphorisms are both lyrical and dramatic in their intensity; and in spite of the riddling philosophical tone of many of them, they are fundamentally poems. Constituted of thoughts or emotions that appear to be struck off at the instant they occur, the aphorisms gain a terrible force and beauty through their spontaneity. As Char says, "Lucidity is the wound closest to the sun"; the poet needs to achieve a painful and shocking clarity, a lightning-stroke of vision. Whatever the subject matter of Char's works, and however densely metaphorical they might be, they always bear on man's position in the world. While he is without religious convictions of any sort, this poet possesses a humane and deeply moral imagina-

tion. His life in Provence has taught him a reverence for the things of earth: flowers, grass, bushes, streams, the various movements of wind and water, the routine of peasant and farmer. The order and simplicity of existence in these country regions provide the feeling of an ancient human pattern which serves as a framework for the values Char upholds. His sequence of little poems about legendary country vagabonds, "Les Transparents," fills the reader at once with an understanding of the pastoral background against which Char has created his poetic universe. A brief and lovely poem about a lark, "L'Alouette," renders his belief in freedom and the miraculous beauty that is natural only to life:

> Extreme ember of the sky and first glow of day,
> She stands, a jewel mounted in dawn, singing the shaken
> earth,
> A chime that is master of its breath and free to choose its
> way.

> To kill this enchantress, strike her with wonder.

The world, and the acts of the spirit within it, complete the province of human experience. Beyond that, there is annihilation and nothingness in Char's understanding. What happens here and now, within the physical and spiritual cosmos of man's mortal condition, counts for everything: "Eternity is not much longer than life."

Death, then, assumes the role of a hated antagonist for Char, and is a constant sinister presence in his poetry. The journal he kept while fighting with the *maquis* in 1943-44, *Feuillets d'Hypnos,* one of the most remarkable war documents of our time, revelas this presence at the margin of daily life. The book follows the same plan of aphorism and prose poem we find in *Partage Formel* and *Le Poème Pulverisé.* Here are jottings on events of the day; notes about the poet's companions; indications of peril and risk at every moment; severe self-examinations; incidents of heart-breaking tragedy; and a pervasive belief in the nobility of human life and freedom—with the poetic enterprise an essential part of that dignity. Poetry answers death because it arises from the details of living; it seizes in speech the mercurial transformations of experience and names them. In the face of annihilation, it gives substance to man's passing thought and emotion. . . . To Char's manner of thinking, literature erupts from the nature of things as they are, is an act bound by moral implication and human concern, though not in Sartre's more restricted sense of commitment. . . . The theme of fraternity runs like a current through all of Char's writings, nor just the war journals, and extends the feeling of community and companionship into the love poems, where the poet gains a more profound relationship with creation through his adoration of a woman. (pp. 45-7)

Though he has the skill of an accomplished craftsman, Char stands outside the institutional and professional areas of the literary life; no one would ever mistake him for a grand man of letters. His poetry itself, as I have already suggested, makes its appearance at the edge of any living situation, on the very fringe of human actions as they occur. Char might say that poetry is the whole manner of being, physical, moral, and imaginative, of a person immersed in a multifarious existence: poems are hieroglyphics or notations expressive of that life. As an admirer of the early Greek philosopher, Heraclitus, Char tries to obtain something of both the precision and the paradox of his fragmentary writings. The juxtaposition of apparently incongruous elements in Char's work reveals a mystery at its heart, and human experience is suddenly illumined by a light breaking from previously unseen affinities and tensions. Such truths do not allow paraphrase, which accounts for the difficulty of doing more for this poetry than indicating constant themes, subjects, attitudes; these poems, unlike Rilke's or Eliot's, do not lend themselves to exegesis. The poetic act projects its author into the future by realizing his desire. But the contradictory nature of this risk lies in the dangerous freedom which the poet enjoys, for he has become the man who invents and tests possibility, the one who refuses to call upon any *external* reserves of belief or creed or dogma. . . . The poet of Char's aphorisms is, of course, primarily himself: he follows his own dicta, his own paradoxes by setting them on paper. In a world "faced with the destroyed god," as he believes, the solitary figure of the poet is transformed into the last priest, the final proprietor of value. Char's art does not partake of the fullness of a culture because that is fast dissolving all about him in mechanical utopias and international aggression; but the poems he writes, while they are the most personal statements, are still universal. They invest with significance, with love and care the objects or the moments of life, preserve and place them in a numinous circumference about man.

Char's true line of descent comes directly from Rimbaud, though he never enters that completely *other* spiritual dimension which was the adolescent poet's habitation. His poems do not fashion a whole universe suggesting the "true life" which in our ordinary lives is "absent." Instead, Char's poems are fragments, snatches of the difficult complex of existence at any moment, words in which such bursts of thought, feeling, and instinct receive a transfiguring power; they are—to use a French word appropriate to them—*témoinages*, testimonials to the perseverance and beauty and potentiality of the human estate. Char does not differ much from the Camus who so admired him: each supports the worth of life before the threat of death as absolute, yet each is also endowed with the same religious impulse, which has to seek its outlet within the limitations of the physical world and the meagre span of an individual existence. As Georges Mounin says in his excellent book [*Avez-vous lu Char?*], Char opposes his common materialist notion of death with the supreme moment of life: a sunlit Grecian noon from whose heights death can be surveyed with "an *objective* serenity." In the prefatory comments to *Feuillets d'Hypnos*, Char speaks of the anonymity and impersonality of these notebooks: "A fire of dry grass might well have published them. . . . This notebook might well have belonged to no one, the meaning of a man's life being so subjacent to his wanderings. . . ." Though he is most assuredly the author, in a more subtle way he is the mediator, for poetry comes into being through him, in a secret collaboration to which he remains just one party. Char's poems are the "elementary poetry," to use Mounin's phrase, of a time, a place, a web of ideas and emotions as these come to focus in language through the writer's presence and craft. The last entry in these diary "leaves" brings together in two brief sentences the entire spirit of his work—a fundamental wish to have his writings give voice to the happenings of life and the things surrounding us, extract their utmost possibility and make them ours:

Within our darkness, there is not one place for Beauty. The whole place is for Beauty.

(pp. 48-9)

Ralph J. Mills, Jr., in Chicago Review *(reprinted by permission of* Chicago Review; *copyright © 1961 by Chicago Review)*, *Vol. 15, No. 2, 1961.*

At a time when the presence of woman held a niggard place in French literature, surrealism revived the theme of love in poetry; Char himself, initially associated with the movement, contributed much to it. To him we owe ten or fifteen of the most gravely moving of modern poems, unabashedly proclaiming the tender beauty of that age-old force.

Some of Char's contemporaries, Breton himself among them, indulged in hyperbolic eulogies, cast in sumptuous poetic prose, of woman as the frail and weak companion who can rescue man from temptation and despair. Nadja and the nebulous feminine figure rapturously lauded in *Arcane 17* are perhaps the intercessors between man and the mysteries of the earth and the unconscious, but they are seldom companions sharing, in lucid sanity, the higher concerns of the author. Enumerations of the woman's beauties or virtues, litanies in praise of her, repeated avowals of man's desperate need of her impart some monotony to the love poetry of Breton, Desnos and even Éluard. Clearly, the neck of eloquence had not been completely wrenched by the earlier generation of symbolists, and the new poets' erotic imagery seemed at times too facile. It was only with René Char that sobriety acquired poetic vigor and muted suggestiveness.

Char's originality as a severe and restrained poet is striking. His goal is serenity, but serenity is a stilled force with him, a composed tension and not a soft lull in which feelings are dormant. It lies beyond struggle and the tumultuous roarings of life, which are at last silenced. In *À une sérénité crispée* (To a Tensed Serenity; 1951) he stated that the greatness of a poet emerges from the number of insignificant pages he leaves unwritten. Interestingly, however, two of the longest of Char's poems remain among his finest, "Visage nuptial" . . . and *Lettera amorosa*, showing that not all eloquence is harmful to poetry and that not all amplification of expression of desire and tenderness deserves to be condemned. The verses that exalt love spurn at the same time all soft and melodious tones, resorting instead to jarring and abrupt rhythms. "O ma martelée" is Char's appeal to the loved one, evoking the incisive and obsessive hammering of a recurring presence and desire. Throbbing, pounding on the mind and the senses, love is a "masterless hammer" pulsating of its own force, dislocating and scattering fragments like twigs (*brindilles*); the poet is himself a stone-breaking Prometheus whose energy cuts up reality ("Pour un Prométhée saxifrage" . . .) and hurls luminous sparks into the distance.

Woman, always present even when she remains absent in Char's poetry, is nameless, undefined in age and features, a captivating force that is never provoking or coquettish. The contrast with more sensuous poets who indulged in erotic variations on the female body, reviving the *blason du corps* of the Renaissance poets, is sharp and total. . . . If, as Valéry once put it, eroticism consists in stressing selected parts of the woman's body rather than the whole, Char is in no way an erotic poet. His allusions to the female presence do not transfigure her into an ethereal, Pre-Raphaelite vision, but what emerges is more the energy that her love inspires than the shape of her beauty. Char remains close to the very earth he evokes, and his settings are composed of bushes, birds and beasts. His affection for the concrete, reduced to its simplest elements, permeates his verse. But both woman and nature emerge from his poetry blended and transfigured into enigmatic and abstract images. Avoiding the vague and spiritual adjectives often found in Baudelaire, such as "mystical," "sublime," "infinite," his verses are more like the fiery reflection of a consuming yearning: "Oh vaulted effusion upon the crown of her belly" . . . ; or, in *Lettera amorosa:* "Tu es plaisir, corail de spasmes" (You are pleasure, coral of spasms). Even where a more specific allusion to female sexuality might be read, as in "L'amande croyable au lendemain neuf" (The credible almond with a new tomorrow), Char remains enigmatic and lofty. In one of his most rapturous and musical love poems he sees himself waking next to the loved woman, filled with a new energy and eagerly "picking the grapes of the fresh sky"; the allusion to woman's breast is remote and almost chaste here, only cautiously reminiscent of Baudelaire's and Valéry's "les grappes de ma vigne" (respectively in "Les bijoux" and "Anne"). Then, in two restrained verses throbbing with emotion, he pursues: "Lying beside you, I move your liberty. I am a clod of earth claiming its flower./Is there a finely worked throat more radiant than yours? To ask is to die!" . . . There are a few equally discreet mentions of kisses in Char; they are very remote from the erotic and complacently prolonged kisses of the Renaissance and Baroque lyrics, or even from the Baudelairean ones. In one of his later, very slim volumes, *Le chien de coeur* (1969), Char includes a five-line poem that remains among his most musical and in which the word *lenteur* is repeated with increasing force until it surges in a kind of climax. The title is "Le baiser".

> Massive lenteur, lenteur martelée,
> Humaine lenteur, lenteur débattue,
> Déserte lenteur, reviens sur tes feux;
> Sublime lenteur, monte de l'amour:
> La chouette est de retour.
>
> (Massive slowness, hammered slowness,
> Human slowness, contested slowness,
> Deserted slowness, return on thy fiery lights;
> Sublime slowness, ascend from love:
> The owl is back.)

Love is a palpitating force that slowly reaches ecstasy here before the nature of birds and sounds can reassert its presence. A long embrace and total surrender live within the repeated sound of the word *lenteur*.

Nudity itself, far from being a theme for esthetic or erotic contemplation, appears grave, figurative, a spiritual presence, in Char's poems. In "Biens égaux" (Equal Goods), originally published in *À une sérénité crispée,* the poet expresses himself in the first person singular. He sketches the setting in which he grew up, his father's garden, his solitude, then the oncoming of mutual love. (pp. 366-67)

Much love poetry with and since the surrealists has portrayed the excitement of desire, a feeling akin to and yet different from the purely physical urge and from the calculated act of waiting meant to inflame the imagination in the delay of fulfillment. Such had been the case with Gide in

his *Fruits of the Earth* and of the "attente infinie" in Valéry's *La jeune Parque.* The word occasionally occurs in Char's poems, always in a deeply sober mood and transfigured into images divested of sensuality. In a poem in *Fureur et mystère* the poet associates desire with the adjective *grave* and symbolizes it by a wheel which brings its periodic recurrence: "La grande roue errante si grave du désir" (The great wandering and grave wheel of desire). One of the nine aphorisms which make up "Afin qu'il n'y soit rien changé" . . . , a series of invocations to the woman, almost in the Petrarchan manner, beautifully declares, "Notre désir retirait à la mer sa robe chaude avant de nager sur son coeur" (Our desire withdrew its warm gown from the sea before swimming on her heart). The lover's desire is communicated to his partner through the old pressing formulas of invocation, "J'aime," "Je t'aime," "Je t'aimais" (in "Visage nuptial"), and through the repetition of the woman's name: Char's traditional reserve is abandoned for once in the evocation of Madeleine, the stylized and pure beauty that emerges from Georges de la Tour's seventeenth-century paintings.

The poet's use of terms of endearment is never childish or light, but always impregnated with nobleness. His use of "bien aimée" is an effective appeal, to which the less usual term "O Dévouée" ("Afin qu'il n'y soit rien changé") or "la Continuelle" (*Lettera amorosa*) is often preferred. In the beautiful prose poem "La Minutieuse" ("Thoroughgo" . . .), in which lives the unreality of a dream, the poet walks, against the background of nature, with his loved one, "between You and that Other who also was You." . . . The "two" women are the double image of his love, twice held in waking and in dream. His hands press on her bare breasts as he walks amidst fields and peasants. The visions of a child-woman and a woman-child blend into the image of a memory called love. What is "her eternal and beloved name" that his soul has forgotten? he asks. The answer is, "Je suis la Minutieuse." No term in English can convey all that is suggested by that word, implying solicitude, meticulous attention to details, effectiveness in humbly fulfilling a task. (p. 367)

If there is here little of the conventional, exasperated sensuousness found in much of the love poetry of Char's contemporaries, there is even less of the banal and declamatory sentimentality of some of the romantics and even of the symbolists. . . . [Tears] are scarce in the poetry of Char, perhaps the most restrained and virile poet in modern French literature. If sensibility is always held in check by the intellect, however, it vibrates in the great love hymns such as *Lettera amorosa*. The adoring quality of his feelings is expressed in concrete terms, in a love that is rendered visible by its own inner force. . . . (pp. 367-68)

The long and meandering poem, replete with mysterious or unpredictable but illuminating images, emerges as a canticle of praise and gratitude to the woman. It does not eschew sensual desire, or the hunger for ardent lips, the exultation of man being the equal of sun and night when standing at the very summit of pleasure. But the prevailing note is one of tenderness, of a pervasive blend of feelings and sensuousness or, as Nietzsche called it, "a rest from passion." Reciprocal confidence reigns between the two partners. The proud male who "stands upright while woman breathes," as in the striking final line of "Visage nuptial," consents to bow down, humbling pride in his love. "Ne te courbe que pour aimer" (Bow only to love) the poet wrote elsewhere, bestowing upon love alone the spark of divinity.

The joy that comes from the nearness of the loved one still lives in the presence of memory. As in the poetry of Shakespeare and Donne, absence enhances the lover's ardor. "You are gone but you remain in the inflection of circumstances" (*Lettera amorosa*). . . .

If in Char's poetry there is only scant insight into woman's mind and spirit, there is also a total absence of the complacent selfishness and the swollen self-importance that other poets at times display in their love praises. Char never consents to humble the loved one or to utilize her as a handmaid to his inspiration. Woman is to him the enticement away from despair, and it is as such that she appears in "La compagne du vannier" (The Basket-Weaver's Companion . . .), a poem that is itself a jewel reflecting the lights of a precious love. "Je t'aimais," utters the humble artisan. "I loved you . . . I brought back from despair a basket so tiny, my love, that it could be woven in wicker work." It is rare to discover in other poets the lovers' determination to draw energy from each other's tenderness and to face the future together, without there appearing at the same time moments of rapturous ecstasy or the complacency of mutual love almost uxorially displayed. Unhappiness and complaints have traditionally offered more fertile sources of inspiration than has the placid contentment of fully reciprocated feelings. Yet there is courage in the effort to hold happiness as an homage to the cherished one and to proffer it as a gift. Char has not recoiled from this. In *Lettera amorosa* he bluntly declares to the woman who has ascended with him the highest pinnacle of joy, "Je ris merveilleusement avec toi. Voilà la chance unique" (I laugh marvelously with you. Therein lies the unique chance), and he shifts from the lyricist's tone to that of the moralist: "I can only be and only want to live within the space and the freedom of my love. We are not together the product of a capitulation or the motive for an even more depressing servitude. Thus do we wage mischievously one against the other a guerrilla war without blame."

Yet love never dwells long in mutual contentment. Life is replete with other forces, and the world of men outside is not excluded. For a time, in the opening lines of "Visage nuptial," the poet's escort is dismissed and the lovers wish to relish their bliss in a solitude peopled by them alone. Elsewhere, even in *Lettera amorosa,* Char, who is a singer of friendship as he is of love, remains aware of the need that the two lovers have of others: "If there were only we two on this earth, my love, we should be without accomplices and without allies." The spontaenous direction of his love poetry is invariably away from regret and the past; it is an impetus that reaches for the moment to come. The inveterate moralist that, in a lofty sense, Char is, opposes or juxtaposes "resistance to fatality" ("Le bulletin des baux" . . .). For a poet who is bent toward the future, love is not an oasis of mutual contemplation or the ephemeral effort to arrest time. For this singer of spiritual energy, to love is to reach forward: "Nous sommes irrésistiblement jetés en avant," he states in "Dans la marche." . . . (p. 368)

In that sense, the one-time ally of the surrealists has remained true to André Breton's admonition to lovers: the lost paradises are not the most enchanting ones; paradises loom incessantly in front of us to be stormed. "How can we live without the unknown in front of us?" asks Char.

The woman is no mere ornamental adjunct to his life, no pleasant pretext for strings of baroque or "precious" metaphors. Even when transfigured by her lover's desire, she remains concrete, endowed with the power to mediate between him and the pollen of flowers, the crickets in the fields, the springs and the majestic oaks ("Hommage et famine" . . .). Only rarely has French poetry been as stripped of all adornment, as grave and as fervent as the three brief stanzas which open one of the very few long poems by Char, the evocation of the three Parcae entitled "Les trois soeurs" (The Three Sisters . . .). . . . Love is not merely a source of poetic inspiration for Char, nor is it the well from which generations of poets before him drew passionate lyrics. Rather, it is the image of a dynamic union in which both man and woman partake of a joy that is a rebirth and a symbol of life. His poems are more an homage to that feeling of total fulfillment than they are the expression of one's limited experience. . . .

As the dean of French poets reaches in 1977 his seventieth year, surrounded in his solitude with the admiration of lovers of poetry in many countires, the restrained force of his verse has added new domains to the expression of passion, tenderness and desire. With grave nobleness he has remained steadily true to the definition of poetry which he once offered: "Le poème est l'amour réalisé du désir demeuré désir." (p. 369)

Henri Peyre, "René Char's Love Poetry," in World Literature Today *(copyright 1977 by the University of Oklahoma Press), Vol. 51, No. 3, Summer, 1977, pp. 366-69.*

In taking leave of coterie surrealism, René Char, half a generation younger than André Breton, interestingly moved in a direction parallel to that of Breton the poet, if not of Breton the surrealist activist. Both continued in the visionary path of Rimbaud, who had taken a new look at nature and at its dynamics; when he bid the Deluges return so that the sorcerer's knowledge of convulsive natural forces might become the substance of the poet's verbal alchemy, he opened a new chapter in the poet's relation with the cosmos.

Calling upon those forces, Breton and Char . . . developed a new kind of nature poetry which, without assuming any particular classification or new label, is an essential segment of modern poetics—one that is not yet sufficiently recognized. From *Le marteau sans maître* (including poems written from 1927 to 1937) to *Le poème pulvérisé* (1947) we follow Char's movement away from playful mating of objects and images to the mastery of a type of vision . . . which becomes thereafter a fundamental and deeply moving mark of his poetry.

Avowedly, nature could no longer be viewed anthropocentrically, and the complicity suggested by a system of anagogic correspondences was to be replaced by a vision consistent with scientific data. Henceforth the poet had to take the initiative in establishing links between his sensibilities and nature if indeed any rapport was to be preserved. The poetics of Breton, Char, Jehan Mayoux, of the Mexican Octavio Paz, the Argentine Aldo Pellegrini, the Chilean Gómez-Correa and the African Léopold Senghor are based on a *naturism* which duplicates in language the convulsive character of natural forces. Philosophically, it is based on the concept of a golden age, not sponsored by exterior divinities but based on our perception of divine manifestations in nature, forgotten and suppressed; for the development of a rational mentality has produced dichotomies that have gradually separated us from the context of the natural world.

In his prose poem ''Jacquemard et Julia'' Char expresses the occurrence of this rupture nostalgically. It is a poem that can be read two ways, one with an eye for the contradictions, such as light and darkness, land and sky, water and aridity. But one can also see that the contradictions which are of the present are set against a past when grass ''knew a thousand devices which did not contradict each other'' . . . and which in their conciliation embraced man as well. So, from the angle of the past all the roads are in concordance, animals in enchantment, time annihilated, errors sheltered, human tears wiped away; the bowed grain finds a direct path to the mouth of the bird. Grass was unkind only to those who were not willing to wander and lose their way. Then an abrupt break occurs in the poem, warning us of the passing of the idyllic golden age; the break is manifest in the very contradiction in language: ''L'inextinguible sècheresse s'écoule.'' ''Inextinguishable'' suggests burning, which proceeds to the next word, ''dryness'' or absence of water, which is contradicted by the next word, s'écoule, i.e., water running. But when the figurative meaning is substituted, the protest of the poet, injected into the language, emerges. The dryness of man's life continues, runs on; for man has made himself ''a stranger to the dawn.'' . . . (p. 380)

However, the poet ends on a note of hope rather than of dejection, for there are still those who recognize the tremors of the grass: ''Cependant à la poursuite de la vie qui ne peut être encore imaginée, il y a des volontés qui frémis-sent, des murmures qui vont s'affronter et des enfants sains et saufs qui découvrent'' (In the pursuit of life that cannot yet be imagined, there are free wills that tremble, murmurings that will be assertive, and children safe and sound who will discover). We are back to the faith expressed in Breton's First Manifesto: that the eidetic power which was taken away from us will someday be restored. The poetry of Char is full of that tenderness of childhood which must be guarded to rediscover the missing links to the circuit of nature where resides a state of grace.

Breton's theory of convulsive beauty was intricately connected with his concept of a cosmography of nature, of the delirium of interpretation which guides man in a ''forest of indices,'' as he explained in L'amour fou. So it was that he linked the flesh of the woman he loved with ''the snows on the summits in the rising sun.'' And in L'air de l'eau, love poems of the same period—which also marks Char's brilliant poetic genesis—Breton had traced the rainbow of his erotic embrace: ''Ta chair arrosée de l'envol de mille oiseaux de paradis / Est une haute flamme couchée dans la neige.'' If we let the sense of these two poetic statements invade us with their full impact, we have at the same time the groundwork on which Char was to build the most resplendent levels of his poetic edifice through verbal resources particularly suited to universal coordinations.

The first of Breton's images fuses the human carnal substance with the element of water, combined with the quality of white/purity, and earth in its highest manifestation of summit, together with fire in terms of sun. The feminine elements of earth and water are invaded by the masculine one of fire, creating fusion and consummation on two levels: human love and cosmic concordance. In the second image again the human flesh is the starting point, and again it crosses barriers of nature's kingdoms: birds drenched in water, and flame in snow. The passage from human love to the cosmos is so smooth, like the flight of birds, that the contradictions of hot and cold, of solid and fluid, of visible and invisible are overcome in the conciliation which represents the fusion of the human embrace. (pp. 380-81)

The collaborative work of Breton, Éluard and Char called Ralentir Travaux (1930) attests to the conjecture that this interweaving of the human with the cosmic must have been reached in consortium by the three poets, who henceforth relinquished overtly or subtly (as in the case of Breton) the more urbane, gratuitous poetry of wordplay and image substitution representative of the earlier surrealist mode. . . . (p. 381)

In a 1931 poem Char declares the love process as the basic poetic process—attraction, gravitation, accolade: '' Dans le domaine irréconciliable de la surréalité l'homme privilégié ne pouvant être que la proie gracieuse de sa dévorante raison de vivre: l'amour''. . . . Further in the collection of Le marteau sans maître we find a poem called ''L'amour'':

Tu ouvres les yeux sur la carrière d'ocre
  inexploitable
Tu bois dans un épieu l'eau souterraine
Tu es pour la feuille hypnotisée dans l'espace
À l'approche de l'invisible serpent
O ma diaphane digitale!

Man's search, expressed in the metonymy of the hunter's stick, is linked with ochre (earth), subterranean water, leaf in sky (vegetal and air), invisible serpent (fauna) and digital flower (flora); in fact, the flower classified as ''digital'' resembles the human finger and thus has a built-in linguistic duplication of the connection between the botanical and the human. The love upon which the poet opens his eye in this intricate design of nature, recipient of the human imprint, turns the notion of the juxtaposition of distant realities into the coordination of realities which lose their distance from each other under the spell that the poet casts upon them. And the adjectives hypnotisée and diaphane qualify the unimaginable union with an ecstatic purity best defined by the title of the poem, ''Love.''

René Char's poetry coordinates the universe in emanations and gravitations that synchronize the human heartbeat with the mysterious tremors which pulsate in the natural world. Since so much of the poet's work is the product of unconscious forces, the distance between art and nature is minimized, making way for interweaving and amalgamation. What Mallarmé called the ''fiction'' of the poet is in the poetry of René Char not the rival of the natural world but very close to nature's own fantasies. Poetry is perceived, then, in Char in ''the fusing angle of an encounter.'' . . . Chance meetings create an image of fusion such as this: ''La lune du lac prend pied sur la plage où le doux feu végétal de l'été descend à la vague qui l'entraîne vers un lit de profondes cendres'' (''Donnerbach Mühle'' . . .). Here we see light (lune), water (lac), earth (plage) and fire (feu) swept into a bed of cinders. In terms of the alchemical process of reducing to essence, we see, then, the interplay of the sidereal (lune), the vegetal (feu végétal) and the liquid (*vague*), a concert of forces creating movement, luminosity and darkness as if it were a contemplation in a hot moonlit summer night just before it gives way to the darkness of sleep and oblivion ("un lit de profondes cendres"): we have grasped man's brief moment of illumination before it turns to darkness. In fact, in the throes of such visions the poet becomes "lord of the impossible" ("A Pain I Dwell In" . . .).

Had not Rimbaud asserted that if flight is impossible, the poet's sole exit is through the alchemy of the word? René Char is of Rimbaud's heirs, and in *Le poème pulvérisé* he dared describe what does not exist and give presence to the indescribable, calling on all earthly forces to nourish his poetic spirit. The terra firma is a source of the light of diamond and of snow; it brushes his being, kindles his flesh. As the invisible becomes visible, so the visible becomes invisible to intensify perception: "La nuit et la chaleur, le ciel et la verdure se rendent invisibles pour être mieux sentis" ("Le bulletin des baux" . . .). He arranges tiers of poetic values, oriented toward the core of a pristine natural force:

> Disposer en terrasses successives des valeurs poétiques tenables en rapports prémédités avec la pyramide du chant à l'instant de se révéler, pour obtenir cet absolu inextinguible, ce rameau du premier soleil; le feu non-vu, indécomposable. ("Partage formel" . . .)

From solid stance he proceeds to fluid passage, whose movements are associated with the dance of butterflies. Thus he gives the reader a sense of passing from one level of motion (water) to another (air). The poet learns to read the microcosm of nature: the storm and garden of its passage are self-contained in the trajectory of the swallow: "Dans la boucle de l'hirondelle un orage s'informe, un jardin se construit." He also knows how to project the microcosm into the macrocosm:

> Les eaux parlaient à l'oreille du ciel.
> Cerfs, vous avez franchi l'espace millénaire,
> Des ténèbres du roc aux caresses de l'air.
>
> (The waters spoke on into the sky's ear.
> Stag, you and you and you have crossed millennia, the space
> From rock darkness to the air's caresses.)
>   ("The Black Stag" . . .)

His fusion of beings and things sometimes reaches gratuitous proportions: "L'encre du tisonnier et la rougeur du nuage ne font qu'un" ("À la santé du serpent" . . .).

If such images were simple practices in the juxtaposition of distant realities, we might be tempted to accept them as a game process like those of Raymond Roussel; and indeed even as such, the versatility might be considered poetic virtuosity and a renewal of the system of analogies. However, in Char's poetry that type of expertise is not the seat of greatness in itself. Poetry is lodged in language, but since the poetic revolution of the nineteenth century it is also the substance of a philosophy and the basis of an epistemology. Of this Char is very much aware. Poet and lover are constantly identified: "Tu es dans ton essence constamment poète, constamment au zénith de ton amour." . . . Poetry is the power of the visionary, giving man new qualifications as

a human being: "Poésie, la vie future à l'intérieur de l'homme requalifié." . . . Poetry becomes the touchstone of the requalification of the human.

In truth, for René Char poetry is an existential stance. It is a *becoming,* a movement into high gear; it is man's only remaining contact with his revised definition of the eternal: "Si nous habitons un éclair, il est le coeur de l'éternel." . . . It is an invitation to return to the natural insights with which other creatures are endowed, to reenter the universal order: "Pouvoir marcher sans tromper l'oiseau, du coeur de l'arbre à l'extase du fruit." . . . Finally, it is a rejection of the mechanical materialism that places man in a system without conscious design, despairingly automatic: "Néglige ceux aux yeux de qui l'homme passe pour n'être qu'une étape de la couleur sur le dos tourmenté de la terre." . . . Char's vast fresco of the natural world is not unlike Paul Claudel's, but without the promises of religious transcendence to the ultimate recognition of meaning. For Char, as for Breton and for a number of other nonreligious mystics, man's creativity has to meet nature's halfway; it is not a question of recognition but of invention of associations, such that each man's universe becomes as complex as his power of cognition, as the elasticity of his sensory tentacles.

Rimbaud, in his poem "Les voyelles," epitomized the spiritual by the color violet, radiant in eyes whose possessor remained ambiguous in the semantic hermeticism of his possessive adjective: "rayon violet de Ses Yeux." Char was to appropriate the color and identify it as the supreme degree of man's manifest divinity. In a very hermetic poem of *Le poème pulvérisé* entitled "Suzerain" he gives us the spiritual autobiography of his childhood: arising to awareness in a crepuscular light, effecting a kind of symbiosis with river, butterfly, weed; and then the death of that world, leaving only a mute Friend. The word "friend" as a luminous phantom plays the role of *Génie* in Rimbaud and *Engel* in Rilke. He teaches the adolescent how "to fly over the night of words" ("Il m'apprit à voler au-dessus de la nuit des mots"), to be free of stationary things like "ships at anchor." At the end he knows that he must leave his hometown to find love and to reach the next stage of his becoming. And strangely, when he attains the next abode, that of *L'HOMME VIOLET* (capitalized by the poet), he is disappointed by what he finds; he observes the same kind of corruption as in "Jacquemard et Julia." He finds a prisoner instead of a fugitive. . . . (pp. 381-83)

But what did the poet want to escape in the guise of the violet man? And where did he want to escape? Certainly not from his corporal existence into an eventual soul-existence! "Tu feras de l'âme qui n'existe pas un homme meilleur qu'elle" ("À la santé du serpent" . . .). Better than the soul-man is the earth-man whom the poet identifies throughout his work. His escape is from a blind assumption of the human space, and it is a penetration of the subjective and objective worlds simultaneously. The poet comes to grips with the non-anthropocentric universe without damning himself as hapless, for he has learned to become part of the network. And thus he is relieved of his solitude and of any sense of drifting. His is neither the ship at anchor nor the shipwreck of Mallarmé's *Coup de dés*. The vision that links man to bird, plant, stone, sun, moon and to the bowels of the earth also turns his eventual demise into a metamorphosis. Fire and water, in their power of transformation and absorption respectively, promote a kind of serenity in the poet rather than a noble but self-consuming despair such as Pascal's. . . .

Let us not forget that René Char is a poet of the 40s and 50s, of that time when existentialism was highlighting *Dasein* as an act of human salvation; but the existentialist notion of involvement related to political action as the sure solace, whereas the poet's existential stance is of a quite different nature of involvement: it is a cosmic embrace. . . . It is deemed a privileged destiny to be able to absorb unto oneself the sun and the wind and to contemplate the kind of eternity Char accords to Antonin Artaud in his memorial to the erstwhile companion of his surrealist days:

Puis renaît plus tard dans la douceur du champignon . . .
Il suffit. Rentre au volcan.
Et nous,
Que nous pleurons, assumions ta relève ou demandions:
   "Qui est Artaud?" à cet épi de dynamite dont aucun
   grain ne se détache. . . .
                              ("Un adieu, un salut" . . .)

All of this explains if not logically, at least poetically, the contradiction of Char's self-assigned epigraph: "vivre, limite immense." . . . Recognizing the limits of the living process, by unfurling the infinite possibilities of the associations of man with his contiguities, Char has illustrated in his poetry what another companion of his youth, Louis Aragon, had stated in *Le paysan de Paris:* the only inconceivable notion is that of limit. . . . Indeed, the unconditional possibilities of passage into the variations of nature in the work of Char illustrate the notion that limit is unthinkable. In the vertiginous layers of existence are gateways to insights, what Char calls "la connaissance aux cent passages." . . .

The naturalism of modern poets like Char is not linked to the romantics' love of nature nor to the sensual courtship of physical realities that are manifest in the poetry of Walt Whitman and in his wake in so many modern American poets. . . . [There] was on the part of nature a guardianship of man, sometimes effective and protective, other times resulting in a failed relationship. (p. 383)

In the case of poets of the category I have called "naturist" —of which René Char is perhaps the most versatile and resourceful living example—nature is a coordinator between the forces in the poet and the forces outside of the poet; whether within or without, they are forces of which the poet is not fully the master. The mystery of those latent powers in him—similar to the blinking of an animal's eye or the burning of a tree or the boiling of a worm in the wood ("Robust Meteors" . . .)—creates the sense of wonder in him, prepares the dialogue between himself and the mute universe. The reciprocity he has known in love is his sole index to the meaning of the universal reciprocity which he considers to be the primal purpose of existence. In repairing the separateness of man, source of alienation and despair, he is releasing the violet man from his prison house to resume his freedom. When the barriers are let down and the contact becomes communication, it is no longer a question of *taking* from nature or asking nature's protection; it is exchange, it is emergence from the labyrinth, it is that existence which Breton called "elsewhere" in the last sentence of the First Manifesto. . . . Char challenges his fellow beings to take stock of the riches within them left inert and in chains. . . . (pp. 383-84)

Char's "elsewhere" is immediate, a series of moments that constantly replenish each other, creating ubiquity out of immobility. It absolves the "I" from the particular to enter into the universal. Rarely does Char have to use the personal pronoun, for his sensibility is the radiance with which he endows the world around him. (p. 384)

Anna Balakian, "René Char in Search of the Violet Man," in World Literature Today *(copyright 1977 by the University of Oklahoma Press), Vol. 51, No. 3, Summer, 1977, pp. 380-84.*

René Char is today the undisputed giant among contemporary French poets. To read Char is to experience the best that modern poetry offers and at the same time to get a glimpse of the directions which poetry may take in the future. Yet to read Char is to face the challenge of entering a dense, elliptical, and fragmented universe. Char is a sketcher of traces, which demand reader activity and creativity. . . . [There] is no given approach to Char's poetic passage—the poem is there, just as a shooting star bursts into a showery pattern and quickly disappears. (pp. 784-85)

Virginia A. La Charite, "An Archipelago of Poetry," in Virginia Quarterly Review *(copyright, 1977, by the* Virginia Quarterly Review, *The University of Virginia), Vol. 53, No. 4 (Autumn, 1977), pp. 784-86.*

*   *   *

CLARKE, Austin   1896-1974

Clarke was an Irish poet, critic, playwright, and novelist. Greatly influenced by Irish myth and legend, Clarke, according to M. L. Rosenthal, had an "identification with Ireland . . . as complete and unself-conscious as with his own family . . . the criticisms he directs against her have the domestic authenticity . . . of a man complaining of wife or mother." Regarded by many to be the greatest Irish poet after Yeats, Clarke wrote poetry and verse dramas with fresh, open rhymes characterized by a linguistic energy and a concern for local and topical matters. (See also *CLC*, Vol. 6, and *Contemporary Authors*, Vols. 29-32; obituary, Vols. 49-52; *Contemporary Authors Permanent Series*, Vol. 2.)

Austin Clarke's repute was a local affair until the publication of his *Ancient Lights* in 1955. The good news was carried beyond the Irish Sea in time for the reception of *Later Poems* in 1961. It is widely agreed that the early poems are not worth reading and that Clarke moved into his stride only when anger made him a satirist. This was my own impression, too, until I went through the poems again on the occasion of the *Collected Poems*, but I am now convinced that the paradigm is inaccurate. Many of the early poems are indeed tedious. . . .

But there are a few good poems in *Pilgrimage* (1929) and the first, premature *Collected Poems* (1936). The first major achievement is not *Ancient Lights* but *Night and Morning* (1938). In fact, Clarke's true work is *Night and Morning, Ancient Lights, Too Great a Vine* (1957), *Flight to Africa* (1963) and a few short poems in an otherwise not very good book, *The Echo at Coole* (1968). The first really memorable poem in the big book is 'Celibacy', from the 1929 volume, and with the 'Six Sentences' from the first *Collected Poems* Clarke found his voice. He showed himself quite capable of losing it again, there are dozens of later poems both false and falsetto, but 'Celibacy' and the 'Sentences' stand in the *Collected Poems* of Clarke pretty much as 'Adam's Curse' stands in the complete Yeats, the place where the reader first hears a genuine poetry as distinct from verse merely going through its own motions. . . .

Clarke always cared enough for [Dublin] to be enraged by its folly. His satires are the work of a city poet: his invocations of rural landscape are regularly praised, though not by me. In his apprentice years Clarke went Yeats's way, writing long poems, reciting 'the thousand tales of Ireland', and generally proceeding on the assumption that the best way to become a poet was by writing like an Irish poet, at great length. . . . An Irish poet who published his first long poem in 1917 would have to sell his soul to Yeats or take care to keep out of his way. Clarke's care took him to the Gaelic metres, a safe place because Yeats had no ear for them.

No Yeats, then, if Clarke could help it; easy enough to understand why he had to guard his inner ear against Yeats's rhetoric. But it is not easy to see why Clarke ran away from Eliot, Pound, the Imagists, the modern French poets, and nearly everything of any importance in the new poetry. . . .

[There] is no evidence of a sustained relation between Clarke's mind and 'the modern movement' in any of its audible forms. He was interested in other poems than his own if they offered him solutions to metrical problems, but normally he taught himself to write by working through the Gaelic poems. He made progress in the art by making mistakes and then correcting them. It took him a long time to discover that he was not created by God to be an epic poet. Belatedly, he divined that God was trying to tell him something, and then he found that he had something to tell God, mainly that he no longer believed in Him. *Night and Morning* is the magnificent result of those communications, a poetry of faith and its fractures, resentments, misgivings, strivings. . . . (p. 69)

[He] spent . . . 15 years working with the Dublin Verse Speaking Society and writing verse plays for the Lyric Theatre Company. Someone ought to have told him that it was a waste of time and spirit. Clarke was not a playwright, he was not even up to Yeats's mark in the theatre. (pp. 69-70)

As a poet, Clarke was fascinated by possibility: it was enough for him that a linguistic act was possible, he did not ask that in addition it be necessary. His mind was full of homonyms, puns, *rime riche,* assonance. He loved making verbs from adjectives: 'fierced', 'futured', a car 'wealthied by', in *Mnemosyne Lay in Dust* (1966) Maurice 'feebled against his holders'. Or making verbs from nouns: stags antler the wind, New York dollars the sky, the sky-blaze noons at Padua. . . . 'Vilified' is nearly always 'villafied', especially when Clarke is sneering at Dublin's suburban pretensions, but also in 'A Centenary Tribute' when he writes of revisiting Yeats's house at Riversdale. . . . We judge these procedures by their results, the cackling does not matter if it yields an egg. Clarke was not given to ambiguity, certainly he did not seek impressions of indefinitely wide reverberation, he liked his words to have several distinct meanings running happily together at the same time but he wanted each meaning to know its own mind and not to confuse itself with its neighbour. He liked to juggle and to keep the meanings simultaneously aloft. His style was not agglutinative, he kept the lines clean, each pointed toward its destination: if a word served two masters, well and good, but Clarke wanted to know each master's name, keeping the record straight. Homonyms pleased him because their meanings went about their business, they did not confound each other, but he took their existence as a good omen and inferred from their proliferation that a poet could still live free. . . .

I think there is more to Clarke's homonyms than that. There is plenty of evidence for associating them with nimiety, natural excess, freedom, but I think they are more powerfully associated in Clarke's poetry with the freedom of sexual fantasy. The conjunction of sex and poetry is common in Clarke, he is an erotic poet, and I would be ready to argue that his high jinks in language are related to standard speech as freedom to constraint: sexual freedoms mostly. (p. 70)

Homonyms are crucial in Clarke's poetry because he loves to find one sound releasing two words; all the better if one of the words stays at home and obeys the rules while the other one runs wild and makes love upon whim and desire. This points to the dominant motif in Clarke's work, the life of freedom and impulse set against the law of institutions. Since Clarke was an Irish poet, the hated institutions were the Church and the State: or rather, the new Church and the new State. His morality is represented by the epic grandeur of the old Irish sagas. . . .

I have never known a poet to get more mileage than Clarke has got from the vagaries of the Catholic Church in Ireland, or the vagaries (no less) of our political masters. He is not, indeed, a disinterested witness. (p. 71)

Every one who irritated Clarke was treated as the personification of some horrible Law or Principle. If he stumbled off a kerb, it meant that he was pushed, probably by the Clergy. He could never distinguish, on any rational ground, between contingency and law, causalities and symptoms. Reading Clarke, I am reminded of something Richard Blackmur said of William Carlos Williams, that it never occurred to him that reality is other than immediately contingent and equal to the actuality. . . .

I am making a fuss about Clarke's dyspepsia to account for the fact that his true work amounts to quite a small list of poems and that he wrote too many poor poems for his reputation's good. The list, for my money, is as follows: 'Celibacy', 'Six Sentences', 'Night and Morning', 'Mortal Pride', 'Tenebrae', 'Martha Blake', 'Repentance', 'The Lucky Coin', 'The Straying Student', 'Penal Law', 'Her Voice Could Not Be Softer', 'Summer Lightning', 'The Jewels', 'Marriage', 'Ancient Lights', 'The Loss of Strength', 'St. Christopher', 'Martha Blake at Fifty-One', 'Japanese Print', 'New Liberty Hall', 'The New Cathedral in Galway', and 'In Kildare Street'. (pp. 71-2)

Denis Donoghue, in The New Review (© *The New Review Ltd., 11 Greek Street, London W1V 5LE), August, 1974.*

Clarke . . . began his literary career as a child of the Revival. His development parallels Yeats's in a number of ways. Both began with the legendary Ireland of the heroic age; both later castigated contemporary Ireland for its failure to live up to the past; both abandoned poetry for verse drama and returned revivified; and both cultivated, in middle age, a picturesque preoccupation with sex—which did Yeats no harm, since he was a Protestant, but involved Clarke in difficulties with the Catholic Church.

The differences between them (aside, of course, from the very much greater scope of Yeats's work) were precisely the differences between the indigenous Gaelic-speaker, sharply observant of the actual physical countryside and concerned to imagine the historical reality of his race, and the idealistic impressionist with his roots in the minor gentry. Clarke was, if you like, the Yeats of Catholic Ireland. When the older man turned to the 18th century, Clarke turned to the Middle Ages, the 'Celtic-Romanesque' monastic culture. . . .

He came into his own with *Night and Morning* (1938) and *Ancient Lights* (1955), volumes separated by nearly 20 years (his years in the theatre) but closely related in theme; and the theme, one to which he constantly returned, was the stultifying effect of conventional morality on the Ireland of his time. . . .

His world has more of Joyce about it than Yeats—the Joyce of the *Portrait,* gaslight and aspidistras, rosary beads and Sacred Hearts. But Clarke was temperamentally averse to Modernism. His technical experiments led back into Gaelic poetry, whose texture he strove to re-create in English; and this, combined with the extraordinary allusiveness of his poems, renders many of them all but inaccessible to the nonspecialist. (p. 518)

> *Derek Mahon, in* New Statesman *(© 1975 The Statesman & Nation Publishing Co. Ltd.), April 18, 1975.*

It is not hard to be intelligent in Ireland, but the things which interest or delight intelligent people there can be too much on a par, a texture rather than a network of avenues. . . . The Clarke pieces [in *Selected Poems*], silly and less, are all one texture because he starts from one texture and works out, which is how the scholar should work it. The verse is corbeled and ornamented with any thing. The shorts lack Landor's waistcoated violence and are not like Yeats or the British, for which we are equally thankful. The long ones are like Quintilian writing verse in his old age, to be read line by line for the riches he simplemindedly put in. If you've lived a while in Dublin the book is about eight times as good. (p. 87)

> *Gerald Burns, in* Southwest Review *(© 1977 by Southern Methodist University Press), Winter, 1977.*

*　　*　　*

CORMAN, Cid　(Sidney Corman)　1924-

An American poet and translator, Corman lives in Japan. His poetry is essentially a poetry of exile, of cultural isolation, and its form is clear, brief, and immediate with great emphasis placed on the sense of word sounds.

Cid Corman is a practiced master of a distinctively modern genre: the skinny poem. A good skinny poem is spare in more than its line lengths (and usually its number of lines—were Poe alive he might explain how a skinny poem of more than, say, thirty lines would be at best a series of related poems). . . . To qualify for the genre, a poem has to look like a skeleton that won its struggle to get out of its fat embodiment. If it says more than it leaves unsaid, it's just

corseted corpulence, pathetically trying to play thin. If it suggests no special logic in its thinness, it advertises a way to cheat editors who pay by the line. Here is one of Corman's honest successes:

> We drink
> to each
> other
> mountain
> flowers
>
> One cup
> leads to
> others
> others
>
> Mind floats
> body
> lies by
>
> Go friend
>
> Tomorrow
>
> Morning
>
> And don't
> forget
>
> Your lute.

The lines of this poem are short and placed as they are for better reasons than a mere predilection for white space. It shows how such simple devices as immediate repetition can be peculiarly telling in a poem so rigorously spare. And it brings to mind another quality shared by many of the better pages in *Livingdying,* an Oriental flavor so strong in some poems that they seem not original works but carefully literal translations. At its worst this flavor may smack of cross-cultural belch, like pseudo-Zen gnomics or Pound pretentiously wagging his pigtail.

> Young strong and willing
> Sword in hand alone
> How much ground covered
> Chang-I to Yu-Chou
> Drank at the Yi's source
> Got to no man's land
> Nothing but old graves
> Of them two high points
> Chuang-Chou Po-Ya rest
> No longer around
> I have gone far—why.

Why indeed. But that isn't typical. Corman lives in Japan, really *lives* there, and in most of his short pieces the Eastern note is earned and genuinely resonant. Few of the wholly successful poems of *Livingdying* are far from the realm of haiku. "The Condiment" is a particularly deft example.

> Grass
> comes over
> the slope
> or nearly
>
> across
> the grass
> the salt of
> shadows
>
> pigeons
> into the

emptying
air.

And there are others (''Willows / pushing buds / I / / only / reach to feel / more'' and ''Of course / life matters. / Twitter / / sparrow, / and let me / know it.'') that exemplify a common feature of American haiku, making overt the connection between thing seen and man seeing.

Geography aside, Corman also lives in America. He has worked his way to the forefront of our native tradition of skinny poetry, a tradition that includes Frost's ''Dust of Snow'' as well as Williams' lean classics, the few achieved miniatures of Louis Zukofsky's work, or for that matter, the funning onomatopoeia of Aram Saroyan's ''crickets / crickets / crickets / . . . .'' When he cares to, Corman can bring off a special blending of haiku-like ellipsis and downright American idiom.

That there
    sky

the tree
    shake

light
    yawn

bird
    song

What you do
    to be

here

What you done
    years

man.

(p. 53)

Robert J. Griffin, in The Nation *(copyright 1970 by the Nation Associates, Inc.), July 20, 1970.*

Cid Corman has long been a poet's poet: a writer neither very profuse—all his books are ''slender'' ones—nor very aggressive, but central. To read Corman is to become conscious of one's breathing, how slightly it separates us from things like stones. The pure language, in minimal lines like those of Williams or Creeley, makes one think of other arts in their purity: a clean tone of harpsichord music, or flute, or lute, or Matisse colors, or *sumi* painting or the Zen archer, shooting well. (p. 271)

Alicia Ostriker, in Partisan Review *(copyright © 1972 by Partisan Review, Inc.), Spring, 1972.*

Cid Corman's characteristic poem of the last 10 years (roughly the period since he went to live in Japan) has a somewhat Oriental look about it: brief lines, measured by syllabic count, with much interplay of tones and accents, usually turning on a point of acute perception. But don't mistake it for the schmaltz that passes as Orientalism in most American translations and imitations. Corman came from New England originally, he lived in Europe for some years before moving to Japan, and I detect in his work a Yankee toughness and existential lucidity that raise it far above trivia. . . .

Corman's questions speak what whole libraries have debated about contemporary experience. And they show his method very well—conflict, balance, compression. . . .

I'd say Corman hits about 10 percent, equivalent to a lifetime batting average of .400 in the ball park. A collection of his best poems, including those from [''Once and for All: Poems for William Bronk''], would be one of the finest works in English from the third quarter of the century. Beyond that, ''Once and for All'' is quite the equal of his earlier books, though perhaps more abstract in substance than some. . . . (p. 12)

Hayden Carruth, in The New York Times Book Review *(© 1976 by The New York Times Company; reprinted by permission), May 16, 1976.*

Sun Rock Man seems above all else a rite of passage, the record of a poet working out his apprenticeship in a foreign country, but in Corman two very different ways of relating to this situation conflict. The book is thus less a study of the evolution of a style than a working out of a contention between outlooks. Many poems are impressive for their craft and their pure externality, the poet a mere agency, a word-journalist, of subjects which speak so eloquently and powerfully in their own right that comment seems superfluous. . . . [There] are five or six . . . accomplished [poems] in *Sun Rock Man*, one asks no more, for they demonstrate what the objectivists (whose influence informs them) meant by ''rested totality.''

And yet, in the end, such poems may rely too heavily on a form of *exotica*, particularly when their content is almost solely a function of the poet's fortuitous appearance on the scene. If places *do* speak to us, nevertheless, they run the danger of becoming terminal *loci* when the poet has taken himself out of his own cultural milieu. Such ''objectivity'' can inhibit the complexity of the poet's response, mainly by preventing him from sufficient accounting for his own presence in the equation of the world he is creating. This certainly seems true with Corman, for cast into the world of *Sun Rock Man*, like a grain of sand in an otherwise perfect oyster of impressions, is Corman's awareness of his own status as outsider, his resources, the choices which are denied his subjects. . . . There is a feeling . . . not only of coming too far but of not coming far enough, an ache to actually enter into that vastness. This mood permeates the last few poems of *Sun Rock Man*, suggesting a leavetaking but not a return. They introduce Corman's later themes, an epiphany to ''that greater speechlessness / leading us all home''; in the work which follows, that ''home'' seems less a physicality than a place, any place, in which the poet can imagine ''speechlessness'' having an echo. (pp. 98-100)

In Corman, facing toward silence—since it cannot respond, only evoke—is a way of drawing off from the self what would pass for style or mannerism. As soulwork, it might usefully be compared to Eliot's notions of impersonality; as vision, it is death-haunted, and yet its consolations are strangely moving. . . . (p. 101)

In the poems of the last six or seven years, the themes are further muted, the attempt to grasp or to make sense of being not so much withdrawn as transmuted into a form of acceptance which has its own nervous energy. (p. 102)

These poems, no longer quests, are certainly different in tone from the anguished work of *Sun Rock Man* with its ache of excess being. Wise in a kind of yielding, they attempt to let things be what they are, what a Buddhist might call ''suchness.'' . . . [The] capacity to maintain, in a kind of semantic juggling act, a multiplicity of meanings . . . is one of Corman's great gifts as a poet. That the meanings adhere to the language at depth and complexity testifies to the visionary nature of Corman's craft. For what is ambiguous about his work manifests itself without obscurity or recourse to private symbolism: it occurs in the service of the recognition, as he says in another poem, that ". . . in time go / words also, however true / Man's life is a conjuring / finally nothing once more."

The air of "finally nothing" pervades . . . *Once and For All, Poems for William Bronk.* Both have an ease and humor, the exile now so much at home in his exile, that past, pain, whatever, are transfigured into a new richness, a new balance. . . . [The] "nothing" in the substance of these poems is the self recognized as a transparency, an agency which works on and gives voice to its interferences. This is decidedly different from our usual liberal or religious ideas that the self is small, hence should be humble; Corman's balance is struck as a kind of arrival, an acceptance into one's condition. Poetic tension comes from the drama and the new knowledge acquired in reconciliation. . . . (pp. 102-04)

Those who are familiar with the work of William Bronk will recognize . . . that Corman's dedication to him of his latest book is a signal, beyond friendship, to shared themes and concerns. In both, what sets them apart from their contemporaries and from much American and English poetry is their metaphysical stance toward what phenomenologists call the "pre-objective" world, the world enshrouded in that silence before concept or name. In Bronk, this seems to have taken the form of Montaigne's "what can I know"; in Corman, the emphasis has been on the nature of the knower. Corman's best poems remind us that the self, of which we are often so glib, is no closer than that world in our understanding. The power of the poems derives from Corman's urge to pare that world, to reduce, to silence language to all but the essential. . . . Such poems have the feel, the completeness of natural objects; they demand as much from one's tact as from one's emotions in that like all otherness they resist our appropriations. Unlike much modern work, they refuse to trade on contemporary anxieties, refuse to be converted into a form of moral coinage—there is barely a word in these poems about the world of "big issues." Nevertheless, they insinuate themselves into our moral consciousness by going to ground, by addressing the self at its most affective point, the economy of its own organization. . . . (pp. 106-07)

What I have said of Corman's poetry strikes me as no less true of his editorship of *Origin;* like the poems, it is an enterprise, a meditation of exile. Its pages testify anew to what makes the American literary scene such a curiosity, such a contradictory set of patterns and influences, that its large-scale movements seem less to have grown organically from well-planted seeds than to have appeared like blisters swollen and agitated by rather small but significant pebbles. (pp. 107-08)

> *Michael Heller, "Soundings Toward a Greater Speechlessness," in* Parnassus: Poetry in Review *(copyright © by Parnassus: Poetry in Review), Spring–Summer, 1976, pp. 98-104, 106-08.*

CORNWELL, David
See Le CARRÉ, John

     *   *   *

COWARD, Noel   1899-1973

Coward began acting at the age of ten; by the time he was twenty he had seen his first play successfully produced. Coward's career was at its apex in the 1920s and 1930s. Capturing the essence of those decades, he wrote technically brilliant, witty, and refined period pieces for the stage. Coward was knighted in 1970. (See also *CLC*, Vol. 1, and *Contemporary Authors*, Vols. 17-18; obituary, Vols. 41-44; *Contemporary Authors Permanent Series*, Vol. 2.)

[Coward's] enthusiastically applauded wit, it saddens me to report, I cannot for some reason or other, despite painstaking hospitality, discover. I can discover, with no effort at all, several amusing little wheezes, but all that I am able to engage in the way of the higher jocosity called wit is a suave prestidigitation of what is really nothing more than commonplace vaudeville humor. This vaudeville humor Mr. Coward cleverly brings the less humorously penetrating to accept as wit by removing its baggy pants and red undershirt and dressing it up in drawing-room style. But it remains vaudeville humor just the same. (p. 207)

Let us . . . turn to the inner machinery of Mr. Coward's "wit." This machinery whirrs entirely, we find, around the stalest and most routinized of humorous devices. Device No. 1, a favorite of Mr. Coward's, is a character's repetition in a later act, for comic effect, of a line spoken seriously by another character in the earlier stages of the play. Device No. 2, believe it or not, is the periodic use of the "go to hell" line. Device No. 3 is the serio-comic promulgation of specious sentimental eloquence. I quote an example: "There's something strangely and deeply moving about young love, Mr. and Mrs. Carver. . . . Youth at the helm! . . . Guiding the little fragile barque of happiness down the river of life. Unthinking, unknowing, unaware of the perils that lie in wait for you, the sudden tempests, the sharp, jagged rocks beneath the surface. Are you never afraid?" Device No. 4 is the employment of a word or name possessed of an intrinsically comical sound. For example, Chuquicamata. And Device No. 5 is—also believe it or not —the causing of a character, who in a high pitch of indignation sweeps out of the room, to fall over something. (pp. 210-11)

Now for the original and profound philosophy underlying Mr. Coward's great wit. I exhibit samples:

No. 1: GILDA: "Why don't I marry Otto?" ERNEST: "Yes. Is there a real reason, or just a lot of faintly affected theories?" GILDA: "There's a very real reason." ERNEST: "Well?" GILDA: "I love him."

No. 2: LEO: "I'm far too much of an artist to be taken in by the old cliché of shutting out the world and living for my art alone. There's just as much bunk in that as there is in a cocktail party at the Ritz." (p. 211)

We now pass to a consideration of the freshness of Mr. Coward's broader humors. Herewith, specimens:

No. 1: LEO: "I remember a friend of mine called Mrs. Purdy being very upset once when her house in Dorset fell into the sea." GRACE: "How terrible!" LEO: "Fortunately, Mr. Purdy happened to be in it at the time."

No. 2: GILDA: "It's very hot today, isn't it?" ERNEST: "Why not open the window?" GILDA: "I never thought of it." (p. 212)

Mr. Coward's "daring sophistication" is still another enchantment of his public and his critics. Let us, in turn, consider this daring sophistication in the light of its most trenchant specimen lines:

No. 1: GILDA: "After all, it [the London *Times*] is the organ of the nation." LEO: "That sounds vaguely pornographic to me." (Regards to Mae West.)

No. 2: GILDA: "The honeymoon would be thrilling, wouldn't it? Just you and me, alone, finding out about each other." LEO: "I'd be very gentle with you, very tender." GILDA: "You'd get a sock in the jaw, if you were!" (Regards to Michael Arlen.) (p. 213)

In order to deceive his audiences and critics into believing that all this vaudeville-hall humor and juvenile naughtiness is excessively recherché stuff, it is Mr. Coward's practice, as I have hinted, to have it spoken by actors in evening dress and to intersperse it liberally with worldly allusions to the more fashionable restaurants, hotels, yachts, duchesses' houses, and watering places. (pp. 213-14)

In order to establish beyond all audience doubt the perfect equilibrium of his sophistication and to persuade it that he is superior even to his own highest flights of philosophical reasoning, it is Mr. Coward's habit to disgorge the philosophical pearls reposing in his mind and then to bring another character to offer a facetious remark about, or to chuckle derisively over, each of the aforesaid pearls. Either that or, by way of passing himself off for a magnanimous intellect, to place his most serious convictions in the mouth of a character who is slightly intoxicated. Thus, let one character speak Mr. Coward's mind about some cynical aspect of civilization, and another like clockwork is ready with some such retort as "That is definitely macabre!" Thus, let a character express a sentiment of some delicacy and another is ready with a deprecation of him as a rank sentimentalist. Thus, let the action turn to normal drama and a character is ready with the mocking exclamation: "Bravo, Deathless Drama!" Thus, let Mr. Coward venture what he considers in his heart to be a first-rate and saucy bit of humor and another character is ready with "That was a cheap gibe!" And thus, let a character express Mr. Coward's sober convictions as to Life and another is in the offing duly to jump in at the conclusion with a facetious "Laife, that's what it is, just laife." And so it goes—always the pseudo-philosopher and commentator taking what he writes with perfect gravity and surrounding himself, fearful and feeling the need of ideational protection, with a procession of minstrel end-men to hop up after each observation and minimize it with a joke.

Mr. Coward occupies the successful place in our theatre today that the late Clyde Fitch occupied twenty and thirty years ago. Both are of a playwriting piece, though Mr. Coward has not yet contrived anything nearly as good as Fitch's *The Truth*. And both have been overpraised and overestimated ridiculously. Where are the plays of Fitch now? Where will the plays of Mr. Coward be when as many years have passed? As in the case of my critical reflections on Fitch in his fashionable heyday. I leave the answer to the calendar. (pp. 214-15)

George Jean Nathan, "Noel Coward" (1935), in The Magic Mirror: Selected Writings on the Theatre by George Jean Nathan, *edited by Thomas Quinn Curtiss (copyright © 1935 by George Jean Nathan; reprinted by permission of Alfred A. Knopf, Inc.), Knopf, 1960, pp. 207-16.*

Four of the most fruitful days of 1929 were surely those that Noël Coward, on a lazy holiday trip around the world, spent writing "Private Lives." The first act of the play, which I don't hesitate to call as nearly flawless a first act for a comedy as any in the language, is said to have been jotted down overnight—formidable proof of the fact, repugnant to puritans, that time and effort have no necessary connection with achievement in the arts. Neither, for that matter, does age—Coward was twenty-nine when he wrote "Private Lives," and he was never to surpass it. . . . [Much] of our pleasure in the play comes from our being allowed to know, from moment to moment, more than the characters themselves are allowed to know. Our laughter springs as much from the sudden glory of anticipation fulfilled as from the witty expression of any ordinary human feeling or—perish the thought!—thought. The first act has a symmetry of word and deed so exact as to be almost uncanny; the two newlywed couples in the swagger hotel in Deauville are made to move through a series of discomfitures as neatly introduced, exhibited, and dismissed as so many magic hoops, cards, coins, and colored handkerchiefs. In the second act, the prestidigitator risks losing control by losing momentum. We perceive that he has time to kill on his way to a third act (in the twenties, a playwright who plotted a comedy in two acts would no doubt have been accused of shortchanging his audience), and we come dangerously close to seeing Amanda and Elyot for what they are—in real life, two of the least delightful people imaginable, with nothing to do but eat, drink, bicker, make love, and congratulate themselves on their isolation from a world unworthy of them. In the third act, the prestidigitator is again in full control; after a flurry of slapstick physical encounters, he rings down the curtain on a breakfast scene that is at once consummately trivial and just the right size. (p. 115)

Brendan Gill, in The New Yorker *(© 1969 by The New Yorker Magazine, Inc.), December 13, 1969.*

Noël Coward's *Hay Fever*, immaculately revived by the author, has been called a comedy of situation; but it isn't really that at all. It is a comedy of characters who are absolutely impervious to situation. This is one of the clear natural differences between farce and comedy. Farce is about people who are preternaturally alert to the outside world, to the dangers behind bedroom doors or the dragons in boilers; comedy is about people with such massively engrossing and indestructible characteristics that the outside world bounces off them like grapeshot off elephant hide. *Oedipus Rex* would be a comedy if, with the plague of Thebes running through the drawing room, the royal family remained blind to their people's agony and thought only about being attractive to each other.

This is pretty much the situation in *Hay Fever*. The Bliss family have invited four wretches for the weekend whom they proceed to wrack with inattention, starting with no introductions, going on to no explanations of a party game at which the theatrical Blisses shine, and ending by leaving them coldly alone with some unpleasant haddock at Sunday breakfast from which the outsiders tiptoe back to London, worn out with histrionics. The Blisses don't notice; they have the survival power of drunks and the hermetic family infatuation of the Greeks. (pp. 242-43)

> *Penelope Gilliatt, "Coward Revived" (1965), in her* Unholy Fools: Wits, Comics, Disturbers of the Peace: Film & Theater *(copyright © 1960-1973 by Penelope Gilliatt; reprinted by permission of The Viking Press, Inc.), Viking, 1973, pp. 242-43.*

I feel no hesitation in saying again what I've often said before: that the first act of "Private Lives" . . . is as nearly perfect as any act of any comedy in English [see excerpt above]. . . . A clue to the nature of the flawless first act of "Private Lives" is offered the moment the curtain rises. We note that the setting is scrupulously symmetrical; a plumb line dropped from the middle of the proscenium arch would split it into halves. Now, set designers ordinarily seek to avoid symmetry, as providing too little to entertain the eye, but in the case of "Private Lives" the stage architecture has obviously been decreed by the playwright; it is a necessary part of the action of his play, and therefore of the highest importance practically as well as symbolically. What we see is, it turns out, precisely what our comedy is about: the hilarious consequences when two people attempt to share equally in a single strong emotion, at no matter what cost to themselves and others.

The setting is the façade of a luxurious hotel in Deauville, sometime in the late twenties. Open French windows lead from a pair of identical suites onto a terrace divided in two by small trees in tubs. . . . Each of the suites is occupied by a honeymoon couple. Amanda and Elyot, divorced for several years, have unwittingly arrived at the same hotel on the same night for the same reason: to celebrate the beginning of new marriages. Modestly, immaculately, the conversations between each of the couples march toward the moment when Amanda and Elyot, alone on the terrace, meet and discover that they are as much in love as ever. The words they speak come close to having the cadence of music; one's ear is as much ravished by the reverberatory silences between words as by the words themselves. We lean forward in our seats, awaiting a familiar exchange as we might await a familiar phrase in an étude. . . .

> *Brendan Gill, "From the Duke of Westminster's Yacht," in* The New Yorker *(© 1975 by The New Yorker Magazine, Inc.), February 17, 1975, p. 84.*

*   *   *

COX, William Trevor
See TREVOR, William

D

DAVIDSON, Sara   1943-

Davidson, an American novelist and journalist, is the author of *Loose Change,* a popular autobiographical novel and television serialization of the growth and awakening consciousness of three women in the 1960s.

Sara Davidson's book of fictionalized reportage, "Loose Change," bills itself as the true-to-life adventures of "three women of the sixties." It purports to be a social history of that tumultuous period seen through the lives of three California women . . . who went to Berkeley in the early 60's, were seniors when J.F.K. was assassinated, pursued the various panaceas of sexual liberation, political activism, spiritual questing and wound up being 30 and disappointed just like most people. As in a novel, the names have been changed except for Sara Davidson who appears as "Sara" in the book. Her story is by far the most authentic and interesting. What particularly distinguishes "Loose Change" from a novel about the same period is its formlessness, its easy topicality, its false sense of conveying history when it is really only dropping the names of historical events, as one might drop the names of famous people. . . .

It is as if the author expected the mere invocation of the events to conjure memories in the reader, to carry their own emotional weight. A teen-ager born in 1963 would read this book in vain, seeking to know how it *felt* to be a college student when the President was assassinated. The author rattles off famous historical events for the reader rather than re-creating them, shaping them and making them come alive.

And yet there is a touching story here, and it is Sara Davidson's own story. Sara (the character, and perhaps the author, too) has an engaging sense of adventure, a willingness to try anything once, a real lust for life. She is a risk-taker, willing to be a fool if in the process she may find enlightenment. . . .

One of the most moving sections of "Loose Change" deals with the author's passage from cynicism to trust and openness through her meetings with Ram Dass, the American guru, formerly Dr. Richard Alpert. Davidson sets out to nail and categorize Ram Dass and other "salvation seekers" and winds up questioning the roots of her profession and livelihood. . . .

The Ram Dass material raises the most compelling ques-

tions in this otherwise rather cluttered book. What good is political radicalism if we don't seek to know and change ourselves? What good is sexual freedom if we find it difficult to love ourselves and others? What point is there to the constant chasing after exotic experiences if, in the process, we lose our own centers? . . .

The lives of all three women are interesting enough, but the telling is often so sprawling that only at odd moments does one feel empathy for them. As a writer, Davidson has a tendency to drown the reader in trivia—like a cook drowning a prime fillet in sauce. We have to know the brand-names of every garment worn by every character, and yet the most important emotional events (deaths, abortions, political assassinations, the disappearance of relatives in fascist countries) are passed over with hardly an effort to describe what anyone thought or felt. There is a heart-breaking shallowness here—heartbreaking because the book might have been so much stronger.

It is not that one wants answers about the 60's and whether or not their particular contribution to sensibility survived the decade, but only that the questions might have been posed more sharply.

It is fascinating to hear Sara Davidson's characters, circa 1968, predicting revolution within a minimum of six months, maximum of six years and then to realize that here it is 1977 and such predictions have already entered the hazy realm of nostalgia—along with Scott Fitzgerald's flaming youth, Hemingway's Paris and the recipes of Alice B. Toklas. What does America do to gobble up incipient revolutions, make their leaders momentarily famous on the cover of *Time* magazine and then throw them into the dustbin along with old soda bottles, aerosol cans and other non-recyclable trash? Why do our most passionate revolutionaries (whether leftist, black or feminist) eventually give up the hope of changing America's ways and turn instead to yogic meditation, Buddhism, "born again" Christianity or Sufism? Why is America the country of the most extravagant hopes and the most profound disappointments? Does the media really have the power to trivialize and thus destroy every important social movement, or does it only seem that way to us? Are changes really occuring at a deeper level? "Loose Change" prompts one to ask these questions; for that alone it is a useful document. (p. 21)

Erica Jong, in The New York Times Book

Review (© 1977 by The New York Times Company; reprinted by permission), May 29, 1977.

Utopianists see the sixties as a time of liberation from sexual stigmas, a time for broadening human perspectives, sharpening the humanist impulse. Glowerers, on the other hand, believe the "liberation" of the sixties was spurious, hedonist, vulgar, and fruitless. Sara Davidson's fascinating portrait of three women, herself included, who attended the University of California in the early 1960s, will not resolve this dispute, chiefly because its narrative details strengthen both sides of the argument. . . .

As a picture of "how it was" to grow up in the sixties, *Loose Change* is vivid and all too believable. But some readers will object that it stops short of making the argument one might have expected from it—that the problems Davidson and her classmates faced were peculiar to their time, and not simply the misfortunes of bright, active women who made unlucky choices. (p. 93)

C. Michael Curtis, in The Atlantic Monthly (copyright © 1977 by The Atlantic Monthly Company, Boston, Mass.; reprinted with permission), June, 1977.

[In] *Loose Change* . . . Miss Davidson proves herself one who eagerly embraced what she experienced as that decade's revolutionary spirit. Her book covers all the familiar landmarks of the 60's. . . .

For Miss Davidson and the others chronicled in *Loose Change*, these sundry phenomena comprised a time of high hope and excitement, one that would usher in a new era characterized by a universal dedication to social reform, open, honest, and loving relationships, a shattering of sexual taboos, and an uncompromising disdain for the grubby pursuit of money, power, and career. That new era never arrived, and in writing *Loose Change*, Miss Davidson hoped to find out what went wrong and why. (p. 70)

For all the tribulations endured . . . , Miss Davidson looks back on the 60's as a time of confidence and exhilaration, and on herself and her peers as a "generation that was special . . . that had sprung from nowhere . . . that had glimpsed a new world where nothing would be the same." She contrasts these great times, with their optimism, energy, and certainty, with the dismal 70's, when young people are caught up instead in a "cross-generational obsession with money and security." Yet even a reader otherwise disposed to give Miss Davidson the benefit of the doubt could not help but notice that her book tends to show that things are in fact the other way around. (p. 71)

What sighs through the pages of this book, as it seems to have done through the lives of these petulant and mindless [characters], is not any buoyant revolutionary spirit but simple self-absorption—that, and an unfailing ability to wind up where the money and glamor are. The only difference in these girls' lives between the 60's and the 70's is that in the 60's they could not acknowledge what they were after, and hence were miserable much of the time, whereas in the 70's they can (if only implicitly) and so have found happiness at last.

As for reality, political and cultural reality, and all those high public events . . . that supposedly gave this period its meaning, these figure in *Loose Change* only as signposts in

a private landscape, seized upon as occasions for self-dramatization on the part of one or another character, or providing Miss Davidson with material for magazine articles. The "revolution" of the 60's is nowhere to be found here, or perhaps it would be more accurate to say that it exists only as a function of the particular mood Natasha, or Sara, or Susie happens to be in on the morning of any particular day. Did it figure any more seriously in the lives of any other members of that generation? Miss Davidson's book gives cause for doubt. But at least we know now what these young women of the 60's are asking of us, as they stride ever resolutely onward to their brave new world: first, what should they wear; second, how should they decorate it. (pp. 71-2)

Jane Larkin Crain, "O Brave New World," (reprinted from Commentary by permission; copyright © 1977 by The American Jewish Committee), in Commentary, August, 1977, pp. 70-2.

Ms Davidson's great success is to have prised out such honest autobiographies from her two friends and then to have retold their stories so vividly and compassionately. Her own story, for all its palpable anxiety to be honest, has a touch of Erica Jong boastfulness about it: all those page one stories, the statutory soft porn wowie sex scene, the glittery life which must be endured, the monster-mother who fucked her up. Ms Davidson was and is an 'over-achiever.'

For all her trying, she nearly misses in 'Loose Change.' Her new-journalistic reliance on faked dialogue, her cliff-hanging chapter endings, and her use of pulpy leitmotifs (Tasha always laughs her 'tinkling laugh'; Rob 'twinkles his blue eyes') threaten to ground the story in coyness. And except for Tasha, whose inner life and recall of it was intense, the stories lack the experiential quality of life or of a good novel. But the book stands as a painful document of what it was like to be young, female, middle class and American during the sixties.

Victoria Radin, "The Nightingales of Berkeley," in The London Observer, November 6, 1977, p. 26.

* * *

**DESTOUCHES, Louis-Ferdinand
See CÉLINE, Louis-Ferdinand**

* * *

DILLARD, Annie   1945-

An American columnist and poet, Dillard is best known for *Pilgrim at Tinker Creek*, for which she won the 1974 Pulitzer Prize in General Nonfiction. (See also *Contemporary Authors*, Vols. 49-52.)

"I am no scientist," says Annie Dillard, "but a poet and a walker with a background in theology and a penchant for quirky facts." In "Pilgrim at Tinker Creek" she offers "what Thoreau called 'a meteorological journal of the mind.'"

The book is a form of meditation, written with headlong urgency, about *seeing*. A blind child the author happened to read about saw for the first time after cataracts had been removed from her eyes. "When her doctor took her bandages off and led her into the garden, the girl who was no longer blind saw 'the tree with lights in it.'" Annie Dillard had found the central metaphor for her book; it is the vision, the spiritual conception, that she will spend her days in solitude tramping the Roanoke creek banks and the Blue Ridge mountainside in search of for herself.

A reader's heart must go out to a young writer with a sense of wonder so fearless and unbridled. It is this intensity of experience that she seems to live in order to declare.

There is an ambition about her book that I like, one that is deeper than the ambition to declare wonder aloud. It is the ambition to feel. This is a guess. But if this is what she has at heart, I am not quite sure that in writing this book she wholly accomplished it. I don't say this, though, to detract from her declared intention in laying herself open to the experience of seeing. It is a state she equates with innocence: "What I call innocence is the spirit's unself-conscious state at any moment of pure devotion to any object. It is at once a receptiveness and total concentration."

But apparently it is an unself-consciousness that can be consciously achieved and consciously declared. And part of her conception of seeing is that in the act of doing it she is herself, in turn, being seen.

"I walk out; I see something, some event that would otherwise have been utterly missed and lost; or something sees me, some enormous power brushes me with its clean wing, and I resound like a beaten bell. I am an explorer, then, and I am also a stalker, or the instrument of the hunt itself. . . . I am the arrow shaft, carved along my length by unexpected lights and gashes from the very sky, and this book is the straying trail of blood."

What happens to that paragraph is what happens to her book. As the episodes begin, we can imagine an appealing young woman standing alert in a meadow, dressed in shirt and pants, holding her field glasses and provided with a sandwich: she is waiting to see, being very patient and still. By the chapter's end, we realize or suspect we are watching a dervish dancing. Receptivity so high-strung and high-minded has phases of its own. The author shows us that it has its dark side too.

"The world has signed a pact with the devil; it had to. . . . The terms are clear: if you want to live, you have to die; you cannot have mountains and creeks without space, and space is a beauty married to a blind man. The blind man is Freedom, or Time, and he does not go anywhere without his great dog Death. The world came into being with the signing of the contract. . . . This is what we know. The rest is gravy."

I honestly do not know what she is talking about at such times. The only thing I could swear to is that the writing here leaves something to be desired. "What's going on here?" is one of the author's refrains. "The creator loves pizzazz," she answers herself.

She is better at stalking a muskrat: "Stalking is a pure form of skill, like pitching or playing chess. Rarely is luck involved. I do it right or I do it wrong; the muskrat will tell me, and that right early. Even more than baseball, stalking is a game played in the actual present. At every second, the muskrat comes, or stays, or goes, depending on my skill." This is admirable writing.

So is her account of the polyphemus moth—first in its co-

coon, then emerging, then crawling away in the presence of a roomful of schoolchildren. It has been directly experienced at what I should say is eye-level. Her account of the migration of the monarch butterflies, which makes the reader see what they looked like coming, how they went over, what they left behind them, what the author learned from the whole event, is precise and memorable.

She can also write straight narrative, showing what the book would have gained in point, direction, and shape from being given a little more of it. (pp. 4-5)

Annie Dillard is the only person in her book, substantially the only one in her world; I recall no outside human speech coming to break the long soliloquy of the author. Speaking of the universe very often, she is yet self-surrounded, and, beyond that, book-surrounded. Her own book might have taken in more of human life without losing a bit of the wonder she was after. Might it not have gained more? Thoreau's wisdom had everything to do with the relationship he saw between nature and the community of man. She read Thoreau, including of course his own meteorological journal of the mind. . . .

[The] author is given to changing style or shifting moods with disconcerting frequency and abruptness. "Thanks. For the Memories." "This oft was thought, but ne'er so well expresed as by Pliny." "The cottage was Paradise enow." You might be reading letters home from camp, where the moment before you might have thought you were deep in the Book of Leviticus.

The relationship between the writer and the reader is fully as peculiar and astonishing as the emergence of the polyphemus moth. It too has got to leave the cocoon, has got to draw breath and assume every risk of being alive before the next step, real understanding, can take place.

But a writer writes as a writer sees, and while the eyes are rolled up, what appears on paper may be exactly what it sounds like, invocation. "Mystery itself is as fringed and intricate as the shape of the air in time." This is a voice that is trying to speak to me out of a cloud instead of from a sociable, even answerable, distance on our same earth. . . .

She concludes her book by saying, "And then you walk fearlessly . . . like the monk on the road who knows precisely how vulnerable he is, who takes no comfort among death-forgetting men, and who carries his vision of vastness and might around in his tunic like a live coal which neither burns nor warms him, but with which he will not part. . . . The giant water bug ate the world. And like Billy Bray I go my way, and my left foot says 'Glory,' and my right foot says 'Amen': in and out of Shadow Creek, upstream and down, exultant, in a daze, dancing, to the twin silver trumpets of praise."

And that's the way Annie Dillard goes. Is the Pilgrim on her right road? That depends on what the Pilgrim's destination is.

But how much better, in any case, to wonder than not to wonder, to dance with astonishment and go spinning in praise, than not to know enough to dance or praise at all; to be blessed with more imagination than you might know at the given moment what to do with than to be cursed with too little to give you—and other people—any trouble. (p. 5)

Eudora Welty, in The New York Times

Book Review (© *1974 by The New York Times Company; reprinted by permission), March 24, 1974.*

In many respects Annie Dillard's book, "Pilgrim at Tinker Creek," is so ingratiating that even readers who find themselves in fundamental disagreement with it may take pleasure from it, a good deal of pleasure. (p. 637)

Annie Dillard has done what many would like but few are able to do. She has organized her life, there in her primarily natural habitat, so that she has plenty of time to spend not only in the field but in the library and laboratory as well. She is the person who has read the books you have always promised yourself to read, from Pliny to Henri Fabre; she knows, though she is not a specialist, more about recent work in biological and physical science than you can hope to learn. And she uses her knowledge well. She describes what she has seen and what she has read; and as long as her eye is clearly on its object, her mind focused on that identity, her descriptions are informative, poetic in the good sense, and often moving.

Inevitably, however, she does more than this: she asks what it all means. The hard, incredible beauty of a monarch migration, the cruelty of a female mantis eating her mate while they couple, the insanity of the pine processionary caterpillar that follows unswervingly a track laid down by its leader and does so even if the procession is in a circle, round and round until it dies of starvation,—what force lies behind such beauties, cruelties, insanities? Is it mindless or intelligent, evil or good? How can one explain, in any moral terms whatever, the frightening wasteful fecundity of evolution? She writes: "A lone aphid, without a partner, breeding 'unmolested' for one year, would produce so many living aphids that, although they are only a tenth of an inch long, together they would extend into space twenty-five hundred *light-years*"—in order that a few hundred may survive. Annie Dillard is appalled. So am I. And not for the aphids' sake either, but because we know the same principle governs and tyrannizes all life, including, as we need not look far to see, our own.

Yet out of these quandaries Annie Dillard always contrives to emerge with a statement of spiritual affirmation, a statement which is, moreover, though expressive of her own sensibility, conventional in substance. Her book has been compared to Thoreau's. For a number of reasons the comparison seems unapt, but it contains at least this much justice, namely, that in essence her view is plain old-fashioned optimistic American transcendentalism, ornamented though it may be with examples from quantum physics and biochemistry. She sees ultimate goodness in everything. Or rather, in almost everything; there is one exception, human self-consciousness, the curse of mankind, she says, which prevents us from attaining to the purity of animal existence, absorbed in greater reality. Only in isolated moments do we jettison self-consciousness and break through, by concentrating our attention sufficiently on exterior phenomena, to a recognition of ultimate goodness. These are our epiphanic moments, pinnacles of life, for which we endure the rest. And because she believes this so firmly, Annie Dillard devotes many pages to what can only be called rhapsody, evocation in words of her own epiphanies. Unfortunately, much of this writing is confused, exaggerated, sentimental, and unconvincing. (pp. 638-39)

Any artist, any artisan, knows that his moments of insight —or outsight—are a marvel; but they occur in, not out of, life. They are gifts, true; but they are given to those who work for them. They are not holiness but the products of holiness. This is the creative struggle, the craftsmanly and prolonged and utterly self-conscious engagement of mentality with experience, from which we derive our humanity, art, knowledge, and—in any meaningful sense—life itself, the essence, the actual goodness (or badness). Annie Dillard's book is a work done in "the deep affection of nostalgia" (her words) for an abstract past, with little reference to life on this planet at this moment, its hazards and misdirections, and to this extent it is a dangerous book, literally a subversive book, in spite of its attractions. To my mind the view of man and nature held by any honest farmer . . . is historically more relevant and humanly far more responsible than the atavistic and essentially passive, not to say evasive, view held by Annie Dillard. (p. 640)

> *Hayden Carruth, "Attractions and Dangers of Nostalgia," in* Virginia Quarterly Review *(copyright, 1974, by the* Virginia Quarterly Review, *The University of Virginia), Vol. 50, No. 4 (Autumn, 1974), pp. 637-40.*

While readers and reviewers of [*Pilgrim at Tinker Creek*], even those in "fundamental disagreement," appreciate Dillard's poetic descriptions of her natural world, they generally question how she is able to celebrate an existence which is often senseless and chaotic to her. As readers of *Pilgrim* know, Dillard uses two major metaphors to reflect her concept that beauty and violence are equal parts of the mystery of creation. . . .

The pilgrim finds what she seeks; no more and no less. Dillard watches the world of nature seriously because ultimately it reflects the rich complexity of human experience. As her narrative develops, Dillard grows comfortable with ambiguity, accepting the senseless ways of nature while scrupulously describing it. Fidelity to horrible detail makes her celebration of life startling, for her style is so careful of the minute that her theme, in comparison, borders on the irrational. How can one be a believer while portraying honestly the chaotic ways of nature. . . .

Dillard is exploring, in truth, not merely the woodland of Tinker Creek, but, more profoundly, what it means to be a believer in God. Her courage is revealed in her daring openness toward nature, the dramatic terms by which she recognizes the Divine. (p. 495)

For Dillard, the world is an epiphany, and the woodlands and waterfalls of Tinker Creek are to be neither ignored nor escaped. The confusion for many readers lies in their misconception that Annie Dillard's terms of existence are mutually exclusive: while believing that one has the choice to accept the world willingly for both its beauty and savagery, she simultaneously claims that there is much about the world that allows no choice. This apparent contradiction is actually paradox. Freedom, for Annie Dillard, lies in choosing the world, not out of pious or pietistic sentimentality, but out of acceptance of one's task to make the world more human by becoming more fully human oneself. The goal of Dillard's work is to make the reader *see,* to hold his eyes open "with toothpicks, with trees." She insists that each person has his own creative capacity to awaken from blindness to a state of perception that discovers the world with new meaning. The problem of celebrating existence lies not in the world, but in man's failure to see with eyes that transfigure. . . .

By surrendering to mystery, Dillard accepts the actual world, even though it remains rationally incomprehensible to her. Her mysticism does not bring her to a vision of another world—*de contemptu mundi*—but rather to a new dimension of life where Tinker Creek becomes a holy land of miracles and demons. By insisting that human beings have the visionary capacity to see both the beauty and the violence of the world with new eyes, Dillard is different from the traditional Transcendentalist. Although the "anchor-hold" at Tinker Creek reminds one inevitably of Walden Pond, Dillard is closer to Melville than to Thoreau. Her awareness of both light and darkness is profound. It is impossible, moreover, to abstract a statement from Dillard that involves the pursuit of utopian or reformist goals; her message, simply and totally, is to honor creation and the mystical revelation of God in creation. The paradise of Emerson as Transcendentalist, on the other hand, is a transfigured world, redesigned by the soul in touch with nature who creates an order analogous to that of nature. . . . Dillard's focus is not so narrow; restructuring the universe is not for her. Although she does not grow to love the Furies more, she accepts their presence.

Living with nature, then, provides Dillard neither escape from life, nor therapy to return to life, nor programs designed to improve the *status quo*. Rather, Dillard's experience draws her more deeply into the mystery of the human condition, and she reveres it. She desires to nourish and protect the holy land, not simply as an ecologist, but as a wonder-struck pilgrim-poet who honors life as a place where "mystery bumps against mystery," where one must search and strive continually to understand existence. . . .

Dillard witnesses to the existential condition as nature reveals it, begging us to see it with her, for freedom to Annie Dillard lies in acute awareness of the terms of life. She does not intend her hermitage at Tinker Creek to stand as a political statement nor to inspire ethical behavior or social reform. If she has a mission, it is purely that of the Christian artist: to offer new insight into human existence. For Annie Dillard, it is significant to feel nature profoundly, for then she is close to asking the ultimate question about being, and, for her, to do this is everything.

In *Pilgrim at Tinker Creek* Annie Dillard reconciles the creative imagination and Christian faith in the Incarnation. She troubles those readers, however, who prefer to interpret her acceptance of the vital tension of existence as the triumph of oversimplification, nostalgia and phony piety. The dialogue will long continue, for Annie Dillard did not begin it. But in an age of disbelief, it is refreshing that the quarrel can even be rekindled. (p. 496)

> *Eleanor B. Wymard, "A New Existential Voice: For Annie Dillard the World Is an Epiphany," in* Commonweal *(copyright © 1975 Commonweal Publishing Co., Inc.; reprinted by permission of Commonweal Publishing Co., Inc.), October 24, 1975, pp. 495-96.*

"Holy the Firm" is a book of great richness, beauty and power and thus very difficult to do justice to in a brief review. On one level it is a 76-page journal of several No-vember days spent on Northern Puget Sound by the author of "Pilgrim at Tinker Creek." "Nothing is going to happen in this book," Annie Dillard writes. "There is only a little violence here and there in the language, at the corner where eternity clips time." She sells herself short.

A moth is immolated in the flame of a candle. A 7-year-old child named Julie Norwich is agonizingly burned in a plane crash. The author buys a bottle of communion wine and carries it home in a knapsack. "Through all my clothing, through the pack on my back and through the bottle glass, I feel the wine. It sheds lights in slats through my rib cage, and fills the buttressed vault of my ribs with light pooled and buoyant."

A great deal happens in this book . . ., and the violence is sometimes unbearable, the language rarely less than superb. . . . One thinks of Gerard Manley Hopkins, among others—nature seen so clear and hard that the eyes tear. One thinks of the conceits of Donne, as in the description of Christ's baptism, where the beads of water become planets and worlds. Even the form is poetic, and the book can be read as a kind of sestina with changes rung on words like salt, flame, holy, moth and nun, with a great reprise in the final image of the artist as one whose face is aflame like a moth's, his feet wax and salt, a being both holy and firm "in flawed imitation of Christ on the cross stretched both ways unbroken and thorned."

Part of what stretches this artist almost to the breaking point is the problem of how to reconcile a world where children must endure ordeal by fire, and all turns finally to ashes, with faith in a god of justice and love. It is Job's problem and Ivan Karamazov's: the problem, finally, of all who echo the cry "Lord I believe. Help Thou mine unbelief." "No gods have power to save," Dillard writes at her bleakest. "The one great god abandoned us to days, to time's tumult of occasions, abandoned us to the gods of days each brute and amok in his hugeness and idiocy." If God exists the question is what is His relation to the world? If He is infinitely other than the world, He is too far. If He is immanent within the world, then He is virtually the god of pantheism and too near, too small. Anne Dillard finds a possible resolution of the problem in something called Holy the Firm, which esoteric Christianity posits as a spiritual substance that is both the ultimate stuff of the world and also in touch with God. If this can be believed, she says, then "matter and spirit are of a piece but distinguishable; God has a stake guaranteed in all the world."

If the explanation seems metaphysical and remote, the reality it tries to explain rings with life in these pages—a world where God is present but invisible, unknowable, but as much part of experience as breath. "A hundred times through the fields and along the deep roads I've cried Holy," she writes. "The air is buoyant and wholly transparent, scoured by grasses. The earth struck through it is noisome, blighted, and salt." She knows only enough of God to worship Him, she says, and maybe that is all that counts.

As for the artist, "his face is flame like a seraph's, lighting the kingdom of God for the people to see.". . . If there are faults to find here, let others find them. This is a rare and precious book. (pp. 12, 40)

> *Frederick Buechner, "Island Journal," in*

The New York Times Book Review (©
*1977 by The New York Times Company;
reprinted by permission), September 25,
1977, pp. 12, 40.*

Julie Norwich was only seven when her father's single-engine airplane unaccountably stalled after takeoff, plunged into a stand of fir trees, and exploded into flames. Julie's father escaped the crash unharmed, but a rush of burning fuel enveloped the young girl's face, virtually obliterating it. . . . [*Holy the Firm*] is a contemplative view of divine intent, a wrestling with the age-old paradox of a merciful God who allows such cruelty to be visited upon his children.

Dillard's own answer seems close to a broadly shared traditionalist view that (as she describes it) "the world is im-manation, that God is in the thing, and eternally present here. . . ." In short, human suffering is neither punitive nor capricious, but a link in the order of things.

In search of a metaphor for this theory, Dillard makes use of the language of an early Christian movement, Esoteric Christianity. . . . General readers will find the theology heavy going (and so will a great many seminarians). But Dillard writes about the ferocity and beauty of natural order with enough grace to survive that objection. (pp. 106-07)

C. Michael Curtis, in The Atlantic Monthly
*(copyright © 1977 by The Atlantic Monthly
Company, Boston, Mass.; reprinted with
permission), December, 1977.*

E

EIGNER, Larry (Laurence Eigner) 1927-

Larry Eigner is an American poet, short story writer, critic, and essayist. The subject of his poetry is immediate experience, which he renders sparely, with a few deft strokes. (See also *Contemporary Authors*, Vols. 9-12, rev. ed.)

[*Another Time in Fragments*] is a major work for Eigner.... Recent thought on the making of poetry has often dealt with the physique of the poet, i.e. muscle into verse young man, the breath determining the line, the total body to be at one with the poem. Consequently, many poets have been fascinated by the apparently disjointed random notations scattered over the page in the poems of Eigner, the spastic. Some have hoped that his palsy enabled him to *see* as others have not. This notion links to the romantic aura of the madman, the privileged state of the psychedelic. A service rendered by this book is that Eigner *in toto* is neither invalid nor superior because of his confinement to a wheelchair. There sits a poet in a chair observing from the window of a house or that of a moving vehicle or those of the world. He has, as Robert Duncan says, come into the full of his poetic voice. He is truly modern in his conception of reality. What he discovers to us is indigenous to mankind. It is uncommon; it is physical. While I welcome the cogent intervals, wish for personal commerce and less selfishness in the poems, I must insist that we have an important poet in Larry Eigner. (pp. 427-28)

> *Andrew Hoyem, in* Poetry (© *1969 by The Modern Poetry Association; reprinted by permission of the Editor of* Poetry), *March, 1969.*

In [*Another Time In Fragments*] the pieces, the fragments, of Eigner's perception have become clearly the elements of an inclusive, unified world. And it is a full, complete world, even if, for most of the poems, the world extends no farther than his front porch. The front porch, the streets near the house—air, winds, trees, sounds—from the porch a world of air, birds, and the mesh of sounds around him. Living on his porch—he is a spastic, forced to spend most of his days in a wheel chair—he has learned to see and hear with a sensitive, untiring coherence. The poems have a thinned feeling of language, a stark bare syntax, and what is left, when he has burned away the undergrowth of the poem, is the object within the poem itself, the thing that had come into his hands to be placed in the poem. As Dr. Williams had it,

"No ideas, but in things." The undergrowth, in another poet's work, would be the poet's self, the identification of self, but Eigner has eliminated it for the object, which has become the poem. The spacing of his poems, as his style has matured, suggests his concentration on the things in the poem. The spaces have the feel, the shape, of the words he's cut away. Lines from almost any of the poems . . . in *Another Time In Fragments* . . . eliminate the useless words that would have involved him in the image. Anything else would have been superfluous. The poetry of China and Japan has this barrenness—and as a method of poetics has long and deep philosophic roots—but most of the younger American poets got it indirectly from the imagists, Pound, and Williams. . . . Eigner's glimpses extend as he looks from one object to the next, and the relationship between the objects often becomes complex; since he doesn't explain anything. He has burned off clarification in the same move toward intensification that burned off the statement of personal involvement in the poem. The work can be difficult—without clarification—but it is compelling. The word usage that colors the object with its sudden intensity can extend to the realization of objects in relation to each other. Since he gives you only the objects you have to follow his implication of the objects to have the whole poem. It becomes like a follow-the-dots puzzle in the Sunday paper. When he gives you enough dots the image emerges with immediate clarity. . . . Dr. Williams, in a letter to Robert Creeley, . . . spoke of Eigner's "perfect ear," then went on, "Not that his text is not at times incomprehensible. That is a minor fault that adds piquancy to the total picture." . . . Much of Eigner's most difficult work can be opened with a reference to its positioning, to its center on his porch in Swampscott, but this is only a single aspect of the poems, and their interior reference is a complex involvement in his emotional frame at the moment of composition. (pp. 107-11)

Eigner's poems, as a moment of his consciousness, have the intensity of that momentary experience. With each thought that becomes part of the texture of the poem there are dozens of associations and external comments. Some of them are close enough to the poem to be involved in it—in the most successful poems to deepen and amplify it—in others the relationship isn't as close. The things, words, objects, in the poem have only the involvement of being in his mind at the moment of writing. It would be misleading if someone tried to give a total coherence to all these passing inferences. Eigner is open to himself in so complete a way that anything is usable as poetic material. The best approach—with a poet who has so few exclusions—is to take the poem on this level of immediate use, and to let any of its more involved inferences develop casually from further readings.

With Eigner's work, to insist that there is a complex series of symbolic allusions through the poems is a confusion of Eigner's method of writing with the allusive poetry of an Eliot or a Hart Crane. His method—in much of the poetry —is of a series of inferences within the poem itself. The motif of the poem is developed through an involvement with the objects of the poem. As a technique it lies somewhere between Eliot's juxtaposition of ideas and Williams' "object in itself." Eigner uses the object—with the allusive inference that is specific with the object—in the kind of juxtaposition that Eliot used with ideas. A shorter poem—#34 —[is] a beautiful poem, complete and intensely felt. Even within its small dimension it has almost infinite suggestion and inference. His small poems often have this sense of developing expression—developing from the concentration on the object and the multicolored spread of reference as the object moves through the intensities of his imagination.

It is the web of suggestion that spins out from Eigner's close cropping of word objects that gives the poetry its immediate use, in a sense gives it feeling of poignancy at the directness of the response to the small things like winds in off the ocean, and the large things like death in the knowledge of stars. The same structured use of object extends into most of his longer poems. Their development is only partially through the pattern of a logical thought process. (pp. 113-15)

Eigner's poetry is so complete, so fully realized, that I don't think he even is concerned with the difficulty of an American, or a vernacular discourse, in the sense that Olson means it. The modern battle for a contemporary idiom has been won so completely that a poet like Eigner doesn't have to consider it. Every poem that he's published breathes in the rhythms and sounds of an American speech, and part of the sensitiveness of the poems is in their use of vernacular expression. The immediacy of an impression is most vividly communicated in an immediate poetic language, and he has always responded with the most direct speech patterns. I don't think a poet has to be "original," since a culture's responses are built into every aspect of its artistic expression, but there are poets who are so individual that their work has a strong personal identity. Eigner, I think, is one of these poets—at least he has the feeling of originality that we associate with the handful of poets whose work is extremely skilled and highly individual. No one else has so successfully combined his use of the small object within a longer, more elaborately developed poem structure. For most of the poets writing in the late 1960's the allusive detail is usually an illustration of one of the poem's concept motifs—or if it's left as itself usually the poem is short. In the intensity of his concentration Eigner is able to develop the longer poem unit, and with his sense of what Dr. Williams called his "ear" there is, at his clearest and most expressive, an underlying sense of unity, even if it's a unity made of fragments.

But Eigner's approach to the poem would be almost useless to someone else as a technique; since he writes with an emotional suddenness. The poem is conceived and written at almost the same moment. He writes many poems, and most of them have the abrupt, gesturing feel of the way they were written. The term he uses himself is "hot"—and the writing process he has described in letters is of immediate excitement in his perception. (pp. 116-17)

Eigner's view as poet is so entire and so complete that he often seems to be unaware of the difficulty. He is involved in the moments with such intensity that he has none of the heaviness of a poet who has to think in terms of the entire range of the poetic experience. Eigner can be laconic when he is most serious, and there is an appealing freshness in his lack of pretense. The object is, after all, only itself, and if it has any other meaning it is only in the poet's conception of the object. With an object you can respond or not—and Eigner leaves you open to make the choice. (p. 118)

> *Samuel Charters, "Larry Eigner," in his* Some Poems/Poets: Studies in American Underground Poetry Since 1945, *Oyez, 1971, pp. 107-18.*

When . . . free verse looks to the poet's inwardness, it may be clear and jagged or imagistically obscure. Such poetry often assumes or speaks of the impossibility, or extreme difficulty, of understanding our experience, yet attempts at least partial understanding, and may reach toward essentializing understanding.

Two poems by Larry Eigner, whose *Anything on Its Side* offers some pleasing examples of the kind, will illustrate respectively the elusiveness and the essentializing. . . .

"An object/words/air/motion/elusive/again." The poem tells of the genre, whose elusiveness is the subject and method of the poem. The relationships, since syntax is absent, are unstated (the "again" is a subtle touch), hence capable of being differently and glancingly seen.

His poetry perceives, drifts, puzzles, suggests, often nicely. It does less well when it attempts to essentialize, as in the poem "Oil at St. A Barbara": "grass-roots/sky-high/violence/earth mined." The "earth mined" suggests analogies between coal- or gold-mining, offshore oil wells, and military landmines set to explode; the rest of the poem lacks that epigrammatic force. The poem relates, with some guessing, to the oil spillage; but the reader has to do the syntax's job; meaning is what syntax is for. (p. 349)

> *Paul Ramsey, in* Sewanee Review *(reprinted by permission of the editor, © 1975 by the University of the South), Spring, 1975.*

Larry Eigner is often successful in manipulating spareness of diction and reticence of statement. His poetry proceeds by ellipsis, indirection, delicacy and precision, for as Eigner says in the introduction to his *Selected Poems,* "I'm cautious, and come on to things by understatement."

The poems focus on the natural world—trees, birds, shadows, clouds, the sea that rolls near his Swampscott, Massachusetts, home. Eigner usually eschews punctuation and capitalization and indicates rhythmic changes by line breaks and a meticulous placing and spacing out of the words on the page. The poems, many of which give me much pleasure, move rapidly; they call to mind the darting motions of birds, which Eigner often writes about. They suggest, often with sparse elegance, far more than they seem to be saying. (p. 173).

Mark Perlberg, in Poetry *(© 1975 by The Modern Poetry Association; reprinted by permission of the Editor of* Poetry*), June, 1975.*

Perhaps because he has spent his life confined to a wheelchair (in his own words, "palsied from hard birth"), Eigner has seemed to be . . . [an] enigmatic personality. . . . Yet his poetry is extremely personal in its imagery, vocabulary, and concerns:

> heirlooms
> in the space age
>   possibly white paper
>   the tree's upward branches like
>   a cone
>   broodings
>   what lines cast shadows
>   airy
>   birds fly around
>   inside of us
>   and the small tree

Eigner's attention to the independent qualities of language makes him a favorite among the poets who object to the dominance of poetry that depends on referentially oriented writing, who call for a new poetry based on the uses of language for purposes other than representation (there have been similar tendencies in the other arts). But Eigner's work is still easily accessible, though often subtle. . . . [His work is] delicate and refined, though his imagery is as concrete and precise as the best descriptive prose.

> time flies
>   birds
>   in odd corners

On rereading, it's clear that Eigner's work will last; it is truly distinct and memorable poetry. (p. 90)

Michael Lally, in The Village Voice *(reprinted by permission of* The Village Voice; *copyright © by The Village Voice, Inc., 1978), February 20, 1978.*

*   *   *

ELIOT, T(homas) S(tearns)   1888-1965

Born in the United States and later becoming a British subject, Eliot is considered by many to be the major poet and critic of our time. With *The Waste Land* came a radical, new poetry, filled with innovative rhythms and woven with foreign phrases and classical allusion. Eliot sought a union of intellect and feeling, frequently dealing with themes of time and disillusionment with the modern world. Initiating a new tradition in criticism as well as in poetry, Eliot wrote from a Christian, anti-Romantic viewpoint, and gave new importance to such writers as Dante, Donne, and the French Symbolists. He was awarded the Nobel Prize for Literature in 1948. (See also *CLC*, Vols. 1, 2, 3, 6, and *Contemporary Authors*, Vols. 5-8, rev. ed.; obituary, Vols. 25-28.)

The Waste Land . . . and the cultural attitude it fostered have fallen out of fashion. The past civilization Eliot taught my generation to mourn would hardly be missed by the majority of today's students who believe firmly in the present and themselves as the tests of relevance and meaning; sexual enigmas are studied and solved in clinics where every effort is made to keep human copulation from being in-

hibited by old mythologies of fertility and regeneration; "the awful daring of a moment's surrender" must seem a quaint line to those who have been copulating since puberty; Coriolanus is the last Shakespearean character anyone wants to revive: *Detta, Dayadhvam, Damyata* would find meaning only in becoming a Third World revolutionary slogan.

The Waste Land is a poem for those who entertain at least the possibility of spiritual action, of a world formed by sin and redemption that is beyond political sentiment and social law. It is a poem for those who would fret and speculate even in the best of times, and who confirm their prisons with each thought, preferring such confinement to the freedom that comes when life is made a matter of rational progress and harmless pleasure. Perhaps after all it is best that the Waste Landers should at no time be regnant, and that there should always be something cultic and comic about those who insist on remembering moments of excellent joy that the majority of mankind has learned long ago to forget.

I, at any rate, by the time the original manuscript of *The Waste Land* was published, had traveled a long way since those days when all one sought was a personal *lacrimae rerum* note. I was glad no one talked about, or quoted from *The Waste Land* any more, for the poem had taken on the aspects of a cultural commonplace to those who had grown up with it, and like many other themes of young adventurous conversations, *The Waste Land* was best left a matter of private memory. Then came the publication of the original manuscript and the discovery of plans, scaffolding, and rough adumbrations that promised once and for all to solve the puzzles of *The Waste Land*. For a long time I put off buying a copy out of respect for the decision I'd made never to enter the poem deeply again. But I, too, had moved with the times, and I had to admit that such a vow now seemed excessive, hysterical even, the sort of romantic reaction which as a literary professional I'd often ridiculed. (pp. 67-8)

I spent days reading and collating various versions of the manuscript. It was a compelling experience in lucidity, a lesson in practical poetics that fully compensated for any feeling of spiritual loss which that part of me still mired in the 50's might have felt. The energy of the intellects that carved, pared down, and shaped the poem infused even the blurred photographs of the original manuscript pages, and far from making one embarrassed by old enthusiasms and reverential feelings for the finished poem, these signs of argument and rough labor proved them justified. The sacrifice of hundreds of almost perfect lines Eliot made to his own and Pound's judgment confirmed his status as a poet almost as much as did the poem that remained. (p. 68)

Jack Richardson, "Looking Back at 'The Waste Land'" (reprinted from Commentary *by permission; copyright © 1975 by the American Jewish Committee), in* Commentary, *August, 1975, pp. 65-9.*

So far as fertility and sex are concerned . . . Eliot's poetry from the beginning presented its readers with failure, impotence, disgust, and even revulsion. Eliot lacked Pound's passion for life. He began for that reason closer to fin de siècle weariness and to the lassitude before and after World War I than did his compatriot. . . . By 1914 the age of the heroic achiever was over. That was, in fact, the truth that

"The Love Song of J. Alfred Prufrock" finally pinned down in a startlingly new and creative way for an entire generation.

In all probability it was a truth "Prufrock" helped clarify in a new and creative way for Eliot himself. Eliot's first wish seems to have been like Pound's—to mock his generation and its pale failures; but that is not what "Prufrock" turns out to accomplish. Eliot's own failure—and it was to be the road he took to all his successes—was that he could not break with what he scorned; his deepest nature pushed him from the start toward participating in his age's shortcomings, and clarifying rather than crusading against them. He moved steadily toward that deliberate choice, though it is impossible to say at what point he clearly made it. By 1911, when he finished "Prufrock," he had already abandoned as had no previous poet the mode of writing which creates, out of words on a page, a "point of view" from which the world can be judged; and he had done so in an effort to seek objective correlatives of word and rhythm that would allow the quite unheroic feelings he shared with his contemporaries to reveal themselves as the feelings they actually were. To the degree that he succeeded, neither he nor his readers knew toward what end his poetry was moving.

To begin with, only one thing about Prufrock himself seemed completely clear: that the words he addressed to his listeners in so slyly conspiratorial a fashion objectified the terrors of a relationship that existed—or failed to exist—between all his arts and artifacts and his sense of time:

> There will be time, there will be time
> To prepare a face to meet the faces that you meet;
> There will be time to murder and create,
> And time for all the works and days of hands
> That lift and drop a question on your plate;
> Time for you and time for me,
> And time yet for a hundred indecisions,
> And for a hundred visions and revisions,
> Before the taking of a toast and tea.

In "Prufrock" nothing actually happens. . . . Prufrock speaks to his listeners as if they had come to visit him in some circle of unchanging hell where time has stopped and all action has become theoretical. He talks compulsively, but his words bear no relation to anything actually present; nothing is real enough to be redeemed or clear enough to judge, and all he speaks of remains clouded therefore in an unreality which Eliot's compelling and hypnotic new poem forced its first readers to experience without having a precise intellectual grasp upon anything at all. Today, with Eliot's subsequent work to guide us, we see more clearly perhaps where the poem leads; but the poem's first readers came to know who Prufrock was only after the fashion he himself insisted upon: by sharing his circle of hell and his journey to nowhere with him, and in the process finding his relation to present time, in some way they could not define, to be their own.

All Eliot's subsequent poetry assumed as its basis Prufrock's desperate failure to exist; but by the completion of *The Waste Land* that existential failure had undergone an amazing metamorphosis. Although Eliot later claimed that when he wrote *The Waste Land* he was not "even bothering whether I understood what I was saying," we are nevertheless tempted to suspect that he must have interpreted central emotions in his poem in Buddhist-ascetic fashion:

that is what "The Fire Sermon" and its footnote clearly suggest. Because we are so tempted, it is important to notice how insistent *The Waste Land* is that any significant desire to escape from time's wheel comes only to those who must intensely experience time's emptiness—to Augustine, Buddha, and Tiresias, not to the typist in her apathy, nor to Elizabeth and Leicester in their gilded boat. *The Waste Land* is a purgatorial poem, as everyone grants; as such its strongest affirmation is that the agony of one's actual life (in all its painfully timid failure) be known and fully accepted: this is what the journey through the sterile land to the empty chapel signifies. And no escape at all is offered. The voice of God that speaks out of the thunder at the poem's end (the clouds are "far distant" and there is, it has been pointed out, no rain) only sends its hearers back to experience once again their failure to give, sympathize, and control, and—as the lines clearly show but never in fact say—to romanticize and so evade those failures still once more in memory and desire. The fragments at the poem's close move in a similar pattern—from Arnaut Daniel's prayer to the quite different order of yearning expressed in the "Pervigilium Veneris," and from there to Tennyson's self-pitying "O swallow, swallow," to end in just two lines with Gerard de Nerval, who is, as Hugh Kenner has said, "enclosed in a mood, in a poetic stance, surrounded by his own symbols." To miss this return to being the shallow creature one is is to miss what was becoming the central motif in all Eliot's endeavor and to see him, as in general his critics have, as moving toward an escape from time when he was in fact moving toward a greater submission to it.

What Eliot was deciding in the years after writing *The Waste Land* was that only in Christian terms and images could time's meaning be made clear. . . . In the years between *The Waste Land* and *Ash-Wednesday* Eliot came to the seemingly paradoxical conclusion that this search [to find meaning in time's movement] (and not the search to escape from this world to a better one) was essential to what had made the West a Christian civilization.

In his exploration of that belief Augustine became of necessity Eliot's primary guide, for Augustine had first called Christianity's attention to the importance of its taking time more seriously than the Greeks had, and he had done so in such a way as to set the course of all subsequent western thought. Like Eliot, Augustine greatly longed to escape from this world to eternity; but Christianity suggested to him that the meaning had become incarnate and this world therefore all-important: all the rest, he said in the *Confessions,* he could find in neoplatonism. Thinking of time as real and important, and not merely the stage on which some already written play is acted out, perhaps over and over in cyclical fashion, he realized that change had to be really change (what Eliot was to call a "new and shocking / Valuation of all we have been"). This meant that only a God out of time, for whom all time is an eternal present, can know the pattern time makes. Immersed in this temporal world at a point where its meaning is only emerging, man lives of necessity in a state of inescapable frustration, caught between his sense of meaning and his sense of meaninglessness, between being and nonbeing, between what is dying and what is not yet alive. One might almost say that Augustine saw all human history as the story of man's response to the tension that results.

This view is the one Eliot adopted, though to prove it is

beyond any question Augustine's would be impossible. . . . (pp. 449-53)

[The] view of time Eliot sought to adopt was Christian in origin and by the time he adopted it a western tradition, and R. G. Collingwood's *Idea of History* (1956) would let me make this point with comparative ease and without worrying about Augustine. It is Collingwood's conclusion that the West's very idea of history was fundamentally remade during the third and fourth centuries A.D. by what he calls (barely mentioning Augustine) "the revolutionary effect of Christian thought." First, the pattern of history came to be thought of as God's and therefore beyond the grasp of the actors themselves: history as a matter of deep currents only coming into clarity, of what seemed to man contingency and accident, of human wishes and actions which all too often revealed their true import only later and in totally unforeseen ways. This view of history's nature and complexity was to persist even after belief in God became an option at best, becoming in time the view that characterizes modern history as a secular discipline. No writer as sensitive to his traditions as Eliot was could have scrapped such a view easily. Indeed it informs *Ash-Wednesday* and the *Four Quartets*.

The second change Collingwood defines is an even more important one. He argues that westerners during the third and fourth centuries A.D. began to think of history as a temporal process that so altered individuals and nations (as God shaped them out of nothing to His will—a process beyond their understanding) that neither individuals nor nations could any longer be thought of as having subsisting natures. Time became change in a radical sense, bringing those total valuations of all we are which Eliot spoke of again and again ("You cannot face it steadily, but this thing is sure, / That time is no healer: the patient is no longer here.") This view of history also persisted after belief in God lost any vital significance for most people, and is our view today perhaps more strongly than ever. Eliot adopted both views, with God still fearfully present in both—to the degree his roots in western thought went deep enough to make him a Christian poet of any relevance to western tradition so that he had to adopt them. Given these views, little else is needed to explicate his poems, except his lifelong and perhaps heretical desire to escape from time altogether; what he got from specific philosophers, eastern or western, is peripheral. (pp. 454-55)

Augustine . . . set an example, as [Etienne] Gilson argues [in *The Christian Philosophy of St. Augustine* (1960)]: an example that has forced those who read him or who come under his influence to turn away from philosophic precision and look back at crucial points upon their own historical reality, where they are compelled themselves to try to understand the historical process in all its ungraspable tension and ambiguity. Augustine's method had then its point, being implicit in the point of view he was exploring. Since we meet the same mixture of philosophic questioning and evershifting personal psychological experience in the opening lines of "Burnt Norton" and again and again throughout *Four Quartets,* and find it used in the same ways, we must consider it an indigenous Christian way of thinking about time which Eliot learned how to renew.

When he wrote *Ash-Wednesday* Eliot probably knew little more about the Christianity he had accepted than the fact that he had accepted it, and that he would seek escape from

the tension it implied in neither attachment nor indifference in neither hope nor despair. *Ash-Wednesday* was as a result a ritual and a prayer: "Teach us to care and not to care / Teach us to sit still."

As Hugh Kenner has said, in *Ash-Wednesday* "every noun, verb and adjective pulls two ways. The heart is lost to the world and in the world. It stiffens with life and with rebellion." The prayer to the lady is full of contrarieties:

> Lady of silences
> Calm and distressed
> Torn and most whole
> Rose of memory
> Rose of forgetfulness
> Exhausted and life-giving. . . .

The speaker's wish is not to escape from this world; it is to accept that state of tension caught between time's meaning and time's lack of meaning in which he finds himself. Despite the purging renunciations demanded and sought, we return at the end of *Ash-Wednesday*—as we did at the end of *The Waste Land* and will again at the end of *Four Quartets*—to earth, time, and the sea:

> And the lost heart stiffens and rejoices
> In the lost lilac and the lost sea voices
> And the weak spirit quickens to rebel
> For the bent golden-rod and the lost sea smell
> Quickens to recover
> The cry of quail and the whirling plover
> And the blind eye creates
> The empty forms between the ivory gates
> And the smell renews the salt savour of the sandy earth.
>   (pp. 455-56)

Eliot now found himself able to work out consciously what he wished to say as he had not been able to do earlier. Prufrock had escaped from present anguish by living self-pityingly and blindly in memory and desire. *The Waste Land* had mixed memory and desire also, stirring dull roots with spring rain to bring its readers emotionally (but with little intellectual clarity) back to the purging possibilities of their earthly existence. Eliot's final poem possessed more intellectual definition than either of these earlier works because it proceeded in full awareness of a fact Augustine had discovered: that it is only through his memories and desires that man knows his life in time at all. Using that knowledge (Eliot now decided), man moves, if he chooses, through a never-ending submission toward freedom:

>   This is the use of memory:
> For liberation—not less of love but expanding
> Of love beyond desire, and so liberation
> From the future as well as the past.

Eliot critics have tended to see the *Four Quartets* as an attempt to relate a mystic's insight into a realm beyond time to his sense of the world in time. That, in part, the poem certainly is; but the modes of relation discovered by starting with this idea in mind become too easily what this way of putting the matter suggests: Platonic, a matter of getting from flux to meaning, of relating the "seemingly-at-first-real" to the "really real." . . . Eliot, disliking time as much as Plato but having become a Christian, found himself like Augustine forced to try to understand this world's importance despite his desire to escape its seeming meaninglessness. The platonic pull is no doubt present in Eliot as in

Augustine, but in both men it is—as both of them say—at war with what they see as the meaning of the Incarnation ("the hint half guessed, the gift half understood"), and so a temptation to be resisted.

In my judgment Eliot decided that time exists as an essential and unending purgation: one in which the fire of this world's agony and the rose of eternal love are finally seen as one, not coterminous but one.... The submission demanded by this view is endless, but—as we are told over and over—once accepted, the end becomes the beginning; the torture, the way:

> We must be still and still moving
> Into another intensity
> For a further union, a deeper communion
> Through the dark cold and the empty desolation,
> The wave cry, the wind cry, the vast waters
> Of the petrel and the porpoise. In my end is my
>   beginning.

The perception of reality expressed here reminds us of another that is not Christian at all: that Greek awareness of the human condition which we find in the *Iliad,* where the mortals, who know that they will die and who taste the bitterness of their insignificance, reach thereby love and significance in ways the gods, who neither die nor truly suffer, do not. Perhaps Eliot's response to life owed as much to this enduring western toughness of mind as it did to the Christian good news. I would not hasten to make that argument, however: Eliot's Christianity may or may not be orthodox; the question is often raised. For him the exploration of man's failure to be in time, which began with Prufrock in the fires of hell and continued through the fires of purgatory with Arnaut Daniel in *The Waste Land,* reached, in "Little Gidding," a vision of paradise where the fire and the rose became one: "A condition of complete simplicity / (Costing not less than everything)": he believed the view Christian:

> Who then devised the torment? Love.
> Love is the unfamiliar Name
> Behind the hands that wove
> The intolerable shirt of flame
> Which human power cannot remove.

Whether Eliot's Christianity was or was not what he thought it, he did differ radically from Pound.... Pound believed Eliot had chosen the wrong one of the "two opposing systems of European morality"; his renunciations sounded to Pound like Atys and emasculation. In *The Idea of a Christian Society* Eliot agreed that our tradition gave us only two options, but did not agree that the choice was between approving of copulation as "good for the crops" or opposing it as "bad for the crops." The alternatives, Eliot suggested, were between believing or not believing in Original Sin—between thinking with Pound that all is united in a single "process" which man can understand and embody, and realizing that man lives in a world where tension rather than unity gives significance to his life. Eliot thought the first view might properly be called "pagan" and the second "Christian." Given these terms, he agreed with Pound that we had to choose between the two alternatives Pound had sketched: "I believe that the choice before us is between the formation of a new Christian culture, and the acceptance of a pagan one." The alternatives were clear: "It must be kept in mind that even in a Christian society as

well organized as we can conceive possible in this world, the limit would be that our temporal and spiritual life should be harmonized: the temporal and spiritual would never be identified.... There would always be a tension; and this tension is essential to the idea of a Christian society, and is a distinguishing mark between a Christian and a pagan society." To desire a pagan society was, Eliot decided—and here he used one of Pound's favorite words—to yearn for a "totalitarianism" in which man would abandon the very agonies that made him fully human: "Totalitarianism appeals to the desire to return to the womb. The contrast between religion and culture imposes a strain: we escape from this strain by attempting to revert to an identity of religion and culture which prevailed at a more primitive stage; as when we indulge in alcohol as an anodyne, we consciously seek unconsciousness. It is only by unremitting effort that we can persist in being individuals in a society, instead of merely members of a disciplined crowd." ... (pp. 457-60)

By the end of the 1930s Pound and Eliot knew that their disagreements were marked and significant. Despite them they shared much, even more perhaps than they realized. Although Eliot sought to affirm a Christianity which Pound rejected, both men were products of a civilization which had for centuries both shaped and been shaped by Christian teaching and Bible reading; and neither could escape the results: whatever they choose to do about it, they shared a sense of time woven into the very fabric of the Old and New Testaments. (p. 461)

Time changed Eliot and Pound more than superficially. Eliot wrote a passage in "Little Gidding" which makes something of what they shared sharply evident:

> Let me disclose the gifts reserved for age
>   To set a crown upon your lifetime's effort.
>   First, the cold friction of expiring sense
> Without enchantment, offering no promise
>   But bitter tastelessness of shadow fruit
>   As body and soul begin to fall asunder.
> Second, the conscious impotence of rage
>   At human folly, and the laceration
>   Of laughter at what ceases to amuse.
> And last, the rending pain of re-enactment
>   Of all that you have done, and been; the shame
>   Of motives late revealed, and the awareness
> Of things ill done and done to others' harm
>   Which once you took for exercise of virtue.
>   Then fools' approval stings, and honour stains.

Eliot saw such final agonies as the last steps in a necessary purgation leading toward beatitude, a view Pound could never adopt. Yet Eliot might as accurately have been foreseeing Pound's final decade as his own; his friend's last years were characterized above all else by the rending pain of reenactment of all he had done and been, and by the shame of motives late revealed and the awareness of things ill done and done to others' harm which he had once taken for exercise of virtue. (p. 462)

To some readers today Eliot's late poetry seems the work of an aged avuncular, the "Grand Old Man" of modern Christian poetry, withdrawn from action with a too clear grasp on everything, talking. Some people see Pound's late *Cantos* as better poetry, believing that their final fragmented and tortured drifting off into nothingness presents rather than discusses from a safe and falsifying distance man's agonies in time. Pound's late poetry and Eliot's certainly differ, but not in so simplistic a fashion. Again what the two men shared is more fundamental than what separated them. Pound all his life intended the *Cantos* to move toward philosophic statement, as he thought the *Commedia* had. At the end his mind failed and he turned back; he spoke afterward of Eliot as "the true Dantescan voice." He may only have meant that his own agon was of a different order; he may very well not have understood his own accomplishment; but his praise for Eliot's late poetry is clear. He made no reservations and was as determined as he had been in 1914: "I can only repeat, but with the urgency of 50 years ago: Read Him."

Pound's plea suggests that we may (perhaps in reaction to the long Eliotic years) be reading Eliot today as shallowly as we read him in 1922. We might begin to reconsider his significance for us by remembering that it was Eliot and not Pound who began his career as a poet as well as ended it in attempting to find verbal equivalents to express what a submission to time's laws would mean in our age. (p. 463)

> *Vincent Miller, "Eliot's Submission to Time," in* Sewanee Review *(reprinted by permission of the editor,* © *1976 by The University of the South), Summer, 1976, pp. 448-64.*

The sense of the aridity of relationships in *The Waste Land,* say, or *The Cocktail Party,* has often been pointed out; and there is the feeling that in his later work Eliot simply retreats from the complexity of human love into a somewhat attenuated and disembodied idea of religious love. . . . The implication seems to be that Eliot, in moving towards a religious sense of life, is lacking in humanity and real vitality. But the case is surely more complex than this. The argument of this essay is that Eliot developed a poetic technique which could explore beneath the surface of his earlier experience and allow its seeds of creative life to grow in a new context. It was a means not of turning his back on the human perplexity of the earlier experience, but of redeeming its creative elements and seeing beneath the aridities of the surface. Eliot's poetic technique is primarily one for creating new patterns out of his experience: certain images or motifs frequently recur in his poetry in changing forms, images which are intensely personal though not necessarily autobiographical. And the way the images recur in different contexts is a way of searching more deeply into their reality and their relationships with life as a whole. In relation to love, it explores new possible dimensions for the word, and in the precise meaning of Johnson's words 'calls new powers into being'; and it does this by never losing touch with what was vital in earlier experience. . . . [By] means of a changing technique Eliot is attempting precisely to give that elusive word [love] a personal meaning, to create it as a reality, a new power.

This change in technique might be characterised as a shift from a predominantly 'imagistic' mode to a predominantly 'symbolic' one. That is, in his earlier poetry Eliot's style is particularly vivid and visual, and also employs structures of narrative or seeming narrative. It uses sharply defined *personae* and actual dramatic situations. It is particularly, as Helen Gardner has suggested, a poetry of the surface. And an important part of the style is the preoccupation with 'gesture' and 'pose' in every sense, the pervasive human

habit of striking, or taking up, attitudes. The later poetry, from *Ash-Wednesday* onwards is more meditative, discursive, and aural rather than visual; it also abandons vivid dramatic 'events' and refers more obliquely to actual, narrative situations. The images of the earlier poetry, like that of the weeping girl, are more briefly and sparingly employed, though they are still important. They take their place as part of a larger structure, in which they are detached for the surroundings of actuality, become more allusive (alluding back to the earlier poetry) and grow in symbolic power. Donald Davie, in an essay on Eliot's 'Symbolism', has written: 'At the bottom of symbolist method, it has been said, is the discovery that words may have meanings though they have no referents. And most of the misreadings of Eliot derive from a failure . . . to recognize this fact about the way language works'. In his later poetry, one might say, Eliot is using words less referentially and more symbolically: the earlier poems seem much more to 'refer' the reader to specific events and situations; in the later poetry the settings are often in the realm of fantasy (as in *Ash-Wednesday* or 'Marina'), or where they are actual, indeed biographical, as in the place names of the *Four Quartets,* these are merely felt to be the starting points for certain meditations. The world of Prufrock and the man in 'Portrait of a lady' are not, certainly to be thought of as biographical: nevertheless they are, as it were, imaginary biographies, scenes from the lives of the *personae.* This technique leads to a very direct confrontation with the problems of the poetic characters. The resulting poetry is often particularly intense, 'as if a magic lantern threw the nerves in patterns on a screen' as Prufrock says, which suggests also the way it sometimes seems to play on *our* nerves rather than our deeper feelings, and the way it is very much concerned with the state of the characters' nerves. The later poetry goes below the vivid and dramatic surface to explore deeper recesses of feeling.

The developing technique is a part of Eliot's changing sense of his own experience, and here one touches on a familiar area of complexity in discussions of Eliot's work. To some it might seem a truism to say that Eliot's poetic effort is to express his experience. To others it might seem positively wrong: Eliot (so the argument would run) is trying to express much more than his own personal experience; and Eliot's remarks against mere 'self-expression' or the expression of 'personality' might be invoked. One could mediate between the two by saying that Eliot is trying to express (and first of all to *discover*) his most significant experience, something which goes below the level of 'self' or 'personality' and may lead him to take completely non-autobiographical forms of expression. But there is a danger here for the poet: in seeking to go 'below' or 'outside' his own personal history he may leave his own authentic experience behind completely. The idea leads in fact to the famous (by now perhaps notorious) statement in 'Tradition and the individual talent' that the poet is simply the neutral medium for disembodied 'poetic' experiences; and to the statement 'The more perfect the artist, the more completely separate in him will be the man who suffers and the mind which creates'. The statement completely belies Eliot's poetic effort, which was to bring the two, the 'man' and the 'mind', into a proper relationship. But that Eliot should make it is explained by the fact that his artistic development is conditioned by the search for a technique which would enable him to stand in the right relation to his subject, neither too close to it nor too far from it. To stand too close involves being too absorbed in a chaos of surface details; to stand too far away involves taking refuge in lifeless abstractions.

For Eliot to make sense in his poetry of the subject of love he had to find a technique which would neither simply dramatise the painful realities of the surface nor retreat into an attenuated idealisation. It had to deal with the elements of his own experience but in a way which brought out the deeper significance of that experience. He moves from a treatment of the subject which is at first romantic and ironic at once, to a treatment which avoids the collision between romanticism and irony (as in 'Prufrock') and in which love is conceived of more selflessly but still personally.... Eliot's concerns are of course more specifically religious in his later poetry, but he ... can be seen as looking for unconventional ways of giving the idea of love a meaning. Human relationships are not strictly a primary concern, but even in a religious poem like *Ash-Wednesday* the experience of relationships are used in an oblique way to create the idea of a relationship with the divine. And in 'Marina' a monologue addressed to 'my daughter' is the medium for expressing a finely achieved sense of relationship with life and creativity in general.

The development of Eliot's technique allows him to use an 'imagery' of personal relationships at certain points as a way of discovering certain religious feelings. The relationships are not focused on so exclusively as in 'Portrait of a lady' or *The Waste Land* but treated in a way which allows their inherent creativeness to emerge, not to be submerged in the surface painfulness of failure. The 'human' does not disappear, to be replaced by the 'divine', but rather the 'divine' as Eliot conceives it draws on possibilities latent in the 'human'. The approach to the wider significance of human life, the 'meaning', allows the human experience to return.... In terms of technique, this ... involves using the imagery of personal relationships in a more oblique way, with less emphasis on their dramatic and often visual actuality. Instead of, as it were, catching or trying to get into sharper focus the details of an experience, 'a gesture and a pose' (which however clear visually or in tone are ultimately baffling), the mind gives itself to a movement in which there are no longer any poses, and in which gestures become indefinite in themselves but significant as part of a whole experience; and in the process lose all elements of artificiality. The precisely seen gestures of the woman in 'Prufrock',... gestures which are so distinct yet so contrived (hiding the woman's feelings behind a frosty politeness)—this kind of precise visualisation gives way to the indefiniteness of, say, the 'familiar compound ghost' of 'Little Gidding', whose presence and words are so significant, but whose identity is indistinct, and whose gestures are vague.... It is the sharp definition [of J. Alfred Prufrock] that I want to emphasise: for Eliot is able to be so sharp and clear just because he is not in the end Prufrock.... One might say that Prufrock is created so that Eliot can express certain feelings or ideas without implicating himself in them too completely.

The poem is the striking of an attitude.... But both the poet and Prufrock are aware that they are striking attitudes, so that we can never criticise them more than they criticise themselves, except of course by point to the limitations of the whole performance.

The equation I want to make is between the 'image' and the 'pose'. Prufrock's images express his attitudes or states of mind, and share their artificiality.... Prufrock explicitly tries out rôles, and then abandons them.... In a similar way, the poet tries out images. (pp. 5-10)

['Portrait of a lady'] is a more searching exploration of the problem of attitude than 'Prufrock', which is content merely to play with attitudes, and through them to half-reveal, half-conceal a human dilemma. It employs far less 'imagery'—disparate and oddly juxtaposed poetic configurations—than 'Prufrock': it deliberately avoids their obliqueness and independent attractiveness. With its greater drama and actuality, the 'Portrait' takes upon itself the task of challenging the poet to define his own attitude. (p. 11)

One might reply [to the critical view that Eliot's poetry is flawed by its absence of love] that Eliot is concerned with little other than 'love'; and that his preoccupation with the subject of relations between the sexes is central to his whole poetic development. The subject is perhaps the leading clue to the unity of *The Waste Land,* a unity which does not have to be substantiated by going outside the poem. Both 'Prufrock' and 'Portrait of a lady' are about the failures of love, which need not be the same as its absence. (pp. 11-12)

Eliot's treatment of love and his poetic use of the 'image' are linked in this way: Eliot's tendency is to stand back from experience in order to be able to deal with it in his poetry. His whole poetic development could be charted in terms of his 'nearness to' or 'distance from' his subject.... An ideal way of standing back or apart from experience is to let it formulate itself in an image, or configuration, which need not be taken from personal history.... In *The Waste Land,* generally, Eliot is ... able wonderfully to objectify and generalise his experience. But these 'fragments' of experience only really leave us with 'a heap of broken images'. The poem offers no solution and no way forward. The technique keeps Eliot (and us) at a distance, however fully we are implicated, in the sense that it simply shows us ourselves and suggests no way of changing. (p. 12)

['La figlia che piange'] dramatises the perplexities of art and memory, the conflict between the artistic desire for form and finality, and the continuing inescapable agency of the memory. In its conflict between formal, idealised yet 'posed' beauty, and the unanswered questions of reality it could be compared with Keats's 'Ode on a Grecian urn' ('O attic shape! Fair attitude!'). It also dramatises the relation between mind and experience (or between 'soul' and 'body'), in a way that offers a radical criticism of Eliot's separation in 'Tradition and the individual talent' of 'the man who suffers' from 'the mind which creates'. Here, in the first stanza, the mind is indeed 'deserting the body', or the experience as a whole, in order to create a simplified and idealised moment of beauty, 'incomparably light and deft', with the resulting faithlessness and preciosity.

This is why the poem seems so central to the questions both of 'love' and 'imagism' in Eliot's poetry. This is a love poem, but I do not think we can say with F. R. Leavis that it is simply 'love in the lyrical sense, with no irony in tone or context'. There is irony in tone and context, but it is not of a destructive kind: rather it questions the power of Eliot himself to achieve a complete view of the experience by trying to catch it in a single image, a single 'gesture' or 'pose'. For the undertaking tends to disembody, idealise and diminish: it removes the poet too far from the experience, and it fails really to give an account of it. (p. 14)

The failure of love is nowhere in Eliot (and might I add, . . . in few other places in modern literature?) so intensely and so personally expressed [as at the end of the second section of 'The Burial of the Dead']. It is almost as if the intensity is too much for the poem to 'bear': the passage closes by falling back into the pathos and melancholy of the Wagnerian lyric, turning the feeling into a more general one and moving it to a distance. It is the great achievement of *The Waste Land* that by its fragmentary and allusive technique it allows poetic moments to take place which would have been impossible to reveal in a more direct approach. The memory rises up here slightly changed, not in any way posed and with no gestures struck, but in the simplest and most natural way. (There are other moments of warm human feeling which seem to me some of the incomparable things of *The Waste Land,* though they are noticed less often than the typist or the girl at Richmond: I am thinking of the passage where Eliot escapes, poetically speaking, from the typist's flat into 'O City, City . . .'; or the response to the question 'What have we given?':

> My friend, blood shaking my heart,
> The awful daring of a moment's surrender
> Which an age of prudence can never retract
> By this, and this only, we have existed

They are poignant *because* they are fragments: because of the sincerity of the poem which will not allow them to be forced into a remedy, which can only close with 'These fragments I have shored against my ruins'.) (pp. 15-16)

The gestures of the earlier poems, those precise but often enigmatic glimpses of actuality, are [in *The Hollow Men*] paralysed and dead. There are no even quasi-biographical or quasi-narrative images in the poem, only disembodied ones. . . . The elements of the earlier poem (the eyes, the sunlight, the garden urn,) are condensed, changed, and broken up, and the mind retreats to indirectness by translating the painful into the beautiful ('the eyes are / Sunlight on a broken column'). The rhythms, the open vowels at the ends of lines, are drawn out, attenuating the experience; the voice drifts off into vagueness. But in the distancing and spiritualising the substance of experience is almost lost. The symbolism of the poem shows a failure (the failure is part of the poem's subject) really to contain the experience. (pp. 16-17)

The actualities of event and incident in the earlier poems are [in *Ash-Wednesday*] renounced for a different kind of poetry, which meditates upon experience in a forward looking syntax, to see if it can construct a life in which it can live, in which life can happen again; as opposed to a poetry which assembles images, trying to make them strong by clarifying them and taking a 'right' attitude to them, in the attempt to shore up an existing building. It is therefore a less dramatic and in a sense less vivid kind of poetry. The vivid moments of *Ash-Wednesday* are presented as fading. (p. 18)

Marriage seems to take its place for Eliot as part of the cycle of the seasons and the years, a rather relentless process of time passing and repeating itself. Eliot can not finally, as Lawrence could, see marriage and procreation as a mystery, but sees it rather as a process essentially of this world and part of the cycle of time which at its most intense moments *Four Quartets* seeks to transcend. Nevertheless, love finds other objects and meanings in the poem. Love of country is one of the strong sentiments behind 'Little Gidding', though it is a love that leads beyond itself. And we are here also made to think again of the preoccupations with liberation from desire and from what is 'actual only for one time / And only for one place', and from the 'faces and places' of *Ash-Wednesday* and previous poems. . . . [In 'Little Gidding' we have]:

> See, now they vanish,
> The faces and the places, with the self which, as it could,
>   loved them,
> To become renewed, transfigured, in another pattern.

What gives the passage its poignancy is the way in which the imperative breaks in on the calm deliberation [of the previous lines about memory and history]. [The] poignant regret at the loss, the keenly felt sense of transience, is somehow caught within the verse and made to serve as a part of the new pattern which Eliot is constructing. In something like the same way, an intense feeling for the 'familiar compound ghost' is generated in the previous passage, even while the 'ghost' is giving the most powerful and pessimistic piece of wisdom in the poem, and as the compound of all Eliot's 'dead masters' bidding farewell to his pupil. The 'ghost' is, in a piece of human wisdom, bidding the poet to pass beyond merely human wisdom; and bidding him to forget the ghost's teaching, and to 'forgive' it; and indeed to pass beyond the ghost himself. The feeling of the poet for the speaker is so mysterious and moving that I do not see why one should withhold from it the word 'love'. It is these experiences which would seem to lie behind the explicit use of the word in section IV of 'Little Gidding':

> Who then devised the torment? Love.
> Love is the unfamiliar Name
> Behind the hands that wove
> The intolerable shirt of flame
> Which human power cannot remove.
>   We only live, only suspire
>   Consumed by either fire or fire.

The lyric in the fourth section of each of the *Four Quartets* is explicitly religious, indeed Christian, and takes this more abstract general form, so that this passage conforms to a predetermined structure. Whether the use of the word 'Love' here, almost a Christian personification, is entirely convincing, depends perhaps finally on the reader's theology, and takes one almost beyond the bounds of poetic criticism. One might feel that the transition is a large one in terms of the predominant language of the poem. Nevertheless it seems indisputable that Eliot has extended our feelings about the use of the word in some of the other parts of the poem. And he does this by never entirely losing the sense of continuity with earlier poems and earlier experience, and other uses of the word. The full examination of this would need a full examination of *Four Quartets* as a whole, but perhaps these remarks will suffice to suggest the wider applications of the word 'love' and the wider examples of the quality of spirit it seeks to define undertaken in the four poems. It also suggest a rare liberation Eliot had achieved from the distracting elements of earlier experience and the way in which nevertheless he had retained a vital thread of feeling connecting with that experience. The last part of this essay goes back one stage in Eliot's poetic career, to examine the particularly fine and beautiful poem 'Marina', in which Eliot seems to be at a rare turning point in his art, the point which seems to enact a moment of transfiguration of earlier experience, a kind of pattern of renunciation which draws into itself faint echoes of the earlier poems in a quite new context, and leaves the poet's feelings free to explore the world of *Four Quartets*.

Eliot's concern with the failure of love in the earlier poems was expressed in terms of vivid glimpses of drama, of gestures and poses which he sought to define and fathom. The poems were fragmentary, but the clarity of outline of those fragments was often intense.... [Their] images are primarily disturbing in their vividness, and the technique which embodies them is somehow confined by its own nature to the disturbing surface. In 'Marina' on the other hand, the images are largely indeterminate, and the precision of feeling is achieved in a different way.... And it is notable that ... the negative and destructive elements of experience are presented not in terms of vivid particularities, but powerful generalisations, which control and hold at a distance the details of the earlier poems. These elements

> Are become insubstantial, reduced by a wind,
> A breath of pine, and the woodsong fog
> By this grace dissolved in place.

—'reduced', it might be noticed, by experiences of the senses, but by those of touch and smell, not by those of sight. And 'dissolved in place' suggests a dispersing of actual scenes of memory, a continuation of the meditation in *Ash-Wednesday* that 'what is actual is actual only for one time / And only for one place'. After the dispersing of the destructive elements of the memory, visual images can return, but in a new way. The faces of the earlier poems, the face of 'fugitive resentment', the 'eyes I dare not see in dreams', the 'blessèd face' renounced in *Ash-Wednesday* have disappeared only to return with a new indistinctness:

> What is this face, less clear and clearer
> The pulse in the arm, less strong and stronger—
> Given or lent? more distant than stars and nearer
>   than the eye.

Visually the face is less clear, but is recognizable on a more profound level. Similarly, the pulse in the arm is felt rhythmically as a gentle undercurrent of physical life in the poet or another, quietly there, but less physically importunate than, say, the 'dull tom-tom' inside the speaker's head in 'Portrait of a lady' or the pulsing insistence of feeling in [the last stanza of "La Figlia Che Piange]:

> Compelled my imagination many days,
> Many days and many hours:
> Her hair over her arms and her
>   arms full of flowers. . . .

And 'the stars' and 'the eye' take up and change images of the earlier poems which embodied the fear of close confrontation ('eyes I dare not meet') and the desire for distance and idealisation ('more distant and more solemn than a fading star'). Here the face and pulse in the arm are closely, intimately felt, but without losing their ideal and mysterious spirituality.

The meaning of these lines depends for its full effect on the rest of the poem. It is as if the images of love from the other poems were understood better by not looking at them too closely, by not scrutinizing them but by letting them

return in their own oblique way. And Eliot does this by concentrating not on the images themselves but on his art. The section about the boat can be seen as a metaphor for the artist's concern with his art: his desire for exactness and specificity is satisfied not by the visual clarity of the images he has been evoking, but by the clarity of this symbol of his 'craft'.... The passage gives a new feeling about the relation of poet, art, and subject. One might see it as a precise symbol for the process he spoke of in *Ash-Wednesday*, 'having to construct something / Upon which to rejoice'.... There is a suggestive play between the concreteness of the boat and the indeterminate area of experience the poet is trying to make his own, between the exactness of the art and the mysterious nature of the experience. (pp. 19-23)

What Eliot has achieved is an art that can be exact without claiming to make the experience it is dealing with exactly understood, in the sense of fixed, summed up, dealt with. It gives up a precise definition of 'gesture' and 'pose' for a seeing beneath the surface. It is a way of manipulating words without manipulating the experience they are trying to convey; a finely developed technique for allowing what was creative in experience to emerge as creative in art. The 'face' of the earlier poems returns in a way that leaves behind its limited actuality 'for one time and one place': it is unidentifiable, general, but still intimate and personal, '*this* face', but not concentrated on in its visual form, and got into proportion by its position between 'this form' and 'this life':

> This form, this face, this life
> Living to live in a world of time beyond me; let me
> Resign my life for this life, my speech for that unspoken,
> The awakened, lips parted, the hope, the new ships.

That final gesture, 'lips parted', quietly takes its place among the more general symbols, not importuning the poet's imagination like the earlier gestures, not theatrical or expressive of one dramatic moment, but rather unwilled and symbolic. It pertains primarily to the life for which the poet is resigning his life, but also, in the total feeling of the close, it seems to express the new feeling of the poet: the hope seems to stir in the speaker himself. In the earlier poetry the preoccupation with vividly recorded gestures was reflected in a technique which involved the striking of poetic attitudes. Here, the facial expression which the poet records and the poetic expression in which he records it are again linked: in seeing life in a new way, the poet shares the life that he sees. And what he sees, what he shares, and what he expresses are the same: not so much a gesture as a reflex, the unwilled reaction to a new sense of wonder.

By concentrating on the construction of his art, rather than on specific images of memory, Eliot brings into being a completely new feeling, and a new object for his feelings. The poem echoes his earlier material, but completely transforms that material. What comes into being is a new birth of the imagination, the 'daughter' to whom the words are addressed. The daughter might be said to represent the new life for which Eliot is 'resigning' his life, and in this sense is 'symbolic'. But 'symbol' is too impersonal a word for the intimate sense of personal relationship achieved in the poem. Eliot has created not just a symbol but a new being, a poetic 'daughter'; and the feeling of love for this 'daughter' is what the poem is about. An object for love has been found not by scrutinising the experiences of the past but by letting them play their part in the construction of the imagination, 'renewed, transfigured, in another pattern'. One has to concede, of course, that Eliot has managed to create this new sense of love by transforming his earlier experience so completely that sexual love is no longer part of his concern here, except as a part of what is 'dissolved'. And yet one has to say too that the feeling in this poem is anything but ascetic, that it is not 'anti-physical'. The 'face' and the 'pulse in the arm' ensure that the feeling is warmly human and intimate. And the feeling for 'my daughter' presupposes, after all, a kind of reconciliation with the human sexuality that brought her into being. Eliot's achievement here seems to be that he develops a highly personal sense of love out of what was initially very unpromising material. A direct treatment of relations between the sexes is not within his scope, except in the early poems of failure. But it is his great achievement that he salvages a distinctly human sense of love from the 'ruins' of the earlier poetry, a sense that does not lose its humanity while moving towards a religious realisation. (pp. 24-5)

> *Martin Scofield,"'A Gesture and a Pose':
> T. S. Eliot's Images of Love,"* in Critical
> Quarterly (© *Manchester University Press*),
> *Autumn, 1976, pp. 5-25.*

Of the themes that occur in both Eliot's poetry and critical prose and in the informal, gossipy "London Letters" [published in *Dial* during 1921 and 1922], a major one is the emphasis on the continuous parallel between contemporary life and antiquity—what Herbert Howarth calls "the continuity of the human predicament." This theme occurs in a large percentage of the essays in *The Sacred Wood,* it is a major unifying device in *The Waste Land,* and it is in fact essential to all Eliot's later poetry. Relating to this continuity—and to its implication of the vital importance of the past to the present and future—is the necessity of the artist's creation of new forms; he must "explore" new worlds in a continuing attempt to establish order and to impose structure. Thus Eliot took the "green and pleasant England" his contemporaries in England were writing of and transformed it into "the dead land," and "this stony rubbish."

Eliot's interest in poetic drama is apparent throughout the "London Letters" and is closely related to his interest in both the "low" art of the music-hall performers and the "high" art of the ballet. The honesty and directness of both the Elizabethan and Restoration drama and the humor of the music-hall comedians were a delight to Eliot; and he considered the music-hall comedian as perhaps the ideal type for performing verse drama. The importance of the audience's participation in any art is emphasized; Eliot deplores the growing apathy and disinterest of the people. He had, of course, already engaged in the formulation of his ideas on poetic drama before the "London Letters" were written. But he expands and redefines many of his ideas in the letters, for this was an ongoing development. The ultimate results of Eliot's interest in poetic drama culminated, at last, in his later plays. His earliest attempt (of record) at putting his ideas into practice was *Sweeney Agonistes* (1932), which shows strongly the influence of the farcical music-hall style. Much of Eliot's theory of verse drama was carried out in *The Rock* (1934), though it was an unsuccessful attempt primarily because of the various limitations, arranged by the producers. (pp. 381-82)

While the "London Letters" cover a brief period in the long career of T. S. Eliot, they are significant because of their comparative "wholeness" and because of their evident importance to Eliot's development during a crucial time in his life. They are representative of the major preoccupations—themes, images, revelations of hints that inspired and directed him as poet and critic—of his poetry and prose during 1920-22. Further, one discerns in these eight documents a great variety in style and in tone; they allow a freedom and a charm foreign to the major criticism. Here, by turns, Eliot is witty, satirical, lyric, prosaic, sad, delighted, and delightful. He frequently demands excellence and is dismissive when he fails to find it; but he is never snobbish or lacking in sympathy for the ordinary working man and woman, quite the contrary. And all this from a writer who is forever being accused of snobbishness and puritanism! (p. 382)

> *Nicholas Joost and Ann Risdon, "Sketches
> and Preludes: T. S. Eliot's 'London Letters'
> in the 'Dial',"* in Papers on Language and
> Literature *(copyright © 1976 by the Board
> of Trustees, Southern Illinois University at
> Edwardsville), Fall, 1976, pp. 366-83.*

*   *   *

ELKIN, Stanley   1930-

Elkin, an American editor, short story writer, critic, and novelist, writes black comedies distinguished by his masterful use of language. (See also *CLC*, Vols. 4, 6, and *Contemporary Authors*, Vols. 9-12, rev. ed.)

Stanley Elkin is our eminent vulgarian, a sensitive receiver at large in access-road America. Having eaten with the Colonel and seen "blockbusters" at Cinemas I through IV, having talked with the nation's innkeepers, Elkin invents *The Franchiser,* a marvelously voiced novel about "the man who made America look like America, who made America famous."

Few writers locate their fiction in popular culture as insistently and perceptively as Elkin does. Pynchon uses popular culture to extend the range of his paranoid systems. Barthelme and others make foolery of our stylized environment. Elkin's bit is finer and goes deeper. He drills desire, how popular culture creates and satisfies need, and he finds flecks of beauty in the roughage.

His first novel, *Boswell,* had celebrity as its subject. *A Bad Man* put the old-movie businessman in an old-movie prison. *The Dick Gibson Show* mixed fairytale with the heyday of American radio. Obsessed with singularity, the heroes of these novels rebel against the ordinary and conventional even while they are motivated by the big ideas of popular culture.

Now, in *The Franchiser,* Elkin makes a man who wants "to costume his country" with "all its ubiquitous, familiar neon signatures and logos," the franchised signs that he, Ben Flesh, is at home wherever he drops out of the interstate grid. Surely this standardization has its economic purpose, is esthetically disastrous, and may be megalomaniacal, but Elkin and Flesh register the pleasant twitch of familiarity—"There's the McDonald's"—that precedes our reasoned objections, the goofy comfort of Radio Shack and Dairy Queen, the vulgar services that link us in America. . . .

The book consists of linked stories from Flesh's past and present. They are not a plot but a Rand-McNally view of man in motion, an atlas of comic and moving encounters. . . . [Elkin's] minor characters are best as chambers for Flesh's voice, intensifiers of his self-awareness, and as figures in the geometry of franchise he has created. Even the Insight Lady, amateur interpreter of everything and one of Flesh's women, is most interesting as yet another dummy for Elkin's voice.

This voice—wheeling, dealing, spieling, yet feeling, too—is, quite simply, the novel, its main attraction and source of all its other achievements. Sentence for sentence, nobody in America writes better than Stanley Elkin. For him, the novel is primarily a place for language, energized and figurative language, to happen. In *The Franchiser,* language possesses the world like a loan shark. The smudged surfaces of America come clean, the shoptalk of business clears, the texture of life in a popular culture beads up.

Elkin's prose is not photography but metaphorical semiotics. When he writes ''popcorn in cylinders large as Quaker Oats boxes, with dollops of drawn butter and high drifts of buff popcorn in the greased glass like a spell of cockeyed weather,'' we re-see the physical and understand through metaphor our small pleasures at the popcorn machine. This kind of signification is stroked throughout the novel to give it an extraordinary density and grain.

Elkin's oral models—sales pitch, speech, reminiscence—give it energy. Even analysis has colloquial vigor and voice's momentum. . . .

Some of this . . . points to the novel's weaknesses. Elkin's collecting deprives him of a large cumulative effect, and his attention to the ''slag of the ordinary'' sometimes seems a waste of perception. But these flaws are on the side of plenitude, the wondrous fullness Elkin shows us (and invents). . . . (p. 27)

> *Thomas Le Clair, in* The New Republic *(reprinted by permission of* The New Republic; © *1976 by The New Republic, Inc.), June 12, 1976.*

The subject of Stanley Elkin's ambitious new novel [''The Franchiser''] is nothing less than the homogenized, manmade surface of America—that coast-to-coast plastic covering of shopping malls and interstate highways, of motels and service stations, of Baskin-Robbins, Burger King and Mister Softee. . . .

The story—such as it is—combines the familiar Elkin ingredients of broad farce, visionary surrealism, sick humor, ethnic humor and a kind of grotesque pathos in the tradition of ''Miss Lonelyhearts.'' (p. 5)

The appetite of readers for Elkin's brand of humor will vary. I laughed (sometimes guiltily) at a lot of it; some of the one-liners are especially funny (''The dishwasher has returned his steak saying it is too medium''). But I had to fight boredom and exasperation with the self-conscious straining apparent in some episodes. . . . A gifted mimic, Elkin can ''do'' hillbilly, Southern, black, Middle-American and the weird electronic jargon of a salesman of audiovisual appliances. But the prevailing dialect of ''The Franchiser'' is . . . freewheeling and exuberant Jewish-American—a tribal dialect in which Eklin can achieve effects worthy of S. J. Perelman and Wallace Markfield. . . .

Elkin is often drunk with words. At its best, ''The Franchiser'' achieves a sensuous poetry evocative not of flesh and sexuality but of the texture of carpeting in movie theaters, of the dazzling orange and turquoise sheen of a Howard Johnson's, of the polished walnut of the caskets in an undertaker's display room. (p. 22)

Unfortunately, abundance too often slides into plethora. Ben—with his magnanimity, his yearnings, his afflictions—is obviously designed as a large-scale character, an epic hero of pop culture, but he is also verbally incontinent. His speeches—some of them splendid set-pieces . . .—too often degenerate into endless tirades that make the reader want to clap his hands to his ears. There has been an element of force feeding in much of Elkin's fiction from ''Boswell'' on. Comic or bizarre situations are protracted self-indulgently until they lose their impact. One learns more than one wants to know about the operation of local radio stations (''The Dick Gibson Show'') or what it is like to inherit a condominium apartment or to copulate with a female bear in heat (''Searches and Seizures'').

This uncomfortable excess is partly attributable, I think, to another weakness in Elkin's fiction. While he can invent wonderful scenes full of madness and power, Elkin seems unable to create a sustaining comic action or plot that could energize the book as a whole and carry the reader past those sections where invention flags or becomes strained. Without the onward momentum of plot—no matter how zany—we are left with bits, pieces and even large chunks that tend to cancel each other out and turn the book into a kind of morass. An insistence upon plot in comic writing (apart from gags or nightclub routines) is no doubt old-fashioned, but it is worth noting that even a Marx Brothers movie has an ongoing action whose complications provide the set-up for any amount of horseplay. The need is especially felt in a book as long as ''The Franchiser,'' where the potentials of situation, character, and theme—very rich potentials—are never fully mobilized into a truly memorable novel. For all of its frenzied motion, ''The Franchiser'' is oddly static. (p. 24)

> *Robert Towers, in* The New York Times Book Review (© *1976 by The New York Times Company; reprinted by permission), June 13, 1976.*

Stanley Elkin is one of a small group of writers, the announcement of whose new works can fill a reader with pangs of anticipation and alarm. . . . [He] resurfaces in each book, a John Gunther of cultural changes, with the latest word on our national dizziness.

Elkin's style is manifest from the first paragraph [of *The Franchiser*]. Not overtly experimental, his syntax is nevertheless crowded with cunning shifts of meaning and extravagant deployments of wit. The purpose of such stylistic pyrotechnics is clear, sometimes even academic. . . . The novel's bravado is to set itself against cultural illiteracy of the untellable in all its forms; when the untellable is the truly monstrous disease of multiple sclerosis, Elkin's verbal triumph is very moving. It may not be an insight into our public mess, but when Ben Flesh observes that his multiple sclerosis is ''always incurable but only generally fatal,'' his grammatical trickery is literally lifesaving. . . .

As a survey of American life, *The Franchiser* is seldom flattering and often offensive. The narrator and leading characters make witless cracks about blacks, Puerto Ricans, homosexuals, the uneducated, the rural, women and their physical functions. . . . [The] reader wonders at the point of all this baiting. . . .

Elkin . . . trivializes some of his moving situations by making them extended puns, the most vulgar form of allegory. (p. 151)

Elkin treats the subject of disease with an imaginative power that has few antecedents. In Proust's great novel, Marcel's grandmother suffers a stroke in a Bois de Boulogne rest room. Later, walking through the park, she tries to thwart her coming degeneration by recalling her past life, exercising the instrument that is about to permanently wind down. In a similar attempt to exert his decaying sensory powers, Flesh tries to discern the denomination of a coin in his hands, when in fact there is no coin. One also recalls Malcolm Lowry's taxonomy of the manic highs and lows of alcoholism, when Elkin tells and shows us "manic rage, anger, petulance, exuberance, exul- and exaltation" as the symptoms of remission. . . .

The Franchiser lacks a political and economic sensibility . . . [and] is best read as a display of literary virtuosity. Elkin's prose rhythms train the reader to expect an eruption of outlandish parallels coincident with the presentation of each new franchise. Yet despite the relentless prolixity of *The Franchiser,* the novel accomplishes something new and wonderful. During the recent summer weeks, only the power of Elkin's vision could make the sensation of humidity seem a blessing. (p. 152)

> *Anthony Heilbut, "Dregs Addicts and Cultural Illiterates," in* The Nation *(copyright 1976 by the Nation Associates, Inc.), August 28, 1976, pp. 151-52.*

* * *

ESPRIU, Salvador   1913-

Espriu, a Spanish novelist, playwright, short story writer, and poet, began his career with an unsuccessful and critically rejected novel. After his initial failure, he concentrated on developing a clear, unadorned poetic style and turned to his native province of Catalonia for his subject matter. Using Catalonia as his focus, he created a mythical world around imaginary villages and wrote critically acclaimed poems which called for unification and understanding among the various peoples of Spain.

Sr. Espriu was slow to achieve a reputation, and his final acceptance coincided with a feeling that the Symbolist phase in Catalan poetry had come to an end. Sr. Espriu's poetry is intensely personal and owes very little to anyone else: though it is highly sophisticated it shows an astonishing awareness of the vocabulary and nuances of popular speech. The maturity of his first book of poems, published in 1946, probably reflects his earlier experience as a prose-writer. Several of the older stories collected in *Narracions* already show what was to become a characteristic polarity in his work: a controlled anger at the false values of the urban middle-classes, and an elegiac tenderness towards the vanishing rural and mercantile community of Arenys de Mar, the "Sinera" of his poems and fiction.

A certain overvaluation of the purely aesthetic, visible in a story like "Letizia", was probably a necessary stage in Sr. Espriu's development. The fact remains that the most suc-

cessful of the early stories are the most human: "Teresetaque-baixava-les-escales", a series of monologues in which the life and death of one woman is made to reflect the decline of the society she represents, and "Conversió i mort d'En Quim Federal", a richly grotesque account of the death of a confirmed atheist whose mistress wishes to be legally married before he dies. . . . "Tres sorores" is a small masterpiece, the nearest thing in Catalan to Joyce's "The Dead". Again, this is a study of a whole sector of society—the genteel lower middle-class of Barcelona—which is living on the edge of an abyss, "a crowd of people whom no Messiah, political or social, would ever redeem". Of the three sisters of the title, one is already dead and survives only in the memory and the daily rituals of the other two. The failure of their hopes and their attempts to maintain their independence are incomparably rendered in the space of a few pages. . . .

The complexity of Sr. Espriu's reactions to the Civil War appeared for the first time in a remarkable piece of dramatic writing, *Primera Història d'Esther*, originally published in 1948. This "improvization for puppets", though not in the first place intended for performance, has since been adapted for the stage with extraordinary success and is justly regarded as a landmark in the postwar Catalan theatre.

One of the reasons for Sr. Espriu's high reputation at the present time is the way in which he has extended the range of his writing in the direction of public issues. This is particularly clear in one of his finest collections of poems, *La Pell de Brau* (1960), a sequence in which the collective situation of the Peninsular peoples is focused through themes and images taken from the history of the Jews in exile. *Primera Història d'Esther* also shows Espriu's highly personal way of combining Biblical themes with traditional Catalan forms of life. By imagining the performance of a play on the Biblical episode of Esther in the small Catalan town of Sinera he is able to superimpose the Old Testament story on the world of his own childhood. Like all Espriu's best work, this depends for part of its effect on the extraordinary linguistic agility with which he creates a situation in which the barriers of time and place are abolished, and where the dead generations of Sinera are as real to the Biblical characters as they are to the author himself. . . .

Sr. Espriu's view of the collective situation is all the more profound for being an intensely personal one. (p. 727)

> *The* Times Literary Supplement *(© Times Newspapers Ltd., 1968; reproduced from* The Times Literary Supplement *by permission), July 11, 1968.*

Salvador Espriu . . . is one of the finest living Catalan poets, a writer of outstanding gifts who certainly deserves to be better known outside his own country. Though he has clearly absorbed his native culture in profound and unexpected ways, he has kept his distance from the poetic movements—Symbolism, Surrealism, Social Realism—which have affected other modern Catalan poets, to the extent that his greatest strengths often seem to come from the qualities of the language itself. As Señor Castellet points out in his preface to *Lord of the Shadow*, Espriu's poetry depends on a series of paradoxes, the chief of which is a constant tension between "the spiritual (almost mystical) experience of a man attempting to renounce the world and . . . the collective and eminently problematical experience of the national community to which he belongs, which constantly demands his presence and his commitment as a citizen''. In practice, however, the search for both personal and collective solutions involves a sense of responsibility towards a language which, in recent years as at earlier stages in its history, has had to fight for its existence against strong political and social pressures.

> *Arthur Terry, "Between Two Worlds," in* The Times Literary Supplement (© *Times Newspapers Ltd., 1976; reproduced from* The Times Literary Supplement *by permission), February 6, 1976, p. 127.*

Hopefully, the intense and indeed terrible lucidity of [Espriu's] poetry will be more widely recognized within his lifetime.

Although the poet's work is very different from that of many twentieth-century writers, it is undeniably modern. If Jorge Luis Borges had a social conscience, he might write like Salvador Espriu. An overriding concern with time and illusion, death and memory, unites the two artists. Fascinated by the image of the labyrinth, both draw upon a diverse array of erudite sources such as the Cabala in their writing.

Of course this comparison has limits. Whereas Borges writes some books with a gauchoesque flavor . . . and others about chimeras and mazes, Espriu consistently fuses the local and metaphysical, injecting a note of contemporaneity and social criticism into even his most philosophical work. Furthermore, . . . he continues to write not in Borges's Spanish but in his own native tongue. From the publication of his first book at the age of sixteen, Espriu has written in Catalan, even during that period in which its use was illegal. Bearer of a proud tradition dating from the thirteenth century, Espriu works the elements of everyday Catalan life (goat paths, fennel) into a profoundly tragic vision of history which remains both individual and communal. . . .

Seemingly simple, Espriu's style is really extremely complex. His latest book, "Holy Week," contains fifteen octosyllabic, six hectosyllabic, five trisyllabic and four tetrasyllabic poems as well as a variety of other verse forms such as tankas and shedokas. Although relying on a limited number of common verbs ("to be," "to see," "to know"), he uses them in a manner characterized by frequent shifts in person and tense. . . .

In looking carefully at Espriu's poetry, one finds references to the Bible; Shakespeare and Dante; Greek, Hebrew and Egyptian myth; Meister Eckhart; Oriental religious writings and Iberian classics. Even these, however, are usually couched in direct, everyday language. Espriu's most common images include night, dust, eyes and sea. His poetry draws heavily on the four elements. . . . Symbols associated with dying are also extremely common. Nevertheless, the poet's "meditation on death" remains intimately associated with life and his own measured hope for the living. . . . (p. 224)

Key monosyllabic words such as death (*mort*) crop up again and again throughout Espriu's work. Often they link one poem to the next, making many of his books series rather than collections of poems. Although the last phrase of one

poem may provide the beginning words for the following, this interlocking is generally more subtle. A word from the beginning or middle of a poem may provide the focus for the next section. Often this element will undergo a significant alteration, as when "our night, heard in fear" in the fourth poem of "The Bulls' Hide" becomes the "night of your hatred" which begins the fifth. Changes like these add a dimension of surprise as well as a certain pleasurable asymmetry to the series.

Just as the same stylistic elements reappear throughout Espriu's poetry, so do common themes. This repetitive linking provides the basic structure for "The Book of Sinera," a representative and particularly beautiful work. . . . [It] reveals the characteristic meshing of abstract universal questions and concrete political concerns which makes Espriu both an intellectual and highly popular poet. . . . Symbol of a personal homeland, the community acquires a mythic force. . . .

The setting for these poems is unrelievedly barren. Espriu creates a sense of winter landscapes swept by winds which scatter the torn fog. Commemorating the passage of an already lifeless present, the poet refers time and again to walls and enclosures, opposing their darkness to "the young sun all wet with sea." Confronted by "this strange sadness of time," memory is powerless. (p. 225)

Though fragrant with the mint and aloes blanketing the hoof-pocked hills, this land remains hopelessly arid. Drenched in blood, the earth remains as thirsty as the men who weep crimson tears. Even the galloping showers cannot alleviate the dryness of its fields, roots, wells, cries or sorrows. Clearly, this aridity corresponds to a lack of liberty. Although freedom is described as "not a glory, but a weight," it remains essential. Over and over, the poet insists that "men cannot live if they are prisoners."

Unfortunately, Sinera is *not* free. The poems therefore prophesy impending death: the end of both an individual life and that of an epoch or a people. . . . Faced with a choice between contemplation and commitment to his countrymen, the poet merges his destiny with theirs. Nevertheless, these two strands (the individual and communal) remain visible even in combination. This dualism suggests a pattern of paired opposites recurring throughout Espriu's poetry. Hope and despair, light and darkness, word and silence, sun and wintry cold, open eye and sightless mouth occur side by side. Often these pairs reinforce one another as variations on the principal theme of life versus death. In this vein, hope equals light, which is also sun, seeing eye and flamelike words which winds extinguish. Similarly, darkness becomes the cold and silent blindness of the mocking beggar. . . .

Although Espriu refers constantly to death and these "words of the void," it would be wrong to consider his poetry melancholy or morbid. "Hopeless," asserts Espriu, "I speak of hope." Although pessimistic, he is never despairing. Speaking of "the worn clothes" of hope as well as those of suffering, the poet suggests that the two may be cut from the same cloth. Though it may be a strange word to describe a poet who by definition has preserved the child's ability to marvel, Espriu is unfailingly adult. Referring openly to the attraction of the bad, he is one of the few writers capable of giving evil its due without giving in to it. . . .

Clearly, the poet's reflection on his losses far exceeds nostalgia. The very gravity of his sorrow lifts it far beyond petty individual lament. Espriu, the Catalan, and indeed the Spanish nation have lived through defeats whose immensity can only be regarded with dry eyes. Their tragedy is of course only a variant on the human tragedy, but history has given peoples such as the Catalans—or Jews—a particularly acute appreciation of its terrible grandeur. . . . (p. 226)

Given the seriousness and difficulty of the situation in which he finds man as well as himself and his country, Espriu's assertion that he has given his life for "some naked words" is not an admission of defeat but an assertion of triumph. The passage of his life "like a wall" has earned him the right to speak with the awful tranquility of one in whom "the light rests" and who, converting crag to song, has already "calmed the darkness." (p. 227)

> *Candace Slater, "The Poetry of Salvador*
> *Espriu: Bare Crag into Song," in* World
> Literature Today *(copyright 1977 by the*
> *University of Oklahoma Press), Vol. 51, No.*
> *2, Spring, 1977, pp. 224-27.*

F

FARIÑA, Richard   1937?-1966

Fariña, an American songwriter, playwright, folksinger, and novelist of Cuban-Irish heritage, was an important figure in the folk music scene of the 1960s. Fariña, who espoused revolution in Castro's Cuba and fought with the IRA in Northern Ireland, was "one of the earliest protest writers to be lyrical as well," according to Lillian Roxon. His song "Pack Up Your Sorrows" is considered a folk classic. (See also *Contemporary Authors*, obituary, Vols. 25-28, rev. ed.)

The style of [*Been Down So Long It Looks Like Up to Me*], which is its least appealing aspect, is derived heavily from J. P. Donleavy: it displays the same edgy levity, the same corrosive strain of guarded self-deception. But Gnossos Pappadopoulis (the hero, "furry Pooh Bear, keeper of the flame") is not simply a little Ginger Man; the flower of a later generation, he is gentler, less decisive, more overtly sentimental, and more innocent. . . .

As a literary work, the value of *Been Down So Long* is slight; its interest as a chronicle of a certain lost hippie scene . . . is limited, if that is what the reader had in mind. But as an expression, highly personal and honest, of the outcome of those feelings of disinterested virtue and existential autonomy once encouraged (though not often proved) by universities, and later condemned as "apathy," Mr. Fariña's book deserves some serious attention. (p. 449)

> *Stephen Donadio, in* Partisan Review *(copyright © 1966 by Partisan Review, Inc.), Summer, 1966.*

[*Been Down So Long It Looks Like Up to Me*] mixes hipster-picaresque with a much more modish, campy style, and seems to be by, for, and about, what Leslie Fiedler calls the New Mutants, whose attachment to normal human attributes is extremely tenuous. There isn't much to it except for a forceful facility in the writing and a horribly accurate ear for the inanities of hipster speech. . . . Mr. Fariña keeps it all going wildly on, in the accepted manner of comic-strip fiction, with lots of way-out names to keep up the merriment: Louie Motherball, Juan Carlos Rosenbloom, Calvin Blacknesse, G. Alonso Oeuf, etc. For all its souped-up gaiety I found it depressing: a bright, cold, cruel, empty book. (p. 28)

> *Bernard Bergonzi, in* The New York Review of Books *(reprinted with permission from* The New York Review of Books; *copyright © 1966 NYREV, Inc.), October 6, 1966.*

Long Time Coming and a Long Time Gone is haunted by a paradox. On the one hand, it displays an almost incredible mastery of moods and styles; on the other, it creates an impression of enormous talent lost in a blur of conflicting identities. In the title story Fariña speaks in the voice of a Southern poor white. Later on he becomes Irish, with strong overtones of Dylan Thomas; then somber Cuban, with echoes of Hemingway at his most pompous, and finally slick New York, in a glossy magazine piece about an encounter with some Birchers at a country fair. A few general themes—death, romance, lurking demons, socialism, the decline and fall of America—remind us that all the pieces were written by the same person. . . . Fariña was a brilliant posturer and a vibrant personality, yet the best work surviving him is his songs. One realizes after reading this book that as a writer of prose he never found a voice of his own. (p. 36)

> *Henry S. Resnik, in* Saturday Review *(© 1969 by Saturday Review, Inc.; reprinted with permission), July 5, 1969.*

Whitman is legitimately associated with a tradition of optimism and occasional naïveté, but he also expresses a characteristic tendency to raise the highest hopes for the future of the country—and then to criticize it mercilessly when it fails to measure up to the standard. The idea of America as a New World Garden of Eden proposes so extreme a conception of society that its realization is almost inevitably doomed. The shift of the American mind to the other extreme is equally predictable, and it brings to the surface expressions of pessimism, determinism, and visions of apocalypse. Major writers of the last decade (including Vonnegut, Brautigan, and Pynchon) have worked almost totally within this apocalyptic mode (an attitude mirrored well in the rock music of the period) and are consequently closer to literary naturalism and what might be called literary Calvinism than has been supposed. Their sense of loss, like Whitman's, is the greater for the image of the American dream which they have carried in their mind's eye. And it focusses on the failure to achieve a humane and democratic culture.

Among the germinal works of this period which have not

received sufficient attention is Richard Fariña's "academic" novel, *Been Down So Long It Looks Like Up To Me*. Although it deals with the university, its themes go far beyond what we have come to expect from the academic novel. And aside from the intrinsic merits of his book, Fariña provides some important insights into the work of Thomas Pynchon, who was his contemporary at Cornell. Pynchon's dedication of *Gravity's Rainbow* (1973) to Fariña is the expression of more than a sentimental connection.

Been Down So Long is in the classic tradition of American literature—a comic quest by a young hero, "the keeper of the flame," obsessed by intimations of death and loneliness, but with a fine seriousness underlying the often fantastic episodes. . . . Invisible, an outcast and isolate in his own land, [Fariña] feels a profound sense of betrayal of the promise of America and its spiritual resources to a mechanistic, mindless, advertising-ridden non-culture which threatens to destroy the environment and its inhabitants. Unlike the writers of the twenties, Fariña sees the situation as the consequence of a conspiracy which emanates from the highest levels of political power—and then goes completely out of human control, even of those who may have seemed to be the prime movers. (There is very little of the passivity and world-weariness we associate with writers of the Lost Generation.) Fariña's hero is reminiscent of the Humphrey Bogart character who proclaims his neutrality and isolation from the conflict but succumbs to the indignation he has tried to control and at last finds himself in the midst of the battle. Mentor University symbolizes for Gnossos [the protagonist] what he thinks he's up against . . . , the microcosmic world of the American university molding its students into consumers of artificial foods and an endless dependence on drugs whose trade names mask what little pharmaceutical reality they contain. The resigned, Gnossos proclaims, are his foes and he combats them with an arsenal of weapons that under cuts the packaged world. (pp. 927-28)

[The] major image is Gnossos the teller of tall tales, the artist as subversive. In response to the conventional world, he invokes a series of references to children's literature, comic books, and radio serials. It is a concatenation of materials from popular culture, the use of which is one of the central characteristics of the fiction of the sixties. . . . Fariña provides a good insight into the use by writers of the sixties of materials from popular culture. . . . [They] symbolize the common heritage of the generation, their only source of communion in a world which offers now only exploitation and the portent of nuclear destruction. We often think of pop culture as "camp" or simply silly, but many contemporary writers place it in a wider frame of reference. It provides a fine shock technique, a thrust at the values of middle class culture. It is similar to the use by a writer like Twain, for example, of folk materials which genteel society considers beneath its notice. The mass media are low on any scale and the young are encouraged to aspire to the "higher arts" as they have been sanctified by book clubs and assorted tastemakers. The heritage of "Western Civilization" is sold to the younger generation; their reaction is to reject it, classifying it as another instance of the hypocrisy of an American culture which pretentiously touts what it thinks is "highbrow." "Classical music," the masterpieces of art, "uplifting" literature are prescribed, but the

real interests of the adult world are more accurately revealed by the perusal of any best seller list. (pp. 928-29)

At the same time, Gnossos' generation has discovered serious and significant meaning in mass media materials. In one sense it is their folklore (as rock becomes their folk music) and despite the objections of professional folklorists there is some truth in the conception. Though hardly anonymous (anonymity being one of the standard requirements for authentic folklore), the mass media are functionally without authorship. . . . The materials, nevertheless, have reached a mass audience and provided it with a stock of fantastic, humorous demigods whose behavior is not very far from the real article. Perhaps equally important, they often operate on a level of brutal honesty and overt violence which exposes aspects of American existence that the official culture will not acknowledge. (p. 929)

[Ralph Ellison has said that] "the blues is an autobiographical chronicle of personal catastrophe expressed lyrically." The statement defines very well Fariña's approach to the form and content of his work, which deals with still another form of invisibility in the United States. "Been down so long it looks like up to me" is a line from a blues well known in a number of variations. . . . Ellison has used the blues as a basis for literary form and it seems to me that, like *Invisible Man*, Fariña's book moves along similar lines. Fariña reveals how well black tradition works for the white American, a point Ellison has tried very hard to emphasize in his own speculations about the relationships between black tradition and American culture in general. (p. 930)

Although there is always the danger of sentimentalizing or distorting the meaning of the black experience (and Fariña guards against this by dealing with the Black Mafia), there is also something the white hipster can learn from it. It helps him to deal openly with the brutal experience of life; it directs him to seek what Melville once called the "usable truth," the awareness that at the bottom of individual existence is a confrontation with evil; it helps him to see that "all men who say *yes*, lie." There is in Fariña's attitude a sense of depravity which is reminiscent of Melville's literary Calvinism.

Gnossos carries close to the surface of his consciousness an image of the monkey-demon, one of several symbols that characterize the power of evil in his world. (The motif is analogous to Pynchon's preoccupation with paranoia.) At the edge of Mentor University's banal community of stupid fraternities, or in the midst of the desert's spaces ("I couldn't even manage a goddamned sunset without a little competition from the Firebird Motel sign"), there are always personifications of evil, banded together in a fraternity of Mafia confidence men, purveyors of drugs, sponsors of orgies, and practitioners of sadistic arts. . . . In fact, he is *their* connection with the kind of energetic and impious personality which they must control. At the same time, they are irresistible to Gnossos, for they provide tantalizing glimpses of the vision he is seeking for himself.

For although Gnossos is not hooked on hard drugs, he relies heavily on mescaline and pot for moments of release from the sickness around him: "You go looking for something simple and the whole cancer of your country gets in and infects it." He tries to use his Greek antecedents to fend off the mass of packaged, dehydrated products which pass for food, but even the bits of goat cheese which he carries in his rucksack are not sufficient. (It is an instance of that complication of pluralistic identities which the American contains and which he often uses to neutralize the impact of a homogenized American culture.) (pp. 931-32)

As in much of the rock music of the period, there is a good deal of *Waste Land* imagery in the fiction of the sixties. But the connection is more with images of desolation and apocalypse than Eliot's sense of the potential redeeming power of the quest. The need for traditional religious values is even less apparent. . . .

Gnossos is not so much cynical, jaded, or deluded as he is aware of the danger that any sincere commitment will be distorted by the organization. Fariña was prophetic in his treatment of the organizational fate of the student movement, for its political aims were "co-opted" or sold out by its leaders. The university itself symbolizes the difference between an academic community and the knowledge factories which turn out the interchangeable parts on their assembly lines and provide an ever-expanding market for the products of off-campus industries. When the dust settled, as Fariña knew, nothing fundamental had changed. (p. 932)

Fariña provides a complex vision—he has written an "autobiographical chronicle of personal catastrophe expressed lyrically," and in a framework that encompasses some uniquely American materials, ranging from folklore to the mass media. But despite some fantastic episodes, his plot line is quite linear and we can see in clearer outline some central themes which are more obscurely developed by a writer like Pynchon who, like Fariña, shows us a devastated spiritual landscape, lighted by explosions of mad, pop humor and similarly destined for destruction. In the background is a vision of what might have been, the dream that has been despoiled. (p. 933)

> *Gene Bluestein, "Laughin' Just to Keep from Cryin': Fariña's Blues Novel," in* Journal of Popular Culture *(copyright © 1976 by Ray B. Browne), Spring, 1976, pp. 926-34.*

*   *   *

FAULKNER, William   1897-1962

An American novelist, short story writer, screenwriter, and poet, Faulkner is regarded as a central figure in the literature of this century. Encouraged by Sherwood Anderson to write about his Mississippi home, Faulkner created the imaginary Yoknapatawpha, a county that became the stage for his view of human existence. As stated in his Nobel Prize acceptance speech, Faulkner considered his major theme to be "the problems of the human heart in conflict with itself." Many of his characters are passionate and violent, but human dignity is contrasted with the decay of the American South, its moral degeneracy and racial tension. Faulkner's complex style unites language with theme and character development through the use of stream-of-consciousness writing, interior monologue, and disordered chronology. Past and present become one, and characters gather significance as they are seen from many viewpoints. In addition to the 1950 Nobel Prize, Faulkner was twice awarded both the Pulitzer Prize and the National Book Award. (See also CLC, Vols. 1, 3, 6, 8.)

Faulkner's metaphysics is a metaphysics of time.

Man's misfortune lies in his being time-bound. . . . Such is the real subject of [*The Sound and the Fury*]. And if the technique Faulkner has adopted seems at first a negation of temporality, the reason is that we confuse temporality with chronology. It was man who invented dates and clocks. (pp. 87-8)

Faulkner's present is essentially catastrophic. It is the event which creeps up on us like a thief, huge, unthinkable—which creeps up on us and then disappears. Beyond this present time there is nothing, since the future does not exist. The present rises up from sources unknown to us and drives away another present; it is forever beginning anew. "And . . . and . . . and then." . . .

In Faulkner's work, there is never any progression, never anything which comes from the future. The present has not first been a future possibility, as when my friend, after having been *he for whom I am waiting,* finally appears. No, to be present means to appear without any reason and to sink in. This sinking in is not an abstract view. It is within things themselves that Faulkner perceives it and tries to make it felt. (p. 88)

Quentin can say, "I broke my watch," but when he says it, his gesture is *past.* The past is named and related; it can, to a certain extent, be fixed by concepts or recognized by the heart. . . . Faulkner's vision of the world can be compared to that of a man sitting in an open car and looking backward. At every moment, formless shadows, flickerings, faint tremblings and patches of light rise up on either side of him, and only afterward, when he has a little perspective, do they become trees and men and cars.

The past takes on a sort of super-reality; its contours are hard and clear, unchangeable. The present, nameless and fleeting, is helpless before it. It is full of gaps, and, through these gaps, things of the past, fixed, motionless, and silent as judges or glances, come to invade it. Faulkner's monologues remind one of airplane trips full of air-pockets. At each pocket, the hero's consciousness "sinks back into the past" and rises only to sink back again. The present is not; it becomes. Everything *was.* In *Sartoris,* the past was called "the stories" because it was a matter of family memories that had been constructed, because Faulkner had not yet found his technique.

In *The Sound and the Fury* he is more individual and more undecided. But it is so strong an obsession that he is sometimes apt to disguise the present, and the present moves along in the shadow, like an underground river, and reappears only when it itself is past. (p. 89)

This unspeakable present, leaking at every seam, these sudden invasions of the past, this emotional order, the opposite of the voluntary and intellectual order that is chronological but lacking in reality, these memories, these monstrous and discontinuous obsessions, these intermittences of the heart—are not these reminiscent of the lost and recaptured time of Marcel Proust? I am not unaware of the differences between the two; I know, for instance, that for Proust salvation lies in time itself, in the full reappearance of the past. For Faulkner, on the contrary, the past is never lost, unfortunately; it is always there, it is an obsession. One escapes from the temporal world only through mystic ecstasies. A mystic is always a man who wishes to forget something, his self or, more often, language or objective representations. For Faulkner, time must be forgotten. (p. 90)

But for Faulkner, as for Proust, time is, above all, *that which separates*. One recalls the astonishment of the Proustian heroes who can no longer enter into their past loves, of those lovers depicted in *Les Plaisirs et Les Jours,* clutching their passions, afraid they will pass, and knowing they will. We find the same anguish in Faulkner. . . .

To tell the truth, Proust's fictional technique *should have been* Faulkner's. It was the logical conclusion of his metaphysics. But Faulkner is a lost man, and it is because he feels lost that he takes risks and pursues his thought to its uttermost consequences. Proust is a Frenchman and a classicist. The French lose themselves only a little at a time and always manage to find themselves again. Eloquence, intellectuality, and a liking for clear ideas were responsible for Proust's retaining at least the semblance of chronology.

The basic reason for this relationship is to be found in a very general literary phenomenon. Most of the great contemporary authors, Proust, Joyce, Dos Passos, Faulkner, Gide, and Virginia Woolf have tried, each in his own way, to distort time. Some of them have deprived it of its past and future in order to reduce it to the pure intuition of the instant; others, like Dos Passos, have made of it a dead and closed memory. Proust and Faulkner have simply decapitated it. They have deprived it of its future—that is, its dimension of deeds and freedom. . . . Faulkner's heroes . . . never look ahead. They face backward as the car carries them along. The coming suicide which casts its shadow over Quentin's last day is not a human possibility; not for a second does Quentin envisage the possibility of *not* killing himself. This suicide is an immobile wall, a *thing* which he approaches backward, and which he neither wants to nor can conceive. (p. 91)

Faulkner's entire art aims at suggesting to us that Quentin's monologues and his last walk *are already* his suicide. This, I think, explains the following curious paradox: Quentin thinks of his last day in the past, like someone who is remembering. But in that case, since the hero's last thoughts coincide approximately with the bursting of his memory and its annihilation, who is remembering? The inevitable reply is that the novelist's skill consists in the choice of the present moment from which he narrates the past. . . . [His] artistry and, to speak frankly, all . . . illusion are meant, then, merely as substitutions for the intuition of the future lacking in the author himself. This explains everything, particularly the irrationality of time; since the present is the unexpected, the formless can be determined only by an excess of memories. We now also understand why duration is "man's characteristic misfortune." If the future has reality, time withdraws us from the past and brings us nearer to the future; but if you do away with the future, time is no longer that which separates, that which cuts the present off from itself. "You cannot bear to think that someday it will no longer hurt you like this." Man spends his life struggling against time, and time, like an acid, eats away at man, eats him away from himself and prevents him from fulfilling his human character. Everything is absurd. "Life is a tale told by an idiot, full of sound and fury, signifying nothing."

But is man's time without a future? I can understand that the nail's time, or the clod's, or the atom's is a perpetual present. But is man a thinking nail? If you begin by plunging him into universal time, the time of planets and nebulae, of tertiary flexures and animal species, as into a bath of sulphuric acid, then the question is settled. However, a consciousness buffeted so from one instant to another ought, *first of all,* to be a consciousness and then, *afterward,* to be temporal; does anyone believe that time can come to it from the outside? Consciousness can "exist within time" only on condition that it become time as a result of the very movement by which it becomes consciousness. It must become "temporalized," as Heidegger says. We can no longer arrest man at each present and define him as "the sum of what he has." The nature of consciousness implies, on the contrary, that it project itself into the future. We can understand what it is only through what it will be. It is determined in its present being by its own possibilities. This is what Heidegger calls "the silent force of the possible." You will not recognize within yourself Faulkner's man, a creature bereft of possibilities and explicable only in terms of what he has been. Try to pin down your consciousness and probe it. You will see that it is hollow. In it you will find only the future. (pp. 91-2)

I am afraid that the absurdity that Faulkner finds in a human life is one that he himself has put there. Not that life is not absurd, but there is another kind of absurdity.

Why have Faulkner and so many other writers chosen this particular absurdity which is so un-novelistic and so untrue? I think we should have to look for the reason in the social conditions of our present life. Faulkner's despair seems to me to precede his metaphysics. For him, as for all of us, the future is closed. Everything we see and experience impels us to say, "This can't last." And yet change is not even conceivable, except in the form of a cataclysm. We are living in a time of impossible revolutions, and Faulkner uses his extraordinary art to describe our suffocation and a world dying of old age. I like his art, but I do not believe in his metaphysics. A closed future is still a future. [In the words of Heidegger:] "Even if human reality has nothing more 'before' it, even if 'its account is closed,' its being is still determined by this 'self-anticipation.' The loss of all hope, for example, does not deprive human reality of its possibilities; it is simply a way of *being* toward these same possibilities." (p. 93)

> *Jean-Paul Sartre, "On 'The Sound and the Fury': Time in the Work of Faulkner," in his* Literary and Philosophical Essays, *translated by Annette Michelson, Rider & Co., 1955 (and reprinted in* Faulkner: A Collection of Critical Essays, *edited by Robert Penn Warren, Prentice-Hall, Inc., 1966, pp. 87-93).*

[Not] until William Faulkner's *The Sound and the Fury* in 1929 did a novelist succeed in incorporating Joyce's techniques into his own artistic sensibility. It is true that Joyce was neither a major formative influence on Faulkner, nor a lasting one: echoes in Faulkner's three novels before *The Sound and the Fury* are minor and localized, and after this novel and *As I Lay Dying,* the influence is barely evident. But in *The Sound and the Fury,* especially in Quentin's section, Joyce is a major influence, and Faulkner's use of Joycean techniques contributes significantly to the novel's success.

Since its publication Faulkner's novel has been repeatedly linked to *Ulysses.* Probably to counter the comparisons, Faulkner expended a great deal of energy denying the possible influence of *Ulysses* on his work. . . . [However, in] this novel and *As I Lay Dying* he attempts to narrate his stories with the help of major technical devices that came directly from *Ulysses*.

Joyce's most significant legacy to Faulkner was the interior monologue. With this technique Faulkner discovered a solution to crucial problems in characterization that had plagued him in his first three novels. *Soldier's Pay, Mosquitoes,* and *Sartoris* all suffer from his inability to create sufficiently complex characters. *Sartoris* represents an important advance over the first two works in its use of the personal and historical past as a context for the present action. But Bayard Sartoris, upon whom the burden of the past-present conflict rests, is too inarticulate to convey the complex pressures acting on him from both his own and his family's past.

Faulkner's unsuccessful characterization in the early novels is related to his use of an omniscient narrator. It is clear from almost all his novels that he prefers third-person, omniscient narration, but in the first three works the use of omniscience impedes characterization, for it results in exterior views of characters who have little to say. Lacking are inside views, except for occasional inchoate attempts to render the characters' thought processes. Then, in three sections of *The Sound and the Fury* and all of *As I Lay Dying,* Faulkner turned to extreme uses of first-person narration; it is as if he saw the need to purge his work of his undeveloped omniscient instincts by eliminating his own voice entirely. Once he gained the necessary discipline, he returned to omniscient narration with much greater control over the inherent limitations and possibilities.

In *The Sound and the Fury* Faulkner combines the use of first-person narration with the decisive additional improvement provided by stream-of-consciousness techniques. The first-person method forces the character to reveal himself to the reader, thereby eliminating the possibility of inarticulateness, but the interior monologue allows Faulkner at the same time to reveal the character's mind far beyond the character's ability to present his own conscious thought processes. (pp. 265-66)

Faulkner's predilection toward omniscient narration might have led him to the technique as employed by Lawrence and Woolf, but he revealed no significant interest in it. . . .

Like most of his contemporaries, Faulkner seems to have read Molly Bloom's soliloquy as a representation of chaos; when he echoes it, his scene is usually a chaotic one. . . . Like Joyce in Molly's monologue, he retains the rhythm of sentences, even as he eliminates punctuation.

This technique appears occasionally in the novels before *The Sound and the Fury,* especially in *Soldier's Pay* and *Mosquitoes.* In the latter it serves primarily to convey emotional agitation, whereas in the former Faulkner uses it for his comic representation of Julian Lowe's ignorant mind. (p. 267)

In both of these novels the technique remains unassimilated within works that are not stream-of-consciousness novels; it either fully reveals the limitations of a minor character's mind or it serves as a temporary excursion into the mind of a major character within a primarily external presentation.

Only in *The Sound and the Fury* does this monologue technique become one method assimilated with others in a narrative in which the events are indistinguishable from the

minds perceiving them. Quentin's section of the novel can be seen as a conflict between two aspects of his mind: his voluntary and involuntary thoughts. . . .

Besides the representation of mental agitation, Faulkner uses the technique as a means of characterization, particularly of Mrs. Compson. (p. 268)

In Quentin's section of *The Sound and the Fury* the technique dominates, even though Faulkner employs first-person narration. Quentin's past-tense reporting of the external facts functions like Joyce's omniscient, third-person narration. To report his character's thoughts, Faulkner, like Joyce, shifts to a direct reporting technique based on the present tense. The similarities can be seen in the opening pages of *Ulysses* and Quentin's section of *The Sound and the Fury,* both of which serve to establish a tone and a set of expectations. Neither "Telemachus" nor Quentin's section begins directly with an interior monologue. . . . Throughout the first six episodes of *Ulysses,* the narration consists primarily of this combination of external description (omniscient, but usually limited to Stephen's or Bloom's perception) and interior monologue.

A parallel development occurs at the beginning of Quentin's section of *The Sound and the Fury.* Quentin himself replaces the omniscient narrator; all of the observations are thus limited to his perceptions. As narrator, he attempts to describe objectively the environment and the events around him, even though this objectivity is nullified from the start by his mind's distortions. The apparent objectivity with which he begins each of the opening paragraphs disintegrates almost immediately into a memory of a conversation with his father. The first five paragraphs work this way, but the fifth becomes more complicated as, inadvertently it seems, Quentin begins to reveal the "stream" of his mind. . . . [The] patterns of association become involuntary, as several thoughts rush into his mind at once. (pp. 269-70)

Structurally, Quentin's section seems in large measure to be modeled on Bloom's day. First, Quentin's "hour upon the stage," like Bloom's, is obviously and explicitly a day: both the opening date and Quentin's obsession with clocks keep us informed of the date and time throughout. The section has both the range of Bloom's day and many of the same mundane concerns. . . . For Quentin, though it is likely that this day is not very different from previous ones (except in its conclusion), the mundane acts take on a ritualistic significance, their simple mechanical nature contrasting with the chaos in his mind. Both Bloom and Quentin spend the day wandering around their cities, and both return "home" at the end. Although Quentin leaves his room again some time shortly after his section concludes, Faulkner carefully ends it at its place of origin and on a relatively calm note. Likewise, the crises for both Bloom and Quentin involve suitors. . . . Quentin's inability to cope with reality is largely summarized first by his desire to literally slay his sister's suitor/lovers, specifically Dalton Ames, and then by his failure to understand why he could not do it.

Although Quentin's section exists as a continuous narrative, there are several divisions implicit within it. Like the episodes in *Ulysses,* these subsections reflect the passage of time during the day and the mind's reaction to the various times of day. . . . As Quentin's day progresses, so does his inability to live in and to focus his mind on present reality, and the passage of time is accompanied by changing narrative techniques designed to reveal the growing domination of the past over the present in Quentin's mind. (pp. 271-72)

As Quentin's section progresses and he becomes more and more immersed in his own thoughts, Faulkner builds upon the basic method and combines it with other Joycean techniques. Both novelists reveal the characters' minds interacting with the outside world by using external incidents to either inspire or cut off an extended memory. . . . Faulkner [also] adopts techniques from Joyce's episode of hallucinations, in which no real action occurs at all, for the presentation of a character whose tormented thoughts are in reality driving him to suicide. (pp. 272-73)

There is an important difference between Joyce's and Faulkner's uses of the exterior-interior monologue technique. Like Quentin, Stephen and Bloom spend large amounts of time recalling or reliving past events, but those events alone do not define the existence of either of Joyce's characters. Most of the thoughts of each are direct responses to external stimuli, "the now, the here" of June 16, 1904. . . . To Quentin, though, the present is nonexistent. The configuration of past events is fixed in his mind, and the present has become only an adjunct to the past. Thus, all of the events of the "stream" of his mind are descriptions of past events or fully remembered conversations. Faulkner employs several of the technical features of Joyce's interior monologue, but he does so to portray not a character balanced between an external and an internal life but one whose present life is completely and fatally engulfed by the past.

Joycean influence in *The Sound and the Fury* is not limited to Quentin's section. A great deal also exists in Benjy's. There Faulkner's use of Joyce's techniques is both simpler and more original, more daring. Faulkner strips one aspect of the interior monologue to its radical essentials by using the association method in a mind that can only associate mechanically, that can make no conclusions or deductions. In *Ulysses* the associations link the past and present in the characters' minds, but in Benjy's monologue Faulkner eliminates all temporal distinctions. Whereas Quentin is all past, Benjy is all present. The artistic principle in Benjy's section is similar to Joyce's in *Ulysses*: fragments and episodes appear early in the section, without explanation, context, comment, or other aids. Elucidation comes later if the reader remembers well. In both cases, the principle of order lies in the author's design rather than in the character's mind (except to the extent that the chaos of Benjy's mind is itself the controlling order). In the use of Benjy, almost by definition, the result is "spatial," since the character lacks all temporal perspective. The result at the end of the section is a picture of Benjy's mind, a still representation of the nature and contents of his consciousness.

It is this extension of some properties implicit in the stream-of-consciousness methods that constitutes Faulkner's original technical achievement here. Yet Benjy and Quentin are balanced by Jason (who shares properties with the first-person narrator of Joyce's "Cyclops" episode) and the omniscient fourth chapter, and *The Sound and the Fury* must, of course, be seen in terms of all four sections. As critics have suggested, devices such as associationism, recurrent motifs, idiosyncratic phrases and rhythms, unex-

plained mental images or ideas, and the basic stream-of-consciousness goal of rendering the contents of a mind all force the novelist away from the direction of storytelling and into the depths of character. This suits Joyce perfectly; Stephen and Bloom are isolated individuals within a society that is presented for the most part in a static picture. Faulkner, however, assimilates these techniques, with their restrictions, into his basic storytelling impulse. Benjy's and Quentin's sections reveal states of being, rather than actions, and they are close to the *Ulysses* model. In Benjy the tension between depth of character and the need to progress in the temporal world does not exist because his mind has no relation to the flux of the outside world. Quentin's section exists essentially to reveal why an event is occurring (or, in the context of the entire novel, why an event occurred eighteen years in the past). The remainder of the novel shifts the balance. Jason's section is a monologue, but there are no interior views, no stream-of-consciousness techniques. In the fourth section, events dominate, reported by an omniscient narrator.

It seems fair to say, with Robert Humphrey, that *The Sound and the Fury* represents the point at which the stream-of-consciousness novel entered the "main stream of fiction." . . . Furthermore, the novel represents Faulkner's own reentry into the "main stream" via the route of modernism. Although Faulkner remained an experimenter throughout his career, after this novel and *As I Lay Dying* he abandoned any attempt to render processes of consciousness directly; his technical experiments became more concerned with sentence formation, point of view, and fictional structure. Outstanding as *The Sound and the Fury* is in itself, as "criticism in new composition" of the interior monologue techniques of *Ulysses* it makes possible Faulkner's subsequent great achievements in omniscient narration in his novels of the 1930s and 1940s. (pp. 275-77)

> *Michael Groden, in* Twentieth Century Literature *(copyright 1974, Hofstra University Press), October, 1975.*

The glitter and flash of the life of [Aubrey Beardsley] would hardly seem an influence upon the literature of a retiring Southern gentleman of homey ways and private means, yet Faulkner's work was to prove that London, Dieppe, and the decadent Nineties were not far removed from Oxford and Yoknapatawpha County, Mississippi. The influence of the aesthetes and decadents upon Faulkner's early work has been noted by several critics, particularly those working on the connections between Faulkner's poetry and the French Symbolists. Beardsley has received less attention from Faulkner students and scholars, but the allusions to Beardsley in three of the novels (*Soldiers' Pay, Light in August,* and *Absalom, Absalom!*) have created a twinkle in a few academic eyes. (p. 339)

[Addison Bross suggests] that Faulkner's interest in Beardsley "may have been, for all his evident admiration, only the passing fancy of those apprentice years." Bross here remains safely within the trenches dug by prior critics such as [William Van] O'Connor and [Michael] Millgate, yet a decadent strain running through Faulkner's later novels seems to justify a venture above ground across this no-man's land of critical opinion. Although surely Faulkner did not remain long within the confines of decadent art, it is likewise true that this influence, particularly that of Beardsley, remained strong through much of his work and helped to form several of his most memorable passages. (p. 341)

[A link is] suggested by the decadent tone, themes, and images of much of Faulkner's work in [his] period of apprenticeship, 1919-29. He decorated the borders of his poem "Nocturne" . . . in a typically Beardsleyan fashion—black and white design, spare line, and familiar images, such as the full moon and flaming candles which were favorite ornaments to Beardsley's drawings (apparently he worked only by candlelight). Millgate notes a similar quality in *The Marble Faun,* Faulkner's book of verse published in 1924, and in his verse from *The Double Dealer* (1925). It is in his early novels, however, as [critics have shown], that we detect Beardsley's presence. . . . It is with his mature works, beginning with *The Sound and the Fury,* that Faulkner becomes the consummate artist, capable of manipulating this decadent strain, no longer dominated by it. Here it is that his own pictorial genius captures the mood and the lines of Beardsley's art and carries that art to its fictional heights.

In *The Sound and the Fury,* a novel of decay, if not decadence, Faulkner makes one apparently explicit allusion to Beardsley. Mr. Compson (who in *Absalom, Absalom!* will suggest to Millgate the "effete disenchantment" of literary decadence) quotes the same Latin epigraph, *"Et ego in Arcadia* . . . which Beardsley had employed in one of his drawings. . . . Beardsley's illustration depicts that same middle-aged decadent gentility which forms the refuge of the *fin de famille* Compson. Faulkner similarly details the cluttered toilet of the younger Quentin's bureau—another familiar Beardsleyan motif.

It is in the elder Quentin's section, however, that the strongest scenes of a jaundiced universe are detailed. His section of the novel, to borrow a chapter title from Weintraub, might easily be headed "The Prevalence of Yellow" —yellow butterflies, yellow moons, yellow mud, yellow leaves, yellow lights. Yellow dominates the landscape and Quentin's narrative as nowhere else in the work (a rough tally yields only four mentions of the color in the other three sections to some eleven references in Quentin's). The connections with Beardsley and *The Yellow Book* are, if not obvious, at least intriguing. . . . It is tempting in fact to draw a rough parallel between Quentin and Beardsley—each lived short lives, dominated by a sense of doom and possible, or imaginative, incestuous relationship with his sister. (pp. 348-50)

Faulkner's next novel, *Sanctuary* (1931), demonstrates perhaps the most parallels with Beardsley's art. Michael Millgate has suggested an "attractive possibility" that the title may be drawn from a line of Herod's in Wilde's *Salome:* "They say the veil of the Sanctuary has disappeared, do they not?" Although this hypothesis must remain in the realm of "attractive possibilities," there exist several other more striking connections with Beardsley, particularly in Faulkner's descriptions of his female characters. Temple, Reba Rivers, and Little Belle all represent types of "the Beardsley woman" who had gained such notoriety in the Nineties. (pp. 351-52)

While *Sanctuary* evoked the decadent glitter of Memphis whorehouses, in *Light in August* Faulkner makes more sparing (though indeed more specific) use of Beardsley's art. He frequently employs the puppet metaphor of *Mari-*

onettes and the *commedia dell'arte* artifice of nineteenth-century aesthetes, and occasionally uses yellow as a metaphor of decay. . . . (p. 352)

Faulkner's greatest work, *Absalom, Absalom!* (1936), bears several resemblances to Beardsley's work, most notably, of course, in Faulkner's description of Bon's mistress and child. . . . (p. 353)

Other resemblances are present as well. Charles Bon in "the slightly Frenchified cloak . . . reclining in a flowered, almost feminized gown" . . . is only a step removed from the youth of *An Evil Motherhood.* The vision of New Orleans' sophisticated (and decadent) opulence recalls several of Beardsley's *Rape of the Lock* illustrations. . . . This same similarity between nineteenth-century Southern decadence and eighteenth-century rococo decoration may be noticed in the descriptions of Henry's bedroom where he lounges "in a gown and slippers such as women wore," which calls to mind Beardsley's *The Dream.* In all, *Absalom, Absalom!, Soldiers' Pay,* and *Sanctuary* seem to be the most prominent instances of Faulkner's use of Beardsleyan design and dress.

It would be a mistake however to limit Beardsley's influence to either these three novels or, as most critics have done, to the early stages of Faulkner's career. The Southern novelist could assimilate most features of the Englishman's art—eighteenth-century, Japanese, Petronian, personal—through most of his career. William Van O'Connor divides the Faulkner canon into three periods—the first of which constitutes his "Beardsley period." From the nineteenth century, O'Connor states, he borrowed "a sense of everything in decay." Although Faulkner did move beyond this decadent aestheticism of the Oxford dandy, he did not abandon it.

The parallel between Beardsley and Faulkner might well be overdrawn—Faulkner could well have arrived at these portraits and themes either from other sources or entirely on his own. Yet Beardsley was available, and for a young artist of Faulkner's ability to ignore the drawings of figures so similar to his own seems unlikely. Then too we have the allusions to Beardsley in the three novels. Perhaps more important, however, is the similar vision of a private and public world in decay—a world of bizarre shapes and shades which draws the audience in to acceptance while at once repulsing, enraging, fascinating. What John Rothenstein says of Beardsley applies equally to Faulkner: "no artist was ever less concerned with the everyday world viewed as a 'slice of life.'" Both artists—the one perhaps a brief intense talent, the other an enduring genius—force this private world upon their tolerant enthusiasts, and both succeed. (pp. 354-56)

> *Timothy K. Conley, in* Journal of Modern Literature *(© Temple University 1976), September, 1976.*

[*The Sound and the Fury is*] certainly the greatest American novel of the century, our prose *Wasteland.*

It is a tragic work, comparable in its dimensions and intensity to the family tragedies of the Greeks, the houses of Atreus and Laios. Faulkner undoubtedly wanted no less a comparison, as we can see from the ways he drew upon Greek and Shakespearean tragedy, not to speak of the death and resurrection of Christ. From Greek tragedy he draws on the themes of incest and the family curse; the techniques of choral commentator and stichomythy; a structure shaped by a prologue of childhood innocence, the agons and death of the tragic hero, and a theophany in the form of the Word. From Shakespeare there are frequent allusions to *Macbeth* and *Othello,* with Quentin an avatar of Hamlet. The work also echoes both Greek and Shakespearean tragedy in the social and cosmic resonance of the deaths in the social and natural hierarchy: grandmother, father-master, servants, animals—even the land, the pasture converted into a golf course. All this points to the validity of a study of the book as a tragedy.

As we would expect, the work is tragic in its form as well as its content. I have just indicated one kind of form: prologue, agon, death, and theophany. I want, though, to offer another tragic form as a way of seeing it. Briefly, I suggest that traditional tragedy—Greek or Shakespearean—is shaped by the following phases: (1) The Breakdown of the Orthodox Order; (2) The Conflict between the Tragic Attitude and the Orthodox, Profane, and Material Attitudes; (3) The Discovery of the Tragic Self; and (4) The Transformation of the Hero, leading to his Transcendence of his Fate. The substance of these phases will be developed in what follows. At this point let me define the four attitudes: the tragic, orthodox, profane, and material. By the material I mean an attitude shaped by expedience and practicality, by creature comforts and social status; it is embodied in figures like Polonius, Osric, and the messenger in *Oedipus Rex.* By the profane I mean an attitude which may be materialist incidentally, but which is primarily the negative, destructive force of evil, as with Iago or Edmund. By the orthodox attitude I mean a prevailing view which unifies life and gives it order, an order codified in religious and moral doctrine, or manifested in stabilizing values such as love, friendship, loyalty, or a code of honor. Examples would include the Chorus in Greek tragedy, Kent, Horatio, Cordelia, and Edgar. By the tragic attitude I mean a new sense of things that begins with the recognition of the breakdown of the orthodox structure, and develops into a tragic sense, a revelation of the mystery of things, that life is irrational, inexplicable. With this sense the tragic hero discovers his ultimate self, that he is a poor, naked, forked animal, born to suffer and to die.

The four parts of *The Sound and the Fury* can be understood in terms of the tragic form I have outlined. The first part, dealing with Benjy, represents the breakdown of the orthodox order; and the three parts that follow are responses to that breakdown; tragic, profane-material, and orthodox, by Quentin, Jason, and Dilsey respectively. The sequence of the parts is the form of the book, and its form is its meaning: the transcendence of the tragedy of the Compson family through enduring orthodox values, this after the failures of the tragic and profane-material responses. (pp. 798-99)

The stream of consciousness may be a technique for reflecting a disintegrated culture, but it is also, as we see, a way of reordering that culture through sense and feeling. It is metaphysically opposed to the time of the new culture, which is public, logical, abstract. This time-by-the-clock seems to unify events, but it is merely an empty scheme by which we peg events; it is mechanical, arbitrary, irrelevant to our existential selves. In time seen as a stream of consciousness, the past is always present; past and present are unified, given value and order. . . . Benjy is the holy idiot, the suffering innocent endowed with redemptive power. He is the touchstone for the humanity of the others. He is the counterpart of Dilsey, who also suffers though innocent, and who is equally linked to the theme of redemption. Both in the beginning and the end—though in strange ways—there is the possibility of redemption. (p. 801)

Faulkner called Jason evil. Perhaps he meant this only in the popular sense of cruelty, perhaps in the theological sense of the absence of good. I am not convinced that Faulkner is right. There is no real commitment to evil even though, in the fourth part, Jason is seen as a Miltonic devil "dragging Omnipotence down from his throne" in the midst of "the embattled legions of both hell and heaven. . . ." But surely this is a comic image. Faulkner may have believed in evil, but there is no evidence that he was able to imagine its depths, neither with Jason nor Popeye. Jason is a comic devil, without the gravity evil calls for. Among Faulkner's many talents, his comic genius stands out; and it is his treatment of Jason as a comic figure, both for his materialism and his profaneness, that makes him perhaps his greatest creation. Comically, he is in the tradition of the obsessed "humor" types of Jonson, Molière, and Dickens, each of whom created his own miser. . . .

[Jason] is the modern, profane man, without roots, absolute in his alienation. But he is alienated comically, not tragically. (p. 807)

Jason symbolizes the emergence and domination of capitalism in the South. His ascendance signifies the end of the feudal hierarchy. The southern past in particular and, therefore, the past in general is meaningless to him. Here, too, he is representative of modern man living in an anxious present which dissolves into a meaningless future made up of an abstract sum of money. Benjy pursues love in an endless moment made up of the past and present; Quentin is pursued by death in an intense present shaped by a tragic obsession with the past. Both feel time; Jason only calculates by it. (p. 809)

[The tragic form outlined at the beginning of the novel] is fully realized in the Quentin section; it also shapes the sequence of the entire work, with one modification. In Greek tragedy—the *Oresteia,* for example—the hero's transcendence is often realized through the mediation of a god. Christ figures in this way in the Dilsey section. This mediation changes tragedy into what we may call a divine comedy, a resolution appropriate to Faulkner's faith in the validity of human life. The form is the same, nonetheless, in both tragedy and divine comedy; in both the hero is transformed by his suffering, and through it transcends his fate. The tragic form is an instance of what is probably Faulkner's most recurrent archetype, that of death and rebirth, and, as such, reinforces the theme which hovers over everything, the death and resurrection of Christ. The death and resurrection is treated in a savagely modern idiom, with irony, parody, grotesquerie: the time sequence is garbled to Saturday, Thursday, Friday, and Sunday; Jason is the one crucified on Good Friday; and an idiot is the symbol of Christ. Yet not for one moment does the work lose its gravity. This tonality—at once grave and grotesque—is of the order of *Lear, The Possessed,* and *The Trial.*

The archetype of death and rebirth reflects Faulkner's preoccupation with tradition, and the grotesque variations on it point to the breakup of that tradition. Cleanth Brooks makes the unreconstructed assertion that *The Sound and the Fury* is not about the breakup of the Old South, only about that of the modern world. It is certainly about the modern world, but it is just as certainly about the Old and New South. We would be mistaken, though, to see it simply as another, if great, novel about the passing of the old order. Its relevance and its power lie in the fact that it presents both the dissolution of a local feudal society and the decline of that capitalistic society which brought on the feudal dissolution. It is out of this double sense of things that Faulkner is at once our most traditional and our most modern writer. This double sense accounts for much of the tension in his work. His traditionalist characters brood over the lost, meaningful past with its texture of ceremony and ritual; they cannot tolerate the empty, profane, and materialistic present, and are left with an energy they cannot use. Out of this cultural dead-end springs their obsessive fury. (pp. 812-13)

> *Isadore Traschen, "The Tragic Form of 'The Sound and The Fury',"* in The Southern Review *(copyright, 1976, by Isadore Traschen), Vol. 12, No. 4, Autumn 1976, pp. 798-813.*

It could be argued that the four most astonishing things about William Faulkner's life were his writing, his drinking, his long years of penury, and his genuine desire for privacy. Perhaps the most astonishing thing about [*Selected Letters of William Faulkner*] is that the reader learns from it very little about either of the first two. Apart from *The Fable*, over which the novelist labored doggedly for some 10 years, the other novels and many of the short stories are treated by Faulkner like some strange children which he admits fathering but prefers not to discuss openly. Forged in another furnace, white hot and remote from the utilitarian and banal need to correspond, they are often described merely as "going well" or, in the later years, "going slowly." (pp. 304-05)

As [Joseph] Blotner's gargantuan *Faulkner: A Biography* told us in 1974, the novelist's life was, in a word, hard. If we needed any further corroboration, these letters provide it but without adding very much to our knowledge of the man holding the pen. (p. 305)

[The data of Faulkner's everyday life does] little to expose whatever it is about the interior space of a great artist that the rest of us seek endlessly to know. The cottage industry that Faulkner "scholarship" has become aims to achieve some of the epiphanies through the usual tools of exegesis and theories about the work, but the best avenues of ingress to the man remain biography, autobiography, and correspondence. (pp. 305-06)

At times in [*Faulkner: A Biography*], and more often in this volume of letters, we suspect something akin to a mild conspiracy working gently beneath the surface of the page. It is not an evil thing, this conspiracy, more like a unilateral decision on [the part of Blotner, the editor,] not to compromise too callously, not to trespass too far into that private self Faulkner guarded so closely—and successfully. This little Mississppian, probably the most private and opaque man of letters in American history, has thus far held all the dogs at bay.

As Faulkner's fame spread, he fought to maintain this privacy and to aver an almost violent separation between himself and his books: . . . [In a letter of] 1949, to [Malcolm] Cowley,

> It is my ambition to be, as a private individual, abolished and voided from history, leaving it markless, no refuse save the printed books . . . it is my aim and every effort bent, that the sum and history of my life, which in the same sentence is my obit and epitaph too, shall be them both: He made the books and he died. . . .

[The] Nobel acceptance speech begins familiarly, "I feel that this award was not made to me as a man, but to my work. . . . So this award is only mine in trust."

It is precisely this unflagging determination to deny access to himself, to reinforce the chasm between man and work, that renders his biography and his letters so enticing. It is his partial success that makes neither book wholly satisfactory. (pp. 306-07)

History will not record this great novelist as a great letter writer—because he wasn't. The overwhelming bulk of the present correspondence endlessly rehashes his precarious financial condition, his contractual difficulties, and his detestation of Hollywood. It is, frankly, often boring and repetitive, particularly if one has read the life with any care. At the same time, in the midst of an existence filled with a good deal of high-grade misery, Faulkner's artistry and personality peep out (that's the problem, we do not carry away any concrete sense of his personality; what, we ask lamely, was he *like*?). . . (p. 308)

> *George H. Wolfe, "Letters of a Private Man,"* in Book Forum *(copyright © 1977 by The Hudson River Press), Vol. III, No. 2, 1977, pp. 304-09.*

*   *   *

FORSTER, E(dward) M(organ)   1879-1970

An English novelist, short story writer, essayist, and critic, Forster is considered a major twentieth-century author. Caught in a continual inner struggle with his homosexuality, Forster used this struggle as a source for his art. Best known for his critically acclaimed novel, *A Passage to India*, Forster wrote prophetically and sensitively of the major dilemmas of our time. (See also *CLC*, Vols. 1, 2, 3, 4, and *Contemporary Authors*, Vols. 13-14; obituary, Vols. 25-28, rev. ed.; *Contemporary Authors Permanent Series*, Vol. 1.)

Mr Forster's place in the canon is an unusual one. He enjoys, securely, a reputation of the most insecure kind—that of a major figure—definitely that—who falls just short—but clearly short—of true greatness. A reputation which might be expected to stimulate objections from all quarters stimulates them from virtually none. No one, apparently, wants to see him promoted into the ranks of the acknowledged masters and hardly anyone wants to see him pushed out of the canon altogether. He is the occasion of no very serious or very interesting debate. When he is praised, he is praised extravagantly but harmlessly. . . . Mr Forster's peculiar reputation rests, it might be guessed, not so much on what he's done as on what he's been taken to represent; and it would be a mean spirit indeed who, given what he *has* been taken to represent, would look with an unfriendly eye upon what he's done.

Looked upon so, Mr Forster has done little more than generate in himself and others an enthusiasm for platitudes. Let us consider two documents, 'What I Believe', Mr Forster's personal manifesto, and *Howards End,* the novel in which he tries most directly to embody the values of the manifesto.

In the essay he says he's in favour of private decencies, personal relationships, people who are sensitive and creative—the lovers, artists and homemakers—good temper, good will, tolerance, loyalty, sympathy, friendship and Love the Beloved Republic and against public affairs, Great Men, force and violence and people who see life in terms of power. . . . We have to take Mr Forster's word for it that he knows not only the words for love and sympathy, but the things themselves. It's only by turning to the novel that we have any chance of bringing the essay's claims into question; it's there we are forced to turn for the knowledge that will make good these claims. And, turning and looking, what we find is not quite a vacancy but yet more fine sentiments and, dominating the palpables of tone, characterisation and plot, an assortment of snobberies and a pervasive self-satisfaction.

The intentions of *Howards End* are explicit and impeccable. It urges its readers to 'only connect . . .' to build within themselves 'the rainbow bridge that should connect the prose in us with the passion' for then 'love is born, and alights on the highest curve, glowing against the grey, sober against the fire' and, like the essay, the novel insists 'it is the private life that holds out the mirror to infinity; personal intercourse, and that alone, that ever hints at a personality beyond our daily vision'. Its heroes and heroines are those who 'attempt personal relations', its villains 'the hurrying men who know so much and connect so little'; its triumphs occur when 'truer relationships gleam'.

But fine sentiments and would-be noble phrases don't even make good feelings let alone good novels. And if, in an essay, a writer can't get away with just naming the things he believes in, how much less so can he in a novel, when his 'beliefs' must be acted out as particular, concrete instances? Talk, for the novelist even more obviously than for the essayist, won't suffice. He must deliver the goods. And if he can't, if he doesn't really own the feelings he lays claim to, his novel will betray him. . . . *Howards End* betrays Forster. He preaches in it love and sympathy and is caught furtively practising the everyday, casual snobberies of any other upper-class Cambridge don of the turn of the century.

The part of the novel that offers the most direct (but by no means the only) challenge to his sympathies is the story of his near working-class figure Leonard Bast. From an essay, 'The Challenge of our Time', one might think him well-equipped to present class relations in England. He says of his own education, for instance, that though it was humane 'it was imperfect, inasmuch as we none of us realised our economic position. In came the nice fat dividends, up rose the lofty thoughts, and we did not realise that all the time we were exploiting the poor of our own country and the backward races abroad, and getting bigger profits from our investments than we should'. But, again as Lawrence said, trust the tale not the teller. It is one thing to describe a case

of social injustice in an essay, and in terms which were, after all, even in 1910, fairly common property, another thing entirely to write a novel in which the characters are seen, have to be seen, not just as illustrations of a thesis but as creatures who, whatever their circumstances, have the same human identity and physiognomy as their author. But Forster, for all his good intentions, can't see that the Basts and he do share a common condition. They are objects to him, objects to feel things for and to have attitudes towards —it makes no difference whether he sympathises with them, feels sorry for them, condescends to them or sneers at them. These apparently divergent feelings belong to a single paradigm, one governed by the powerful unconscious assumptions of an upper-class world-view which divides the world into 'us' and 'them'. Whatever Forster 'feels for' the Basts he feels securely as one of 'us' regarding 'them'. The Basts are nothing, have nothing, represent nothing that could bring into question for Forster himself and his world. And having no authority over their author they are dead as characters.

Forster's good intentions are, on their own terms, genuine enough. (pp. 222-25)

But the good intentions only work as a leavening upon the snobbery. The 'facts' of Leonard Bast's 'case' are obviously meant as social criticism but, as presented, they draw our attention, not without creating a certain risibility, to Mr Forster as commentator rather than to society as commented-on. Leonard, Mr Forster tells us, was 'inferior to most rich people, there is not the least doubt of it. He was not as courteous as the average rich man, nor as intelligent, nor as healthy, nor as lovable' and his wife Jacky is 'brutally stupid'. Not only is Leonard deprived of his livelihood by an unjust and all-powerful social machine and not only is he without the cultivation of the Schlegels but, additionally, he has none of the rude vigour, physical or psychological, of the middle-class barbarians like Charles Wilcox, without whose spirit 'life might never have moved out of protoplasm'. (p. 225)

The other boundary of [Bast's] social world, the proletarian 'abyss' where his origins are among the 'submerged', is only a threat and a teror to him. . . . Somehow, he has entirely escaped being influenced by his family background. We are told certain things about it—that a grandfather was a Lincolnshire farm-labourer, his father a Cockney tradesman, a brother a lay-reader and that two sisters married commercial travellers—but none of this information is active *within* Forster's characterisation of him. It is only supplied at all because Forster thinks he ought to give him a genealogy. Once he has given it he promptly forgets it because he doesn't know how to use it. Leonard isn't seen as a son or brother at all let alone one born into a particular class. The point isn't that Leonard is presented as one thing when he ought to have been presented as another, that his presentation is 'unrealistic', but that what is missing from him as a person isn't presented by Forster *as* missing. Properly speaking, it isn't missing from the character but from the book. *Howards End nowhere* contains any sense of what the alternative to Leonard might be. Leonard doesn't have merely an incomplete relation to his family and class presented as such but no relation at all.

He is without any moral or emotional history because Forster, although he would like to be writing about 'a real man', can't help running off another version of that comic

Cockney stereotype which is (perhaps 'was') so indelibly printed on the middle-class imagination. . . . Forster wants to be generous towards Leonard, wants to present a young man with a sense of honour and of self, but the materials available to him are woefully inadequate. Leonard's would-be Cockney is stilted and inanely self-preoccupied, the sense units short and repetitive and the vocabulary picked up from the 'Music Hall' or a dictionary of Cockney English, picked up and thrown down in a heap without any sense of how, when or where the words are used. It's a fair measure of Forster's linguistic insensitivity that it's not clear whether 'in trouble' does or does not mean 'pregnant'.

Forster's tone, characteristically, is condescending, and at its worst when he is paying Leonard compliments: 'the naive and sweet-tempered boy for whom Nature intended him', 'no one felt uneasy as he tiptupped along the pavements, the heart of a man ticking fast in his chest', 'within his cramped little mind dwelt something that was greater than Jefferies' books—the spirit that led Jefferies to write them'. The trouble with these remarks is not, perhaps, so much their snobbery as their simple fatuity:

> it is an adventure for a clerk to walk for a few hours in darkness. You may laugh at him, you who have slept nights out on the veldt, with your rifle beside you and all the atmosphere of adventure pat. And you also may laugh who think adventures silly. But do not be surprised if Leonard is shy whenever he meets you, and if the Schlegels rather than Jacky hear about the dawn.

This from someone who is supposed to be a major modern English novelist, preceded in importance only by Conrad, James, Lawrence and Joyce, someone often compared to Lawrence and Jane Austen. It's difficult to say what is most ridiculous about the passage, its sloppiness about the darkness and dawn, its willingness to take adventures on the veldt seriously, its arch pretence that we might meet Leonard Bast or, what we are presently concerned with, its condescension for clerks. (pp. 226-28)

[Forster's] dominant attitude to the Basts is made up of a distaste for the unattractive surfaces of working-class life and an amused superiority at its bad taste. . . .

The presence in the tone of the condescension and the contempt is, of course, bound up with the absence from the characterisation of any 'solidity of specification'. . . . Forster condescends towards the Basts because they are stock figures for whom condescension is the stock response. His compassion and concern for people such as they is nothing more than feeling sorry for them for not being like himself. He both pities and admires Leonard but he pities him for lacking his own spiritual and moral advantages and admires him for wanting them. It is not Jane Austen whom he resembles but Emma Woodhouse: she too, thinks 'a very narrow income has a tendency to contract the mind, and sour the temper. Those who can barely live, and who live perforce in a very small, and generally very inferior, society, may well be illiberal and cross'. At bottom, Forster's response to the Basts is the same as hers to the poor cottagers of Highbury: 'These are the sights, Harriet, to do one good'. . . . (p. 229)

That Forster's concern for the victims of social injustice is

make-believe is evidenced not only by his presentation of the Basts but also by the relationship their story bears to the rest of the novel. What really matters to Forster is not the fate of the Basts but that of the Wilcoxes and Schlegels. The Basts are just a side-show. The imaginative centre of *Howards End* is the division between and reconciliation of its two middle-class families. Whether the reconciliation between Wilcox and Schlegel, 'prose' and 'passion', that Margaret Schlegel works for and the novel welcomes is seen as one between social groups, the entrepreneurs and the intelligentsia, or psychological types, or whether it is read as a command to the individual to lead a whole life, it is equally irrelevant to the problems of the Basts, which are caused by an unfair division of wealth and labour and which cannot be solved without upsetting the life led by the Schlegels and, one might add, the public of *Howards End*. (p. 229-30)

Far from wishing the removal of the injustices the Basts suffer from, *Howards End* wants to see preserved a world that permits the kind of 'personal' life enjoyed by Margaret Schlegel—even if the price is being reconciled to the necessity of the Wilcoxes and the injustices attendant upon the circumstances in which they flourish. Margaret in an argument with her sister Helen says,

> If Wilcoxes hadn't worked and died for thousands of years, you and I couldn't sit here without having our throats cut. There would be no trains, no ships to carry us literary people about in, no fields even. Just savagery. No—perhaps not even that. Without their spirit life might never have moved out of protoplasm. More and more do I refuse to draw my income and sneer at those who guarantee it.

In these remarks, as in so many others, it's hard to sort out the bad faith from what is merely inept. Margaret avoids (and Forster avoids) having to comment on the morality of the social relationships that subsist under capitalism by appealing in a very general way to the desirability of 'progress'; she gives the credit for 'progress' to the entrepreneur class and measures 'progress' by the security of existence enjoyed by 'us literary people'. Her last sentence could be anybody's recognition of what side his bread was buttered on but it's presented to us as the mark of her moral lucidity. Forster puts no distance between himself and this would-be clear-headedness; on the contrary, he shows it triumphing over Helen's muddy-minded liberalism. Helen not only gets worsted in the argument but by the end of the book has come round to 'appreciating' Henry Wilcox just as Margaret does.

Forster *is* critical of the Wilcoxes (that is to say, he often sneers at them) but he is critical not so much of their social role as of their personal inadequacies. Yet were Henry and Charles Wilcox the most loving-hearted and cultivated of men, their economic relationship with the Basts would still be a suspect one. Denying the Wilcoxes any likeable personal qualities isn't a social criticism; it's merely an intellectual's snobbery. It *obscures* the social significance of business, is an evasion of those very issues which, pursued, might have led Forster to see the role of the Schlegels, his rentier figures, as a parasitic one. As it is, he has it both ways. He sneers at the Wilcoxes for lacking the cultivation he's got and admires them for having a certain kind of confidence and power which he's without but which makes his kind of life possible—and admires them for this, moreover, in the language of *Room at the Top:* Charles is 'dark, clean-shaven and seemed accustomed to command', Henry is 'one of those men who know the principal hotel by instinct' and whose 'management' of practical things is always 'excellent'. As people, the Wilcoxes may be unattractive but as representatives of the capitalist spirit they *are,* as Lawrence said in a letter to Forster, 'glorified'.

Forster's failure with the Basts and the social issues their story raises is hardly attributable merely to a lack of first-hand experience. Nor is it necessary to explain it in Marxist terms as a 'necessary' consequence of his 'objective' class position. It seems to me a failure of intelligence and imagination, a failure to be a good enough novelist. Forster's presentation of his middle-class characters is just as coarse as that of his lower-class ones. (pp. 230-31)

Forster's authorial comments regularly show only a perverse pleasure in scoring off his characters. It is one thing to dramatise a character who is 'rubbishy', say Mrs Elton in *Emma,* which requires both that one be a novelist and have a grasp of the possible other case, quite another to invent characters only in order to call them names. (p. 232)

In Forster's account of the Basts his lack of curiosity in the lower classes creates a moral vacuum which is filled by the stock snobberies of a rich man; in his account of the Wilcoxes his lack of curiosity in businessmen creates a vacuum which is filled by the stock snobberies of an intellectual and aesthete. The Basts and the Wilcoxes are unreal. And Forster's sympathy and respect for them are unreal. But the moral failure isn't *additional* to the artistic one. The possession of sufficient moral imagination to put oneself in the place of the unfamiliar and to deal with it generously . . . is the very condition of being able to give it an air of reality.

Forster's failure with his middle-class characters isn't limited, though, to the morally unfamiliar, to the Wilcoxes. He fails just as badly with the Schlegels too. The Schlegel sisters and Mrs Wilcox are just as unreal as the Basts and the other Wilcoxes. Forster can no more give the air of reality to upper-class decency and cultivation than he can to upper-class business or lower-class aspiration. And in this instance the failure to cope with the supposedly familiar, the supposedly humane and sensitive Schlegels, is identical with the failure to cope with the unfamiliar, with the Basts and Wilcoxes. Not himself having a sufficiently sensitive and generous imagination to render the Basts and Wilcoxes decently, how could Forster ever have successfully embodied sensitivity, decency and imagination in the Schlegels? His failure with the Schlegels is not so much a failure to recognise the place of private decencies and personal relations in the larger social context (his is *not* the case of Jane Austen) but a failure to represent them at all, a failure to know what they really are. Forster's grasp of the private life as embodied in the Schlegels and Mrs Wilcox (the very heart of his book) is every bit as unsure as his grasp of business life and the life of the lower classes. There is no more knowledge of love, sympathy, affection, etc. in the portrait of the Schlegels than in 'What I Believe'. There are merely gestures on a larger scale, gestures whose import has equally to be taken on trust, gestures that are hopelessly inadequate for the job they are asked to do. (pp. 232-33)

Put to the test of embodying his 'beliefs' in a novel Forster is too much the creature of his upbringing, and not enough of a novelist, to do more than display, side by side, the aimless good intentions and the incurable snobberies of a no-doubt kindly but fundamentally self-regarding, upper-class English intellectual of the turn of the century. *Howards End* has the interest of a social document but none, that I can see, of the interests of a novel. The most interesting question about it is how it got its reputation, and particularly its reputation as a novel which embodies a spirit concerned with what is 'decent, human, and enlarging in daily conduct'. A large part of the answer must be, presumably, that its American readers are typically innocent of English life, particularly our class system, and are often infatuated with our upper classes, and that its English readers, being exclusively middle-class, find their own world-view mirrored in it. One enjoys reading a fairy-story, the other enjoys looking at a flattering portrait of himself. Both, no doubt, find agreeable the mildness of its social criticism and the generous vagueness of its solutions—only connect, let truer relationships gleam, build that rainbow bridge, and all may be well.

A Passage to India seems to me equally unreal, equally as factitious and unneccessary a novel. Its characters are equally stereotyped and its incidents just as merely illustrative of the stereotyped. Reading it, I have the impression, as new characters and incidents are introduced, of watching a series of *exempla* pass by, of listening to a succession of 'points' being made in illustration of the double thesis that the principled Anglo-Indians are coarse and the unprincipled Indians sensitive. Neither side seems to me to be dealt with with any greater understanding than the Wilcoxes and Basts. Aziz seems to me just as insensitive and prejudiced a portrait of a member of a subject race as Leonard Bast is of a member of a lower class. He even shares Leonard's taste in paintings: 'Aziz in an occidental moment would have hung Maud Goodmans on the walls'. Robust, self-sufficient Indians have as little place in Forster's world as robust, self-sufficient Cockneys. Forster's Indians 'are deprived of their adulthood, live in a perpetual childhood'. The phraseology of his 'positives' in *A Passage to India* is just as empty and unfulfilled as of those in *Howards End:* 'the sanctity of personal relations', 'the fire of good fellowship in their eyes', 'the divine lips of beauty', 'centuries of carnal embracement', 'a sense of unity, of kinship with the heavenly bodies', etc. *A Passage to India* seems to *me* as comprehensively *not* a novel as *Howards End,* fully as much a thing of unrealised intentions. (pp. 234-35)

Duke Maskell, "Mr Forster's Fine Feelings," in The Cambridge Quarterly *(copyright © 1971 by the Editors), Spring, 1971, pp. 222-35.*

The publication in late 1971 of E. M. Forster's long-withheld novel of homosexuality together with the writer's death in 1970 means that a revaluation of both man and author is in order. The 1960's provided several substantial works of scholarship and criticism and a good range of shorter pieces—testimony to Forster's reputation and continuing impact as a literary, and perhaps spiritual, presence. The emergence of *Maurice* from its Edwardian dormancy puts these works to the test and suggests once more that a figure of such artistic subtlety and comprehensiveness as Forster is not readily delimited by even the best efforts of scholarship. The fine elusive quality in the better novels now more than ever seems to hover about Forster himself; one can only believe the man delightedly foresaw this as not the least part of his legacy. The "Terminal Note" provided by Forster and published with *Maurice* is itself a minor gem. For devotees of Forster's life and career the adventure has only begun. (p. 157)

The revelations in *Maurice* should result in more sensitive and acute readings of the short fiction (for example, "The Story of a Panic"; "Other Kingdom"; "The Story of the Siren") and novels other than those now before us. It should be possible to come somewhat closer to the center of Forster's writings, to locate more nearly the point of balance among societal pressure against homosexual disclosures, Forster's own valuing of restraint and artistic indirection, and the Freudian dimensions operative beyond the novelist's awareness. Where individual fictions, or passages within them, appear to violate or embody inadequately Forster's esthetic, it may well now be possible to come to the reasons. In short, there is much to be hoped for from Forster's posthumous gift. (p. 158)

To see *Maurice* as an undisciplined apologia for its creator's homosexuality or as a work compromised by its "happy ending" into sentimentality is to misunderstand its subject and structure.... *Maurice* is in fact more nearly a novel about the barriers to love in a largely sterile and class-ridden society than it is a description of achieved communion and consummation; if love is to have a chance, it must elude the societal negations which reach out to destroy it. At novel's end Maurice and Alec Scudder are only at the threshold of their relationship; whether or not their love can sustain itself through the years is left to the reader's imagination. This last is perhaps the true subject matter of the homosexual novel, and Forster makes no pretense to it.

The removal into the greenwood as a way of preserving psychic health and the promise of love—and Forster's norm of the personal relationship—is a theme we believe we know a great deal about today; more agonizingly than Forster likely could have sixty years ago, we know both the absolute need for a renewal and the unlikelihood of securing it.... Forster's novel may well be more illuminating for its insight into a declining culture than for its probings of homosexuality.... What we as readers must do is to attempt to make the imaginative leap into the very texture of the late-Edwardian world as Forster gives it and then to respond to the moral and spiritual modulations within this texture. We cannot validly wish ourselves into a *Maurice* somehow disassociated from its temporal birthing, cannot insist upon a voice uncommitted to the givens of syntax and diction.

A major difference between *Maurice* and the other novels is the former's lack of a richly conceived interplay of characters both central and peripheral, both "round" and "flat." It is precisely this omission of a dialectic at once subtle and expansive, "realistic" and spiritually resonant, which constitutes the chief disappointment in *Maurice*.... At their best Forster's characters achieve a largeness which outgrows their allegorical functions, important as these often are, and introduce elements of the vital and the unexpected. We find little enough of this in *Maurice*. The novel centers upon its main character to a degree not found in Forster's other fictions; and although Maurice's two lovers,

Clive Durham and Alec Scudder, are crucial to the action, they do not typically come to us, or engage one another, from within the kind of webbed richness developed in the other novels. With the evolution of Maurice from varying degrees of sexual "normalcy" to the gradual recognition of his own nature, to the final full-bodied commitment to Alec as the driving impetus of the novel, the work advances with a straightforwardness foreign to Forster's previously published fictions. The use of the enriching episode or complicating action is at a minimum. Unlike the evocations of Italy in the Italian novels, the treatment of Greece in *Maurice* is subordinated almost entirely to plot convenience. As well, Forster's superb capacity to evoke a sense of place and mood, notably in *Howards End*, remains in abeyance; neither Cambridge nor the estate at Penge are captured concretely and convincingly in *Maurice*. One may say that the artistry of *Maurice* is marked more by directness and economy than by richness and involution.... *Maurice* is a line drawing and not a painting, so to speak, and must be adjudged on its own terms. Or, venturing elsewhere for a metaphor, one may say that the novel proceeds more nearly by means of rhythm and melody than by harmony and counterpoint—the way of Indian rather than Western music.

Given the conventions and restrictions Forster employs in *Maurice*, I would suggest that the novel possesses the artistic vigor and integrity sufficient to place it a shade above *Where Angels Fear to Tread* and perhaps *A Room with a View* and somewhere below *The Longest Journey*. *Maurice* appears to possess a greater artistic finish than *The Longest Journey* but lacks the largeness and vision of the latter. That *Maurice* will ever be found to challenge either *Howards End* or *A Passage to India* seems unlikely indeed. What Forster says about the true test of method (point of view) is applicable to evaluation of the work of fiction as a whole: it resolves itself "into the power of the writer to bounce the reader into accepting what he says." And though authorial intrusion is at times present, I find that *Maurice* wins through to suspension of disbelief. We know from Forster's disclosures in the "Terminal Note" and from other sources that the choice of subject matter in the novel went to the very center of the man's being, was the most sensitive he could have considered. In the fictions given to the public in his lifetime, Forster's felt need for concealing his homosexuality provided in all likelihood a disciplining force which facilitated the gaining of the distancing and detachment essential to the artist. From the evidence of the novels we know how successfully Forster the man subordinated himself to the obligations of the artist. Not always of course; one thinks for example of problems with characterization of Mr. Emerson in *A Room with a View*, Gino of *Where Angels Fear to Tread*, and Rickie Elliot in *The Longest Journey*. (pp. 158-61)

Forster's strategy for securing distancing in *Maurice* is revealed in the "Terminal Note": "In Maurice I tried to create a character who was completely unlike myself or what I supposed myself to be: someone handsome, healthy, bodily attractive, mentally torpid, not a bad business man and rather a snob." This statement shows acutely just how far Forster believed he had to go in order to gain necessary detachment. Being deeply in love, how best to write perceptively about love; being a homosexual, how best to hold one's self in abeyance in order to image forth the truth of homosexuality and not violate the high ends of art. The answer is this: the writer holds his protagonist at bay by drawing into him some of the very elements which negate his attractiveness. Thus we find a Maurice who is a good bit of a philistine and something of a Wilcox, who reminds us of Sawston and all that that implies, and who leads us to Forster's words as to the "slowness" of the "typical Englishman," for example. In short, a homosexual protagonist more nearly a John Bull than an apostle of Bloomsbury! And the strategy is effective; for the most part the tonalities and ironies surrounding Maurice prevent any sentimental collapse of character into author, any special pleading for homosexuality. Similarly, a careful distancing between Maurice and reader is sustained. The reader is not permitted any easy empathy with the main character; indeed he is not encouraged to like young Hall very much until the action is well under way. It is a mark of the finesse and control in this novel that the reader's identification with the protagonist is so tightly bound up with imagistic and thematic unfolding; there is relatively little "unearned" emotion within the pages of *Maurice*. . . . One should add that a price is paid in *Maurice* for its tightly controlled and thinned-down esthetic posture: the novel does not achieve the "difficult rhythm" admired by Forster. Few novels ever do achieve this, one may well argue. Forster demonstrated that he was capable of it in *A Passage to India* and possibly in *Howards End*. *Maurice* suggests something of an over-reaction in the direction of the scrupulous, perhaps; it strikes one as being so consciously written a novel that elements of grandeur and elusiveness have difficulty abiding therein. . . . The beauty offered by *Maurice* is rather obviously a circumscribed one but it is real.

In *Maurice* as in the other novels Forster's imperative of the personal relationship, the need for a mutuality of feeling and understanding which transcends the formidable and dehumanizing barriers of modern society, lies at the thematic center. But Forster well perceived that the introduction of a homosexual protagonist made severe demands on the general reader; were the latter made to accept the main character's special bent too quickly or insistently, he almost certainly would recoil in suspicion and doubt before completing a reading of the book. Thus the protagonist must not appear to be favored by the author; the reader must be won over slowly if he is to accept Maurice long enough to realize that his homosexuality is a valid instancing of the human and the personal. The reader is introduced to Maurice in a low-keyed, almost off-hand manner; Maurice is at first simply "Hall, one of the older boys" soon to be dispatched to public school at Sunnington. Maurice's school chums believe him to be brave, but this is a "great mistake—he wasn't brave: he was afraid of the dark. But no one knew this." . . . One should note that the last quotation serves not only to deflate Maurice but to introduce imagery of darkness, a major motif of the novel. (pp. 161-62)

Ironies operate through much of the novel to facilitate Maurice's distancing. The depth which comes gradually to the young man's personality is carefully counterbalanced by descriptions of his shallowness and foolishness. . . .

We know that Forster's other novels cannot be adequately described in terms of a narrowly conceived realism; in them we find symbolic infusion, stylistic and mimetic heightening, and the authentic elusiveness of spirit. It should not be surprising, therefore, that *Maurice* also flies above the literal and the earth bound. (p. 163)

An excellent way of gaining insight into the style and tonality of *Maurice* is to turn to a novel written within several years of it, Max Beerbohm's *Zuleika Dobson*. With qualifications, what Beerbohm did with Oxford Forster did with the Cambridge portions of his own novel. The presiding point of view toward the action, the stylizing of the characters, the verbal rhythms, show interesting similarities. And one remembers that Forster, in discussing *Zuleika* as an example of "fantasy," expressed considerable admiration for Beerbohm's novel as "a highly accomplished and superbly written book whose spirit is farcical." The theme of *Zuleika* "is treated with a mixture of realism, wittiness, charm and mythology" by Beerbohm, Forster argues (*Aspects of the Novel* . . .). The element of wit in *Maurice* is subdued (but effective), and the mythological dimension is largely transmuted into a natural piety; but the similarities otherwise are many, and they help us into the ambience of Edwardian England.

Forster's artistry is further evidenced in *Maurice* by skillful use of tonal variety. For example, Chapter Thirteen has something of the idyll about it as Maurice and Clive abandon Cambridge for the day and lose themselves in the countryside; the young men are able for the time to put aside the rigidities of societal forms and converse naturally and with a degree of spontaneity. Chapter Sixteen shows the two friends together at Penge and effectively contrasts the restraints and decorum of the household with the intimacies exchanged by Clive and Maurice in the delicious privacy of the study. . . . Chapter Twenty-Five brings together elements of farce and melodrama and balances them astutely against the intensities of Maurice's passion. Chapter Thirty-Seven leads the reader more directly into Maurice's growing desperation and need for a responsive personal relationship while maintaining careful distancing through its style. Chapter Forty-Three, one of the best executed sections in the novel, blends imagistic and thematic energies with the near-farcical in a manner which leaves little doubt of Forster's artistry and control. The Forty-Sixth and final chapter ties motifs and ideas together in an economical and persuasive manner; crucially, the protagonist of the concluding pages is a figure who has earned his worth and interest for the reader.

Much of the validity of *Maurice* derives from the fact that the homosexual interest at the novel's center are not made into self-justifying ends but rather are tied closely into three major concerns of Forster's thought. These are the belief in the vital importance of personal relationships; the critique of the spiritual inadequacies of modern society; and the belief in the regenerative powers of nature. Forster's great themes are not explored in *Maurice* with the incisiveness or richness found in his best fictions, but they nevertheless are effectively and suggestively presented. The major patterns of imagery in the novel (those of the heart, darkness, and sleep) operate so as to give concrete force both to thematic statement and resonance. Additionally they complement the distancing techniques discussed above and effectively mediate Forster's deep personal involvement with his subject matter and protagonist and the disciplined evocations of the successful work of art. Forster's command of himself and his art is superbly demonstrated in his containment of his protagonist within the imagistic dialectic. From an initial fear of the "darkness" within both himself and world, Maurice evolves toward increased understanding and then to a final profound commitment to his "dark" lover Alec.

Forster shows us that the normative relationship must be based upon a mutual awareness of the depths and fullness of the principals; "sleep" and "darkness" are vital to the health and growth of the "heart." Both Clive and the major institutions of the society have sought to withdraw into the sterile "light" of the class structure, the narrowly rational, the ego-driven. Forster's words about birth and death as the "two darknesses" within which man moves are not without relevance here *(Aspects of the Novel. . .).* At the novel's end Clive remains cut off from both his authentic selfhood and reality (nature's rhythms); in the "stupidity of his heart," Clive fears the evening darkness—even as he perceives that Maurice has become "essential night." . . . Forster provides further articulation of the immense gulf separating the former lovers in the minor motif of the night-blooming primrose.

Maurice's imagistic ties not only with the "heart" and passion but also with the vitalities of nature validate his role as symbol of life's energies. Maurice will not marry or produce children, but he likely will achieve a fecund spiritual relationship with Alec; in contrast there is little to hope for from Clive. Dante notwithstanding, Alec and Maurice will come far closer to mutuality and happiness in the green-wood than to the retribution of endless circularity; and the rain that falls on the pair will be wet enough. As if in defiance of the *Inferno,* Maurice and Alec earlier leave "the enormous and overheated" British Museum and pass "the library, supposed catholic," seeking out the rain and darkness. . . . The socially conditioned shame and alienation from self which have worked upon Maurice for so long a time begin to give way. Yet—in the most perceptive moment of the novel—all is not as it should be: ideally the life of society and the "life of the earth" . . . would be one; there would be no necessity to flee to the greenwood, to become an "outlaw" as Maurice and Alec must. To win through to spiritual wholeness, to the "heart," at the price of repudiating societal existence is to pay a heavy price indeed. Forster leaves no doubt that the bifurcations of head and heart, convention and passion, are spiritually debilitating; and, again, not simply because they militate against homosexual expression but more importantly because they threaten all personal relationships. In Clive, Anne Woods (the surname suggests an ironic refraction of the greenwood), and the vacuous Mr. Ducie, Forster sketches in the distorted humanity emanating from a decadent society. Ducie's echo of the *Pippa Passes* refrain—"It all hangs together—all—and God's in his heaven, All's right with the world" . . . reinforces the point. Not by chance one of Clive's sisters carries the name of Browning's young innocent. Through these allusions Forster suggests that the society encountered by Maurice is no less brutal and false than that surrounding the poet's Pippa.

Maurice offers yet further evidence of Forster's high commitment to artistic discipline and excellence; the homosexual themes and concerns put both man and artist to a severe test and Forster met the challenge well indeed. *Maurice* is not without flaws, but these are minor and do not threaten the overall success of the novel. In the final analysis, I would argue, we need make no more concessions to this novel than to many others conceived and written in a period so remote from our own; I believe that *Maurice* will hold its own in the critical battles which are certain to swirl about it. For there are moments when even the rhythms and vision of *A Passage to India* seem to rise

from the page and one knows that the essential Forster is not far away. (pp. 164-67)

> *Douglass Bolling, "The Distanced Heart: Artistry in E. M. Forster's 'Maurice',"* in Modern Fiction Studies *(copyright © 1974, by Purdue Research Foundation, West Lafayette, Indiana, U.S.A.), Summer, 1974, pp. 157-67.*

'Here was a protest and a feeble one, and the more congenial for being feeble', said Forster of Prufrock, and his novel of 1924, *A Passage to India,* suggests more fully how feebleness can seem to Forster like an unexorbitant bit of honesty. For in this novel the experience and dismaying surprise that Forster has stored up for the reader is to approach the India of the English Raj through Mrs Moore and Miss Quested with a set of good, tolerant, liberal feelings whose inadequacy is then shown up. Humanity, it seems—Christianized or Moslem—has not quite enough stuff of good will to patch over multiplicities, egotism, or chaos, but whether that shows us something about the great universe or, more likely, Forster's easily-wearied, preconceived sense of sympathies between people, is not clearly displayed till after the events that follow the Marabar Caves incident. Earlier, through Fielding's eyes, at the tea-party fiasco, we have seen the break-down of liberal good feeling, with Aziz 'shoddy and odious', Mrs Moore and Adela Quested 'both silly, and he himself and Heaslop both decorous on the surface, but detestable really, and detesting each other'. But it is not until Adela and Fielding meet again, in reconciliation after being on opposite sides during the trial of Aziz, that we have such an explicit statement from the author to make it plain that it is the inadequacy not just of 'good will' but of human 'personality' that the failure of feeling, the break-up, has revealed.

> A friendliness, as of dwarfs shaking hands, was in the air. . . . [Their] words were followed by a curious backwash, as though the universe had displaced itself to fill up a tiny void, or as though they had seen their own gestures from an immense height—dwarfs talking, shaking hands and assuring each other that they stood on the same footing of insight.

We would be wrong to think that Forster offers a view of his characters similar to the perspective from which Eliot's wit presents Prufrock ('Do I dare / Disturb the universe?'). Dwarfs they may be, and impoverished is the meaning of human kinship and sympathies, but what this represents, as Forster's novel later shows, is not an adverse judgement on the paltry or enfeebled state of relationships but the reconstituting, in an emotionally minor form, of the outmoded liberality whose failure is signalized by the decline and death of Mrs Moore. . . . [What] the movement of Forster's novel really suggests, however, as the nonchalance of Hamidullah and Fielding over Mrs Moore is succeeded by holy unfastidiousness of Professor Godbole in the 'Temple' section, is that the minor form of inadequate response is the smaller enactment of the diffuser, more disillusionable failure to feel on a larger scale. A disappointed compassion for general mankind, all the thin-spread humanism in shreds, comes to look in this novel very much like its smaller version, the sterile lack of feeling for the particular human being. . . . Godbole represents Forster's dubious sense of humanistic inadequacy as it re-emerges to gain for itself all the loose religiose credit attaching easily to one whose failure or meagreness can be made to look like an almost universality of embrace. The dead Mrs Moore becomes part of Godbole's embracing vision, not as a remembered 'personality', but an object among many in his call to God to come. 'This was all he could do. How inadequate! But each according to his own capacities, and he knew that his own were small.' Paltriness and universality are deviously interchangeable, and by the same hidden aversions in Forster that cause him to invent Godbole to embody the duality, so it is his humanistic-religiose joke to see Mrs Moore mistakenly (yet rightly) transformed by popular legend into a goddess and to settle carefully for a view of the ceremonies and reconciliation-in-collision by Indians and English on the lake which is emotionally not defined at all: . . . 'Looking back at the great blur of the last twenty-four hours, no man could say where was the emotional centre of it, any more than he could locate the heart of a cloud.' At the 'emotional centre', blurred over, one suspects, is an unexamined aversion towards the involving demand in human relations. . . . (pp. 6-7)

> *Richard Swigg, in* PN Review (© PN Review 1977), 1977.

* * *

FOWLES, John 1926-

Fowles, a British novelist, short story writer, and poet, depicts the struggle of the individual to overcome society's pressure to conform. This often takes form in the machinations of a representative of the *hoi polloi*, who attempts to confine and control the protagonist. *The Collector* and *The Magus*, both of which were made into movies, are examples of his fiction of manipulation. (See also *CLC*, Vols. 1, 2, 3, 4, 6, and *Contemporary Authors*, Vols. 5-8, rev. ed.)

The Magus is an allegory of the manner and meaning of the search for self-realization. To convey this process in Nicholas Urfe, who is both the narrator and protagonist of the novel, and to convey to the reader his own need for the quest, the novel makes use of ideas and images drawn chiefly from four different models of experience: from mythology, psychology, philosophy, and mysticism. The mythical pattern is that of the quest, return, and discovery, with a consistent analogue in the metaphors of place and travel which shape the three-part structure of the plot. The frequent parallels of Nicholas to the great heroes of mythology and literature are obvious, as is the maintenance of the image of the maze. The most important psychological model for Nicholas's experience is the Jungian process of individuation, of "becoming an 'individual'," of "becoming one's own self," "'coming to selfhood' or 'self-realization'." In this model the maze comes to represent the unconscious, and Nicholas's struggle consists in a confrontation with his own inner center. The philosophical way is that of Kierkegaard and Sartre, the novel being profoundly existential in both word and deed. Both existentialism and Jungian psychology stress the need for the knowledge and acceptance of self, though in one the self is created and in the other it is discovered. At times in *The Magus* the two models of experience coalesce in the same passages. . . . Lastly, the occult way is revealed by the process of becoming a magus, an image which, we are reminded by the epigraph to the novel, comes from the Tarot, but which also appears as one of the archetypes of the collective uncon-

scious. The Tarot teaches the connection of the magician with the divine, while for Jung 'magical' seems merely another term for 'psychic'. Nevertheless, the mystical and the psychoanalytic metaphors of the self are here closely related. (pp. 916-17)

Fowles has managed to involve the reader in [the] "mysterious present and concrete feeling of excitement," thus making his fantastic story credible. The sense "of being in a situation where anything still might happen" is not even relieved at the conclusion, which, we are told, is but "another mystery." . . . [The] fact that the novel leaves the reader with a question suggests that its structure is designed to enact the truth it proclaims. The emphasis of the novel is quite clearly on beginnings, not endings; on the moment of choice which initiates action, not on the natural or determined outcome of that action. It is the quest that the novel promotes, not the destination; living in the labyrinth, not finding a way out. . . .

One of Fowles's major achievements lies in having endowed the ancient mythic pattern with a structure of meaning in the terms of contemporary existentialism and depth psychology, creating a mythic novel which speaks with urgency and power to a contemporary audience. (p. 919)

> *Barry N. Olshen, "John Fowles's 'The Magus': An Allegory of Self-Realization," in* Journal of Popular Culture (*copyright © 1976 by Ray B. Browne*), *Spring, 1976, pp. 916-25.*

Consideration of *The Magus* properly begins with *The Aristos*, a book of philosophical aphorisms written in the years during which Fowles wrote the novel, although later heavily revised. (I use the original 1964 version as representing Fowles at the time of *The Magus*.) It is the quarry from which the fiction's philosophy is mined, though nothing of fictional art is suggested in its bare and somewhat awkward reasonings. *The Aristos* is a peculiar book, not only in substance but in motive: it seems outlandish that a gifted young author should want to publish his notebook and express a number of traditional and semi-original ideas about life and the world in 246 pages. The aphorisms are modeled on the surviving fragments of the pre-Socratic philosophers, particularly those of Heraclitus. Such early practitioners could set down an entire philosophy (granted its difficulties of interpretation) in what amounts now only to a few pages—presumably because they stood at the beginning of the Western world-view. In taking up this stance while placed near the end of the Western tradition, Fowles is asserting a need to go back to origins, to reassert elementary ideas.

Fowles specifies, moreover, that he is not going to talk about the world but about *his* world: he subtitles the book *A Self-Portrait in Ideas*. This mind emerges as a synthesis of surprising contradictions: it presents the image of a socialist, humanist, atheist existentialist with strong aristocratic and individualist tendencies—rather of the Ayn Rand sort. The author emerges as a man who wants to see the social order rationalized and yet sees the deep irrationalities which are its splendor and misery. He is also a man with a particular gripe against the modern age, as an age of overcivilization and of over-kill, but who sees its spectacular possibilities for mental and personal liberation. As in *The Magus*, the urgent fiat posed by *The Aristos* is "thou shalt be free,'' and, as we come to discover, that is the most out-rageously difficult demand that could be made of us. Yet our special position as inheritors of all the ages gives us a strong chance to claim such freedom, and the novel applies the myriad arts of the West to the task of freeing a repre-sentative modern man. (pp. 298-99)

Fowles's vision of the absent or dead god of modern theol-ogy and poetic tradition is a humanized one. In *The Ma-gus,* a man has grasped that god—whatever his ontological status may be—leaves man free but that men insist on erecting a divine governance in order to escape from their own possibility of freedom. This man decides to play god for the men of his day, commanding them to be free by first asserting and then gradually withdrawing his control of their lives. That is the God-game, as played in the novel. It rests on the notion that a man can teach another man to be free by playing god to him and then revealing that he is not a god, that there is no god and that each man must be his own god.

The Aristos further enlarges on Fowles's views of life and the after-life and on the relation between them that might be called "myth." It is only in the modern world that we have, potentially, the capacity to make this life—insofar as it is a bodily affair—decently human for all. "The great myth of the afterlife has stood between us and reality" . . . both as a confession of man's incapacities and as a stumbling-block to his possession of his physical world. . . . Yet perhaps we can use . . . [myths and rites] . . . to organize the mystery of the world we *do* live in. *The Magus* is a retelling of clas-sical myth—the Orpheus legend—according to a structure derived from the presumed pattern of the "mystery" reli-gions. These cults aimed at making the Orphic legends op-erative in eschatological salvation; in *The Magus* an indi-vidual is morally saved by going through the process established in Orphic religion.

Why stop with Orphism, since it is instrumental, not doc-trinal? Fowles uses in this educational process a wide vari-ety of occult lore, from the Tarot deck to the mystifications of de Sade. It is never clear how much one approach is to be believed—that is, all are to be played out and known by their fruits in personal growth. Such syncretism leaves Fowles open to the reviewers' charges that he has made a modish bouillabaisse of his mythical sources. Despite the enormous investment in mythical and other strains of im-agery that flow into *The Magus,* Fowles's educational art is ultimately quite simple. He himself scorns avant-garde mystifications in other novelists and poets . . . and has ex-pressed his approach to art in an account of a trip to the mythical realm of the Muses: "I climbed Parnassus once, and between the mundane village of Arachova and the lovely summit, quite as lovely as the poets have always had it to be, there is nothing but a slope; no abysm, no gulf, no place where wings are necessary." . . . The realm of art is . . . part of the human, not the occult, scene. Not only the artist but the ordinary man who is the subject of his art needs to discover this humanly accessible, natural realm. The hero and heroine of *The Magus* are shown making the same trip and experiencing Parnassus in an eminently mun-dane and winning way. It is not a sheer cliff, Alison and Nicholas discover, but a long climb. Man is on the moun-tain with the muses, with the great poets, with those who live at the top: there are no secrets of the trade, only the various forms of mental blindness by which men manage to

obscure from themselves their own freedom and the bounti-fulness of their world. (pp. 300-01)

The . . . novel—like life itself—is to be conceived not as a regression to an occult, religious or mythic world-view, but as a symbolic experience, in which man learns to interpret the signs given by the world. The artist is not to descend to mystification, but he can learn to distil the core of truth from the traditional forms of self-obfuscation that men have chosen. The magic is useful only as something to be stripped away, and eventually we are to transcend those forms and come into the harsh light of reality where we can learn to live. Yet there will remain a sense of mystery, not added by the magus-figures, but built into the world and adding to its attraction for us.

We see from the outset that Fowles wants to initiate his reader in the same provocative and artificially mystifying way chosen by the magus-figure who initiates the novel's hero. (pp. 301-02)

The imagery surrounding the dramatic process enacted in the novel does not point . . . to a pattern of education through torment, through successive encounters with suffering—either one's own or that of others—although the hero gets a full treatment in these respects. It is rather a pattern of education through rebirth, returning to sources, discovering the meaning of one's name (Urfe, Orphée), and reordering the past—developing new transactions with what is already given in the self but not yet fulfilled. The or-phaned hero acquires more intense feelings toward father- and mother-surrogates than he ever enjoyed with his par-ents; he learns how to love the woman who had already been given him, and whom he had let slip away; he comes to enjoy the freedom which he had always claimed and never exercised. (p. 303)

Returning to origins and discovering one's name and race traditionally requires a journey in quest, and another pas-sage marked for the hero in an idiom he will presumably understand is from Pound's Canto XLVII:

> Yet must thou sail after knowledge
> Knowing less than drugged beasts. phthengometha
>   thasson.

The archetype, with its reference to Odysseus, marks the striving of men from the ancient Greeks to the modern, the effort to return home and come into one's own. Moreover, the advice is that of Pound's Tiresias, who challenges Odysseus' state of bondage to Circe, sex, and present pleasures; it is an injunction to deny oneself in order to find oneself, to lift the veil of illusion and see what is there, to become fully a man in raising oneself above the animal. All these things the hero undertakes to do in choosing to pur-sue the sender of these messages; source-hunting here be-comes a parody of the quest, and the interpretation of one's own nature becomes an advanced problem in literary criti-cism. (p. 304)

Nicholas' scepticism, while it is one of the hindrances of his education, is also an appropriate stance before a world ultimately without gods. Man must live sceptically, in doubt, and attuned to the metaphoric illusoriness of myth and other cultural modes, as Fowles has indicated in *The Aristos.* . . . As Nicholas comes to recognize more of the behind-the-scenes trumpery of the magus' artifice, he is not the less but the more ready to acknowledge the home truths delivered in the course of its mystifications. Revelation and demystification come packaged together, just as truth and illusion usually come to us inter-twined; sometimes by conscious design the illusion can act as symbolic medium for the truth, but only when our scepticism is trained to operate selectively upon it.

While the tools of literary criticism are never far from hand in *The Magus,* the art most dramatically employed is that of the theater. Conchis is a master not only of interpretation but scenario—an "Empson of the event," as Nicholas says. . . . He is mountebank, impresario, master of revels, *psychopompos,* and movie director, if not puppeteer. While these images have been used to describe Fowles the novelist in his manipulation of character, Conchis has only scorn for fiction: "The novel is dead. As dead as alchemy. . . . Why should I struggle through hundreds of pages of fabrication to reach half a dozen very little truths?" . . . Incorporating Fowles's parody not only of his own art but also of contemporary reviewers' clichés, the passage is significant in mingling the arts in which Conchis is engaged: fiction, alchemy, and dramaturgy are all called upon, but the last, being most kinetic and efficient for education, is most in evidence. Conchis also comments on Forster's dictum, "Only connect": "Fiction is the worst form of connection" . . .; and Nicholas sums up his position as follows: *"Words are for facts. Not fiction."* . . . The vulgar interpretation of this position would be that language in fiction is at a second remove from reality and that reality must be imitated or expressed directly in action to have cathartic effect. . . . The ultimate comedy of Conchis' position is, of course, that it is spoken inside a novel; Fowles is not about to abandon his art, although he may chafe at his bondage to it and curse its limitations. (pp. 306-07)

One of the assumptions of [Conchis'] dramaturgy is that all the world's a stage and all men actors—the only choice being to play one's own play or another man's. Yet this assumption is comprehended in a more basic one: if role-playing is seen to be a universal phenomenon, it becomes part of the foundations of the world and thereby a means of access to them. The ancient ties between religion and drama are here reasserted, as Nicholas' participation in a series of mock-events is given meaning by their approximation to religious acts designed for the illumination, testing, and strengthening of the soul.

Yet Conchis' educative ritual bears the suspect odor that it does partly because of its absorption in theatrical modes. There is barely an effort made to prevent Nicholas from sensing "an air of stage management, of the planned and rehearsed. . . ." The ground for Conchis' self-revealing technique is his intention to demystify, to reveal the ultimate absence of gods and other mythic equivalents of stage-managers for human life; to do so, he must implant a distaste for manipulation on the occasions where Nicholas is manipulated for his own advancement. But there is also a flair for the theater in Conchis—fulfilling his role of magus as "Magician, or juggler, the caster of the dice and mountebank in the world of vulgar trickery," as the epigraph from Waite's *Tarot* has it. . . . It is with evident relish that he pursues his "meta-theater," in which his characters are allowed to be *"mysteries to him as well"*—though he names his new mode with a conventional term in calling it a "comedy." . . . But in the end this imitation of the Baroque masque . . . , with its deities, spectacles, and machinery, is

returned to reality, or at least to the realm of the fictions by which men live: "The masque is a metaphor" . . . , as Conchis tells Nicholas. Through his response as audience and in his interpretive powers as actor, the hero will learn to be his own playwright, eventually composing the script of the final scene in which he wins his freedom and his beloved. (p. 308)

[The] second phase is marked by greater suffering (much of it sadomasochistic) for the novice and greater freedom in the means employed: Nicholas must not only know but feel, so that he can act on his knowledge. . . . [The] connection of the education with the Orphic myth behind the Eleusinian mysteries becomes explicit at this point. Since Orpheus, despite his derelictions, had passed through the underworld and gathered its lore, his myth was readily connected with the eschatological instruction at Eleusis and in many other cults in the ancient world. Similarly, since Alison had been able to part from Nicholas without looking back, in contrast to his weak-willed behavior throughout their affair, she becomes an inspiration for the defective will of the latter-day Orpheus, who must be trained to love well and to recover his beloved. The main theme of the later Orphic cults, liberation from the cycle of reincarnation by learning the appropriate mystic lore, becomes in this demythologized version the pursuit of liberation from the bondage of egoism and of modernity, and the discovery of oneself, one's world, and the possibility of existential freedom in it. To anticipate: the final phase of Nicholas' learning will take him to a woman who identifies herself as a Demeter-figure, a mother who underwrites his rebirth, an earth that he has come to know and possess. The connection of Conchis' mysteries with the Eleusinian worship of Demeter will be fulfilled at that point. But first Nicholas must learn more of his world. To teach him the reality of the land in which he has been content to respond to the beauty of landscape only, he must be brought by elaborate means to confront its people and their historical experience. . . . Not only is Nicholas brought face to face with the reality of human wretchedness and the bare fact of pain, he is invited to suffer the doubt and claim the freedom involved in Conchis' choice of the principle of *Eleutheria,* even at the cost of immense loss of life. (The later re-enactment of this choice, when Nicholas is offered the chance to flagellate his tormentor during the disintoxication scene, is a somewhat formalized occasion for applying the lessons learned earlier.) The only danger of this remarkable sequence is that it brings recent history so movingly forward that it tends to diminish the universality of the hero's experience; there is even a hint of the tendentious in Conchis' summary of the story: ". . . the event I have told you is the only European story. It is what Europe is. A Colonel Wimmel. A rebel without a name. An Anton torn between them, killing himself when it is too late." . . . Fowles has here introduced the side of modern experience which Anglo-Saxon literature has failed most flagrantly to confront.

The horror of the war and the supposed calamity of Alison's death bring Nicholas to the next stage of the mysteries, the most elaborate sequence of costumed masque-scenes and the most flamboyant sadomasochistic fantasies. It is all a Black Mass, a descent into the underworld. . . . The experience and its personae are intentionally obscurantist, yet have the effect of an initiation. . . . (pp. 310-11)

The most obvious parallel to the educational process conducted through role-playing is the therapeutic technique of psychodrama. While the ends of growth and liberation and the means of projection and catharsis are in many ways similar in the psychiatric and the fictional dramas, the distinguishing element here is artistry—and, perhaps, humor. Conchis is concerned to create a set of theatrical forms, coyly alluding to their artificiality but at the same time making them highly finished and refined. This consideration is expressed in the brilliant parody of a medical demonstration which occupies much of the climactic disintoxication sequence. As the actors run through their roles of experimental clinicians—parading the jargon and expertise of the psychiatric clan in wonderful style—their director makes a point of acknowledging the esthetic quality of their experiment. . . . Other elements of the disintoxication process point to the artful element at work even in this moment of apparent scientific objectivity, for example, the degradation of the "subject" follows the forms of the similar scene in the "Circe" section of *Ulysses,* in which Bloom is classified and flayed by psychiatric and medical categories. . . . (pp. 311-12)

In this sequence, *The Magus* approaches nearest to the realm of pop culture—so close indeed that it may be said to justify the scorn that the well-behaved critical mind will be likely to display toward it. (p. 312)

The sensation of being left alone with one's freedom is powerfully summarized at this conclusion to the second part of the novel: "What was I? . . . I dismissed most of the Freudian jargon of the trial; but all my life I had tried to turn life into fiction, to hold reality away; always I had acted as if a third person was watching and listening and giving me marks for good or bad behavior—a god like a novelist, to whom I turned, like a character with the power to please, the sensitivity to feel slighted, the ability to adapt himself to whatever he believed the novelist-god wanted." . . . The power of this passage derives from its reflex action on the novelist himself: as the hero learns to reject life lived as a character in fiction—a metaphor of all cultural constructs for a non-existent external controlling force—so the novelist who writes the novel reveals at last that it is only a construct, and a particularly pernicious one in its power to delude the reader, though a necessary deviation on the path to truth. (From this standpoint, Fowles's later success, *The French Lieutenant's Woman,* is merely a series of footnotes to this keen perception of the mysteries and banalities of his art.) (p. 313)

Given only the bare materials of the earth for his salvation, acting out the pattern of his life as he alone can conceive it, acting *as if* there were gods or other spectators out there (there are, for they are we), the hero must become no longer actor but stage-director, the character his own novelist. . . . (p. 314)

Avrom Fleishman, "'The Magus' of the Wizard of the West," in Journal of Modern Literature *(© Temple University 1976), April, 1976, pp. 297-314.*

Jamesian in sensibility, [Fowles] has avoided both conventional rosiness and absurdist blackness, placing his tales either in the realm of the faintly fabulous—as in *The Collector* (1963), *The Magus* (1966), and much of *The Ebony Tower* (1974)—or in a time not our own—as in *The*

French Lieutenant's Woman (1969), set in the Victorian Era. There's no doubt though that Fowles's hopes for us run high: His heroes are tested not for ordinary decency but for the depth of their consciousness and the grace of their morality. As for sentimentality, Fowles's rigorous intellect, his yen for myth and artifice, and his elegant reflectiveness haven't lent themselves to it.

Now Fowles has written *Daniel Martin,* a "realistic" novel set in the present with a daringly happy ending. Daniel Martin, in the thick of what he self-mockingly calls "male menopause," is a very successful, very disenchanted British scriptwriter living in Los Angeles, away from his roots. He would qualify as Fowles's ideal reader and perhaps even alter ego, since at the novel's end the narrator calls himself Daniel's own "ill-concealed ghost." . . .

[The] plot could easily become a soap opera or a sentimental movie perhaps entitled *The Second Time Around.* But its potential for triviality is exactly what Fowles seems to enjoy outwitting.

The novel's weight lies in Daniel Martin's sensibility, the prism through which all events are filtered. As an added twist, Fowles makes him an aspiring novelist: Screenplays always "betray the real thing." Dan wants to write "the real history of what I am"—Fowles's novel, of course, meaning to be just that. But, echoing Fowles, he feels that fashion dictates that "only a tragic, absurdist, black-comic view . . . of humanity" is considered artistically "serious," and from such a perspective the events of Martin's own life fall short. One night, however, Dan has a moment of epiphany: "To hell with cultural fashion; to hell with elitist guilt; to hell with existentialist nausea; and above all, to hell with the imagined that does not say, not only in, but behind the images, the real."

If Fowles were totally comfortable with this insight, *Daniel Martin* would be thoroughly brilliant. Instead, he seems to fear that his sentiment might be mistaken for sentimentality, particularly in this, his least stylized, least distanced novel; so Fowles defends himself and diffuses the novel's power with red-herring digressions, a syntax that occasionally obscures meaning, and far too much intellectual muscle flexing. . . .

To maintain the standard illusion that the novel isn't a novel, [Dan's] Scottish girlfriend is allowed to wonder "Who'd ever go for a character called Daniel Martin?" For his part, Dan is permitted to compare the "real" lives around him with fictional lives in Beckett, Jane Austen, Kafka, and Samuel Richardson. And, presumably because of the preoccupation with the objective versus the subjective, there is an otherwise pointless shifting from third person to first person and back again.

But nothing in *Daniel Martin* couldn't have been fixed by a good editor, and its flaws dwindle in the face of the informed humanism Fowles has aimed for and fundamentally achieves. The closing lines of the novel deliberately redirect us back again to its first line and its theme: "Whole sight; or all the rest is desolation." . . . As Fowles implied in *The Aristos,* literary despair often seems more knowing, more comprehensive than joy. But in *Daniel Martin,* John Fowles, without either sentimentalizing or overlooking, succeeds in conveying an affirmative vitality that can hold its own against bleakness any day. Its vision is one even Daniel Martin would not be embarrassed by.

Elizabeth Stone, "Put on a Happy Face,"
in The Village Voice *(reprinted by permis-*
sion of The Village Voice; *copyright © by*
The Village Voice, Inc., 1977), September
12, 1977, p. 41.

John Fowles's reputation as a highly readable and resourceful storyteller has carried with it the hint that as a
novelist he was slightly suspect—that books as tricky and
teasing as "The Collector" (1963), "The Magus" (1966)
and the rightfully admired "The French Lieutenant's
Woman" (1969) somehow lacked the deeper sincerities and
purposes of more serious fiction. Such an account will no
longer do, if it ever did. This new, long, ambitious novel
["Daniel Martin"] must be judged his best piece of work to
date and is a masterly fictional creation, dense with fact. In
its overall tone and sympathetically critical engagement
with its hero, "Daniel Martin" follows along naturally from
the title story in Fowles's collection "The Ebony Tower."
. . . And, as in that story, the themes and ideas of this new
novel only emerge through the voice of a narrator of immense tact and charm.

The charm needs to be emphasized and can be heard
whether the narrator is introducing English country curates
or American film producers. As with Fitzgerald's Nick
Carraway in "The Great Gatsby," one feels good about
listening to this humorous, quiet, carefully observant voice
speaking in a range of tones, ironically or directly, about
the look on a person's face or the kind of shirt he's wearing, as well as about larger matters—political, cultural or
sexual. Yet just because the narrator shows so much urbanity and charm, Fowles worries about it and moves the
novel beyond him to study the sorts of compromises, falsi-
ties, cowardices that are necessary for that urbane social
tone to be achieved and maintained. . . .

Fowles is not much interested in building a plot where one
thing inevitably leads to another, or where ingenious and
seemingly impossible combinations are brought to combine. . . . In fact, one of the attractive things about the
book is its leisured, ruminative pace—nothing need be left
out for the sake of getting on with it. So when the narrator
tells us about his youthful botanizing, one of the few things
he could do which his clergyman father approved of, he
goes into full-named detail. . . . (p. 1)

Such facts are the sweetest dream that labor knows; and
their presence is crucial to some of the best poetry in
Fowles's novel, as is the clearly autobiographical resonance felt here and elsewhere.

But, as with any Fowles novel, matters of precisely named
fact are not the only matters explored. Around these relatively unexceptional characters and plot are deployed other
kinds of speculation and argument. . . . (pp. 1, 42)

Though perspective is an important worry for any post-
Jamesian or Conradian novelist, Fowles is particularly obsessed by it in this book. There is much political debate, on
a spectrum from embattled Toryism to Marxist Third-
World analysis, with Dan always the man in the middle
seeing and seeing through both sides, then feeling guilty
about it. He writes for the movies but comes to realize—as
part of his re-education—that "no novel about the English
that can be successfully filmed is a true picture of them";
and he imagines "something dense, interweaving treating
time as a horizontal, like a skyline; not cramped, linear and

progressive." Something like "Daniel Martin," and also
involving extreme nervousness about first-person narrative. . . .

Here I think one must complain a bit and be less interested
in Fowles's narrative games than he. "To escape the first
person, and become one's own third" is Dan's purpose, or
fantasy; he distrusts the murkiness of an authorial "I" and
aspires instead to see himself as others see him. That aspiration is a mad one, yet Fowles keeps so aspiring, moves
his narrative arbitrarily from first to third person—often
abruptly or fussily—and the result is needless murkiness.
There are shiftings of perspective, as when we see Dan
through the literary efforts of his mistress in America,
which are interesting enough in themselves but don't contribute greatly to the novel as a whole. And at times the
narrative fails by a portentous straining after Significance, a
too-quick readiness to jump on any fact and read it symbolically, make it reveal a pattern deeper and larger than empirical individual experience. A very un-English way to behave, as Fowles well knows, and so he feels the more
compelled to behave that way, to construct a book more
discontinuous and hard to swallow than your average good
read.

Yet a very good read it is too, most so when it relaxes and
operates unembarrassedly in the distrusted first-person
mode. The novel's finest section ("Phillida") is an extended, beautifully developed account of Dan's first passionate love with the daughter of an "educated yeoman"
from Thorncombe. In it, as in the hero's remembered childhood and his conversations with the important women in
his life, Fowles gives us wonderfully sensitive and entertaining portraiture, writing as an old-fashioned novelist interested in nothing more than that mystery of felt life. His
superb sense of timing, his learning and lore, his thoroughly
cultured state of being someone who couldn't lost his esthetic sense if he tried—these gifts are employed to engage
and charm the reader, even as they are contemplated ironically or analyzed sociologically or just apologized for.

When at the end of a chapter late in the book, Dan seems
to have failed to move the woman he wants above all others
to move, he is still able to fall asleep with a wan smile, "potential being making peace with actual being. One would
survive, being English; knowing to the farthest roots of
one's existence that it was all, finally, a comedy." There is
a lot to be said for this point of view, but only if the novelist
is able to make "being English" an important alternative to
other serious potentials in the book (America, Lukacs,
being young and absolute) that are also created as more
than labels. Recently Marvin Mudrick has spoken of what
he calls "the silliest, least interesting, and most influential
of twentieth century critical dogmas: that books are machines with nobody inside." "Daniel Martin" makes it
quite clear that however ingenious John Fowles's manipulations look to be, the body inside the book is strongly identifiable, is of a man whose humanism and whose English-
ness, for all that can be said against them, turn out finally to
be just worth it. Which means, for the reader, very much
worth it indeed. (p. 42)

William H. Pritchard, "An English Hero,"
in The New York Times Book Review *(©*
1977 by The New York Times Company;
reprinted by permission), September 25,
1977, pp. 1, 42.

Since publication of *The French Lieutenant's Woman* . . . , and certainly since *The Ebony Tower* . . . , it has seemed that John Fowles is the only novelist now writing in English whose works are likely to stand as literary classics—the only writer in English who has the power, range, knowledge, and wisdom of a Tolstoi or James. He is a master stylist, we've known since *The Collector* . . . , and he has the talent, much underestimated these days, for telling suspenseful, interesting stories.

Storytelling—the rigorous attention to plot that characterized the nineteenth-century novel and that characterized, also, *The French Lieutenant's Woman,* Fowles's superb fictional exploration of the philosophical background and moral implications of the nineteenth-century novel—is not prized by some of our serious writers because in their rather too easy, too fashionable commitment to existentialist notions of human freedom, they underestimate the force of the past. . . .

But existentialism tells a half-truth. It is true that we must make choices, change our lives; but it is not true that we can ignore the inertial power of all that has brought us to where we are. This is a theme John Fowles has treated before, especially in *The Magus* . . . and *The French Lieutenant's Woman;* it is the central dramatic problem in his new novel, *Daniel Martin,* Fowles's best book so far. Here, as in all his work, Fowles explores the problem partly by analysis of the ways in which the arts—especially the art of fiction—can limit or liberate our emotions and ideas (that is, our lives) and partly by brilliant close analysis of the psyches and histories of lifelike human beings. (p. 22)

Fowles's novel is about more than the search of a cast of beautifully rendered individuals for an authentic past and future. As Daniel and Jane search out where their lives went wrong, so the novel as a whole seeks an understanding of where our Western civilization went wrong and how we who carry the burden of history can redeem our age, find a future worth living. As individuals can forget or deny their beginnings, so humanity as a whole can forget its Eden, sliding into the persuasion—now popular with novelists and philosophers—that from the start the universe has been a dung heap. Fowles shows that both philosophers and writers are engaged in the same effort: serious writing about reality aimed at preserving what is of worth in human life. . . .

Daniel Martin is a masterpiece of symbolically charged realism: every symbol rises, or is made to seem to rise, out of the story. This is true even of those symbols that would seem in another writer's work to be most obviously message-laden. (p. 23)

By the end of *Daniel Martin,* the daring of Fowles's symbolism will become downright awesome: a false and shoddy resurrection of history's buried life in the raising of a temple that would otherwise perish behind the Aswan Dam (the dam itself a symbol here, a masterpiece of technology that, like the atom bomb, threatens the civilization it serves and at the same time prevents total war, since an Israeli bomb on the Aswan Dam would destroy most of Cairo and shut down modern Egyptian civilization); an accidental assemblage, on a Nile touring boat, of vividly individualized representatives of Western history's alternative "empires" —British, French, American, East European—while on the banks stand impoverished and diseased fellahin, the de-

tritus of ancient Egypt; or, most stunning of all, the terrible desert desolation of ancient Palmyra. "What an extraordinary place," Jane says. Dan comments: "End of the world." But they are not quite right. Fowles writes:

> It was the weather, they decided; it took all the serene aura out of classical antiquity, reduced it to its constituent parts, its lostness, goneness, true death . . . and the contrast of the reality with the promise of the name: Palmyra, with all its connotations of shaded pools, gleaming marble, sunlit gardens, the place where sybaritic Rome married the languorous Orient.

The "weather" not only in a literal sense but in psychological and philosophical senses as well: bad emotion and bad philosophy have reduced antiquity to "its constituent parts." Jane and Daniel—modern humanity—have lost the ability to see life whole. Like Rome and the Orient, like male and female, reason and emotion, opposing principles must marry. And in a sense, miraculously, in the waste of Palmyra, Jane and Daniel do.

At the end of the novel, looking at a self-portrait of Rembrandt as an old man, Dan sees, and Fowles spells out, the secret: *No true compassion without will, no true will without compassion.* It is through culture, through the arts' gropings of history, that we learn to see who we are, where we are, where we can go and cannot go. Without will, the artist's—or any other person's—conscious determination to love and to save (the impulse stirred in Dan by his philosopher friend's coerced promise and self-sacrifice), we cannot rise to compassion. And without compassion, without real and deep love for his "subjects" (the people he knows and, by extension, all human beings), no artist—no person—can summon the will to make true art or a true life. He will be satisfied, instead, with cynical jokes and too easy, dire solutions, like those in shallower novels about individuals and history, such as John Barth's *End of the Road.* In *Daniel Martin,* Fowles defines what art requires, what life requires. It is the first line, and the implied last line, of the novel: "Whole sight; or all the rest is desolation." (pp. 23-4)

John Gardner, "In Defense of the Real," in Saturday Review (© *1977 by Saturday Review Magazine Corp.; reprinted with permission), October 1, 1977, pp. 22-4.*

John Fowles has revised *The Magus*!? . . . [News] that Fowles has tampered with his olympian 1965 novel surely warrants the above exclamation point.

And prompts the question mark. In the foreward to the revised version, . . . Fowles explains that he was never satisfied with this first novel. . . . "Even in its final published form," he writes, "it was a far more haphazard and naively instinctive work than the more intellectual reader can easily imagine."

Fowles has, indeed, improved upon himself—and anyone deciding to read *The Magus* for the first time should probably choose the new version. But he has also outsmarted and, what's even more astonishing, misread himself to the point that the various adjustments and superior craftsmanship of this second grooming won't be what draw Fowles's lovers ever deeper into a rereading of the book. No, what will intrigue them (us) is Fowles's unacknowledged and presumably unperceived reason—his self-critical foreword notwithstanding—for such a curious literary enterprise. (p. 87)

In rendering his book the same but different, Fowles has made changes that fall into four distinct categories. . . . These categories are as follows:

(1) *Stylistic*. There is a multitude of small changes, especially in the first part of the book, and most of them make no never mind—deletions of a word or phrase here and there, and such substitutions as ''rarely'' for ''never,'' ''all women'' for ''a mystery,'' and ''a polite scepticism seemed best'' for ''I decided to pursue a course of polite scepticism.'' These changes do ease the narrative flow somewhat, but the alterations in scenes and characters is sometimes puzzling: Why have certain flashbacks in Conchis's life been put back a year? What purpose is served by the expanded and rearranged references to Nicholas's predecessors on the island, Leverrier and Mitford? Still, if they make Fowles happy, why not?

(2) *Character*. One of the problems of the 1965 *Magus*—the only problem if you had asked me at the time—is that Alison, the Australian airline stewardess whom Nicholas loves, leaves, and tries to reclaim, is strident and off-putting to the reader, and never more so than when she should be building the sympathy needed if the ordeal Nicholas undergoes on her behalf (and, of course, his own) is to seem worthwhile. Fowles's deletions of some of her early dialogue go far toward correcting this problem; and Alison, in the new version, is much more acceptable, even likeable.

(3) *Erotic*. ''The erotic element is stronger in two scenes,'' Fowles writes in his foreword. ''I regard that as merely the correction of a past failure of nerve.'' This rectification of erstwhile prudery takes the form of a couple of love scenes that are not necessarily beneficial to the quality of the writing: ''Her mouth reached towards mine, as if she could speak better with lips now than in words. But just as we were becoming drowned in each other, unaware of anything but our joined mouths and close-pressed bodies, we were stopped.'' The change is, however, notable for the manner in which, to accommodate new penetrations, Fowles further modulates his already ingenious series of episodes. Julie, the mysterious twin who lures Nicholas into Conchis's traps, now lures him into a few more by dropping one of her roles sooner. She gives Nicholas a few more turns in the game of blind man's bluff that is at the bottom of the intrigue of *The Magus*. In other words, in beefing up his novel . . . with these scenes, Fowles has found a way to surpass a surpassing story.

(4) *Clarifying*. Yes, Fowles fans, our man has gone about trying to clarify what we all wanted clarified—the ending. Here, again from the foreword, is what he has to say about it: ''Though its general intent has never seemed to me as obscure as some readers have evidently found it—perhaps because they have not given due weight to the two lines from the 'Pervigilium Veneris' that close the book—I accept that I might have declared a preferred aftermath less ambiguously . . . and now have done so.'' Actually, I wouldn't say he has. Even though Nicholas is walking away from Alison as the first version ends, I was always optimistic about their future. Now Nicholas and Alison are ensnared in a literary stop-frame that says nothing cogent to

me of their eventual situation. This is fine for Keats, but not for the kinetics of Fowles. As for the ''Pervigilium Veneris'' refrain, which is printed in its original tongue, Fowles is right. If I understand the lines correctly, they make the promise, or at least hold out the hope, that those who have never loved will. But when our author says readers haven't given the lines ''due weight'' isn't he being kind or patronizing? (pp. 87-8)

[What] Fowles has done is this: He has gone over something twice in order to get it right—and isn't the process of analysis of actions in order to correct them what *The Magus* is all about? (One recalls the lines he quotes from Eliot's *Little Gidding*—''And the end of all our exploring / Will be to arrive where we started / And know the place for the first time.'')

Fowles's theme has dictated his behavior, or, put another way—given that Fowles believes in (is obsessed by?) his theme—the surprise of his having reworked his book is that we are surprised. It should have been predictable, not only because of what he has written here, but also from what his other work tells us. The novella, ''The Ebony Tower,'' which gives its name to the 1974 collection of stories, is a variation, a reworking of *The Magus.* So is last year's *Daniel Martin,* insofar as it is about a man, who, by journeying to a foreign country, is able to revive a previously failed love affair. Isn't Fowles also echoing the fine gimmickry of *The French Lieutenant's Woman* (1969) by supplying more than one ending to *The Magus* (for two endings are what it now has—both will continue to coexist)? And, to take his fictive game of theme and variation one step further, can't *The Magus* be seen as a reshuffling of one of the books Fowles says influenced him, Alain-Fournier's *Le Grand Meaulnes*? . . .

Throughout much of his work Fowles worries the question of freedom of will (e.g., the new ending), but a more recurrent titillation of his is the interplay of life and art. By rewriting *The Magus* he uses his art to provide himself (and his readers) with evidence of what he seems desperate to believe life will always offer: The second chance. Fowles, indeed, is the novelist of the second chance, of the youthful mistake corrected, of if-at-first-you-don't-succeed . . . , of honest and long toil leading at last to a happy conclusion. You have to love him for it.

The only catch is that *The Magus* rewritten is, of course, a prelude to *The Magus* reread. Ironically, and despite the now smoother story-line, a second perusal may not be what *The Magus* can sustain. ''I should add,'' Fowles writes, ''that in revising the text I have not attempted to answer the many justified criticisms of excess, overcomplexity, artificiality, and the rest that the book received from the more sternly adult reviewers on its first appearance. I now know the generation whose mind it most attracts, and that it must always substantially remain a novel of adolescence written by a retarded adolescent.''

He may have known this, and some reviewers may have known it, but I didn't—nor did I want to. Now I know it. The philosophizing, the poetastering that can afflict Fowles's lesser writings (*The Aristos,* which is Philosophy 101 packaged as after-dinner mints; *Poems,* which is what the poetry Nicholas Urfé burned must have been like) is all too apparent. I missed it the first time around—let the ideas fall where they might—because I was turning pages so fast to see what happened next.

Although Fowles seems to have read everything there is to read and mulled most of it over, I can't see that he has assimilated it so that his ideological stance works its way easily into his fiction. When he deals with the histories of philosophical and literary thought, his references tend to float around in the prose like croutons in soup. He isn't, on the strength of his novels, an intellectual, so why intellectualize when there's so much better he could be doing? He is a superb story-teller; what higher praise could he want, how could he tire of hearing it?

Paul Valéry observed that you don't finish a work of art, you abandon it. Glossy as *The Magus* is now, as improved for the new reader, I kind of wish that Fowles had followed Valéry's advice. (p. 88)

> *David Finkle, "John Fowles Takes a Second Chance," in* The Village Voice *(reprinted by permission of* The Village Voice; *copyright © by The Village Voice, Inc., 1978), February 20, 1978, pp. 87-8.*

*   *   *

FRISCH, Max   1911-

Frisch is a Swiss novelist, playwright, and architect. Translated into many languages, his writings involve not only themes of personal identity but social concerns, such as dictatorship, anti-Semitism, prejudice, and justice and injustice. (See also *CLC*, Vol. 3.)

Both Wilder and Brecht greatly influenced Zurich's Max Frisch, who employs forms typical of Brecht's epic theater and who shares his deep moral commitment. He does not, however, share Brecht's naive faith in Marxism. Frisch called one of his plays a *"Lehrstück ohne Lehre"* (a didactic play without a lesson) and critics have accordingly dubbed Frisch a Brecht without Marxism. Frisch constantly warns against man's inclination to create false images of a person, a race, or a nation. He maintains that the attempt to say anything definitive about "the Jews," "the Russians," and others can result only in brutal distortion. This thesis is particularly evident in his novel *Stiller* and in the play *Andorra*.

Frisch's early plays, *Nun singen sie wieder* (*Now They Sing Again*, 1945), *The Chinese Wall* (1947), and *Als der Krieg zu Ende war* (*When the War Was Over*, 1949), deal with problems of the immediate postwar life. His next play, *Count Oederland* (1951), depicting the transformation of a representative of law and order into an anarchist, has generally been understood as a rather inadequate explanation of the events of the Hitler era, which shows that every common man has a certain potential for violence and cruelty. *Don Juan or The Love of Geometry* (1953) is Frisch's first comedy. Here Don Juan possesses none of the qualities usually attributed to him. Instead of seducing women he is constantly seduced by them. . . . Frisch's dominant theme is visible even in this comedy: Don Juan realizes that women merely love in him the image they have created of him.

The Firebugs (*Biedermann und die Brandstifter*, 1956) is the parable of a man who thinks he can appease those who want to destroy his world. In a city plagued by arsonists, the rich and hypocritical Biedermann shelters two firebugs in his home. . . . [He] lets his world catch fire because of his unwillingness to resist the forces of violence.

The climax of Frisch's work is his play *Andorra* (1961), a study of prejudice. Here a teacher brings his illegitimate son Andri to his homeland of Andorra, telling his fellow citizens that the boy is a Jewish child whom he rescued from the dangers of the anti-Semitic neighboring state. The boy grows up and gradually experiences the racial prejudice of the entire community. Andri is molded into the stereotype image the people of Andorra have of the Jews. As the armies of the neighboring anti-Semitic state invade Andorra, the teacher reveals his son's true identity. But Andri thinks his foster father is trying to save him and refuses to accept the story. He has been convinced that he is Jewish and that he possesses all the "Jewish" qualities people have observed in him. The enemy executes Andri as a Jew. In the ensuing trial, the people of Andorra declare themselves not guilty of Andri's death. But obviously their latent prejudices have led to Andri's violent death as much as has the open anti-Semitism of the invaders. (pp. 397-99)

> *Diether H. Haenicke, "Literature Since 1933," in* The Challenge of German Literature, *edited by Horst S. Daemmrich and Diether H. Haenicke (reprinted by permission of the Wayne State University Press; copyright © 1971 by Wayne State University Press), Wayne State University Press, 1971, pp. 350-404.*

Max Frisch is . . . a meticulous storyteller, a discriminating selector of the relevant from the batches of irrelevant. His best works—the plays *The Firebugs* and *Andorra* and the novel *I'm Not Stiller*—are intelligent comedies, intricate fables without morals. In discussions of Frisch's literary antecedents and sources, his name travels in the lofty company of Brecht, Kafka and Mann. Frisch acknowledges these influences. But what is most interesting about his writing are Frisch's consistent attempts to define precisely in what ways he is *not* Brecht, Kafka and Mann.

Who Frisch's characters really are is the central and unresolved question of his plays and novels. Who Max Frisch is, the kinds of relationships he conducts, the kinds of political beliefs he affirms, the kind of writer he wishes to be, and the kind of writer he is, are the questions around which Frisch has shaped his two most recent works: *Sketchbook (1966-1971)* and *Montauk*. In *Sketchbook* Frisch writes primarily about his political and social concerns, but oddly, it is a more personal, more intimate and engaging book than *Montauk*, a work which Frisch determined would be about his private life. (pp. 27-8)

Frisch confesses that he is exceedingly uncomfortable with the confessional form. The stated subjects of [*Montauk*], his "life as a man," his fame, his literary ambition, his inquiries into his past relationships with women, his relationships with his mother and daughter, are nearly all subverted by the self-consciousness of a writer too cautious and suspicious of his readers to be candid about his emotions. . . . [It] is a nightmare to Frisch to think of giving up his own life to the myriad of possible interpretations other people make. It is a nightmare not to be able to control what readers think.

Montauk is Frisch's written record of his attempts to make peace with his nightmare. He wishes to stop directing and censoring his experiences, to see and feel his life as he really lives it, to capture what he calls the "thin current moment." As a writer, however, Frisch has no feel for the "thin current moment." (p. 28)

Montauk is very uneven going. Frisch's writing about his past is dramatic and convincing in a way that the present moment of his book never is. He complains of feeling tyrannized by memory. It devours his present. But Frisch's loss is the reader's gain. What rings true in *Montauk* reads like Frisch's fiction, and what does not read like fiction, does not ring true. (p. 30)

> *Laurie Stone, "Living in Quotations," in* The Nation *(copyright 1976 by the Nation Associates, Inc.), July 3, 1976, pp. 28-30.*

If one accepts the premise that "God is the living spirit in each human being," then any kind of typecasting, any kind of limitation placed on human individuality and human development borders on the sacrilegious. And this is precisely the way in which such transgressions are presented in Frisch's major works.

The conflict between the stereotyped, fixed image of a person and the life force which permeates this person is the nucleus of several of Frisch's plots. The resolutions of this basic conflict vary: Stiller finally learns to accept himself and his wife in peaceful resignation. In *Andorra* the image-making deteriorates from the level of the individual to racial prejudice by an entire nation and eventually to collective murder or at least acquiescence in it. In *Mein Name sei Gantenbein* (1964; translated as *A Wilderness of Mirrors*) the perspective shifts somewhat, since the author does not present one definite conflict or plot, but several possibilities of plots. . . . Frisch succeeds admirably in his aim of "showing the reality of a persona by having it appear as a white spot, outlined by the totality of the fictions that is possible for this persona." . . . *Gantenbein* is undoubtedly Frisch's best novel. It closes with a definite affirmation of life, apparently in all its vicissitudes.

Throughout his career as a writer Frisch has integrated personal experiences into his imaginative works. If one uses Flaubert's famous dictum that the author "should be omnipresent but nowhere visible" as a standard in judging how well Frisch integrates fact and fiction, then one can easily demonstrate a progression toward perfection. His first novel, *Jürg Reinhart* (1933/34), is a traditional and obviously autobiographical Entwicklungsroman whose protagonist, an innocent youth with a pure heart, develops into manhood. This theme is reechoed and the same telltale name reappears in *Die Schwierigen oder J'adore ce qui me brûle* (1942; The Difficult Ones). In both of these early novels the author's personal preoccupations stand out too clearly; the facts simply have not been molded into fiction. On the other hand, in *Stiller* (1953/54; translated as *I'm Not Stiller*) there are several passages, descriptive as well as incorporating action, which are almost verbatim repetitions of Frisch's diary entries covering his stay in the United States and Mexico, and yet they fit perfectly into the narrative fabric. Moreover, they are probably the most beautiful texts in the whole novel. It is clear at this point in his development Frisch had become a *poietes*, a maker, a truly creative artist. (p. 228)

Reading through the "Complete Works," one is frequently surprised by the vast amount of nonfictional material which they contain. Much of this material is political in the original sense of the term; it is concerned with the polis, with

the problem of how people live together, with the problem of order in society. Here, as everywhere in his works, Frisch's statements, even his polemics, are well-reasoned: they always present the pros and cons of an argument; they never fail to recognize the complexity of modern life. . . .

Today his polis encompasses the world. No matter whether he is concerned with the fascist putsch in Greece in 1967, with the suppression of dissident intellectuals in the Soviet Union, with the American invasion in Cambodia or with the Swiss trade in arms, his plea is always for humaneness, for justice, for a pluralistic and free society. But while he has a keen understanding of the large political and sociological forces which determine our lives, it is safe to say that from his beginnings to the present Frisch has been primarily concerned with the individual. . . .

[It] is a pleasure to report that Max Frisch is working on a new drama which will take place in Hades and which will show a sociological cross-section and a philosophical summary of our century. May this work appear soon and may it be followed by many others! (p. 229)

> *Franz P. Haberl, "Max Frisch: A Retrospective," in* World Literature Today *(copyright 1977 by the University of Oklahoma Press), Vol. 51, No. 2, Spring, 1977, pp. 227-29.*

*   *   *

FROST, Robert   1874-1963

One of America's most celebrated and widely read poets, Frost wrote poems depicting rural New England life in traditional verse and a seemingly simplistic style. Concerned with the human ability to develop an individual identity in a world bent against the individual, Frost was a poet who, according to Elizabeth Jennings, used "the pastoral mode as a vehicle for his inquiries into the nature and meaning of life." Frost's recognition as a great poet has lasted for more than fifty years and he won the Pulitzer Prize in Poetry four times. (See also *CLC*, Vols. 1, 3, 4.)

The main difficulty in assessing, as in enjoying, Robert Frost is the extreme interdependence of his poetic virtues and vices. The agricultural canniness-within-canniness, the cracker-barrel philosophizing and the manly-coy flatness of tone yield so many dead acres it comes hard to admit these very qualities produce the best of the crop. And the best is so extraordinarily good, while so similar in *persona,* verse-method and aim, as to make the reader doubt whether the worst can be quite as bad as he thinks. Yet surely it is.

Which is not to say that Frost is a poet who does one thing either marvellously well or abysmally badly. He is a versatile writer, not only exploiting narrative, dramatic, lyric and argumentative forms in a wide variety of ways but accomplishing a multiplicity of effects. For instance, in addition to the major lyrics, "The Death of the Hired Man" is surely one of the best short stories of the century, "The Witch of Coös" and "Paul's Wife" important contributions to ghost and science fiction, and "To Earthward" a love poem that in tenderness, reach and music ranks with the best of the age. . . . [Views] have always been sharply divided on the point where the Frostian virtues, over-indulged, descend into self-caricature. . . . At [an] extreme of opinion on Frost's colloquial method is Yvor Winters's Johnsonian pronouncement that since poetry is very obviously not conversation, there is no virtue in its being conversational. That, in Frost's case, is surely wrong; his folksy tone may dilute and deaden longer poems, and it certainly makes for some heavy-handed satire, but it works to marvellous effect in many of the lyrics, especially when riding in unlikely harness with a very different sort of language: his own brand of high romantic rhetoric. In a similar way Frost's craggy pragmatism and determinedly no-nonsense pose co-exist with a habitual and unreigned mysticism. . . .

[Another] vulgarization that turns good Frost into bad [is] the over-exploitation of his genuine (and considerable) charm, the determination to please at all costs. The eagerness to displease is so prevalent in contemporary poetry that one feels Frost might be pardoned his more agreeable weakness; nevertheless it is a cloying defect and something more than that. . . .

[Ian Hamilton contends in the introduction to *Selected Poems*] that Frost, by hogging the stage with his honest-to-goodness homely old wiseacre act, obscured—and deliberately obscured—his true, unbeautiful and superbly treated subject. Whether or not Mr. Hamilton is entirely right in this (however phoney the *persona,* is it not often put to remarkable poetic uses?), he is surely correct, with Lionel Trilling, in identifying that subject as the terminal desolation of life, the futility at the root, with the poet "yearning for the conditions to be otherwise". At the still centre of Frost's world is a terrifying blankness, caught unforgettably in such pieces as "Acquainted with the Night", "Neither Out Far nor In Deep" and that extraordinary poem, "The Most of It".

> *"Bad and Best," in* The Times Literary Supplement (© *Times Newspapers, Ltd., 1973; reproduced by permission), October 19, 1973, p. 1278.*

Robert Frost in conversation and in his letters vacillated from one extreme to the other in religion, and his attitudes were more changeable than Aleutian winds. From youth to age he may have moved from some belief to skepticism and back toward belief, but at any given moment he could turn in any direction. . . . Biographers and critics use a word like *essentially* before *Christian* to describe Frost, but in his maturity, I believe, he never precisely described himself as Christian. He did maintain that he was orthodox, but how he defined orthodoxy may be a question. (p. 445)

Frost's statements about his religious beliefs and God are often enigmatic. Moral or intellectual or otherworldly terms cause ambiguity. At first glance what he says may seem to be certain and orthodox; a second look raises doubts. Often Frost reveals faith only in the possibilities of man. He describes the condition of the believer without regard for the divinity of the thing believed. His equation of the soul with decency and integrity affirms morality but denies religion. (p. 446)

Frost's statements of disbelief reach far greater extremes than his affirmations. Only an outright atheist could subscribe to some of them. Religion is "All froth." Despite the constant search for something in nature, the poet once concluded that "there's probably nothing 'up there' but a stockpile of nature observations that came from earth." Almost promising never to believe, Frost described himself as "safely secular till the last go down." And he stated that he had "never had a religious experience." He said that he

"never prayed except formally and politely with the Lord's prayer in public." In short, any statement about Frost's religion at one time contradicts something he said at another time.

Frost's poetry does not reflect the wide variety of his prose statements about religion and God. The poems fall into only two chronological and religious categories. Those of some belief come mainly early and late in his life. They are weak artistically, and their religious assertions are superficial general statements without convincing and serious personae, without the concrete imagery and the emotional tensions of the better poems. Many of them seem to follow conventional patterns of prayer without the poet's making them a vital part of his poem. Frost could be sincerely religious, but the bad verse raises questions, rightly or wrongly, about his belief. It is difficult to see depth of faith in a shallow well of poetry. The poems of doubt come mostly in the middle of Frost's career; they are figured intricately in concrete images, groping personae, and dramatic tensions. (p. 447)

All Frost's poems that treat religion reach some middle height, some point between the realms of spirit and matter. Then the poet wavers between two poles, unhappy with mere matter, afraid of pure spirit, discontent with a middle, aware that no metaphor can perfectly combine matter and spirit. (p. 448)

Several of Frost's narrative and dramatic poems like "The Mountain" have obscure and subtle origins in religious belief. The meaning of "Maple" depends upon Frost's excellent use of a Biblical allusion and a religious subject. The chief character spends her life trying to discover why she was named Maple by her mother, who died shortly after childbirth. . . . Maple's mother left a maple leaf as a bookmark in a Bible. The girl reads the two pages, removes the leaf, and loses the place. . . . With the name and the maple leaf the mother had tried to leave her child an understanding of a relationship between herself, the child, God, and nature. The relationship is never comprehended by the child, who, as a representative of a generation of disbelief, puzzles over enigmas without solving them. Faith in one generation gives way to excessive and futile seeking in the next. (p. 451)

The strongest and most obvious indication of which direction Frost's lyric poetry would take in his middle years is found in "Birches," which has been popular not only because of the beautiful imagery early in the poem but also because of the directness of the conclusion. Religion begins to come to the surface:

> I'd like to get away from earth awhile
> And then come back to it and begin over.
> May no fate willfully misunderstand me
> And half grant what I wish and snatch me away
> Not to return. Earth's the right place for love:
> I don't know where it's likely to go better.
> I'd like to go by climbing a birch tree,
> And climb black branches up a snow-white trunk
> *Toward* heaven, till the tree could bear no more,
> But dipped its top and set me down again.
> That would be good both going and coming back.

"*Toward* heaven" but never *to,* never all the way. Frost fears transcendence. Despite all the apparent moralizing ("earth's the right place for love"), this passage is one of the most skeptical in Frost. He contemplates a moment when the soul may become completely absorbed into a union with the divine. But he is earthbound, limited, afraid. No sooner does he wish to get away from earth than he thinks of "fate"—rather than God. And what might be a mystical experience turns into a fear of death, a fear that he would be snatched away "not to return." He rejects the unknown, the love of God, because he cannot know it, and he clings to the finite: "Earth's the right place for love."

Between 1920 and 1923 Frost made the most significant change of his entire career in the form of his poetry. He clearly divides *New Hampshire* into fifteen narrative-dramatic poems at first, followed by thirty lyrics. The dividing poem is "I Will Sing You One-O," possibly chosen because it exactly sets the course for the prevailing subject and manner. This poem marks a sharp shift to lyrics which solemnly inquire into the place of man in the cosmos. It is a pivotal poem in the last complete collection of poems published in his lifetime. It is transitional in his entire poetic career.

After lying awake long at night listening for the sound of a clock striking the hour, the speaker of the poem at last hears clocks in a tower and in a steeple say "'One!'" These two clocks represent two established orders: The civil or human (the tower) and the religious (the steeple). Both derive their concepts of time from the natural order ("the sun/And moon and stars"), the only reference by which man, civil or religious, may attempt to establish a scheme of time based upon an ordering principle outside himself. But man's view of time and the eternities is so limited that his clocks are unreliable, "unfettered":

> They left the named
> And spoke of the lettered,
> The sigmas and taus
> Of constellations.

That is, the eighteenth and nineteenth brightest stars of constellations, the remote and unknowable.

> They filled their throats
> With the furthest bodies
> To which man sends his
> Speculation,
> Beyond which God is. . . .

No matter how far man extends his exploration in the mysteries of astronomical space, God is even farther away, beyond the apprehension of mortals who attempt to establish time and fathom truth. The distance of man from God and of finite time from the eternal is emphasized perhaps by the remoteness (two lines intervene) of the feminine rhymes *God is* and *bodies,* which seem, however, to belittle God more than they exalt man. The humor usually associated with double rhyme becomes ironical and satirical. In *God is* the possible existence of the eternal is linked with a term which connotes extreme finiteness, *bodies.*

The next lines suggest the impersonality of God by describing the stars as "The cosmic motes/Of yawning lenses." . . . Frost . . . regretfully states the limitations of his own belief, and he sings of the absence of an ordering principle. What appears to be order in astronomical distance is violent chaos. . . . If man finds more "whirling frenzies" as he penetrates deeper into space, he also finds disorder and lawless energy omnipresent in time, in history, and in all man's attempts to see God . . . . (pp. 453-55)

The subject matter of Frost's lyrics is usually the place of the individual in his universe. The best poems treat three levels of being—man, nature, ultimate. No poem treats less than two of these three levels. Few develop relationships between man and man, between one individual and another. The speaker or the poet is usually the only major character in the poem. In the best lyrics communication between man and nature or man and the ultimate is uncertain if not impossible; in the lesser ones communication between levels of being is certain, especially between man and nature. The best poems are based upon disbelief. They hint in unexplained images of possible relationships between levels of beings; the lesser poems make explicit statements—disbelief embodied in poetic figures is more credible than belief asserted in direct words. The better poems often establish the speaker as a dramatic vehicle, a concrete persona in a defined moment of time; the lesser ones present meditations which are uttered by an unknown and undescribed speaker. The better poems deny the pathetic fallacy, the existence of mind in nature or human characteristics in nature; the lesser ones contain implausible personifications, accept the reality of the pathetic fallacy and the human qualities of the natural world, make weak and forced analogies between different levels of being. Finally, the speakers of the better poems are able to arrive at no certain beliefs or conclusions; in the lesser poems the poet or the speaker becomes didactic.

Frost's greatest accomplishment as a lyric poet, then, occurs in poems with concrete imagery and concrete situations which represent an intense yearning for faith which never comes. (pp. 455-56)

Frost's best-known lyric poem, "Stopping by Woods on a Snowy Evening," confronts many kinds of being and experience: woods (nature); the village; a horse (the animal world); promises (duty and obligations to some social world). This poem hardly defines the attempt to communicate with the ultimate; but much of its beauty derives from the concreteness with which Frost embodies the mysteriousness of the ultimate in the dark beauty of a silent natural world. For once he contemplates without asking for explanations. He stops "Between the woods and frozen lake/The darkest evening of the year." Much of the appeal of the poem may be attributable to its acceptance of beauty without finding or asking for truth in the woods, which "are lovely, dark and deep."

The range in the quality of the poems in Frost's last four volumes (*A Further Range, A Witness Tree, Steeple Bush,* and *In the Clearing*) is wide. The worst poems reduce the old subject and the old manner to absurdity, even while Frost seems momentarily to be near acceptance. Generally, the nearer the poet seems to be to faith, the more absurd his figures of speech are. (p. 457)

There is never a deep love of God in the poetry of Frost. His greatest poems reveal a fear of God, a fear of the absence of God, or frustration at the limitations of man. The loss of poetic vision and imagination in Frost's late years corresponds with a decline in his interest in cosmic questions. On one page in *Steeple Bush* he argues facetiously that his love of the stars in this world ought to save his soul in the next. . . . And on the page facing this poem he uses the same stars as an argument that man is only a scientific and material phenomenon. . . . The late poems on the subject of faith vacillate more than ever in attitude and state the opinion of the moment in explicitness, generality, and obviousness.

Even in his late period Frost wrote about a half-dozen great poems. "Design" leaves out the human level altogether and effectively treats Frost's theme in a miniature world. The "dimpled spider, fat and white," the white heal-all, and the moth act out a terrible travesty of the evil design of the universe, "If design govern in a thing so small." If design does govern such a small thing, then the universal plan can be only evil. If design does not govern here, the implication is that man is also created without design. God's eye is no more on man than it is on the moth and the sparrow. In "Design" Frost found an objective correlative for his theme which enabled him to terrify without reducing his meaning to statement.

In "Neither Out Far Nor in Deep" a single-minded group of people on the seashore "look at the sea all day." . . . Many critics of the poem interpret it as a satire on the illimitable desire of man to know despite his limited capabilities: Frost is said to ridicule "blind persistence in seeking beyond the horizon at the neglect of present realities" in a "witty epigrammatic treatment" and with a tone of "quasi-jocular cynicism." The trouble with these interpretations is that they reverse the thematic and developmental patterns of the poetry of Frost's entire career. Most of his best poems attempt to look out far and in deep, and the finiteness of man was no hindrance to Frost's own wishes to perceive. The thrust of the last stanza, furthermore, and the tone hardly support the argument for satire. The simplicity of the entire poem well represents the single-mindedness of the yearners for truth. . . . Every poetic device of the poem makes it a chant of simplicity, longing, need, and unanimity. "Neither Out Far Nor in Deep" represents not satire, but the poet's and mankind's deepest spiritual need.

Frost was never able to write a poem at a moment of intense belief—if he had such moments. Without exception, I believe, his good poems come in the shadows of yearnings and doubts. His great lyric and dramatic poems never place much confidence in nature or in God. His only significant deep belief was in the possibility of man and especially in his capacity to suffer and to endure adversity. In technique, he appeared to preach more and more, to become wiser and wiser; in subject matter he shallowly accepted obvious truisms or hid his skepticism behind the facade of the moralizing of a grandfatherly sage, a good gray poet. (pp. 458-59)

> *Floyd C. Watkins, "Going and Coming Back: Robert Frost's Religious Poetry," in* South Atlantic Quarterly *(reprinted by permission of the Publisher; copyright 1974 by Duke University Press, Durham, North Carolina), Autumn, 1974, pp. 445-59.*

Frost was no more eager than any other poet to define poetry, but when he spoke about it he generally used such phrases as: "a way of grappling with life," "a little voyage of discovery," "a way *out* of something." All these phrases represent poetry not as entity but activity, and, more specifically, as "a way," that is, as method. In the essay "Education by Poetry," Frost suggests that in coming close to poetry the student enters the world of metaphor and, through metaphor, learns what it is to think: "it is just putting this and that together; it is just saying one

thing in terms of another." He is not speaking of trivial comparisons but the most profound thinking humans engage in. "Unless you have had your proper poetical education in metaphor," he writes, "you are not safe anywhere. Because you are not at ease with figurative values: you don't know the metaphor in its strength and its weakness. You don't know how far you may expect to ride it and when it may break down with you. You are not safe in science; you are not safe in history." . . . The figure Frost uses to describe metaphor in this sentence is itself worth attending to: we "ride" our metaphors. Metaphor should be construed not merely as an identification of resemblance but as an instrument used to get somewhere, a tool for thinking, the vehicle, perhaps, on which the poet undertakes his "voyages of discovery." Poems become methods of moving toward new insights on the strength of the poet's figures. (p. 66)

Love, belief, and poetry. Frost . . . associates these three, and through that association he expresses the same vision of poetic activity that Stevens articulates in "A Primitive like an Orb" [see especially Cantos 4, 5, and 6]. Frost often used love as an analogy for poetry, as, for example, in saying that "the figure a poem makes . . . is the same as for love." . . . But love is more than an analogy for poetry; it is also Frost's name for the positive force that impels poetry, the energy behind all true thinking. In "Accidentally on Purpose" love is called the basic instinctual force that underlies "intention, purpose, and design" in the universe. (p. 79)

For Frost love and poetry function as twin figures of the creative activity in which man commits himself, with "passionate preference," to a certain tacit foreknowledge that he has and, by believing in it, brings it to fulfillment. In "Education by Poetry" he wrote that, in connection with learning about thinking, "the person who gets close enough to poetry, he is going to know more about the word *belief* than anybody else knows, even in religion nowadays". . . . Like the relationship of two people in love, the process of poetic thinking demands the act of "believing the thing into existence," and in poetry as in love one learns that the indwelling of the human spirit in its forms is essential to all creation and to all knowledge. Like Stevens, Frost came to see poems as individual embodiments of a single, central activity. (pp. 79-80)

Frost's best treatment of the role of belief and commitment in establishing truth appears in "Directive," a poem about returning to some basic source of wholeness and strength, "beyond confusion." It begins with an introspective journey through a landscape of desolation, marked by waste land imagery which makes it seem doubtful that this journey can lead in a valuable direction. Yet a guide appears, vague and phantom-like at first but increasingly more concrete and personal toward the end of the poem. By the final lines it is clear that the guide is the poet, and the source of wholeness he discloses is a fundamental power within the self. The poet is a guide to the life of the imagination, to the "broken drinking goblet like the Grail" taken from the children's "house of make-believe." . . . Like the teachings of Christ, poetic truth depends on commitment and faith. The power Frost guides us to in "Directive" is the power of belief in ourselves and our figures, the power of poetry itself as a method of thinking and knowing. (pp. 81-2)

Todd M. Lieber, "Robert Frost and Wallace Stevens: 'What to Make of a Diminished Thing'," in American Literature *(copyright © 1975 by Duke University Press), March, 1975, pp. 64-83.*

In the popular mind Frost appears in the guise of a gentle nature poet who writes poems which the common man can understand—poems free of those dreadful complexities and sexual allusions found in much modern poetry. How this image can persist in the mind of anyone who has read such a terrifying poem as "Out, Out—" I do not know. But most people have not read "Out, Out—" and others of its tone. When such appreciaters encounter Lionel Trilling's theory . . . that their sweet cracker-barrel philosopher conceives of an essentially "terrifying universe," indignant sparks fly. These people have made Frost in their own image and cannot bear to have the mirror cracked.

To anyone who has read all of Frost's poems with an open mind, however, Trilling's conclusions become inescapable. Frost's landscape is bleak. His doctrine is disturbing. That doctrine appears most clearly in two poems which are central to an understanding of Frost, *A Masque of Reason* and *A Masque of Mercy.* . . . These poems were published in 1945 and 1947, when Frost was in his seventies and had had time to formulate his ideas about life. These poems are overtly doctrinal and should give us a good look at that bleak Frostian landscape.

Using a method similar to Thornton Wilder's in *The Skin of Our Teeth,* Frost bases his two masques upon Biblical stories but sets them in modern time. *A Masque of Reason* tells the story of God's encounter with Job and Job's wife on Judgment Day. Jonah's story forms the basis of *A Masque of Mercy.* Stated simply, the theme of both masques is the choice between reason and unreason. In the *Book of Job,* . . . Job learns that man must not expect to be treated logically. . . . God is a free agent, not bound by mere man's conceptions of the way the world should be. The "discipline man needed most/Was to learn his submission to unreason." So it is that *A Masque of Reason* affirms *unreason.* The world, says Frost through God, is not run by any laws which man's reason can grasp. Job should not expect God to heed his plea, "The artist in me cries out for design." A man who probes deeply finds that there is no design at all, that God is forced to admit, as He does to Job, "I was just showing off to the Devil."

The lesson for Jonah in *A Masque of Mercy* continues the theme of reason and unreason. Man cannot demand logical treatment, in the form of strict justice. In this case, God's injustice is manifested, not in hurting the innocent, but in showing mercy to the guilty. The reasonable virtue, justice, falls before the unreasonable virtue, mercy. (pp. 453-55)

[Is] there anything disturbing in what I have said so far? Job and Jonah learn to accept unreason. They find that man's ideas of justice and logic are small and insignificant in God's plan. Both learn that faith surpasses reason, and Jonah comes to realize that God's mercy and love are greater than man's justice and logic. If these are heresies, Thomas Aquinas was a heretic. The ideas summarized here are not at all disruptive but are to be found among very traditional Christian beliefs. These conventional doctrines in the masques lead Harold Watts to conclude erroneously [in "Robert Frost and the Interrupted Dialogue"] that the

masques "must, in the 'Frost story,' stand for a sad acceptance of traditional stereotypes." However, an understanding of the total system of belief in the two masques suggests that Frost denies the traditional stereotypes. Indeed, seen from a traditional point of view, Frost is a heretic.

First, Frost does not give the traditional justifications for having faith and avoiding the doubts of reason. The faithful receive no promise of salvation. The door slams in Jonah's face.

Second, Frost's portrayal of God is deliberately and shockingly unorthodox. In *A Masque of Mercy,* God is a friendly little being who deserves respect but is something of a bungler and is overly idealistic. . . . In *A Masque of Reason,* Frost's God looms largest—and smallest. He struggles out of the Burning Bush and "pitches throne," the throne being a "plywood flat, prefabricated." A blunderer, He cannot prevent the throne from collapsing under Him. His speeches are most undignified. . . . God here is no more than human. He is, in fact, a puny and insecure being with an inferiority complex. In an attempt at dignity, He clambers back onto His throne to meet the supercilious Devil. The end of the masque is significant for Frost's conception of God: Thyatira gathers God, Job, and the Devil all together to take a snapshot of them with her Kodak. She treats all three alike, with no reverence, and they all appear side by side in the picture. God, Man, and Satan are of equal status in this masque.

The status of God is crucial to the interpretation of *A Masque of Reason.* Marion Montgomery argues [in "Robert Frost and His Use of Barriers: Man vs. Nature Toward God"] that Frost's "presentation of a cavalier God is a deliberate device [which shows] . . . not lack of reason or justice in God, but rather man's stubbornness and lack of understanding. It is like man, especially in our day, to see God 'pitching throne with a ply-wood chair'." I believe, however, that Frost is trying to show not man's misunderstanding of God, but God's lack of superhuman perfection. Throughout his poems, Frost treats God with little awe. . . . John Ciardi, who knew Frost personally, believes that the poet gave up all thought of religion. The portrayal of a humanized and fallible God colors the whole masque. According to traditional doctrine, the world cannot be understood in terms of mere man's ideas of order and logic because God is very great and has a plan beyond the comprehension of man; here, the mystery arises only because God is too small for one man to comprehend by his present reverent ways of thinking. As Job says:

> I expected more
> Than I could understand and what I get
> Is almost less than I can understand.

This new God makes necessary a new doctrine. If God is a fool, the whole edifice of ancient justifications collapses. The comforting old landscape grows bleaker and bleaker. Frost has removed from it the hope of salvation. He has debased God until He can be spoken of without a capital letter. What next? The universe. Frost's universe is lonely and terrifying. In both "Choose Something like a Star" and "The Most of It," Frost's lone speakers seek an answer to loneliness but find that the universe never answers in a language which man can comprehend. Man is alone in a gigantic, echoing universe. (pp. 457-59)

What is left in the darkening landscape? People. But people are no source of comfort in a Frostian landscape. In most of Frost's shorter poems, only one person is present. Both the masques present several important characters; however, they serve to underline the loneliness of Job and Jonah. (p. 459)

I believe that Frost is saying, "The universe is indifferent. God, if He exists, is weak. There is no justification for your efforts beyond your own purposes for them. Make up a meaning for yourself if you need to think you have a purpose. If it is a lie in the absolute sense, that is all right so long as you find it meaningful." Frost has dealt with this problem before. A terse sonnet, "Any Size We Please," portrays the loneliness of every man and the tragicomic necessity to make one's own world. (p. 460)

In Frost's poetry, people who make their own worlds usually go about it in one of two ways. Some merely get by, endure.... But others of Frost's characters acquire a kind of heroic quality in the process of making their own worlds. It does not matter that their chosen purpose cannot be supported by an absolute standard of validity, that it cannot be affirmed by religious and universal consent. Such people make a commitment and act upon it. Jonah makes such a commitment when he almost sees the shining gate and says,

> I want to run
> Toward what you make me see beyond the world.

Although he fails to reach his goal, Jonah's example inspires Keeper. Until Jonah's death, Keeper has been one of those who simply get by. He is a coward, not because he is wrong about God or about the meaninglessness of everything in the absolute, but because he has let his awareness of the absolute truth prevent him from making an attempt at human heroism. Suddenly Jonah's example teaches him that Jesse Bel was right in glorifying courage, for we need firm courage to overcome the fundamental insecurity of the human condition....

Frost has left us with a bleak landscape indeed. The universe is indifferent to man. God is a well-meaning but bumbling being. There is no promise of salvation or of any reason beyond our own for our efforts. And other men are of little help. If a man merely gets by in such a world, that is well enough. But if he adheres to some kind of purpose, commits himself to a set of values in the face of universal indifference, he achieves a measure of heroism. Still, such a one is likely to fail in the absolute judgment—his best sacrifice may be found unacceptable in Heaven's sight. (p. 462)

I believe that Frost did not freely choose to cultivate soundness and balance [as George Whicher contends]; he felt forced to take the position he did, and it was not a rational or comfortable posture. His aversion to that bleak outlook which he found inescapable made him increasingly melancholy and marked his later poems, in which he shows how little he relished [his] pessimism.... And Frost begins to laugh more and more, to laugh when laughter seems a desperate shield against despair. "Bursting Rapture" and "U.S. 1946 King's X" conjure up a mocking, scornful laugh at the possibility of nuclear destruction. In the face of the ultimate denial of human dignity, Frost offers no solace, no cosy cracker-barrel certainties—only bitter laughter.

[Frost's doctrine] is, in fact, a caricature of the old doctrine of faith and reason, justice and mercy. It leaves man the burden of accepting unreason without the assurance that, by doing so, he will be "saved." The perfect complement to Frost's doctrine, which is a parody of ancient beliefs, is his form, which is a burlesque of conventional forms. The two poems under consideration are called "masques." Traditionally, a masque was an elaborate poetic drama, containing music, song, dance, costumes, and spectacle. Frost's masques are "anti-masques." There is no elaborate spectacle, no dance, no song, and even no drama—Frost is essentially a meditative rather than a dramatic poet. Full of debate over abstract ideas, the two masques contain hardly any action and little characterization; if presented on stage, they would probably fall as flat as God's plywood throne. They are all talk. And such talk! It has no dignity.... Both masques are full of outrageous puns. (pp. 463-65)

The undignified tone is even more apparent when casual conversation and puns are joined by a multitude of mocking literary allusions.... [And there are] light barbs on every side—hits at psychiatry, Socialism, and *The New Yorker*. Frost has chosen a form and style of language perfectly suited to the purpose of his content. The form is a mockery of serious form because the content is a mockery of men's old illusive comforts about life. In order to tear down the hypocritical platitudes which lull men into complacence, Frost has created a new form by the process of "committing an outrage" on several conventional literary forms. (pp. 465-66)

The Man of La Mancha has so distorted Cervantes' intentions that its theme song glorifies the "impossible dreams" of a simplified, idealized Don Quixote. Dickens's horrifying London of *Oliver Twist* has undergone the magic of movie-industry metamorphosis and emerged as a nineteenth-century Fun City, from true nightmare to sweet dream. Robert Frost has too long suffered the same cosyfying falsification. It is time to read him with an attentive ear, one attuned to chords that are not warm, nostalgic, friendly, harmless. It is time to take him out of the junior high schools, to stop stopping by woods on a snowy evening, to read him as a mature poet who has shown the courage to describe unflinchingly the bleak landscape facing the twentieth-century reader. (p. 466)

Roberta F. Sarfatt Borkat, "The Bleak Landscape of Robert Frost," in The Midwest Quarterly *(copyright, 1975, by* The Midwest Quarterly, *Kansas State College of Pittsburg), Summer, 1975, pp. 453-67.*

Frost's *In the Clearing* was celebrated as a great public event, with an appropriate burst of sentimental and patriotic flourishes. His late elevation to the post of fireside bard to the American people and laureate of the Kennedy administration, officiating at the vaunted marriage of Poetry and Power, had certain comic overtones, for he was anything but "progressive" (in the liberal Democratic tradition), his characteristic vision could scarcely be described as optimistic, and in the main body of his work, forgetting the embarrassing doggerel towards the end, he was to be seen as hermetic, idiosyncratic, and egocentric—qualities that he shared with many other famous poets.

Even in his decline one gets occasional flashes of the intrinsic Frost, as when he notes, of butterflies, in "Pod of the Milkweed": "They knock the dyestuff off each other's wings," after which he appends his undeceived reflection,

"But waste was of the essence of the scheme." In the title-poem ("A Cabin in the Clearing") the speakers are Mist and Smoke, and the subject of their dialogue is the uncertainty of the human condition. The final lines, though too stiffly articulated, carry a recognizable beat and moral: "Than smoke and mist who better would appraise / The kindred spirit of an inner haze."

One of the most profound of his aphorisms stresses the necessity coupled with the difficulty of making choices: "Nature within her inmost self divides / To trouble men with having to take sides." The theme is a recurrent one. Years before he had written in lines that every schoolboy thinks he understands: "Two roads diverged in a wood, and I—/ I took the one less traveled by, / And that has made all the difference." What, in passing, could be more artful than that suspended first person singular? This traveler's pride in his ability to confront his fate and to make up his mind, despite the persistence of the "inner haze," induces him to call one of his last lyrics, "Escapist—Never." The title has a ring of defiance, perhaps a hollow ring. As the poem reaches its climax we are given a momentary glimpse of a redemptive pathos: "His life is a pursuit of a pursuit forever. / It is the future that creates his present. / All is an interminable chain of longing." (pp. 252-53)

> *Stanley Kunitz, in his* A Kind of Order, A Kind of Folly *(© 1935, 1937, 1938, 1941, 1942, 1947, 1949, 1957, 1963, 1964, 1965, 1966, 1967, 1970, 1971, 1972, 1973, 1974, 1975 by Stanley Kunitz; reprinted by permission of Little, Brown and Co. in association with the Atlantic Monthly Press), Atlantic-Little, Brown, 1975.*

As far as I can tell, no one has explained the relationship between Frost's two dramatic narratives "The Witch of Coös" and "The Pauper Witch of Grafton," which he published together in 1923 under the title "Two Witches." "The Witch of Coös" has been very widely praised (Randall Jarrell called it "the best thing of its kind since Chaucer"), frequently anthologized, and thoughtfully discussed. "The Pauper Witch of Grafton," however, has received very scattered praise and only fragmentary explanation.... A close study reveals that not only are these poems mutually illuminating to a startling degree but that they were surely written as companion pieces and ought to be seen as a single poem formed like a two-panelled picture. "Coös" is a study of sexual failure between one kind of witch and her husband, and "Grafton" a study of sexual triumph between a different kind of witch and her husband.... I find "Grafton" as good a poem as "Coös" and richly deserving of explanation, but strange to say, I understood its sexual psychology and symbolism before I understood that of the more popular "Coös" and was led by this discovery back to "Coös" and to a grasp of its barely explored plot, psychology, and symbolism....

[It has been noted that] the protagonist of "Coös" has been unable to distinguish between her terrifying fantasies and reality, whereas the protagonist of "Grafton" has an excellent understanding both of herself and of others' reactions to her. This as yet undeveloped insight is, I think the clue to the earlier failure of critics (and myself) to see the complementary nature of the poems, for the obsessional material of the witch in "Coös" needs to be both uncovered and synthesized by the reader, whereas the psychology of

"Grafton" only requires a synthesis of attitudes (her own and others') that the witch herself understands. (p. 69)

The core of the contrast between the psycho-sexual histories of two marriages leads to differing manipulations of point of view. In "Coös" the focus tends to be inward—however random—for the protagonist and less so for the other characters. In "Grafton" the focus for the protagonist tends to be outward and for the other characters inward. "Coös" centers on the supposed witch's fantasies; "Grafton" on the fantasies and authentic reactions of other characters to the witch....

Although "Coös" is occasionally referred to as a tale of the supernatural, most commentators recognize that the witch describes fantasies based on painful and persistent feelings of guilt about her infidelity to her husband and her assistance in hiding the fact of the lover's murder by helping to bury his corpse below the cellar floor. (p. 70)

Frost's own scepticism about psychoanalytic explanations and his reticence about all matters sexual should not keep us from acknowledging in him a deep intuitive knowledge of such things and a partly unconscious recording of them in symbolic action and detail. More troublesome than Frost's supposed rejection of psychoanalytic paradigms are the hazy outlines of this grim love-triangle, but the witch's confusion and incomprehension are the cause of this haze and once it is penetrated, sharper lines become visible. The woman and her husband are sexually inadequate to each other. She is frigid to him and he has inhibitions which make it difficult to penetrate or relax her defenses. Thus they shore up each other's inadequacies. The wild lover can and does penetrate these defenses but he arouses enough guilt in the woman either to lend to his betrayal or to compound her turning against him when her husband discovers the adultery. The exact action remains somewhat obscure. (p. 71)

The description of the cellar with its snow- and sawdust-packed doors and windows is symbolic of the woman's repressed sexuality and of her perverse pleasure in an unconscious pact with her husband to remain tight within the confines of their marriage. The skeleton is a symbol of the sexuality that both of them have repressed. Her "I knew them—and good reason" about the bones suggests sexual intimacy, haunted guilt, and obsessive perplexity. The continuing description of the bones and their behavior is a marvelous melange of ambivalent motifs. That the bones waited "for things to happen in their favor" is a recognition that they are now part of her mentality and that she had once encouraged them when they were part of her lover. The description of the bones as a chandelier and as a chalk-pile that brushes "chalky skull with chalky fingers" combines suggestions of burning, of grotesquerie, and of puzzlement. The chandelier connects with the later images of fire in the skull, the grotesquerie with her desire to reduce her guilt to a fanciful game, and the puzzlement with her desire to know what the dead are keeping back and why she is haunted. The chalk-pile also shows her great reluctance to acknowledge the lover's sexual superiority to her husband. Her desire to "bring the chalk-pile down" with her husband's aid suggests a wish to lay the ghost of guilt and to deny the lover's superiority. The husband's taking hold of her is a gesture of fright, not of intimacy, and it occurs in a lighted room where neither of them can see the skeleton. His gesture reinforces the sense of his minimal masculinity, but his inability to hear the phantom skeleton is a reminder that it is less a threat to him than to her. But the skeleton symbolizes more than guilt and bafflement. "A moment he stood balancing with emotion / And all but lost himself" suggests a sexual commitment desperately beyond social bounds. . . . Her pursuit of a finger piece in her button box shows the attempt to control her obsessions and connects to images of old man, infant, and chandelier as unsexed. If the bone she searches for were really in the button box it would belong to a game in which it could be found and defined. The opposition of the woman's puritanical impulses and the lover's sexual force is repeated in "So that it looked like lighting or a scribble / From the slap I had just now given its hand," and the "scribble" reinforces the idea of the lover as a messenger from another mode of experience—in this case, the sexual, though I think in the poem as a whole this connects with the "something the dead are keeping back." (pp. 71-2)

Probably the most difficult and ambiguous symbol in the poem is the skeleton's ascent from cellar to attic. Most probably this action represents the bursting out of both the woman's buried guilt about her double betrayal of her husband (the adultery itself and adultery as an accusation against his sexual failure) and her continued perplexity about the significance of the whole involvement: Why did she yield to the lover? Why is she still unable to entirely regret her yielding? Why does she share the lover's puzzlement about her betrayal? When she hears the bones "come down the stairs at night and stand perplexed" she is reenacting her own puzzlement. A skeleton in the attic is worse than one in the cellar. In the cellar it is undetected and kept out of consciousness. In the attic it is close to the bedroom and to consciousness, continually haunting, and—insofar as its presence is described—it must be accounted for. The accounting is a strange melange of puzzlement, falsification, and psychological revelation. . . . Tormented by guilt and by perplexity about the meaning of the passionate relationship which she helped betray, she teeters at the borderline of ultimate realization. (pp. 72-3)

The couple in "Grafton" have experienced deep love rooted in sexual satisfaction and that satisfaction sheds a permanent glow through the gloom at the poem's end. The couple in "Coös" not only failed to have such a communion but suffered through cruel act and persistent guilt over an experience which dramatized their sexual-love failure. (p. 73)

[The witch of Grafton's] descent in life was from great and enviable personal and sexual power to social rejection and isolation. Her "It doesn't seem as if I'd had the courage / To make so free and kick up in folks' faces" does stress the pathos of her situation, but more importantly it shows that her life was unlike the witch of Coös, for the Grafton witch did play a kind of joyous game of button, button in which sexual elements were delightfully discovered in not-very-hidden places as part of living her deepest nature. She may be disappointed, but she has gained something partaking of the permanent—knowledge that her nature brought deep fulfillment to herself and her husband. The poem ends on a balance between that triumph and her present plight, but surely her memories show that she could say with Frost in "I Could Give All to Time": "And what I would not part with I have kept." Her memories are precious. Those of the witch of Coös are dreadful. The metaphysical dimen-

sions of both poems are sketchy, but they do suggest a contrast between dooms and triumphs of memory, and quite possibly imply dimensions of such failure and success extending beyond this life.

Quite probably the downbeat in "Grafton's" last six lines has limited comprehension of its portrayal of triumph. Perhaps Frost was playing the fox in showing us two lonely old women who are both social-butts to a degree but are actually in contrasting situations. When we see the greatly differing bases and nature of their loneliness, and of their scoffed-at social positions, we are led back to contrasting portraits of psychological fragmentation and integration. "Coös" is a poem largely about holding back. The woman and her husband hold back from each other. The cellar, house, and attic present images of containment. The pursuit of bone as button suggests confinement. The something the dead are holding back represents a kind of knowledge but also a containment like that of the sexual failure. The poem ends with a blank confrontation of time and an implied empty gaping of the grave. In "Grafton" images of openness, expansion, and liberation abound. The Grafton witch lets both her husband and us into her secrets. Her liberation keeps her desirous of life and concerned about her husband and his love—both past and the possible present and future. The Coös witch vaguely and desperately fumbles with the facts of unfulfillment. The Grafton witch has earthly ills but goes on living with a center of faith. The poems offer another contrast on the social level. Even though she has taken a lover at one time, the witch of Coös is socially more conventional than the Grafton witch. She and her husband have conspired to conceal from the world their sexual problems and a murder. The Grafton witch is straightforward about her sexual powers and needs, but has a less savory reputation. Thus the two poems taken together make an ironic comment on society's capacity for bumbling judgments about interrelations between sex, society, and morality. (pp. 77-8)

Mordecai Marcus, "The Whole Pattern of Robert Frost's 'Two Witches': Contrasting Psycho-Sexual Modes," in Literature and Psychology (© *Morton Kaplan 1976*), *Vol. XXVI, No. 2, 1976, pp. 69-78.*

[Why] did Frost become such a migrant and meandering talker? What propelled, for it does seem finally a compulsion, this inherently most private of men to conduct more of his mental life in public than even naturally effusive men generally do? It could be suggested that it was the only outlet of this nature which he permitted himself. He was not an abundant letter writer, that safety valve for so many disciplined men, and gave Dr. Johnson as an authority for not doing so. . . . Moreover, Frost was not, in any sense, a "confessional" writer in his poetry and would be horrified at this aspect of the Lowells and Sextons of our day. Also, one hazards the guess, based on a good deal of observation, that Frost had many acquaintances but few, if any, intimates. He could suffer fools gladly (meaning professors and students!) but not equals though he made a humorous show of being an "equalitarian" who wanted to "associate only with his equals."

If [his] Bread Loaf talks often in their unfettered expansiveness and garrulity seem to be giving us both the baby *and* the bath, in complex men like Frost we must search for multiple reasons. Assuredly a principal one may be that, with utter confidence in their reception, he is testing his conceptions and their possible range, chewing his intellectual cud in public. Many of the ideas that go into the poems are found in the talks, loosely scattered and sometimes as cloudy as nebulae. We have had peripatetic poets, like Wordsworth, who thought out their poems on solitary walks, but few who could do it so successfully on the platform, giving us like a scattered bill of fare the nutrition that would sustain the poems.

Thus there is a kind of prodigal indulgence, an almost bohemian recklessness in the grasping imagination of these talks. One wanders into other territory to see Frost as one of Henry James's "greedy feeders," a man who believes his digestion can handle almost any intellectual topic. Consequently, a certain animus of appetite crops up, and one remembers a bull-like look which could come into the face of the shaggy-eyed poet when he was opposed, as if most of the fodder belonged to him by right of superior force. Anyone who could move the feast so entirely according to whim, so bent on taking possession of the world through language, is bound to have some of it come back on him, and there is no doubt an occasional flatulence in Frost just as Edmund Wilson pointed out that in the work of the Master there was a certain "Jamesian gas." (pp. 451-52)

Not infrequently, though introduced so as not to be noticeable to his audience, an element of guilt seems to motivate the mock-confessional tenor of the intellectual display as if so guarded a man must expose his intentions a little in spite of himself. It is as though this man who purified himself so powerfully and incorruptibly in the best of his poems should show, at least glancingly, that he was humanly and normally corrupt. The "darkness" of Robert Frost does come through despite the folksiness, the cuteness, the ostensible rational discourse of the surface and, in fact, helps to dramatize the soporific effect of what the poet himself called his "preliminary indulgences." (p. 452)

[Frost] was perhaps the greatest poet-performer of our times, a master whose timing was almost as good as his text. "Style," he once said, "is the way a man takes himself," and he was adept at making his listeners accept him at face value. And it was not a "low" performance either, though it contained elements of vulgarization. Few poets can successfully stage and sustain the uncanny way in which Frost could walk the thin line between candor and corn, facetiousness and farce, the platitude and the apperception. He once told me, almost as if in justification after having "assassinated" the reputations of most of his contemporaries, that the primary element of poetry was conversation about others, and in his public and private appearances, he came across as the Great Gossip, both cosy and caustic, and not many will deny that few can command our attention like one who insinuates that he knows the secrets of others as well as of the universe—Old Wives' Tales, except that the teller is masculine, and we are reminded that Frost said that poetry may be a feminine thing and for that reason he generally preferred it written by a man. As one story leads to another, one may turn a little uneasily like the man shifting with the log in "An Old Man's Winter Night," but this may be the price we must pay for having been "acquainted with the night" which seems to be, underneath the japes and the jokes, what "gossip" is most nearly all about. (p. 453)

Charles Edward Eaton, in The Georgia

Review *(copyright, 1976, by The University of Georgia), Summer, 1976.*

Along with Whitman, Dickinson and Stevens, Frost has a place among the greatest of American writers. We know something about the lives of all these poets and they were all isolated souls. Dickinson was fierce in her detachment, Whitman troubled by it, Stevens at perfect ease. Frost is really in a different class: a more hateful human being cannot have lived who wrote words that moved other human beings to tears. . . .

There is a cant about "the dark Frost" and a cant about "Frost, the tragic poet." On the occasion of his 85th birthday Frost heard himself lauded, in an after-dinner speech by Lionel Trilling, as a bearer of bad tidings for civilization—as one who, like Sophocles, fulfilled the proper role of the poet. Frost was visibly shaken for days afterward. At last someone had called his bluff on the popular audience—and at a public ceremony. But he may have been shaken too because he had succeeded in yet another lie. Frost wrote out of the darkness in himself, and said so. He knew nothing else. But here was a critic of reputation, with enormous gravity and tact, calling that darkness a universal condition and praising Frost for having revealed it. Once more he found himself where he wanted to be: before the others yet thoroughly hidden from their view.

What meaning, if any, does this life have for the art that came from it? Frost carried the dream of self-reliance farther than his heroes, Emerson and William James, would have dared, or wished. His recovery of his own axis was a project that had no end, and it made him the bleakest of lords. To realize this does not make his poems less astonishing. It does allow us to read them more truly and severely as what they are. At the end of "To a Moth Seen in Winter" Frost spoke for himself.

> You must become more
>   simply wise than I
> To know the hand I stretch
>   impulsively
> Across the gulf of well nigh
>   everything
> May reach to you, but cannot
>   touch your fate.
> I cannot touch your life,
>   much less can save,
> Who am tasked to save my
>   own a little while.

The lines can be read, many of us once read them, as a touching confession of humility and even modesty. But, if we think of Frost's own life, we can hear him biting off every word. He is signing off. As we survey 90 years for the most part so mean and so desperate, the artful and endearing "a little while" seems the only lie. (p. 28)

David Bromwich, "Nedwick's Season of Frost," in The New York Times Book Review *(© 1977 by The New York Times Company; reprinted by permission), January 16, 1977, pp. 4-5, 28.*

Frost's poetry of "home" is a dramatization of the human costs and human benefits of decorum. As a reader becomes more intimate with the poems, however, it is hard to resist what seem like solicitations to think of social or psychological or domestic decorums as somehow synonymous with poetic ones. How much "extravagance" is possible within decorum; how much can be mediated by it; what extremities are induced by the constraints or failures of mediation; and what, in case of failure, are the prospects beyond decorum or mediation except nothingness or madness? These are issues central to English poetry, especially since 1800, and to the great Americans, Whitman and Stevens. One of the reasons Frost has not been taken as seriously as Stevens is in part explained by the fact that though he can be found working within some of the same dialectical oppositions, he chose resolutely, even defiantly, to work also within the circumstantially or topically familiar, as if from a list of the hundred most famous poetic and novelistic situations. So insistently ordinary, so particularized is the domestic drama of his work that it appears to be written *against* that kind of poetry which is an interpretation of itself and of its potentialities. Of some importance, too, when it comes to the understandably Anglophilic bias of literary critics, is the fact that Frost chose a landscape . . . which does not have anything storied about it. . . . It was a landscape without poetic or sublime associations and Frost got credit for being able even to report on a region and a people so uninspiring.

Frost was treated mostly as the brilliant poet of the average human lot, and that attitude continues . . . to stand in the way of efforts to give him credit for being a great poet precisely because it was within that human lot that he found the glories and plights of poetry itself. . . . (pp. 136-37)

[While] it is possible . . . to infer from Frost's poems an interest in the drama of poetic "making," he is some of the time even tiresomely determined not to surrender the human actuality of his poems to a rhetoric by which action is transformed immediately into ritual, as in the account of the boy stealing the boat in *The Prelude*. Where such enlargement of rhetoric occurs in Frost, it redounds almost invariably to the disadvantage of the speaker; he must face the opposition both of nature and of the decorum, however pliant, which Frost establishes between himself and the reader. . . . Having met the challenge that no one can turn certain kinds of New England and especially household experience into metaphor, he then, with an exquisite pride, wants to show that he does not choose ostentatiously to extend his metaphor into a fashionable literariness. A great poem like "Home Burial" thus has to win its way, with a lean and sinewy and finally irresistible necessity, to a reading that tells us not only about lives but about Frost's own life in the writing of poetry and about his rescue of a life for poetry out of his own desperate need for circumscriptions.

He is a poet who finds his freedom of movement out of a sense of restraint: the movement to one extreme is provoked by the imminence of the other. "The Wood-Pile" is like a sequel to "Home Burial," with the man in this instance wandering from a "home" that seems little more than an abstraction to him and to us. More a meditation than a dramatic narrative, it offers the soliloquy of a lone figure walking in a winter landscape. (pp. 137-38)

[There] is a recognition of a wintry barrenness made more so . . . by a reductive process by which possibilities of metaphor—of finding some reassuring resemblances—are gradually disposed of. . . . It is as if the wintry prospect . . . , a cold clarity without redeeming deceptions, has in itself been an achievement of the imagination. . . .

[The] speaker in "The Wood-Pile" shapes, from his very opening words, a human presence for us in his sentence sounds, his voice; he makes us imagine him as someone in a human plight "far from home." (p. 139)

The voice of this man ("So as to say for certain I was here / Or somewhere else") cannot be expected to test the poetic potentialities of what is seen and heard and can even less be expected to cheer itself up by indulging in the hyperbolic or the sublime vocabularies. There is an informality even in the initial placement—"out walking . . . one gray day"—of the spondaic effect of "gray day," as if it were a scheduled occurrence (like "pay day") and of the possible metaphoric weight in what he says, as in the allusion (but not really) to the lack of adequate support he can expect in this landscape ("The hard snow held me, save where now and then/ One foot went through"). Such anxious and innocuous precision about the relative hardness of the snow or the size and contour of the trees is humanly and characterologically right. It expresses the kind of paranoia that goes with any feeling of being lost and of losing thereby a confident sense of self. (pp. 140-41)

From its opening moment ["The Wood-Pile"] becomes a human drama of dispossession, of failed possessiveness, and of the need to structure realities which are not "here." . . .

The only probable evidence of structure that he does find, already put together, is the "wood-pile," a forgotten remnant of earlier efforts to make a "home" by people who, when they did it, were also away from home. The pile of wood . . . once more excites [the speaker's] anxious precisions. He still needs to find some human resemblances, evidences in zones and demarcations for the human capacity to make a claim on an alien landscape. (p. 142)

If the speaker "resembles" anything at the end of the poem, it is the wood-pile itself, something without even a semblance of consciousness; it is wholly self-consuming. As in "Desert Places," another poem about a lonely man walking in a landscape of snow, the man in "The Wood-Pile" could say that "The loneliness includes me unawares." . . . He is on the point of being obliterated by the landscape, rather than allowed to exist even as an observer of it, much less a mediating or transcending presence. . . . For Frost's lonely walkers, far from "home," nothing can come from such nothing, and they therefore must try to speak again and in such a way as to make known an ordinary human presence. (p. 144)

Frost's whole theory of "sentence sounds" is implicitly a way of taking an exception to transcendental vision and to the Sublime as an alternative to the discovery of barrenness: "I cultivate . . . the hearing imagination rather than the seeing imagination though I should not want to be without the latter." . . . Barrenness, poetry, the mind of winter are posited as conditions of life and of poverty. . . . [In Frost] these same conditions are held [in a] . . . dialectical tension. "Home" exerts such a simultaneous restraint on and incentive to "extra-vagance" that anyone who feels it must become pugnacious in the expressed need for ventilation, for some degree of imaginative license. Hence the sharply . . . individuated and personalized tone of Frost's poems.

They cannot scare me with their empty spaces
Between stars—on stars where no human race is.
I have it in me so much nearer home
To scare myself with my own desert places.

The self-assertion here is implicit in the slangy schoolyard tone of "They cannot scare me." . . . It is typical of Frost that he would bring, without any signaling, a fashionable-sounding phraseology of self-diminishment into combination with that kind of vernacular voice which draws its strength from a sense of rootedness, no matter how unfertile the soil. (pp. 145-46)

Voice is the most important, distinguishing, and conspicuously insistent feature of Frost's poetry and of his writing about poetry. There is scarcely a single poem which does not ask the reader to imagine a human character equivalent to the movement of voice, and there is no other poet in English of whom this is so emphatically the case. Behind the theory of "voice" and "sentence sounds" that he presented wholly as a literary choice, behind his related insistence that poetry was as good as it was "dramatic," there is a psychological and moral imperative. It can be most simply described as a revulsion against the idea of human transparency. Under any and all circumstances he would resist becoming a "transparent eyeball." It would mean getting lost. This was never an agreeable prospect for him, despite little hints to the contrary in "Directive," and there are therefore no poems by him of visionary afflatus. There are, however, close to terrifying poems about wandering off, losing the self, or belonging nowhere. (pp. 146-47)

True "realization" for Frost occurs *after* the man who went outdoors comes back in. "I opened the door so my last look / Should be taken outside a house and book." Thus Frost begins a poem called "One More Brevity," in his last volume. But the "look," while a perfectly "extravagant" one, in that it is beyond both "home" and literature, is really a way of assuring himself that the stars are in place so that he may sleep more securely: "I said I would see how Sirius kept / His watchdog eye on what remains / To be gone into if not explained." "Intensifications" while "out of doors" are not in themselves a true form of "realization," so far as Frost is concerned, since the very nature of metaphor involves for him a constant pressure, *at some point,* against intensifications and the excesses that go with them. Quite charmingly, while the man is looking up at the star Sirius a dog slips by "to be my problem guest: / Not a heavenly dog made manifest, / But an earthly dog of the carriage breed." This is a fine example of what Frost means when he says "I would be willing to throw away everything else but that: enthusiasm tamed by metaphor." . . . (pp. 148-49)

In Frost, the ideal aspect of metaphor exists only that it may be tested. Metaphor is an education by which the reader learns to be "at ease with figurative values," at ease not to luxuriate but the better to know "how far [he] may expect to ride" a metaphor "and when it may break down with [him]." . . . (p. 149)

Frost asks us to be [two] kinds of readers; and his unique difficulty is in the demand that we be common and literary all at once. Which is a way of suggesting . . . the great difference sometimes between Frost, whose extensive literary allusiveness is always less apparent than are his allusions to clichés, and any of the other great figures of the first half of this century. (p. 152)

"On the Heart's Beginning to Cloud the Mind" and "The Figure in the Doorway," are about houses looked at with some sort of ulterior, "creative" intention by a poet-observer from a passing train. The poems are placed next to one another in *A Further Range,* which also includes "Desert Places," "Design," and "Provide, Provide." All these are meditations on bleakness, a subject of increasing frequency in Frost's work beginning with his fourth volume, *New Hampshire.* They are different from earlier poems about the failures of "home" to nourish the imagination in that the narrator is disengaged and relatively dispassionate. The houses are discovered by accident, and it is implied that the viewer is somebody who wanders less in a search for signs and embodiments than to amuse himself with the possibility of their existence. (pp. 154-55)

[In "The Figure in the Doorway" a] vision of the "great gaunt figure" filling the cabin door prompts little more than superficial reportage. Four lines in a row begin with the repeated "he had"; the man's possessions are then as dutifully listed. It reads as if the speaker were determined not to make anything out of what he sees. Beyond these measurements, all we learn about the man is the merest guesswork. . . . [There] is scarcely any scene at all here; there is no material for poetry except what might be guessed *if* the spectator were in a position to watch long enough. This, then, for all its self-discipline, also becomes a "surface flight," and the best he can do with the image of the giant man in the doorway is to make a "tall tale," in a grotesque sense of the term, about what might happen at some future time: "And had he fallen inward on the floor, / He must have measured to the further wall. / But we who passed were not to see him fall." (p. 158)

["The Most of It"] is the most powerful of what might be called his spectatorial poems, those in which a wandering figure tries to locate a "home" by the exercise of vision, the making of metaphor, or the making of sound to which an answering call is expected. . . . "The Most of It" is a poem in which "life" is being asked to do some or all of a "poet's" work. The request is illegitimate, and it is made not by Frost but by the speakers or spectators—or would-be poets—in his poems. If their calls on "life" have a pathos of innocence, they also elicit that Frostean exasperation which is aroused by anyone who acts politically, or poetically, as if the world owes him a living, or as if it is easy to be "at home in the metaphors" one contrives about the world. (pp. 159-60)

Significantly, the poem following "The Most of It" is "Never Again Would Birds' Song Be the Same." There, the world itself has already been made our "home," partly by the fact that the "birds" "from having heard the daylong voice of Eve / Had added to their own an oversound." It is a sound that still "persists" in the wilderness which is of our present moment. But her "sound," her "voice," was not, we have to remember, directed to birds at all in any naive expectation that they would answer her in kind or in any other way. The birds simply heard her voice as it was "carried aloft" from the intercourse between Adam and Eve, the "call or laughter" of their daily life together before the Fall. To the extent, then, that the sound of birds has been crossed with and become an echo of human sound, it is not to be confused with the kind of sound the man in the opening lines of "The Most of It" requests as an answering call from the wilderness around him. Keeping the universe alone, he is an Adam without an Eve. (p. 160)

In the best and simplest sense ["The Most of It"] is exciting for the largeness of its embrace, and because the man is beautifully anxious that "life" be allowed to exalt and enrapture itself. So that even without knowing classical literary analogues in echo literature, and all that is implied therein about man and his relation to the universe, any reader feels the presence and pressure here of a great human tradition and a great human predicament. In the expansive gestures of inclusiveness made at the outset, in the efforts to bring a universe into the focus of the self and its immediate environments, the poem is about the attempt to "make" a home by demanding a "return," a coming back of sound enriched and transformed by its movements out into the universe. If the man or "life" asks too much, then the response which they do get by the end of the poem is at least to that degree more powerfully informative about the nature of things than if they had asked for too little. If the aspiration is always to bring "home" what would otherwise be unseen, an element left to chaos, then at least the effort should show not only what can but also what cannot be given house room. (pp. 166-67)

"Never Again Would Birds' Song Be The Same" is quite properly located between two poems in which human sound fails in an attempted transaction with nature. It is as if the young man and the woman of "The Subverted Flower," the last of the three poems, were in a post-lapsarian world where flowers and sex have the power to transform them into beasts, while the man alone in "The Most of It" is in the world without an Eve of any kind, and where the only form of animal life which can be heard, seen, or imagined in response to a cry of loneliness is so alien as to be called "it." In both poems the world is devoid of love, and consequently, as Frost would have it, of the power to realize a human extension, "someone else additional to him," a metaphor, like Adam and Eve, that would augment the human animal and allow it to make a human "home." These three great poems are profoundly about finding a "home" in the largest sense—by propagating the self through love, through the metaphorical discovery of self in another. "You must have read the famous valentine / Pericles sent Aspasia in absentia," Frost writes at the end of the late poem (1951) "How Hard It Is to Keep from Being King When It's in You and in the Situation." And he then gives his version of the valentine:

> For God himself the height of feeling free
> Must have been His success in simile
> When at sight of you He thought of me.

Simile or metaphor is the act of love, the act of writing poetry, and also evidence in each of these of how something as frighteningly big and potentially chaotic as the "universe" can be "kept" to a human measure. In the disproportion between these two words, "universe" and "kept," is both the pathos of "The Most of It" and a clue to Frost's sense that his own personal and poetic salvation lay in facing up to the full cost, in poetry and in daily living, of the metaphors he makes. "Earth's the right place for love," we are told in "Birches," and while there are times when the speaker of that poem would "like to get away from earth awhile," his aspiration for escape to something "larger" is safely controlled by the recognition that birch trees will only bear so much climbing before returning you, under the pressure of human weight, back home. (pp. 171-72)

Richard Poirier, "Soundings for Home"

(originally published in The Georgia Review, *Summer, 1977), in his* Robert Frost: The Work of Knowing *(copyright © 1977 by Oxford University Press, Inc.; reprinted by permission), Oxford University Press, 1977.*

*   *   *

FUGARD, Athol   1932-

Fugard is a South African dramatist. His plays feature a small cast of characters whose minds are probed by Fugard. Although Fugard depicts lives of desolation and ennui, he is most concerned with apartheid and its consequences. He collaborated with John Kani and Winston Ntshona on three of his most recent works, *The Island, Sizwe Bansi Is Dead,* **and** *Statements after an Arrest under the Immorality Act.* **(See also** *CLC, Vol. 5.)*

Though there have been plenty of books, films and documents in the past 20 years outlining or illuminating different areas of repression and distortion in South African life caused by apartheid, the . . . plays by involving Athol Fugard . . . [provide] the first sustained attempt to show British theatre audiences the terrible effects of the régime in human terms, reaching into the most personal areas of life. (p. 40)

The Island is, perhaps, . . . [more] explicitly political [than *Sizwe Bansi Is Dead* or *Statements After an Arrest Under the Immorality Act*], as it deals with two detainees on Robben Island, where hard-line opponents of the South African government are kept. The monotonous, soul-destroying, back-breaking routine of their lives is, if anything, rather too emphatically established at the play's outset in a lengthy mime by the two [characters] involved . . .; and the play goes on to explore their relationships with their basic situation and with each other, fluctuating between hope and despair, mutual affection, exasperation and jealousy. (p. 41)

The play cannot help but be moving on account of the conditions it depicts, particularly at its tremendous emotional climax. Thematically and artistically, it has affinities with Beckett's *Godot* and is none the worse for that. . . . But, ultimately, the play does not quite reach the level of *Sizwe Bansi,* if only because the characters are not individually delineated and believable to the same degree.

Little remains to be said about *Sizwe Bansi Is Dead,* which has received unanimous and justifiable critical acclaim. . . . All that I would like to add is that the play has everything the most demanding theatregoer could conceivably wish for: a strong story-line, with tension and humour nicely balanced; very individual and profoundly conceived characters; . . . and a political and social significance informing every line of the text without ever becoming blatant or overt. (pp. 42-3)

Statements deals with the clandestine love affair between a white woman, a librarian, and a coloured man, the headmaster of a local school, married to someone else. ('Coloured' in the South African sense of the word, meaning 'mixed race'). As most people know, sexual intercourse between people of different races is forbidden in South Africa; and the tension of the situation arises mostly from this fact and partly from Errol Philander's guilt caused by his adultery. . . .

Despite its many excellent moments . . . *Statements* is, in many ways, the least satisfactory of the three. It is the most obviously a 'play' . . . , constructed on fairly conventional literary lines. . . . Fugard fails to clarify the relationship between Errol and his wife and how it affects his relationship with Frieda the librarian. Also, the role of the policeman stands like an afterthought tacked onto the play, never organically involved with the action. . . .

Overall, one feels far better informed at the emotional level as a result of these plays about the grim texture of life for some of the oppressed South African people. Fugard's main strength lies in his ability to create plays on two levels: the bedrock economic and political one and the personal one of characterisation and relationships. These two levels subtly impinge and interact on each other, creating works of art that are emotionally as well as politically convincing. (p. 43)

> Jonathan Hammond, "A South African Season: Sizwe Bansi, The Island and Statements," in Plays and Players (© copyright Jonathan Hammond 1974; reprinted with permission), March, 1974, pp. 40-3.

It is hard to look at *Sizwe Bansi Is Dead* as a mere play; it is both more and less than that. One of a brace of theater pieces by the white South African dramatist, Athol Fugard, it was created in collaboration with John Kani and Winston Ntshona, the two blacks who constitute the entire acting company. Significantly, the program describes these works as "devised" rather than written, and *Sizwe* is indeed a device. It is, essentially, three documents stapled together. . . .

Let us not pretend that this is drama, or even literature. It differs from Fugard's best plays, *The Blood Knot* and *Boesman and Lena,* where the structure is much more homogeneous and harmonious, the characterization fully three-dimensional, and where, though the references are South African, the relevance is universally human. Here the construction is rambling and diffuse, and though there is much human savor, the main focus is on specific South African injustice. What is laudable, though, is that *Sizwe* is not just agitprop; that the people, even if they are of a circumscribed place and time, come before the propaganda. So perhaps we can best describe it as poster art. When it is affixed to buildings, fences, or barricades, it is a poster, a call to arms or other organized action. Decades later, when it and others like it are hung in exhibition on museum walls, something else will become apparent: a certain artistry, and maybe even a modicum of art.

Despite these strictures, I do not consider *Sizwe Bansi* unrewarding or uninteresting, except for some *longueurs* in the third section. Fugard, an intelligent, magnanimous, and brave man, and his two first-rate actor-collaborators . . . have breathed much juicy authenticity into their "device." A new motto may arise from it, to supersede the South African government's "Divide and Conquer!"—"Devise and Overcome!" (p. 87)

> John Simon, in New York Magazine (© 1974 by NYM Corp.; reprinted by permission of New York Magazine and John Simon), December 2, 1974.

Athol Fugard's *Boesman and Lena,* which was presented in New York four years ago, is one of the best new plays I have seen in my life [see Kauffman's comments, *CLC,* Vol. 5]. . . . (p. 16)

[*Sizwe Bansi Is Dead* and *The Island*] are drawn from the innermost feelings of three gifted and committed men. So it's something more than sad to report that, for me, both plays are disappointing. . . .

The chief trouble is simultaneously the chief emotional asset: the conditions out of which these plays grow. The facts of South African apartheid are as well known, in essence, as they are ever going to be to those who are interested in knowing them; and these plays do little more than elaborate, without deepening our insight into, those facts. And even those facts are interfered with by the staginess, old and avant-garde. . . . Even more disappointing, because more centrally relevant to the work of making plays out of this material in the first place, is that they illuminate so little imaginatively. . . .

As for Fugard, I've known no one in my lifetime who has worked with greater passion in the theater, but apparently his very passion can misguide him. I presume to think it has done so here. He is a director of strengths, but he is a writer of much greater strengths. He has opted in these past few years to work with actors in "devising" plays: he had his reasons—passionate, I'm sure—for doing this, but the result is wasteful of his best talents. This devising of plays with actors is a function of directors who cannot write original work—sometimes greatly gifted ones like Andrei Serban. But I hope Fugard, a writer, will write. In these plays devised with actors he has slipped into theatricalisms like none I can recall in his other work. These new works, compared with *Boesman and Lena,* are somewhat superficial because they are artistically insecure and essentially didactic, and are thus only about the troubles of South African blacks.

I'm aware of the risks in that "only," but I stand by it, particularly after rereading *Boesman.* . . . (pp. 16, 26)

> Stanley Kauffmann, in The New Republic (reprinted by permission of The New Republic; © 1974 by The New Republic, Inc.), December 21, 1974.

Sizwe Bansi Is Dead and *The Island* . . . have received considerable praise, but the critics of the popular press have stressed the politics of these plays in a way that does them a disservice and that reveals much about prevailing (mis)conceptions about the relationship between "politics" and art. These *are* political plays, but are not one-dimensional, undramatic, or inartistic as is sometimes implied by the pejorative use of "political" to imply a limitation in a work of art. The critic short-circuits his analytical function by simply naming a play "political" and dismissing it out of hand, if its politics are "bad," or damning it to faint praise for good intentions, if its politics are "good." (p. 116)

Because Athol Fugard speaks openly about the conditions in South Africa that he abhors, and because his plays are set in his homeland and confront the inhumanity spawned by its laws and values, it is facilely assumed that he is a propagandist and that his plays are mere devices. Art, dramatization, and suggestion are supposed to have been replaced by politics, explication, and emotional marching orders. Fugard, however, can no more ignore the conditions in which he lives than could Faulkner ignore slavery. Fugard's link to his homeland is complete. He cannot conceive of living or working elsewhere, and this intimate tie is evident both in his portrayal of blacks living under apartheid, and his description of the exquisite mating of co-bras. . . .

Fugard and his actor-collaborators implicitly and pro-foundly understand that political values and processes per-meate their lives and must, therefore, be reflected in their work. "Politics" is not simply added on to a pre-existing work, nor is it an independent element solely intended from the start. Kani [one of Fugard's collaborators] has said that "it is for the audience to call a play political, not for the artist to intend it so . . . these plays are called political be-cause they show our lives, not because we are politicians." (p. 117)

Like Ibsen, Fugard might claim, "I am less the social critic and more the poet than people seem generally inclined to believe." He is a kind of despairing pessimist, an agnostic whose faith resides in human beings and the making of theatre. He is not a writer with a cause; would any propa-gandist state, "I'd like to believe that a play can be a signif-icant form of action but I've never been able to convince myself?"

Sizwe Bansi Is Dead opens with a long monologue by Styles, a factory worker turned photographer, whose speech is interrupted, finally, by the visit of a customer who calls himself Robert Zwelinzima. In a flash-back Rob-ert, now called Sizwe Bansi, visits Buntu who, during a night of drunken revelling, discovers the body of a dead man. Sizwe's own identity book prohibits him from working or living in the city and he is convinced by Buntu to switch books with the dead man, Robert Zwelinzima, whose book is in proper order. In *The Island,* John and Winston prepare *Antigone* for a concert at the prison where they are confined. John is called to the warden's office and informed that an appeal has been successful and he is to be released in three months. Ecstatic at first, the friends re-alize that their close relationship will soon end since Win-ston has been sentenced to life; they present *Antigone* nonetheless.

Sizwe Bansi has attracted more attention than *The Island* (and has been performed more frequently) but is marred in several ways. It is discursive at times, and some of its components are unassimilated, but the subject is powerful and suggestive. . . . It is only in retrospection that one real-izes the accomplishment does not quite equal the potential of the material. The focus created by the opening mono-logue, and Robert's visit to Styles's studio, is dissipated in the second half of the play, particularly in the seemingly interminable carousal of Sizwe and Buntu.

The central image of a photograph—that snapped by Styles and the one on the identification card—is poignant. A pho-tograph affords a kind of immortality, perhaps the only kind possible to a black South African. Styles calls his studio "A strong-room of dreams. . . . That's what I do, friends. Put down, in my way, on paper the dreams and hopes of my people so that even their children's children will re-member a man. . . ." (pp. 117-18)

Unfortunately, the photographic image is insufficiently sus-tained, obfuscated in a torrent of words and emotion.

The play also suffers from some over-explanation and an inconsistency in the character of Sizwe. As a newcomer to the city from the government established "homeland," Sizwe is unfamiliar with the difficulty of finding work or

living quarters without the appropriate stamps in his book. Buntu tediously explains the bureaucracy of Influx Control, computerized records, permits, licenses, Native Commis-sioners, and government living quarters—but Sizwe's illit-eracy can explain only a part of his innocence. It seems, finally, unbelievable, particularly when he is utterly con-fused by the opportunity of changing his name. While this underscores his association between name, identity, dig-nity, and manhood it reaches a preposterous level when Sizwe becomes confused by the imagined effect a change of name will have on his relationship with his wife and chil-dren. Near the end of the play he states: "A black man stay out of trouble? Impossible, Buntu. Our skin is trouble." This rings a bit hollow, coming from a man who appears so naive and backward and who, seemingly, has never before experienced the impact of the laws and regulations.

Sizwe Bansi is also somewhat formless and rambling at points. . . . (p. 118)

While discursiveness might seem an inherent danger of the collaborative and improvisational process which resulted in these plays, *The Island* is structurally integrated, tightly controlled, and sharply focused. . . . Kani and Ntshona use their own names in *The Island.* . . . (p. 119)

Both plays contain aurally haunting moments: A siren blasts as John and Winston exit; Sizwe repeats again and again his new identification number and the repetition be-comes an insistent chant, so earnest that one understands the daily significance of this number to the man. Both plays also use the audience. Styles's opening monologue is openly addressed to it and he is assisted at one point by a volunteer. While this is generally a self-indulgent device, there is none of the usual tension and anxiety created when the spectator is startled from his voyeurism and asked to relinquish his anonymity. . . .

Fugard's characters are never the one-dimensional stick figures implied by those who see these plays as political tracts. *The Island* is the story of political prisoners, but also of the loving bond between two men. Styles's mono-logue in *Sizwe Bansi* on the Ford plant seems to imply an indictment of the capitalistic base, yet in his struggle for some degree of independence and integrity he turns to pri-vate enterprise. True, he has few alternatives, but he ag-gressively protects his investment from the curiosity and reach of a customer's children. (p. 120)

Fugard has stated that he is addicted to the actor and that it has been an obsession throughout his career. Fugard im-plies that it is for the actor that he writes. In both these plays he has helped create original and full-bodied charac-ters equal to those in his previous work. These collabora-tions also resemble Fugard's previous plays in at least two other ways—the characters, despite their plight, maintain an infectious and incisive sense of humor, and variations on the play-within-the-play technique are used.

Whatever the desperate conditions of their lives, Fugard's characters are able to laugh—at themselves, at their sur-roundings. Sometimes it is the laugh which keeps one from the brink of insanity, but more often it is a simpler bemuse-ment, an ability to see and embrace incongruities. (pp. 120-22)

Fugard's characters often engage in self-conscious play to escape themselves or their wretched environments, and their fantasies may lead to an epiphany of self-recognition. Indeed, in a pervasive and painful sense black South Africans are forced to play a role—that of the happy, contented and obeisant semi-human he is thought to be. . . .

In all of Fugard's plays the imagination is a certain road to an equitable and happy world of dreams. In *The Blood Knot,* Morrie and Zach relive their childhood in an escapist ride in an imaginary car. Milly and her lodgers in *People Are Living There* give a party at which, she insists, they must have a good time (whether or not they actually do). Lena pretends to understand the words of the Old African speaking a foreign language in *Boesman And Lena.* In *Statements After An Arrest Under The Immorality Act* the lovers explain how they would spend their last forty-three cents on a day with no tomorrow.

Sometimes characters play by intentionally deceiving others: in *Hello and Goodbye* Johnny leads Hester to believe their father is still alive; in *Sizwe Bansi* the foreman is dependent on Styles for the translation of his instructions to the "boys" and, by Styles's cunning, is made a dupe in the process. In the photography studio, Robert strolls down a make-believe avenue lined with imaginary office buildings, a cigarette in his hand, a pipe in his mouth. John and Winston have a nightly ritual of placing imaginary telephone calls from their cell to their friends back home.

The presentation of *Antigone,* however, is a return to the conventional use of a formal play-within-the-play and its use is more calculated than playful: Insight and comprehension have preceded rather than followed the act of play. The parallel between Antigone, John, and Winston is clear: Whatever the higher law might be, each has contravened the inhuman, immoral, and arbitrary law of the state and is held accountable. This use of a political play within a larger political play raises the question of the relationship between art and politics. (p. 122)

Antigone is not saved, nor Creon deposed, but a statement is made—a dramatization, not a call to arms. The mere ability and strength to make such a statement marks a change from the impotence of Fugard's previous plays. There is a clear shift from the complete powerlessness of *The Blood Knot* in which Zach has no choices and Morrie has some, but does not take them. Mary Benson, an exiled South African, has written, "the characters in Fugard's plays are vital metaphors of human survival." They endure, without self pity. In *Sizwe Bansi* and *The Island,* however, survival is not simply the result of Promethean forebearance or saintly patience. The characters of these two plays begin to take an active hand, however tentative, in their own fate and future. Styles has opened a business and Sizwe breaks the law in order to support himself and his family. There is no call for revolutionary upheaval. For the time being at least, Sizwe uses the system for his own benefit; though somewhat dim-witted he is not impotent, nor as pathetic as Milly, Lena, or Zach. In *The Blood Knot,* the brothers are passive, saved by fate from a confrontation with a white woman. In *The Island,* John and Winston openly present *Antigone* to the prison dignitaries. Characters have developed a sense of pride and are even willing to defy the laws—Winston was imprisoned for burning his passbook in front of a police station.

Since *Sizwe Bansi* and *The Island* are collaborations it is impossible to attribute changes from the earlier plays to a change in Fugard's perceptions. Indeed, this may suggest that the changes are not of his own making. He has been working with improvised theatre since 1967. Although useful, collaboration has been a stage of his development which he has now left to return to the privacy (and security?) of pencil and blank paper. He admits that collaboration does not always allow the opportunity to aver the personal statements he wants to make, "Yes, there is some difference between what I want to say and what we have said." Perhaps, strange as it may seem, *Sizwe Bansi* and *The Island* are more optimistic and hopeful than is his own vision.

Some critics have complained that the material of *Sizwe Bansi* is well known by now and that nothing new has been added. It is true that we have heard before the plea for dignity, "I'm a man brother" and know, intellectually at least, the horror of prison life. However, *Sizwe Bansi* and *The Island* make us experience these things deeply. They authenticate experience outside our own. The subjects are far from hackneyed within the context of these plays because they are so forcefully driven by felt experience. These plays *are* well-known in one very important sense—they are human statements, not political treatises; we respond to them immediately.

The Island and *Sizwe Bansi Is Dead* appear so pervasively political because the reality, the milieu, in which they are rooted, is so overtly political. Our society is equally political, though less obviously so because of its subtle (but perhaps more insidious) benign neglect, and pale of normality, equality, and legitimacy. (p. 123)

> *Russell Vandenbroucke, "Robert Zwelinzima Is Alive," in* yale/theatre *(copyright © by Theater, formerly yale/theatre 1975), Fall, 1975, pp. 116-23.*

Dimetos seems, at first, to be far removed from the hard political clarity of Fugard's earlier plays concerned with apartheid. It is set in a 'remote province' and based on an obscure myth which Fugard found mentioned in the notebooks of Albert Camus. The Dimetos of the myth had a 'guilty love' for his niece who hanged herself; so indeed does Fugard's Dimetos have a guilty love for his niece, who also hangs herself. The stage Dimetos, an engineer who has fled from the city to the country, becomes aware of his passion when his niece removes her dress to clamber down a well and help him rescue a horse. When an emissary from the city comes to try to lure Dimetos back, Dimetos uses the unwitting man to help arrange the near-rape of his niece. It is the niece's discovery that her uncle watched the assault from a lemon grove that leads her to kill herself, and, quite some time later, the emissary, Danilo, returns and accuses Dimetos in the all-too literal words of Camus, of having had a 'guilty love'.

In the myth, some time after the hanging, the body of a beautiful woman is washed ashore and Dimetos, finding the body, falls in love and goes mad as he watches it decay. In the play, Dimetos has fled with his housekeeper to a remote beach where a sea-creature one day crawls upon an off-shore rock, dies and decays. Dimetos, the engineer who fled the city, now reduced to collecting shells for trading, gradually lets the smell of putrefaction drive him mad, and his geometrically ordered universe shatters. In order that the collapse of his universe might be understood, much of the first act is given to demonstrating engineering principles, with Dimetos propounding gravity as a law (the word is crucial) that holds the universe together, or demonstrating knots or a system of pulleys. (pp. 26-7)

It has been said that the play is too neatly a dramatisation of Camus's paragraph. I suggest that on the contrary it is too energetically concerned with all the possible implications and motivations of the simple events outlined. Most of the first act is fleshy exposition which elaborates Dimetos's history while coyly hiding the logical occurrence of place names with inexplicit phrases such as 'our bustling little metropolis'.

It seems to me that the action begins more than halfway through the play, virtually at the point where the heat of the solstice, drink and proximity bring Danilo to attempt his assault on the niece. Little of the detailed dramatic justifications carefully built into the story are necessary from that point on. To be sure, it is necessary to establish that physical laws have ordered Dimetos's existence, it is useful to know that Dimetos taught his niece the knot she used to hang herself with, but little more of the dialogue in the first hour prepares one for the claustrophobic last act.

The power that is in the play arrives with the carcase on the rock. As the almost perceptible odour of rotting oppresses Dimetos and his housekeeper, it cracks the rigid structure of their lives and opens up the play to Fugard's preoccupations. Although the play, despite its evident Afrikaner distrust of cities, is not overtly political, there are similarities to the political plays. Fugard's anti-apartheid plays were not so directly concerned with the politics of situations as with his characters. It is the roles of individuals, whether in relation to the laws of physics or laws of government, which concern him. Dimetos's failure is to come to grips with the lawless nature of his desire. . . .

For all its failings, *Dimetos* is undeniably the work of a major playwright. (p. 27)

> *Ned Chaillet, "One Play Down," in* Plays and Players (© *copyright Ned Chaillet 1976; reprinted with permission), August, 1976, pp. 26-7.*

The plays of Athol Fugard offer an opportunity to explore some of the political and artistic tensions in the work of one of Africa's leading writers. Furthermore the nature of the society in which Fugard is writing, repressive and philistine, censorious and neurotically suspicious, lend to the tension innate in any literature a particular exigency and a singular sharpness. As an outsider reads any work of South African literature he is conscious of this underlying reality: art produced in such hostile circumstances must be vulnerable to political temptations and aesthetic dangers which are in equal measure aesthetic temptations and political dangers. (p. 167)

Fugard's commitment to change hasn't wavered . . . , but what has undeniably altered [since the late fifties] is his sense of the relation between his work in theatre and his political engagement. The two introductory essays written for *Three Port Elizabeth Plays* and *Statements,* in conjunction with the plays themselves, constitute some fascinating evidence about the dynamics of literature's political life in contemporary Africa.

From 1961 to 1968 Fugard was at work on what he now sees as his 'Family Trilogy', his large reputation outside Africa being built on these three plays. During those years Fugard had been preoccupied with domestic, familial relationships, this stage of his work being summarized in a Notebook entry for September 1968:

> The thought today that *Boesman and Lena* is the third part of a trilogy, that together with *The Blood Knot* and *Hello and Goodbye* it should be called *The Family.*
>
> *First* [in *Blood Knot*] brother and brother, then child and parent [*Hello and Goodbye*], and now in *Boesman and Lena,* parent and parent, man and woman.

The completed trilogy forms a powerful and moving exploration of the tensions generated from intimacy; it is, beyond doubt, a major theatrical achievement. Racial injustice, the currency of daily human impoverishment under apartheid, is never far away from the action and dialogue of the trilogy, but is hardly presented explicitly. In these plays the reality of a statutory inhumanity is a ceaseless murmur at the level of their 'sub-text'; it is present only in the assumptions and perspectives of the characters. . . . (pp. 168-69)

After completing *Boesman*—whose intentions were in reality *opposed* to apartheid—Fugard seems to have become dissatisfied with the domestic realism of the trilogy and his three later plays are marked by changes in content and in dramatic style. Fugard's themes have moved from the family outwards, to the various ways in which a harsh society impinges upon the individual's freedom. In *Sizwe Bansi Is Dead* it is the pass laws and their limitations upon the freedom of man as a worker; in *The Island,* the draconian penal system; and finally, in *Statements After an Arrest Under the Immorality Act,* the effect of sexual prohibitions upon man's erotic and emotional growth. (p. 169)

Fugard's career can thus be viewed in terms of the changes in his subject matter, from presenting man as a unit in a family structure to the more recent portrayals of him as a citizen; in such a reading, the internally generated pressures of the home have been replaced by the external tensions of the statute book and law courts; familial abrasions become forensic assaults enforced by police and warders. Alone, though, an account of Fugard in these terms is incomplete, since it neglects to note how the forms and structures have also developed as a vehicle for political dissent. In the earlier plays, and particularly with *Hello and Goodbye* and *Boesman,* Fugard has recorded with characteristic overtness the difficulties he experienced with 'plotting'. Incident and dialogue: these were at the heart of Fugard's creative blockages, and they had to be resolved because of the dictates of the form in which he had chosen to express himself. In the drama which derives from Ibsen and Chekhov, the verbalized and linear plot is the means by which the playwright embodies his intuitions. The word is here paramount and when the verbal, narrative vocabulary has been discovered, when the ideas and images have been given flesh, the resulting, complete text is the writer's security.

Simultaneously with the development from an indirect, implicit material to the explicitness of *Sizwe Bansi,* there was a growing feeling in Fugard that the whole *form* of the domestic plays was now no longer suitable: 'My work had been so conventional: it involved the *writing* of a play; it involved *setting* that play in terms of local specifics; it involved the actors *assuming* false identity . . . 'It is as if Fugard now felt, after *Boesman and Lena,* that all the battles he had fought to 'plot' those plays with lucidity were now irrelevant. And even, moreover, as if the earlier search for verbal clarity had, paradoxically, only led to an essential ontological falsity, an inauthenticity. The orthodox dramatic form now no longer seemed worth 'retailing'. The conventional modes of western realism, that had served so well in relatively open societies, appeared to Fugard inseparable from his own failure to give full expression to the living texture of life in a totalitarian state. And so, with the inspiration of Grotowski's theories and of his own practice since 1963 with the Serpent Players, Fugard abandoned the complete, 'prefabricated' text, conventionally offered to the actors at the outset of rehearsals, and began to work under no constraint from the exigencies of plot and sequential dramatic logic. In this new process, which was to result in *Sizwe Bansi* and *The Island,* plays of a startling polemical candour, the writer remains essential, because it is his images—'at least an image, sometimes an already structured complex of images about which I, as a writer, was obsessional'—that are the seedbed of the play. The process involves devolution and decentralization: not abdication. The writer, in other words, gives his actors what Fugard calls a 'mandate', which is not a plotted, structured text but a cluster of images on which they work. The actors created their own 'texts' in rehearsals and these were moulded and disciplined as if in the preparation of a conventional play. The result has been, in Fugard's account, 'as if instead of first putting words on paper in order to arrive eventually at the stage and a live performance, I was able to write *directly* into its space and silence via the actor'. This, in summary, has been the collaborative genesis of *Sizwe Bansi* and *The Island,* and, in part, of *Statements,* which, though plotted conventionally, was rehearsed with similar techniques. The new political incisiveness of these three plays rests, therefore, upon formal and stylistic modulations in Fugard's art as well as upon a more publicly accessible group of themes.

The degree of political acuity won by Fugard's use of a dramatic form unconstrained by narrative demands, in which he can write 'into space and silence' without being diverted by the linear, temporal exigencies of episode, is exemplified in *Sizwe Bansi Is Dead* (1972). Of the three representatives of Fugard's new dramaturgy recently published in one volume, it is this play which most effectively blends the creativity of the players, John Kani and Winston Ntshona, with the writer's power of shaping, of plotting, the actors' own text of mime and reminiscence. The mimetic and reminiscential have always been large constituents of Fugard's theatre—as in, for example, the 'car-ride' scene of *The Blood Knot.* Indeed such passages, though potent in themselves, have sometimes threatened to absorb imperialistically the advancing narrative. Now, though, in the last three plays, Fugard seems able to view them more dispassionately, because they are the product not of his solitary creativity but of the communal pressures generated in the rehearsal room. Prolixity and verbal repetition had had to be controlled by the author alone in *The Blood Knot* and *Hello and Goodbye,* two plays with, we know, an autobiographical poignancy. Latterly, however, the altered, public genesis of the 'Political Trilogy' has enabled Athol Fugard to gain an objective, critical distance, the result of which is a new brevity and economy. The devolution involved in

moving away from a complete, quasi-patristic text, for which the writer was solely responsible, to a theatre built from the unexpected catalysts which are then moulded by the writer, has furnished Fugard's company, as he has noted, with 'a much more immediate and direct relationship with [its] audience'.

In a South African context the political implications of this loss of obliquity don't perhaps need to be spelt out in full. That articulation of verbal harmonies, the total effectiveness of dramatic realism for which Fugard had wrestled until *Boesman,* is seen only to lead to an art which was mediate and muffling. This modification has involved a radical reappraisal by Fugard of the effectiveness of realism, a form which since the fiction of the last century has been generally directed to political dissent, cultural agnosticism, and individual emancipation. . . . But to the artist working in a society which defiles semantics, which rewrites, for instance, the rich associative power of the word 'homeland', the cybernetics of realism, a mode rooted in historical and verbal confidence, must appear problematic. A society becoming increasingly repressive, despite its recent attempts to mouth the vocabulary of international docility, places strains upon the artist's viable forms of communication. It is not simply that the themes of literature change shape under these pressures: forms, and styles must also develop. The 'Family Trilogy' of the sixties . . . had been founded on the paramountcy of the world. . . . The trilogy's plots . . . had been diachronic, moving steadily from, say, Hester's sudden return in *Hello and Goodbye* to her parting from Johnnie at the conclusion. Now, though, in the later trilogy, the structure of the action is often flexibly synchronic. The word, similarly, is subordinate to the power of the images: the flashed photographs of interracial intimacies in *Statements;* the photo of the labourer in *Sizwe Bansi,* emasculated by the pass laws and snatching at dignity by smoking a pipe and a cigarette at the same time. (pp. 169-72)

In Fugard . . . we can discern a certain pattern of development from realism to a species of 'Imagist' art, much less concerned with the exfoliation of characters within a dense, fully rendered environment. Fugard has indeed recorded his interest in Pound's definition of the 'Image' as 'that which releases an emotional and psychological complex in an instant of time'. The playwright's account of the genesis of the three plays in *Statements,* as well as the plays themselves, underline the similitudes between Fugard's recent work and the earlier Imagism of Pound and Ford. However, it is remarkable how the earlier aesthetics of Imagism, implicated with an elitist, apolitical ideology, has been transformed by Fugard into the vehicle of a progressive, deeply dissenting theatre. The kinetics of literature's political life is, we should recognize, complex and only to be established after attention to both form and content. These recognitions and attentions are, I would suggest, a fundamental necessity to the critic of a literature which is, north and south of the Caprivi Strip, so firmly plaited with the events and pressures of the political life. (p. 172)

Robert J. Green, "Politics and Literature in Africa: The Drama of Athol Fugard," in Aspects of South African Literature, *edited by Christopher Heywood (copyright © 1976 by Christopher Heywood; published by Africana Publishing Company, a division of*

*Holmes & Meier Publishers, Inc.; reprinted
by permission), Africana, 1976, pp. 163-73.*

In South Africa . . . the inability of black and white to love each other is legislated by the state, so a South African play on the subject has to be a political play. Athol Fugard's *Statements After an Arrest Under the Immorality Act* is a play that would rather be about love, but is about politics by force of circumstances, and, by the nature of those politics, is a horror play. On a library floor, a white spinster librarian and a married Bantu school teacher lie in the nude, after lovemaking, and talk—about life, learning, and libraries, about the course of their love affair and the works of Sir Charles Lyell, about reasons for existing and modes of action. (The black man quotes a line from Lyell that has important meaning for him): "No vestige of a beginning and no prospect of an end.") There is a noise outside the shuttered library; the white woman worries about a nosy neighbor—and very abruptly a white man, a detective-sergeant, appears at the side of the stage and reads from a police report: The two people are under surveillance, and the scene we have been watching is the night of their arrest. . . .

I don't know if Fugard himself . . . had the idea of presenting the play as one continuous scene, with interrogation, trial, and punishment all happening with the characters still in the library, he desperately holding onto his clothes, she clutching a sheet around her, trapped at the moment when the state interrupts their lives. The power of the image is awesome, though Fugard's language doesn't always support it. A genius with the poetry of petty naturalism, he strives for a higher language here and stumbles a few times on his way to it. At the end, he regains his stride with a fine monologue: The white woman, in prison, is learning to grow and to strengthen her spirit.

But the black man has suffered more than imprisonment. I don't know how to convey the effect of his final speech, except to say that there are certain parts of human life that have always seemed closed to art, because they are unimaginable, and for a writer's imagination to leap over one of these barriers is a special kind of triumph. This speech is the nightmare of a black man who has been castrated by a white state and dreams that he is called before the Last Judgment to account for the loss of his testicles. If this is political art, it is on that high level where a political stance renders a major service to art and to the human spirit, making us feel inside something we have always thought was impossibly distant from ourselves. (p. 91)

Michael Feingold, in The Village Voice *(reprinted by permission of* The Village Voice; *copyright © by The Village Voice, Inc., 1978), February 20, 1978.*

G

GLASSCO, John   1909-

A Canadian poet, novelist, and short story writer, Glassco won the Governor General's Award for Poetry in 1971. Although the subject of his verse varies from psychological insight to praises of rural life, his novels basically center on eroticism and fetishism. He has also written under the names George Colman, Jean de Saint-Luc, Miles Underwood, and Sylvia Bayer. (See also *Contemporary Authors*, Vols. 13-16, rev. ed.)

Thomas Hardy is the poet we are most apt to cite as combining a traditional poetics with a skeptical temperament. If there is a dominant influence to be found in Glassco's work it is that of Hardy; and it is to Glassco's credit that he more than once succeeds in achieving effects as powerful as the master's own. (p. 51)

The knowledge most of us in the United States have of Canadian poetry is unfortunately sketchy. Readers wishing to remedy this lack of acquaintance could begin to do so very pleasurably with Glassco's *Selected Poems.* (p. 53)

> *Robert B. Shaw, "A Voice from Canada," in* Poetry (© *1975 by The Modern Poetry Association; reprinted by permission of the Editor of* Poetry), *April, 1975, pp. 50-3.*

Seeking to pinpoint the "essential Glassco" and attempting to systematize his work is a frustrating task. Over a writing career of forty years he appears in numerous different guises. At one moment he's "Nijinsky's faun, fresh from some sylvan adventure" [as Leon Edel characterized him in his introduction to Glassco's *Memoirs of Montparnasse*] and the next he's the bearded old man on the mountain hurling down his tablets of doom. There's the profligate youth chronicling the escapades of the lost generation and the reclusive poet wrestling with death and consciousness in the Eastern Townships, the mischievous master of erotica and the elder statesman of Canadian letters. (p. 28)

Both Glassco's prose and poetry are enhanced by his great power to recall totally a situation and reconstruct its mood. In the *Memoirs* this is accomplished by the use of a dramatization of dialogue which does not even pretend to be a verbatim account of the actual conversation. The author simply withdraws and lets the characters reveal themselves. It is Glassco's greatest ability and the one which gives his scenes such economy and freshness. (p. 29)

The John Glassco of the *Memoirs* was not a mature artist. He had an admirable style, complete technical command of the language, lots of anecdotes to relate, but could only speak with authority on youth. John Glassco the poet was a long time in developing, and when he does emerge, he reveals a sensibility and a wisdom of age, a vision of life that no young man could have. It is a poetry of the end of life, inspired by the imminence of death. All his best poems are written from the vantage point of a hilltop, where the "future is abolished" and where for a prolonged moment a man can turn and survey the past laid out before him. The experiences and the emotions, the goals and the motivations are sifted through in the light of the harsh, newly-realized truth of death.

The intolerable loss of consciousness must somehow be made tolerable. The place of the individual's ego must be rethought so that death can be seen as a culmination of life rather than a contradiction. It is this process of sifting and rethinking that is the inspiration and which provides the raw material for John Glassco's later career as a poet.

The poems which spring from this special sensibility are of two main types. There are the long meditative poems which deal with consciousness and the workings of the mind. They recreate and analyse at length a mood or emotion. The psyche is isolated and we see it again and again assaulted by love, ambition, sensuality, or the awareness of approaching death.

The other category consists of shorter, tightly-wrought poems built around symbols in the external world. Included here is most of the townships poetry. The images, concrete, familiar and prosaic, are brilliantly manipulated by the poet. Old houses, crumbling barns, and deserted homesteads are perceived through an eye which alternately sees in them horror and tranquility, corruption and beauty. (pp. 31-2)

Success in Glassco's poems lies in finding a permanence, not in cheating death but in finding values which will make a whole life complete unto itself within the brackets of birth and death. The conventional, socially approved goals and dreams don't work. Many of the poems, like the first, are tragedies, but tragedies are the result of mistakes, and a mistake implies the failure to perceive and follow the correct course. (p. 33)

Some of the poetry tends to be a bit didactic, and the poet

is always at his best when least visible. His themes are best revealed by his characters in . . . poems such as "The Death of Don Quixote" and "The Web" who can speak with more conviction and more freedom than the poet can permit himself. (p. 34)

The older poet has attained the overview which was denied to the youth. The experience of living and dying is encircled, organized, and reduced to its essential facts.

First there is man's place in nature, where the race may survive, but each individual is doomed. Then there comes the problem of making a meaning between birth and death, that brief period of consciousness. And consciousness itself, that unique gift, is a two-edged sword which permits man to see and learn, but also creates the ego and gives birth to dreams and visions that are unattainable and doomed to frustration. The only commitment that is worthwhile is to another human being. Self-sufficiency is abandoned; the individual ceases to be isolated and becomes part of the chain which is immortal. (p. 39)

The prose works do not reveal the complete Glassco, but then neither does the poetry. It has been argued that the verse is the more serious, and so it is if by serious one means grave and humourless. Glassco's reverence for the form excludes all amusement and makes the poetry more earnest than the man. There is another side to Glassco which delights in the absurdities of life and has the will and the ability to make us laugh. The comic vision revealed in the simple, elegant prose of the Memoirs and Erotica is no less of an accomplishment and of no less artistic value than the very different vision presented in the poetry. (pp. 40-1)

> *Charles Murdoch, "Essential Glassco," in*
> Canadian Literature, *Summer, 1975, pp. 28-41.*

Glassco . . . is a superb writer, probably the subtlest prose stylist in Canada today. . . .

The limitation of the genre [of the novella; Scobie is reviewing *The Fatal Woman,* a collection of three novellas] is the limitation of the concept of the Fatal Woman itself. The Fatal Woman is a sexual fantasy of long, even of archetypal standing, but like all such fantasies it is limiting and ultimately dehumanizing. Glassco links its modern forms with the sensibility of Romanticism, which he describes—in the most fascinating piece of intellectual speculation in the book—as "a kind of disease," which results in a "sick" art. In this sense, the obsession with the Fatal Woman is a sickness, a deformity of normal human experience. (p. 108)

"The Fulfilled Destiny of Electra" and "The Black Helmet" are much more successful [than the third novella, "Lust in Action"]. Both set up a hermetic environment within which Glassco can explore the equally enclosed mental landscape of obsession. Even when the external world intrudes, at the end of "Electra", in the shape of two bewildered police officers, the intrusion is effortlessly assimilated into the myth, becoming the instrument by which the self-destructive destiny of the central male character is fulfilled.

The limits of the closed world set up a complete dramatic situation, which should be, in Glassco's view "static" or "motionless". The tension should then vibrate between the fixed points of the characters' hieratic roles, rather than

derive from any forward thrust of narrative action. The preface tells us that Glassco considered he had come closest to achieving this in "The Black Helmet"; even so, "it was clearly a failure."

It is clearly nothing of the kind. It is a complex and subtle narrative structure, in which Glassco contrives to provide an ironic context for his presentation of obsession while at the same time preserving a sense of that obsession's intensity. This is achieved by alternating the narrative between the hero's diary, in which he both records and analyses his devotion, and the ironic overviews provided, at one remove, by the goddess Artemis and the structural myth of Endymion, and, at the second remove, by the implicit presence of the author himself, John Glassco, in all his superbly delicate indelicacy.

These different layers of awareness are continually producing subtle effects. . . . (p. 109)

> *Stephen Scobie, "Glassco's Muse," in*
> Canadian Literature, *Summer, 1975, pp. 108-10.*

* * *

GÓMEZ de la SERNA, Ramón   1888-1963

Gómez de la Serna was a Spanish poet, dramatist, essayist, and novelist who is best known as the inventor of a new genre, the *greguería*, a kind of serendipitous parable.

El teatro en soledad, written in 1911 by Ramón Gómez de la Serna, and Pirandello's *Sei personaggi in cerca d'autore,* written about ten years later, are strikingly similar in many significant ways. Coincidence cannot be the explanation, and it is extremely unlikely that Pirandello knew about Ramón's play, which was published in an obscure Spanish journal. The key to the explanation of this phenomenon may be found by turning to Paris during the "Banquet Years" and especially to the cubist school of painting. (p. 59)

El teatro en soledad is a very important document in the history of pre-Pirandellism in Spain. The first twenty of the eighty pages are devoted to the "Depuración preliminar" in which Ramón describes his state of mind . . . and his purpose in writing the play. . . . He also speculates about literature in general, rejects almost all manifestations of the Generation of '98, meditates about artistic creation, and gives his opinions about the future of literature. . . . In short, this part of the manuscript is a type of literary manifesto. (p. 60)

Like *Sei personaggi, El teatro en soledad* is a play which serves to dissect the theater and the techniques employed destroy theatrical illusion by showing people and elements which should remain behind the scenes. There are several levels of reality; in fact, in the list of characters the participants are separated into two groups in both plays: characters and actors. In addition, the author and the spectators, who were to become so important in Pirandello's theater-within-the-theater trilogy, are discussed. The characters are even more important in Ramón's play than in Pirandello's, since the stage belongs to them completely during most of the play. The actors and characters do not occupy the stage simultaneously as they do in Pirandello's play, and the actors are unaware that the characters exist; however, the characters have a critical attitude toward the actors very similar to that shown in *Sei personaggi.*

The actors in Ramón's play are presented as a rather sorry lot: poorly dressed, unattractive, and disagreeable. They converse about several problems associated with the mixture of levels of reality, such as when they criticize Enrique, an actor, for playing only himself instead of his role. After the director has left, the actors complain about his control of them . . . , a complaint rather similar to that found in *Questa sera si recita a soggetto.* (p. 62)

The characters who arrive after the actors and stagehands have left for the night constitute the core of the play. They are autonomous characters, just as Pirandello's *Sei personaggi* are, and they are also searching, because they are characters without a drama. But unlike Pirandello's characters, they do not even have a story; indeed, they are self-sufficient and do not want an author. They appear to be searching for an absolute expression of true drama.

In both plays the stage itself, stripped of illusion, occupies an important position. Although many details are reversed, the first stage directions of the two plays give similar impressions. (p. 63)

In *Sei personaggi in cerca d'autore* the main desire of the characters is to represent their drama on the stage. They suffer when the actors try to play a scene from their life because it lacks authenticity. . . . The characters of *El teatro en soledad,* even though they are also actors, have a similar problem. . . . Later they further discuss the difficulty of representing true emotions on the stage. . . .

The theater-within-the-theater techniques used by Pirandello, which even include such extreme devices as participation by spectator-actors, interruptions, and scenes in the lobby, have led to the decrease or destruction of aesthetic distance. That is, the observer is no longer separated from the art form he is contemplating—he becomes a part of it and is thus unable to view it with the necessary detachment. It is interesting to note that Ramón, who foreshadows Pirandello in so many ways, also touches on this problem. For example, the director tells the actors that their untidy appearance upsets the audience. After he has left, one of the actors observes that when their collars become detached during a performance, it distracts some spectators who involuntarily look at their own collars to make sure that they are in place. Similarly, a young actress remarks that she was afraid the director would mention that during the performance she was smiling at her *novio* who was in the audience. In both cases the audience has overidentified with the actors and thus cannot contemplate the work of art as such. However, there is also a reverse side to this phenomenon—a strong audience-actor *rapport* which enhances the actors' performance. (p. 64)

In addition to the technical innovations in these two plays, the moods in them are extremely similar. . . . In *El teatro en soledad* the intellectual dialogue almost always has an undercurrent of passion, which yields a tone remarkably similar to that of Pirandello's plays.

Since most of the innovations found in Ramón's play can be explained by applying cubist aesthetic theories, it will be necessary to show his close involvement with the artistic environment of the time. Ramón made his first trip to Paris in 1906, the year in which Pablo Picasso began "Les Demoiselles d'Avignon." . . . Much more important, however, was Ramón's residence in Paris from 1910 through 1911, the most significant period for the development of analytical cubism. He frequented the Bateau-Lavoir, the birthplace of cubism, and became acquainted with many of the leading artists of the day. Ramón himself enjoyed drawing and illustrated many of his writings. He was greatly interested in the artistic innovations of the epoch, and his 1931 book *Ismos* bears witness to this.

In the prologue of *Ismos,* Ramón [indicates that] he reacted to the August 1910 Exposition des Indépendants as one would to sighting the coast of a new continent. . . . He enthusiastically reveals that this was a turning point in his interest in art. . . . (p. 65)

In *Ismos* Ramón gives evidence of his commitment to the new attitudes. Of course twenty years had passed since he wrote *El teatro en soledad,* however, certain evidence in the play itself indicates that when he was writing it he was experiencing the same emotions that he more maturely described in *Ismos* which is a very personal study of the epoch then ending. (pp. 65-6)

Ramón states that he has always been a "vanguardista" and that he is especially a "porvenirista." In a discussion reminiscent of Lessing's *Laocoön* he ponders the relationship between literature and art. He believes that literature is even more capable than art of capturing the new aesthetics . . . , and goes on to explain the limitations of painting as compared to the wide possibilities of verbal expression.

He tells how painters' techniques can also be applied to literature. . . . He believes that it is necessary to devour innovations, use them, and continue on to new things, for repetition is monstrous in art. (p. 66)

In the *Historia de las literaturas de vanguardia* Guillermo de Torre points out that the term *cubism* is always used hesitatingly by literary critics. . . . However, the present analysis of *El teatro en soledad* shows that with almost mathematical certainty, cubist aesthetic theory applied to the theater would produce techniques such as those found in Ramón's play and later in Pirandello's. For example, the cubists' abolition of the single viewpoint, their showing the object from a multiplicity of angles, would correspond to the different angles from which the stage is viewed. At one moment we are in the rafters with the stagehands, looking toward the stage, at another we contemplate the empty auditorium with the electrician; we see the author from the actors' point of view and then the actors from the characters' viewpoint, and so on. Also, the cubists broke up volumes. A cubist playwright dissects theater, almost destroying the very medium he is using to convey his art. The collage, which involves the attachment to paintings of "real" items such as newspapers or cigarette packs, would, of course, correspond chiefly to the "life" brought into cubist-oriented drama in the form of spectators, ushers, or stagehands. The superimposed planes so important in cubist paintings become the many planes of reality manifested in the theater by various forms of theater-within-the-theater technique. In essence, both cubism and Pirandellism are intellectual arts, both strive for maximum possibilities of expression and a new confrontation with the materials at their disposal, and both participate in the "art-about-art" trend.

El teatro en soledad, besides being a cubist play in technique, contains imagery of cubist origin, and there are many interesting details in the play which prove that Ramón actually had pictorial representation very much in mind when he was writing it. In the "Depuración preliminar" there are numerous references to painting. These pages, although obviously a literary manifesto, are unintelligible in parts if one does not consider the artistic background of the time. (pp. 67-8)

Ramón speaks about perspective in a manner which suggests painting rather than literature. . . .

He realizes that he is adapting artistic theory to literature, and finally he actually formulates a literary theory based on these concepts. . . . (p. 68)

In the play itself there are also numerous details which suggest cubism. The names of the characters sound like the titles of cubist paintings: "La vieja amarilla," "El de la nariz vinosa," "El de chistera," "La de la frente lunar," "La de los aretes," "La de la boca violeta," and "El recio de pómulos." (Some of Picasso's titles are "Mujer en verde," "Señora del sombrero negro," "Mjuer con abanico," "La señora del manguito," "La mujer del moño.")

Some of Ramón's character descriptions are verbal sketches of cubist paintings. (p. 69)

Several critics have suggested that Pirandello transposed cubist inspiration into theatrical terms. MacClintock comments on Pirandello's changed point of view and compares it to contemporary painting and poetic techniques. He explains that art does not necessarily resemble reality as most know it. Picasso "takes the elements of a form as he sees it and jumbles them into a pattern which has nothing to do with what we see." He believes that Pirandello's philosophy of drama is the same:

> So to Pirandello the drama is also a self-contained medium of expression with conventions of its own and its own justification; the action need not be based upon facts (which are illusory), it need not contain a thesis or teach a lesson, it need not even be probable if only it is psychologically and philosophically true.
>
> (pp. 70-1)

The fact that Ramón's play, which was directly inspired by the cubist school of painting, contains many of the same elements which later appear in *Sei personaggi* certainly supports [the critics'] contention that Pirandello was also influenced by the new philosophy of art. Pirandello was strongly inspired by the parallel philosophical and psychological currents of the epoch, while Ramón shows more concrete influence of cubist painters. Ramón wrote his rather tentative practice piece at the beginning of an epoch during one of the most exciting years of discovery and development of cubism. Luigi Pirandello wrote his masterpiece several years later at the end of the cubist epoch; although art would never be the same, the official denotation of cubism would no longer be applied to subsequent paintings. Ramón was young and greatly inspired by the new movement when he wrote *El teatro en soledad,* while Pirandello was a mature and experienced writer when he wrote his play. Ramón's drama has been forgotten except by a few scholars, while *Sei personaggi in cerca d'autore* is recognized as one of the most significant plays of the twentieth century. Both plays, however, directly reflect the spirit of their age as it appeared in the plastic and literary arts. (p. 72)

Wilma Newberry, "Ramón Gómez de la Serna," in her The Pirandellian Mode in Spanish Literature from Cervantes to Sastre *(© 1973 State University of New York), State University of New York Press, 1973, pp. 59-72.*

Ramón Gómez de la Serna, or simply "Ramón," as some critics refer to him and as he preferred to be called, is fast becoming recognized in North America not only as an outstanding innovator in literary creation who was one of the most representative Spanish authors of the period between 1914 and 1936 but also the one who illustrated perhaps better than any other the universal Spanish intellectual (and humorist) of the twentieth century. Julián Marîas went even further a few years ago when he maintained that in Ramón's generation only three men reached the status of genius: Ortega in philosophy, Picasso in art, and Ramón in literature.

The "great Ramón Gómez de la Serna," as Octavio Paz has called him, has among his many publications a work on the major "isms" that came into being between the two world wars, and his own ideas, style, and name have been associated with many of them: Ultraism, Cubism, Dadaism, Surrealism, even Futurism. Some critics accept him as a precursor of many of these "isms" as well as an influential figure who had a major impact on the forms and direction his Spanish literary contemporaries and followers were to take. (pp. 237-38)

Indeed, during the greater part of this century, Ramón, a prose writer, largely through his use of metaphor, imagery, and other figurative devices more consistently than any poet in Spain lived up to Aristotles' dictum, namely, that the poets' mission is to discover similarities between things, a "mark of genius" Ramón flaunted to the fullest in the *greguería,* a new literary genre he named in 1909 and of which he became the first conscious cultivator. Poets have always been aware of the infinite possibilities of analogy, and Ramón Gómez de la Serna like them has ventured to take daring steps that join clashing and contrasting extremes thereby enlarging the scope of analogy. The power to startle consistently with surprising analogies is one of the major artistic achievements of the *greguería.* The expression of this surprise, shock, and astonishment is one of the main objectives of this literary "invention" which, together with his reputation as a humorist, will perhaps be Ramón's greatest and most lasting claim to fame. For, although his total literary output is massive, it is the *greguería* . . . that made him famous back in the Twenties and Thirties, long before his total literary production was known. And the *greguería,* often *inédita,* continues to appear even after his death. . . . (p. 238)

Ramón, in breaking with the set forms of literature, has had lasting success with the *greguería* as it survives, and its form together with his vision of the world which evolves from a personal and humanistic attitude based in part on the personification, animation, and humanization of things is partly responsible for this survival. (p. 242)

Richard L. Jackson, "The Status of the 'Greguería' of Ramón Gómez de la Serna," in Modern Fiction Studies *(copyright © 1976, by Purdue Research Foundation, West Lafayette, Indiana, U.S.A.), Summer, 1976, pp. 237-42.*

GRAU, Shirley Ann   1929-

An American novelist and short story writer, Grau is a regionalist author whose territory is the South. She is noted for her precise characterizations and her ability to convincingly present multiple points of view. (See also *CLC*, Vol. 4, and *Contemporary Authors*, 1-4, rev. ed.)

The Wind Shifting West [is a collection of] eighteen stories ranging in setting from an unspecified South to the east coast. The stories are thoroughly professional throughout, completely competent from beginning to end, but slightly disappointing: I sometimes felt that I'd read several of them before under many different professional names and in many magazines.

On the other hand, Miss Grau certainly knows what she's about, she knows how to build a scene, she knows how to move her characters around and how to dispose of them at the proper time. She is at her best, it seems to me, when her angle of vision is that of a girl or a woman, as it is in the very good title story of a wife's casual introduction to adultery with her brother-in-law; or in "The Beach Party," in which a teen-aged girl is introduced to dates and to death; or in what seems to me her best story, "The Way Back," a relatively brief, unpretentious and completely convincing depiction of the end of an affair.

The collection is also highlighted by two effective, low-keyed stories centering around white-black relationships and problems. "Eight O'Clock" depicts a racial disturbance as viewed through the eyes and consciousness of a young black child; "The Other Way" concerns the only black child in a recently-integrated class.

When she tries too hard or strays too far from the usual, I find Miss Grau less convincing. "The Patriarch," reminiscences of an eighty-five-year-old egoist, is entertaining but seems preposterous. "Three," about a college student, her husband, and the ghostly apparition of her first husband who was killed in Vietnam, is a valiant effort that doesn't come off; "The Last Gas Station," surreal and apocalyptic, I found silly and unconvincing; and "That Lovely April," the author's fling at old-fashioned "sothren gothic," generates some early tension and suspense but ends up a bore. (pp. 723-24)

> *William Peden, in* Sewanee Review *(reprinted by permission of the editor,* © *1974 by The University of the South), Fall, 1974.*

[*Evidence of Love*] is an elaborated study of a father and a son whom [Grau] first introduced in *The Patriarch*, a short story published several years ago. Spare, and dry to the point of aridity, the narrative portraits emerge in three separate sections related, in turn, by Edward Milton Henley, . . . his son Stephen, . . . and Stephen's wife, Lucy. . . .

As the contours of these three destinies take shape, one waits, with mounting impatience and finally in vain, for something in the proceedings to catch fire. Though the *idea* of the novel is engaging enough—allowing for immediacy and detail in the self-portraits, variety in the incidents and in the settings their reflections recapture—the totality is curiously flat and uninspired. To be sure, the book has its moments; sparks fly especially in Lucy's section, perhaps because the author is most in touch with the rhythms of a female sensibility. It is difficult to say exactly what goes wrong in *Evidence of Love*. Peopled with characters resur-

rected from a previous work, the novel is obviously an investigation of lives [Grau] has found compelling. Alas, there is very little here to make us agree that she should have found them so. (p. 28)

> *Jane Larkin Crain, in* Saturday Review *(© 1977 by Saturday Review Magazine Corp.; reprinted with permission), February 19, 1977.*

I have never experienced the appeal which many other readers have discovered in Grau's work: Grau always has seemed to me a pedestrian, distinctly effortful novelist. *Evidence of Love* strikes me as her least impressive book. The history of a rich Louisianian, his son, and his daughter-in-law, the novel means, I gather, alternately to shock and to console us. The excesses of Grau's characters are tame enough, though, involving as they do nothing more terrible than coldness, blasphemy, calculation, egotism, lust, sexual unconventionality. This will seem a provocative catalogue of energies but in Grau's heavy hands all the quotients of psychologically aberrant behavior somehow do not occasion response. Gide's Michel, Conrad's Kurtz, Mann's von Aschenbach conceive of their own extremity as a resource and a project. Grau's Edward Milton Henley wants only, like an errant schoolboy, to feel entertained. Stephen Henley wants simply to be left alone. Lucy Henley wants just to want something. Nor is Grau significantly less puerile than her tedious characters. The novel is scarred by repeated authorial pronouncements upon the fragility of love, the evanescence of life's structures and meanings, the general vapidity of humankind. For example, Grau has the novel's heroine remark about her daughter-in-law: "She thinks exactly what every nearly middle-aged mother of two children thinks . . . Nothing at all." An arrogance so comfortable as this—authorial as well as fictitious—hardly can seem to us authoritative upon the subject of love and its evidences.

Whether she undertakes to unsettle us by dismissing the possibilities of love or to console us, as she tries to do in the novel's third section, by approving of the diversity and resilience of the human spirit, Grau manages only, I fear, to define the pronounced limitations of her own sensibility. I know of no other established American writer who teaches one less. (p. 444)

> *Peter Glassman, in* The Hudson Review *(copyright © 1977 by The Hudson Review, Inc.; reprinted by permission), Vol. XXX, No. 3, Autumn, 1977.*

*   *   *

GRAY, Simon   1936-

A British novelist, editor, short story writer, and playwright, Gray is a master of the double entendre and comic situation. Gray's dramas are often seemingly domestic, but they transcend domesticity to deal with the conflict between individual expression and repressive social institutions such as the church, government, and marriage. (See also *Contemporary Authors*, Vols. 21-24, rev. ed.)

Ben Butley—tattered, battered super-anti-hero of Simon Gray's play "Butley"—is coming adrift at his moorings. . . .

Butley is a very interesting man, and his tragedy is beautifully and crisply funny.

Mr. Gray has written about this half-baked academic with astonishing compassion. Butley goes around "spreading futility." He slouches like a lost soul, and yet uses his wit like a sledgehammer to ward off the world and reality. And despite his glorious and desperate faults, he remains oddly likable and strangely sympathetic. Even his pompousness and mad egotism have been made in some way attractive.

Mr. Gray has devised his comedy with considerable adroitness. Butley is caught at the very pinpoint moment of his final deflation. His life is subsiding around him. Where Mr. Gray has been particularly clever is to give his declining slob all the funny lines. He fights against all comers like a cornered Bugs Bunny full of wisecracks and with a splenetic humor. You can see the tarnished brilliance of the man, the fallen hopes, the eroding self-distrust that spews out a fine comic bitterness upon the world. Unfulfilled and unforgiving, Butley makes his last stand with style and venom.

What the play has caught is a specific mood and style. Here is the spiteful humor of a university common room combined with a rootlessness and lack of purpose that seem currently endemic among the foolishly wise. Even Butley's sexual leanings are, at the very least, ambivalent, and he rails at the world to no purpose. He hates himself in a very chilly climate. . . .

"Butley" is no major contribution to dramatic literature, but it is that sadly rare thing—a literate and literary comedy with a heart.

> *Clive Barnes, in* The New York Times *(copyright © 1972 by the New York Times Company; reprinted by permission), November 1, 1972, p. 54.*

Simon Gray has written novels as well as plays, but in the novels the playwright is always trying to get out. Descriptive commentaries turn into stage directions, scenes into scenarios, dialogue into a means of dramatic progression. What results is a curious fictional sterility, a coruscating way with words that cuts, amuses, and extends itself so long that it becomes as arid as it is acid, eloquently forgettable. The telescoped form of the drama, however, gives Gray the appropriate medium for his sharp tongue. There his social conscience comes alive and his bizarre picture of domesticity becomes an engrossing metaphor of contemporary life.

The novels read now like Robertson Davies reruns, sneering wittily at provinciality, but possessing no superior society very firmly as a substitute. . . . [The] structural double-entendre [displayed in *Simple People*], ironic but serious, was to become one of Gray's technical trademarks. His wit derives frequently from the clash between the stock responses we give a tired metaphor and the jolt we experience on recognizing its original exactness. But the resultant laughter seldom calms a problem or absolves anyone of his responsibilities; instead, it intensifies the underlying issues, forces an audience to realize the serious implications of the disparities that it has first perceived simply as amusing incongruities. The macabreness of Gray's wit contributes to the same effect. . . . (p. 163)

The novels distantly amused the mind; the humour of the plays sears it. . . . (p. 164)

More compassionate than Gray's earlier plays, *Spoiled*

shows his increasingly relaxed command over the techniques of stage drama and the developing breadth of his social views. Domesticity is merely an immediate landscape in which to probe the limitations of love and the enervating effect of fear. The metaphor's implications reach far, into government, religion, and all other forms of social intercourse, where the ethics of action is brought face to face with the politics of belief. At the end of the play, in the long staring silences between Richard and Joanna, still nothing has been resolved. The society they typify has not found ways to forgive itself for being human, and the understandings that might illuminate, the perceptions that might explain, the sympathies that might relate, are all sacrificed to the gods of public propriety and private fear. Formulas always intervene to deaden language, and institutions to inhibit contact. All of the plays of Simon Gray work with this dilemma in mind. As Hawkins puts it in *Dutch Uncle*, "How can a city live, if a city's lost its faith, and has its horrors locked in its households?" But Hawkins himself is no answer. The law, the church, and the school alike have failed the private person in his striving to live. If their authority still wins out, it does so partly because the private person does hesitate to express himself. Paradoxically, that failure of expression also *becomes* an expression—of a selfishness that inhibits communication as much as the institution does, and so contributes to social malaise. The circle locks again. Gray does not—perhaps cannot—break it. All he can do as an accomplished playwright is invest the moral dilemma with life, involve his audience in his characters' choices, and mordantly, with genuine sympathy for the humanity of man, provoke them all into appreciating the ambivalence of what they do. (pp. 171-72)

> *William H. New, "Household Locks: The Plays of Simon Gray," in his* Dramatists in Canada: Selected Essays *(copyright © 1972 by The University of British Columbia), University of British Columbia Press, 1972, pp. 163-72.*

[Simon Gray's *Otherwise Engaged* is] a wonderfully funny, incisively wise play, better even in impact and structure than his excellent *Butley*. . . . (p. 88)

What splendid writing, what elegant plotting and character-painting Mr. Gray has given us, what lovely compliments to the alert and intelligent among our theatergoers! His play discourses, with utmost insight and drollery, on a basic malaise of our time: the deceptive ease of communication that technology has placed at mankind's disposal, and the tragic ease with which we hurl words at one another without making contact. His protagonist, Simon Hench, sits surrounded by modern communication gadgets: his beloved hi-fi onto which he aches to plop his latest Wagner album, his telephone, his answering machine. These are his refuge, an electronic armor into which he can retreat. Words to him are like transistors on a circuit board. He is an editor and he has, therefore, learned to line up words neatly and solder them immaculately into place. His only distress comes when words are used on him with some of their connections loose. He chooses not to respond to verbiage, no matter how important, merely to fiddle with its grammar.

Simon is man en route to robot, yet the author portrays him triumphant. (p. 91)

> *Alan Rich, in* New York Magazine *(© 1977*

by NYM Corp.; reprinted by permission of
New York Magazine and Alan Rich), February 14, 1977.

Simon is something of an enigma—Simon Hench [the protagonist of Otherwise Engaged], that is, the character, though Simon Gray, the author, is something of an enigma too. Is he (Simon Hench) deliberately cruel, or is his indifference uncalculated and sincere? And more crucially, is he (Hench again) really undamaged by the damage he does to others, or is his continued impassivity at the end only a facade? Is it good or bad to be Simon Hench; is he truly serene, or just empty? When he finally sits down to listen to his Parsifal records at the end, is Parsifal really all he needs, or merely all he has left? Is this a play of the Triumph of Solipsism, or the Failure of Solipsism? Mr. Gray isn't saying, which is one reason why his play reverberates so in the mind.

Otherwise Engaged can be repetitive and predictable, but it is never boring; Mr. Gray is too clever for that. Simon Hench uses a gravely playful, subtly nasty sort of wit to keep people at a distance. . . .

Mr. Gray clearly has a good deal in common with Harold Pinter. Otherwise Engaged is less elliptical, less disorienting, more accessible, less "heavy" than Mr. Pinter's plays, but both writers tend to see human relationships as power games, and both are skilled in the deploying of charged understatement. . . .

The evening belongs firmly to Mr. Gray, whom I mistrust as being too much on Simon's side, looking down with condescending pity on the "plops" of the world. I reject the implication that "plops" at school are condemned to be "plops" forever; some people do graduate. Not, apparently, however, Mr. Gray. Otherwise Engaged has a smell about it of old boarding-school obsessions, erotic and otherwise (especially a faintly nasty psychic sadomasochism), as if the playwright shares with his characters the very upperclass-English trait of never having outgrown his schooldays. Mr. Gray fails the Holden Caulfield test for writers; it is hard to imagine anyone coming out of the theatre after a performance of Otherwise Engaged wanting to go call up the author. Still, he has written an entertaining play, and its enigmas did stir my feelings about feeling.

Julius Novick, "Looking Down on the Plops," in The Village Voice (reprinted by permission of The Village Voice; copyright © by The Village Voice, Inc., 1977), February 14, 1977, p. 81.

Engagement, responsibility to one another, seems to be one of the principal motifs of Simon Gray's Otherwise Engaged, but this seeking among my fellow journalists for ulterior motives concerning the charming, amiable, middle-class Simon's civilized responses to the passions of his fellows strikes me as a bit too much of poking around in the woodpile. I see Simon not as "otherwise engaged" in the sense that he is turned off to responsibility, but rather as having, like Augie March or Mary Chase's Elwood Dowd in Harvey, the marvelous ability to accept people as they are. All around him are people "otherwise engaged," in ego-tripping, in strategies for cornering power or despair. I suppose the extent to which Simon (hero as opposed to author) denies the validity of Freud's pleasure principle makes him dangerous, or at least irritating to others, but he seems to me a treasure. (p. 69)

Arthur Sainer, in The Village Voice (reprinted by permission of The Village Voice; copyright © by The Village Voice, Inc., 1977), February 28, 1977.

Simon Gray, the author of Butley, reveals his identity in his play through literary allusions. He is, like Butley, a lecturer in English at Queen Mary College, London. Through Butley, Gray uses literature and its conventions to satirize his profession. In fact, signs of this profession permeate the play, even in its structure. Observing the classical unities, Gray presents the disintegration of Ben Butley's personal and academic life in one day. On that day, Butley sheds his wife, Anne, and their infant daughter, Marina; he pushes his colleague and former student, Joey, from him into a homosexual marriage, and he chooses to continue his professional career without students or scholarship. The action of the play is in one place—the office that Butley shares with Joey. All of the action revolves around Butley and his reactions to others who enter his office. (p. 374)

Ironically, Butley never leaves his profession; as he moves farther from contact with others, he becomes more literary. His control of symbols, his timing, and his epigrammatic wit at first serve to identify him as a neoclassical satirist. And, like Swift and Pope, Butley can be obscene or turn a phrase so that it becomes obscene. His literary references become double entendres. . . . Our inclination is to prefer Butley and to laugh with him, but he prevents us from getting too close just as he prevents others in the play from getting near him. We are distanced by his wit, by his literary allusions, and by his academic barbs. (pp. 375-76)

In a perverse manner, Butley demonstrates those qualities we believe essential to the English professor: sensitivity, kindness, perceptiveness, eloquence, but he uses them on this day to annihilate, destroy, or dismiss those around him and to reject and sever his professional ties. He may appear to be casual as he dismisses Edna, his colleague, because she "weighs on his spirit" . . . or run to locker-room obscenities as he asks about Joey's lover, Reg, but the laughter is shaded by our realization that we are part of Butley's target and that we are intimidated by him.

Gradually, we identify with his victims. We understand that Edna is mediocre; we recognize that she is much like us, that she is the establishment in all its pallid weight and that Butley alone sees her with contempt. . . . [Butley ends an exchange with Edna] with a misreading of Denham's line from "Of Prudence": "We may our ends by our beginnings know." The literary allusion assumes a silly sagacity that reflects Butley's view of Edna. Butley uses the allusion to ridicule Edna, whom he believes has subverted literature. (pp. 378-80)

After Edna leaves, Butley's rage bursts forth in one of the most compelling of misquoted literary allusions from Yeats' "Second Coming": he says of Edna, "She never did understand her role. Which is not to finish an unpublishable book on Byron. Now the centre cannot hold. Mere Edna is loosed upon the world." . . . He is surrounded with rubbish —Joey's, Edna's, Miss Heasman's [Butley's tutorial student]—and yet, ironically, the rubbish he sees is not only tolerated by his society but also rewarded. The work of his students, like Edna's and Joey's work, is uninspired, pedestrian. It is part of a ritual that has lost its meaning. Miss Heasman's persistence is to Butley a madness akin to

Edna's tenacity. Both Edna and Miss Heasman are ambitious and competent, but they deaden rather than inspire. As Butley judges and rejects the students' papers, he is drawn to nursery rhymes that still have vitality. . . . His statements have continuity in the images and ideas that suggest the conceits of the metaphysical wits. The last cliche, ''But then they took pride in their work . . . '' is followed by a twisted literary allusion from Alexander Pope that retains its original meaning. With the identification of his life as a disease [''This hash, my life . . . this long disease, my . . .], Butley becomes more isolated, and the tone of the play becomes blacker.

His isolation intensifies as he searches for moments that must have been significant to him, but he cannot recapture them. He turns to his marriage and his daughter. Butley's recollections merge with his recollections of T. S. Eliot. His quotations are now accurate; there are no silly or barbed misquotations. Though the words have remained intact, his emotions have changed. Eliot is an ordered, neoclassical poet of the twentieth century whose youthful despair and wit matched the sensibility of the younger Butley. Now, unlike the later Eliot, Butley finds no hope or redemption. Butley's recollections begin here with his infant daughter and Eliot's poem ''Marina,'' which reflects Butley's past hope for regeneration, love, and peace. . . . The passage from ''Marina'' is broken by a brief passage from Eliot's ''Lines to a Persian Cat'' in ''Five Finger Exercises.'' Butley stops short of the allusion to suicide implicit in, ''O when will the creaking heart cease.'' However, he does mention his inability to relate to others. The Eliot poem bridges Butley's literary past with his literary present manifest in *Cecily Parsley*. The poem has the imagery and rhythm of a nursery rhyme, but it has the message of despair. (pp. 380-83)

Act II opens as Butley confers with Miss Heasman, who reads a dull, inept paper on *A Winter's Tale*. Her eagerness for the right words, however clumsy, leads Butley to new cruelties.

> MISS HEASMAN. 'The central image is drawn from nature, to counterpoint the imagery of the first half of the play, with its stress on sickness and deformity. Paradoxically, *A Winter's Tale* of a frozen soul—'
> BEN. Bit fish mongery, that. . . .

Her comments obliquely define Butley's own state of being as it has been revealed in the first half of the play; he is isolated and detached. His soul is frozen. Butley's response is a quick dismissal. He identifies the student's easy platitudes and echoes Hamlet's response to Polonius' moral certainties. . . . (p. 384)

Earlier in Act II, Butley seemed to identify with Hamlet as he challenged Miss Heasman's turgid but morally regenerative analysis of *A Winter's Tale*. Here [in an exchange with his rival, Reg], Butley seems to identify with another Shakespearean tragic hero—Antony. Though the comment is witty, it is poignant as well. The lapse into self-pity does not last. Instead, the humor increases with one of Butley's final games. . . . Butley begins to lose control as he alienates us when he goes beyond our sense of evil and decorum and offends us as he offends Reg. The revelations continue, leaving Butley more and more isolated. With each, Butley

responds with a rage that drives others even farther away. (pp. 385, 387)

The echoes of neoclassicism, the echoes of Prufrock suggest that once Butley had been a teacher; once he had seen in life something positive and redemptive.

Then, from Edna, Butley learns that Joey is leaving their office for one beside Edna's. As Edna leaves, she greets Gardner [Edna's tutorial student], the source of her vexation, with some grace, and Butley is left alone with Gardner, who, instead of wit, displays a kind of nastiness. . . . Butley finds the passage from Eliot's *East Coker* that Joey had read years before and he asks Gardner to read it. As Gardner reads, Joey walks in.

> GARDNER (*reads*). 'In that open field
> If you do not come too close, if you do not come too close,
> On a summer midnight, you can hear the music. . . .

While Gardner reads, Joey completes the cruel task of gathering his books and papers; their relationship is ended. (p. 388)

The poetry of Eliot no longer functions for Butley as it once had. The evidence has mounted from the time the curtain rose and revealed, ''on the wall a . . . blown-up picture (photograph) of T. S. Eliot, with a smear across it and one of its corners curled.'' . . . The picture is a relic, soiled and ignored. Eliot's poetry conjures memories but no longer inspires. At the end of Act I, Butley identified Marina and Anne with Eliot and rejected them. The poetry linked him with Joey as well, but Joey has gone, and Butley finds that he cannot begin again.

Like Eliot, Butley had been a teacher, though now he avoids teaching. Just as once poetry was vital to Butley, so, too, was teaching. The painful recognition that the vitality has gone causes Butley to turn from Gardner and Eliot to his nursery rhymes. (pp. 388-89)

The play concludes with an action, a visual metaphor, that italicizes the theme of Butley's wasteland:

> GARDNER *puts the Eliot down, goes out.*
> BEN *puts the book back, sits at the desk, turns off the desk lamp and tries feebly three times to turn it on again.* . . .

Butley has forgotten all but the words of literature, especially the words of Eliot. He has left himself in darkness. His efforts to illuminate his life through literature or relight his dying relationships with Anne, Joey, and Gardner were feeble and unsuccessful. At the end of the play, Butley is alone. He has noted wittily his relationship to tragic heroes. He has even alluded once to suicide. He recognizes his fall from the grace of husband, lover, and teacher to the state of pitiable, lonely man who baits and ridicules others mercilessly.

Butley has as much laughter as any comedy could evoke, but it is a laughter generated by literary allusions, by wit, and by skilled word play that were used as weapons of defense and attack. Butley's skill is verbal, and for a while his wit captures our sympathies and our admiration, yet he manages to create a distance so that ultimately he is isolated from us, too. The effect is at first baffling, confusing; we are invigorated by a man whose intellect and sensitivity lead him to see more in life and in literature than most of us but whose intellect and sensitivity turn sour. Where Butley once saw value in Eliot, Joey, Anne, he now sees nothing.

We are left with words that force laughter and distance; we are left alone with wit. Unlike Eliot who finally found his way out of the wasteland through a regenerative faith, Butley cannot or will not be redeemed and defies redemption despite the words of literature. The satire is black. If we admire Butley and his view of himself and those around him, we will see him as he sees himself—a Hamlet or an Antony beset by betrayal and mediocrity. If we see him as others in the play see him, we see an irresponsible, wasted man who is not tragic but pitiable. In either case, the disintegration of Ben Butley's personal and academic life is revealed adroitly and economically through a satiric tone that echoes the controlled, but furious, satires of the neoclassicists. Simon Gray has indeed effectively used allusions to literature to undermine the illusions of academe. (pp. 389-91)

> *Sophia B. Blaydes, "Literary Allusion as Satire in Simon Gray's 'Butley',"* in The Midwest Quarterly *(copyright, 1977, by* The Midwest Quarterly, *Kansas State College of Pittsburg), Summer, 1977, pp. 374-91.*

* * *

GREENE, Graham 1904-

A British novelist, short story writer, editor, children's writer, essayist, and playwright, Greene is a highly respected and widely read author. Greene's literary world is one of paradox and seediness where the sinner is often the saint, the idealist a destructive agent, and evil is everywhere while innocence is suspect. Greene's Catholicism figures prominently in his fiction, providing him with a system of concepts, situations, and symbols that he uses to dramatize human nature. (See also *CLC,* **1, 3, 6, and** *Contemporary Authors,* **Vols. 13-16, rev. ed.)**

"Le pécheur est au coeur même de chrétienté. . . . Nul n'est aussi compétent que le pécheur en matière de chrétienté. Nul, si ce n'est le saint." ["The sinner is at the very heart of Christianity. . . . No one is as competent as the sinner in Christian matters. No one, unless it is the saint."] As a general proposition these words of Péguy are highly suspect, not to say offensively slick. Naked paradox can be self-defeatingly clever. But when Graham Greene attaches this paradox, as epigraph, to *The Heart of the Matter,* then indeed we must test Péguy as seer and Greene as novelist. In my opinion Greene's book succeeds triumphantly as fictional case in support of Péguy's generalization. Major Scobie (quite apart from his view of himself) is a fine example of good and evil interwoven and interdependent—so fine an example as to demonstrate the need for Purgatory, realm or condition of salvation-with-a-difference. (p. 711)

My own contention, which still needs urging despite our level of critical sophistication, is that some knowledge of Catholicism is legitimately required of anyone reading this book, but that, whereas knowledge may or may not be joined to religious belief, the only area wherein people can understand one another as literary critics is that region wherein the believer suspends belief and the nonbeliever disbelief, even as each brings his knowledge critically to bear upon the text. (p. 712)

[The] trouble is that some readers overreact to the real need to apply Christian knowledge, hence inadvertently prejudge what *ought* to be found in the book, and then devalue the book as literature because of the supposed gap between fictional elements and an extraliterary notion of Christianity.

The terrain is slippery because, together with the necessity of starting out with some knowledge of Catholic Christianity, goes the attendant responsibility for allowing the fiction to reshape or force attention upon some perhaps obscure corner of that theoretical knowledge. It is worthwhile to point out that Scobie is asked about Christianity and happiness (as if Greene were anticipating some questions), that he distinguishes on one occasion between "happiness and love," that he sees no chance for happiness in a miserable world . . . , and that for him happiness and peace are always impressionistic dreams of solitude, of quiet, changeless, cool darkness—whereas his waking world is cluttered, torrid, complicated, impermanent, and sad. But while he despairs of ever reaching peace himself, the novel is the psychological account of his efforts to gain it for others. Joy (happiness, peace) is decidedly at stake, then, by virtue of its conspicuous absence; and Scobie's relationship to it is conditioned by character and peculiarly tied to his sense of God, Louise, Helen, and his own creatureliness. Perhaps a shorter answer is that, while joy may indeed be available to the Christian, his belief alone is no guarantee of joyfulness —any more than lack of joy need point to heterodoxy. (p. 714)

[We] should notice a frequent complaint that Scobie's dilemma is artificial and thus fails of sufficient force. The objection is that if Scobie loved God he would bring himself to end his affair (if indeed he could have begun it), and that continuing in it proves that he cannot love God but is merely using God in order to enjoy his own guilt and make Helen Rolt suffer in his masochistic toils. . . . And Helen Rolt herself . . . tells Scobie, "'If you really believed you wouldn't be here'" [i.e., with her]. Scobie's answer is the only one he can give: "'But I do believe and I am here. . . . I can't explain it, but there it is'." . . . His insistence does not prove itself, of course, but it does show him aware of an obvious accusation. As "proof" that he believes in and loves God, even while he keeps a mistress, nothing can be offered except a close look at his behavior and intentions. That is, he does not fully "explain" his motives (and, as we shall see, the narrator's distance compels us to see Scobie's motives differently from the way Scobie sees them), but his actions *show* the mixed motives without which his choices make no sense. (pp. 714-15)

Just as George Tesman and Judge Brack are ironic victims of their own conviction that "people don't do such things," and are left to reconsider what people will do (and why), many a reader of *The Heart of the Matter* is left either to consider motives he may not be familiar with, or to abandon the book as incompatible with his own way of reading. My point is that anyone making the second choice should be aware of the comment he thus makes upon his own limitations, rather than upon a book's own terms.

Among this book's own terms is that omniscient point of view which, though it can give us the introspections of Helen, Harris, or Wilson, spends so much of the narrator's time rendering Scobie's attitudes that many readers take the book straight, very nearly as Scobie's account of how the novel's events add up. Such a confusion destroys one's experience of the novel, although we must certainly attend carefully to Scobie's self-reading as we get it from the narrator and from Scobie's first-person letters and diary. It is one thing to refer to this loosely as "Scobie's novel," and another thing to allow ourselves to ignore that distancing point of view which should make us contrast Scobie's awareness and the insights of others. To miss this opposition is to suppose Scobie's knowledge of Catholic Christianity complete, to overlook his ironic misreadings of his own character and motives, and inevitably to flounder about wondering what to do with the *post mortem* ending.

Scobie's views and the narrative point of view not only differ, but call attention, at least by implication, to different points of Catholic doctrine. This is the main reason why literary point of view must be kept straight in the present instance. To take Scobie at his own estimate leads to several erroneous conclusions: that Father Rank's last words—to the effect that Scobie perhaps loved no one but God—are only a collapsing agreement with Louise in her bitter accusation that Scobie's love of God was a self-loving devotion preventing his loving anyone else; that Father Rank finally therefore thinks Scobie's damnation more likely than he had just been arguing; that the unhappiness of both Louise and Helen indirectly testifies to a sinner's inability to achieve anything good for anyone, and indirectly supports Scobie's conviction that suicide would damn him. But it seems clear that narrative omniscience militates against accepting Scobie's view just as it prevents any other character's view from being solely final. We have to balance attitudes—Scobie's, Louise's, Helen's, Wilson's, Father Rank's, the Church's (the last two are of course compatible, but are related as particular interpreter to general legislator)—as omniscience requires. And when we do so, we find both that Scobie makes some important mistakes unawares and that some of these are a sound basis for supposing him ultimately saved.

A look at his mistakes is, in fact, a useful way to see his character and motivation, apart from what he may think both to be. What the narrator makes plain is that Scobie, for all his thoughtfulness and sensitivity, is not a reader of books. What needs adding is that he is not intellectual and not even especially intelligent, in spite of his insights and his spontaneous invention of an adventure story for a young boy. In being very nearly anti-intellectual, Scobie is not only like some other of Greene's protagonists—the whiskey priest, Pinkie, Mr. Brown—but is also one who proceeds by feeling and intuition, and whose *knowledge* of doctrine and whose ideas in general he himself will often tend to distrust (as he distrusts God) and discard (as he generally strips his life bare of all save feelings for others, God included). (pp. 716-17)

He is, however, a fictional character named Scobie, and one whose important oversights and other mistakes—such as those just mentioned—are perfectly motivated by his being a simple man (simple both deliberately and indeliberately) and are supported by a number of other plausible miscalculations. He reminds himself briefly and self-surprisingly that no human can plan another's life . . . , but because this is an *idea* he typically forgets it and continues to follow feelings. . . . Moreover, his reason for assuming himself beyond the pale is his conviction that he knows what he is doing at all times and hence is beyond being pitied. This is one of his root mistakes, this presuming upon his own knowledge and hence upon virtual exemption from what he regards as the universal human condition; and, as will become clearer, this gross mistake is the best evidence of what is called invincible ignorance and thus of eventual redemption.

There are other mistakes, of quite different kinds, on which his characterization is heavily based. His habit of seeking justice, for example, cannot be readily broken; that is, he is not *adept* at crookedness (an observation bearing to some extent upon Scobie as sinner). He imagines himself clever at covering his affair with Helen, though in fact Louise and others know of it. He is a dupe in Yusef's effort to frame a case against Tallit. He finds it hard to believe in Wilson's duplicity. He cannot even manage the deceitfulness required to fake his diary entries convincingly and thereby cover his suicide. Importantly, he quite miscalculates the effect of his death upon Louise, Helen, and (I argue) God. Such mistakes are sometimes thrown up as evidence that Scobie is too weak to hold a big theme together, or to serve as the character demanded by Péguy's paradox, or to represent anything important in God's plans. But it seems to me that Scobie is beautifully designed to deny all such charges, and that his very mistakes testify to his real devotion to justice and to his genuine desire to die for others. Only such a confusedly simple man could miss so much; could push himself ahead on such limited evidence; could believe in the efficacy of his acts as unshakably as this oddly innocent man does.

How may such innocence be reconciled with what Scobie does to Louise, Helen, Ali, God? The question may be posed in various ways, but what it usually means is that innocence does not sin, does not violate those it professes to love, and only *seems* to inhere in a character bathed in romance or sentimentality. Such accusations must be faced, and we will do well to see how facing them involves us in the sins Scobie commits.

By "innocent," then, I mean ignorant; but of course Scobie is ignorant only after reaching a certain level of awareness. (pp. 717-18)

The book achieves its sinner-saint tension by making vivid the terrible consequences of sin—consequences which should prevent our seeing Scobie as sentimentally conceived and portrayed, and which should demonstrate that the book earns its right to borrow Péguy's words by hammering away at the ruin all around Scobie. Ignorance, then, can save a sinner; but even invincible ignorance is measured and relative, and therefore blocks neither sin nor the consequences thereof.

Among Scobie's mistakes lies the believably unintelligent supposition that Louise, Helen, and God will soon forget him when he's dead, and will cease to be pained. This no doubt can seem an unlikely supposition, given Scobie's awareness that, alive, he means enough to all three of them to be tormenting them in their various demands for his love. But the book makes fine use of this seeming improbability to drive home yet again the fact that Scobie really thinks little of his own value. He is a genuinely humble man, the more so because he would no more think himself humble than he would be able to see himself as the hubristic God-player of a standard theological textbook. Innocence again (i.e., something he cannot know) operates in his favor. As always, the intention makes the difference, and Scobie's intention is not to escape a mess or to relieve his own pain, but to relieve the pain he causes others—to relieve it even as he goes to what he thoroughly believes will be unending pain for himself. . . . (p. 720)

But what of Scobie's treatment of Ali? This is clearly not an intentional betrayal (and thus in a sense not a betrayal at all), but at the same time the book carefully places the event—both in contrast to Ali's earlier role in Scobie's dream of peace, and after Scobie's sacrilegious reception of the Eucharist—to demonstrate the grounds of Scobie's sense that the devil is now taking care of him since he has sinned against God. . . . All of Scobie's sins are betrayals in some sense, certainly; but the prominence of this particular sin is in Scobie's seeing it so clearly for what it says of his vision of peace, of Ali's trust, of his own exercise of responsibility. The event is powerful, as it must be to waken Scobie from lethargy that could indeed carry him into mere self-pity, and to intensify his sense of the pain he continues to cause those who, unlike Ali, survive in their trust of him.

Ali's death is the most important evidence for the probability of Scobie's choosing suicide, precisely because Scobie can from here on see no future but a painful one for anyone who trusts him. But would he do this to God, of Whom he is intensely conscious? This is inevitably the first and last hurdle to the book's exemplifying Péguy's paradox, and the narrative clears this hurdle despite a certain weakness here.

The weakness is in the barest suggestion that Scobie supposes himself to be contemplating a death that is no more the *sin* of suicide than was Christ's crucifixion for others. . . . This brief suggestion that perhaps there may be an acceptable "out," together with Scobie's telling God that he was deterministically created with a sense of responsibility . . .—these two points to some extent weaken my argument for invincible ignorance, since they seem to say that Scobie knows and thinks more than the rest of the book allows, and that perhaps O'Faolain is right to say that Scobie gambles on God's being merciful to him. But, while these two occurrences are embarrassing to the rest of Scobie's psychology, they by no means outweigh the poignance and frequency with which Scobie takes all the blame, characteristically, upon himself and suffers finally the sure conviction that his despair assures damnation. . . .

Once this inconsistency is admitted, we can concentrate more levelly on Scobie's abiding attitude toward God. For Scobie, God is dominant and omnipotent not so much by virtue of being Creator or lawgiver as by virtue of His crucified helplessness, humiliation, suffering for others, and supreme need signified by public exposure on Golgotha. God's infirmity is a measure of His powerful appeal to Scobie. . . . And in fact Scobie's discussions with God, after he receives the Eucharist in sin, are clear evidence, not only that the God Scobie innocently plays is another version of his own character, but that only Scobie's brand of naiveté could leave untouched an underlying goodness which that naiveté firmly believes itself to be destroying. . . . Scobie's vivid awareness of the crucified Christ (an awareness that the narrator emphasizes in juxtaposing broken rosary, dead servant Ali, and servant-God now betrayed by servant-Scobie, . . . drives him to despair of entrusting his problem to the divine helplessness and of presuming to increase God's burden; and despair leads to suicide. But despair and hence suicide are rooted in a pity

so convincing and so preposterously beyond any human's prerogative *consciously* to exercise that it is transformed into love (charity) which in turn is motivation sufficiently intense and dominant to alleviate Scobie's sinfulness and thus to argue his need for purgatorial suffering rather than his damnation. Most briefly, then, Scobie's sins are real and not to be wished away; but what looks to him and the textbooks like the gravest sin of all is precluded by love. Scobie kills himself for love of God and of creatures made and seen in God's image. And the crowning evidence of extenuation is his very inability to imagine such a case as the omniscient narrator is making or to see anything but damnation for himself. Thus, if betrayal (like any serious sin) requires *full* knowledge and consent, it is clear that Scobie does not betray God: he only *thinks* he knows all that the book enables us to know of his choice and its basis, when in fact it is that invincible ignorance which preserves him. He must pay for sins and he pays a great deal all through the book; but his sins are not what he thinks. He intends both more and less than he can know. (pp. 721-23)

What this omnisciently narrated book does is force readers to see that Father Rank, who we have no reason to think knows more of Scobie's case than he says, and who certainly knows less than we do, has the literally last and thematically perfect word. . . . We are not to assume that Father Rank is aware of more than he says. He is a good priest making a necessary distinction between a general teaching and man's inability to apply that teaching to any particular case. But what Father Rank does not know has filled this book, so that *we* know how to take his words. Father Rank does not know that the novel makes sense of the advice to "love God and do what you will," but we must know this, just as we must see that only invincible ignorance of any glib presumption underlying the advice is the final clue to Scobie's motives and his destiny as an "obscure saint." . . . (pp. 725-26)

The details of Scobie's moral career reinforce and make meaning for his final "Dear God, I love . . .". . . . This inadvertently finished sentence says what Father Rank implies at the end: "charity (i.e., love) covers a multitude of sins." Scobie's love is not without objects, but, being the love of God and embracing God's creatures, it has so many objects that no one can presume to supply a predicate for him. (p. 726)

Joseph Hynes, "The 'Facts' at 'The Heart of the Matter'," in Texas Studies in Literature and Language *(copyright © 1972 by the University of Texas Press), Winter, 1972, pp. 711-26.*

At the end of *The Symposium*, Plato reports that Socrates was heard to insist "that the genius of comedy was the same as that of tragedy, and that the writer of tragedy ought to be a writer of comedy also." Socrates' comment here has been variously interpreted and much disputed, and so seems a proper introduction to a discussion of the genre of Graham Greene's *The Comedians* (1966). Written by an author who has tried more than half a dozen genres . . . *The Comedians* was reviewed widely and has received scattered commentary more recently; but there has been much indecision as to its generic nature. The novel's title suggests classification with comic spirit, but its action argues for a darker category. (p. 139)

[The] emphasis upon localizing the novel within the bounds of a specific genre distorts what in fact Greene seems to me to be doing: *The Comedians* is not so much a novel based upon the decorum of a specific genre, as, rather, a *parody* of two genres, farce and comedy.

This parody of the farcical/comical parallels Greene's normal method of parodying melodrama. . . . Indeed, *The Comedians* contains all the technical equipment of melodrama: murder, assassination, suicide, revolutionary activity, flight-for-freedom, grotesque setting, miraculous rescue, and so forth. . . . Greene shifts somewhere in the course of his novels to a parody of the tragic mode. Since what Greene does with farce and comedy is similar to his handling of melodrama and tragedy, some discussion of these latter two modes is justified.

Now melodrama is, of course, tragedy stripped of its serious dimensions; melodrama is ultimately not serious. Melodrama emphasizes wild action, contrived scenes, rapid pace, sentimental situations—all in and for themselves and their emotional appeal, and not to disclose any "deeper truth." The villain is categorically evil, and the hero outrageously good. Moreover, in melodrama there is no moment of tragic vision, no insight into life: in short, no recognition scene. What Greene does by parodying melodrama is to show us what the world is (a dangerous place to live in) by showing us what it is not (simply melodrama: danger that is not really dangerous). That is, the real danger appears in disguise, for Greene hangs his serious comments upon the scaffolding of the pot-boiler. The reader picks up quickly the melodramatic formula, then is jolted somewhere along the line by the realization that it is all really a very serious matter once one scratches the surface. And because it is serious, it is not really melodrama at all. The real dangers of the world are made to seem all the more dangerous for their appearance in the mask of the non-serious, so that Greene by his use of parody duplicates for the reader the disguised form of the world's dangers.

And at this point, with the realization of elements of high seriousness in the novel, the reader begins to suspect that he is in fact confronted with a tragedy. But when he comes to the recognition scene, he is inevitably faced with a baffling ambiguity, so that it is impossible for him to decipher for sure if the protagonist is successful or not. The "resolution," in brief, consists of a parody of tragic recognition, and the reader is never certain whether or not the protagonist has achieved insight. This pattern can be traced in novel after novel of Greene.

Understanding this, it is not difficult to understand Greene's parody of farce and comedy. Farce, of course, stands in the same relation to comedy that melodrama does to tragedy. For farce too is stripped of serious meaning. It employs many of the same devices used in melodrama—emphasis upon wild action, plot contrivances, rapid pace, caricature; but whereas melodrama evokes tension from these devices, farce evokes laughter. Now comedy takes over from farce elements that evoke laughter and provide them with serious underpinnings. In the end, the foolish and deceitful are unmasked, and the equilibrium of society is set aright once again. What Greene does in *The Comedians* is to have Brown, the narrator, establish an essentially farcical pattern through which the serious elements of the story eventually penetrate to transform the farce into a grim comment upon Brown's life. (pp. 139-40)

Brown's use of farce becomes . . . a sort of unintentional parody, and it is made clear after a while that the "joke" is not a joke pure and simple, that hiding behind it is a very serious matter, made all the more serious by its being hidden within the seemingly meaningless. Yet the devices of humor continue; it begins to appear that we are perhaps witnessing a comedy, and we are given all the trappings of a successfully resolved comic plot in which the life-inhibiting forces are unmasked and cast out all ends "as you like it." But this, of course, is precisely what does not happen, for Greene's parody of the comic formula reverses the normal mode of resolution. This is not really comedy, for the ludicrous and meaningless rampagings are not corrected in the end, and in fact are made all the more ludicrous and meaningless by being cast into the comic mode, which suggests that they will be transformed into something good and happy.

Before the development of Greene's parody in *The Comedians* can be traced in greater detail, the character of the narrator, Brown, must be understood. For it is Brown who uses farce and comedy as pat metaphors for his view of the world. Brown's difficulties are said by himself to go back to his loss of religious belief instigated by his role as Frère Laurent in a college production of the French version of *Romeo and Juliet*. . . . The actor's urge to play a role, however, is something he can never replace with a true conception of self. Lacking a clear notion of his mother's background; not knowing who his father is or even if his name really is Brown; feeling that having been born in Monaco "'is almost the same as being a citizen of nowhere'" . . . ; Brown is a case-study of the so-called identity crisis. Brown notes that the dramatic director at the college "taught me adequately enough the secrets of make-up" . . . , and his life since that time consisted of little else than shifting roles to meet the particular situation of the moment. Indeed, Martha refers to Brown as a "prêtre manqué" . . .—a "failed priest"—as if Brown had never really gotten himself untangled from the role of the foiled Friar Lawrence.

Lacking orthodox religious belief, Brown accepts the Manichean heresy . . . , and sees God as "an authoritative practical joker." . . . Brown's own life is thus conceived by himself as being nothing really serious, as being, rather, a farce or a "confused comedy" (. . . Brown throughout uses the two words, farce and comedy, interchangeably), and not the "very serious affair" it was in childhood, when God was "incarnated in every tragedy"; and the Haiti setting is the "extreme point of comedy." . . .

Again and again Brown returns to his pet metaphor. His affair with Martha, he feels, is not serious, it is only "a sub-plot affording a little light relief" to the "tragic theme" of Haiti politics. . . . Their affair is nothing beyond an "act" belonging "too closely to the theatre of farce." . . . Unlike Marcel, neither Brown nor Martha "would ever die for love. . . . We belonged to the world of comedy and not of tragedy." . . .

But not only does Brown deny any significance to love, he conceives of virtually the whole of his life as consisting of a "game" whereby he peddles a particular version of himself for the right price and can therefore call himself a "comedian." . . . Brown's view of the world as a sort of farcical/comedy is itself, however, only a thinly masked disguise for avoiding commitment to responsible action. (pp. 141-42)

What Greene will do is to have Brown, the narrator, render his own story in such a way as to bring the farcical/comical elements to the fore. Brown will try to convince the reader that his lack of involvement is justified due to the non-serious nature of his existence, and he will do this by presenting his life as a combination farce-comedy. But Brown's own narrative mode, we shall see, undercuts itself; for the ultimate seriousness of the story slices through the veil of comedy, and what emerges is a grim parody that is really not funny at all. As comic narrator, then, Brown is only failing at another of the roles he has been unable throughout his life to pull off successfully. (p. 142)

As narrator, Brown attempts to create a facade of comedy over his own interpretation of life. The nightmare of the outer world—the Haiti background never far off throughout the book; but if Brown, looking back over a period of his life when "I still regarded my future seriously" . . . , can convince the reader that his life is in fact a sort of joke that should not be taken seriously, he can justify his failure to engage in the wider troubles of the world. Brown's narrative technique, then, will be to emphasize those comic elements which lend a non-serious air to his personal existence. . . .

Brown throughout the narrative sustains use of metaphors of drama to give the impression that he is really only involved in a stage play, a fiction we should not take seriously. Time and again Brown conceives of his own actions as if they were determined by the script of some unnamed playwright. (p. 143)

All of these elements of the comic spirit Brown brings to bear to certify his early point, "Life was a comedy, not the tragedy for which I had been prepared." . . . This delusion is, as I have argued, the foundation for Brown's belief in an uncommitted way of life. As a "comedian," then, Brown can slide into detachment on the basis that "I am not a hero" and "I was never brave." . . . Nothing less than virtually the whole of the story of Brown's own wretched existence, however, works against the validity of this belief. Brown has tried to trick life into becoming something it is not, a low-grade comedy, but he has tricked only himself. Martha, who at times seems the novel's most morally lucid character . . . , turns Brown's own drama metaphors against him in a perceptive attack that exposes Brown's ugly mental habit of projecting onto others roles that do not coincide with their personal natures:

> Darling, don't you see you are inventing us?
> . . . You won't listen if what we say is out of character—the character you've given us. . . . To you nothing exists except in your own thoughts. Not me, not Jones. You're a Berkeleyan. My God, what a Berkeleyan. You've turned poor Jones into a seducer and me into a wanton mistress. You can't even believe in your own mother's medal, can you? You've written her a different part. My dear, try to believe we exist when you aren't there. We're independent of you. None of us is like you fancy we are. Perhaps it would not matter so much if your thoughts were not so dark, always so dark. . . .

Brown has turned others into what they are not—fictions of his own twisted intellect; he has turned life into something

it is not—a meaningless joke; he has turned himself into something he is not—a comedian. (pp. 144-45)

The parody of the farcical/comical, however, is not contained solely within the deluded mind of the narrator, Brown. His own methods, as story-teller, of characterization and plotting seem to be attempts to reinforce his mental viewpoint as "comedian." That is, Brown as narrator attempts to create for the reader the stock characters and the essential plot-devices of comedy. But his efforts backfire: a comic interpretation of the characters and of the plot is blocked by the action containing them, reducing to unintended parody the very devices by which Brown is trying to thrust upon the reader his twisted perspective.

Perhaps the most obvious character-type in *The Comedians* is the *miles gloriosus*—the braggart soldier, represented by Jones, whose model may be Shaw's Bluntschli. . . . Traditionally, of course, the boaster is exposed and held up for ridicule. This normal pattern is maintained temporarily; for Jones eventually admits that in fact he was rejected by the army due to flat feet, his only contact with the military being as a checker of "transport and travel vouchers for third-class entertainers." . . . Indeed, Jones has never seen a dead man, and he vomits when he finally does see one. . . . Yet in the end, Jones achieves heroic status. He receives a stone monument, which, Philipot says, "will be a place of pilgrimage" . . . ; further, Philipot will not only contact "the British ambassador, [and] perhaps a member of the Royal family" . . . about Jones's heroics, but he will even "write about him to the Queen of England" . . . : all this even though Jones has died an apparently meaningless death because his flat feet failed him. . . . Indeed, his death seems itself to parody the grandly romantic ending of Hemingway's Robert Jordan: Jones "could hardly move because of his feet. He found what he called a good place. He said he'd keep the soldiers off till we had time to reach the road—none of them were anxious to risk himself very close. He said he would follow slowly, but I [Philipot] knew he would never come." . . .

Another stock comic character is the tyrant-figure, the usurper of power. Usually this unruly figure controls the state of affairs at the start of the action, but in the end he is unmasked, stripped of power, and replaced with a more benevolent ruler. The Tontons Macoute—Duvalier's bogey-men—represent a group of tyrant-figures. Especially interesting here is the nefarious Captain Concasseur (French, *concasser*: "to break or crush"), who tells Brown, "You have a sense of humour. I appreciate humour. I am in favour of jokes. They have a political value. Jokes are a release for the cowardly and the impotent." . . . The bogey-men have typical disguises, their sunglasses, which they wear even at night. They are shorn of their power, first psychologically, by Mrs. Smith's incredible rescue of Brown . . . , then physically, by means of Philipot's equally incredible rescue of both Brown and Jones . . .—here, Concasseur receives the traditional unmasking when his sunglasses are smashed. Yet even though Concasseur is killed, Philipot's revolutionary activities fail and nothing has really changed.

The Smiths seem to be a parody of the young lovers from romantic comedy. They have about them an air of the courtly: Smith, for instance, "looked around the saloon before he stood aside so that his wife could enter under the arch of his arm, like a bride under a sword. It was as though he wanted to satisfy himself first that there was no unsuitable company present." . . . Their relationship is greatly admired by Brown: "I have never known in Europe a married couple with that kind of loyalty." . . . Yet unlike the traditional young lovers of romantic comedy, who are associated with Spring, the Smiths, aged and childless, seem to represent Winter-figures. (pp. 145-47)

Northrop Frye has distinguished a recurring comic figure he labels the "plain dealer, an outspoken advocate of a kind of moral norm who has the sympathy of the audience." In *The Comedians* this "plain dealer" would be represented by Dr. Magiot. He is drawn throughout the story as a benevolent man who speaks out against the suicidal activities of the revolutionaries even though he supports their goals: "Go on living with your belief, don't die with it" . . . ; the revolutionaries "may be heroes, but they have to learn to live and not to die." . . . His final letter to Brown states an idealistic desire to wed Communism to Catholicism. . . . And yet upon second look Magiot appears to be less than a model of right thought and action. He is presented as a man out of his own time and place, thrice associated with the world of ancient Rome. . . . Magiot's sitting room is described as "Victorian" . . . , and his garden contains a tree that looks "like an illustration in a Victorian novel." . . . This sense of removal from the present indicates that, for all his espoused commitment, Magiot is really a man detached from current realities. . . . His attitude toward Marxism is extremely sentimental: he speaks of "the Marxist dream of a far far future. . . ." And not only does he slither away for cover in a moment of possible danger, leaving Brown exposed . . . , he dies a martyr's death in direct violation of his own credo that one must live if one is to be an effective agent of good.

A liberal sprinkling of minor characters are also to be found in comedy—the clever servant, for example, represented in *The Comedians* by Joseph, who is able to mix the finest rum punches anywhere. Joseph seems also to have affinities with the tricky slave of Roman comedy, for the Smith's continually prattle their disapproval of Brown's treatment of Joseph, "as though [Brown] were a southern plantation-owner." . . . The tricky slave is traditionally a hatcher of plots, yet Joseph's "plot" to help Dr. Philipot escape goes awry when Joseph mistakes Brown for the Tontons Macoute, a mistake that motivates the doctor's suicide. . . .

Another typical comic figure is the buffoon. Luis, the cuckold, would seem to fit this role: "'let us all be comedians together,'" he chants. "'Perhaps even Papa Doc is a comedian. . . . We mustn't complain too much about being comedians—it's an honourable profession'." . . . Yet Luis himself generates little comedy (the normal function of the buffoon), and even recognizes that he is a "bad comedian." . . .

The stock comic rogue finds its type in *The Comedians* in the ship's purser, a ribald fellow whose life centers around jokes, sex, liquor, and a petty power struggle to match the ship's captain. He is, however, perhaps more grotesque than he is comic. His use of prophylactics for balloons has already been mentioned. When Brown asks him about a certain prostitute, the purser answers, "'I always eat off the same plate. How are Mr. and Mrs. Smith?'" . . .

As for the comic nature of the plot, it turns upon the most antique formula of all, "lover's gifts regained": boy wins girl, loses girl, regains girl. The parody in Greene's novel of this type of plot is not difficult to perceive. To begin with, the lovers are hardly young: Brown is sixty and Martha about thirty-five. . . . The plot may be viewed, additionally, as a parody of the plight of the *senex*-figure—an aged man who is in some way renewed in the course of the action even though he must lose the love game to youth; but Brown, of course, is anything but renewed by story's end.

The resolution of the comic plot generally involves detailed, intricate plotting, schemes of all sort, and what not. This pattern of resolution is suggested in the complicated escape of Jones, which will break the "triangle," allowing Brown and Martha to be together. However, Brown's plotting carries with it lurid overtones. Motivated by Brown's own senseless jealousy, the escape is conceived of by Brown as a "trap" . . . with which to get rid of Jones even if it ultimately means death for Jones. Jones does escape (only to be killed shortly thereafter); but Brown is forced to flee to Santo Dominico, so that his plotting only ends with his separation from Martha.

In comedy, if one device fails, decorum allows for the implementation of further contrivances to unite the lovers. Hence, in *The Comedians,* the coincidental meeting of Brown and Martha in Santo Dominico. Yet this meeting concludes with the final separation of the lovers. Further, it seems to be a grim parody upon the traditional wedding ceremony that brings all together at comedy's end. Here the final setting is indeed a church, but the occasion is a funeral. Martha takes Brown "by the hand and led me into a side chapel: we were alone with a hideous statue of Saint Clare. . . . 'We had reached an end [Martha says], hadn't we, you and I?'" . . . Death of body and of love, then, and not rebirth of love, ends all as the final curtain falls on *The Comedians.*

Besides these traditional elements of structure, comedy includes a significant social dimension. Frye has observed that in comedy, the theme is the "integration of society, which usually takes the form of incorporating a central character into it." . . . That is, comedy is a mode in which at work's end the morally divergent characters are included into the social body so that the life-promoting forces triumph. But at the end of *The Comedians,* Jones is dead, Martha is headed for Lima, and Brown is employed as an undertaker, a servant of the forces of death. Undertaking, Smith asserts, is a "'valuable social service'" . . . , and so the parody of the theme of inclusion into society of the comic protagonist is brought to the fore.

Moreover, laughter is seen by Bergson as a "social gesture," a "corrective" by which society transforms death-promoting forces into life-promoting ones; laughter is society's tool for setting itself aright once its equilibrium has been tilted. . . . Yet in *The Comedians* it is clear that there is, in fact, no power capable of redeeming the destructive impulses at work both within man and within society.

By way of concluding remarks, we may consider Brown from the perspective of the traditional view that perceives an inability on the part of the Englishman to ridicule his own follies. (pp. 147-150)

What Brown, as narrator of *The Comedians,* attempts is to follow this tradition. He will, that is, try to present himself as a laughingstock, and he will do this not in self-ridicule of traits in need of correction, but in self-defense of his fear of "involvement." But, like his other strategies, this one too ends in unintended parody; for Brown, like his fellow Englishmen (although Brown's ethnic background is uncertain, he is counted as a British subject in Haiti) . . . , is really hiding his true self from both his own conscious mind and from ourselves as audience. Illusion, and not reality, has triumphed in *The Comedians,* and the joke really is on Brown. (p. 150)

> *Michael Routh, "Greene's Parody of Farce and Comedy in 'The Comedians',"* in Renascence (© *copyright 1973, Catholic Renascence Society, Inc.), Spring, 1974, pp. 139-51.*

Graham Greene divides his work into serious literature and 'entertainments' and I, for one, have always preferred his entertainments to his serious literature, largely because the former are free from the Catholic shop-talk of the latter. The 'entertainments' also reflect Graham Greene's passionate interest in old crime and spy stories, those humble but vastly pleasurable and unpretentious types of straightforward story-telling which could often serve as models for more ambitious but also more boring forms of literature. It was a splendid idea of Graham Greene's to follow the [recent triumph of] *Sherlock Holmes* with a revival of E W Hornung's counterpart to the great detective, that equally great gentleman amateur cracksman and test cricketer, A J Raffles. If Holmes had returned from the Reichenbach Falls, why should not Raffles rise from the dead of Spion Kop?

William Gillette's *Sherlock Holmes* was melodrama seriously meant; Graham Greene's *Raffles* is nostalgic pastiche, but none the worse for that. For lovingly tongue-in-cheek parody is a far more conscious, deliberate genre than naïve melodrama, it operates on more and subtler levels of irony and reflectiveness. And certainly Graham Greene is a better writer and a more accomplished artist than William Gillette could ever have been.

By lovingly reconstructing the late Victorian milieu, moreover, Graham Greene is enabled to say a great deal, indirectly, about his own time by contrast as well as tragic irony. In the figure of the ageing Prince of Wales on the eve of becoming Edward VII he finds a brilliant spokesman for much that needs to be said about the virtues of *his* society and, by implication, the barbarisms of ours. And at the same time he enables us, enlightened, liberated denizens of a 'permissive' age to laugh about the barbarisms of that period, its naïve patriotism, imperialism, love and sport and stuffiness.

Greene's Raffles is a far more sophisticated character than E W Hornung's; he is a philosopher, albeit a hedonistic one, as well as an elegant thief. And Graham Greene has put him into the world of Oscar Wilde and Lord Alfred Douglas, so that he becomes part of a *fin de siècle* aesthetic circle. . . .

The plot is secondary to all this. . . . If the plot had been more ingenious, the play would have been less frothy, less light-heartedly rambling, less of the delightful entertainment which it triumphantly proved to be. (p. 30)

> *Martin Esslin, in* Plays and Players (© *copyright Martin Esslin 1976; reprinted with permission), February, 1976.*

In "In Search of a Character" Greene has referred to "the abiding temptation to tell a good story"; a temptation fully indulged in ["The Human Factor"], as in its predecessors, "The Confidential Agent," "The Ministry of Fear" and "Our Man in Havana." But the story is not the point, it is told only for the sake of the characters, to give them something to do and many things to suffer so that we may come to know them. Character, Greene's abiding concern, is disclosed in thoughts, attitudes and feelings more accurately than in deeds. "We are saved or damned by our thoughts, not by our actions," Greene writes in "The Lost Childhood," where his text is the fiction of François Mauriac. If Greene's fiction has a moral, it is that our ethical judgments are inept if they are directed upon a man's actions. By their deeds ye shall know them? No, not by such things, mere external appearances, false clues. Maurice Castle [the central character of "The Human Factor," a British double agent leaking information to the Russians,] is a traitor. Nevertheless, he is a good man because his motives are selfless, his feelings are pure.

Greene's fiction has a design upon the reader to make it impossible for him to condemn Castle. Castle's mother condemns him, but she knows nothing of mercy, charity, love. In Greene's "The Heart of the Matter" Scobie says that he liked West Africa because "here you could love human beings nearly as God loved them, knowing the worst." Greene admires only the kind of love which is animated by that knowledge. The purpose of his fiction is to tempt us with characters whom it is easy to dislike, despise, patronize, condemn. But we indulge these responses only when we hold ourselves aloof from Greene's art. When we yield to his rhythm, we accept his characters, knowing their worst. If we do not accept them, the reason is not that they are beyond redemption but that our moral judgment is premature; we are not sufficiently patient, we are too eager to see our judgments enforced.

But all this raises a problem. How does Greene avoid the limp conclusion that we are all innocent, a conclusion not much more convincing than that we are all guilty? . . . Greene deals with [this problem], as an artist, by reducing the list of sins and withholding punishment. But one sin remains, and is unforgivable. The cardinal sin is not to care. (p. 1)

The epigraph to "The Human Factor" is a text from Conrad . . . : "I only know that he who forms a tie is lost, the germ of corruption has entered into his soul." By such loss, we live; by that germ of corruption, we are purified. Castle has formed a tie with [his wife] Sarah. The tie is likely to destroy both of them. . . . "The Human Factor" is concerned with ties, connections, lines, limits. One of Castle's code-books is "War and Peace," and he refers to a passage about the line between Denisov's troops and the French, a line which "one dreads to cross, and longs to cross." The Conrad who suffuses Greene's imagination is the author of "The Shadow-Line" and "Victory" and "Heart of Darkness," fictions about the terrible crossing of lines between security and terror, and the need to cross them.

Some people care; in Greene's fiction these are saved, or at least made worthy of damnation. Logic would say that those who do not care cannot be saved, and must be cast into outer darkness. But Greene is not intimidated by logic, and loves to show its force refuted by pity. In "The Lost

Childhood'' he sees the logic refuted not in Conrad but in Henry James. ''The final beauty of James's stories,'' he writes, ''lies in their pity. 'The poetry is in the pity.''' Not pity for those who deserve it: no effort of imagination, patience or care is required in such cases. Whether we are of God's fraternity or the Devil's, we are punished in our own way: this is the source of James's pity. ''It is in the final justice of James's pity,'' Greene asserts, ''the completeness of an analysis which enabled him to pity the most shabby, the most corrupt, of his human actors, that he ranks with the greatest of creative writers.''

Greene says nothing of James's analysis except that it is complete, but his implication is that a moral analysis is dismally inadequate, esthetically incomplete, until it is brought to the point at which pity is lavished upon everyone. If there is a question of judgment, James allows his characters to judge themselves, and he pities them for their severity. If they are incapable of punishing themselves, or unable to know the worst of themselves, he pities them for their poor disabilities. Writing of James's achievement, especially in the short stories, Greene is also writing of himself and of the morality he intends.

It is not difficult to pity Castle: what else could one do with him, a victim of care, devotion, love? The minor characters are harder to pity. . . . [We] have to deal with Cornelius Muller, a sinister chief of the secret police in South Africa, who tried to blackmail Castle by threatening him with the Race Law. (pp. 1, 43)

Muller is one of Greene's most impressive achievements in this novel: a mere thriller writer would have kept him sinister in the old way, even in London and Berkhamsted. . . .

''The Human Factor'' is the work of an old master in a genre congenial to his interest and talent. Greene has done many other things, more exacting fictions of crime and punishment, sin and redemption. This is the kind of book he could now write with one hand tied behind his back. But he has chosen to use both hands and to do it with finesse. It is not meant to be ''War and Peace,'' or even ''The Heart of the Matter.'' Twenty years ago Greene would have called it an entertainment rather than a novel, making a distinction which he has recently given up. It is simply, but not too simply, a good story, a novel about the void between thought and action. Winners take all, but the all is nothing. Losers lose all, but the loss is providential, a form of grace. (p. 43)

> *Denis Donoghue, "A Novel of Thought, Action and Pity," in* The New Yorka Times Book Review *(© 1978 by The New York Times Company; reprinted by permission), February 26, 1978, pp. 1, 43.*

Maurice Castle, [*The Human Factor*'s] protagonist, exists in the relative freedom of London, but as a prisoner of loyalties at odds. The dilemma for Greene's heroes has remained consistent: how retain integrity when the very nature of the word posits ''oneness,'' isolation? His men do well enough alone. But such self-protective isolation is threatened in the novels—drastically, disastrously—by the force of love. The individual can battle a system, perhaps, but his battle-line will be breached by compassion. . . .

The plot here is well-made as always; Greene digs up what he plants. Chocolates that figure in the first chapter are

sure to figure elsewhere; Castle's incidental-seeming bulldog is central to a later incident. A series of literary referents wind through the text; Tolstoy and Browning recur. . . . Reality and fiction meld so that Kim Philby and James Bond can complement each other; the tedious details of spywork create an exploded cliche. ''We've never been very James Bond minded here. I wasn't allowed to carry a gun, and my only car was a secondhand Morris Minor.''

This absence of permission is one hallmark of Greene's world; his celebrants are dutiful, and a marriage celebration ends in argument over the hostesses' shattered china owl. (p. 32)

Castle is a fortress of rigid defenses, yet pinned. The chess terminology is intentional here; we are very much in the world of double agenting, encoded messages and the mirror image. . . .

Importantly among Greene's gifts, I think, is the ability to express ''doubt and even denial,'' to play both sides of the game. It's why he commended Bishop Blougram's chessboard—wherein a contestant must do just that—and why he writes so readily of the double agent's role. Yet the book does seem flattish and faded; corruption is routine. There is a sense of weary manipulation throughout; the ''kings'' and ''bishops'' of this game are hemmed in by regulations also —behaving at country shoots and funerals and clubs with much the same enjoined precision as do their threatened ''pawns.'' . . . Everywhere we sense this weariness, nor is it necessarily intentional. . . .

Perhaps it's that Greene has written of such sacrifice before, or that the genre of which he's past-master has a present master as informed as Le Carré. Or possibly it's the echoes of those incisive earlier efforts. Yusef of *The Heart of the Matter* is a more persuasive villain, say, than Dr. Percival or Muller here, and the love of Maurice Bendrix for *his* Sarah in *The End of the Affair* seems both more baffled and comprehensive than that of the present Maurice. To one who takes pure pleasure in the *oeuvre* entire, however, such recapitulation is a gift.

Graham Greene should long since have been accorded the Nobel Prize. He is ''integrity's'' laureate, whether Stockholm accepts him or not. What living English author can lay claim to greater eminence or to have interested more readers in more ways? . . . In this half-a-century, Greene has been both an unstinting craftsman and the unswerving advocate of decency. If *The Human Factor* cannot take its place with masterpieces such as *The Heart of the Matter, The Power and the Glory,* or *The Comedians,* it nonetheless is first-rate work—an instruction as well as ''entertainment,'' an artful spy story and publishing event. (p. 33)

> *Nicholas Delbanco, in* The New Republic *(reprinted by permission of* The New Republic; *© 1978 by The New Republic, Inc.), March 11, 1978.*

*   *   *

GREGOR, Arthur   1923-

An Austrian-born American children's writer, editor, and poet, Gregor is primarily known as a mystical, introspective poet. (See also *Contemporary Authors,* **Vols. 25-28, rev. ed.)**

Like other peoples who have lived in times of general calamity, we have become accustomed to the kind of mysticism that proclaims itself in raucous and unintelligible, not to say psychedelic, terms. It is a well-recognized aspect of social deterioration. Consequently we are refreshed to find a mystical poet who still speaks to us about his experience with the assurance of candor and simplicity:

> I see a firing squad.
> you, a young sailor
> tied at your wrists.
> Churchbells are raging as if
> all of the wind of the sea
> had swept into steeples.
>
> I see an entire city kneeling,
> a girl throwing open a window
> tossing you a rose.
> The bullets, and you are swaying
> as though tied to a mast
> at sea in the wildest storm. . . .

In such terms Arthur Gregor invokes the Immanence behind the world's facade—the Prince, the Stranger, "you who opened the glass door." And in equally simple figures —trees, city streets, a concert hall—he praises the moments of his spiritual vision. Rare moments: and the poems do not always succeed, for what he is trying to write is the most difficult of all kinds of poetry. But his successes are moving and genuine.

Partly, Gregor's maturity is that of any poet who has written for twenty years, and who derives from the great tradition of the purposive imagination, roughly definable in reference to such poets as Stevens, Éluard, Gottfried Benn. For Gregor, metaphor remains all of poetry; psychedelic theory to the contrary notwithstanding, no direct re-creation of mystical intuition is possible. Hence most of his failures are poems in which he succumbs to the risk of metaphor and crosses over entirely into symbolism, the manipulation of "objective correlatives," while his successes are poems in which he lets his objects speak for themselves. Or perhaps we should say, more accurately, that his successes come from the times when his dream, his vision, has presented itself in sufficiently concrete terms. Given the abstractness of the human mind, such occasions are bound to be rare.

Partly, however, Gregor's maturity, which is also his modernity, is a question of his particular mystical point of view. Speaking bluntly, far more bluntly than the poet himself would condone, if a God exists He must be a sorrowful God, not merely because He is aware of the pain of the world but because He is an expression of it. His root is in our suffering. Paradoxically, only in the bliss of heaven could a thoroughgoing atheistic materialist sustain himself. This Gregor knows, and he writes, in a poem addressing his own consciousness as it first moves toward transcendent awareness:

> What you must know before
> you enter this domain
> and learn the ways of which
> we shall not speak is this
> first truth of what you are:
> a sorrow, a sorrow
> begging for home. Or you
> would not have come so far.

Of course most of us—95 per cent, I imagine—cannot live in Gregor's world. Not that we are materialists in the old sense; but in spite of calamity we remain secularists and existentialists, believing that the meaning of reality lies, not behind a veil of objective chaos, but within our own breasts. Yet having said this we must add two further points.

First, we are exactly the ones who are the most faithful readers of poets like Gregor. For one thing, we are always seeking an outlet—an acceptable outlet—for our own unquestionable religious feelings; and for another, in our determined reasonableness we cannot choose to deny ourselves the advantage—the emotional service, so to speak— of mystical beauty. Hence we are the best, most persistent readers of Yeats, for instance, although we are easily annoyed by the vulgar elements of his occultism. In Gregor we have a lesser poet; but we also have one who abstains from the crudities of the Rosy Cross in favor of a base in the broad and pristine, but no less knowledgeable, tradition of overt neo-Platonism.

Second, we cannot fail to be impressed by the staying power, not only of this tradition but of the individual poets within it. In contrast to the sensualists and eroticists and naturalists, they age beautifully, vigorous to the end. Whereas the sensualist's insight merely closes in on him, inevitably, leaving him with only bombast as his senses wane but his artistic technique matures, the Platonist's insight is, in Gregor's words, "without horizons," i.e., unpredictable and expansible; its source is everywhere. In twenty years Gregor has produced only three small books. But very probably he is just now hitting his stride, beginning to find the means to accommodate any experience to the particular demands of his vision. What will his progress be? Through the next twenty years, at all events, many of us will watch it with special interest. (pp. 473-74)

> *Hayden Carruth, "Mystical Candor," in* The Nation *(copyright 1967 by the Nation Associates, Inc.), November 6, 1967, pp. 473-74.*

Arthur Gregor is surely one of the most deeply spiritual poets of our time. The development of his art can be viewed as the cultivation of a purely transparent medium in which language becomes a vehicle for transmitting moments of luminous being. To many readers, his poems may appear to be moving toward a total absence of style, the condition of stylelessness. Yet he is an experimental stylist in the truest sense. In Gregor's work, we find the nearest approach in American poetry to what Susan Sontag has identified as "spiritual style" in the films of Robert Bresson. To a generation of readers accustomed to a garish obtrusiveness of style, Gregor's style is apt to seem invisible. Simply to compare Gregor's style with the bland, featureless style of most poetry in translation, poetry without any face, is to be struck with the distinctive serene beauty and simplicity—the austereness—of his lines. . . . A special quality of Arthur Gregor's writing is his power to hold a long sentence in breathless suspension over many lines, lines which instill the feeling of softness, gentleness, lightness. In Gregor's medium, tone must be perfectly pitched and mood everywhere sustained, since any slip in rhythm or phrasing will be accentuated by the stark crystallinity of his line movement, and may be picked up instantly by the careful reader.

Gregor's fervent preoccupation with images of subtle and delicate movements in nature is indicative of a search for living correlatives to the stillness-in-motion he aspires to in the refinement of his poetic line:

> Silence shivers as if touched by sounds
> subtle as the air that holds
> the heron's spread blue wing . . .

Gregor has evolved a poetic manner that serves as a frictionless conveyor for his thought. Ideas in the poems are as inseparable from the style of their expression as wave from water, wind from air. Because Gregor's work is more a poetry of ideas than we are accustomed to reading today, it is easy enough to make the mistake of dismissing him as merely a philosopher-in-verse. But these poems are not doctrinaire; rather, they employ ideas as one of many elements in the service of projecting an inner luminosity of being. Philosophy is subordinate to the stream of intensely devotional feeling running through most of the poems.

In a few pieces, ideas do dominate the poetry. Similar motifs may be employed repeatedly, and the weaker poems fail to give any new life to the theme. Philosophy must be lifted above a minimal threshold of linguistic and imagistic adventurousness to become poetry, and some poems lag much below that minimum. Another of the difficulties in Gregor's art is the tendency to sameness in line length and line movement. He evidently has a nearly irresistible affinity for shorter lines, perhaps because they nearly always so aptly facilitate the free flow of his mind.

But in his longest and best poem . . . [in *Figure in the Door*] ("The Unworldliness that He Creates")—he achieves an altogether new line movement: supple, pulsing, taut or slack by turns, long or short, adaptable to multiple rhythms. The new mode intersperses prose passages in a matrix of expanding sentences of poetry, sentences that employ a Whitmanesque paralleling of clauses is sequence to encircle a larger and wider landscape of vision. The one constant in the poem—which marks a perfect arrival and fulfillment of many of the central motifs in the book's philosophy—is the movement from beauties of art, nature, urban scene, into the space in the persona's being in which all "things he looks upon achieve themselves."

Gregor's power to envision for the reader the quality of spiritual beauty in strangers, "foreigners," is an ideological mainstay of many of his poems. He seems to be proposing a theory of personality which gives a new validity to the romantic axiom of love-at-first-sight by annexing it to its antithesis of classical restraint:

> On your way home you stopped to shop,
> looked around as you were going in,
> and recognized yourself in me
> some steps away. Then you went in
> and I went on. Of course the outcome
> could have been otherwise, but not
> what had already taken place.
> That we had seen each other in
> each other's face without disguise,
> had beheld what is not yours nor mine:
> a nameless recognition we might not
> have reached, had our shyness and
> each other's namelessness been breached.

Again and again, Gregor dwells on the kinds of recognition

—the radiances—that are possible only between strangers, the momentous flash in the eyes of "the figure in the door." The sensibility in the poems is one that has learned to guard against the damages—the subtle losses—that result from frail intimacies. The fashionable glamor that attends all forms of personal involvement today leads to serious, though nearly imperceptible, injuries to the self. Gregor revives the power in us to respond to beauties in people that transcend their worldly personalities. This impersonal —or transpersonal—beauty is, for Gregor, the supreme reality. (pp. 606-08)

> *Laurence Lieberman, in* The Yale Review *(© 1968 by Yale University; reprinted by permission of the editors), Summer, 1968.*

Basic Movements by Arthur Gregor is a book of nerveless, unemphasized poems, both delicate and sure. . . . They suggest a competence not overtly demonstrated. . . . Gregor is a contemplative poet, and again, "things" are dissolved and merged in the poems. I find them too rarified to evoke any fullblooded response in me—Shelley without the blaze and ethereal wings. One minor defect is the tendency to archaisms—"Unto," "forth," "therin," giving a suggestion of falsity that belies the poems. In key and mood this book resembled Kenneth O. Hanson's *The Distance Anywhere*. These are poems of a man puzzled but not confounded. The Greece poems are refreshingly different from Lawrence Durrell's, breezy but never enchanted. They are place poems and travel poems by one who never leaves himself behind, as if he looked through the wrong end of a telescope. (p. 869)

> *Jack Bevan, in* The Southern Review *(copyright, 1970, by Jack Bevan), Vol. 6, No. 3, Summer, 1970.*

Few writers have sustained such purity of intention combined with virtuosity of form, or have grown in craftsmanship as has [Arthur Gregor] without losing—to borrow the title of one of his finest and most ambitious poems—"the unworldliness that he creates." Yet, why should such a steadfastness through all the changes of fashion in poetry be a reason for praise? Does that not somehow show an impoverishment of the imagination, or perhaps a failure to deal with experience? Have we not come to expect the romantic in his forties to have gone sour, to have hardened himself against the sudden approach of the beautiful, to cherish irony of vision more than purity and simplicity of tone? Not so Arthur Gregor. In the long, meditative, deeply personal poem "Horizons West" with which he concludes [*Selected Poems*], he reflects, in a wilderness solitude, on his early errors of commission and omission, on the persons who helped to shape his life—parents, friends, his brother, women:

> The women
> whose care and laughter pursued me,
> whose fear of what I strove to
> experience, whose insistence on
> demanding from me what I
> did not want, made me escape them.

> (p. 230)

From the beginning, in the poems written while he was in his early twenties and published in his first collection *Octavian Shooting Targets* (1954), Gregor has demonstrated a brilliant virtuosity of diction, a sure mastery of the most subtle verbal music. . . . The daring shifts of syntax and atmosphere, the bravura technique which dazzlingly compresses ancient and contemporary decadence into a powerful montage, make such poems as "Ritual" and the book's title poem as fresh and exciting today as when they were first published. In these first works Gregor sounded the themes that would continue through the entire body of his work: exile and wandering, the loss of beloved persons and places, life in Vienna before Hitler, the second World War and the new Diaspora. There was a cultivation, too, of conventionally romantic images: swans, places, fountains, the sea, mandolins, and legendary gardens, "princes who have missed their cue, who have no other chance and have no other chance." Mediterranean elements, Oriental strains, and the effect on his work of the poets he has most admired—Eliot, Rilke, Wallace Stevens—were also in evidence.

Three years later, Gregor published *Declensions of a Refrain,* a small and beautifully-made volume in which these early themes were struck again: travel (Venice at night, and Siena); the persistence of the sensual in music; gardens, birds, and boats arriving and departing. At the same time there was much less pyrotechnic display, the poet was less likely to establish himself in the rooms of the palace than in the quieter corridors of his mind. The title poem shows him working—to use a musical analogue—in a sonata form. Of the longer poems and variations, this poem is surely his most successful. Beginning with a quiet statement—"More or less is a relative gesture / as in gain or loss," it fuses dream and personal recollection with Gregor's continuing sense of the presence of history, as he invokes the ineffability of human greatness, our defiance of states and kingdoms and princes; and always there is the journey, this time

> from dream to dream
> to a first calm that overcame me
> in that distant harbor, the sun
> at dawn more enormous and barbarous
> than when it set in the Arabian sea.

As the poem drives forcefully toward its resolution of what the poet has heard in Bach and seen in Cézanne: the mystery hidden deep within the human spirit, in "caves that rest in them / and stir like a burning marvel."

At this point in his career, Gregor had gone beyond his early facility, beyond his technical mastery of what might be regarded as the mathematics of poetry, the lines and stanzas as perfectly balanced as equations, to achieve an apparently effortless synthesis of the meditative and lyrical strains of his talent. *Basic Movements* (1966) continued the synthesis, confirmed the simplicity and directness of Gregor's diction (adjectives are always used sparingly in his work, and he resists the temptation to overload his syntax, writing, as a consequence, some of the purest and loveliest lines in contemporary poetry), while deepening the resonance of his music. . . . In certain poems, he reaches the almost wholly intangible, tantalizing indefinable quality of meaning, as in "Twenty or So," where he seeks to recapture the nature of a look which meant more to him than experience itself, was experience itself. The epigraph for the volume—"In the world, not of it"—defined both his estimate of his own situation and his ambition for his art. (pp. 230-32)

Much has been said of Gregor's resemblances to Rilke and Hofmannsthal, and of certain affinities in his work to Constantin Cavafy, of whom he has spoken admiringly. It is true that he has combined elements of the European tradition with an American sensibility, but by the time *A Bed by the Sea* was published last year, he had found such serenity in his point of view, such complete control of his skills, that any conflicts between his heritage and the discords of contemporary American life have been completely resolved in the unity and purity of his work. He writes now without the masks and elaborate defenses of the more vulnerable artist he was in his youth. He writes with a clarity and transparency which leaves no place for either self-deception or self-conscious artifice. . . . (p. 232)

One has only to read "The Statue," an indisputably great poem, to understand Gregor's triumphant acceptance of himself as both man and poet, or "The Release" to realize the maturity and profound dignity with which he confronts suffering in himself and in humanity. In these last poems, even his sense of playfulness has been liberated. Though he has always had a finely-balanced sense of humor in his personal relationships, humor has seldom figured in his poetry. Now, in "Variations," he plays ruefully with his own romantic imagery:

> Everything alive is sensitive.
> If not a phoenix, a dove,
> (all right, a pigeon) lifts from
> the fire of autumn leaves.

The acceptance is most simply expressed in "Words of a Pilgrim":

> Nothing matters to me but
> inner accord.
> Come, beasts,
> I'll face you if I must.
> I'll walk through the dark with
> the unfulfilled, the lost.
> Let their terror be my cry.
> What is hidden
> shall come forth.
> Light insists
> nothing shall be missed.   (p. 233)

Robert A. Carter, "Pilgrimage of the Imagination," in Modern Poetry Studies *(copyright 1971, by Jerome Mazzaro), Vol. 2, No. 5, 1971, pp. 230-33.*

Arthur Gregor's [*A Bed by the Sea*] will reward a careful reading; those who prefer Grieg to Vivaldi and Renoir to Dürer will like it. The landscape of the poems seems one in which pastel-shaded forms out of Fragonard blend slowly to the heart-wounding sobs of long-winded violins: a mixture of rococo and early symbolism. You can be sure that Irving Babbitt, for one, would not have liked it at all, and it is hard to see how anyone (who is unwilling to surrender himself to this sort of mood music) could be taken with such a poem as "Worldliness"—

> Worldliness is your enemy.
> Never think otherwise.
> It does not tolerate for long
> love that you love.
> From where springs the pure lament
> played on ancient instruments?
> To what is a sob a response?
> Trumpets lift our spirits up. To where?

The world is entangled with
continued decay and death.
It courts but abhors
the opposite it needs.
Entrapped in its laws
it ravages love,
hacks at truth,
weeping, weeping it must do
what is incumbent upon it to do!

How moving to think
that from time to time
a white horse does come
bringing a beautiful
redeemer in human form.

The conclusion to that poem, in addition to the discomfort to the aesthetic sense that it achieves by reviving one of the deadest clichés of romance, outrages simple common sense. . . . [It] seems a small request to ask to be spared poems containing beautiful redeemers in human forms on white horses. I do not think that what I have said represents a willful and cruel misreading of the poem; I am even more repelled by the "aesthetic" response to human suffering that one finds in other poems in this volume, in "The Release", for example: "the feeling that / deep sorrow resides / in everything I look at / makes me more alive"; "Only in the midst of / pure suffering / will I release my cry!" I am not quoting out of context; the poem makes it clear that he is writing about the suffering of other people: "What moment moves us more / than when we realize / another's sorrow as our own?" I am not objecting to sympathy and compassion; I merely mean that I am appalled that Gregor should suppose that the suffering of other people constitutes the best condition for the composition of poetry; reducing this line of thinking to the absurd is not difficult: one only has to imagine a poet who was unable to compose, whose aesthetic sense slumbered, until he was urged into song by the spectacle at My Lai, and thereupon found himself able to produce things of beauty that were joys forever. It's like the men who ran the concentration camps and then went home to read Rilke (as Auden tells us). I do not truly believe that Gregor goes very far in this direction, and I hope that these remarks do not make anyone who is fond of his poetry ill.

The book as a whole appears to be a record of a kind of voyage of the soul—which coincides with a good deal of actual travel. In the course of his meditations, Gregor seems to be considering the question of where to live, in the mind as well as in the world, and he entertains alternatives which are all escapes of one kind or another: into an old-fashioned romantic *tour d'ivoire;* or into a life of (refined) sensations rather than thoughts, with which Keats was briefly enamored; or into some museum of the heart or intelligence. Many lines suggest the idea of escape, or perhaps of withdrawal: "Abroad again, adrift on foreign shores"; "Intentionally or not, I have courted loneliness"; "That on waking / you depart from / your true home / that the world / is not for you"; "Worldliness is your enemy"; and, in the opening lines of the book, "I must surround myself with / intangibles again." Travel poems are, of course, perfect vehicles for such meditations. Much of the charm of travel is its endless superficiality, the emotional relief of knowing nothing whatever of the lives of the persons one encounters. Gregor, though, does garner some-

thing more useful than mere hedonistic rambling would produce. In the conclusion to the poem "At-Homeness in the Self", he writes—

In view of the recognition
that repeated travel brings—
that experience is a transparent fabric
thin and scattered by a wind—

love alone is valid,
love the only link.

Death renders numb all concepts.
Swallows, the Italians call *rondini,*
continue a perpetual round
when heavy bells are tolled.

In time each drops to earth,
but swallows do not change.

The dance continues.

The self remains throughout.

(pp. 488-90)

H. T. Kirby-Smith, Jr., in Sewanee Review *(reprinted by permission of the editor,* © *1972 by The University of the South), Summer, 1972.*

Arthur Gregor came to this country from Vienna when he was fifteen, and in certain respects his writing bears the mark of his origin. His normal method is to spread out a series of images and allusions, often rooted in European culture, and let the meaning arise from the resulting impression, assisted by commentary. This means that Gregor has no use for conciseness or the kind of meter that would allow him to put every syllable in its place; his verse is loose and soft because he wants it that way. (p. 494)

His associative, impressionistic manner . . . leads him to subjects that are inherently vague, such as fog, shadows, clouds, haze, or dreams, which recur again and again. There are emotionally convincing poems about sterility and artifice, among other things; and it is true, as most of the quotations on the dust-jacket affirm, that Gregor is interested in spiritual matters; but I have trouble finding distinguished individual poems in this collection [*Selected Poems*]. To imagine *The Faerie Queene* without its meter, allegory, or plot would give some notion of Gregor's book as a whole; the interest is pictorial and thematic, not verbal. Nearly every line is aurally commonplace; the rhythms are prosaic, there is not much rationale to the line breaks, and little of interest happens among the words themselves. . . . [The] tone throughout the book is homogeneous, like a long, muted reverie. This kind of writing, to which cliché and even melodrama are endemic, would probably become much sharper if recast as prose; though the short poem makes hardly any formal demands at present, it does tend to encourage self-indulgence. To those who prefer dense texture in poetry, Gregor's work will seem very loose-woven indeed. (p. 495)

Raymond Oliver, in The Southern Review *(copyright, 1973, by Raymond Oliver), Vol. 9, No. 2, Spring, 1973.*

One finishes reading [*The Past Now: New Poems*] with a heavy heart. In Gregor's earlier work the temporal world was always capable of offering illumination. . . . But in the course of this new book the temporal world loses its brightness: expectation and hope "have left me" and are replaced by "a look of loss / as people, cars stream by / and the appointed hour / has long been passed." Gregor is famous for his expression of the tension in man created by the opposing lures of the postlapsarian world and the absolute world of Otherness. Near the close of *The Past Now,* however, that tension gives way to a diminishing interest in the former world: "Hushed sounds on the stair, / the careful closing of a door / do not concern me now." At the end, "light across the lake withdraws."

The theme of loss is equally prominent at the start of the volume but there its treatment is significantly different from its subsequent employment: "Only by feeling close to that / which we can never reach / but lasts are we / enlarged and comforted." For Gregor the essential man is not *homo ludens* or *homo faber* but *homo desiderans,* man the desirer. . . . [Deprivation] is an opportunity for the deepest communion with the self. Similarly, suffering is the way of renewal: "wounds can open up, / the scream erupt like a birth." The paradoxes here—vain pursuit is in truth fulfillment, wounds are transformed into fruitful wombs—echo the familiar paradoxes of religious precepts (give and ye shall receive) and theology (Christ's "defeat" on the cross as redemptive triumph). By the end of the book such conversions of death into life, of absence into presence, seem less probable, less possible. "Yearning guided me, / now it is gone." In Gregor's terms, that means an entire self is gone.

All of this is not to say, however, that *The Past Now,* because of its course, disappoints; on the contrary, it is a gripping, dramatic record of a man living between the two outposts of hope and despair. . . . Gregor's work is the unimpugnable testimony of a pilgrim. It transcends "mere" literature, recalling Ford Madox Ford's dictum that "the last thing literature should be is literary." (But after purgatory, what *paradiso*? Bodilessness, a number of poems suggest. Allen Tate's concept of "the angelic fallacy" seems useful for an exploration of this book.)

These poems can perhaps be read singly but they gain considerably from each other, like chapters of a narrative (thus poem titles have not been cited here). The story the poems cooperate to tell is ultimately that of a man divided between the heroic attempt to complete the circle (i.e., repair the terrible rupture represented by the expulsion from Eden) and the conviction that he is fulfilling his fate most when he is *not* completing the circle but only striving, in passage, to do so. By the end of the story, not only has the heroic attempt failed but that conviction, which could sustain him in hard times, has weakened. A tone of weariness and finality becomes dominant. One trusts that the finality is more apparent than real and that the title of the book is prophetic, that the harmony of the past will somehow manifest itself to the pilgrim in the present moment, accessible and now. May the manifestation be in the form of more poems like these.

Highly recommended. A book of purity, integrity, and distinction. (pp. 365-66)

Philip Dacey, "Outside the Garden," in Prairie Schooner *(© 1976 by University of Nebraska Press; reprinted by permission from* Prairie Schooner*), Winter, 1975-76, pp. 365-66.*

The poetry of Arthur Gregor could scarcely differ more from that of Howard Moss, in temperament, in tone, in the stuff of which it is made. And yet . . . Gregor and Moss have in common certain characteristics which help to account for the stature of their poetry. They are two of the best poets we have, in a period in which the writing of poetry has become an epidemic. The qualities they share are a highly disciplined intelligence, the sense that a poem is not a happy—or unhappy—accident, and a concern with those buried human relationships so sparsely evident on the surface upon which we maneuver our lives. In the welter of guess-what-happened-to-me-last-night verse, their poetry speaks only to someone willing to listen. (p. 346)

"Spiritual" is a word so bedraggled by abuse as to be suspect; but to apply it to Gregor's poetry is to restore its strictest usage.

In *Octavian Shooting Targets,* published more than twenty years ago, history, roots and memory are the book's essence. The tone, since then, has become increasingly clear and rich, but it is still true that no poem is severed from roots which go deep into the human past. The consciousness of the European heritage is still strong, but now the sources of heritage are discovered in a wider and deeper field than can be represented by any limited provenance.

Poetry such as this is a threatened species. Reading Gregor, we become conscious of what its even temporary loss would mean. The book's title [*The Past Now*] is accurate. In Gregor's work, the past is never the past; it is alive in every aspect of the poem. The danger for poetry which has a strong spiritual force at its center is that the poems may become remote from the immediate and tangible. Gregor's most impressive accomplishment is his ability to make the spiritual intensely apprehended by the senses.

In this poetry, the inherent image is that of the pilgrim; his memories, the exhilarating or harrowing aspects of his journey, and the constant presence of his expectation—all are packed into the poem's texture. (pp. 346-47)

Gregor's is such uncautious poetry that the reader, crammed by wary practitioners of "relevance," has a clear sense of the poet's intention of engaging major issues. Where, in one's life, is the godhead? In which moments is one authentically alive, and capable of receiving the extraordinary? Must a vision of peace and concord be abandoned because these things never wholly existed, however briefly? To take on this scale of intention is to work in high altitude without a net. (p. 347)

One of the reasons for the book's lack of soft spots is the direct, stripped dignity of its speech—the opposite of that strenuously obscure style of poetry which attempts to distract from its tiny, jaded core. The lines of *The Past Now,* rarely long, flexible as the tones of a human voice, create with the reader a one-to-one encounter. It is poetry for which we should be very grateful indeed. (p. 348)

Josephine Jacobsen, in The Nation *(copyright 1976 by the Nation Associates, Inc.), October 9, 1976.*

H

HACKER, Marilyn 1942-

An American poet now living in England, Hacker is a recipient of the National Book Award. Her poems, which are highly personal and often surrealistic in nature, have been acclaimed for their deft rhymes and juxtapositions. (See also *CLC,* **Vol. 5.)**

Marilyn Hacker's poems have a breezy, loquacious, bouncy toughness to them, ingratiating in spite of their faults, which very likely accounts in part for the two important prizes, the Lamont and the National Book, given to her first volume only last year. It was called "Presentation Piece," and now already we have this new one, "Separations." A case of striking while the iron is hot? Is the new book made up of poems that were left out of the first one? Or does she really write so much and so fast? I have no idea, and probably it doesn't matter.

Except that the new book does contain, unmistakably, poems she might have been well advised to withhold. Dull poems, too long, and some damnably obscure. It is obscurity of both kinds: the kind that comes from reticence about private affairs (in which case why publish at all?) and the kind that comes from insufficient thought (in which case why not wait till the materials become clearer?). One can't help thinking another year or two between books would have been a good idea.

But the annoying poems are a minority, and one shouldn't, at this point anyway, dwell on them. I think all readers who aren't categorically opposed to traditional forms will find most of her new book a real pleasure. Hacker writes in free forms sometimes, but she especially likes sonnets, she writes a lot of them, tough sonnets, humorous or half-humorous, with very skillful interweaving of true rhymes, off-rhymes, and no rhymes, and she likes sestinas too, and villanelles, and even canzones, the hardest of all foreign forms. I don't see how anyone who knows versification can help but admire and relish her abilities. Notice, for instance, how remarkably well she disguises the padding needed in any rhymed poem to make the lines come out right. With great syntactical diversity and with an immense vocabulary from which to choose her padded words, she makes the unnecessary seem not only necessary but natural, which is half the art of the poetic artificer.

Add to this her thematic adultness and intelligence, her compelling poems of lust, anger and grief, her sense of experience truly lived, and you have a formidable poet to contend with. "Separations" is the work of a woman whose body and mind are functioning at high intensity, perfectly coordinated. You can't draw the line between sensation and idea—a rare achievement. (p. 12)

> *Hayden Carruth, in* The New York Times Book Review *(© 1976 by The New York Times Company; reprinted by permission), August 8, 1976.*

Marilyn Hacker writes too much, doesn't blot many lines (or at least many poems) and adopts at times, perhaps unconsciously, a hopped-up early Lowell manner ("What do you know of me? I am alone. / The turning sockets on the rack of bone / rotate like the cogged hubs of jointed wheels.") and a tough-sexy lyricism which isn't irresistible ("I kissed his eyes, mouth, feet. I kissed his knees, / Ate honey from the flower between his thighs / and felt it rise with sap against my tongue. He was so young . . ."). But more often than not she cares about the figures her poems make, and writes urgently, sometimes delicately, about separation, a state peculiarly interesting for the poet who not only—as woman or as man—is separated from somebody else, but must also write about being separated from somebody else. The poem where this situation is treated most complicatedly and movingly is "Somewhere in a Turret," too long to quote in full but which begins like this:

> Somewhere in a turret in time,
> castied and catacombed in but
> still on a tan street that
> ends with a blue-and-white gingerbread house,
> those rooms are still filled
> with our pictures and books. On the sill
> our black-and-white cat hums after a fly.
> It is getting light. When we come in,
> no one will ask you to leave, no one will send me
>   away. . . .

There are enough good moments in these poems [in *Separations*], enough feel of and for cities, rooms, textures, to convince me that Marilyn Hacker is somebody to be reckoned with who will give us more and better. (pp. 456-57)

> *William H. Pritchard, in* The Hudson Review *(copyright © 1976 by The Hudson*

Review, Inc.; reprinted by permission), Vol. XXIX, No. 3, Autumn, 1976.

Although there are still a few poems which betray her apprenticeship, sounding like exercises or baring influences, Hacker extends her technical mastery and increases her self-confidence measurably in *Separations*. Spinning out sonnets, sestinas, villanelles, canzones, couplets, fixed and free forms, lyrics and narratives in generous portions, she displays an impressive virtuosity and vitality of language.

All of this technical skill is in the service of a dark, somewhat sordid urban vision which is sometimes lightened, but more often further darkened, by love. Raking her forms across the separations of death, distance, and unreturned love, Hacker attempts, as she says, to "maul the pain / to shape":

> . . . Hating words, I fumble words
> into a bridge, a path, a wall.

The book is pervaded by a sense of disappointed aubade, a wakening to a cold and grimy morning after a night of love remembered more for its pain than for its comfort. . . . (p. 292)

Hacker can strike other notes as well, as in *Imaginary Translation, After Catullus,* the marvelous sestina *La Vie de Chateau,* or . . . in *Occasional Verses*. . . . But despite these other tones and voices, the great preponderance of poems are somber and preoccupied with loss, most of them winding their way around eventually to the same conclusion —"Predictably, it's cold." And it is in this preoccupation and narrowness of vision that my troubles with this poetry lie; for while I admire the sureness of technique, I keep asking myself why it must be all that damp and dreary, unrelieved by any of the ordinary compensations of life. These poems have, as Richard Howard has said of another poet's work, "the conviction of sordor without the conviction of grandeur", and so, exhausted by all the mauling and fumbling, dirtied by stained sheets and grimy streets, I come away from the book feeling as if I should take a bath. Hacker, in short, takes her losses too seriously, nursing her grievances and dwelling on them with the single-mindedness of a Malvolio, and Olivia's advice would seem to apply to her as well: "To be generous, guiltless, and of free disposition, is to take those things for birdbolts which you deem cannon bullets." The power of language that Hacker possesses deserves a more balanced vision. (p. 293)

Robert Holland, in Poetry (© *1977 by The Modern Poetry Association; reprinted by permission of the Editor of* Poetry), *February, 1977.*

*   *   *

HARRIS, MacDonald (pseudonym of Donald Heiney) 1921-

An American editor, critic, novelist, and short story writer, Harris attended the U.S. Merchant Marine Academy and spent much of his youth at sea. His stories reflect, in subject and theme, his attachment to the sea, and they are often humorous in the vein of Evelyn Waugh. (See also *Contemporary Authors,* Vols. 1-4, rev. ed.)

[*Trepleff*] is a strange novel, propelling a reader forward pell-mell and totally absorbed, but never providing a solid footing. Experiencing it is an exciting but precarious business, like running along a fictional tightrope. Hence, while *Trepleff*'s separate merits are many, and it is far better than most novels these days—in fact, it is very fine—the book as a whole never reaches the level of the assured, sometimes brilliant writing in its parts.

For one thing, though its central subject is a man who marches steadily from a position of affluent respectability to a state of semi-idiotic nothingness, its tone sways hither and yon from dead seriousness to slapstick comedy, from high lyricism down to existential coolness, with intermittent squiggles of mood as unexpected as they are indescribable, as if Mac Donald Harris was never quite sure what attitude he should have about his own creation. For another, characters don't develop, they leap from this to that, sometimes sans motive or credibility. And always there is the nagging question, what to make of them?

As perhaps might be expected from such a complex balancing act, Trepleff, the hero, ends up in a sort of combined prison-hospital-insane asylum, those final refuges of so many of today's weak but saintly heroes. Yet when he asserts in the last pages that he is not some kind of isolated freak, that there are many destinies like his, the statement echoes the haunting feeling a reader has had all along about the fundamental significance of Trepleff's zany adventures and concerns. . . .

By way of clarification, Trepleff is a character in Chekhov's drama *The Seagull,* and since role-playing is still another major theme in this theme-packed novel, the name works as both a title and an identity for the protagonist. . . .

Trepleff's decline is mated with his roles. As Trepleff he marries, less for love than out of pity, a girl already pregnant by another man. As Sinclair Lewis's Arrowsmith he becomes a $60,000-a-year psychiatrist, the epitome of scientific rationality and square living. As a quasi-Christ he ruins his career by making dutiful love to one of his most pathetic patients. As Trigorin, the heartless novelist in *The Seagull,* he manipulates a rich widow into supporting him, finally driving her to suicide. Basically, however, Trepleff is Trepleff, compassionate and desiring love, doomed by fate and an inner demon to play multiple parts, and as a result to suffer fears, separations, and even crucifixions in each of them.

These are the steps in the action and its principal theme: the inability of men to care, and the pain they cause to themselves and others when they try. Yet any sequence of related episodes and any solid foundation of idea falsifies the nature of this crazy-quilt odyssey. What will stick in the mind are the best of its moments: Trepleff ransacking his own house for loose cash; Trepleff trying unsuccessfully to drown his dog because it insists on fornicating around; shoeless Trepleff being thrown out of a swank Paris hotel; Trepleff in Rome, interrogated by the police about a murder that never happened; Trepleff working out a *modus vivendi* with Nadia, the widow, in one of the queerest love-hate relationships in a long while. . . .

Such episodes as these are handled with a mature style, with wit, energy, intelligence. For such traits a reader should be willing to be a bit out of kilter, to live in a house of fiction where, as Trepleff puts it, the walls are not quite straight. (p. 31)

Robert Maurer, in Saturday Review (©

1969 by Saturday Review, Inc.; reprinted with permission), December 20, 1969.

The fact that [*Trepleff*] is a work set in contemporary American society with a prefiguration from Chekhov's *The Seagull* might invite certain speculations about the parallels between the twilight of late-Imperial Russia and the present condition of the United States. But this is not generally an academic work, of the kind Thomas Mann would write; it belongs rather to the picaresque tradition. (p. 228)

[The] novel begins with what seems to be a classic reenactment of Chekhov's play, with the producer of this amateur dramatization logically playing the role of Trigorin and even having an appropriate affair with the girl cast as Nina. By the time the (unnamed) narrator, playing Trepleff, comes to her, the Nina figure—Syd—has been jilted by the producer just as Trigorin abandons Nina; but Syd is even left bearing a child as a result of the encounter. The notion of imitation takes on a new nuance in *Trepleff* because of the method of acting employed. Egon, who has Trigorin's part and also produces the play, is a great believer in the Stanislavsky school of acting. . . . There are some splendid parodies of method-acting techniques in the first chapter, but the notion is introduced for more serious effects too. The reader is encouraged to feel that the method fails: a certain tension remains between character and role, and this discrepancy the novel develops.

The first intimation of the complications to come emerges with the narrator's feeling that Syd is "badly cast" as Nina. Nina's profound unhappiness contrasts with Syd's easy nature. Already the narrator has expressed misgivings about the acting technique; he is critical of the power the producer has, reducing the actors to mere puppets, and he describes the end effect as "a form of controlled schizophrenia." When it comes to following the set prefiguration, the hero is particularly recalcitrant; the very fact that he marries the girl playing Nina is a sign that the *Seagull* motif has been introduced as much to be departed from as to be followed.

The Trigorin figure leaves the modern Nina to have an affair with the actress playing Masha. And this makes Syd so angry that she rejects any previous sympathy she may have had for her role: "O, that Nina, what a fool she was." What Syd here criticizes is the passivity of Chekhov's characters, showing an impatience with the way some of the Russian figures behave which emerges again and again in Harris's novel. The narrator, too, reacts against his role in the play. He even has a positive prefiguration to contrast with the ineffective role of Trepleff forced upon him. Having read Sinclair Lewis's *Arrowsmith* at a receptive point in his life, the narrator "decided that it was [his] destiny to be a scientist like the hero of Lewis's novel: dedicated, truth-seeking, idealistic, a white-clad figure moving among the sick and alleviating pain with the sure touch of [his] fingers." Hence, when he refuses to become the parody of the Russian superfluous man, his concentration fixes once more on his youthful goal. "Now I saw that the thing was simple, much simpler than I had ever dreamed. I didn't have to be Trepleff, I didn't want to be Trepleff. I wanted to be Arrowsmith: cool, knowing, competent, Olympian, but sympathetic." . . . Looked at in the terms evolved in this study, the first chapter of *Trepleff* shows the same link between serial condensation and psychological development as was seen in Hans Erich Nossack's *Nekyia*. As he

progresses, the central figure moves from one prefiguration (Trepleff) to another (Arrowsmith), But in *Trepleff* this sense of development engendered in the first chapter eventually proves illusory.

Before his marriage breaks up (he is a little too willing to "alleviate pain with the sure touch of [his] fingers") and before the prefigurations are shuffled once more, we have in a sub-plot a further veiled parallel to the course of Chekhov's drama. The narrator one day resolves to destroy his dog Ernest, a decision which in itself mars the general idyll he has constructed for himself. (Ernest has been enjoying a devastating love-life with the high pedigree bitches of the neighborhood, a motif which in fact itself prefigures the hero's path in later parts of *Trepleff*.) . . . Symbolically, it is an event reminiscent of Trepleff's first suicide attempt in *The Seagull*. Or, looked at another way, the attempt at killing the dog is a parody of the killing of the seagull in Chekhov's play. The outcome of either reading of this episode is the feeling that the narrator-hero of *Trepleff* is a rather unlucky, if not downright incompetent individual. (pp. 229-31)

The real starting-point of *Trepleff* is the image of a successful professional man with a happy married life—a stereotype of security from which the narrator gradually escapes. The catalyst comes when the hero slips into an adulterous relationship with one of his more frustrated clients, assuming the role of lover partly to rescue her from a state of permanent, unloved insecurity. . . . The hero's realization that he is becoming something of a Trigorin in the way he manipulates people comes closer to the turn his character is now taking. He is in the process of becoming an anti-hero, a role which reaches its nadir when the ex-psychiatrist, professionally struck from the register and deprived of all his money by his ex-wife and his "victim's" lawyers, ends up playing the part of gigolo to a rich American lady on her yearly visit to the fashion-houses of Europe. Although the novel is generally most explicit in naming prefigurations for the main protagonists, this lady is not related so openly to any Chekhovian character, yet it is clear from the outset that she is the modern equivalent of Mme Arkadina. (pp. 231-32)

By the time he reaches Europe, the hero has stood in a number of different relationships to the *Seagull* prefiguration: he has resembled Trepleff by falling in love with a Nina, but he has differed from this initial prefiguration by actually gaining the girl. Then, the more he refuses to play the part of Trepleff, the closer he comes to resembling Trigorin. With the further refinement that in his eyes the opposite of Trepleff is not always Trigorin (for this is a nineteenth-century antithesis), but Arrowsmith, we find a certain schizophrenic element entering the work. It can be seen, for example, in the narrator's attitude to his "mistress," though she is this in name only: "Part of me hated her and part of me desired her, but the most intelligent part of me, the clear unemotional detached Trigorin part, admired her." From this point onwards, whenever the narrator feels the urge to take stock of his demoralizing position, that of gigolo to his self-centered traveling companion, he turns to his Chekhov: "I was beginning to respect her, in at least part of my mind . . . but what happened to Trigorin? You call this manipulating people, all this carrying packages and running up and down stairs with her coat?" The narrator has difficulty in relating his present predicament to the prefiguration. "It seemed to me I had a slight problem here but not really. Trigorin was still around but he was collecting data. After a while he would figure out what to do with the data. At least that was what I told myself. It was possible that I was kidding myself but I didn't think so." Psychotic overtones begin to emerge, for there is a complicated network of doubts and protective motivations here which the ramifications of the motif do much to highlight.

The more wilfully his "mistress" behaves, the more difficult it becomes for the narrator to reconcile himself with the image of Trigorin which he seems to prefer at this stage in the proceedings. When he finally asserts himself, after taking a great deal of humiliating treatment from Nadia, the narrator very quickly finds himself evicted from the hotel where they had been staying together. (pp. 233-34)

The hero's revenge finally comes when he invidiously reminds Nadia of her age and plays upon her fears of growing old, and hence being no longer fashionable. He does this by taking her to see a gruesome collection of skeletons and bones in a crypt just off the Via Veneto in Rome. ("It reduced Helen of Troy, Romeo and Juliet, Petrarch's sonnets, all poetry and all human aspirations to something for a dog to gnaw on.") The narrator is very proud of the fact that he has found Nadia's Achilles' heel and has been able to wound her grievously there. (p. 234)

At this juncture, the Chekhov prefiguration is given a new twist and applied afresh, to Nadia. With the narrator endeavoring to reestablish himself as something of a Trigorin, Nadia starts to resemble Trepleff. Once more, there are no explicit references to this effect, but her double suicide attempt—the first unsuccessful one, in Rome, leaving her with a bandaged head like Trepleff's—makes the change of prefiguration abundantly clear. That the fragmentation and condensation of prefigurative roles no longer respects sex differences, but has a woman playing the role of Trepleff, might at first sound quite radical. Very few novels have worked with female prefigurations referring to male characters or vice versa. But this reversal is far from out of place in *Trepleff,* for the narrator's place as gigolo at this point in the plot is in itself an effeminate role, and the domineering behavior Nadia displays makes her suited to a man's part. (p. 235)

If the narrator is generally well aware of the appropriate counterparts in *The Seagull* to various characters in his story, the fact that nothing is made of either of Nadia's successive prefigurations—first Mme Arkadina, and then Trepleff —becomes a significant aspect of his attitude towards her. Why he makes no reference to the Trepleff parallel is perhaps easier to answer. He was himself for a long time closely linked with this figure, and he is to return to it at the end of the novel. To admit that his treatment of Nadia has reduced her to playing the role of Trepleff in a melodrama of his own making would be tantamount to another "vicarious suicide," from the hero's point of view. By not mentioning the Trepleff correspondence, at the point where it becomes fragmented to include Nadia, the narrator manages to distance himself substantially from a woman with whom he in fact has dangerously much in common. He probably does not mention the Arkadina prefiguration for equally self-protective reasons. At the time when he begins to make a pass at Nadia, while crossing the Atlantic on the first-class ticket he forfeited all his remaining funds to buy,

the hero likes to think of himself as Trigorin, the manipulator of people. (In other words, he has in mind the Trigorin who is capable of loving and leaving Nina.) On the other hand, Trigorin's relationship with Mme Arkadina is a more complex matter. She is on the whole far more of a manipulator than he is, and for this reason it would not be very flattering for the narrator to think of Nadia as Mme Arkadina and to start pondering what his relationship with her means in the light of the Trigorin-Arkadina analogy.

So far, Nadia and her prefigurations have been considered in terms of what I have called plot-motivation. One can see that there are good psychological reasons why the hero, who is also the narrator of the novel and therefore in a position to suppress things unfavorable to his image of himself, should not want to consider what analogies exist for Nadia. But there are also good aesthetic reasons why the reader should not be constantly presented with a clear-cut analogy in this part of the narrative.

The hero's progress in the novel is from an integrated position in contemporary society to what at first appears to be a traditional outsider's role: that of parasite upon the more nauseating sides of the very society that he appears to reject. Nadia, with her fear of death and her constant preoccupation with preserving her fading beauty and keeping up a cosmopolitan appearance, with her Europe-fixation, her matriarchal posturing and her complex frigidity, becomes almost a parody of aspects of a society that the ex-psychiatrist has left behind. The hero seems to be, as a result, a figure from the picaresque tradition, for the picaro too lives off the society he rejects. There are passages reminiscent of *Felix Krull,* of Gide and Kerouac, to reinforce the stereotype employed. We tend to identify with the narrator even, as much because of his ubiquitous humor as because of the first-person perspective maintained throughout. It therefore comes as something of a shock—and perhaps a further literary parody—to find that *Trepleff,* like so many other novels of recent years, is being narrated from a lunatic asylum. . . . The relevance of this shock revelation to the *Seagull* motif lies in the fact that the Chekhov prefiguration reappears at precisely the same juncture as we realize that the hero is more than the traditional outsider, that he is in fact already suffering from acute schizophrenia. At this point he regresses to the *persona* which had been imposed upon him in the "controlled schizophrenia" of the amateur production of *The Seagull.* He "becomes" Trepleff once more. (pp. 235-37)

[The] modern Trepleff finds himself certified and put away amongst those stock figures who believe themselves to be Napoleon or Joan of Arc. The ultimate variation on the *Seagull* motif in the novel is that the narrator claims to be looked after by a certain Dr. Dorn (the name of the doctor in Chekhov's play). The final part of the novel is given over to the kind of intimate, solipsistic understandings that the mad sometimes share with their attendants:

> Dorn is the only one in whom I have confided my secret and for this reason he is careful not to let anyone overhear when he calls me by name. When he appears in the doorway, a smile already forming under his soft moustache, he glances around behind him before he greets me: "Good morning, Konstantin Gavrilovich." And we both smile, pretending it is a joke, although we

both know it is not a joke but our secret. If anyone overheard us, of course, we could pretend it was a joke and in this way the secret would not be discovered. "What did you do this morning, shoot a seagull?" "No, I shot at one, but missed." "If you kill one you must lay it at my feet." "I have already laid one at your feet. The one I killed because she threw my shoes out of the window."

Primarily the narrator means Nadia, but he might also be talking about himself. For in his insanity he has come to identify fully with what was merely an objective correlative in *The Seagull,* and he lays himself at the feet of Dr. Dorn. The suicide is now no longer vicarious; but it is essentially a mental suicide. The schizophrenia is no longer controlled, as it was in the college dramatic production but inescapably psychotic. The *persona* has become an identity.

The link established in *Trepleff* between imitating a prefiguration and becoming fixated by the role to the point of mental aberration is also a theme in *Doktor Faustus* and *Passages.* Other novels of recent years, such as Zelazny's *The Dream Master* and Spencer's *Asylum,* use the reenactment of myths as a way out of madness: offering a therapeutic reversal of the *idée fixe* through psycho-drama. Whereas Thomas Mann could still see the reenactment of a myth as a noble goal, it has been presented as a negative process in various recent novels. (pp. 238-39)

The extent to which myths have been shown in this chapter to confuse the outline of the plot, rather than put it into focus, also reflects a change in attitude to myths that appears to have taken place since the beginning of the century. . . .

Attitudes to myths, inside or outside literature, . . . have changed in recent times, with a certain anti-myth reaction setting in. Yet this change in attitude has not led to the disappearance of mythological motifs from contemporary fiction. At most, they have been more often used in a pejorative way. Such prefigurations appear to have remained part of a standard method of telling a story and commenting on it at the same time from a different perspective. (p. 240)

> *John J. White, in his* Mythology in the Modern Novel: A Study of Prefigurative Techniques *(copyright © 1971 by Princeton University Press; reprinted by permission of Princeton University Press), Princeton University Press, 1971 (footnotes deleted for this publication).*

[*Bull Fire*] is a Baedekker of symbolic history. . . . [The] images in *Bull Fire* run riot until they cloak the narrative in a gauze as heavy as a classical dictionary. I had begun the novel with great expectations. The language has great power, and I was immediately drawn into the promise and texture of the child's life which opens the book. (p. 406)

All of [the convoluted happenings] would have been perfectly proper in the straight and well-told story which lies somewhere beneath all of [the] mythology, but there are too many portentous overtones as it exists now. . . . Mr. Harris follows the outline of myth, and has produced only a sketch. This is a great pity, since his prose can be both lyrical and effective. He captures moods and landscapes with

great finesse, but they remain only an adjunct to the well-heeled plot. (pp. 406-07)

> *Peter Ackroyd, in* The Spectator *(© 1973 by The Spectator; reprinted by permission of The Spectator), September 29, 1973.*

[In "The Balloonist"] Gustavus Crispin, a Vernian inventor and scientist, together with a positivistic American journalist and a demure young Frenchman who knows Virgil by heart, tries to reach the North Pole [by balloon] in 1897. . . . Crispin is . . . the narrator, and it is his oddball, icily narcissistic way of telling things that lifts "The Balloonist" above the level of old-fashioned adventure yarn to that of ruminative elegance.

Sometimes Crispin seems the commonplace mind at full stretch, coming up with resonant banalities ("The contents of the mind are infinite in their convolutions and at any given instant couldn't be encompassed by a hundred encyclopedias"), but more often, as if transfigured by some daydreaming hubris, he stages slow-motion inspections as his mind freewheels. . . .

Suave work, this, done with mirrors and mellow sardonicism. "The Balloonist" proves that epiphanies of sheer finesse are more sensual than the complacencies of the pissoir, and more worth writing about as well. (p. 38)

> *Paul West, in* The New York Times Book Review *(© 1976 by The New York Times Company; reprinted by permission), November 7, 1976.*

It is into ten days of July 1897 that Macdonald Harris puts [*The Balloonist*] with "Hommage à Jules Verne" on the dedication page. But I had read the book, and with lessening mystification and growing admiration, before I read the blurb on the jacket or noticed the dedication. Of course the period and the balloon brought Verne to mind, but I was surprised to learn from the blurb that this is a "witty" (as well as "richly sensual and ingenious") novel, and that Gustav's love affair with Luisa is "hilarious" (as well as "stormy and tender") and that their earlier balloon trip across the Gulf of Bothnia was "delightfully comic". I wasn't finding, looking for or wanting chuckles. . . .

On the surface it is three explorers in a balloon, hoping to navigate it to the north pole and back from and to Spitzbergen. One of them, the narrator, a Swedish major called Gustavus Crispin, is a "magneto-electrical aerographer". Another, Waldemer, is a journalist and the third—well, that's even less clear so far. . . . Theodor seems to be there because the balloon's ups, sideways and downs demand three live bodies of about that weight overall. Theodor modestly disappears behind hummocks of ice to answer the call of nature, as the author puts it.

Off they go, with some homing pigeons for a link with civilization, and every time Gustav curls up in his reindeer coat to sleep, he dreams: preferably erotic dreams, preferably of Luisa. These dreams lead him into a romantic past and several European countries. Less than half the book is airborne exploration. When, in that exploration, a windless, dumb cold eventually grounds them hundreds of miles from nowhere, dreams outnumber waking actions. One has heard that to die of cold is a marvellously merciful last journey, fed on psychedelic fantasies of warmth and love and salvation (the mother bird's skeleton found sitting on frozen eggs). I took it that the slow freeze-up was the author's deliberate patterning, and thought it highly successful.

Some of the waking action (Waldemer's bear-hunt and near-death on the ice-cliff, Theodor's near-death from the killer whales) is written with vivid imagination, too. But Gustav and Luisa in warm double beds on dry land is a more lasting picture than any of the arctic action, or even the cold comforts of coupled bodies drifting into oblivion. But why did Gustav secretly remove Waldemer's message out of the capsule on the pigeon's leg? And what did he read in it when he had removed it? Or have I been drifting into oblivion myself? If so, I have enjoyed it very much.

> Richard Usborne, "A Cold Going," in The Times Literary Supplement (© Times Newspapers Ltd., 1977; reproduced from The Times Literary Supplement by permission), May 13, 1977, p. 580.

*   *   *

HAWKES, John   1925-

Hawkes is an American novelist, playwright, and short story writer. Jonathan Baumbach calls Hawkes "something of a naturalist in reverse"; in his experimental fiction he outlines and defines life as a surrealistic, often terrifying, dream world. Hawkes has said that his novels attempt to renew the form of that genre. According to critic Albert Guerard, in whose writing class Hawkes wrote his first novel, *The Cannibal*, he is "perhaps the most original American novelist since Faulkner." (See also *CLC*, Vols. 1, 2, 3, 4, 7, and *Contemporary Authors*, Vols. 1-4, rev. ed.)

John Hawkes is perhaps the most consciously traditional of all the modern fabulators. He is also the most experimental, the most *avant-garde*. (p. 59)

In Hawkes we have the picaresque strand, with its traditional cruelty and violence modified by its passage from a proto-realistic form to a surrealistic one. In this line of development Céline is a crucial figure and his *Journey to the End of Night* a crucial book. This work is so important because in it Céline seemed to recognize, more deeply than anyone before him, a natural tendency in picaresque toward a grotesque exaggeration of misfortunes: an intensification of everyday troubles into an ironic vision of a distorted cosmos, where a poetic injustice reigns, which destroys all who do not learn to accommodate themselves to it. (pp. 60-1)

Considering Hawkes as a picaresque writer, we can begin with the obvious fact that his affinities with the picaresque tradition are not mainly formal. He has accepted some of the dark premises of the picaresque attitude, but he has moved very far indeed from the loose and episodic picaresque form, with its simple, chronological string of events in the life of a roguish individual. In addition to Céline and the early picaresque writers, Hawkes admires Nathanael West, Flannery O'Connor, Faulkner, and Nabokov. His admiration for the last two, in particular, suggests the kind of delight in formal and verbal dexterity that is the essence of fabulation. For a modern writer, such care for form almost inevitably involves the rejection of any too easy adoption of the forms of his predecessors. (pp. 66-7)

John Hawkes is closer to the French in [his revolt against realism] than any other modern writer I can think of. He has written more criticism than most first-rate American

writers do, and he has been readier than most to explain his work seriously in interviews and discussions. In doing this sort of thing, Hawkes has created something like a polemical position for himself. Perhaps because he has done it in this piecemeal and roundabout way, his statements seem unusually free of the self-serving public relations gimmicks that one associates with Robbe-Grillet's frequent position papers. At any rate, I have selected for some serious consideration a statement about his work that Hawkes made in [an] interview for *Wisconsin Studies in Contemporary Literature*.... This statement should help us to see how Hawkes situates his work against the background of previous fiction, and where he would wish us to find the "unique" qualities he mentioned in acknowledging Faulkner's influence on his work.

> My novels are not highly plotted, but certainly they're elaborately structured. I began to write fiction on the assumption that the true enemies of the novel were plot, character, setting, and theme, and having once abandoned these familiar ways of thinking about fiction, totality of vision or structure was really all that remained. And structure —verbal and psychological coherence—is still my largest concern as a writer. Related or corresponding event, recurring image and recurring action, these constitute the essential substance or meaningful density of my writing. However, as I suggested before, this kind of structure can't be planned in advance but can only be discovered in the writing process itself. The success of the effort depends on the degree and quality of consciousness that can be brought to bear on fully liberated materials of the unconscious. I'm trying to hold in balance poetic and novelistic methods in order to make the novel a more valid and pleasurable experience.

This statement tells us a good deal, and there are aspects of it which I believe we can accept without reservation as illuminating. There are others about which I feel we should have some reservations. (I am always suspicious, for instance, of suggestions that fiction can get along without plot. Both Robbe-Grillet and Hawkes sometimes claim to have eliminated or suppressed this element in their fiction, but when I read them I find myself responding to an intense, forward-moving pressure, a real narrative flow. And this, I say, is what makes their works stories rather than poems. They may have abandoned certain conventions of plotting, but I do not think they have abandoned plot.) But the statement is certainly as good a way into Hawkes's special world as any other, especially if we understand all its implications. What I propose to do is examine three parts of the statement in some detail, working out some of their implications, in hopes that they will serve to illuminate our later and more specific consideration of Hawkes's practice as a fabulator. One is the question of plot *vs.* structure. A second is the notion that structure is developed by a process in which consciousness works on materials liberated from the unconscious. A third is the notion that this structure (which can be seen as a balance between poetic and novelistic methods) should lead the reader to a valid and pleasurable experience.

Each of these three parts of the statement points toward a different object. Structure directs our attention to the internal coherence of the works themselves, and beyond that to the art with which they have been put together. The relationship between consciousness and unconsciousness emphasizes both the connection of the works to the psychological processes of the author—along with his understanding of them—and by extension to all mental processes; Hawkes means to use conscious thought and art to illuminate the unconscious, to show us things about ourselves which may be locked in our own unconscious minds, avoiding the scrutiny of our consciousness. Finally, the notions of pleasure and validity point directly to our experience as readers—in two different ways. Hawkes feels that him aim is to produce a "more" valid experience. More valid than what? More valid, I should think, than that of the "conventional" novel, and perhaps more valid than our experience of day-to-day living as well. (pp. 68-70)

He is suggesting that the validity he is aiming for—and the pleasure he hopes to give—are functions of his attempt (a) to balance poetic and novelistic methods, and (b) to apply conscious consideration to materials from the unconscious. Thus "validity," in this context, becomes both a matter of art and of life, of form and of content. It involves discovery and creation simultaneously. (p. 71)

A notion something like the old surrealistic method of "automatic writing" seems to lie behind Hawkes's formulation. . . . Except that André Breton and the surrealists would have been horrified at the thought of allowing consciousness to work on these precious materials. Hawkes, on the other hand, insists that a valid structure in fiction depends on the combination of conscious thought with materials from beyond consciousness—just as a successful psychoanalysis depends on the analyst's skill in first helping the patient expose and liberate the sources of his anxieties or neuroses, and then (almost simultaneously) in making a valid interpretation of the symbols through which these materials are manifested. Hawkes has modeled his manner of proceeding as a fabulator, apparently, on the techniques of psychoanalysis. Thus his works are most likely to find their justification in terms of psychic value. (p. 72)

At this point we have considered . . . two of the three aspects of Hawkes's statement. We have yet to consider the distinction between plot and structure. This is a very slippery area in narrative theory, and it will probably be well to set out a few guide-lines before plunging into it. There is a sense, of course, in which we immediately understand the point Hawkes is making about his fiction. He has certainly turned away from orthodox plotting. And he has turned in the opposite direction from a writer like John Barth, who has chosen to emphasize plot more than the realistic novelists did, rather than to reduce its role in his fabulations. But there is a kind of counter-movement in both these turns. By his exaggeration of "plottiness" in a work like *The Sot-Weed Factor,* Barth finally causes us to take his plot more lightly than we might take a less rococo arrangement of events. (p. 73)

Similarly, by reducing the overt plottiness of his fiction, Hawkes generates an intense reaction to such elements of plot as remain there. If Barth gives us the sense of being on a great roller-coaster ride, in which we move up and down —but always safely on a track, Hawkes seems to place us in an emotional quick-sand where we struggle painfully for every inch, and finish with a sense of great achievement when we lie gasping on firm ground a few steps from where we began. Thus by driving his plot underground Hawkes has made it less visible but no less important. His work *is* poetical, in his sense, of course. That is, it is a tissue of recurring and corresponding images and verbal patterns which are emotionally and intellectually meaningful. But his fabulations are not poems; they always depend on some sort of narrative impetus to keep the reader moving. The recurring beads are held together by a string of plot. The buried string of events attracts our attention and draws us toward it, so that we prize it all the more when we have discovered it and experienced it. The dislocations of time and space in Hawkes's work serve the same purpose that they do in Conrad, Ford, and Faulkner. They involve the reader in the constructive process, making him help to create the story. (pp. 73-4)

I have chosen *The Lime Twig* for fairly extended treatment because it seems to me representative of the controlled wit and power which animates Hawkes's mature work. But before turning to it, I wish to pause a moment over an early and somewhat neglected piece: his first long fiction, *Charivari.*

Charivari is militantly *avant-garde,* not in the philosophical sense employed by Hawkes in speaking of a perpetual avant-gardism, but in the more trivial sense of formally shocking. . . . Perhaps we have in this work an excess of conscious effort working on an insufficiency of materials liberated from the unconscious. It is, then, not a great performance, but it has a special importance for us because it reveals so much about the roots of Hawkes's fiction. It also has the special charm that often accompanies youthful precociousness. (pp. 74-5)

The book's aggressiveness begins with its title: a word to be looked up. Unlike Hawkes's other titles which are words to be understood in context, this word provides a context for understanding the book.

> Charivari. . . . A serenade of "rough music," with kettles, pans, tea-trays, and the like, used in France, in mockery and derision of incongruous or unpopular marriages. . . .
>
>   The OED.

This particular *Charivari* is a surrealistic examination of the marriage of two "typical" well-to-do modern people. The married couple are a pair of forty-year-old children, faced with the fact that the "bride," after fourteen years of marriage, has become pregnant. The ground plan of the narrative covers two days in the lives of the married couple— two days mainly devoted to a houseparty of West/ Fitzgerald and Waugh/Huxley tone and dimensions. In the course of these two days both husband and wife make forays away from their home, where the party is in progress. The husband rides a bus into town, considers picking up a woman who resembles his wife, and is finally brought back home like a runaway child in his father's limousine. The woman drowns in a wild storm. The wife too makes a childlike limousine voyage—accompanied by her mother—to have her pregnancy verified (with overtones of abortion) by a doctor who finds it hysterical (or aborts it) much to everyone's relief. (pp. 75-6)

The two excursions from the party are used by Hawkes as ways of illuminating the suppressed fears and desires of Emily and Henry. These two, racked by a fear of growing up, of living as adults and hence of dying, represent aspects of the modern cult of youth. And the entire work, borrowing its hallucinatory technique from surrealism and such originals as the Circe episode of Joyce's *Ulysses*—where hallucination is employed mainly to act out sexual fantasy —can be seen as a bitter satirical fantasy of the Nathanael West variety. It also has a good deal in common with the early Albee play *The American Dream*. Both Hawkes and Albee, in these early works, seem to have found surrealism a handy vehicle for attacking contemporary mores. Later on, one suspects, they became dissatisfied with using such a powerful weapon on such easy targets. Both the Albee play and *Charivari* are full of delightful exuberance and joy in the mastery of technique—the joy of the fabulator realizing his skills. But their display of skill invites us to question their employment of it. . . . *Charivari* is in itself quite good indeed—more interesting than Albee's *American Dream* I should say—and in it we can find some clear examples of the attitudes and techniques which, in more refined form, shape the later works. One of the most important attitudes, one, in fact, which seems to be a governing attitude throughout all of Hawkes's work, is the attitude toward cruelty in fiction which the narrator of *Charivari* formulates with a bold directness and simplicity that we shall not find elsewhere in his fiction:

> And have you heard, or do you think we are likely to hear what very private shames and resentments and misgivings these people are harboring? May we be cruel enough?

Something like this purpose seems to animate all of Hawkes's fabulation. The cruelty and brutality of the work are there in order to expose private shames and resentments. But this statement in *Charivari* is a bit too complacent about locating the shames and resentments in the characters only—"these people." A sense is established of reader and narrator conniving to expose "them." In the later works the exposure involves *us* as well as *them*. Here the reader's psyche is insulated from emotional complicity by a curtain of satiric detachment which Hawkes drops between reader and characters. . . . *Charivari* . . . is less picaresque in spirit than Hawkes's later work. It is a satire of manners, really. And Hawkes's growth as a writer has involved developing beyond satire. His cruel and clever wit finds its true scope in works like *The Lime Twig* and *Second Skin,* where it functions more circumspectly and humanely. (pp. 76-8)

The source of his narrative power, it seems to me, is located at the point where his cruel wit and delicate sensibility converge to generate the special tonal qualities which mark his best work. I think we have some of his best work in *The Lime Twig.* . . .

To trace the interconnections between cruelty and tenderness in *The Lime Twig,* I must try to concentrate closely on the texture of particular passages, but in the context of the work's total structure. To do this I am going to consider a fairly large block of narrative, Chapters 6 and 7. . . . (p. 79)

The central event of . . . chapter [6] is the beating of innocent Margaret Banks by the brutal mobster Thick. Margar-

et's attempt to escape has given this sadist an excuse to go to work on her with his rubber truncheon. . . . We know why Thick does this; the question is why does Hawkes feel obliged to devote a chapter to it, why does he present it so elaborately, why, in fact, does he present it at all? Is this a perverse indulgence, a wallowing in brutality for its own sake?

These questions should be considered from two aspects. One has to do with the function of this chapter in the narrative as a whole: the degree to which it can be accounted for in terms of specific contributions to the larger scheme. The other has to do with the way brutality and cruelty are presented here; in comparison with other works which present us with the cruel and brutal, to what extent does this work seem wantonly sadistic? The second question, if answered satisfactorily, should help us to answer the first. The more clearly we see what is going on when Thick beats Margaret, the better we will be able to understand the relationship of this scene to the rest of the book.

First of all, we need to remind ourselves that there are beatings and beatings—many ways of actually hurting people and many ways of describing or representing any such occurrence in literature. . . . [Joyce's] main effort [in presenting beatings in *A Portrait of the Artist as a Young Man*] is to render the physical pain undergone by Stephen and the associated emotional pain: the "hot burning stinging tingling blow," the "fierce maddening stinging tingling pain," followed by "a palsy of fright" and the "scalding cry" and "scalding tears" which well up in Stephen to his "shame" and "rage." Joyce's rendering of physical pain here should help us see how little Hawkes is concerned to render it: in fact, how carefully he avoids it. It is not Margaret's pain but her situation as helpless victim which Hawkes is rendering. Joyce's simile of Stephen's hand crumpling like "a leaf in the fire" is just one detail in a whole sequence of high-temperature imagery Joyce uses as the most potent means of evoking pain. (Hell is fiery for the same reason.) Hawkes, however, emphasizes the coldness of the weapon and its ugly sexuality ("hard and solid as a length of cold fat stripped from a pig") and in his most elaborate image compares the sound of the blows to "a dead bird falling to empty field." This image is telling us more about Margaret's situation as lonely victim than about the sound it is ostensibly aimed at rendering. Sympathetic fear, not empathetic pain, is the emotional effect actually sought by the prose in this passage. (pp. 82-4)

Hawkes has worked in a number of ways to frustrate any attempt we make to descend into mere sentimentality here. He is, as in all his best work, trying to construct what Rilke called a "bridge barely curved that connects the terrible with the tender." And even in this scene, the bridge of his sympathetic perception is braced and stiffened by his cold and grotesque wit. Margaret's relief . . . at the thought that Thick has his truncheon and will not be reduced to his favorite substitute is—even under the circumstances—comic: "she thought that a wet newspaper would be unbearable." The pitiful inadequacy of this response to her situation, which is unbearable in any case, is pathetic. But Margaret's maintenance of her own prim perspective under these terrible circumstances, the incongruous rigidity of her mental processes, qualifies the pathos of her situation. Her perception of Thick as a sort of naughty child also has in it a bizarre mixture of appropriateness and incongruity. His truncheon makes "her think of a bean bag, an amusement for a child," which is partly just an inadequate response to the threat in the instrument, derived from Margaret's innocence, and partly a very shrewd perception of Thick's childishness. This sort of complication, which prevents any easy sentimental response to these brutal events, is also in evidence in the complicity of understanding (as between mother and naughty child) between her and Thick. The paragraph just preceding the actual beating is an extraordinary one:

> Then something happened to his face. To the mouth, really. The sour sweat was there and the mouth went white, so rigid and distended that for a moment he couldn't speak: yet all at once she knew, knew well enough the kinds of things he was saying—to himself, to her—and in the darkness and hearing the faint symphonic program, she was suddenly surprised that he could say such things.

Innocent Margaret is surprised that Thick can think the things she attributes to him. He does not speak aloud, but she understands whatever sadistic ravings are implied by that white, rigid, distended mouth. And so do we. She is surprised that Thick "could say such things." We are surprised that Margaret can find words for thoughts that so surprise her. But we know what she means he means. By her understanding she becomes a kind of accomplice to this crime of sadism. And by ours we share that guilt.

A further dimension, also partly comic, is added to these events by the matter-of-factness Margaret maintains throughout. A touch of pride enters into the way she conceives of her experience. She is "like a convent girl accepting the mysteries . . . and no matter how much she accepted she knew it now: something they couldn't show in films." To conceive the inconceivable elements of her experience she tries to frame it in religious or cinematic terms. It is like an initiation into inconceivable "mysteries," and it is too outlandish to be put on the screen. These terms, again both pitifully inadequate and curiously appropriate, make Margaret's situation both poignantly accessible to us and ironically distanced from our own situations. Thus Hawkes, by intertwining comic and pathetic elements, has generated a situation so fraught with tones and attitudes that no simple emotional reaction is adequate to it. (pp. 86-8)

Margaret's destruction, of course, is "undeserved." In the picaresque world this is the way things happen; rewards and punishments are incongruous and inappropriate. But this is not a purely picaresque world. Things happen in a curiously dislocated way, but there is also a kind of logic at work, a kind of plotting behind the apparently random sequence of events which makes the events more meaningful than they could be in a merely episodic structure. In the chapter we have been considering, Margaret suffers because of Michael's involvement with the people who make her suffer. Not only does she become hostage and victim so that the gang will have maximum control over Michael, but, specifically, some of what she suffers has been directly and immediately caused by Michael's actions of the same night —actions which are presented to us *after* we see their results so that we apprehend them colored by their consequences. We are forced to see them ethically.

In Chapter 7, Hawkes chronicles Michael's activities of the same night we have been considering in Chapter 6, and in his presentation he takes care to give us a number of ways to synchronize the two chapters and understand their interrelationship. (p. 88)

[The] rape of Margaret is the final violence of the sixth chapter. And among our other reactions it leaves us wondering whether there might have been any particular reason for Larry's cruelty here; we wonder why he "meant" to cut Margaret. The next chapter provides our answer, but not at first. It begins earlier, at "2 A.M. of the last night he spent alive," with Michael cavorting in bed with Larry's girl Sybilline. Her task has been to keep Michael docile and amused until the race is over, but she has apparently exceeded the call of duty, having "given a single promise and three times already made it good." And this is only the beginning of a night of surrealistic sexual activity for Michael. Before the evening is over he also contents the widowed landlady; Annie, the girl next door; and finally even Dora. (p. 89)

[After] Michael retires to engage in his final sexual activity of the evening—this time with Dora—Larry, with his torso bare except for the bullet-proof vest, visits Margaret. By giving us the timing of the two chapters so precisely—one beginning at four, the other at two—Hawkes helps us to make the necessary synchronization. But he also uses another device, which reaches out beyond synchronization for the book's larger implications. In each chapter we have a bird on a branch. In Chapter 6 Margaret hears it just before Larry enters. . . . In Chapter 7 Michael hears its mate. . . . (p. 90)

The birds serve to link the two chapters and the two characters. This evening with its bizarre and strenuous activities has seen them both receive initiation "into the mysteries." In their separate beds they have explored the world of violence and sensuality. Margaret's excess of pain and suffering has been ironically balanced by Michael's excess of "pleasure." But they are both doomed. It is the last night for both. They are like birds lured to a lime twig and stuck fast for destruction. The two chapters end almost simultaneously. Little Monica discreetly runs out of Margaret's room as Larry begins his assault, only to be shot by the absurd constable. Michael, pricked by one of the pearls Sybilline lost in his bed, fingers it idly and drops it ("lost the pearl for good") just as the constable's shot explodes in his ears.

Michael has become like one of those characters in folk literature (often doomed), who have their wishes granted. Annie's appearance at the orgy is simply the result of Michael's having lusted after her—the girl next door—at one time or another. The whole involvement of Michael and Margaret with Larry and the gang is the result of another wish fulfilled—a dream: "his own worst dream, and best, was of a horse which was itself the flesh of all violent dreams." Hencher is the fairy godmother who grants Michael his wish. The destruction that ensues has been lurking in Michael's dream all along. "If wishes were horses, beggars would ride," our folk wisdom tells us. And when Michael's wish takes on the form of horseflesh, Michael rides out to his destruction. He "rides" sexually throughout that long pre-race orgy. And he races out across the track on the day of the Golden Bowl to throw himself in the path of the destructive energy he has unleashed, to bring to a halt the terrible motion of his dream fulfilled. This act of self-destruction redeems Michael, returns him from the brutal dream world of Larry and Syb to the ordinary world of humanity. (pp. 91-2)

In *The Lime Twig* Hawkes has gone well beyond the easy satire of *Charivari* to a richer, more complex mode of narrative. By pruning somewhat his surrealistic exuberance, and coming to terms (even if somewhat ironic and parodic ones) with fiction's need for plot, he has achieved a controlled intensity of effect which bridges beautifully the gap between terror and tenderness. This effect is based partly on the balance he maintains between the delicately serious and the grotesquely comic, and partly on the way he has ordered the flow of information about the events of the story as they enter our consciousness. He demands a resolutely alert reader, willing to pay close attention to detail and piece out from dislocated hints the real fabric of events: what has happened, what is happening, and what is going to happen.

In the two chapters which I have been discussing, the order in which the fictional events enter our consciousness has much to do with our attitude toward them and toward the whole narrative. (pp. 92-3)

In *The Lime Twig* the very language in which events are described conspires to suggest connections and correlations with other events. Thick's truncheon, sounding like "a dead bird falling to empty field," is subtly and ironically connected to Michael's flinging aside the widow's whalebone stay "as he might a branch in a tangled wood." Birds and branches are woven all through *The Lime Twig,* making a tapestry of images which elaborates on the motif of the title. Michael is ominously greeted by a "tiny black bird" . . . as he stands near his and Margaret's bed at the beginning of the day in which he becomes involved in "this crime." Lying in bed and plotting, Hencher hears "a little bird trying to sing on the ledge where the Kidneys used to freeze." . . . This interweaving of images around the title motif . . . must be the sort of thing Hawkes had in mind when he spoke of introducing a poetic structure into his work in place of the traditional plot. But this structure in *The Lime Twig* is subordinated to the more peculiarly narrative structure of multiple suspense which gives the story its driving force.

One of the things I am trying to suggest here is that this kind of book, which seems so foggy and dreamlike, is actually as neatly and tightly put together as the electrical circuitry of the human nervous system. In his perceptive introduction to the book, Leslie Fiedler makes one emphasis which I should like to reverse. He suggests that Hawkes "does not abandon all form in his quest for the illusion of formlessness." I should like to go much further, to say that not only are there what Fiedler calls "occasions for wit and grace" in the book, but that it has been plotted with a grace and constructed with a wit that makes the whole story not a "random conjunction" but a true fabulation—a more satisfying piece of work than any casual construct, no matter how full of occasional graces, might be. The revulsion inherent in facing the shadow of terror is turned into a pleasurable experience for Hawkes's readers precisely by means of his care for form. It is the form—and the sense it gives us of connections and correspondences, along with the feeling of controlled movement from tension to stability—which makes such terrible materials not merely bearable

but beautiful. This is what makes Hawkes a fabulator like the one described in the fable: capable of rejoicing us when we are heavy. The joy that goes into the fabulation is returned to us in the reading. And it is for this joy that we must be grateful, even to the darkest of fabulators. (pp. 93-4)

> *Robert Scholes, "Fabulation and Picaresque," in his* The Fabulators *(copyright © 1963, 1966, 1967 by Robert Scholes; reprinted by permission of Oxford University Press, Inc.), Oxford University Press, 1967, pp. 59-94.*

Animated by a spirit close to that of the medieval demon, [the archetypal Harlequin] continually breaks the laws of society and nature—but not out of rebellion and not toward the end of gleeful destruction. Sharing the innocence and underlying shrewdness of Socrates and Folly, he does not reaffirm a primal order. Apparently simple-minded and naïve like the buffoon, he is acutely aware of his situation and of himself. Harlequin thrives in chaos but to build rather than to destroy. His creations are silly, precarious, evanescent; but they bring positive pleasure and are a source of positive values. The world Harlequin inhabits is as irrational and menacing as the one left us by the medieval demon or the *sottie* fool. Harlequin has no illusions about this world but nevertheless affirms the greatness of the human spirit that can, in the words of William Faulkner, "not merely endure . . . [but] prevail."

Harlequin is fully aware of his situation, his nature, and the potentialities of his role. . . . John Hawkes's *Second Skin* [is] well suited to explore the modern manifestation of Harlequin, his situation, nature, and role; for . . . Hawkes's focus on psychological reality [is an ideal complement]. (pp. 102-03)

Second Skin is the "naked history" of a fat, bald, fifty-nine-year-old ex-skipper of a small naval vessel, who undergoes a series of physical indignities and psychic outrages. They begin with the suicide of the Skipper's father, an undertaker, who shoots himself in a lavatory while, outside the locked door, his young son tries to distract him by playing Brahms on a cello. The father's suicide is a signal, an omen. And it is with a mixture of guilt, foreboding, and latent incestuous love that the Skipper accompanies his daughter, Cassandra, on her honeymoon trip in an old Packard loaded with black-market tires; holds tight to her hand on a dark desert as three soldiers strip, bury their gear, and then, naked except for their steel helmets, take turns kissing her; chaperones her at a high-school dance on their cold Atlantic island where he is tricked into the belly-bumping contest as she goes off with Red, Bub, and Jomo; and escorts her aboard the *Peter Poor* where he is forced below while Red makes love to her on the deck and the boat heads for the rocks. Wraithlike and passive Cassandra is drawn from him until finally there is the drag race on the moonlit beach as the Skipper tries to save her from Jomo. No lights, no muffler, no windshield, accompanied by Miranda with her skirt billowing and her long black hair stinging his eyes, the fat, bald Skipper drives desperately, skillfully, up and down the rock-strewn beach, forces his antagonist into the sea, and leaps to his daughter's rescue—only to find that it is a decoy, that it is Bub wearing Jomo's baseball cap. And so there is one more race. Near exhaustion, the Skipper plunges through the deep sand to the lighthouse, climbs the steel stairs, and reaches the top to find a neat pile of his daughter's clothing. The chase is over. Cassandra is down below on the sharp rocks.

Described with detachment, terror, parody, and slapstick, each outrage contains abortive love and frustrated heroism. The central outrage in the novel takes place during the war, aboard the U.S.S. *Starfish,* when a youth named Tremlow inspires the crew to mutiny by dancing in a grass skirt and violates the Skipper over a water keg. Throughout the novel Tremlow's name is continually recalled, as are the main images of the mutiny; for instance, the steel ladder the Skipper climbs to the pilothouse becomes the ladder he is carried down on the *Peter Poor* and the steel stairs of the lighthouse. The emphasis on the mutiny suggests that the senseless experience of the war was responsible for the violence, the perversion, the frustration, and the absurdity of the Skipper's world. It is the war that the father signals with his suicide shot, and that is symbolized by the black-market tires on Cassandra's honeymoon and the soldiers on the desert. It is the war's absurdity that is dramatized when the Skipper finds his son-in-law killed during a homosexual affair, on the day the fighting ends. It is the war's echo that we hear as Miranda listens to the "Horst Wessel," snips off the baby's rubber nipples with kitchen shears, and conspires in Cassandra's destruction. The war is not even forgotten in the lyric pastoral scenes on the last tropic island, where the Skipper—still wearing his old naval cap and sneakers—has become an artificial inseminator and lover of the dark-skinned Catalina Kate.

Not only is war seen as the condition of life, but death is at the center of the [world] of . . . *Second Skin.* (pp. 104-05)

The Skipper is haunted by the suicide or the potential suicide of each member of his family. The plot of the novel, although fractured in its presentation, moves from the death of Skipper's father to the mutiny on the *Starfish* to the death of Cassandra on the cold Atlantic island to a final celebration of birth in a tropic cemetery. "We melted wax and stuck candles everywhere we could on the dark stone, I jammed lighted candles among the weeds in the center of that listing shape. The little flames were popping up all over the grave and suddenly the unknown soul was lighting up Sonny's smile and mine and Kate's, was glowing in Kate's eyes and in the soft sweat on her brow."

There is a "heart of darkness," then, in the [world] of . . . *Second Skin;* but . . . the Skipper [isn't] allowed to face it in the manner of Kurtz or Marlow. For the [world] of . . . Hawkes [is] not like Conrad's. . . . [Unlike] the earlier heroes, . . . [the] Skipper [accepts his role] as clown and [his] own foolishness with complete awareness. [He is] aware that war is the condition of life, that there is a heart of darkness which is all the more terrifying because it precludes the heroic posture. Moreover, [he is] aware of [his] own [nature] and of [his] potential in the [role] of clown. For this reason we can place [him] in the tradition of Harlequin.

The nature of the clown is best described by Enid Welsford, who concludes her study [*The Fool: His Social and Literary History*] by illuminating the twofold human contradiction that he epitomizes.

> In the first place we are creatures of the earth, propagating our species like other animals, in need of food, clothing and shelter and of the money that procures them. Yet if we need money, are we so wholly creatures of the earth? If we need to cover our nakedness by material clothes or spiritual ideals, are we so like the other animals? This incongruity is exploited by the Fool.
>
> (pp. 106-07)

The clown's function is also described by Miss Welsford, when she points out that in contrast to the tragic hero his role is not central; "he usually stands apart from the main action of the play, having a tendency not to focus but to dissolve events." (p. 108)

John Hawkes . . . works with a vulnerability that is psychological. Skipper follows more in the tradition of Oedipus than that of Lear, of Tristram Shandy than that of Gargantua and Pantagruel. Throughout the novel he is driven to save each member of his family and the image of himself as son and father, even at the cost of outrage and indignity. But he fails to save his father, mother, and wife; and his paternal overprotectiveness helps drive Cassandra to her suicide. What Hawkes suggests with his clear psychological and literary allusions is that Skipper is driven as well by a natural desire for his father's death and for a relationship with Cassandra that could only be achieved by the destruction of her as a daughter. Further, the outrage and indignity expose and lacerate his vulnerable psyche, but they also bring him the same natural and ambivalent satisfaction achieved by Dostoyevsky's Underground Man. They assuage his feelings of guilt, they bring him a substitute pleasure, they provide for his only possible expression of free will.

Soft and sensitive, Skipper is immeasurably vulnerable in a world whose past and present is irrational and violent. [Following] in the tradition of Harlequin, he is able to live in such a world by accepting his role as clown. . . . He is capable of love, whether the dark love for his daughter and the mutineer Tremlow, or the natural love for his granddaughter, his Negro messboy, and his island mistress; and he is capable of courage. But he recounts his "naked history" with sufficient detachment to see himself as a "large and innocent Iphigenia betrayed on the beach" (by a father starting off a senseless war) and spared to love and fight and live in his hapless way. His power is unobtrusive; his mode of attack is an apparent helplessness or escape. Skipper wills, with at least one part of his psyche, the destruction of his father, his tie to the past, and of his daughter, his tie to the present. The destruction is accomplished by what is at the same time heroic gesture, clownish impotence, willful helplessness. The escape is an ever-present fantasy, a warm tropic island where he can establish a society and a family that is psychologically ideal, where all the polymorphous forms of love are given free reign, where violence is transmuted into play, grotesqueness into lyricism.

While the traditional clown stands apart from the action to dissolve it, . . . Skipper, like so many clowns in modern literature, [stands] at the center, and in two ways, as [hero] and as [narrator]. Still, [he retains] the power to dissolve events. When the clown stood apart from the main action, there was a balance between his world and the world from which he stood apart—between appearance and reality, the ideal and the actual. The structure of the comic play can be developed with fantastic intricacies and convolutions just because of its essential equilibrium. But with the clown at the center of the action the equilibrium and balance are destroyed. Appearance and reality, the ideal and the actual blend and mix. (pp. 112-14)

Hawkes's clown . . . dissolves reality. An *eiron* with no *miles gloriosus* to expose, he strips *us* of our preconceptions and forces us to question our attitudes toward all of the characters, the world they inhabit, and finally the world we inhabit. And he accomplishes this through the style and structure of the story he narrates. A distinctive feature of all Hawkes's novels is the extraordinary landscape, which despite its dreamlike quality conveys a sharp impression of surfaces and local detail, and despite its strangeness is distinctly the world we know. His earlier works, which take place in [varied] settings . . . , achieve their power through a surrealist shifting. *Second Skin* achieves its power, and its far greater range of style, experience, and emotion through comic dissolution, through its central focus on the clownish hero/narrator.

The novel's kaleidoscopic structure is composed of three major patterns. The first pattern contains what we can call the present time. Here the Skipper attempts to save Cassandra in settings variously calculated to explore and reveal his psychic states. . . . The second pattern contains the recollected past, running from the father's suicide in the bathroom to the mutiny aboard the U.S.S. *Starfish*. And the third pattern contains the imaginary future upon a "wandering island . . . unlocated in space and quite out of time." Here the Skipper makes love to the warm and dark-skinned Catalina Kate, and here he reigns as Artificial Inseminator of the Cows. . . .

The three patterns serve to reveal the sensitive and fertile mind of the hero. And the hero/narrator, the clown at the center of the novel's action, continually dissolves his narrative in such a way as to keep us aware of their interrelationship—of the fact that interrelationship is what the story is about. (pp. 114-16)

Skipper surfaces the contradictions of modern man's psychological reality. . . . Hawkes reveals him as destroyer and creator. . . . Hawkes takes us deep inside the psyche of a bald, fat, bumbling ex-skipper to transvalue the values of love and courage. . . . [The] transvaluation [is not] based on an underlying primal order, as it was with Flannery O'Connor. Rather it is based on a hard, clear view of a world that offers no ultimate stability, meaning, or source for these values, except what can come from man's existential will and choice. This situation is explored to its limits . . . where the hero does not merely accept but actively chooses the role of clown. . . . (p. 116)

> *Richard Pearce, in his* Stages of the Clown: Perspectives on Modern Fiction from Dostoyevsky to Beckett *(copyright © 1970, Southern Illinois University Press; reprinted by permission of Southern Illinois University Press), Southern Illinois University Press, 1970.*

[The] writing of John Hawkes produces in us a . . . violent reaction: attraction and repulsion, the irreconcilable opposites. Of one's uncontrollable responses to Hawkes' work, Earl Rovit writes [in *Modern Fiction Studies*, Summer 1964]: "The reader is deeply violated and aware at the same time that it is only through an unwilled but willing want of himself that the violation takes place." . . .

Hawkes' dreamlike world . . . paralyzes us with fear, at the center of which is the perception of our own complicity in evil. The ravishment of the reader is like that of the viewer of malignant pornography. The world Hawkes shows to us is impossible; we reject it and live in it. His characters are abhorrent to us; they are ourselves. . . .

John Hawkes is generally classified as a modern Gothic writer. Inasmuch as gothicism played a large role in the development of the Decadent movement, it became inextricably linked with decadence. Because of the interrelationship of gothicism and decadence we see both in Hawkes. . . . With Hawkes it can be no accident that elements of pornography are contained in work that relies on gothicism and decadence for actions, characters, and atmosphere. (p. 151)

In *Pornography and the Law,* . . . a book written by two psychologists, eleven "major criteria" for obscene books are listed. Of the eleven, eight are applicable to the work of Hawkes. . . . If we were to accept these statements as a methodology for determining what constitutes obscenity or pornography, we would find the fictive and dramatic world of Hawkes a pornographic one. But although Hawkes does meet those criteria and frequently another requirement that a book is aphrodisiacal which keeps "before the reader's mind a succession of erotic scenes," . . . he does not attain what are considered all the structural requirements of pornography. For example, the "true" pornographer, if he uses background scenery, treats it erotically. Hawkes' scenic descriptions, though sometimes highly suggestive or filled with sexual symbolism, are often also non-erotic.

The plot of a Hawkes play or novel may be simple or complex but almost always sexuality in multiple forms is focal. . . . Rovit observes that "things are happening or failing to happen, but action takes place in a fragmentized void virtually unconnected to psychological motivation or controlling idea." . . . The close relationship between such technique and pornography is difficult to overlook.

If motivation for behavior is also lacking, there is yet one more instance of the similarity to pornography where character depiction is extremely limited. Once again Hawkes' work falls on both sides of the line. Although *Second Skin* and *Blood Oranges* have at least one character, the narrator, who is shown in depth, this is not true of *The Lime Twig,* in which all the characters possess a flatness, a stereotypical quality that is characteristic of the pornographic film or novel.

The narrator and major character of *Blood Oranges* calls himself a "sex singer"; his very existence depends on the sexual act, which is intended to obliterate time, to negate dissolution and death. (pp. 152-53)

The linkage of sex and death is as old as primitive literature. Hawkes uses this liaison far more savagely in *Second Skin* and *The Lime Twig* [than in *Blood Oranges*].

From first page to last in *Second Skin,* sex and death are central. The narrator of this novel is a man who has lived his life with suicides, his father's, his wife's, his daughter's. He has also lived in a sex immersed world (though he himself is somewhat asexual), where sex is degenerate, vicious, and omnivorous. . . .

". . . what pornography is really about ultimately, isn't sex, but death," writes Susan Sontag. "It's toward the gratification of death, succeeding and surpassing those of eros, that every truly obscene quest tends." . . . In *The Lime Twig*, the most brutal of all Hawkes' work, gothicism, decadence, and pornographic elements are brought together in a terrifying vision of death and nothingness. (p. 153)

To label John Hawkes as a pornographic writer would be as naive as it was to so classify D. H. Lawrence and James Joyce. Yet both Lawrence and Joyce had far fewer elements of pornography in their work; furthermore they drew characters who searched for meaning, and existences that had creeds. But writers do utilize pornography as a means of revealing their perceptions of life. . . . John Hawkes uses the elements of pornography to show us a world bereft of light. Like a progenitor of black humor he perceives twentieth century life to be absurd, and in its absurdity obscene. By definition, that which is obscene is pornographic. (p. 154)

Helen S. Garson, "John Hawkes and the Elements of Pornography," in Journal of Popular Culture *(copyright © 1976 by Ray B. Browne), Summer, 1976, pp. 150-55.*

Since Skipper of *Second Skin,* all of Hawkes's narrators have been "voyeurs of the incredible," leading privileged, self-indulgent lives, totally at ease in what Cioran calls the banality of the abyss. Out of such indolence they seek to create, to *devise*, the perfect pornographic fantasy, the liberation of love. But their fantasies always depend finally on sexual envy and humiliation, and their erotic aspirations are bounded by the cosmic humiliation of death. The narrator of *Travesty* is a cerebral holy fool, so intent upon manipulating his destiny that he is bound to kill himself trying. . . . [He] talks compulsively; his is the only voice we hear. In fact, I'm inclined to doubt that there really are two other people in the car. We have only the narrator's word for it. He may after all be driving alone, imagining the presence of Chantal and Henri; it would certainly be in keeping with his obsessive self-esteem—the Many in the One.

Although his entire life seems directed toward "clarifying" his situation, his obsessiveness constantly muddles things. He agrees with the poet that "imagined life is more exhilarating than remembered life." But his monologue is a tissue of remembrances. His dream of "design and debris" is a travesty of poetry. He envies the fictive and empathetic powers of the poet, and from this devises his own ultimate manipulation of reality: the well-made death. It never occurs to him that even when poetry is most destructive, most abrasive and critical, it is nonetheless generative, a brute life-force. Likewise, although he tries to be as graphic and as realistic as possible when describing erotic events of the past, his clarity is purely theatrical, worrisome in its detail, and cold as fish. In his obsession with pornography he is the compleat academic. His eroticism is staged reality at best: we can almost see the klieg lights burning offstage. His enlightened self-awareness has bled him of instincts.

No one publishing fiction in America today has Hawkes's ability to curl back the edges of sexual self-consciousness and sexual brinksmanship. His recent fictions dramatize what it's like to have eroticism on the brain, like an imaginary disease, and how self-absorption (which is becoming more and more a high fashion of American culture) can program instincts out of existence. Hawkes might have been a minor author in the literature of cruelty were it not

for his obvious commitment to the possibilities of comic redemption. As an imaginative act (and it's a brave one, I think) *Travesty* desperately seeks to discover and reveal new sources of passion, to point toward new possibilities of love in our pitilessly abstracted and self-conscious age.

Hawkes's control is astonishing. *Travesty* is presented to us as a kind of photographic negative which we, in the act of reading, transform into a positive image. The stillness, the uncanny stasis, of this book suspends the reader in a pure present: the book goes so many places without seeming to go anywhere at all. Even as the narrator's car hurtles through time and space, his monologue creates a languid, sensual, apparently timeless slot in time. It is Hawkes's deft way of impersonating the disturbing presence of the past. The *novella* form, which Hawkes handles with such delicacy and wit (much like the great Italian writer Sciascia), is designed to suit these effects. For *Travesty* is a book of passage, from obsession to oblivion, and the danger of such a journey is intensified by its brevity. We catch detailed glimpses of roadside scenes along the way ("one of the strongest gratifications of night driving is precisely that you can see so little, and yet at the same time so very much") and must attend to Hawkes's concentrated, sometimes telegrammatic, use of metaphors (the narrator's wife is named Honorine, and their country home is called Tara). Every phrase, every sentence of *Travesty* contributes to its comic nihilistic rush.

The book's last words carry an ominous resonance: "But now I make you this promise . . . there shall be no survivors. None." They refer of course to the end of the narrator's luxurious romance with death and clarity. But I also hear Hawkes himself telling us that this marks the end of one major stage of his imaginative career. *Travesty* rounds off, concludes, obliterates the complex journey into the dark territories of sex and death which the earlier two novels [*The Blood Oranges* and *Death, Sleep, and the Traveller*] had begun. The coherence, which the narrator of *Travesty* seeks but does not find, is realized by Hawkes himself, the poet-novelist who redeems "imagined life" from academicism and gives it to us in all its dangerous clarity. It's a wholesome but provocative gift. (pp. 222-23)

W. S. Di Piero, " 'Design and Debris': John Hawkes's 'Travesty'," in The Southern Review *(copyright, 1977, by W. S. De Piero), Vol. XIII, No. 1, Winter, 1977, pp. 221-23.*

*   *   *

HAYDEN, Robert   1913-

Hayden, an award-winning American poet, deals with the black experience in America. His poems revolve around concepts of suffering, and his use of alliteration and complex sound structure has often resulted in comparisons between his work and that of Wallace Stevens and Hart Crane. (See also *CLC*, Vol. 5.)

Hayden has always been a symbolist poet struggling with historical fact, his rigorous portraits of people and places providing the synaptic leap into the interior landscape of the soul, where prayer for illumination and perfection are focused on the oneness of mankind. Having committed himself to the improvement of language, he has sometimes been falsely accused of timidity of commitment to the black struggle because of his refusal to "politicize" his work for expedient and transient goals. But it is Hayden's poetry that best captures the Afro-American tradition of the black hero. . . . Hayden is the master conversationalist and handler of idiom; his perfect pitch is always pointed toward heroic action and his central images are almost always an embracing of kin. He has never abandoned his people. . . .

Though Hayden has not written about his mother directly, it is her voice [in "Angle of Ascent"] that informs his love of detail and spice; he alludes to her passing in "Approximations" ("In dead of winter/wept beside your open grave./Falling snow."), an approximate haiku fused with his own experience. He has been critical of his own slow pace in turning out poems, of what he has summarized as "slim offerings over four decades." But his own assessments should include the *teachableness* of this volume to an increasing public audience. . . . Hayden is the poet of perfect pitch. . . . (p. 34)

His experiments with the ballad form have produced singular achievements—*ballads in spirit* in the language, with dramatic tension and economy that adapt to his personal view of history. . . . Hayden's "The Ballad of Nat Turner," written before the Turner controversy of the late sixties, demonstrates how he does this, dwelling on the high points of the mysterious and archaic roots of black folk rhythms.

His search for kinfolk is the permanent condition of his poetry and his personality. . . .

"Angle of Ascent" is a book that is told. The title comes from the poem "For a Young Artist," which grew out of a conversation with a young musician set upon "astral projection," the attempt to live and create on the highest spiritual plane. Hayden's answer is to find transcendence *living among the living.* In "Stars" Sojourner Truth "Comes walking barefoot/out of slavery/ancestress/childless mother/following the stars/her mind a star," giving testimony to Hayden's living "angle of ascent/achieved." (p. 35)

> *Michael S. Harper, in* The New York Times Book Review *(© 1976 by The New York Times Company; reprinted by permission), February 22, 1976.*

Hayden's poetry [has] been ghettoized along with the work of the other "Black poets." For proof that this situation remains true, one need merely look to the magazines that have so far reviewed *Angle of Ascent* and notice that most, if not all of them, have felt that the book had to be reviewed by another black.

But Robert Hayden has always wished to be judged as a poet among poets, not one to whom special rules of criticism ought to be applied in order to make his work acceptable in more than a sociological sense. His stance . . . has been well known for a long time both to militant blacks and to "liberal" whites. Thus, if the latter have relegated Hayden to the literary ghetto along with the other Black poets, the former have seen him, if not as an "Uncle Tom," at least as a reluctant resident. Perhaps this situation will best explain why Hayden has been ignored.

Yet Hayden has written as much out of his ethnic background as has anyone else. . . . [He] is a paradigmatic poet of the English language who has been true to his roots and history, though not circumscribed by, or limited to, what is merely racial, ethnic, or personal. (p. 200)

Used in the proper circumstances, [understatement, or *litotes,* a] universal technique, can be one of the most effective in the poet's toolbox. Robert Hayden has written one of the most touching contemporary poems utilizing litotes, "Those Winter Sundays," one of his best-known poems also. . . . (p. 207)

[In discussing "black technique in poetry," in his introduction to *Understanding the New Black Poetry*, Stephen] Henderson defines his neologism "mascon": "a massive concentration of Black experiential energy." . . . But it is not the techniques that make [Hayden's poems] Black—*it is how the techniques are applied.* There is "mascon" in the poems, but the "massive concentration of Black experiential energy" is a function of *style*, not [of what Henderson calls Black poetic] structure. (p. 209)

Hayden is usually not content merely to be influenced by a form, he transforms it into something uniquely his. Though "The Ballad of Nat Turner," for instance, looks typographically like a traditional ballad, and might even fool the casual reader into thinking that it is one, in fact it does not rhyme as most ballads do, it consonates; and, though repetition is sometimes used as a substitute for rhyme, there is no ballad refrain. Some stanzas do not even consonate or have repetition, yet the whole poem has the effect of a unified narrative song. This is a masterful wedding of tradition with personal style. (p. 212)

No poet I know of is so capable of couching the American Black's experience and situation, emotion and ambience in language that is accessible to everyone. . . .

[Hayden builds a context for "cue-words"] which provides the alien reader with points of reference which will allow him to understand some of the overtones with which the cues are laden. Hayden does . . . [this] in poem after poem—he cares about the reader, whoever he may be. . . . (p. 216)

One of Hayden's finest poems is full of 19th-century Negro southern dialect: "The Dream" alternates narration regarding a character named Sinda with Black letters from the Civil War front. It is the most effective dialect poem I have ever read, though Hayden claims that many people have misinterpreted it. This puzzles me, and the only reason I can think of for it is that the unexpected person dies. (p. 217)

There are wisdom, art, and the science of language in the poetry of Robert Hayden. His work is unfettered in many ways, not the least of which is in the range of technique available to him. It gives his imagination wings, allows him to travel throughout human nature. Yet he is in no way untrue to his personal heritage, nor to the heritage of American blacks. His style is Protean, capable of change and growth as he develops from book to book, poem to poem. If his work has been overlooked in the past, it has been for the smallest of reasons; it is because he has been willing to be neither a propagandist nor a dweller in a literary ghetto. He has preferred to be a poet. (p. 219)

> *Lewis Turco, "'Angle of Ascent': The Poetry of Robert Hayden," in* The Michigan Quarterly Review *(copyright © The University of Michigan, 1977), Spring, 1977, pp. 199-219.*

HEINEY, Donald
　　See HARRIS, MacDonald

*　　*　　*

HERBERT, Zbigniew 1924-

A Polish poet, Herbert came to the forefront of Polish litera-ture with the relaxation of political suppression in 1961. Her-bert's poems have as their subject matter everyday objects and mythical fantasies, and they are imbued with great wit and nonsense. Although his poems seem to be simply mischie-vous, they are actually careful, studied indictments of the repressiveness of totalitarianism, and the poet uses his out-ward buoyancy to enhance sanity and survival in a world that is bleakly impersonal.

The most distinctive quality of Herbert's imagination is his power to invest impish fantasy, mischievously tender non-sense, with the highest seriousness. His humorous fantasy is the armor of a superlatively healthy mind staving off po-litical oppression. Fantasy is an instrument of survival: it is the chief weapon in a poetry arsenal which serves as a care-taker of the individual identity, a bulwark against the men-tal slavery of the totalitarian church and state. Rarely, in Herbert's work, does the tone of solemnity displace that of buoyancy, even in the most scathing political/religious sat-ire; and surprisingly, the veneer of whimsicality in the most bitter poems heightens their power of outrage. Herbert's indignation gathers potency from being held in abeyance, half-hidden behind gentle ironies.

Some of Herbert's poems seem too calculatedly manufac-tured, but they are intended for *use,* not for show or orna-ment. They would compete with our viable objects-in-use to become indispensible components of our living space: a stool, a pebble, a wooden board,

> my imagination
> is a piece of board
> my sole instrument
> is a wooden stick,

or a wooden bird,

> it lives now . . .
> on a dry stalk
> on one leg
> on a hair of wind
> on what tears itself away
> 　from reality
> does not transform itself
> into an image.

The very strategy of poetic metaphor-making is held by Herbert to be suspect, a device prone to falsifying of our last resources—inner and outer. It is a distraction from the vigilant search for the "one word" that can accurately name—and thereby protect—those modest few perishables needed to sustain our sanity, and, with better luck, our love. Everything in the mind, everything in the poem, is trimmed, stripped down, geared to preserving in our lives the few simple valuables that are left after so unthinkably much has been taken away. So many irreplacable jewels—the hair, the skin, the fingers, the genitals—have been torn from the flesh of the living before the poet's eyes. The po-etry resists the ornamental grace of literary artifacts, the holy sanctity of the altar, the musical lyricism of song; we must look to other poets for artfulness, for holiness, for melody. Herbert gives us instead the habit of long looking

for what is true, what is durable, what is still blessedly touchable in our narrowing life-space, and will not give way under the annihilating pressures of totalitarianism.

Herbert's most characteristic heroism is the refusal to settle for any substitute—artistic, political, religious—for the ser-viceableness of kind acts, kind words, kindliness (unnoticed usually) even in objects. He tells us he would rather be transformed in death to "rock, wood, water, the cracks of a gate . . . the creaking of a floor" than to be reborn an angel. And he means it, literally. Conventional divinities ("shrilly transparent perfection") take a merciless thrashing in Her-bert's poetry. In poem after poem, he obviates any last false hope of squaring the political butchery of the concen-tration camps with the "paradise" of the after-life. In *At the Gate of the Valley,* the next world is simply projected as an extension into the beyond, into eternity, of the living deaths of the camps. Priest, angels, gods—all are flunkeys to a ruthless and sadistically anti-human divinity. They are public relations underlings, soft-selling the old dead religion to ghosts from whom every last precious memento will be taken away. . . . (pp. 52-3)

> *Laurence Lieberman, in* Poetry (© *1969 by The Modern Poetry Association; reprinted by permission of the Editor of* Poetry), *April, 1969.*

[Zbigniew Herbert] is an *avant-garde* poet whose experi-ments and precise, restrained rhythms have sent Polish prosody off in a new direction. Trained in law, he is a man with a passion for classical literature and for history, and with all the intellectual tautness associated with a poet like T. S. Eliot. Yet his verse is unremittingly political. In the circumstances, it could never have been otherwise. (p. 142)

Clearly, he is not political in the conventional sense: he does not purvey, in suitably touched-up forms, the predi-gested truths supplied by any party. He is political by vir-tue of being permanently and warily in opposition. Yet that, too, is a misleading, over-dramatic way of putting it. His opposition is not dogmatic: during the Nazi occupation he was not, to my knowledge, a Communist, nor during the Stalinist repression was he ever noticeably even Catholic or nationalist. Herbert's opposition is a party of one; he re-fuses to relinquish his own truth and his own standards in the face of any dogma. . . . (p. 143)

Most of Herbert's poetry is concerned with reasons for being neither terrified nor convinced, and with his strate-gies for survival.

Most important of these strategies is irony. Yet Herbert's irony has nothing to do with the dandified, touch-me-not distaste—by Eliot out of Laforgue—which was fashionable among the post-Symbolist poets of the twenties and the American academics of the forties. For that irony was, in essence, a slightly less than noble art of self-defence; it pro-tected those who wielded it from emotions they felt they would be better without—feelings for other people, the temptations of commitment. In contrast, Herbert's irony is neither elegant nor embattled. . . . Irony of this kind is a two-edged weapon, which turns on the poet as readily as on the world outside. It is based on a sense of his own ineffec-tual fragility when faced with the steam-roller of political force. It is, in short, the irony of a vulnerable man. In his love poems, like 'Silk of a Soul' or 'Tongue', it inhibits nothing; it simply helps him gently to preserve a sense of proportion, the watchful compassion of a man who, like his 'Pebble', has come to terms with his own limits. . . . Herbert's irony is in the service of an ideal of balance and repose. It is not a safety device which ensures that the outer world will impinge on the poetic only in discreet, carefully regulated doses; it is, instead, a way of focusing the whole mass of his experience so that 'to the end [his poems] will look at us with a calm and very clear eye'.

This sense in his verse of a strong and steady light, which, without denying the shadows, somehow makes them easier to tolerate, is the core of that 'classicism' always invoked to describe his work. There are also other related qualities: for example, his preoccupation with the Greek and Latin classics, cannily modified so that contemporary experience is constantly held in the long, cooling perspective of myth. Then there are his subdued, chaste rhythms and spare language, which leave no room for romantic excesses. . . . Herbert's poetry is also classical in the tautly intellectual control that edges it continually towards some Platonic point of rest, some poise of art and understanding. In poem after poem he strains cunningly towards the moment of final silence. . . . (pp. 144-46)

[The] tension between the ideal and the real is the backbone on which all his work depends. It is what allows him to be at once classical and insistently political. For everything he writes is founded on the realization that poetry, by its nature, is idealistic, hopeful or, as William James put it, 'tender-minded', while the situation in which he must function as a poet is savagely 'tough-minded'—pragmatic, political, destructive, controlling. . . .

To some degree, this tension places him firmly in the tradition of Polish literature, which has developed during the last two centuries despite constant domination by one foreign power or another. But where most Polish poets derive some support from their fierce nationalism, Herbert seems to work without any illusions at all. He is a poet of complete isolation. Soon after the thaw he wrote an ironic ode to his desk drawer; the theme was simply that now he was able to publish all the work he had kept locked away for so long, he no longer had anything to write about. According to the code of Herbert's politics of isolated opposition, even publication is a betrayal of standards, a loss of dissident freedom. (p. 146)

A. Alvarez, "Zbigniew Herbert" (originally published in The Review, *1967), in his* Beyond All This Fiddle: Essays 1955-1967 *(copyright © by A. Alvarez; reprinted by permission of Random House, Inc. and Candida Donadio & Associates, Inc.), Random House, 1969, pp. 142-47.*

[Herbert] draws his metaphors not from particular Polish poets or from the particular events of Polish history, but either from everyday objects—stools and pebbles—or from a common body of European culture: the Bible, Greek mythology, Thucydides, Tacitus, and Shakespeare. Herbert's originality lies in the way his mind works upon this common body of knowledge. (p. 245)

Herbert is a political poet, but the word political may be misleading for it brings to mind the bad verse of the thirties, verse damaged by causes: some of Auden's, some of Spender's, and many poems by a host of minor Marxist poets. The political poet who deals directly with the events of contemporary history usually plays a losing game. His moral outrage will probably overwhelm his poetry, making it self-righteous, predictable, and shrill. . . . Although Herbert's poetry is preoccupied with the nightmares of recent history (the lies, pretensions, and horrors of totalitarianism), it is not public speech. Herbert never advocates this or that cause and he never moralistically "cries" about contemporary experience. He approaches his subject obliquely; wandering among the ruins caused by such destructive forces, Herbert looks for objects that remind us of our stubborn desire to survive and remain sane. Subdued and casual, his poems shun both hysteria and apocalyptic intensity. To answer chaos with chaos, Herbert implies, is to succumb to the very forces we should resist.

Herbert's obliqueness and restraint derive in part from his use of biblical and Greek mythology. The lens of myth reduces the glare of contemporary experience, placing it in a perspective that enables him to look at it without losing his sanity and sense of humor. In several of Herbert's poems the language of religion becomes a metaphor for the language of the totalitarian state. Angels are flunkeys of the highest power and Paradise is the Utopia that supposedly exists. (pp. 246-47)

Herbert's use of myth liberates him from the confines of particular historical events. The satire is not directed at one totalitarian regime, but at all such regimes. At the same time the use of myth fleshes out the thin bones of the satire, making it sly and elegant, not obvious and heavy-handed. Furthermore, Herbert's satirical humor is a way of resisting the dehumanizing and impersonal language of the state—the so-called higher truth of its ideology. Keeping a sense of humor means keeping a private language and avoiding the total politicization of the self. After all, "they"—the solemn angels of the state—never laugh.

Of course such humorless angels can be frighteningly effective. They can compel belief or they can compel guilt. A chilling poem, "Preliminary Investigation of an Angel," brings to mind the forced confessions of Stalin's purge trials, when even the most loyal members of the Communist Party were forced to confess their guilt. An angel—one who is a faithful member of the heavenly hierarchy—naturally thinks that he is spiritual and "innocent." The state, however, judged him as material and guilty, and so he slowly metamorphoses before our eyes. . . . No one can resist the inquisition of the state, not even such a faithful member of its hierarchy. (p. 247)

It is only after the angel has been broken by the state that he becomes real, and his reality undermines the unreal "spiritual" perfection of the totalitarian order. Because of its ruthlessness and suspicion, the system creates its own opposition, creates such a "simple prophecy." Icons of a "faith" different from that of the state, the drops of wax deny the "gluey agreement."

A similar parable is adumbrated in a poem that makes use of Greek myth, "Apollo and Marsyas." Apollo, with his "absolute ear," pipes the song of the state on his flute and therefore cannot lose the contest he has with Marsyas. The latter, who dared to challenge Apollo, is flayed alive, yet

> only seemingly
> is the voice of Marsyas
> monotonous
> and composed of a single vowel

> Aaa . . .

In reality, the howling of Marsyas provokes a shudder of
disgust in Apollo, who is "cleaning his instrument," and
the victorious god begins to walk away from the flayed satyr, wondering

> whether out of Marsyas' howling
> there will not some day arise
> a new kind
> of art—let us say—concrete
>
> suddenly
> at his feet
> falls a petrified nightingale
>
> he looks back
> and sees
> that the hair of the tree to which Marsyas was fastened
> is white
> completely . . .

Like the drops of wax, the petrified nightingale and the
white "hair" of the tree are a new kind of concrete art that
grows out of the inquisition of the state. The latter two are
deformations of nature that testify through their grotesque
metamorphosis to the terror of the state. (pp. 248-49)

Herbert's obliqueness and restraint . . . , derive not only
from the use he makes of myth, but also from the attention
he pays to concrete things. In "At the Gate of the Valley,"
a poem in which the Last Judgment is seen as a parable of
mass extermination, Herbert says:

> those who as it seems
> have obeyed the orders without pain
> go lowering their heads as a sign of consent
> but in their clenched fists they hide
> fragments of letters ribbons clipping of hair
> and photographs
> which they naïvely think
> won't be taken from them . . .

The objects that these people clutch make them individuals
and not the statistics of a holocaust. Although threatened
by a final solution, the victims refuse to give up their possessions. The disaster may be enormous but the responses
to it are personal; the final solution happens to particular
individuals at particular places and times. (p. 249)

Herbert's particularity is . . . an attempt to clear the atmosphere of verbal smoke and fog—the smoke of literary hysteria and the fog of totalitarian lies. The poet wants to learn
how to use words carefully again, and therefore he focusses
on objects. The pebble, he says,

> is a perfect creature
>
> equal to itself
> mindful of its limits
>
> filled exactly
> with a pebbly meaning . . .
>
> > —Pebbles cannot be tamed
> > to the end they will look at us
> > with a calm and very clear eye.
>
> (p. 250)

The pebble and the stool also work as analogies, implying
both a basic human stubbornness ("Pebbles cannot be
tamed") and an attitude toward life and art that might be
called classical. . . . Clarity and emotional restraint: these
are classical virtues. Herbert's classicism, however, does
not mean that he has removed himself from the present and
that he looks at it in a sadly disillusioned manner from the
ivory tower of the past. His classicism is a prescription for
survival and sanity in the present—a method for swimming
in the destructive element and not going under.

Herbert's clearest statement of his classicism is found in
the poem "Why the Classics." Here he contrasts Thucydides, who honorably accepted the responsibility for his
unsuccessful expedition to Amphipolis, with "generals of
the most recent wars." . . . Unlike Thucydides, generals of
the most recent wars evade the responsibility for their actions. Wallowing in self-pity, they break down and call everything a mess, say that everyone (and therefore no one) is
responsible for the failure. They cannot make distinctions.
(p. 251)

Self-pity for Herbert resides in our inner voice. In a poem
called "Inner Voice" he says:

> he is of no use to me
> I could forget about him
>
> I have no hope
> a little regret
> when he lies there
> covered with pity
> breathes heavily
> opens his mouth
> and tries to lift up
> his inert head.

The inner voice, full of "syllables / stripped of all meaning," tempts us to lie down and cry. Herbert tries to ignore
this siren song, but he does so with "a little regret." Crying
is the easiest thing to do. . . . The classics show us how to
resist such a temptation. Listening to Marsyas' howl, Herbert does not respond with a whine. Instead he disciplines
himself by looking at objects—calm things of "great immobility" that "reprove us constantly for our instability."
Such objects survive disaster; the classics help us to do the
same thing.

As a classicist Herbert does not heed his incoherent inner
voice; and as a classicist he makes very few claims for poetry. In "A Knocker," his art is "nothing special," and his
imagination is a

> piece of board
> my sole instrument
> is a wooden stick . . .
>
> I thump on the board
> and it prompts me
> with the moralist's dry poem
> yes—yes
> no—no.

The symbol for his imaginative powers is not, as it was for
the romantics, a fountain; it is a wooden stick. And myth
for Herbert is not, as it was for Blake, a sign of the gods
within the mind, an example of the inexhaustible fertility of
the human imagination. Myth for Herbert is an order that
we can turn to in order to get away from the anarchy of the
self. It provides us with a way of placing contemporary
experience in a larger perspective. Finally, unlike the romantics, Herbert writes the "moralist's dry poem"; he is
neither a prophet nor an unacknowledged legislator.

Another aspect of Herbert's classical frame of mind is his skepticism about language itself. Throughout his poetry there rumbles an *ostinato* of linguistic despair. The poet can only thump his board, aware that words themselves are inadequate to convey the horrors of contemporary experience. (pp. 252-53)

But of course we must say something, and such a chaotic situation requires the voice of a Fortinbras, not a Hamlet. Hamlet's language is full of tragic intensity, but it is an intensity that arises from his despair and self-pity. Fortinbras, the man who arrives after the disaster and tries to make some sense of the ruins, is Herbert's hero, even though his task is a prosaic one, and what he does will never be worth a tragedy. In "Elegy of Fortinbras" the soldier says of the prince:

> The rest is not silence but belongs to me
> you chose the easier part an elegant thrust
> but what is heroic death compared with eternal
>   watching
> with a cold apple in one's hand on a narrow chair
> with a view of the ant-hill and the clock's dial
>
> Adieu prince I have tasks a sewer project
> and a decree on prostitutes and beggars . . .
> I go to my affairs This night is born
> a star named Hamlet We shall never meet
> what I shall leave will not be worth a tragedy . . .

Fortinbras speaks with a good deal of regret, for he knows that Hamlet's "heroic death" is the "easier part," and as such it is tempting. By dying Hamlet avoided the mediocre tasks of survival; by dying Hamlet did not have to compromise himself. As Fortinbras says of him: "you believed in crystal notions not in human clay." By dying Hamlet kept his crystal notions intact.

Like death, exile is also the "easier part," for it keeps us away from the contaminations of mediocrity. The proconsul of "The Return of the Proconsul" does not want to choose the easier part; he does not want to accept the death-in-life of exile. He wants to return to the emperor's court although he knows that there he must compromise himself. At the beginning of the poem, he confidently announces his decision to return and "see if it's possible to live there." . . . The proconsul's dilemma is agonizing: he cannot accept the "death" of exile nor can he bring himself to return to the emperor's court, where he would—at the least—become a mere flunkey. His decision to return, repeated several times in the poem, is only an *ignis fatuus* of his mind. He desperately wants to be convinced, yet he remains unconvinced: he continually postpones his return. Although at the end of the poem he says that "I've decided to return to the emperor's court / yes I hope that things will work out somehow," we believe that he will never return. His pathetic delusion, however, compels our admiration, for he cannot accept exile—the easier part. He never stops hoping that things will work out better somehow and then he will be able to return. Herbert's poem must not be read as a comment on real exiles, but as a parable about the man who always faces towards life, although he has more than enough reasons for turning towards death.

Will things work out better somehow? Such is the proconsul's hope, not the poet's. In the prose poem "When the World Stands Still," Herbert does say that "after a while the world moves on. The ocean swallows and regurgitates,

valleys send off steam and . . . there is also heard the resounding clash of air against air." Yet, as in "The Longobards," the possibility always exists that a new barbarian force will overrun the cultivated valley:

> An immense coldness from the Longobards
> Their shadow sears the grass when they flock
>   into the valley
> Shouting their protracted nothing nothing nothing.

Hearing those apocalyptic and inhuman shouts, we can either choose the easier part or try to survive. Herbert, with his resolute and unsolemn stoicism, prescribes in a prose poem some "Practical Recommendations in the Event of a Catastrophe": "Place yourself as far as possible from the centre . . . before the whirling motion as it gets stronger from minute to minute begins to pour in towards the middle . . . Keep your head down. Have your two hands constantly free. Take good care of the muscles of your legs."

Like Fortinbras, Herbert does not choose the easier part; he does not yield to the mere process of disintegration. Instead, like Fortinbras, he tries to bring order to a situation that seems beyond ordering. "Such a sight as this," as Fortinbras says in *Hamlet,* requires a disciplined and measured voice, one mindful of its limits and filled exactly with a pebbly meaning. (pp. 254-56)

> *Stephen Miller, "The Poetry of Zbigniew Herbert," in* The Rarer Action: Essays in Honor of Francis Fergusson, *edited by Alan Cheuse and Richard Koffler (copyright © 1970 by Rutgers, The State University of New Jersey; Rutgers University Press, New Brunswick, N.J.), Rutgers, 1970, pp. 244-57.*

One of the major themes in *Pan Cogito* is the identity of the self; this can be seen as a deepening of the quest of [Herbert's] earlier volume, *Studium przedmiotu* (Study of the Object; 1961). The opening poems of *Pan Cogito* ask the questions "Who am I? Where do I end and others begin?" and they introduce the idea of the complexity of the self. Why do we have features which we have consciously rejected, which we do not recognize as our own? Mr. Cogito says of his image in the mirror, "But it is not me!" In these poems the personality is seen as radically unharmonious and dependent on elements over which we have little control, such as familial and racial heredity and history. The complexity of the self is given a deeper and more personal content in the beautiful poem "Remembering My Father," where the father has a double appearance: first as a judging, severe and all-powerful Jehovah of the Old Testament; later as a very fragile and suffering Christlike figure. In "Sister" the very *principium individuationis* of the personality is threatened, since a change of identity seems as "simple as changing a place at the table."

The poems dealing with the problem of identity are among the most autobiographical and personal in all of Herbert's poetry. In his earlier poems he paid little attention to the self; his concern was usually addressed to others, and the self's harmony was assumed. Much of the stringency of the earlier poems' moral stance depended on this concern for others; Herbert was rarely self-conscious or self-indulgent, and his references to himself were usually ironic. At first glance in reading *Pan Cogito* it might appear that the strong, clear moral alternatives of the earlier poems are compromised by this new complexity. This is not the case; the moral stance is deepened, not diluted.

If Herbert discovers in himself traces of others and feels menaced by biological and historical determinism, he has at the same time an acute awareness of his separation from other human beings. In his earlier books Herbert frequently used the pronoun ''we'' with a feeling of great solidarity and compassion for others, while in his recent work he tends to use the first-person singular pronoun. This is surprising—the ability to identify with other people and to put himself in their skins is one of Herbert's most striking traits. However, in ''The Alienations of Mr. Cogito'' Herbert sees others as stones confined by the limits of their own skin. . . . (p. 210)

The choice of the stone to express a sense of separateness is not surprising. . . . Herbert has always been interested in inanimate objects, but not because they are inhuman. On the contrary, he tends to find human traits in objects (rather than vice versa) and to discover a community of interest between humans and objects. . . . In *Pan Cogito* there are at least two striking poems about objects, ''Sense of Identity'' and ''To Take Objects Out.'' Far from praising the stability of objects, in these poems Herbert stresses an opposite quality which he finds in them, changeability. . . . For Herbert, objects never represented an escape from the human; he continues to be intrigued by them and to study them, finding unexpected new qualities and aspects of reality. He humanizes them and at the same time respects their fundamental opacity. There is no longer an abyss between man and inanimate objects; on the contrary, there is a new sense of identity with them based on the realization of human fallibility. Herbert is engaged in breaking down the barrier between the human and the inanimate and in extending the limits of the human, what might be called a long-term project of reclamation of the inanimate.

In *Pan Cogito* there is a poignant acceptance of imperfection and defeat. The stern moralist . . . has become more tolerant of weakness both in himself and in others. Poems like ''Mr. Cogito Reads the Newspaper,'' ''Mr. Cogito and Pure Thought,'' ''The Everydayness of the Soul'' and ''Mr. Cogito Laments the Pettiness of Dreams'' show human ideals, dreams and feelings as limited, largely practical, often petty and incapable of great flights. In Herbert's earlier poetry the blame for much of the mediocrity of modern life was placed on historical forces and politics rather than on the individual. Now the individual appears in all his weakness. However, this is neither tragic nor exasperating; in these poems there is an acceptance of imperfection and defeat which contains little bitterness. At most there is irony, but it is relatively gentle and totally unlike the mordant irony of an earlier political poem such as ''Report from Paradise.''

This acceptance of imperfection and defeat is important because it provides a matrix for one of the most important philosophical themes of the book: the attack upon transcendence. In earlier poems like ''Anything Rather Than the Angel'' and ''The Paradise of the Theologians'' Herbert attacked bloodless abstraction and favored ''the creaking of the floor'' over ''shrilly transparent perfection.'' This attitude is carried a step further in what are some of the finest poems in Herbert's latest volume, ''Mr. Cogito Tells about the Temptation of Spinoza'' and ''Georg Heym—the Almost Metaphysical Adventure.'' Another poem written after *Pan Cogito*, ''Beethoven,'' continues the same argument. Herbert now attacks transcendence head on, in its philosophical form in the ideas of Spinoza, and in its poetic form in the ideas of Heym. The attack is carried out with great skill and intensity of feeling. It could be said that non-transcendence—or imperfection—itself becomes a ''transcendent'' goal in the place of transcendence. But this is avoided in a number of ways: by playfulness, irony, humor, lack of traditional form and punctuation and by the absence of the high rhetoric of literary tradition. And finally, the use of the device of Mr. Cogito—who is often a mock persona—underlines the impurity of the poems. (p. 211)

There is much historical erudition in his poetry . . . ; yet the past is rarely used in opposition to the present. Instead, it is a natural extension and continuation of the present. The historical personae are remarkably similar to the living people we know. They are rarely ''Aesopian'' allegorical devices, nor are they symptoms of an unwillingness to face the present directly, a charge occasionally leveled against Herbert. For Herbert, history is ourselves, and historical figures act in essentially the same space as we do, with the same psychology and ethics. Past and present are contemporaneous. The historical dimension of Herbert's poetry seems to arise with complete spontaneity. This gives many of his poems considerable universality and is probably the key to his ability to be such a remarkably public poet. (pp. 211-12)

Herbert's long residence abroad, both in West Berlin and the United States, partly explains his use of the pronoun ''I'' instead of ''we'' and his frequent self-observation. Far from the political situation in Poland and the painful memories of World War II, Herbert was for the first time alone with himself. In addition, the presence of art, which was so important in his earlier collections of poems and in the collection of essays *Barbarzyńca w ogrodzie* (Barbarian in the Garden), fades into the background. Now the poet is no longer a ''barbarian'' from the Slavic world making a pilgrimage to the ''garden'' countries of Western Europe, primarily France, Italy and Greece. In the more industrialized countries Herbert apparently found that art had less relevance to daily life; he was living in a different world where many of his earlier concerns were ignored or considered to be abstractions.

It should be said that Herbert's reaction was not only one of opposition. If the United States was unsure of its identity as a country, Herbert also became less sure of his own as an individual; he questioned his earlier historical orientation, and the clear opposition of the barbarian to the garden, of totalitarian backwardness to civilization, is no longer as assured and striking as in his previous volumes of poems. It now has to be worked out in philosophical terms, and this is what Herbert does in the middle section of *Pan Cogito*. He defends Aristotle, logic, form, Homer and Horace—what perhaps might be called the mainstream of Western civilization—against the Orient, magic, chaos, artificial paradise and artificial hell, what he calls ''the art of aggressive epilepsy.'' In the poems of dialogue with the United States, Herbert's Cartesianism and rationalism are most prominent. The sense of a ''garden,'' however, of a place most favored by civilization, is lost.

Finally, we must ask why Herbert created the figure of Mr. Cogito and what his identity really is. Several critics have begun their discussion of *Pan Cogito* by considering this problem, assuming that it is the key to the book and that once it is solved, a judgment can be made about the volume as a whole. For this assumption to be true, however, Mr. Cogito would have to be an allegorical persona representing a fixed value or point of view, analogous to Valéry's Monsieur Teste, Pound's Mauberley or Eliot's Sweeney. However, this certainly is not the case. The mood and humor with which Herbert uses the figure of Mr. Cogito varies greatly—even more so, for example, than John Berryman's treatment of his "Henry." Herbert employs many tones and speaking voices in his poems, and so does the fictitious Mr. Cogito. They range from the serious, biblical language of "The Envoy of Mr. Cogito" to the humorous, light "Mr. Cogito on Virtue" with its references to Elizabeth Taylor and pop music. Often Mr. Cogito's presence is stated only in the title of a poem but nowhere else, or only in an epigraph, as in "Houses of the Outskirts" and "Caligula." These poems could clearly dispense with their epigraphs or the reference to Mr. Cogito in the title without any esthetic damage. Often Mr. Cogito's "presence" is pure bluff or playfulness on Herbert's part; he is a mock persona or pseudo-persona and is not to be taken seriously. This playfulness is not new: although Herbert is a severe moralist, he is frequently whimsical and humorous. Often Mr. Cogito is little more than a device permitting Herbert to refer to himself with a third-person pronoun. At other times Herbert's famous irony is at the heart of the existence of Mr. Cogito—tongue in cheek, he is clearly *not* to be believed in, he is only a parody. Frequently it is clear that Herbert is making no effort to modulate or disguise his voice; he is both spontaneous and personal. And in the past many of Herbert's mouthpieces have been ironic: figures such as the Proconsul and Fortinbras spoke in the contemporary idiom of the twentieth century with an evident and disabused knowledge of its holocausts. In this list of personae (a long one) Mr. Cogito is probably the most ironic.

The relationship between the author of the book and Mr. Cogito is never decisively or satisfactorily settled. The ambiguity of the Mr. Cogito poems, the constant shifting between third- and first-person verbs, is already peresent in the name "Mister," indicating a third-person form of address, while *cogito* is the first-person singular form of the verb *cogitare.* Both from the stylistic and from the grammatical point of view, Mr. Cogito is a combination of the self and others. This ambiguity reflects the major philosophical theme of the volume: man's identity and the problem of his relationship to others. (pp. 212-13)

If the reader should ask why Herbert needs to use a device or figure such as Mr. Cogito at all, the answer is the need to "objectify". . . . Even when Herbert is most personal, he is always talking about the outside world and about its reality. The personal tone is a vehicle for approaching the world as directly as possible; on the other hand, to call attention to his own ego, to his separateness, would confine the poem and diminish that broad reality he observes so intently, so unflinchingly.

Mr. Cogito is clearly a little man, and some have called him petty. His concerns are frequently ordinary and practical; he enjoys reading sensational newspaper articles, he tries transcendental meditation and fails, his stream of consciousness brings up detritus like a tin can, he needs advice, and so on. However, this ordinariness is largely involuntary—Mr. Cogito has average impulses. This is different from being only average, and he does not stop there.

Mr. Cogito is a device allowing Herbert to admit this ordinariness we all share, to establish it and, once this is done, to build upon it. Herbert wants to underline ordinariness and imperfection because he wants to deal with practical, not transcendent, morality. The poems of *Pan Cogito* consistently apply ethics not only to action but to the possible, viable action of everyday life, taking human failings into account. The poems are tolerant and humane in their approach, and they are less categorical than the earlier poems, embracing a greater range of contradictions. They are both more personal and more general, which gives striking modernity and depth to the volume.

Herbert does not call for extraordinary exploits of resistance, which is in keeping with his attack upon transcendence. The earlier poems were usually terse and sudden, going straight to their target without digressions; the poems in *Pan Cogito* are less swift and terse, yet they are about heroism no less than the earlier poems. Herbert addresses the problem of how the ordinary man in the modern world, without any superhuman powers, can achieve the heroism of a Hector, a Roland or a Gilgamesh. The "Envoy of Mr. Cogito," which concludes the volume, considers the problem of how an average individual can find a stance, an acceptable attitude, which is not shameful when compared with those of heroes of the past. Herbert claims this is possible, and to demonstrate, he uses a person who is anchored in practicality, who is above no one and who is of the measure of anyone and everyone. If Mr. Cogito were extraordinary, Herbert's claim would be less convincing. Surely those who have complained about Mr. Cogito's pettiness and grayness have missed the point, because if he were more remarkable he would be less universal. Herbert is casting his nets widely, and in poem after poem Mr. Cogito does achieve heroism in his ironic, low-keyed manner. The poems have a great, deliberate burden of everydayness, of ordinary, intractable reality, to carry.

The ultimate irony of these poems is that, in the final analysis, Herbert seems to say that we must act against human nature. Suffering does not release us from certain duties— of acting according to our conscience and against human nature. One must accept, but here the awareness—the *cogitans,* intellectual awareness—is important. One must be aware of one's own human nature and limitations; one must not do violence to them. One must accept, consent and *then* overcome them. (pp. 213-14)

Herbert argues for the acceptance of suffering without big words and dramatic gestures, for a deflation of attitudes. It is needless to say that such acceptance is far more "heroic" and difficult than would be the case if it were accompanied by rhetoric, by ethical inflation and melodrama. In *Pan Cogito* the moralist is also a humanist, but the humanist is also a moralist; in the book Herbert struggles to create a fusion of the two. (p. 214)

Bogdana Carpenter and John Carpenter, "The Recent Poetry of Zbigniew Herbert," in World Literature Today *(copyright 1977 by the University of Oklahoma Press), Vol. 51, No. 2, Spring, 1977, pp. 210-14.*

*   *   *

HERSEY, John   1914-

An American journalist, essayist, and Pulitzer-Prize-winning novelist, Hersey was born in China. He writes of the major

social events and problems of his time, producing contemporary histories that are probing accounts of the world he perceives. Hersey's work is characterized by the journalist's thorough analysis of his subject as well as the novelist's ability to tell stories that have a certain poetic conviction. (See also *CLC*, Vols. 1, 2, 7, and *Contemporary Authors*, Vols. 17-20, rev. ed.)

Hersey shows himself at the peak of his form in this love story [*The Walnut Door*] that positively shimmers with vitality and controlled suggestiveness. (p. 38)

[The] story is tender, deep-rooted, and ... subtly grained.... It is a novel of erotic discovery in the best sense because in the widest sense. Moreover, it bears an upbeat message for our fear-ridden and somewhat frenzied generation. (p. 39)

> *Peter Gardner, in* Saturday Review (© *1977 by Saturday Review Magazine Corp.; reprinted with permission), September 17, 1977.*

Throughout his long and meritorious career, John Hersey has been an author of the public kind. By that I mean that through his previous 18 books, 11 of them novels, Hersey has sought always to measure and define the impact of public events—often of the most massive and cataclysmic variety—upon the private character and mores of the individuals he has written about.... But while no one has ever denied his craftsmanship—Hersey's ability to combine strong plot lines with meticulous research into the subjects that have concerned him—his reputation in literary circles has suffered at the hands of reviewers who do not care to be preached at in a novel, or who have found his parables thin, his allegorical tendencies unconvincing.

Accordingly, although Hersey has spent much of the past 20 years at Yale, his alma mater, and has more intellectual energy than whole regions of the Modern Language Association, his work has not been made the object of academic enshrinement and very likely never will. Probably this does not bother Hersey overmuch.... [He] has always aimed for an audience broader than the one literary eminence customarily brings. His novels teach themselves.

Even so, "The Walnut Door" seems to mark a kind of departure. The focus of this novel is the curious personal relationship between two pampered children of the educated middle class; therefore Hersey's ability to define character in this book is more important than the events he describes. To a point Hersey succeeds quite well. (p. 9)

Hersey's mastery of plot is as sure as ever; very few readers who begin the novel will fail to complete it.

But narrative facility can detract as much as it adds: By using the technique most familiarly seen in the thriller—quick, often truncated, vignettes from the point of view of one or the other character, and always in the present tense—Hersey inherits the shallow characterization that often goes with it. Why [Elaine and Eddie, the novel's two central characters are] drawn together so compulsively, and why, in the final analysis, we should care about them for over 200 pages remains unclear....

Hersey's attempts to juxtapose private life against the public events of the past two decades establishes little more than that all Americans in their mid-20s remember Lee Harvey Oswald, Sirhan Sirhan and Vietnam....

Ultimately though, "The Walnut Door's" main flaw is that Hersey has made his protagonists' fecklessness too convincing. Each seems less an actor than one acted upon, less a survivor of a difficult time than a victim of his or her incapacity for serious choice. All that remains in them is sexual melodrama—the anodyne of their class and time. But Hersey handles sensuality unconvincingly; what makes these characters compelling to each other will remain a mystery to most readers. One almost wishes he had appended a moral; it would be interesting to know what he makes of it all. (p. 48)

> *Gene Lyons, "What Remains Is Sexual Melodrama," in* The New York Times Book Review (© *1977 by The New York Times Company; reprinted by permission), September 18, 1977, pp. 9, 48.*

[*The Walnut Door*] fairly glows with the author's fundamental humanity. Hersey's decency is both transparent and transcendent. He cares about matters that deserve to be cared about, and he writes about them with palpable passion. Scarcely a subject of contemporary moment has escaped his attention; he has written about everything from overpopulation to racial discrimination to the student revolution to war, and in every case he has written with his heart and mind firmly set in the right direction....

But as a novelist Hersey has been less successful [than as a writer of nonfiction], artistically if not commercially. Like so many writers whose deepest motivation is political belief, he tends to be didactic and simplistic when he turns to fiction. His symbolism is too obvious, his characters too ordinary, his situations too pat.

The Walnut Door suffers under all these difficulties. It is rescued from being either boring or trite by an inner tension that Hersey sustains rather successfully, but it has too many problems to work well as fiction. It is a variation of sorts on John Fowles's early, and far more effective, novel, *The Collector*, in which a young woman is held captive and abused sexually by a curiously demented man. It is intended, clearly, as a parable about the real and imagined fears of contemporary urban existence, but the parable overwhelms the story....

[As] a work of fiction *The Walnut Door* lies down and dies. The two central characters are only mildly interesting, it becomes too obvious too soon what is going on, and the tone of the novel is all wrong. Hersey has obviously kept in touch with the young folk from his vantage point at Yale, but his efforts to capture their argot and culture are clumsy, if endearingly so. Like a middle-aged man with a wig or a woman with a facelift, he is trying to occupy the country of the young, and it doesn't work. Despite its good intentions, to read *The Walnut Door* is to wince.

> *Jonathan Yardley, "Lost in the Country of the Young," in* Book World—The Washington Post (© *The Washington Post), October 16, 1977, p. E5.*

*   *   *

HIRAOKA, Kimitake
See MISHIMA, Yukio

*   *   *

HORGAN, Paul   1903-

An American editor, playwright, historian, essayist, short story writer, and novelist, Horgan is a regionalist writer of the American Southwest. Horgan won the 1955 Pulitzer Prize in History for *Great River: The Rio Grande in North American*

History. His works, in which his Catholicism figures promi-nently, are characterized by attitudes of charity, optimism, and a belief that spiritual forces are at work in life. (See also *Contemporary Authors*, Vols. 13-16, rev. ed.)

Though he is a Catholic writer, Horgan is more devoted to explaining human dignity achieved through experience than he is to specifically "religious" answers. Somewhat like the whiskey priest in *The Power and The Glory*, his characters are more than Catholic, for they embody the experiences universal to the growth of the human spirit.

In some ways "Death and the Children" is a prototype of the most significant of Horgan's writings. Its theme, even its characters and setting, are those which become impor-tant in his works, both short stories and novels. Death it-self, the central fact of this story, does not become a major theme for Horgan, though it is often used. A shattering per-sonal experience, of which death is perhaps the most pow-erful, is the core of many of his most important writings; and the use of childhood, and specifically of a boys' camp, is to recur again in later works. It appears that Horgan is not interested in childhood as such, just as he is not really concerned with death, but he used it as the most appro-priate symbol of man's growth through experience. His children are only secondarily children; first they are the embodiment of the human soul struggling toward under-standing and expression. (pp. 10-11)

In *Things As They Are*, Horgan writes more openly than in any other work of his concern for the cruelty and deceit that make up a part of the world of human relationships. Cruelty and deceit are recognized in his other novels, but the emphasis is on his characters' mastery of them, and not on their existence, as in this book. His use of the first per-son is competent, but does not display the same adeptness at characterization as some of his other stories. (p. 23)

Paul Horgan is known as a regional writer, and in fact most of his fiction has been set in the Southwest. In a broader sense, however, the major themes of his novels are not those of a regionalist, and his chief concern is with charac-ter.... His plots are often well-conceived in themselves, but invariably they are extensions of, or vehicles for, the expression of character. (p. 27)

In attempts to master new aspects of fiction, Horgan was far more ready to experiment with point of view, time span, or characterization than with literary technique. Prose, in his works, is the vehicle for carrying plot and atmosphere and is well-trained and facile, but not original. (p. 29)

> *James M. Day, in his* Paul Horgan *(copy-right © 1967 by Steck-Vaughn Company), Steck-Vaughn, 1967.*

[Two] motives—to transform the commonplace into the legendary, to find the beauty behind the banality—appear to me to be the generating forces of ["Whitewater"], as they are the generating forces of much art. The great Romantic and post-Romantic poets, from Wordsworth to Wal-lace Stevens, have in various ways sought to redeem the actual world from banality. It is no mean chore for the nov-elist, who runs the same risks as the poets—the chief risk being that because of insufficient heat, or light, or energy, the banal remains banal, the typical only typical, the aver-age only average, and the sought-after legends and beauty emerge only fitfully, if at all. Mr. Horgan has bravely and not altogether successfully run this risk.

"Whitewater" is mostly the story of young [Phillipson] Durham and his yearning to escape the provincial deadli-ness of the small plains town.... The outline of his life, of his story, is [a simple one].

It's an artful simplicity, too. Horgan is a writer who has clearly controlled and restrained his powers of language and thought to create a classically familiar story, and he has told it with great economy, even elegance. Much of our life is accurately rendered: the achingly familiar corniness and turbulence of adolescent emotion, the hopelessly ambigu-ous desires of parents for their children's future, the suffo-cating oppressiveness of small town life. Every man who grew up in the sticks will recognize at least part of himself in Phillipson Durham.

And that, of course, is where the trouble lies. The point at which the familiar becomes the cliché, the evocation of universal experience somehow turns out to be a depressing recital of things too well known—that point is reached fairly early in Mr. Horgan's narrative, and the reader never really finds his way to the beauty and the legends he might have hoped to discover....

Ordinary life and ordinary people aren't *that* ordinary, pre-dictable, finished, and Mr. Horgan presumably knows it. At one point, Victoria says to Durham, "And if you only think about it, life is bigger than art, and we have a lot of life in our town." What went wrong? Somehow Mr. Hor-gan's considerable art doesn't measure up to Victoria's fine and truthful words.

One knows that even the most commonplace lives are more unpredictable, more mysterious, less finished than Mr. Horgan's art allows. Only rarely does he animate Victoria's description of the town, most strikingly perhaps in the de-scription of a fishing trip on Whitewater Lake. Phillipson and Billy hear voices floating across from the next island, they swim toward the island to investigate, are shot at and swim back without ever finding out who the voices be-longed to or what they were saying. This episode stays with Phillipson into his adult life, and he never ceases to wonder what it was he could not hear that night.

I imagine it is something like those voices we ourselves want to hear in a novel like "Whitewater." But we come away all too certain that we've heard more than enough.

> *James Boatwright, "Flawed Quest for the Beauty Beyond Banality," in* The New York Times Book Review *(© 1970 by The New York Times Company; reprinted by permission), August 27, 1970, p. 5.*

Paul Horgan's *Whitewater* has so much going for it that I am surprised it has not gone farther....

It is hard to fault Mr. Horgan for doing everything right. When he mentions Belvedere he tells us that it has a popu-lation of 5,453, and I approve of facts. In the opening scene he describes "Fourth Island in Whitewater Lake, which backed up Whitewater Dam, on the Whitewater Draw, forty-nine miles from the town of Belvedere, in Orpha County, in West Central Texas." If we praise that kind of thing in Defoe, we must praise it in Mr. Horgan, it comes from good motives. But it does not ring true. After a while, these details in *Whitewater* begin to sound like abstrac-tions, arithmetic drifts off into metaphysics. I think the rea-son is that Mr. Horgan's sense of life is generic rather than individual, he takes an interest in people only because they constitute Man; or so the fiction suggests. . . .

[In *Whitewater*] Mr. Horgan tries to . . . tell a commonplace story in such a way that it becomes legendary, and the colloquial style becomes sublime. But the trouble is that legends cannot be forced, they come or they do not. Mr. Horgan coaxes the commonplace to transfigure itself. . . . There is a feeling, toward the end of the book, that Mr. Horgan is putting in the significance which the story itself failed to give; details are underlined, glossed, pondered, lest they die as details.

Henry James, considering the novel as a picture of life, said that it is not expected of a picture that it shall make itself humble in order to be forgiven. But Mr. Horgan's picture makes itself grand in order to be noticed. Judging from the style, I conclude that Mr. Horgan has misgivings about his fiction. He worries that perhaps it will not mean enough or mean it abundantly. He has good will, good nature, powers of reflection, and he cares about the quality of life; what his writing lacks in *Whitewater* is nonchalance, the ease which succeeds difficulty. He writes as if there were nothing, no release, beyond difficulty. (p. 23)

> *Denis Donoghue, in* The New York Review of Books *(reprinted with permission from* The New York Review of Books; *copyright © 1970 NYREV, Inc.), November 5, 1970.*

History-as-nightmare may be something from which none of us will ever awaken, but in books like Paul Horgan's *Great River: The Rio Grande in North American History* we get a rousing good shake and a fighting chance to open our eyes. Not that Horgan's vision is as glibly rosy as that of many another chronicler of the Southwest. On the contrary, throughout the epic sweep of *Great River* (from prehistory to the 20th century) one is fully aware that greed, cruelty and madness have been the acolytes of every change and movement, every rise to power and fall from grace. But what sets *Great River* apart and is its finest virtue is Horgan's ability to inspirit human events with the flavor and feeling of the land that spawned them. The stage he sets is broad, permanent. In the background one feels the steady pulse of the land and its river; they endure. At least until the coming of the railroads and the automobile, the land invariably conquered its conquerors. (p. 31)

The scope of the work is shaped by neither political nor cultural boundaries. Its territory is defined only by the river that snakes 1900 miles from the snowcapped mountains of southern Colorado through desert, canyon and plain to the swampy margins of the Gulf of Mexico, and on this continent is exceeded in length only by the Mississippi-Missouri system. The river and the dry wilderness at its sides provide the thread to unite the centuries of human experience there; culture, armies and law do not. (pp. 31-2)

[Critics] were by no means unanimous in their praise of the book. Some found it arty and accused it of being too "pretty" for history. One critic at the *New Yorker* summarized many of his fellows' misgivings. "An odd thing happens to writers who live in the high country," he wrote, ignoring the fact that the Rio Grande, like any major river, must flow through the lowest land in its region. "They see the mountains, the sand, the stars, the cactus, the wrinkled Indians and they begin to babble about 'time' and 'space.'"

He may as well have said that history is at all times obliged to be sere and sober and that there is no place in it for poetry or enchantment, even such as the people who are its subject may have felt in their own lives. Happily, that is not Horgan's point of view. As the river is animate and mysterious in the mind of the Pueblo and of many who followed him to its banks, so it is evoked in Horgan's graceful prose. . . .

Four "books" make up the whole of *Great River*. . . . One book is devoted to each of the four peoples who successively dominated the history of the Rio Grande: Pueblos, Spanish, Mexicans and Anglo-Americans. Horgan . . . lends his considerable imaginative power to the task of recreating the quotidian reality of each of those peoples. . . .

In Books III and IV the tempo of the work rapidly accelerates. . . .

The mad pace of events is matched by the extraordinarily high level of excitement sustained by the writing. But there are also interludes of quiet where the rhythm mellows and Horgan continues the practice established in Book I and II of devoting long chapters to the social history of the river's people. . . . The result is as good a digest of the American frontier experience as one may hope to find.

There is one problem. As a tool for further research on the Southwest, *Great River* is not much help. Although the bibliography is marvelously complete . . . , specific sources for material in the text have been omitted in the interest of not "diverting the attention of the reader." Hence frustration. One wishes he had left more tracks (as he did so well in *Lamy of Santa Fe*, in a separate section of "Notes"), yet compared to the immensity of his achievement, that is a niggling complaint. . . .

Great River concludes with some rather awkward commentary on the changes that the present century has brought to the Southwest, but it is not as though Horgan simply runs out of steam. . . .

Horgan ends his history with a kind of mystical optimism and gestures vaguely toward the future. He does not quite seem to know what to make of a civilization that builds Los Alamos and the bomb and that no longer finds itself bound to the life-giving power of the Great River. In that, he is certainly not alone. (p. 32)

> *William deBuys, in* The New Republic *(reprinted by permission of* The New Republic; *© 1976 by The New Republic, Inc.), February 7, 1976.*

Horgan is an excellent craftsman and a skilled delineator of character, large and small; he commands an elegant yet unobtrusive prose in which the events of ["The Thin Mountain Air"] seem embedded, unfolding before the reader almost as if he were watching the action in a *makimono*, a Japanese scroll. If the story, finally, seems to add up to little more than itself (and the pleasure it gives on the way), for Horgan's many admirers this will once more be enough. (p. 36)

> *Ivan Gold, in* The New York Times Book Review *(© 1977 by The New York Times Company; reprinted by permission), September 11, 1977.*

Paul Horgan . . . once complained that contemporary novelists inhabit "the age of the case history," in which style is reduced to fashionable psychological "jargon." Horgan himself prefers unfashionable jargon. In one scene of *The Thin Mountain Air,* he has Richard, the aggressively lyrical adolescent narrator, describe his mother with a reference to "that ageless and formless foreboding which women harbor for those they love."

This is the third "Richard" novel in a series . . . that explores what Horgan has called "the pervasive U.S. fictional theme: leaving boyhood." As in the earlier novels, Richard is burdened with guilt, nostalgia . . . , and an overload of epiphanies. . . .

Ironically, [the novel's] promiscuous "moments" are less compelling than the physical surroundings in which they are set. Horgan's sense of place is as palpable and magical as ever: New Mexico's "immense sweep of light, heat, water, and vision" has considerably more life than its ranch hands, who, as Richard admits, speak "the professional cant of cowboy fiction." Horgan wants us to believe in the "rude lyrical humanity" of these people, but what we *do* believe in is the majestic inhumanity of his mountains, deserts, and skies. (p. 40)

> *Jack Sullivan, in* Saturday Review *(© 1977 by Saturday Review Magazine Corp.; reprinted with permission), September 17, 1977.*

* * *

HUGHES, Ted   1930-

Hughes is an English poet, playwright, editor, and writer of books for children. He is a nature poet in the sense that his poems express, in their descriptions of wildlife and landscape, the brutal savagery of nature. (See also *CLC*, Vols. 2, 4, *Children's Literature Review*, Vol. 3, and *Contemporary Authors*, Vols. 1-4, rev. ed.)

[The] real limitation of Hughes's animal poems is precisely that they conjure emotions without bringing us any nearer to understanding them. They borrow their impact from a complex of emotions that they do nothing to define, and in the end tell us nothing about the urban and civilised human world that we read the poems in. If they reach back, "as in a dream", to a nexus of fear and sensation, this is just the point and the reason why they frequently fail as poetry: one difference between dreams and art is that art deepens our understanding while dreams on their own do not. Larkin's horses are more profound than Hughes's, in fact, because they show us something about the relationship between the horses' world and our own instead of just frightening us with theirs.

Hughes's poetic world is really a prehistoric world of natural violence, where humanity has only the barest fingerhold: when the poems are not about animals they are often about inanimate nature ("October Dawn"), and they give no place to emotions and experience of an essentially human kind. In this sense Hughes is a nature poet, a kind of tough mid-century Blunden (compare their pikes or their Octobers), and makes no serious attempt to face the "full range" of his experience: the experience and emotions that control his poems are frequently those that we share with animals, and these are evoked "as in a dream" more often than they are explored. It would be one thing to write a single poem or two out of this idea, but to make it the domi-

nant theme of an entire output is quite another. When Hughes makes a direct attempt on human experience the result is often catastrophic: when people feature in the poems they serve as occasions for the poet's own cocksure imagination ("Famous Poet", "Vampire") or comfortable romanticising ("A Woman Unconscious") and never imply a real human engagement or any of the self-doubt that this might sometimes carry with it. It is always hard for a poet to write about people, because there is a deep and perpetual antagonism between human individuals and the poetic images through which we attempt to understand them. But this is what gives poetry its work and its justification. With Hughes the victory goes simply and completely to the images . . ., and the result is a cruel absence of compassion and a profound denial of the capacity for growth, love and uniqueness which makes human beings human (and not simply one more species of animal). Hughes's poems are often very fine technically, with sharp detail and imagery and a tense motion perfectly suited to their dramatic content ("Pike", "Esther's Tomcat", especially). . . . But their most important lesson, it seems to me, concerns what can and cannot be done in an idiom which is decreasingly workable and relevant today and which involves, with Hughes at any rate, a lack of any essential commitment to the human world and its conflicts. (pp. 10-12)

> *Colin Falck, in* The Modern Poet: Essays from 'the Review', *edited by Ian Hamilton (© Ian Hamilton), MacDonald, 1968.*

Hughes's desire for language free of any gentility is akin in motive to Baraka's stress on the brutal side of white America's consciousness, and he took intellectual clues from a book on shamanism and from certain interests of Vaska Popa's. But anyone can see how much his earlier poetry, whatever it's *about,* is intimately in search of a language so hard and fierce it will taste of blood. His animal poems in *Lupercal* are concentrations of that search, projections of a sophisticated and even decadent neo-primitivism. When he broke out of their thematic grip, he still kept the same aim of making the intensity of his language, in itself, his symbolic means. "Cadenza" [in *Wodwo*] . . . is perhaps Hughes' most purely lyrical poem despite its violent buffoonery at the very end. It consists of a series of images, proliferating in singing couplets after the one-line opening stanzas, evoked by a violin solo. The images are of death-terror, lost love, and mourning. They make for a dazzling surrealist elegy, and the rhythmic idiom inevitably recalls, because it echoes and summons up their very tone and pitch, the voice and tone of Sylvia Plath's poetry, especially the title-poem of *Ariel.* Her miraculous buoyancy and, simultaneously, her suicidal death-consciousness reverberate in many of the lines and couplets of "Cadenza." (p. 60)

In *Crow,* Hughes tries to suppress that voice which stamped itself into his own spirit even while Sylvia Plath was going through the terrible phase, at once passionate and charged with deadly hatred, defined by the poems in *Ariel.* Husband and wife, as young poets developing together with a definitely reciprocal influence on one another despite their quite individual minds and styles, had shared a desire to be ruthlessly true to their perceptions and to the demands of language. One can actually see, in certain poems of the *Crow* sequence, a continuation of that reciprocity. They present both a fused voice and an ongoing dialogue. Meanwhile, the larger vision of the sequence as a whole pushes toward a kind of negative transcendence, archaic, archetypal, anti-lyrical, and obliterative of personality. The process by which Hughes creates a context for "the plainest and ugliest language" while guiding the interplay of opposites into what he calls "a bit of an epic" makes *Crow* an improvisational structure just as surely as are the superficially more diffuse great American sequences. (pp. 60-1)

Hughes's work . . . is of the same order as some of the most interesting American work of the age. It represents a formal ordering of a kind that the best American poetry has been after for a long time but that British critical hostility has made it difficult for English poets to pursue. Such a triumph is always internationally significant, and the explosive violence in Hughes's poetry seems especially expressive to Americans at this moment. (p. 61)

> *M. L. Rosenthal, in* Salmagundi *(copyright © 1973 by Skidmore College), Spring-Summer, 1973.*

Many of the younger British poets have . . . turned to myth as a vehicle of personal expression. One of the most gifted, Ted Hughes, has invented his own myth in the figure Crow, a primitive creature depicting the human consciousness exposing its own visions of immortality and love as evasions of the ever-present reality of death and the violence of man's history. Crow's world [in *Crow*] is as stark as Beckett's, even closer in its atmosphere of total desolation to that of *Endgame* than *Waiting for Godot,* and he himself, like Beckett's mythical figures, is a composite of unconscious drives and yearnings reacting without order or comprehension to an equally chaotic nature. Reduced even further than Beckett's characters to the level of pure appetite, lust, aggression and rage, Crow, like them, acknowledges both classical and Christian mythical figures, only to interpret their deeds through the perspective of his own narcissism and despair. He consumes them and, stripped of their exalted roles, they become part of his essence. Toward God, his adversary, he is equally violent.

Hughes's various techniques—mock ballads and songs, ritual questions and incantations, direct accounts of battle and carnage that suddenly take on the mad logic of dreams, imitations of the contents and tone of Genesis that conclude in savagery and violence—all expose the deepest layers of consciousness struggling not only to survive the constant threat of extinction, but even to retain its fantasy of power and control. At the end of "Examination at the Womb-Door," having answered a long series of questions with the repeated word "*Death,*" Crow is asked the last one: "But who is stronger than death?" The ambiguity of his reply typifies the distortion of myth which is its essential means of revealing the consciousness that conceived it: "*Me evidently,*" he says, and he has passed the test.

In many of the poems of this volume, Crow's elemental probing, staring, prophesying, struggling and weeping have the effect of genuine mythical narrative, but there are times when he seems more a manifestation of Hughes's self-conscious efforts to establish his creature's unqualified rage as a mythical force than a conveyor of general psychic conflict. This self-consciousness in the use of myth to depict extreme possibilities of mental experience occurs in much of contemporary poetry. (p. 13)

> *Lillian Feder, in* Books Abroad *(copyright 1974 by the University of Oklahoma Press), Vol. 48, No. 1, Winter, 1974.*

[Ted Hughes's *Selected Poems 1957-67*] is scarcely the occasion for thorough revaluation of his work, but one may hazard a few thoughts after reading this selection of pre-*Crow* poems. . . . [Enough] individual poems can be found in *The Hawk and the Rain* and *Lupercal* "The Thought-Fox," "The Horses," "Wind," "Meeting," the fine "October Dawn," and the even more impressive "November," "Thrushes," and "Pike"—to support an account of Hughes as an authentic minor poet. Most of these display, in addition to the natural forces encountered, an "I" that encounters them with piety, fostered alike by beauty and by fear. Such respect is felt strongly within the speaking voice's rhythms of presentation—not in dramatic shifts of tone . . . but in the sure grip and force of assertion. . . . (p. 229)

But what would he do when he ran out of animals, went the joke. The answer was to let Crow stand for everything in the universe that isn't mind or soul, then write increasingly simplified "cartoon"-like poems in which you assume the voice of God and don't stay for question or answer. . . . [We] look to the poet to provide us with more complex, various, and interesting versions of experience than we ourselves can come up with. Hughes seems to me humanly deficient in his vision of things. . . . For me . . . [*Crow* is a disaster]: the humanly tentative, relatively flexible moments of seeing in the earlier books are no more; the poetry is now sensationalistic, bloody but unsustaining. And there looks like more coming—his latest sequence is called "Cave Birds."

I am also aware that Hughes's progress could be seen quite otherwise. . . . But the performance of *Crow* is of the sort that polarizes readers into comparably cartoon-like extremities of posture; so it is good to have this selection remind us that it was not ever or always thus in Hughes's organized violence upon language. (pp. 230-31)

> *William H. Pritchard, in* Parnassus: Poetry in Review *(copyright © by* Parnassus: Poetry in Review*), Spring–Summer, 1976.*

Hardly any of criticism's established systems of value, most of which are one way or the other neoplatonic, prove adequate for dealing with Ted Hughes's poetry, either as frames or as starting points. More obsessively than Lawrence, Hughes demands that we forget everything, moral value included (and moral and intellectual temporizing especially), in order to perceive the extent to which our assumptions about the nature of existence are crude illusions of perspective, innocent epistemologies based upon fastidiously selective habits of perception. Even to say that is to imply a conventional humanistic agenda which Hughes appears to have moved beyond. In fact he has divested romanticism of all its notions of sentimental humanistic utility, and it seems to me that this represents a quantum progression even beyond Lawrence. . . . Hughes is nothing if not committed, and he goes his way, pressing toward apocalypse this century's hardened antihumanistic pessimism.

It is not an accident that his poems are unpeopled, and it seems unlikely that he will one day cast off his shaman's raiment and disclose himself to have been R. D. Laing in disguise. There are reassuringly lyrical moments, most recently in *Season Songs,* but even Hughes's lyricism is gothic and is motivated chiefly by weather and beasts and stones. . . . The question that he . . . [broods] over is whether achieving it is worth the cost, even where existence without it is worth less. Like Beckett, Hughes has the forbearance, and the cynical distrust of mere aesthetic form, to leave the question unresolved.

The mode of being which clearly is not worth living is the effect of the enlightenment extended into our time: vital relationships suppressed at all levels of experience by the rule of intellect. . . . For Hughes it would seem that the modern predicament is an effect . . . of our powers of sympathy having gone awry, become abstract rather than affective, so that in denying "essential human subjectivity" in the interest of protecting others from ourselves, we have ceased to be selves at all and have broken off our continuity with the forces of nature, which are by definition brutal. (pp. xciii-xciv)

It seems inevitable that Hughes will be intelligible mainly to the St. Georges of the world and that his energies, like Blake's, will in the end be harnessed to serve rationalism's vested interests. Perhaps the nearest thing to revelation we can hope for now is that occasionally a modern reader will look up from a volume of Hughes's poems onto a cold geometry of architectural glass and prestressed concrete and feel momentarily insecure—or perhaps, glumly, very much like a clockwork orange. (p. xcvi)

Vereen Bell, in Sewanee Review *(reprinted by permission of the editor,* © *1976 by The University of the South), Summer, 1976.*

The Anglican Reverend Nicholas Lumb has a surprising way with him. It seems

He is starting Christianity all over again, right from the start.
He has persuaded all the women in the parish.
Only women can belong to it.
They are all in it and he makes love to them all, all the time.
Because a saviour
Is to be born in this village, and Mr. Lumb is to be the earthly father.

He is eventually killed by outraged husbands after a quasi-theoriomorphic ritual orgy which goes murderously wrong.

The whole plot of this long narrative poem is not quite so simply hilarious. Lumb is some sort of duplicate of Lumb from "the other world"—the substitution is effected in a nightmarish prologue. The real Reverend Lumb stands up at the end on the west coast of Ireland and leaves a notebook of opaque poems on a rock—and these form the conclusion of *Gaudete.* Yes, the whole as a whole is perplexing. "Poets in our civilization . . . must be *difficult.*"

But the central action is splendid, available, and generally fine writing. It would be tempting to recommend starting a first reading here but for the fact that the mysterious and bloody prologue (whatever its ultimate point) productively complicates one's response to the clear people, clear events and potential humour of much of what ensues. It causes the action to be attended by a continuous and disturbing ambiguity.

Form and technique are fascinating. The poem we are told was originally intended as a film scenario. It is comprehensible that Ted Hughes might try one. He has that sure poetic instinct that heads implacably for the particular instances rather than ideas or abstraction; he has an especial talent for evoking the *visual* particular; he has an avowed belief in the inability of words to match experience. . . .

Thoughts and conscience take the shape of visualized fantasies and dreams. The story-line picks its way from picture to picture. We follow (for example) a woman moving from room to room, we focus on a drop of water on a tap, on mirrors, a conifer through the window, an orange vase . . .; "she stares towards her husband's medical reference library, to numb herself on its dull morocco". . . .

Poetical narrative is borrowing cinema's distinct method of narrative: cinema's method of switching scene and "point of view", cinema's method of suggestive particularizing, cinema's method of getting across action, thought and emotion.

It might not have worked (Antonioni's scripts incidentally make uproariously awful reading). But Ted Hughes has produced a strange bastard form that does work, often brilliantly. It works not simply because he is a fine writer. It is because he has such an acute sense of the suggestive power of specific visual images and the ability to evoke them in words. . . . *Gaudete* is obviously a very different work from Hughes's other poetry, but it indulges one of his most familiar talents. It ranks I think with *The Hawk in the Wind* or *Lupercal* (high praise)—though I must admit to preferring the earlier work. . . .

Like all good writers Ted Hughes has good qualities vulnerable to caricature; and like all good writers he occasionally caricatures himself. His style characteristically involves wonderfully violent bombardments of basic words. But these can tend towards overkill, to excessive agglomeration and unproductive mixed metaphor. . . .

If a tendency towards an occasional self-defeating extravagance be admitted, his own theoretical pronouncements supply a clue to the cause. Hughes has a strong sense that words cannot match what one actually feels and sees. In *Words and Experience,* for example, he writes as follows: "There are no words to capture the infinite depth of crowiness in the crow's flight. All we can do is to use a word as an indicator, or a whole bunch of words as a general directive. . . . And a bookload of such descriptions is immediately rubbish when you look up and see the crow flying." So we get our bunches of sometimes despairing and ineffectual words—he tries too hard. But not often: mostly his work belies his own pessimism. And (more important) Ted Hughes can do more than reproduce experience. The theorizing mentioned above suggests a rather cramping view of the relationship of art to life; but luckily his poetry in general does not. Art can imitate the form, art can be better than life.

Oliver Lyne, "The Lecherous Reverend Lumb," in The Times Literary Supplement *(© Times Newspapers Ltd., 1977; reproduced from* The Times Literary Supplement *by permission), July 1, 1977, p. 800.*

[The] narrative poetry of Ted Hughes . . . seems with each book to grow more rigidly violent in matter and style.

Though the first few pages [of "Gaudete"] present a Mithraic baptism in which live bulls are disemboweled above the spread-eagled victim of a ritual flagellation, the violence of expression exceeds that of incident.

A radio "squirts out a sizzle of music," while bees at apple blossoms are "groping and clambering into the hot interiors of the blood and milk clots." When a lady is excited, "a lump of boiling electricity swells under her chest"; later, a man hears his daughter, pregnant by Lumb, playing piano: "Her hands seemed to be plunging and tossing inside his chest." Even the foundation garments are done in hot purple: "the hot silken frailties, the giant, gristled power, the archaic sea-fruit inside her, which her girdle bites into."

From such hysteria there is nowhere to go; so, when Lumb sees that an entire street has become a mass grave, he is "too astonished to speak," a characteristic, excruciating anticlimax. "Powerful," chime the reviewers' blurbs, and Hughes courts the adjective with bloody persistence. His language and characters both resemble ponderous items of antique military engineering, futile rams and engines, so manically overbuilt for power that they cannot budge: fantastic artifacts of peacetime generals.

Such writing is bad not because it tries to make violence seem erotic, stimulating, morally "powerful," but because it makes violence and eroticism both seem merely literary and boring. In fairness to "the most powerful and original voice in English poetry today" (according to the London Times Educational Supplement), I should say that the book has to do with dark ritual truths, the prime core of the abnormal. . . . So, for some readers the violence may be justified by deeper rewards; but as for me, I can't find anything under all that ketchup except baloney. (pp. 4-5)

> *Robert Pinsky, in* The New York Times Book Review *(© 1977 by The New York Times Company; reprinted by permission), December 25, 1977.*

In his continuing examination of violence and its role in the world, Hughes does not choose sides for or against the forces that are set in opposition to each other, except in a few particular situations. For the most part, violence is an accepted fact of life that exists as the connecting link between all creatures in the history of the earth from prehistoric times to contemporary England. . . . Again and again Hughes stresses the subtle connection in the primitive drives of the wind, the jaguar, the soldier, of all creation. . . . [The] animal world is used by Hughes as a means of gaining greater insights into the human world. (pp. 92-3)

Hughes does begin with the assumption that violence is an inherent element of all being, but this does not involve the glorification or propagation of violence through his poetry. Instead, Hughes sees that because the mainstream of twentieth-century thought, modern liberalism, has been unwilling to admit that man's nature in some way partakes of a primitive violence, man has become unable to cope with this element in his world. Like other elements of life, says Hughes, violence *in vacuo* is morally neutral and only takes on qualities of good and evil from its social and historical environment. (p. 93)

[Hughes's] speaker is more often a created persona than the voice of the poet. Another technique that effectively removes both reader and poet to a distance from the poem is the choice of the animal world for symbols of primitive violence and force. Ironically, by shielding himself in these ways from charges of insensitivity, Hughes opened himself up to criticism from another source. His detachment has been interpreted as a rejection of compassion and involvement with human affairs. . . . Such criticism ultimately falls short of coming to terms with the poetry. The elements that Hughes employs to gain detachment were used by Donne and Milton, by Eliot and Yeats. Detachment implies neither insensitivity nor disengagement. (p. 94)

[His] continual accents upon large and complex patterns of behavior give his poetry a sense of . . . depth. Primitive myth and symbol are integral elements of his poetry, as seen in the titles of two of his volumes: *Lupercal* and *Wodwo*. His later volume, *Crow*, shows Hughes moving more consciously in this direction. The crow is a frequent figure representing discord and strife in folk iconography. He is called the Great Crow or Crow Father in both Eskimo legends and in American Indian myths. While the effect is closer to the mythmaking of Yeats or the restructuring of myths by Lawrence, the technique is nearer to Hardy's in *The Dynasts,* where the reader is shown the forces of the world at work, moving both through and beyond the limitations of man. (p. 95)

His primary concern is with violence as a primitive force that is invested in every form of life. It is here that his tone of assertion is present, for the one dominant theme that emerges throughout his poetry is that this mythic violent force is inherent in the very essence of being, from the wind and rocks to humankind. The basic conflict in life revolves on man's attempt to deal with these forces, which on the one hand are subhuman but by that very token are beyond man's capability to subdue. Man must come to terms with this element in his nature, not through suppression or escape (both of which are impossible), but through accommodation. In a sense this demands a Lawrentian "lapsing-out," for man's consciousness and intellect are the basic obstacles to a successful accommodation. Hughes sees the intellect's indulgence in the life of violence as a perversion of the primitive instinct for violence that still persists in the animal world. It is at this point that the poet shows regret for what he sees to be lacking in the modern expression of violence. Violence in nature is actually a positive force, but when man imposes the intellect upon it, he makes it into something destructive. Under these conditions Hughes becomes an apostle against violence. But he emphasizes the distinction and points to the source of the pollution. His emphasis is finally positive, with the assertion that man must commit himself to life in spite of what he might consider the destructive consequences of violence upon life. (p. 96)

What we notice in [the] earlier poems that tell of violence in the natural world is a direct, sincere voice, the voice of an observer who knows that his detached descriptions are sufficiently effective for his purpose. But the poems in *Crow,* having as their subject a mythical force rather than an actual animal, take on a cynical tone that is echoed in the bitter laughter heard in many of the poems. The poet's vision has crystallized and unified, and the certainty with which he now approaches his theme demands a unique strength. (p. 97)

His response [to violence] tends to be analytical rather than emotional, and he is more interested in the nature of the violence than in man's reaction to it. The poetry of Hughes is not of the immediate historical moment and as a result is not in . . . danger . . . of becoming dated. (p. 99)

Man is the creature who has been excluded from the violence of nature, for his violence is no longer instinctual but planned and intellectualized. Recognizing this rift between the two worlds of violence, Hughes in poem after poem sets out mental scouting parties that explore the forms of violence that still link man to the other world: birth, sex, war, and death. He sees these experiences as means for man to reestablish his connections with his primitive origins. (p. 101)

Crag Jack is a symbol of all men who have lost identity with their violent origins and who have partial insights into their unconscious instincts. Hughes is frequently preoccupied with examining these insights, always asking if it is possible, after birth and childhood, to make some kind of accommodation with the violence in his nature. This search provides much of the tension in his poetry, for the release that he expects to come from indulging the instincts (in sex, in war) is usually frustrated by the very fact that his characters are human. He never advocates the abandonment of humanity in pursuit of one's instincts, and his characters often find it impossible to straddle the civilized and the instinctual worlds.

One of the connectors that he examines is the sexual union, and the poet's response is typical of the philosophical dilemma in which he frequently finds himself. The sexual act, we might expect, should be represented in his poetry as a viable connection with the instinctual world. But Hughes is above all honest, and love and sex are seldom positive forces in his work. Rather it is man's inability to be both man and animal at the same time that dooms the sexual response. For in accommodating oneself to his sexual instincts, he submits to a primitive and thoroughly selfish impulse, or, by avoiding them, he is drawn into ugly repressions. (p. 102)

There is constant tension and confrontation between man's intelligence and the powers represented by Crow. Hughes sees one of man's basic failings to be his continuous effort to objectify "evil," or in Crow's amoral world, the black forces. "Crow's Account of St. George" is one of the most horrifying poems about human relationships in our language. It begins with the premise that man is misdirected in attempting to see a logical order in the universe:

> He sees everything in the Universe
> Is a track of numbers racing towards an answer.

Because of this orderly universe, he is led to believe he can control and master those elements that he finds hostile. . . . The mistake soon becomes evident; by projecting the evil outside man, it remains undetected as it grows within and around him. Once he begins to search out evil, he encounters it everywhere—the blackness is omnipresent. (p. 109)

Because man has become isolated from what Hughes sees as his true nature, the poet offers for a solution an accommodation with his violent nature that depends upon his ability to fuse the intellectual and instinctual. All attempts to overcome the outbreaks of violence from below result either in defeat for the human element ("Two Wise Generals") or at best in a standstill that promises continuing struggle in the future "Thistles"). Since there seems to be

no danger of man's abandoning intellect and consciousness, Hughes directs his attention to an accommodation that man must make with the instinctual part of his nature. In the effort to achieve this balance, he must abandon himself to or at least consent to the violent forces within him and accept his consciousness not as a help in this matter but as a burden. He seeks a way to relieve the tensions of poems like "Secretary" and "Incompatibilities," tensions that frequently result in unresolved frustrations. He recognizes the validity of submitting to the destructive element, while at the same time realizing the necessity of emerging as a whole human being. Two sides of this essential problem are explored in the title poems of *The Hawk in the Rain* and *Wodwo*. The former shows the man caught between the two forces and unable to resolve the tension; the latter depicts a symbolic accommodation that releases this tension. (p. 110)

The thrust of violence can be positive or negative; in "The Martyrdom of Bishop Farrar" the poet's metaphysical concern with violence finds a workable metaphor that stresses the revitalizing powers of violent action. . . . Preaching a lesson of man's basic brutality and the necessity for accommodation with this part of one's nature, [the poet] must necessarily come into conflict with traditional social values. But his success as poet does not rest in his retreat from violence but in exploring this as his theme. The poet finds greater credibility among his readers not in avoiding this issue (like the neohumanists) but in pursuing the study of violence in man's nature. Those who try to frighten people away from violence are leading people astray: "An ignorant means to establish ownership / Of his flock!"

Those who try to escape the implications of living in a violent world are generally shown to be failures. Man may attempt to substitute wisdom, shrewdness, ideals of brotherhood, for the forces of his violent nature, but his attempts prove futile. (pp. 115-16)

Frustration seems to be the tone of a number of poems illustrating the theme of man's destructive nature, the frustration being barely controlled by a poet who feels his audience does not dare to listen to him. "Criminal Ballad" presents the education of what Hughes would consider the romantic humanist, the man who insists on defending his vision of a happy world. But as he vigorously protests the beauty of the world, this very act bloodies his hands, marks his participation in the destructive acts he struggled against. His initial response is to weep for the loss of his imagined world, until he realizes that the real world is absurd and cruel, and nothing he will do can change it; so "he began to laugh." This is a difficult lesson to have set before us, but Hughes insists that we face the situation nakedly. In this sense, his poetry becomes a rending of the veil, the veil of illusion that allows us to remain in happy contact with nature, with our fellow men, with ourselves. Any attempt to alter this reality, or any effort to contend with the dark forces is futile and ridiculous—the traditional concept of the mythic hero who might come to destroy the black force and make the world safe for mankind is absurd. "The Contender" who devotes his life to this crusade has in the end only "his senseless trial of strength" as his reward. (p. 118)

Although Hughes sees the attempted escape from violence as an escape from life, and the intellectual's circumvention as a sign of weakness and ineffectual temporizing, he never assumes an assertive stance that indiscriminately approves of all violent acts. Hughes seldom creates circumstances that lend themselves to a strong criticism of violence, but there are several striking poems in which this occurs. From these poems we understand what he finds offensive in the modern expression of violence and how he feels an essentially healthy instinct has been perverted in modern history.

His basic complaint is that modern violence has ceased to be a function of those instinctive urgings that he writes about in most of his poetry. "The Ancient Heroes and the Bomber Pilot" contrasts ancient and modern wielders of violence, stressing that what is lacking in the pilot is the sense of personal self-expression in his acts so that they become totally destructive both in reference to himself and to his victims. The ancient heroes on the other hand found healthy expression in their violent acts. . . . The bomber pilot . . . is a highly sophisticated instrument of war, trained to kill by command, not from need or desire. Contrasting his own actions and motives with his ancient counterparts, he is mortified: "The grandeur of their wars humbles my thought." (pp. 122-23)

Nor is man greatly concerned with individual suffering and violence. In "A Woman Unconscious" man's modern consciousness is preoccupied with universal destruction, which is a substitute for his concern with private tragedy. It is no longer a question of one warrior fighting another. . . . The bomber pilot could make the enemy capital "jump to a fume," but he would be insensible to the suffering of the thousands burned alive. Hughes seriously challenges this loss of values in an atomic age, and cries out with more immediate passion than is usual in his poetry. . . . (pp. 123-24)

While registering the frustration, the despair, and the moral indignation [aroused by contemporary society], Hughes never retreats from what the majority of his poems describe as man's commitment to life, his association with primitive nature. His final accents are positive, for Hughes asserts that the human spirit, not only in spite of the violence of its nature, but also because of it, must always turn towards life, never away from life.

Hughes quite clearly expresses this part of his philosophy in a short three-stanza poem that is almost lost in the middle of *The Hawk in the Rain:* "Invitation to the Dance." This is an extremely important poem in a discussion of Hughes's attitude towards violence, for while acknowledging that the essence of life is touched with violence and brutality, it asserts that these elements should not deter us from committing ourselves to a full and active participation in life. (pp. 125-26)

The ultimate value of Hughes might be [that he had] the strength to stand up and endure in the face of violence. . . . [He] fulfills that famous prescription of Faulkner: "The poet's voice need not merely be the record of man, it can be one of the props, the pillars to help him endure and prevail." (p. 127)

His ability to involve himself with violence and to handle it with an exciting poetic technique distinguishes him from those contemporaries who retreat to the security of safe traditional technique and conventional minor themes. (p. 129)

Lawrence R. Ries, "Ted Hughes: Acceptance and Accommodation," in his Wolf Masks: Violence in Contemporary Poetry *(copyright © 1977 by Kennikat Press Corp.; reprinted by permission of Kennikat Press Corp.), Kennikat, 1977, pp. 92-129.*

I

IONESCO, Eugène   1912-

French dramatist Ionesco is a leading figure in European avant-garde theater. His work reveals his obsession with the absurdity of life, of death, and even of the play itself, creating the "anti-play." Ionesco's plays are typically humorous on the surface, but have dark undercurrents of horror beneath. A common theme is man's alienation and the difficulty of communication. His characters speak in ridiculous clichés and fragments, creating what Ionesco calls "a theatre of violence—violently comic, violently dramatic," a surreal caricature of life. (See also *CLC***, Vols. 1, 4, 6, and** *Contemporary Authors***, Vols. 9-12, rev. ed.)**

Both early and late in Eugène Ionesco's drama occur aspects of the comic that were analyzed by Henri Bergson in his classic study *Le Rire*. . . . Specifically, I refer to Ionesco's *Le Piéton de l'air,* for its hero is his only one, the Bérenger of *Rhinocéros, Tueur sans gages,* and *Le Roi se meurt.* In the first two plays of the cycle, Bérenger is the special person, the unique individual. In *Rhinocéros,* he is the only person who does not become an animal, who does not conform. Briefly he thinks perhaps the others are right, but soon he discovers that he wishes to remain human. . . . In *Tueur sans gages,* Bérenger is the most innocent, the best, the purest person, who initially believes the Architect in the City of Light and who tries to reason with the Murderer at the end. Bérenger is the human being capable of thought, and it is his tragedy that the world is not what it should be. Trying by logic to talk the killer out of murder is fruitless; appealing to ethics or humanity in today's world is pointless, suggests Ionesco, at least in that pessimistic play. Bérenger is out of place, but tragically, not comically. (pp. 297-98)

Ionesco admits that, as with the theatre of Feydeau, his own plays, *Les Chaises* and *Le Nouveau locataire,* show a mechanism gone awry and adds that in *La Leçon,* this phenomenon, centering on language, leads to the tragic. (p. 301)

The setting for *Le Piéton de l'air* is a dreamy landscape replete with a fanciful cottage; the scene itself is Bergsonian, for the philosopher once described the relationship between comedy and dreams as one in which both share a dislocation of logic. Into this setting comes a naughty little boy who hits two old ladies with a ball. His parents repeat profuse excuses that the child is loath to make and then repeat a series of compliments to the parents of a well-behaved little girl. "Madame" and "Monsieur" and a series of "Sorry, sorry" speeches are pronounced by the four English parents. The stress on the nationality recalls *La Cantatrice chauve*. Like automatons the two old ladies, also very British, cry, "Oh! quel vilain petit garçon!" when he thumbs his nose at his unobservant parents. The inadvertent, the absent-minded, and the distracted are subjects of comedy, according to Bergson . . . , and one can laugh at the child's parents without taking the boy's rudeness seriously.

In the stage directions and dialogue between Ionesco's hero and an interviewer occur two other devices discussed by Bergson: the play on words, in which two similar sounds recur with variations, and the celebrated Jack-in-the-box. . . . After they both repeat singular and plural versions of *question*(s), Ionesco establishes the ridiculous variant "journal-journaliste" and the excuse that a paper has nothing to do with reporters, all of this dialogue punctuated by the reappearing and disappearing head of the hero. . . . And a little later, when Bérenger confesses he has realized he "had no reason to write," the newspaperman picks up the words and twists them in a funny and timely way, into a spoof of metaphysical anguish. . . . (pp. 301-03)

Still playing tricks with language, this passage leads Bérenger into explaining his difficult choice between nihilism and existentialist action. According to Bergson's distinction between the humorous and the witty, wit makes us laugh at a third party or at ourselves and thus gives an added dimension to the comic. . . . By that definition, Ionesco's dialogue in [this] scene . . . is, then, not only humorous but witty, for the parody is directed at Sartre's philosophical discourse. It is significant too that Bergson counts professional jargon as material suitable for exploitation by comic dramatists. . . . Bérenger talks inflatedly of renewing himself internally, of the course of events, and of the relationship between neurosis and truth. As Bergson says, making small things big and deflating great issues are satirical techniques. . . . (p. 303)

Still another Bergsonian example of comic absurdity is the reduction of the sublime or divine to the ridiculous or mundane, spirit debased to matter. . . . In *Le Piéton de l'air,* the silly reporter assures Bérenger of a sizable check for his philosophical musings, in return for the anguish he has voiced aloud, cheapened, popularized, publicized. . . . Perhaps the effect produced on the spectator is a twisted smile as he recognizes the irony of Bérenger's situation.

If treating big issues as trivial produces *le rire jaune,* the reverse contributes to heartier laughter. Bergson noted that attention to small details rather than momentous matters makes us laugh because there is a disproportion between the cause and the effect. This contrast is successfully exploited by Ionesco when Joséphine regrets the premature announcement of her father's funeral ceremonies and decides to send out [an "announcement of the resurrection"]. Actually more is involved here. Not only is it silly to worry about announcements, but to juxtapose such a powerful, theologically-charged word as "résurrection" with "announcement" accentuates the lack of proportion. The event of magnitude—life rather than death—is reduced to the trivialities of printing and mailing; the holy is denigrated to the worldly. Rebirth phrased in Christian terms is cheapened to the physical—to ink and paper. So too Bergson notes that the mood is lightened whenever attention is called away from the spirit to the body, from the mental to the physical.

Bergson's theories are explicitly recalled when one reads Ionesco's stage directions describing John Bull "comme une énorme marionnette" [like a large puppet], slowly taking off his hat, wiping away perspiration both in it and on his forehead, putting back the handkerchief, then donning the hat again, "*turning slowly toward the public,*" and after this series of gestures, standing with his legs apart, arms behind his back. . . . By his very name, John Bull is allegorical or caricatural; by his movements he is less than human and therefore capable of eliciting laughter.

Automatism recurs shortly thereafter as the little English girl starts to sing, really to utter "*des trilles, exactement comme ceux d'un petit rossignol mécanique*" [trills exactly like those of a little mechanical nightingale]. . . . These trills are repeated several times by all the English people, and the mechanical musical display is paralleled by a visual one, while the English fathers merely smile. Normally a person smiles because, spontaneously and thus without coaching, he finds something pretty or amusing. When a smile is natural, it is delightful; when artificial, it is laughable rather than lovable. (pp. 304–05)

Although Ionesco's use of repetition [in one scene] provokes a comic response, his similar practice has a different outcome in [another scene]. Bérenger, his wife Joséphine, and their daughter Marthe, left to their French selves, repeat a number of phrases in lyrical, oneiric vein. They speak of turning around, rejoicing, holding hands without thought or worry, looking at the trains that pass like toys. But as they do not repeat verbatim, they do not seem like automatons. . . . Rather they are human beings. . . . (p. 305)

Ionesco is not writing to a thesis, however, and for that reason does not limit his sympathetic characters to one lofty type: the spiritual, imaginative, and intuitive. Bérenger has all these qualities, but Joséphine is very likable even though she is more of a rationalist than either her husband or daughter. In fact Joséphine hopes Bérenger will return to writings couched in clearer (i.e., duller) prose. She is more fully aware than he of space and time. She wants factual answers to questions about columns and nothingness; she says quite honestly whether something is visible to her, whether it seems impractical or wonderful or strange.

Because Joséphine lacks hypocrisy and possesses a refreshing frankness, she must be ranked with the other sympathetic characters, her husband and child. Despite her complaints, she does not resemble the Madeleine of *Amédée.* (p. 306)

At the same time, because Joséphine does display a diminished sensitivity in comparison with her loved ones, she is a pivotal figure in Ionesco's play, who occupies an intermediate point between her family and the automatons. Furthermore she provides Bérenger and Marthe with the opportunity to expound their visions of the marvelous. Joséphine is quizzical and skeptical yet receptive to those explanations which stand up to the scrutiny of sense and the senses. When the column and the tree alternately appear and disappear, the couple discuss nothingness, will power, and the divine intoxication of a certitude that life is beautiful. As a person Joséphine requires precision of thought and Cartesian proof, but her love for Bérenger permits her to accept the possibility that he may be right. She would prefer to base life's beauty on oxygen and reason but sees, like her daughter, a shining bridge of silver and calls out therefore to Bérenger her approval of his views. (p. 307)

When Bérenger returns in the nick of time, he describes the Apocalypse, the end of the world in flames, the guillotined people, and the whipped victims. . . . The English automatons lose interest . . . when he speaks of "Mud, fire, blood." . . . He knows all is Nothingness . . . , but of what interest is that to machines? From beginning to end of Ionesco's strikingly theatrical *Le Piéton de l'air,* the puppets contrast with the human, the dullards with the dreamers. These disparate elements fuse and blend comically to lighten the spectator's metaphysical anguish through the use of the very devices that Henri Bergson analyzed. The value of the play lies precisely in its comic aspects. . . . (p. 309)

[This] play is not metaphysical but comic and, just as Bergson described that genre, social in nature, using satirical and farcical techniques. . . . Bergson . . . was right about inversion, for the topsy-turvy does makes us laugh. . . . *Le Piéton de l'air* is not a parody, bitter like Adamov's *La Grande et la petite manoeuvre,* but an outright *féerie.* Rather than representing the mixed genres of Ionesco's absurdist plays and even his later ones, *Le Piéton de l'air* is pure fantasy and laughter. Even the apocalypse reported by Bérenger does not destroy the underlying mood of the comic. After all, such masters as Molière and Shaw allowed serious thoughts to enter their theatre without writing tragedy or philosophy. No bow to these latter dramatic categories is in order, so much as is a curtain call for Henri Bergson. (p. 310)

Charlotte F. Gerrard, "Bergsonian Elements in Ionesco's 'Le Pieton de l'air'," in Papers on Language and Literature *(copyright © 1973 by the Board of Trustees, Southern Illinois University at Edwardsville), Summer, 1973, pp. 297-310.*

L'Homme aux valises is a dream play. As such it is projected out of linearity onto the vertiginous spiral of the time/ space continuum. This does not mean, however, that the atmosphere is unreal, vaguely symbolist; on the contrary, it is characterized by that peculiar sharpness and vividness of detail which is inherent to the dream state. In the latter, we are not surprised to meet our ancestors and talk with them as though they were contemporaries, and we can be at the same instant in Paris and Venice simply because Paris is Venice and Venice Paris. As Jung explains: "Dreams . . . are the facts from which we must proceed."

Ionesco, who is deeply indebted to Jungian analysis, is aware that he is working with archetypes. In this play, however, he is conscious of dealing with what he calls "cultural archetypes." (p. 21)

The man carrying luggage is an eloquent symbol for the state of estrangement and spiritual exile which characterizes contemporary man. To wander aimlessly, to be exiled and self-exiled, to lose one's roots, one's papers, one's name and identity, such is our lot. We are all men without shadows. . . . L'Homme . . . is never given a name so that he is both Everyman and NoMan, the latter being the way in which Odysseus identifies himself to the Cyclops. . . . (pp. 23-4)

The protagonist of *L'Homme aux valises* is doomed to travel through [wars, revolutions, and catastrophes] in search of his personal and ancestral past. (p. 24)

If one of André Breton's noble obsessions was the creation of "the dream-text," then it can be said that in *L'Homme aux valises* Ionesco pursues his self-declared program of creating an oneiric universe upon the stage. Like the Surrealists who were his masters Ionesco believes that an interpenetration occurs between the conscious day life and the subconscious night existence, for dreams contain fragments of the day's impressions, and the latter are encrusted with bits and pieces severed from the psyche's intense activity in its nightly revels. To use one of Breton's own titles, the two modes of apprehension must be viewed as "des vases communicants." (pp. 24-5)

Two themes constitute the leitmotivs of Ionesco's *L'Homme aux valises:* the loss of one's identity, and the hope of survival on the very brink of dissolution. (p. 29)

L'Homme aux valises is an attempt to dramatize the search for the presentness of life, such as it was experienced at the Mill, with its seasons "spread out in space." Even Baudelaire, Ionesco's favorite poet, could not persuade the dramatist that "this world is a hospital where everyone is possessed by the desire of exchanging his bed." (p. 33)

L'Homme aux valises ends with a fête, a particularly threatening one, at once a child's vision of post-war Paris, and an intimate sexual fantasy. (pp. 33-4)

The final image of this play is that of l'Homme sitting on one of his valises in the midst of a busy throng. Suddenly everyone of the dancers turns into a traveler, each carrying one suitcase. They seem terribly busy as they rush from one side of the stage to the other. Some begin to pile up their luggage around the protagonist who does not move, watching this hustle and bustle with a bemused smile. An Ionesco-logue is reminded of the end of *Le nouveau locataire,* with the tenant literally buried under the pile of furniture carried up by the movers. Here, however, the familiar mechanism of proliferation, one of Ionesco's favorite devices, is used to a different end. The sudden immobility of l'Homme does not suggest death as much as a state of contemplation. It is as though, after much searching and running, the protagonist had at last reached the center of the mandala, and this only as a result of his

final renunciation, his transcendence of desire. The suitcases carried by the others symbolize their life. Some are still rushing headlong, others set down their existence at the feet of the sage. He watches, at once *solitaire* and *solidaire* like Camus' Jonas. It is a splendid image of the artist as the eternal Adam. . . . [This is] the ultimate metaphysical image, that of Man as inveterate dreamer, and by this very fact, perfect mediator. As Wandering Jew, he brings to his fellow-creatures the wisdom of centuries of suffering, and the knowledge that comes from a refusal to be committed to the transitory. To be truly present to oneself, and to others, one must be of No Place and of Every Place, to be No Man and Everyman. Only then can one found relations based on mutual reverence for the spirit, though it be assigned to this grotesque and vulnerable dwelling, mortal flesh. As Ionesco declared in the course of an unpublished lecture delivered in March 1976: "The reason for writing is to cast up to heaven our cry of anguish, and to let other men know that we have existed." (pp. 34-5)

Rosette Lamont, " 'L'Homme aux valises':
Ionesco's Absolute Stranger," in Performing Arts Journal *(copyright © 1976 Performing Arts Journal), Fall, 1976, pp. 21-35.*

No one familiar with their work would seriously ask whether Beckett or Ionesco belonged by rights in the liberal or radical or conservative camp. Such loose, time-worn labels do not fit their case. Their productions clearly show that their envisagement of the human condition transcends the values and the motives implicit in the vocabulary of politics that move men to act. Ionesco's plays, for example, point up the futility of all human striving. His characters find it impossible to justify their existence. His metaphysical drama of the absurd "reveals existence as having no reason to exist and the unjustified as existing in superabundance. In short, the world is superfluous." Ionesco's plays breathe a spirit of utter disillusionment with all terrestrial affairs. They entertain no possibility of hope through the agency of politics and sound no evangel of redemption. (pp. 186-87)

Though he admires Breton, Ionesco is no Surrealist. He belongs, in fact, to no school. It is not likely that a genuine believer in the absurd will be a follower of some literary movement. The literature of the absurd is, by definition, *sui generis.* Unlike Surrealism, it does not surrender the principle of control or deny the need for form. Spontaneity is essential, but the energy that streams forth from the cornucopia of the unconscious must be expressed with lucidity. The work of art, be it Surrealist or absurdist in inspiration, calls for selectivity, the imposition of order and form.

Apolitical in his *Weltanschauung,* Ionesco is not the type of writer who can be dragooned into espousing a set of abstract ideas, noble causes, utopian projects. He will not march in military formation in the ranks of the Left or the Right. . . . He has no intention of converting the theater into a political forum, a sounding board for ideologies. He despises both the formal theater and the theater of ideas. Realism, especially Socialist realism, furnishes only a truncated, impoverished version of reality. He believes in the truth revealed by the heart of desire, the truth of dreams. In his diatribe against the theater of ideas and the thesis drama, he warns of the danger of allowing the theater to be perverted to political ends. Though he does not deny that all drama is "social" in content, this is not tantamount to saying that it must be Socialist in its orientation. The art of the drama at its best gives expression to moments of luminous insight, intuitions and epiphanies that reach far beyond the temporal plane or the exigencies of the historical situation. (pp. 187-88)

Ionesco is intransigent in his opposition to the politically committed theater. He draws an important distinction between being "social" and being politically partisan. He is no admirer of Brecht's propagandistic plays or his gallery of exemplary "heroes." Ionesco proceeds to unmask the true character of "Brechtian man," who is one-dimensional. The politically committed playwright furnishes a distorted and fundamentally false picture of a given historical period because his ideology restricts his field of vision. This is the purblindness common to ideologists and people "stunted by fanaticism." Metaphysical in his perception of "realities" that transcend the categories of time and the pleasures of history, Ionesco seeks to capture intimations of the universal. The great plays of the past convey this sense of the inevitability of death. Empires perish, kings are hurled from their thrones. Nothing endures. It is this haunting, inescapable experience of mortality, when contrasted with man's obdurate and irrational longing for eternity, that gives rise to the tragic vision. (p. 188)

Ionesco is not taken in by the specious argument that everything under the sun is affected by politics. He insists that the distinction between ideology and reality, propaganda and art, must be reinstated. The economic society that the revolutionary activists hope to establish moves us in the direction of social conformism and "the world of alienation." Just as Valéry waged a bitter, lifelong campaign against the mystagogic ideas of Pascal, so does Ionesco concentrate his attack on the dramaturgic theories of Brecht, especially the theory of *Entfremdung* that Brecht attempted to apply to his later plays. Brecht sternly forbids —and endeavors to prevent—any emotional participation on the part of the audience. The spectator is denied the pleasure of empathy; he is not allowed to identify himself with the characters Brecht presents. (pp. 189-90)

Ionesco is the antithesis of the didactic writer. For him as a playwright, political and economic problems are of secondary importance. Why should he be preoccupied with them since he knows: "(1) that we are going to die, (2) that revolution saves us neither from life nor from death, (3) that I cannot imagine a finite universe, an infinite universe, nor yet a universe that is neither finite nor infinite." Since everything in the world seems to him arbitrary, contingent, absurd, he eschews the partisan spirit. Too many ideologies are at bottom rationalizations of hidden aggressions, outlets for the destructive instinct. "The saviors of mankind have founded inquisitions, invented concentrations camps, constructed crematory ovens, established tyrannies." To call for "commitment" on the part of the writer is, in effect, to deprive him of his creative freedom. . . . An anarchist as well as absurdist at heart, Ionesco resists the aggressive designs of the professional revolutionaries, who demand that the artist, to save his soul, give unconditional obedience to the Cause, the anointed Leader, the Party. He has repeatedly stated that he has no faith at all in the Revolution. Today, Ionesco contends, it is the Left that provides the most shocking example of ideological tyranny. (pp. 190-91)

What Ionesco finds singularly lacking in this age of political fanaticism is the metaphysical vision, the hunger for the absolute. It is unfortunate that the fever of contemporary politics has supplanted the archetypal quest of man for the absolute. (pp. 191-92)

For Ionesco the supremely ironic fact that we shall soon turn to dust renders everything else in the world insignificant by comparison. Why burst into a frenzy of anger, resentment, and vindictive hatred? Why not fall into silence? For the convictions we so passionately defend—all this will be utterly forgotten in the grave. How account for the thanatophobic upsurge that leads twentieth-century man to indulge in idolatry of the State, the Nation? Why should anyone worship the State, which is only an abstraction, an administrative system? It is not God but an idol made of clay. It is a spurious entity. But this abstraction is endowed with the attributes of the sacred and invested with the power of dispensing justice, or what it mistakes for justice. As Ionesco demonstrated with trenchant dramatic force in his play *Rhinoceros*, for those who were transformed into rhinoceroses "the State has become God." . . . It is these pernicious abstractions, the hypnotic mumbo jumbo of politics, that are chiefly responsible for the alienation of the modern self.

It is the knowledge that all men are doomed to die that fills Ionesco with a nameless but oppressive anxiety. This obsession will not let him go. How can it be, he wonders, that he is still afraid of death, how can it be that he does not "fervently desire it?" . . . He cannot reason his way out of these painful existential dilemmas. . . . Though he realizes that there is no answer to the tormenting enigma of existence, Ionesco will never stop asking the same question: why? This is the type of non-sense question that the logical positivists have proscribed. Ionesco interrogates the universe of death. Precisely because there are no answers does man persist in asking this question. "We are here. We don't know what that means." . . . (pp. 192-93)

> *Charles I. Glicksberg, "The Politics of the Absurd," in his* The Literature of Commitment *(© 1976 by Associated University Presses, Inc.), Associated University Presses, 1976, pp. 186-93.*

What was obvious in *L'Homme aux valises* is . . . the dramatists's slow but persistent turn to the classical tradition. (p. 732)

At first glance, there is nothing very much different in [the play] from standard Ionesco-type situations. The problems which beset the main protagonist are those of numerous other characters encountered in his plays. What is different is the language used. Words, which in the classical tradition are imbued with meaning, and have direct relationships between them and the objects or concepts to which they refer, are, to a surprising extent, those which Ionesco writes in his play. If *L'Homme aux valises* is still reminiscent of the Ionesco of old, it is because the language used must be adapted to the oneiric situations it describes. Such an adaptation results, of course, in what the author called "un langage un peu déformé, un peu irréel." Although it is no longer necessary to have a code and to decipher its elements, the dialogue nevertheless retains a complexity which is at times baffling and which requires a more than average intelligence for immediate comprehension. (p. 733)

[Ionesco] extracts from words all the marrow which they contain, all that they hold as known and unknown, and almost always every nuance in between. Words are no longer used merely as tools, they are abused as slaves. They are qualified by other words or phrases, they are broken down, compounded, sucked dry of meaning, which may then be reinforced, altered, or even contradicted altogether. The thought-processes of the hero using them are thus always *becoming,* as befits the oneiric situations within which he moves. There is neither logic nor an entire absence of it, there is no reality but there is a border to it, and one can look beyond and see its landscape even if one remains nevertheless incapable of crossing the frontier. This is as close as Ionesco gets, in *L'Homme aux valises,* to the classical tradition. . . . Language, then, if still "un peu déformé," if still "un peu irréel," still relates to the characters. . . . (p. 734)

That Ionesco who would manueuver language in order to destroy it seems relegated to the distant past. The dramatist who devised characters without thoughts, or with no thoughts worth expressing, or with expressions that berated all attempts at thinking; the playwright who camouflaged, changed, contradicted, and even abolished thought by his language, has now gone a step further, or rather backwards. . . .

Ionesco's style in *L'Homme aux valises* . . . seeks to convey distinctions, degrees of subtlety and of truth, for the dream images he describes are necessarily fleeting and therefore in dire need of being slowed down by careful, punctuated, and dissecting analysis. To proceed differently would be to make of the spoken or written word a less than concrete manifestation of the ordering and interrelationship between images. Not that oneiric images are usually ordered or connected. But whatever link there may be is given a degree of precision hitherto unencountered in Ionesco's plays.

Precision, of course, is a word that can be understood differently in different contexts. When applied to Ionesco's style in *L'Homme aux valises* it should not lead one to think that it is really possible to summarize the work, or to know exactly what is going on. In fact, there is really no story to summarize, there are only very few details which can be pointed out, and vagueness persists. . . . In his latest play one begins to recognize that a character's discourse on stage can validly encompass the maximum extension of both meaning and form just as it could validly, in an earlier play, degenerate into engaging and extremely comical repetitions of the word *chat.* (p. 735)

> *Alfred Cismaru, "Ionesco's 'L'Homme aux valises': The Absurdist Turned Classic," in* French Review, *April, 1977, pp. 732-36.*

*   *   *

ISHERWOOD, Christopher   1904-

Isherwood is an English-born novelist, playwright, translator, short story writer, and screenwriter who is popular for his largely autobiographical accounts of pre-Nazi Berlin and for his detached, humorous observations of men and manners. Critic Frederick R. Karl speculates that "perhaps no novelist . . . seemed better equipped . . . to catch the peculiar tone of his times." As a young man, Isherwood was a member of the Marxist group that included Spender and Auden; the latter first convinced him to go to Berlin. Isherwood and

Auden later collaborated on a number of plays. Isherwood's works reflect his interest in film and its techniques, such as flashbacks and time shifts. While living in California, he wrote movie scripts and *Prater Violet,* a novel about the film industry. His *The Berlin Stories,* adapted by John Van Druten for his *I Am a Camera,* was the basis for the musical and film *Cabaret.* Isherwood became a U.S. citizen in 1946. (See also *CLC,* Vol. 1, and *Contemporary Authors,* Vols. 13-16, rev. ed.)

Lions and Shadows is the most unpretentious exhibit in the vast gallery of Romantic and post-Romantic works that chart the development of the artist as a young man. It is also the only one of Isherwood's books that he has chosen to acknowledge as autobiography, although the novels as well appear to reflect, more or less accurately, the events and experiences of his life. Indeed, the preface to *Lions and Shadows,* typically, invites the reader to treat the book as if it were fiction, but it is clear that, even where the work in untrue to fact, it is faithful to the inner struggles it exposes. For this reason and because it does in fact reveal in a form least affected by the requirements of fiction Isherwood's typical themes and concerns and his characteristic manner of expression, *Lions and Shadows* holds a central place in Isherwood's career and provides the best introduction to all of his writings, especially to those highly ironic novels of the nineteen-thirties, which are still the foundation of his reputation.

In his note to the reader, Isherwood announces his theme with the statement that "this book is about the problems of a would-be writer"; he goes on to add: "The style is the man." . . . The two statements are not completely coordinate, since the first takes into account both the protagonist and the narrator and the nature of the development from one to the other, whereas the second refers to information that can be inferred about the author-narrator alone. The latter, however, although less immediately obvious, is ultimately the more central figure in the book: at first sight simply bland, neutral, and cool, the familiar detached and impartial spectator of modern literature, the narrator supplies, in his observations and evaluation of the "education in the twenties" that transforms his younger self into the more sophisticated, thirty-three year old author of the thirties, not only the angle of vision but also the moral values that the reader adopts in his interpretation of *Lions and Shadows.* The clue to his own personality and to the "implied authors" of all the early novels lies, as Isherwood's epigrammatic sentence indicates, in the style or, more broadly, in the technique of the work—in the shaping voice that is everywhere, if lightly, felt, as the major presence of the book. (pp. 475-76)

[Purple] passages or "literary" effects are rare in Isherwood's writing. Certainly his diction is simple; what needs to be added is that the words are frequently deployed in such a way as to produce in the reader a sense of incongruity that is as potent as but less obtrusive and less blatantly grotesque than what one takes away from the early novels of Aldous Huxley, where comparable strategies are employed. The use of domestic and animal imagery in juxtaposition with the human and the natural, to choose typical examples, generates a series of small shocks, the effects of which are at times simply humorous, at times more unsettling. . . . [The result is to make the reader] apprehend the texture of daily life as somewhat ludicrous, uncomfortable, even repellent.

Most descriptions in Isherwood's work are in fact written from an angle that is oblique to ordinary perception. Not only the ordering and arrangement but also the choice of words serves to bring about a slight but constant displacement of the reader's expectations, and it is Isherwood's accomplishment that even the most apparently random word or phrase contrives to fantasticate the entire passage of which it is a part. (p. 476)

Lions and Shadows has its moments of exuberance, if not quite of intensity, and it is on certain levels at least a very funny book, but its persistent mode is deflation, its instrument the self-inflicted and barely noticeable pin-prick. Diction, however, plays only a part, perhaps the smaller part, in creating the distinctive tone of the book; more elusively and, from the reader's point of view, less consciously, syntax gives shape to the author's vision. It is generally assumed that Isherwood's sentences are as simple as his vocabulary. Many are, and a typical one tends to organize a single impression, thereby imparting to the style of the book an effect of dryness and spareness and providing a formal equivalent to the discontinuities of perception that characterize the narrator's mind. On the other hand, the ear, even sooner than the eye, will convince the reader that in almost any paragraph of *Lions and Shadows* there is to be found a number of long and complicated and, more rarely, of complex sentences. Of course, neither length nor complication is at variance with a style that is colloquial and familiar. Isherwood's sentences are never formally rhetorical or architectonic; the mind that they reflect is one in process, thinking discursively, as if in the midst of conversation, adding to, qualifying, or making more vivid some initial statement or observation. . . . (p. 477)

One more point needs to be made about Isherwood's style, specifically about the impact of an entire paragraph. Here it is not a question of diction or syntax but of the variety among and the concatenation of the sentences that compose the larger structural unit. The principle, however, is roughly the same: one is conscious of, or at least made to feel, a constant shifting among the kinds of sentences, a slight detachment of each from the others, a tendency to produce an effect of decrescendo toward the end. Everything follows, but nothing is explicitly related; an invisible hiatus fills the space after every period, producing for the reader the time needed to adjust to the minute but constant shifts of direction he is expected to make. Connectives, implicit or explicit, are rare in Isherwood's early prose, where one is forced to jump, so to speak, rather than glide from one stop to another. (p. 478)

Style and the narrative technique that duplicates in another area its essential features, the tone that they combine to produce, with its perpetual slight mockery and denigration, its understatement and tea-tabling; and, as we shall see, point of view—all help to translate and in turn point to a vision of the world that can best be described as ironic. Irony in this context is not to be understood as an isolable literary technique. For modern man it is a characteristic sensibility, a response, like sentimentality in the eighteenth and nineteenth centuries, to a growing loss of faith both in the reality of the external world and in the authenticity of the self. (p. 480)

All irony demands the complicity of the reader and assumes a level of intelligence at least equal to the ironist's own. Isherwood's in particular calls for a degree of sustained attention without which even the most alert are likely to be betrayed into the mistaken belief that the apparently neutral and transparent narrator is simply the recorder, reporter, or, most famously, in *Goodbye to Berlin,* the camera that he purports to be. What is reflected by these various stances is, in the first instance, not methodology but psychology, not the supposedly bland empiricism of the scientist or the literary realist but the involuntary detachment of the outsider. Whether or not it is intentionally ironic, it is significant that the narrator adds—in apposition to his description of his younger self as "the would-be novelist"—the phrase: "the professional observer". . . . Isherwood's books take as their leading theme the failure of involvement and communication, the failure to establish contact between the self and the world. Viewed in this light, the seeming transparency is seen actually to be a mask and a shield: "Henceforward," the narrator says late in the book, "my problem is how to perfect a disguise." . . . (p. 481)

The difficulties of penetrating the perfected disguise are three-fold. It has already been suggested that the narrator calls little *overt* attention to himself. The lightness of his touch and the refusal to dramatize himself make him the most unobtrusive of guides through what he calls "the vast freak museum of our neurotic generation." . . . Furthermore, there is a remarkable consistency in maintaining the tone of the book: "the wry, the sotto-voice,/Ironic and monochrome," as W. H. Auden puts it in one of his poems. Irony is pervasive, not occasional; there are no excursions into sentimentality, as in Forster's novels, or into anger, as in Huxley's. Few modern writers exhibit in their works a more uniform texture or provide fewer jolts to the reader's absorption in narrative surface. *Lions and Shadows* is in fact a study in low relief: all of the characters, incidents, and objects that make it up are viewed from the same distance and with the same amount of interest. So in his opening note, Isherwood refers to the "caricatures" he has drawn, and, although he is at that point indicating primarily the lack of correspondence between his characters and their real-life models, there is some validity in the remark. Later in the book, he comments: "I was, and still am, endlessly interested in the outward appearance of people—their facial expressions, their gestures, their walk, their nervous tricks . . . ". . . . Characterization, in other words, is largely external; there is little probing of minds, little effort to lay bare the inner life.

Isherwood's conception and articulation of his characters bears little resemblance to the methods of the modern psychological novel. Here, as elsewhere, the approach is oblique; the reader is presented with surface and left to infer depth. The characters in *Lions and Shadows*—and in all of the novels where the protagonist bears Isherwood's name—are less individuals in their own right than facets in the first place of the protagonist and then of the narrator-author. Everyone whom the young Isherwood meets throughout the course of *Lions and Shadows* is in some way an objectification of a quality, good or bad, that is inherent or potential in him; each is what he might be, what he revolts against, or what he is. Necessarily, since the record of his thoughts and actions supplies the narrative interest of the book and his development, its unifying thread, the protagonist receives more attention, but the difference is one of degree, not kind. Ultimately, he, like the others, is part of the network of clues that refers back to the narrator who is recording his education.

[The] primary theme of the autobiography is . . . the need to transcend the limiting boundaries of the ego and to establish some authentic relation not only with other isolate individuals but with the world at large. (pp. 481-83)

Lions and Shadows . . . is a study in limitation and, more ambiguously, in growth. Its irony is directed most consistently at those fundamental traits that lead to the deficiencies and subterfuges of the protagonist and especially at their successive manifestations: the aberrations of conduct which keep him at the borders and not at the center of life. The nature of his character and conflicts is articulated most fully by means of two recurrent symbols—Mortmere and The Test—which correspond to the evasions and the failures of the protagonist. . . . (p. 483)

Both symbols point to the protagonist's underlying fear, which in turn finds expression in two repeated images, the one expressive of his complete rejection of and revolt against the adult world, the other of his retreat from it: the nursery and acting. (p. 484)

The ultimate desire, never consciously acknowledged and perhaps never fully understood in *Lions and Shadows,* is to lose the the self, to destroy with one gesture personal identity and its reflection, the "nursery prison," the world as threat and punishment. In fact, the loss of the self, the abnegation of individual identity, is the goal toward which all of Isherwood's work strains. (p. 486)

It is the nature of Isherwood's irony to equivocate, to register the simultaneous awareness of different possibilities without choosing among them. Like so many other open-ended books of the twentieth century . . . *Lions and Shadows* offers at its close a sense not of completion and certainty but of speculation and doubt, posing most insistently the question of whether there is any *substantive* difference between the Christopher of the late twenties and Isherwood of the thirties. The evidence of technique indicates that there is not. (p. 487)

Both Christopher and Isherwood are . . . ironists, to use that term as I have defined it. "The goal of satire," Auden has . . . written, "is reform, the goal of comedy acceptance." One might add that the goal of irony is neither the one nor the other, but understanding. . . . Self-analysis is what, on one level at least, *Lions and Shadows* is, and it is also what Christopher achieves as a result of his education. Problems are posed, difficulties acknowledged, but of any significant change beyond the perfecting of a disguise there is no evidence.

To say that irony seeks understanding and liberation is not to deny that there is implicit in it a point of view toward the very things it wishes to rise above. The search is born out of precisely that vision I earlier tried to describe: the sense of failure that is anterior to the undertaking, the disappointment that precedes the event. (pp. 487-88)

The final irony of *Lions and Shadows* is that its very existence disproves its thesis. Style is the man and it is the artist too, and conduct shapes all three—but to different ends. Isherwood's autobiography is a validation of itself rather than of the life it records, an ambiguous testimony to the triumph of the aesthetic over the moral. "Day after day," Stephen Spender writes about Isherwood in his own autobiography, ". . . I witnessed that transformation taking place in his mind, where the real becomes the malleable"

and where, it might be added, the refractory is given satisfactory definition in the timelessness of literature. (pp. 488-89)

> *Alan Wilde, "Irony and Style: The Example of Christopher Isherwood," in* Modern Fiction Studies *(copyright © 1971, by Purdue Research Foundation, West Lafayette, Indiana, U.S.A.), Winter, 1970-71, pp. 475-89.*

Critics and scholars love to reduce writers and their work to fit into the limits of neat epithets or thematic headings. I suppose if I had to submit Christopher Isherwood to such a treatment, the obvious choice would be *Sexuality and Spirituality.* This seemingly incongruous duo recurs throughout his writing, though rarely so happily united as they have been in the latter half of his own life. . . .

It has been stated often and wrongly that Isherwood is obsessed with sexual perversion, that the majority of his characters are maladjusted people on the fringe of society, tragic freaks of shoddy demi-mondes. Statistically that is nonsense, though it is certainly true that many of Isherwood's most memorable observations (I hesitate to use the word 'creations', as so many of his characters are so clearly based on actual human beings who have strayed across his field of vision) are practitioners of minority sexual tastes. (p. 343)

There is . . . a traceable development in the approach of his novels to sex, as if each time he has felt justified in going one little step further, swimming with the current of enlightened public opinion rather than leading it. To my mind, therefore, his significance in this field comes from the way he has helped to make respectable topics previously unmentionable in polite society. . . .

In the first of Isherwood's novels, *All the Conspirators* (1928), sex is presented only obliquely, hinted at as a motivating force behind personal relationships, but seen only through the lens of those relationships. As in much other fiction of the period, Freud hovers in the background. Much of the talk about sex remains on an undergraduate, pseudo-intellectual level, such as Allen Chalmers' 'casual' remark: 'I wonder . . . whether the desire to photograph puffins during the love act could be classified as any form of sexual mania'. . . . (p. 344)

The young people in *All the Conspirators* are arrested adolescents par excellence. Nobody in the book really radiates physical confidence, despite their bravura. Philip Lindsay, indeed, exudes insecurity and an inability to assert his masculine individuality, a result, we are led to believe, of the pernicious influence of his mother. (Isherwood, in these early works, shows a clear awareness of the fact that smother is an anagram of mothers.) It took Isherwood a good many years to work out his resentment against his own mother, the dominent influence in his development, as his father had been killed while he was young. He finally exonerated her in 1971 with the positively loving portrait in *Kathleen and Frank.* One is acutely conscious of the fact that his attitude to mother-son relationships obscures his vision and presentation of all women characters in the early books. These women exist not so much as characters in their own right, but as demanding attenders on the male characters, often tyrannical or brainless and frequently shallow. (pp. 344-45)

Women gain more status and credibility in *The Memorial* (1932). Mary Scriven is shown to be an admirable member of the older generation, capable of both human compassion and organising efficiency. Lily Vernon is more in the Mrs. Lindsay mould, destructive in her love for her son Eric. Both she and Mary Scriven have lost their husbands either in the War or through desertion, so that as in *All the Conspirators*, there is no picture of a couple married, happily or otherwise. However, we do know that Lily's twelve-year relationship with the late Richard was seen as a blissful one.

Only two other women appear in the novel as important characters: Mary's daughter Anne (who remains as shadowy as Philip Lindsay's sister Joan in *All the Conspirators*), and that much more interesting individual Margaret Lanwin. In the more direct parlance of today, I suppose one would refer to Margaret as a fag-hag, the first of a series of women who appear in Isherwood's work and world, serving as friend, confidante, honorary sister or mother to the gay protagonist, and more often than not getting emotionally involved with him. Despite the futility of her emotions and desires, Margaret's relationship with Edward Blake is a beautiful one, and gives the Isherwood reader the first opportunity to witness some of the more admirable traits of feminine nature.

Edward Blake, of course, is the first overt homosexual in this fictional canon, a bundle of paradox. He has a brilliant war record, is athletic and witty, but also prone to depressions and vulnerable to alluring, worthless boys who will desert him. He even attempts suicide, in the rather Freudian way of thrusting a gun in his mouth—and fails. The lot of the homosexual is shown to be a dismal one, and curiously remains so throughout Isherwood's work. (pp. 345-46)

During his time in Berlin, Isherwood undoubtedly passed The Test, clambered over the barrier presented by his own adolescent problems vis-à-vis sex and life in general. The exact nature of these problems can be gleaned from his early autobiographical volume, *Lions And Shadows*. But in Berlin he was largely freed, and the liberation brought about a noticeable improvement in his presentation of what makes people tick. *Mr. Norris Changes Trains*, published in the States as *The Last of Mr. Norris* (1935), greatly widens the gamut of the author's characters. He has become more confident in his descriptions of individuals and their sexual tastes, aided no doubt by a stylistic shift to objective, documentary observation of striking individuals met during his three and a half years in the period of the Nazis' rise to power. (p. 346)

Norris, along with the other characters in the book, benefits from a closer attention to detail on Isherwood's part. Physical characteristics are painted in briskly but astutely, often centering on the eyes, those betrayers of personality and sexual taste or mood. (pp. 346-47)

Feminine sexuality is largely ignored in *Mr. Norris*, apart from thumbnail sketches of those prostitutes who serve their clients' various whims. Fräulein Schroeder, the landlady, does emanate a certain earthiness, but this is never explicitly sexual in Isherwood's eyes. But the hard-as-nails British journalist Helen Pratt is a new phenomenon: a female liberationist, precursor of the bra-burning brigade, who 'loathed being reminded she was a woman except in

bed'. . . . One senses Issyvoo's distaste for her. Yet that is not because she is a woman, but rather that she has thrown over the graces of her sex to play the dirtiest of men's games. She is also a journalist—the most damned profession in the novels—and, more seriously, she is hostile to Arthur Norris, to whom Isherwood (partly represented in the narrator William Bradshaw) shows considerable loyalty.

Thus one feels the sudden force of innovation in *Goodbye to Berlin* (1939), where, for the first time, the reader is presented with a credible woman, who works from basic feminine desires—Sally Bowles. It is no mere quirk of fate that she has remained Isherwood's most famous creation, for she is the most alive, the most normal and identifiable of the whole range of unusual personalities. (p. 347)

Side by side with the burgeoning of Isherwood's understanding of women, as witnessed in the Berlin stories, comes a greater frankness about the sexual attractiveness of the male. None of the early creations emitted much sexual appeal (or if they did, it is not evident from the text), whereas in *Goodbye to Berlin*, there is a strong undercurrent of animal sensuality, particularly among the working class. . . .

Despite the fact that the homosexual content of the Berlin stories must penetrate even the most blinkered reader's mind, Isherwood does not commit himself one way or the other. He has not yet come out of the closet, as he would later describe the process. He disguises his own sexual stance by the very inclusion of a Christopher dummy character in the novels, a narrator who observes everything going on around him with a positively asexual detachment. (p. 348)

Christopher's ambiguity remains in *Prater Violet* (1945), that much-awaited novel which broke Isherwood's fictional silence during the War, a period where he was putting in order his own spiritual house, devoting himself latterly to the Vedanta movement, working on translations of religious texts, and even for a while practising personal abstinence. In *Prater Violet*, sexuality is relegated to a place of minor importance so as not to detract from the basic aim of portraying the film director Berthold Viertel (Friedrich Bergmann in the book). Isherwood nonetheless derives a certain pleasure, shared with the reader, by hiding his own sexual life from this honorary father figure. . . . [In] *Prater Violet*, Bergmann's romantic ideal of love is held up as an appealing contrast to Christopher's empty affairs: 'Women are absolutely necessary to a man . . . he needs them like bread. I do not mean for coitus . . . one needs their aura, their ambiance, their perfume'. Or again: 'Love is like a mine. You go deeper and deeper'. . . . (pp. 349-50)

There is always a time delay in Isherwood's career between his experiencing a phenomenon, and his writing it out. This gestation period is frequently several years, as if his literary nature had to catch up with his real-life self. Thus his own self-questioning about the compatibility of sexuality and spirituality, largely a feature of his life in the forties, only really emerges in 1954, with the publication of *The World in the Evening*. . . . It is significant that Stephen treats the boy fairly shoddily, as Isherwood takes a dim view of bisexuals or married men who have male peccadilloes on the side. . . . [It] is a poor book, as even Isherwood admits, a failure during the transition period in his career from a European to an American environment. I would be tempted to dwell no further on it if it were not for the curious pair of homosexual lovers represented in it: Bob Wood and Dr. Charles Kennedy.

Considering Isherwood's personal life, which has included several longish relationships, . . . it is most curious that he does not treat the phenomenon of proper homosexual relationships in his books. Nearly all homosexual encounters and couplings in his fiction are brief, animal affairs doomed to failure. The one happy homosexual 'marriage' in his *oeuvre* is referred to in *A Single Man,* but even there George and Jim's bliss is shattered by Fate with the latter's untimely death. So, Bob and Charles in *The World in the Evening* appear as the only male couple in the ten Isherwood novels who actually seem to have some chance of making a go of it. Their portrait is not over-edifying, largely due to the silliness of Bob Wood, who may have been intended as an endearingly goofy, fun-loving American kid, but who in fact comes over as yet another retarded adolescent fairy. Isherwood had sadly not yet learnt to be fluent in American youth English.

Why is it that so many of Isherwood's homosexuals have such blatant psychological weaknesses and deficiencies? . . . Eventually one is forced to the conclusion that basically the sort of people and situations that stimulate the literary side to his being *are* the failures of the emotional world, and that this generalisation (despite the weakness of all generalisations) is just as valid for the *hetero*sexuals as well. Death, it seems from CI's novels, is the only reward for happy relationships.

Perhaps the realisation of the failure of *The World in the Evening* was one reason why Isherwood reverted to an earlier format for his next novel *Down There on a Visit* (1962). . . . Maybe the most interesting thing about the book as a whole . . . is the change in Christopher from his early Berlin days. One is conscious of the older Christopher narrating the adventures of his younger self, claiming detachment, but in fact so clearly a product of the young man who, for the first time, admits to actually taking part in some of the more unusual goings on that are described. (pp. 350-51)

Isherwood's last novel, *A Meeting by the River* returns to the theme of sexuality and spirituality, though not so much in combination as in competition. There *is* one character who seems to embody both aspects, Patrick's wife Penelope, but she remains offstage. So the forces are polarised in the two brothers Oliver and Patrick, the one preparing himself for the acceptance of vows in a Hindu monastery, the other bursting with sexual vitality, and fresh from a very physical affair with a young boy student from the West Coast. Oliver is seen resisting sex (he has been, and still is, emotionally and sexually attracted to his sister-in-law), understanding of other people's desires, but determined to leave the carnal world. Patrick, on the other hand, must remain sexual; his struggle is to decide exactly how. In the end, he goes for the security of his marriage and family, ditching his boy lover in a despicable lack of feeling (one gathers it is not the first time). Again the uncomplimentary portrait of the wicked bisexual, hypocritical and selfish! Yet one feels Isherwood understands both sides, that even if he disapproves theoretically of a person's sexual or emotional behaviour, he nonetheless accepts it in reality, and sympathises, with a tolerance and understanding sadly lacking in most people on either side of the sexual fence. (p. 352)

Jonathan H. Fryer, "Sexuality in Isherwood," in Twentieth Century Literature *(copyright 1976, Hofstra University Press), October, 1976, pp. 343-53.*

J

JARRELL, Randall   1914-1965

Jarrell was an American poet, critic, editor, translator, and novelist whom Robert Lowell called "the most heartbreaking . . . poet of his generation." Jarrell's work presents a sensitive perspective of the condition of modern man and his culture. Jarrell also wrote several delightful, poetic books for children. (See also *CLC*, Vols. 1, 2, 6, and *Contemporary Authors*, obituary, Vols. 25-28, rev. ed.)

"We have lost for good," Randall Jarrell once wrote, "the poems that would have been written by the modern equivalent of Henry VIII or Bishop King or Samuel Johnson; born novelists, born theologians, born princes." We might add, born critics: because Jarrell . . . can be said to have put his genius into his criticism and his talent into his poetry.

That talent, in the course of his life, grew considerably. . . . If we reconstruct, from [*The Collected Poems*] . . . , the boy Jarrell growing into the man Jarrell, we can see the progress of his peculiarly double nature, one side of it charming and comic, the other vulnerable and melancholy.

The poems Jarrell wrote before World War II—roughly before he was 30—are on the whole forgettable, but they foreshadow his continual risky dependence on history, folk tale and art: many of the later poems are retellings (of history or biography), redescriptions (of a Dürer etching, a Botticelli canvas, the Augsburg Adoration), or reworkings of a myth. That dependency in Jarrell never died; he was, nobody more so, the eager audience to any book or piece of music that captured his wayward interest; his poems in which the scene is a library are hymns to those places where we can "live by trading another's sorrow for our own."

His first steady original poems date from his experience in the Air Force, when the pity that was his tutelary emotion, the pity that was to link him so irrevocably to Rilke, found a universal scope:

> We died like aunts or pets or foreigners.
> (When we left high school nothing else had died
> For us to figure we had died like.) . . .
> In bombers named for girls, we burned
> The cities we had learned about in school.

Jarrell brings us his adolescent soldiers with their pitiful reality of high school—high school!—as the only notching-stick of experience; he brings us the veteran "stumbling to the toilet on one clever leg of leather, wire, and willow," with the pity all in the *faute-de-mieux* weird boastfulness of "clever"; he brings us the bodiless lost voices in the air—"can't you hear me? over, over—"; and, for all its triteness now, he brings us the death of the ball turret gunner.

The secret of his war poems is that in the soldiers he found children; what is the ball turret gunner but a baby who has lost his mother? The luckier baby who has a mother, as Jarrell tells us in "Bats," "clings to her long fur / by his thumbs and toes and teeth . . . / Her baby hangs on underneath. . . . / All the bright day, as the mother sleeps, / She folds her wings about her sleeping child." (p. 5)

Jarrell has often been taken to task for his sentimentality, but the fiction, recurrent in his work, of a wholly nonsexual tenderness, though it can be unnerving in some of the marriage poems, is indispensable in his long, tearfully elated recollections of childhood. The child who was never mothered enough, the mother who wants to keep her children forever, these are the inhabitants of the lost world, where the perfect filial symbiosis continues forever. The nostalgia for childhood even lies behind Jarrell's aging monologists—the Marschallin, the woman at the Washington Zoo, the woman in the supermarket—and gives them at once their poignancy and their abstraction.

For all his wish to be a writer of dramatic monologues, Jarrell could only speak in his own alternately frightened and consolatory voice, as he alternately played child and mother. It has been charged that Jarrell's poetry of the war shows no friends, only, in James Dickey's words, "killable puppets"—but Jarrell's soldiers are of course not his friends because they are his babies, his lambs to the slaughter—he broods over them. In his final psychic victory over his parents, they too become his babies as he, perfectly, in this ideal world of recovery memory, remains *their* baby:

> Here are Mother and Father in a photograph,
> Father's holding me . . . They both look so young.
> I'm so much older than they are. Look at them,
> Two babies with their baby.

His students are his children too, and the sleeping girl in the library at Greensboro receives his indulgent parental solicitude. . . .

The student—"poor senseless life"—is nevertheless finally the pure and instinctual ideal. . . . (p. 5)

[His] guileless taste requires a guileless style, and Jarrell found it late, in the gossipy, confidential and intimate manner of "The Lost World," his recollections of a childhood year in Hollywood:

> On my way home I pass a cameraman
> On a platform on the bumper of a car
> Inside which, rolling and plunging, a comedian
> Is working; on one white lot I see a star
> Stumble to her igloo through the howling gale
> Of the wind machines. On Melrose a dinosaur
> And pterodactyl with their immense pale
> Papier-màchê smiles, look over the fence
> Of *The Lost World*.

That childlike interest—in the cameraman, the artificial igloo and the cartoon monsters—was the primitive form of Jarrell's later immensely attractive enthusiasm for all the pets he kept in his private menagerie. Nobody loved poets more or better than Randall Jarrell—and irony, indifference or superciliousness in the presence of the remarkable seemed to him capital sins. In one of his last poems, "The Old and the New Masters," he takes issue with Auden, arguing that in any number of paintings the remarkable sufferer or redeemer is not tangential but is rather the focus of the whole:

> . . . everything
> That was or will be in the world is fixed
> On its small, helpless, human center.

Those lines could be the epigraph to these collected poems; and yet there are dimensions of Jarrell that we could wish for more of. One of his talents is to rewrite, in a grim way, nursery tales, so that we see Cinderella finally preferring the cozy female gossip of the fireside to life with the prince, or we see Jack, post-beanstalk, sitting in a psychotic daze by his rotting cottage, "bound in some terrible wooden charm . . . rigid and aghast." Another, and perhaps truer, Jarrell writes a disarming poem of pure pleasure ("Deutsch Durch Freud") on why he never wants really to know German; it's so much nicer only to know it halfway, via Rilke and lieder:

> It is by Trust, and Love, and reading Rilke
> Without *ein Wörterbuch*, that man learns German
> . . .
> And Heine! At the ninety-sixty *mir träumte*
> I sigh as a poet, but dimple as *ein Schuler* . . .
> And my heart lightens at each *Sorge*, each *Angst*
> . . .
> Till the day I die I'll be in love with German
> —If only I don't learn German . . .

In lines like these, all of Jarrell's playful wit is coming to surface, that wit which dazzled us from the pages of his energetic criticism, but which often falters under the (very Germanic) melancholy of "The Complete Poems." The refugees, children, recluses, soldiers and aging women who inhabit his verse might have left more room in it for their satiric and resilient creator, but Jarrell kept his two sides very distinct. . . . He cannot be said, as a poet, to have invented new forms, a new style, or new subjects, in any grand way; but he made himself memorable as a singular man, at his most exceptional in denying his own rarity:

> How young I seem; I am exceptional;

> I think of all I have.
> But really no one is exceptional,
> No one has anything, I'm anybody,
> I stand beside my grave
>   Confused with my life, that
> is commonplace and solitary.

So one late poem says, but it had begun, in a flash of the boyish Jarrell *brio,* with a woman in a supermarket "Moving from Cheer to Joy, from Joy to All." Zest, down to a zest for the names of detergents, stayed mixed, to the very last, with the tears of things. (pp. 5, 42)

> *Helen Vendler, "Randall Jarrell, Child and Mother, Frightened and Consoling," in* The New York Times Book Review (© *1969 by The New York Times Company; reprinted by permission), February 2, 1969, pp. 5, 42.*

Jarrell . . . strikes me as a poet whose poems are primarily the poems of a prose writer. There is nothing invidious about this remark, for it is true also about Hardy and about Lawrence. . . . Jarrell, as in that fine poem, the title poem of one of his later volumes, "The Woman at the Washington Zoo," or even more in the much longer second poem in that volume, "The End of the Rainbow," goes on till he has finished what he has got to say: as prose writers do. It is detail, texture, modulations of thought and feeling, what one of the anthologies I am reviewing calls "open forms," that attract us in general, not the sense of finality. And perhaps I am wrong about the nature of prose: one stops not because one has said everything, but because one has said enough for the time being. (p. 297)

> *G. S. Fraser, in* Partisan Review (*copyright* © *1970 by Partisan Review, Inc.), Vol. XXXVII, No. 2, 1970.*

[*The Third Book of Criticism*] confirms one's view of Randall Jarrell as an excellent, a positively useful critic of a rare kind, combining the 'common touch' (i.e. knowing exactly where to lay his finger) with a deep and intimate understanding of the workings of literature, and a range of information which one is not quite tempted to call 'scholarly'. His procedure and his tone are fully present in the essay on Wallace Stevens here, even in a few short quotations from it. Thus, on *The Auroras of Autumn:* 'transcendental, all too transcendental études; improvisations preserved for us neither by good nor by bad, but by middle fortune'; returning to them, he managed 'after a while' to feel that he had not been as familiar with the poems or as sympathetic to them as he ought to have been, 'and there I stuck. Whatever is wrong with the poems or with me is as wrong as ever . . .' The essay complements and follows up the essay on Stevens in *Poetry and the Age*. . . . 'G. E. Moore at the spinet,' he then commented, having remarked that 'it is the lack of immediate contact with lives that hurts his poetry more than anything else.' Despite the gravity of his strictures, and despite the apparent easy looseness of his discourse (he actually seems to be enjoying himself as he writes), what he says throughout makes you positively eager to read Stevens—which, in my experience, is peculiarly rare in criticism of this poet. (p. 124)

The Third Book also contains a shrewd, entertaining piece on Robert Graves, in which warm and seductive appreciativeness coexists with a firm grip on literary standards and human values—it is marred only slightly by the rhetoric, almost gush, which is the price Jarrell occasionally pays for his sense of freshness and discovery—and a powerful investigation of early Auden, first published in 1941 but by no means limited in its application, even, indeed, prophetic. . . . Words fail me here . . . Auden, he goes on to say, was 'like someone who keeps showing how well he can hold his liquor until he becomes a drunkard . . . Reading *Another Time* is like attending an Elks' Convention of the Capital Letters.' Finally, Jarrell admits to feeling embarrassed by the 'ungrateful return' he is making. 'But analyses, even unkind analyses of faults, are one way of showing appreciation'—they are, the way he does them. Here, as so often in his criticism, one thinks of Kipling's mother and her reply (Jarrell quotes it in *A Sad Heart at the Supermarket*) when the son was angered by her criticism of his poems: 'There's no Mother in Poetry, my dear.'

What a splendid quoter Jarrell is! So quick with the telling reference, not dragged in for the sake of showing off, not sitting there wondering what it is doing, but throwing light for miles around. His 'Introductions' are truly introductory: here is the new reader and there is the literary work, and (whether you go all the way with him or not) they always lead you near the heart of the matter. (pp. 124-25)

Just as common feeling informs his best poetry, so what underlies Randall Jarrell's criticism is common sense—that quality derided by frothy phonies who have failed to notice how uncommon it is—strengthened and clarified by exactly remembered reading, considerable knowledge of what is essential to know, and his own experience in the art of writing. (p. 125)

> *D. J. Enright, "A Glad Heart," in* The Listener *(© British Broadcasting Corp. 1975; reprinted by permission of D. J. Enright), January 23, 1975, pp. 124-25.*

[Jarrell's] work is fundamentally romantic, for it presupposes a natural splendour, a primitive integrity, from which the barrier of our jaded senses keep us. The individual's past—and the past of the race—are the repositories of true experience.

At the same time, Jarrell always involves himself deeply in the literal, for his major concern is with how reality fails to live up to the expectations his commitment to the ideal has created. As he makes Irene Rosenbaum say in [*Pictures from an Institution*], 'Nostalgia is the permanent condition of man.' Jarrell's work glorifies otherness, but it always remains grounded in realistic detail; what interests him is how we come to grips with the sense of deprivation amid the thinginess of the present.

'A Girl in a Library', the lead poem in the *Selected Poems* (1955), is largely concerned with our alienation from an unknown, but imagined state of grace; it is also representative of several other typical features of Jarrell's poetry. The narrator, a more-or-less unbodied voice, muses about a young Home Economics major who has fallen asleep over her book, and sees in her a modern, i.e., diminished, New World version of the ancient myth of regeneration. (pp. 113-14)

In 'A Girl in a Library' as in much of Jarrell's work, literature offers an almost religious salvation from alienation, for it purveys a vital consciousness through which the dross of reality can be translated into authentic experience. Myth is

the pure heaven of the totally actualized, the standard by which our poor lives conducted in the worthless present are measured. The sad, thoughtful awareness of the unbridgeable gap between the inheritors of transmitted values and the new breed of mass-manufactured philistines, between the Old World and the New, which shapes the poem, is characteristic of Jarrell. Also characteristic are the personae: the pensive, almost histrionic narrator who observes without acting and speaks with a Godlike finality, and the young woman, emblematic of a victimized, limited state of being. (p. 114)

Jarrell's sentences begin simply enough, but they modify and expand as they continue, until they fill line after deceptively complex line. This exuberance, which works in concert with the extraordinary, almost prosaic naturalness of Jarrell's diction, makes his poetry attractive and accessible, but it is also responsible for weaknesses in his style. As John Crowe Ransom put it, 'I don't know if the combination of prose properties and poetic properties in the same piece is as good as either prose or poetry by itself; the prose and the poetry seem to adulterate one another.'

Jarrell's early poems are more formally intact, and adhere to the conciseness such precision requires. But they strike me as alien to his fundamentally earth-bound, discursive voice. Jarrell cares about the small stuff and nonsense, the messiness of this life; the ideal is a recourse to which he resorts when his love is not returned, which is almost always. Conventional form was a perfection into which his vivid sensitivity to organic disorder could not accommodate itself. In plotting the longer poems, which are, to me, most expressive of Jarrell when he is most himself, the reader needs to imagine an exploratory conversational logic pervading the total composition. Poems like 'A Girl in a Library' and 'An English Garden in Austria' and 'Woman' are complexes of interwoven ideas and attitudes, in which extracts from raw experience are juxtaposed with generalizing and mythic elements. (Compare, for example, Coleridge's conversation poems.) (p. 115)

In the Second World War . . . Jarrell found a subject drawn from direct rather than literary experience, one that was capable of both encompassing and broadening his concerns. Jarrell's own tour of duty in the Air Force brought him face to face with the repressive impersonality of corporate organization, a force whose debilitating influence he had not yet explicitly come to terms with. The political nature of the *anomie* that fills the isolated lives of his earlier characters comes to light in his poems of barracks and battlefield. The result was the most powerful and compassionate poetry to come out of the war. (p. 116)

The grisly irony [of the poetry] reminds one of Auden, an inevitable influence on Jarrell's work of this period, but there is a horrible closeness to the event which Auden would not have ventured. Jarrell's best war poems, and the best part of many of the others, are . . . rich in dramatic tension, and grounded, as his best work always is, in vivid detail. His ubiquitous generalizations earn their significance from gorgeously terrible descriptions of carnage and fear. . . .

Jarrell's post-war studies of the world of the military-industrial complex manifest a deepened understanding of the severely circumscribed situation of the modern individual. The glorification of change is transformed into a consciousness of the losses for which time and man are together responsible. Change occurs, ceaselessly, but usually in the form of degradation, a further distancing of the dreamer from the attainment of his most basic desires. Man no longer merely exists in an alienated state, but the possibility of a return to innocence, too, has to be relinquished in the long run. . . . (p. 117)

[The] perspective offers no hope for salvation; man appears . . . as a powerless victim, betrayed not only by society, but by nature, too. Significantly, Jarrell frequently chooses women as the protagonists of these poems of cultural protest. A glance at 'Woman' and 'In Nature There is Neither Right Nor Left Nor Wrong', which begins, 'Men are what they do, women are what they are', will show that his conception of femininity was more or less traditional, and to present-day readers, stereotypic. According to the received view, women were the frailer and more vulnerable sex, and Jarrell would appear to have capitalized on that commonplace in representing mankind's defencelessness through female characters.

Most frequently, Jarrell's women, though conscious there is something wrong in their lives, are unable to define precisely or to respond creatively to their predicaments; they are merely witnesses to their victimization. It is to children, the humans closest to their state of original grace that Jarrell looks for inspiration, to those who, because they have lost the least, remain endowed with many of their innate faculties. For them, according to the romantic programme, the world is a *Märchen;* myth *is* reality. Through a child's eyes, change regains its redemptive properties. . . . The major poems of Jarrell's last period are devoted to the pursuit of that childlike clarity of vision. (p. 118)

'A certain number of years after, / Any time is Gay, to the new ones who ask', Jarrell says in 'Thinking of the Lost World', the concluding poem in the last book of poems he was to publish. His true theme here, as it can be argued to be in much of his work, is the creative act itself, the imaginative attempt to bridge the gap between the ideal, (which is itself the product of imagination and its handmaiden memory) and the imperfections of what we see with jaded adult sight as poor fact, and out of which our conception of the ideal has to arise. The poet, still endowed with something of his childhood brilliance, can restore us, if only partially and momentarily, to a fuller consciousness of the limitless potential of fact. . . . (p. 119)

In the end, reality has the final say. Jarrell's early death broke off the ongoing tug-of-war between fact and imagination which preoccupied him throughout his career; the ecstatic resolution of 'Thinking of the Lost World', to this reader at least, doesn't comprehend the anguish and irony of his social poetry.

Jarrell wrote about imperfect persons in real places. . . . He tried to show us finer, more brilliant, more whole than the vagaries of time allowed us to seem. The age was against him, of course, as any age would have been; the intensity he championed belonged beyond it, as his work said, in the realm of art. Great poems, he wrote in 'The Obscurity of the Poet', 'manage at once to sum up, to repudiate, and to transcend both the age they appear in and the minds they are produced by'. Jarrell's poems masterfully sum up and repudiate their time; no more accurate index of the silent anxiousness of America at mid-century exists. A few of

them—and 'The Island', 'The Death of the Ball Turret Gunner', 'The Dead in Melanesia', 'The Woman at the Washington Zoo' and 'Thinking of the Lost World' are merely five—also succeed in transcending both their era and the despondent, yearning intelligence that brought them into being. In these poems, and in some of his sympathetic appreciations of other poets, Jarrell achieved that synthesis of enthusiasm and disinterestedness, that realized ideal, toward which his whole work was a striving, and earned himself a lasting place among the significant American writers. (p. 120)

> *Jonathan Galassi, " 'Hansel and Gretel in America,' The Dynamics of Change and Loss in the Poetry of Randall Jarrell," in* Poetry Nation *(© copyright* Poetry Nation *1975), No. 4, 1975, pp. 111-20.*

Randall Jarrell . . . has been widely regarded as having written some of the most memorable poems of the Second World War. His *Death of the Ball Turret Gunner* is among the most frequently anthologised poems to have come from battle experience in the 1939-45 war and it is one of the most bitter condemnations of war's waste and futility to have been written in the past half century or so. . . .

Jarrell sees war as totally destructive and pointless, the circumstances wholly degrading, robbing the individual of all that separates him from the predatory beasts, an evil . . . in the natural harmony of things, achieving nothing. There are no victors in Jarrell's view of war, only victims, among whom he would number the survivors as well as those who, like the flak-smashed ball turret gunner, was '. . . washed . . . out of the turret with a hose.'. . .

Jarrell is an uneven poet, rarely dull but, in his wartime verse, quite often given to prolixity and he sometimes permits his language to clot, the violence and inconsistency of imagery to run riot, and he cannot always control a tendency to muddle the abstract and concrete so that, instead of the powerful statement he wishes to make, he obscures his subject and blurs his effects. At this stage in his poetic development he does not seem to have realised that the verb and noun are the muscle and bone of language and qualifying words—adjectives and adverbs—are the flesh. A too generous endowment of flesh leads, of course, to obesity, and some of Jarrell's earlier poetry of the war does seem overweight. (p. 190)

One feels that, far too often, Jarrell has found it necessary to pad out the pentameter with unnecessary verbal baggage. He is generally happier with the shorter line though in *A Pilot from the Carrier*, he handles the pentameter with much more assurance, he eschews the abstract and keeps his eye on the hard details, conveying the physical sense of the parachute descent with admirable skill. . . . (p. 192)

Among the many poems which deplore the inescapable reduction of man to either animal or instrument by the calculated process of military training and by the uniformed civilian's enforced acceptance of the murderer's role, the cruel larceny of all sense of personal identity, is *Mail Call*, and here Jarrell is at his formidable best. The scene-setting is masterly: the visual sharpness of the flung letters, the irony that sees each missive just escaping the clutching hand of its intended recipient; then the meditation which follows the initial imagic statement develops naturally and movingly to the conclusion with its haunting ambiguities:

'The soldier simply wishes for his name'. Quite literally he wants to hear his name called by the distributor of mail; perhaps less consciously, but no less urgently, he wishes to re-establish contact with the world beyond the limbo of army existence, to hear from some one to whom he is a name, a unique person, not just a number and a function: he 'wishes for his name' because he longs for the restoration of identity that has been stolen from him by his absorption into a military unit. (p. 193)

The theme of military man reduced to the level of animal or object is often repeated or hinted at in other poems but it is only in one, *Eighth Air Force,* which examines the condition of the soldier whose humanity has been diminished and bestiality fostered by his training and environment, that we find at least a hint that he is not irredeemably reduced, that there might even exist a certain nobility and self-sacrifice in his acceptance of his role as killer, that traces of his former innocence and gentleness remain, and, above all, he is not to be judged and condemned.

> If, in an odd angle of the hutment,
> A puppy laps the water from a can
> Of flowers, and the drunk sergeant shaving
> Whistles *O Paradiso!*—shall I say that man
> Is not as men have said: a wolf to man?
>
> The other murderers troop in yawning;
> Three of them play Pitch, one sleeps, and one
> Lies counting missions, lies there sweating
> Till even his heart beats: One; One; One.
> *O murderers!* . . . Still, this is how it's done . . .

The wolf, the murderer, cares for a puppy; there are flowers in the water-can and the song whistled, however ironically or thoughtlessly, is one of spiritual aspiration; a simple game is played, a vestigial childness and simplicity persist; one of the 'murderers', who evidently has only one more mission to complete before his operational tour is over, lies in an agony of apprehension. The resolution of the poem is neither facile nor consolatory. Jarrell half-accuses himself of lying—or of casuistic self-justification—then bows to historical necessity in a conclusion that is sadly resigned yet dignified:

> Men wash their hands, in blood, as best they
>   can:
> I find no fault in this just man.
>
>   (pp. 194-95)

Apart from a couple of his rather weaker poems, *Transient Barracks* and *The Dead Wingman,* where there might be detected a faint glimmer of affirmation, in the first, a cautious and drab celebration of an airman's return to his homeland and, in the second, a recognition that personal affection and loyalty can survive the dehumanisation of service-life and combat conditions, Jarrell's war poetry becomes progressively more bitter and despairing. *The Range in the Desert* ends uncompromisingly:

> Profits and death grow marginal:
> Only the mourning and the mourned recall
> The wars we lose, the wars we win;
> And the world is—what it has been.
>
> The lizard's tongue licks angrily
> The shattered membranes of the fly.
>
>   (p. 195)

Field Hospital, a firmly moulded and verbally chaste poem, ends with its subject, a wounded soldier, 'comforted', but the comfort is that of oblivion and, from the pain and desperation that informs so much of Jarrell's war poetry, the reader might reasonably assume that, for the poet, dreamless sleep is the only possible refuge from the senseless and destructive realities of war. (p. 196)

Only rarely does Jarrell turn to the brief satirical poem but when he does he handles it with great accomplishment. . . .

> There set out, slowly, for a Different World,
> At four, on winter mornings, different legs . . .
> *You can't break eggs without making an omelette*
> —That's what they tell the eggs.

The war, which could be the First World War, the Second, or indeed any war in Jarrell's view, achieved nothing. In his reversal of the old adage, millions of eggs were broken—that is to say, millions of lives were lost—and the only consequence was incalculable suffering, humiliation and waste. There is no mistaking the intensity of Jarrell's pain, pity and despair nor the inflexibility of his truthfulness. There are moments in his war poetry when the force of his passion results in confusion and overstatement but far more frequently it is directed and controlled through a technical assurance that has produced some of the most relentless indictments of the evil of war since Sassoon and Owen. (pp. 197-98)

> *Vernon Scannell, in his* Not Without Glory: Poets of the Second World War *(copyright © 1976 Vernon Scannell), The Woburn Press Ltd., 1976.*

* * *

JOHNSON, B(ryan) S(tanley)   1933-1973

Johnson, a British novelist and poet, was an experimental writer concerned with exploring the relationship of fiction and truth. He took his own life a few weeks after completing *See the Old Lady Decently,* **a fictionalized account of his mother's death. (See also** *CLC,* **Vol. 6, and** *Contemporary Authors,* **Vols. 9-12, rev. ed.; obituary, Vols. 53-56.)**

For ten years, in seven novels and a number of shorter pieces, Johnson single-mindedly and belligerently pushed at the frontiers of the novel and prowled the shifting and nebulous borders between fiction and fact. He was centrally concerned with the relationships of the writer to his material as well as to his readers. . . .

In the Prelude to *Travelling People* (1963) Johnson promptly announced his departure from the convention of employing only one style throughout. With the example of *Ulysses* probably in mind, he compared the use of one style exclusively to "eating a meal in which each course had been cooked in the same manner. The style of each chapter should spring naturally from its subject matter." (p. 58)

The plot [of *Travelling People*] is not remarkable; what lends interest to the novel is the collection of styles, including that of ironic detached expository narrative, extreme fragmentation with suggested headlines in the manner of the Aeolus episode of *Ulysses,* sections of interior monologue, quotations, scraps of conversation, and letters. In all, Johnson was concerned, however diffusely, with the relationship of the author to his material; his forthright intrusions into the narrative were the first in what were to be a consistent series of sallies at the reader. Although a number of the individual elements Johnson employed in the novel seem derivative, the combination of them into the central substance and structure of the book is essentially a new venture—or was at the time. (p. 59)

In [*Alberto Angelo*] Johnson carried forward his serious concern with form and style by structuring the novel in five parts: Prologue, Exposition, Development, Disintegration, and Coda. In the Prologue, which is largely in the form of dialogue, we learn that Albert is an architect who teaches while working for his degree. He designs buildings no one builds. He believes, however, that one day they will insure his immortality. The Exposition moves stylistically from first person through second person to third person and then repeats the pattern. The Development consists of short sections of first-person narrative with juxtapositions of dialogue, quotations from a book on Gothic architecture, and stream-of-consciousness comments upon the dialogue. Advertisements for a Madam Mae, spiritualist and advisor, are inserted, as are poems and brief comments about Albert by some of his students. Sections of two pages are cut out. This array conveys the disorder of Albert's life and . . . reflects Johnson's continuing and deep conviction about the chaotic nature of human experience.

The crucial moment of the novel comes at the end of the third section, when a third-person narrative resumes briefly: "Part of the trouble, he thought, was that he lived and loved to live in an area of absolute architectural rightness, which inhibited his own originality and resulted in him being—OH, FUCK ALL THIS LYING!" The author has leapt angrily out of the book at us, bringing the section to an abrupt close, if not collapse. The section entitled Disintegration starts in the next breath, with the author continuing to boil over in the middle of a sentence:

> —fuck all this lying look what im really
> trying to write about is writing not all this
> stuff about architecture trying to say some-
> thing about my writing im my hero though
> what a useless appellation my first character
> then I'm trying to say something about me
> through him albert an architect.   (pp. 59-60)

[The] novel has, at least in part, a didactic aim: it must be "a vehicle for conveying truth," and to help achieve this goal, the novel itself as concrete object must be brought into play, for "every device and technique of the printer's art should be at the command of the writer." The cut-out pages, for example, suggest some of the possibilities inherent in such methods. (p. 60)

In his next novel, *Trawl* (1966), Johnson turns even further within and actively embraces solipsism. He, Bryan Johnson, as himself, is his principal character. The open lines are indicative: "I . . . always with I . . . one starts from . . . one and I share the same character . . . are one. . . . one always starts with I." (p. 61)

To Johnson, *Trawl* was "all interior monologue, a representation of the inside of my mind but at one stage removed; the closest one can come in writing." . . . With this statement Johnson arrives at his true subject: the inside of his own mind. For this reason, *Trawl* represents a crucial phase of his work and perhaps in more ways than Johnson himself was aware. Following the self-announced liberation from "lying," the novel is one of the early and most impor-

tant instances in the contemporary novel of the author's use of himself as his own principal character, a device that Mailer, for instance, was to employ a few years later in *The Armies of the Night*. Johnson was clearly attempting to be painfully sincere and honest in this confessional novel, and his straightforward delineations of past pain and deprivation are, in many passages, convincing and effective. One can only wonder if Johnson, in view of his single-minded insistence on "truth," was fully aware of the ironic complexities of the book. It reads like a fairly conventional contemporary novel of recall, in which the central character tries to come to terms with his present situation in the light of his past. *Trawl* even has a happy ending, the implications of which, remembering Johnson's insistence on the randomness of experience, are interesting.

The major issue which the book raises, perhaps unintentionally, concerns the relationship between fiction and fact, the besetting issue of all Johnson's work. . . . For all the flux of experience here encountered and recounted, frequently tellingly so, one's final impression of the novel is that it is—and Johnson would have despised the description —highly and artfully patterned and, in its movement from suffering to exorcism, almost pat.

His next book, *The Unfortunates* (1969), came in a box. It consists of twenty-seven sections, or chapters, temporarily held together by a removable wrapper. (pp. 62-3)

[In] a note on the wrapper we are told that in this novel Johnson tries to solve one of the novelist's chief problems: "how to represent the random workings of the mind within the enforced consecutiveness of the book." He later described the novel as being "as nearly as possible a re-created transcript of how my mind worked during eight hours on this particular Saturday." He felt that he "went some way" in combatting the artificial sense of order imposed by the conventionally bound book by his use of the loose sections in a box, and that "In this way the whole novel reflected the randomness of the material; it was itself a physical tangible metaphor for randomness and the nature of cancer." . . . Again, complications crowd. What of the second, third, or fourth reader? Is he receiving the book in random order or a predecessor's order? Indeed, is the term "random order" self-contradictory?

What comes through most forcefully in *The Unfortunates,* however, is not the question of order but of grief. The book is an elegy of sorts, often eloquent and moving. The author is preoccupied by death—his friend's and inevitably his own. He cannot finally understand death but only feel pain, and this realization persists to the end. He is left with a sense of loss. The fact of the death is important, although, again, final causes elude Johnson, as they did in *Trawl*. (pp. 63-4)

In each successive novel Johnson, apparently, was determined to try something new. What was yet to come was no exception: *House Mother Normal* (1971). (p. 64)

Again, typography and the physical form of the book function to reinforce its theme. Each line of each chapter corresponds in time to the same line in each of the other chapters, an attempt at simultaneity which has occasionally humorous ramifications: the final chapter has several blank pages—the character has dozed off. Johnson has implied that he was interested in this novel in commenting upon the kinds of distinctions society makes between normal and abnormal and gives ample evidence of his skill in blending and blurring the categories. His feel for character is manifest, and he has merged humor and compassion, coarseness and pathos. He was also clearly interested in making certain, as he does through the [character of the] House Mother, that we know we are reading a book, that we are in the presence of a literary device. (pp. 64-5)

Once again we find [in *Christie Malry's Own Double-Entry* (1973)] an arbitrary structural device, here that of double-entry bookkeeping. The plot is interspersed with five "Reckonings," in which central aspects of the story are listed either as debits or credits, with various amounts of money assigned. The basic idea is that young Christie Malry, a "simple person," takes a correspondence course in accounting and learns the double-entry system, which becomes his "Great Idea." (p. 65)

The matter-of-fact and thoroughly dispassionate style [of the novel] effects a kind of humor, ironic and frequently ribald, which permeates the pages and gives some strikingly surrealistic glimpses of modern life.... In frequent interludes the author and his character comment on the novel form, tending to keep us aware of the artifice and screened off from morbidity—but not completely. If, as Christie says at one point, the novel "should now try simply to be Funny, Brutalist, and Short," and if this one qualifies for the first and third terms, it achieves the quality of the second as well. It is at times frightening in its depiction of a psychotically adversary relationship between the self and society and in its account of inexorable psychic disintegration. It is, finally, after the laughter has died out, a disturbing book and, it may be, a disturbed one.

Johnson's final novel, *See The Old Lady Decently* (1975), was published posthumously. From the introduction by Michael Bakewell we learn that Johnson intended the book to be the first volume of three, to be collectively titled *The Matrix Trilogy*, of which the individual titles were to form a complete sentence: *See The Old Lady Decently / Buried Although / Amongst Those Left Are You*. The first volume was the only one completed, but central themes were to link the three: the mother's death, the decay of the mother country, and the renewal aspect of motherhood.

The themes are carried forward in separate sections of *See The Old Lady Decently:* a kind of fragmentation with which we are now thoroughly familiar in Johnson's work. Some sections are labelled as fiction, others consist of the memories of people who knew his mother, Emily, and still others constitute a kind of brief guided tour of Britain, from the earlier periods of growth to present decay. The mixture of different materials expresses Johnson's conviction that experience is finally inscrutable.... (p. 66)

Among the major themes of the book is that of the archetypal Anima. Quotations from Erich Neumann remind us, in one passage, of the essential function of a "matriarchal world of the psyche" in balancing a "patriarchal development of the male intellectual consciousness."... Johnson clearly posed considerable difficulties for himself in his concept of the novel and the remaining, never-to-be-written volumes of the trilogy—problems that were never completely solved. At times the structure tends to come unglued, perhaps because it is too elaborate for the relatively brief work to underpin. The novel is only 139 pages long, a rather brief compass for an attempt to deal with history,

archetypes, and the basic rhythms of human experience. Yet the sense of universals in the concrete particulars of experience is impressive, so that, given the completion of the other two volumes, the scheme may well have come off.

At times we may grow weary of learning more than we want to about the author's gastric and family situations at various moments, yet as Bakewell points out in his preface, Johnson insisted at an early stage that the writing of the novel must itself be one element of the novel. We must, therefore, think of it as an artifact in which process and product are of equal importance, an artifact in which the disjointedness may be the central point. (pp. 67-8)

[Johnson's] poetry, for the most part, is spare, conversational, and frequently wry. Johnson indicated, at the end of one volume, an interest in experimenting with meter and in another place summarized the major themes of his poetry as being the "corroding effect of time, decay in general, unrequited love, unforgiveness, solipsism." Several of these terms, particularly the final one, connect the poetry and the fiction. (p. 68)

The perception of experience as chaos or flux and the ultimate failure of attempts to impose pattern upon it find expression in a variety of ways [in Johnson's work].... In most of his novels, the structural devices are arbitrary, as the use of bookkeeping categories in *Christie Malry's Own Double-Entry*. The rigid ordering into set labelled sections, in several of the novels, emphasizes the artificiality of the rendering. The stuff of experience is at best but barely contained in these prescribed categories—and sometimes not at all, as when it boils over in *Albert Angelo*.

The concomitant conviction that fiction is lying, the subject of the tirade in *Albert Angelo*, is given considerable play in several other novels, most notably *Trawl* and *The Unfortunates*, in which the attempt is to get completely away from the "falsity" of fiction by dealing with "actual" events in the lives and deaths of "real" people. Further emphasizing the artificiality of literary representations of experience is Johnson's use of typographical and graphic devices so the reader will be in no doubt that a book is a book, not a slice of life. The gray and black pages in *Travelling People*, the cut-outs in a few pages of *Albert Angelo*, the loose-leaf sections of *The Unfortunates*, the spacings and blank pages in *House Mother Normal*—all are attempts to present the book as artifact; while conveying nondiscursive elements concretely, they also emphasize the separateness of literature from life.

Johnson's frequent practice of speaking directly to the reader reinforces the sense of artifice. The convention itself is certainly as old in the English novel as Fielding and Sterne, from the latter of whom Johnson quotes on occasion, yet his own use of the convention is frequently distinctive. At times, such as in *Travelling People*, he launches discussions of some aspects of the novel.... At times we find whimsical and humorous asides to the reader, either by the author himself, as when he intersperses details of his family life and activities with the narrative, or through the mouths of his characters.... (pp. 70-1)

Sometimes the author and his character merge in these insertions. In *Christie Malry's Own Double-Entry* Johnson says: "I shall now attempt a little dialogue between Christie and the office supervisor, as if it had happened"; Christie, in the ensuing scene, tells the office supervisor that there is not much time to arrange his mother's funeral because "It's a short novel." Not only do writer and reader share the realization that the work is fiction, so do some of the characters. The light-heartedness of most of the observations creates an intermittent atmosphere of good-humored whimsicality: "Be quiet, I think to my neighbors. Some of us are writing masterpieces." Although reinforced by occasional jokes, limericks, and ribald stories, the light-heartedness is only intermittent and sometimes seems labored, for death broods over much of Johnson's work, either as subject or as the inevitable conclusion to chaos. In many of the novels, a central character dies either at the end or before the beginning of the novel, the death serving as the occasion for the book—and rather typically death is caused by cancer. In each instance, death is represented as arbitrary, random, untimely. . . . (pp. 71-2)

To attempt a definitive assessment of Johnson's importance would be clearly premature, not only because he was so recently with us and died before giving us all the novels he had intended, but also because he leaves us with several fundamental matters unresolved. For example, his obstinate and naive contention that fiction is lying is difficult to understand or accept. When he first voiced this dictum, in *Albert Angelo,* he provoked a controversy, but Johnson stuck to his guns and continued to insist on his point of view, although it was conveyed with some modifications in *House Mother Normal.* His insistence, in retrospect, is doctrinaire and curious. Any writer knows that he fabricates not only fiction but, to a certain degree, reminiscence as well, that the imagination is highly selective in compiling even what purports to be unvarnished recollection. As Johnson's own *Trawl* testifies, we are all obsessed with that blessed rage for order which comes into play when we attempt to render human experience in any form, and which results inevitably in some sort of pattern, whether discovered in or superimposed upon the material.

Still, Johnson has performed a useful service with his blunt statements, by refocussing our attention upon what is undoubtedly the crucial aspect of the creative process, the link between the raw material of experience and the consciousness through which that material is filtered and by which it is shaped and articulated. If he obstinately and combatively oversimplified, he made that relationship impossible to take for granted, and his insistence on being as true to life as his talent would allow him carries with it a homely and useful enjoiner against the facile falsification of experience.

Another difficult and related problem is posed by his stubborn insistence upon solipsism, which inevitably comes into conflict with his insistence on telling the truth. The only truth available to the solipsist is the inside of his own head, so that the full flux of experience is never in view, having been blotted out, and what remains is largely a view of the writer's interior landscape at a given moment. To fix on this, and this alone, as the appropriate subject for a writer is to deteriorate into self-indulgent narcissism. Fortunately, Johnson's own practice frequently belies his preachments; he had a very keen eye for the life around him, if his characterizations and descriptive passages are any measure. Again, the contradictions are never quite reconciled.

His compulsive novelty, evidenced by the various forms into which he cast his novels, becomes, finally, tedious.

Yet he probably could not, in justice to his tenets, have written any other way. He had rejected the Dickensian novel as no longer appropriate, and to undertake one just to prove he could write it would have been, for him, a pointless enterprise. While we might share the slight exasperation of one of his reviewers who voiced the feeling that with Johnson a better novel "seems to be just around a corner which he doctrinally refuses to turn," we must realize that, to Johnson, experimentation was not something to be simply gotten out of one's system so that one could get back into the main stream but was, indeed, the main stream. We must, in short, take him as he is.

He was stubborn and unregenerate, and these very qualities help make his work significant. For he was not satisfied with the form he inherited. He rejected what to him was an outworn legacy, and he stretched the form to accommodate and give voice to the stuff of the contemporary world. He never let us forget how important the novel is. Whether or not he dealt with them effectively and successfully at all times, he knew very well what the crucial issues of the novel are, and he was right to insist, however extremely, upon their primacy. If he seemed to spend an inordinate amount of time alternating between fist-shaking and nose-thumbing, he was also, at the same time, steadily pointing with his other hand toward the frontier. (pp. 72-3)

> *Robert S. Ryf, "B. S. Johnson and the Frontiers of Fiction," in* Critique: Studies in Modern Fiction *(copyright © by James Dean Young 1977), Vol. XIX, No. 1, 1977, pp. 58-74.*

What is it that makes an experimental novelist? There are many possible motivations, but among them must always be the desire for self-projection in a more total, more arresting form than that available to more conventional writers. Self-projection has usually been a risky business, and until recently the threat of ostracism hanging over the experimental writer was very real. Now it is so no longer. The upsurge of experimental art in the 1960s revealed that experimentation had become a recognised form of publicity-seeking. This is the background to B. S. Johnson's career. Johnson was never shy of self-advertisement —one remembers the advance publicity for his novel-in-a-box, *The Unfortunates* (1969)—but the show he put on was as much one of anxiety and vulnerability as of virtuosity. It was uncomfortably typical of Johnson that the 'random order' effect in *The Unfortunates* should seem superfluous in a novel of painfully literal honesty, that his one popular success with *Christie Malry's Own Double-Entry* (1973) should be achieved in apparent contravention of his own principles, and finally that his most ambitious artistic project, the *Matrix* trilogy, should be curtailed by his suicide. It was as if Johnson had reintroduced the risk into experimental writing by publicly setting himself tasks which were in fact impossible.

One should beware of arguing that any artist deliberately courted failure. And yet while artistic failure is commonplace, a record of ostentatious 'failures' like Johnson's must surely be rather rare. During his lifetime, he was most commonly seen as a brilliant writer thrashing around in a trap of his own making. I shared this view, but have more recently come to feel that there was method and not artlessness in Johnson's constant disappointment of the reader's, and his own, expectations. Reread in sequence, his novels can be seen to exemplify a peculiarly British form of self-punishment. Johnson's imagination is of the manic-depressive type, the mania resulting in bold experimentation and extravagant comedy, and the depression in the gloomy, morose self-examination of his more intimate novels such as *The Unfortunates* and *Trawl* (1966). This in itself is not so very remarkable; if they did no more than project a personality, Johnson's novels, though certainly arresting, would hardly stand out as unique. What makes these novels significant is that they are shaped in accordance with a conscious aesthetic, and this aesthetic . . . has a deep historical correspondence with the particular kind of personality-structure that Johnson's writings reveal.

'Telling stories is telling lies . . . I am not interested in telling lies in my own novels.' This thesis which Johnson nailed to the door of his house of fiction provoked a barrage of refutation from critics, even the most sympathetic. It was denounced as an expression of hostility to art and a deliberate shackling of the imagination. It was seen as a denial of its author's own gifts and a pernicious example to others. This sort of misunderstanding may have been inevitable, since Johnson was at once a vociferous member of the avant-garde and an extreme individualist. But Johnson's version of the Eighth Commandment was devised for his own purposes, not for the general reformation of contemporary fiction. In arguing this, I wish to stress a point that I do not think any previous critic of Johnson has made—that his objection to 'telling stories', so far from being revolutionary, is the traditional objection of English Puritanism. Thus Johnson's originality was not a matter of mere innovation; it was that his innovations, together with other aspects of his art, reveal how far the Puritan tradition survives as a means of making sense of the contemporary world. (pp. 45-6)

B. S. Johnson was an aggressively anti-religious writer. Whatever its roots may have been in his personal experience his anticlericalism speaks of [an] . . . austere, . . . vulnerably religious temperament. . . . Christie Malry, the hero of Johnson's penultimate novel, tries to prosecute his parish church under the Trade Descriptions Act—after all, they claim to have 'the answer to all problems, personal, political and international'—and eventually has to be cautioned by his girlfriend for his 'obsession with knocking religion'. Christie, an urban guerrilla, is an inverted Christ-figure, and so is Haakon, the scapegoat hero of Johnson's play *You're Human Like the Rest of Them* (1964). The play ends with Haakon's parable of locusts and lizards: the futile resistance of the locusts which are being fed to lizards in a cage is seen as the only protest open to man in the face of a vindictive deity:

> The only thing a locust could do was
> To make itself an awkward thing to eat
> By sticking out its arms and legs and wings
> To make itself an awkward thing to kill
> So shall I: I have to die, but by God
> I'm not going to pretend I like it
> I shall make myself so bloody awkward!

Anti-Christian attitudes like these play a regular and certainly not a very profound role in Johnson's writings. But it is within the context of an acknowledged anti-religious obsession that Johnson will be seen to exemplify some underlying patterns of the Puritan intelligence. (pp. 47-8)

Johnson's renunciation of fiction was . . . not so much a principle to guide the novel-reader as a standard against which to measure himself. Superficially he may have hoped to change contemporary fiction but deep down, it would seem, he was setting himself tests he did not believe he could pass. While the exploitation of selfconscious devices in his novels was often playful, it could also be anguished and hurt. The bilious emotional outburst which interrupts the narrative near the end of *Albert Angelo* (1964) is far removed from the suavity with which a practitioner such as John Fowles exploits the convention of the novel with a thwarted ending. Johnson's principles provide for many comic moments, but they also produce anguish when he cannot live up to them and guilt when he contravenes them without the reader knowing. In *Aren't You Rather Young* he expressed his private struggle in terms that any serious writer could understand: 'I feel myself fortunate sometimes that I can laugh at the joke that just as I was beginning to think I knew something about how to write a novel it is no longer of any use to me in attempting the next one.' If we see his aims as, in some sense, unattainable the joke here will seem rather precarious. Johnson's self-deprecation is compounded by the fact that, once he had declared in public that he hated telling lies, he had done his best to make the reader suspicious of every novel he wrote. Any success of his will seem hypocritical since he has substituted an impossible technical standard for the impossible moral standards of religious Puritanism.

Johnson's attempts to reconcile fiction and truth was explicit in his first novel, *Travelling People* (1963). Here he announced his intention to expose the mechanism of the novel, by means of interludes, jokes and stylistic variation, in order to eliminate deception between writer and reader. *Travelling People* was well received, but Johnson later called it a 'disaster' because it was 'part truth and part fiction'. . . . His next novel, *Albert Angelo*, contains an extraordinary exercise in self-abasement when the hero, a supply teacher, sets his secondary-modern class an essay on 'What I think of teacher'. The answers make a brilliant series of parodies, but then Johnson interrupts the narrative, denouncing his fictional structure as a sham and confessing that 'teacher' is himself. There followed *Trawl* and *The Unfortunates*, novels of mordant self-examination in which the narrator broods over his futile love-affairs and over a painful bereavement. In *House Mother Normal* (1971) and *Christie Malry*, by contrast, Johnson abandons the autobiographical mode and portrays masterful and self-confident main characters whose behaviour arouses outright revulsion or, at best, a guilty and sneaking admiration. These are novels which cauterise normal human reactions, and only on reflection does their moral purpose become apparent. Such purpose is hidden as if Johnson were ashamed to take credit for it, preferring to be allied with his protagonists as scapegoat-turned-villain. Finally there was to be the *Matrix* trilogy, announced as his major work—a double humiliation in that his determination not to tell lies seemed likely to reduce the narrative to a random montage, and in that he did not live to complete it. (pp. 48-9)

The correspondence between technical and psychic exploration is a working hypothesis which points us towards the real matter of Johnson's art. What was the 'dredged-up material' in his case? He himself wrote of his work as a systematic, rational struggle with technical problems, while I have initially approached it as a process of public self-humiliation. In fact it is the presence of a continuous moral vision that emerges from rereading the novels, although Johnson rarely spoke of that vision. Without such a vision, it would in any case be otiose to speak to him as a Puritan artist. (p. 50)

House Mother Normal, a 'geriatric comedy' set in an old people's home, is a technical *tour de force* consisting of nine interior monologues, each taking up twenty-one pages and covering exactly the same stretch of time. Every line in a given monologue corresponds to the same moment in each of the others. The strict scheme is handled with such ingenuity that we can identify with each of the inmates in turn, while putting together the complex jigsaw of events during the Social Evening which takes up the allotted time-span. The novel has a powerful *memento mori* effect, not least through Johnson's use of blank spaces to indicate periods of pain, mental confusion and unconsciousness. Here a typographical trick which was first exploited in *Travelling People* is put to serious and dignified use. The book is an intimate reminder that—in Johnson's final words—'worse times are a-coming, nothing is more sure'.

There are two aspects which seem to require some explanation. The first is the curiously sensational role played by House Mother, a role which ends with her stripping for the benefit of her senile charges and performing a sexual act with her dog. Then there is the correspondence of the novel with Johnson's principle that 'Telling stories is telling lies'. Admittedly, House Mother, like Albert Angelo, is finally exposed as an invented character:

> Thus you see I too am the
> puppet or concoction of a writer (you always knew
> there was a writer behind it all? Ah, there's
> no fooling you readers!). . . .
>
> So
> you see this is from his skull. It is a diagram
> of certain aspects of the inside of his skull!

But, unlike the earlier novel, we are not told *why* she has been invented. At first reading her exhibitionism seems gratuitous and Johnson's purpose remains unclear. At the simplest level, he is no doubt using sexual titillation to sustain an air of suspense about actions which have to be reported nine times over. Beyond this House Mother is used to make a point about 'normality'. Johnson himself wrote that 'The idea was to say something about the things we call "normal" and "abnormal"', but it is doubtful if the point needs such heavy underlining. There may be an error of judgement here, but at least House Mother will not seem the product of cynical sensationalism when we examine the attitudes contrasted in the novel more closely.

House Mother holds her position because society tries to ignore old age by calling its victims 'geriatric' and shutting them away in institutions. She is a petty tyrant with total control over the inmates, and has found how to derive a range of emotional satisfactions from her charge. These satisfactions must be perverse because a healthily sensual individual would not have taken on her job in the first place; this, at least, is what Johnson seems to imply. None the less she is an ordinary person and therefore combines various more or less understandable forms of corruption with an energetic habit of self-justification. We are put off from the beginning by her false, ingratiating tone of address; though ironically her voice introducing the narrative is also

the authorial voice. . . . House Mother exerts maternal authority over her patients, but the reality from which she wants to shield them is that of disillusionment with God. Yet she is not a believer, only a hypocrite who believes in maintaining the holy lies on which respectable society is based. Johnson's attitude to her is indicated when he concludes her list of clinical features with a diagnosis of 'malignant cerebral carcinoma (dormant)'. But it must be added that she is also a narrator-figure, whose initial plausibility he is at some pains to establish.

Unlike her patients (whose self-absorption ranges from states of reverie and self-admiration to heavy pain and extreme catatonia) House Mother is always appealing to an audience. Her monologue has a rhetorical purpose; she is an inveterate liar because she is a deliberate story-teller using her fantasies as a means of subduing and imposing on others. These fantasies have become an adequate substitute for reciprocal human relationships, so that she is content with her unenviable profession and content also with a sexual partner who is her dog. As individual psychology this may be fairly lurid, but House Mother must be understood as a surrogate figure whom Johnson invests with his own guilty compulsion to be a writer and tell lies to command the attention of others. Yet the reader who responds to the hints of moral condemnation in the way I have done has himself been manoeuvred into the position of the Puritan externalising his own guilts and finding a scapegoat for them. The subtlety of the novel lies, I think, in Johnson's realisation of the humanity that is fought over by these warring ethical alternatives. (pp. 50-2)

In *Albert Angelo,* the hero prepares a homily to his class on 'the dignity of humankind'. They are unmoved and—in one of the novel's alternative endings—dump him unceremoniously in the Thames. The value of stoicism is sardonically affirmed throughout Johnson's novels. . . . Suffering in Johnson's writing is both intensely personal and a general experience. The dignity of the old people in *House Mother Normal* is partly theirs as members of the generation that fought on the Somme, and who have survived only to face death again in the modern equivalent of the workhouse. As individuals they are not all very attractive, but their memories, whether of war or love or gaiety or bereavement, convey a fortitude which will enable them to meet whatever is in store for them just as they have done in the past. Unlike the reader they are simply unmoved by House Mother's exhibitionism and, whatever the causes of disgust that arise with the decay of the body, they are simply in need of material, and not of spiritual, help. In this novel Johnson has both dramatised the Puritan compulsions of bodily loathing, moral condemnation, guilty self-righteousness and keeping up appearances, and has transcended them by means of a more fundamental, non-rhetorical assertion of human dignity.

House Mother Normal, I believe, will stand as Johnson's finest work. I have argued that it makes subtle use of Puritan reactions, but it is in the middle-period novels *Trawl* and *The Unfortunates* that we find the more narrowly Puritan obsessions. *House Mother Normal* is a statement of the truth of non-rhetorical (and in this sense non-fictional) individual consciousness. Its interplay of nine interior monologues must be technically unique. In the two earlier novels the interior monologue is used in a much more traditional way, to convey the confessional meditations of a single character suffering from remorse of conscience. It was here that Johnson gave full rein to the solipsistic tendencies inherent in his hostility to 'fiction'. (pp. 53-4)

The gloomy, alienated viewpoint of *Trawl* is continued in *The Unfortunates*. This is a tribute to a friend who died of cancer. . . . It introduces the theme which was continued in the later novels. . . . The theme contrasts sharply with the whimsical randomness that results from putting the novel into a box. . . . Johnson's idea is to allow the reader to participate in his own uncertainties about structuring the novel; but in fact the demonstration is pointless because it makes one feel that the structure does not matter. In my experience there is no way of re-ordering the twenty-seven different sections so as to introduce a previously hidden element of surprise. *The Unfortunates* is not a truly random work because we are never tempted to doubt the common source of the separate discourses constituted by each section. the author provides a 'First' and 'Last' episode, and the intervening sections are all interior monologues produced by a manifestly continuous first-person narrator, who is a journalist reporting a football match in a Midlands city. Given the uniformly confessional content of the novel, the fact that Johnson himself may have pieced it together from different episodes written at different times is really of no significance to the reader.

The one aspect in which Johnson's self-consciousness is triumphantly justified is the reporting of the match itself. Stuck to the bottom of the box is a facsimile of a football report signed 'B. S. Johnson' in the house-style of the *Observer* newspaper. The headline 'Sub inspires City triumph' is, of course, a Johnsonian pun calling attention to the drastically truncated form of the report as it appears 'in print'. The section which shows how this report is produced handles material which would have appealed to Balzac by means of the comic techniques of Joyce and Sterne. The narrator's interior monologue during the game is interspersed with the sentences he notes down in draft. There follows a transcript of his phone-call to the editorial desk during which he dictates his copy. The section combines the formal incongruities involved in the production of a 'text' with a highly authentic picture of a journalist at work; it could be seen as a portrayal of alienated labour with the journalist's professional skill balanced against his personal boredom and resentment. But his exposure of the mechanism of hack writing must make up for the absence of any real exposure of the process of writing *The Unfortunates* itself. The various forces that may have determined the latter text remain conjectural and implicit. (pp. 54-5)

In his middle period Johnson failed to solve the conundrum of the non-fiction novel that he had set himself. Both *Trawl* and *The Unfortunates* have the form of a kind of pilgrimage, a successive discovery of the pain and nullity of the world of experience. The pilgrim has as his goal certain immanent truths but these must either be confined to the self (as in *Trawl*) or falsely objectified in terms of another (as in *The Unfortunates*). The effective result in either case is solipsistic—a dramatisation of the writing self which questions everything except its own justification. In *House Mother Normal* and *Christie Malry* Johnson broke away from this pattern, cauterising the 'I' of his fictions by creating characters who represent the anti-self and become scapegoats drawing upon themselves the weight of Puritanical loathing. The result is that the figure of the novelist

comes under reflexive attack in these novels, but at the price of creating a fictional structure akin to traditional comedy, where the hero's bizarre and misguided modes of behaviour are in sharpest contrast to the implied securities of writer and reader. It follows that Johnson could no more escape the accusation that he is using a lie to root out a lie than could, say, Cervantes in *Don Quixote*.

Christie Malry is an urban guerrilla waging an isolated, solipsistic war with society. Trained as a bank-clerk, he adapts the method of double entry book-keeping to his own purposes; every debit entered by the outside world against his own name must be balanced by a corresponding credit. The idea of life as a vale of book-keeping, in which the account one can render of one's own life corresponds as exactly as possible to the balance that is written up in heaven, is one that is dear to the Puritan imagination. The difference between Christie and the 'Johnson' of the earlier novels is that the discharge of conscientious duty makes him not a novelist or a self-punishing solipsist but a Jacobean revenger. He reduces the debt that society owes him by expedients that range from pilfering stationery to blowing up a tax office and poisoning London's water supply. The result is an acrid little tale, written with tremendous verve and punctuated at invervals by the balance sheet which shows Christie's own reckoning of his 'current account'. Finally, with his debt-collection getting more megolomaniac and his methods of reckoning increasingly farcical Christie is struck down by cancer. The revenger has at last turned scapegoat, and before he dies he just has time to turn his dissatisfaction on the narrator: '"In any case," he said, almost to himself, not looking at me, "you shouldn't be bloody writing novels about it, you should be out there bloody doing something about it."' So we are back to the hideousness of cancer, and its unfairness—an unfairness which will not be wiped out when the doctors discover a cure. In *House Mother Normal* and *Christie Malry* Johnson has resolved the unfairness of cancer in the one (ineffectual and lying) way to which the novelist has access: by creating victims who for all their entertainment-value are finally so monstrous that cancer is what they deserve. The fiction of 'poetic justice' serves to bring home in a grim and farcical way the injustice—the lack of any balance-sheet—in life.

The creation of a scapegoat may be satisfying to the Puritan conscience, but what after all is it worth? Christie's sturdily anarchist values, his effortless success as a revenger and his capacity for uncomplicated erotic enjoyment may form the basis of the novel's comic exuberance, but the exuberance is superficial and behind it we sense the author's helpless and sardonic detachment. The idea that Christie ('Christ'?) deserves his fate does not compensate, except in the terms of his own dehumanised 'book-keeping' attitude to human relationships, for the pain and bewilderment that are present as surely as in *The Unfortunates* and *Trawl*. The book ends with the 'Final reckoning,' which is obviously a parody of the Last Judgement at which the entries in God's Book are to be revealed. (pp. 55-7)

Johnson was a conscious disciple of Beckett and Joyce, and his place in modern fiction may be best ascertained by invoking the category which Hugh Kenner has proposed for these novelists—that of the 'stoic comedians'. (p. 57)

Johnson's principle that 'Telling stories is telling lies' is what makes the space available for his novels a confined one. In many ways he is a 'stoic comedian', a minor follower of one of the major modernist schools. But there is one crucial difference between Johnson and the giants who figure (whether rightly or wrongly) in Hugh Kenner's pantheon. Johnson's literary attitude, unlike theirs, is that of a humanist. In Beckett's fiction the tedium and sterility of life is experienced by a succession of fictional personae, behind whom their creator lurks, noncommittal and unseen. Johnson is a confessional, not an impersonal artist, and the sterility and tedium are felt by him as a private burden or obsession. His first-person narrators are not distanced but transparently autobiographical, and the burden of inadequacy and guilt are his own. Against his occasional lugubriousness should be set the fact that he was able to be very direct about his reasons for writing:

> I think I write because I have something to say that I fail to say satisfactorily in conversation, in person. Then there are things like conceit, stubbornness, a desire to retaliate on those who have hurt me paralleled by a desire to repay those who have helped me, a need to try to create something which may live after me (which I take to be the detritus of the religious feeling), the sheer technical joy of forcing almost intractable words into patterns of meaning and form that are uniquely (for the moment at least) mine, a need to make people laugh with me in case they laugh at me, a desire to codify experience, to come to terms with things that have happened to me, and to try to tell the truth (to discover what is the truth) about them. And I write especially to exorcise, to remove from myself, from my mind, the burden [of] having to bear some pain, the hurt of some experience; in order that it may be over there, in a book, and not in here in my mind.
>
> *(Aren't You Rather Young . . .)*

This statement has an admirable simplicity, which not one of the great modernists would have managed. It may be modelled on Orwell's 'Why I write'. Perhaps so confidently discursive a tone speaks too much of the journalist-novelist, and throws into question Johnson's position as an experimental artist? Johnson himself would seem to have felt unhappy about it, since he went on to provide an alternative, more poetic but also much balder statement. The interest of this second statement lies in the last of the three motives which he lists for writing down an interior vision: 'so that I would not have to repeat it'. Even here, one would guess that the idea that he could exorcise his experiences, and avoid repeating them, may itself have come to seem a lie: one of life's unavoidable, and yet unjustifiable, fictions.

B. S. Johnson is like Bunyan's pilgrim, condemned always to go on writing in the hope of getting rid of the burden on his back. English seventeenth-century literature exemplifies two of the ways in which a writer may respond to the overwhelming presence of evil and death in the world. The first is the way of the Jacobean dramatists, with their farcical and morbid connoisseurship of evil, revenge and the suffering of the innocent; a way that is broached in *Christie Malry* and *House Mother Normal*. The second is the confessional impulse of the isolated soul searching for what is lasting among the ephemeral phantoms that assail him; this is what Johnson pursues in his middle-period novels. I would suggest that these are two sides of the lurid, isolated and self-punishing Puritan imagination. To see Johnson in these terms is to suggest that, for him, experimental writing was the authentic expression of a deep-rooted artistic individualism. Despite his anti-religious obsession Johnson succeeded in reviving the characteristic religious form which British individualist consciousness has taken. His Puritanism offered a standpoint from which—except in *Travelling People*—he could at all times attack merely fashionable or respectable values. A corresponding tendency to solipsism was most adequately countered in *House Mother Normal*, which exploits the forms of Puritan consciousness in such a way as to transcend and negate them. But if Johnson's reputation as a minor novelist continues to survive it will owe as much to his revival and exploration of the Puritan conscience as to his membership of the contemporary avant-garde. (pp. 57-9)

> *Patrick Parrinder, "Pilgrim's Progress: The Novels of B. S. Johnson," in* Critical Quarterly *(© Manchester University Press 1977; this abridged version © Patrick Parrinder 1978), Summer, 1977, pp. 45-59.*

* * *

JONES, Gayl 1949-

Jones is an American novelist, poet, and short story writer. Both the form and subject matter of her work are drawn from the black oral tradition. Her writing is powerful, the rhythms of black jazz and blues giving cadence to her poetry and prose. (See also *CLC*, Vol. 6.)

This ["Eva's Man"] is the blues that lost control. This is the rhythmic, monotone lamentation of one woman, Eva Medina, who is nobody I have ever known.

You gather from the name that she, this woman, embodies bad news for men. (Cf. the Garden of Eden and also the stone consequences, so to speak, of Medusa.) You further surmise that this alleged Double Trouble, this demented black woman invented by a black woman writer, is supposed to renew or revise some pretty traditional ideas about the female. And, in case you miss the first two heavies, there's another signifying figure in the story, name of "Queen Bee": so much for the apparent aims of this experimental, gruesome narrative.

In addition, there is the very real, upsetting accomplishment of Gayl Jones in this, her second novel: sinister misinformation about women—about women, in general, about black women in particular, and especially about young black girls forced to deal with the sexual, molesting violations of their minds and bodies by their fathers, their mothers' boyfriends, their cousins and uncles. (p. 36)

Did Eva skip school, altogether? How was it when her mother bought new winter clothes for her, or didn't? Did her family never attend a wedding celebration or a christening? What happened about birthdays, in her house? In this short work of bedeviled compulsion, there is sex or there isn't. There is absolute loneliness by one's self or there is the elliptical loneliness of brutal, mute coupling; accidents of exploitation that bespeak no history, no promise.

Miss Jones delivers her story in a strictly controlled, circular form that is wrapped, around and around, with ambivalence. Unerringly, her writing creates the tension of a problem unresolved. . . .

As for the Eva/Medusa/Queen Bee facets of the tale, they arise and disappear. But, at the last, they do not mesh into illumination. Rather than renew or revise ideas about the female, these chapters perpetuate "crazy whore"/ "castrating bitch" images that long have defamed black women in our literature.

And I fear for the meaning of this novel. What does it mean when a young black woman sits down to compose a universe of black people limited to animal dynamics? And what will such testimony, such perverse ambivalence, contribute to the understanding of black girls in need of rescue and protection?

What will it mean to that great crowd of the everlastingly curious who wonder about black women, our consciousness, capacities and want? Is Eva Medina the new Bigger Thomas minus the enemy white world? Is this a second "Fear of Flying," the crawl and the scream of a fantasy that will sell well?

At the end of this novel, Gayl Jones says to the reader, *"See what they are doing with this woman."*

I must ask Miss Jones, *"Who is she?"* (p. 37)

> *June Jordan, in* The New York Times Book Review (© *1976 by The New York Times Company; reprinted by permission), May 16, 1976.*

Gayl Jones' first novel, *Corregidora*, was a small, fiercely concentrated story, harsh and perfectly told. It was about the arrangements between black men and black women, and also about heritage. Original, superbly imagined, nothing about the book was simple or easily digested. Out of the worn themes of miscegenation and diminishment, Gayl Jones *excavated* the disturbingly buried damage of racism. *Eva's Man* is a deepened exploration of the woman's inner life: of the pressures, the cruelties, the imposed expectations. Like the first work, part of the interest of *Eva's Man* lies in its having no relation to the polemical tradition of "Black Literature."

It hardly matters, in this novel, that Eva Canada is black. Structurally unsettled, more scattered than *Corregidora*, *Eva's Man* is extremely remote, more troubling in its hallucinations. This story is spoken—screeched or moaned would be closer to the tone—by Eva who is incarcerated in a ward for the criminally insane. . . . The personal exploitation that causes Eva's desperation is hard to appreciate. Her rage seems never to find its proper object, an adequate form of expression, except, possibly, in her last extreme act. The first novel concerned itself with a violently incestuous chronicle, a legacy of rape and abuse dating from Brazilian plantations; and these things make the pathological frigidity and inherited psychological damage of its heroine understandable. But Eva's terror is too deep, strangely recessed. Memory, here, assumes a shattering tyranny. . . .

[What] is offered the reader is somewhat insufficient: the torment [Eva] suffers as a woman is not unusual, unfortunately, due to its frequency. No, this is not meant to depreciate the daily nature of a woman's pain; but not all women become schizophrenic, destructive. Both novels are relentlessly about fornication and sex, as an act, as a burden,

central to the plot of existence, a dialogue between the deprived. The most private and reduced relations between the characters is all that is needed to indicate their social oppression. There is a continual sense of suffocation in these novels, as if their lives took place in a closet. The stasis and isolation are haunting. . . . Gayl Jones' novels are, finally, indictments against black men. The women are denied by convention what Angela Davis has called "the deformed equality of equal oppression." (p. 27)

The *paranoia* of [Eva's] soliloquy is reminiscent of some novels concerning homosexuals. Both Baldwin's *Giovanni's Room* and Vidal's *The City and the Pillar* end in murder, as if mutilated or troubled sexual identities had only the *grisly* as their fate. The lesbian overtones of *Eva's Man* are intriguing. Only the women seem capable of reflection, affection without completely impure motives. . . .

Gayl Jones places her heroines between victory and defeat where deprivation is a narcotic. Though they are women of intense and complicated feelings, their severity suggests an impasse. How does one sustain or add to the pitch of these books? There are hints of fragmentation and strain in the conception of *Eva's Man*. And there are risks in offering the novel as a form for poetic and violent tirades of the solitary self: the limitations of tradition are exchanged for the narrowness of inaccessibility. Opaque, flat, peculiar, in her fiction Gayl Jones has presented problems that are living, historical and important additions to the current American —not just black—scene. These novels are genuinely imaginative creations. (p. 28)

> *Darryl Pinckney, in* The New Republic *(reprinted by permission of* The New Republic; © *1976 by The New Republic, Inc.), June 19, 1976.*

Femaleness as experienced by American blacks was Gayl Jones' subject in her first novel, "Corregidora," and "Eva's Man," her second, continues the exploration with a sharpened starkness, a power of ellipsis that leaves ever darker gaps between its flashes of rhythmic, sensuously exact dialogue and visible symbol. Ursa Corregidora's meandering voice has become the softly mad voice of Eva Canada. (p. 74)

Miss Jones, at twenty-six, is an American writer with a powerful sense of vital inheritance, of history in the blood. Evil is no idle concept to her. . . . [Evil] permeates the erotic education of Eva Canada. . . . Though everything in Miss Jones' fictional world becomes a symbol . . . , and though in this novel her repetitious, dreaming dialogue and fragmentary, often italicized scenes verge on mannerism, we never doubt the honorable motive behind her methods— the wish, that is, to represent the inner reality of individuals who belong to a disenfranchised and brutalized race. Real fish swim in her murky waters, though she does not always land them. Her heroines are unable to respond, and, as T. S. Eliot pointed out in connection with "Hamlet," an inability is hard to objectify. *"An owl sucks my blood. I am bleeding underneath my nails. An old owl sucks my blood. He gives me fruit in my palms."* We have not been persuaded Eva could think this; the author is pushing images through her. It is expressionistic, but expressive mainly of literary strain. And in her troubling nullity Eva is surrounded not so much by other characters as by amateur psychotherapists, all nagging at her silence. Miss Jones apparently wishes to show us a female heart frozen into rage by deprivation, but the worry arises, as it did not in "Corregidora," that the characters are dehumanized as much by her artistic vision as by their circumstances. (pp. 74-5)

John Updike, in The New Yorker (© *1976 by The New Yorker Magazine, Inc.), August 9, 1976.*

Eva's Man is a heavily repetitive, possessed *female* fantasy that works as a vindictive counterpart to the male-controlled vagina dentata. Eva, the "savage woman," murders her lover by dental castration and becomes enough of a celebrity to essay a proletarian remembrance of things past. This short novel should have been shorter or clearer about its interests and grounds. There is a hollow heartiness about its lantern slide—say rather litany—of Southern ghetto misadventures, female variety. But the litany, if not false in any of its terms, is false in its effect of monotony and monochromaticism. As Coleridge observes, "images, however . . . faithfully copied from nature, and accurately represented in words, do not of themselves characterize" the artist. The images, the imagination here lacks fundamental play and proportion and relation and conviction.

Eva is a character with the mentality of a child ("I tell them I'm not getting things straight") in the body and the social complex of an abused adult woman. The real interest of her story is not in its details, but in her nature, in the question whether the numbing squalor of her experience has left her a nature. Jones is perhaps essaying a metaphysics of squalor, but *Eva's Man* too much resembles a tour of squalor with its beatings, shootings, sodomy, cockroaches, deformity, child molestation, and people "biting [their] own umbilical cord." Eva's is a world with no motive, no value, no consequence even—her imprisonment for murder is incidental to her opportunity for another off-beat encounter. The question arises whether her deed is spontaneous combustion from all the numb repressions and oppressions heaped in the privacy of Eva's soul, or a freak of sensual abandonment, or an act of dumb retaliation for her whole life or only for the lover's leaving her moved while he just moves on, or a radical repudiation of being touched and humanly culpable, i.e., vulnerable again. Only the last possibility gives the novel any real depth or resonance, and it is not substantiated. Jones combines Eva with Medusa in the novel, as if the pristine mother and the primordial horror were one. But this seems gratuitous, uncorroborated in the story. Jones's homicidal neutering . . . may criticize and deny what appears a gratuitous male power, but it does so by the grossest form of flattery, imitation. (pp. 150-51)

Michael G. Cooke, in The Yale Review (© *1976 by Yale University; reprinted by permission of the editors), Autumn, 1976.*

K

KAWABATA, Yasunari   1899-1972

Kawabata, a novelist, short story writer, and critic, was the first Japanese author to receive the Nobel Prize for Literature. Numerous deaths in his family left Kawabata virtually alone at a young age and impressed upon him the loneliness and impermanence of life, a view often reflected in his work. He was respected not only as an author but as a patron of younger Japanese writers such as Yukio Mishima. (See also *CLC*, Vols. 2, 5, and *Contemporary Authors*, obituary, Vols. 33-36, rev. ed.)

In [*House of the Sleeping Beauties*], Kawabata poignantly explores the intimate thoughts of an old man searching for the meaning of his existence. In his sensual yearnings, erotic fancies, and subtle attempts at self-deception Eguchi probes back to the source of life. But the quest is a failure; he ends a lonely old man, chilled with the knowledge of his aloneness.

The novel is at once traditional, from one called the "most Japanese" of writers, and modern—as modern as geriatrics, senior citizens, and "Sunset Villages." . . . The something "Japanese" about Kawabata is a meditative, sympathetic, sometimes wistful, and highly evocative understanding of nature, or rather, of the subtle interplay between nature and human existence. It has deep roots in the heritage of Japan's past, both religious and literary, from Buddhist reflection and Shinto mystique as well as their artistic calling card, the haiku poem. Thus, in *House of the Sleeping Beauties,* the wrist of one of the sleeping girls brushes over old Eguchi's eye and the scent brings "rich new fantasies." The old man's thoughts are like a poem; "just at this time of year, two or three winter peonies blooming in the warm sun, under the high stone fence of an old temple in Yamato." . . . The flowers in turn suggest old Eguchi's daughters. This passage, and others like it, illustrate what one critic has described as the "painfully delicate nuances and almost immeasurable subtlety peculiar to Japanese art and literature."

But even for Japanese readers the Nobel prize winner's works sometimes appear strange and even uninviting. Is it because Kawabata's sad, fragmented world is also a world of resignation, of quiescent Buddhism? Is the voice of this most Japanese of Japanese authors the voice of the past? . . . The answers are not easy to obtain. . . . In any case, however "traditionally Japanese," however much "of the past," and however puzzling, Kawabata's artistry has much which declares its timeliness and relevance for the present.

What indeed could be more relevant—to any age—than loneliness, the hopelessness of love, alienation? From the frustrated lovers of *Snow Country* to the dreamily desiring man in "One Arm," Kawabata brilliantly evokes the poignancy of thwarted love. His other major themes too are universally appealing. The "darkness and wasted beauty" which "run like a ground bass through his major work," represent an integral part of the heritage of both East and West. Again, old age and death too preoccupy Kawabata. He said after World War II that he could write only elegies, and in keeping with this resolve wrote such works as *The Sound of the Mountain* and *Thousand Cranes. House of the Sleeping Beauties* can be added. Puzzling then, he may be, in great part no doubt due to his poetic, elliptical style, but Kawabata is very much relevant, "contemporary" in the sense that universal themes are always contemporary. And his major themes are all presented in *House of the Sleeping Beauties*.

Like Tanizaki's *Diary of a Mad Old Man,* Kawabata's works reveal the inner workings of an old man's mind, recording his efforts to make the erotic most of his last days. But Kawabata's novel has a sinister note, and the crimson velvet curtains of the sleeping beauties' room create a setting which might have come from one of the macabre works of Edgar Allan Poe. The sinister note is sustained, for death suffuses the narrative; from the opening pages where one reads that "the wind carried the sound of approaching winter" to the final lines where the dark girl's body is dragged downstairs, the reader suspects death. And death comes, as inevitably as it must soon come to old Eguchi. Kawabata's artistry manifests itself in the way he combines the suggestions of death with bits of setting, builds up suspense, and uses indirection to achieve a unified tone. The result would satisfy Poe's criterion for the ideal short story, one which has a "unique or single effect." The effect in this case is a feeling of inevitability, a gloomy sense that something is coming to an end, and that at the end death waits. (pp. 19-21)

The opening words of his story are a warning which at once suggests danger and a strange eroticism. Old Eguchi is "not to put his finger into the mouth of the sleeping girl, or try

309

anything else of that sort." . . . Kawabata quickly adds the sinister note. The house has a "secret," and a locked gate, and when Eguchi arrives, all is silent. The woman who admits him has a strange and "disquieting" bird design on her obi (kimono waist band). Images of death soon accumulate. The secret house is near the sea, and the sound of the waves is violent. . . . The winter season and the nearby sea, both archetypal symbols of death, suggest the mood. Eguchi, before entering the room of the sleeping girl, recalls lines from a poetess who died young: "the night offers toads and black dogs and corpses of the drowned." He wonders if the sleeping girl will resemble a drowned corpse. . . .

Small wonder that old Eguchi begins this first visit to the secret house with "apprehension" and an "unpleasant emptiness." As the reader first suspects, then gradually realizes with deepening awareness, that "emptiness" is Eguchi's own. For the old man's series of visits to the House of the Sleeping Beauties is a series of confrontations with himself, a set of experiments in self-analysis in which his identity is very much at issue. What could force one to be more intensely introspective than a meeting where the other person is only a presence, a body, and where one's musings, questions, charges are met only with silence or the slight movement of a hand? (pp. 21-2)

Nearing seventy years of age, Eguchi is like the secret house seems to be when the waves roar, perched on the edge of the cliff above the sea. Yet still clear of mind, and still virile to some extent, he grows irritable at any suggestion that he might be senile or helpless like other old men who visit the house. "I'm all right," he growls at the woman of the house when she cautions him to be careful of the wet stones and tries to help him, "I'm not so old yet that I need to be led by the hand." . . . But his vision is that of one in his last extremity. "An old man lives next door to death," he says in the final chapter. . . . And what is it to be an old man, in one's last extremity? (pp. 22-3)

Kawabata divides his narrative rather formally, into five chapters. Unlike the familiar dramatic form, however, the final section is not a denouement; rather, the story builds to a climax which comes only in the last pages. In each of the first four chapters, Eguchi visits the secret house and spends the night, each time sleeping by the side of a different girl. (p. 23)

One can see in the structure of the narrative both progression and thematic unity. Eguchi's visits to the secret house follow the deepening season; autumn turns to winter and the fall rains become sleet and snow. The final visit is made in "dead winter." The suspense too deepens, as Eguchi's thoughts become increasingly serious and macabre. Part of the subtle build-up is the old man's gradually increasing desire for stronger medicine and the growing urge to join the sleeping beauties in their death-like sleep. Unity is achieved by the concentration on character—primarily old Eguchi—and on place, by the continual piling up of sensuous imagery. Eguchi is in turn aroused, soothed, stimulated, troubled, and calmed by the touch, smell, and sight of the soft flesh beside him in the red room. Again, unity is heightened by the recurrence of like or similar images; virginity, sexual experience, pregnancy, and babies vie or blend with the thoughts of flowers, parts of a woman's body, blood, and the sleep of death. Like Nathaniel Hawthorne, Kawabata is especially deft in his use of color. The house of sleeping beauties is a house of whites, reds, and blacks: the whiteness of skin and milk, the redness of velvet curtains and blood, the blackness of night, death, and the dark sea.

Like Hawthorne too, Kawabata symbolically probes the human heart. Indeed the crimson-curtained room is both heart and womb. It is heart, where an old man living a death-in-life confronts his paradoxical opposite, a young woman who is life-in-death; here he relives his past loves and puzzles over his existence. Eguchi probes deeper and deeper into his consciousness or "heart" as he returns repeatedly to the secret house. And it is womb; in its warm comfort, Eguchi's thoughts turn to baby's milk, pregnancy, sex, blood, and death. It is a feminine world, where the women of Eguchi's life parade through his dreams and reveries. Maternal in its appeal, the crimson room lures him ever deeper in thought and farther back in time, inevitably, to the first woman of his life, his mother, in whom the notions of babies and breasts, his hopes, fears, and anxieties, the sensations of blood and death have their source.

On a cold night in the dead of winter Eguchi makes his fifth visit to the secret house. An old man has died while sleeping beside one of the beauties, and references to that death dominate Eguchi's conversation with the woman of the house. Eguchi is startled to learn that this time there are two girls. In another Hawthorne-like touch, Kawabata makes one dark, the other fair. . . . As drowsiness overcomes him, his thoughts turn to the first woman of his life; "Now at sixty-seven, as he lay between two naked girls a new truth came from deep inside him. Was it blasphemy, was it yearning? He opened his eyes and blinked, as if to drive away a nightmare. But the drug was working. He had a dull headache. Drowsily, he pursued the image of his mother; and then he sighed, and took two breasts, one of each of the girls, in the palms of his hands. A smooth one and an oily one. He closed his eyes." . . . His mother had died when Eguchi was only seventeen. He recalls the grief and terror of that scene. "'Yoshio. Yoshio.' His mother called out in little gasps. Eguchi understood, and stroked her tormented bosom. As he did so she vomited a large quantity of blood. It came bubbling from her nose. She stopped breathing. . . . 'Ah!' The curtains that walled the secret room seemed the color of blood. He closed his eyes tight, but that red would not disappear." . . .

Thus Eguchi, an old man standing on the brink of senility/death, yearns to return to the source from which he first gained reason and life. In his "last extremity" he lies symbolically cradled with the protective covering of the two girls, and, clinging to their breasts, journeys in thought to a time of security and warmth. In the blood-red room the dark and light girls, their feet intertwined . . . encircle the old man like the yin and yang of totality, and he longs with incestuous longing to penetrate again that comforting oneness, that matrix which is a mixture of life, hope, escape, and death. But his memory of mother is primarily a memory of suffering and death; the breasts that haunt his memory are withered, and no fresh milk will come from them. And so Eguchi dreams a succession of nightmares, erotic dreams of his honeymoon, of coming home to mother, and of blood-red flowers. He awakens to find the magic circle broken: the dark girl, of whom he had first murmured, "Life itself," . . . is dead. Eguchi emerges from the warm, dreamy, illusory sleep to feel the cold press upon him for the first time. It is as if part of himself has died. (pp. 25-8)

The reader who has come to identify with Eguchi will share something of the chilled numbness which characterizes the old man in the final scene. One has a sense of near paralysis, of having been reduced by events to a state of catatonic immobility. . . . The suffocating or numbing effect again illustrates Kawabata's narrative skill. He achieves it by filling his short work with countless examples of paradoxical or contradictory thoughts and appearance/reality opposites. They emerge, sometimes several to a page, throughout the novel. The result is tension, and for the reader, the feeling that he is pulled in different directions, none of them clear, or . . . the feeling that he is trapped, immobilized by the certainty that death is inevitably approaching but that he can only remain fixed and gasp for air.

The contraries are apparent first in the nature of the story itself. Ugly old men sleep beside beautiful young girls; the young girls are alive, yet death-like in sleep. They are real persons, but the situation is artificial. The opposites of life/death, old-age/youth, ugliness/beauty, and reality/illusion continue throughout. Eguchi's thoughts expand these themes. . . . [He] wonders if there is anything "uglier" than an old man lying beside a drugged girl. The woman's repeated admonitions about "rules" add further tension. (pp. 28-9)

The tension of opposites increases on subsequent visits. Eguchi thinks he will not return to the secret house, but does. He feels guilty about his first visit, but acknowledges that "he had not in all his sixty-seven years spent another night so clean." . . . Eguchi expects the same girl, but gets another, one whom the woman describes ironically as "more experienced." To his protestations about "promiscuity," the woman mockingly refers to gentlemen she can "trust"—but then adds laughingly, "And what's wrong with being promiscuous." . . . Eguchi has thought that sleeping girls represent "ageless freedom" for old men; he now wonders if the secret house conceals the "longing of sad old men for the unfinished dream, the regret for days lost without ever being had." . . . (p. 29)

On his third visit Eguchi hears that the girl, though sleeping, is somehow supposed to be "in training." The sight of the young girl's body saddens him and evokes a death wish; he longs for "a sleep like death," but hovers between this desire and the desire to stay awake for enjoyment. Aroused by the presence of the girl, he contemplates an "evil" deed, then stops to consider what evil might really be, and what evil he might have done in his life. The girl, he imagines, might even be a kind of Buddha. His thoughts thus lead ironically to another contradiction: she is temptation to evil, yet her "young skin and scent might be forgiveness" for sad old men. The contradictions continue through Eguchi's last visit which begins with steaming tea to counteract the freezing cold. But now death dominates the atmosphere and the crimson curtains seem like blood. What has begun as a curious search for new pleasure and vitality has ended in death; the girl Eguchi calls "life" is dragged lifeless down the stairs of the secret house.

Thus Eguchi learns—for even an old man must learn—the brittleness of his existence, the subtlety of self-deceit. The young flesh beside him is real enough: real to the hand, the nose, the eye, the ear, the mouth; it is the illusion of youth that deceives. The thin-lipped woman of the house, like some ancient hag-guardian of the hell of self-delusion,

mocks those who enter her domain. Her callous remarks and actions, like the artificial light which must remain on throughout Eguchi's nights in the crimson room, reveal the cold secrets of the house of the sleeping beauties. For Eguchi, the safe warmth of the womb is no escape; the only "escape" is death itself. The comfortable oneness of things has been broken. In his last extremity he stands, a chilly old man asking questions of himself. (pp. 29-30)

Arthur G. Kimball, "Last Extremity: Kawabata's 'House of the Sleeping Beauties'," in Critique: Studies in Modern Fiction *(copyright © by* Critique, *1970), Vol. XIII, No. 1, 1970, pp. 19-30.*

Early in his career Kawabata Yasunari . . . was a member of the Neo-Perceptionist school. . . . The existence of this group, as a part of Japanese literary history, is not so interesting or important in itself: its creed, like those of the Naturalists, the Anti-Naturalists, and other groups, derives from imported avant-garde European manifestoes, and, like most, suffers from poor digestion of same. . . . Kawabata's position in the group was not a dominant one. Nonetheless, when looked at as a serious attempt at enlarging the novelistic possibilities of the Japanese language, the modernist practices of the group must be recognized as vital in the formation of Kawabata's style.

Kawabata's main contribution to the group's platform, "The New Tendency of the Avant-Garde Writers" (*Shinshin Sakka no Shinkeikō Kaisetsu*), published in 1925, makes a plea for the new—new perception, new expression, and new style—and strongly emphasizes the importance of sense perception for the novelist. While not being very precise in his "epistemology of expressionism," and dodging most of the hard problems of his theme, Kawabata does spell out the need for a new language to replace the existing "lifeless, objective narrative language." "Dadaist," "Freudian," "free associative," "subjective, intuitive, and sensuous" expression—all such terms are left undefined, but in the context of his discussion they do suggest a coherent feeling for a certain style. He would have a language for the novel that would reflect immediately the inchoate state of a man's thoughts, feelings, and sensory experience. Instead of syntactically complete sentences, the characters (or the narrator) ought to be allowed to speak sometimes in fragments, which will not only suggest more accurately the author's view of the particular situation but will give the reader a fuller picture of the characters and their surroundings. (pp. 96-7)

The imprint of Neo-Perceptionism on Kawabata continues strong in those works written over the ten years following this "modernist" manifesto. . . . The deformation of idioms, such as in the sentence "an illness entered the core of the body" in "Needle and Glass and Fog"; a long interior monologue, very much after Molly Bloom's, in "The Crystal Fantasy"; the predominantly nominal and asyntactic construction of *The Red Gang of Asakusa;* the hundred miniature "novels" later collected into one volume as *The Palm-Sized Stores* . . .—these are the most conspicuous examples. Determinedly "modern" too are their themes and settings. The characters are typically urban "new types," whose life style is self-consciously "Western." (p. 99)

I do not mean, of course, that in these experiments Kawabata succeeds in creating anything like the cosmopolitan as a type of person recognizable across all linguistic and cultural borders. The notion of a cosmopolitan is itself quite specific to modern Western culture. The fact is, in the complexion of their feelings and emotions his characters are unmistakably Japanese. "The Crystal Fantasy," for instance, puts the cosmopolitan wife in the context of a tension between her medical and scientific interests and her sexual fantasies—in itself an unlikely situation for a Japanese woman of the time—and yet her relationship to her husband at once defines her as Japanese. There is a very uncomfortable gap in the work between its intellectual intention and its actualization by a sensibility formed out of the traditional expectation and response. Whatever stylistic feat Neo-Perceptionism may have achieved here, one realizes, it is not so much surrealistic in effect as *haiku*-like, still imbued as it is with the age-old associations and conventions despite its being set in a modern frame of reference. . . . For all its youthful wrongheaded theorizing, Neo-Perceptionism taught Kawabata a great deal about the possibilities of Japanese for prose fiction. . . . (pp. 99-100)

One of Kawabata's earliest and least experimental stories, "The Izu Dancer" . . . , stands up better than his modernist attempts. . . . "The Izu Dancer" is a first-person story of a trip to the country. . . . [The] voice here is lyrical throughout, and not mediated either by irony or by manipulation of time between the events and the telling. The student-narrator's experience is set in the fresh provincial scene by means of an evocative, slightly nostalgic language which is neither elaborate nor learned. . . . "The Izu Dancer" has the forthright appearance of a single unadorned episode. (p. 100)

The atmosphere of freshness and innocence enveloping "The Izu Dancer" comes, I think, from Kawabata's utterly simple language which sets the experience down among the trees and clean air and wet grass of a country resort. In contrast to the urban environments of his Neo-Perceptionist works, the setting of this story recalls the province of the traditional *haiku*. There is also the circumstance that Kawabata, instead of explaining the characters' thoughts and feelings, merely suggests them by mentioning objects which, in a country setting, are certain to reverberate with tangible, if not identifiable, emotions. . . .

Snow Country (Yukiguni) combines elements of Kawabata's Neo-Perceptionism with his *haiku* style of juxtaposition and understatement. The first thing that must be mentioned in this connection is the curious evolution of the work. (p. 102)

What is extraordinary [about the work] is of course Kawabata's free attitude about the wholeness and unity of a piece of literature. First, it took fourteen years for the story as a whole to be completed; second, the sections were published in different periodicals with little expectation that readers would have access to any section previously published; third, the final addition and revision, coming years after the earlier tentative completion, brought considerable changes in the text. All this seems to indicate that Kawabata had a sense of the novel as a temporally changeable entity built on the autonomy of each part. . . . With a work of this sort, the search for "structural unity" is likely to end in one's grappling with the author's mere schematization, a ghost of the story, rather than with the energy and movement of the artist's spirit-quickening words. (p. 103)

Another way of getting at the situation is to stress the essentially temporal nature of Kawabata's art. Instead of spatially schematizing the continuity, planning a unique shape like a sculpture, Kawabata just lets his language flow in time, lets it weave its own strands, almost come what may. The "shape" of the novel is thus not architectural or sculptural, with a totality subsuming the parts, but musical in the sense of a continual movement generated by surprise and juxtaposition, intensification and relaxation, and the use of various rhythms and tempos. The *renga* form is often mentioned in connection with Kawabata and for good reason: it too is characterized by frequent surprises along the way and only the retrospective arrangement of the parts into a totality as they approach a possible end.

Snow Country recounts the love affair of a writer, Shimamura, with a resort geisha as it develops over a period of some twenty months during which he is intermittently a guest at a mountain spa. The story opens in the winter with Shimamura about to begin his second stay, but the sequence is interrupted shortly after his reunion with the geisha by a long flashback describing their first encounter the previous spring. After that, the story progresses in chronological order to the end, telling of the rest of his current stay and of a third visit the following fall. The seasonal order is thus from winter to spring, back to winter, then to fall which is passing slowly into winter. Not a complicated sequence, certainly, and yet the long flashback, together with numerous brief references to earlier events throughout the rest of the book, effectively disrupts the single sequentiality and thus creates a subtle sense of passing time. In fact, the persistent back-and-forth time motion is just confusing enough to lead the author himself into a miscalculation of the total time (three visits in "three years") but the "error," not at all seriously misleading the reader, has the salutary effect of reinforcing the novel's diffuse sense of time's passage.

The flow of time which defines the shape of *Snow Country* is also an important thematic element, established at the very beginning by the celebrated mirror image. Shimamura struggles to remember the appearance of the girl he will soon see again. Only his tactile recall is strangely vivid: the forefinger of his left hand suddenly feels "damp from her touch." In this frustrating state of sexual immediacy yet final remoteness of the loved one, he sees a woman's eye "float up before him." It is the reflection in the coach window of a girl sitting opposite him.

> In the depths of the mirror the evening landscape moved by, the mirror and the reflected figures like motion pictures superimposed one on the other. The figures and the background were unrelated, and yet the figures, transparent and intangible, and the background, dim in the gathering darkness, melted together into a sort of symbolic world not of this world. Particularly when a light out in the mountains shone in the center of the girl's face, Shimamura felt his chest rise at the inexpressible beauty of it. . . .

The montage of the girl's face transparent over the continually moving landscape provides a good visualization of the book's main motif—the passage of time and man's continual struggle to slow it or pin it down to something substantial, or at least an image of something substantial. Shimamura, like anyone else, is continually compelled from the past to the present, and from here into the future, but he lives the present as though it were a somehow lasting extended stasis, the experience of beauty occasionally shocking the moving darkness into a radiant stillness.

Kawabata's handling of the mirror image is characteristically delicate. The reader is not let in on the full "symbolic" import of the superimposed image on the train window, and only after spending a considerable time with Shimamura is he allowed to discover—retrospectively as it were —that Yōkō, the girl in the train window, is enmeshed in various relationships with Komako, Shimamura's geisha. The two girls complement each other to create the fullness of womanhood—one static, more timeless, less individualized (the name *Yōko* meaning "girl of leaves"); the other, dynamic and more fully alive in time (*Komako*, "girl like a colt"). (pp. 104-06)

Komako is one of very few life-sized and full-bodied female characters in Kawabata's novels. Uninhibitedly passionate, but she knows the futility of it all. She really loves Shimamura, but does not expect their relationship to proceed beyond a casual once-a-year arrangement. Time and again, she is described as "clean" or "pure" (*seiketsu*), as though she somehow embodied the crystal purity of the mountain snow. But at the same time, red is the color most often associated with her. Her character resonates on the poles of this oxymoron of purity and fire, carefully underlined by the mirror image at the beginning and the fire scene at the end. I find it remarkable that Kawabata is able to flesh out the logic of such a character into a real person, yet he does so, keeping her fire and ice somehow in balance. The other characters, principally Yōko and Shimamura, tend to be fainter embodiments. Against the bodily tactile realization of Komako, the intense and ethereal Yōko is hardly tangible. We are frequently told about her beautiful eyes, and her voice which seems to "come echoing back across the snowy nights." . . . Yōko, thus disembodied, is the other half of a woman, the spirit or soul of a woman, always eluding men's reaching hands, always fragile and more than a little mysterious. Just as her voice seems an echo, her whole person appears not to belong to this world either. She is a fairy-tale figure, a symbolic marker, living not by her own will and desire but at the beck and call of the heroine—that is, to fulfill the logic of the drama.

Yōko's characterization deficits are thus fairly well justified by the central time-stasis paradox in the novel, but Shimamura's insubstantiality as a character is not so easily explained. Although the story is in the third person, it is told almost entirely from Shimamura's point of view. So much so, for instance, that the narrator does not even identify Komako by name until their reunion is fully told and a quarter of the story is well over. . . . Thus, despite its third-person form, *Snow Country* is essentially a first-person novel. Similarly, if there is little distinction between character and narrator, neither is there much room between character and author. With "The Izu Dancer," a lyric inviting no ironic examination of the narrator's experience, this problem never arises. *Snow Country,* not being a lyric, calls for some critical investigation of Shimamura's point of view. Had this been provided, as in a dramatic monologue, we would have had clues to the author's stance toward the hero. As it is, the story remains disturbingly inconclusive in its judgment on its principal character. (pp. 106-07)

Shimamura's behavior toward Komako, too, is left suspended finally in the novel's attitudinal limbo. . . . Shimamura is fully sensitive to the moral implications of his relationship. He knows he will never marry her and he feels some guilt about this, even if he never acts on it. There is overall a kind of neutrality in the book regarding Shimamura's character which a "moral" interpretation is bound to misrepresent.

Despite the fact that *Snow Country* gives great prominence to the Tanabata legend, the scene of the starry heavens that concludes the novel is not clear enough in its significance to serve as a gloss on the work. According to the legend, Kengyū and Shokujo loved each other so much that God turned them into stars placed on either side of the Milky Way (conceived of in the myth as a river, Ama no Kawa). . . . In the last scene of *Snow Country,* Shimamura, hurrying with Komako to watch a burning building, feels the "naked" Milky Way "wrap[ping] the night earth in its naked embrace" . . .; the next moment it seems to flow "through his body to stand at the edges of the earth" . . .; and finally "the Milky Way flow[s] down inside him with a roar." . . . The overwhelming galactic image here is very much like the rainbow in D. H. Lawrence's novel which operates as a symbol of promise of sexual fulfillment. The double message comes with the Kengyū-Shokujo reference which appears to emphasize the anguished separation of the lovers.

What I have come to believe is that Kawabata is ultimately indifferent to moral considerations in art. He will always, for instance, shift the narrative line so that the human action or situation is implicitly compared with a natural object or event which has in itself no single definite meaning at all, though it may be powerfully evocative of certain emotions. Take the passage describing the dying moth . . . or the one concerning the *kaya* grass . . .: they are there not so much to interpret and comment on the hero's action as to break the line of the story, or drop a hint that no matter what the characters may be up to, the world around them is always present but uninvolved, insensible, and not really attended to often enough. He reminds us to stop and look. The kind of resigned sadness or loneliness one always feels in Kawabata's novels comes, it seems to me, from his acceptance of man's helplessness before such a comprehensive flow of things in time. It is not all sadness, of course, because Kawabata finds quiet pleasure in this acceptance. (pp. 108-10)

Yet [Kawabata] does interpret [the world]. Time flows through the process of his work, and he, having abandoned the effort to make particular judgments all the time, sees men and women on a larger canvas than human actions and their consequences can provide. Kawabata sings the tune he picks up from the changing world just as he hears it. In this way the accepance of things as they are becomes, in Kawabata's hands, a vital act of interpretation.

As we have seen from the discussion of the window-mirror and the fire, *Snow Country* employs Neo-Perceptionist techniques consciously distilled in the spirit of *haiku*. But there are numerous other image-markers in the novel which act to animate and intensify the narrative movement. Such images at times approach the gratuitous. . . . Yet we can't help but see that the use of the near irrelevancy is the strong new feature in Kawabata's art. . . .

[A] kaleidoscopic succession of images . . . [may effectively suspend] the narrative progress and [force] us to pay attention to those large margins in the canvas of life. [In several] passages in *Snow Country,* Kawabata's use of one-sentence paragraphs strongly suggests the *haiku,* or the *renga,* a technique which will become a dominant feature of *The Sound of the Mountain.*

Overall, as compared with his earlier works, the verbal surface is more sedate in *Snow Country,* yet there are several residual experimentalist expressions. . . .

> The innkeeper had lent him an old Kyoto teakettle, skillfully inlaid in silver with flowers and birds, and from it came the sound of wind in the pines. He could make out two pine breezes, as a matter of fact, a near one and a far one. Just beyond the far breeze he heard faintly the tinkling of a bell. He put his ear to the kettle and listened. Far away, where the bell tinkled on, he suddenly saw Komako's feet, tripping in time with bell. He drew back. The time had come to leave. . . .

The metaphor of the wind in the pines is so intricately developed, changing to the sound of a bell, and then to Komako's steps, that we can almost see Komako herself dancing among the pines. The real and the fantasied are so closely woven that we realize with a start that Komako's appearance is only in Shimamura's consciousness. "The time had come to leave" is remarkably convincing as the reader is awakened from the reverie he has been allowed to share. (pp. 110-12)

Once again, the flow of time that propels *The Sound of the Mountain* is inseparable from the substance of the novel. Written almost entirely from the point of view of Shingo, a man past sixty, it establishes at once that his memory of recent events is fast declining, while the people and events he recalls from the remoter past are becoming more and more vivid. As he shuttles back and forth between Tokyo and the suburbs, he remembers his home village, the girl he secretly loved there in his youth (his wife's older sister, long dead), and particularly the flaming maple tree she used to take care of. Against the general background of present dissolution, the remembered past offers him rest, solace, and solidity. But his life does have its present, too. More and more he sees the beautiful girl of the past in his daughter-in-law, Kikuko. If there is anything like a plot in the novel, then, it can be found commuting between these well-matched poles of the past and the present, death and life, with no perceptible advantage on either side.

Dissolution and death are everywhere around Shingo. (p. 113)

If the balance of life and death has something to do with what *The Sound of the Mountain* is all about, the movement of the novel, its ever passing present, is also, paradoxically, a stasis, since it is all largely within Shingo's consciousness. The three locales—Kamakura (where the family resides), Tokyo (where Shingo and Shinichi [his son] work), and Shinshū (their country home)—function less as distinct settings than as spatial correlatives of Shingo's present and his past. More, even Shingo's workaday motions around Tokyo and Kamakura serve as occasions for reminiscence which set off at a moment's notice his reveries on long-lost things. . . .

Always at the center of Shingo's time-crossed consciousness is his daughter-in-law, Kikuko. She is his "window looking out of a gloomy house," and he connects with the past and the present only through his love for her. (p. 114)

Kikuko is Kawabata's eternal untouchable woman, his Izu Dancer, his Yōko, exquisite and elusive. Once again we see that an approach to Kawabata's work in the expectation of meeting a fully realized female character is bound to be disappointed. Nor is Shingo, for that matter, a fully developed character. As is true of *Snow Country* and most other Kawabata novels, *The Sound of the Mountain* does not operate on ordinary novelistic logic. Rather, the play and performance of the images of things and their settings—whether related or unrelated to the characters—animate and move the novel. In the usual novel . . . imagery serves mainly to reinforce the logic of the plot as it comments on the human drama. In *Light and Darkness* the night that envelops the hero toward the end—his dark night of the soul, as it were—suggests a crisis that might lead him to the "light" of self-knowledge. The image is there to amplify, intensify, and elaborate on the character's experience, not as it would be in *The Sound of the Mountain,* to dilute or deemphasize action. Of course, elsewhere in Kawabata's work, too, one can find imagery that functions in this fashion. But *The Sound of the Mountain,* which is written for the most part in very brief paragraphs, moves at crucial points from image to image by a series of leaps. And these leaps are the novel's movement, the batteries that energize it.

> The moon was bright.
>
> One of his daughter-in-law's dresses was hanging outside, unpleasantly gray. Perhaps she had forgotten to take in her laundry, or perhaps she had left a sweat-soaked garment to take the dew of night.
>
> A screeching of insects came from the garden. There were locusts on the trunk of the cherry tree to the left. He had not known that locusts could make such a rasping sound; but locusts indeed they were.
>
> He wondered if locusts might sometimes be troubled with nightmares.
>
> A locust flew in and lit on the skirt of the mosquito net. It made no sound as he picked it up.
>
> "A mute." It would not be one of the locusts he had heard at the tree.
>
> Lest it fly back in, attracted by the light, he threw it with all his strength toward the top of the tree. He felt nothing against his hand as he released it.
>
> Gripping the shutter, he looked toward the tree. He could not tell whether the locust had lodged there or flown on. There was a vast depth to the moonlit night, stretching far on either side.
>
> Though August had only begun, autumn insects were already singing.
>
> He thought he could detect a dripping of dew from leaf to leaf.

Then he heard the sound of the mountain.

It was a windless night. The moon was near full, but in the moist, sultry air the fringe of trees that outlined the mountain was blurred. They were motionless, however.

Not a leaf on the fern by the veranda was stirring.

In these mountain recesses of Kamakura the sea could sometimes be heard at night. Shingo wondered if he might have heard the sound of the sea. But no—it was the mountain.

It was like wind, far away, but with a depth like a rumbling of the earth. Thinking that it might be in himself, a ringing in his ears, Shingo shook his head.

The sound stopped, and he was suddenly afraid. A chill passed over him, as if he had been notified that death was approaching. He wanted to question himself, calmly and deliberately, to ask whether it had been the sound of the wind, the sound of the sea, or a sound in his ears. But he had heard no such sound, he was sure. He had heard the mountain.

It was as if a demon had passed, making the mountain sound out.

The steep slope, wrapped in the damp shades of night, was like a dark wall. So small a mound of a mountain, that it was all in Shingo's garden; it was like an egg cut in half.

There were other mountains behind it and around it, but the sound did seem to have come from that particular mountain to the rear of Shingo's house.

Stars were shining through the trees at its crest. . . .

Obviously, Shingo's experience is being described by the narrator from Shingo's point of view. But it is not at all clear what this litany of objects—the moon, Kikuko's dress, the locusts, the sound of the mountain—and the precision with which they are observed really amount to. Only free association of an aging man's night thoughts? For that, the bright moon, the dress hanging on the line, the screeching locusts and, of course, the sound of the mountain have something too ominous about them. A direction is being felt out, but where? The transitions between the very autonomous paragraphs are disjointed (hardly any conjunctions are used) and it seems that the sequences could stop at any time. In fact, with each new paragraph, we feel a surprise, however delicate, at still a new turn in the train of thought. It is not the suddenness of a new percept that surprises, although the sound of the mountain is indeed unexpected. "The moon was bright," "Though August had only begun," "Not a leaf on the fern," "Stars were shining"—the paragraphs, highlighting the objects of his consciousness, nonetheless gradually move away from the interior of his existence toward the container of all the drama—the world around, the wide margins of the novel.

As for Shingo's hearing the sound of the mountain, there is a mimetic aspect to it, certainly. First, the fact of his hearing the sound is stated unqualifiedly. Next, his causal inventory is given—windless night, nearly full moon, motionless trees, and the rustling leaves of the fern. Then, his more generalized question "If it is not the sound of the waves?" is answered, followed by a description of the sound as like "wind, far away." The next paragraph brings the question back to himself: isn't the sound coming from his own body? With his denial of every such possibility, the sound suddenly stops. Shingo is frightened. In this longest paragraph in the passage, he is said to "want to" ask the same questions again; that is to say, he can no longer ask since he already knows the answers. The fearfulness of the experience is underlined by the reference to the "demon." Thus, Shingo's psychological reality is available to us here: an aging man's fear of death by some inexplicable and possibly diabolical natural event. And yet the attractiveness of the passage does not depend entirely on the mere representation of the old man's state of mind. The man and his presence approach transparency as we begin almost to hear *through* Shingo the ominous sound of the mountain. Shingo himself is not really very substantial in this moonlit reality; rather it is his instrumental role in making accessible the wide world that spreads around him. For Shingo, as for Kawabata, the awareness of the large margins of the world around human beings and their actions, the large area of silence that stays intact despite human speech and the words of the novel—that is what powerfully informs his mind.

Shingo is no Leopold Bloom, whose stature and massive weight can carry the burden of everyman everywhere, in the whole city of Dublin and beyond. Mrs. Dalloway—or Mrs. Moore, for that matter—might be a closer analogy, with her delicacy and apparent fragility. But as a character Mrs. Dalloway has a rich and substantial interior life; she has angst and terror and tenderness, frivolity and sensuality, and an overall self-awareness embracing both her past and her present. Shingo as a character shies away from such definition, and it is only his remarkable sensitivity that identifies the context of his personality within the novel.

Kawabata's achievement, it seems to me, lies in just this, his keen awareness of the objects around men that exist in themselves as solidly as people do. Objects, in the world and in the world of the novel, are somehow or other related to people, but Kawabata seldom makes the connection between them explicit for us. With each of his brief paragraphs self-contained in this way (and, I should perhaps add, with each of the brief installments also self-enclosed), these objects tend to stand autonomous. Although he continually invites us to make our own efforts to connect, he stops short of giving us the keys to the house. . . . What I would call Kawabata's nominal imagination is apparent even in his earliest work. The objects here are not organized syntactically. He does not relate them, with verbs and conjunctions, into a sentence, a proposition, but just leaves them as he finds them. Exactly in the same way, *The Sound of the Mountain* reaches out and gathers objects into a narrative, but refuses to hook them into a chain of cause and effect, a plot. They are assembled but unconnected. What emerges, then, is not an argument—which any construction of plot (the whole cause-effect complex) implies—but a perception of the world and an acceptance of it as perceived, one thing at a time. It is a world parceled and scattered in a way more ruthlessly than even the broken family and society in *The Sound of the Mountain* can justly reflect. Yet even while referring to the myriad objects in the margins of human existence, Kawabata manages to be happy in the radiant beauty he finds there.

Kawabata's art is always immediately recognizable. . . . [It] is finally traceable to the traditional sensibility of sadness (*aware*) over the transience of men and things, as exemplified by Lady Murasaki, Sei Shōnagon, and countless other writers and poets. As such, it is not easy to talk about in modern critical terms. . . . What is so convincing to me about Kawabata's art is the vibrant silence about it; the delicate strength in the leap of images, and finally, in his refusal to connect things into an easy meaning, his embrace of the shambled world. The lack of "structure," often mentioned as though it were a blight on his work, is Kawabata's way of adjusting the novel to the flow of time so that art can survive and teach men and women to survive. (pp. 115-20)

For Kawabata, the margins of life blend imperceptibly into that yawning voiceless world and are finally commensurate with it. (p. 121)

> *Masao Miyoshi, "The Margins of Life," in his* Accomplices of Silence: The Modern Japanese Novel (*copyright © 1974 by the Regents of the University of California; reprinted by permission of the University of California Press*), *University of California Press, 1974, pp. 95-121.*

[The] distinctive mark of Kawabata's sensibility is there from his first work, "The Izu Dancer" . . . to his latest and final novel, *Beauty and Sadness*. Like his famous works, *Snow Country* and *Thousand Cranes*, his new fictions create an extraordinary tension between inanition and eroticism; and an uncanny discrepancy between theme and tone. As in Kafka, in Kawabata the narrative voice remains dispassionate while it relates events of terrible and aberrant passion. "The Izu Dancer" tells of first awakening; set in the mountains, where a lone student falls in love with a young dancing girl, it seems romantic—except that the girl is younger than we thought, a child, and the student curiously drifting into an ambiguous relationship whose consequences we might wish not to foresee. For the consequences of passion in Kawabata are never finite nor innocuous; they create an insidious web that draws in another generation, entangles it, and perhaps even, as in *Beauty and Sadness*, destroys it. Kawabata's geometric design is a quadrangle that emboxes the father and his mistress and his son, and another woman, usually nubile, an innocent or an avenger. . . . Kawabata recounts . . . lurid events with the utmost limpidity, with purity of style and cleanness of line. He strips his art to the simplicity of a Japanese landscape painting. Such simplicity, however, has the power to shock and menace. For the art of [*Beauty and Sadness*] is inextricable from the sexual obsessions that become perpetuated through art. . . . [Obsessions] become inescapable, and art seems not a transcendence but a permanent enslavement to the past. (pp. 317-18)

> *Blanche H. Gelfant, in* The Hudson Review (*copyright © 1975 by The Hudson Review, Inc.; reprinted by permission*), *Vol. XXVIII, No. 2, Summer, 1975.*

The Lake is a short and ostensibly simple book, worked in the haiku tradition both in its economy of words and in its sudden bright fusions of ironic opposites. But the style articulates a surprisingly complex structure which allows for a multiplicity of effects. Like all Kawabata's work *The Lake* is haunted by a sense of perverse injustice and wasted beauty which sets up reverberations in the mind of the reader long after the book is finished. (p. 21)

> *Sebastian Faulks, in* The Spectator (© *1977 by The Spectator; reprinted by permission of* The Spectator), *February 26, 1977.*

The Lake (1954), in this version at all events, is a pallid production, and admirers of the earlier *Snow Country*, presumably the book which (together with Kawabata's good works in the literary world) did most to attract the Nobel Prize, will do well to discount it. It has all or nearly all the weaknesses of modern Japanese fiction and, apart from the account of a firefly-catching party, none of the strengths. Gimpei and his ugly feet could have come from an ungifted beginner's effort at science fiction. Emotions (though the word is too emphatic) float in a vacuum, actions lack motivation, characters lack character, and we are asked to identify with a figure even more boring than unlikable—no, that is unfair, we are asked nothing. The novel gives off a musty generalized air of ugliness, misery and perverseness. No one can be blamed for anything, praised for anything, or pitied for anything. This is the famous Japanese "sadness" at its most autonomous, its most casually uncausal.

> *D. J. Enright, "Wrong Foot Forward," in* The Times Literary Supplement (© *Times Newspapers Ltd., 1977; reproduced from* The Times Literary Supplement *by permission), March 11, 1977, p. 261.*

[In] *The Sound of the Mountain* plot is less important than theme, and the themes are developed and enriched by the use of image, parallel and symbol. The title itself embodies a cluster of events and associations that dominate the life of the protagonist, Ogata Shingo, and illustrates the way in which his sensitivity to the details of nature and domestic life illuminate his larger concerns. . . .

[The imagined sound of the mountain is] a hint of Shingo's impending death, though he does not die during the novel and may not for some time.

[This theme] and others, such as Shingo's reflections on his failures as husband and father, the questions he raises to himself of heredity and rebirth, his meditations on the relation between art or illusion and reality, and others overshadow anything resembling plot in the novel. . . .

The real sense of the book is built on a cumulation of image and episode; recurring deaths and pregnancies, reference to objects of art, the emotions that the changing seasons call up, and so forth. The novel unfolds through Shingo's perceptions of nature, his experiences of recurring ideas and dreams and his growing awareness of his imperfections and those of his family. That he is still sensitive to the subtlest of details heightens our apprehension of his approaching death, but at the same time the delight he takes in the sight of sunflowers, the sound of locusts and the taste of expensive tea signals renewal as well as decline in his life. (p. 207)

The images in his dreams and thoughts arouse him more

than the living presence of a woman. . . . It is only memory or thought that awakens him. For example, as he thinks that if he "had married Yasuko's sister, then probably he would have had neither a daughter like Fusako nor a granddaughter like Satoko." This provokes a reaction so strong as "to stir in him so intense a yearning for a person long dead that he wanted to rush into her arms."

At this point, it is helpful to remember some of Kawabata's literary interests. Linked verse (renga) depends partly for its effect on the repetition or carry-over of an image from one verse to the next. In *The Sound of the Mountain* events which have no apparent logical or temporal connection come together in Shingo's mind because of a common image or thought, such as [a] puppy. Therefore the cumulation of such objects, events and ideas works thematically without Kawabata's ever stating a theme explicitly, and repetition provides transition and unity without his having to tell dates or show specifically why he moves the action from one time to the next. An image such as two trees leaning toward each other, seen a second time, will recall the original context. If the weather or season changes, so might Shingo's mood or attitude toward that context, thought or idea.

Haiku would also come to a Japanese reader's mind in this connection. Haiku poems each contain references to seasons, and traditional haiku involve only natural phenomena and the implied emotional responses to them. Each chapter of the novel opens with some reference to a season: the songs of autumn insects, a storm that is traditionally associated with the 210th day of the year, and so on. Since many natural events are transitory (cherry blossoms, moonlight, locusts), they inevitably produce sadness and reminders of our mortality. Yet melancholy is pleasurable, perhaps one of the most appealing of moods to the Japanese. That is why fall is the favorite season: it suggests more than any other the passing away of life. Moreover, the novel begins and ends in the autumn; the year has run full cycle, and so, perhaps, have other elements of Shingo's life. . . .

The links are too numerous to list, but one cannot help but draw together ideas of loss and recall of memory and premonitions of death in conjunction with the segment of his life which was the most poignant to him. At times those memories seem more alive for him than the immediate affairs of his family, except for the merging of birth and death. . . . (p. 209)

Thus, although *The Sound of the Mountain* is not distinguished by a clear plot line, suspense, climax or denouement, the cumulative effects of imagery, repetition and parallels work together to provide theme and build a total picture of a man aging in the midst of his memories and concerns. They reveal the gradual disintegration of Shingo's mind and his sense of personal failure in a life that is outwardly successful. In spite of his bitter disappointment with himself and his family, the same bright and touching stimuli to his senses that signify his decline also comfort and renew him. We hear the sound of the fishmonger's knife, feel the lonely chill of autumn and share his fear when one day he finds he has forgotten temporarily how to tie his tie. We see the gingko buds, the sunflowers and the gourds that Kikuko is arranging at the end of the novel on a level of acute appreciation and awakened awareness, just as we also see them as symbols surrounding the waning de-

sires and nostalgia of a man growing old with the ends of his life untied. (pp. 209-10)

Mary Dejong Obuchowski, "Theme and Image in Kawabata's 'The Sound of the Mountain'," in World Literature Today *(copyright 1977 by the University of Oklahoma Press), Vol. 51, No. 2, Spring, 1977, pp. 207-10.*

*　　　*　　　*

KHERDIAN, David　1931-

Kherdian is an American poet. His family, their Armenian heritage, and his childhood play an important part in his poems, especially in his early work. (See also *CLC*, Vol. 6, and *Contemporary Authors*, Vols. 21-24, rev. ed.)

Of the four books of his own poems that Kherdian has published under the Giligia imprint, *Homage to Adana* is probably his best. At least it contains more of those poems he does best, the Armenian poems, remembrances of his childhood and family. They are personal poems, simply dealing in conversational language with the commonplace. Kherdian has captured the dignity and suffering not only of his Armenian ancestors, but of immigrant people everywhere. He touches on the poignancy of fathers abandoned by their "unruly preoccupied children" uninterested in the language or culture of the old country. And then:

> Years later these grown children
> seek out aging old men who knew
> their fathers and carry Armenia
> in their fallen faces. Armenia!
> Each regards that country now as his home.

These poems and others like them from *On the Death of My Father and Other Poems* reflect Kherdian's experience of identifying with a more defined and therefore solid background of his heritage, an experience not uncommon among second generation Americans. (pp. 41-2)

[The poems in *On the Death of My Father*] reflect his growing interest in nature and his own domestic life. These poems foreshadow not only *looking over hills*, but also *The Nonny Poems* and the poems he is currently working on. Having received his start by mining his family and past, Kherdian is now branching out. The newer poems show a maturity in style. They are economical and much surer in execution, but the nature poems from *looking over hills* have lost something of his warmth. (p. 42)

Charles L. P. Silet, "David Kherdian and the Giligia Press," in Poet and Critic *(copyright © Department of English and Speech, Iowa State University), Vol. 9, No. 1, 1975, pp. 39-44.*

Like the Chinese art that with a few lines and bits of color suggests a vista, the poems in [*Any Day of Your Life*] present with few words profound experiences of natural life. . . . [Kherdian's] language has actually grown more taut than before, without becoming tense. This is because the work suggests peace without slackness. It is wrought by a poet who can write with truth of "my silent eye in the changing light." It is a certain kind of "silent eye," the kind which seems to have learned the silence which the Old Testament urges us to seek: "Be still and know . . ." And the miracle, if I may continue the metaphor, is thus performed. It is the silence between and even within the poems which now achieves what the poet hoped for when he was a beginning poet: ". . . to feel rooted in my own life / I must sit still and let my life gather about me." The occasional danger in this kind of writing lies in presenting a piece so thin as to be invisible. Happily this occurs only rarely in any of Kherdian's poetry.

It would be simple to note that these latest poems are part of the ongoing words that capture what happens in the man's life: the reading of a book; the pleasure of being alone; the enjoyment of companionship with his wife and their cats; the remembering of his Armenian background and tradition. Truly, *Any Day of Your Life* gives us days which are remarkably like the days of any one of us, if we made poetry of them instead of poses of ourselves. What has occurred here is dual growth: growth in actual life into the spirit of the life about him, as well as growth of the life in the poems, giving to us who momentarily share his life the wonderful mating of life and poetry that takes place in "The Anniversary Song." Although the poems in this volume can be felt and understood without knowing his earlier books at all, it is necessary to know them to realize fully "the changing light" that has come to the poet; for the light is not only the metaphor for changing times and ways. It suggests, as well, the ancient meaning of light, which is wisdom through perception. Without being in the least theological, moralistic, or didactic, the poems give to a jaded, shaken-up time the realization of the miracle of any day of your life. (pp. 54-5)

> *Alice Moser Claudel, in* The New Laurel Review, *Spring, 1976.*

Kherdian gives life to Chaucer's important category "for the nones" in his *Nonny Poems,* as well as to many other basal English musings, most of them hymeneal, most of them on harmony and offspring, art and life. The lyric poet's gasp from Sappho to Poe is there and so is the playful title "Ah, Nonny, Nonny." The heavy side of Chaucer's "nones" is in Kherdian's frequent allusions to writing ("my art"; "my poems"; "my scratchings"); the nuns and the solemnities of the Nonae can be heard in New York artists' love and marriage; in the "creatively ordered" apartments; in the middle limbo of beads, incense, frantic subway rides, and wasted family ill will. The lighter, but not empty, "nonce" is in the minimalist second half of the book. The New Hampshire sequence, in retrospect, is indifferent even to the tribal self-realization of the poet, who was becoming more and more Armenian as he was making his English more real historically, as he came to engage more styles of poetic introspection from Wyatt to Auden. The New York section can be read rather pleasantly as homeopathic exorcism of like by like. . . . New York, mimetically, is the plerosis on eggplant and pilaf, gnomic transitions, pride, even learned art. New Hampshire's just seasons, on the other hand, is the phase of kenosis, the place in perfect consonance with the verse, and equally mimetic: No tensions, no possessions—"Through / the day it snowed / and all day we waited / at the window / in confusion and want."

Kherdian's second personal collection (*Any Day of Your Life*), sustains the "want" and spareness of the New Hampshire sequence in the *Nonny Poems,* but clearly slides into the euphonic second helpings of the ruby-crowned kinglet, the Israel of fact and fiction alliterated by

Charles Reznikoff's name, and by the Christmas anagram in the Basic Book of Organic Gardening. Poems for the liberal cultural native. His cognac, the Buddha hour for cats, afghans, Brubeck playing Brubeck, and Kherdian is back in the ads of the *New York Review of Books*. Perfect cartoonist's matter, if it were not for the late triple rictus of the *American Poetry Review* in the inventory of the modest pleasures of the sensitive intellectuals of the sixties. The exceptions are worth noticing. The allusions to language are not the diaristic dramatizations of someone who tries to remember his vocation; as soon as they occur—and they are good things for the poems to be working up to—the poems end: "I clear my throat / for the perched birds / to hear / and begin my speech.". . . There is genuine refinement again of the anecdotal and the introspective in a poem called "Again": "'Genius is hard / work,' I say aloud, and write / it down, ending this poem / only to begin the next." (pp. 175-76)

> *Stavros Deligiorgis, "Ethos/Ethnos," in* Parnassus: Poetry in Review *(copyright © by Parnassus: Poetry in Review), Spring–Summer, 1976, pp. 175-82.*

[*Any Day of Your Life*] is a continuation of Kherdian's *The Nonny Poems . . . ,* in which he lovingly recorded his courtship and marriage with Nonny Hogrogian. *Any Day of Your Life* extends their experience out into the countryside, retaining the comfortable, domestic warmth of the Nonny poems while echoing the nature studies of Kherdian's *looking over hills*. This time, however, it is nature in context, in relationship with the two of them, and it makes for a much more satisfying collection.

Much of what is appealing about this new volume of poems is the gentle acceptance with which Kherdian experiences life. It reminds one of his earlier poems about his childhood and youth among his Armenian family. Perhaps this generosity comes in part because Nonny, too, is Armenian. But primarily, this acceptance appears to result from their relationship and is reflected in Kherdian's maturing command of his idiom. It is a small world he explores, one full of love and nature. It is a quiet, domestic world of seed catalogues and planning for spring, of baking bread and of writing poems. He writes about the seasons of life and man's need for and closeness to the earth, "our final comfort / and friend."

Like the Nonny poems, these verses explore the private and close world of lovers, claustrophobic but for the insistent intrusion of the seasons and the expansive joy which true intimacy can bring. These are love poems, for Nonny, for nature, for the undeniably human longing for warmth and comfort. (pp. 39-40)

The poems give a permanence to life as well as a pre-eminence. Locked together, Kherdian's images preserve for us fleeting glimpses of lives well-lived. (p. 40)

> *Charles L. P. Silet, in* Poet and Critic *(© Department of English, Iowa State University), Volume 9, Number 3, 1976.*

*   *   *

KIRKWOOD, James   1930-

Kirkwood is an American novelist and playwright. His own experiences have often formed the basis for his works. In 1976 he was one of the five recipients of the Pulitzer Prize in

Drama for the book for the musical *A Chorus Line*. He says of himself, "I have the outlook of a survivor. Whatever I've gone through, good and bad times, it tells me that I will survive. I write from that belief." (See also *Contemporary Authors*, Vols. 1-4, rev. ed.)

Gilford Academy, the setting of James Kirkwood's hilarious and terrifying novel, "Good Times/Bad Times," and its deranged headmaster, Mr. Hoyt, should become classics of the prep-school genre, just as Notre Dame is the definitive cathedral and Quasimodo its inevitable bell-ringer. . . .

The novel is a long, explosively honest letter from young Peter Kilburn to his attorney, the man who will defend Peter in a murder trial. If the letter is also a confession, it certainly is not the sort of tidy, legalistic document so beloved by district attorneys. Peter tells his lawyer everything, as a good client should, and his tale is neither *mea culpa* nor a cop-out. He tells it as it happened, in an adolescent diction so precise and so accurate as to be spooky. . . .

[Peter's] loose-jointed but lucid narrative, and his point of view—sometimes sophisticated, sometimes naive, but always crisp—are what make the novel such a joyful taste of Heaven and a shattering glimpse of Hell. (p. 77)

> *Richard Bradford, in* The New York Times Book Review *(© 1968 by The New York Times Company; reprinted by permission), December 8, 1968.*

James Kirkwood's "P.S. Your Cat Is Dead!" amounts through artistic miscalculation to two plays for the price of one, and this is nearly always less of a bargain in a theatre than it is in a supermarket. . . . Go and laugh at Mr. Kirkwood's many excellent jokes in the first act and, during the second act, ponder with gravity his preaching on the subject of sex, which he wishes to free from the usual tiresome discriminations in respect to gender. "Bother gender!" says Mr. Kirkwood, and I happen to think he is right, but he has chosen the wrong occasion for such a sermon; his audience, having been encouraged to do nothing but laugh until the first-act curtain falls, is astonished upon its return to discover that the first item on the agenda has become the reform of unthinking heterosexuals.

Mr. Kirkwood's comedy takes place on New Year's Eve, and I confess that I've a weakness for plays that make use of that particular holiday; one knows that *some*thing is bound to happen, be it only the ringing of nearby church bells or someone drunkenly exhaling "Auld Lang Syne." We are in a delightful loft in the Village. . . . The occupant of the loft is a thirty-eight-year-old actor named Jimmy, and he is in trouble. He has just been dropped from a play, his role is being written out of the TV soap opera that provides his daily bread, and his girl has decided to break off their relationship. It is she who appends to her note of farewell the postscript that his cat is dead. Nor is that all, for what he doesn't know upon arriving home is that a burglar is hiding under his bed. . . .

The plot of the play revolves around the relationship that develops between the two men. At first, Jimmy, having captured Vito, is tempted to turn him over to the police, but it occurs to him that he will gain greater satisfaction from punishing Vito on the premises. Starting as adversaries, they soon perceive that neither of them will be able to hold the upper hand for long. Thanks to Vito's persist-

ence and in spite of Jimmy's reiterated objections, a bond begins to form. In the first act, the bond is largely a matter of gags, both sight and verbal; in the second act, when we have learned that Vito is bisexual, the gags diminish and a serious demand for affection begins. By the end of the play, though Jimmy and Vito go to sleep in separate beds, they are no longer separate. (p. 103)

> *Brendan Gill, in* The New Yorker *(© 1975 by The New Yorker Magazine, Inc.), April 21, 1975.*

[The characters of *A Chorus Line*] are mostly refugees who dread having to return to the outside world either by failing or by aging. The border between psychic needs and creative impulse is always fuzzy; and this show makes clear that most of these people are here, have suffered to get here, are suffering to stay, at least as much out of hatred of their pasts and past selves and the glare of daylight as out of their love of dancing and the theater.

None of this is startling or deep, some of it is show-biz corn, but most of it is authentic, even some of the corn. And almost all of it is well done. (pp. 20, 31)

> *Stanley Kauffmann, in* The New Republic *(reprinted by permission of The New Republic; © 1975 by The New Republic, Inc.), June 21, 1975.*

Self-revelation, of course, is not new in drama. When Oedipus confesses his sins, or when Lady Macbeth mutters guiltily, their confessions relate to both plot and character. But in modern confessional drama, there often are no plots. Confession has come to exist for its own sake.

Nor do these plays bear much relation to traditional autobiographical drama. O'Neill at least bothered to transform the members of his family into viable dramatic characters, but today's playwrights often simply plop remembered parents, siblings, and friends onstage. Instead of writing scripts, they have even been known to transcribe actual dialogue from tape recordings.

An excellent example of current confessional drama is *A Chorus Line* . . . , a glossy, virtually plotless musical about aspiring dancers. . . . [*A Chorus Line*] is set at an audition for a musical. Between dynamic rehearsal numbers, the spotlight singles out one anxious hopeful after another, and each in turn talks about his or her past, present, or dreams of the future.

For the most part, these personal confessions reveal a vast desert of conventional emotions and motivations, as well as a fairly high proportion of male and female homosexuality. . . .

A Chorus Line is a hit primarily because it's fast, polished, and relentlessly entertaining, and also because it sounds the way an audience wants a confessional play to sound—real. Since the cast is made up of bona fide dancers, rather than actors and actresses who pretend to be dancers, there is a ring of authenticity to begin with. One long, exceedingly banal discussion of why dancers dance, and what they do when they can't dance any longer, sounds so realistic, so utterly undramatic, that it almost seems the cast has forgotten its lines and is improvising. (p. 50)

> *Barbara Mackay, in* Saturday Review *(© 1975 by Saturday Review/World, Inc.; reprinted with permission), August 9, 1975.*

Some Kind of Hero is not panoramic, grand, [or] epic like
. . . but the big social message is clear enough . . . : our society is unredeemable, hence the individual had best rush
out and make it on his own. Making it for this particular
hero, Eddie Keller, means pulling a couple of holdups for
which we are apparently supposed to respect him more: he
is brave, determined, resolute in the face of continuing long
odds. . . .

So Eddie Keller is profound in being "some kind" of hero
rather than the usual kind. Kirkwood is certainly anxious
not to tell us outright *what* kind but as the story progresses
he can't keep it from us. Eddie is a hero because he is normal. He is a sensitive, sexually precocious (all heroes of all
kinds now have to be sexually somehow precocious) young
soldier who meets the enemy and is captured, jailed near
Hanoi for four years and released unharmed to return to the
US as a momentary usual hero; then relegated to poverty
and trouble by a variety of forces from a bad daddy to a
thankless Pentagon but never allowed by his creator to
react to those forces unpredictably, that is, react to them
the way an all-American boy wouldn't. During his miscellaneous adventures on two continents he meets one POW
who is a good guy, one military medico who is a good guy
and one girl who becomes his wife, but otherwise the not-
large cast consists of grotesque including his mother (paralyzed by a stroke), a tyrannical jailer, a hooker who is so
sexually precocious that she has a room full of whips and
other useful items and a number of subordinate eccentrics
who enforce Eddie's normalcy by contrast. (p. 35)

And of what does normalcy consist? Aside from sexual
potency, which is basic, the main normalcy ingredient
would seem to be a wholly desirable capacity to feel warmly, hopefully toward others. Eddie is meant to be a man
with lovely honest feelings in a world not distinguished for
lovely honest feelings. He even has lovely honest feelings
toward his country, and when his plane flies in over San
Francisco at dusk he discovers that his life, which has
"been in black and white for the last four years . . . has
turned Technicolor again." He is in other words an apple-
pie American at heart and we should be grateful, the drift of
the text suggests, for his existence.

The apple-pie drift is even strong enough to have caused
one critic, quoted on the jacket, to go slightly ga-ga, saying,
"You will root for, cry with and cheer Eddie on"; but since
the cheering, if there is to be any, must include cheering for
Eddie as he lifts approximately 100 grand from a couple of
strangers it is a cheering for an individual who has a
nowhere-questioned prerogative to determine what apple
pie *is*. That prerogative would seem to include the right to
kill though no one is actually killed, and it is the prerogative
that probably chiefly distinguishes the "some kind" of hero
of our time from the old heroes who lived by laws beyond
themselves. Eddie is a most representative modern American hero in his assertion of the prerogative, and his creator's insistence that Eddie remain a good guy when he asserts it is a representative modern putdown of all possible
institutional prerogatives. Onward and upward with Eddie
and his gun. (pp. 35-6)

Some Kind of Hero . . . shows no scruples at all about violence for the private good, none, that is, unless the introduction of Eddie's Ma constitutes a scruple.

Yes, Ma. For Eddie, it turns out, is not working wholly for

himself as he battles the bad world and picks up his 100
grand. He is working for himself *and* Ma. . . . Without Ma
and the girl, I suppose, he might be criticized for being selfish. (p. 36)

Reed Whittemore, "American Pie," *in* The
New Republic *(reprinted by permission of*
The New Republic; © *1975 by The New
Republic, Inc.), August 16 & 23, 1975, pp.
35-6.*

A Chorus Line . . . is Broadway's most celebrated and
talked about show in years. . . .

It isn't an easy show to write about, unless you simply
want to settle for a parade of such adjectives as "exhilarating," "innovative," "luminous," "explosive" and "poignant," all of which it has been called and all of which it is. It
has a very simple idea at its core—or, more appropriately—
heart. Day after day, year after year, the "gypsies," the
chorus kids of the theatre, troop from audition to audition,
rehearsal to rehearsal, show to show, for the most part unidentified and unrecognized, certainly uncelebrated by other
than their peers. Yet, they are individuals, every bit as individual as the Carol Channing, Pearl Bailey, Gwen Verdon
or Zero Mostel who's taking the applause a foot or two in
front of their chorus line. . . .

There isn't much around for these "kids," and what there
is has been rapidly diminishing. Some, perhaps most,
dream of becoming a star, and all live with a haunting fear:
"What do you do when you can't dance any more?" (p. 40)

[*A Chorus Line*] prompts both laughter and tears. (p. 41)

Catherine Hughes, in America *(© America
Press, 1976; all rights reserved), January 17,
1976.*

*   *   *

KUNDERA, Milan   1929?-

**Kundera is a Czech poet, playwright, novelist, short story
writer, musician, and filmmaker. Although his work has
been banned in Czechoslovakia since 1967, his satiric fiction
is more personal than political. (See also *CLC*, Vol. 4.)**

Kundera's fiction is outspoken, but never polemic. His
basic concern is with the tricks people play on themselves
rather than on the state, and a man may make a fool of himself under any political system; for Kundera, the central
arena for the absurdity of humankind is the relations of men
and women. Even though the short stories of *Laughable
Loves* were published in Czechoslovakia in 1968 at the
height of liberalization, they are almost entirely apolitical.

Life Is Elsewhere, completed in June 1969 after the reform
movement had crumpled, either took more chances or simply led in more dangerous directions. It makes some
pointed remarks about imprisonment and torture during the
years after the war, and pokes bitter fun at the childishness
of revolutionary fervor. Its misguided hero's act of Party
loyalty leads to his girl friend's imprisonment and probably
to her brother's death. Whether or not Kundera realized
that his novel would be refused publication, he has not re-
canted; thrust into official darkness, now he is bled of all
his standing by each relentless little tick of an *apparatchik*
of the gross new hardline bureaucracy.

Still, *Life Is Elsewhere* is not a political novel, but the fictional biography of a lyric poet. Indeed, Kundera intends to be general as well as specific: he gives us the biography of *all* lyric poets, and the comedy lies in the specific application of the general rule. . . .

Kundera always finds his comedy in the gap between a man's postures and his real relation to the world. And since the lyric poet eternally poses and is always out of touch with reality, he is the perfect comic character. . . . Lyric poetry has the fleeting genius of immaturity, and the poet dramatizes situations he fails to understand, nevertheless transforming them into rich verse. The one girl with whom Jaromil goes to bed is a mousy clerk he accidentally acquired while pursuing her attractive friend. It scarcely matters. He becomes a Communist revolutionary, since "the more I make love, the more I want to make revolution—the more I make revolution the more I want to make love"—a slogan from the student uprising at the Sorbonne, cited by Kundera. Any girl will do, any revolution. Within and behind the comedy lies the implication that Communism is a homely girl indeed.

Since Kundera's short stories are studies in motivation, their characters are as fully and carefully drawn as those in his novels. His world is made up of people, and he wastes no time on scene painting. Trapped in their own poses, his characters are forced to learn more about themselves in order to break free, and sometimes these dives into the dark waters of the psyche go beyond comedy altogether. (p. 1248)

Most of the stories have a lighter tone. . . . If "The Hitch-hiking Game" had the taut lines of Roman Polanski's *Knife in the Water,* "A Symposium" is an internalized bedroom farce like Ingmar Bergman's *Smiles of a Summer Night.* (pp. 1248-49)

> *Charles Nicol, "Writing Well in the Wrong Places," in* National Review *(© National Review, Inc., 1974; 150 East 35th St., New York, N.Y. 10016), October 25, 1974, pp. 1248-49.*

Kundera's new novel, ["The Farewell Party,"] like much of his previous work, reverses our expectations in unsettling ways, and once we have accepted conditions we did not expect in the first place, reverses them again and again, until we see that the prevailing terms of the understanding were contained all along in the fine print while our attention was slyly deflected elsewhere. Who would expect of a contemporary Czech novel the atmosphere of sexual farce more suited to the French or Viennese turn-of-the-century stage?

"The Farewell Party" seems washed in that light. The health spa and fertility clinic that is the setting is only a four-hour drive from the unnamed "capital," but it might as well be in another, timeless, world. . . .

Sexual comedy, . . . burlesque; or so it seems. Throughout, the tone holds icily to that of high comedy, elegant, worldly, just as the narrative gracefully weaves its patterns until the inevitable design is wholly achieved. But in Kundera's work, comedy and farce, although they are persistent elements in his sense of life and practice of art, are always subverted and transformed by darker, more ambiguous tones. (p. 4)

Kundera . . . has fashioned the kind of novel still possible

for an Eastern European writer who declines to submit in the face of crushing penalties. As if oblivious, he remains faithful to his subtle, wily, devious talent for a fiction of "erotic possibilities . . . and enterprises" (Philip Roth's phrase in introducing the American edition of Kundera's stories) in a setting "beyond justice." . . . "The Farewell Party" is the kind of "political novel" a cunning, resourceful, gifted writer writes when it is no longer possible to write political novels. (p. 18)

> *Saul Maloff, in* The New York Times Book Review *(© 1976 by The New York Times Company; reprinted by permission), September 6, 1976.*

At the outset this new novel by [Kundera] sounds much like a bedroom farce. A famous jazz trumpeter, Klima, is a confirmed womanizer deeply in love with his wife. . . . Ruzena, a nurse at a spa celebrated for its gynecological miracles, calls Klima to say that as a result of a one-night stand . . . she is pregnant by him. Pregnancy is in a different category from philandering . . . , so Klima hares off to persuade her to have an abortion. The next few days see a fair amount of bed-hopping.

The Farewell Party plainly doesn't aim, as much current European fiction does, to be a self-justifying aesthetic or lyric event, whatever that may be. But, to begin with, it is at least informative. So, even beyond the iron curtain people tell lies to avoid marrying people to whom they have told lies to get into bed. . . . One touch of shabbiness makes the whole world kin. . . .

The whole world is kin. But—we are casually told—Jakub, the political dissident soured by his misfortunes, is unofficial ward to a girl whose father, his friend, was executed. This is the sort of passing remark one doesn't too often meet with in Anglo-American writing. . . . The turns and counterturns of Czech communism since 1948 form the other strand in Kundera's work. . . . This strand is counterpointed with the "private life," the hopes and needs, exploitations, and treacheries, of sexuality. The counterpointing is so complicated (perhaps the Czech has too much to tell) that it is hard to grasp the final significance of this tangled music.

The similarities between *The Farewell Party* and *The Joke,* Kundera's celebrated first novel, are striking. And not confined to similarities of generalized irritation, distaste, and at times disgust. According to Jakub, the saddest discovery of his life is that the victims of history are no better than their oppressors, for the roles are always reversible: and so it is advisable simply to blame everything on the Creator for making man the way he is. Otherwise, "to come to the conclusion that there is no difference between the guilty and their victims is to reach a state where you *abandon all hope.* And that, my dear, is a definition of *hell.*" In *The Joke* Kostka meditates on Ludvik, the hero and victim of the "joke," a figure much like Jakub, another political unfortunate, another soured survivor: "You have never forgiven mankind . . . such general bitterness toward people is evil and sinful. It has become your curse. *Because to live in a world in which no one is forgiven, where all are irredeemable, is the same as living in Hell.*" Both Jakub and Ludvik know that this is so: the knowledge doesn't help them very much.

As for humor, the true and harsh joke of *The Joke* is not so much the joke of the title—the facetious postcard, "Optimism is the opium of the people!" which Ludvik as a student sent to his girlfriend and which led to his expulsion from the Party—as the joke arising out of Ludvik's attempt to avenge himself on his opportunist persecutor, fifteen years later, by seducing the man's wife. . . . Ludvik brings off the seduction, only to find that the couple have lived separately for the past three years and that his erstwhile enemy now has a young and much more attractive girlfriend —much more attractive to Ludvik, too. . . .

The humor in *The Farewell Party,* which even has what resembles a happy if somewhat farcical ending, is considerably lighter and less abrasive, and derives chiefly from the activities of Dr. Skreta, whose specialty is curing barrenness in wives. This he does by means of injections from his private sperm bank. It is truly an agreeable relief to see the melancholy Jakub, about to say farewell to his native land, noting how many little Skretas there seem to be around. (p. 49)

Dr. Skreta and the clinic are likely to remind us of Hofrat Behrens, Dr. Krokowski, and the International Sanatorium Berghof of Thomas Mann's *The Magic Mountain.* People at the Berghof, Herr Settembrini remarked, were possessed of two ideas, and only two: "temperature—and then again temperature"—by the second temperature meaning a fervid preoccupation with local amatory activities. . . . But where *The Magic Mountain* has Goethe and German music behind it, *The Farewell Party* has only tawdry destructive ideologies and a jazz trumpeter. (pp. 49-50)

While *The Farewell Party* commands one's intellectual respect and admiration, to read it is not wholly a pleasure. The sourness, the glum cynicism consequent upon disenchantment and alienation, come through too strongly, or too repetitively; there is an excess of soul-searching, whether self-accusatory or self-justificatory; it has the air of a cold-hearted metaphysical puzzle whose terms are either incomplete or not clearly enough set out. How far these impressions are due to inadequacies and injustices in translation I cannot say. But, for instance, Bartleff hardly seems much of a saint, or mysterious, or special, when he says of the dead Ruzena, "You have no notion what a fine person was locked inside of her." Novels may be very different from lyric poetry, but style tells with them too.

The richness of *The Magic Mountain,* its "meticulous" solidity and its diversity of viewpoints, in a sense leave the reader where he was—though they leave him much better informed. . . . Not so in *The Farewell Party,* which, whatever its truthfulness, is finally lowering in both its explicitness and its clever irony. The world of *The Magic Mountain* could go somewhere, anywhere—the world of *The Farewell Party* and *The Joke* doesn't look to be going anywhere at all. Many readers will be ready to accept this as inevitable and commiserate with its truthful author. I am not sure about this response. Perhaps literature needs to be something more than simply and solely true to the facts. (p. 50)

D. J. Enright, "The Disenchanted," in The New York Review of Books *(reprinted with permission from* The New York Review of Books; *copyright © 1976 NYREV, Inc.), September 16, 1976, pp. 49-50.*

L

LARKIN, Philip   1922-

**Larkin is an English poet, novelist, and essayist. The subject
of his poetry is his personal experience, the setting that of
common provincial life. Larkin has consistently rejected what
he feels to be the obscure symbolism of contemporary poetry
and its focus on aesthetic problems. His concerns are humanistic, and a recurrent theme is man in his relationship to nature. (See also *CLC*, Vols. 3, 5, 8, and *Contemporary Authors*,
Vols. 5-8, rev. ed.)**

Philip Larkin husbands his talents charily. *High Windows*,
his first volume in ten years, contains only two dozen
poems and his total output has been sparse. This poetic reticence is appropriate to his effort to face modern life objectively and honestly; he does not spin out words for their
own sake. Behind the individual poems lies his awareness
that the universe is ultimately empty, like the high windows
of his fine title poem. His acceptance of impending oblivion
causes him to see the everyday pursuits of people, including himself, with irony and elegiac sadness. Larkin is
distinctly of our time, yet the verse itself is traditional and
ordered. His tone is cool and his emotions in check—there
is no rage here against the dying of the light.

His longer poems are often confrontations with mutability
and death since for him the recognition of death is the beginning of wisdom. "To the Sea" and "The Old Fools" are
successful examples in this collection, but he is most explicit in "The Building," a description of a hospital that
becomes a meditation on death. . . .

[A] sense that life is finite and rounded with oblivion underlies all his poems, but he is not usually so solemn [as he is
in "The Building."] Slang and comic irony enliven many of
his shorter poems, such as the very clever "Annus Mirabilis." Often, as in "Vers de Société," a light beginning
gives way to a serious conclusion. "This Be The Verse"
begins like a jingle and is sprightly in meter throughout, although it develops the grim idea that our psychological mis-
eries increase from generation to generation. His subjects
are contemporary, but his verse has a traditional quality in
its use of tight structures and in his diction. Often he manages to combine the right smack of the Elizabethan plain
style with the wit of later times. (p. 270)

Larkin depicts himself as a detached observer, affectionate
towards life but not a swimmer in the mackerel-crowded
seas. In "Posterity" he imagines his biographer complaining at being stuck with "One of those old-type *natural*
fouled-up guys" whose work does not come from "out of
kicks or something happening." In "Money" his unspent
bank account reproaches him, "I am all you never had of
goods and sex./You could get them still by writing a few
cheques." But his awareness that experience is fragile and
transitory prevents him from regretting very deeply his
alienation from it. This becomes clear in "Money" when
he turns around the equation he draws between his savings
and "goods and sex"—like money the things of this world
cannot ultimately prevail:

> I listen to money singing. It's like looking down
>   From long french windows at a provincial town,
> The slums, the canal, the churches ornate and mad
>   In the evening sun. It is intensely sad. . . .

For me, his ability to face and live in a world of limited and
uncertain meaning is provocative; he accepts what drives
other poets to evasions or despair. I was attracted to
Larkin by the wit and beauty of his verse, but I have come
to value more its clear-voiced honesty at a time when many
of us conceal ourselves in rhetoric or retreat into silence.
(p. 271)

> *Stephen S. Hilliard, "Wit and Beauty," in*
> Prairie Schooner *(© 1975 by University of
> Nebraska Press; reprinted by permission
> from* Prairie Schooner*), Fall, 1975, pp. 270-
> 71.*

Philip Larkin describes ["Jill," his] first novel, originally
published in 1946, as "in essence an unambitious short
story." This is a modest remark, and the modesty is not
misplaced, for "Jill" is indeed a quiet, gray, inconclusive
little book, with a gray hero, and a plot so slight that
readers might be forgiven for thinking, as I did, that the
final blank pages of the volume were a mistake of the print-
ers, and that some dramatic denouement had been accidentally omitted. But this is not so: the inconsequential ending
is deliberate. Some might expect this of Larkin, the poet of
half-tones and gray moods, suburban melancholy and accepted regrets, but in fact the poet is much better at conclusions than the novelist: most of Larkin's poems, at least in
his last three volumes, are remarkable for their devastating
and bitter punch lines. In "Jill," there is much of the
gloom, little of the bitter precision of wit.

Nevertheless, it is an interesting book for several reasons. It was written when the author was 21, and has some most accomplished passages of descriptive prose—notably the hero's visit to his bombed hometown, Huddlesford. (Larkin's own birthplace was Coventry, one of the most heavily bombarded towns in Britain.) At the least, it is a noteworthy piece of juvenilia by one of England's finest poets. It also has, according to the American critic James Gindin, the first example of "that characteristic landmark of the British postwar novel, the displaced working-class hero." . . .

As a working-class hero, in fact, John is singularly spineless: unlike the defiant and ambitious characters that people the novels and plays of Amis, Wain, Braine, Osborne, Wesker, he seems all too keen to learn the ways of his social superiors, even when those ways [are] repulsive. . . . None of the joys, all the embarrassments of youth are carefully catalogued. Maybe this is Larkin's point. Being young was not much fun in those days, for that kind of boy. In a poem published recently, "Annus Mirabilis," the older Larkin deplores the fact that the younger Larkin missed out on the good times, and was too old for the wonderful year of 1963, when the Beatles and sexual intercourse were invented. Times have changed, and "Jill" is certainly a useful sociological record by which to date those changes.

But perhaps the most curious section of this volume is Larkin's own introduction. There are, in fact, two introductions, one written in 1963, and a postscript to it, composed specially for this edition in 1975. Anyone interested in the history of attitudes and ideas will find these compelling reading. In the 1963 section, Larkin sets out, ostensibly, to explain wartime Oxford to the American reader. . . .

In the 1975 addendum, Larkin remarks that despite all efforts to dissociate himself from the feeble John, he still finds readers identify him with his own creation. This annoys him, as does, apparently, the passing of the collegiate system that his own novel renders so unattractive. And, finally, he disclaims the myth that he was himself a scholarship boy. . . . [It] is worth remarking . . . that it is an extraordinary thing for an Englishman to say. . . . One wonders what the 1984 introduction will have to say about British education. (p. 5)

> *Margaret Drabble, in* The New York Times Book Review *(© 1976 by The New York Times Company; reprinted by permission), May 16, 1976.*

[This] lyrical little novel ["A Girl in Winter"] . . . still ranks as one of the best embodiments of pre-Second World War manners and turns of speech, and of the particular charms of the English shrubs and mists that grace the landscapes of Turner and Constable. . . . The book's main flaw is that the reader is led to expect an up-to-date account of the family [with which the central character, Katherine, had been involved], which never comes. . . . Despite this defect, Mr. Larkin's painterly descriptions of green country lanes, weathered punts, and soft English skies, and his wry ones of such native types as a braying colonial hunter who speaks with "leaden sincerity" and a girlish spinster who looks like "a large tea-rose gone well to seed," more than justify the reissue of this minor classic. (pp. 209-10)

> *The New Yorker (© 1976 by The New Yorker Magazine, Inc.), December 6, 1976.*

[The] readiness to proclaim [Larkin] as the true voice of our contemporary English experience, the instituting of him as Laureate of the Ordinary, make up the agreed basis of his general acceptance in a manner that brings one fact home with depressing clarity: the place which Larkin occupies in the esteem of many, as spokesman of the English sensibility, has not had to be arduously won—changing our consciousness, for instance, that we may appreciate the language of *his*—but is there and ready for him more by default than by pronounceable achievement, like an inheritance which at last, in slow, permeating obviousness, can no longer be denied him. The meek shall inherit the earth, but only, it seems, when the great have left it, together with our contentiously vital scepticism, or when the humane mind of an age is too worn down, enervated, or badly frightened to enable it to challenge not only the dubious humility of a Larkin but the kind of accepting vision which could possibly conceive of him as a major poet. For what essentially disturbs, beyond the fact that his poetry is found important or congenial, is the existence of the larger phenomenon which such popularity confirms—that is to say, the lineage of commonplace writing (and defences of it) to which contemporary acclaim of Larkin should point us back.

Larkin's kind of success is only possible because he has precisely tuned his poetry till it now speaks with perfect confidence for that tradition of inadequacy, where failure to feel becomes a virtue, which has been evident in English poetry since Hardy but which has a more far-reaching lineage. If, as now, one tries to trace some of the gradations in this line of descent, it should quickly become evident that commonplaceness exerts its charms more calculatingly, and, in English writing of the last fifty years, has been more subtly apologized for, than may be realized. . . . The view from Larkin's train offers 'no historical perspective, no measuring of present against past', according to Davie [in *Thomas Hardy and British Poetry*]—'Canals and smashed cars come along with hedges and cattle simply because they come along like that in any railway journey through England, as we all know'—but though, in that comment, we can see how the null, the deathly indiscriminateness of the poetic mind, has enough appearance of the bright and the living to be given the credit of honest reporting, Davie's intelligence does not make Larkin's supposed observing power the main reason for finding him attractive. How it is that Davie, with his real sense of literary and historical perspective in which Larkin's poetry is set—'Those slow canals have wound through many a poem about England since T. S. Eliot's *Waste Land* . . .'—can come to rest, so welcomingly, on a poet who shuns any such wider cultural visionings, is suggested by the assumptions of this sentence: 'And precisely because poem after poem since *The Waste Land* has measured our present (usually seen as depleted) against our past (usually seen as rich) Larkin's refusal to do this is thoroughly refreshing—at least, we recognize with relief, we can take all that for granted, take it as read.' There seems, oddly enough, the implication in this remark that Larkin's 'refusal' to make a well-worn contrast is positively there with enough strength to take us into a refreshed, unblinking sense of the present, whereas the poetry suggests nothing as vital as a 'refusal', more a failure to care, or see why he should have to care, about the past *or* the living present. On Larkin's train we have the appearance of movement through the present, the sensation (if not the profounder sense) of perceived contemporaneity, as if the life-motion, by which we might feel the past active in our present, has been degraded to an unknowing, uncaring transience.... [The] relief which Larkin's poetry affords to Davie, I suggest, comes from finding in work of such lowered expectations (Larkin's 'level-toned acceptance of that England as the only one we have') a refuge for the idea of civilization, of self-control and courtesies, which is threatened by those forces manifested in the confessional, 'extremist' poetry of Lowell, Sylvia Plath, or Berryman, and cheered on to the breaking-point by Alvarez. In the light of such poetic claims, it is what Larkin does *not* seem to claim, rather than the self he does possess, which makes him have for Davie the credit of lowered-sights modesty, the semblance of the civil, honest-speaking voice. In fact, the negation which Larkin so carefully specializes in could only be imagined as fit ground, the repository of civilized values, by someone who has arrived at him, as Davie has, in refuge from the loud, chaotic, confessional voices which he hears from Lawrence to the present. But the endorsement of Larkin has more significance to it than the act of preferring the small-visioned but seemingly civilized poet to the vigour of others—where vigour, in Davie's confusing of it, is not distinguished from the brash, the apocalyptic, the civilization-denying forces. Larkin, or Larkinism, is what one inevitably does arrive at if one is driven to occupy a far smaller ground for a liberal idea of civilization than it originally and confidently seemed to embrace. It shows not that civilization and the impetus which has created it can be actually contracted to the modestly miniature, the negativity of small decorums and poignancies. Such a concept of the civilized seems to betray the idea, not preserve its force, and it suggests that one's idea of the civilized may from the very beginning have been narrower, more straitened, and less sympathetically vital, than it is eventually disclosed to be. (pp. 3-4)

A seeming contemporaneity of vision, a compassionate-looking embrace of the English present, together with a carefully gauged lowering of sights: these represent the poles between which [Larkin's] writing fluctuates without any . . . emotional clumsiness.... The persuasiveness of a kind of poetry that can . . . provide the appearance of modest wisdom suggests how well Larkin, in his grasp of commonplace writing, has cleared away without regret much that Auden clings to. (pp. 10-11)

Indeed, what marks Larkin off so distinctly from Auden's fumblings about the value of being ordinary is the deathly inadequacies which his contempt and clarity of purpose bring him to celebrate. His is not just the case of the Philistine mind which yearns for some semi-tragic prestige to gloss over his own reluctance to see beyond his undeveloped, withered feelings: Larkin's Philistinism is, more unpleasantly, an aspect of a very purposeful mind dedicated to the breaking down, the dissolving away into multiplicity, ambivalences, of direct or definite feeling.... [This] is what strikes one about the *déjà vu* quality of Larkin's poetry: the re-cycling of feelings that seem both sprightly and stale at the same time.... Larkin's 'posthumousness', the falsely life-like concreteness with which he puts together the picture of lives meeting in novelistic congruence, is not something that is ever quite faced for what it is. The formalism, the semblance of solidity and disillusionable ideals, may be a brightly-lit montage of effects that Larkin drains the light from into a fade-away flatness, a sense of life's

cheats, but the shining, clichéd falsity of those pictures of the ideal exert a continuing fascination which the disillusionment feeds off—a tawdry focused framework which the unfocused haze of resentment and nullity cannot abandon, and thereby show itself as truly dead.... What life *is* Larkin has not the positiveness to suggest; what it negatively is not, in dulled equivocalness, is his real concern and one that depends on the over-lit falsity of promises and idealism to verify. The sensibility never ultimately has to *be* in its times, whatever the appearance of truth-telling anecdotalism.... (pp. 11-12)

'The commonplace needs no defence', says Plomer but it needs Larkin's special ability, his power of creating religiosity out of emotional dissolution, the total numbing of distaste for the vulgarized, to make a defence not seem necessary. Aboard the train in 'The Whitsun Weddings', the poet cannot be placed by us in any exact state of educated or class-consciousness: borne along on 'this frail / Traveling coincidence', and watching the newly married couples getting on the train to London and the wedding parties seeing them off . . . the poet, as in other poems, can seem (except for the stereotypes and over-tinted lighting) almost inside his moment, almost tolerantly among the world of relationships. But as London approaches, that approximated sense of coherence, of human solidarity, breaks up: a 'slackening ache' takes over, a braking movement which, as in 'Here', signifies that sapping of momentum 'That being changed can give'. It is not Yeatsian 'change', the perception of one movement ending and another newly beginning, but the simple process of deadening that now emerges as the foremost motive:

> We slowed again,
> And as the tightened brakes took hold, there swelled

> A sense of falling, like an arrow-shower
> Sent out of sight, somewhere becoming rain.

To make a slackening of coherence look like something religiously beneficent, the disintegrative become energetically fecundative, is a piece of brazen suggestiveness on Larkin's part which is very characteristic. But equally manipulative is the kind of reader's response which can construe from Larkin's equivocal emptying of the present's significance, 'out of sight, somewhere becoming rain', the liberality of the agnostic who modestly keeps life's options open.

There is no modesty of that kind here, and it will not do, therefore, merely to see Larkin, as Alvarez sees him, as a postwar Welfare State embodiment of the 'gentility principle' in English conventionality—a writer whose attitude to death (unlike that of Sylvia Plath where 'death appeared as a positive act, an intense confirmation of identity') makes it 'nothing more than a dank tailing-off . . . the logical end to the denials he habitually practises in his work', a thing only frightening 'because it lies outside routine and amiable comfort.' Larkin's deathly, disintegrative consciousness is more persuasively and wilfully at large in the poetry than may be evident to a critic who wants to confine it behind a class-category of clerkish, timid suburbanism, while reserving the name of courage for those who actively embrace death. Larkin's 'posthumousness', with close links to Sylvia Plath's kind, is a phenomenon which is representative of a continuing diminution of feeling that carries on from the War and which has become almost an unremarked feature of poetic and dramatic consciousness. (p. 12)

Richard Swigg, "Descending to the Commonplace," in PN Review (© PN Review 1977), Vol. 4, No. 2, 1977, pp. 3-13.

* * *

Le CARRÉ, John (pseudonym of David Cornwell) 1931-

Le Carré, an English novelist, is best known for his fiction of espionage. His work is characterized by an elegant prose style and a subtle insight into human character. (See also *CLC*, Vols. 3, 5, and *Contemporary Authors*, Vols. 5-8, rev. ed.)

For Le Carré, who sees nothing glamorous in espionage, the spy is not autonomous. The spy is a thing, created in dull security meetings and controlled by a board of drab directors.... The double and triple agent becomes the truly absurd hero because, as a puppet, his only choice is to be a comedian, to act out his empty loyalties in order to show contempt for each of them. Le Carré is the best of the espionage lot, probably the best writer in the form after Graham Greene. His conclusions are close to what other serious fiction has been telling us about the world we have to live in, that it is physically shabby and seedy and spiritually sterile, without love, faith, or hope. (pp. 57-8)

> *Robert Gillespie, in* Salmagundi *(copyright © 1970 by Skidmore College), Summer, 1970.*

Unfortunately, ... charity ... is needed [in reading *The Honourable Schoolboy*] in order to cope amiably with this deadeningly spun-out display of unassimilated guide-book info mixed in with all the stock Le Carré ploys. The central suspense line is thoroughly ungripping, not to say lethargic, and the Research thrusts itself from almost every page in the form of huge, inert slabs of topography and local colour. There's an unbelievable amount of sheer debriefing in the book, and many a character exists solely to pass on to us some necessary piece of Eastern lore. Embedded in all this are the main characters, Smiley and Westerbury. Smiley remains as shadowy as ever; he's been cuckolded a few more times since we last met but that's about the extent of his development. Westerbury, though, does signal an attempt by Le Carré to extend and deepen his characterisation of the unillusioned agent-figure, the battered pursuer of goals that must not be too closely called in question. Le Carré has never been much good at dealings between individuals (it's a novelty when he equips a member of the cast with more than two or three identifying traits) but he has always dangled vague romantic prospects before the noses of his run-down, manly types. In this book, he makes the mistake of permitting some fruition, and thus involving the manly one in weighty introspection. The result is depressingly cartoon-like—and all the more so in the operations-room atmosphere that provides the context for these intermittent flourishes of Sensitivity and Insight.

Much of all this could be swallowed if the book had any pace, but the things that are wrong with Le Carré, at the level of seriousness he no doubt feels he's aimed for here, totally debilitate the book's appeal as a run-of-the-mill espionage yarn. (p. 415)

> *Louis Finger, "The Manly One," in* New Statesman *(© 1977 The Statesman & Nation Publishing Co. Ltd.), September 23, 1977, pp. 414-15.*

Le Carré's contribution to the fiction of espionage has its roots in the truth of how a spy system works. If in Ian Fleming's James Bond novels we meet fantasy and embrace it with a willing suspension of disbelief, in books like "The Honourable Schoolboy" we approach a truth, or at least a plausibility that must be accepted even if we would prefer to reject it. The people who run Intelligence totally lack glamour, their service is short of money, they are up against the crassness of politicians. Their men in the field are frightened, make blunders, grow sick of a trade in which the opposed sides too often seem to interpenetrate and wear the same face; they have no notable dexterity with women, they vomit, and, when they get hurt, the hurt lasts.

Since le Carré wants to present espionage as actuality, he is not at liberty to invent fantastic schemes of global takeover, villains like Milton's Satan, mad ingenuities of torture or girls of lubricous voluptuousness.... Le Carré must also cling to real places, where real espionage situations are available. The world available to the British spy who (unlikely story) is not called in to assist the C.I.A. is shrinking very fast. Only Hong Kong seems to be left, and that is where the greater part of the action of this novel takes place. (p. 9)

Le Carré is so concerned with planting his story in a wide field of credibility that he spends far more time in mowing the field than in spudding in his shoots. This is a very long book for its subject, and there is scene after scene—usually back in London where the Circus operates—in which the old fictional principle of Ockham's Razor (less is more) is relentlessly eschewed. On the other hand, le Carré has learned something about dialogue that is not apparent in the earlier books. His Hong Kong Chinese sound like the real thing, as do his Americans—the Cousins, as the Brits call them—and the horrible Bolshies and Yellow Perils of the Circus (so the specialists are facetiously called) speak like many varieties of Brit. But the dialogues go on forever, as if boredom were an essential adjunct of learning the real truth of how intelligence operations are set up. Le Carré is like the film director Stanley Kubrick of "2001: A Space Odyssey": if you're bored in this fictional situation, therefore this fictional situation is real life. Sometimes, bizarrely, I seemed to be reading a novel, like those of Wyndham Lewis, in which every character is solid but not one of them moves.

From the very start, le Carré seems determined to put you off these characters: they're unattractive, therefore they must be real. The facetiousness—cliché-laden and often brutal—of much of their speech, and of the *récit* surrounding it, sets one's teeth aching. As we move with steamroller slowness to the dénouement, we move also toward the region of a conventional and satisfying spy story.... And before that, we've had some efficient evocations of Laos, Northeast Thailand and Phnom Penh. And, always, the marine, cartographical, ballistic and procedural technicalities are faultless....

Does [this book] have anything to do with literature? In the sense that literature is recognizable through its capacity to evoke more than it says, is based on artful selection, throws up symbols, suggests a theology or metaphysic of which the story itself is a kind of allegory, the answer has to be no.

[Le Carré remains] ingenious, veridical, documentary

rather than imaginative. There is nothing wrong with that, but it is probably better for a novelist's Soul? *Soul?* Souls are for the running dogs' Baptist missions. (p. 45)

> *Anthony Burgess, "Peking Drugs, Moscow Gold," in* The New York Times Book Review *(© 1977 by The New York Times Company; reprinted by permission), September 25, 1977, pp. 9, 45.*

It is difficult not to overpraise [*The Honourable Schoolboy*], this new (and, apparently, concluding) installment of the voluminous history of the British spymaster George Smiley and his brilliant secret service, known as the Circus. It has, most certainly, its faults. It runs to well over two hundred thousand not always necessary words. Its plot— the tracing of a high-ranking Chinese turned Russian spy— is devious but essentially thin. Its opening chapter—a drunken romp at the Hong Kong press club—is embarrassing. And so is the author's fondness for stylistic mockery. . . . But these fade in the glorious sunshine of its virtues. It has a compelling pace, a depth beyond its genre, a feeling for even the least of its characters, a horrifying vision of the doomed and embattled Southeast Asia left in the wake of the Vietnam war, and a dozen set pieces—following, fleeing, interrogating—that are awesomely fine. (p. 163)

> *Mollie Panter-Downes, in* The New Yorker *(© 1977 by The New Yorker Magazine, Inc.), October 3, 1977.*

John le Carré's *The Honourable Schoolboy* . . . has its enervating moments. Local color sometimes yawns into travelogue. Romantic interludes seem pasted in. The ending is contrived. And it's foregone that George Smiley, the failed-priest bureaucrat of the British Secret Service . . ., will survive. . . .

The plot of *The Honourable Schoolboy* is superbly elaborate and, except for the end, so adroitly worked out that it can fool us into overrating its importance. . . . This is structure, scaffolding; that it's wobbly in one place doesn't matter much. The real novel is inside.

That is, inside George Smiley's head. He perceives always the anomalies of his life's work, but with a difference. The spy business may be peripheral. It is often extremely stupid, and sometimes comic in a rueful way. But he doesn't claim much tragedy for it. When things go wrong, it's a matter of circumstance. People are buffeted by ambition, physical needs, exhaustion. What might seem tragic is merely these circumstances getting in the way of the simplest (or most complex) of intellectual intentions—these and chance and the relentless passage of time. The hours and days troop by—here now, then irretrievably gone; their pace is inflexible, utterly beyond the most minor modification by man. We grow older; spies grow older.

In this context, the great questions—What is loyalty? What is honor? What rights and responsibilities go with having even momentary effect on others?—do not lose their potency, but are simply addressed within humbler dimensions. The questions, not the action, the violent skullduggery and derring-do (of which there is plenty), provide the tension in the book, are its engine of suspense. (p. 103)

This is a very rewarding tale: so much is *told*. It's old-fashioned in a sense—le Carré wants to intrigue and entertain, not to whine. It's an escape in the classic mode: You lose yourself in it, suspensefully but cozily. But you don't lose yourself entirely; a bit of the reader's future is mortgaged, too. (p. 105)

> *Eliot Fremont-Smith, "Thriller of Dignity, Diller of Distaste," in* The Village Voice *(reprinted by permission of* The Village Voice; *copyright © by The Village Voice, Inc., 1977), October 24, 1977, pp. 103, 105.*

[*The Honourable Schoolboy*] is about twice as long as it should be. It falls with a dull thud into the second category of le Carré's books—those which are greeted as being something more than merely entertaining. Their increasingly obvious lack of mere entertainment is certainly strong evidence that le Carré is out to produce a more respectable breed of novel than those which fell into the first category, the ones which were merely entertaining. But in fact it was the merely entertaining books that had the more intense life. . . .

The Honourable Schoolboy brings the second sequence to a heavy apotheosis. A few brave reviewers have expressed doubts about whether some of the elements which supposedly enrich le Carré's later manner might not really be a kind of impoverishment, but generally the book has been covered with praise—a response not entirely to be despised, since *The Honourable Schoolboy* is so big that it takes real effort to cover it with anything. At one stage I tried to cover it with a pillow, but there it was, still half visible, insisting, against all the odds posed by its coagulated style, on being read to the last sentence.

The last sentence comes 530 pages after the first, whose tone of mythmaking portent is remorselessly adhered to throughout. "Afterwards, in the dusty little corners where London's secret servants drink together, there was argument about where the Dolphin case history should really begin." The Dolphin case history, it emerges with stupefying gradualness, is concerned with the Circus (i.e., the British Secret Service) getting back on its feet after the catastrophic effect of its betrayal by Bill Haydon, the Kim Philby figure whose depredations were the subject of *Tinker, Tailor, Soldier, Spy.* The recovery is masterminded by George Smiley, nondescript hero and cuckold genius. . . .

This novel didn't *have* to be tedious. The wily schemes of the Circus have been just as intricate before today. In fact the machinations outlined in *The Spy Who Came In From the Cold* and *The Looking Glass War* far outstrip in subtlety anything Smiley gets up to here. Which is part of the trouble. In those books character and incident attended upon narrative, and were all the more vivid for their subservience. In this book, when you strip away the grandiloquence, the plot is shown to be perfunctory. There is not much of a *story.* Such a lack is one of the defining characteristics of le Carré's more recent work. It comes all the more unpalatably from a writer who gave us, in *The Spy Who Came In From the Cold,* a narrative so remarkable for symmetrical economy that it could be turned into an opera. . . .

To start with, the prose style is overblown. Incompatible metaphors fight for living space in the same sentence. "Now at first Smiley tested the water with Sam—and Sam, who liked a poker hand himself, tested the water with Smiley." Are they playing cards in the bath? Such would-be taciturnity is just garrulousness run short of breath. On the other hand, the would-be eloquence is verbosity run riot. Whole pages are devoted to inventories of what can be found by way of flora and fauna in Hong Kong, Cambodia, Vietnam, and other sectors of the mysterious East. There is no possible question that le Carré has been out there and done his fieldwork. Unfortunately he has brought it all home.

But the really strength-sapping feature of the prose style is its legend-building tone. Half the time le Carré sounds like Tolkien. You get visions of Hobbits sitting around the fire telling tales of Middle Earth.

> Need Jerry have ever gone to Ricardo in the first place? Would the outcome, for himself, have been different if he had not? Or did Jerry, as Smiley's defenders to this day insist, by his pass at Ricardo, supply the last crucial heave which shook the tree and caused the coveted fruit to fall?

Forever asking questions where he ought to be answering them, the narrator is presumably bent on seasoning myth-omania with Jamesian ambiguity: *The Lord of the Rings* meets *The Golden Bowl*. Working on the principle that there can be no legends without lacunae, the otherwise omniscient author, threatened by encroaching comprehensibility, takes refuge in a black cloud of question marks. . . .

Fatally, the myth-mongering extends to the characterization. The book opens with an interminable scene starring the legendary journalists of Hong Kong. Most legendary of them all is an Australian called Craw. In a foreword le Carré makes it clear that Craw is based on Dick Hughes, legendary Australian journalist. (p. 29)

Le Carré used to be famous for showing us the bleak, tawdry reality of the spy's career. He still provides plenty of bleak tawdriness, but romanticism comes shining through. Jerry Westerby, it emerges, has that "watchfulness" which "the instinct" of "the very discerning" describes as "professional." You would think that if Westerby really gave off these vibrations it would make him useless as a spy. But le Carré does not seem to notice that he is indulging himself in the same kind of transparently silly detail which Mark Twain found so abundant in Fenimore Cooper. . . .

In his early novels le Carré told the truth about Britain's declining influence. In the later novels, the influence having declined even further, his impulse has altered. The slide into destitution has become a planned retreat, with Smiley masterfully in charge. On le Carré's own admission, Smiley has always been the author's fantasy about himself—a Billy Batson who never has to say "Shazam!" because inside he never stops being Captain Marvel. But lately Smiley has also become the author's fantasy about his beleaguered homeland. . . .

This novel still displays enough of le Carré's earlier virtues to remind us that he is not summarily to be written off. There is an absorbing meeting in a soundproof room, with Smiley plausibly outwitting the civil servants and politicians. Such internecine warfare, to which most of the energy of any secret organization must necessarily be devoted, is le Carré's best subject. . . .

Outwardly aspiring to the status of literature, le Carré's novels have inwardly declined to the level of pulp romance. He is praised for sacrificing action to character, but ought to be dispraised, since by concentrating on personalities he succeeds only in overdrawing them, while eroding the context which used to give them their desperate authenticity. Raising le Carré to the plane of literature has helped rob him of his more enviable role as a popular writer who could take you unawares. Already working under an assumed name, le Carré ought to assume another one, sink out of sight, and run for the border of his reputation. There might still be time to get away. (p. 30)

> *Clives James, "Go Back to the Cold!" in* The New York Review of Books *(reprinted with permission from* The New York Review of Books; *copyright © 1977 NYREV, Inc.), October 27, 1977, pp. 29-30.*

*   *   *

LERMAN, Eleanor   1952-

An American poet, Lerman depicts in her poetry the seediness and despair of the underside of an American culture that is caught up in drugs, lesbian love, and violence.

If volumes of poetry carried letter-ratings the way movies do, then "Armed Love" would deserve at least a double X. In their glimpses of life in a drug-torn Lesbian ghetto, the poems talk to us in a voice that wavers between self-deprecation and self-righteousness. At its clearest, its tone is absolute candor.:

> I guess some of us are born to be charming and
> run gaily by the evening shore for
> feminine deodorant commercials while the rest of us
> end up poor and incoherent
> babbling about drunken visions
> and dying with people we don't know

Such terrifying simplicity, such hunger for love are bound to unnerve us and stir us. . . . Much of the time, though, the raw facts just remain on their page like meat left in its butcher's paper, untouched by deep understanding or by art. At too many crucial moments, the poet falls back on words like *shining, incredible* and *terrible;* on sentimentalities like *your frail dreams, my terrible dreams* and *your shining, dancing heart.* "The Graceless Years," one of the grimmer failures, is about the speaker's obsessive desire to slash her own throat; and another poem, about doing "terrible things" to a girl named Angelica, lamely concludes: "I hate to think / what all this means." Although Eleanor Lerman has an infectuous contempt for "clean living," for the dull typing jobs farmed off on women and (in general) for North American civilization, it would take the skill and intelligence of a Sylvia Plath meaningfully to relate her private agonies to those of a larger world. (p. 6)

> *X. J. Kennedy, in* The New York Times Book Review *(© 1974 by The New York Times Company; reprinted by permission), February 17, 1974.*

Eleanor Lerman's book *Armed Love* is about Lesbian promiscuity, drugs, theft, suicidal threats, psychological and perhaps physical torture of people, disorder, mockery of real and fraudulent ideals—also passion, also love. It attacks moralists with wit and polemical skill ("Graduate School"), yet the moral understanding is greater than Plath's or Berryman's, whose desperate poems have granted their authors fame. The rhythmical movement is dislocated, representing brokenness of view, jumps of impression, hysteria, events collided and ungrasped. Such a technique is common in modern poems, but seldom so successful as here. The poems are clear in wildness, disturbing, brilliantly lighted, often felt as wholes. "Shotgun Days" is an extraordinary blues poem; the last poem in the book and "Will Someone Who Is Not Guilty" are not easy to forget; and "The Alchemist Lost to Human Gifts" and "As in a Dream I Would Yet Remain" are starkly beautiful and tender. (pp. 404-05)

> *Paul Ramsey, in* Sewanee Review *(reprinted by permission of the editor, © 1974 by The University of the South), Spring, 1974.*

[*Armed Love*] looms like a defensive banner over the lesbian world [Eleanor Lerman] portrays. Monologues, encounters, details, read like data from a sordid casebook.... [The] hell that unfolds appears pasteboard. The reasons are technical.... [Her poems] would not survive critical scrutiny as heterosexual love poetry. How, then, as lesbian poetry? It is neither parody nor burlesque of conventions. It is, forgive the pun, straight. The injection of mock rhetoric ... into otherwise simple diction, blurs the tone. Genuineness of sentiment becomes suspect.

A dual pattern emerges in the imagery of Lerman's poems. The normal world is presented in flat nominatives—"The candy bride my mother kept for me / in a blue tray with all those bangly earrings";—while the deviant world is suggested by remote, arcane metaphors: "I had revealed the translation of the Martian obelisk / and promised you the crushed disk of the star-mined silver." Because the two modes are not integrated, the poems lack a tension necessary to dramatize suffering. (p. 3)

> *Norma Procopiow, in* Book World—The Washington Post *(© The Washington Post), May 26, 1974.*

Eleanor Lerman is most enthusiastic indeed about presenting her life and loves. Her New York is ... disastrous ... and her humorous efforts to overcome her situation are [, in *Armed Love,* somewhat] energetic. Fresh resilience rather than wry weariness is her hallmark. Sometimes she flaunts a heroic Lesbianism in the fatuous face of the establishment. At other times she reveals all the vulnerability and romanticism of a sensitive girl in her very, very early twenties. She can be lighthearted, toughminded, fierce, tender, mystical, and romantic, primarily over her beloved Frances. At times she is a little too exhaustive on the subject of *Armed Love:* after a while the attitudes she strikes or the mystical/romantic language she slips into become too familiar.... And despite the limitations of her subject matter, with the very narrow focus on herself and her fantasized, shifting roles in a limited milieu, she has written what is for me [an] exciting [book]. (p. 59)

Ms. Lerman runs into a bit of trouble with her paradoxical armed love. One of its aspects is the violence directed towards her lover, expressed sometimes by the vampire image that emerges and submerges in the book. Another is uncontrolled violence undertaken on the beloved's behalf, an upending of chivalric values: "In Your Movements I See Drownings" and "I Will Teach You About Murder" are particularly explicit. The drive towards absolute secular power is allied to the motif of the alchemist reshaping the world for his beloved. And at a third level tyrant and alchemist merge into fantasies of power over the whole universe ("Finally I See Your Skin"):

my mouth cracks open and planets start to pour out
universes form and begin to show
signs of life

These seem to be perilous, drug-induced hallucinations which lead her farther and farther from an exploration of the true nature of her relationships. Her vocabulary changes and we are suddenly in the mystic misty realm of romance, fairy tale, astrology, and science fiction, with a dash of dream and film imagery. Her sharp sanity dissolves in too much drifting and warring, light and dark, gold and silver, and the amalgam starts to cloy. I prefer the clear vision of "As in a Dream I Would Yet Remain." The scene of the poet cradling the trusting Frances against the river wind is desolate, but it has the kind of life-giving perceptiveness that her cloudier visions of a mystic love do not. Here they are simply two youngsters lost in one of our "intricate american cities."... (pp. 60-1)

> *Sally M. Gall, in* Shenandoah *(copyright by* Shenandoah; *reprinted from* Shenandoah: The Washington and Lee University Review *with the permission of the Editor), Fall, 1974.*

Violence, blood, and shooting "your way out of / the women's museum" haunt *Armed Love*—the title is suggestive—like persistent aches. One comes to think of Lerman as a sort of latter-day Rimbaud, "babbling about drunken visions" as she bleeds metaphors in dark doorways, or perhaps as a member of some literary SLA, a guerrilla in the wars of love and art.

Yet at the same time, though she's a notable scholar of cruelty and despair, her poetry is tender, witty, elegant, even beautiful. For along with the anger that drives poets like Spivack and Swenson, she inherits the sheen and music that distinguished, say, Garrigue.... Here ... is an intensity of vision that tells us we're in the presence of something wholly authentic—love poems, hate poems, horror poems, written with scalpels on the nerve-endings. (pp. 53-4)

Lerman's revelations glow in the dark, wickedly phosphorescent. Like all visionary "babblers", she's a shameless braggart, a charming liar, an elegant lover, a Casanova of the imagination.... (p. 54)

> *Sandra M. Gilbert, in* Poetry *(© 1975 by The Modern Poetry Association; reprinted by permission of the Editor of* Poetry*), October, 1975.*

Suppose someone came running at you screaming "Yes! Yes! How romantic it was! See how carefully we died for each other! See her teeth still embedded in my hands!" How would you react? Would you be interested? At first, yes, startled and therefore engaged. But suppose the screamer merely continued repeating that same aggressive invitation. Suppose you realized that she was alluding to the death, or departure, of her lover, and you saw that there were not, in fact, any teeth embedded in her hands. You might feel pity or a bit disgusted by her hyperbole and solipsism; you would hope that she'd feel better soon, and that she would get professional care if her frenzy persisted; but your interest would probably wane rapidly, and soon you would leave her alone.

The speaker of one of Eleanor Lerman's poems ("Romance, I Think, Must Remain'') describes herself screaming those words, and though this speaker intends a bitter irony about her painful addiction to her love-relationship, the effect of Lerman's poetry on the reader is much like the effect that hysterical accoster would have on you if you met her in the street.

There was much to admire in Lerman's *Armed Love* when I read it two years ago. It seemed a bravely naked book, far more alive than the tidy intellectual constructions of the other young poets I had in hand. My impulse was to defend *Armed Love* against the kind of disapproval summarized so well by X. J. Kennedy [see excerpt above].

There is a raw-meat quality to Lerman's work: it shows no signs of academic curing, no workshop seasoning, nor does it smell like any dish cooked in the kitchen of a major American poet past or present. But what lies thick and red on the page is not a catalogue of facts—Lerman's poetry is too (literally) fantastic for that—but of emotions, volatile and potentially lethal. Lethal, because they threaten to overwhelm the poet; and lethal too (I have to admit now, having read *Come The Sweet By And By*) because they threaten to bore the reader to death.

It becomes apparent reading through *Armed Love* that the author is a lesbian; yet this is never openly stated. It would be possible (though not easy) to construe every utterance as that of a heterosexual person sympathizing with the oppressed. This central reticence amid such voluble anger and resentment is disappointing, but it reminds us how dangerous an open acknowledgment of unorthodox sexuality is still felt to be in our society. Lerman shows she is aware of the political nature of sexism, though she wishes she didn't have to think in political terms. . . . Despite her political consciousness, *Armed Love* is not an indictment of America, or of men. . . . [She] seeks an individual rather than a collective-political identity: ''They can't simply belong to the community of women.'' *Armed Love* dives again and again into personal misery. Lerman shies away from any generalization and is tempted to reject thought altogether. (pp. 235-36)

One of the distinctions of *Armed Love* is that all the poems emanate from the same place, the same small world—violent, claustrophobic, sex-obsessed, hopelessly urban. This sort of unity invites redundancy, but it gives us carnivores something to sink our teeth into. After reading *Armed Love* I felt I had been taken somewhere, to a special place with uncommon noises and colors.

Now, however, Lerman's second collection has appeared, and it forces me to take a jaded second look at her talent. . . . [*Come The Sweet By And By*] has no overarching scheme, and if it differs from *Armed Love* by being less New York-oriented and more concerned with memory, this difference does not amount to a unifying identity. *Come The Sweet By And By* mostly sounds like *Armed Love*, Part Two: there is no reason to believe that these poems were written after those in *Armed Love*. Perhaps the two collections are merely two arbitrary handfuls from a gigantic pile on Lerman's desk. This is no crime, of course, but it's disappointingly unambitious: a mere encore when one hoped for a fresh concert.

Unless you linger patiently to analyze a single Lerman poem, the poems in *Come The Sweet By And By* tend to merge into one endless demented monologue, with pauses only for breath. If you read three or four poems in a row you are lulled (despite the vigor and pain of the voice and the extremeness of the imagery) into a dazed, non-discriminating mood whose dominant thought is merely, What will she think of next? Lerman's mind jumps from image to image, situation to situation, and attitude to attitude, almost never sustaining one tone or metaphorical scene for more than five consecutive lines. Each poem seems to be an almost random grouping of five or six image-clusters and dramatic attitudes (e.g., pleading, mourning, suspecting, berating, deriding) which are linked, if at all, only by a general emotion (yearning, or regret, or resentment) which reappears often enough in the poem to seem its basic impulse.

If you resist being dazed, however, the rather limited pleasure of being repeatedly surprised disappears and you grow frustrated as you try to dig into an individual poem. Lerman's poems are particularly frustrating because her use of long lines and (often) complete grammatical sentences seems to guarantee that she will make clear narrative sense, or at least that a given poem can be heard as the controlled utterance of a rational speaker who is willing to converse with the reader. Instead, you find that the poem is not like rational conversation at all; not only is it not prosaically expository, it also refuses metaphoric coherence. You face the job of studying the poem's various images to see if they ultimately can be shown to reflect a *particular* state of mind which would make the speaker interesting as a *particular* character. None of Lerman's characters sounds very trustworthy; they coyly dodge the reader's questions. In giving her poetry its illusory surface readability Lerman resembles one of her characters, ''pretending it's going to be a normal day / when I know it's going to be a mood piece / from start to finish''. The reader should be warned by the fact that Lerman never uses periods, although she does often capitalize the first word of each new sentence. In Lerman's universe, nothing ever ends; indeed, nothing ever even stops long enough for the poet to ask herself whether something—an idea, an outcry, a poem—has been finished.

Poetic form holds no charm for Lerman—she never uses rhyme, metrical schemes, or traditional verse forms. Perhaps she has grimly decided that such pleasant techniques are unavailable to honest poets in the modern world—''If only there were reason to believe / in some ancient artistry,'' she laments in ''Nuns, Geometry, Grief.''

Nor is Lerman always artful in her diction. At times her language strays so far into prosiness that it begins to sound like poor, overblown essay-prose. . . . In such lines the writing works neither as poetry (bringing emotions and ideas to life before our eyes) nor as exposition (developing a clear thought); rather, it sinks to the level of notebook jottings which have value only to the jotter, if even to her. Every poet has wanted to write lines like the two below, but most of us have been wise enough to destroy the poems in which we succumbed to the temptation: ''I can't stand it any more / everything goes on on on on on.'' (pp. 237-39)

[For Lerman] the reader (other than her lover) is eternally an outsider, an intruder who can't adequately sympathize. In *Come The Sweet By And By* Lerman echoes *Armed Love*'s resentment of society's intrusions upon her private life. She wants to be free to immerse herself in the joys and griefs of her personal relationships, but an awareness of public issues and struggles such as the feminist movement cannot be banished from her mind. . . .

As in *Armed Love,* most of the poems in *Come The Sweet By And By* refer obliquely to problems in the love-relationship between the speaker and a mysterious ''you'' whom she addresses. This common set-up for a poem nowadays (and in Donne's day too, indeed) always runs the risk of shutting out the reader, making him feel like an unwelcome eavesdropper unable to crack the lovers' code. (p. 240)

There are, happily, a few exceptions to the above remarks about Lerman's solipsism, notably ''Poet For Time.'' This too is an address to the poet's lover, but here her tone is calm, melancholy but not morbid, warmed by an affirming spirit of love that emerges freely. This spirit, unlike the doubts and fears that energize many Lerman poems, seems to foster (or at least permit) a lovely clarity. The poem deals directly with the problem all lovers have of accepting the fact that their beloved has a past that excludes them. This unavoidable and quite reasonable truth can seem terribly unjust to a person in love, and Lerman expresses both the pain and a mature response to it in ''Poem For Time.'' It may be judged a simple poem, but it has the virtue of being candidly simple, and it achieves poignancy in such clear lines as these. . . . Similarly, scattered throughout Lerman's work are brief moving evocations of lovers' mutual dependence. . . . (pp. 240-41)

But too much of the time Lerman remains evasive, as if she must address her lover in their verbose code because she knows we are going to overhear and, despite her drive to understand her love problems (the poems are full of anxious question marks), she doesn't want *us* to get too sharp a picture of them, lest we employ our insight against her as part of society's repression of unusual love. . . . [In ''Return''] Lerman seems to be aware that much of her language does not come across to the unknown reader, and to admit that her first intention is to communicate with her beloved. She fears the reader, she fears her own memories, and she fears poetry—because all of these are forces calling upon her to impose order on her emotions. Lerman thrives on painful passion. She doesn't want anything to be wrapped up neatly and put away; she cherishes the vibrant irresolution that washes over from one fiercely unhappy poem to the next: ''Is it possible perhaps, never to be completed?'' she asks in ''The Common Fate Of Objects.'' Apparently she sees completion—of the self and of the poem—as synonymous with death. But she courts the other kind of death that comes from submission to chaos and the misunderstanding that flows from chaos; too many of her passages die on the page because the poet has not cared enough about our comprehension. (pp. 241-42)

> *Mark Halliday, ''Passionate Jottings,'' in*
> Parnassus: Poetry in Review *(copyright ©*
> *by Parnassus: Poetry in Review), Spring–*
> *Summer, 1976, pp. 235-42.*

Eleanor Lerman is an important new poet, and a strange avatar of Emily Dickinson. *Come the Sweet By and By,* her second book, moves so far beyond the tortured power of her first volume (*Armed Love*) that one hardly believes she has reached this level of rhythmic competence and emotional wisdom so quickly. . . .

The traumatized settings are familiar enough. What distinguishes her work in this mode is its humaneness, as if ordinary people in very typical American places, doing commonplace things, had unexpectedly discovered themselves and their environment to be possessed. The poems record how people try to maintain their most basic human feelings —love in particular—despite the fearful sense that the world they live in is out of their control. The theme is announced in the strange and lonely narrative which opens the book, with its wonderful dislocating pun on ''bows'' in the first line:

> The Texas girls make deep and
> courtly bows for each other
> in chambers adjoining the ballroom
> Their silence is secretive and
> serious . . .
> The never-to-be husbands stand
> together
> waiting for them in the carpeted
> hallway
> whispering across clear, ribboned
> boxes of white carnations
> about how ephemeral and
> unladylike
> the debutantes' bodies have
> become
> And will they ever walk through
> that doorway again?
>
> (''The Texas Girls'')

This goodbye to the empty love rituals of debutante balls also establishes the book's world, which is feminine. . . .

Most of the poems in the book are scenes—in scattered American localities, and often while travelling—of these lovers trying to get by and (to borrow a peculiarly appropriate old-fashioned term) cleave to one another. . . . [As] the book's title suggests, the poems are haunted with a sense of final things. Love in these poems, as Ms Lerman has also said, is a way of ''getting by—no matter how strange, difficult, absurd or grievous are the circumstances you find yourself in, there must be a way to survive them''. Love here occupies small and suffocating areas, and seems a seed fallen among the thorns and stony places of typical American scenes. Nevertheless, as all the poems show, such love does not seem to need to fall upon a rich ground to live. It sprouts, survives; and it even translates its surroundings. Every day seems lived as if it were the last day, which is cherished as a weird promise of yet another final meeting ''on that beautiful shore'' in the sweet by and by. Lerman's people are ''waiting for time to be repealed.''. . .

Always about to die, for love; to occupy such a position continually is a manoeuvre of terrible desperation, a hunt among stones (''but we are running out of surplus marrow / and have had to utilize the family pain supplies / Eventually we will be too crippled to separate''). Living this way, in poetry, is a way of showing what being alive means (''we go together, you and I / to make the summer games for us all'.'). The device is like the romance conventions of fairyland, which in fact these poems continually reproduce. Fairyland (terrible, wonderful, impossible) is not itself our attachment, or what we are meant to long for; it is the occasion for revealing precise and memorable images of true human attachments. This is why the enamelled surfaces and ritual localities and events in these poems are so important, and why they would evaporate to nothing if they were not the manifesting (and disappearing) frame for all the common, small talk. The power of these poems issues out of that necessary marriage of the strange and the piteously familiar.

> *Jerome McGann, "The Love That's Left,"*
> *in* The Times Literary Supplement (©
> *Times Newspapers Ltd., 1976; reproduced*
> *from* The Times Literary Supplement *by*
> *permission), December 10, 1976, p. 1563.*

*　　*　　*

LEVINE, Philip 1928-

Levine is an American poet, critic, and editor. His poetry is peopled with unhappy, unlucky characters depicted at the dramatic moment of personal defeat. (See also *CLC*, Vols. 2, 4, 5, and *Contemporary Authors*, Vols. 9-12, rev. ed.)

[Philip Levine's] immensely moving *The Names of the Lost* . . . is essentially a book of belated elegies for the Spanish anarchists, but Levine has the control of pathos necessary to prevent any mere study of the nostalgias. *For the Fallen,* an elegy for the Durruti brothers, may be the finest of these poems, but every page of the book is marked by a severe and appropriate eloquence. (p. 23)

> *Harold Bloom, in* The New Republic *(re-*
> *printed by permission of* The New Republic;
> © *1976 by The New Republic, Inc.), No-*
> *vember 20, 1976.*

Deeply emotional, [Philip Levine's verse in *The Names of the Lost*] avoids sentimentality through its simplicity. Modern writers, the best of them included, tend to indulge themselves in fancy rhetoric about the dark night of the suburban soul, or new losses of innocence in the face of this wicked world. Levine's plain style is like a drink of cold water after a diet of soft drinks. His liturgical cadences never pontificate. . . .

From the detritus of past and present suffering, Levine can continue to scent a God who is "the odor of light / out of darkness, substance out of air / of blood before it reddens and runs." This uncompromising vision is more Biblical in spirit than all the optimistic freedom and space of Rosenberg's interpretations. *The Names of the Lost* sings with the Psalmist that even in seeking answers, we can accept the ways of a God beyond our understanding. (p. 17)

> *Phoebe Pettingell, in* The New Leader (©
> *1977 by the American Labor Conference on*
> *International Affairs, Inc.), January 17,*
> *1977.*

[The] power to look around and see and the strength of a living syntax have distinguished Philip Levine's poetry at its best. In "Not This Pig" (1968) and "They Fed They Lion" (1972), he awakened and moved readers with poems meant to be read. That is high praise when so much recent poetry seems sealed off from what people see or how people might speak when moved—sealed off either by coy mannerism or by the standard poetic diction of a chic reticence. . . .

Into that antiseptic, surrealist kitchen came Levine's recognizable pig. . . . [The pig] does not explain God's ways to man, but it is human, and a real animal, part of an American terrain that Levine has seen with unglazed eyes. The material itself invites literary cliché: the lower-middle-class

Detroit of Levine's childhood; the slaughterhouses, grease-shops and smeared rivers that are part of the country; the sweet, uneasy California suburb that is another part. The list itself is a cliché, but Levine can overcome that because like the pig these things are not seen as "material," but as life; the poet's prejudices are political and moral, not literary.

That said, it must be admitted that Levine's work is uneven and that its failing is the maudlin. I understand the maudlin to be not a degree of feeling, or even a kind of feeling, but the locking of tone into a flaw or groove, running there without the capacity for modulation of emotion: a single, sustained whine, piercing but not penetrating. In other words, if Swinburne used the same adjectives for a sunset and a woman, Levine sometimes uses the same ones for a dead fish and a lost war. (The poems not directly of America often draw on Levine's experience of Spain, particularly Barcelona and its enduring aftermark of the Civil War.) As with women and sunsets, there may be good reasons for using the same terms, but the reasons must be thought out and felt through, somehow.

What staves off the maudlin in any art is continuity of thought, a sustained choice to speak with all of one's mind. The best poems by Levine meet that intellectual risk, or make peace with it, as in (for example) "Silent in America," "Animals Are Passing From Our Lives," "Baby Villon," "Salami," "They Feed They Lion," all from the two volumes I have named.

The new poems of "The Names of the Lost" renew and heighten the accomplishments and conflicts that I have tried to outline here. The mood is (as the title implies) more obsessively elegiac than ever. . . .

"1933" disappointed me, seemed duller because the poems had become more impressionistic and orphic, less rather than more willing to make the mind known.

To be more specific: I cannot say, amid the technologies of death, deliberate and inadvertent, that America, Barcelona, the world are any less horrible or less fit objects for elegy than Levine says. But often his horrors feel too much the same; to grow old, to drink bad water, to bomb Dresden, to eat sick animals, to be shot by Fascists, if they are understood too similarly have been understood too simply.

[In "The Names of the Lost"], as in "1933," the tendency to hold a poem together from its beginning to end only by a thin, vibrating wire of emotion seems extended. Is it odd or inappropriate to find poems deficient in *thought*? The monotony of feeling and repetitiousness of method produce a dark, sleepy air not so different, after all, from the Stone-Breath-Light-Snow surrealism. With the exceptions of "New Season" and "Another Life," the poems of "The Names of the Lost" are both more vatic and looser than earlier work; if not quite trivializing the mood of "They Feed They Lion," then making it more formulaic. (pp. 6, 14)

> *Robert Pinsky, "The Names of the Lost,"*
> *in* The New York Times Book Review (©
> *1977 by The New York Times Company;*
> *reprinted by permission), February 20, 1977,*
> *pp. 6, 14.*

[In *The Names of the Lost*] Levine is concerned with historical events—the wars of this century, the Depression, the Spanish Civil War—but only as they impinge on his growing up in Detroit, on the lives of his relatives and friends. This is personal poetry given wider reflection, history brought into the autobiographical mode, and sometimes usurping it. A poem like "On the Murder of Lieutenant José Del Castillo by the Falangist Bravo Martinez, July 12, 1936" is followed by a piercing lament, "For the Fallen." "Belle Isle, 1949," a re-creation of an experience (swimming) from Levine's own boyhood, is set amid poems speaking of the wider human contact. The most impressive quality about Levine's poems in this collection is his use of language. . . . "The flowers drying in the garden are the body. My wife raises the fallen arm and binds the forehead. She goes on her knees before a rose blackened at the center, she rests in the shadow of sunflower. At 8:30 there is a carnival of blue morning glories; the mockingbird squawks their sudden thought, the hummingbird steals their intuitions. If I love the body that is yours for a time, wild phlox, marigold, weed, if I love the cactus that holds on and the thistle burning alone, if we are our bodies, naked. . . ." Reprinted without line divisions to give the full effect of the speaking voice that Levine creates, this passage is just one of many in which the poet manages to bring divergent images into a single focus almost before the reader notices, because the movement through the words has been so effortless, so effective. We enjoy reading these words because they are chosen with grace, with art.

And finally, perhaps, that is the insistence of the contemporary poet—that readers remember that the heart of any poem is its language. (p. 94)

> *Linda W. Wagner, in* The Ontario Review *(copyright © 1975 by* The Ontario Review*), Fall–Winter, 1977–78.*

* * *

LOWELL, Robert   1917-1977

Poet, playwright, translator, editor, and critic, Lowell is considered to be the greatest American poet of his generation. Acknowledging the influence of Williams, Ransom, and Tate, Lowell considered himself a "formal" poet, especially in contrast to poets of his generation such as Ginsberg or Ferlinghetti. Lowell's concern with the past and with tradition is evidenced in the subject matter of his drama: he used themes from Melville and Hawthorne in his Old Glory dramatic trilogy and translated Greek and Roman classics in a modern idiom. Throughout his career, Lowell remained an innovative stylist, constantly exploring the possibilities of poetic expression. His work is characterized by a strength and vitality controlled by his innate sense of form. (See also CLC, Vols. 1, 2, 3, 4, 5, 8, and Contemporary Authors, Vols. 9-12, rev. ed.; obituary, Vols. 73-76.)

"Life Studies" is probably one of the four most important volumes of new poetry in English since *Four Quartets*. One reason for this judgment would certainly be that Lowell had profited from the other three: *Paterson, The Pisan Cantos,* and *Howl and Other Poems.* (p. 96)

Lowell also showed an extraordinary ability to profit by the advice given him over the years by people like Frost, Eberhart, Tate, Blackmur, Jarrell, Fiedler, Bewley, and Arrowsmith. Fortunately for him, these critics agreed in estimating his strengths and weaknesses. They all said he had a great talent for the strong metrical line, the rich image, and the complex mosaic structure. Some frankly envied his hereditary grasp of the New England mingle of European and American materials. In different ways all pointed to the same shortcomings: a lack of lovingness, inability to manage narrative, ventriloquism, "monotonous violence" in prosody and in imagery, imagery that reflected a bleak Protestant temper even while alluding to the most unctuous or baroque Catholic emblems. Lowell countered these strictures (or turned defects into virtues) in the fifteen poems of Part IV of the *Life Studies* volume by using strategies new to his work.

First, he took up in them the familiar subject matter of the American writer, his own early childhood and youth. Second, by opening his prosody to free verse, he moved like many other poets in the fifties into the camp of William Carlos Williams (whose work he had always, in fact, admired). Not so obvious, but vital to the enthusiastic reception of the volume as a whole, were two other strategies which are outstanding in the series of fifteen "Life Studies" poems and are not to be found in such concentrated form elsewhere in Lowell's writing to date. They serve to set these poems off as a distinct work. First, "Life Studies" . . . is not a connected narrative, but it has a very strong mythic structure: a combination of the two Freudian myths of maturation and the family romance. The reason no one has pointed out these schemata, I suppose, is that both myths have been so widely internalized by now that we take them for granted. What I call the Freudian maturation myth might at first seem, indeed, only a behavioral platitude. But Freud's insistence upon genital adulthood and social responsibility, adopted by Lowell in "Life Studies," is a quite particular model for the life scheme and self-valuation of many poeple today; in this sense it is a myth. And finally, as if in answer to those who charged him with dour rigidity of feeling, Lowell adopted a comic strategy for "Life Studies," pitching it in the seriocomic (at times almost black) vein that has so widely supplanted the tragic in recent writing. (pp. 96-7)

[The] comic vein of "Life Studies" is wry, not ebullient. Were it not true in this way to Lowell's mind and experience, the series of poems could hardly have been so successful. Just as characteristic, I should say, is the fact that Lowell's comic vein is rhetorically well supported, on a theory of the comic that, again, owes much to Freud. . . . To Freud, a certain kind of laughter is the final proof of adulthood: when we can react to a punishing or humiliating situation with a laugh instead of a moan of despair, we are saying, "I am too grownup to allow this to distress me!" Laughter of adulthood is an assertion of superiority and at the same time a healthy release of otherwise destructive pressure.

Lowell's use of the secular Freudian myths succeeded where he had formerly achieved but limited results with "plots" drawn from Christian salvation dogma or dream-ridden psychodrama. In "Life Studies" his version of the family romance centers in the maturation story of Robert, Junior. The odds are against his achieving adulthood, for his mother has been so overpowered by her own "Freudian papá" that she inevitably sets about castrating her weak husband, Robert, Senior. The son has no proper father figure to model himself upon; but he unconsciously falls into two relationships, both comic, that save his virility even while they dangerously imperil his maturation. First, he and his Grandfather Winslow pair up; later, Robert carries on an intrigue with his mother so as (symbolically, in the

Freudian sense) to cuckold his father. At last, both parents die; Robert is the victim of psychic crises, but "Life Studies" ends on a firm, and comic, note of resolution and redemption. He, too, is now a parent, his wife no castrater but on the contrary a redeemer, an Alcestis; he finally comes to share the primitive, vital instinct for self-survival and self-perpetuation found in the maternal animal. Because his own life is vitally related to his child's, it has a value grounded in the continuity of all life.

There is an exact congruence between this "plot" and the basic Freudian theme and variations involving the individual's struggle to become a mature adult in the setting of his family and society. It is confirmed in detail by the prose autobiography, "91 Revere Street," in which Lowell tells the story of his life from beginning school to early adolescence. The result is, therefore, anything but a confessional piece in the crude sense of an unguarded outpouring of anguish and guilt. On the contrary. "Life Studies," like the works of St. Augustine and Rousseau, is the effort of a skilled rhetorician to persuade his audience that he has in fact survived his trial. (pp. 97-8)

One of the rhetorical functions of the comic in "Life Studies" is to show that the poet's genealogical ties to the colonial past are a mixed blessing. If, as it has been said, people envy Lowell for his lineage, let them realize that the actual personal links were a considerable handicap, humanly speaking. The poet shows us the ambiguities of his family history as the rhetor might do, to capture the goodwill of a largely plebeian audience. The rhetorical advantage of the Freudian myth so insistently employed in "Life Studies" is that it works with an audience that needs only to be human. (p. 102)

In the "Life Studies" series his adoption of a new, resolute stand toward life achieved a poetic presentation . . . largely by means of the Freudian myth of the psyche's progress from infantile Oedipal hostility and narcissism to the verge of adulthood and responsible paternity. Insofar as mine is merely an "interpretation" of "Life Studies," it may or may not be of much value. It is of greater critical importance, I think, to recognize that these fifteen poems are a literary entity, requiring the critic to treat them as such. If I can succeed in persuading the reader to entertain the possibility that "Life Studies" is a comic work, that too has some importance. What I should like most of all to accomplish, however, is to invite attention to the nature of the changes Lowell made in his style, because an understanding of these changes helps us to appreciate the problems of contemporary poetry more fully. I believe, in fact, that the redemptive movement in "Life Studies" is to be found in the evident renewal of the poet's speech, as well as in the progress his persona makes toward adulthood in the Freudian sense. (pp. 105-06)

> *George McFadden, "'Life Studies'—Robert Lowell's Comic Breakthrough," in PMLA, 90 (copyright © 1975 by the Modern Language Association of America; reprinted by permission of the Modern Language Association of America), January, 1975, pp. 96-106.*

In the twentieth century we prefer to think of our poets as rebels and innovators, and it is not difficult to fit Lowell into these categories. At the same time he remains very much a traditionalist, nourished by his New England roots, steeped in the classics, preoccupied with technique, shored up by Christian and post-Christian values. (p. 248)

If he were less of a traditionalist, his sporadic radical decisions and statements . . . would be less meaningful. Though he is not a man of action, he has a great intuitive gift for symbolic gesture. And though he is more deeply committed to the past than most contemporaries, the vibrant touch of his poetry is on the nerve of the modern. At one time Lowell was regarded as a New England poet, but despite his family connections he is no Yankee versifier and is not to be classified among the regionalists. . . . His abortive conversion to Catholicism, the influence of which dominated his early work, must be considered among his radical dissents. He remains an essentially Protestant spirit.

Lowell is fascinated by "the prose grip on things." In *Life Studies,* which looms as one of the watersheds of modern literature, he attempted to recapture a portion of the territory that poetry has for so long yielded to the novel. In *Notebook,* now retitled *History* in its expanded form, he has aimed at closing the gap between public and private events. One of his signal intuitions is the connection between terror as a fact of our political life and as a principle of the imagination, what Burckhardt in his study of the Renaissance called "terribilità," a term equally applicable to the sculpture of Michelangelo and the politics of Cesare Borgia. The two dominant figures in his landscape are Milton's Lucifer and Captain Ahab, "these two sublime ambitions," as he defines them, "that are doomed and ready, for their idealism, to face any amount of violence." In his poetry Lowell investigates states of crisis as permanent aspects of being. His work is invested with the quality of a mind that suffers history. Evil, guilt, and power are his insistent themes. Sometimes he magnifies the trivial to satisfy his taste for enormity. (pp. 248-49)

One of the disarming features of Lowell's work is that it does not pretend to aspire to the condition of an absolute art. He tells us the time in the right kind of voice for the day. He does not try to overpower us with a show of strength; instead, with his nervous vivacity, he hurries to build a chain of fortifications out of sand, or even dust. A revisionist by nature, he is forever tinkering with his old lines, rewriting his old poems, revamping his syntax, and periodically reordering his existence.

"It may be," he has remarked, "that some people have turned to my poems because of the very things that are wrong with me, I mean the difficulty I have with ordinary living, the impracticability, the myopia." Nobody else sounds quite like that. He makes us excruciatingly aware of the thrashing of the self behind the lines; of the intense fragility of the psyche trying to get a foothold in an "air of lost connections," struggling to stay human and alive. He is a poet who will even take the risk of sounding flat or dawdling in the hope that it might be true. What we get from these poems is the sense of a life . . . a life that has been turned into a style. (pp. 249-50)

> *Stanley Kunitz, "Poet of Terribilita," in his A Kind of Order, A Kind of Folly (© 1935, 1937, 1938, 1941, 1942, 1947, 1949, 1957, 1963, 1964, 1965, 1966, 1967, 1970, 1971, 1972, 1973, 1974, 1975 by Stanley Kunitz; reprinted by permission of Little, Brown and*

Co. in association with the Atlantic Monthly Press), Atlantic-Little, Brown, 1975, pp. 247-50.

Violence is Lowell's essential subject, terrible in its variety (of time, of place, of motive, of nature) and terrible in its unchangingness. . . . From his earliest poems to his latest, he has been preoccupied with violence. The national violence that is war, in poems about Napoleon, the Somme, Alexander, Hitler, Hamburg, the American Civil War, the Cuban missile crisis. The supra-national violence that is myth, in poems about the Gorgon, Odysseus, Clytemnestra. The domestic violence that is nagging or infidelity or divorce or murder or the war between children and parents. The personal or psychic violence that is nightmare or madness or suicide. Lowell has written poems on all of these and more. I cannot imagine a kind of violence, a time and a place for it, that he has not imagined on his and our behalf.

'I am against violence,' he said in an interview. 'If I were still Calvinist, I would call it *the* hell-fire.' And at once we are aware, as Lowell is, of the problems and paradoxes. For you do not have to go along with the lavish dilution of the word 'violent' (like that of the word 'obscene') to acknowledge that the burning-glass of hell-fire is a violent doctrine, violent in its extremity and in its inflictions.

So we have to ask, too, how Lowell manages to avoid, if he does, the nemesis that lies in wait for all imaginings of violence—even or especially the denunciations of violence: that to imagine it may be to minister to it. Isn't Lowell famous for the violence of his ways with language, with poetic forms, with writer-reader understandings? And how can there be an art which preaches non-violence and practises violence? . . .

Lowell has thought hard, and felt deeply, about violence. His own life . . . is contemporary with that of the words 'non-violence' and 'non-violent' (both born 1920, fathered by—and mothered by—Gandhi). The last half-century has tried to make imaginable an opposite of violence and an alternative to it, has tried to create 'the principle and practice of abstaining from the use of violence'. The attempt is noble in its aspiration; grim in its recognition that our century stands in hideous need of such a word and concept; inspiring in that it has at least partially succeeded in bringing to birth and to life such a word; and dispiriting in that it has succeeded only partially. . . .

Lowell's sense of violence and of 'the war of words' is evident in the first sentence of his most famous early poem, 'The Quaker Graveyard in Nantucket', which uses the word 'violently' but has just previously tranquillised it by using it of the sea's 'breaking' (when the sea breaks violently, it is mercifully intransitive—it breaks, it does not necessarily break anything); and Lowell then calms the word again, but sinisterly, by following it at once with the image of night as a hostile convoy. . . . About recent violence Lowell has said: 'Other things are boring for these young people, and violence isn't boring.' Yet Lowell as a poet stands in a tense relation to boredom—how can he create non-violent excitements that will not be incitements? (p. 314)

'In the Lowell country,' one of his critics, Marjorie Perloff, has said, 'objects never touch gently; there is always a head-on collision.' But often in a Lowell poem there are not two realised presences which can collide; in the absence of one of the terms, the collision remains a perpetual possibility only in a world of speculation. 'In a day when poets long to be irresistible forces, he is an immovable object,' said Lowell's best critic, Randall Jarrell. Lowell may yearn, of course, to be both, but he knows what a collision there would have to be, and he allows only one of the terms a collidable reality. . . .

Phrases in Lowell like 'hit the streets', or 'strike for shore', or 'clashing colours' or 'clashing outfits', at once evoke a potential violence (they have both a violence of expression and a hardened unfeelingness, such as we hear by now in a cliché like 'a sickening thud') and also are phantasmal, precipitating no real pain of violence—it is streets that are hit, not people, and colours that clash, not people. So I think that those critics of Lowell are right who feel a disconcerting unreality in his violence of expression, but wrong when they make this an accusation against the poetry. 'She thundered on the keyboard of her dummy piano': that thunders on neither a real piano nor a dummy one, and itself constitutes a strange art of the shadowily unimaginable or inaudible. The unreality is sometimes an evocation of an absent reality, imaginable but not here fully imagined; and the point of this is to escape the very collusion with violence of which hostile critics have accused him. . . .

Like all poets, Lowell is sensitive to such potent absences; a recent poem, 'The Airport', can say 'Your absence is presence', and we know what loving pressure this has and is about. Lowell's poems have always been alive with these vigorous spectral combats, at once violent (they disturb) and non-violent (one sense cannot strangle itself). So one characteristic response to Lowell's phrasing has always been to wonder for a second if you are misreading it. The early poems are muscular with these ripples of misconstruction. . . .

The characteristic early or middle poem by Lowell has such a combative fending off, like that of a pugnacious referee in the ring, necessarily pugnacious, perhaps, in his peace-keeping. There is a description of Hermes and his wand, 'His caduceus shadow-bowing behind him', which calls up and fends off 'shadow-boxing'—the perfect image for that combative non-combatancy of Lowell's which yet is not hollow or rigged, but is a brave, imaginative attempt to deal with the problems of an uncollusive imagination of violence.

But Lowell has grown older, and his sense of how to deal with combat and violence has calmed and changed. In *Life Studies,* his turning-point, the extraordinary autobiographical prose of '91 Revere Street' was devoted largely to the paradoxes of his father's life in the navy and at home, mostly both at once. Lowell as a child loved toy-soldiers, he tells us; and his father is loved as a toy-sailor. '91 Revere Street' should be read as an affectionate (not scornful or cutting) evocation of the absurdities and decencies of a civilianised military world. 'As a civilian he kept his high sense of form, his humour, his accuracy, but this accuracy was henceforth unimportant, recreational, *hors de combat.*' *Hors de combat* is the right Lowell phrase for a violence acknowledged but not entered upon.

In the very first poem in Lowell's first British volume, *Poems 1938-1949,* 'The Exile's Return', the liberating soldiers 'ground arms'. Lowell has come to distrust even the violence with which arms may be grounded—the violence of the command or of the butts hitting the ground—and his most recent poetry is an attempt to advance non-violence by a less violent staving off or holding at arm's length or coming between the combatants. So 'the war of words' has been replaced by something calmer, a contrariety of ideas expressing the old avoided combat in terms of a sentiment not a wording. . . .

Lowell's forthcoming volume, *Day by Day*, is about his recent life in England, his marriage, his memories of family and school, his present home in Kent and the necessity now to move from its lavish sprawl. The poem called 'The Day' begins with a new sense of the *hors de combat*, which depends less upon a contrariety of phrasing or diction and more upon the image of a harmlessness of violence:

> It's amazing
> the day is still here
> like lightning on an open field,
> terra firma and transient
> swimming in variation,
> fresh as when man first broke
> like the crocus all over the earth.

'Broke', but like a flower bursting up and open, not like a destruction or a fracture or a disease; 'like lightning', but 'on an open field'. There is an openness of violent non-violence about the very idea. . . . These recent poems of Lowell's which have appeared in magazines suggest that in *Day by Day* there will be the promise of a new safety provided for him and by him, and that the attempt to create a positive non-violence, one that recognises what it is up against but finds ways of not allowing itself to be up against it in any kind of punch-up, will take new and more gentle forms and words. . . . [New] efforts of imagination are made by the poet whose art is an art of conscientious objection. . . . (p. 315)

> *Christopher Ricks, "Robert Lowell at 60,"
> in* The Listener (© *British Broadcasting
> Corp. 1977; reprinted by permission of
> Christopher Ricks), March 10, 1977, pp.
> 314-15.*

Lowell has written in these ten years a number of verse sequences containing poems good, not so good, and indifferent. These are sonnet-length productions, for the most part, and, caught up as they are in the flow of sequences that pursue a decidedly uncertain course, they are not likely to draw to themselves the kind of attention once directed at classic set-pieces like "Skunk Hour," "Falling Asleep Over The Aeneid," or "For The Union Dead." A part of Lowell's audience has tended to lose touch with him as readers have become less secure about the isolable merits of individual poems—as they have found him more elusive, less committed to the creation of memorizable classics than to the discovery of fluid forms adequate to contain the shifts in his own temper and interests. It may well be, of course, that Lowell has not done his best writing in these years, but many readers seem primarily troubled by the fact that they do not really know how to tell what are and are not the palpable merits of the verse he has in fact produced. How is one to judge a sequence moving only in parts, sometimes casual almost to the point of uncaring? Lowell 'trained' his audience to expect classics, which he nicely provided in book after book for more than twenty years.

Most of his readers could not be asked to shift gears and read the later volumes—*Notebook, For Lizzie and Harriet, The Dolphin,* and others—as though a brilliant poetic graph of lived experience were ample substitute. That many of the individual items in the late sequences stand with the best Lowell has done; that the sequences as a whole press the reader for a quality of sustained and discriminative attention few long poems can claim, were not possibilities every loyal reader has been willing to confront.

There is more. It has become possible to say that Lowell does not write the kind of poetry an American poet ought to write. . . . Lowell, it would seem, has chosen to respond to the wrong poetic modes, to challenge the wrong forbears, to revise the wrong ratios. (pp. 4-5)

Robert Lowell is the contemporary poet who has most persuasively established the status of the poem as classic, he is the figure who may most appropriately guide us back in the direction of the text itself. . . . If Lowell's recent books have not, for some of us, ministered to the expectations aroused by earlier books, they have surely spoken with sufficient authority to many readers and to a whole generation of younger poets. It is the object of this special tribute to Robert Lowell to redefine attention to poetry as primarily attention to poems, and to indicate that Lowell's work—more than the work of any other recent poet—continues to repay the kind of close study we consider appropriate in our approaches to Stevens, to Yeats, and to Pound. (pp. 5-6)

> *Robert Boyers, "Preface: For Robert Lowell, on His 60th Birthday," in* Salmagundi
> (copyright © 1977 by Skidmore College),
> Spring, 1977, pp. 3-6.*

[One] can't think about literature in the twentieth century *without* thinking about the body of Lowell's work. He has stayed alive as a poet by never drawing a line around what a poem can or should be. Again and again, his style has changed in an attempt to deal with intractable, unfashionable, or intolerable subject matter. He has kept his poetry close to the intuitions, concerns, obsessions that dominate his mind. Many of us would be terrified to face or write the record of our lives. He says at the end of *The Dolphin:* "my eyes have seen what my hand did." . . .

His whole career has been an embodiment of the traditional formal possibilities of English—in terms of meter, rhyme, stanzaic form, even genre—as well as an unending argument with the expressive limits and assumptions of the language. Perhaps this is why critics are often at first bewildered by his new work, and compare it unfavorably to his next-to-last. (p. 54)

I think I am not alone in feeling that—personally, and as a nation—one way we have come to understand and judge ourselves is by reading Robert Lowell. (p. 55)

> *Frank Bidart, "On Robert Lowell," in* Salmagundi (copyright © 1977 by Skidmore
> College), Spring, 1977, pp. 54-5.*

"Quaker Graveyard" is not a political poem. I had assumed that it was, that its rage against the war and puritan will and the Quakers of Nantucket who financed the butchery of whales was an attack on American capitalism. But a political criticism of any social order implies both that a saner one can be imagined and the hope or conviction that it can be achieved. . . . I went back to the poem looking for the vision of an alternative world. There is none. There's grief and moral rage but the poem imagines the whole of human life as sterile violence . . . and it identifies finally with the inhuman justice of God. . . . (p. 57)

[The poet is] forced to step outside the human process and claim the vision of some imperturbable godhead in which the long violence of human history looks small. But in "Quaker Graveyard" it is important to say that is the position the poem *finally* arrives at because it is a poem of process, and of anguish. Warren Winslow drowns, the Quakers drown, the wounded whale churns in an imagination of suffering and violence which it is the imperative of the poem to find release from, and each successive section of the poem is an attempt to discover a way out. (p. 58)

It is possible, I suppose, to object to the brilliance of the writing. Charles Olson is said to have complained that Lowell lacquered each of his poems and hung it in a museum. But this judgement, like the 'confessional' revolution envisaged by the professoriat, seems to be based on the sociology of Kenyon College or the fact of meter or Lowell's early models, on everything but a reading of the poems. Finish in poetry is, as Olson insisted, a question of form following function. "The Quaker Graveyard" is brilliantly written. . . . But its brilliance seems neither dictated nor wrought; it is headlong, furious, and casual. There are moments that hover near grandiloquence—"Ask for no Orphean lute . . ." but they didn't bother me then and don't much now. (p. 60)

In the speed of the writing, the syntax comes apart; it dissolves into emotion, into music and the subterranean connections among images. Throughout the poem it is characteristic that the important associations occur in subordinate clauses or compounds so breathless that you have to sort your way back quite consciously to the starting point. This resembles the syntactical strategies of the French surrealists, particularly Desnos and Peret. The main clause is a pushing off place and the poem makes its meaning out of its momentum. It's a way of coming to terms with experience under pressure and not some extrinsic decision about style. (pp. 61-2)

The current taste is for the explicit, however weird. Surrealism comes to mean the manufacture of peculiar imagery and not something in the sinews of a poem. The fish in "For the Union Dead" are a midpoint in this levelling process. They are transformed into sharks and then into cars as "a savage servility slides by on grease," but the delivery is slower, the context narrative and topographical. It is pretty much the same image as in "The Quaker Graveyard," but it has been clarified like broth. . . .

And this won't do for Lowell because the power of his imagery has always been subliminal; it exists as the nervous underside of the thing said. (p. 62)

[The tone in "Fourth of July in Maine"] has to do with rendering. . . . It is not the experience but a way of handling the experience. The imagery accumulates its desolating evidence, but in such a way that the terror in the poetry is perceived while the novelistic pathos is felt. The subterranean images, whether "consciously wrought" or not, are intellectual. In this way, it is exactly a metaphysical poem as nothing in *Lord Weary's Castle* is. (p. 64)

[To see how "The Quaker Graveyard" works], look at the third section of the poem. If you ask yourself how the language or the thought proceeds, it's not easy to say. First sentence: All you recovered died with you. Second sentence: Guns blast the eelgrass. Third sentence: They died . . . ; only bones abide. Characteristically, the Quaker sailors appear at the extremity of a dependent clause; then their fate is seized on, midway through the section, as a subject, and the stanza unravels again into violence as the sailors drown proclaiming their justification. And it does not seem arbitrary. It seems inevitable, because this hopelessly repeated unravelling into violence is both the poem's theme and the source of its momentum. Hell is repetition and the structure of anger is repetition. In this poem history is also repetition, as it is the structure of religious incantation. They are all married here, desperately, and the grace of the poem has to exist in modulation of tone. This modulation, like the different textures of an abstract expressionist painting or like the very different modulations, that create the texture of Whitman's poems—"Song of Myself" comes to mind—is the grandeur and originality of "The Quaker Graveyard." Not theme, not irony or intimacy or the consciously wrought, but absolute attention to feeling at that moment in the poem's process. (pp. 65-6)

Lost innocence is not the subject of the poem. There is a kind of pleading between the poet and the innocence of his cousin, the ensign who went to the war and did his duty. "All you recovered . . . died with you". But the innocence of the child, of the ensign, of the figureheads is only one syntactical leap away from the stupidity and self-righteousness of the Quaker sailors . . . who are swallowed up without understanding a thing. Their eyes are "cabin-windows on a stranded hulk / Heavy with sand." (p. 66)

[The] killing of the Whale [is] also an image of the crucifixion of Christ, but in the poem this act is the source and culmination of evil. "When the whale's viscera go . . . its corruption over-runs this world." There is no sense here of the crucifixion as a redemption. I can imagine that three or four pages of theological explication could put it there, but it isn't in the poem. Typologically the legal torture and murder of the man-god is not the fall; in the Christian myth it is not cruelty and violence but pride and disobedience through which men fell. One can make a series of arguments, threading back through the blasphemous pride of Ahab to the dominion given man by God in the epigraph to the poem, and emerge with a case for cruelty as a form of pride, but cruelty is not pride. They're different things, and it is cruelty and death, not pride and the fall, that preoccupy the poet, no matter how much of Melville or theology we haul in to square this vision with orthodoxy. (p. 67)

Sexual wounding: it is certainly there in section V, both in the imagery and in the way the section functions, literally, as a climax to the poem. This is the fall, the moment when corruption overruns the world. And the rhetorical question, "Sailor, will your sword / Whistle and fall and sink into the fat?" wants to make us all complicit. The passage is Calvinist in feeling; every day is judgement day. . . . In sexual imagery, not only the penetration by the death lance but the singing of the stars, the dismemberment of the masthead, we are all judged. . . . [We] look at the sickening cruelty it actually describes. It's a relief and much easier to talk about myth or symbolic sexuality. This is an image of killing written by a pacifist who was willing to go to prison.

It makes death horrifying; it makes the war horrifying, and the commerce of the Nantucket Quakers whom Melville reminded his readers to think of when they lit their cozy whale-oil lamps. ''Light is where the landed blood of Cain . . .''.

But, just as there is disgust with the mothering sea in the bilge and backwash throughout the poem, there is a deep abhorrence of sexual violence, of sexuality as violence. . . . The fact is that there is an element of cruelty in human sexuality, though that isn't the reason for the Puritan distrust of sex. The Puritans distrusted sexuality because the sexual act dissolved human will for a moment, because—for a moment—men fell into the roots of their mammal nature. You can't have an orgasm and be a soldier of Christ. Thus *Samson Agonistes*. And the Puritan solution, hidden but real in the history of imagination whether in Rome or the Enlightenment, was to turn sex into an instrument of will, of the conscious cruelty which flowered in the writings of Sade. It is there in our history and Lowell is right to connect it with the annihilative rage of capitalism. Flesh is languor (''All of life's grandeur / is something with a girl in summer . . .'') but it is also rage. It marries us to the world and the world is full of violence and cruelty. This is part of the bind of the poem which is also the Calvinist bind of determinism and free will. The way out is not-world, an identification at the end of the poem with the ''unmarried'' Atlantic and the Lord who survives the rainbow-covenant of evolution. (pp. 68-9)

Pound says somewhere, sounding like a surly Matthew Arnold, that a history of poetry that's worth anything ought to be able to point to specific poems and passages in poems and say here, here and here are inventions that made something new possible in poetry. This is one of those places.

Its occurrence makes emotional sense because it follows section V. It is the peace of the satisfaction of the body's rage, a landscape of streams and country lanes. The nineteenth century would have described the writing as chaste or exquisite and I'm not sure we have better words to praise it with. It's wonderfully plain and exact:

> Our Lady, too small for her canopy,
> Sits near the altar. There's no comeliness
> At all or charm in that expressionless
> Face with its heavy eyelids. As before,
> This face, for centuries a memory,
> *Non est species, neque decor,*
> Expressionless, expresses God: it goes
> Past castled Sion. She knows what God knows,
> Not Calvary's cross nor the crib at Bethlehem
> Now, and the world shall come to Walsingham.

This is another temple, not the god of sorrows but the goddess of an almost incomprehensible peace. It appears to be the emphatically Catholic moment in the poem. . . . But I don't think it is Catholic, or not especially Catholic, and that is its interest.

The crucial phrase is ''past castled Sion.'' Lowell is not after sacramental mediation but a contemplative peace beyond any manifestation in the flesh, beyond thought or understanding, and most especially beyond desire. This isn't incompatible with Catholic theology, but it's not central to its spirit which is embodiment: the Orphean lute and the crib at Bethlehem. This apprehension of God, of a pure, calm, and utterly clear consciousness, belongs

equally to all mysticisms, Christian or otherwise, and it has always seemed to me that the figure of Our Lady here looks a lot like Guatama Buddha. It is the embodiment of what can't be embodied. This is a contradiction, but it is one that belongs to any intellectual pointing toward mystical apprehension. It is the contradiction that made the world-denial of Buddhists and Cathars at the same time utterly compassionate toward and alert to the world and flesh and makes the Buddhist Gary Snyder our best poet of nature. This is not the rejection of the world which the last lines of the poem suggest; it's something else and for me it's something much more attractive as a possibility of imagination.

But how does it square with the last lines? I don't think it does. Nor does it contradict them. That's the aesthetic daring of this section. What the Lady of Walsingham represents is past contention. She's just there. The method of the poem simply includes her among its elements, past argument, as a possibility through which all the painful seeing in the poem can be transformed and granted peace. She floats; everything else in the poem rises and breaks, relentlessly, like waves. (pp. 70-1)

[Hearing Lowell read ''Near the Ocean''] I began to understand the risks attendant on backing away from the drama and self-drama of *Lord Weary's Castle*. Pain has its own grandeur. This disenchanted seeing was not serene neutrality—it was not serene at all; it had the clarity of a diminished sense of things not flinched at. (p. 72)

> *Robert Hass, ''Lowell's Graveyard,'' in* Salmagundi *(copyright © 1977 by Skidmore College), Spring, 1977, pp. 56-72.*

The unchanging element of Lowell's poetry was that whatever he was writing about in whichever one of his many styles, the words loomed everywhere as if in some huge magnifying lens of etymology and idiom and sound—and yet were always in the stream of English speech.

Lowell's genius and his grinding labor brought to verse in English not only technical mastery on a scale otherwise scarcely attempted in this century, but then his courage and honesty brought, to crib from myself, ''a new generosity and dignity to the whole enterprise of poetry.'' He was not afraid of mistakes and made plenty of them, or so it seemed to me, in the mulled-over *Notebooks*. (pp. 14-15)

> *John Thompson, in* The New York Review of Books *(reprinted with permission from* The New York Review of Books; *copyright © 1977 NYREV, Inc.), October 27, 1977.*

In his prime, and occasionally in his last volumes, Robert Lowell was one of America's five-star poets. And what made him great, more than his dramatic instinct or his bristling sense of language, was his soldierly dedication to honesty, to reporting what was, to cutting through all the posturing and triviality to the meaning of events. One misses him. One wishes he were sending dispatches from the afterlife; they would be so perceptive, unsentimental, reliable.

> *Carll Tucker, ''Soldier Lowell, 1917-1977,'' in* Saturday Review *(© 1977 by Saturday Review Magazine Corp.; reprinted with permission), October 29, 1977, p. 64.*

[The generation of American poets to which Robert Lowell belonged] were pioneers of guilt. Not the fashionable Fifth

Avenue malaise of the Fifties; I mean the real thing. Night after drunken night, all night, they talked about "responsibility." If there was a god they were sinners. If there was not a god they were still sinners. Why? It is not easy to say; I am sure the answer will occupy many volumes in years to come. But one thing is clear. They had inherited from their elders—Eliot, Pound, Stevens, Williams, Auden, even Frost—an enormous metaphysical awareness, an enormous apparatus for moral, psychological, and aesthetic inquiry, without anything to use it on. They were in a vacancy ("the unredeemable world"). They had neither faith nor doubt, neither art for its own sake nor the natural environment. Everything had been used up. . . .

Guilt gave way to humiliation.

And humiliation craved more guilt. Lowell was a voracious feeder on criticism. No matter what you said against his poems, he took it in, enlarged it, and gave it back. Yes, he said, *mea culpa, I can't* integrate my metaphors, my language *is* unnatural, my poems *are* self-indulgent, I *don't* know foreign languages, and my translations *are* awful. But he went on doing the same things to the end, just as he went on denying, obliterating, his own best talents. He had a brilliant critical mind and refused to write criticism; he could probably have been the best epigrammatist in English since Ben Jonson and he refused to write epigrams.

New England puritanism was what fueled Lowell. He was born to it, though if he hadn't been he would have found something else—guilt invents its own crimes. . . . If existence itself is presumptuous, then existence in a theocracy whose rationale has departed, a brutal witch-killing theocracy at that, is an iota worse. Melville and Hawthorne had known it, and Lowell knew it even more keenly, looking from the cold vacancy of modern spiritual nihilism with all its intellectual technique. He had no recourse but to study himself, his own existence. Who was he? *What* was he? Could something better be invented? Perhaps poetry could accomplish that.

Even in his early poems, in *Lord Weary's Castle* (1946), notwithstanding their devotional Catholic fomentation, the secular personal element had been not only evident but the most genuine part, as Lowell himself saw afterward. In *Life Studies* (1959) he turned to candid, open autobiography, and in all the books since then his self-searching continued, however his styles varied. One notices the commonness of glass in all this poetry—windows, eyeglasses, fish tanks—and of photographs too, reality caught and objectified through a glass lens. Lowell always seemed to be up against a transparent barrier, either inside looking out or outside looking in. And what he got, what we get, are only snapshots: Lowell the child, Lowell the awkward lover, Lowell the agonized moralist—static and already yellowing. The man himself is elusive, the warm living organism, always

somewhere on the other side of the glass. This is true as much of his inner being as of his outer; both are objectified and fragmented, tiles of a broken mosaic. One can read all his poems, first to last, and in spite of the self-confessions, self-advertisements, and what some call self-betrayals, one still will not know what kind of person Lowell really was.

Yet perhaps just because of this, some poems, even a good many, are very moving. They are truly pathetic, with the pathos of the lost and undiscoverable self, guilt that finds no expiation because it finds no terms in which to conceive its own criminality. (pp. 110-11)

Lowell's new book, *Day by Day* . . . , was published a short time before his death. . . . The book is a miscellaneous one, almost jumbled, and I expect reviewers will vary considerably in their opinions of it—as they usually have with Lowell's earlier books, for that matter. Many of the new poems seem extremely self-indulgent, not only in their reverting continually to the poet himself and his repetitive, now sometimes trivial, complaints, but also in their obscurity of private reference. . . . Some poems are awkward, others slack. But a fair number, it seems to me, are quite good, and a few very fine. . . . The book is in effect a summation of Lowell's whole work, since it contains poems in most of the styles he has used before, and . . . consequently it is in some respects a clarification, even a justification, and is valuable on these grounds alone; . . . it is a more genial, easier performance than *Notebooks* or *History*. . . . (pp. 111-12)

I have had many letters from other poets recently, both from well-known poets and from the very young, writing their responses to his death with remarkable unanimity of feeling. They all say that although they dislike elements of his work and deprecate the worst aspects of his influence on American poetry in general during the past two decades, they are deeply upset by the news of his dying, much more deeply than they would have expected. I feel the same. It is because I see myself in Lowell. I see all of us—poets of latter-day America—in him. He was truly the figure of the embattled artist (though one uses such post-romantic terms with reluctance now), the artist fighting a degraded society, a cruel history, an absurd universe, and most of all a sense of lack in his own being, fighting in complete honesty and utterly refusing to compromise. . . .

Lowell was a great flawed poet (for greatness always has its flaw and often depends on it). Without doubt he was a great exemplar. (p. 112)

Hayden Carruth, "An Appreciation of Robert Lowell," in Harper's *(copyright © 1977 by* Harper's *Magazine; all rights reserved; excerpted from the December, 1977 issue by special permission), December, 1977, pp. 110-12.*

M

MacBETH, George   1932-

A Scottish poet and novelist, MacBeth is noted for his innovative use of word associations and juxtapositions. His verse is both ritualistic and personal, his fiction experimental and erotic. (See also *CLC*, **Vols. 2, 5, and** *Contemporary Authors,* **Vols. 25-28, rev. ed.)**

George MacBeth's cluster of nasty, surreal images go with a sardonic lilt these days. I don't care for the places in [*In the Hours Waiting for the Blood to Come*] where they are marshalled with the old intensity (as in the title-poem), but it would be wrong to miss the skill with which, in something like 'Elegy for the Gas Dowsers', MacBeth brings off a sustained parable of decay, a genuine eco-nightmare for our time. Even so, the best poems are the most relaxed. 'The Poet's Life' is by far the best of those, a neat session of self-revelation and self-mockery which makes one of the most entertaining poems he has given us for some time. (p. 60)

> *Alan Brownjohn, in* New Statesman (© 1975 The Statesman & Nation Publishing Co. Ltd.), July 11, 1975.

[A] specialist in subhuman detail with nightmare overtones is George MacBeth, but his piquantly titled *In the Hours Waiting for the Blood to Come* may come as a disappointment to some of his old fans. The blood, foetuses and shocking fables are still there but the tone is more coolly sardonic than usual and the book ends with an amiable sequence called 'A Poet's Life' in which he coasts drily along for almost 20 pages without reaching once for an interesting bestiality. Whether MacBeth is mellowing it's probably too early to say but when he leaves off his snakeskin boiler-suit and appears *in* (more or less) *propria persona* as a member of human society the results are often satirically enjoyable. Presumably

> urged by the social, he strays to the
> savage. He dreams

is the key so far as MacBeth's own poet's life is concerned, but it looks as though he may at last be getting tired of carrying his horrors around with him like a charismatic shock-wave. (p. 62)

> *Colin Falck, in* The New Review (© The New Review Ltd., 11 Greek Street, London W1V 5LE), August, 1975.

''The Samurai'' bears almost exactly the same relationship to a readable espionage tale that it does to serious fiction. Which is to say, none at all. . . .

[Evidently] the editorial handicappers promoting ''The Samurai'' have noticed that writers of undeniable seriousness and quality have been appearing on the best-seller list almost as regularly as the sensationalists. So they are trying to have it both ways by marketing this half-baked, witless muck as ''an entertainment'' by a serious and well-known poet. It is difficult to imagine any other reason why a writer of talent and sensibility would put his real name on the cover. So, as stuffy as it is to take the literary high-road these days, I earnestly hope that MacBeth feels perfectly wretched about it for months. . . . (p. 10)

> *Gene Lyons, in* The New York Times Book Review (© 1975 by The New York Times Company; reprinted by permission), August 10, 1975.

Poet Macbeth's first novel [*The Samurai*] is an episodic allegory that is part sensually violent thriller and part metaphysical pornography. What there is of a plot centers on a band of modern *ronin* trying to reinstitute the ancient Japanese ethos of perverse purity through death and their destruction by a group of British agents whose own purification comes through perverse sex, acts which are not merely symbolically equivalent but, ultimately, identical. The story is basically unconvincing, and is bogged down by excessive eroticism, but Macbeth is so adept at portraying the subtle exoticness of it all that one cannot help but become involved and engrossed. (p. cxlii)

> Virginia Quarterly Review (*copyright, 1975, by the* Virginia Quarterly Review, *The University of Virginia), Vol. 51, No. 4 (Autumn, 1975).*

Sinning and salvation . . . have their place in *The Survivor*, in which a second-world-war Japanese pilot crash-lands on a Pacific island, survives and promptly proceeds to atone for his incestuous relationship with his daughter by grinding through an undiluted stream of nightmare 'illusions'. . . . The careful inwardness of the description is overlaid with somewhat obscure asides about *tsukas* and *kashiras*, and with an ill-defined air of significance. A doubtfully efficient means of expiation. (p. 60)

Susannah Clapp, in New Statesman (©
1977 The Statesman & Nation Publishing
Co. Ltd.), July 8, 1977.

George MacBeth, as both impresario and practitioner of
poetry, has shown over the years an occasional tendency to
become infatuated with the sensational, eccentric and fash-
ionably barmy, though this too eager readiness to explore
the new-fangled has usually been counterbalanced by a
shrewd awareness of what is imperishable in traditional
English poetics. . . . I was not surprised that [The Survivor,
Macbeth's novel,] should be formally "experimental", intensely cinematic, with its use of flashback, cross-cutting,
dissolves and zooming shots, nor that it should eschew realism for something more oblique, ambiguous, surreal, that it
should be much concerned with physical violence and unorthodox sexuality, but I was not quite prepared for its almost crazy resolve to spare the reader nothing in the way of
human perversion. . . .

[The] direct descriptions of sexual activity . . . are not very
different from the ill-printed stuff that was popular among
the troops in the Middle East during the Second World War
—"Her hands slid forwards and up the stiff pole of his organ . . ." is a fair example of either, though in fact it comes
from The Survivor—and too much of the novel consists of
just this kind of writing.

Vernon Scannell, "Japanese Wha Hae," in
The Times Literary Supplement (© Times
Newspapers Ltd., 1977; reproduced from
The Times Literary Supplement by permis-
sion), July 15, 1977, p. 849.

*   *   *

MALAMUD, Bernard   1914-

**A novelist and short story writer, Malamud is considered a
leading author of fiction which is Jewish-American in subject
and character. Aware of man's possibilities for regeneration
and salvation, he has been described by Herbert Gold as
"Dostoevsky tempered by Chagall's lyric nostalgia for a lost
Jewish past." (See also CLC, Vols. 1, 2, 3, 5, 8, and Contemporary Authors, Vols. 5-8, rev. ed.)**

Mr. Malamud is neither naturalist nor impressionist, and he
is not even dull; his fancy, confined neither to the limitations of the sensitive observer nor the narrow world of
"real experience," manipulates the details of his fable in
the interests of surprise and delight.

The epigraph of [The Natural] might well have been that
melancholy popular phrase, "He could of been a hero!" It
is about heroism that the story turns: the obligations of the
heroic and its uses. For Roy Hobbs, the protagonist, the
problem is the proper and pious use of his gift, that natural
(or magical) talent which has its meaning only in its free
exercise, the gratuitous, poetic act. For the fans, which is
to say for us, the problem is our relationship to the hero
and the question of whether he can survive our bribes and
adulation, make the singular, representative act which
alone can fulfill us, before we corrupt him into our own
sterile image. For in truth, we need almost as desperately
to hate and destroy the hero as to love and live by him; our
self-hatred is projected as ferociously onto the representative figure as our reverence before our own possibilities. To
say that in our world (the world of the Judge who pays for
the defeat of the team he owns and the depraved dwarf in

the stands ready to hoot down with his automobile horn
defeated excellence) the hero fails is scarcely necessary.

Mr. Malamud finds in baseball the inevitable arena in
which to play out our own version of this drama: part ritual
and part commerce and part child's game, bounded by stupidity and corruption and sung only in the clichés of the
sports writers, there yet survives in its midst a desecrated
but indestructible dream of glory. The ball team of The
Natural is real, its slumps, its fans, the absurd psychologist
who comes to hypnotize the players, their charms and
spells; and being real, it is comic. The details are the details
of something which remains stubbornly a fact for all of its
abstract meaning, not of a contrived device which functions
only for the sake of that meaning.

Having said this, I dare confess at last that behind the literal fable, there is the presence of a legend, of the Grail
Legend. Mr. Malamud reaches out with one hand to Ring
Lardner and with the other to Jessie Weston. If this is outrageous, it is the sort of outrage I enjoy. . . . [The] hero,
slain once with a silver bullet and miraculously resurrected,
returns in a time of drought to a disease-ridden team called
the Knights, presided over by a manager called Pop Fisher,
etc., etc. (pp. 324-25)

Mr. Malamud has in The Natural found, not imposed, an
archetype in the life we presently live; in his book the modern instance and the remembered myth are equally felt,
equally realized and equally appropriate to our predicament. It is this which gives to his work special authority
and special richness; for he has not felt obliged to choose
between the richness of imagined detail and that of symbolic relevance. He is out of the trap! It is for this reason
that I have been moved to ignore the small failures of technique and consistency in his book and to say quite simply,
"Hurrah!" There is no real way to pay for the pleasure a
work of art gives us; but one can at least record that pleasure and his gratitude. (p. 325)

·   ·   ·   ·   ·

In his second novel [The Assistant], Bernard Malamud has
turned away from the rich playfulness, the free use of myth
and magic which made of his first book, The Natural, so
welcome a sport in the dim world of contemporary fiction.
It is impossible, I think, to appreciate the kind of discipline
and self-denial which motivates the muted style of The Assistant without a knowledge of the earlier work, and a consequent awareness that Malamud is doing what he does
because he chooses to, not because he lacks the fancy to
conceive anything else or the invention to accomplish it.

He is playing a dangerous game in The Assistant all the
same; and in the earlier portion of the book, his resolve to
treat gray lives grayly, to render dull conversations dully,
threatens to succeed only too well. The material he deals
with seems at first depressingly familiar: we have read before of the lives of poor Jews, proprietors of groceries and
candy stores, just as we have encountered before Jewish
writers, plagued by an ideal of imitative form and impelled,
in the face of their material, to give us not the poetry of
banal lives but their banality.

Long before we have reached the end of the book, however, we realize that, though muted, the poetry is never denied and that Malamud's theme remains here what it was in
the more extravagant The Natural: the Absurd—here spe-

cifically the absurdity of existence in its most commonplace forms. It is odd how the subdued tone, the show of "realism" in Malamud take us in, as life itself takes us in, with its routine surfaces. We tend to accept on the level of mere realistic observation and reporting an account, say, of a young man wedged perilously in a dumbwaiter shaft watching the daughter of the man he has robbed but loves strip for a shower; or the description of the same young man crouched in guilt and fear and hunger in the basement of a store, feeding frantically and in secret on stolen bottles of milk.

A slight shift in emphasis, a slight heightening of tone—and we would be face to face with some quasi-surrealist image of the Underground Man, not unlike, perhaps, the hallucinatory opening of Ralph Ellison's *The Invisible Man.* But Malamud has chosen to create the least melodramatic of all possible versions of the Absurd: a vision of the commonplace as absurd. (pp. 326-27)

One is even tempted to say, on such grounds, that Malamud has with this book entered into the main Jewish-American tradition in the novel, taking up the frustrated experiments of writers like Fuchs or Nathanael West, ignored in the thirties in favor of "the proletarian novel," and overshadowed by the inflated reputations of Steinbeck and Dos Passos and Farrell. In a strange way, Malamud's novel *is* a belated novel of the thirties. It is not, I think, definitely located in time; but one imagines its events as happening in the dispirited years of the Depression. Only in that context does the struggle of the poor Jew, Morris Bober, to keep his store open achieve a proper sense of desperation, or the desire of his daughter Helen to go to college touch a full note of pathos.

But how different *The Assistant* is from any novel *written* in the thirties! The kind of politics which informed the "proletarian novel" is, of course, quite gone, as is the note of hysteria, the apocalyptic shrillness which characterizes all novels of the period, whatever their politics. Not even the humor of West or Fuchs is present, neither the half-mad belly laugh nor the self-deprecatory giggle by which such writers came to terms with terror and desolation. Indeed, Malamud's book is willfully, almost perversely humorless, even as it is apolitical. Helen Bober and her Jewish boy friends may talk the same stilted, hyperurban speech (indeed Malamud is masterful at reproducing it) as that of Arthur Kober's "Dear Bella" and her beaus; but here *it is no joke.*

Just as Malamud will not permit us the luxury of righteous indignation and political protest before the prospect of an honest man incapable of earning a living or a warmhearted girl cut off from the possibilities of love—so he will not let us snicker or guffaw at their plight either. He compels us to contemplate the absurdity of their situations—and that of Frank Alpine, the Gentile who alternately robs and aids them—with the pure response of *pity*. Beside this, politics and humor are revealed as rival opiates of the people: devices to prevent the confrontation of the full and terrible ridiculousness of human loneliness and desire, unsuccess and death. His is a book and a viewpoint essentially (questions of doctrine aside) *religious*.

The quite unpredictable, though distressingly up-to-date, absurdity of *The Assistant* belongs to the nature of its religiousness. We live in a time of an at least nominal revival of interest in religion, and the appearance of conversion stories surely surprises no one. *The Assistant,* however, is concerned with a conversion *to* Judaism—a theme by no means usual. . . . Malamud's Frank . . . is painfully impelled toward Judaism and accepts it as he accepts pain itself. After he has rescued Helen Bober from assault and more than half-raped her himself; after he has been cast out by Morris and has witnessed his quietly heroic death; after he has taken on himself the burden of the store which becomes in the novel scarcely distinguishable from the burden of life itself—Frank takes the final step. "One day in April," the book concludes in its characteristic low key, "Frank went to the hospital and had himself circumcized. . . . The pain enraged and inspired him. After Passover he became a Jew." As a happy ending, a springtime close for a story which begins in the chill of autumn, it is all quite ridiculous. Surely nothing is more conducive to titters and bad jokes than the notion of the circumcision of a grown man; and to *become* a Jew when it is hard enough to remain one—nothing could be more improbable.

At first glance, such a conclusion seems more sentimental than absurd; but it is saved from sentimentality by a further turn of the screw, a final note of the ridiculous. Frank becomes a Jew without knowing in any explicit way what a Jew is; and we are asked to accept his conversion knowing as little as he what he is converted to. What *is* the content of Jewishness as Malamud understands it? . . . It is apparently nothing more than what an unlearned immigrant, who has not been in a synagogue in twenty years, but whom *everyone* would agree in calling a Jew, happens to live by.

Morris Bober is the book's exemplar of Judaism: a man who not only sells but eats pork who knows scarcely anything of the Talmud, who can hardly answer when asked what a Jew is. Yet it is he, through the example of his life, who converts Frank Alpine, to whom being a Jew means practically taking on the responsibilities of Morris: his wife, his daughter, especially his accursed, ill-paying store. The nearest thing to an explicit definition of Morris' Jewishness is spoken by a rabbi called in after his death, a rabbi who has never known him and who improvises in broken English a eulogy on the basis of hearsay and the conventional lies one says in honor of the dead.

Yet in this speech, the novel reaches its climax of poetry and pity and truth. It must be read entire and in context for its full impact, though its sense can be resumed in a few excerpts:

> My dear friends, I never had the pleasure to meet this good grocery man that he now lays in his coffin. He lived in a neighborhood where I didn't come in. . . . He caught double pneumonia from shoveling snow in front of his place of business, so people could pass by on the sidewalk. . . . He was also a very hard worker, a man that never stopped working. . . . Fifteen, sixteen hours a day he was in the store, seven days a week, to make a living for his family. . . . This went on for twenty-two years in this store alone, day after day, except the few days when he was too sick. And for this reason that he worked so hard and bitter, in his house, on his table, was always something to eat. So, besides honest, he was a good provider. . . .

When a Jew dies, who asks if he is a Jew,
we don't ask.

Is this, then, what Jewishness has become for us, our world
—not at its worst but at its human best—"to take care of
the store?" One is reminded of the oldest of Jewish jokes,
of the dying man who blindly asks for all his family one by
one, and when he discovers all are present, cries out,
"Then who's taking care of the store?" Is this, after all, a
joke not on the dying man, as we have always thought, but
on *ourselves* who laugh at it? Is that ridiculous deathbed
cry the cry of a *lamedvavnik,* one of the hidden just for
whose sake the world is preserved? To believe it would be
absurd. (pp. 327-30)

> *Leslie Fiedler, "Malamud: The Common-
> place as Absurd," in his* The Collected Es-
> says of Leslie Fiedler *(copyright © 1971 by
> Leslie A. Fiedler; reprinted with permission
> of Stein and Day Publishers), Stein and
> Day, 1971, pp. 321-30.*

[A reader familiar with Bernard Malamud's works expects
to meet] Malamud's variant of the Yiddish *shlemiel:* the
fool-victim, who is the butt of fate and men, bungling his
way through life, but who somehow manages to endure it
all, helped by his foolhardy persistence and his wry grim-
aces and shrugs. Among other strands that enter into the
fabric of a Malamud novel or story there is the all-too-hu-
man female character—one hesitates to dub her 'heroine'—
whose gift of love tends to be a dubious blessing. The male
protagonist's personality and destiny are often given depth
and scope through the motif of the double; this is not exactly the Romantic *Doppelgänger,* but rather two characters whose destinies are linked in various ways, sometimes
in a (spiritual) father-son pattern. The heroic-unheroic action will very likely take place in an atmosphere of isolation
and imprisonment, the ghetto being a prototypical setting.
The past will most certainly play a small but important role
as a means of creating depth and resonance; it may appear
as history, legend or myth. Touches of a pastoral world—
trees, flowers, birds—will hint at possibilities of freedom,
purity and innocence. The *shlemiel* will never really be attuned to these happier strains; nevertheless there will most
probably be a movement in his development toward a qualified rebirth, a limited redemption, which will have to be
bought with suffering and commitment. This might be the
commitment of the artist, and the satisfaction of wholehearted dedication will be balanced and often outweighed
by anguish and doubts of purpose and ability. Malamud
always lightens the sombre picture with humour and wit;
this is achieved by colourful 'Jewish' echoes: self-depre-
cating jokes and home-made sayings and proverbs which
tend to reduce tragedy to something trivial and commonplace. The 'Jewish' accent may reach us also through the
immigrant's imperfect handling of English (especially English syntax). Suffusing all these various elements of the
Malamudian novel there will be the author's unsentimental
humanism and his belief in man in spite of the odds.

All these properties of the Malamudian craft can be found
in *The Tenants,* some as mere rudiments, others as essential parts of setting, character, action and tone. Harry Lesser, the novel's Jewish writer-protagonist, whose very name
suggests inadequacy, reveals his kinship to the Malamudian
shlemiel in his fatal misses in his relations to other people:
he loses his girl, and he fails to establish an enduring con-

tact with a fellow writer, the black Willie Spearmint. There
is nothing compelling about Lesser, scarcely anything attractive; he is nondescript (in fact, Malamud hardly describes him at all, except for a few traits, such as thinness
which, considering Lesser's ascetic habits of living, would
seem all too natural.... Malamud no doubt never envisaged any ties of affection between his protagonist and the
reader; the main thing for us may be not to write Lesser off,
not to give up hope for him—which may mean also for ourselves.

Here lies a possible crux for the reader: with a protagonist
like Lesser, who is totally undistinguished and average except for his one great passion in life—the art of writing—the
ordinary, non-artistic reader may fail to be deeply engaged
in the issues presented through the novel's characters and
action. Lesser's dedication to his art is, at least for the
present reader, made to seem only one special kind of dedication, not easily transferable to other forms of commitment. This problem can be seen in relation to another question: does the novel afford an element of redemption, or at
least a glimmer of hope? Or does it end in utter darkness
and pessimism, as some critics have concluded?

Whatever the outcome of the blundering protagonist's
struggle to complete his novel and to relate to other people,
his very commitment and his mulelike endurance are certainly *meant* to redeem him somewhat as an individual.
Malamud makes Lesser insist on art's redeeming function
and on the total commitment that is demanded of the artist.
(pp. 85-7)

[Levenspiel, Lesser's landlord,] is deaf to all this talk of
art: 'Art my ass, in this world it's heart that counts.' Who
knows but that on the lower frequencies Levenspiel speaks
for the reader?

Irene, who is willing to love Lesser, is, like others of Malamud's women characters, slightly bruised by her earlier
experiences; she is not particularly bright or interesting, not
talented enough for the acting career she has chosen or
drifted into. Since nothing is allowed to be perfect in Malamud's fictional world, the best he can do for Irene is to
describe her as 'verging on beautiful.' ... A nice Malamudian touch is the suggestion of a slight physical defect,
both ludicrous and pathetic, that in Irene appears as
pigeon-toedness. In Malamud's women such imperfections
often add to their sexual attraction. ...

The woman character in *The Tenants* is less important than
the second man in the love triangle: Lesser-Irene-Willie.
She represents love, which in the end Lesser gives up or at
least postpones indefinitely, and the chance of a rebirth
through life, not art.... It doesn't seem possible for him to
combine 'life' and art. His final choice is less compromising
in this respect than any earlier Malamudian protagonist's
has been. This may be a new note which might make the
shlemiel less of a *shlemiel*—and Lesser *is* less *shlemiel*ish
than, say, S. Levin of *A New Life*—and more of a tragic
hero. But once again, the reader's acceptance of such a role
for·Lesser hinges on whether Malamud has managed to
make the writer's commitment to art seem a noble choice.
S. Levin, for one, appeared committed enough when he
accepted the burden of a slightly superfluous woman, two
adopted children and an insecure future.... [He] flung into
his future wife's ex-husband's grinning face his challenging
explanation of why he took himself such a load: 'Because I
can, you son of a bitch.' ... (pp. 87-8)

Malamud uses seasonal changes as symbols: love and hope, as well as nature and human beings, are revived in spring. Irene's faked-blonde hair is going back to its normal black, her eyebrows are recovering their natural shape. True to his customary pattern, Malamud lets most of the book's action take place in winter. (The misery of cold appears to be more awful to him than sweltering heat.) The time scheme of *The Tenants* is carefully worked out. The scene opens onto a cold wintry Manhattan. We move through the end-of-year season, through January and February; suddenly there is promise of spring: by now Lesser has been aroused out of his hibernation through yearnings of life and love . . .; it's April at last. But spring also unleashes the violence of revenge: Willie causes the destruction of Lesser's manuscript. As if to suggest the total blankness of Lesser's despair after this tragedy, the months of late spring and summer have neither contours nor distinguishing traits, and the imperceptible shift from April to autumn takes place within the space of a couple of pages of the novel. Then it's once more winter, and January, and finally again, unaccountably, spring, but this time without the love, the leaves and the flowers. The question is whether Malamud's novel ends here, and consequently the time scheme, too. (pp. 89-90)

Nature is thus included in Malamud's store of archetypal myths of life, death and rebirth, of love and hatred. The pattern might turn out a bit too neat: spring—rebirth—love; but often Malamud avoids banality and sentimentality by twists of irony. . . .

Spring is never given its romantic due; it is most typically reduced to a bare mention of spring '[flaring] with leaves and flowers.' . . . It is wholly characteristic of Malamud to puncture the nature lover's fond hopes with a barb of wry humour. . . .

Nature symbolism is used to point up the terrifying wilderness of the urban slum. (p. 90)

[The] ironic contrast between visions of pastoral calm and beauty and the shabby, imperfect actuality of New York City is employed to great effect in the opening section of the book. Malamud gives his writer free rein to envision a blissful, post-novel existence. . . . [After Lesser's fantasy flight to an idyllic seashore], the phoniness of Lesser's dreams and his diction is shown up by being contrasted with the actual protagonist, his setting and his situation. As if directed by a sardonic moviemaker's camera, our view is turned from the free-wheeling birds rising against 'the lucent sky' (images of birds being very frequent in Malamud's work), and now closer to the birds, identifiable as gulls and blackbirds, 'mewling' and 'shrilling'. The camera moves down, down, until it stops on the prosaic house, the lonely man. The final Whitmanesque view of the island of Manhattan (with its Shakespearean imagery) is false and ridiculous, and the focus shifts quickly onto what is today's reality: 'Ah, this live earth, this sceptred isle on a silver sea, this Thirty-first Street and Third Avenue. This forsaken house. This happy unhappy Lesser having to write.' (pp. 90-1)

The Tenants is a novel almost entirely set in the present—no matter what tense Malamud uses for his narrative—and the only other timesphere it hints at may be the future. (This possibility depends on how one reads the ending of the novel.) It is above all the great poets of the past—

named or unnamed—that, by way of allusion, quotation or parody, provide ironical counterpoints to Lesser and his strivings. . . . Willie Spearmint defiantly manipulates his own name to make it reverberate with Shakespearean echoes: 'Bill Spear' and 'Blind Willie Shakespear' (also a Miltonian echo?). . . . All these literary allusions seem natural with a subject like that of *The Tenants;* they may indeed be natural to the point of obviousness, and nothing beyond that. On the whole, they seem to me to fail in creating the resonance that Malamud may have sought, and the humorous-ironic contrasts they may be intended to afford do not always come off.

Humour there is, of course, in this novel, but it plays a less prominent role here than in most other works by Malamud. . . . Malamud's gift for comedy may be seen in a mock-epic vein. . . . [There] are phrases suggesting Yiddish sayings and proverbs; they are often put in a strikingly simple language, words being repeated in a consciously simple-minded manner. . . . But in this novel such phrases seldom do the trick; they tend to be rather mechanical and mostly fail to create a humorous effect. Instances of such failures seem to me to be the following: 'The empty hall was empty' . . . and 'A wedding is a wedding.' . . . (pp. 91-2)

Dreams and reveries play an important role . . . in *The Tenants*. Indeed, of all Malamudian characteristics, this one feature is what gives *The Tenants* its very particular mark. On the realistic level it seems understandable that Lesser, a writer living a very isolated life, should indulge in fantasies of various kinds. Toward the end, when he is more desperate than ever, when he feels as if he is almost losing control of himself in anger and paranoia, his fantasies become hallucinations. . . .

[The] element of surrealism is extremely important in *The Tenants* and . . . gives a strong clue to the meaning of the book. . . . [The] main means by which, in this novel, Malamud achieves an effect of surrealism is his very skilful handling of the grammatical category of *tense*. A subsidiary means is the occasional substitution of a first person perspective for the normal third person narrator. (p. 93)

To start with, Malamud proceeds in a fairly orthodox manner, here and there breaking the past-tense narrative with present-tense insertions of various types and lengths. On the most 'normal' level, the present tense is employed to render Lesser's thoughts, fragments of an interior monologue, which are not set off from the narrative proper by quotation marks or other devices which might distinguish between narrative, dialogue and interior monologue. The present tense is also used for descriptions and explanations of the writer's present situation. . . . [The] shifts are smooth and will probably not confuse any reader. . . . Malamud avoids a blend of outer and inner view at this early stage of the novel; thereby he puts off the fusion of past and present, and of outer and inner perspective, that, like the skilful manipulator he is, he will perform later on in the book. (p. 94)

The earliest scene where the present tense is employed for an effect verging on the surrealistic is one where Lesser and Willie, sitting on the floor of Lesser's kitchen, smoke pot and chat about writing. . . . Here are fragments of dialogue and glimpses of hashish visions. . . . (p. 95)

The present tense is next used, in an orthodox fashion, to

paraphrase and summarize the work in progress that Willie has asked Lesser to read and criticize, and also for the writer's reflexions on this manuscript. . . . Lesser and Willie's discussion of the black's book constitutes the first confrontation between them, indicating their contrary literary and human positions. This section . . . is almost exclusively in the present tense. To Lesser (as to Malamud surely), Willie's disregard of form, at the expense of raw experience, is unacceptable; a gulf separates the two writers: one wants universal significance, the other seeks action here and now through 'black writing'.

Following this confrontation, Lesser has an erotic dream of love with a black girl, [presented in the present tense]. . . . [Malamud's] method of creating a smooth transition from fantasy to reality, which is a preparation for a complete blurring of the line dividing the real from the unreal, is in evidence also in this dream. . . . And here reality intrudes upon the dream: 'Willie raps on the door'. The transition from present to past tense is performed equally smoothly [in the succeeding section]. (pp. 95-6)

Malamud maintains this subtle blend of (predominant) past tense and (occasional) present tense, of direct dialogue and indirect speech, of third-person focus and 'I' focus. . . .

About halfway through the novel Malamud makes increasing use of 'abnormal' shifts of tense, occurring even in the middle of sentences, but the reader is now accustomed to these changes. One instance is the scene where Lesser for the first time happens to meet Irene alone. . . . This is the first section where the present tense is used exclusively for regular narrative and dialogue (the past tense being here employed for glimpses of Irene's and Willie's pasts). Is it that 'love' affords a parallel to 'dream' in quality and significance? (p. 96)

As the tension increases [after Willie learns of Lesser's betrayal] the shifts from past to present become more frequent and more abrupt; they can be said to parallel Lesser's growing fear and nervousness. The present tense is employed for his anguished thoughts of Willie's revenge. These lead to a feverish fantasy. . . .

From now on shifts of tense and alternating focuses on 'he' or 'I' are more frequent and more 'disorderly'; this development corresponds to Lesser's increasing desperation and anguish. . . . His manuscript destroyed, Lesser sits down at his desk, doggedly working at a reconstructed and, as he hopes, better version of his book: 'He sits at his desk . . . typing as fast as he can. He hopes this time to do a better job than he had done in the previous draft Willie Spearmint had so heartlessly burned.' . . . Immediately after this, a new section begins with the never-ending action: 'Lesser writes.' . . . These two sections resemble the opening section of the novel: the action and the mood are the same, Lesser isolated in his dilapidated ivory tower, engaged in his eternal struggle to finish his book. Seasons pass, monotony reigns supreme. Again there are hints of a quest for rebirth. Endurance and hope battle with despair ('. . . he will, he will' . . .). (p. 97)

Direct dialogue is growing increasingly scarce; much of the action is internalized in Lesser's mind. His growing nervousness, which is caused by doubts about his book, by his loneliness and suffering, expresses itself in fantasies of fear. It is clear that he is slowly becoming unhinged; paranoia threatens. One year has passed since we first saw Lesser

strapping on his timepiece in mock-heroic fashion. (pp. 97-8)

The reader by now doesn't know for sure whether Lesser is imagining things or not; this is where Malamud's careful and skilful manipulation is beginning to do its remarkable work. He is making it more and more difficult for us to distinguish between reality and fantasy. We cling to bits of information that seem to prove to us that things exist also outside of Lesser's mind. (p. 98)

[Lesser's wedding dream] unfortunately seems less well integrated into the novel as a whole than the other reveries-dreams-nightmares which are described in the book. The two traditions—black African and white Jewish—hardly amount here to more than folklore, and it is rather more phony than funny. The humanistic wisdom—which we so sorely need—appears a bit implausible in the context. It is after all Lesser who provides the material for the dream, and we haven't earlier detected such wisdom in him or in his book. This may be Malamud speaking out of turn.

From now on the reader has less to go on in deciding whether events are merely imagined by Lesser or whether they actually take place. It is possible that the writer fancies he catches a glimpse of Willie on the stairs: 'Frightened imagination? Optical illusion?' . . . This is preparation for our uncertainty about the final encounter between Lesser and Willie. Tenses shift often now; the narrative switches almost imperceptibly from an external ('he') to an internal ('I') point of view. The dramatic tension increases markedly from a moment indicated by the following: 'One winter's night they meet on the frigid stairs.' . . . They stare at each other, they talk, they part. We ask ourselves: did this actually happen? Or is it another of Lesser's frightened imaginings?

Malamud's mastery is fully evident on these pages which take us from the actual world to a surreal one. We cannot tell exactly at what point we step across the dividing line. It seems perfectly 'natural' that the writer has hallucinations: he is on the verge of a temporary bout of insanity, which has been brought on by physical and psychical exhaustion, by fear and guilt. His paranoia is acute. . . . (pp. 98-9)

The conflict is approaching its end, as Lesser, mad with rage, destroys Willie's typewriter with an axe. This act is described in the past tense, which by now . . . is the 'non-normal' tense. . . . [The] brief concluding sections of the novel, the contours of space, time, action and thought are blurred by the devices that Malamud has so masterfully handled all along: present and past tense intermingle, 'he' and 'I' interchange. The rapid switches create an impression of chaos and despair. (p. 99)

We have reached the final section of the narrative; here is also the last confrontation between the black and the white. This scene is enacted in an atmosphere of pure surrealism. . . . The setting is clearly surrealistic. . . . Just as the 'grassy clearing in the bush' is fantasy, so is the meeting, and—this is the crux of the present reading of *The Tenants* —so are the castration and the killing. The novel ends, not in real killing, but in an imagined act of violence, which is perhaps meant to have a cathartic result, but, more importantly, which is intended as a reminder and a warning.

In this surrealistic scene, the past tense is used to great effect: this 'normal' narrative tense has, through Malamud's manipulation throughout the novel, been transformed so as to function here as a vehicle for the unreal. Or, perhaps more accurately, the past tense serves to redress somewhat the imbalance that exists between the realistic narrative and the surrealistic setting and action, just as, earlier in the novel, the present tense often lent a slightly fanciful shimmer to the ordinary and the actual.

The last sentence of this surrealistic section ["Each, thought the writer, feels the anguish of the other."] clinches the case: the present tense verb sums up the meaning of the imaginary confrontation. The writer, Lesser (and perhaps this applies to Malamud too), has emerged out of the imagined tragic encounter, with a new insight. Here is suggested a sort of limited 'redemption': it implies a recognition of 'the other' and an insight into his anguish. But this redemptive value is reduced by the qualifying reporting-tag, 'thought the writer'. Lesser (and Malamud) can only speak for himself with any authority. Never in the book have we been allowed to enter into the black's mind. The only exceptions are the few instances in this concluding surrealistic scene; here a kind of identification with the black is hinted at on the part of the writer-Malamud. 'Each knew where the other was,' it says, and 'Neither of them could see the other but sensed where he stood. Each heard himself scarcely breathing.' This 'trick' of Malamud's further enhances the surrealistic impression. It all takes place in the writer's mind. (pp. 100-01)

After the *'hab rachmones'* passage [which, seeming strained, largely fails], there is no ending proper; the book never gets its 'promised end', neither Lesser's book, nor Malamud's. For we are once more back at the opening section where we find Lesser waking to finish his book. The tragic conclusion that we have just rehearsed exists in Lesser's mind as a vague, saddening memory. . . . And this I see as Malamud's message: to remind himself and us of 'the other's' anguish and of the necessity to keep this memory alive.

So the beginning of *The Tenants* is also the end and a new beginning. This is a novel without an ending. And herein lies the only real hope Malamud gives us in an otherwise pessimistic book: the antagonists are locked in a fatal struggle, but there is hope because the writer—who serves as a prototype of man constantly trying to reach the end—never gives up. The conflict between black and white is naturally at the focus of attention, but Malamud obviously wishes to extend the scope of the book's meaning to include other confrontations in hostility and fear.

One question remains: Supposing that Malamud wishes to remind us all of the plight of 'the other' and to speak for endurance and commitment, has he succeeded in this aim? Can we identify with Lesser the writer? Can we accept his dedication to writing as a model for our individual commitments in other fields of life? The present reader must admit: no. Malamud does not fully succeed in making the writer's efforts seem worthwhile. Lesser never becomes interesting. Perhaps because his antagonist and double, Willie Spearmint, is never seen from inside, there is, as a result, a lack of balance in the main conflict. If Malamud wishes to speak to us (white) readers, he has not been very helpful in affording us new insights into 'the other'. Willie is mostly a stereotype, with a mask no doubt very much like the one of pride and arrogance that certain young blacks wear these days. When Malamud breaks through the mask, he reveals,

not so much another human being, as another writer. But the ordinary reader probably would prefer to recognize a *semblable,* rather than an *auteur.*

The Tenants could be read as an oppressively pessimistic novel with a totally tragic ending. It has been my line of argument that Malamud has provided the minimum of 'outlet' that the general reader seems to ask of a fictional work, and that this minimum of 'redemption' is expressed in the idea of the never-ending effort. . . . I have attempted to show that the tragic conclusion is *not* the actual ending of the story, but that the circularity of the plot and the structure reflects the artist's commitment to his art, as well as his duty to remind himself and us of 'the other', be he black or white. This is a worthy aim for the novelist, and we listen with sympathy to Malamud's wise and humane message. (pp. 101-02)

> Brita Lindberg-Seyersted, "A Reading of Bernard Malamud's 'The Tenants'," in Journal of American Studies, *April, 1975, pp. 85-102.*

Bernard Malamud's first story in the Fidelman sequence, "The Last Mohican," is a pivotal work in the author's writing. Since it utilizes themes and techniques found throughout Malamud's first three novels, *The Natural, The Assistant,* and *A New Life,* and in most of the stories collected in *The Magic Barrel* and in *Idiots First,* the story is representative of the author's early period; in addition, "The Last Mohican" is a seminal story for the motifs and concerns of some of Malamud's more recent fiction, including *The Tenants* and, most obviously, *Pictures of Fidelman.* The technique in the story of the double, for example, in which one character teaches the other self-knowledge, is similar to that of *The Assistant,* while the motif of the stolen manuscript reappears as a central component in the plot of *The Tenants.* Because it holds such a crucial place in Malamud's canon, a correct understanding of "The Last Mohican" is valuable for any analysis of the author's work in general. (p. 397)

The story concerns Arthur Fidelman, who arrives in Italy intending to write "a critical study of Giotto, the opening chapter of which he had carried across the ocean." When he enters Rome, the art student is approached by the inimitable Shimon Susskind, a Jewish refugee. Though Fidelman gives him some money, Susskind is unsatisfied. "'In your luggage,' he said vaguely, 'would you maybe have a suit you can't use. I could use a suit'." . . . Fidelman, budgeting to make his money last long enough to finish the book, refuses to give the refugee his spare suit. Nevertheless, Susskind continues to shadow Fidelman's movements and to plague his thoughts. The refugee is literally a *luftmentsh:* when the student asks him how he lives, Susskind replies, "I eat air." . . . After Susskind appears surreptitiously in Fidelman's room to renew his suit for the student's spare one, without success, Fidelman discovers his manuscript missing. He suspects the refugee, naturally, and searches Rome for him, but the formerly ubiquitous Susskind has disappeared. Fidelman finally locates him months later, selling Christian articles in front of St. Peter's, and follows him to "an overgrown closet containing bed and table" . . . , but not the manuscript. Finally, the answer comes to Fidelman as he dreams of a fresco by Giotto of Saint Francis of Assisi giving his cloak to a poor knight: "San Francesco dona le vesti al cavaliere povero."

... Like Frank Alpine in *The Assistant,* Fidelman receives enlightenment from St. Francis, in this case through the agency of Giotto's art. Waking, the student immediately carries his suit to Susskind, reenacting the charity of the saint. Though the refugee suspects that the suit is being offered in trade for the manuscript, Fidelman assures Susskind that he wants "nothing at all" ..., and leaves the rat's nest.... The relationship between art and life—a common theme in Malamud—is at least this clear from the story: one who cannot act charitably and humanely in life cannot really appreciate, or has not sufficiently understood, great art, which has compassion at its root. Giotto's painting of the charity of St. Francis was unintelligible to Fidelman while the student could refuse to consider giving his suit to an impoverished refugee; the spirit of that charity was missing from the manuscript and from the student himself until Susskind helped him to enlightenment. Fidelman sees this, and calls after the fleeing refugee, "'Susskind, come back,' he shouted, half sobbing. 'The suit is yours. All is forgiven'." ... The story ends with Susskind, having educated the student, running out of sight; Fidelman is left equipped with genuine compassion.

Few critics have presented readings similar to this, and none has pursued his beyond the story's literal level. Many more have misunderstood even these superficial aspects of Malamud's story. Sheldon Norman Grebstein, for example, describes Fidelman on arrival in Rome as "respectably dressed and with the worthy ambition to become an art critic." ... The worthiness of being a critic is also dubious in "The Last Mohican." Fidelman only chooses that profession after he is "a self-confessed failure as a painter" ..., and the movement of the story tends to restore his artistic powers; the relationship of the artist to life, central to all the Fidelman stories, does not apply to an art critic. (pp. 397-99)

The refugee's qualifications for teaching Fidelman self-knowledge arise from the characters' intimacy as doubles. This is clear from Susskind's first appearance: standing outside the Rome railroad station, "Fidelman experienced the sensation of suddenly seeing himself as he was, to the pinpoint, outside and in, not without bittersweet pleasure"; shortly afterwards, the student "became aware that there was an exterior source to the strange, almost tri-dimensional reflection of himself." ... Not only does Susskind's presence show Fidelman his true, innermost self, but the double first appears beside the statue of another famous pair, Romulus and Remus. A further identification with Susskind is also found in the student's name: especially in Yiddish, there is little orthographical difference between "Fidel" and "peddle."

Susskind, much more in the story than just Fidelman's double, is hardly the "dirty, sponging, obnoxious immigrant," or the "shameless parasite," that some critics have described. This misunderstanding of Susskind's character may originate with Fidelman himself, who concludes from the insufficient evidence of the peddler's first "shalom" that he is "a schnorrer." ... Accepting Fidelman's appraisal, however, is a critical error; Malamud has taken great pains in "The Last Mohican" to distinguish between peddling and begging. Susskind never begs in the story, nor is he ever termed a beggar by the narrator.... Susskind may seem to be asking for money, but in fact his questions are carefully worded not to ask for more, but to ask, hypo-

thetically, why more shouldn't be forthcoming. If this is hairsplitting, it is Malamud's distinction as well as that of Susskind; those who have seen in the peddler the archetype of "Susskind the Beggar" have misunderstood both his character and his function in the story.

The difference between begging and accepting charity is finely delineated in the scene at the trattoria. At first, Susskind watches Fidelman eat "with rapt attention." ... Initially, Susskind does not refuse the food; his first reply is one of acceptance. But acceptance with "thanks" is different from asking with "thanks yes." Asking is begging, and Susskind refuses to beg; when he must commit himself, if only by a simple "yes," the refugee goes hungry. Susskind even avoids asking for the student's spare suit. "In your luggage," he questions Fidelman during their first meeting, "would you maybe have a suit you can't use. I could use a suit." ... The refugee thus presents Fidelman with two premises: Fidelman has a spare suit, and Susskind needs one. The charitable conclusion, that the student should give Susskind his suit, is never voiced by the peddler. (pp. 399-400)

Susskind's identification as a peddler begins with his first name, Shimon, in English Simon. When Fidelman finally finds him after months of searching, Susskind is engaged in simony, "selling black and white rosaries to all who would buy." ... Though the profession is inauspicious, and rather ill-suited for saving Fidelman's soul and heritage, Malamud's imagery elevates peddlers to the level of angels. Until Susskind is located selling rosaries, only two types of beings fly in the story: there are the "flights of angels" Fidelman sees one night after overtaxing his eyes in the Vatican museum ..., and the "fly-by-night peddlers" amongst whom he searches for Susskind.... Fidelman, who travels to Rome by boat and train, never flies, but Susskind, who "had an odd way of standing motionless, like a cigar store Indian about to burst into flight" ..., is consistently associated with flying and angels. (pp. 400-01)

Though Susskind does not beg, he does demand; he comes "instead of an angel," but he comes as a Jew. For Malamud, Jewish consciousness makes certain demands; and as Susskind tells him, Fidelman is responsible for them "because you are a man. Because you are a Jew." ... Fidelman's primary problem is that he has rejected his own Jewish culture, but is unable to assimilate into that of the Italians. His gift of the suit at the end of the story is not merely a sign that he has understood Giotto's painting; by that point, he also understands—and accepts—himself and his people.

The conflict between Italian and Jewish history begins immediately upon Fidelman's arrival in Rome. Viewing the Baths of Diocletian, he mutters to himself, "Imagine all that history." ... The word *imagine* is repeated three times in as many lines, drawing attention to the student's distance from the history of Rome. Later, walking along the banks of the Tiber, Fidelman defines history in his thoughts as "the remembrance of things unknown" ..., playing on the translation of Proust's title. The history of the Jews is also present in the world of "The Last Mohican," embodied by Shimon Susskind. Like a microcosmic Diaspora, Susskind lived in Israel "once" ..., and has also fled from "Germany, Hungary, Poland. Where not?" ... That history, however, bores Fidelman; he says to Susskind, "Ah, that's so long ago." ... The remark contains a double irony, both parts at Fidelman's expense. Compared to the history of ancient Rome, of course, the recent horrors of Nazi persecutions, as represented by Susskind the individual, hardly occurred "long ago." In contrast, the history of Susskind, representative of the Jewish people, is far longer than that of Rome, to which Fidelman is attracted because of its apparent antiquity. (p. 401)

Of all Jewish history, it seems only "Israel interested Fidelman" . . . ; the student identifies with Israeli victors, but refuses to acknowledge the centuries of Jewish victims. To Malamud, however, the lessons of persecution are at least as valuable as the rewards of success; Fidelman must therefore accept his heritage as a Jew to gain a full understanding of himself. To discuss this process of acceptance, we must return to Fidelman's search for Susskind.

After the refugee takes the manuscript, Fidelman is unable to work. The absence of his chapter exposes a vicious circularity in the student's character: he always "needed something solid behind him before he could advance, some worthwhile accomplishment upon which to build another." . . .

While searching to recover the chapter, Fidelman begins unconsciously to identify with his double, Susskind. He wears "a blue beret with his trench coat and a pair of black Italian shoes" . . . , which are, as Richman has noted, "the very clothes Susskind wears." He also searches in the ghetto, and even visits an Italian synagogue, where elements of Jewish and Italian history are intertwined in the beadle's story of a son "killed in the Ardeatine Caves." . . . When Fidelman finally does locate the peddler, he follows him "all the way home, indeed the ghetto," and returns later to search Susskind's hovel, "a pitch black freezing cave." . . . The destitution in which the refugee subsists appalls Fidelman; "from the visit he never fully recovered." . . . (p. 402)

Subsequently, Fidelman has his dream in which a Dantean "long-nosed brown shade, Virgilio Susskind" guides him through the underworld of his own subconscious. . . . The shade's taunt, "Why is art?" not only twists the title of Tolstoy's essay to force a perception of humanity on the student, but also poses a more personal question about the existence of Art Fidelman. The climax of the dream, Fidelman's vision of Giotto's painting, is an example of Malamud's genius in synthesizing his themes. The scene of St. Francis giving away his cloak integrates Susskind's need for the suit with Fidelman's desire for self-knowledge and appreciation of art. Moreover, the use of Giotto as the painter is simultaneously the central and yet the most understated element of the synthesis. The Italian word *giotto,* "foundry," is traditionally the etymological root of *ghetto.* The first official ghetto, proclaimed by Pope Paul IV in 1555, was "located on the malarial west bank of the Tiber, near the *giotto,* the gun factory." (pp. 402-03)

Malamud's ambiguous use of Giotto's name in place of its paronym is also reversed within the story; the beadle's advice to "look in the ghetto" . . . , foreshadows the student's dream of Giotto's fresco.

The story operates on several levels, connected by verbal ambiguities, on each of which Fidelman progresses from alienation to reconciliation, with art, humanity, his Jewish heritage, and himself; in each instance, Susskind's intervention, in a dream or otherwise, provides the fundamental

stimulus for Fidelman's amelioration. Most critical misreadings have originated with an undue sense of parasitism. Similarly, in "The Mourners" (*The Magic Barrel*), "The Death of Me" (*Idiots First*), and *The Tenants,* readers have mistakenly seen Gruber, Marcus, and Levenspiel, respectively, as the innocent victims of ruthless demands perpetrated by someone only marginally connected to them, as an employee or a tenant. Susskind's association with Fidelman, either as a man or as a Jew, is even more tenuous; but in this story, and in the others, no one is victimized except by himself. Only under Susskind's tutelage can Fidelman regain "the remembrance of things unknown" in the Jewish past so essential to his own present.

Due emphasis must also be given to this story, and to all of Malamud's work, as universal art, transcending the issue of Jewishness. The author's statement that "all men are Jews," is particularly applicable to "The Last Mohican," where all men are Shimon Susskind. Fidelman sees his search for the refugee as an attempt "to know man" . . . , and the cry when he is found—"ecco, Susskind!" . . . —reinforces the peddler's role as humanity personified. Ultimately, Fidelman's insight, by which he becomes himself and Everyman, is also available to the reader, both despite and because of Malamud's ethnocentric approach. (pp. 403-04)

> *David R. Mesher, "The Remembrance of Things Unknown: Malamud's 'The Last Mohican'," in* Studies in Short Fiction *(copyright 1975 by Newberry College), Fall, 1975, pp. 397-404.*

In *The Fixer,* all the themes which Malamud had introduced in his earlier works were refined and brilliantly reworked into their most powerful, controlled, and effective statement. . . . In our view, some of the most significant [themes] are a search for a new life in the manner of the *Bildungsroman,* i.e., a focus on growth and development from boyhood to manhood; the prison motif; the necessity for moral involvement, or freedom vs. responsibility; the value of suffering; the ritualistic and mythic elements in life; the search for a father or a son's displacing of a "father," or the scapegoat or orphan motifs; and a consuming concern with Love, Mercy (*Rachmones*), *Menschlechkeit.* (p. 1)

The theme of a new life involves the protagonist's leaving his home in search of change, a second chance, new opportunities. Sometimes the change brings good, sometimes not.

On the surface, the change may involve only different surroundings. But the change should—if it is going to be a good one—involve a growth in the person from boyhood to manhood, that is, a giving up of the selfish concerns of youth for an involvement in the problems of mankind, an acceptance of life's responsibilities.

In *The Assistant,* Frank Alpine's conversion to Judaism becomes such a change. But for Roy Hobbs, the failed hero of *The Natural,* the change in his physical surroundings does not include this necessary interior growth, and thus he is a failure.

S. Levin, in the novel *A New Life* . . . , goes West to a new career in new surroundings and freedom. What he finds, eventually, is a third new life when he gives up the Greek dream of freedom for the Jewish acceptance of responsibility and moral entanglement.

When Henry Levin, in "The Lady of the Lake," changes his name to Henry Freeman to escape his Jewishness, this denial of his past leads to the loss of his beloved, a concentration camp survivor, who says she has suffered too much for her heritage to betray it. Because Levin-Freeman refuses to accept his Jewishness, his "change" brings him no good.

In his search for the increased opportunities outside of the prisonlike confines of the *shtetl*, Yakov Bok [in *The Fixer*] shaves off his beard and changes his name. This change brings disaster. Ironically, however, inside the actual prison, Yakov learns that the purpose of freedom is to create it for others. His change brings moral growth. By refusing to confess and betray Russian Jewry, he accepts responsibility for the Jewish community and becomes actively involved in the fate of his people. This novel, among other things, shows the growth of the hero.

In Malamud's fictional world, there is always a prison. It can lie in the physical environment—a grocery store, a tenement, an artist's garret, a bordello, a *shtetl*, or a real prison cell in a dungeon. But it can also lie in being imprisoned by one's own self and within one's self, being confined by one's ineptitudes and thus becoming a victim of one's own self.

Furthermore, some critics have said, Malamud's central metaphor of Jewishness *is* the prison, a perfect symbol for the human and most particularly the Jewish condition. Metaphorically, the prison becomes an acceptance of life's limitations and responsibilities in this sense. Thus, ironically, in imprisonment there can be freedom. (pp. 2-3)

[The] Malamud *schlemiel* appears to realize a variety of themes and motifs. And the *schlemiel* operates powerfully in the recent stories collected in *Rembrandt's Hat*.

Whether the *schlemiel* epitomizes the born loser, the hard-luck guy, the poignant misfit, or, collectively, world Jewry, he has a long and honorable history. One can trace him back to the nineteenth-century Yiddish writers who gave us types like Tevye the milkman, and extend it to the New-World Herzogs and Fidelmans. The *schlemiel* is a composite of history, legend, myth, and folklore. And underlying all is the comic element. More often than not the comic figure of the *schlemiel* seems to be a victim, but because he and his creators redefine his world, in the end he achieves the moral victory often denied to others. (pp. 3-4)

We believe that [Malamud's] definition of Jewishness includes such universal human virtues as moral obligation to one's fellow man and the community; acceptance of responsibility; being involved in the suffering of others; and learning from one's own suffering. (p. 4)

A great deal of Malamud criticism has been devoted to discovering and analyzing his use of myth, ritual, and symbolism. . . . Much of this complex analysis is dependent upon a close examination of the texts; unfortunately, popular commentary on Malamud's fiction often ignores the intricate symbolism and the patterns of meaning which Malamud so painstakingly weaves into his work.

If one works for a moment with Yakov's name and the idea of the scapegoat, some of the complexities and nuances become apparent. We are all familiar with the old Hebraic use of scapegoat—literally a live goat; the meaning is extended to a person or group bearing the guilt for a larger

group. The name Bok means goat, and Shepsovich means son of a sheep. The charge of ritual murder against Yakov is really an indictment against the entire Jewish nation, Yakov simply being the "accidental" victim standing for all Jewry.

Seasonal patterns of myth are also apparent in *The Fixer* and are quite important in *The Natural, The Assistant,* and *A New Life.* Certain events occur appropriately at specific seasons, thus leading the reader to tie the present to the sweep of history and to ancient myths and rituals.

We believe that one of the most important of the mythic elements involves the search for a father—either real or spiritual, within or outside of oneself. Although the theme is found frequently in Greek literature and in the folklore of all peoples, historically the search for a father is central to Jewish writings. Beginning with the Jewish patriarchs—Abraham, Isaac, Jacob—it finds a further expression in the story of Moses and the Exodus, and runs through the great history of biblical kings where, between the ambivalent Davids and Solomons, we have hostility and acceptance, hate and love. Overarching all is the tension between the acceptance and the rejection of the Father of us all—the One God. In this sense Malamud is a very Judaic writer, who tends, ironically, to undercut the Christian themes that appear in his work. Most of his heroes or anti-heroes or *schlemiels* are still young, and are either orphans or have a vague, ineffectual father somewhere in their backgrounds.

In almost all cases we have men who are free spirits, who insist upon freedom—but at the same time are destroying themselves because of that freedom. They have no purpose, no goal. And there is no one to guide them; there is no authority. So, even though Frank Alpine and S. Levin and Yakov Bok don't realize it, they are really looking for that authority or guide which is represented by a real or substitute Father and/or God. Frank Alpine accepts and then becomes Morris Bober. S. Levin accepts responsibility as a father. Yakov Bok accepts Raizl's child as his own. Even Harry Lesser accepts Willie Spearmint as a brother-son. Perhaps one of the most important elements in Malamud's handling of this theme is that the Yakov Boks accept themselves, their families, their communities; they step out of a nebulous history in limbo into the Judaic tradition of Abraham, Isaac, Jacob—and the covenant with God. Whether or not they would approve this formal Judaic tradition, they have indeed become *menschen.*

This brings us to the humanity or *menschlechkeit* in Malamud—love, mercy (*rachmones*). It is more than a coincidence that . . . *The Tenants* . . . ends with a struggle to the death by two writers—Harry Lesser (a Jew) and Willie Spearmint (a black man). The final thoughts in the novel are given to the Jew—Harry Lesser: as both men die, Harry is convinced that "each . . . feels the anguish of the other." Then Malamud writes "THE END." After this formal ending, we have the chorus of the Jewish landlord:

> "Mercy, the both of you, for Christ's sake . . .
> *Hab Rachmones,* I beg you . . .
> Mercy Mercy Mercy. . . ."

Mercy is then repeated more than 100 times.

We should recall too the final scenes in *The Fixer:* Yakov . . . imagines his confrontation with the Tsar—the so-called father of Russia. "*Rachmones,* we say in Hebrew—mercy, one oughtn't to forget it,'' Yakov says to the Tsar. Because the Tsar had no *rachmones,* he was destroying the Jewish people; therefore, Yakov, who in his imagination destroyed the Czar, was leaving the way open for the reappearance of the true father of the Jews and all people—the God of Mercy, the God who has *Rachmones.* (pp. 5-7)

> *Leslie and Joyce Field, "Malamud, Mercy, and Menschlechkeit," in* Bernard Malamud: A Collection of Critical Essays, *edited by Leslie and Joyce Field (© 1975 by Prentice-Hall, Inc.; reprinted by permission of Prentice-Hall, Inc., Englewood Cliffs, New Jersey), Prentice-Hall, 1975, pp. 1-7.*

[One] of Malamud's major strengths is his ability to bring together in harmonious conjunction a large variety of disjunctive schools and styles. For example, his handling of the Yiddish-inflected English dialect of his characters seems to be unparalleled in Jewish-American writing. It is a dialect that possesses the Old World "heart" within the quick impatience of New World forms. But not until *A New Life* and *The Assistant* appeared was Malamud able to show that he was equally at home in the novel as in the short story. *The Natural,* his first novel, was more in the nature of a metaphysical *jeu d'esprit*—even to the counterpun of the title itself—than a fully developed novel. To be sure, *A New Life* is a Jewish picaresque while *The Assistant,* because of its more melancholy undertones, is antipicaresque. But Malamud's syncretism is a prime characteristic of these works, for in them he shows his ability to handle a variety of themes and techniques, and be at home in all of them.

The mythic pattern in *The Natural* is that of the Waste Land—a dry (baseball) season of no wins, the hopes (or prayers?) for rain (victory), and the "romantic agony" in their attempted attainment. Roy Hobbs, the baseball hero, is the "knight" in search of the holy grail of a game (or quest), which in this instance involves not the winning of a lady's favor but the World Series. And even the lady assumes the role of *la belle dame sans merci* when she "kills" Roy in the first of his incarnations, so that he may rise again "reborn." Roy's "knighthood" of course is derived from the ball club he is associated with; for Malamud, quite consciously, if somewhat heavy-handedly, has dubbed them the Knights. Admittedly, all of this fits too neatly into the mythic grail-quest pattern and the "victory" which is eventually Roy's. Yet as mechanical in its parallel of the medieval romance as it may be, or as derivative of T. S. Eliot's "Waste Land" as it obviously is, the end effect is to further illustrate Malamud's use of syncretism.

The Natural is replete with readily recognizable mythic elements. Any alert undergraduate in the humanities, or major in English or in anthropology, should be able to pick out such obvious symbolisms as the knight's search for the holy grail of his redemption through victory, a victory genuine in Hobbs's case because it is made all the more meaningful by his rejection of a false, as well as a cheap one. And an intelligent sophomore should be able to note both a father figure in the person of Pop Fisher, the club manager, and his symbolic function as a psychologically maimed Fisher King. Thus, though Malamud is no T. S. Eliot, he has woven Eliot's widely disparate Waste Land/grail motifs into this first novel—even though these occasionally seem to be more superimposed than fully integrated.

Further, Malamud's syncretism is roomy enough to include such diverse strands as the proletarian, the mythic, and the Dostoevskian. His ability to fuse such disparate elements within a single novel may best be seen in *The Assistant.* In this work there is the entirely successful synthesis of the proletarian strain—a fable of blindness and discovery—and of the mythic: the death of the father, Morris Bober, and his resurrection through his "son," Frank Alpine; and there is the Dostoevskian, in Alpine's sin against Bober—his participation in the robbery of the old man's store—a sin which will later lead to Alpine's repentance and redemption through his love for Morris's daughter, Helen, and his final conversion to Judaism, a conversion which would presumably include the acceptance of the prophetic and social values of that religion.

Malamud's syncretism has also drawn upon the best, or most useful, aspects of that split tradition—the Jewish-American and the Graeco-Hebraic—and brought them together in his novels and short stories as few other Jewish-American writers have done. Not even Saul Bellow, the most formidably intellectual of the lot, has succeeded in weaving these strands into his work quite as naturally as Malamud has done. Further, while Malamud . . . expresses the redemptive vision of a Dostoevski, the ambiguity of a Hawthorne, and the psychological probings of a James, he has also adopted the surrealistic mode of a James Joyce—a technique which the later Fidelman stories exemplify. Like Joyce, Malamud combines, though not always as successfully, the syncretism of Hebraism and Hellenism, and the fusions and the tensions that grow from both when they are polarized as symbolic antipodes. Thus he renders, like Joyce, the Hegelian unity of opposites. The result is the quintessential Irishman within the quintessential Jew: put another way, the Jew in Malamud, as in Joyce's Leopold Bloom (possibly the greatest portrayal of a Jew by *either* a Jew or non-Jew in twentieth-century fiction), has become the Jew-as-Everyman, just as Bloom, the Irish-Jew, becomes Bloom the Everyman-as-Father.

Pictures of Fidelman is the work that perhaps best exemplifies this Hebraic-Hellenic tension. . . . Fidelman's inner split—the Hellenistic side of his Jewish self—lies in the tradition of classical criticism. In a sense, Fidelman discovers or rediscovers his Jewish soul through Hellenic means, and is thus finally able to recognize the universal Everyman within himself and within the "two cultures." (pp. 76-8)

Comedy, satire, humor, wit all run through Malamud's best work. . . . [However], the comedy rarely manifests itself in the black humor of the alienated soul within a larger alienated society. Perhaps the one exception to this in Malamud may be seen in his novel *The Tenants.* For even behind the most alienated of Malamud's Jews stands an order, a sense of continuity, in spite of the non-Euclidean leap into the New World, that makes the Jew a part of a larger, long-lived tradition. In Malamud the victim-schlemiels, no matter how comical they may appear to be, are more the objects of our compassion than of our derision. (pp. 78-9)

> *Sam Bluefarb, "The Syncretism of Bernard Malamud," in* Bernard Malamud: A Collection of Critical Essays, *edited by Leslie and Joyce Field (copyright © 1975 by Sam Bluefarb; reprinted by permission of Sam Bluefarb), Prentice-Hall, 1975, pp. 72-9.*

A New Life is a Western, or more accurately a neo- or meta-Western, which is to say, a Western written by an author (typically in a university, where such literature is studied) aware of the tradition, the genre, and therefore a book about that genre as well as about life in the West. It is helpful, I think, to remind ourselves that at the same moment at which Bernard Malamud's meta-Western was appearing, another book was being published, very different in every other aspect, but like *A New Life* academic in its origins and its relationship to the tradition of the classic or pop Western. Moreover, like Malamud's novel it, too, is set in the landscape of Oregon, and Oregonians move through its pages.

I am thinking of Ken Kesey's *One Flew Over the Cuckoo's Nest*. . . . (p. 212)

What I intend to suggest (assuming that every genre embodies an archetype, at whose heart is a characteristic myth of love) is that the erotic center of Kesey's novel re-embodies the archetypal Eros which underlies the most American of all fictional forms. I have spent a good deal of my life writing about that myth, from my early essay "Come Back to the Raft Ag'in, Huck Honey" to a relatively late study called *The Return of the Vanishing American,* and I like to think there remains scarcely a literate American who is not aware of its structure and meaning. It seems to me, therefore, sufficient at this point to say merely that it is a myth of transitory and idyllic love between two males in the Wilderness, one a White refugee from White civilization, the other a non-White member of a group which has been exploited or persecuted by his White lover's people. White Women, who represent the world of Law and Order from which the renegade White Man is in flight, when they appear in this myth at all, appear as the Ultimate Enemy. Whenever we find such pairs at the center of a fiction, whether they be Twain's Huck and Jim, Cooper's Natty Bumppo and Chingachgook, Melville's Ishmael and Queequeg, Saul Bellow's Henderson and Dafu, or Kesey's Patrick McMurphy and Chief Bromden, we are in the presence of the true Western. (pp. 212-13)

The West is a metaphor for, a mythic name of, the Unexplored wherever it may be: the retreating horizon, the territory that always lies just ahead of where we happen to be, waiting to be penetrated by anyone willing to light out ahead of the rest. (p. 213)

Malamud . . . is not sufficiently misogynist to write a real Western. Indeed, no one can truly understand or love the West, as it has been mythologized in hundreds of novels and thousands of films and T.V. scripts, who does not hate Respectable White Women, the enforcers of civility and normality—for Kesey, the Nurse, and for most of his forerunners, the Schoolmarm.

But S. Levin *is* a schoolmarm who likes to think of himself as bringing Culture and Liberal Humanism to the Barbarian West, meanwhile dreaming of promotion and tenure, making it as a Professor, and, who knows, maybe even someday as Chairman of a Department of English. . . . He has no vision of the West as an alternative way of life, an altered mode of consciousness, radically different from all we had imported from Europe and reconstructed in the old urban East. . . . Levin ends up, therefore, not by riding off alone, as in the Western movies of my childhood, or dying in the liberating, murderous embrace of his Indian buddy,

as in Kesey's book, but by marrying Madame Bovary and heading out for San Francisco . . . to live happily—or unhappily—ever after. (pp. 213-14)

Malamud's novel is in this sense an anti-Western disguised as a meta-Western, or at least a travesty Western. It is a tale about failed Westering, the failure of a refugee Easterner to become a Westerner because he could not abide being reborn in heroic loneliness. . . . What remains obscure in *A New Life* is whether it is the West which fails S. Levin or S. Levin who fails the West, or both. In any case, Malamud's novel is, or at least tries to become comic. It belongs, therefore, not, like Kesey's, to the sentimental tradition of Owen Wister, Jack London, and Zane Grey, but to one whose first eminent practitioner was Mark Twain, who also had gone West hopefully, then retreated in amused despair to write a book, get married, and make his fortune. (p. 214)

[As] long as *A New Life* remains a burlesque account of a buffoon with a fedora hat on his head, an umbrella in his hand, and a copy of James Joyce's *Ulysses* under his arm, a *shlemiel* who cannot really believe that the Pacific is really out there over the next range of mountains, and who has never seen a mountain ash or heard of a potluck picnic, a *nebechel* who, in a world where men have gone from horse to automobile to airplane without ever touching the ground, cannot even *drive* (which is to say, is by the definitions of the place, impotent), it is not just hilarious, but moving and true. . . .

As long as S. Levin remains the absurd anti-hero on whom kids pee and nervous housewives spill tuna-fish casseroles, I love him and believe in him; as I do, too, when he fails to make it with a barmaid in a barn, or with his aging and anxious officemate on a desk—fleeing bare-assed and flustered, while sexual defeat piles on sexual defeat. The archetypal Eros of the travesty Western is *coitus interruptus,* the unconsummated act of love. . . . But when Levin finally makes it under the trees with a faculty wife, my credulity grows strained, my interest wanes, and disconcertingly, the West even as a physical setting begins to disappear from the book—along with anything like a genuine confrontation of East and West.

Self-pity, self-righteousness, and a sneaky kind of self-adulation take over from a healthy irony and sense of the ridiculous as the book slips into what may well be the least rewarding of all American fictional sub-genres, the Academic Novel. (pp. 214-15)

Up until the cop-out point, *A New Life* had provided for me, who have never seduced or decamped with the wife of a Dean or Chairman, real vicarious satisfaction. (p. 215)

S. Levin is not untypical in his total shlemielhood, though there can have been few who came like him to an Ag School without knowing it, or for that matter, without knowing quite what an Ag School was. But he is typical of more than the westward bound academics of the Fifties; indeed, insofar as *A New Life* records the misadventures of a luckless bumbler, it belongs to a genre with which Jewish writers were concerned long before any of them had heard of Tom Mix or Gary Cooper or John Wayne, a genre with roots in Yiddish folk culture, whose most eminent old world practitioner was Sholem Aleichem. Moreover, it has influenced the Jewish-American novel, especially in its comic erotic scenes ever since the time of Daniel Fuchs and Nathanael West. But this means that insofar as *A New Life* is about the Shlemiel in Love or Out West or in the University, it belongs to the mainstream of Jewish-American fiction.

So why then is S. Levin not a Jew, not really, *really* a Jew, either in his own consciousness, or in that of his colleagues, students, goyish lovers, and haters? He seems in this respect less like Malamud's earlier and later protagonists, and more like, say, the leading character in Arthur Miller's *After the Fall,* of whom I once heard a departing spectator remark, "If his mother is Jewish and his father is Jewish, how come he ain't Jewish?" (p. 216)

Yet our anti-hero's name, after all, is Levin, S. Levin, Seymour Levin as he calls himself, or Lev as Pauline calls him (only the hostile, indifferent, and insensitive call him "Sy" in an attempt to acclimatize him). A Jewish name in all its changes, one is tempted to say, if there ever was one. But the epigraph from *Ulysses* with which Malamud prefaces his book, sends us off on what seems a deliberately planted false scent; by equating the name with a perfectly good old English word meaning "lightning"; and directing us to a novel about Dublin written by an Irishman. "Lo, Levin leaping lightens / in eyeblink Ireland's western welkin."

Upon further consideration, however, the Joycean allusion turns out not to be so false a scent after all—suggesting that the ambiguous Jew at the center of this American parable of a Stranger in a Strange Land is derived from a goy's portrait of his own aging, foolish self as an Imaginary Jew, or if you like, a mythological one. And there turn out to be stream-of-consciousness passages attributed to S. Levin in this academic novel which sound like pastiches or parodies of L. Bloom's ruminations on his way from and to home on Eccles Street. Moreover, the word "western" in the passage cited provided Malamud, I am convinced, a clue for the geographical translation of Bloom lost in Ireland to Levin disoriented in the American West. It is a notion that smacks of the Graduate School, but it is as fraught with pathos and pure comedy as that other classroom inspiration of Malamud's to replay T. S. Eliot's version of the Grail Legend in Ebbets Field, which makes for all the best effects (and they are very good, indeed) in *The Natural.*

If there is another place in the world besides Ireland where the immemorial conflict of Jew and Gentile can be played out as comedy, burlesque, farce rather than tragedy, it is precisely the American West. Here, quite as in Ireland, the mythological hostility of two cultures joined and separated by a common myth, is not associated with a long history of bloody pogroms as in Russia or Poland or the Middle East, or with an attempt at total genocide as in Germany. It can therefore be presented in a tone scarcely more serious than vaudeville skits like Gallagher and Shean or hits of the popular comic theatre like *Abie's Irish Rose.* The very notion of the Western Jew is like that of the Irish Jew a joke in itself. (p. 217)

In the early chapters of *A New Life,* Malamud seems on the verge of blending successfully the comic folk traditions of the *shlemiel-shlimazl* and the tenderfoot-dude, and combining both with Joyce's burlesque version of the Wandering Jew as cuckold, masturbator, and peeper at underdrawers: a culturally displaced person, who in a world of drinkers cannot drink, only talk on soberly as everyone else

proceeds to get joyously smashed or laid or both. But finally Malamud fails, as his book fails to be funny enough, perhaps out of timidity or pedanticism or squeamishness, or perhaps because (influenced not by what *Ulysses* is, but what it had come to seem in the hands of the academic critics) he wanted to write an Art Novel, a Great Book, instead of an Entertainment or a Travesty. At any rate, out of lack of nerve or excess of ambition, he turns S. Levin into a cuckolder rather than a cuckold, a successful lover of women rather than a beater of his own meat, a heroic defender of the Liberal Tradition, which is to say an insufferable prig like Stephen Dedalus rather than an unloved, loveable victim like Leopold Bloom.

The giveaway, the final offense against the original conception of the book, and its potentiality for becoming the first real Jewish anti-Western . . . is that there is neither anti-semitism nor an ironical defense against it to be found in its pages. And how can there be, if there are no real Jews, and for that matter, no real goyim either, which is to say, no mythological Westerners. There is not even an ultimately and dangerously appealing *shikse,* in a deadly sexual encounter with whom . . . the protagonist of the Jewish American Novel must test his manhood and his Jewishness. . . . Poor Pauline. She cannot ever really become the Deadly Stranger Woman, that Faye who always seems Greener on the other side but has to be satisfied with the role of the Loathly Lady—if big feet and no tits are enough to qualify her for even that mythological role.

After she speaks the magic word "Jewish," however, and it is only she who is permitted to say it, the action promises to turn around, the tone of the book to change from that of condescending satire (the sort of goyish satire endemic to all academic novels), which only puts down the other, to true Jewish irony, which is directed first of all against oneself and one's people, and, at its most intense, against one's God. It is the tone of the Book of Jonah, prototype of all Jewish humor, with its wry comment on the ambiguous meaning of being chosen, i.e., having no choice. When Pauline has finished explaining to Levin that she needed him, wanted him because, however he may have avoided that label, he *looked* Jewish, Levin responds dryly, "So I was chosen," and for the first time in many pages I am moved to laugh. (pp. 217-18)

Immediately thereafter, in any case, he gives himself a new name, or rather reclaims an old one, but this strange rebaptism is even more ambiguous. "God bless you, Lev," the woman he has chosen goes on to say in real or burlesque or merely trivialized benediction. And at that point, he chooses to disavow the name he has allowed her to call him unchallenged throughout, rejecting along with it the cryptic initial S., by which his author had designated him, and "Seymour" as well—that ridiculous pseudo-Anglo-Saxon appellation, which like Irving, stirs a snigger in polite anti-semites. Nor does he want any longer to be known as "Sy," an assimilationist nickname, as American as apple pie. "Sam, they used to call me at home," he says; and "God bless you, Sam," she responds in a kind of continuing litany.

The conjunction of "call me" and "Sam"—short, of course, for Samuel—seems too apt to be unplanned, evoking for me the image . . . of the first of the Hebrew Prophets, who when God called him by name, answered, "*Hineni,* here I am." *No,* I want to say, don't do it! It's too pat, too easy, too slick, somehow, too *Christian* a conversion. And then I tell myself, "Come on, Malamud knows what he's doing. If his hand is on his heart a little melodramatically, his tongue is firmly in his cheek, to take the curse off by undercutting the pretentiousness of the Biblical allusion." But I'm not sure, even though S. Levin does say "Sam" and not "Samuel," making it possible for us to recall, as we close the book, not the solemn passage in *Kings* but the jocularly anti-semitic song, "Sam, you made the pants too long." I certainly would prefer to take it this way, for such a reading makes *A New Life* in conclusion what it promised to be at the start, really Jewish and funny as hell. (pp. 218-19)

> *Leslie A. Fiedler, "Malamud's Travesty Western," in* Novel: A Forum on Fiction *(copyright © Novel Corp., 1977), Spring, 1977, pp. 212-19.*

*　　*　　*

MALRAUX, (Georges-) André　　1901-1976

Malraux was a French novelist, diplomat, philosopher, critic, and art historian. Avoiding strictly personal considerations in his writings, Malraux chose to deal with universal themes of the irrevocability of death, human suffering, isolation, dignity, and the search for absolutes. Best known in literary circles for his *Man's Fate* and *The Conquerors*, Malraux, an existentialist, saw violence as an unavoidable and elemental aspect of the human condition, for violence is action, human action, before a world that is both inane and solitary. (See also *CLC*, Vols. 1, 4, and *Contemporary Authors*, Vols. 21-24, rev. ed.; obituary, Vols. 69-72; *Contemporary Authors Permanent Series*, Vol. 2.)

The highest forms of art, argues Malraux [in his *Psychologie de l'art*], are precisely those which underscore the moments of crisis when man becomes acutely aware of his destiny. The universally tragic feeling of revolt is attributed to art as its most noble and ultimate function, both in Malraux's approach to art and art history and in his conception of character, structure, and imagery in relation to his novels. (p. 799)

[If] Malraux discovers in the highest artistic achievements of all ages the desire to justify and defend the self against the finality of death, it is largely in the wake of the collective protest of Romanticism that his attitude is most easily understood.... Romanticism expressed a profound distrust of all that the majority of men held dear: reason, justice, love and decency. Malraux exhibits a strong attachment to this spirit of Romanticism as we find it in Dostoievsky, Tolstoy and Nietzsche, especially the last, because they embody the Promethean challenge of the universal order of things.... The French writer's thinking contains the mark of a sustained reaction to the rational dissolution upon which the whole of Romanticism was founded, and it is this very reaction which, couched in artistic terms, has exercised such a profound effect on many of his fictional heroes.

Malraux measures the greatness of man by the dignity and courage that accompany his artistic efforts in reducing the universal chaos to some kind of human order which he can make meaningful. That Malraux attempts to make man's life meaningful through revolt demonstrates an obvious affinity with Camus who, in *Le Mythe de Sisyphe* and *L'Homme révolté*, rejects suicide in favour of revolt be-

cause the latter offers the only posture capable of investing man with some sort of coherence, however fragile. Thus, Malraux sees man as unaided by the gods, impelled by his own imperious will and giving permanency and meaning to his own being by imposing coherence on incoherence, form on formlessness, justice on a sense of betrayal. What attracts Malraux is less the mystery of life than man's recalcitrant attitude in face of that mystery.... The fundamental artistic impulse in man is not to create beauty or harmony, and least of all to stimulate pleasure in the onlooker or reader, however paradoxical this may appear, but rather to deny victory to the nothingness hovering menacingly over each existence.

The general framework of art conceived as a revolt against nothingness and as an *anti-destin* illuminates the different aspects of Malraux the revolutionary writer, the activist as well as the aesthete, the adventurer and politician as well as the novelist. The quest for the eternal in art, novel writing and political activity, merges into one and the same phenomenon, which explains the very special place he grants to the political revolutionary in his novels.... Malraux assumes a unique role as revolutionary thinker and novelist since he is unquestionably one of the first modern French writers to confer upon the novel the power of indictment against what he considers to be the meretricious values and behaviour of Western civilization, and put that indictment into practice. He illustrates as sharply as any writer the intimate relationship existing between art and politics, literary concern and a social conscience, and this relationship marks him off as a romantic thinker. (pp. 799-800)

Les Conquérants (1928) and *La Condition humaine* (1933) cannot be considered as novels of communist propaganda although they contain much material and fervent debate supporting Marxist ideology, but as novels of man viewed in his extreme condition, in the compulsive act that brings him as close as possible to the experience of death. Malraux expresses an adherence to the principle of communism but not to the order and discipline it implies; in other words, he declares himself against capitalism but not for communism. This is why Garine, the protagonist in *Les Conquérants*, although presented as the leader of the propaganda machine in the revolt of 1925 in Canton, is not in fact a communist at all. If anything, he is a fascist. He clings obstinately to his individualism, realizing himself in so far as he exercises constraint over others. His Nietzschean will to power eliminates all necessity for the transformation of society....

Political revolution appears to the early Malraux as the most acute and urgent form of expressing the need for constant movement, the restless regeneration of the self, the refusal to adhere to fixed opinions. In other words, freedom means nothing save the urge to achieve freedom which, once acquired, is transformed paradoxically into a static condition, while it is precisely at this point that Malraux sees the theme of revolt to be rooted in the Western tradition, as opposed to the Eastern vision of the world epitomized by Buddhism, for instance. In his *Psychologie de l'art*, he contrasts Eastern and Western civilizations in their Buddhist and Christian expressions, manifesting a predilection for the latter which he extols as a dynamic movement, characterized by the eternal awareness of the creative act and the will to power that promotes it. Western art, comments Malraux, is an art of active participation, affirmation of self in motion, in diametrical opposition to the passive, somnolent state of the Buddhist accepting his fate as decreed by the gods. . . . What seems contradictory in Malraux's Eastern quests is his search for a revolutionary spirit in a land that had never known it, and his abandonment of a civilization whose very essence is intimately associated with the ideal of perpetual movement, recreation and revolt. . . . (p. 801)

What invests Malraux's writings with such a thrilling resonance is that the man of action can gain access to the reality of action only by living the conquest of art, which explains why many of the dialogues in *L'Espoir*, for example, emerge from a background of gunfire, smoke and permanent threat of death. Political revolution constitutes an indispensable ingredient in the development of the novels with a regard to their characters and structure because it offers an immediate and compelling arena for the discussions that transcend it. The art of the novel is the means by which Malraux expresses himself against the injustice of existence, man's inhumanity to man and even political ideologies tending to diminish his grandeur. The art becomes all the greater as Malraux opposes danger in all its forms, and despite all the aggressiveness and violence of the novels, Malraux is really creating a defence against existence, instead of an affirmation of it. (p. 802)

Malraux exhibits less an adherence to communism than an aversion to fascism. . . . It was a curious quirk of fate that, once installed in de Gaulle's post-war government, Malraux found himself subject to accusations of fascism. It is arguable that his cult of the Nietzschean will to power, his ideal of the heroic adventurer detaching himself from the herd, and his doctrine of authority, brought him dangerously close to fascism. Yet, the concepts of France as a supreme cultural force and of the will to power in its aristocratic and artistic acceptation form part of what he calls a cultural democracy founded on art as an *anti-destin*. (pp. 802-03)

Les Conquérants, La Condition humaine and *L'Espoir* all terminate in failure, and so for that matter does *La Voie royale,* because in the final analysis, political revolution proves no more than a myth. T. E. Lawrence had demonstrated the same point before him. Armed revolution, even if successful, cannot deliver man from death, the supreme scourge, and there is certainly nothing permanent about it, which, by way of contrast, underlines the ultimate value of art that can confer upon man a sense of eternity. . . . Malraux did not write novels of communist propaganda any more than he could have written fiction in the service of the Gaullist cause. He wrote novels, prompted by the deep desire to create. He wanted above all to . . . give birth to an artistic reality capable of resisting the eternally present image of death. If all art constitutes a revolt against man's fate, Malraux incarnates his revolt in Perken (*La Voie royale*), Garine (*Les Conquérants*), Kyo (*La Condition humaine*) and Kassner (*Le Temps du mépris*), as well as in numerous figures in *L'Espoir,* in order to live through the creative act his rebellion against death. Damocles never felt existence so intensely as when he saw the sword above him hanging from a horse-hair, and likewise, Perken never affirms life more than when he approaches the abyss of death. The fascination with death which may be focussed most keenly by the thoughts and impressions of the revolutionary mirrors the hero's defiant attitude *vis-à-vis* the

cosmic forces arrayed against him. The mortal threat providing the texture for Malraux's novels stimulates the development of the highest and noblest qualities in man. . . . Man must choose the moment when he wishes to die and refuse fate the right to choose for him. . . . The hypnosis of death is transformed into the supreme test for the man of action who dies participating actively in his last moments because it is the noblest manner of defying the decrees of fate. (p. 803)

The concept of revolt assumes increasing dimensions with each of Malraux's novels. Thus, the gun-running adventurer Perken in *La Voie royale* pits his indomitable will against the challenge of death in the form of the Moï natives and the Cambodian jungle. Garine, while refusing to identify himself with the communist ideal [in *Les Conquérants*], at least allows himself to be caught up in a movement greater than himself, and which he cannot therefore control. [In *La Condition humaine*] Kyo and Katow associate themselves more fully with the Revolution, creating what has become one of Malraux's most exalted and dynamic themes—*la fraternité virile*. The movement from individual to collective revolt continues in *L'Espoir* until man is seen to resist not only the tyranny of his oppressor but also that of the huge, unsympathetic and impartial universe. This seems to explain why, for all its disjointedness, *L'Espoir* is, in many ways, a more successful novel than the preceding ones since it combines three distinct levels of revolt, the individual against death, the collective against human oppression (the Franquist invaders) and a broader collective resistance against the horror of the cosmic spaces. . . . René Girard comments upon *L'Espoir*'s cosmic style and panoramic vision which lift man from the daily and limited sense of the finality of death and from the political arena, to an implacable, eternal darkness which gives it its backcloth. The intensification of the theme of revolt is correspondingly reflected in man at three distinct technical levels. Firstly, the characters express explicitly their discontent in dialogue form. . . . Secondly, the characters appear joining battle with the enemy in a limited action. . . . Finally and most significantly, man in his capacity as pilot assumes the tragic combat with the unheeding universe as he rises up into the infinite spaces. . . . Although Malraux had used the infinity of space in *La Condition humaine* as a technique for heightening the feeling of the human struggle, the description of plane warfare in *L'Espoir* (the Spanish civil war was probably the first war to provide an arena for the plane as a constant means of combat) lends a new dramatic quality to the strife. Man's puny revolt in the face of the 'sérénité géologique' and the 'astres morts' becomes all the more admirable because it is situated for the first time in an actual infinity of space. (pp. 805-06)

[If] the keenest moments of revolt are translated by violence and action, the sharp, staccato movement of sentence, paragraph and chapter renders a sudden, recoiling mechanism, an unexpected impression of imminent danger and the unpremeditated urge to combat that danger. Malraux's vivid, elliptical style, written in the same jolting vein as Hemingway's, and for similar reasons, plunges the reader into a vital, forward movement. . . . The strong passion for the abrupt, often half-finished and self-contained sentence informs the general construction of Malraux's novels. . . . [His] scene construction . . . is really composed of a series of isolated images, unlinked by a proper, transitional sentence or sentences. The elliptical nature of Malraux's sentence and scene construction suggests a naked confrontation between man and an inimical universe, while it is precisely this constant jabbing effect that lays emphasis on man's recalcitrance. Malraux's refusal to conform to a world order, whether it be based on God, nature or reason, emerges from his sentence and scene construction which aims not at Flaubertian beauty, harmony and equilibrium, but at the very opposite, that is disjointedness and the magnification of the act of rebellion.

Although the style of *Les Noyers de l'Altenburg* differs considerably from that of the preceding novels, the theme of revolt still remains as the central preoccupation. The stress is transferred in the last of Malraux's novels, less successful on account of its excessively intellectual and discursive content, from the spatial dimension of the universe to the historical and artistic development of man. Set in the context of passing time reflected in the three Berger generations, that is, the narrator, his father Vincent Berger and his grandfather, *Les Noyers de l'Altenburg* is organized around a group of eminent intellectuals invited to a colloquy to discuss . . . [whether there exists] a permanent characteristic in man, despite the varying opinions, the changing civilizations and the fatality of death? The only answer that appears to crystallize in the complex discussion is that the one irreducible and invariable feature in man is not that he protests at his sensitive and vulnerable position in a universe of disorder, but that he has been able to transmit to succeeding generations from the most remote past an artistic expression of resistance to the fatality of time and death, and that this resistance has assumed a definite and permanent shape in the Western tradition. Vincent Berger underlines the centrality of the Christian presence in the Western tradition because it highlights the essential suffering of man in terms of original sin and man's refusal to conform to that suffering. Christianity's most important function, 'c'est d'avoir installé la fatalité dans l'homme' . . . , and it is the sense of the fatality of sin in the individual life which elicits the rebelliousness in man's nature. One of the greatest factors in the history of Western art is that man has continually refused to acknowledge the implications of original sin, namely that he must needs depend on a Creator to absolve him and that the rejection of God's presence in the individual's life constitutes sin. The artist is a direct descendant of what Camus in his *L'Homme révolté* calls 'Les Fils de Caïn', endeavouring to deny God his supreme privilege as Creator, attempting by the very creative act to supplant God Himself. . . . Malraux's attribution of the Promethean motive to artistic creation accounts for what many critics agree to be one of the finest of the novelist's images, that of Nietzsche who, following the onset of madness in Turin, is brought back by train to Basle by Franz Overbeck, his real life friend, and Walter Berger who relates the episode. Passing through the darkness of . . . [a] tunnel, Nietzsche starts singing his poem *Venice* the words of which rise invincibly above the clatter of the train. For all the mediocrity of his singing, Nietzsche's song is 'sublime', capturing the very essence of artistic life and feeling, translating the dignity and rebellion of the overman who assumes a dimension all the greater because he finds no final answer to the prison of life symbolized by the blackness of the tunnel. Nietzsche reacts in exactly the same way as Cervantes, Daniel Defoe and Dostoievsky who all experienced the more frightening aspects of prison life. Appropriately, Malraux does not interpret *Don Quixote, Robinson Crusoe*

and *The Idiot* as mere transpositions of prison life but much more as a refusal in art form to bow before man's humiliation and shame. It is because the three novels in question were written by authors having undergone the extreme suffering of prison life that they are the very novels Walter Berger's friend would have selected to help him resist the prison atmosphere. . . . Significantly, the New Testament is rejected as a companion for prison life, no doubt because, emphasizing the virtues of love and humility, it does not inspire the creative impulse and the heroic desire to conquer the world. . . . Malraux's movement of revolt is deprived of an ultimate ethical meaning, despite his apparent concern, in the 1920s and 1930s, for the disinherited and the persecuted. . . . It is at this point that the essential difference becomes clear between Malraux and Camus (a figure who inevitably comes to mind in any consideration of revolt in a contemporary French context), for the latter, in his role as moralist, seeks what unites men. . . . In contrast, Malraux singles out what is unique in man, what marks off the achievements of a particular individual from the rest, and these achievements are always interpreted by him as the artistic expression of the most dignified part in man, his radical dissent when faced with his ultimate fate of death. Malraux's urge to revolt appears to discard the needs of the common herd, rooted in a kind of romantic titanism where the will to create is all and otherness becomes nothing. The writer's conception of the artist, which is equally valid in any interpretation of the novels . . . , presents the individual creating, by dint of sheer will-power, an artistic form capable of resisting the passing of time. Man assumes art as his final defence in an implacable universe, investing it with a Nietzschean, warrior-like quality causing him to scorn the ethical passion. This bellicose element in Malraux's art philosophy finds its most fitting context in the background of war and revolution, filling the novels with frenzied action and violence. The fundamental instinct of action which is revealed as man's privileged method of smothering temporarily his metaphysical problems and the only reality able to impart meaning to life, indicates the astonishing discovery of the Greeks who were the first people to ascribe to art the concepts of movement and conquest. Claude's archaeological quest in *La Voie royale*, the frantic demoniacal urge of Tchen in *La Condition humaine*, the Altenburg colloquy, together with Malraux's books on art philosophy, all point to the questioning of the significance of the world which, when exposed as hostile and even inhuman, elicits from man the sole authentic attitude, that of revolt which confers upon him his fundamental glory as creator—for Nietzsche and Malraux the highest form of man in the present era. (pp. 806-09)

R. Batchelor, "André Malraux and the Concept of Revolt," in The Modern Language Review *(© Modern Humanities Research Association 1972), October, 1972, pp. 799-809.*

Following the Second World War, when André Malraux turned from novels to aesthetics and politics, he often had occasion to speak of History, with a capital "H." Although he has not always been absolutely consistent in his vocabulary, for him History seems to be rather closely linked to the Destiny or Fate against which men gain their fullest measure of dignity by rebellion. However, in the period before 1939—when he was known primarily as a brilliant young novelist—it was history with a small "h" which was most central to his concerns. This preoccupation became evident with the 1928 publication of his first serious work, *Les Conquérants,* based on certain contemporary incidents in China; it reached a climax nine years later in what many critics consider to be his masterpiece, *L'Espoir,* centering on the early months of the Spanish Civil War. (p. 345)

[When *Les Conquérants* appeared] some critics immediately protested that Malraux's novel was not so much a work of creative fiction as it was a "rapportage," a direct presentation of certain individuals and events that the author had come to know first-hand during his 1924-25 stay in Asia. Other commentators went to the opposite extreme, loudly denouncing the book as a gross falsification in which the real facts of history had been altered or tailored to suit Leftist propaganda needs. The degree to which the author was actually a creative artist serving an aesthetic and ethical purpose (while using historical events as the materials for his creation) was obviously central to the discussion. During the next decade this whole question grew even more important—and more hotly debated—as Malraux produced a number of other novels that were closely linked to contemporary happenings. (pp. 345-46)

[Speaking of *Les Conquérants,* Malraux] denied that he had falsified history, and he emphasized the basic authenticity and accuracy of his novel. . . . [Admittedly], Garine was not a real person but a literary creation in the best sense of the term: an amalgamation of a number of actual and imagined personalities. As a hero, he epitomized the spirit of one type of revolutionary leader involved in the rebellion in China.

Most important of all, Malraux's comments about *Les Conquérants* clearly indicate that he had used the historical real in his novel not only for aesthetic and political reasons. For him, no work except one closely linked to history could be so meaningful to modern readers on an *ethical* level. (p. 346)

[This] whole matter was increasingly complicated by the fact that Malraux himself came to play a larger and larger role in certain contemporary historical events. Indeed the facts of history, together with the legends of his personal biography, often became so closely linked to his literary creations that it became almost impossible to study the relationship between art and reality in his works. This is particularly true in the case of *L'Espoir,* his most overtly historical novel. (p. 347)

Malraux has always incorporated a great deal of real history and personal experience into his literary works. But he is first and foremost a literary artist whose creative imagination always modifies or transforms the real into the components of a work of art. Thus, [an] actual incident [, that] of the Olmedo farmer, undergoes a number of changes before it finally emerges as a central element in his novel, *L'Espoir.* (p. 351)

There is no extraneous or peripheral material in [his 1937 *Literary Digest*] account of the Olmedo raid, not even information about the flight to the target area or comments about weather conditions encountered en route, nor does it contain any lyric or personal elements. The narrative is a strictly factual presentation of the destruction of an important military target. In tone and content it is probably very close to the official report of the mission which Malraux—as observer on the original Olmedo sortie and the com-

mander of the Escadrille—must have turned in to his superiors at the War Ministry in Madrid. Certainly the text offers no hint of the literary use that he would subsequently make of the incident. (pp. 353-54)

[In a later *Collier's* version, a] change in the role of the farmer and in the importance of the bombing raid to the Republican cause suggests that Malraux was now beginning to see events like the Olmedo sortie not as isolated incidents, but as part of a bigger whole—the unity of all those who were fighting against Franco and what he represented. As yet, however, this broader dimension of the text appears only briefly.

The *Collier's* version is also noteworthy for the new tone which is evident in much of the narrative, a tone which might best be characterized as Romantic. The purely factual—almost journalistic—earlier *Digest* account here takes on lyric color when Malraux depicts certain high points of the mission, as—for example—in the long passage cited above describing the flight over the clouds. This kind of writing—like certain parts of *La Voie royale* and the account of the 1934 Saba flight—reminds us that Malraux has always been someone for whom experience (particularly exciting experience) is attractive in large part because it gives rise to powerful new sensations. Indeed, many of the major experiences of his life doubtless presented themselves to him initially in strongly emotional terms, whose "higher" meaning was not perceived or sought until later. In his sense, one may consider the *Collier's* text as kind of lyric version or transformation of the real Olmedo raid. The Romantic "I" of the narrator is central, and the flight is experienced in large part as a vivid personal adventure. Malraux has not yet placed it within the framework of a larger whole, nor given it the philosophical resonance that characterizes his mature novels. (pp. 358-59)

The incident of the Olmedo farmer in its final literary form appears in the first half of the third chapter of the concluding portion of [*L'Espoir*], a section originally entitled "Les Paysans," but subsequently modified to "L'Espoir." (p. 359)

Most of the minor alterations that Malraux makes in this final adaptation of the Olmedo incident are essentially stylistic in character. . . . However there are several major changes that deserve closer examination. The first of these is purely factual. . . . Just why did Malraux wish to make the Olmedo raid a part of [a later campaign, by changing its date and location]? The reason seems clear. The original event had taken place very early in the war. The exaggerated accounts in the Spanish press cannot hide the fact that it was really just one more minor skirmish in the unsuccessful Republican attempt to stop Franco's advance toward Madrid. However, by the spring of the following year (when Malraux was actually writing his novel), the celebrated Loyalist victories . . . seemed to indicate that at last the tide had really begun to turn against the Fascists. Now the Republicans could reasonably begin to hope that they would eventually win the civil war. By re-dating the Olmedo event Malraux is able to use it to help generate the feeling of optimism he wanted for the final section of his novel. (pp. 363-64)

To center attention on the actual destruction of the field, Malraux trims his text to eliminate a good deal of the peripheral or descriptive material found in the previous *Col-*

lier's version. His pruning is most evident in the section dealing with the flight over the mountains, where several pages are reduced to little more than a paragraph.

In focusing his text in this way, Malraux also gives it a somewhat different tone from the version which had appeared in the American magazine. This change is in keeping with the new meaning he sees in the incident. By removing many of the passages of description and personal reflection, he no longer presents the raid as a kind of lyric personal adventure, but rather as a major military mission. Here again this is particularly evident in the revision of the text describing the flight over the mountains. But while almost nothing of the previous lyricism of the passage remains, the philosophical overtones of the experience—only barely suggested before—now are emphasized. Malraux wishes to point up the sense of human solidarity—the unselfish fraternal commitment to a higher common cause—which the mission represents.

Indeed, it is to emphasize this fundamental message of the novel—and to prepare its most striking formulation: the scene of the descent from the mountain—that Malraux makes a final and highly significant alteration in the original Olmedo material. He changes the basic plan of the mission so that it will require a pre-dawn takeoff. This, in turn, necessitates finding some way to light the airfield for the pilots. A major proportion of *L'Espoir* centers about certain individuals, each of whom in some way represents one of the various factions supporting the Republic. But Malraux evidently felt that he had not adequately presented the largest group of those who were involved in the struggle—the vast laboring masses of rural Spain, the farmers upon whom the burden of war fell most heavily. He admired the quiet courage and steadfastness with which these long-suffering individuals faced their harsh destiny, and he decided that they would figure in the climax of his novel in a direct and dramatic way. Magnin's search for vehicles with headlights to illuminate the field provides just such an opportunity.

As Magnin returns to his base to prepare the takeoff of the mission. he passes through a village he had visited several hours earlier. In the central square he sees some men ... who carry huge sacks into a building evidently being used as a warehouse. It is a group of volunteers unloading a shipment of food. When Magnin asks why such heavy loads must be carried on men's backs, he is told that no other transportation is available.... He is very moved by this show of solidarity [because all vehicles had been sent to help light the Republican airfield.] ... Thus the addition of this incident to the original Olmedo material enables Malraux to portray the Escadrille and its flyers as the delegates "de toute la paysannerie d'Espagne." When one of the planes crashes on the return from this mission, it is particularly fitting that it be these same farmers who shelter and protect the wounded pilots; it is also they who bear them in a long cortege down the mountain, expressing their respect, affection and gratitude with the simple gesture of a silent salute. Most critics agree that Malraux's belief in the brotherhood of suffering mankind has had no finer literary expression than in this climatic scene near the end of *L'Espoir.*

Art is often defined as a transformation of the real. Malraux is a man who has had many exciting and unusual experiences in his life, but as an artist he always transforms and adapts them to fit into the larger whole of an aesthetic creation. For him, as for all artists, the *real* is less important than the truth that underlies reality.... Malraux's book makes it very clear that he himself had transformed his experience as a squadron commander in Spain not only into a work of art, but into a "conscience," a fuller awareness of the dimensions of the human condition. The successive changes he made in the single incident of the mission to Olmedo faithfully mirror such a higher ordering and confirm once again his lifelong commitment to certain humane values. (pp. 364-66)

> *Walter Langlois, "The Novelist Malraux and History," in* L'Esprit Créateur *(copyright © 1975 by* L'Esprit Créateur*), Fall, 1975, pp. 345-66.*

Malraux throughout his life has mixed truth with untruth the way painters mix oil colors with turpentine. And when dealing with ideas of an exalted, all-circumscribing sort, he may well often remind us of an automobile which has sixteen cylinders and no steering wheel....

What we are dealing with in this peculiar case is the lie as a source of vital energy: as an indispensable part, in other words, of the persona that drives a writer to write....

Malraux is not in the class of Stendhal as a novelist, and we may doubt that he was in the class of Chateaubriand when it came to diplomatic realities; but the claims which he makes for himself are in many cases so dotty as hardly to call for rebuttal. Pending a final judgment on the career which they seem to have helped to make possible, we can most profitably regard them as a kind of pneumatic make-believe with which Malraux has felt the need to support himself. (It would also, by the way, be a mistake to assume that because some of his claims are untrue all of his claims are untrue. No man who gets the Croix de Guerre four times over, between 1944 and 1946, can be altogether a fraud.)

The matter of Malraux's Great Thoughts is likewise one on which judgment can be passed too hastily. One problem is that Malraux is a lifelong allusionist....

We may even suspect that the allusionism is a device for never staying long enough in any one place to be able to tell sense from nonsense. It may or may not be true, as Malraux said already in 1922, that "we shall understand more about the Greek genius by comparing a Greek statue with an Egyptian or an Asiatic statue than by getting to know any number of other Greek statues." What is true beyond a doubt is that this belief absolves us from the discipline that is required if we want to discuss one Greek statue in relation to another Greek statue. This nonchalant aerial purview has got Malraux in trouble with art historians. "There is no evidence," E. H. Gombrich wrote in 1954, "that Malraux has done a day's consecutive reading in a library or that he has even tried to hunt up a new fact."

But when that has been said it remains true that along with much that is gaseous and impenetrable in Malraux's writings on art, as on everything else, there are surprising observations that come not from "a day's consecutive reading in a library" but from the first-hand experience of one of the oddest men of this century. Malraux writes like a man who wants to write what he once called "the first complete history of mankind" and believes from time to time that he almost has it within his grasp. Whence the giddy, all-risking character of the adventure which he proposes to us, and the difficulty—and, in some cases, the resentment and the exasperation—with which we debrief ourselves at the end of it. (p. 10)

[Malraux] is, as he has often said, someone who "married France" or "had a contract with France." On the other hand, he knows that the world is growing up—not without all the difficulties which that phrase implies—and he takes a long view of the incidental adjustments which have to be made. . . . There is nothing narrow about his allegiances, and in the end it may well be the notion of "one world, one civilization" which is closest to him. But he is also a shrewd observer of the world as it actually is. "For all your talk of negritude," he said to Senghor, "it is for Senegal that you live. The notion of nationhood was born here, now, and today. Nietzsche has got the better of Marx."

Malraux did nothing for the theater when he was minister of culture, but in his own writings he is a great stage director. *Hôtes de Passage* includes one of his finest short historical romances: the story of how he looked into the suggestion that a piece of textile which had been offered to the Louvre was stained with the blood of Alexander the Great. The narrative skill, the heightened sense of the past, the headlong commitment to what might have been—all these may make us regret that Malraux has for so much of the last thirty years been more a public figure than a writer.

This feeling will be enhanced if we turn to *Lazare*, a book prompted in the first place by a disagreeable few days in the Salpetrière hospital. . . . [In] the first part of the book he represents a famous but now almost irrecoverable episode from *Les Noyers de l'Altenburg*, the novel or part of a novel which he wrote during World War II and published in Switzerland in 1943. (p. 13)

Malraux was one of the first consequential writers to be influenced by the cinema. In *Lazare* there is an image of a runaway horse that is as vivid in its way as the image of the dead white horse which slides down the bridge in *October*. Malraux uses the quick cut, the close-up, the long shot, the slow pan much as Pudovkin and Eisenstein used them in the films that he saw in his early twenties. But the long passage has also a moral power which can be called "Tolstoyan" without exaggeration; Malraux convinces us that this was the moment at which something went irreversibly wrong with mankind. . . .

Reading *Hôtes de Passage*, we . . . find something obnoxious in the insouciance with which in May 1968 Malraux goes on talking of old times in Spain with a fellow-survivor of the period while civil servants come in and out with bulletins of the fighting in the streets. "Four Hundred and Fifty Wounded," one message reads. "Nobody killed yet. Rather interesting, isn't it?" and the two old gentlemen go on with their chat. It is as if Malraux for ten years had been so dazzled by the lights around his lectern that he never once looked at the actual French men and women who turned out to hear him. . . .

For Malraux, certain beliefs are indispensable to a full human life. If those beliefs are not defined, they cannot be acted upon and will die. The difficulty with this particular belief is that it has been so often perverted. . . . But that is no reason to discard it. Fraternity of the kind that Malraux had in mind finds an unmatched beauty of expression in

Verdi's operas, for instance. When tenor and baritone are united we sense immediately that something of incalculable importance is being set before us by a man whose basic instincts are entirely good. Fraternity as it has been systematized in our century is almost always a curse: so much so that we shrink from the word. But there are concepts which should be formulated against all the odds, and this is one of them.

Malraux has never been odder, more eloquent, more completely himself, than in [his] late works. Anyone who has ever managed to get beyond the first pages of *The Psychology of Art* will treasure, for instance, the long passage in *Tête d'obsidienne* in which Malraux discusses the concept of the "museum without walls" with Picasso. Malraux had not yet gone into print on the subject, but Picasso knew that what he had in mind was "not a Museum of Preferences, but a museum in which the works of art choose us more than we choose them." No one could have been more sensitive to that idea than Picasso. (p. 14)

> *John Russell, in* The New York Review of Books *(reprinted with permission from* The New York Review of Books; *copyright* © *1976 NYREV, Inc.), March 4, 1976.*

As he observes in "Picasso's Mask," a pompous yet deeply informative tribute to the genius of modern art: "I was twenty-two when I met Braque, and sixty-two when I transformed the colonnade of the Louvre into two wings for the vigil of his funeral service." . . . Although Malraux's great period of art appreciation did not begin till around 1938—after such political novels as "Man's Fate" and "Man's Hope" and his combat against fascism in the Spanish Civil War—his attempt since then to formulate a grand and aggressive apologia for modernism never ceased.

"Picasso's Mask" continues an epic venture that has made pictures and statues from all over the world speak with each other and to us. Malraux's animating force is remarkable; and this time it is the turn of Negro art to be given its voice. Malraux's secret is that he does not try to fix the exact or historical meaning of works that may be, in any case, "beyond history," but views them instead through the paintings of artists who have been influenced by them and so helped them to survive. The present book reconstructs Picasso's discovery and appropriation of the tribal arts after seeing African masks at the old Trocadéro museum early in the century.

"Picasso's Mask" is also, however, a meditation on a skull. Haunted by the analogy between primitive art and the "austere style" of painting after Cézanne, Malraux recalls a death's-head of black quartz in Mexico City's National Museum. This "obsidian head" is encased in a glass shrine backed by a mirror, so that those who look at it see their reflection and death's image together. As if it were a Black Virgin, Malraux surrounds this pre-Columbian fetish with votive memories of his visit to the private collection Picasso bequeathed to France, and with an elaborate account of the sumptuous Fondation Maeght show on "Malraux and the Museum Without Walls" in 1973, the year of Picasso's death. (pp. 25-6)

In the most original pages of this book, Malraux returns to the subject of oriental art and wonders if our present style of painting can absorb the impact of such Japanese masterpieces as Takanobu's portrait of the statesman Shigemori (ca. 1200).

For Malraux what matters is not the esthetic or the beautiful, but the distortions of an art rising from death like fetishes or ruined statues—an art surrounded by the dark halo of an unknown function we somewhat helplessly define as "sacred" or "demonic." His own prose, paradoxically, is not at all austere, but baroque, time-obsessed and aswim with strange names and places. Yet it may survive its thesis, which is now a commonplace. The modern movement, Malraux insists, produced in conjunction with photography a new way of understanding the art of the past. Picasso's changeable style expressed a capacity for metamorphosis which has now overtaken all originally divine or cultic objects. It has transformed gods into museum pieces, and by resurrecting *as art* all those primitive sacred images, it has created a new, world-wide and humanistic culture. (p. 26)

Joseph Conrad's ["Heart of Darkness"] was an actual influence on Malraux; but I allude to it here because it helps to raise a question about his achievement. This conspicuous redemption and reappropriation of art is, as we scan Malraux's opulent books, shadowed by a doubt. May not his idealistic view of the *fraternity* of primitive and modern prove merely that the modern works are fetishes too? Not only in the sense that Picasso expressed when he said that the African masks were "intercessors" against unknown or threatening spirits, and that his "Demoiselles d'Avignon" was—likewise—an "exorcism-painting." But also in the sense that they are commodities, whose value resides in our wish to own them as investments or display them for that purpose. (p. 27)

One honors Malraux's missionary fervor on behalf of magic masks, nail-studded fetishes and fertility objects, but one cannot overlook the fact that the esthetic revolution he celebrates is also a revolution in an art market that has become more sanctimonious and profitable than the ivory trade. (p. 28)

> *Geoffrey H. Hartman, in* The New York Times Book Review *(© 1976 by The New York Times Company; reprinted by permission), December 12, 1976.*

Most writers, and indeed probably all of us, would like to know what happens beyond that bourn from which no traveler returns—provided, of course, we could in fact return to tell our traveler's tale. This desire was exceptionally strong in André Malraux, who was death-obsessed all his life and never ceased referring to our mortality in his novels, his art criticism and his autobiographical writings. If any "hack of academe" cares to do a comparative word-count of the use of *mourir* and *la mort* in Malraux's works, he or she can be confident of discovering that the late Gaullist Minister for Culture holds some sort of record. I can think of no other writer who so constantly tried to measure life against death, or who has written so vividly about killing and dying.

Without being heartless we can say, then, that he was no doubt quite lucky, in 1973, to experience a dress-rehearsal for his own extinction three years before he actually died at the age of 75. He became afflicted with a disturbance of the cerebellum accompanied by a high temperature; rushed to the hospital, he lay there suspended for a time between this world and the problematical next. We are to understand that, like the inveterate writer he was, he had taken his notebook with him and had made jottings which were later worked up into "Lazarus." According to the Gospel of St.

John, the original Lazarus said nothing when he emerged from the tomb; and all the painters who have dealt with the scene show him as being bloodless and ghostlike. What is so striking about Malraux's Lazarus is the volubility and the full-blooded intellectual glee with which he recounts his experience. Nearer my death to thee and the more urgently lyrical I become. . . . (p. 12)

The book may, at first sight, seem rather incoherent, because it supposes a knowledge of Malraux's past and an acceptance of his usual literary procedure. When illness interrupted him, he was busy on his memoirs, "Le Miroir des Limbes" (The Mirror of Limbo), of which "Lazare" now forms the final section in the Pléiade edition of his works. These memoirs are unique in that they make no attempt to distinguish between the original "facts" of his life as they may have existed and their fictional representation in the works. It is almost as if Malraux had forgotten what he had lived through in reality as distinct from what he had experienced imaginatively in writing his novels; or as if on principle he refused to see any dividing line between the real and the imaginary. He therefore works chunks of his novels into his memoirs, with the hero or heroes acting as projections of himself; or again, he writes up certain episodes of his life—for instance, his discussions with de Gaulle at Colombey-Les-Deux-Eglises—as half-fictional purple-prose passages of significant exchange. At any moment, too, he may make sudden cross-references to some part of the mythic pattern of his career: his adventures in Indochina or the Spanish Civil War; his search for the lost city of the Queen of Sheba; his Resistance experiences and his arrest by the Gestapo; his conversations with Nehru, Mao, Trotsky, et al. He sees himself unashamedly as a great man, and he operates instinctively on the level of the sublime, like the two Romantic predecessors he most obviously resembles, Chateaubriand and Victor Hugo.

This explains why one quarter of "Lazarus" has nothing to do with his stay at the Saltpêtrière hospital, but is a long extract, with some minor modifications, from Malraux's last novel, "Les Noyers de l'Altenburg." . . .

The logical relationship between [an episode from "Les Noyers d'Altenberg" depicting the first German gas attack on the Russian lines during World War I] and Malraux's own predicament in facing death from natural causes is not clear to me, and perhaps it is not meant to exist. On general principle, I think it is a mistake for Malraux to reintroduce sections from his novels into his memoirs; they gain nothing through being removed from their original contexts. The more relevant part of "Lazarus" is a long debate with the doctor who is looking after him, a debate that may have some foundation in fact, but also has all the signs of being an exemplary "imaginary conversation," reminiscent of Malraux's encounters with de Gaulle.

It must be confessed, however, that in spite of the lofty, excited tone in which Malraux writes, nothing that he or the doctor says on the subject takes us much further than Pascal's acute sense of the mystery of life and death, or of the Absurd which that philosopher experienced before making his leap into faith. In other words, "Lazarus" as a title is slightly meretricious, slightly mythic, in keeping with Malraux's usual penchant for self-dramatization. He has not really gone over the edge into death and come back again; he has stayed on the hither side of extinction, and what he has to tell us we may already have read elsewhere, or even experienced for ourselves in less extreme circumstances. All of us, in moments of illness or on waking in the small hours, may have felt that pure sense of being, "I-without-the-ego," which he defines as the threshold of death. All of us at some time may have reflected that, even if man were immortal, life would not be more comprehensible, so long as "God" did not let us into the secret of why we are here at all. Malraux poses the fundamental question again and again, and gives it a vast, universal human resonance to make up for the absence of any divine reply. (pp. 12-13, 36)

John Weightman, "No News from Beyond," in The New York Times Book Review *(© 1977 by the New York Times Company; reprinted by permission), September 18, 1977, pp. 12-13, 36.*

*   *   *

MAMET, David   1948-

Mamet is an American playwright. His plays reflect a wry sense of humor and their dramatic language, often obscene, reveals the loneliness and fear he finds in our culture.

If the style of "Sexual Perversity" derives from Beckett and Pinter, its content connects it with the satiric tradition of the Second City, Nichols and May, and early Feiffer. . . . In a series of beautifully spare and controlled—and funny—short scenes, Mr. Mamet addresses himself to a question that was also of interest to his satiric predecessors: what do young (and youngish) middle-class urban single Americans do about sex? Mr. Mamet's answer is that mostly they talk about it, because each sex is scared out of its mind by the other. In Chicago, he suggests, by far the most common sexual perversity is fear. And Chicago is clearly not alone in this respect. Mr. Mamet knows that all the mouthwash in the world will not take the worry out of being close. . . .

Mr. Mamet doesn't know as much about how women are afraid of men, as he does about how men are afraid of women. Bernie is his triumph: a leisure-suited swinger . . . who regards all women with avid crudity as sexual material to be discussed, evaluated, fantasized about—from a safe distance. Mr. Mamet's stylistic virtuosity is not just a matter of snappy patterns; inside Bernie's rhetoric of lubricious appreciation, he shows us this man's terrible rage at female sexuality, that mysterious force that is so much more than he can deal with. Bernie's macho attitudinizing is a mask, made transparent for us by the playwright's art, for horrified repugnance.

The point about Bernie is not, I think, that he is a "latent homosexual" (whatever that means), but that—like Joan—he is scared, scared, scared. Bernie is not such a freak—his name is legion in every singles bar in the country—and elsewhere. . . .

Some people have been offended by the misogyny and sexism in "Sexual Perversity," but it seems to me highly insensitive—or, in another sense, highly oversensitive—to take Bernie's fantastic crudities as the play's statement. On the contrary, this is a compassionate, rueful comedy about how difficult it is . . . for men to give themselves to women, and for women to give themselves to men. It suggests that the only thing we have to fear, sexually, is fear itself—our own, and other people's—but fear itself is plenty.

Julius Novick, "The Real Perversity Is Fear," in The Village Voice *(reprinted by permission of* The Village Voice; *copyright © by The Village Voice, Inc., 1976), August 16, 1976, p. 95.*

Mamet is someone to watch. More specifically, Mamet is someone to listen to. He's that rare bird, an American playwright who's a language playwright. In the country of incessant obbligatos accompanying all activity—music in offices and elevators, tapes in cars, radios in restaurants—Mamet has heard the ultimate Muzak, the dissonant din of people yammering at one another and not connecting. He is a cosmic eavesdropper who's caught the American aphasia.

Not that he's the proverbial tape recorder, picking up speech like lint. Mamet is an abstract artist; his characters speak in a kind of verbal cubism, they address one another with the forked tongues of paranoia, insecurity, hostility, desperation. "American Buffalo" . . . has three lumpencrooks . . . in a junk shop plotting to rip off a coin collection. They are brutes who need each other, but their words are like punches that almost casually build to real violence. "Sexual Perversity" is like a sleazy sonata of seduction involving two couples. These plays are relentlessly profane; Mamet is the first playwright to create a formal and moral shape out of the undeleted expletives of our foulmouthed time.

"A Life in the Theatre" is the most accessible and engaging of these plays. It deals with two actors, [Robert and John]. . . . [We] see these dim thespians playing snippets from hilariously bad plays, changing their costumes, putting on their makeup, until the banal plays and the banal life become interchangeable. In one play Robert is a revolutionary, waving a flag and shouting inanely: "The people cry for truth, the people cry for freedom from the vicious lies and slanders of the age . . ." During the next scene at the make-up table, Robert mulls over greasepaint: "What is it? . . . texture, smell, color . . . Meaningless component parts (though one could likely say the same for anything) . . . But mix and package it, affix a label . . ." John: "Would you please shut up?" This touching, pointedly ironic little play says a lot about the relationship between reality and theatre. . . .

Mamet's ear is tuned to an American frequency, transmitting the calls for help, at once funny and frightening, which much of our speech barely disguises behind its bravado.

Jack Kroll, "The Muzak Man," in Newsweek *(copyright 1977 by Newsweek, Inc.; all rights reserved; reprinted by permission), February 28, 1977, p. 79.*

I was in an especially optimistic frame of mind as I made my way, one evening last week, to the première . . . of David Mamet's new play, "American Buffalo." I had been delighted by Mr. Mamet's earlier work, "Sexual Perversity in Chicago." . . . Here, thought I, is a young man . . . fresh from the fabled Second City and bringing to us its authentic voice of coarsely uttered hope and satiric protest. I assumed that once Mr. Mamet had mastered the art of making his skits accumulate into a true play, we would be in for an exceptional treat. . . .

Alas, "American Buffalo" is so far from being a treat that my disappointment may have led me to dislike it more than it deserves. . . . It is a curiously offensive piece of writing, less because of the language of which it is composed—every third word is either scatological or obscene: street language attempting in vain to perform the office of eloquence . . .—than because it is presumptuous. The playwright, having dared to ask for our attention, provides only the most meagre crumbs of nourishment for our minds. Three characters of low intelligence and alley-cat morals exchange tiresome small talk for a couple of hours, and the play stumbles to a halt in a monosyllabic colloquy intended to convey the message that life, rotten as it is, is all we have. Well, yes; no news there. And no news even on the level of information, for the characters onstage appear to know no more about their squalid means of survival—burglary, cheating at cards, and the like—than we in the audience have long since learned from reading the papers and watching TV. (p. 54)

> *Brendan Gill, in* The New Yorker *(© 1977 by the New Yorker Magazine, Inc.), February 28, 1977.*

David Mamet is apparently listening to America's lower class. The news he brings back in his new play, *American Buffalo* . . . , is that Americans living on the dark underside of small business and petty crookery speak of macho frustrations almost entirely in four-letter words. . . .

Mamet is imitating a hundred Bogart, Cagney, Robinson, and Brando movies, and he's not bad at the job. His dialogue has some of the vivacity missing from those movies. They were better at plot, however. . . .

Mamet has seen too many lowbrow movies. With friends like [him] words don't need enemies. (p. 37)

> *Gordon Rogoff, in* Saturday Review *(© 1977 by Saturday Review Magazine Corp.; reprinted with permission), April 2, 1977.*

*   *   *

MATTHIAS, John   1941-

Matthias is an American poet, critic, and editor. With the publication of his second collection of poetry, *Turns*, Matthias was heralded by many critics as the next of our poets to reach major status. (See also *Contemporary Authors*, Vols. 33-36, rev. ed.)

Matthias can be cryptic, mannered, sometimes exasperating, footling or just flat, occasionally incomprehensible; but if he is prone to abuse his talent, the talent itself is finally an impressive one. It is not his ostensible themes that present difficulty. Ranging from friends and family, through American politics, and attempts to relate himself to an English cultural heritage, to a searching engagement with abstruse questions of aesthetics, metaphysics, historical consciousness, Matthias's subject-matter shows an admirably enterprising range and seriousness. One problem for the reader is, however, that it is when he is at his most accessible that Matthias tends to be wooden and perfunctory: in his 'protest' poems, or some rather rambling epistles to friends. . . . (p. 55)

Not that Matthias can't be deft and pointed. 'A Painter' is a delightful and telling evocation. . . .

[While] retaining an air of knowing what he is up to, Matthias is often much more cryptic, elliptical, extravagantly mannered in form and idiom. The results can be silly, as in 'New York Power Crisis':

Do not use electric lights
Do not use electric chairs

   Demand is over 7,000,000 kilowatts

The new conductor broke his long baton
The hopeless tenor coughed up blood in his beard

That's the poem, folks. But Matthias is not only a poet very conscious of literature and culture in the sense that his poems bristle with names, references, allusions to the notable dead; he is obsessed with the textures, resonances, historical evolution and associations of words. . . . What's certainly true is that Matthias's fascination with language and the historical stimulates him to exceptionally daring enterprises involving technical experimentation and ventures into arcane reaches of aesthetic and other conceptual thinking, which can prove as fruitful, and in a strikingly original way, as they may at first seem extravagant. What are we to make of this opening to his long title-poem, 'Turns: Towards a Provisional Aesthetic and a Discipline'?—

The scolemayster levande was the toun
and sary of hit semed everuch one.
The smal quyt cart that covert was and hors . . .
to ferien his godes. To ferien his godes
quere he was boun.

The onelych thyng of combraunce (combraunce)
was the symphonye
(saf a pakke of bokes)
that he had boghte the yere
quen he bithoght
that he wolde lerne to play.

But the zele woned (zele woned).
He neuer couthe ani scylle.

I'd read *Jude the Obscure* recently enough to cotton on to this—Matthias's poem doesn't let on for some pages that it is the opening of Hardy's novel being transmuted, or 'turned', into Middle English. But why? . . . From this starting-point Matthias's conundrum of a poem ramifies into speculation about aesthetics, 'transmutations' of all kinds, 'turns' of meaning and history; modulating in form into the prose of a prosaic modern world half-way through; at times *merely* 'contrived', fiddling with quibbles, seemingly whimsical; yet over-all contriving to stimulate, by no means pointlessly perverse. By its close the 'scolemayster' figure emerges as a symbol for all the 'unproletarianised obscure', not required to produce commodities for the markets of a commercialized age, travelling with his 'pakke of bokes', an 'intermediary' in capitalist society: ' . . . the shape of his life is determined by the nature of society: the nature of his art seeks to determine the shape of society by administering to its nature.' He retains his 'Hermetic privilege'—to practise arcane arts such as those so cherishingly exemplified in this extraordinary poem itself, and belonging to all times. Beginning as the subject of a perverse-seeming linguistic exercise, he 'turns' through the poem into a rich and vital symbol for the artist himself. (p. 56)

> *Andrew Waterman, in* PN Review *(© copyright PN Review), Vol. 4, No. 4, 1976.*

The importance of *Turns* . . . lies in the fact that not only is it the first British collection from this major poet, but it was mostly written or given birth to there, while the poet was staying here.

To class a poet as major, when he has yet to apparently prove his merit (can only two books justify this?) in numerous publications, needs expansion. If one applies the criteria of not only human appeal but also intellectuality and a wide field of poetic vision and emotion, regardless of language, then Matthias is a major poet. He is a writer of range and immense versatility of style, language and poetic intention. He writes in epic vistas, though not necessarily in epic quantities or style.

His work is experimental, but only in that it seeks to elucidate meaning or plumb new intellectual deeps—he is not a gimmick-seeker or a mere charlatan (they are in ample abound these days [in English language poetry])—by his usage and juxtaposition of languages within the European tradition, and with much mediaeval English married to contemporary American English.

[*Turns*] cuts across nations and history, cultures and time with all the quick movement of the best of surreal poetry— yet it is not surreal *per se*. Matthias is one of the most important of very few efficient poets of his generation (under 40) on either side of the Atlantic, writing in English. His book is a revelation in the real meaning of the word. It is essential to any reader who cares for and believes in the power of poetry and its continued evolution. (p. 6)

> *Martin Booth, in* Tribune, *January 30, 1976.*

[In *Turns* Mr Matthias exhibits a] controlled yet flexible style: for example in the skilful counterpointing of the "monographs on / Mahler" and "the still & deadly music of the I.R.A."; of the intended victims, "diplomats on holiday in / Devon" and the actual victim, "lap of an astonished secretary / dreaming of her lover". The last phrase shows irony finely controlled by pathos. Elsewhere there is a memorable curt summary of America's riot squads: "The other guys are faster and they draw."

What a brief quotation cannot show is this poet's ability to bring together and give order to a wide range of experience.... [*Turns*] moves fluently through American violence, reminiscences of friendship, a heart check-up, his father's death, the poet's need for an ordered background, and finally England. Mr Matthais [is able] "to make things fit together that don't but should". *Turns* encompasses the order of art and the painful or grace-giving accidents of life; seriousness and wit; America's present, Russia's Stalinist yesterday, England's distant past; experiment and tradition.

Mr Matthias is eclectic, polyglot, often abstruse. Some of his titles are irritating ("Double Derivation, Association, and Cliché: from The Great Tournament Roll of Westminster"), and some of the poems are obscure, quirky exercises, partly redeemed by his splendid ear for the music of words. But excessive virtuosity is forgivable in our stark poetic scene, and I admire very much the way life—his own and other people's—presses into his poems. He has something to say and a way of saying it. *Turns* is an exciting, richly promising collection. (p. 697)

> *D. M. Thomas,* The Times Literary Supplement *(© Times Newspapers Ltd., 1976; reproduced from* The Times Literary Supplement *by permission), June 11, 1976.*

[*Turns*] is full of the ways in which the poet and the reader will get on with one another, and with the poems. Common and uncommon, "vulgar" and hermetic, the poems derive from a "word hoard" guarded and sometimes squandered by the poet. Double meanings, double derivations, and double sonnets mark the poet who is digging down and half oriented when the book ends—the position and yet not the position from which the entire book is written. Recovery is the object and subject of the poems, the kind of excavation we encounter in the work of the British poet Geoffrey Hill. We go back to earlier centuries, to other languages, to arts and works other than poetry, to figures and countries as various as we could ever dream. (p. 181)

Turns repeatedly gives the impression of having caught before us on the page a word, a phrase, a line, maybe a poem—an "architecture of sounds" against "disintegrating space." Lest we mistake the text for the gloss, or the artifact for its context of significance, Matthias sees to it that we note periphery and center, stopping place and road. (p. 182)

The book is carefully divided into three parts, and the third ends with a poem written from a new home (in England) and under a new aesthetic and discipline ("provisional") which finds a language for lyric and elegy. Matthias is able to write a poem for a man (painter) he "never really knew" because the widowed wife has the details (the text and context of love) the poet needs. That concluding poem—"Epilogue from a New Home: For Toby Barkan"—joins poems like "For John, After His Visit: Suffolk, Fall" and "Clarifications for Robert Jacoby . . ." as major art. These establish Matthias as a poet who understands Ezra Pound, W. C. Williams, Charles Olson, and Robert Duncan as poets who view the poem as a field visual and aural, natural and crafted through which the poet moves. Although the second poem I mention is full of thrusts at Robert Lowell's poems in *Life Studies*, the parts that succeed best and which make the poem significant are those where the poet gives up parody for finding a style that is his own. Sometimes, Matthias is able to come upon what he needs by means of one of those famous accidents or mistakes in literature the critic would never want changed:

> Like? in a way?
>   the flaw in the printer's eye
> (the typesetter's, the proof-
>   reader's) that produced and then
> Let stand that famous line
>   in Thomas Nash's poem about the plague,
> "Brightness falls from the air",
>   when what he wrote was, thinking
> Of old age and death, "Brightness
>   falls from the *hair*."

From history, philosophy, literature, and other disciplines, the poet learns how words can be "execution" and "penance." And how society and the poet as one level always are at odds. Particularly attracted to the medieval period, Matthias keeps before him a death's head to remind himself of the way that flesh and words eventually go. Whatever "turns" the poet can make may not be "enough," but they are "maneuvers" he can at least make. When they are made as brilliantly as they sometimes are here, I see the kind of "survivor" Matthias wants himself and his art to be. (pp. 182-83)

> *Arthur Oberg, in* Western Humanities Review *(copyright, 1977, University of Utah), Spring, 1977.*

MAURIAC, Claude   1914-

Mauriac, a French novelist and essayist, is the son of Nobel Prize-winning author François Mauriac. His fiction, which is in the New Novelist tradition, is a curious and complex presentation of simultaneous perceptions and points of view.

Claude Mauriac is engaged, in his novels, in justifying the "increasing presence . . . of writer-heroes in the works of writers." And so he, himself, is triply present in his own books—twice as a man named Bertrand Carnéjoux, who is both the object of his observations and the subject who makes them, and once as Mauriac himself who intrudes into his own novels to discuss them and himself, and to rub elbows with the other characters. He has written a suite of four novels thus far, three of which have by now appeared in English. Together they are titled *The Interior Dialogue* (though Carnéjoux calls *his* suite *Communication*) and they concern the mysterious and tricky technique of communication with others, and among one's selves.

From a technical point of view, Bertrand Carnéjoux, the hero-writer-subject, the "I" of all Mauriac's remarks, is fascinated by movie-making and philosophical treatises. His novels and Mauriac's are an amalgamation of these two elements: the first represents a move toward extreme realism in which the author seeks to "invent" the minimum and achieve "exactitude" in beauty; and the second represents an attempt to comprehend whatever unity underlies the multiplicity of events and persons. Mauriac and Carnéjoux, his alter-ego, are also heirs to Proustian investigations of the transcendence of time—the discovery that consciousness is not chronological, but immediate as well as cumulative.

Mauriac speaks often of the "reality of time"; that man lives both within and out of it. The sum of facts, therefore, both defies and annihilates time and is symbolic of the complicity between man's temporal engagements and his eternalness. It is this existentialist theme that Mauriac's novels invade.

The same characters appear and reappear in all of his novels, but they do not change, that is, they bear perpetually the same relationship to each other. At the bottom of all this lies a personal obsession about the inevitability of solitude and the mystery of communion (thus, the "interior" nature of the "dialogue"). One Mauriac personage affects another, if he does, principally by being a constant reminder that each is entirely replaceable for the other, that all men are interchangeable, all women are fatal, that each encounter is a reminder of our habitual aridity. Conversation is to be understood as simultaneous monologue.

All Women Are Fatal was the first of Mauriac's novels. . . .

[It recounts] four episodes in the life of Bertrand Carnéjoux (the name literally means flesh and games) at the ages of 33, 38, 42 and 25, in that order. Each is an account of specific event when, in a crisis of passion, an act of love or a loss of affiliation or desire, the impossibility of love is especially typified.

All these failures are symbolized by sexual encounters because, one supposes, they represent an ultimate attempt to contact another human being. But sex is a poor religion for, unlike his father François, Claude's preoccupation is not with morality in the traditional sense . . . but with metaphysical man. To put it another way, with man's ability to transcend the limits which enjoin him from any real joy. (p. 20)

In *The Dinner Party,* in which eight people monologue simultaneously to themselves and each other, he has joined far more complex observations, and in *The Marquise Goes Out at Five,* Mauriac evokes, during the time span of one hour, not only the mind of Carnéjoux in its entire cogitative spectrum, but an extremely complicated environment.

By the third book, one knows a great deal about the mind of Mauriac and Carnéjoux and, also, the convolutions of style and manner have been elucidated. Significantly, in the *Marquise,* Carnéjoux has retired from the world to contemplate, not his pleasures but the meaning of his pleasures. In this book and in his fourth, *L'Aggrandissement,* Mauriac again employs a virtuoso scheme by which his is triply present: "a novelist, animated by a novelist whom I, myself a novelist, have put into a novel." In the fourth, the novelist prepares a book, evokes a former book and in so doing makes a present one. This attempt to dramatize both subjectivity and objectivity at the same time, to treat them at once on all three levels of abstraction is a major conception.

There is, of course, the inherent danger of monotony. The incessant analysis and mass of detail may have the cumulative effect of a telephone book. . . . We see more but we do not always see better.

However, like his literary mentor Nathalie Sarraute, Mauriac's lucidity transforms the minutiae into a tremendous equation. "Man," he concludes, "has his states of grace which escape any chronicle"; but his own chronicles admit their shadowy existence. Mauriac is by no means an easy writer, but his vision is particular and severely absorbing. (pp. 20-1)

> *Alice Mayhew, "All Things at Once," in* Commonweal *(copyright © 1964 Commonweal Publishing Co., Inc.; reprinted by permission of Commonweal Publishing Co., Inc.), September 25, 1964, pp. 20-1.*

As much dominated by rigorous intellect as his father's books were by violent, instinctive passion, [Claude Mauriac's] first piece of fiction, *Toutes les Femmes sont fatales* (1957), is meticulously composed, full of scrupulous correspondences and subtle balances—"A true mind-teaser for careful readers." The words are from the book itself, for Claude Mauriac likes to have his narrator, who discusses a work he is planning to write, provide the key to the one being read: "One could begin reading my book anywhere, reading and rereading it in any order one might choose. An essay more than a novel. Fictional essay, perhaps, a genre that needs to be invented." . . . That sort of thing makes for a fascinating game of patience, but there is another side to the coin—what fascinates a reader's rational intellect might not attract one with a creative mind.

Told in the first person by Bertrand Carnéjoux, the character who provides the major link between this and the three subsequent books, *Toutes les Femmes sont fatales* consists of four separate interior monologues, each one covering a brief period of time, but the entire set spans about fifteen years. Through his eyes and mind one also meets, among a host of others, most of the characters who will figure prominently in the later fiction, but one is not much affected by what is hardly more than a succession of names. That, at any rate, is all they represented to me. There is little rapport between them and the narrator who ruminates on his anxieties in Rio, Paris, New York, and prewar France—little rapport, it seems, beyond matters of sexual involvement. Within the text's frame of reference, this is as it should be. (pp. 133-34)

What informs all four sections, saving them from being merely the record of a retarded adolescent's search for personal gratification, is Carnéjoux's constant preoccupation with death, his realization that he will grow old and die without the world's being the poorer for it. Flitting from one woman to the next, he seeks, beyond physical pleasure, what he calls "the frontiers of death." . . .

While Claude Mauriac makes use of some relatively new techniques introduced by other writers, among them Dujardin, Gide, and Joyce, his first novel is not exactly revolutionary. (p. 135)

Le Dîner en ville (1959) showed far greater originality. The setting is a snobbish apartment on the Ile-Saint-Louis in Paris during a formal dinner party. The book opens with the guests' entrance into the dining room and closes as they leave the table to go back to the salon for coffee. Plot is characteristically nonexistent. The apartment is that of Bertrand Carnéjoux, now married to Martine, the daughter of one of his former mistresses. Six guests have been invited, and they are either single or have come alone, for a variety of reasons engineered for the sake of providing more revealing material. With the same aim, Mauriac also arranged for an unlikely combination of age groups, including a young student and an ancient, although hardly respectable, woman. There is no narrator involved, and the book consists exclusively of a supposed transcription of the conversation and thoughts of those eight people seated around the table. But the lack of descriptions or narrative statements is not its main originality. Marguerite Duras' *Le Square,* published four years earlier, one remembers, was almost entirely in dialogue form. *Le Dîner en ville* includes not only conventional dialogues and interior monologues but also interior or "silent" dialogues. Ironically, the disappearance of the narrator is somewhat illusory, for he has been resurrected in the guise of an omniscient transcriber who records not only the dinner conversation but the thoughts of each and every guest. First-person narration, third-person narration with central intelligence, interior monologue—all had a vague claim to realism. Mauriac's technique, in theory, has none. In practice though, it affords a greater illusion of reality, partly because of its newness, partly because the reader has been granted godlike powers to see (or hear) things "as they really are." Such aggravating problems dealing with fictional realism are not laid to rest until writers of the next generation, like Sollers, Ricardou, and others, reject the concept of literature as mimesis.

Claude Mauriac's "recording" technique is endowed with one additional feature, which might have been considered a drawback but actually fitted his purpose quite well: as the transcription is supposed to be authentic, with no editorial matter added, there is no external way of identifying the person who thinks or speaks. Since, according to Mauriac's postulate, all men and women are basically alike, the anonymity of the guests conforms to reality. There are, nevertheless, distinguishing characteristics, superficial as they might be, that permit identification in many if not all cases

—manner of speech, obsessions, professional competence, and so forth. Such features also prevent the reader from getting lost among the eight table talkers and transforms the text from the puzzle it might have become into something eminently readable. (pp. 136-37)

Removing Carnéjoux from his former position as narrator also adds to the dimension of *Le Dîner en ville.* Previously, his obsession with sex and death had an egotistical tinge. He said that all men were like him, but in the text he was the only one to say so. Here, the obsessions are shared, emerging clearly out of the several interior monologues. (p. 138)

In *La Marquise sortit à cinq heures* (1961) the setting shifts to the Carrefour de Buci, a busy Paris intersection on the left bank, filled with detailed and confused activity. It is between the hours of five and six on a warm afternoon, late in the summer of 1960. Once more there is no conventional narrator, only what appear to be transcriptions of dialogues, interior dialogues, and interior monologues. Bertrand Carnéjoux is still the central character, and he spends the hour watching the street scene from his balcony. But something has happened to him. He is separated from his wife, has renounced his mistresses, and resigned from his editorial positions to devote himself to the writing of his next book, which one is now reading. He has apparently become fully aware of the futility that characterizes human activity, including his own, and in contrast with the attitude of his earlier representations he has become reconciled to it. "I am conscious of my nonexistence at the same time as I realize theirs. I am detached from our ephemeral lives. Ever since, I have left women, children, newspaper, and relative wealth in order to devote myself, no longer to my pleasures, but to the understanding of what my pleasures meant." . . . He has taken over the role of outsider that belonged to the student in *Le Dîner en ville.*

The situation, however, is a bit more complicated, for Claude Mauriac is becoming more and more self-conscious in his own role as author and needs to have Carnéjoux's thoughts focus on problems of the writer. The main character becomes split: Carnéjoux's *alter ego* Desprez, an erudite historian, who is watching from a balcony on the other side of the intersection, assumes the part of commentator that Carnéjoux, in his statement, has led the reader to expect. The link between the two is made clear by their identical physical stance above the Carrefour de Buci as well as by their sharing the same cleaning woman. If the name "Carnéjoux" suggests the idea of toying with flesh, "Desprez" is close enough to *dépris* and its connotation of being freed from a bond or a habit. He could be said to represent Carnéjoux's new self, one who fully accepted the Saint-Germain-des-Prés revelation, for the name also echoes the last two words in the name of the church. (pp. 138-39)

Such a concentration of time into the fictional hour during which the action of the book takes place is what expands the scope and interest of *La Marquise sortit à cinq heures* far beyond what had been attempted in *Le Dîner en ville.* Desprez can account for "at least eight centuries of Paris life, at this precise spot" . . . , and he discloses a frightening record of crime and injustice throughout those centuries. Everything that is read by a character is of course reproduced in the text. (pp. 139-40)

What emerges is of course a strong indictment of Western

civilization. Such a condemnation, intellectual in origin, is given an emotional hue by the pervasive presence of children, both on the Carrefour de Buci and in the literature of the past. Carnéjoux's daughter, Rachel, whom Martine has brought to visit her father, serves as catalyst for the reader's feelings. (pp. 140-41)

These devices are much the same that Michel Butor had used in *Degrés,* which appeared a year before *La Marquise sortit à cinq heures,* in a very different context, but with essentially the same effect of arousing the reader. There is also a difference in the handling of the episodes. Butor is more discreet, less prone to call attention to what he is doing, while Mauriac cannot help explaining everything, constantly tugging at the reader's elbow. (p. 141)

The themes of injustice and suffering subsume the theme of death that has been carried over from the previous works. Many more characters from different walks of life help to express the universal fear of death posited by Claude Mauriac. (p. 142)

Mauriac's characters like to think of themselves as full of love and sorrow for others: "Me, such a noble heart!" . . . exclaims a woman poet. . . . The anxieties of all these people are not limited to their fear of death. They are all wrapped up in themselves. (p. 143)

Such anxieties, as they were in *Toutes les Femmes sont fatales,* are usually translated into sexual terms, only they are now applied to a host of characters instead of being nearly monopolized by Carnéjoux, who, in this book, appears strangely ascetic.

His main task is to express himself on the techniques of fiction. He does this first, as in the previous work, as a writer thinking and dropping hints about the book he is writing and about fiction writing in general. But earlier, Carnéjoux was a character who was also a writer, and his other activities were in the foreground; now he is a writer and nothing else. What he had to say in the past about the book he was planning threw light on the one being read. In *Le Dîner en ville,* when he talked about "Le Plaisir grave," one had the impression that it resembled *Toutes les Femmes sont fatales,* and one feels that "Le Déjeuner au bistro" has much in common with *Le Dîner en ville.* In *Marquise sortit à cinq heures,* however, it becomes increasingly obvious as one progresses through the book that it is precisely the one Carnéjoux is working on. The far greater frequency of his reflections on his craft are partly the cause of that impression. How the convention that forms the basis of this work is gradually exploded becomes a more important consideration.

In *Le Dîner en ville* an identical convention was strictly adhered to. Here, Mauriac begins by respecting the framework of his *carrefour* and of his hours. Then, a first, plausible exception is made for historical texts, and next, texts about Algeria are brought in. What goes on in the street is supplemented by what happens inside the various houses. Historical persons who have lived on the spot are followed by others who merely passed by. These are succeeded by fictional characters who could be connected with the *carrefour* (the eighteenth-century Manon Lescaut, for one) and by real persons who simply might have passed by, "Anonymously and without leaving any evidence," for it is reasonable to assume that "they *all* have one day or another passed through this intersection . . . Voltaire, Bonaparte,

Hugo." . . . Finally, a fictional character is introduced who lives somewhere overseas and happens to be thinking about the *carrefour,* the name of which he can no longer remember.

The process is not without analogy to one Butor used in *Degrés* when, by introducing the concept of negative relationships, he managed to integrate all the students and teachers of a *lycée* into his system of family relationship groups. That is, of course, quite legitimate, but one of its consequences can be, as it is here, to call attention to the fiction *qua* fiction and to the close connection between what Carnéjoux is thinking and what is actually taking place, that is, to his creating the events that he pretends to be recording. The impression is completely confirmed by the instance in which he notes what another character has thought, in an interior monologue that has just been transcribed with the obvious intent of using it in his book—which he has just done. . . . What is clearly meant by Carnéjoux's being the author of the book we are reading is that he has now become Mauriac—a harmless supposition, since he has, early in the text, divested himself of nearly everything that made him the fictional character of the two other works. He has become the omniscient narrator and Claude Mauriac's surrogate. In the last few pages, Mauriac gives the show away by stepping into the text himself: "Novelist brought to life by a novelist that, as novelist, I have myself placed in a novel where, nevertheless, nothing has been invented." . . . As usual, he must carefully explain what was becoming evident.

This explanation does not really mar the ending of the book. It matches the tone of this and previous works and brings matters to their logical conclusion. At one point Carnéjoux admonishes himself, "I must carefully avoid adding commentaries, no matter how short, to my quotations" . . ., but Mauriac does precisely the opposite by means of Carnéjoux's remarks on fiction writing. In another respect, he is like Nathalie Sarraute: not only does he want to control carefully what goes into his work, he also wishes to restrain the reader and make sure he does not take out of the work more than was intended. As he intervenes is *La Marquise sortit à cinq heures,* he stresses what he considers to be the link between the fiction and the reality. (pp. 143-46)

The title of this third work refers of course to Paul Valéry's saying that he would never write such a preposterous sentence as "La marquise sortit à cinq heures," which had been publicized by André Breton in his surrealist manifesto. . . . Because the marquise is a middle-aged, male homosexual, it acquires an ironic twist, but that is a minor point. Valéry, in attacking that kind of narrative statement, was condemning what he thought was trivial and traditional in the mass of contemporary fiction, but in effect he was attacking a symptom rather than a disease. The judgment weighed heavily in the minds of writers during the thirties and forties, and Claude Mauriac deserves some credit for reversing it, so to speak—showing that even such a statement as "la marquise sortit à cinq heures" might be used in a serious work. . . . As Mauriac writes, in the guise of Carnéjoux: "In the present as in the past, the anecdotes to which my fictional essay will be boiled down will have no importance at all. And yet, they will make up my only reliable asset." . . . (pp. 146-47)

He undoubtedly shared the apprehensiveness of many older

novelists when faced with Valéry's dictum. Even though he used the anathematized statement to show that the poet had been mistaken, his last sentence, "The marquise did not go out at five," is an unwitting justification of Valéry's distrust. In emphasizing the reality that lies at the source of his fiction, he not only refuses to recognize the creative power of language but, by laying bare the mechanisms of his work, he has in one sense retreated from the position assumed by traditional novelists, who, like Balzac, might have considered their fiction more important than reality. (p. 147)

L'Agrandissement (1963), the final volume of the series featuring Bertrand Carnéjoux, is something of a letdown. As the title suggests, this work is an enlargement of a detail of the preceding one, and it consists of a long interior monologue attributable either to Carnéjoux or to Mauriac himself, spun in the length of time required by the Carrefour de Buci traffic light to turn amber to red, green, and amber again. In his monologue, Carnéjoux (let us suppose it is he) creates and expands on what he had previously pretended to record, to the extent, for instance, of projecting the lives of passing *lycée* students forward to the time when they have become old *lycée* professors. He also reminisces about aspects of his own life, and he thinks, as usual, about the art of fiction. If it does not provide an exciting esthetic experience, it certainly is not uninteresting. I might even say that it generates considerable intellectual enjoyment. (pp. 147-48)

The handling of time in this tetralogy is both logical and fascinating in its progression. From an extended time sequence involving a narrow subject, Mauriac moved on to a more restricted framework in time (one evening) and a broadened subject. Next, by limiting the time to one hour, he extended his scope tremendously. In the fourth fictional work, reducing the framework to approximately two minutes might have permitted an enlargement encompassing the infinite depth of the human psyche. But if that does not take place—perhaps because Mauriac lacked genius, perhaps because the human psyche lacks depth—the experiment was well worth undertaking. In any case, it marks a point beyond which the Carnéjoux series could not logically be continued.

Claude Mauriac broke the cycle with *L'Oubli* (1966), which was greeted by several enthusiastic reviews but in my opinion had best be forgotten. The mock detective-story plot that holds things together, involving cliques of novelists, was probably meant to be taken as light satire and high-level amusement. Actually, it is more grotesque than burlesque and somewhat embarrassing in its inanity. Too bad, because an excellent idea lies at the center of the narrative. A boy of twelve and a girl of seven play together in spite of their parents' forbidding them to, and during their play they discover something very important. Both are obsessed with the incident throughout their lives, although neither one can remember what was discovered and said or who the other one was. When they meet again much later, both, separately, think of the incident but do not connect it with each other, and they part never to meet again.

Ideas, however, are not sufficient to make a work of art, and this one gets lost among the nonsense. It does serve to remind us that most of Mauriac's characters have had a traumatic experience in their childhood or youth that haunts them from then on. That, and other obsessive ele-

ments as yet unnoticed, will perhaps emerge more clearly when his fictional work is complete—assuming that he does pursue it—giving it a greater dimension than his intellect had allowed. What is clear is that his esthetics remains traditional. (pp. 148-49)

It appears that he cannot bring himself to abandon the myth of the individual creator, perhaps even the genius, with inspiration manifesting itself in some gifted individuals. Nor does he like to think that the writer might not be responsible for what he writes, that he might be conveying the realities of his culture, civilization, or class more than anything really his own. One should also add, with respect to another prejudice manifested in this last quotation, that the wealth of meaning a reader might extract from an aleatory work of art does not reflect credit on the author—that, again, is an individualistic fallacy. It enriches the reader and, if that reader is a critic, many other readers as well. For Mauriac, however, the reader's function is less to create than to decipher. (p. 150)

> *Leon S. Roudiez, "Claude Mauriac," in his* French Fiction Today: A New Direction *(copyright © 1972 by Rutgers University, The State University of New Jersey; Rutgers University Press, New Brunswick, N.J.), Rutgers, 1972, pp. 132-51.*

Claude Mauriac's *The Marquise Went Out at Five* (1961) [is] one of the most interesting novels to come out of the fervor of fictional experiment in France during the past fifteen so years. . . .

[All] serious novelists must confront the arbitrariness, the necessary falsification, of the worlds they invent through words. In his critical writings, Mauriac has coined the term *alittérature* to describe this intrinsic problematic of literature. All literary creation worthy of the name, now and in previous ages, is seen as a reaction against the inevitable falsity of antecedent literature, a restless devising of strategies to escape being "just" literature. I think the idea is more historically accurate than the notion of a contemporary literature of exhaustion, and *The Marquise Went Out at Five* is a persuasive demonstration of its efficacy as a rationale for the continual renewal of literature.

By the conclusion of the novel, Carnéjoux, the novelist as self-observing observer, imperceptibly gives way to the author of *The Marquise Went Out at Five*. The evoked world of fiction, revealed as fiction, shrivels up, and, as at the end of many of Nabokov's novels, the fabricator of the fiction himself stands in its place. . . . Mauriac, it should be noted, does not in the end make the facile gesture of some contemporary novelists who simply shrug off their own fictions as, after all, mere fictions: he avows the artifice but affirms it as a means of mirroring "life's sensations, feelings and thoughts," fiction seen as perhaps the only way to get at a whole range of real human experience. (pp. 226-27)

All this might be mere cleverness if the novel did not have the impelling sense it does of the urgency, the philosophical seriousness, of its enterprise. What drives Bertrand Carnéjoux, and behind him Claude Mauriac, is an acute perception of two concentric abysses beneath the artifice of the novel—history and death. *The Marquise Went Out . . .* attempts to exhaust the human experience intersecting [a] carefully delimited time and place. But as Carnéjoux and his inventor realize, such an undertaking is "doomed to failure" because "the unity of actual time . . . [is] surrounded, penetrated, absorbed . . . by the infinite pullulation of innumerable past moments." . . . Though Mauriac explicitly compares the achronological method of composition here through a long series of separate "takes" with the methods of a film-maker, the effect is precisely the opposite of cinematic composition in Robbe-Grillet because Mauriac accepts and works with the essentially time-soaked nature of language as a medium of art. (pp. 227-28)

Some readers may feel that Mauriac is too explicitly direct in the way he reveals . . . fundamental matters of motive and design in the making of his novel, but the fiction itself bears out in concrete detail what otherwise might seem portentous assertion. A writer, about to vanish like every human being born, has only words to grasp with at some sort of tenuous, dubious permanence. Words console, words are the most wonderful of human evasions; but the writer, using them as truly as a writer of fiction can—which is to say, with a consciousness of how their enchantment transmutes reality into fiction—comes to perceive profoundly what words help us to evade. The seriousness and the ultimate realism of the novel that mirrors itself could have no more vivid demonstration. (pp. 228-29)

> *Robert Alter, in* TriQuarterly 33 (© *1975 by*
> Triquarterly), *Spring, 1975.*

Le temps immobile is not an account of M Mauriac's novels, nor of his critical writings, and it has relatively little to say about his family. It covers the period from 1958 to 1975, and is concerned mainly with three men who played a dominant role in his life during those years, General de Gaulle, André Malraux and Michel Foucault, and the discussions and episodes which they inspired or originated.

Naturally, one other person is also constantly present, and that is the author's father, François Mauriac. Not only was Claude Mauriac dominated by his presence and his memory, he was often made to serve his father's needs. . . .

But it was because of François that Claude Mauriac has constantly been surrounded by the distinguished and famous, and it is this which has enabled him to write a journal which other people will want to read. There are always those who like to hear anecdotes, and all that M Mauriac has had to do is to record the stories which he heard in the course of the day. . . . To this extent M Mauriac has published a book which is bound to be successful.

But it has two aspects which are unusual. The first is its variety. It begins with de Gaulle's return to power and the establishment of the Fifth Republic. M Mauriac wonders whether he is to be appointed to de Gaulle's staff, as he was in 1944. But the appointment does not materialize, and it is as a spectator only that he watches the new regime. . . .

In the second, longer half of this volume, M Mauriac describes a direct and active life in the politics of protest: the small intellectual, groups who form associations, hold meetings, pass resolutions, investigate injustices and combat authority. Here the concern is with the scandal of prison life, with the atrocities committed against Algerian immigrants, with the terrible housing conditions in certain parts of Paris, as well as with the larger injustices to be laid at the door of particular governments.

The Mauriac who patiently interviews Algerians in the hope of finding out the exact truth about some incident, and who spends so much of his time drafting statements which are ignored by most of the press, seems very different from the man who hangs on to every reminiscence which a garrulous Malraux is prepared to proffer. . . . Thus this is a journal of particular interest and distinction.

Its second unusual aspect, however, is less satisfactory. M Mauriac claims to be preoccupied with the problem of time, a preoccupation which takes the form of interposing the record of events from one year to another, so that at certain moments there is a deliberate confusion of narrative. . . .

The method is meant to be significant for his life, and to resemble artistically a *montage,* in which the observer becomes aware of intricacies that would otherwise be concealed. But it looks more like a device than a principle, and in spite of M Mauriac's insistence, one has the impression that the method is secondary to the matter.

> *Douglas Johnson, "The Best of Company,"
> in* The Times Literary Supplement (©
> *Times Newspapers Ltd., 1976; reproduced
> from* The Times Literary Supplement *by
> permission), September 17, 1976, p. 1161.*

*   *   *

MAURIAC, François   1885-1970

Mauriac is a French novelist, essayist, journalist, playwright, and poet. Although a Roman Catholic, much of his work exhibits strong existentialist ties. Mauriac imbued his works, especially his novels, with a pervasive concern with sin. He won the Nobel Prize for Literature in 1952. (See also *CLC*, Vol. 4, and *Contemporary Authors*, Vols. 25-28; *Contemporary Authors Permanent Series*, Vol. 2.)

[To] the non-Catholic it may seem strange that Mauriac should have such a strongly Protestant sense of religion in a Catholic country. . . . This nominal adherence to the Catholic faith is manifest in Mauriac's novels by his protagonists' general failures to perform the traditional obligations of their religion. It is also manifest in their very personal response to sin and evil, in contrast to the much more communal response one normally associates with Catholicism. . . . For Mauriac's characters, mankind's sins may rest on their shoulders, but each man, not mankind, must work out his own redemption; the communal Church seems less crucial than the individual soul. Moments of recognition in which they sense this personal responsibility come to many of Mauriac's people. The curé who helped consign Jean Péloueyre and Noémie to a grotesque marriage, in *A Kiss for the Leper,* suffers through an epiphany of enormous, archetypal guilt: "The curé was a man of scrupulous conscience . . . and he questioned with relentless rigour the motives which had led him to act as he had done. . . . Each time that he thus sat in judgment on himself, he ended by pronouncing absolution, but that did not prevent him from endlessly reopening the enquiry. . . . Had he really been an obedient servant of the Lord, or was the real truth that a poor parish priest had usurped the functions of the Eternal God?" And the almost totally evil Félicité Cazenave, who virtually murders her daughter-in-law, suffers a moment of personal and religious aloneness in *Genetrix* in the same way as her son had earlier: "Suddenly she started up. 'Somebody's walking in the garden!' Had she really heard somebody walking? . . . It was borne in upon her that this momentary terror had been the young woman's [her son's wife's] companion night after night. Coincidence? . . .

Chance? . . . '' Laughing off her sense of guilt and alien-ation, Félicité remembers how the ''Terror'' had once driven away the priests, and here Mauriac offers an image of religion that characterizes the rather Old Testament tenor of faith in Mauriac's work: ''At the beginning of the previous century the children of the Landes had had but one religion, that of the implacable and fiery sun; had known but one Almighty, the blaze that burned the pines—a swift-moving, unapproachable God who left in the wake of his progress a host of smoking torches.'' For Mauriac, this more or less pagan God of the Landes is not essentially different from the Christian God he imagines in his fiction, for that God is no less powerful, implacable, inscrutable. In short, Mauriac's image of religion is close to the Dutch Jansenism whose doctrines of predestination, natural de-pravity, and irresistible grace seem so much more Calvinist than Catholic. (p. 160)

[The] violence is greater in the intent of his characters than in their physical actions. Félicité Cazenave, of *Genetrix,* for instance, intends mortal violence toward her daughter-in-law, but it is not action but inaction that causes Ma-thilde's death: Félicité does nothing to help the girl after she has a miscarriage and contracts puerperal fever, but the violence the fever does to the girl is no match for the vio-lence Félicité *would* do. (p. 161)

In Mauriac there is a tendency to avoid overt physical vio-lence . . . : the violence is not of event, but most frequently is one of language, of metaphor and simile, really of *style.* (p. 162)

[Imagery] of battles, fire and heat, martyrdom and death, rain and storm pervades Mauriac's best fiction. In *Gene-trix,* where—as in much of Mauriac—every emotion is a *passion,* with all its connotations of violence, a favorite image is of enmity, ''the legacy of fire,'' between mother and son, of a fury that swept through the mother ''like a fire, burning up her will to renunciation even before it had come fully to birth.'' But in this tale the most pervasive imagery involves warfare; the human relations in the Oedi-pal triangle of mother-son-wife are all seen in the language of armed conflict: the side of the house where Mathilde lives is the ''enemy wing''; mother and son together are ''like two ancient frigates''; the son Fernand is a ''captured fortress,'' ''a piece of property snatched from her by anoth-er's hand and which she must recapture by violence.''

In the end—and this is frequently true of Mauriac—the people do less violence to each other than to themselves. Hence, where the language of warfare clearly suggests the destructive violence of human relationships, the imagery of passion and fire and heat that dominates, say, in *The De-sert of Love* just as clearly suggests the internal violence of Mauriac's characters. . . . Much of the problem with Mau-riac's people in this work is their lust, not for real, but for imagined flesh—fantasy, imagination, drama, role-playing being vastly important here and elsewhere in Mauriac; it is the internalizing of love—a *self-consuming* Narcissism—that drives and corrupts. . . . The urge to self-destruction that haunts these people . . . is neatly imaged by Mauriac as ''that species of madness which compels those whose clothes have caught fire to run.'' The desert of love Mau-riac shows us here—and elsewhere—has been created by that same kind of fire. (pp. 163-64)

James M. Mellard, in Renaissance (© *copy-*
right, 1974, Catholic Renascence Society, Inc.), Spring, 1974.

Thérèse [of *Thérèse Desqueyroux*] is a totally untypical Mauriac heroine, bearing no resemblance whatever to most others and only slight resemblance to two of her fictional sisters. Mauriac devoted his talent exclusively to depicting provincial life in southern France and his cast of characters is drawn principally from the Bordeaux area bourgeoisie. What sets Thérèse apart from the other women of her mi-lieu is her knowledge of a certain fact of French provincial life. She would like to communicate the following idea to her daughter Marie, but the same information could be profitably communicated to all the wives and sweethearts of Mauriac's sensitive young men. . . . In Mauriac's nov-els, literary creativity is unquestionably the most important activity for any person, and women, or so it seems, inter-fere regularly and decisively with that activity. This inter-ference takes a particular form, depending on whether the woman in contact with the poet is wife, sweetheart or mother. (pp. 15-16)

Mauriac coined a phrase in his first novel *L'Enfant chargé de chaînes* that describes magnificently the whole group of women who, as wives, interfere with literary pursuit on the part of their husbands. The phrase: *petite âme ménagère.* When Thérèse referred to her daughter as a ''future com-mère d'Argelouse,'' this is her own expression of the same idea. The *petite âme ménagère* distrusts, fears, resents lit-erature, especially poetry. In *Le Baiser au lépreux,* when Mauriac is explaining why Noémi cannot come to grips with her feelings, he states that she had never opened any book except her prayerbook and that no fiction could now help her understand her own heart. A key word in Mau-riac's vocabulary is *abrutissement,* that state of mental atrophy sought after by all of Mauriac's provincials who lit-erally bury their minds in business affairs, or, in the case of the women, in housework, children and servants' quarrels. When a *petite âme ménagère* and an intellectually inclined young man meet and marry, the result is disaster for the male and sometimes for both marriage partners. (p. 16)

Mauriac's fictional sweethearts have a very special role to play in his novels. When one considers the totality of his fictional work, it becomes obvious that, like his fellow Bor-delais Michel de Montaigne, Mauriac considered friendship between two intellectual men the most perfect relationship on earth, incorruptible and uncorrupting, free from the ca-prices of the flesh. The role of the woman, a true *femme fatale,* is to disrupt this relationship, distract that member of the pair who is the potential intellectual, and metaphori-cally carry him off to the world of the flesh, of business af-fairs, of property, of *abrutissement.* . . . This oft-repeated pattern is most sharply defined in one of Mauriac's later novels, *Les Chemins de la mer.* Pierre and Denis have been lifelong friends. Pierre is a poet, Denis has a vocation to intellectualism. He shares Pierre's deep love of poetry and keeps himself informed of the progress of Pierre's po-etic efforts. After his father's disgrace, Denis chooses to marry the ignorant and coarse Irène, daughter of a farm-hand, and becomes one of those whose life is a ''chemin mort qui ne mène à rien.'' (pp. 16-17)

In the first two stanzas of ''Bénédiction,'' Baudelaire gives us a description of the poet's mother that is startlingly simi-lar to Mauriac's description of that character. According to Baudelaire, when the poet's mother discovers her son's inclination, she shakes her fist to heaven and curses the moment she conceived "her expiation." This situation, in varying forms and patterns, occurs in every novel in which a poet's mother is alive and on the scene. (p. 17)

In the light of this short study, it is tempting to see in François Mauriac a male chauvinist of gargantuan proportions. He seems to despise women. However, if one realizes that Mauriac is chiding women for hiding in the house, excoriating the practice of loss of self in offspring, if one realizes that a woman who, for instance, returns to school would get nothing but praise from Mauriac, the tag no longer seems appropriate. Let us consider Thérèse Desqueyroux. She jumps into a disastrous marriage with a male version of the *petite âme ménagère,* attempts to kill him, and yet retains all of her creator's sympathy. Thérèse is intelligent, she loves to read, she has no illusions about herself, she refuses to sacrifice to the family honor, she maintains a fierce individualism when all the women in her family expect her to live in and for her daughter, and she probably has a vocation to write. One night, Thérèse has a dream which illustrates both this vocation to writing and the yearning for sexual love which interferes with that vocation both in Thérèse and in Mauriac's intellectual males.... Mauriac loves her, despite the fact that she fails to develop her talent. He faults her for squandering her time on chimeric love affairs much as he chides his male intellectuals for wasting their time on women as sex objects.

In *L'Education des filles,* Mauriac made it clear that the subtle brainwashing of women ... was primarily responsible for all the marital, all the maternal woes in his novels. I use the phrase "in his novels" judiciously, for Mauriac-novelist can appear to be in maddeningly total disagreement with Mauriac-essayist. Even within *L'Education des filles,* there appear to be contradictory opinions expressed. Mauriac both chides and sympathizes with the *bourgeoise* whose entire universe is populated by children and servants.... Mauriac has been called ... a divided novelist whose art is the dialogue between the contradictory voices of his own self. We see this dialogue, this artistic tension, especially in his fictional treatment of women. They fail in his novels because they conform to one of his wishes as expressed in one of his essays.

Within the novels, there is a very clear double standard which Mauriac applies when determining the purpose of reading. For men, intellectualism is an end in itself and literary creativity, the most exalted occupation.... But for women, reading is ordered to a higher good. Women should read in order to be able to love men better.... There are, in Mauriac's novels, several startling "conversions" in which a woman, unsatisfactory for various reasons, picks up a novel and immediately is transformed from an ignorant shrew into an intelligent and passionate lover. The most notable example of this is Brigitte Pian of *La Pharisienne.* Brigitte's characteristics before she grew interested in literature suggested the title of that novel.

The year before Mauriac died, a new novel of his appeared in which, at last, he had finally created his perfect woman. Jeannette Seris in *Un Adolescent d'autrefois* was preparing herself, through study under the curé's tutelage, to be a good wife for Alain Gajac, the poet-hero of the novel. Even more hopeful and optimistic was Mauriac's creation of a poet's mother who, while not an intellectual herself, had advised Jeannette to study, read, meditate. (pp. 18-20)

Kathryn E. Wildgen, "Dieu et Maman: Women in the Novels of Francois Mauriac," in Renascence *(© copyright, 1974, Catholic Renascence Society, Inc.), Summer, 1974, pp. 15-22.*

* * *

McGAHERN, John   1935-

McGahern is an Irish novelist, screenwriter, and playwright. Like Joyce, McGahern is exacting in his portraits of the Irish experience and his use of the language, and, like Joyce, his countrymen have both honored and banned his work. He is concerned with individual action in society, and he places his protagonists in conflict with their Irish backgrounds. (See also *CLC*, Vol. 5, and *Contemporary Authors,* Vols. 17-20, rev. ed.)

There is such a strong family likeness between Joyce and John McGahern that it is almost too obvious to be worth remarking on. To wander from McGahern's new novel, *The Leavetaking,* into *Portrait of the Artist, Exiles,* and the first hundred or so pages of *Ulysses* is like listening to four movements of a single symphony. There are changes of pace and emphasis and key, but the theme, whatever variations are played upon it, remains essentially the same; and McGahern's and Joyce's prose styles bleed imperceptibly into one another like the voices of kissing-cousins. (p. 77)

McGahern's writing works in collusion with Joyce's, drawing strength from the echoes it evokes. It is not a case of imitation or pastiche so much as a bold statement of a common concern. At his best, McGahern writes so beautifully that he leaves one in no doubt of his equality with Joyce: the similarities between the two writers spring from a sense of tradition which is thoroughly and profoundly shared. And that is something which one is so unused to encountering in 20th-century literature that it is tempting to mistake what is really a glory for a shabby vice.

For the novel's formality, its assured seriousness, its air of ritual are dependent on this conviction that it is possible to share a history and a language. Every phrase gathers weight and darkness from the past on which it feeds so confidently. The heart of the book is the sequence in which the child watches his mother die of cancer and spies from a distance on her funeral. It is written with extraordinary purity and exactitude and it makes the desolation which it records at once fiercely unique to the child in the novel and universal. It would be barbarous to give a quotation from it, but it should be said that its rhythm is as stately as that of a requiem, its vocabulary has a dignified simplicity, yet it is always miraculously alert to the particular. A wren flitting among the branches of a laurel interweaves with the mourners and altar boys, bringing the general tragedy of everybody's dying into sudden unbearable sharp focus. McGahern has a genius—and that word does not overstate what he does—for mediating between the deep currents of feeling which belong to myth and history and the exact texture of the moment, seen so freshly that it comes off the page in a vivid cluster of sensations.

As long as *The Leavetaking* stays in Ireland, it reads like a masterpiece. Its landscapes, set in Leitrim and Dublin, build up powerfully, soaked in the grey drizzle of Catholicism and its priesthood. The young man and the boy he once was grow from this dank country mutinously and inevitably. When people talk, they do so in sentences as brief and formalised as versicles and responses. Every paragraph of McGahern's writing is able to draw on a deep reservoir of nuance.

But, quite unexpectedly, the novel suddenly goes adrift when it moves to London and the love affair with the American girl. One symptom of this is the new explanatory amplitude in the dialogue. . . . We have been suddenly ejected from that world where everything is known, and needs only to be hinted at to come alive, into a place, a country, a state of mind, where everything needs to be explained. And McGahern, so brilliant on the familiar, turns out to be surprisingly clumsy when it comes to dealing with strangers. He simply has very little gift for making people talk outside the phatic code of the family. And Ireland in his work is a vast extended family of dull relations who know too much about each other for their own comfort. England, a neutral territory, is a place of long creaking sentences and incomprehensible characters. The girl's father, who gets too much space to himself in the crucial middle of the book, is a ramshackle creation out of cultural science fiction, a bug-eyed monster. The girl herself is too beautiful, too tender, too evanescent to be real; a dream or a muse rather than a person.

On *things*—the feel of walking on a street or sitting in a room—McGahern's splendour is undiminished. But this leads to some very odd effects indeed. One watches a real cigarette and a real glass of beer in ghostly motion against a background of real furniture and a real floor. But the people who activate these objects are at best smeary, at worst transparent. It is as if out of Ireland they had ceased to exist except as shadows in suits of clothes.

Yet *The Leavetaking* asserts a quite opposite truth: that only by leaving can life begin. Its moral force is all directed towards exile; but its style stays stubbornly at home, refusing to budge from the landscape out of which it has grown. It asserts a salvation in the marriage between two separate refugees—a sacramental marriage which supplants all the hopeless pieties of Irish history. . . . But the wife is a ghost-bride. One feels at the end that the man's leavetaking is really just as solitary as Stephen Dedalus's was; that his wife is a phantom in his breast. In Joyce she was called Art; in McGahern she is said to be an American divorcée, but the language of his novel is too truthful to be fooled by such a thin disguise. Strangely, with honour, and often with immense power, *The Leavetaking* eventually turns itself inside-out. Like Joyce and Flann O'Brien, McGahern reveals that leave, however much it may be ached for, cannot be taken. (pp. 78-9)

> *Jonathan Raban, in* Encounter (© *1975 by Encounter Ltd.), June, 1975.*

McGahern's primary concerns are . . . social: he is interested in depicting the features of contemporary Irish life, both rural and urban, and in the novels he focuses on a conflict between one central character and the social environment. . . .

The Barracks is set in a small village in the west of Ireland. At the center of the novel is the Reegan family: Elizabeth, her husband (no Christian name given), and three children —from Reegan's previous marriage. From the outset, McGahern suggests that the family's environment has an atmosphere of tension and drabness about it. . . . (p. 5)

Elizabeth Reegan is not a young woman; she is in her late thirties and fears that she may have cancer. She realizes that her marriage to the village police sergeant was based on an illusion: she believed that she could find love and happiness in the small world of the village, but she now questions her decision. . . . Her dream—or illusion—has been shattered. She is trapped in a family and a community where she can find no personal solace, no answers to the questions she is continually asking herself. As she concludes later, she is "shut in a world of mere functional bodies." . . . Elizabeth's preoccupation now is to try to understand the meaning of her place in the world. With her fine sensitivity she has divined that whether she has cancer or not, whether she dies or not, "nothing could ever change" . . . , the world will go on. She needs to understand, to find out what life is about.

These somewhat vague aspirations McGahern succeeds in making credible for Elizabeth. Through flashbacks we discover the complex nature of her past. . . . (pp. 6-7)

Not only by her dreams has McGahern set Elizabeth apart from the other characters in the novel. She is a deeply sensitive person, fully appreciative of the natural beauties around her, but she is unable to share her feelings with others. (p. 8)

To a large extent, however, McGahern has ordained that the bleakness of a sensitive woman's life will be emphasized by placing her in a withering environment. (p. 9)

Little relief is given from the emphasis on Elizabeth's alienation from this restricting community, a community in which the unusual is suspect and the commonplace exalted. . . .

Irish society, Thomas Kilroy asserts, "is a very restricted and restricting society with little room to manoeuvre, no elaborate scales and . . . novelists are at their best when they are recording with accuracy these features of Irish society." His comment certainly applies to *The Barracks*. That drabness and pressure to conform within a village community is only part of the picture. McGahern is also concerned with national issues, and his opinions on Irish society in general emerge through his depiction of some of the characters. . . .

Reegan is a somewhat enigmatic figure. He has been a country sergeant for many years and now at fifty sees no possibility of further promotions. . . . Reegan's hopes have not been fulfilled, and he complains about younger men being promoted ahead of him and talks about "this balls of a country." . . . McGahern does not make clear, however, whether Reegan's failures are due to character weakness or to some fault in Irish society as a whole. (p. 10)

McGahern is more successful, however, in deriding the bourgeois mentality of some of his minor characters. The mockery of the woman in the hospital who had risen into the middle classes is one example. . . . One feels that McGahern almost enjoys exposing the pretentiousness of the woman. (p. 11)

The conclusion of the novel contains no relief for the central character; the harshness of McGahern's vision is unrelieved. On one occasion, as Elizabeth enjoys the fragrance of roses, she reflects on her understanding of love:

> Things had to be taken in small doses to be

enjoyed, she knew; but how that means of measurement degraded and cheapened all passion for life and for truth, and though it had to go through human hell, a total love was the only way she had of approaching towards the frightful fulfillment of being resonant with her situation and this was her whole terror and longing. . . .

Such total fulfillment has never been hers, and she knows it never will be: she cannot break out of the confines of her existence. Elizabeth is not being fatalistic, rather she is accepting what is inevitable for her. (pp. 11-12)

The vision of despair continues to the end; Elizabeth's death is followed by Reegan's final battle with Superintendent Quirke and his resignation from the force. No lifting of the gloom, no expression of hope for the future of the ex-policeman and his family. . . . (p. 12)

In several respects John McGahern's second novel, *The Dark,* has a great deal in common with *The Barracks.* They have similarities in location, family grouping, and in the isolation of what Kilroy called the "suffering, sensitive figure at the center." The location is again the rural west of Ireland, an area of small farms and villages dominated by the "river" (the Shannon). The Mahoney family consists of a father and several children (three, one boy and two girls, are featured, another similarity with *The Barracks*). The wife is dead and rarely mentioned; the father is a small farmer—in these aspects *The Dark* could be regarded as a continuation of the first novel. More significant, however, is the fact that young Mahoney (we never know his first name) is, like Elizabeth Reegan, a character apart in temperament and in sensitivity from the other characters. The differences between the two novels lie principally in novelistic techniques, especially those presenting the central character.

We first meet young Mahoney in a brutal confrontation with his father. He is accused of saying "fuck" and is taken upstairs to be whipped before his sisters. The barbarity of the incident is unmistakable—the father is compared to an animal—and we are directed immediately to the cruelty and lack of affection in the household. Succeeding short chapters reinforce the initial impression: the Mahoney family is one without real affection or love. As a result, the growing boy keeps his innermost thoughts and hopes to himself. He is isolated within his own family.

Although Elizabeth Reegan and young Mahoney differ in many respects, they share a sensitivity to nature, a sharp intellect, an awareness that life is not simple, and most importantly a dream. Elizabeth's dreams of a life of love and happiness, first with Halliday and then with the village police sergeant, came to naught—and in the chilling reality of approaching death she tried to come to terms with the meaning of her life. Mahoney, too, has dreams, first of becoming a priest and then of acquiring a university scholarship. As with Elizabeth, the failure of the first dream leads indirectly to the growth of the second. The difference between the two is one of perspective: Elizabeth was looking back, remembering and reassessing the dreams she had had; a young boy must look forward and try to comprehend what life will mean for him. Although the difference in perspective leads to problems with the form of the novel, we should examine how McGahern presents the boy's first dream.

In Chapter Five we find young Mahoney looking at a Memoriam card for his mother and reflecting:

> On the road as I came with her from town loaded with parcels and the smell of tar in the heat I'd promised her that one day I'd say Mass for her. And all I did for her now was listen to Mahoney's nagging and carry on private orgies of abuse.
>
> I'd never be a priest. I was as well to be honest. I'd never be anything. It was certain.
>
> There was little to do but sit at the fire and stare out at the vacancy of my life at sixteen.

The promise, the dream of saying Mass for his dead mother, is followed by an admission that he will never be anything. A temporary feeling of failure and frustration is understandable and in character for a sixteen-year-old boy, but McGahern, trying to emphasize again that pessimistic vision, goes further—the note of despair about the boy's future is an indication that McGahern has predetermined that he will fail. (pp. 12-14)

Although young Mahoney occasionally feels attracted to the priesthood because he desires the special powers conferred on a priest, . . . he sees it as fulfilling a more basic psychological need. . . . Like Elizabeth Reegan, he is concerned with establishing a meaning to life before he leaves it—but on another level . . . he is searching for security, something which he feels does not exist in the secular world and which he has certainly not found in his own family.

The culmination of the first part of the novel comes when the boy visits a clerical cousin, Father Gerald, for the purpose of deciding whether he will become a priest or not. (pp. 14-15)

The scenes at the priest's house are among the best in the novel. McGahern effectively reinforces the atmosphere of tension between the two people by setting the scenes during a period of unusually hot, sultry weather. He also, here more than elsewhere, enriches the prose with symbols and patterns of imagery. Young Mahoney sees the priest's house as full of an "utter sense of decrepitude and dust" . . . ; the bookcases are full of tomes—only one book, Tolstoy's *Resurrection,* has "more green leaves and living light of day about it than the dust and memory of the others." . . . The garden around the house is a "green prison" . . . ; life, in the shape of vans, cars, people talking, goes past outside—but within the house and garden all was quiet: "here was only interest of the graves." . . . In the descriptions of the church and garden mention is frequently made of the "cactus" and the "bellrope dangling before the church door." "Bellrope" recalls that moment in Chapter Four of *A Portrait of the Artist as a Young Man* when the priest twisted a blindcord around his finger as he discussed the priesthood with Stephen. McGahern, like Joyce, appears to associate the priesthood with the strangulation of life. "Cactus" initially appears to be incidental, but Mahoney wonders if it has "religious significance" and concludes that "to look at the yellow cactus long enough was to come to silence and fear." . . . It is associated in the boy's mind with the aridity of the priestly life and, with the "artificial roses and lilies" . . . , becomes identified with death. As though in affirmation of his decision not to become a priest, young Mahoney turns away from these symbols of death towards the "red rose of life" and the "tree of life." . . . Although the use of somewhat conventional symbols would support the view that McGahern is not innovative, he nevertheless employs the symbols effectively: the texture of the prose is enriched and so, too, is our understanding of the complex mental torments in the mind of the protagonist.

The Dark, however, is not without its technical faults. Principally, these center on the inappropriateness of the confessional form for McGahern's pessimistic vision. The absence of flashbacks, made necessary because of the youth and inexperience of the protagonist, . . . [reduces] the effectiveness of the presentation. . . . Furthermore, McGahern places the boy in a hostile but unreal environment. . . . One often feels that McGahern is determined to force his bleak world on the reader—the scene must be gloomy, the minor characters must be frustrated, and come what may, young Mahoney must live out a life of despair. In addition, McGahern seems unsure of the confessional form; he varies his narration, for example, from first to second to third person. Presumably, he wishes to make the reader more intimate with the deepest thoughts of the protagonist, but such variation in narration is not successful.

In the second part of the novel the boy is involved in working for a university scholarship. . . . Although the dream is based on an illusion, McGahern does not allow his character to experience any joy at the thought to taking up a successful career. The university "dream" is thought of rarely and then only in vague idealistic terms. Emphasis is placed on the drudgery of cramming, the uselessness of most of the subjects, and the boy's continuing gloomy introspection about the future. Mahoney feels trapped—feels that he is a prisoner in a hideous system.

The final chapters, dealing with the aftermath of the exams, the award of the scholarship, and the rejection of the university, are complex but not altogether satisfactory. . . . The authorial uncertainty in these final chapters is all too evident. (pp. 15-17)

One searches in vain for a . . . reasonable explanation of why [Mahoney] fails to come to terms with university life. Remembering Elizabeth Reegan's understanding of her loneliness and alienation, we expect the boy to try to articulate some understanding of how the local community has moulded him in a certain way. . . . The relative poverty of the Mahoney family could obviously be linked to the boy's mental torment over his decision to leave the university, but such social points are not considered by McGahern. Since the emphasis remains firmly on the gloom and futility, the presentation of young Mahoney's character in the second half of the book is narrow and incomplete.

In focusing his attention on the protagonist, McGahern has neglected the presentation of that rich environment from which Mahoney comes. It was successfully presented in *The Barracks* and is so again in *The Leavetaking;* similarly, the wider implications of the darkness in Irish society is examined in these two novels but not in *The Dark.* Our view of "the lonely frustrated figures" who make up the other characters is limited; we see little of their personal opinions. . . . The novel presents no awareness of local and national mediocrity, so pervasive in the earlier novel and so appropriate a context for the sufferings and mental anguish of its protagonist.

The Dark has many good things in it: the enriching of the prose with symbols and the exploration of Mahoney's rejection of the priesthood. But much of it is unsatisfactory: the poise of the earlier book is missing; the assurance with which Elizabeth Reegan was presented is not carried over to *The Dark;* the problems with the confessional form are never overcome; the presentation of the minor characters is incomplete; and in the second part of the book McGahern has allowed his pessimistic vision to distort his presentation of the central character. (pp. 18-19)

The central character [of *The Leavetaking*], Patrick Moran, has many of the qualities already associated with McGahern's major protagonists. He is from the west of Ireland, the product of a small village; his father is a callous police sergeant, his mother a refined, sensitive individual (she dies of cancer while the boy is young); his many sisters are mostly unnamed. Patrick is sensitive and imaginative, has a feeling for the beauties of nature, and is opposed to the restricting parochialism of Irish society. Patrick's conflict with the society is important for the plot—although the plot is not of great significance. Because he gets married in a registry office, he loses his job teaching in a Dublin school: the Catholic hierarchy will not accept anyone who deviates from its strict ethical principles. McGahern's antipathy for this bourgeois Catholic society is again in evidence, and through his first-person narrator he handles the portrayal of the society with skill and subtlety [in the words of Peter Straub]: "*The Leavetaking*'s most convincing moments have to do with the protagonist's awareness of Irish aridity and confinement."

The "awareness" is evident at the very beginning of the novel. The opening scenes are set in a Dublin primary school, and from the narrator we begin to visualize the society from which he is about to take leave. . . . McGahern's "precision of observation" is nowhere more in evidence than in these opening pages. Details of characters and scene contribute to a picture of that constricting society which is convincing, not exaggerated nor distorted.

Patrick's victory in the final scenes of the novel also involves McGahern in criticizing the society but with a maturity in the presentation. McGahern does not resort to frustrated, unrepresentative figures as he did in *The Dark.* The headmaster and the parish priest—both involved in Patrick's dismissal—are amiable men; they are not perverted or even vicious, but simply people upholding a system they are unwilling or unable to change. Nor does McGahern place his central character in a position where he has to resort to feeble excuses or blame Fate in order to justify his actions. Patrick's actions spring directly from his personality—he makes no bitter outbursts against the absurdity of the decision to dismiss him. . . . The absence of strident criticism reinforces the impression that such a society is beyond salvation. Like Stephen Dedalus, Patrick's solution is to escape.

The theme of *The Leavetaking* is again concerned with dreams. The incident in Patrick's childhood which stands out in his memory is the promise to his mother to be a priest—the same promise that young Mahoney made to his dying mother. The dream was his mother's, never Patrick's, and when he cannot live up to his promise he turns to teaching: "out of guilt I chose second best. I followed her footsteps to the Training College." . . . The dream of a pleasant life in the country, happily married to a girl who conforms to his mother's image, is then contemplated and rejected. The girl did not love him. After a period of futility, a period in which sex but not love is important to him, he comes eventually to discover a new dream: "If I was lucky I'd find someone I liked as well as loved, the dream of a friend and a beloved in one, a person as well as a body." . . . He attains his dream through a relationship with an American girl, Isobel, dealt with in the second part of the book. It is the first occasion in a McGahern novel that a personal dream has been realized.

Throughout *The Leavetaking* one is constantly aware of the importance of time. The novel opens and closes on the same day, the day of Patrick's dismissal. In the body of the novel are the memories, the recollections of the past, the telling of events that have led to this day. The novel ebbs and flows in time, from the recounting of events that happened two generations ago down to the mundane affairs in the present-day classroom. (pp. 19-21)

John McGahern is concerned not just with the passing of time but with the influence of time on the memory and the imagination. He presents his schoolteacher as a man coming to terms for the last time with his past life and all the social forces which have made him what he is. The re-creation of the past involves imagination as well as memory:

> My mother's dream for my life, the way that life happened down to the schoolroom of this day, my memory of it and the memory of her dream, and so the tide is full and turns out to her life; and what a coffin this schoolroom would be without the long withdrawing tide of memory becoming imagination. . . .

The lyrical rhythms of the prose with the balanced sentences and the long drawn-out sounds reinforce a nostalgic tone. The concern for memory and how it can lead to an imaginative re-creation of the past are uppermost in the character's mind. . . . The fascination which Patrick displays for the power of memory and imagination is of more than passing interest. One is made aware of the character's past life and of his desire to understand it before he leaves it.

John McGahern discussed some years ago the importance of images in reaching an understanding of what our lives mean. He saw our lives taken up with the search after "the one image . . . the lost image that gave our lives expression, the image that would completely express it again in this bewilderment between our beginning and end." Images are of great significance in *The Leavetaking,* working at different levels in the novel; for example, certain episodes in Patrick's memory can be regarded as "images." His early conversation with his mother about becoming a priest has traditional images of mother caring for child. . . . Such symbolic associations give these episodes a representative quality; McGahern is underlining the universal implications of Patrick's experiences.

Of course, the more conventional images work through the language and need to be explored in some detail. The opening paragraph of the novel begins: "I watch a gull's shadow float among feet on the concrete as I walk in a day of my life with a bell, its brass tongue in my hand and think after all that the first constant was water." . . . The "shadows" and "gulls" figure prominently in Patrick's mind in the opening sections of the novel. The gulls are, first, asso-

ciated with escape—Patrick's escape from this restricting community; for Stephen Dedalus, too, birds symbolized flight from Ireland. They undoubtedly also remind Patrick of Howth where his love awaits him in rooms overlooking the sea. The gulls swooping down for scraps of food have been seen as "greedy shadows in turmoil, an Irish nation in miniature." The image of "shadow" is more complex. Although they are here seen "floating," elsewhere they are "calmly crossing" . . . ; later they are "thinning and drifting over the trees." . . . The movement of the shadows has an intoxicating effect; they provide a contrast to the squawking and shrieking of the gulls and the noise of the boys in the school playground. As the shadows drift across the playground, Patrick "drifts away from the classroom" . . . into his reveries, and gradually the shadows take on a deeper significance. The young boy found himself more in sympathy with his mother, "away from the cold shadow my father cast" . . . an early memory which he recalls. The "shadow" from his mother soon became cold, too, after the first leavetaking:

> A shadow was to fall forever on the self of my life from the morning of that room, shape it as the salt and wind shape the trees the tea lord had planted as shelter against the sea, for in the evenings they do not sway as other trees in the cooling wind, but stay stubbornly bent away from their scourge the sea, their high branches stripped of bark and whitened, and in the full leaf of summer they still wear that plumage of bones. . . .

The shadow is now associated with death and with the sense of guilt which shapes Patrick's life as relentlessly as the salt and wind shape the trees. At the end of Part One he reflects that by this evening his life "would have made its last break with the shadow and would be free to grow without warp in its own light." . . . The religious undertones in these passages are unmistakable; one notes immediately that the rhythms in the language with the carefully balanced clauses are reminiscent of the Psalms. The references to "bones," to trees resisting the wind, and to life growing "in its own light" have Biblical connotations. Patrick sees himself as living in "the shadow of death" from which he will emerge after this last day at school. (pp. 22-4)

A liveliness and lightness about the prose in Part Two contrasts with the wistful tones of Part One, appropriate for the protagonist's change of fortune. On the night of his dismissal Patrick can state with assurance: "The gulls' shadows will not float this evening on the concrete. The sky has filled. I can see it is already raining out on the bay." . . . The shadows have dispersed; Patrick and Isobel are ready for their flight.

The use of "bay" and "raining" calls our attention to another reference in the opening paragraph—"the first constant was water." The image of water is one which gathers accretions of meaning as the novel develops. When Patrick's mother confirmed his suspicions that Santa Claus did not exist,

> It was the first break in the sea of faith that had encircled me, for what if God were but the same deception. I shuddered as if I already felt that the journey would be dark and inland through sex and death, the sea continually withdrawing. . . .

The constant "sea of faith" has been broken. Patrick foresees that he will have to set out on a journey, a journey of darkness towards death. We can also note that "sex" is associated with death, but "love" with light. . . . In the closing scene of the novel Patrick sees himself as setting out on a new sea:

> The boat has slipped its moorings and is leaving harbour to trust to the open sea: and no boat needs so much trust to put to sea as it does for one body to go human and naked and vulnerable into the arms of another. . . .
>
> (p. 25)

McGahern has . . . succeeded with the form of [*The Leave-taking*]. As in *The Barracks* his use of flashbacks for the revelation of the past of the central character is appropriate for the explication of the central theme: that a man can successfully resolve to cut the ties of family, country, and heritage—and set his life on a new course.

Some critics have noted similarities between John McGahern and James Joyce. . . . McGahern's vision, however, has not always encompassed the possibility of happiness outside Ireland. Elizabeth Reegan had lived in London, and young Mahoney knew that for a "fiver" any fool could go to England—their lives were no happier for such experience or knowledge. The malaise in Irish society of the first two novels is intimately linked to McGahern's deep and almost bitter pessimism—he will not countenance any escape for his protagonists. A lifting of the gloom, however, has occurred in the latest novel. McGahern, like Joyce, may continue to look to his native land or, like his character Patrick Moran, seek for inspiration elsewhere. (p. 26)

> *F. C. Molloy, "The Novels of John McGahern," in* Critique: Studies in Modern Fiction *(copyright © by James Dean Young 1977), Vol. XIX, No. 1, 1977, pp. 5-27.*

*   *   *

MEGGED, Aharon   1920-

An Israeli novelist and short story writer, Megged is among the generation of writers who began their literary careers after the establishment of the Israeli state. (See also *Contemporary Authors*, Vols. 49-52.)

Jonas, the hero of Aharon Megged's novel, *Living on the Dead,* is a young writer in thrall to the Zionist past represented by Davidov, legendary pioneer and nation-builder whose biography he has been commissioned to write. He has signed a contract committing him to this task and he sets about it by methodically retracing the career of the dead man, at the same time compulsively reenacting some details of it in his own life. But the biography will never be written. Jonas's attitude to history is, to say the least, ambivalent. From time to time he seeks oblivion and escape from his responsibilities in the "Cellar," a place of convivial resort for the bohemia of Tel Aviv. And in the end he does succeed in losing the notes and documents which he has so laboriously collected. But history will not be mocked. As we see him at the end of the novel, Jonas is awaiting trial for breach of contract, and "so long as this trial hangs over my head, I cannot start anything new." (pp. 74-5)

Living on the Dead [is] a "Dybbuk" story, one calling to mind the archetypal theme of the figure of the living

haunted by the spirit of the dead which occurs in so much Romantic and post-Romantic literature of the past century. From this point of view the novel can be said to be in the symbolic mode. But the symbolism, though clear, is far from wooden; *Living on the Dead* is an absorbing and vivid representation of Israeli life in the 60's, and its descriptive truth is never overthrown by the weight of an artificial symbolic structure. (p. 75)

> *Harold Fisch (reprinted from* Commentary *by permission; copyright © 1972 by the American Jewish Committee), in* Commentary, *August, 1972.*

The teasing paradox common to such varied authors as Barth, Biely, Borges, Pirandello, and Unamuno is their consummate literary reminder that words are static and therefore fatal. Sticks and stones can merely break bones, but some of the most engaging works of recent decades read as if "Warning: texts can be hazardous to your health" had been printed on every page.

Among this international choir clamoring for silence, Aharon Megged's *Living on the Dead* (1965) deserves a prominent place. Its author's eighth book, it is a highly sophisticated yet gripping exploration of just what it means, in philosophical, social, and personal terms, to write a novel. As its title suggests, the work employs life and death as central metaphors for its thematic concerns. Furthermore, *Living on the Dead* is set against a contemporary Israeli background which provides unique variations for its familiar themes. . . . [Megged] casts his Janus gaze back at the earlier, European-born pioneers who came to the Land with nothing but faith and will, and ahead to a later, sabra generation sometimes pictured as having everything but faith and will. How to portray this flow of history without freezing the flow is the challenge faced both by Megged himself and his fictive author Jonas Rabinowitch.

Living on the Dead is Jonas' own first-person account of his inability to write a biographical novel. He has been commissioned to produce a work drawn loosely from the life of the late national hero Abrasha Davidov. Davidov, laborer, farmer, politician, and soldier, resembles one of those legendary dynamos, like David Ben-Gurion. . . . Though he continues receiving monthly payments from his publisher as specified in their agreement, Jonas nevertheless finds that he simply cannot write the book. In an effort to forget his literary obligations, Jonas attempts to lose himself in a life of sensual abandon. But a humiliating law suit for breach of contract with his publisher forces Jonas into an anguished scrutiny of his attitudes toward the burden he has assumed. The result is the book we read, the story of how he came not to write the book he intended. As in Samuel Beckett's trilogy, in which each speaker is most concerned simply to tell us how little he wants to speak, *Living on the Dead* erects the trope medieval rhetoricians called *occupatio*—refusal to sustain a description—into a basic structural principal of a sustained narrative.

Like his Biblical namesake, Jonas would gladly choose Tarshish over Nineveh, facile comfort over the austere duty of a prophet's life. . . . However, as much as he is drawn to spending his days sleeping and his nights in bacchanalian adventures which leave him oblivious to everything, Jonas is still haunted by a stern call. Megged's fiction is too modern and realistic to rely on such devices as the

Muse or a burning bush, but the forces urging Jonas to return to his mission as writer are no less compelling. (pp. 232-33)

The courtroom episodes suggest elements of both Kafka and Lewis Carroll. An impersonal system of justice here confronts a frail individual and imperiously interrogates him about his own worthiness. Prosecutor and judge are vivid reminders to Jonas of the destiny he has tried to elude—both as an aspiring writer who has lapsed into silence and as a young Israeli who would avoid coming to terms with the ghost of a pioneer. At the same time, though, this very curious trial is conducted with an earnest disregard for its own manifest absurdities. A simple civil suit, the case occupies many months of the court's calendar, and by the end of the book there is still no prospect of conclusion. . . . Jonas remains unimpressed by the casuistry of either prosecution or defense. His painful ambivalence toward the Davidov project cannot be resolved judicially. (p. 233)

Jonas' title [for an uncompleted novel] *Hero of Our Time* of course recalls Lermontov, and, in its inquest into the nature of literary creation, *Living on the Dead* never allows us to forget that it is itself artifice. The reference to a nineteenth-century Russian writer, like the epigraphs from assorted poets beginning each chapter, foregrounds the work. It subverts mimetic illusions and calls our attention to the fact that we are, after all, reading a novel, one throughout confounded by the relationship between fiction and the experience it transmutes. . . .

Examples of necrophagia, of living on the dead, are scattered throughout this novel, from poets who seem to cultivate experiences in order to convert them into inert stanzas to a nation fond of worshipping its heroes dead. (p. 234)

Jonas is consumed by the realization that he himself is the most voracious necrophage in the drama. . . . [Like] those scholars who bide their time until such lives as Stravinsky, Pound, or Picasso are completed before rushing out with the definitive study, Jonas, beneficiary of the publisher's monthly check, is in a real sense feeding himself from a dead man. . . . Furthermore, if creation is but imitation, Jonas, like Plato, arrives at the guilty awareness that all artists are liars. No matter how faithful he attempts to be to the spirit of a figure who can no longer speak for himself, to describe is to distort. As with Sartre's historian Roquentin, who amasses abundant data on the life of the Marquis de Rollebon but discovers there is no core to the personality, every version of Davidov that Jonas assembles is irreconcilable to every other. While schoolchildren idolize the Zionist hero, his widow provides a bitter account of neglect —"can a man love the whole Jewish people, the whole human race, and not love his own family?" (pp. 234-35)

Jonas' sense of unworthiness, both as an individual and as writer, to undertake the Davidov project is only part of a complex ambivalence he feels. Though he eagerly accepted the assignment, he loathes it as an oppressive burden. He admires and detests Davidov and sees himself as both parasite and victim. "I had meant to write about a dead man, and he was stifling the life out of me.". . . Some of the tensions here can be attributed to the artist's love-bout with his raw material, the Romantic sculptor's delight in and impatience with the intractable marble. But the figure of Davidov also has a special hold on Israelis in general and on Jonas in particular.

As artist and as citizen, Jonas is an extension of an intimidating tradition he feels helpless to elude. . . . The spoken Hebrew language lay dormant for hundreds of years, from the onset of the Diaspora until revived at the beginning of the modern Zionist movement. Because of its extraordinary history, Hebrew lacks the accretions of centuries of usage found in other languages. As a result, it is difficult to write a paragraph in Hebrew which does not link its author directly to ancient texts, to what is The Tradition. . . . [Allusion] of some sort [is] unavoidable, and allusion affirms complicity in a tradition. For a modern Hebrew writer like Jonas, whose very name destines him to a prophetic mission, silence would be the only desertion.

Like the Hebrew words which are the writer's self-betraying tools, Davidov embodies the nightmare from which Jonas dreams of awakening. He is also the patriarch who must be buried before the sons can feel free. (pp. 235-36)

Davidov is buried, but Jonas survives. Indeed, he survives by recounting it, by living on the dead. Yet the very fact that he continues to write about this figure he both loves and hates as violently as if Davidov were his father only demonstrates the stranglehold the old man continues to exert on the young one. Every word he pens, even guilty explanations of why he cannot produce the book he was commissioned to do, only implicates him further in a relationship to history he seeks to deny. The only way he can finally exorcise this *dybbuk* of tradition is by completely ceasing to write.

Yet as long as the noisy trial, confronting his artistic and civic conscience, goes on, Jonas cannot rest in silence. Prosecution and defense continue parading obscure legal precedents, and Jonas' lawyer gleefully assures him that it could last for years. Jonas' weary reaction, the final sentence of the novel, is: "The fool does not understand that, so long as this trial hangs over my head, I cannot start anything new.". . . Jonas never does emancipate himself from his burden and never does resolve his ambivalence toward his literary mission and toward his nation's history. Aharon Megged's *Living on the Dead* thus remains open-ended, continuing to haunt readers throughout the world whose lives it has entered. (pp. 236-37)

> *Steven G. Kellman, "Portrait of the Artist as Necrophage: Aharon Megged's 'Living on the Dead'," in* Modern Fiction Studies *(copyright © 1976, by Purdue Research Foundation, West Lafayette, Indiana, U.S.A.), Summer, 1976, pp. 231-37.*

As one of the leading short story writers and novelists of the generation of Israel's War of Independence, Megged has depicted the varied aspects of life in the new state, from war themes to the kibbutz and urban life.

In his more recent novels Megged has gone a step further and has dealt in depth with the value system of Israeli life. Two of these novels, *Living on the Dead* (1970) and *Fortunes of a Fool* (1962), which are available in English translation, are among those in which he has raised searching questions about Israeli society. Megged has experimented with new techniques and has absorbed the influences of writers such as Kafka and Agnon.

In an apparent effort to venture outside familiar territory, Megged has endeavored in [*Ha-atalef*] to deal with a worldly theme. However, in so doing he has strained the credulity of the reader. The novel's protagonist Gershon Rieger . . . grows up in a small settlement during the Mandate period in Palestine. He is obsessed with the idea of achieving complete Jewish sovereignty over the land and is led to extreme acts. (p. 328)

The novel is written in the form of letters from Rieger to a former teacher, Yardena, for whom he had developed a crush as a teen-ager. The flow of the narrative is interrupted by several shifts in time, resulting in a montage effect. Perhaps Megged would have us believe that Rieger was led to his extreme acts of fanaticism because of his early frustration in love. If so, his purpose is beclouded by the mass of extraneous detail in his novel. (pp. 328-29)

> *Jacob Kabakoff, in* World Literature Today *(copyright 1977 by the University of Oklahoma Press), Vol. 51, No. 2, Spring, 1977.*

*   *   *

MEWSHAW, Michael   1943-

Mewshaw is an American novelist, short story writer, poet, essayist, and critic. His prose is characterized by witty dialogue and sensitive character portrayals. (See also *Contemporary Authors*, Vols. 53-56.)

By the time you finish ["The Toll"] (and there's no way you *won't* finish it!), you'll feel splayed, flayed, disembowelled, deep-frozen, parched, lousy, expatriated, exodontiated, racked and probably tattooed. "The Toll" is one of the most thoroughgoing strippings-away of man's pretensions to humanity since "Last Exit to Brooklyn"—but this time on the level of pure action and impure motives, noble rhetoric curdled into yellow bile, idealism boiled down to gutsurvival, flower children rotting on a compost heap. . . . (p. 36)

The "girl" is named Bert, and I wish Mewshaw had omitted her so that we wouldn't be subjected to those Robert Jordan-Maria couplings in the back seat of Ted's Renault, not to mention all the mooning about sex and reality, about "when they touched, it was as though more than their bodies met." And I'll bet you haven't heard the following dialogue-exchange since the last time you saw Glenn Ford and Rita Hayworth: "Can we trust him?" "We have to."

But these lapses are harmless breathers, and most of this juggernaut-fiction speeds like nemesis on wheels. You can smell and taste the Moroccan setting, and you almost wish you couldn't. The brutal four-day action of maneuvering, escape, chase, evasion, confrontation and subanimal murder grows like nightshade from the talk about boredom being the cancer of the age, about nothing being worse than the laws of absolute nullity, and from the gradual recognition that these middle-class freedom-fighters stink with deception and self-indulgence and doom themselves by refusing to acknowledge the existence of limits. . . . The high body count in "The Toll" is not the reason for its grim fascination. Mewshaw's talent is. (pp. 36-7)

> *James R. Frakes, in* The New York Times Book Review *(© 1974 by The New York Times Company; reprinted by permission), March 24, 1974.*

Michael Mewshaw's *The Toll*, which can be read by those new to this writer as a straightforward and jarring thriller, in many ways grows out of his last novel, the widely praised *Waking Slow*. Here, violence is . . . direct. . . . [The] book is built about a botched caper, and ruthlessly plays out its own implications. What animates *The Toll* and puts its gory collisions and mishaps into the class of serious fiction is its political despair. The novel absorbs the usual theoretical underpinnings of the thriller, that value is invented and local and the world a primal disorder, and makes these notions its very subject. I suppose it could be compared to Polanski's film *Chinatown* in this respect; as in that film, good intentions, experience, passion and foresight, the qualities which should create cases of order, come to nothing. . . .

My greatest single reservation about *The Toll* is that in places it's a trifle over-literary. . . . Still, a book with a very high charge. (p. 261)

> *Peter Straub, in* New Statesman *(© 1974 The Statesman & Nation Publishing Co. Ltd.), August 23, 1974.*

It is good orthodox philosophy and good literary theory at once that all knowledge begins with sensation and that one's images must be firmly fixed in reality. A novel by Michael Mewshaw, *Earthly Bread*, demonstrates the continuing problem of trying to write fiction within the specific limits of one's culture.

Mewshaw will follow, if he can, in the tradition of Catholic comic novelists—O'Connor, J. F. Powers, Walker Percy. His situation is current in the highest degree. A Paulist priest, undergoing a crisis of belief of his own, gets caught up in an attempt to de-program a Jesus freak. The parents of the new convert ask him to accompany the de-programmer they have engaged so that he can provide the necessary "Catholic influence." . . .

The priest, Father Amico, increasingly wonders just what the phrase "Catholic influence" might mean under the circumstances. Mewshaw has chosen as matter for his fiction something dangerously off the top in terms of contemporary controversy. Perhaps it is not wise to expect much genuine spiritual meaning to be derived from the fuss over standard culture versus counter-culture. (p. 503)

The problem of belief, Mewshaw's intuition appears to tell him, may well have to do with the impact on our senses of the world as we have built it for ourselves. Father Amico complains when he catches himself in a moment of emptiness, "I discovered myself concentrating on the Musak, that ubiquitous aural intrusion, the wallpaper of music. Once back in America, my eyes and ears gorged omnivorously on all manner of insipidness, while my mind tried to avoid more troublesome matters." . . .

[Everything] that is seen works a hardship on our higher aspirations. Even in the greater open spaces of the West it is our electronics that supplies the images. . . . And the rest is a long line of motels, bars and junk food stands. The priest furnishes his room out of stuff acquired with savings stamps from the Redemption Center. Who can believe anything with all this around? At this point the novel comes closest perhaps to some kind of realization. . . .

Symbolism has traditionally been a part of religious art. In *Earthly Bread*, however, symbolic figures are almost always used for purposes of satire and parody. . . . Mewshaw, like many of his contemporaries, is determined to use the dreck of our culture as part of his novel. The problem in all cases is that it may take an especially fine imagination to keep one's novel from becoming part of the dreck. In Mewshaw's instance, the task might be to transform the symbolism one step beyond a mere satire on how we live our lives to a point of religious affirmation so that it is the signs of an omnipresent God that appear to be ubiquitous. . . .

Once the action moves to a motel room where the de-programmer has taken the Jesus freak, whom he has more or less kidnapped, the novel settles into a series of debates over science and religion and rationality and irrationality. The priest is plainly on the side of the boy, who has taken the new name Tiagatha, and against the de-programmer, Meadlow. Meadlow is pure villain. One of the difficulties of the novel is Mewshaw's inability to separate himself substantially from the counter-culture so as to entertain the notion that de-programming may, in fact, be an accurate, if brutal term—a recognition of a kindred system in its contempt for free will. The religious spirit, one Thaddeus, whose apostle Tiagatha has become, is not around so that although we are provided a grim picture of Meadlow's methods we never see the other's influence at work.

What begs to be considered is that the Jesus revival is at bottom more a rebellion against a set of middle-class values than a closely specified religious creed. Sure enough, the interview with Tiagatha's parents takes place in their expensive suburban home. To say that Christianity has always been in revolt against materialism hardly effects the distinction. If the boy had joined the Hare Krishna movement, it is difficult to see that it would have made any difference to the narrative outcome of the book. Someone with a real stake in living a spiritual life might well find himself caught between the mutually treacherous forces of pseudo-belief and nonbelief. . . .

The impression throughout the novel is that Father Amico is being hounded by God. In the end he is finally able to bring himself to pray.

> . . . In my own room the lone sound was the murmur of the air conditioner, as ceaseless in the performance of its duty as those Carmelite nuns who pray night and day so that every moment all over the world there will be devotion to God.
>
> Once I had undressed and switched off the lamp, I dropped to my knees and added my solitary voice to the world-wide whisper.

What the priest prays over and over again is one word, "Jesus." The scene has its intensity of feeling with the idea of a single prayer being added to the "world-wide whisper," but what kind of irony is intended in connecting the prayers with that great comfort maker, the air conditioner? (p. 504)

> *Eugene Chesnick, "Fiction and Religious Credibility," in* The Nation *(copyright 1976 by the Nation Associates, Inc.), November 13, 1976, pp. 503-04.*

Michael Mewshaw has a gift for depicting the infinite incongruities of modern American life. In *Waking Slow* he evoked, in a thousand tiny details, the sense of California as a living parody of itself. His new novel, *Earthly Bread*, has similar qualities. There is the same whiff of fear—

> The dog greeted me by sniffing up the inseam of my trousers until his growling snout was wedged in my crotch.
>
> "Don't bother about him", she said. "He won't bite."
>
> "But he breathes hard, doesn't he?" . . .

But in this novel, Mr. Mewshaw has forgone the panorama, and concentrated instead on an intense conflict between opposing faiths. The plot is simplicity itself. . . . [Tommy Hoover] has joined a group of Jesus freaks. The Hoovers have hired the noted "deprogrammer" Noland Meadlow to straighten out the boy's head, but Mrs. Hoover would be grateful if Fr. Amico could extend a Catholic influence over this procedure.

What happens during the deprogramming is the main business of the book. Fairly predictably, the real conflict is not between Meadlow and the boy, but between Meadlow and Amico as the representatives of fate and free will respectively.

[Various] contrivances gradually make it apparent that landscape and incidents must be read symbolically. Fr. Amico's feet are washed by the Hoover boy; he wakes one morning to find a scorpion in his sink; the sun burns ever more fiercely; Meadlow's self-sufficiency begins to crack. Along with this, there is a tendency to underline doctrinal points. Halfway through the contest, Amico notes: "I recognized now what a deprogramming really was—an exorcism in which God, not Satan, was cast out", something most readers will already have worked out for themselves. Yet, for all that, there is considerable wit and energy in the dialectical exchanges, and, as in all the best religious works, sin wins, outright. (p. 740)

> *David Nokes, "Sin Wins," in* The Times Literary Supplement *(© Times Newspapers Ltd., 1977; reproduced from* The Times Literary Supplement *by permission), June 17, 1977, p. 740.*

*   *   *

MILLER, Henry   1891-

Miller is a self-educated American novelist, essayist, and critic who has long been involved with searching for truth and freedom. Many of his best-known and most controversial works, such as *Tropic of Cancer* and *The Rosy Crucifixion* trilogy, are autobiographical; in them he describes his quest, which culminates in a rejection of modern civilization, but with an eventual realization about personal truth. Karl Shapiro says of him, "As a spiritual example he stands among the great men of our age." However, due perhaps to the frank sexuality and scatological language in his writings, and to his somewhat dissatisfied attitude with America, his reputation has only lately been changing from notorious to influential and well-respected. (See also *CLC*, Vols. 1, 2, 4, and *Contemporary Authors*, Vols. 9-12, rev. ed.)

When Henry Miller settled down in Paris in 1930, it was with no mere sense of being an expatriate. He believed he had died and been reborn. From this time he dated his birth as a creative artist and the beginning of the "auto-hero," "Henry Miller," whose past and present being he was to examine throughout the whole decade of the Thirties which he spent mainly in Paris. From this time he became a citizen of the universe, occupant of that "enormous womb" which reached to and included the most distant stars. And from this time he began once more to be an American. He felt that he was American in a sense of the term that would have been meaningful to the great transcendentalist writers of America's literary renaissance. In *Democratic Vistas* Walt Whitman had tried to formulate anew what he felt to be the motivating ideals of America, and Miller's work gave expression to similar vistas: a recovered awareness of the roots of democracy in spiritual community; a reorientation in human as distinct from commercial and technological values; the effort to liberate individual identity from conformist pressures and from the "City"; the acceptance of change and of suffering; faith in individual creative power as a force for transforming society; and—here, perhaps, most of all like Whitman—a profound acceptance of love and of death. (p. 221)

As Thoreau moved to Walden Pond, Miller moved to Paris for fear that he would awake one morning and find that he had not lived. He wished to possess himself and to be aware. And like Thoreau's *Walden,* Miller's *Tropic of Cancer* is a mythic birth of personality, a self sculptured into full separateness from the cultural clay that would have leached away the individual nature. Miller saw the threat to individuality as more terrible than mere dissolution in its action: "By simple external pressure, by force of surroundings and example, by the very climate which activity engenders one can become part of a monstrous death machine, such as America, for example." (p. 226)

While Miller frequently raged at America's highly technological society, he believed that the root of its troubles lay in a pseudodemocratic political and social structure, one in which the common man's worst qualities flourished, power and riches were garnered by a few, and there was no foundation of respect "for the sacred human individual who aggregate makes a democracy and in the ultimate will make divinity." (pp. 226-27)

In the process of creating the material out of which he assembled *Tropic of Cancer,* Miller sought with hatred and contempt to cut away from himself those portions of his identity which he conceived as being the cancerous "City," and to bring into recognizable being his separate and unique personality. The narration is autobiographical, but only if one allows for the possibility that dreams, wishes and lies are essential parts of the central consciousness. Although the narrator is in Paris, he is cutting himself free of the disease of civilization which he had absorbed in America; he has reached Cancer, "the extreme point of realization along the wrong path," "the apogee of death in life," and must reverse his course. The novel begins abruptly, and unlike the stream-of-consciousness novels which seek to reproduce an *apparent* discontinuity of thought and an *apparent* dissociation from reality *Cancer,* in form and subject, responds to the narrator's effort to be true only to his nature as animal and as god and thereby to betray his cultural conditioning.

Order, system, pattern, these are aspects of the disease which must be destroyed. All taboos must be challenged because they are taboos; the only authoritative totem is the self. Miller was to describe America as "the schizophrenic Paradise" and as "a far-flung empire of neurosis"; in *Cancer* what is given is the process of analysis through which the author heals himself. Other American characters in the novel, like biblical scapegoats, are heaped with the narrator's afflictions and abandoned to the devils of the American wilderness. A young Hindu, infected with the virus of America, demonstrates that "America is the very incarnation of doom. She will drag the whole world down to the bottomless pit." The auto-hero's temporary job as proofreader of the stock market section of the Paris edition of the *Chicago Tribune* (a job Miller actually held) provides a metaphor of his indifference to the statistical heart of American life.

While Miller hires himself out when it becomes absolutely necessary to earn money, he contrives to make each job serve his purpose of self-creation. The making (of the self, of the book) is always going on. Like Hemingway, he, too, has arrived at a sense of life as play: "Cease laboring altogether and create! For creation is play, and play is divine." Play has its own law, spontaneous and compulsive, operative always at the borderline between exterior and interior life. Early in *Cancer* Miller states his Dadaist determination not to let will, ethical or aesthetic, affect his creation, to make no resistance to his fate, and to pass, as it were, out of the menagerie into the jungle.

He had found himself becoming, in New York, "a city, a world of dead stone, of waste light, of unintelligible motion, of imponderables and incalculables, of the secret perfection of minus," whereas he wished to become "a wild and natural park," where people go to rest and dream. (pp. 228-29)

In his efforts to become a writer, Miller had copied pages of the work of Hamsun, Dostoievski and Céline, fascinated by the way in which these authors could create a protagonist who threaded his holistic way through frenzy like the eye of a hurricane. While Miller shared the destructive need of these authors, he did not as yet possess the deep, upwelling strength—a different kind of strength in each case—which enabled them to hurl their anathemas. With *Cancer* Miller for the first time got off "the gold standard of literature," and instead of creating from what he had drawn from the "City" and "Man" sought to be incorruptibly true to his inner generation. . . .

In creating the disorder of *Cancer,* he created the rebellion of his actual life; he opened the black spring, the "dark, mysterious realm *in the absence of which nothing could happen*"; he made himself into the sublime, absurd rebel who, he believed, was closer to Divinity than was the saint with his revelations in that the rebel was responsive to the sources of human nature. (p. 230)

Miller's concern with change and his contempt for the institutions of western civilization are not necessarily related. He felt that contemporary institutions were particularly destructive of the human spirit, but his concern was almost exclusively with changing the individual—almost exclusively with the creation of that individual, Henry Miller. As an American in Paris he found it possible to stay free of institutions, and to live as though governments, religions, laws, political organizations, social movements and the rest did not exist. (p. 231)

Being concerned with self-fulfillment, Miller felt that the men devoted to social reform were caught in an imaginary wheel rolling clockwise into the future. In their concern with the problems of arranging life to come they failed to solve the problem of living; their action was evidence of individual failure. Miller believed in "spreading" nothing—

neither gospel, nor education, nor the wealth, nor brotherhood. To try to do so was to interfere with the sacred privacy of others. He saw "the brotherhood of man" as a permanent delusion common to idealists everywhere in all epochs; it always fails because it reduces men as individuals "to the least common denominator of intelligibility." Individuals and peoples, he believed, can only be helped—and should only be helped—after suffering has played its necessary part in the resurrection of the spirit. (p. 232)

The struggle of the creative artist is not with politics and social reorganization; it is a personal and religious effort to make life a poem. Such an effort, because it is creation, is play, "which just because it has no raison d'être other than itself is the supreme motivating power in life." Instead of trying to impose his ideas of order upon the world, the individual had to learn acceptance, to put himself in order with the world. How? "Through art then, one finally establishes contact with reality: that is the great discovery." (p. 233)

Although the autobiographical material of the *Tropics* might suggest otherwise, even in the Paris years he was an avid reader and absorbed much of what he read into his creative process. The growth of his theme of the disease of American life found rich nutriment in the prophecies for western culture made by Nietzsche and Spengler. Civic decay, he discovered, had been richly imaged by the French symbolist poets. Joyce, Proust, Lawrence, Céline, all were converted to use in Miller's varied denunciations. A civilization was dying and Miller said bad cess to it in hundreds of pages purportedly dealing with Shakespeare's *Hamlet*. The prospect of the decline and fall of America was to Miller something to be regarded with great joy, for only through its suffering and death could America be reborn. The nation, too, must have its rosy crucifixion. To elaborate this fundamental theme, Miller absorbed Walt Whitman (albeit first through parallels drawn from Balzac novels) into his process of creative realization.

Miller was struck by the similarity between the view of France given in the 1830s by Balzac in *Louis Lambert* and *Seraphita* and the view of America expressed in 1870 by Whitman in *Democratic Vistas*. Even more striking to Miller was the coincidence of Balzac and Whitman's views with his own view of America in the 1930s. In exploring these related views, especially Whitman's concept of death, Miller arrived at his deepest understanding of the relation of America to his "being." Unlike the successive generations of Americans who have gradually come to a recognition of the virtues of many elements in Whitman's poetry but still cannot truly accept his views of love and death, Miller at once absorbed these views into his own. What America needed, both agreed, was great poems of death.

To Whitman and to Miller it was essential to sing of death in its relation to divinity and to democracy. The civilization dominant in the United States, in the estimation of both men, had lost the sense of death wherein each man, individually, knew his death as passage—a stage in the process of being—a part of divinity being restored to the whole. Out of their separate experiences, both men had arrived at the conception of America as *idea*. America was an idea synonymous with the idea of "Religious Democracy." Like Emerson they believed each individual to be "part or parcel of God," and in this divinity and in this being part of a whole lay the essence of democracy. (pp. 233-34)

The special sense in which, for Miller, Whitman was "America" was expressed in *Cancer* as follows: "Whatever there is of value in America Whitman has expressed, and there is nothing more to be said. The future belongs to the machine, to the robots. He was the Poet of the Body and the Soul, Whitman." When Miller ends *Tropic of Cancer* he is at rest where the Seine leaves Paris and flows on toward the sea. "I feel this river flowing through me—its past, its ancient soil, the changing climate. The hills gently girdle it about: its course is fixed." He is one of Whitman's "identified souls," at one with the flowing river of Man's past, part of nature and part of divinity. In leaving his homeland he was not the man who ran away from something, but "the man who ran *towards* something"—toward those timeless democratic vistas that had the local and temporary name of "America." (p. 235)

> *Harold T. McCarthy, "Henry Miller's Democratic Vistas," in* American Quarterly *(copyright © 1971 Trustees of the University of Pennsylvania), May, 1971, pp. 221-35.*

Miller is not an artist. He never knows when to stop. He suffers from logorrhea, writing on and on about a scene with gusto, detailing sights, sounds, smells (especially smells), using many long words found only in dictionaries and more than a few that did not use to be in order to capture the essence of a scene, which he has the talent to do. But after he's captured the feeling of the moment he goes on and on speaking until the very sound of his written voice obtrudes and drives the sense of scene away to leave only the sense of that irrepressible voice. (p. 251)

Nor is that the end. Having overwritten a scene in one book, obviously to his dissatisfaction, too, Miller returns to it in another book. And so *Quiet Days of Clichy* repeats episodes from *Tropic of Cancer,* and *Tropic of Capricorn* is regurgitated *ad infinitum* and *ad nauseam* in *The Rosy Crucifixion*. He admits freely, of course, that all of his writing is more or less autobiographical.

Miller himself boasts of his antiart: "This," he says on the second page of *Cancer*, "is not a book, in the ordinary sense of the word. No, this is a prolonged insult, a gob of spit in the face of Art. . . ." Nine pages later he continues this assault on form: "I have made a silent compact with myself not to change a line of what I write. I am not interested in perfecting my thoughts, nor my actions." . . . They all ramble hither, thither, and yon. Although the *Tropics* have symbolic underpinnings, these are not apparent. *Cancer,* for instance, as the name implies, is supposed to depict the corruption abounding in the world: "No matter where you go, no matter what you touch, there is cancer and syphilis. It is written in the sky; it flames and dances, like an evil portent. It has eaten into our souls and we are nothing but a dead thing like the moon." . . . But such simple statements are few and usually lost in the rush of sensation, are contradicted by their opposites: sentences that capture life, feeling, activity. There certainly is both symbolic and actual death all around, but we cannot become very concerned with it when Miller barges through it, barely acknowledging the existent pathos in his enormous gusto for life. His Whitmanesque acceptance and his emphasis on the comic or the mystic make the tragic seem negligible, insufficient—certainly not the center of attention, *Cancer*'s title notwithstanding.

Miller's books start in hectic *medias res* and end, except for flights of expectable but not really prepared-for mystic affirmation, the same way. There is no pattern, no order, no real conclusion; in *Cancer,* what does the ominous hint about Collins mean; does Fillmore ever get to New York, sane; what happens to Ginette; does Miller keep the money that Fillmore gave him for her? These questions would perhaps be impertinent if Miller hadn't the skill he has of bringing these characters and their problems to life on the page. We're not all as dead as he sometimes accuses us of being, and he creates in us empathy for these characters which goes frustrated, sympathy that gets short shrift, as when he says of Max (of *Max and the White Phagocytes*): "I have no idea [what became of him]. I presume he was killed by the Germans when they overran France." (pp. 252-54)

He sings of life, praising it, wallowing in it, while constantly depicting its dregs, filth, dirt, despair, and disease. His energy does convince me, or at least underscores my own sense of life's possibilities, but he rubs my face in the dirt so much while saying it that the message remains somewhat overpowered by the stench in my nostrils and the bad taste left in my mouth. There are also the wonderful grotesques he introduces us to, moving them on stage at random, then off again. Which brings me back to what I said before—Miller is not an artist, for an artist deals with form, selection, and order, and Miller does not. (p. 254)

[When] Miller says, "The terrible emphasis today upon plot, action, character, analysis, etc.—all this false emphasis which characterizes the literature and drama of today— simply reveals the lack of these elements in our own life," he's right. . . . And it's for [this very reason] that I seek order in art, balance there if nowhere else, man as artistic, if not artist-as-man, giving something a definite and satisfying shape. Which Miller does not. And, of course, I do not simply wish that all literature be Pollyannaish in nature, but I do wish that what Miller wrote was more like literature. Whole chunks of his books could be omitted, for the segments present are discontinuous and are not linked at all by causality and only vaguely by chronology. He wants to re-create life as he lived it, with no moral judgments. I disagree: I think an author should indicate, if only by negation, how life should be lived. And I think that writers should shape their material. Writers as diverse as Keats, Wallace Stevens, and Hemingway wrestled with the problem of passion and form. Even someone as hedonistic in his poetry as E. E. Cummings is far from formless, and, in fact, depends upon our knowledge of standard forms and plays against them for the effects that he gets.

Miller despises forms. He's an anarchist, and not just in literature, which is why I consider his philosophy dangerous. Not his preoccupation with sex. Certainly sex is an important if not central element of life, as Freud said, and as Lawrence and Miller have campaigned to allow authors to say. And while we can't hold these individuals responsible for the freedoms they initiated, from *Peyton Place* to *Portnoy's Complaint,* had their messages been heeded and sex been accorded its natural, not illicit or sordid, place in our existence, the hang-ups described by more modern writers might not exist. Moreover I agree with Miller that what he writes is obscene, but not pornographic: he graphically describes sexual intercourse and the evacuation of excrement, but his purpose is not to excite or titillate. Once the shock

is over—and it was only a shock when Miller was hard to obtain, no longer—Miller is not that exciting. The *Tropics* are not books one (or at least I) cannot put down; the discontinuous segments even invite such a reading. In fact, such passages as that where Miller watches a whore trying to earn fifteen francs from Van Norden, is not at all prurient: it's terribly sad and depressing. (pp. 255-56)

No, the sexual portions of Miller do not disturb me as much as his anarchy does, his celebration of life, energy, passion, ecstasy, and his condemnation of anything that restricts free enjoyment. He almost worships passionate, powerful speakers, men like Katsimbalis, but unfortunately demagogues, manipulators of emotion from Hitler to George Wallace frequently speak with more passion than more quiet, reasonable men like Adlai Stevenson or Eugene McCarthy. Miller worships energy, explosions of energy, that result in ecstasies of sadism, and the only things created are more pain and confusion. (p. 256)

Miller is the prophet of the Apocalypse, to which we may well be headed: he describes the causes of our self-destruction well, and I agree with him about them. But I neither agree that we ought to rejoice at our world's collapse, bad as it is, nor do I believe as he does that it will be replaced, if there is a planet left on which to replace anything, by something better, finer, and true. That's why I'm frightened by such statements as "Until this colossal, senseless machine which we have made of America is scrapped there can be no hope." (p. 257)

Miller admired Nietzsche, but probably the equally apocalyptic *Zarathustra,* rather than *The Genealogy of Tragedy.* There Miller would have found the Dionysian qualities he loves. But he would have been reminded that Dionysian energy led not only to creation, but to orgies of dismemberment, guilt, insanity, and death. The art of which Nietzsche spoke blended this Dionysian force with Apollonian control, which gave it shape, which gave it form—the qualities which Miller's writing and thought drastically lack.

In *Cancer* again he says that he is not attracted to men who express themselves perfectly; rather, "Show me a man who over-elaborates and I will show you a great man!" . . . A neat pat on the back for his own logorrhea. In *The Time of the Assassins,* he says, "I call that man poet who is capable of profoundly altering the world"—which makes the greatest poets of this century Josef Stalin and Adolph Hitler. He is a pacifist, but he is for violence. In his own words he is antiart; in Ihab Hasan's terms, antiform. He is a revolutionary who sees the task of the artist—he uses the term though he denies art—as the need "to overthrow existing values, to make of the chaos about him an order which is his own, to sow strife and ferment so that by the emotional release those who are dead may be restored to life . . ." . . . (pp. 257-58)

Peter L. Hays, "The Danger of Henry Miller," in Arizona Quarterly *(copyright © 1971 by the* Arizona Quarterly*), Vol. 27, No. 3, Autumn, 1971, pp. 251-58.*

Miller . . . pretends that he is examining erotic folly and romantic heartbreak [in "Insomnia"], but old hands will know better, for the detail of his courtship of Hoki Tokuda is merely incidental to the parable of the divine clown in the fallen world which for forty years has informed every word he has written. The book is slight, a fragment only of the

Henry Miller of the grand manner, and perhaps it can stand as little more than an appendix to the single Work of which his entire life and art have been the making. But it is an expression of the same energy that gave us "Capricorn" and "The Colossus of Maroussi," and it is rich with the excess that leads a certain kind of fool to the Palace of Wisdom. Above all, it can make us proud of Henry Miller, who bears so gaily his burden of flesh and years. (p. xl)

Virginia Quarterly Review *(copyright, 1975, by the* Virginia Quarterly Review, *The University of Virginia), Vol. 51, No. 2 (Spring, 1975).*

*   *   *

MISHIMA, Yukio (pseudonym of Kimitake Hiraoko)   1925-1970

Mishima was a prolific Japanese novelist, essayist, and playwright who was obsessed, both in his life and his art, with what he called "my heart's leaning toward Death and Night and Blood." As a child he was fascinated by pictures of samurai warriors committing ritual suicide. Mishima in his work combined elements of both Eastern and Western literature with a desire for a return to the perfection of the past; he created a literature, often autobiographical, which dealt with such contemporary questions as the human capacity for evil and the meaninglessness of life. After an unsuccessful attempt to incite the Japanese army to riot for a return to imperialistic tradition, Mishima committed *seppuku,* the ritual suicide; it was the only act, he felt, that could affirm his personal convictions and that could make him comprehend his own existence. (See also *CLC,* Vols. 2, 4, 6, and *Contemporary Authors,* obituary, Vols. 29-32, rev. ed.)

Despite its distinguished tradition in Japan as the *shi-shosetsu,* or "I-novel," raw autobiography in the guise of fiction was a genre Yukio Mishima dismissed with a contemptuous smirk. Like Kafka, who once noted that writing an autobiography would be as easy as recording one's dreams, Mishima was convinced that confessional writing exercised neither the imagination nor the craft to shape it into art, merely one's propensities for self-indulgence. Yet, he submitted to the considerable attraction it must have held for him on several occasions. . . . [His] early *Confessions of a Mask* (1949) can be cited, as can *Sun and Steel,* written some twenty years later. Neither conforms strictly to all *shi-shosetsu* conventions, however, the former because its material shows evidence of tight artistic control, the latter because its character as abstract discourse excludes much of the quotidian in which the *shi-shosetsu* usually revels. But both works lay bare the essential forces at play, or at war, in Mishima's puzzling psychology.

What emerges most clearly from this psychology is a conflict between two antithetical modes of being, both equally seductive for Mishima. To establish one's existence either within the confines of mentality or to do so within the confines of physicality—that was the dilemma at the center of his thinking about himself. And so consuming was his obsession with it that hardly one of his artistic productions escapes being invested with the problem, whether on the level of theme, characterization, or style.

Early in *Confessions of a Mask,* following an etiological foray into the background of the protagonist's psycho-sexual makeup, there occurs an incident immediately identifiable as one of those core events from which a lifetime's preoccupations can be seen to spring. The protagonist, a

frail, introspective, and excessively sensitive young boy stands before the gate of his family's house, watching with transfixed fascination as a parade of young men carrying a festival shrine on their shoulders passes before him. Unexpectedly they turn in his direction, crash into the garden, and proceed to destroy it in an outburst of physical intoxication. Terrified, the boy rushes into the house, where from a second-floor balcony he observes with "unaccountable agony" the men's expression of "obscene and undisguised drunkenness."

Some twenty years later, after intermittent treatments of this pivotal episode of his childhood in his work, Mishima returned to it near the beginning of *Sun and Steel* (1968), a work entirely occupied with the mind-body conflict. . . . It is apparent . . . that the boy in the scene from *Confessions of a Mask* represents mind, observing with equal amounts of repulsion and attraction the physical activity of the body, represented by the young men carrying the shrine.

The scene is a figurative projection of the rift between body and mind, muscle and brain, passion and reason, romantic abandon and classical order, that for Mishima defined the two poles between whose claims he fashioned his life. It made it the intense affair it obviously was: at worst, the thrashings of a man hopelessly entangled in irreconcilable conflicts: at best, the admirable explorations of someone exhausting every means at his disposal to find some irreproachable basis for his existence, some foothold in a soil unsusceptible to the erosions of his own psychological vacillations or his culture's compromises with values not native to it. (pp. 41-2)

[One finds] Mishima's fictional worlds . . . replete with grating conflicts, ideologies hotly contested, emotions in clashing opposition, in short, the aura of battle. But whatever the set of characters or narrative manner, the various battles remain, at bottom curiously similar. The reason is that the deepest conflicts generated in his art are worked out with the mind-body duality as the point of contention.

What readership Mishima has acquired in the West by way of translation is partly due no doubt to this characteristic of his fiction. Despite a Japanese literary tradition that acknowledges duality, the aim of artistic production and enjoyment, no less than the aim of the Zen *koan,* was to shatter the earthly habit of thinking in opposites. (p. 43)

[It] must be remembered that in the artistry of the Japanese poet or in the ideal behavior proposed by the philosopher, the paramount concern was the resolution of the duality, not the substance of the conflict itself. It was the lyricism of an attained harmony that comprised the substance of the work, not the drama of unresolved conflict. What helps to explain his enthusiastic reception in the West is the drama in Mishima's literary manner, the drama intrinsic to a matter and mind, body and soul, flesh and spirit dualism—an idea the West has lived with since at least Plato. (p. 44)

Consider the scene again: the solitary observer on the balcony and the sweaty, ecstatic group of men down below; the dispassionate, rational mind spinning words, and down in the garden, the violent, rapturous body in action. The former is associated with weakness, timidity, fear, the latter with strength, ecstasy, sex. All of Mishima's work, and the life he so intimately bound up with it, can be seen as an attempt to relinquish as a predominant perspective the Apollonian heights of the balcony and thereby to disentangle himself from the web of words that he believed falsified a pure perception of the external world while it corroded the purity of physical action. He wanted to look at the world not solely from a position of rationality inspired by fear, but from a position of communal abandon inspired by an acceptance of destruction, chaos, and death. This perspective alone could provide, as he maintained in *Sun and Steel,* the tragic view of life, the only view he believed to confer dignity and nobility on man. Digging at the obscure roots of human motivation, he discovered, like Nietzsche, a failure of nerve at the origins of the urge toward rationality, a cowardly trembling before the wild, primitive, animalistic frenzy of man's deepest instincts. Dispassionate rationality he excoriated as a makeshift bulwark against man's fear of himself, granting a false comfort in the face of pain and suffering, turning at last into a denial of death itself, cheating it of meaning, glory, and beauty.

The fly in the ointment was that, of course, Mishima as a writer could not reject words. They were what he had started with, based a career on, found himself, voluntarily or not, deeply involved with. (pp. 44-5)

As a writer, commitment to words was the *sine qua non* of his being. But words, he complained, falsified a pure experience of physicality's ultimate reality. . . . [Mind] undoes action, while body strips words of their essential and legitimate function as tools in the ordering of reality. As the thematic strands of so much of his fiction demonstrate, Mishima, conferring equal value on mind and body, found life a slow corruption of each by the other.

His deepest need was an existence of unwavering intent, uncomplicated by contrary claims to his allegiance. But neither was it possible to choose the body and live like one of the beautiful, mindless, young men who swagger through his stories as regularly as Genet's hoodlums do his, nor was it possible to choose the mind and live like one of the intellectuals who talk of beauty but stalk his fiction like flabby, wrinkled ogres. (p. 45)

That such an obsessive quest for personal fulfillment should find expression in his artistic output seems only natural, especially since art itself constituted one of the terms of the conflict he tried so desperately to resolve. That it also proved a felicitous influence is more difficult to establish. In fact, though Mishima's art is inconceivable without the various imprints of his *idée fixe,* whatever faults mar his books can often be directly traced to his obsession with the mind-body duality.

Almost every one of his works contains some permutation of this dichotomy. Except in the pages of *Sun and Steel,* a bald statement of the theme is rare. But it emerges from every book whose set of characters Mishima divided between those he endowed with the qualities he associated with mind and those he endowed with the qualities he associated with the body. Set in opposition (as, in his own mind, were the philosophical principles they stood for), these are the people who engender the tension from which any particular story derives its impetus.

The unfortunate consequence is that often the merit of a work depends almost exclusively on how well the duality is integrated into and not simply imposed on the stuff of his fiction. This means that Mishima achieved his most consistently acclaimed work either by restraining his tendency to exaggerate, or, what may amount to the same thing, by

immersing all theoretical considerations of the duality sufficiently within the human context so that his characters do not reduce to mere caricature whatever situational and human complexity he intends.

His *The Sound of Waves* (1954), for instance, limited in scope and ambition, shows none of that strenuously intellectual debate or wrenching emotional stress so prevalent in his other work. . . . Evil, in the form of two characters who represent the mind principle, remains on the periphery, failing to corrupt the pure love between its Daphnis and Chloë-modelled lovers. (p. 47)

After the Banquet (1960), places the mind-body conflict solidly within the framework of a socio-political situation. . . . Due in part to the politically-charged atmosphere surrounding his characters, providing a dimension through which the working out of the conflict could be refracted, Mishima managed here not to appear to slight the human complexity of his central characters. (pp. 47-8)

Despite a delectably nasty plot, [*Forbidden Colors,* (1951-53)] must be judged one of the most stilted and contrived he wrote. In it, the mind-body duality is so accentuated, so obviously pushed and dragged to the forefront by whatever devices of plot, scene, and character seem serviceable, that the entire enterprise creaks like some ancient and cumbrous machine. (p. 48)

Mishima seems to have envisioned human nature as ranging along a spectrum that at one extreme concluded in pure physicality, and at the other in pure mentality. Both of course are hypothetical modes of being, but figures such as Omi in *Confessions of a Mask,* Saburo in *Thirst for Love* (1950), and all those young toughs, farmhands, and soldiers who pass through his pages without a name, approach as nearly as possible what Mishima meant by living exclusively within a pure sense of their own physical presence. In his characteristic narrative manner as omniscient author (after the first-person account of *Confessions of a Mask*), Mishima never divulges their thinking; they exist within the silence of their muscles, often only as objects of erotic reverie, living in what in *Sun and Steel* he called "the world of those who are 'seen'" . . . , those who find proof of their existence in the gazes of others, or in their own gaze before a mirror. At the other extreme are those who approach a mode of being in which only a pure sense of their own consciousness is experienced. Such people derive their sense of existence from their own introspection, their thinking about themselves, and the proof of their existence lies in words. (pp. 48-9)

The archetypal situation in Mishima's fiction, the one for which the balcony scene in *Confessions of a Mask* served as prototype, involves the "solitary, humanistic man of letters" who, suspecting his dealings with words empty, false, or simply insufficient to give himself a firm sense of his own existence, turns his attention outward and finds himself enthralled by some arresting vision of physical perfection. And in his efforts to appropriate the experience of that mode of being, he corrupts it, kills it, or is destroyed himself. . . . [An explication of this idea is found in a passage from *Sun and Steel:*]

> Admittedly, I could see my own muscles in the mirror. Yet seeing alone was not enough to bring me into contact with the basic roots of my sense of existence, and an immeasura-

ble distance remained between me and the euphoric sense of pure being. . . . In other words, the self-awareness that I staked on muscles could not be satisfied with the darkness of the pallid flesh pressing about it as an endorsement of its existence, but . . . was driven to crave certain proof of its existence so fiercely that it was bound . . . to destroy that existence. . . .

That is to say, once there is self-awareness of the muscles, once the ''seen'' and the ''seeing'' occur in the same person, the ''euphoric sense of pure being'' vanishes. To close the gap between ''seeing'' and the silent, impassive sense of existence granted by muscle, a blow must be dealt ''to the realm of the senses fierce enough to silence the querulous complaints of self-awareness.'' (p. 49)

In *Forbidden Colors,* however, as in most of his books, this dialectic takes place between two figures, not within one. Mishima intentionally avoided the portrayal of just one hero. . . . [However,] both Shunsuke and Yuichi [the two characters of *Kyoko's House* (1959)] strike us as caricatures, mechanical, puppet-like creations, arbitrarily manipulated by the psychological needs and philosophical ideas of the author. (p. 50)

Despite its failure to provide characters who go beyond the limits of their categorization, *Forbidden Colors* does foreshadow the terms and the movement of the dialectical pattern worked out more satisfactorily in later novels such as *The Temple of the Golden Pavilion* (1956). In this work, which succeeds where *Forbidden Colors* fails, the ''world of those who are seen'' is represented by a temple, an inanimate structure which partakes of that world by virtue of its extraordinary beauty. . . . The working out of the dialectic does not strike the reader as too ruthlessly excessive here, perhaps because from an inanimate object we expect none of the human complexity an ''organic entity'' implies. . . . (pp. 50-1)

[The] stark terms in which Mishima saw the world dictated that the love-hate relationship between ''seen'' object and ''seeing'' subject, carried to a point of ultimate confrontation, had to end in death. And when, within *one* person, consciousness elevates ''seen'' object and ''seeing'' subject to a level where they balance with equal weight and value, the ultimate gesture must be, as Mishima came to realize as he pursued his relentless logic, an act of both suicide and murder at once. (p. 51)

By the time he began the tetralogy [*The Sea of Fertility* (1969-71),] Mishima had either abandoned his program against creating characters as ''organic entities,'' or had mastered the technique of doing so. In any case, there is no one in *The Sea of Fertility* as perfunctorily drawn as Shunsuke and Yuichi in *Forbidden Colors.* But while the dialectic at the heart of his themes may be sanctioned by tradition and the dialectic at the heart of his characters made credible by craft, the mind-body problem (or better in this context, the word-action problem) lying also at the heart of style led him to a kind of language which flaws his work as surely as did his earlier renunciation of what Forster called ''round'' characters.

Once more Mishima adheres to his formula of assigning his major characters to either side of the mind-body question. And reverting to the body principle as it applies to the

human rather than to something inanimate like a temple, the emphasis falls on passionate action rather than on physical beauty alone. As the account of the balcony scene in *Sun and Steel* makes clear, those who belong to the world of the ''seen'' are also those who ''do.'' (p. 52)

[The] nature of Mishima's language often subverts the credibility of the intense emotional ferment meant to be seen at the root of the events depicted. . . . In the give-and-take between form and formlessness, in whose process Mishima felt to reside the central impulse behind his aesthetics, one or the other may gain the upper hand, seriously compromising the finished work.

The one element of form conspicuously at odds with Mishima's favorite subject matter is his style. The rigid cast of his language—the stately rhythms, the solemn tones, its general grace and decorum—often works against the passionate nature of the people and circumstances his novels take for subject. . . . [He] postulated for his art a rupture between form and content that allied Apollonian concepts of lucidity, restraint, and calm with the former and Dionysian concepts of spontaneity and turbulence with the latter. And here, too, the gulf is unbridgeable. In at least the first two volumes of *The Sea of Fertility* he attempted to tell romantic stories with romantic characters through a framework of classically conceived rhetoric. The attempt is not wholly successful. Both Kiyoaki and Isao—characters through whom Mishima intended to celebrate the sense of ecstatic abandon stemming from a physical, as opposed to a mental, relationship to existence—remain somewhere behind his screen of words, too weak in novelistic presence to leap out at us from the confining texture of his language. And for that reason, despite the considerable effort Mishima expended to show how motive leads to act, they fail to infect the reader with a sense of their passion. This would not be the flaw it is, if he did not offer them as his ideal human type precisely on the strength of that passion.

Not due to a lack of skill, however, the problem is the result of a deliberate stylistic program. In the final pages of *Sun and Steel* Mishima spoke of driving language to emulate the body. And since, as he maintained there, the body's ideal destiny was to attain a tragic heroism through participation in group action, words should likewise aspire to that heroic, public quality. (pp. 55-6)

While his Western counterparts strove for an exact formulation of their discoveries on the frontiers of human consciousness, Mishima strove for the language of the public hero, not the language of the private explorer of a personal vision. And while the Western writer despaired over the resistance language mustered against precision, Mishima's distress sprang from his own inability to pull language back, to make it innocent again, to cleanse it until radiant with the poignant simplicity and universality of *samurai* or *kamikaze* pilot utterance.

Despair was inevitable because, notwithstanding his distaste for the modern, Mishima could not escape being a product of his age, sharing with his Western colleagues an overriding concern with self, world, and the consciousness that mediates between them. The psychological and philosophical complexities that such issues involve, however, do not lend themselves to expression in the simple utterance of Mishima's ideal, just as the ''weighty solemnity,'' the ''ceremonial, grave pace'' . . . of it undermines an adequate expression of the youthful passion of his romantic characters. (pp. 56-7)

[There] was little that mattered more to Mishima than beauty. Hardly a major character in the entire *oeuvre* is not concerned with it. Mizoguchi of *The Temple of the Golden Pavilion* provides the best example—his very being revolves around the meaning of the temple's beauty. That meaning is elusive—at one time, beauty hints at the eternal, at another, the ephemeral. But Mizoguchi concludes that beauty synthesizes contradictions, and ultimately equals nothingness. (p. 57)

The beauty Mizoguchi pursued is at once a phenomenon that synthesizes opposites, hints at the unknown, and signals nothingness. Ultimately, it is connected with death. Have we not here a clue to solve that puzzling ending of *The Sea of Fertility*? With allowances made for their respective temperaments, is Honda not another Mizoguchi? Gazing at the temple, drawn by intimations of perfection toward the realm of the absolute, Mizoguchi finds nothingness at the heart of beauty. And does not Honda [the central character of the last three volumes of *The Sea of Fertility*] in the temple garden, recalling his past with its threefold look into ideal human life, come to a recognition of the nothingness at the heart of human endeavor? If so, *The Sea of Fertility* does not end with the despairing negation some Western critics have found in the conclusion. Rather than pulling the rug out from under Honda's feet, Mishima plucks the wool from his eyes, removing the veil of ignorance and forcing him to experience the void underlying everything. (pp. 57-8)

"Nothingness was the very structure of this beauty," Mizoguchi says of the Temple of the Golden Pavilion. With an ingenious stroke, Mishima succeeded in incorporating that nothingness into the very fabric and design of his last work. As paradoxical as it may sound, it may be said that he redeemed his life by suicide and his art by installing within it its own negation.

To divest mind of its self-reflective power and prevent the body from slipping into decay, and, furthermore, to reach thereby a point where some ultimate and pure experience of each coincided—what more impossible task could Mishima have set for himself? No wonder some have seen in the cultivation of his dualistic world view nothing more than a pretext to act out a diseased craving for self-destruction. Certainly someone less obstinately intense would have repudiated an idea that argued more and more persuasively for death. And certainly someone less serious about his art would not have dared end his *magnum opus* on a note so literally effacing. Let us match seriousness for seriousness and think of his mind-body fixation as a gigantically conceived spiritual exercise through which he hoped to encounter not simply oblivion but a condition receptive to the ecstatic embracing of nothingness. Perhaps in his self-inflicted death he found such a moment. And it is somewhat of an artistic triumph that, despite his inability to fuse theorizing and the requirements of fiction, those last pages of *The Sea of Fertility* manage to impart a masterly analogue of the nothingness he yearned for. (p. 60)

Dick Wagner and Yoshio Iwamoto, "Yukio Mishima: Dialectics of Mind and Body," in Contemporary Literature *(© 1975 by the Board of Regents of the University of*

Wisconsin System), Vol. 16, No. 1, Winter, 1975, pp. 41-60.*

The Sea of Fertility spans the whole period of modern Japanese history, from 1873, in the early years of the Meiji Era, up to the 1970s. One of the book's two major themes is the dissolution during that period of the old aristocratic culture and the values which it supported. . . . (p. 61)

The other major theme of *The Sea of Fertility* is the dissolution of the individual, but this is not immediately apparent in the first volume except in an abstract discussion about history and the individual will between the hero, Kiyoaki, and his school-friend confidant, Honda. *Spring Snow* is the most appealing of the four volumes, on the face of it a straight-forward "old-fashioned" novel about the doomed, idyllic love-affair of Kiyoaki—a Byronic version of the young Mishima—with the beautiful and impeccably aristocratic heroine, Satoko. Mishima paints the period details, particularly the traditional ceremonies, costumes and scenery, with loving care; and he is masterly at setting them off against the Rolls-Royces, billiard-tables, trivial conversation and cheap values of a Japanese Edwardian society. The book ends in a blaze of romanticism with Satoko entering a Buddhist monastery and Kiyoaki dying of tuberculosis almost at its gates. . . .

For the remaining three volumes the main viewpoint shifts to Honda. He becomes, as it were, Kiyoaki's ghost, a walking memory of the handsome selfish youth who died at the age of twenty, surrounded by the dispiriting signs of a new age but himself enclosed as in a mediaeval garden by his deliberately impossible, deliberately high-flown and archaic romance. In order to convey Honda's ghostliness, Mishima uses the idea of reincarnation. Thus through each of the three volumes there is a fresh body on to which Honda's consciousness can fasten. In the story Honda becomes convinced that Kiyoaki has been reborn when he sees the familiar pattern of three moles on each of the three bodies in succession. This is the "fairy-tale" element of the book . . . which was no doubt partly responsible for its cold reception. But the importance of the idea structurally is that it separates a rational, sleepless consciousness, upon which the compromising reality of modern life constantly impinges, from a series of nonrational physical ideals which die almost at the moment they flower and whose perfection is impervious to everyday reality.

Here then is that absolute division between the classical awareness and the romantic being, or to put it another way between the writer's mind and his psychological need, which seems to be basic to an understanding of Mishima's nature. (p. 62)

John Spurling, "Death in Hero's Costume: The Meaning of Mishima," in Encounter *(© 1975 by Encounter Ltd.), May, 1975, pp. 56, 58-64.*

There is always something curiously cerebral about the erotic obsessions and fantasies which Mishima depicts. . . . Mishima is at his best in coolly showing people so driven by fantasies that their violent acts are accompanied by disturbing sexual excitement. He becomes unconvincing and artificial when he attempts to link these fantasies with political ideologies or philosophical doctrines. Even the Buddhism and Shintoism which appear in Mishima's last work . . ., *The Sea of Fertility,* are like doctrines carefully studied and put to use by a foreign writer; rather than anything lived from within.

How are we to account for the banality of some of his novels such as *The Sound of Waves,* or the unbelievably shoddy quality of the arguments in his right-wing political tracts? Perhaps these are better understood in the light of his cult of the deliberate. He felt that the intentionally preposterous was better than the accidentally mediocre.... To be able to publish such a simple tale, written in a popular style, was itself, for Mishima, a superior act. Indeed, he described the book, according to [John] Nathan, as a "joke on the public." And one suspects that some of Mishima's crude political writing was also something of a joke on the public, an exercise in creating for himself a public image and in manipulating popular reactions to it. But of course the simplistic effects he achieved in such novels as *The Sound of Waves* and in his tracts are no less a failure for having been deliberate. Nor was his work helped by his longings for what he misleadingly called "purity"—which for him is nothing more than a single-minded and total absorption in an emotion or belief; the more implausible the belief and more destructive the emotion, the "purer" Mishima considered such absorption to be.

Two autobiographical novels, *Confessions of a Mask* and *Kyoko's House,* reveal his fascination with the workings of self-deception. He tried to show how those who play-act can remain aware that they are embracing illusions, and by that very awareness keep a precarious contact with reality....

[In] his best works Mishima was a great craftsman of Japanese prose, and deep down he seemed to be a sensitive and vulnerable man. (p. 49)

> *Hidé Ishiguro, "Writer, Rightist or Freak?" in* The New York Review of Books (*reprinted with permission from* The New York Review of Books; *copyright* © *1975 NYREV, Inc.), December 11, 1975, pp. 48-9.*

Three years before his suicide, Mishima wrote at length on his interpretation of *Hagakure,* a seventeenth-century treatise on the ethics of the samurai trade, and the influence the book had had on his career. Readers seriously interested in Mishima's work will certainly find this an important statement. It will interest, if not altogether enlighten, even readers merely curious about what Kathryn Sparling, the translator, sums up as "Mishima's death for the sake of an emperor who had no interest in him, for a cause to which he knew he would contribute nothing—and by his own hand." (pp. 96-7)

> *Phoebe-Lou Adams, in* The Atlantic Monthly (*copyright* © *1977 by The Atlantic Monthly Company, Boston, Mass.; reprinted with permission), September, 1977.*

* * *

MOJTABAI, A(nn) G(race)   1938-

Mojtabai is an American novelist. (See also *CLC,* Vol. 5.)

Did you read, and if you did, have you been able to forget "Mundome," A. G. Mojtabai's first novel? ... "Mundome" made a small critical splash and then sank into the customary oceanic depths reserved for promising but unspectacular first novels....

["The 400 Eels of Sigmund Freud"] bears no resemblance in subject matter to the first [novel]. Where its sibling relationship is evident is in its fine, reserved, simple prose which also distinguished the first book. Mojtabai is able to make a kind of verbal mezzotint out of such materials as the death of a mad woman's parrot.... (p. 7)

The novel works well, and if it is not quite the full-bodied performance that A. G. Mojtabai seems on the verge of presenting us with, it is still, in its alembic form, a fine, intelligent and moving work. (p. 8)

> *Doris Grumbach, in* The New York Times Book Review (© *1976 by The New York Times Company; reprinted by permission), May 30, 1976.*

[A] summer community of high-school trainees dedicated to the ideals of scientific humanism is the subject of ... *The Four Hundred Eels of Sigmund Freud.* ... Despite the title, the founding father is mentioned only once....

A witty and tantalizingly subtle portrait of derangement, *Mundome* was a brilliant début. [Mojtabai's] second novel, though superbly controlled and perceptive, is also more predictable, a highly polished performance without the vitality and astonishment of *Mundome.* ...

[Somehow] the novel doesn't have the tragic resonance that Mojtabai has aimed for. Her eye for the pretensions and sweetness, the cosmic yearning and disorderly intelligence of the precocious young is acute but also rather chilly.... Mrs. Mojtabai is spare and cryptically suggestive to a fault. In her ruthless trimming of anything that smacks of fatty excess, she has also shorn away some of the living tissue as indispensable to her story as the eels of Sigmund Freud. (p. 16)

> *Pearl K. Bell, in* The New Leader (© *1976 by the American Labor Conference on International Affairs, Inc.), June 7, 1976.*

Science's dream of Utopia is blind to the most urgent needs of human beings. A sensitive child will be brutalized at an authoritarian school. These themes, you say, have for a century or so been overworked in fiction, but A. G. Mojtabai does not agree with you. She exercises both in ["The 400 Eels of Sigmund Freud"]. (p. 93)

Mojtabai's story is all prelude to a crisis or a moral greater than the tired one she produces. A dreadful competence suffuses her novel when what was needed is punch, brilliance or originality. Unwilling or unable to create a situation that is truly harrowing or resonant, she attempts to compensate by underlining her characters' fatigued perceptions: "The real trouble was that nobody, but nobody, in that madhouse had any sense of humor." Perhaps her story might have been tauter had she limited her perspective to one ... point of view. By giving us everybody's musings she has made a short novel seem far too long. (pp. 93-4)

> *Peter S. Prescott, "Prelude to Crisis," in* Newsweek (*copyright 1976 by Newsweek, Inc.; all rights reserved; reprinted by permission), June 7, 1976, pp. 93-4.*

[In *The 400 Eels of Sigmund Freud*] the writing is good enough to create a final dissatisfaction with the novel, which seems to promise more than it gives. Looking for emblematic truth by means of concrete occasion, A. G.

Mojtabai ends up with a beautifully caught occasion which is slightly too concrete to carry any distance beyond itself, too full of mice and science and what looks like autobiographical reminiscence. It is not enough to make an emblem, it makes only a delicate story rather thinly clothed in implications. (p. 10)

> *Michael Wood, in* The New York Review of Books *(reprinted with permission from* The New York Review of Books; *copyright* © *1976 NYREV, Inc.), June 10, 1976.*

["The 400 Eels of Sigmund Freud"] opens with all signs pointing in the direction of the gothic.... But although there is a bit of violence toward the end of the book, that's not where it ends up at all—to the extent that it ends up anywhere. As in the author's first novel, "Mundome," it is once again human nature facing a dead end that seems to fascinate her.... The book simmers along like a savory stew, with various interesting people ... surfacing briefly and then disappearing. But nothing comes together very much, and whereas "Mundome" had a mysterious, disturbing quality about it, this one seems merely unthought-out and disconnected. (p. 84)

> The New Yorker *(© 1976 by The New Yorker Magazine, Inc.), July 5, 1976.*

*   *   *

MONTALE, Eugenio   1896-

The greatest living Italian poet, Montale is also a translator, journalist, and critic. Montale began his career as a poet of landscape, but under the influence of Valéry and the symbolists he broke away from the staid conventions of Italian poetry of the twenties to produce a richly symbolic verse with cryptic, unconventional lyrics. The obscurity of his poetry led critics to name him along with Ungaretti and Quasimodo as the founders of the poetic movement known as hermeticism. His love of music, as well as his poetic philosophy, is revealed in the following quote: "I wanted to free the music in words, apply them to reality, and in transcending mere depiction capture what is essential." The sea is a frequent symbol, exile and uncertainty are common themes, and despair and desolation are recurrent moods in Montale's poetry. In awarding him the Nobel Prize for Literature in 1975, the Academy cited his pessimistic but "indelible feeling for the value of life and the dignity of mankind." (See also *CLC*, Vol. 7, and *Contemporary Authors*, Vols. 17-20, rev. ed.)

[The] Swedish Academy's reference to [Montale's] "deep pessimism if not negativism" and an ancient and misleading custom in the English-speaking world of linking his work to Eliot's—seems to me to miss the vein of ironic humor, often self-directed, and satirical fantastication evident in his most recent poetry (e.g., 1961-72: *New Poems* represents about half of it).... (p. 341)

The materials for Montalean humor are, I think, much the same as the materials of his central myth expressed thirty years ago in the following manner:

> It seemed to me I lived under a glass bell, and yet I felt myself close to something essential. A subtle veil, a thread just kept me from the ultimate *quid*. Absolute expression would have meant the breaking of that bell, that thread, the end of the illusion of the

world as representation. But this was an unreachable limit.

If this recalls the solipsistic nightmare of Eliot's wasteland prisoners—

> We think of the key, each in his prison
> Thinking of the key, each confirms a prison

and the accompanying gloss from F. H. Bradley to the effect that "my experience falls within my own circle, a circle closed on the outside," there is nevertheless a vital distinction to be made: in Montale's world the circle is not entirely vicious, the blockade can be run, the limit may be not only reached but surpassed. In the earlier poems this rule-proving exception, this passage permitted from contingency to "something essential," this "liberty, miracle, fact that was not necessary" (as he put it in the great "Chrysalis" of 1924), is for certain others only; the poet sees himself as witness, transfixed and prevented from participation in the miracle his poetry serves. In later poems however the *direction* of passage is discovered to be more benevolent: centripetal that is—if we take the self as center—as well as centrifugal. Which is to say that a chosen few from Montale's life-experience—those evoked by his famous *tu* for instance, or the stormy angel Clizia, or more recently his companion-wife La Mosca ... may return from beyond the barrier bringing those who must, like the poet, remain behind care and renewed courage to endure with decency. For Montale, who only half-mockingly styles himself a Nestorian (Nestorius was a fifty-century "heretic" who taught the fundamental humanity of Christ), believes that the other order—the one we call divine—must submit to incarnation, to metamorphosis into flesh and blood, in order to fulfill itself.... Like Hölderlin he feels that the possibility of ... recognition [of "divinity incognito"] is the privilege of poets. (pp. 341-42)

[The] pre-1960 Montale is above all a dramatic poet, the poet of (the italics are his own) "*this* individual, in *this* place, in *this* situation," and the product is matchless: a powerful and impassioned vocal music moving through its various specific occasions of ecstasy and anguish, metrically intricate, *ore rotundo*. The new manner is very different.

It lies in what I shall call a distancing or de-dramatizing of the subject (as with a telescope reversed) by various stylistic means, ... all of which contribute to the vein of humor lightening the latest work [*New Poems*]. Something of this more casual, free-floating, "prosaic" and *désengagé* mood may be caught in the Italian titles for the poems of this phase: *Satura* (miscellany, mixed-bag-including satire, gallimaufry) and, of course, *Diario*. I do not mean that earlier Montale lacked humor, far from it, but the vein is much more in evidence here. Perhaps it is the appropriate voice for a certain sort of old age and retirement: the poet was 72 when he wrote "Divinita in Incognito." But the ghosts of Yeats and Ungaretti are there to give me the lie....

[Both Hardy and Montale] composed sequences arising from the death of their wives, Hardy in the *Veteris vestigia flammae* (vestiges of the ancient flame) of 1912-13, Montale in the *Xenia* (guest-offerings) of 1964-67. But if the occasions are similar the differences in situation and response and therefore tonality are far more striking.... Hardy's vestiges haunt and taunt him—the original air-blue gown is gone forever or survives in mocking memory only. Whereas

Montale, technically bereft and bemused, most unelegiacally hosts a persisting if elusive presence flickeringly *there* in the charmed clutter of what he calls La Mosca's relics . . . which manage to encapsulate and maintain her essential being. . . .

One aspect of the comic touch in late Montale is precisely [his] sense of the insubstantiality in the world of the so-called living, our ongoing "human show" landing its capsules on the moon, consoling itself with Teilhard de Chardin, packing a murderous Olympics. As he notes to his guest, La Mosca,

> We had studied for the hereafter
> a token of recognition, a whistle;
> I'm now trying to modulate it in the hope
> that we're all already dead without knowing it.
>
> (p. 342)

Robert Lowell writes that . . . [Montale] "was strong in simple prose and could be made still stronger in free verse." I agree with the first point—Montale's muscular, dramatic flair plus his intelligence and sharp wit make his verse, *unlike* Leopardi's or Ungaretti's for example, reasonably available in a "simple prose." On the other hand free verse is surely not a "stronger" medium for any but the latest batch of poems. . . . (p. 344)

> *Joseph Cary, "Count Your Dead: They Are Alive," in* The Nation *(copyright 1976 by the Nation Associates, Inc.), October 9, 1976, pp. 341-42, 344.*

Although never prolific, . . . [Montale] built up a reputation for the tense integrity, the evocative power, and often the inner anguish of work produced at one of the most difficult times of Italian history. One can draw strength from difficulty, and Montale has always been aware of the paradox that, as he says, he 'would not want to live at any other period' and yet his inspiration to write could come only from a feeling of 'discord with surrounding reality'. Hence, no doubt, the characteristic mixture, in his first three volumes, of bleakness ('Eastbourne'), and haunting recollections ('The Customs-Officers' House') and self-questioning ('Arsenio'), and yet, also, deep current of thrusting life ('The Eel'). As he wrote in some striking lines in a later poem ('Blow and Counterblow'):

> Hardly out of adolescence
> I was flung for half my life
> into the Augean stables.

Out of such alienation came a poetry of pent force and brooding intensity. The 30 years from *Ossi di Seppia* to *La bufera e altro* (1956) are the years of his strongest and most enduring work; but after his wife died in 1963, he began to write a series of elegies for her, and in doing so, started off another phase of poetic activity, which saw publication as *Satura* (1971) and *Diario del '71 e del '72* (1973). It is from these two collections that [*New Poems*] has been made.

Satura contains the best-known of these recent poems, the elegiac sequences called 'Xenia I and II', together with other poems reminiscent of his wife, and various reflective and ironic pieces; the *Diario,* as its title implies, is largely a repository for occasional poems, often satirical, but again sometimes elegiac. In this latest phase, Montale writes with an easy assurance, often of everyday things. The pages have much reference to persons and places, many words and phrases from other languages—English, French, German, Latin—inserted without italics, many minute and stinging signals of the here and now and of the there and then of an actual past. In general, the tone is lighter than that of his earlier work, engaging, surprising, mocking, but now and again very touching, as it records some detail of loss or kindness or cruelty or pity.

> *Edwin Morgan, "Quartet of Straws," in* The Listener *(© British Broadcasting Corp. 1976; reprinted by permission of Edwin Morgan), October 14, 1976, p. 484.*

[Characteristically] throughout [Montale's] poetic career he has sought in the miscellaneous events and articles of daily life a satisfying image of his own condition. What is remarkable is less his ambition than his success in marrying the public with the private—evident more than ever in [*New Poems*], in which personal reminiscence and metaphysical speculation find natural metaphors in radio announcements, chiming clocks and even the moon landing. He does not identify with mass culture and its institutions or with modern technology. Indeed, he is sceptical of their worth. But the refusal to believe in them need not be a refusal to use them. . . . The telephone, the television and the photograph are successful in communicating, among other things, a sense of our individual isolation. In any case, he doesn't believe in himself—he speculates in 'The Ghost' whether, after all, the phantasm 'is not the lost original and I its facsimile'. In 1960, he wrote of his wartime collection, *La Bufera e altra,* which he thought his best. 'It vividly reflects my historical as well as my human condition' and his unhappy love affair described there becomes, as the loss of a child to Ungaretti, a part of the tragedy of the war.

The love poems in that volume anticipate in many ways the two 'Xenia' sequences in *Satura,* written after his wife's death and about her. Naturally, the fragmentary poems of Xenia are an occasion to remember, but they are also an occasion to make a poignant contrast between the passages of historical time and the nature of personal time—'tempo cronologico' and 'tempo psicologico' he calls them in a note to his collection of essays, *Auto da Fé.* What is historically over survives in the memory and many of the other poems in *Satura* ('Time and Times', 'Here and There', 'The End of 1968', *etc*) turn on the disparity between public and private time—most beautifully expressed in 'The Arno at Rovezzano'. . . . Montale's peculiar tone derives from his ability to live with the disparity—his poems themselves recognise they are only momentary reconciliations. . . . [His] scepticism provides a firm basis for poetry. 'Neither in God nor in Marx', the title of one of his essays, asserts that uncertainty is the main characteristic of the post-war crisis in Italy and uncertainty is the major theme of these latest poems. But uncertainty is not indifference—the characteristic feature of Italian inter-war poetry, according to the critic Russi. It is the possibility of facing life without illusions about meta-physical certainties—a legacy from Croce. . . .

Unlike the T S Eliot of the *Four Quartets,* Montale's qualifications and reservations ('They say . . .') reflect an acceptance of the absurdities of the poet's position in an age where values are in the hands of the mass media, controlled by capitalist interests. . . . But the impossibility of a lasting synthesis is itself a reassurance that individuals suffer differently. Unlike Eliot, too, Montale's river is not a god but history, to be viewed dispassionately and not accepted, and what redeems its heartlessness is the light reflected on its surface as it turns a bend. There it becomes personal history—Montale is the historian of the moments history misses ('We Went') or does not acknowledge ('After a Flight' and 'Two Venetian Pieces').

Not surprisingly, in view of this, Montale's favourite mode of expression is through apparent paradox which reveals a new ground for hope. . . . The fragments that Montale succeeds in shoring up do not imply a fragmented world but only their modest role in the synthesis. Montale shares with Croce a wish to base metaphysical speculations on particular, commonly accessible experiences. Even what is repugnant has its part to play. Although Montale, the critic, acknowledges that Italian poets have been hampered by their tradition, and although he rejects D'Annunzio, the precursor of Fascism, he learned from his metrical experiments—the same catholic taste recommends Gozzano . . . as well as Pound and Petrarch. . . .

Montale's tone [in the 'Xenia' poems] is suggested by quoting T S Eliot's definition of Marvell's 'wit'. The effect of such parallels is to remove the poet from the world in which he lives and to place him in a hermetically sealed and alien tradition. Anglo-Saxons persist in seeing Pound's fascist propaganda as an eccentric aberration: it was, in fact, in the context of Italian culture, not unreasonable. Not that social and cultural history are necessary to appreciate the poems, but the implication that his work is purely literary, merely a further link in the tradition, softens the impact. . . . Ironically, the more contemporary a poet is, the more his culture matters to us. In his notes Singh [the translator] explains the allusions and rare words but the reader would never guess that they are a central part of Montale's desire to create a common language of images. (p. 48)

> *Paul Carter, "Passionate Sceptic," in* Books and Bookmen *(© copyright Paul Carter 1976; reprinted with permission), December, 1976, pp. 48-9.*

Montale, despite the efforts of [translators], is still not an English poet in the way in which Homer, say, was to Keats (in Chapman's version) or Rihaku is to us (in Pound's). Montale is up for grabs. But some of [Edwin] Morgan's versions (*Sarcophagi I & II; Bring Me The Sunflower; Eastbourne*) manage to reenact Montale's astonishing clarity; that of 'a sunflower's open face / and rabbits dancing lightly round and round. . . .' (p. 86)

> *James Greene, in* London Magazine *(© London Magazine 1977), February-March, 1977.*

Montale in these poems [*New Poems*] composed in his seventies—and still so firm an enemy of anything limiting the mystery of the imagination—is still forever questioning the status of imaginative truth. It is as if each poem starts from a gentle "And so what" in response to a thought or perception, and ends by handing the question over to the reader. For if Montale's work has long offered "occasions" or "epiphanies" it is the puzzle of such moments that holds him. His is the wisdom of a man witty, intelligent and reductive, in no doubt of what is false but driven by a sober obsession to seek what is true. Occasionally a set piece will allow him to relish the wit of the paradoxes which fill his mind, as in 'L'Élan Vital' where the materialist finds god

only in the 'antiteleological' thunder of the universe and then has his speech silenced by the roar of a jumbo jet; or 'In The Courtyard' where public events break into the indolence of spring with news that a specialist in tumours has been elected to parliament. But in the more personal poems the paradoxes are undramatic, denied the relief of conclusiveness, teasing through their passive refusal to give emotions the security of a rational source. This is most evident in the many poems to his dead wife Mosca, including the rightly celebrated 'Xenia I & II'. . . . These poems are of memory, which has the capacity to make both the living poet and his dead wife equally alive. The events take place in his mind but they are created of physical properties—touch, sound, sight, taste, smell. (p. 76)

Mosca's myopia, telephone calls, a tin shoe-horn, friends, places and fragments of conversation are quietly re-traced as sources of contact. Images are allowed to become metaphors then brought to earth: literal details, such as the names of wines, Inferno and Paradiso, can be wittily elevated and reduced. The sceptical intelligence evaluates, weighs, but does so in an atmosphere of tender recollection. . . . (p. 77)

> *Desmond Graham, in* Stand *(copyright © by Stand), Vol. 18, No. 2 (1977).*

Montale is a kind of anachronism, and the extent of his contribution to poetry has been anachronistically great. A contemporary of Apollinaire, T. S. Eliot, Mandelstam, and Hart Crane, he belongs more than chronologically to that generation. Each of these writers wrought a qualitative change in his respective literature, as did Montale, whose task was much the hardest. . . .

A stern metaphysical realist with an evident taste for extremely condensed imagery, Montale managed to create his own poetic idiom through the juxtaposition of what he called "the aulic"—the courtly—and the "prosaic"; an idiom which as well could be defined as *"amaro stile nuovo"* (the bitter new style), in contrast to Dante's formula which reigned in Italian poetry for more than six centuries. The most remarkable aspect of Montale's achievement is that he managed to push forward despite the grip of the *dolce stile nuovo*. In fact, far from trying to loosen this grip, Montale constantly refers to or paraphrases the great Florentine both in imagery and vocabulary. His allusiveness is partially responsible for the charges of obscurity that critics occasionally level against him. . . .

The maturity that Montale displayed in his very first book —*Ossi di Seppia*, published in 1925—makes it more difficult to account for his development. Already here he has subverted the ubiquitous music of the Italian hendecasyllabics, assuming a deliberately monotonous intonation that is occasionally made shrill by the addition of feet or is muted by their omission—one of the many techniques he employs in order to avoid prosodic inertia. If one recalls Montale's immediate predecessors (and the flashiest figure among them is certainly D'Annunzio), it becomes clear that stylistically Montale is indebted to nobody—or to everybody he bounces up against in his verse, for polemic is one form of inheritance.

This continuity through rejection is evident in Montale's use of rhyme. Apart from its function as a kind of linguistic echo, a sort of homage to the language, a rhyme lends a sense of inevitability to the poet's statement. Advantageous as it is, the repetitive nature of a rhyme scheme (or for that matter, of any scheme) creates the danger of overstatement. To prevent this, Montale often shifts from rhymed to unrhymed verse within the same poem. His objection to overstatement is clearly an ethical as well as an aesthetic one—proving that a poem is a form of the closest possible interplay between ethics and aesthetics.

This interplay, lamentably, is precisely what tends to vanish in translation. Still, despite the loss of his "vertebrate compactness" . . . , Montale survives translation well. By lapsing inevitably into a different tonality, translation—because of its explanatory nature—somehow catches up with the original by clarifying those things which could be regarded by the author as self-evident and thus elude the native reader. Though much of the subtle, discrete music is lost, the American reader has an advantage in understanding the meaning, and would be less likely to repeat in English an Italian's charges of obscurity. . . .

Perhaps the term "development" is not applicable to a poet of Montale's sensitivity, if only because it implies a linear process; poetic thinking always has a synthetic quality and employs—as Montale himself expresses it in one of his poems—a kind of "bat-radar" technique, i.e., thought operates in a 360 degree range. Also, at any given time a poet is in possession of an entire language and his preference for an archaic word is dictated by his subject matter or his nerves rather than by a preconceived stylistic program. The same is true of syntax, stanzaic design, and the like. For sixty years Montale has managed to sustain his poetry on a stylistic plateau, the altitude of which one senses even in translation.

New Poems is . . . Montale's sixth book to appear in English. But unlike previous editions which aspired to give a comprehensive idea of the poet's entire career, this volume contains only poems written during the last decade, coinciding thus with Montale's most recent (1971) collection—*Satura.* And though it would be senseless to view them as the ultimate word of the poet, still—because of their author's age and their unifying theme, the death of his wife—each conveys to some extent an air of finality. For death as a theme always produces a self-portrait. (p. 35)

The protagonist of the *New Poems* is preoccupied with the attempt to estimate the distance between himself and his interlocutor and then to figure out the response "she" would have made had she been present. The silence into which his speech necessarily has been directed harbors, by implication, more in the way of answers than human imagination can afford, a fact which endows Montale's "her" with undoubted superiority. In this respect Montale resembles neither T. S. Eliot nor Thomas Hardy, with whom he has been frequently compared, but rather Robert Frost of the "New Hampshire period," with his idea that woman was created out of man's rib (a nickname for heart) neither to be loved nor to be loving, nor to be judged, but to be "a judge of thee." Unlike Frost, however, Montale is dealing with a form of superiority that is a *fait accompli*—superiority *in absentia*—and this stirs in him not so much a sense of guilt as a feeling of disjunction: his persona in these poems has been exiled into "outer time."

This is, therefore, love poetry in which death plays approximately the same role as it does in *La Divina Commedia* or in Petrarch's sonnets to Madonna Laura: the role of a

guide. But here quite a different person is moving along familiar lines; his speech has nothing to do with sacred anticipation. What Montale displays in *New Poems* is that tenaciousness of imagination, that urge to outflank death, which might enable a person, upon arriving and finding "Kilroy was here," to recognize his own handwriting.

But there is no morbid fascination with death, no falsetto in these poems; what the poet is talking about here is the absence which lets itself be felt in exactly the same nuances of language and feeling as those which "she" once used to manifest "her" presence—the language of intimacy. Hence the extremely private tone of the poems in their technique and in their close detail. This voice of a man speaking—often muttering—to himself is generally the most conspicuous characteristic of Montale's poetry, but this time the personal note is enforced by the fact that the poet's persona is talking about things only he and she had knowledge of—shoehorns, suitcases, the names of hotels where they used to stay, mutual acquaintances, books they had both read. Out of this sort of *realia,* and out of the inertia of intimate speech, emerges a private mythology which gradually acquires all the traits appropriate to any mythology, including surrealistic visions, metamorphoses, and the like. In this mythology, instead of some female-breasted sphinx, there is the image of "her," minus her glasses: this is the surrealism of subtraction, and this subtraction, affecting either subject matter or tonality, is what gives unity to this collection. (pp. 35-6)

Death is always a song of "innocence," never of experience. And from the beginning of his career Montale shows his preference for song over confession. Although less explicit than confession, a song is less repeatable; as is loss. Over the course of a lifetime psychological acquisitions become more real than real estate. . . . [The] poems that make up the present volume are full of references to Dante. Sometimes a reference consists of a single word, sometimes an entire poem is an echo—like No. 13 of "Xenia I" which echoes the conclusion of the twenty-first Song in the *Purgatorio,* the most stunning scene in the whole *Cantica.* But what marks Montale's poetic and human wisdom is his rather bleak, almost exhausted, falling intonation. After all, he is speaking to a woman with whom he has spent many years: he knows her well enough to realize that she would not appreciate a tragic tremolo. He knows, certainly, that he is speaking into silence; the pauses that punctuate his lines suggest the closeness of that void which is made somewhat familiar—if not inhabited—because of his belief that "she" might be there. And it is the sense of her presence that keeps him from resorting to expressionistic devices, elaborate imagery, catch-phrases, and the like. She who died would resent verbal flamboyance as well. Montale is old enough to know that the classically "great" line, however immaculate its conception, flatters the audience and is a kind of shortcut to self-deception. He is perfectly aware of where his speech is directed. (p. 36)

New Poems provides an idiom which is clearly new. It is largely Montale's own idiom, but some of it derives from the act of translation, whose limited means only increase the original austerity. The cumulative effect of this book is startling, not so much because the psyche portrayed in *New Poems* has no previous record in world literature, as because it makes it clear that such a mentality could not be expressed in English as its original language. The question "why" may only obscure the reason; because even in Montale's native Italian such a mentality is strange enough to earn him the reputation of an exceptional poet....

New Poems ought to be read and reread a number of times, if not for the sake of analysis, the function of which is to return a poem to its stereoscopic state—the way it existed in the poet's mind—then for the fugitive beauty of this subtle, muttering, and yet firm stoic voice, which tells us that the world ends with neither a bang nor a whimper but with a man talking, pausing, and then talking again. When you have had such a long life, anticlimax ceases to be just another device.

The book is certainly a monologue; it couldn't be otherwise when the interlocutor is absent, as is nearly always the case in poetry. Partly, however, the idea of monologue as a principal device springs from the "poetry of absence," another name for the greatest literary movement since Symbolism—a movement which came into existence in Europe, and especially in Italy, in the Twenties and Thirties—"Hermeticism." (p. 37)

Montale has the reputation of being the most difficult poet of [the Hermetic] school and he is certainly more difficult—in the sense of being more complex—than Ungaretti or Salvatore Quasimodo. But for all the overtones, reticence, merging of associations or hints of associations in his work, its hidden references, substitutions of general statements for microscopic detail, elliptical speech, etc., it was he who wrote "*la primavera Hitleriana*" ("The Hitler Spring").... [The] "hermeticist" label became glued to Montale's back, and he has, ever since, been considered an "obscure" poet. But whenever one hears of obscurity, it is time to stop and ponder one's notion of clarity, for it usually rests on what is already known or preferred, or, in the worst cases, remembered. In this sense, the more obscure, the better....

Montale seems to be the last person to disclose his inner processes of thought, let alone the "secrets of his craft." A private man, he prefers to make the public life the subject of his scrutiny, rather than the reverse. *Poet in Our Time* is a book concerned precisely with the results of such scrutiny, and its emphasis falls on "Our Time" rather than on "Poet."

Both the lack of chronology and the harsh lucidity of language in these pieces supply this book with an air of diagnosis or of verdict. The patient or the accused is the civilization which "believes it is walking while in fact it is being carried along by a conveyor belt," but since the poet realizes that he is himself the flesh of this civilization's flesh,

neither cure nor rehabilitation is implied. *Poet in Our Time* is, in fact, the disheartened, slightly fastidious testament of a man who doesn't seem to have inheritors other than the "hypothetical stereophonic man of the future incapable even of thinking his own destiny."...

It is a tempting and dangerous thing to quote Montale because it easily turns into a full-time occupation. Italians have their way with the future, from Leonardo to Marinetti. Still, this temptation is due not so much to the aphoristic quality of Montale's statements or even to their prophetic quality, as to the tone of voice, which alone makes one trust what he is saying because it is so free of anxiety. There is a certain air or recurrence to it, kindred to water coming ashore or the invariable refraction of light in a lens. When one lives as long as he has, "the provisional encounters between the real and the ideal" become frequent enough for the poet both to develop a certain familiarity with the ideal and to be able to foretell the possible changes of its features. For the artist, these changes are perhaps the only sensible measurements of Time.

There is something remarkable about the almost simultaneous appearance of [*Poet in Our Time* and *New Poems*]; they seem to merge. In the end, *Poet in Our Time* makes the most appropriate illustration of the "outer time" inhabited by the persona of the *New Poems*. Again, this is a reversal of *La Divina Commedia* where this world was understood as "that realm." "Her" absence for Montale's persona is as palpable as "her" presence was for Dante's. The repetitive nature of existence in this after-life-now is, in its turn, kindred to Dante's circling among those "who died as men before their bodies died." *Poet in Our Time* supplies us with a sketch—and sketches are always somewhat more convincing than oils—of that rather overpopulated spiral landscape of such dying yet living beings.

This book doesn't sound very "Italian," although the old civilization contributes a great deal to the accomplishment of this old man of letters. The words "European" and "International" when applied to Montale also look like tired euphemisms for "universal." Montale is one writer whose mastery of language stems from his spiritual autonomy; thus, both *New Poems* and *Poet in Our Time* are what books used to be before they became mere books: chronicles of souls. (pp. 38-9)

Joseph Brodsky, "The Art of Montale," in The New York Review of Books (*reprinted with permission from* The New York Review of Books; *copyright © 1977 NYREV, Inc.*), *June 9, 1977, pp. 36-9.*

N

NAIPAUL, V(idiadhar)S(urajprasad)   1932-

A novelist, essayist, short story writer, and author of travel books, Naipaul was born in Trinidad of Indian parents and has resided in England since 1950. His early works drew praise for their clear prose style and delicate sense of humor. Critics have lauded his ability to capture with wit and compassion the West Indian dialect and life style. (See also *CLC*, Vols. 4, 7, and *Contemporary Authors*, Vols. 1-4, rev. ed.)

[The] most arresting quality of Naipaul's sensibility [is] his acute sensitivity to sights, sounds and smells. When the object of his attention is the physical world, the result has been some superbly evocative descriptive writing. But when the object is the human body and its functions, the sensitivity tends to become a fastidiousness which at times, especially in connection with female sexuality, borders on revulsion and which contributes to the distinctive atmospheric tincture with which much of Naipaul's writing is suffused. This fastidiousness is responsible for some of his finest effects, for example the atmosphere of pervasive horror that is gradually built up in *In a Free State*. But it is also responsible for some of the most gratuitous, like the page-long description of a stranger's eating habits at the end of *The Mimic Men*. On balance, it is hard not to regard Naipaul's congenital fastidiousness, the Brahmin cast of his sensibility, as a mixed blessing for his fiction and as a more important creative determinant than he once thought his colonial background was.

Both Naipaul's sensibility and his experimentation with schemata are evident in *Guerrillas*. . . . The setting is an unnamed Caribbean island, for all practical purposes Trinidad, and the plot is obviously based on the career of Michael de Freitas, the Trinidadian black-power leader. One of the novel's most striking features is the willed exteriorization of the picture of Trinidad, the one place on earth Naipaul knows intimately from the inside. The island is seen almost entirely from the point of view of transient whites; representatives of its East Indian community, the macro-subject of Naipaul's first three novels, appear *en passant* in only one scene; and the novel's three principal foci—sex, race and a white, outside point of view—are the very elements which in 1958 Naipaul said that, for reasons of artistic integrity, he was not able to use in making his Trinidadian subject matter more appealing to the non-West-Indian reader. (Concerning the first of them Naipaul said

that he lacked sufficiently wide experience, disarmingly adding that his friends would laugh and his mother be shocked.) (p. 75)

Naipaul is as pitiless concerning [the three central characters in *Guerrillas*] and their interrelationships as he is tireless in his notation of the sweat, dirt, heat, and ugliness that surround them. All are pathetically limited and inauthentic; each misunderstands and misinterprets the others and wrongly thinks he or she figures largely in the others' thoughts and fantasies. All mime the gestures of either revolution, humanitarian concern or romance with an awkwardness that ill conceals their inadequacies and essential hollowness. All are emotionally, spiritually and intellectually impoverished, burnt-out cases like the drought-stricken, sun-scorched landscapes and like the island itself, which seems to Jane (nothing in the novel gainsays her view) 'a place at the end of the world, a place that had exhausted its possibilities'. A fourth character, who at least aspires to authenticity and self-fulfillment, and whose views may to a degree be taken to have authorial sanction (though Naipaul is too scrupulous a writer to have a spokesman for himself within his novel), tells Jane and Roche that they will never change, that the life they have lived in the past is the life they will live in the future; the remark is as true of Jimmy as it is of the two other dead souls. (p. 76)

Resemblances between *In a Free State* and *Guerrillas* could be multiplied, for the central situations as well as the central characters are similar: heat, sweat, colonial relics, abandoned industrial estates, and ugly corrugated buildings are the background to the explosion of a volatile political situation which is obliquely glimpsed by the white couples who exist 'in a free state' of non-alignment but are nevertheless tested by events. In each work, the political upheaval follows the same pattern: racial strife among the principal non-white factions; demagogy, incidental persecution and exploitation of non-white minority groups; and evidence of American intervention. But while the subject matter is similar, the schemata are different. *In a Free State* has the resonant spareness, the single emotional key (the sustained sense of mounting fear and horror) and the parabolic dimension (too overtly hinted at in its opening sentence—the work's one false step) which are characteristic of the novella form and make not inapposite comparison with Conrad's *Heart of Darkness*. . . . *Guerrillas*, on the other hand, has affinities with those novels of Graham

Greene in which *deraciné* white characters are placed in violent third-world settings. There are telling similarities in sensibility between Greene and Naipaul which have been insufficiently remarked by the latter's commentators: the exact understated prose with its dispassionate registration of the distasteful, sordid and ugly; self-exile and its attendant peregrinations; the preoccupation with failure—both individual failure and the failed cultures of the decaying parts of the world both writers seek out. In *Guerrillas*, generic similarities to novels like *The Quiet American, The Comedians* and *The Honorary Consul* underscore temperamental affinities.

Recognition of differences in schemata facilitates an understanding of why *Guerrillas*, for all the fine things in it, is a less successful fiction than *In a Free State*. In the first place, Naipaul has unsuccessfully attempted to get into his novel the parabolic drift and the cumulative force of his novella. The novel's title and its epigraph—Jimmy's statement that 'When everybody wants to fight there's nothing to fight for. Everybody wants to fight his own little war, everybody is a guerrilla'—indicate the intended parabolic dimension. But this is never more than notionally realised because while guerrilla activity is often talked about by non-participants it is insufficiently concretised. 'Guerrilla' remains a symbolic conception unrooted in the realistic surface of the novel. Similarly, while Naipaul tries very hard to have the landscapes of *Guerrillas* convey the heightened intensity of the landscapes of *In a Free State*, he is unable to do so successfully because the greater length of the novel form dissipates effects that can be concentrated in a shorter form.

While failing to adapt features characteristic of the novella, Naipaul has at the same time failed to utilise effectively the elbow-room that the larger form of *Guerrillas* affords. Extended inside views of all three central characters are offered, but only Jimmy's characterisation is thereby enhanced. Despite interior detail and background information Roche is no more complexly realised than Bobby [of *In a Free State*], and rather less well focused. And the characterisation of Jane, the most compelling and original figure in the novel, is actually weakened by the inside views and the background information. It is Jane's externals, her speech, gestures and actions, and what they are made to convey about her inner being, that make her so memorable and disturbing. And while a great many of the novel's pages are given over to talk about politics, violence and revolutionary activities, little is done to dramatise them. Even Jimmy, a political force and a committed revolutionary, is characterised almost entirely in sexual terms, and his bold attempt to bend a mob to his political will—a key turning point in the novel—takes place off stage and is summarised in a few sentences.

What might account for the imperfect success of *Guerrillas*? Part of the reason may lie in the novel's dependence on a single documentary source, the story of de Freitas. Another part may have to do with the choice of a genre requiring a strong story line, a certain amount of action and a sense of political and cultural place to explore an essentially static situation—the relations between Jimmy, Roche and Jane. One reviewer of *Guerrillas* suggested that Naipaul was too interested in the historical mood and not enough in the human motive; but the opposite is surely the case. A great deal of time is spent in the creation of a mood

appropriate to the psychological exploration of the central characters, but only in a few places . . . is much attention paid to the creation of an historical mood. A third part of the reason may have to do with the pressure of Naipaul's growing obsession with sexuality. . . . (pp. 77-8)

It is hard to imagine a more unpleasant or a more negative ending [than this novel's]; yet when one looks back over the novel it is seen to be neither unprepared for nor inappropriate. For the dominant subjects of *Guerrillas* are the repellent unwholesomeness of Jane and Jimmy, and the weakness of Roche, to which the political and public dimensions of the novel are not made as quantitatively ancillary as they are qualitatively so. The three longer fictions Naipaul has published since 1967—*The Mimic Men, In a Free State* and *Guerrillas*—have all mixed sexual and political concerns. In *The Mimic Men* the sexual theme was recessive, the political and colonial themes dominant. In *In a Free State* the two concerns were given equal weight and held in a mutually vivifying tension; in *Guerrillas*, perhaps in spite of Naipaul's intention, revulsion with sexuality has become dominant. It remains to be seen what the next fictional product of this remarkable writer's increasingly exacerbated sensibilities will be, but one certainly does not expect a return to the 'comprehensive humanity' and piety of *A House for Mr Biswas*. (pp. 78-9)

> *Kerry McSweeney, "V.S. Naipaul: Sensibility and Schemata," in* Critical Quarterly (© *Manchester University Press), Autumn, 1976, pp. 73-9.*

Written in a style reminiscent of early Graham Greene, littered with repetitive symbols of futility and despairing, discontinuous dialogue, *Guerrillas* is another of Naipaul's novels exploring the deeper significances of culture and order. Brought up in the expatriate high Hindi culture of Trinidad and fascinated by the island's chaotic Creole society, he has always had an acute sense of the relationship between cultural achievements and the power of history. If Hindi culture could not survive its uprooting to the Caribbean, the freedom of Creole society is illusory, consisting of fantasies and extravagant gestures, but producing nothing of lasting value. The ironies of the early novels result from compassionate awareness that those on the fringes of the empire can only struggle for momentary local recognition.

Naipaul's own expatriation to England taught him that the center no longer held. His subsequent novels and travel writings have been studies in the ambiguities of freedom that occur when there is no clearly defined system of power and of moral authority. If in London the newly independent nations appear to be at the center of action, in the Caribbean Jane [protagonist of *Guerrillas*] learns "that she had come to a place at the end of the world, to a place that had exhausted its possibilities." The withdrawal of the empire, rather than initiating a new era, is the start of chaos. The only clear values are the old imperial ones that remain under attack, as they were under colonialism, because history has left no other options. Without a culture there can be no order.

Naipaul has long been treated with suspicion in the third world, where his meditations on culture, order, and history are felt as subversive. It is possible that when Naipaul's work is better understood in metropolitan centers, it will also be treated with circumspection, since it radically questions our modern assumptions about the dignity of freedom and the autonomy of the self. To understand Naipaul's vision as essentially conservative would, however, be as incorrect as claiming Conrad was a reactionary. The often noted similarity between the two writers is that they have understood the nugatory achievements and moral anarchy that are common to those on the fringe of a stable civilization. (pp. 129-30)

> *Bruce King, in* Sewanee Review *(reprinted by permission of the editor, © 1977 by The University of the South), Winter, 1977.*

[Naipaul uses the English language] with singular purity and some disdain, as if the words on the page are more cryptic in their plainness than the reader knows. Reading him, I feel that the words are reduced from some intensely anxious communion with himself. But they get into his books as the subtly disturbing tattoo that a good plain style can work on the reader. He hates "showy, complex" words.

No other novelist in English of Naipaul's range, virtuosity, flair—there are not many—could say, as he does in "A Wounded Civilization": "The novel . . . is a form of social inquiry." His novels are about the struggle for existence in a world still colonial in feeling despite the breakup of the old Western empires. His style will hardly remind you of Dickens's prose operatics or Balzac's impasto. But the indignation just under the surface takes you back to so many great 19th-century "novelists of society" that I was not surprised to hear him say that reading Balzac was as delicious as eating chocolates. By contrast, the "hippies" he has seen travestying Indian religious practices are suffering "intellectual anorexia."

Naipaul's own fiction is as unmistakably on the side of the victims as it is contemptuous of Western pilgrims seeking to "complete themselves." As a documentary reporter he reminds me more of Dickens on American manners and Chekhov on Sakhalin Island's prison colony than of Norman Mailer on the steps of the Pentagon. He is totally without ideology. He is not sentimental, as anyone can see from "Guerrillas," about the new "rebel" movements in the Caribbean. But the old-fashioned passion against exploitation can be felt in "The Loss of El Dorado," Naipaul's history of the Spanish and English imperialist "adventure" around his birthplace in the Caribbean. And since he is just as confident a loner as Nabokov, is as historically pent-up as Solzhenitsyn, is as funny/sad as Beckett, I mind as much as he does the fact that he is not better known, that he is always asked to tell his own story over again as some lesser writers are not.

It must be admitted that no other novelist is quite so embedded in old history—British imperialism—and at the same time is so sharp an observer of what in "A Wounded Civilization" he calls "the shattering world." History as irony without solution, history without obvious redemption, history as a mass "shattering" of traditions all help to explain Naipaul's powerful quietness as a writer. He is the novelist as thinker. The tragic sense that permeates his books can be felt in him even when he is most casual and "English."

Camus said that "we are all special cases." But I cannot think of another novelist in English today whose "special-

ness" brings home the old political world that broke up after 1945. There is a quality of historical compression to Naipaul's style, his books give off a suggestion of *his* being cornered, that I ascribe to political fate. He and his characters are still living the old storybook of British imperialism.

The sense of displacement has given Naipaul an ominous sense of place. . . . History is more real to him than political "attitudes." History judges victims as cruelly as oppressors. "A Wounded Civilization" is an often mordant criticism (as is Naipaul's best novel about Trinidad, "A House for Mr. Biswas") of Indian moral smugness, which for some reason permits tremendous violence and even social contempt to the point of genocide. (p. 7)

What we have in Naipaul's writing is something essentially different from the self-conscious "psychological man" who dominates current American fiction and, so far as I can see, occupies much of its wisdom. Naipaul has little interest in *North* America because it does not figure in his historical experience. The novel as "a form of social inquiry" is something he has lived as well as written. So my deepest sense of him is that he recognizes himself as a historical effect and that he has used this in his writing with something like the British power that once awed poor Indians in Trinidad. (p. 20)

Naipaul's great subject *is* the old imperialism, the leftovers that make up his world. The past is never dead, said Faulkner; it is not even past. History has many cunning passages. V. S. Naipaul is one of those passages. . . .

He is the most compelling master of social truth that I know of in the contemporary novel. But it is clear today, as it was not to Dickens, Balzac, all those lost realists, that you shall know the truth and it shall *not* make you free. (p. 22)

> *Alfred Kazin, "V. S. Naipaul, Novelist as Thinker," in* The New York Times Book Review *(© 1977 by The New York Times Company; reprinted by permission), May 1, 1977, pp. 7, 20, 22.*

*　　　*　　　*

NEMEROV, Howard　1920-

An American poet, novelist, short story writer, critic, editor, and playwright, Nemerov is best known for his poetry which blends traditional lyricism and ironic detachment. (See also *CLC*, Vols. 2, 6, and *Contemporary Authors*, Vols. 1-4, rev. ed.)

[Nemerov] has always been, very individually, one of the best poets of his generation, but with the emergence of his *New and Selected Poems* it becomes necessary to class him outside the category of a mere generation; for the book makes it clear that he is one of the best poets writing in English.

Nemerov's early poems were like marvelous tricks, brilliant in themselves, but each in a sense isolated from the rest. In some of them it almost looked as if he were setting himself difficult problems in style and tone for their own sake. . . . But the value of the apprenticeship served in the early poems becomes apparent in his succeeding work: for rhetoric is now an instrument with which he can pry open what he pleases.

He is at equal ease in the modes of epigram, comic poem,

meditation, and narrative, yet his work in each is now clearly related to his work in all the rest. His style has great range. He can write [an] abstract statement . . . which is careful and qualified, and derives much of its strength from Renaissance writing. . . . He can also, however, elaborate images in [a] much more casual, seemingly random manner. . . . What the two [styles] have in common, perhaps, is an easy authority of tone, by means of which particular observation is generally placed and generalization is seen in relation to a particular context.

The latest poems, occupying more than the first quarter of the book, are the most exciting. For from traditional materials he has fashioned a kind of blank verse which I believe to be, in Pound's sense, an invention. Its most striking characteristic is the almost continuous use of runovers. . . . The effect in Nemerov's poems, in say "Mrs. Mandrill" or "Death and the Maiden"—two of the best—is of an unceasing flow, an unchecked movement *without* looseness or breathlessness: the unit of the line is never destroyed or forgotten (though it is true, as often in blank verse, it has become less important than the unit of the paragraph), and the constant use of runovers, instead of causing the disintegration of form, has created a new form. I find this a technical invention of great importance, and have little doubt that Nemerov will have his imitators within a few years. What is more, the speed at which the verse moves enables the writer to introduce a great many juxtapositions of detail which would seem forced in a slower-moving verse. Seemingly discrepant images are caught up and absorbed by the swift movement to bring about a continuous enrichment and qualification of meaning.

There is in fact a concentration of experience without the loss of richness and variety that concentration can involve.

Most of the poems in this selection possess a similar authority, and are composed—to apply to him one of his own phrases—with "a singular lucidity and sweetness." It is a distinguished and important book. (pp. 586-88)

> *Thom Gunn, in* The Yale Review *(© 1961 by Yale University; reprinted by permission of the editors), June, 1961.*

Mr. Nemerov's finest poems have always had a peculiar freshness, a buoyancy and a hush all their own: in "Runes," a quiet meditative lyric that ought to survive any change of fashion, and in *The Blue Swallows,* his most elegantly sustained volume, Mr. Nemerov placed himself among the few poets of his generation identifiably blessed *with a character*. Yet it has to be allowed that his connection with poetic tradition is strongly visible and at times uneasily specific, from Auden to Yeats.

And now to Frost. Because the typical poem in *The Western Approaches* is a poem that takes its verbal energy, its motive and moral, from the air one first breathed in Frost, generally late Frost. (p. 1028)

[Hardly] a nature poem in the book—many of its best poems are about trees and seasons—can be read without some shake of the head: one is seeing double. "The Consent" has to do with the fall of leaves from ginkgo trees, suddenly, in a single night. "If this," asks the poet, "Can happen thus, what race shall be exempt? / What use to learn the lessons taught by time, / If a star at any time may tell us: *Now*." One trusts these lines, from the second and generalizing stanza, since the first has provided a cue with exquisite description. Nevertheless, the poem strikes one as a footnote to "Spring Pools": as do many others in this volume.

But I realize that I have begun to sound grudging, and that is not what I meant at all. "Every idiom has its idiot," a wise man observed. Few are lucky enough to have an employer as nimble as Mr. Nemerov. His dealings with his own latest idiom are sometimes, indeed, so intelligent that his poems become a second nature to Frost's. To learn something new in an old language is of course to learn something new. Here and there, it is true, Mr. Nemerov likes to play with words, to play the words like an instrument, to have his way with them; in his epigrams—which I do not especially care for—he only seems fierce; what drives him, as a rule, in his unhappiest moments, is a free-floating nervous energy, the need to behold a thriving creation of lines joking at each other or words joking within a line, to make a more impressive tension from what started as a tic. But, in any case, he errs on the side of plenitude. Over large stretches of *The Western Approaches* Mr. Nemerov resumes activity as the very serious and very American poet who emerged in *The Blue Swallows*—whatever he finds useful to keep himself going is useful to his readers—and we are simply grateful to have him among us. (p. 1029)

> *David Bromwich, in* The Georgia Review *(copyright, 1976, by the University of Georgia), Winter, 1976.*

Howard Nemerov's poetry in *The Western Approaches* is a poetry mostly of saying rather than singing, even when it speaks of the power of traditional, transcendent song. The saying includes some skilled modes of speech, in some of the best poems, notably "Learning the Trees" and "A Cabinet of Seeds Displayed" (the kinship of subject is nearer essence than accident), reaching a firm and fair contemplation, mastered in technique, with an important, reverberant something to say. The reverberation comes from understanding quietly won. The book also offers fine poetry of physical description, and some high song.

The book, then, is important in itself, and in its place in the development of one of America's best and most highly reputed men of letters. Since the book is important, I shall take it seriously and, thus, disapprove some. Mostly I shall attempt to define what constitutes Nemerov's typical style, attitude, metrical convention.

His style, in deep intertwinings with attitude, is witty, analogical, speculative, and uncertain. Yet it is also nostalgic and reverential, especially toward great past poetry and music; also slangy, chatty, obscene; with some unusual combinings. The uncertainty underlies, interlaces, and unlaces much of the rest.

The uncertainties also affect his criticism. He is one of the best living practical critics, wonderfuly responsive, astute, discerning. He is, argument by argument, one of the best living theoretical critics; he defends very ably diverse and contradictory theories of literature and criticism. . . . He does not choose between the varied theories. Typical remarks are "grains of salt will be handed out by the ushers" or, more centrally, speaking of poetry: "Sacrament or con game? As impossible as unnecessary to decide." But that will not serve. Some poems are beautifully sacramental, the outward and visible sign of an inward and spiritual beauty; some are very like con games; the former are preferable.

The uncertainties affect the poetry, especially in the ways jokes intersect or bethump the meanings. His convention is more settled in *The Western Approaches* than in the earlier work; the disruptive joke and the crude clash of levels of propriety occur less often. Rather than such vacillations, what is typical in the newer poems is a cool yet gloomy distancing from the subject so that the ironies, analogies, and whatever are not so much funny or sad as just there. The tone is mild, amused, resigned, factual, observant, speculative, cool yet consistently uncertain of itself, somehow ghostly, everyday, yet unified.

A highly typical poem is "Fiction," which has admirably clever jokes and emblemings of fate and religious lostness. Do we laugh? Do we cry? No, we watch, unsure just how to respond. The tone is a balancing, almost a vanishing act. (pp. 130-31)

"The Backward Look" has perhaps the greatest variety, gracefully modulated among the various tones: quiet reflectiveness, satiric counterposings, love of the warmly ordinary, the cold severity of space, gathered terror, nostalgia for Dante's more certain vision; the factual, many-analogied precision of the close: "We take our dust and rocks and start back down." The poem also has a grand completeness of structure; it is one of the best poems on space travel we are apt to have.

"Boy with Book of Knowledge" starts with talk, remembering tenderness, a little joshing, appropriate to the boy's youthful enthusiasm, then moves into the fierce and holy presence of the last two stanzas, probably the greatest poetry—in theme, resonance, depth, precision—that Nemerov has ever written. . . .

"The Consent" is also a remarkable poem. I swore off the adjective *brilliant* some years ago . . ., but hereby revoke my pledge. The poem is brilliant like fireworks (if every fluttering fan of light stayed perfectly in descending place), brilliant as a starry night, brilliant in order and persuasive rhetoric. The ending is deeply moving, even though it crosses (tends to cross—however jolting, the conclusion is hypothetical) some of my deep convictions. (p. 136)

The book may well be Nemerov's best book of poems, which ranks it high. Too much is still too ready of wit, merely and pointlessly if cleverly speculative, self-mockingly relaxed, curiously analogical. Who else but Nemerov would devote a whole, rather carefully written poem to asking whether the fishing hook or the question mark is upside down? But, then, who but Nemerov would be apt to notice the reversed likeness? It's the lively and observant intelligence that occasions the problem. Nemerov is conscious of the difficulty and has answered the charge "that my poems are jokes, even bad jokes" by saying "I incline to agree, insisting however that they are bad jokes, and even terrible jokes, emerging from the nature of things." The pun on *bad joke* is a pretty good joke, but not a sufficient defense. At least to me his jokes seldom sound expressive (as those of Randall Jarrell's sometimes do) of a desperate-absurdity-locked-into-the-tears-of-things.

The convention he usually adopts is, all in all, too deliberately and casually talkative, too uncharged and uncertain. Uncertainties can be the stuff of strong poetry, in Shakespeare, Donne, Dickinson, Hardy, Hopkins, Tennyson, Winters, Jarrell. Nemerov's uncertainties do not emerge so; they link in special ways with his linguistic wit, his speculative and analogical gifts, to tune down his poems from often reaching his best effects. Even in his best poems he dallies with the slacker strings too often.

But—it's quite a' *but*—the intelligence is just of a different order than that at work in most books of poetry; the fun can be lively fun; the self-putting-down can be genuinely amusing and finely perceptive ("Du rêve, de la mathématique, et de la mort" is my favorite of that sort); the linguistic and metrical skills prompt admiration, even admiration in the older sense: he's awesomely gifted. The best work—excellent physical description; the controlled variety and feeling of "The Backward Look"; the intricate, precisely registered intelligence that in "A Cabinet of Seeds Displayed" reaches contemplative poetry of the first rank; the greatly haunting conclusion of "Boy With Book of Knowledge"; the fine completeness of "The Consent"—requires high praise and much gratitude. For Nemerov more than most poets, his best is the enemy of his many-skilled normal; he is too near to poetic greatness to step modestly away. (pp. 137-38)

> *Paul Ramsey, "To Speak, or Else to Sing,"*
> *in* Parnassus: Poetry in Review *(copyright*
> © *by* Parnassus: Poetry in Review), *Spring-*
> *Summer, 1976, pp. 130-38.*

In an 1892 review, W. B. Yeats defined "noetry" as "descriptive of verse which though full of intellectual faculty, is lacking in imaginative impulse." Noetry was then "a term of most constant utility." Recalled, it is serviceable for describing what Howard Nemerov has been writing recently [as in *The Western Approaches*]. It is not that his verse lacks imaginative impulse, but that it is artfully ideational. Formerly a fidgety, near-sighted stepsister, noetry has come of age as a fascinating companion for solitary nights.

Noetry relies without shame on mental constructs. Nemerov, sometimes compared to metaphysical poets, offers numerous examples. "Two Pair," for instance, links the odds of poker, two laws of thermodynamics, and two holy testaments (with, of course, couplets) to reach the turnstile where mind is left to itself. That limbo, fated or self-chosen, is Nemerov's Parnassus. Others may have their soulful landscapes, heartbreaks, headaches, and pretty things: Nemerov has modern *ideas* pretty much to himself and turns them back where others begin.

> Of making many books there is no end,
> And like it saith in the book before that one,
> What God wants, don't you forget it, Jack,
> Is your contrite spirit, Jack, your broken heart.

Lines like these are indicative of Nemerov's calculated deflation. Disinclined to strut for the ivory stages, disdaining untethered imagination, he is skeptical to the quick. . . . Elsewhere he punctures mythologies, psychology, the nation's auto craze, and spelling conventions.

Nemerov's *Gnomes and Occasions* (1973) gave ample warning that his taste for poetic economy was running to epigram. The course continues. . . . (pp. 272-73)

> *W. G. Regier, in* Prairie Schooner *(© 1976*
> *by University of Nebraska Press; reprinted*

by permission from Prairie Schooner*), Fall, 1976.*

Howard Nemerov . . . has interested himself in the elaboration of a distinct tradition in English poetry: that of the secular contemplative lyric. For Nemerov, . . . the sources of poetry lie "far out in the sea of tradition and the mind, even in the physiological deeps", as he puts it in *The Measure of Poetry,* a prose poem in his latest collection [*The Western Approaches: Poems 1973-75*] which explains a great deal about his attitude and method of composition. For Nemerov, measure is an elemental order, which he compares to the rhythm of the tide, and which is acted upon in the process of writing by "the objects which are to appear in the poem". This dynamic working relationship between basal constancy and individual variousness yields "moments of freedom, moments of chaos", "relations which it may be that number alone could enrage into being"; that is, without the underlying, reassuring sense of order provided by rhythm, we perhaps could not afford to tolerate wildness, nonsense, fine excess.

This is not a reading of the world with which everyone will agree; but even a superficial appraisal of this witty and deft collection, Nemerov's ninth, will reveal that *The Measure of Poetry* is a distillation of long experience, and not empty theorizing. In more than seventy expertly lucid, pungent, and economically-managed lyrics, Nemerov makes use of "the objects" of contemporary upper-middle-class life—its games, its gadgets, its intellectual enterprises—as well as of nature, as occasions for an unending flow of gently ironic observations on the flux of personality in the continuum of history. Nemerov is both urbane and humane—not always necessarily a congenial combination; he is Horatian in his perspective, academic in his precision. His poems do something we're not accustomed to these days: they aim at the articulation of what it is not unfair to call a kind of rarefied commonplace, "What oft was thought, but ne'er so well express'd". . . . (pp. 164-65)

[His] kind of calm straightforwardness goes against the noisy self-advertising mainstream of current writing, and it deserves praise and attention for that. There's genuine intelligence and feeling here, and the fact that the verse doesn't call attention to itself—except, perhaps, by dint of its polish—is part of the point. *The Western Approaches* affords pleasures close to those which belong to music that is playful, various, and elegantly resolved. (p. 165)

Jonathan Galassi, in Poetry (© *1976 by The Modern Poetry Association; reprinted by permission of the Editor of* Poetry*), December, 1976.*

*   *   *

NERUDA, Pablo (pseudonym of Ricardo Eliecer Neftali Reyes y Basoalto)   1904-1973

A Chilean poet and diplomat, Neruda was active in various social and political movements. The recipient of the 1971 Nobel Prize for Literature, Neruda celebrates in his poetry love, nostalgia, experience, and the interior life. He is considered one of the finest surrealist poets of our time. (See also CLC, Vols. 1, 2, 5, 7, and Contemporary Authors, Vols. 19-20; obituary, Vols. 45-48; Contemporary Authors Permanent Series, Vol. 2.)

Pablo Neruda's *Odas Elementales* are particularly interest-

ing for their fusion of a considerable amount of social doctrine and of many subjects traditionally considered "unpoetic" into very effective poetry. . . . Neruda's choice of poetic subject has made certain poetic techniques particularly apt. For it is evident that personification, catalogues, and the creation of foil relations between large parts of poems (frequently structured dialectically) are techniques common to most of these poems.

Nevertheless, as hasty equation of the dialectic structure common in Neruda's poetry with the dialectic form of his Marxist social doctrine (generally progressing from past to present to a more or less hortatory future) would certainly be an oversimplification. For these poems are odes, and their dialectic structure also corresponds to the traditional division of the Pindaric ode into strophe, antistrophe, and epode. The two influences would appear to complement and reinforce each other, the form of the ode perhaps supplying the tripartite structure, the Marxist doctrine the tendency toward the temporal division into past, present, and future.

Such a structure is readily apparent in "Oda a las Américas." . . . The strophe and antistrophe correspond to the typographical division between stanzas one and two, and their temporal division into past and present. But Neruda's dialectic here is somewhat complicated by his concern with universalizing his poem. This concern causes him to call upon America primarily in terms of the beauties of its nature, especially at the beginning, and only to present a more explicit and direct vision of its people in the middle section. . . . For America as a continent with its natural beauties has a greater direct appeal for the reader, regardless of national, class, or ideological affiliations, than a more partisan class or historical approach, say exclusively through the Pre-Columbian Indians, could possibly have. At the same time, specific historical, class, and even certain chauvinistic appeals to a Pan-Latin Americanism, must be and are made in the poem to fill both doctrinal and exemplary needs. This results in some tension and ambivalence between the two directions, finally united at the end.

It is evident from the prominent place nature has in this poem, and from its first lines, where the oceans are said to have kept the continent pure and intact in a more or less military metaphor ("guardaron"), that we are here in a world similar to the beginning of the *Canto General*, where nature is called upon to resist the Spanish conquerors and to act as one with the Indian defenders. A different emphasis, however, is apparent in this poem. Whereas in the *Canto General* nature's purpose was primarily to protect the largely helpless Indian civilizations, here it is clearly the other way around, and in the latter part of the poem there is a fairly explicit reproach to the Latin Americans for allowing their beautiful continent to be plundered by the new conquerors. . . . (pp. 41-2)

Much of the ambivalence evident in the second part of the poem over just where the real value of the Americas lies, whether in the unspoiled beauty of its nature, or in its people, is undoubtedly due to the poet's personal sense of outrage and disappointment at what he feels to be the complete failure of Latin Americans to achieve viable and independent political and economic institutions. A resolution of all ambivalence finally occurs when the speaker makes clear in the last section of the poem that the continent's treasure includes both the land and its people. . . . The dialectic between nature's purity and man's misery and corruption finally resolved in a new man in harmony with nature also presents a specific Latin American formulation of the general Marxist dialectic of past versus present to synthesize in an ideal future. (p. 42)

[Neruda] seems . . . to be opting for the sentimental view of the Pre-Columbian Indian as the noble savage living in a largely paradisiacal environment, who is now come to woe at the hands of foreign invaders, rather than for a more orthodox Marxist dialectic, which would see Pre-Columbian America in a more objective and perhaps less rosy light. . . . Neither the *Canto General* nor most histories would suggest that the Indians under Spanish rule, or any considerable part of the population of these countries since independence has been much better off than they are now. The cause of this logical inconsistency, apart from what is perhaps some simple carelessness in the poem's elaboration, appears to lie in Neruda's political beliefs. These seem to have dictated the creation of an earlier, golden age, to act as a foil to the present state of affairs, and so to portray that state as negatively as possible. That golden age is conveniently not specified. The resulting lack of a clear subject to make possible the creation of a dramatic antithesis or foil considerably reduces the effectiveness of this last image, and leads to the simplistic visualization of these countries in terms of editorial page cartoon images as caricatures of mouths, rather than of their suffering inhabitants. (pp. 43-4)

In addition . . . to the structural use of foils for the creation of the dialectic and the general polemic and extra-literary foils of exploited-exploiter which pervade the poem ideologically, Neruda manages to create another, a very emotional foil relation between the polemic eloquence of his narrative voice which reproaches and contrasts with the shameful silence of the Latin American reader. This final foil relation reaches out beyond the poem itself, seeking to resolve the poem-reader dichotomy in the synthesis of the reader's direct action against the postulated common enemy.

In "Oda a la pobreza," Neruda uses similar techniques, but structures his poem about a central dichotomy between himself, the poor of the world, and a poverty personified much like the figure of a medieval vice. The poem is divided into the past of the poet, when he himself was persecuted by poverty, and the present, when he relentlessly hounds poverty wherever he can find it. The foil relation is thus dramatized into a personal confrontation between the narrative voice and a personified enemy. The explicit appearance of the narrative voice as the rhetorical "I" in the poem greatly increases the vigor and force of the poem, adds to the effectiveness of the contrast, and serves as a sincerity ploy to capture the sympathy of the reader for the speaker and his cause.

Catalogues serve an important function in the poem. The enumeration of the objects which he first associates with poverty . . . is essentially metonymic, but the more extended catalogue of his persecution of poverty toward the end of the poem . . . is so amplified as to create its own world, a world of the future where poverty is already substantially defeated. . . . [The] tremendous sense of action and the images of positive, constructive work seem already to represent the desired millennia. . . . The structure of the poem, then, while essentially a dichotomy between the poet

pursued by poverty in the past, and the poet now pursuing it in the present, nevertheless manages to arrive at the suggestion of a synthesis, where poet and people together construct a world without poverty.

In "Oda al caldillo de congrio," a poem much lighter in tone, Neruda is presented with a problem which is roughly the opposite of that in "Oda a las Américas." There he had to make specific a very general subject, along with a good deal of potentially unacceptable social doctrine. Neruda's program in these poems includes subjects considered inherently unpoetic. This is implied in the title *Odas Elementales,* and here takes him into that area of the expository presentation of cognitive material which is usually avoided by most good poets. This poem is a poetic recipe.

Besides the able creation and manipulation of images and rhythms, Neruda manages to generalize the subject by certain specific poetic techniques in combination with the humorous tone. Thus we progress by syntactic association and juxtaposition . . . [until we approach] bathos. . . . To insure that the reader has not been completely swept away, and that he remembers the tenor of these witty hyperboles, the poem's subject appears again . . . for a final juxtaposition.

But this poem is not typical of the manner in which Neruda handles such a problem in these poems, just as the lack of polemic content and social doctrine is not typical. The link between polemic content and the combination of foil, personification, and catalogue is therefore made more apparent in this poem by a prominent diminution of both foils and personification. Catalogue structure is, of course, inherent in a recipe. Much more common is the solution in "Oda al átomo," where he strongly personifies and dramatizes a specific, scientific concept, the atom, puts it into a social setting, and creates foils into a dialectic structure, all through amplification and catalogues of pathetic, emotion-arousing imagery with exemplary value. . . . (pp. 47-8)

Whatever focus Neruda uses in these poems, in nearly all of them foil, personification, and catalogue are key structural elements. This is undoubtedly in part due to the epic mode of most of the poems, which calls for generous amplifications and broad, emotive contrasts. More specifically, personification allows Neruda to bring into a specific dramatic framework both the abstractions of his social doctrine (as in "Oda a la pobreza"), and very specific, somewhat unpoetic subjects (as in "Oda al átomo"). Foils are used to organize his material into the dialectic perspective of his doctrine. And the catalogues serve mainly to universalize by amplification and thus to create the distinctly epic mode of these poems.

Neruda's ideology also creates some interesting similarities between these poems and much medieval doctrinal poetry, especially the *Everyman* morality play, where foil, personification, and catalogue were also key structural elements for the exposition of an ideology whose dichotomy between good and evil was even more absolute than that of Neruda, and which supplied no synthesis as it refused to countenance any true dialectic between good and evil. It is indicative of Neruda's talent as a poet, however, that whereas in the plays the resolution of the dichotomy always occurs within the character of Everyman himself, and the audience remains largely passive, Neruda often manages to focus his dialectic upon the reader himself, who is then called upon to provide the synthesis by direct action. (pp. 48-9)

Walter Holzinger, "Poetic Subject and Form in the 'Odas Elementales'," in Revista Hispánica Moderna, *XXXVI, 1970–1971, pp. 41-9.*

Pablo Neruda is fecundly dead. His poems keep coming into English, sometimes bruised and tattered by the translator's egotistical ineptitude and sometimes decently clad, as in [*Fully Empowered*]. Almost always enough survives the metamorphosis to serve as an invigorating example of how a truly universal poetic consciousness goes about its business. . . .

A difficult poet Neruda may be; but he never, to my knowledge, wrote nonsense. Fifty or more years ago, though, even his friends had trouble with a line like, "I am sad, but I am always sad," considering it either unintelligible or unnecessarily repetitive. When asked to explain himself, that sad eyed young poet from the South wrapped himself tighter in his railman's cloak and kept his own counsel. But when hostile critics of *Veinte poemas de amor y una canción desesperada* (1924) laughed long and mockingly as they recited, "I don't love her anymore, that's true, but perhaps I love her," Neruda tried his best to explain in *La Nación.* "For ten lonely years my poetry has obeyed differing rhythms and conflicting currents. Joining them, braiding them together, unable to find a permanent essence because it doesn't exist, I've composed *Twenty Love Poems and a Desperate Love Song.* . . ." (p. 100)

Quite early, Neruda seems to have realized that an integral poetry, more like Rimbaud's than Baudelaire's, must aim to reproduce or represent that level of authenticity below censored consciousness at which mind operates in endless alternations and concatenations of contraries. These are the differing rhythms and conflicting currents he alludes to. Fidelity to his own feelings had forced Neruda to do violence to the niceties of language and to defy the logic of identities which, because it ignores time, can maintain that A is always A. What the critics were laughing at was a natural consequence of this precocious poet's discovery that you can be sad now, and then again sad; you can love this way and that, but never in the same way consecutively. In *Twenty Poems,* love and unlove, trust and mistrust, Mary-sunlight and Mary-shadow alternately beat out a rhythm which is locked in time and which cannot come to rest in any permanent essence *because nothing of the sort exists in time* and nothing at all can exist outside it. (pp. 100-01)

Like William Carlos Williams, Neruda . . . learned to kill the explicit sentence, but with weirdly different results. [*Residence on Earth* is, according to Neruda,] "a heap of very monotonous, almost ritualistic poems, full of mystery and sorrows like the poems of the old poets. Something very uniform, like a single thing attempted without success."

What is this *single thing* attempted without success? . . . Intellect, Neruda is saying, has deprived poetry of its substantiality, has removed it from the arena of existential struggle so that it can no longer give sustenance. Neruda wants to re-endow the poetic message with substance and sustenance. He wants to "penetrate life and make it prophetic." But for the time being he can do no more than establish an authentically self-expressive language that accurately registers a relentless and desperate attempt to refloat a monstrously barnacled universe of human aspirations that

has foundered in time. He has the language now, but no credible and life-empowering dream to make it fully intelligible, and the only form is the pressure of the effort itself. Forget this, and the pre-political poems of the *Residencias* (1925-47) seem opaque and aphasic; remember their intention, and they become unbearably articulate in a way as yet unavailable in English. (p. 101)

What is the most moving about the later Neruda is not his occasional political stridency, but the enormous generosity of his vision and his unfailing sense of humor. "You learn poetry," he said in 1956, "moving step by step among things and beings, never isolating, but rather containing them all within a blind expansion of love." *Fully Empowered* (1962) is a triumphant expression of this all-encompassing expansiveness. Here is the house, whimsically built from the stars down; here is a child that needs washing; here are thistles and clocksmiths, friends and enemies, all have a place in this finally convincing Nerudian universe where, as Rilke has it, song is existence itself. You read these poems and you ask yourself sometimes: "Didn't Brother Pablo say this better somewhere else?" And the answer is, "Maybe, but never mind, no one ever said it better, ever." (p. 102)

Luis E. Yglesias, "Out of Some Rumbling Wholeness," in Review *(copyright © 1976 by the Center for Inter-American Relations, Inc.), Spring, 1976, pp. 100-02.*

Attached to the end of a literary career that spanned five decades and that gathered to itself, like moss to a rock, more than 40 volumes of poetry, prose, verse drama, and translations, Neruda's *Memoirs* is not so much a summing up, a culmination of a life, as it is simply one more chapter added to his continuous revelation of himself. He was first driven to poetry, he says in *Memoirs,* by youthful shyness, a sort of "kink in the soul" that intensified both his sense of innate human solitude (the common inheritance of so many Latin-American writers) and his own particular separation from those around him. Thereafter, self-disclosure in poetry seemed to him one way of smashing whatever barriers were raised between himself and his fellowman. . . .

Pablo Neruda's *Memoirs,* therefore, is not his first conscious venture into the confession of how he lived, who he was. His poetry is as progressive as it is prodigious, and it moves through stages in which he was—among other less definable things—a romanticist, a surrealist, an erotic lyricist, a symbolist, a realist, a political revolutionary. Through all these multitudinous sea changes, however, the constant is Neruda himself, and in some works he is pointedly autobiographical. . . .

Neruda professes in *Memoirs* to have been, always, too simple a man, which was both his honor and his shame. He was born not to pass judgment, he says, but to love. From the start, his life's education was anti-literary and anti-intellectual, taking its source from instinct rather than from reason, arousing in him a suspicion of all fixed ideas, precepts, structures, and sects—including those of the Communist dialectic, which he subscribed to with reservations. His problem in his voluminous confessions, therefore, seems never to be W. B. Yeats's mystery of how to locate within his many-sided complexities a "unity of being," nor is it how to construct any vast Yeatsian synthetic "vision." Like Walt Whitman, his acknowledged model, Neruda seems at peace with his metamorphoses and contradictions. ("Pablo is one of the few happy men I have known," Ilya Ehrenburg once wrote about him.) His problem, rather, is how to fix in language the person he was at any given moment; the task, he wrote in *Black Island Memorial,* is never-ending. . . . (p. 19)

The result of Neruda's approach to his remembrances is a book of lapses, of airy interstices, but also of fullness—a sort of distilled essence of himself in both substance and form. He never seems prompted to play the part of sage, of the comprehensive thinker who somehow captures his life and era with trenchant abstractions; and except in isolated parts, *Memoirs* seems hardly to have been written at all, if we think of writing as language that is tight, sparse, impeccably fashioned, consciously structured. "Our [Latin] American stratum is dusty rock, crushed lava, clay mixed with blood," Neruda says, attributing his style to his continental heritage. "We don't know how to work in crystal." Perhaps for these reasons, it is doubtful that *Memoirs* will ever appear on a list of great literary autobiographies. Much more certain is its destiny as a book of uses. It is the starting point for all future biographers. It will serve as a rich mine of support for those who share Neruda's political views. . . . The chapter "Poetry Is an Occupation" is invaluable for students of Neruda's work, and innumerable short portraits of writers and artists should serve scholars as a bottomless source of opinions and quotations. . . .

The drama of his position in Latin America, he once said, didn't permit him the luxury of being uncommitted; and he felt strongly that even poetry that professed to be impervious to politics was thus political to the roots. "Everyone has to choose a road," he said in an interview with Robert Bly, "a refined and intellectual way, or a more brotherly, general way, trying to embrace the world around you, to discover the new world." Neruda's choice was the second one. It was, in a word, Whitman's. (p. 20)

> *Robert Maurer, "A Confession of Life," in* Saturday Review *(© 1977 by Saturday Review Magazine Corp.; reprinted with permission), February 19, 1977, pp. 18-20.*

Neruda must have written these marvelous, exasperating memoirs fitfully during the last [, busy] decade of his life. . . . Neither his publishers nor his editors say so, but it would be one explanation for their discontinuity and unevenness. . . . Another explanation may be that these are, after all, memoirs: the reader must be thankful for whatever the writer is pleased to remember. But the most persuasive explanation, whatever the manner in which they were written, is that Neruda could not have performed differently—a poetic genius trying in an unaccustomed medium to fit the prose of his life to the persona he created in more than 60 volumes of poetry. (p. 3)

[Many] of these anecdotes, vignettes, prose poems, are succulent leaves that we should not do without. Some of them have the charm and humor and mystery of his best poems. . . . He manages, too, despite his self-absorption, to come up with some charming portraits, some done with love, some with malice, of Ehrenburg, García Lorca, Juan Ramón Jimenez, Rafael Alberti, Nehru, Miguel Hernández. He is master in all this, as in his poetry, in making the homely, neglected detail vividly new, the grand mysteries intimate. . . .

Only the knowing will discover some of his malice and obtuseness in his memoirs. (p. 18)

[Still] Neruda . . . must be forgiven his disingenuousness, malice, vanity and egoism—he was a brave man who wished us well and generously left us an incomparable body of poetry, the finest in Spanish in this century. (p. 20)

> *Frank MacShane, "Neruda in New York," in* The New York Times Book Review *(© 1977 by The New York Times Company; reprinted by permission), March 13, 1977, pp. 3, 18, 20.*

*   *   *

NISSENSON, Hugh   1933-

Nissenson is an American short story writer, novelist, and essayist. Contemporary Jewish life forms the subject matter for most of his fiction. (See also *CLC,* **Vol. 4, and** *Contemporary Authors,* **Vols. 17-20, rev. ed.)**

Hugh Nissenson established himself as a writer of consequence with two volumes of short stories, "A Pile of Stones" (1965) and "In the Reign of Peace" (1972). All these stories except one dealt with Jews. . . . All of them were written with fine control, in a style distilled, compassionate, just. And dominating most of these stories was one agony: the existence of pain and cruelty and evil in a universe that itself exists within a divine mind.

Now Nissenson has written a short novel ["My Own Ground"] pursuing that theme further. (p. 6)

The teeming, struggling, yet communal old East Side life saturates these pages. The conflict between the precipitate claim that has been laid to new territory and the realization that full adjustment is yet to come—this is a deep countertheme. (As the title indicates.) The true action is the persistence of evil and chaos, taking somewhat new aspects in the potential New Paradise. (pp. 6-7)

[The] book has some feeling of discomfort, of maladjustment.

The first cause of this discomfort is the form that Nissenson has chosen. Because everything must be set down by [the narrator], a great deal that has happened "offstage" must be recounted to him. The book is full of narratives—of past lives and of recent doings. This cools the immediacy of the events, and it also leads to some similarity of diction. . . .

All this tends to some flatness of characterization, a touch of the stereotype. . . .

Fundamentally there is some strain between the material and the novel form itself. This is felt early, in the first 50 pages, before the shape of the main action—which compensates somewhat—begins to be clear, but it never completely disappears. Unavoidably the suspicion arises that the dimensions of the novel are being forced on a substantial short story, that the author thinks the way to write a novel is to distend a story. A lot of the material . . . could have been condensed or omitted. More important, Nissenson, especially hampered by his structural device, has not yet mastered the differences in characterization between the story and the novel. In his stories he handles his people well, "people," as Frank O'Connor said of short-story characters, "whose identity is determined by their circumstances." But the characters in a novel face more options and go through metamorphoses. Nissenson's people here are stretched, rather than developed.

Does Nissenson feel some sort of obligation to "move up" from the story to the novel? I hope not. He is a fine writer of stories and, for one reader at least, could just go on writing them. He is not—not yet—an equally good novelist, though of course nothing is precluded to a man of his abilities. (p. 7)

> *Stanley Kauffman, in* The New York Times Book Review *(© 1976 by The New York Times Company; reprinted by permission), April 4, 1976.*

[In *My Own Ground,* Nissenson is] not simply concerned to recapture unsavory types, who in any case can be found in Yiddish language literature itself. There is a long tradition of conflict between *proste* (vulgar) and *edel* (refined) types in both Jewish life and literature. For the first time, though, I believe, we are being shown Jews who are utterly debased spiritually....

[The] vulgarity is all in [the] characters, never in [the] prose. Nissenson, moreover, gives *My Own Ground* the literary structure of a descent into the underworld....

Nissenson's Hannele ends by committing suicide in horror at her own degradation.... It seems that the old tradition is inescapable, after all. (p. 30)

> *Peter Shaw, in* The New Republic *(reprinted by permission of* The New Republic; *© 1976 by The New Republic, Inc.), April 10, 1976.*

My Own Ground is a slender museum. Hugh Nissenson's themes are elemental and abstract. I sense that he's been laying off on his bets. Look, Nissenson implies, maybe you won't agree with or understand the premise of my novel, but at least you'll pick up some hard information.... Objects, events, processes, their authenticity will stand guarantee for less researchable matters: passion and spirit and human worth.

My Own Ground isn't a Jewish novel. It's too Jewish for that. The Jewish novel, so-called, has always been a second- or third-generation artifact. Nissenson's people are still East European.... Guilt, high-class ethical refereeing, those are primary themes of modern Jewish fiction. But guilt, to adapt Wordsworth's formula, should best be recollected in tranquillity, not at the presser's bench. A Bellovian or Malamudian hero has leisure; he's in the business of judging, himself and civilization. Usually, usually reluctantly, he chooses involvement, crashes America as if it were some goys-only social club. (p. 737)

Young Jake Brody, Nissenson's first-person protagonist, seems more a utensil than a hero. It will be for his children to write the Jewish novel.... He's a double immigrant, from Russia, from the Lower East Side. In second- and third-generation Jews, I think, emigration—particularly to materialist America—was cud for a leisurely guilt.... But Jake Brody is a survivor; he doesn't choose involvement. He just sees. Though Jake has tranquillity enough in Elmira for recollection, there is little feeling and less guilt. As Jewish heroes go, he's a disgrace to the profession.

Hannele, Rabbi Isaac's daughter, is an ethical mercury switch. One week she wants to get *shtupped* by Schlifka,

the pimp, or some client of his; one week she'd prefer sexless housekeeping for Roman Osipovich, an ascetic Marxist. Jake doesn't judge Hannele. Anyway, religion has been outmoded along with homemade purgatives; American genius will manufacture some gutta-percha replacement for the Talmud. It's significant that Jake speaks both English and Yiddish: he functions, throughout, as an interpreter; his narrative style has the self-effacing, precise tone of simultaneous translation. Jake, too, can switch on and off. He'll accept money from Schlifka, who has set him on Hannele's tail. He'll accept lectures from Osipovich, without any commitment. It's the habit of interpreters to noodge events. Jake forces a brutal confrontation between pimp and Marxist, but these are learning experiences, as your child might push its roly-poly, one side, then another, to see how far it will go. Hannele commits suicide: her disinvolvement. Jake heads for Elmira, which, with all due respect to that city, is somewhat analogous.

I don't judge either. I accept Jake's attitude; hell, what's wrong with being a survivor? The tone has aptness to it. But then, as if he distrusted himself, Nissenson hauls Jake back from Elmira for a big Dream Sequence. Typical stuff: earth mother, cannibalism, birth, hot-housed psychodrama. I happen to think you should get one buck off every novel that sports a Dream Sequence.... It clanks here; the terse, impartial narrative is spoiled. Nissenson seems guilty for Jake. The second or third generation has intruded after all. (pp. 737-38)

> *D. Keith Mano, "The Genuine Article," in* National Review *(© National Review, Inc., 1976; 150 East 35th St., New York, N.Y. 10016), July 9, 1976, pp. 737-38.*

In his last collection of remarkable stories, *In the Reign of Peace,* [Hugh Nissenson] explores some agonising paradoxes of Jewish life. To summarise the deep unease many of them express, is to minimise the dense, layered effect of the stories—nevertheless, the metaphysical sticking-point is: the truth of the Torah may well shine on the uncouth harshness of much of Israeli experience, or on the monstrosity of the years of the Holocaust, yet to many, it seems to beam no actual light at all. Could it be inapplicable? Are there different sorts of realities? Of course to require a clear understanding from the Torah about the recalcitrance of post-Auschwitz reality could be a demand for no less than a new Revelation, and even the most sensitive of writers are left groping for insights. So perhaps it is no surprise to find that [*My Own Ground*] has been set in a simpler, earlier time, in the Lower East Side of New York in 1912. New York, where Hugh Nissenson was born in 1933, is therefore presumably the ground—in the sense of place and of spiritual foundations—which is his own.

My Own Ground, written in the first person by the youthful Jake Brody, an orphan of 15 working as a presser for fourteen hours a day, is a backward glance, a place to begin from, a tale of the "days before the flood"—pre-Great War. But the illusion that those days might somehow have been kinder ones is soon shattered.... This evocation of the Lower East Side is quite without sentimentality, recognising human degradation and violence, and might at first seem only a sharp, pornographically frank, disheartening tale.

But the transforming power of the imagination, to which all

aspirations and fantasies belong, is the key to the underlying meaning of the book, and its real strength. All the people in it were transplants from the corrupt ground of Europe, where they had been nurtured by the Law, fed on Jewish folk-lore, and finally uprooted by the viciousness of Jew-haters, and the brutalities of the Pogroms. Hugh Nissenson must have listened to many tales in his life, as he captures the physical flavour of memory with chilling accuracy. . . . (pp. 48, 50)

In the concluding pages, Jake dreams a fearful tale compounded of many of the elements of cruelty, blood and death, experienced in his childhood in Umersk, and later in New York. The gruesome dream is no more ghastly than what actually happened. There can be no real explanation of either. Jake's last response is only tears. The kindly Mrs. Tauber wipes them away. "And the Lord God will wipe away tears from off all faces," said Isaiah. The ache of the waiting for that time, the desolation before that time, are both implicit in those last quiet moments. (p. 50)

> *Margot Lester, "The Price of Redemption," in* The Jewish Quarterly *(© The Jewish Quarterly 1976), Autumn, 1976, pp. 48, 50.*

O

OATES, Joyce Carol   1938-

Oates is an American novelist, short story writer, poet, playwright, and critic now living in Canada. Her work is peopled with lonely characters engaged in a vain search for love and self-knowledge in an indifferent world. Violence forms a motif throughout Oates's work; her characters are its victims as well as its perpetrators. A serious artist, Oates has yet to write a major work. (See also *CLC,* **Vols. 1, 2, 3, 6, and** *Contemporary Authors,* **Vols. 5-8, rev. ed.)**

Oates writes prose of striking directness and simplicity. Everything she writes bears the marks of a terrific imaginative pressure. That pressure is also the clue to her astonishing productivity. . . . The model of the driven writer, she invests everything she touches with the qualities of her own voice, which is nervous, fast, febrile and hot as an iron. I'd unhesitatingly say that she is one of the most important living American writers, and sadly underestimated here [in England].

In the 24 stories of *Marriages and Infidelities,* dealing with adultery, death, murder, madness and obsessive relationships (a central theme for her), Oates creates a series of metaphors for American life, perhaps urban life, overridden by a panicked sense of unreality and hidden violence—violence which is about to happen. She can be very frightening, but is never merely sensational; nothing seems plotted simply for effect. Also, she reports an American reality seldom seen in fiction by a woman—the American of the working and lower middle class. Bus stations, the cosmetics counter at Woolworth's, Saturdays spent on crowded, gritty beaches, the smell of beer in a roadhouse parking lot: Oates has total recall of these details. And she is entirely unafraid to extend her normal manner, so that a number of these stories exhibit a stunning technical courage. (p. 261)

> *Peter Straub, in* New Statesman *(© 1974 The Statesman & Nation Publishing Co. Ltd.), August 23, 1974.*

[*The Poisoned Kiss and Other Stories from the Portuguese*] are as 'Portuguese' as Mrs Browning's sonnets. They were inspired by an imagined Portuguese writer, 'Fernandes', who suggested images and stories to Miss Oates in a series of waking visions. Interestingly, it was not a case of possession or trance so much as of polite insistence from one part of her brain, which (usefully) interfered

with neither her teaching nor the rest of her writing. There is no specific attempt to evoke Portugal, or indeed to present any close description; but despite the greater degree of abstraction, these stories come from the recognisable Oates territory of obsession and extremity, solitude and violence. . . . Miss Oates perhaps had more compunction about interfering with her Portuguese muse than with her native one; and some of the pieces are not so much brief as fugitive. But the longer ones (especially a neat tale of a writer discovering himself to be an unconscious plagiarist) have scale enough and a spare, intriguing power. (p. 685)

> *Julian Barnes, in* New Statesman *(© 1976 The Statesman & Nation Publishing Co. Ltd.), May 21, 1976.*

The Joyce Carol Oates phenomenon has begun to jangle the nervous system of the literary establishment. Her name, once mentioned with reverence among the literati, is now increasingly spoken in jest. Her problem, imply the critics, is that she writes too much.

A work of art, these days, from conception to birth, must be years in the making. But Oates populates the literary world with a new one every nine months, and the critical feeling seems to be that if she can produce offspring as easily as an Irish washerwoman, then what she does can't be that good after all. As a result, *The Assassins* has caused only a minor literary stir. Had it taken three or four years to write the very same novel, however, I am convinced that it would have been greeted with boundless critical enthusiasm. . . .

[It has a] story line . . . that should dazzle any with-it contemporary critic, as should the novel's theme and structure.

"Why insist upon chronological experience?" asks Hugh near the beginning of the book; obviously, he is speaking for the author herself, who certainly does not thus insist, but who flirts with time very artfully indeed, darting back and forth, in and out, yet always skillfully holding together the particularities. And she flirts with reality as well, offering differing and conflicting perceptions of shared experiences in a way which adds somehow, not only to the action, but to the characters themselves. (p. 965)

[Oates's] style reflects her own instinctive and automatic perception of human experience. That style has not been painfully contrived with an eye toward literary fashion, as is often the case with her peers. There has been no time. Her last book of short stories was published in March, and this novel is nearly six hundred pages long. And yet she has contrived it perfectly. When her critics suggest querulously that she slow down and rewrite, I cannot imagine what they have in mind. Stylistically, she is irreproachable.

Having said that, however, I still find myself troubled by the central Oatesian failing, a failure of vision. I may be on shaky ground here—certainly most contemporary critics would say so. If, after all, the woman's perception of the universe is that it is ultimately senseless, chaotic, and demented, then we can hardly ask her to write us sane and rational novels. Shaky ground indeed, even when we label that perception a defect, for the modern novel has been encouraged to move so far down the path of obsessional derangement that any attempt to herd it back up would be as silly as asking a contemporary double-knit politician to adopt the programs and mannerisms of Calvin Coolidge.

And if I were called upon to criticize the modern novel for the path it is taking, I would certainly not begin with Joyce Carol Oates; for, again, unlike so many of her faddish contemporaries, when she shows the universe to be maniacally malign, she seems really to mean it. In contrast to, say, a Pynchon novel, an Oates work leaves the impression that the author honestly sees nothing in the scheme of things to prevent her from being arbitrarily hacked to death. . . . Literary trends and the Oatesian vision have happily collided, creating, if not great art, at least the genuine article. (pp. 965-66)

> *Patricia S. Coyne, "Thinking Man's Break-fast," in* National Review (© *National Review, Inc., 1976; 150 East 35th St., New York, N.Y. 10016), September 3, 1976, pp. 965-66.*

The dazzling multiplicity of writings by Joyce Carol Oates may bewilder, impress, or dismay her readers. Stories, novels, poems, essays, plays, stream from her demonic imagination with a fecundity unsurpassed by any of her contemporaries. . . . She seems to share with Robert Penn Warren and Iris Murdoch the ability to reach both a broad, general audience and the realm of the intense literati. But along with such abundance of invention comes the risk of failure or deep flaw: thus Oates's brilliant success in her recent volume of stories *The Seduction* is simultaneously offset by her unreadable novel *The Assassins*. . . . [One] of the stories, "A Posthumous Sketch," shows Oates in her best vein of horror, enigma, compassion, and awareness of mysterious psychic currents that invest human relationships and their relation to the outer universe. But the other piece of prose, "The Child-Martyr," is a total failure—a labored effort at grotesque religious allegory.

The poems show a more consistent excellence; only a few fade out into incoherence or flatness of phrasing. . . . Despite such flaws, the theme of the book is well expressed in the opening poem, "Broken Connections," where the image of a dead telephone line strikes a motif found elsewhere in the book, as in "Lovers," where we find two people physically separated, yet locked together by the ringing and the silence of the telephone, or in the fine short poem "Two Insomniacs". . . . The tautness of the simple language here, conveying the bitter longing of the lovers, is an instance of the risks that Oates will take and win. Usually

her successes are more strongly involved in concrete detail. . . . (pp. 114-15)

Oates is not only trying to convey, in her abrupt, tenuous apprehensions, the sense of broken connections everywhere; she is at the same time suggesting the need to mend connections. . . . (p. 117)

The wonder-working of the volume resides in her success in convincing us that connection is possible through the fabulous beasts that we are, or create, by our verbal powers. She quotes Heidegger in one epigraph: "it is not we who play with words, but the nature of language plays with us." That is to say, in terms of this poetry, language lies at the core of our humanity, demanding our response and creation, so different from the limited forces found in outer nature. . . . Meanwhile, her gothic imagination has a distinctive way of twisting the potentially sentimental into a horror; thus a kiss becomes "Our mouths together, a communion of wounds"; snowflakes become like "insects swollen with white blood"; walking on the beach suggests "faceless mouths beneath our feet, sucking-sighing"; and even the annual American exercise of returning Christmas gifts on December 26 reveals a cry of anguish for a gift of love lost and unreturnable. . . . Nevertheless, in the penultimate poem of the book, the human "I" apprehends a strange unity, after the manner of an ancient Greek saying, "All things are full of gods." . . . It is a good account of the impact made by this entire (and it is a whole) book. (pp. 117-18)

> *Louis L. Martz, in* The Yale Review (© *1976 by Yale University; reprinted by permission of the editors), Autumn, 1976.*

Joyce Carol Oates in *The Assassins: A Book of Hours* gives an elaborate but also feverish and intensely shallow rendition of the problem of women and violence. She returns to the alarmist, even paranoid spirit of the end of *Them,* and commits herself to the subject of violence with a relentlessness that all but invents a violence of length. The book is a sort of triptych with the central character, in every sense, being Yvonne, the woman who attracts, causes, suffers, imagines, and dismisses violence. She marries into the Petrie family (an odd conflation of the Buckleys and Kennedys, with the Karamazovs thrown in). One brother, Andrew, is a politician, one, Hugh, is an artist, and the third, Stephen, is a religious fanatic. . . . The story is in some respects a whodunit whose limpness is supposed to be a sign of a psychic or spiritual involvement. But the adagio parade of suspects assumes rather than substantially assuring that the reader will consider it worthwhile to have done in the ultra right-wing Andrew Petrie, or urgent to associate the deed with members of his family or various faintly limned pseudo-political types.

But fear of extermination may be the donnée of the story—Hugh and Yvonne and Stephen and Andrew all evince it—as well as other common traits that make the multiplication of characters seem a generic cliché rather than an intrinsic need. One cannot be sure how much the story owes to *The Paranoid Style in American Politics,* but surely the self-importance that is wedded to paranoia appears repeatedly in the caricaturist Hugh and the caricaturish Stephen (the former thinks he is an Artist omnipotent, the latter calls a spade a spade and thinks he is God). In some respects the story is too blatant, too much given to the inconvertible and incontrovertible terms "must" and "will." Its ironies, where one might imagine them, are imprecisely wielded or facile, as in the equating of "God" and "catastrophe," or in all too readily slipping, in its own idiom, into "the most outrageous, merciless scenarios."

Behind the surface solidity of the story's violence there seems to lie a disbelief in the solidity of persons and things, or a rank impatience with them. The violence bears paradoxical witness to this, as heads are blown off and limbs hacked away and the world itself apparently becomes a "galaxy of tiny secret writhing seething bits, deathly white, ferociously alive, utterly silent." Even casual thoughts and gestures suggest a universe of insolidity; the ripping up of a letter resembles the "wiping out" or "obliteration" that Hugh and Yvonne wish for whatever inconveniences them. . . . (pp. 148-49)

It is this casual thought of ultimate violence that eventually dominates and virtually defines *The Assassins*. The book rather emptily envisions the wiping out of sex differences, and the coming of "some messianic androgynous youth," but its loyalty goes to the negative apocalypse implied in the notion that the only alternative to the physical act of "writing" is "chaos" (biographers and structuralists take note). Perhaps there is a parallelism with the notion that the alternative to "violence" is "nothing."

Finally, the Oatesian brand of violence betrays not so much a deficiency as a denial of human life. It is revealing that *The Assassins* is centrally populated by impotent men and frigid women. The novel makes repeated pseudo-apocalyptic use of the pronoun "it," without strict identification. Instead of marshalling, this amounts to the neutering of all experiences, and the reader is left with a suspicion that the novel's violence is primarily engendered by the state or act of neutering. One of the early moments of *The Assassins* presents a picture of the human person as a head without adequately developed genitals (to say nothing of the heart). It is, one discovers, a frequent, key image, and a sinister cousin to the Oatesian neuter "it." There would have been a certain fascination—especially in light of the conventional association of man and intellect, woman and emotion—if Joyce Carol Oates had been here exploring and evaluating the modern intellectualist bias. But in her use of the *caput sine genitalibus,* she seems rather to be exhibiting that bias, and so illustrating the position that "the brain finds itself seriously threatened by an enemy of its own making. It is its own enemy." It is at any rate the enemy of everything else in Oates's vision, and proof that while the genitals cannot give rise to brains, the brains cannot give rise to life (or at times compelling fiction). (pp. 149-50)

> *Michael G. Cooke, in* The Yale Review (©
> *1976 by Yale University; reprinted by per
> mission of the editors), Autumn, 1976.*

Joyce Carol Oates has written her best novel in years. "Childwold" has tenderness for the courage of people locked by social class and sexual desire into a noose-embrace. In this tale of a poor farm family—a blowsy mother whose many children have many fathers, her 14-year-old daughter, Laney, and Kasch, an anguished intellectual who loves them both—Oates reaches the power of statement and compassion that marked ["them"]. . . .

Miss Oates has remained fascinated by poverty as a form of exclusion and self-exclusion from the significant world. But

her social awareness surfaces in "Childwold" as a poor kid's anxiety. (p. 8)

Childhood is the fragile barrier against the future as a have-not or a killer. The novel's tight Oedipal triangle opens into a triple alliance against age and aggression as each person tries to turn the biological clock back towards innocence. . . .

Miss Oates's verbal brilliance bares characters who are driven by blind impulse through the pitifully few parts they can play. I think she rhapsodizes the incomprehensibility of their lives too lovingly. She virtually pleads for their blindness as a way of not seeing how little real mystery there is in lives that seem predestined to be unhappy. Fate could have written this primal drama of mother, daughter and rich man. And the novel's major flaw is exactly an almost superhuman, torrential flow of words that washes out the individual voice and often makes it difficult to tell who is saying what. The rapid-fire flashbacks that open the novel are its least effective part, offering little more than jumbled scenes of violence recollected with nostalgia. But "Childwold" is more brilliant than its beginning.

Protective, sacrificial love as a weapon against greater despair has gone out of fashion, particularly in the novel. But Joyce Carol Oates has made it new again. This insistent writer can call us back, through her dense psychological and social detail, to rural America in a spiritual and economic depression. The characters of "Childwold" inspire the terror and recognition once aroused by those monumental "lonelies" of William Faulkner and Carson McCullers. Passing over the current sense of sex as a matter of problem-solving, "Childwold" turns back the clock toward a tradition in which life is decipherable only through the code of compassion. Miss Oates has mastered that code and penetrated the morbidity of her view of life as a life sentence. (p. 30)

> *Josephine Hendin, in* The New York Times
> Book Review (© *1976 by The New York
> Times Company; reprinted by permission),
> November 28, 1976.*

Having forged past the wind-rocked bed, the weightless moon, and the threshing walnut tree on the first page [of "Childwold"], I can report that, while Oates remains true to the style of her opening, she includes enough in the way of character and action to allay the suspicion that the publisher is trying to palm off a runaway lyric poem. Nevertheless, despite the soothing traces of a novel, a certain question may arise in the minds of unsuspecting readers aware of the author's renown but unfamiliar with her previous work (I generalize from my own position); namely, What is she getting at?

Closer acquaintance with Oates indicates that there is no easy answer to that question. The clearest thing about her is the vehemence of her feelings: clearer than her view of life, an inconclusive mixture of sentimentality and disgust; clearer than her high-strung poetic prose; clearer than her characters, settings, or plots, which are cloudy with hidden meanings. Oates is primarily a conveyer of overwhelming emotion. . . .

[It] seems to me that her infatuation with the mystery of the universe, and with the manifold ways of expressing that mystery, is the main weakness of ["Childwold," "them," and ''Do with Me What You Will'']. In the two earlier novels, Oates lavishes considerable thought and verbal facility on creating some memorably eccentric characters and then lets them wander away from her after five hundred pages or so, to the mixed confusion and relief of the reader, exhausted by the absence of likelihood. There is a passage in ''Childwold'' that seems to describe the philosophy at the bottom of this aimlessness:

> *By merest chance.* Infinite universe, infinitely expanding, Principle of Indeterminacy, *merest chance,* in one direction the maggot-swarming corpse with that idiot's tongue, in the other direction a ninety-five-pound angel, gray-eyed, fair hair curly. . . .
>
> (p. 74)

In ''Childwold,'' as in the two other books, the characters are permanently imprisoned in themselves, moving at random through a merciless world. Except for Kasch, who, serving as a stand-in for Oates, thinks and acts almost exclusively on a metaphysical plane, the characters have no motives, no expectations, no interests, and what I would call a meagre sense of reality. They live only on the borrowed energy of the author's attention.

Oates's strong points as a writer are the doggedness of her pursuit of subconscious thoughts and feelings and the ritualistic distance she keeps in celebrating the grimness of life, which gives power to her vision even when her verbal extravagance gets out of control. . . . There is a Principle of Indeterminacy at work in Oates's choice of words as well as in the lives of her characters.

Oates underestimates the value of ordinary life and language. The more conventional structure and the leisurely pace of ''them'' and ''Do with Me What You Will'' establish an illusion of direction that at least intermittently conceals the fact that there is no inner or outer force to define and give weight to the characters and events. But even in ''them'' she writes:

> Like all lives, Jules's was long and richly tedious, vexed with prodigious details of physical existence he would have been ashamed to record, were he writing his own story: his story would deal with the spirit exclusively. . . .
>
> Of his experiences as a boy there hasn't been much time to speak, and anyway we have enough of these memories in other books. Of the many thousands of hours spent around kitchen tables—those eternal kitchen tables of the poor!—there is not much to say.

Oates now leans farther away from the substance of physical existence, toward its shadows, and from that oblique standpoint she has produced a novel that is the less interesting for its lack of those prodigious details. *Prodigious* details? Lying in ambush for the meaning of the universe, ''Childwold'' is distinctly languid. (pp. 74, 76)

Susan Lardner, "Oracular Oates," in The New Yorker (© *1977 by The New Yorker Magazine, Inc.), January 3, 1977, pp. 74, 76.*

The plan of *The Assassins* is legitimate and easily grasped. The narrative center, the controlling force of the book, is Andrew Petrie, though he is seen only in memory and in the effect that he has had on the other characters. We are told of Andrew's death in the opening pages and then we follow the mental peregrinations of Andrew's brother Hugh, his wife, Yvonne, and another brother, Stephen. From these loci of observation, which are highly subjective and which shift from time to time into pure stream of consciousness, we move into the lives of other characters, watch a dozen subplots unfold, and learn at last who actually pulled the murderous trigger. But this disclosure is anticlimactic, incidental almost to what has gone before, and like *Do with Me What You Will* and other recent books in Miss Oates's canon, the novel simply trails off—a welcome end to a dreary 568 pages.

From a technical standpoint what goes wrong first of all is the character of Andrew. He is a rich man with pretensions to politics and learning, a conservative who can command at least a limited amount of power. That he is not Miss Oates's sort of chap is clear from the outset, which is all well and good except that by not giving the devil his due she deprives her novel of its proper foundation. Andrew is flat, unrealized: he is snide when he should be cruel, mean when he should be evil. There is no sense of his flesh, of what tremors he caused when he walked the earth, no physical presence. As a consequence all other elements of the story suffer.

Hugh is a neurotic cartoonist, in love with Yvonne and on his way to insanity and suicide. But to what end this decay of the mind, the filthy apartment, the deteriorating talent, the growing paranoia, the psychedelic visions? If we could be sure—or even think—that Andrew when alive sowed the seeds of self-destruction in Hugh, then the novel might begin to cohere; but no such thing is ever rendered. Yvonne was a poor girl who had to make her own way, and she intends to make her way still, but she neither grieves nor shows a calm indifference. She aims to survive, which is a typical ambition in the work of Joyce Carol Oates, but the impulse to survival has no palpable connection with Andrew or with much of anything else that goes on in the story. Stephen is the most detached character of all; his narrative drifts and at times flounders in confusion; he seeks his own identity, but who has deprived him of the certainty of self in the first place, and how can we be sure that he has found himself in the end? In the final scene of the book, he is on the road with his sleeping bag, but what this has to do with Andrew's death or Yvonne's life or any of the other lives and deaths in the book, I cannot tell you.

Yet even this basic incoherence is not the worst that can be said about *The Assassins.* Other novelists have been unable to construct long narratives—Thomas Wolfe comes to mind —but the best of them have made up for weaknesses in structure and sometimes in characterization by the sharpness of their perceptions and the energy of their prose. In *The Assassins* one discerns a great weariness as if the author were half-asleep at the keys: the job seems to have been done by rote: inspiration and even desire appear to be lacking. And one might guess that such was the case. Those who have followed Miss Oates's career know what she can do—or could do when she first started writing. The sheer terror that is generated in ''Where Are You Going, Where Have You Been?'', the worlds that are created in such books as *A Garden of Earthly Delights* and *them,* and the impoverished and abused and brilliantly realized heroines of these same fictions testify to the scope of Miss Oates's talent. Reading the books of her youth for the first time, we had a right to expect more than she is giving us in her maturity. Surely she is writing far too much; surely she owes herself and us more self-discipline. (pp. 116-17)

> *Walter Sullivan, in* Sewanee Review *(reprinted by permission of the editor, © 1976 by The University of the South), Winter, 1977.*

Not "Stories," but "Tales," the subtitle says; as in Poe's "Tales," or Hawthorne's mossy old "Twice-Told Tales," or as in lurid mass-market paperbacks with titles like "Tales of the Supernatural." Because "Night-Side," Joyce Carol Oates's new addition to her dozen or so books of fiction, presents a gallery of people haunted, spooked, driven mad or victimized in general by invasions from outside the sane, rational borders of consciousness. (p. 15)

[These] are not literal ghost stories, but Oates has borrowed from the creepiness and disorientation of that genre to give a distinctive emotional color to her otherwise rather clinical studies of mental disorder.

Good old mental disorder and distress. Maybe the otherworldly tone of "Night-Side" is unusual in today's serious fiction, and even something of a departure for this author—although hauntings have turned up before in her writing, notably in "Wonderland" (1972)—but the subject of borderline sanity is one in which Joyce Carol Oates has been demonstrating a handy competence from way back. If there's a difference between the strange mental worlds here and those Miss Oates has taken us to before, it is that the pain pervading the new book is peculiarly lonely and private. Her most considerable works to date, for example, "Wonderland" and the National Book Award winner "Them" (1969), have been, to some extent, *social* novels, in which personal suffering ran deep, but was shared, too; was somehow familial or communal. In ["Night-Side"] . . . there's hardly an instance of two people understanding one another. The book is lined with sharply isolated madnesses, like jars on a shelf; discrete little psychoses and neuroses, with the lids on.

Oates's way with madness has two strengths: (1) She's clear-minded and sensible about disordered psyches, yielding not at all to the irresponsible, romanticizing tendency that's rightly been criticized in the recent craze for potboilers and films about insanity. The sources of anguish in Oates's people are neither too simple nor mysteriously abstruse: clues to a diagnosis are usually there somewhere, if you look. (2) Crucially, she has the knack of convincing us that individuals in the extreme states that interest her must actually think and feel as she says they do. And because it's convincing, the writing is involving and disturbing and real. Few contemporary writers can match the credibility and experiential power of Oates at her best. In almost all the stories these powers get a showing, and in five or six, Oates is at the top of her form. (pp. 15,18)

Fighting off needs and memories and subrational horrors is the action of "Night-Side." Mostly it's a fight the characters lose. At an inevitable moment, the lie is given to the glib rationales that support their sanity and they are brought up hard against what they can't suppress or deny. A quality of melodrama attaches to these revelatory moments, just as there is something melodramatic and overfamiliar about the underlying thesis that rationality itself is a fraud, an evasion of deeper, darker truths about the self. But there's such a thing as superior and intelligent melodrama—such as Poe's and Hawthorne's. Joyce Carol Oates's melodrama is first-rate, and, unlike other people's, it makes sound psychological sense. (p. 18)

> *John Romano, "A Way with Madness," in* The New York Times Book Review *(© 1977 by The New York Times Company; reprinted by permission), October 23, 1977, pp. 15, 18.*

* * *

O'CASEY, Sean   1880-1964

An Irish playwright, O'Casey was largely responsible for changing the focus of Irish drama from peasant comedies to highly realistic urban dramas. His strong social and political sentiments are evident in many of his plays, which are concerned with the Irish rebellions against England. In O'Casey's plays vibrant and effective female characters far outnumber males, who are often portrayed as weak and conventional. (See also *CLC*, Vols. 1, 5.)

In admiring O'Casey's faithful rendering of dialect . . . we might tend to overlook the very conscious control he exercised in its use, particularly in his later plays. Increasingly he employed dialect to serve clearly-defined purposes in his dramatic design.

A comparison between any of O'Casey's earliest plays and any 'realistic' play of the same period shows a marked difference in the treatment of language. T. C. Murray and Lennox Robinson used language as the barest instrument of plot and characterisation: it might express feeling or mood but is rarely allowed to obtrude. O'Casey, on the other hand, in these early plays shows a preoccupation with language and an obvious belief in its power to transform reality. (p. 387)

In these early plays, however, O'Casey does occasionally depart from an exact imitation of real or conventionally real speech at heightened moments in the drama. Mrs. Tancred and Juno employ the language of the Catholic missal, Bessie Burgess the words of a Protestant hymn. A more common method of departing from the speech of the streets or the popular tradition was the employment of a form of balanced language which probably owed more to Shaw than any other source. This occurs mainly when the author is clearly speaking his mind through a character. Thus, when Davoren is reproving Shield for his superstition, he exclaims:

> . . . You know as little about truth as anybody else, and you care as little about the church as the least of those that profess her faith; your religion is simply the state of being afraid that God will torture your soul in the next world as you are afraid the Black and Tans will torture your body in this.

This balanced language he continued to use throughout his career as a dramatist and usually for the same effect as in the early plays. His use of dialect, however, became gradually more selective and was subject to more subtle changes than in any of the early 'realistic' plays.

In *Within the Gates* there are three layers of speech. At the bottom is the Cockney speech of the chair attendants and the Disputants, whereas the other characters employ standard speech. Now, this does not appear to be a simple differentiation of class, as it might be in a more realistic play. The Young Woman and her mother and father (the Atheist) clearly all belong to the lowest stratum of society. But, while the mother and daughter speak in standard English, the father's speech is generally indicated as Cockney. O'Casey seems to have indicated Cockney speech as an arbitrary theatrical convention, purely as a distinguishing mark of the Disputants and the chair attendants. It is merely a device for highlighting their ignorance or stressing the inanity of their argument. (pp. 388-89)

Sometimes within the same play O'Casey uses a dialect to reinforce two contrary attitudes of mind. When he is clearly in sympathy with the sentiments of O'Killigan in *Purple Dust*, he often expresses those sentiments in the Irish vernacular as a sharp contrast to the language of Stoke and Poges. Yet the Canon, who normally speaks in an approximately standard form of English suddenly reverts to dialect in a moment of passionate bigotry:

> Help us to curtail th' damned activity of the devilish dance halls! Open a dance hall, and a month or less the innocent disthrict becomes worse than your Leicester Square. . . .
>
> (p. 389)

The Dublin dialect itself is often with O'Casey an indication of a commonsense, earthy attitude to life to which he presumably would subscribe. In *The Bishop's Bonfire*, to take one example, the speech is often ordinary Dublin dialect and this is generally used when the characters, forgetting their social roles, behave as normal human beings under stress. (p. 390)

Nevertheless, O'Casey's use of the Dublin dialect in some of his later plays is both flexible and subtle enough to suggest other moods. In *Behind the Green Curtains*, the Dublin dialect predominates. O'Casey, however, uses this dialect for both realistic and symbolic purposes. In the first scene its use is clearly realistic, and Lizzie, Angela and the others who intervene in the conversation, speak in broad Dublin speech.

In the second scene particularly (though not exclusively) McGeera, McGeelish, Horawn and Bunny use the dialect for a purpose other than realism. All of these characters are the supposed representatives of Ireland's cultural life. One would therefore expect them to speak in an approximately standard form of English and certainly in a grammatically correct form. It is worth looking, therefore, at the language used in the argument between McGeera and McGeelish just after the latter has filched the incriminating book from Chatastray's drawer:

> MCGEELISH. Youse are takin' the scandal lyin' down. What are we goin' to do about it? (*He has kept the photograph and has continued to stare at it while he talks*) God, what a revelation! A leader of piety and upright thought, and now look at this!
>
> MCGEERA. Divil a one's gettin' a chance to look at it, except yourself. If Chatastray

saw the model in real life, then, bedammit, I envy him!

> MCGEELISH. As practisin' Catholics youse make me sick. Renan the Atheist and this nude girl. . . .

Now, this extract is a typical sample of the language used by these characters and it is obvious that the dramatist is employing a familiar satirical method. Just as the meanness of their actions is revealed through the act of rifling Chatastray's property, so the lower register of speech reveals the vulgarity of their minds. The satirical diminution is achieved not only through the use of dialect but perhaps even more through the tone. The short exclamatory burst—'What are we goin' to do about it? God, what a revelation!'—suggests the vulgarity of minds too eager to destroy another's reputation.

The same dialect, however, as we have seen before, can reveal in the same play a contrary characteristic as when Reena lapses into familiar Irish speech in her sympathetic recital of Chatastray's virtues.

A close scrutiny of O'Casey's use of dialect, therefore, shows clearly that he seldom in his later plays used dialect merely to lend verisimilitude to the setting. His use of dialect is always conscious and he exploits it for the purposes of mood and attitude. Of course, it is mainly Irish speech that he puts into the mouths of his characters, since his own vision of the world is nearly always related to contemporary Ireland. For this reason his use of dialect can at one moment imply meanness and parochialism, at another, generosity and love of life: the world that is and the world that might be, O'Casey's constant theme. (pp. 390-91)

> *J. A. Snowden, in* Modern Drama (*copyright © 1972, University of Toronto, Graduate Centre for Study of Drama; with the permission of* Modern Drama), *February, 1972.*

The national theme must be given due weight in any assessment of [*Juno and the Paycock*] as a tragedy. At the same time, it must be acknowledged that the play gives more attention to the domestic themes concerning "Captain" Boyle's expectation of a legacy and Mary Boyle's expectation of marrying a school teacher, Charles Bentham. (p. 3)

The national and domestic themes of the play are linked and unified by a number of important parallels and resemblances. In the national theme, the slogan declaimed by Johnny Boyle, "Ireland only half-free'll never be at peace while she has a son left to pull a trigger" . . . shows how the great hopes of Irish unity and independence . . . have been thwarted by the partition of Ireland and the civil war which it has precipitated. Correspondingly, the domestic theme of the legacy deals with great expectations which are thwarted by a disappointing partition, because Boyle's hopes of affluence coming from the property left by his cousin William Ellison, are dashed when it is revealed that the will has been so vaguely formulated that the legacy must be partitioned between all of Ellison's first and second cousins, wherever they may be, and that none of them is likely to get anything worthwhile from it. In the other domestic theme, Mary's high hopes of marrying Bentham come to a sad end when he discovers that the Boyle's legacy is worthless, breaks their engagement without warning and departs for England.

The national and domestic themes of the play also acquire unity and depth from the fact that each of them involves the breaking of fundamental human relationships, treachery, and desertion. In the national theme, Ireland is split by the warring factions of Free Staters and Diehards; Johnny Boyle is guilty of treachery when he betrays Robert Tancred, and is subsequently deserted by his former comrade. . . . In the domestic theme, the Boyle family is split by Mary's disgrace and the loss of the legacy; Boyle and Johnny turn against Mary viciously and treacherously when they hear of her plight. . .: Boyle's callousness and his delayed revelation of the worthlessness of the legacy impel Juno and Mary to desert him. The family, like the nation, breaks up. Relationships supposedly based on love and friendship dissolve even more quickly. Bentham and Jerry Devine both profess love for Mary, but they betray their high-flown spiritual and humanitarian creeds when they desert her in her time of need. (pp. 3-4)

Early in the play, a connection between the Irish nation and the Boyle family is humorously implied when Boyle talks about his rights as a husband and boasts that Juno will have to take "an oath of allegiance" in the "independent Republic" that he is going to proclaim. This connection acquires a tragic potentiality, however, when the "Troubles" of Ireland are equated with those of the family in Boyle's peevish comment, "More throuble in our native land" . . . when he is asked to hear the result of Mary's visit to the doctor. This tragic potentiality is realised when Juno, too, uses the key-word "troubles" after hearing that Johnny has been taken away by gunmen: ". . .is me throubles never goin' to be over?" . . . The association of the Boyle family, Ireland, and "throubles" blends the tragic with the satiric in the final episode of the play when Boyle in his tipsy meanderings identifies himself with Ireland's plight, "The counthry'll have to steady itself . . . it's goin' . . . to hell . . . Irelan' sober . . . is Irelan' . . . free." . . . (p. 4)

The structure in which these themes are embodied is highly original. One of the distinctive characteristics of *Juno* as a tragedy is its modulated movement from the apparently comic to the grievously catastrophic. Perhaps no tragedy provokes as much laughter as *Juno* does. But the laughter gradually diminishes as the tragic implications of the action deepen, and from the outset O'Casey counterpoints the mirthful with the satirical and with even starker considerations. (p. 5)

The characterisation as well as the structure of *Juno and the Paycock* is finely calculated. It is based upon a continuous contrast between the masculine and the feminine personages, from which the women emerge as far superior to the men because of their capacity for love, altruism, and wisdom. The men in the play are all deluded, self-centered, and hypocritical. In the political plot, Johnny Boyle's glib slogan, "Ireland only half free'll never be at peace while she has a son left to pull a trigger". . . , ill-becomes one who has recently betrayed a fellow-Diehard and is far transcended by Mrs. Tancred's rejection of violence when she appeals to Christ to "Take away this murdherin' hate . . . an' give us Thine own eternal Love!" . . . In the love story, Bentham and Devine, for all their high-flown philosophies, are both snobs. Mary Boyle, for all her faults, has a capacity for genuine passion which they lack, as we realise when she tells Juno, "Mother, the best man for a woman is the one for whom she has the most love, and Charlie had it all." . . . (pp. 6-7)

The most detailed contrast between the feminine and the masculine, however, is the one between Juno and Boyle. The title of the play indicates the importance which O'Casey attached to this contrast. It was Boyle himself, we find, who nicknamed his wife "Juno" because of various events connecting her with the month of June. . . , but he did not realise that "Juno" was the Roman name for the goddess who presides over justice and loyalty in family life and safeguards women, marriage, childbirth, and finances. Juno Boyle tries to uphold the same ideals and protect the same things in the play. The chariot of the goddess Juno was said to be drawn by peacocks, but in the play Boyle is more hindrance than help to his Juno, and is described as a peacock ("Paycock") chiefly because of the *consequential* strut of his walk and the colossal vanity of his character. . . , which remains incorrigible, though many forces besides Mrs. Madigan try to pull "some o' th' gorgeous feathers out o' your tail." . . .

There is humour as well as satire in O'Casey's portrayal of Boyle: his command of words and his resilience are comparable to Falstaff's. His catchphrase in Act One—"I've a little spirit left in me still" . . . is an exquisite understatement. As the action of the play develops, however, we are made more and more conscious of the tragic consequences of the complacency and self-absorption which cause men like Boyle to live in a world of dreams, illusions, poses, and lies. (p. 7)

The selfishness at the heart of Boyle's poses emerges more and more ominously in his reactions to death, war, and the life inside his pregnant daughter. . . . The truly tragic character is often distinguished by the fact that he comes to recognise hard truths through the stress of suffering. But Boyle never suffers and it is one of the great ironies of the play that he applies his catchword "chassis" (i.e. "chaos") to things which are disintegrating—his family, his country, his world—without recognising the bitter truth of his description. (pp. 7-8)

Unlike Boyle, Juno becomes a stronger and wiser character under the stress of tragic circumstances. From the outset, she is an unconscious devotee of the goddess Juno in her efforts to preserve the family in which she is the only wage-earner; she provides food, gives Mary sensible advice, comforts Johnny, tries to keep a tidy home and to get Boyle to work. She scolds him for laziness and deflates his talk of having been a seafaring captain when she reveals that he was "only wanst on the wather, in oul' collier from here to Liverpool." . . . Whereas Boyle uses these fictions to cushion himself against reality, Juno faces it and responds compassionately and constructively to the problems of their time. Boyle says religions have had their day "like everything else". . . , but Juno tells Bentham that if people "ud folley up their religion betther there'd be a betther chance for us." . . . Boyle says the war is "the Government's business," but Juno passionately reminds him of how many men in the adjoining tenements have been killed or maimed, and declares, "if it's not our business, I don't know whose business it is." . . . Only Boyle's pride is affected by Mary's plight, but Juno's altruism enables her to see that Mary may have forty years of bitterness to endure. . . . When Mary bewails the fact that her child will have no father, Juno comforts her with her glowing declaration, "It'll have what's far betther—it'll have two mothers." . . . Juno speaks for all mothers of her generation in Ireland when she ends her last speech by re-echoing Mrs. Tancred's poignant words: "Sacred Heart o' Jesus, take away our hearts o' stone, and give us hearts o' flesh! Take away this murdherin' hate, an' give us Thine own eternal love!" . . .

Juno's wisdom connects her with the classical goddess. Her sufferings connect her with other great feminine archetypes. In Irish folk lore, Ireland has long been symbolised by a maternal figure, Cathleen ni Houlihan. When Juno asks ". . . is me throubles never goin' to be over?" . . . she embodies the sufferings of the mythical Cathleen. When Boyle peevishly compares her to "Deirdre of the Sorras". . . , we recall how Deirdre in the ancient myth abandoned the self-centered King Conchubar of Ulster to create a finer life elsewhere, and that Juno abandons Boyle to make a better life for Mary and her unborn child. By various means, Juno is also connected with "Our Lady of the Sorrows," the Virgin Mary, who, like Mrs. Tancred and Juno, lost a beloved son. In the middle of the rear wall of the Boyle's living-room is a picture of the Virgin, and for most of the play attention is drawn to it by the votive light that burns beneath it. Johnny is anxious to keep the light burning . . . ; he identifies his safety with it. Mrs. Tancred's invocation of the Virgin in her lament in Act Two also concentrates attention on the picture and the light, which become even more significant in Act Three, when the votive lamp *gleams more redly than ever* . . . and then suddenly *flickers for a moment and goes out*. . . . When Mrs. Madigan enters soon afterwards with the news of Johnny's violent death, the scene takes on the religious quality of an inverted annunciation as Juno stands beneath the picture and the spent lamp and re-echoes Mrs. Tancred's invocation to the Virgin.

This symbolic use of the votive light and the picture is characteristic of O'Casey's brilliant stagecraft in Juno, whereby he succeeds in charging simple properties of a naturalistic kind with a deeper meaning which is sometimes poetic in quality. At the beginning of the play, the mirror and the books by Ibsen on the table symbolise two forces at work on Mary Boyle; her vanity and her genuine desire to improve her mind. In Act Two, every available spot is ornamented with huge vases filled with artificial flowers . . . , an addition to the furnishings symbolic of the vulgarity and extravagance of the hopes inspired by the Boyles' prospect of a legacy. But O'Casey creates his finest stage-image in Act Three, when all the upholstered furniture acquired on credit is taken away, so that Boyle and Joxer stagger at the end into a room whose bareness and emptiness provide a stark visual symbol of the general chaos proclaimed by the very last words of the play. The movement of the stagecraft of the play from naturalism to symbolism accords with its tragic method, in which political and domestic themes are more and more closely integrated so as to subject the characters to tests which determine their capacity for discriminating between appearance and reality, between the choices that make for sympathy, altruism, and life, and those that lead to selfishness, anarchy, and death. (pp. 8-9)

William A. Armstrong, "The Integrity of 'Juno and the Paycock'," in Modern Drama *(copyright © 1974, University of Toronto, Graduate Centre for Study of Drama; with the permission of* Modern Drama*), March, 1974, pp. 1-9.*

Sean O'Casey simultaneously mimics and modifies some distinguishing dimensions of myth, both Christian and pre-Christian, in his *Within the Gates* (1934), a modern morality set amidst the vanishing greenness of a crowded London park, and in his *Cock-a-Doodle Dandy* (1949), an Aristophanic allegory situated in a drought-seared, fence-enclosed Irish garden. Indeed, O'Casey's mythopoeic imagination achieves a marriage of myths in these two dramas as Christian clerics collide with fertility figures, maypole dancing challenges formal Christian worship, and ancient fertility symbols like the silver shaft and the cock's crimson crest contrast with the pious parishioners' cross and rosary beads. O'Casey's basic intent, however, seems to be a desire to use myth both structurally and satirically: (1) to employ myth as a means of organizing his dramas into ritual sequences, and (2) to employ myth as a satiric stratagem which accentuates the difference between the function of mythico-ritualistic elements in the lives of ancient and modern man. Emphasizing the degenerative adaptation of antique mythical patterns—patterns designed to restore potency to people and provinces—O'Casey apparently laments modern man's reluctance to enter joyously into the rites of revivification which could redeem and revitalize both self and society, the sick soul and the modern wasteland. (pp. 11-12)

It is in the constantly evolving natural settings in both plays that we first discover the birth-growth-decay pattern so prominent in various vegetation and fertility rituals designed to mirror the fundamental rhythm of nature. Cyclical in design, O'Casey's dramas are clearly arranged in a ritualistic fashion so as to serve as symbolic representations of the birth and death of one year and one day. The four scenes in *Within the Gates,* for example, move us from the splendor of spring to the starkness of winter. Scene I unfolds in the park on a clear spring morning as birds search for food and build nests, fowl swim in the water or preen themselves on the banks, and yellow daffodils search for the sun. A chorus of young boys and girls, representing trees and flowers, enters to sing "Our Mother the Earth is a Maiden Again." A sexual union is suggested as the Earth Maiden seeks out her bridegroom, the Sun, in the "lovely confusion" of birds, blossoms, and buds. Scene II occurs during a summer noon yet the colors are now chiefly golden glows tinged with gentle reds. The daffodils have been replaced by hollyhocks which cluster beneath the shrubbery. Red and yellow leaves flutter to the ground and the sunflowers are "gaunt" in Scene III, set on an autumn evening. It is a cold winter's night in Scene IV and the bare branches of the trees form strange patterns against the black canopy of the sky. Only the light from three stars penetrates the chilly darkness.

A similar yet drastically abbreviated cyclical pattern is visible in *Cock-a-Doodle Dandy* as we move from morning brilliance to evening darkness. Scene I takes place in the garden in front of bog owner Michael Marthraun's house on a glorious summer morning as tough grass, buttercups, daisies, and sunflowers struggle to retain their vivid vitality in the midst of a long drought that has tinted the vegetation with a deep yellow hue. It is noon of the same day in Scene II and although a strong breeze causes the Irish Tricolor to stand out from its flagpole, the "sunshine isn't quite so bright and determined." Scene III occurs appropriately at dusk of the same day now much colder. The vivid reds, greens, and yellows of the earlier scenes have now been replaced by sombre hues. As the sun sets, the flag pole and house stand black against the sky; the sunflowers have also turned a "solemn black" and the evening star is but faintly visible.

The discernible changes in the landscape are correlated with corresponding changes, both physical and psychological, which the two young women, Jannice and Loreleen, undergo as they interact with others, especially the two clergymen. In Scene I of *Within the Gates* Jannice, despite her concern for her fainting spells resulting from a defective heart, is identified as a courageous and sensitive person whose main desire is "for a bright time of it." She affirms: "If I have to die, I'll die game; I'll die dancing!" In Scene II Jannice is still hopeful and tenacious as she seeks the Bishop's support in arranging a marriage with Ned, the Gardener, and she assures the Dreamer that she has not forgotten his "sweet song" with its carpe diem thesis. Jannice is both faltering and frantic during the cold greyness of the autumn evening in Scene III. Often pale and short of breath, she is increasingly fearful of the fiery torment which she thinks she must endure because of her many transgressions. In the final bleak winter scene, Jannice, breathing erratically with a fixed look of fear on her face, must be supported by the Dreamer in the dancing which she attempts. Drained of energy, she finally collapses and dies as the Bishop assists her in making the sign of the cross.

Yet O'Casey's young woman may not have danced and died in vain. Shortly after her demise the purple-black sky begins to change as it is pierced with golden shafts of light, "as if the sun was rising, and a new day about to begin." Moreover, the Old Woman predicts: "A few moments of time, and Spring'll be dancing among us again . . . the birds'll be busy at building small worlds of their own . . . the girls will go rambling round, each big with the thought of life in the loins of young men. . . ." The seasonal sequence prepares to repeat itself. (pp. 12-13)

As two women of beauty, passion, and vigorous affirmation, Jannice and Loreleen emerge as fertility figures whose function is to restore or release energies in both the withering wastelands and their infirm inhabitants—the dead souls. Moreover, the names of both contain mythopoeic overtones. The name Jannice links O'Casey's dancing protagonist with Janus, the Roman god of doorways and the special patron of all new undertakings. As god of beginnings, Janus' blessing was sought at the beginning of each day, month, and year, and at all births, the beginning of life. Jannice is, therefore, O'Casey's guardian of the park gates, and is the fair maid alluded to in the May Day rites in the early moments of Scene I as the chorus of young boys and girls sing "Our Mother the Earth is a Maiden Again."

Like her Roman namesake, Jannice is also a woman with two faces or two distinct aspects to her person. At intervals she thinks of prayer, penance, and self-denial; at other times she favors wine, song, dancing, and sexual self-indulgence. Anxious to emphasize this dichotomy in his heroine, O'Casey thereby links Jannice with Diana, another Roman goddess with two faces. Diana was . . . the guardian of flocks and fields, the chaste goddess of the hunt. Hence hers was largely a migratory life of abstinence. Yet Sir James Frazer points out in *The Golden Bough* that Diana evolved from earlier, more primitive fertility figures in ancient vegetation ceremonies. Thus Diana, "as goddess of nature in general, and of fertility in particular," also came to be regarded as "a personification of the teeming life of nature, both animal and vegetable." Hence Diana was associated with both chastity and sensuality.

Although Diana was frequently depicted with a bow, quiver, and javelin, she was also sometimes identified with a crescent. It is not accidental, therefore, that O'Casey repeatedly stresses the fact that his Jannice has a black crescent on her head and a scarlet one on her hip. Jannice's mother, for example, mentions this detail twice in Scene IV, reminding us again of the psychic ambivalence of the heroine. Additionally, the Dreamer reinforces this woman-nature, fertility goddess motif in Scene II when he compares Jannice's legs to the fresh, golden branches of a willow, and her breasts to gay, white apple blossoms. Again in Scene II he states that Jannice's hand resembles a lovely, blue-veined, pink-tipped lilly.

As a fertility figure, Jannice is pursued by many of the males in the park, but it is Ned the Gardener who celebrates her physical beauty in song. Moreover, it is the Gardener's singing that inspires the group of couples to sing of an earlier garden when Adam first saw Eve's "beauty shining through a mist of golden hair." Additionally, it is the Gardener who carries the black maypole, ancient phallic symbol, that is to be used in the folk dancing designed to make England "merry again." Moreover, it is the Man with the Stick who lectures the Gardener about the maypole as "symbol" in Scene I, informing him that "It represents life, new life about to be born; fertility; th'urge wot was in the young lass [Jannice] you hunted away." It is appropriate, therefore, for the chorus of young girls and boys dancing around the maypole to sing the folk song "Haste to the Wedding" because Jannice repeatedly insists that she must have a husband, child, and home to be fulfilled. Ironically, the Gardener does not really want to make things grow; he shuns marriage and so must carry a black maypole, symbolic of his denial of life's creative urges.

Loreleen's name likewise evokes myth. Like the Lorelei of German legend, she is given the alluring traits of a temptress who would lure men to their ruin. In Scene III Father Domineer associates her with the snake and the Garden of Eden. Both Father Domineer and bog owner Marthraun agree that it is the "soft stimulatin' touch" of woman's flesh and the graceful, provocative movements of "good-lookin' women" like Loreleen which place men in peril. Yet Loreleen would tempt men to live not die—would tempt men and women to reject domestic drudgery and Christian duty for dalliance and dance. As defender-performer of the Dionysian dance, Loreleen is likened to a "flower" that has been blown by a winsome wind into a "dread, dhried-up desert." Because she is responsive to the fundamental rhythms of life, especially sexual and instinctive, she is consistently identified with the color green. When she arrives from London in Scene I she wears a dark green dress and a "saucy" hat of brighter green; when she departs in Scene III, refusing to be suffocated under Father Domineer's black clerical cape, she wears a green cloak over her shoulders, an external sign of her inner vitality. Moreover, Loreleen, like Jannice, is associated with the color scarlet—a color which hints at both passion and piety —voluptuous woman and fallen woman—in both plays. If Jannice has a scarlet crescent on her hip, Loreleen has a scarlet crescent on her hat, an ornament which resembles a cock's crimson crest, and it is the crowing cock, with his vivid colors and agile movements, who is obviously an incarnation of the eros of life that animates both men and nature in *Cock-a-Doodle Dandy*.

If the two questers resemble fertility figures, the two clerics remind us of the sick fisher king whose illness brings a blight—a plague—to the land. The Bishop in *Within the Gates*, a man of sixty, has lost much of his vitality, and O'Casey indicates that his powers are "beginning to fail." Comfortable, complacent, and hypocritical, he refuses to involve himself in the sordid stress and strife of daily life. . . . His encounters with Jannice, however, help him discover his deficiencies, and he manifests new energy, humility, and compassionate purpose in his actions at the play's close. Jannice has assisted at his rebirth, which bodes well for future park visitors.

Such is not the case with Father Domineer in *Cock-a-Doodle Dandy*. An inflexible father who would frighten people into obedience, Domineer defends tradition against individual talent while raging at the carnal desires of men. A bigot and a bully, he has a restricted and restrictive religious code distinguished by an abnormal, Jansenistic fear of the flesh. He surrounds himself with unthinking sycophants who assist him in his activities which include physical abuse, exorcisms, ceremonial marches, and caustic, non-Christian tirades. Loreleen can not enlighten and liberate this cleric, and so the spiritual desolation must remain to stifle the conforming souls of Nyadnanave. The clerical chains remain to choke or confine those who lack the courage to rebel and depart like the young woman in green.

If the two clergymen remind us of the fisher king and his drought or pestilence-plagued land of pre-Christian myth, the two young men who perform choral functions in the two dramas—the Dreamer in *Within the Gates* and the Messenger in *Cock-a-Doodle Dandy*—resemble the wandering minstrels of earlier historical interludes. With his soft, broad-rimmed hat and vivid orange scarf, the Dreamer lives off the land, wandering from place to place to peddle his poetry. He gives money to Jannice from the advance which he has received on a book that is to be published, and he patiently strives to diminish Jannice's fear of hellish punishment. After Jannice's death he asserts that God will find room for one "scarlet Blossom" among his "thousand white lillies," and he hopes that future children will "sing and laugh and play where these have moaned in misery." The Messenger wears a silvery-grey coat adorned with a pair of scarlet wings, green beret and sandals, carries a silver staff, and leads the strutting cock around with a green ribbon. Hence he resembles the messenger—attendant to the gods of Greek and Roman myth. Yet his name Robin Adair links him with the Robin Hood romances. With his accordion and gentle airs, this Ariel-like figure finally departs with maid Marion, affirming that passionate young men and women will always obey the impulse to circumvent clerics to engage in the ancient and exhilirating fertility rites of spring.

It is apparent, therefore, that O'Casey both contrasts and commingles ancient ritual and modern, ironic romance in these two ceremonial, song-seasoned dramas, utilizing a congeries of provocative mythical constructs to impose design upon his material and to accentuate his satiric indictment of modern man's spiritual decline. (pp. 14-17)

Certainly the ritual—the patterned pageantry of the past—is transparently present in both of these plays, but the romance is not. True, lovely maidens, wearing gay garments and rehearsing high hopes, dance spiritedly but all too briefly through a green, pastoral world, but the handsome, knightly male, with his heightened ethical awareness and love of comradeship and challenge, is largely absent, replaced by sycophants, false seers and gombeen men. Merriment and marriage have given way to migration and martyrdom. And it is the mythical patterns which become the objective correlatives in these ritual-romance dramas, facilitating the audience's cognition of O'Casey's bias for an age with a greater fondness for and commitment to faith and frolic than our own. (p. 17)

> *Ronald G. Rollins, "From Ritual to Romance in 'Within the Gates' and 'Cock-a-Doodle-Dandy'," in* Modern Drama *(copyright © 1974, University of Toronto, Graduate Centre for Study of Drama; with the permission of* Modern Drama*), March, 1974, pp. 11-17.*

O'Casey's pugnacious defense of his writings, which gave him a reputation for arrogance and churlishness, sometimes makes [*The Letters of Sean O'Casey*] tedious and embarrassing, even to those who love him. Occasionally [the letters] shamed O'Casey himself. But the strength and consequences of his passions also give the correspondence a Shakespearean quality. The effect is heightened by the evidence of his patience and integrity in dealings with individuals who patronized or manipulated him—and profited from his first three plays either personally or on behalf of their organizations.

Time and the correspondence also show that O'Casey's major judgments were acute to the point of prophecy. Politically a realist as well as a humanitarian, he predicted the global successes of socialism, especially if there were repeated wars. He foresaw the consequences of dividing Ireland, and the impossibility of "classless" nationalist struggle. He challenged the exaltation of reckless violence a half century before Conor Cruise O'Brien, and was likewise misunderstood by many. Modern practice has vindicated O'Casey's crusade for fantasy and innovation, although his own later plays are still criticized harshly. Outraged by British philistinism, he sought to educate critics and public alike by pressing the merits of O'Neill, Joyce, and Eliot (*Murder in the Cathedral*) before they were well known or institutionalized. It is unjust to obscure O'Casey's farsightedness, as critics of this correspondence have done, by recalling only the strident means by which he was driven to express his views. (pp. 389-90)

> *Irma S. Lustig, in* South Atlantic Quarterly *(reprinted by permission of the Publisher; copyright 1976 by Duke University Press, Durham, North Carolina), Summer, 1976.*

*   *   *

OLSON, Charles 1910-1970

Olson was an American poet, literary critic, and essayist. While rector and instructor at Black Mountain College in the early fifties, Olson greatly influenced the group that came to be known as the Black Mountain Poets—Robert Creeley, Denise Levertov, and Robert Duncan among them. His concept of poetry is known as Projectivist verse, in which the

poet strives to replicate both the "acquisition of his ear *and* the pressures of his breath." For Olson, the typewriter was the perfect instrument for this verse, for it forces the poet, as the bar and measure force the composer, to record "the listening he has done to his own speech" with accuracy and fidelity. (See also *CLC*, Vols. 1, 2, 5, 6, and *Contemporary Authors*, Vols. 15-16; obituary, Vols. 25-28, rev. ed.; *Contemporary Authors Permanent Series*, Vol. 1.)

No poet could have been more patriotic than Olson was; not in the jingoistic sense, of course, but in the Whitmanian sense. . . .

Olson's aim in "The Maximus Poems" was to present Gloucester, as it is and was, and then to assimilate it into the Whitmanian spirit of America, as he saw it, and into the entire religious fabric of history from Egypt and Mesopotamia to the present, with excursions also into Far Eastern sources. Yet it was more than this. Ultimately he aimed to celebrate mankind. . . .

"The Maximus Poems" was a huge and truly angelic effort; it needs prolonged reading and extended commentary. Here, all I can do is record my feeling that Olson succeeded only in parts. The whole is a failure.

The trouble is incoherence, more and more so toward the end. One wonders to what extent drugs were responsible, especially when one notices a half-hidden reference to "speed" in one section. But surely the more crucial incoherence was Olson's self-dividedness, between his democratic faith, his deeply rooted generosity, good nature, and spirituality on one hand, and what his eyes saw on the other, the degradation of America. He could not resolve it. His two sides, pragmatic and spiritual, were at war. No matter how he strove, writing under streetlamps late at night on the Gloucester waterfront, jabbing the notebook with bursts of rhythmic speech, he could not find the word that could tie his or his nation's warring parts together.

He saw the same conflict in Ezra Pound and could not resolve it there either. "Charles Olson & Ezra Pound," comprising the notes and records Olson kept for about two years when he was visiting the older poet at St. Elizabeths Hospital in Washington, D.C., is one of the most fascinating literary documents we have. . . .

The book says more about Olson than it does about Pound, showing us Olson for what he was, warm, generous, intelligent, without an ounce of viciousness, as likable a man as anyone would care to meet. Yet it does not show us that these qualities helped him as a poet. Which is to say, it goes to the heart of the poetic enigma.

We are left with a great poem in its fragments, "The Maximus Poems," which we place together with the best work in "Archaeologist of Morning" . . . to make a very creditable body of work. Should we ask for more? . . .

I wish he could somehow have been content with description, for the descriptive parts of "Maximus" are the best, they alone sustaining the real force of the poem, and who knows how much more the poet might have achieved if, paradoxically, he had been willing to set this limit on his imagination? (p. 35)

> *Hayden Carruth, in* The New York Times Book Review *(© 1975 by The New York Times Company; reprinted by permission), November 23, 1975.*

For Olson there were only three proper areas for the study of myth: "initiatic cosmos," "the world of nature," and "the celestial world." Mythology was not reference, not metaphor, it was an "inner inherence" that one had to learn in order to give oneself control over time and space—"the retardation of eternity." It was in this sense that Olson was a poet; he believed poetry to be the articulation of order. (p. 45)

The delight Olson felt, whenever reminded by his followers that he was extraordinary, seemed to create in him a conscious ability to become ever more extraordinary. His constant awareness of the universal must have enabled him to expose or reinforce that universal in his every action. Why? Is the adulation and presence of followers so necessary? Olson, as so many other heroes before him, could pronounce laws and be assured of obedience. Yet he himself was free to disregard his own decrees. Olson could mock his own theories, and he did; whenever and for whatever reason, Olson could contradict himself. He was completely in power—or, at least he thought he was. Olson was dependent upon the admiration of his disciples; without it, his creativity declined. But by exerting his genius and, thereby, cultivating followers, Olson, in one sense, deprived his followers of creative freedom. And so, of course, he did not die. Great men do not die in their own times.

Olson was a genius, an incomparable teacher, but he was also overpowering. In his presence, few could maintain their individualities; they were, literally, overwhelmed. Olson did not promote growth in his students; he did not nourish them; they, especially those who were . . . sensitive . . . , could only wither in the presence of his intense, unmitigating light. (p. 46)

> *Zora Devrnja, in* Poet and Critic *(© Department of English, Iowa State University), Volume 9, Number 3, 1976.*

Knowledge to Olson was a compassionate acquisition, an act of faith and sympathy. He meant primarily that knowledge is the harvest of attention, and he fumed in great rages that the hucksters prey on our attention like a plague of ticks. In his first thoroughly Olsonian poem, "The Kingfishers," a *canzone* that divides decisively Modern from Post-Modern poetry, the theme states that when our attentions change our culture changes. He uses the firm example of the Mayan cultures, overgrown with jungles. The Mayan shift in attention was culturally determined: every fifty-two years they abandoned whole cities in which the temples were oriented toward the planet Venus, which edges its rising and setting around the ecliptic. The new city was literally a new way to look at a star (this is one meaning of "polis is eyes").

There is history (Waterloo, Guadalcanal) and there is the history of attention (Rousseau, Darwin). The kind of knowledge that shifts attention was Olson's kind of knowledge. He was interested in the past because it gives us a set of contrasts by which to measure events and qualities. (pp. 253-54)

Olson's argument throughout his poetry is that awareness is an event caused by multiple forces, setting multiple forces in action. No force is ever spent. All events are lessons. No event can be isolated.

Olson therefore evolved a kind of poem that would at once

project historical ponderables (for history is the ground for all his poetry) and allow him free play for contemplation and response. (p. 255)

If we allow for the sections of [*The Maximus Poems*] that quote historical documents, and for the occasional jeremiad, we can go a long way toward understanding them by noting that they are variations on Keats' nightingale ode. They are for the large part written at night (by a Timonish Endymion *en pantoufles,* or an insomniac bear with clipboard wandering about Gloucester, caught from time to time in the spotlight of a police cruiser), they share the imagery of bird and flower (cormorant and nasturtium here), fierce seas and bonging bells (buoys on Cape Ann), and they meditate on resonances of the past that can still be heard. (pp. 255-56)

Olson's spiritual barometers and seismographs give readings that we have to live with for awhile before they begin to render up sense. His view of mankind reaches into the backward abysm. Geologically the world is in the Pleistocene still, the age that evolved the horse, elephant, and cow more or less as we know them. And man. And the arrangement of the continents as they now are.

From *Maximus IV* forward Olson has introduced the subject of continental drift. (p. 257)

Two hundred million years ago there was one continent, so the theory runs, named Pangaea, and one ocean, Panthalassa. (Has geology ever sounded more Ovidian?) A northern land-mass, Laurasia, split away from the southern landmass Gondwana a hundred and thirty-five million years ago. Another twenty-five million years, and India wandered away from Africa. The last of the continents to divide was the one that became Antarctica and Australia.

The long and perilous voyage that brought Europeans into America as a second migration, 150,000 years after the Indian came here from Asia, could at one time (if any men were about) have been made by taking a single step.

Throughout these last Maximus poems [Volume III] Olson keeps gazing at the offshore rocks, especially Ten Pound Island. That it was once at the bottom of an icesheet that lay across Europe is a fact rich in mythological tone. The severing of the continents is itself a comprehensive symbol of disintegration, of man's migratory fate, of the tragic restlessness of history. (pp. 257-58)

What has happened to American culture (Melville observed that we are more a world than a nation) is a new disintegration that comes hard upon our integration. . . . [A] cooperation between greed and governments is far too mild a monster for Olson's vision. He would have agreed with De

Gaulle that we are the first civilization to have bred our own barbarians. . . . (p. 258)

The *polis* is gone; no one can imagine that there are any American cities left. The towns have died at their centers and thrown up a circular scab around themselves, a commercial carnival. We know all too well what Olson is talking about, if not what he is trying to teach us. These poems are more frightening in their implications than the last of the *Cantos,* than Dr. Williams' diagnoses.

I have not been able here to give any notion of the wideness of these new Maximus poems—the horizon they survey is vast—nor of their depth, which goes back into various histories (the Hittite, Egyptian, Greek, Roman, paleolithic) in new and bright ways (Olson's eyes were open to everything and very little got by him). Nor have I mentioned their religious concern. The best way to offer a summation is to note that a movement is closed by them, a movement that began with Thoreau and Whitman, when America was opening out and possibilities were there to be stumbled over or embraced. Olson is the other term of this moment. He is our anti-Whitman (like Melville before him). He is a prophet crying bad weather ahead, and has the instruments to prove it. (p. 259)

> *Guy Davenport, "In Gloom on Watch-House Point," in* Parnassus: Poetry in Review *(copyright © by Parnassus: Poetry in Review), Spring–Summer, 1976, pp. 251-59.*

If we take as the definition of the classical writer the one who objectifies his material, pushes it outside the self, presents it in some inherited or given pattern . . . and the romantic as the one who infuses into his material as much of the self as he can manage, the forms dictated by every idiosyncratic ripple of individuality, his material virtually a sexual partner, into whom he must plunge all! all the body! all the self! . . . then, by these definitions, the progression of *Maximus* is from Charles Olson, the man who started writing about Gloucester when he was in North Carolina, to some extent objectifying it, and who told me, when he moved back to Gloucester, he was nervous about the move, uncertain he could get *at* Gloucester when he was that close to her—from such a man, the progression is to the *Maximus* of Volume Three, who is utterly identified with and fused into Gloucester . . . a man who becomes The Last of the Great nineteenth-century Romantics. (p. 272)

> *Paul Metcalf, "A Seismic Rift," in* Parnassus: Poetry in Review *(copyright © by Parnassus: Poetry in Review), Spring–Summer, 1976, pp. 260-74.*

P

PERELMAN, S(idney) J(oseph)   1904-

Perelman is an American humorist whose work parodies American characters and culture. In addition to books and essays, he has written several Hollywood screenplays—notably the Marx Brothers' *Monkey Business* and the Academy Award-winning *Around the World in Eighty Days*. (See also *CLC*, Vols. 3, 5, and *Contemporary Authors*, Vols. 73-76.)

To most of the self-confessed hacks who spent years writing shabby screenplays, Hollywood was a nightmare to be escaped from as soon or as frequently as possible. . . . Another response to the Hollywood experience was that of S. J. Perelman and his close friend and brother-in-law, Nathanael West. These writers found in the show business milieu both an ideal metaphor for American culture in general and a set of rhetorical and structural techniques suitable to their own fictional interests. Also it was the films of the Marx Brothers that both Perelman and West most curiously approached in their fiction. The object of Marx Brothers satire is the medium the brothers employ—show business itself, and often show business in its most preposterous, because most untrue-to-life, manifestation—the Hollywood movie. In certain ways this strategy is also employed by Perelman and West. . . .

It is tempting to speculate that though Perelman was one of the writers of *Monkey Business,* the first Marx Brothers film that was not a remake of a stage play, it was the Marxes who helped mold Perelman rather than the opposite. (p. 660)

In the illogic of the Marx Brothers films, there is a constant fluctuation between the conversion of routine situations (like lighting cigars) into extended rituals and—what is more frequent—the conversion of pompous productions (like operas and society dinners) into back-alley capers. The lowly is exalted; the lofty is trivialized. Unlike the comedies of Chaplin, for example, or Laurel and Hardy, the films of the Marx Brothers are little concerned with domestic or political satire. Their satirical objects are the theatrical productions of society. The pomposities they demolish are the creations of people unable to conceive of their lives other than as roles in formulaic show business productions. . . . Except when such roles are taken by the brothers themselves, the performers assume with absolute vacuous seriousness the behavior of movie stereotypes. They become unintentional caricatures of caricatures. In the Marx Brothers films, then, the show biz world is *the* world; the mask is the face; Hollywood is reality.

The same is essentially the case in many of S. J. Perelman's stories—not simply the large number which deal explicitly with Hollywood, but also those concerned with such demimondes as fashion and clothing (a Perelman obsession), medicine, publishing, travel, advertising, and even farming. Where Perelman fundamentally differs from the Marx Brothers is that he introduces to the show biz setting not a group of irreverent and destructive eccentrics, but a naïve worshipper of the fraudulent scene. Usually nameless, the Perelman protagonist craves success, but in his gullibility invariably is defeated by the conscienceless frauds who rule whatever papier-mâché empire it is that he seeks to invade.

The Marx Brothers always win. Their brashness makes them invulnerable to fraud. The Perelman protagonist, though sometimes bemused and jaded by hypocrisy, is helplessly vulnerable. His jokes and puns are most often at his own expense. He is the schlemiel temporarily seduced by impresarios with such names as Harry Hubris, Stanley Merlin, and Tony Morningoff, or bright-eyed sexpots like Elaine Strangeways, Xanthia Mothersill, and Bitsy von Auchincloss.

The Perelman hero's sole defense is language—a unique composite of irrelevant erudition and show-biz badinage. (Perelman's style, incidentally, obviously derives from the basic form of American Jewish monologue humor, the *shpritz* . . .). Perelman's hyperbolic rhetoric, an absurd extension of the linguistic exaggeration common to the performers who entrap the hero, is his only way of surviving. (pp. 660-61)

Still Perelman's language entraps him as well. Like the actions and thoughts it conveys, it calls attention to its own falsity. . . .

Unlike the Marx Brothers, the Perelman persona never knows he is playing a role. (p. 662)

Like Nathanael West's feeble protagonists . . . Perelman's narrators are compelled to be victims. They are eminently seducible by power and glamor, but they fall short in what both writers seem to judge the only effective weapon in the Hollywood situation—that is, brutality. Now brutality is what Groucho Marx possesses in abundance (as, in their pixieish ways, do Chico and Harpo). All of Groucho's roles show him as shrewd, unsympathetic, reveling in his own frauds, and cruel. He is tolerable because he is clever and funny, while his victims are fools; but he is a man without conscience. In Perelman's stories, the Groucho-like figures are leaders of the establishment, the movie moguls and clothing store entrepreneurs whose bravado and unscrupulousness are at the service of fakery. It is to the point, I think, that S. J. Perelman despised the Marx Brothers and took little pleasure in writing for them. (pp. 662-63)

In story after story, the Perelman protagonist finds Marx Brothers monkeyshines intolerable—intolerable because irresponsible. But his rages and retaliations are futile. (p. 663)

Perelman's perspective is invariably that of the victim. In many of Perelman's "scenarios"—those playlets within narratives that he has been writing for half a century—the comedy revolves around role reversal; that is, the character who is conventionally in a servile position assumes dictatorial control. (pp. 663-64)

Perelman has written hundreds of short stories, nearly all variants on the same subject: the hyper-literary naïve who becomes entrapped into actual or quasi-show business situations dominated by manic tyrants. The prototype of his settings is generally Hollywood. His descriptions of Hollywood types and dwellings, resembling those of West in the first chapter of *The Day of the Locust,* are so abundant in his fictions as to seem obsessive. They repeat with increasing disgust and detail Perelman's first published description of the Hollywood scene. . . .

Like West, Perelman relates external confusion and hypocrisy to the psyche of the movie people, who can live only by assuming bizarre roles, which are constantly being replaced by other bizarre roles. Surely it is appropriate that it was Perelman who devised the basic plot of *Monkey Business,* in which the Marx Brothers, as stowaways on an ocean liner, evade capture through constantly changing props and costumes. When Groucho puts on the captain's hat, he is the captain. (p. 665)

I think that the essential affinity between the Marx Brothers films and Perelman's preoccupation with stylistic incoherence is in the matter of language. Marx Brothers dialogue doesn't make sense. Part of their comedy is their verbal caricaturing of a culturally nonsensical society. Why should words convey reality when nothing else does? In the Marx films, as in Perelman's stories, everyone is costumed. Like the stooge figures in the Marx films, the Perelman personae sustain illusions that reality conforms to plots (often movie plots), that such matters as purchasing a house or proposing marriage can be managed with a fair degree of verbal accuracy. The Marx Brothers and the Perelman "leeches" reject such an assumption. The demolition of language is the ultimate significance of Perelman's own style—itself the most extreme cultural melange of his fiction. In its way, it is as bizarre as a Hollywood lot in its shiftings from the literary pretentious to Yiddish slang to advertising and show business argot. The pathetic Perelman narrator, unlike Groucho, tries to give a verbal order to his befuddling and maddening experiences, but the only language available is that of assorted artificial cultures. In such societies as Perelman depicts there is no such thing as a non-artificial culture, and no one is more immersed—be-

cause more observant and more obsessed—than the Perelman narrator. (pp. 665-66)

Perelman's comic victims are in a sense "cheated," but they are cheated of nothing more than illusion; to them distinction and pretense seem quite sufficient goals. (p. 672)

> *J. A. Ward, in* The Southern Review *(copyright, 1976, by J. A. Ward), Vol. XII, No. 3, Summer, 1976.*

There are at least two distinct types of laughter that the writing of S. J. Perelman produces in the reader, the Honk and the Yurble. Of these, the Honk is the more frequent. It might be the effect of a line of dialogue ("He opened a vein in his bath." "I never knew baths had veins.") or one of his intricately bizarre openings ("Every so often, when business slackens up in the bowling alley and the other pin boys are hunched over their game of bezique, I like to exchange my sweatshirt for a crisp white surgical tunic, polish up my optical mirror, and examine the corset advertisements in The New York Herald Tribune. . . .") or one of his all-purpose endings ("We bashed in his conk and left him to the vultures."). The Yurble is caused by Perelman's linguistic cobbling, as for example when "a panoply of porn" becomes "a pornoply" or he asserts "I hold no buff for the briefalo" or he gathers a cast that includes Gonifson, Hornbostel and Groin, and the atmosphere begins to resemble that of Nighttown with Leopold Bloom cruising through its surreal precincts.

In a sense, the humorist is like the man who hijacks a jumbo jet and its 300 passengers by threatening the pilot with a 10-cent water pistol. The arsenal is simple—technique matters, manner is everything, and fury helps. Mr. Perelman is good on the grotesque, because he is great at his tetchiest and best when he is angry. A movie such as "I Loved You Wednesday" or "The Texas Chainsaw Massacre," a magazine like House and Garden, the book "Oh, Doctor! My Feet!" by Dr. Dudley J. Morton, or practically any inedible sandwich is enough to set him off. But he is never more furiously comic as when dealing with a specific geographical location, whether it is a house in eastern Pennsylvania (about which he wrote an entire book, "Acres and Pains") or a back street in Kowloon. . . .

"From bar mitzvah on," Mr. Perelman writes at the start of "Eastward Ha!", "I had longed to qualify as a Jewish Robert Louis Stevenson." It is one of Mr. Perelman's more modest claims, but after reading "Unshorn Locks and Bogus Bagels," an account of his stay in Israel, one tends to think that he is in grave danger of being read out of the tribe for his having brought such ill tidings to Zion. "What magic, what ingenuity and manpower it had taken to recreate Grossinger's, the Miami Fountainebleau and the Concord Hotel on a barren strand in the Near East!" In Tel Aviv he came across a brand of perfume called Chutzpah. He describes this as a breakthrough even Dr. Chaim Weizmann ("himself a chemist") would have applauded: "Not a soul in history, from Helen of Troy to Helena Rubinstein, had ever thought of pure, unadulterated gall as a cosmetic." He notes in passing that the best hotel in Jerusalem—if not in the whole country—is run "by a family of Baptists." But Perelman is nothing if not fair-minded, and I cannot think of anyone better equipped to describe the troglodyte face of Yassir Arafat—indeed, I believe he has already done so, with devastating results.

Typically, because he hated the place so thoroughly, the Israel piece is one of his funniest. Discomfort, pomposity, bad service, importuning natives, hideous weather—anything vile makes Mr. Perelman's prose sing with mockery. Years ago, miffed in this present book's companion volume, "Westward Ha!" he was forced to leave "enough baksheesh in Santa Sophia to gild the transept"; and who but Perelman would have titled a comedy "The Rising Gorge"? In his disgust resides his eloquence. His experience of the Soviet Union in "The Millennium, and What They Can Do With It" is pure acid. Nothing went right, yet the result is not a tantrum but a glorious backhander in which everything he saw from Moscow to Yalta is dismissed. "Yalta contains sanitariums that ignite more hypochondria in the onlooker than the Magic Mountain . . . that Chekhov managed to glean any literary nuggets from Yalta is merely added proof of his stature." In Iran, which is . . . one of the earth's nightmares of unspeakable modernity and uncompromising barbarism, Mr. Perelman lets fly, but always with grace: "the demented thoroughfares" in Teheran are terrifying, "as a result, there are only two kinds of pedestrians . . . the quick and the dead."

It is only when Mr. Perelman is describing a dear friend or a well-loved place that his voice drops and one hears his so-rarely-used tone of gratitude or good will. In Penang, the colonial buildings and warehouses and dockside life "typified for me the magic of Kipling's Far East." It sounds like sarcasm; one waits for his swift deflation, but none comes—it is, almost incredibly, nostalgia. This is unexpected, but perhaps not all that odd, for like the references to Daddy Browning and Peaches, Joshua Slocum, Tazio Nuvolari, the Three Stooges, the reminiscences of Rhode Island and Hollywood, the exact price of brooms in Tzmir and words like "mazuma," "chicken-flicker" and "simoleon," there is room in Perelman's prose style for nearly everything. It is not so strange that in her introduction to a Perelman collection some years ago, Parker was at a loss for words. Perelman is incomparable.

> *Paul Theroux, "No Buff for the Briefalo," in* New York Times Book Review *(© 1977 by The New York Times Company; reprinted by permission), October 2, 1977, p. 9.*

In pebble glasses and high choler, S. J. Perelman, that word-besotted humorist, has again [in *Eastward Ha!*] set out to traduce the globe. Perhaps the countries of the world deserve the lumps they take at Perelman's practiced hand—they so rarely live up to the traveler's feverish imagination. In his earlier *Westward Ha!* Perelman went, well, west; now he heads in the opposite direction. . . .

One can hear his host of readers asking, "Is *Eastward Ha!* vintage Perelman?" The real question is whether they will be satisfied with a belly laugh every few pages or so and a lot of chuckles in between or whether they will be ingrates. For me, Perelman's names alone—Nauseatrauma for the manager of the Jakarta Stilton, Phee Line Miaow for a Siamese room boy, the Star & Kreplach for a Scottish pub—are worth the price. (p. 35)

> *Ralph Tyler, in* Saturday Review *(© 1977 by Saturday Review Magazine Corp.; reprinted with permission), October 15, 1977.*

Clearly the most irascible traveler since Smollett, in

[*Eastward Ha!*] Perelman lets fly with somewhat diminished zest at the unfortunate denizens of Edinburgh, Paris, Moscow, Tel Aviv and Points East. The veins of other travelers—at least at the beginning of their journeys—course with blood: only Perelman boasts ichor. If the State Department doesn't already have an official Ill-Will Ambassador, they should create the post just for him. . . .

It would be pleasant to report that *Eastward Ha!* is as fine a performance on the Perelman as its predecessor *Westward Ha!* but such, alas, is not the case. Despite such splendid inventions as the musician who "played some instrument, I think the hullabaloo, in a rock group calling themselves The Damp Squibs," the language is less outrageously baroque; some clichés, like "scarcer than hen's teeth" go unsavaged; phony words like "dichotomy" are used in all seriousness, and our most erudite humorist even forgets for the nonce that humidity, no matter how oppressive, is still measured in percentages, not degrees. Worst of all, the book boasts a mere two illustrations by the incomparable Al Hirschfeld, royal iconographer to Perelman as Holbein was to Henry VIII.

Perelman addicts will be somewhat disappointed, I think.

> *Richard Freedman, "Perils of Perelman," in* Book World—The Washington Post *(© The Washington Post), October 30, 1977, p. E7.*

*   *   *

PINSKY, Robert   1940-

Pinsky is an American poet whose work is characterized by vivid imagery and a clear, straightforward poetic voice. (See also *Contemporary Authors*, Vols. 29-32, rev. ed.)

[Robert Pinsky] suffers at times from a shockingly complacent wounded-academic-falling-through-the-rye complex, and his worst stuff could have floated up from the very bottom of *New Poets of England and America* (1957 edition). Most depressingly, he commits the error of supposing that he can write poetry about the garbage heap from an unregistering deadpan. The title poem of *Sadness and Happiness,* however, gives one a jolt. It is indeed about the garbage heap, but its moods are extraordinarily varied, its resonance, through every turn of colloquial frankness, always clear and sure. Mr. Pinsky has written a long autobiographical poem about the confused yet mostly satisfying present tense of his life, and, because he holds everything at a distance, he makes the confusion exhilarating. To call "Sadness and Happiness" the best of its kind would be fatuous since there is nothing else like it. I am the more surprised when I note that Mr. Pinsky seems to have derived his method from the dreary backwash of Robert Lowell's *Notebook.* . . . [In "Sadness and Happiness" one sees] how surely and regularly this poet's high spirits are able to steer him away from self-pity. At all events Mr. Pinsky strikes one as—to steal a phrase from Coleridge—brow-hanging, shoe-contemplative, strange: and one comes to like him for it.

He is also, Stevensianly, the poet of "houses and cars, trees, / grasses and birds; people, incidents / of the senses": his admiration for landscape, always slightly abstract, comes through in a few of the short lyrics as well. But equally, and with a loping self-confidence, the poet of streets, "as a Salvation Army band marches / down the middle, shouldering aside / the farting, evil-tempered traffic, / brass pitting its triplets and sixteenths / into the sundown fray of cops, gesturing / derelicts, young girls begging quarters, / shoppers and released secretaries.'' The obvious complaint against Mr. Pinsky is that his respect for the prose of life has allowed him to concede too little to the poetry. Yet he seems to understand this, and to find his own temperament odd enough to follow anyhow. (pp. 1025-26)

There will be those who find Mr. Pinsky just too dry, too cautious and ''squint-eyed,'' and they will be only angered by the descent he claims. To me, his slow and even circular journey was reviving: I hope he will move further in the direction of ''Sadness and Happiness.'' Mr. Pinsky is in no danger of becoming fashionable, but he needs, as other poems of his indicate, to grow wary of the state of mind known as relax and collapse. (pp. 1026-27)

> *David Bromwich, in* The Georgia Review *(copyright, 1976, by the University of Georgia), Winter, 1976.*

Public, discursive, witty, ironic when not downright sarcastic, intelligent, at home with ideas and cultural references, sardonic, lightly formalistic: call them Roman. I don't mean Virgilian, of course, nor Horatian either; more in the lighter line from Catullus to Propertius that has influenced so much of American verse in this century, though 99 percent of those influenced have never read their models. At any rate, this is the kind of poetry offered to us [in ''Return Your Call'']. . . . (p. 18)

> *Hayden Carruth, in* The New York Times Book Review *(© 1976 by The New York Times Company; reprinted by permission), April 4, 1976.*

The feeling that, somehow, American poetry has entered a new era of confidence is borne out by . . . *Sadness and Happiness,* the first book of poems by Robert Pinsky. . . . Pinsky is the most exhilarating new poet that I have read since A. R. Ammons entered upon the scene. He has a crisp, unfaltering technique, a firm grip on images, a sense of humor, and above all, something to say. He speaks for a new generation that has ceased to complain about the shopping centers and the model homes, the garages and the parking lots and the transit systems; he even likes psychiatrists. The whole of the modern world is for Pinsky a region where the soul, yes the Soul, has to face its mysteries; and the outer conditions for him are no worse or no better than they ever were for any generation. What matters is

> how love falters and flags
> When anyone's difficult eyes come
> Into focus, terrible gaze of a unique
> Soul, its need unlovable. . . .
>
> (pp. 126-27)

Form is difficult, as Beardsley might have said to Yeats, but form is what the soul demands for Pinsky, and he tries to find it everywhere. . . . (p. 127)

[The] showpiece of the whole book is the long, concluding ''Essay on Psychiatrists,'' humorously cast in the divisions of a formal disquisition or classical oration, while musing along in those familiar tercets of our day: Invocation, Terms, Proposition, Identification, Comparisons, Historical Instance (the *Bacchae* of Euripides as example: which

is the true psychiatrist, Pentheus or Dionysus?), Consideration, Dismissal, a Footnote, a Generalization, more Examples, two Perorations, and a Conclusion—all couched in an ample, easy-going manner that includes everything from comic strips to Walter Savage Landor on Happiness and Yvor Winters on the course of English poetry. And the conclusion? ''That 'psychiatrist' is a synonym for 'human being'''—

> All fumbling at so many millions of miles
> Per minute and so many dollars per hour
> Through the exploding or collapsing spaces
> Between stars, saying what we can.

In his peculiar and original combination of abstract utterance and vivid image Pinsky points a way toward the future of poetry. (pp. 128-29)

> *Louis L. Martz, in* The Yale Review *(© 1976 by Yale University; reprinted by permission of the editors), Autumn, 1976.*

[*Sadness and Happiness: Poems*]—with its stark title, at once embracing and reductive—is an engaging [book]: its voice is open to complaint or acclaim, its strategies are straight-forward, its intelligence and sympathies are poised, its topics notably ''normal''—the way we live now, fraying into the future: our eyes lowered, our jaws squared, our minds wary, our hearts exhausted. As a poet [Pinsky] is most successful where he is most generous—though not with the length of his attention. His extended poems on the game of tennis and the profession of psychiatry are catalogues for easy conclusions: tennis is like life, psychiatrists are like us. His other poems, while occasionally as discursive, are more tentative and probing, but they too prefer exaggerated gestures, which he grounds in drab remembered places or contemporary circumstantial scenes. . . . (p. 505)

[Like] a suburban Rilke, Pinsky is impatient to discover how

> Against weather, and the random
> Harpies—mood, circumstance, the laws
> Of biography, chance, physics—
> The unseasonable soul holds forth

As if the actions of this world were mere pretense, Pinsky bullies his subjects until they yield the vague comfort of a moral. It is an indication of his distrust of his own dramatic method, which seeks to imitate the world—to *mime* in art's foreign accents—only to realize he has duplicated rather than transfigured what he longs to change. . . . His concern for the contours of experience imposes on him the ''tyranny of the world visible,'' which he at once indulges and resents, and so finally submits to, submits us to. But his admirable, if strenuous, intellectual persistence rarely succeeds in clarifying or refining his dramatic material into poetic vision—as, say, the early work of James Wright did with such natural conviction. Pinsky speaks in a large, outspoken voice, anxious to proclaim formulas of and for our condition, which he details with trenchant precision. The only problem with his poems—and it is the primary risk of such dramatic poetry generally—is that they more often assume rather than earn the lessons they draw us toward.

Given the monochrome of his material and the flat earnestness of his tone—and we must grant any writer his given— Pinsky is still capable of exciting moments: acts of attention within any one poem's dramatic appeal. But they are moments isolated from one another and from any cumulative force the book may have had apart from its author's engaged and engaging personality. (p. 506)

> *J. D. McClatchy, in* The Nation *(copyright 1976 by the Nation Associates, Inc.), November 13, 1976.*

* * *

PINTER, Harold   1930-

Pinter, one of England's leading dramatists, has also written poems, short stories, screenplays, dramatic sketches, and criticism. In his plays there is an ever-present anxiety, a sense that nothing is certain. The seemingly meaningless conversation that is characteristic of his dramatic dialogue reveals a sense of the absurd akin to that of Beckett. The absurdity of atmosphere contrasts vividly to the naturalistic settings of his plays. (See also *CLC*, Vols. 1, 3, 6, and *Contemporary Authors*, Vols. 5-8, rev. ed.)

Pinter has chosen to be the great "mystifier," whose plays are famous (notoriously so, even to the point of parody) for their meaningful silences, their unanswered questions, their ambiguities, their symbolism admitting a multiplicity of interpretations. But this anarchic privilege of making his plays mean whatever one wants them to mean (traditionally, they are parables of "the human condition," taking place anywhere, at any time) does a considerable injustice to the achievement and particularity of *No Man's Land*.

The title . . . has its historical resonance, of course, taking us back to World War I, when the phrase was descriptive of that bleak, blasted space on the Western Front between the German trenches and the trenches of the Allied Forces. But Pinter is not writing a "war" play, . . . and his setting is not a battlefield but a very handsome drawing room, elegantly furnished—a great sweep of four windows in a semicircular bay, curtained in green velvet—in a fashionable quarter of London. . . . What do we find there?

Two men in their sixties, Hirst and Spooner, the former nattily dressed and evidently the host, for he is pouring drinks, the latter in "a very old and shabby suit; dark, faded shirt, creased spotted tie." Hirst . . . is a successful man of letters, very rich and very drunk—in fact, an alcoholic on his way, in this first act, to total incoherence and stupor. Spooner . . . is also a man of letters, sprightly where Hirst is ponderous, gabby where he is taciturn, and a failure where Hirst is so notably, in his expensive drawing room, a success. In fact, Spooner is the epitome of the potentially gifted writer who has talked his gift away over countless pints in countless pubs.

When the play begins, Hirst, pouring whiskey at the cabinet, asks, "As it is?" and Spooner replies, "As it is, yes please, absolutely as it is." This casual exchange of stereotyped phrases—precisely what one says in such a situation, the offer of a drink in someone's house—might serve usefully as the motto, or epigraph, or signpost for Pinter's play: "as it is," the true subject of *No Man's Land*. The crucial question, then . . ., is quite simply, "What does Pinter mean by 'as it is'?" To which one might fairly reply, the condition of life, "now and in England." (p. 102)

Hirst and Spooner—the one a success, the other a failure—are merely opposite faces of the same social coin: both belong to the class of gentlemen, as their accent (still a decisive indicator in English life) immediately proves. And both are powerless. They are the captives (in a quite literal way) of Hirst's guardians/nurses/caretakers—Foster, a man in his thirties, and Briggs, a man in his forties. When these two, who complete the cast, enter in the middle of the first act and begin to speak, we know, thanks to the decisive indicator, that almost certainly they are thugs, and certainly not gentlemen. . . . They are new men, flat, quasi-transatlantically accented, sinister, and outside the boundaries of class. . . .

Poor drunken Hirst, poor gabbing Spooner, measured against the threatening, hinted-at realities of Foster and Briggs—how frail and anachronistic they seem, survivors from a discarded history. "All we have left," says Spooner, "is the English language," and together he and Hirst are allowed by their creator to offer a virtuoso display of language in action, resonant, allusive, echoing (deliberately) Henry James, T. S. Eliot, and others of the pantheon, the conventions of upper-class theater dialogue, on the battlefield and in the drawing room. So we have Hirst and Spooner featly footing it among echoes—resorting to parody, the form that remains to them after the substance has gone—and able, as if by magic, to become a variety of stock characters in any number of stock situations. (p. 103)

But mastery of language is no salvation, when it becomes an end in itself. And in due course, the real end comes; Foster and Briggs are finally in control: "Nothing else will happen forever." (pp. 103-04)

> *William Abrahams, in* The Atlantic Monthly *(copyright © 1976 by The Atlantic Monthly Company, Boston, Mass.; reprinted with permission), February, 1976.*

One of the least likely working dramatists one tends to think of in terms either of palpable surface artifice or deliberate literary borrowings is Harold Pinter, and yet his latest play, *No Man's Land*, reveals both of these characteristics. . . . *No Man's Land* indeed emerges lobsterlike, its skeleton on the outside with the flesh hidden deep within. . . . [A] close examination of the literary affinities and the formal characteristics may demonstrate that *through* its structure the meaning of *No Man's Land* is dramatized. In other words, the shape of the play is what it is about.

The form of *No Man's Land* is inextricably linked to its literary antecedents—Beckett's *Endgame* and, primarily, Eliot's "The Love Song of J. Alfred Prufrock." (p. 291)

In trying to "get the structure right" in *No Man's Land*, Pinter seems to have raised form to a position of preeminence and hence conspicuousness, perhaps, it might be argued, at the expense of some other aspects of the drama.

The principal carrier of the play's structure is its dialogue (supported by the deliberate diminution of such other components of drama as plot, and both physical and dramatic action). Two elements of the highly formalized speech are largely responsible for giving the play its peculiarly noticeable shape: 1) clearly evident and, at times, rhythmically stressed patterns of verbal repetition, and 2) a coherent, unified fabric of imagery emanating from or related to a controlling metaphor of stasis embodied in the play's title, the twice-stated definition of that title . . ., and Brigg's monologue on the difficulty of getting out of Bolsover

Street. . . . While linguistic patterning is familiar enough as a device of Pinter's to give his plays shape, the inclusion of an insistent, pervasive system of images conveying a single impression seems uncharacteristic. Of course, linguistic repetition and a single system of related images, themselves frequently the content of the repetitions, are closely allied structural devices, and both may be seen as natural developments from literary antecedents of the *No Man's Land.*

The stasis in both *Endgame* and "Prufrock" is created by unresolved and, hence, balanced tensions between recollected memories of the past and ongoing life—such as it is —in the present, resulting in the virtual inaction of the characters trapped between these polarities. (p. 293)

Endgame gives little of its dialogue to *No Man's Land,* but instead chiefly yields up larger elements of dramatic construction: visual stage imagery, patterns of movement (or non-movement), and relationships between topics in the dialogue and the surrounding dramatic action. A room with a single entrance and curtained windows is nothing new in Pinter (*The Room, The Caretaker*), but place front and center in that enclosure "a strong and comfortable straight-backed chair" . . . from which one character plays most of his scenes and *Endgame,* as Irving Wardle observed, seems not far behind. Nor does it seem entirely coincidental that just as Hirst remains for the most part frontally seated like Hamm, the other three characters, all of whom at one time or another assume the role of his servant, usually remain standing and relatively mobile in the manner of Clov. In both plays, too, there is extended dialogue concerning either memories of the past or the prospect of remaining stationary in the future, these passages coming at the very time the characters involved are attempting to cope with problems confronting them in the present. (pp. 293-94)

In the verbal fabric of *Endgame* and *No Man's Land* one finds almost no direct analogues save one that appears deliberately and significantly chosen. To say that both plays contain numerous passages of repeated phrases or linguistic patterns is to suggest a very loose connection of small value. This general similarity is simply a further demonstration of something already known: Pinter's acknowledged literary indebtedness to Beckett. (p. 294)

[The] cadences of Spooner's speech . . . are suggestive . . . of the heavily stressed rhythms of Eliot's poetry. . . .

The creation of . . . overall atmosphere by Pinter fairly primes the listener to be alert for specific reminiscences of Eliot and, further, has the effect of sharpening the very faintest of echoes to the degree that they make their impact in but a single viewing of the play. Twice after the first and famous "For I have known them all already, known them all," the speaker in "Prufrock" recalls specific aspects of a remembered past (eyes and arms, . . .) using identical sentence structures. So too Spooner, in similar rhythms, four times reiterates things from his past, each time beginning, "I have known this before." . . . (p. 295)

Whereas such passages in *No Man's Land* are demonstrably rhythmic as well as imagistic borrowings from "Prufrock," the rhythmic similarity is absent from an analogue structurally and thematically more crucial to the play as a whole. No fewer than four times does Hirst recount or allude to *dreaming* of a person drowning in a lake . . ., almost an inversion of the last line of "Prufrock," "Till human voices *wake* us and we drown." . . . The visual picture is

the same, and the sensation of inanimate suspension in a fluid element is a vivid metaphor for the condition of stasis which makes up a large part of the form *and* meaning of both the poem and the play.

That stasis is indeed the controlling metaphor of both "Prufrock" and *No Man's Land* is, I believe, finally evidenced by the opening lines of each. Eliot's famous image of "a patient etherised upon a table" . . . establishes the mood of equipoise, of a precarious balance between life and death, present activity and recollected past, as much as the first exchange between Hirst and Spooner—literally just about how the latter wants his drink—sets the tone of immobility and suspended animation in the rest of the play. (pp. 295-96)

Though specific verbal repetitions and images of stasis from Beckett and Eliot may be said to be the cornerstone of the architecture of *No Man's Land,* they in no way make up all the structural components giving the play as a whole its specific shape. Apparently eschewing or underplaying most other elements of dramatic construction, Pinter builds upon his models by creating his own elaborate linguistic structures and a greatly expanded imagery of static balance and stagnation. Before examining these two key formal devices, however, one cannot simply dismiss those aspects of drama seemingly neglected in the play; the very effect of their neglect is too great for such dismissal. (p. 296)

While it may be said to have an "end" (perhaps), *No Man's Land* is not clearly tied to anything resembling a usual "beginning" or "middle," even in the dramatic world of Harold Pinter. . . . There is virtually no development of alteration of either character or situation from curtain to curtain in *No Man's Land*. (pp. 296-97)

With plotting and action kept to a minimum (and their effect thus achieved in a rather negative way), it remains for the linguistic structures and imagery (both verbal and visual) to give shape to *No Man's Land* and, through that shape, to convey its principal theme. It has already been noted that Pinter's chief linguistic device in this play is repetition; the forms this takes are several. One is the reiteration of a single sentence or groups of sentences such as Foster's parrot-like "What are you drinking? . . . How are you? . . . How are you? What are you drinking? Who are you? . . . Who are you, by the way? What are you drinking?". . . . Each repeated question serves not to advance the situation but actually to keep things precisely where they are. By rattling on in a monologue and not letting Spooner answer him until the final repetition, Foster has effectively frozen their encounter at a particular point in time, not allowing it to progress any farther. A similar device is the refrain-like repetition of sentences syntactically the same but varying slightly in content. (p. 297)

Just as the play begins with "As it is?" and ends with Hirst's "I'll drink to that" . . ., assenting to Spooner's reiteration of the title definition . . ., *No Man's Land* from start to finish is packed with verbal imagery and direct statement suggestive of various aspects of the condition of stasis. (p. 299)

[Miscellaneous] images of stagnation (lost, time-blackened tennis balls . . .), bondage (chains, bonds, lack of freedom . . .), and entrapment (quicksand . . .), to cite only a few, permeate the play, but three larger "systems" of imagery or explicit statement help unite the more diverse individual images into the coherent single impression of stasis which forms the structure of *No Man's Land.*

The first of these systems is a series of related images, phrases, and even clichés projecting the idea of an "eternal present" very much in the existential sense—a time of timelessness beyond (or trapped within) the confines of normal chronology. (p. 300)

The second larger device bringing cohesiveness to the multiplicity of impressions of stasis is not, like the first, a series of passages scattered throughout the play. Rather, it consists of four pages of intensely concentrated dialogue . . . just prior to the final curtain, whose topic is the frightening and irreversible implications, physical and metaphysical, of changing the subject "once and for all and for the last time forever." . . . The two most profound results of this act, it emerges, are "that there is no possibility of changing the subject since the subject has now been changed" . . . and "that nothing else will happen forever. You'll simply be sitting here forever." . . . In short, as if by now it need be said at all, the results are complete and irrevocable stasis.

The third, and also most powerful, most explicit of these larger constructs embodying the play's controlling metaphor, consists of the title itself and the two virtually identical definitions of that title in the dialogue. Placed as they are, once fairly early in the first act and then at the very close of the second act, these definitions function almost as a frame to contain most of the other varied and sometimes elusive visual and verbal structural components. They also serve as direct thematic statements to which the ideas about stasis refer as they are conveyed through the formal aspects of the play. (pp. 300-01)

There is no suggestion, either in the shape of *No Man's Land* or in the more explicit statements that it makes, that anything external to a man—whether societal, cosmic, or metaphysical—is responsible for thrusting him into a state of suspended animation, of, perhaps, an everlasting equipoise between past memories and an eternal, though inactive, present. Quite to the contrary, most of the play's evidence points squarely to the person himself for creating—or, if not creating, at least allowing—his own condition of stasis. . . .

The reason for this volitional entrapment or stagnation may be the same as the reason for characters' desiring the security of a room in other of Pinter's plays: fear. Here it is a fear of flux, of change, of encountering and perhaps being rebuffed by the unknown. By comparison, a life of quietude, even to the point of total immobility, is relatively safe and, hence, comfortable—though one may occasionally be disturbed by memories of what he was. (p. 302)

The stasis . . . which is one of the themes of *No Man's Land* is its dramatic and verbal structure as well. This structure of stasis operates partly through minimizing plot and action but mostly through constructing a complex of linguistic repetitions, visual and verbal imagery, and direct statements such as the title definitions which remain unchanged and unchanging from beginning to end. There is no movement or progression from one kind of imagery to another; there is not even an intensification. The verbal component of the play is static from the opening "As it is?" to the closing "I'll drink to that," and it is the very stasis of the structure, quite close to the surface of the play, which carries the meaning of *No Man's Land.* (pp. 302-03)

John Bush Jones, "Stasis as Structure in Pinter's 'No Man's Land'," in Modern Drama *(copyright © 1976, University of Toronto, Graduate Centre for Study of Drama; with permission of* Modern Drama*), September, 1976, pp. 291-303.*

Too many of the commentators on Pinter, faced with the playwright's refusal to explain himself, impose meaning on him, usually a kind of quivering metaphysics far too spongey for the dramatic solidity he puts on stage. By now everyone knows (or should know: there are always a few baffled people in the audience demanding a tune they can whistle) that what is happening on Pinter's stage and to whom will not be explained. Even so, audiences are drawn into the best of his plays, moved sometimes by emotions that they cannot define for themselves. Pinter is a playwright first, a creator of dramatic events, the implications of which float free for the viewer to trap, take home, domesticate, do with what he will.

The event in *No Man's Land* is a favorite one with Pinter. An outsider, a stranger, who may or may not be a stranger really (*v. Old Times*), is introduced into a static social or familial situation—as the derelict is in *The Caretaker,* the wife in *The Homecoming.* After several acts of remarkable talk—threats, cajolery, reminiscence, aborted philosophy—in which the intruder or the status quo appears to be in danger, the play ends, usually with a restatement of the original situation or a variation on it, as in *The Homecoming.* In *No Man's Land* the outsider is a down-at-heels poet, or perhaps a pub busboy who sounds and looks like one. . . . Hirst, obviously affluent, apparently a successful literary man, brings Spooner back to his house, to a fascinating circular room (tower? prison? hospital? tomb? home?), one of those enclosures in which Pinter so likes to trap his characters. They are joined by Hirst's servants (keepers? guards?), another of Pinter's menacing comic pairs, descendants of McCann and Goldberg in *The Birthday Party,* who spend a good part of the play tormenting Spooner, as Mick does the old man in *The Caretaker.* for the most part, Spooner appears to be invulnerable to their barbs, until toward the end of the last act when he makes a determined plea for a permanent place in this strange ménage—a place which he holds in any case since the Hirst establishment has its only reality on stage and Spooner, as abrasive presence, has been a part of it since the play began. His intricate connection with the small group is clear at the final curtain—not so much an ending as an abrupt breaking off of the action—when Hirst accepts Spooner's restatement of the "no man's land" that Hirst and all of them inhabit.

Pinter characters are regularly beset by uncertainty about their identities—Stanley's shifting history in *The Birthday Party,* the old man's lost papers in *The Caretaker*—and about their memories, as in *Landscape, Silence* and *Old Times.* "I am I," says Spooner proudly, making his pitch for a job as well as a stranger, a supplicant as well as a free man, a busser of pintpots as well as a poet. As with the present, the past. There is a marvelous sequence in the second act, almost a parody of Oxcam-Home Counties gossip, in which the two old men begin to remember or invent old triumphs, old scandals; each one tries to top the other until Hirst is ready to horsewhip Spooner for an insult to a woman whom neither of them may ever have known. . . . [Memories], in Pinter and in fact, have a way of borrowing from fiction. This sliding sense of reality only emphasizes that the theatrical moment is the closest in reality anyone can come to in a world with a redactable past and an unknown future. Any future here, as the age of the poets and some of their lines ("last lap of a race") suggest, is death. . . .

No Man's Land . . . falls short of the best of Pinter—too many Pinteresque echoes perhaps, tinging immediacy with artifice. Still, *No Man's Land* has substance, characters, wit, verbal dexterity—all that one has come to expect from Pinter—and it would be foolish to let the memory of earlier achievements stand in the way of the new play. Dangerous, too, for if I understand Pinter correctly, I may have invented the early Pinter plays in retrospect. (pp. 20-1)

> *Gerald Weales, "Absolutely As It Is," in* Commonweal *(copyright © 1977 Commonweal Publishing Co., Inc.; reprinted by permission of Commonweal Publishing Co., Inc.), January 7, 1977, pp. 20-1.*

Five or six years ago we used to go to Pinter plays straining to find the profound meanings beneath his brilliant surfaces. Now we've twigged that Pinter's plays are nothing *but* surfaces, and after all the variations he has spun, the surfaces no longer seem so brilliant. It's fun, up to a point, to be teased by Pinter's enigmatic little games, and there's no doubt Pinter has a great sense of mimicry and a terrific ear for revealing idiom. But ultimately I'm turned off his work for the same reason I stay away from those revues that feature the collected songs of a certain composer. When I go to the theatre I want not just the production numbers but the play they were built into. Pinter's chamber concerts are like production numbers without a context.

Pinter creates verbal ping-pong matches for performers. . . . [*No Man's Land*] is simply a vehicle to show off an incredible pair of actors. . . . (p. 63)

> *Martin Knelman, in* Saturday Night *(copyright © 1977 by* Saturday Night*), January-February, 1977.*

No Man's Land is a play about . . . "long perspectives": a battle between two men, one trying futilely to escape the isolation of the artist's perspective, the other trying, equally futilely, to gain it.

Both men are, appropriately, poets, men who strive to make words immortal. Hirst, in whose house the play takes place, is a distinguished poet and a "man of letters," while Spooner is a failure—as he explains it, "I was one of the golden of my generation. Something happened." Spooner has joined Hirst for a nightcap and a chat, but it soon becomes apparent that his host is not all there. (p. 160)

It takes . . . every bit of Hirst's concentration just to stay anchored to the present. His first line—"As it is?"—is as much a declaration of his intent to stay fixed to the present as it is a query to Spooner concerning whiskey. Spooner, on the other hand, longs for immortality. . . . The action of the play is a series of strategical maneuvers by Spooner in an attempt to ride Hirst's coattails into immortality.

In *Old Times* Pinter showed how memories can be deliberately revised to suit whatever situation arises. Remembering becomes an act of aggression: the power of a memory lies in its ability to wound another, and the ac-

tuality of a remembered experience becomes secondary. . . . In *No Man's Land* memory bears a similar relationship to the present. Spooner struggles to become Hirst's partner in timelessness by imposing biographical details on the latter's past. He wants to share Hirst's past so he can merge his life with that of a successful poet. As in *Old Times*, the "truth" of a memory is determined entirely by its effectiveness in the present. (pp. 160-61)

[The] "truth" of a fiction lies in its attractiveness, its ability to convince: Spooner equates accuracy with "essentially poetic definition." . . . Hirst [wards] off Spooner's attempt to create a mutual memory while reinforcing his isolation. A few moments later Hirst, perhaps exhausted by this effort, loses his tenuous grip on the present and collapses (literally) under the weight of his accumulated past:

> No man's land . . . does not move . . . or change . . . or grow old . . . remains . . . forever . . . icy . . . silent.

Hirst's no man's land is the zone where past and present, memory and reality, are indistinguishable. (pp. 161-62)

[Hirst] thwarts Spooner's attempts to tamper with his life once and for all, but in doing so he also backs himself into a state of permanent stasis. . . .

The poet is again trapped by his own words. The scene takes on the existence of a work of art, in which "nothing else will happen forever. You'll simply be sitting here forever." Hirst's entire past and present begin to blend and settle around him, and he hears the sound of birds: "I hear them as they must have sounded then, when I was young, although I never heard them then, although they must have sounded about us then." He returns to his dream of a person drowning, the dream in which Spooner had identified himself as the drowning man. "But I am mistaken," he says this time. "There is nothing there."

In altering his dream this way, Hirst remembers Spooner out of existence, as in *Old Times*, where one character "murders" another by saying "I remember you dead." Ironically, Spooner's one successful attempt to incorporate himself into Hirst's life is used against him. Spooner's defeat is total. His existence to Hirst both as poet and man has been denied. Excluded from the still life formed by Hirst and his keepers, he numbly repeats an earlier speech of Hirst's. . . . Spooner has finally been forced to the realization that he can only be a witness to art, a parasite. A describer. (p. 163)

> *Craig Latrell, "As It Is," in* yale/theatre *(copyright © by* Theater, *formerly* yale/theatre *1975), Spring, 1977, pp. 160-63.*

*   *   *

PLATH, Sylvia   1932-1963

American poet, novelist, and short story writer, Plath, sometimes called an "Extremist" for her poems of despair and death, collected fragments of her life and created from them a poetry both intensely personal and technically complex. She will probably be best remembered for her autobiographical novel, *The Bell Jar*. She has written under the pseudonym Victoria Lucas. (See also *CLC*, Vols. 1, 2, 3, 5, and *Contemporary Authors*, Vols. 19-20; *Contemporary Authors Permanent Series*, Vol. 2.)

The courting of experience that kills is characteristic of

major poets, and even if we discount the artist's hindsight, Sylvia Plath seems to have been so preoccupied from the beginning.

> Breath, that is the first thing. Something is breathing. My own breath? The breath of my mother? No, something else, something larger, farther, more serious, more weary. . . .

That breath, discounting our own hindsight now, is both the echo of her future voice, as well as her first sense of 'Otherness', with whom, in a variety of guises, she will argue the possibility of existence throughout her life. (p. 21)

On the occasion of the birth of her brother, her first rival, her second sense of 'Otherness', the sea provides a sign—an antidote to the loss of her specialness. (p. 22)

The confrontation of 'Otherness' requires that imagination become equal to experience. She appropriates the sea by collecting from it a banquet set of seachina; she accepts her brother by resurrecting her own totem of him. All babies come from the same place. There is no division between the world and her wilful representation of it. 'The state of being in love threatens to obliterate the boundaries between ego and object . . .', Freud warns us.

Her mind and the world, her sea and the real sea do not divide until she is nine. Then:

> My father died, we moved inland.
>
> (pp. 22-3)

These formative years, the dialectic they propose, conforms to critical preoccupations all too nicely. Freudian analysis is perhaps inescapable—sibling rivalry simultaneous with guilt at the father's death, the vengeful urge to get back to the father through the mother, the lovingly expressed Death-wish. (p. 24)

For Sylvia Plath, that sense of 'Otherness'—the larger, weary breath which accompanied her from the very first—takes varying form and voice as she matures. Her entire body of work can be seen as dialogue with an 'Other', but it is not a dialectic in any academic sense, for her voice and her interlocutor metamorphize as the context of her private quarrel is enlarged.

In avoiding irresponsible gossip about that *Other,* we should recall that generation of critics which obscured Emily Dickinson's poetry either to identify or protect 'real people'—the ostensible correlatives of her work. Not only did this excite the very excesses it meant to control, but reduced the finest love lyrics by an American of her century to a sensationalistic confessional.

The cult which obscured Emily Dickinson's poetry in its posthumous appearance has much in common with that which now attends Sylvia Plath's work. Similar legends surround their respective objects of affection. It was suggested that Emily held her father in something more than esteem, that her nephew bore the wish-fulfilling burden of her childlessness. Potential suitors appeared as eligible young house-guests only to be banished by a tyrannical father and subsequently die of a broken heart, or as a married man of the cloth, whose sinful proposals Emily herself dismissed. (pp. 24-5)

The point is that although each 'character' in fact existed,

and may indeed be traced through specific poems, this love poetry is best understood as the reverberations of sensibility against actuality—a poet's unity of fancy more than a woman's case-history. For both poets, the brother/father, husband/lover relationships are finally significant as they effect the poet's chosen *personae*—just as it is the poet's imitative sea and not the real sea which attracted Sylvia from the first. Such a distinction has nothing to do with protecting 'real people', but only to distinguish poetry as craft from autobiography. This is not unimportant, for the irony and grief of Sylvia Plath's poetry issues from the tension between her imagination and experience, the urge to make them one again. (pp. 25-6)

Further, we can best understand Sylvia's obsession with death, not in terms of a Freudian post-mortem, but rather from within a poetic tradition that extends back through Emily to Anne Bradstreet and Edward Taylor, a tradition in which the imaginative realization of dying is the determining, climactic experience of living. (p. 26)

No American poet of her era treated the theme of love with more candour than Emily Dickinson, and Sylvia Plath carries the tradition to equal heights at mid-century. What lifts their work above the commonplace is the totality of their affections and the fastidiousness with which they express them. Both cut through popular sociology by acknowledging the terrifying ambiguity of the female role, and then by universalizing their very feminism. That is to say, by rejecting the traditional pose of the 'heroine', they give us the woman as 'hero'—a protagonist who not only undergoes the central action of a work, but a character whom men as well as women may view as an actor in a destiny possible for them.

The essential difference between their approaches binds them all the closer. For while Emily was obsessed with the paradox of *giving* love in a Christian context, Sylvia Plath, in her day of abstract philanthropy and evanescent relationships, dramatizes the difficulty of knowing or *accepting* love. (pp. 26-7)

Sylvia subjects secular classical models to the same firm scrutiny as Emily did the biblical. Both took seriously Whitman's dictum to find an aesthetic which would 'meet modern discoveries face to face'.

'The Bible is an antique volume / Written by faded men', Emily tells us playfully, and Sylvia echoes her in 'On the Decline of Oracles'. . . . (pp. 27-8)

Like Emily, she sensed that the Gothic was simply an importunate regurgitation of the classical mode, and a nostalgia particularly crippling to a female narrator. Within the gothic or classical traditions, one could be merely a 'heroine'. A poem might possibly be both oracular and feminist, but it was a personal medium or nothing.

In fact, Emily is in many ways the beginning, and Sylvia the culmination of the movement whereby the imagination, sated with the abstraction of myth, is driven back to the concrete. Emily astounds us because she presages the Imagist manifesto, and Sylvia does because she demonstrates how flexible that tradition is when metrical lyricism and narrative momentum are restored to it.

There is, of course, a price the modern poet must pay, in terms of perception, if not vision. When adopting the *persona* of Electra, for instance, [Sylvia] admits ruefully that in order to give magnitude to her father's memory, she must 'borrow the stilts of an old tragedy'. But while she goes through the motions of self-mockery, and while she is at first simply turning a cliché upon itself, she is gradually asserting her own strict vision. (pp. 28-9)

Abstraction and archaic usage are not limited to classical models or gothic sentiment. Indeed, for the contemporary poet, the debt to an immediate past may be more burdensome. Sylvia Plath's work is most remarkable in its struggle with modern influences.

Her first published work was thoroughly researched, initially employing that most complicated of French forms, the Villanelle. Her final work is spontaneous, achieving her own definition of greatness, 'born all of a piece . . . poems possessed . . . as by the rhythms of their own breathing . . . .'

The development between these two periods is astounding, in that her ability to deal with larger themes and her technical virtuosity keep precise pace with one another. She experiments with an extremely wide variety of forms and modes.

Yet, as with Emily, the despair at not being equal to her craft remains a constant theme. (p. 30)

Her development does not derive from the adoption of a specific *persona* as yet—but from that ability to find cosmic truths in the minutiae of private life. This is no peculiar feminine construct, but the gift of Emily's Transcendental heritage. Not the Emersonian variety, of course; for him the oversoul was a premise, not a discovery. But rather Thoreau's microscopic vision that the structure of the self suggests the structure of the universe, that nature is an organic externality of the soul. Such an ontology is quite apparent in a poem like 'Sculptor'. (p. 31)

Sylvia's immediate predecessors treated nature according to the laws of their own perception, 'as things-in-themselves'. In late Stevens, for example, the poems become, not descriptions of 'things' at all, but an epistemic description of the process of poetic perception. In Sylvia's case, she at times carries the process one step further; that is to say, she overcomes the tension between the perceiver and the thing-in-itself by literally becoming the thing-in-itself. In many instances, it is nature who personifies her. As she began in awe of the ocean's breath, she gradually assumes it. (p. 33)

[Within] her own context, such an identification represents the poet's triumph over 'Otherness'. (p. 34)

She published *The Bell Jar* under the pseudonym of Victoria Lucas (echoing the nationalities of both husband and father) because she apparently did not consider it a 'serious' work. What she felt, I would guess, was that it was *too* serious—that is, it recorded autobiographical data not completely absorbed and transformed by her art. Nevertheless, it remains a remarkable work in many respects.

In the first place, it is one of the few American novels to treat adolescence from a mature point of view, although the narrator is an adolescent. Secondly, it chronicles a nervous breakdown and consequent professional therapy in nonclinical language. And finally, it gives us one of the few sympathetic portraits of what happens to one who has genuinely feminist aspirations in our society, of a girl who refuses to be simply an *event* in anyone's life.

Essentially, this is the record, in a strange blend of American and British vernacular, of a female Holden Caulfield driven to self-destruction by despair with the alternatives adult life apparently offers. Except that Esther Greenwood is both more intelligent and less mannered than Holden, and her conflict the more serious one between a potential artist and society, rather than the cult of youth versus the cult of middle age. Further, Holden Caulfield, for all his charm, is a psychotic; which is to say, his world is the pure world of his own distortion, and no conflicting interpretation is allowed to obtrude upon his narration. The fascinating and terrifying technique of *The Bell Jar*, on the other hand, is the continuous conflict between the real world and the narrator's desperate reconstruction of it. It chronicles what that first flight to the ocean previewed.

We can guess from the background how her problems were clinically defined; what is more interesting is how she chose to make aesthetic use of her 'illness'—which *personae*, in fact, could successfully mediate between the world of external truth and her own more profound, if nemesic vision. (pp. 35-6)

In any event, it is clear she does not become sick as a consequence of *seeing* the 'awful' truth—indeed her imagination functions as a necessary counterweight to reality—it is when her vision is ignored, that it becomes only internalized and not projected, that her 'health' degenerates. (p. 36)

Gradually the eccentricity of her perception, her candour, her fastidiousness, isolate her from the 'real world'—her mother, her fiancé, her peers, her job with *Mademoiselle*. The bell jar descends, isolating her in the vacuum of her own ego—'The silence depressed me. It wasn't the silence of silence. It was my own silence . . .'. She is closeted with nothing save her own fierce irony—what remains remarkable is her resistance to simple praise or blame—she is determined to record her very inability to communicate. And in her hands, the crisis of adolescent identity is given both a rare dignity and perspective. (p. 37)

[Either] as a novel or a case history, *The Bell Jar* is abortive. Indeed, as a hopeful premise plotted on the curve of her life, it is ironically tragic. Nevertheless, it can be valued as a poet's notebook, a holding action of the imagination against the tyranny of both fantasy and flat fact. For this novel was written not to regain her psychic balance, but to transform the opacity of language, the tyrannous headlines, into her own medium. (pp. 42-3)

Indeed, all the characters in the book are finally reduced to the verbal equivalencies which express their various approaches to life—her mother to shorthand, her suitor to Gray's *Anatomy*, her professor to *Finnegans Wake*, her psychiatrist to professional jargon, her father to his epitaph, herself to her own epigrammatic wit, inhumanly equal to every situation. The characters stagnate in their own limited language as the narrator develops her own. The topic sentences of each lead paragraph are curiously condensed and isolated, implying that if they were compiled vertically, we would have an associative free verse poem, and not a novel at all. The prose of this book is the testing ground for the poems which will outlast it. And the book ends how and where it does, I would guess, not because she is cured, but because her talent has matured. (p. 43)

To explain her poetry in terms of feminism is as inadequate as describing her illness as schizophrenic, yet it is impossible to ignore the thrust towards the *persona* of the 'new woman' which emerges from *The Bell Jar*. She remains among the few woman writers in recent memory to link the grand theme of womanhood with the destiny of modern civilization. The lucubrations of a Mary McCarthy, a Simone de Beauvoir remain merely officious by comparison. (pp. 43-4)

The conflicts are charted: the co-ed and the recluse; the mother and the mistress; the wife and the poetess. What begins as an affinity for the New England spinster tradition evolves a domestic fury. . . . What begins as a Baudelairian lament for the father . . . becomes an epiphany for her own kind. . . . What begins as ironic detachment in *The Bell Jar* becomes an active vengeance in 'Stings'. . . . What begins as the paradox of sex and marriage becomes nothing less than the conflict between art and life. . . . What begins as the jealousy of another's birth becomes the jealousy of death itself. What begins as an embarrassing curiosity has become an awful certainty, or more briefly—Electra becomes Clytemnestra. (pp. 44-5)

She is a very different woman in the last long year of her life. . . . She has moved beyond the *persona* of the 'new woman'. 'Deflection' is how she chose to describe the confrontation between experience and art.

It is with the same calculated indifference, and at a period of similarly repressed crisis, that Emily Dickinson begins to dress 'all in white'. It is simply a modern reversal of style on Sylvia's part to accentuate her sense of specialness with severe hair and Victorian puffiness, as 'the magician's girl who does not flinch'. (p. 46)

Emily chose to pose as an angel to emphasize her witchcraft; Sylvia adopts witchcraft to approach heavenly perfection. (p. 47)

The last poems are written with an intensity and rapidity which cause her friends to fear for her; they remain one of the most astonishing creative outbursts of our generation. I believe they will be recognized as a breakthrough in modern poetry—perhaps even more importantly, as a break of poetry *from* the modern—for she not only rewedded imagist technique to the narrative line, but demonstrated that our present division of poetry into the 'academic' and 'beat'— 'cooked and uncooked' in Robert Lowell's words—is historically arbitrary. She showed us that the poet can still deal with the most mystical elements of existence without sacrificing any precision of craftsmanship. In the last poems, there is not the slightest gap between theory and realization, between myth and the concrete particular— they utterly escape the self-consciousness of craft. Her experience and her art are again indivisible, as they were when she lived by the sea. (p. 49)

We must constantly be attuned to the shifts in *personae*— whether she speaks as the poor, plain bright girl of *The Bell Jar*, or the archetypal Jew of 'Daddy'—for this movement is the dynamic principle of her art. It is essential to both biographical fact and the measure of her poetry to see these shifts in role as a poet's search for the most authoritative voice possible. She is not relating herself to history or to any systematic philosophy in these last poems, any more than she related herself to nature in her early work. She is using history, like nature, to explain herself. It is the Transcendental vision that history is within ourselves, and that history is the flux of Compensation. (pp. 50-1)

Hers is extremist poetry, to be sure, and as such, we cannot tell how well it will wear. But one thing is certain; if the literature of this decade has focused on the Apocalyptic vision, in both its prophetic and parodic forms, then this poetry is the definitive—exhaustive—statement of that vision.

It must be left to others to fit the development of her *personae* more precisely against the details of her private life, as clinical/biographical information and more poetry, possibly, becomes available. But they should be careful about delimiting her art in either psychological or historical terms. In this regard, I am not sure that 'confessional' is the appropriate term for the late poems, even though her concerns frequently parallel those of Lowell and Sexton. For there seems to me to be a definite effort to move *beyond* the anguish of the self in these poems, towards the establishment of a new, more impersonal, editorial, even prophetic voice. While the 'self' still remains at the centre of the poem, it is nonetheless a different self, one more powerful, less biographically identifiable; a voice at one remove from the crises it invokes. (pp. 52-3)

Are we surprised that such fierce talent could develop in [Northampton], Massachusetts and Cambridge, England? Had she been incarcerated, exiled, undiscovered, executed, we could understand her as a part of the extreme twentieth-century violence which most Anglo-American poets have been personally spared. We might then see her as heir to Mayakovsky, Rimbaud, Lorca, Rilke, more than Emily Dickinson or Wallace Stevens. Yet this is the very point. For in absorbing, personalizing the socio-political catastrophes of the century, she reminds us that they are ultimately metaphors of the terrifying human mind. Sylvia Plath is, above all, a poet of the cold-war; not that conflict of pseudo-ideologies, but of the private guerrilla warfare we carry out against each other every day. Remember the conflagration behind the Fourth of July!

In the very last poems, death is pre-eminent but strangely unoppressive. Love and Death, all rivals, are resolved within the irreversability of experience. (p. 53)

The ultimate *persona* is that of transcendence. . . . (p. 54)

Sylvia Plath evolved in poetic voice from the precocious girl, to the disturbed modern woman, to the vengeful magician, to—*Ariel*—God's Lioness. She ends a long way from the 'wingy myths' she first rejected. Like Emily, she becomes the Spirit's apprentice. Not God himself; . . . but rather Pythia, Cassandra, the Whore of Babylon—harbingers of the apocalypse—those whose words defy both divinity and congregation.

If, through her art, Emily practised valour in the dark of a hopelessly constricted life, then Sylvia likewise demonstrates the integrity possible in a life hopelessly overblown. Both heroines of the peripheral, they conquer the 'incalculable malice of the everyday', and precisely an existence is what they pay. (pp. 54-5)

> *Charles Newman, "Candor Is the Only Wile—The Art of Sylvia Plath," in* The Art of Sylvia Plath: A Symposium, *edited by Charles Newman (copyright © 1970 by Charles Newman and the estate of Sylvia Plath), Indiana University Press, 1970, pp. 21-55.*

It would not, I believe, be going too far to say that the sea, and more especially the idea of death by water, is the central image of the whole of [*The Colossus*]. The poet returns to it obsessively, again and again.... One of the subtlest identifications of the sea with death occurs in 'Man in Black', a tautly written poem which is one of the very best in a volume which is now in some danger of being underrated. (p. 93)

The distinction which critics usually make between the poems in *The Colossus* and those in *Ariel* is that there is something much swifter, more abrupt, more sardonic about the latter. Frequently, as in the famous poem 'Daddy', there is a kind of bitter jesting on the edge of hysteria. It is interesting to see how far these characteristics have already developed in the eleven poems which are brought together in *Uncollected Poems*. (p. 94)

In *Uncollected Poems,* the obsession with the sea is unabated. In 'Blackberrying', for example, the poet describes how she suddenly comes upon it, after following a sheep-path.... The poems which go to make up *Ariel* duly continue the use of sea and water-imagery, though other symbols have now come to join this one, and perhaps manage to take precedence over it. The watery death-wish has not changed at all.... (p. 95)

It is interesting to see how the new symbols in *Ariel* link up with this long-established one. The book, for example, has many references to the moon—'bare', 'merciless', with a light that is 'cold and planetary'; a thing 'beautiful but annihilating', a creature who 'abases her subjects'. At one point the poet tells us that:

> ... the moon, for its ivory powder, scours the sea.

The connections are so obvious as to need little stressing.

Another important set of symbols in *Ariel* is connected with the idea of 'the black man'.... But surely we have met the 'black man' before—in the pages of *The Colossus*? Fairly clearly, he must also be the 'Man in Black' in the poem of that title.... This hypothesis is strengthened by the fact that we seem to find him again, still walking towards the sea, in the first section of 'Berck-Plage'.... As one studies the relationship of the 'black man' image to the sea-imagery, it rapidly becomes plain that the sea-imagery itself has certain striking peculiarities. For example, the sea is usually thought of as hostile, and sometimes, contrary to tradition, it is thought of as male. 'Full Fathom Five', by its very title ('Full fathom five / Thy father lies ...') makes the connection between the ocean and the hated father. Where the sea is not hostile, as I have already noted, it represents nothingness, oblivion, abeyance—things which the poet both seeks for and fears. She does not venture into it or on to it, but watches from the shore. 'Daddy' is a striking poem—perhaps the most striking Sylvia Plath ever wrote—but its theme of ritual killing, of total exorcism—does not ring quite true to the rest of her work.

Indeed, it seems apparent that one of the reasons why that work makes such a tremendous impact on the reader is through its cunning, obsessional harping on a comparatively limited number of themes and situations.... These themes and situations exist as plainly in the early poems as they do in the later. Most of them are unresolved. (pp. 96-8)

There is no question that Sylvia Plath developed considerably as a poet. She was the very opposite of an idle writer—she was extremely ambitious, and she took a close interest in her craft. The basic themes, the basic materials of her poetry (some of them almost too frightening for anyone to confront) were there from the very beginning—it was simply that she learned to deal with them more truthfully, more incisively and more originally. If extremism was involved, I suspect it was involuntary—something planted a long time beforehand in the psychic mechanism. In *The Colossus* she is struggling, for the most part, with precisely the same problems that she confronted in *Ariel*, and the development between the two books ... must be attributed to something other than merely the problems themselves. (pp. 98-9)

> *Edward Lucie-Smith, "Sea-Imagery in the Work of Sylvia Plath," in* The Art of Sylvia Plath: A Symposium, *edited by Charles Newman (copyright © 1970 by Charles Newman and the estate of Sylvia Plath), Indiana University Press, 1970, pp. 91-9.*

[For] all the freshness of perception they reveal, [Sylvia Plath's] poems are essentially emblematic. They derive their meaning, both profound and sometimes literal, from an underlying code, in which objects and their qualities are endowed with stable significations, and hierarchized. It is indeed only because such a pre-ordained scheme (probably unconscious to a great extent) existed that such a large output, of such quality, was made possible. The reader cannot but perceive such a system, however dimly, and has to adopt it while he reads; for without such a feat of identification—sometimes difficult because of the highly personal interpretation Sylvia Plath put on certain objects already accepted, with other meanings, as current symbols—many poems remain impenetrable, or at least lose most of their harmonics.

This code is extremely rigid, inasmuch as an object, once charged with a given signification, never forfeits it: the moon, the snow, the colour black, always have the same function. But the attitude of the poet can vary, and thus introduce some ambiguity: the colour red, the colour blue, can play different parts in various contexts. The child as theme and the child as subject appear in very different guises. But such differences are minimal, and we can only admire the inexhaustible freshness of inspiration which allowed infinite variations on such fixed themes.

Recognition of this fact also sheds light on what Sylvia Plath was attempting to do in her poetry. She was not trying to render each experience by means uniquely suited to it, but rather to dominate such experiences by making them fit (sometimes with difficulty) within a previously adopted framework, which automatically results in their being integrated in a scale of values. Indeed, there is evidence, from those poems which seem more directly biographical in inspiration, that the same could be said about her approach to her life itself, many events having no doubt been experienced on the symbolical and mythical plane as well as on the personal, at the time they occurred. This, to some extent, applies to all of us, but without the rigidity of connotation by which the poet seems to have hoped to control the violence of her reactions.

This reduces considerably the relevance of whether some allusions are personal or not, and here the poet showed us the way in her analyses of her own poems, 'Daddy' or 'Fever 103°'; and furthermore, as we shall see, subject and object, torturer and victim are in her poetry finally indistinguishable, merely lending the depth of their existence to all-powerful entities and symbols. This is not to say that biographical details are of no importance; but it should be realized that Sylvia Plath was, both consciously and unconsciously, constantly trying to establish the distanciation without which there can be no art. Thus the obscurity of some poems never springs from the fact that we do not know what personal experiences were their immediate cause (even when it is plain that there were such experiences), but from our inability to grasp the central structure according to which the clusters of images are arranged. Were the poet's private mythology more flexible, definitive impossibility to understand would follow; fortunately, this is not the case, and even poems like 'The Jailor', or 'The Other', which are written in a kind of symbolical shorthand, can eventually be made to yield their wealth of overtones.

Sylvia Plath's effort to achieve a necessary distanciation in her life and her art is also revealed in a fund of cultural imagery, which is greater than appears at first sight: classical reminiscences, references to historical events, contemporary allusions, numerous Christian anecdotes and symbols, philosophical concepts, legends (such as that of the vampire) and superstitions (such as that of the cracked glass as a portent of death). But the subject of the poems is never anything but an individual experience. The starting point can be a sensation ('Cut, 'Contusion'), an action (going to the cellar in 'Nick and the Candlestick'), an abstraction brought to mind by a given circumstance ('Kindness'), or, very often and in a way which affords us a glimpse into the working of her poetic self, an object which is used as a peg for a fluid symbolism ('Balloons', or the whole sequence of the bee poems). The primary object of experience is then explored at leisure, and all its symbolic potentialities reviewed, only to organize themselves finally according to familiar categories, with man firmly in the centre. Nature, reality, the world, are only in appearance interrogated as potential sources of meaning; for this meaning has been chosen once and for all, and henceforth they will only be used for their expressive possibilities. The mood is never collective; although the poet projects her private experience on a wide background, the speaking voice remains individual. Nor does this distanciating generalization ever imply that the subject of the poems is intellectual; indeed, this refusal to acknowledge the intellect as a 'positive' value will be seen to have far-reaching and tragic consequences.

Within such limits, however, Sylvia Plath's particular way of experiencing life is shown to have been an interplay between the particular and the general, which finds expression in the vast range of her vocabulary and images. The juxtaposition of the sublime and the homely, the 'poetic' and the scientific (words like *carbon monoxide, acetylene, ticker-tape, adding machine*), is no accident: it reveals a constant and vivifying exchange between depth and surface. 'A Birthday Present', 'Stings' are, among other things, a reflexion on the ambiguous nature of the Poet, the most common and the most unusual of beings, nearest to Nature and farthest from it.

There *is* indeed in the world of Sylvia Plath . . . an intuition of a kinship between poetry and death; yet, and this is what radically separates her from the great Romantic prototypes,

this intimacy with death never gives rise to positive, fundamentally religious, feelings. In spite of a certain masochistic complacency, death always appears as a terrifying conclusion. At the most, it has a kind of saving nobility which favourably contrasts with a prosaic life.

Thus we must be aware of the danger of romanticizing a poet who would have been outstanding in any circumstances; yet it is inevitable that one should start a review of themes and images with the major theme of vulnerability, for the impression derived from even a cursory reading of her poetry is that of an overall threat. The mood is virtually always negative (we shall see that even the few optimistic poems call for a significant reservation), and ranges from mere foreboding to hopeless revolt and utter despair. In such an atmosphere, clichés assume a new significance, as in the beginning of 'Totem':

The engine is *killing* the track, the track is silver,
It stretches into the distance. It will be *eaten* nevertheless.

Its running is useless.
At nightfall there is the beauty of *drowned* fields. . . .

The living flesh is felt as essentially vulnerable. . . . Small animals are butchered and eaten, man's flesh can undergo the final indignity of being cut to pieces and used as an object. . . . Subjects and metaphors include a cut, a contusion, the tragedy of thalidomide, fever, an accident, a wound, paralysis, a burial, animal and human sacrifice, the burning of heretics, lands devastated by wars, extermination camps: her poetry is a 'garden of tortures' in which mutilation and annihilation take nightmarishly protean forms. . . . On the realistic plane, there is a feeling of an almost unbelievable luck if nothing untoward happens. . . . But on the psychological plane, the mind cannot but see a sign of its own fragility in this very multiplicity of symbols. Disintegration threatens, all the more because of a past history of breakdown. This word is [in 'Daddy'] to be understood literally:

. . . they pulled me out of the sack,
And they stuck me together with glue. . . .

[An] obsession with catastrophe is in itself the most potent force of disintegration; it sometimes takes the form of revolt and despair, and at other times of almost an infatuation with death. We shall see that it finally vitiates and destroys every foundation of hope. In some poems, she seems to show an awareness of herself as primarily self-condemned, 'the slap and the cheek, the wound and the knife', as Baudelaire put it, and in none better than 'A Birthday Present', in which the speaker is seen to impose on a mysterious event the meaning which he expects and fears, as often happens in nightmares.

In this respect, two of the numerous dangers which threaten in her poems occur with a symbolic frequency. The first is the threat of stifling or strangulation, in which an obstacle stands between life and the person, finally destroying the latter. . . . The second is the threat of destruction by small enemies, outside or inside the body. . . . Death by fumes or carbon monoxide shows how the first threat is reducible to the second, since chemical death is due to changes in the small units of the body. Typically blood is almost always presented in a plural form, as the 'blood berries', the 'blood bells of the fuchsia' or a 'bowl of red blooms' ('Tulips', 'Years'), as if the individual was made up of smaller units endowed with a spontaneity not necessarily in agreement with the conscious self. Thus the ambiguity found in 'A Birthday Present' is echoed in 'Cut', where the thumb is called a 'saboteur', a 'kamikaze man', and the blood is an army of a million soldiers about whom can be asked:

Whose side are they on?

(pp. 101-07)

Broadly speaking, we can say that the dialectic of life and death is the sole subject of the poems. The poet's existence is presented as a cosmic drama in which these two great principles are confronted, and their struggle is expressed in patterns whose structure is accordingly antithetic. The life-principle is colour, pulsating rhythm, noise, heat, radiance, expansion, emotion and communication. Death is the other pole: darkness, stasis, silence, frost, well-defined edges and the hardness of rocks, jewels, and skulls, dryness, anything self-contained and separate or which derives its positive attributes from some other source, instead of generating them freely—for death is absence, nothingness. Such is the framework on which the poems base their innumerable variations.

The natural symbol of life is 'the beautiful red' ('Letter in November'). It is the colour of blood, the life-fluid, which expresses emotion by its pulsating centre, the heart, in its turn comparable to a wound which reveals life, or to the mouth, which kisses and screams. . . . (pp. 107-08)

Classically, death is black and so is foreboding, which heralds it. . . . But white is also an absence of colour, and is indeed the symbol of death in some civilizations. This, coupled with the other attributes of death, makes the moon the perfect symbol for it: it shines in the night, its light is borrowed, its shape regular, well-defined and self-contained, and its bald light turns everything into stone—such are the aspects which are repeatedly stressed in poems like 'Medusa', 'Elm', 'The Moon and the Yew Tree', 'Childless Woman', 'The Rival', 'The Munich Mannequins', 'Paralytic', 'Edge'. They form a constellation which obviously transcends any personal application; although certain poems do seem to have been written with someone definite in mind, their relevance for an understanding of the poet *herself* is unquestionable, and is in fact stated in 'The Moon and the Yew Tree':

The moon is my mother. . . .

'Flat' is often used, as in 'Tulips', to express a superficial contact with life, when shapes seem two-dimensional as they do in moonlight. (pp. 108-10)

The moon is also a suitable symbol for sterility because of its circular shape, the most perfect of all, and because it rules the flux of menstrual blood. In the latter, death is in the midst of life, which is cut from its rightful end, according to Sylvia Plath. . . . (p. 110)

[Once] we have realized what the moon symbolizes, we can easily recognize the same connotation every time some attribute of the moon is used to qualify some object or event. This leads to underlying associations and derived meanings which can be extremely cryptic if one is not aware of their derivation. (p. 111)

Words like 'pearl', 'silver' or 'ivory', which can be used to describe moonlight, always announce some untoward event or indicate a condemnatory judgment, as in 'A Birthday Present', 'The Munich Mannequins', 'Childless Woman', 'Totem', 'Contusion', the 'sticky pearls' on 'Lady Lazarus', etc. Thus again with snow, which is cold, white, made of regular units, and melts to nothing, thus revealing its kinship with absence, death, as in 'Night Dances' or 'Wintering'. In this light, an antithesis which was startling at first seems perfectly normal: the Munich Mannequins are

Intolerable, without mind.
The snow drops its pieces of darkness,

Nobody's about. . . .

The moon is also 'bald and wild', and 'bald' is another word laden with negative connotations, as in 'The Munich Mannequins', and the 'bald and shiny suit' of the self in 'Totem'. Bald light and glare can mean the inhuman, as in 'The Hanging Man', the coldness of science, and the proximity of death. (p. 112)

Most of Sylvia Plath's ideas seem to have needed to be translated into her personal and specific poetic language in order to become integrated to her mental universe. Of course, a general congruence between object and concept determines the adoption of a symbol; but once this is done, the concrete qualities of these symbols react in their turn on the messages and opinions they embody. (p. 115)

The idea of sacrifice as the central notion of religion has deeply impressed the poet; sacrifice either of the heretics, or of the most precious and most innocent; the golden child in the poem above, the tortured Christ in 'Elm', or his suicidal 'awful God-bit' in 'Years'. Because of an identification in which the sadism attributed to the deity is fused with a masochistic drive, the idea of redemption actually has death as a consequence, as appears in 'Brasilia'. . . . (p. 119)

Shine, glitter, mirrors, which are or cause reflections, like the moon, are always used in a derogatory manner. And this in turn has a bearing on the status of another symbol, that of the smile.

It is sometimes used to signify tenderness, a gentle and unalloyedly positive feeling; but it soon becomes a negative sign, because it is commonly used without sincerity, in order to reassure oneself or the others that everything is all right, as in 'Lady Lazarus'. . . . Henceforth, coupled with glitter, it symbolizes deceit, the Maya, the illusion to which all the comforting manifestations of life are shown to belong in the end. (p. 121)

It is only normal, and highly significant, if in spite of all this the ever-changing face of the mirror is still used as a symbol for life which is preferred to fixity; the shattered mirror is then a metaphor for death. (p. 122)

Evil and nothingness are ubiquitous in Sylvia Plath's poetry. Her positive themes are therefore presented against a negative background, with an undertone of frightened defiance, as being capable of holding death and failure at bay. We shall see that even in those poems which at first sight appear untouched by menace or the obsession of death, the choice of details and adjectives betrays an underlying defensiveness, and implicit contrast. And this can be said even with regard to the few poems on the subject of children, for all other positive themes contain possibilities of degeneration and disillusion.

The child is, in principle, the fountainhead of all life and hope. His self is not yet 'bald and shiny', he is 'vague as fog', and 'Trawling (his) dark as owls do' ('You're'): a vagueness imbued with infinite possibilities, before which the parents are humbled: 'your nakedness / Shadows our safety' ('Morning Song'). He is akin to the elements, the sea, the wind, the clouds 'with no strings attached and no reflections' (as written elsewhere, in 'Gulliver'). (p. 123)

This is not to say that the image of the child never appears in poems whose general tone is one of foreboding and even despair.... Even in a poem like 'Balloons', where the image, already encountered in 'Morning Song', recalls 'oval animal souls', the balloons are opposed to 'dead furniture'; in 'Nick and the Candlestick' the child is like a faltering candle in a frozen cave full of murderous fishes.

Furthermore, the obvious justification of one's existence which the child brings is not always potent enough to appease the guilt of the egotist, as appears in the poems on the childless woman or those which show the dead children as appendages to the dead woman. In 'Fever 103°', guilt actually evokes the image of a 'spotted', dying child, whereas in 'Nick and the Candlestick', the blood bloomed clean in him. We might say, to summarize, that as a subject the child is positive, but that as a theme it is often combined with others which greatly diminish this positive value, and can even make it completely negative; the child-theme is then used to reinforce guilt, fear and despair.

Much the same could be said about another theme, that of the lulling comfort of everyday life. Kindness supplies another 'necessary fluid', a 'poultice', and busies itself 'sweetly picking up pieces'. Love, in its beginnings, evoked 'a green in the air' which 'cushioned lovingly' the poet. And so does daily life.... But what happens when interest wanes and the endless stream of life-symbols dries up? The environment of daily life, when evoked like an incantation in such circumstances, is no more than 'dead furniture', fragmented and powerless:

> I survive the while,
> Arranging my morning,
> These are my fingers, this my baby.
> 'Little Fugue'

and in 'Tulips', the mood of which is the lowered vitality which makes the individual unable to cope with life:

> They have swabbed me clear of my
>   loving associations ...

> I watched my teaset, my bureaus of linen, my books
> Sink out of sight, and the water went over my head.
>   (pp. 124-25)

To the maimed self, therefore, daily life cannot give back wholeness, only crutches, a frequent symbol ('Berck-Plage', 'The Applicant'). And death can actually be welcome, since it frees one from this useless lumber, useless, yet irreversibly acquired, for man is the prey of an 'adding-machine'. (p. 127)

We have seen that purification can be achieved in death, in which the scattered personality is seen as gradually withdrawing towards its vital centre and abandoning its tainted externals, as in 'Fever 103°', in 'Tulips' and in 'Paralytic':

> I smile, a buddha, all
> Wants, desire
> Falling from me like rings
> Hugging their lights.

Echoes are often used as a symbol of these externals, since they are a degradation of sound, a repetition travelling away from the original event. Thus in 'Words', in which emotion, animation, life, were contrasted with the unchangeably bare skull and the fixed stars, a second constellation of images confirms the meaning of the first: the words are 'Axes / After whose stroke the wood rings', while echoes travel off from the centre. But the words by themselves are powerless once the central intention which informed them has gone.... (p. 128)

Love is ... subject to three forms of degradation and disappearance: the petrification of daily life and meaningless forms, the dissolution into glitter, the transfiguration which depersonalizes both object and subject. There is in fact no place here for adult relationships: in *Three Women* the Girl is unmarried, the Secretary has a bloodless relationship with her husband, although she finds at the end that she has become 'a wife'; but the Wife herself never says anything at all about the father of her child—this male baby is her only 'lover'.

Nor does the awareness of her difference and of her gifts seem to have given the poet much reassurance—certainly nothing comparable to the notion of giving birth to a child. The lack of any trace of a feeling of achievement seems, on the evidence of the poems alone, to be explained by the fact that, although the poetic urge flows irrepressibly, this generosity is suicidal, it is in the nature of a wound.... So, although a divine visitation is wished for in the midst of everyday life, and although the poet cannot help feeling some pride and some nobility in her calling, she always conceives it as another of those numerous disintegrating factors which threaten her, and incomparably the most potent and terrifying. In fact, it is in this connection only that we can detect a genuine feeling of the divine, and a religious attitude which is on the contrary conspicuously absent in all mentions of a conventional deity. This seems at least one of the possible interpretations of 'The Hanging Man'. This in itself is evidence of great purity in poetic feeling; but if we turn to the part in which the poet can feel [herself] to be to some extent responsible for her art, dominating poetry as a craft, instead of being dominated by it, there is merely disenchantment, and especially when looking back on the achieved poem, always inferior in its very achievement to the ideal one. This seems to be the subject of 'The Night Dances'; in this poem, we can see that the uniqueness of the living flesh is placed, in her scale of values, *a priori* above the cold, impersonal 'mathematics' of poems. The child is elemental like the clouds, the poem is an artifact, whose beauty and regularity remind one of snowflakes, which will melt to nothing. Perhaps we are here given the rare sight of an exceptionally gifted poet who did not believe enough in poetry.

But in addition there seems to have been, in her particular case, another disturbing factor: a profound uncertainty about the possibility of reconciling womanhood and intellect, whether the origin of this is to be sought in long-standing sociological or psychological causes, or in the special circumstances which preceded the writing of the last poems. Among the latter was the birth of her son, which, we are told, was followed by a great burst of creativity; if so, this may have been the sign of a release from a guilt associated with her vocation. (pp. 130-31)

To conclude, we can say that the symbolic net which Sylvia Plath casts on the world of perception has above all a personal value, and that we must consent to a partial identification with her if we are to enjoy her poems to the full, and even to understand them. Ultimately, however, her work stands on stylistic merits alone. And it is remarkable that the devices she uses, although we can to some extent list and classify them, are almost as varied as the thematic content is rigid. The ease of composition to which she has testified in connection with her last poems shows that the unconscious processing of her material was formal as well as thematic, for the felicitous rhythmic and phonetic inventions, which perfectly render the finest intentions are innumerable. . . . [Among] the dramatic and unexpected cuts which are such a striking feature of her poems, some are particularly evocative. (p. 133)

Generally speaking, the cuts tend to induce a strong narrative tension, chiefly due to a counterpoint between grammatical and rhythmic structure, and sometimes, when the rhythm becomes obsessively marked, or in the last line of a five-line stanza, there is a feeling of foreboding very similar to many piano accompaniments of romantic ballads such as Schubert's, as in, for instance, 'The Arrival of the Bee Box'.

Apart from the thematic value of sibilants, which we have discussed above, the same freedom is observed in the sounds as in the rhythm. We might just detect an embryonic thematic function in a few others, such as the fullness and gaiety of the child's world in 'a creel of eels, all ripples', the vagueness of 'oval animal souls', or 'trawling your dark as owls do', the gaping chasm of death in 'the flesh the grave cave ate', or 'your dark amputations crawl and appal', or the hollowness of deceit in

> Lies and smiles. (. . .)
> And he, for this subversion,
> Hurts me, he
> With his armoury of fakery.

The general tone is very rarely purely elegiac, since we have seen that the effort to dominate experience and the fear of fighting a losing battle result in most poems being built on a feeling of duality and antagonism. Stylistically, this ambivalence results in a Laforguian juxtaposition of the sublime and the homely, of compassion and hatred. It is noticeable that, just as the first line often states boldly the subject and the dominant tone of the poem, the last line is often markedly prosaic, at variance with the prevailing rhythm, as if there was, at the end of each of these efforts to shape experience into patterns and thus dominate it, a loss of faith and a return to a shapeless and hopeless existence, a feeling of the uselessness of effort. Yet the fact that we are always strongly aware of an individual voice speaking to us, even from the midst of despair, is a testimony to the poet's achievement. . . . The poet must re-enact in his life the struggle between anarchy and order, and it is doubtless a silent but profound awareness of this duty which accounts, in Sylvia Plath's poems, for the essential ambiguity of the themes and the protean presence of death. (pp. 133-35)

Annette Lavers, "The World as Icon: On

Sylvia Plath's Themes," in The Art of Sylvia Plath: A Symposium, *edited by Charles Newman (copyright © 1970 by Charles Newman and the estate of Sylvia Plath), Indiana University Press, 1970, pp. 100-35.*

Sylvia Plath's poems in [*Warnings from the Grave*] (which were written immediately after the birth of a child, and shortly before she committed suicide) come out of a consciousness which is unique [and] immensely forceful. . . . Their power, their decisiveness, the positiveness and starkness of their outline, are decided not by an identifiable poetic personality expressing herself, but by the poet, a woman finding herself in a situation, out of which she produces these disconcerting, terrifying poems. The guarantees of the authenticity of the situation are insanity (or near-insanity) and death. All the way through we feel that the last thing the poet cares about is her book, her name, whether she will get a critical accolade, a Book Award, a Pulitzer, a Guggenheim, or whatever. She is writing out of a pure need of expression, certified, as I say, by death. The miracle is an effect of controlled uncontrolledness. As one reads on, one begins to seek the dark places which provide the structure of the control, the landmarks among which the poetry is moving. There is the German and Austrian background (Sylvia Plath was born in Boston in 1932 of German and Austrian parents), feelings about her German father (which correspond rather to those of Theodore Roethke about his), concentration camps, her daughter, and her son, her husband (the English poet, Ted Hughes), the Devonshire landscape, villagers, the sea. Probably at some later stage, critics will chart this autobiographic territory. One will be grateful when they do this, but one can be grateful also that they have not done so already. Part of the impressiveness of these poems is the feeling they give the reader of finding his way darkly through a dark and ominous landscape. (pp. 200-01)

[Nature in Plath's poems] is not in the least alleviating, it is not outside the poet, it is not the great furniture of the continuity of the seasonal earth, on which the distraught mind can rest. Or if there are some externals in these poems (they do give one a strong panicky feeling of kitchens, utensils, babies, gardens) they exist in an atmosphere where the external is in immediate process of becoming the internal, opposites identical with one another.

The same fusion of opposites applies to the feelings expressed. Sylvia Plath's imagination does not, like D. H. Lawrence's, merely oscillate between feelings of love and of hatred. With her the two attitudes seem completely fused. (pp. 201-02)

Considered simply as art, these poems have line to line power and rhythm which, though repetitive, is too dynamic to be monotonous. Beyond this, they don't have 'form'. From poem to poem they have little principle of beginning or ending, but seem fragments, not so much of one long poem, as of an outpouring which could not stop with the lapsing of the poet's hysteria. In this respect they have to be considered emotional-mystical poetry, like the poems of St. John of the Cross, in which the length of the poem is decided by the duration of the poet's vision, which is far more serious to the poet than formal considerations.

They are like nothing more than poems of prophecy,

written by some priestess cultivating her hysteria, come out of Nazi and war-torn Europe, gone to America, and then situated on the rocky Cornish Atlantic coast. One does not think of Clytemnestra as a *hysteric*; one thinks of her as hysterical for very good reasons, against which she *warns*. Sylvia Plath would have agreed with Wilfred Owen that 'all a poet can do today is to warn'. But being a woman, her warning is more shrill, penetrating, visionary than Owen's. Owen's came out of the particular circumstances of the trenches, and there is nothing to make us think that if he had not been on the Western Front—the mud and blood into which his nose was rubbed—he would not have warned anyone about anything at all. He would have been a nice chap and a quiet poet. With Sylvia Plath, her femininity is that her hysteria comes completely out of herself, and yet seems about all of us. And she has turned our horrors and our achievements into the same witches' brew. (pp. 202-03)

Stephen Spender, "'Warnings from the Grave'," in The Art of Sylvia Plath: A Symposium, *edited by Charles Newman (copyright © 1970 by Charles Newman and the estate of Sylvia Plath), Indiana University Press, 1970, pp. 199-203.*

The last poems of Sylvia Plath draw their compulsive intensity not so much from their element of naked confession but from this assumption that in a deranged world, a deranged response is the only possible reaction of the sensitive mind. This is seen in her poem 'Daddy'.... The rhythm of a poem such as 'Daddy' has its basis in nursery rhyme, and in this respect may be compared with the rhythms used by the witches in *Macbeth* or, more recently, by T. S. Eliot in *Sweeney Agonistes*—a dramatic fragment surprisingly close to Sylvia Plath's poem in feeling and theme. The rhythmic patterns are extremely simple, almost incantatory, repeated and giving a very steady return. The first line, for example, 'You do not do, you do not do', with its echoes of the witches winding up their sinister spell, 'I'll do, I'll do, and I'll do' or T. S. Eliot's repetition of 'How do you do. How do you do' denies the affirmation of the marriage service which is later introduced into the poem, 'And I said I do, I do', and suggests a charm against some brooding but largely undefined curse. As in nursery rhyme, the force, almost compulsive, of the rhythmical pattern of the poem gives a sense of certainty, psychologically a sense of security, to a world of otherwise remarkably haphazard and threatening events. The dilemma of the old woman who lived in the shoe, of Dr. Foster, or of Miss Muffet terrified by the spider, is largely contained and appears acceptable and almost reassuring in the comforts of an incantatory rhythmical pattern, for order is imposed, often, indeed, superimposed, on an otherwise fortuitous and even terrifying reality. Also the subject of the nursery rhyme tends to accept his situation with something like a matter-of-fact stoicism; often he seems to co-operate with the events that beset him.

The effectiveness of 'Daddy' can largely be accounted for by Sylvia Plath's success in associating the world of the poem with this structure of the nursery rhyme world, a world of carefully contained terror in which rhythm and tone are precariously weighed against content to produce a hardly achieved balance of tensions.

Sylvia Plath's *persona* exemplifies, she has said, the Electra complex and is involved in the classical psycholog-

ical dilemma of hatred for her mother, with whom she identifies herself, and love for her German father whom she rejects as tyrannous, brutal and life-denying. The animus that sustains her is both directed towards the father and driven in on herself as if, in the wish to prove her love for those who persecute her, she must outdo them in persecuting herself. The area of experience on which the poem depends for its images is rawly personal, even esoteric, and yet she manages to elevate private facts into public myth, and the sheer intensity of her vision lends it a kind of objectivity. The detachment she achieves in this sudden, terrifying insight into a private world of suffering and humiliation far from dragging the reader into a vortex of suffering and humiliation curiously releases him into a sense of objectivity and freedom from such emotions. The central insight is that of the *persona*, her awareness of her own schizophrenia, of herself as a victim, a centre of pain and persecution; but there is also awareness of a love/hate relation with those responsible for persecuting her. It is this insight into her schizophrenic situation that gives the poem its terrifying but balanced polarity; the two forces, persecutor and victim, are brought together because the *persona* cannot completely renounce the brutality which is embodied in the father/lover image without also renouncing the love she feels for the father/lover figure. The love/hate she feels is the very centre of her emotional life without which she can have neither emotion nor life. In this sense she can be said to co-operate with those that persecute her and, indeed, to connive at her own suffering. As in nursery rhyme, the heroine loves her familiar terrors.

The main area of conflict in the poem is not that covered by the relation of persecutors and persecuted but is within the psyche of the persecuted herself. It is between the *persona* as suffering *victim* and the *persona* as detached, discriminating will. In this poem the diseased psyche takes the place of sensibility and the problem is to establish the relations between subconscious psyche and conscious will. Torn between love and violence, the *persona* moves towards self-knowledge, the awareness that she loves the violence or, at least, towards the recognition that the principles of love and violence are so intimately associated one with the other that the love can only express itself in terms of the violence. By accepting the need for love, she exposes herself to the pain and humiliation of a brutal persecution. The traditional associations of love with tenderness, respect, beauty, and so on, have been utterly destroyed; love is now associated with brutality, contempt and sadistic ugliness. Love does not bring happiness but only torture, 'the rack and the screw'. Moreover, far from admiring the traditional qualities of a lover, the poem insists that:

> Every woman adores a Fascist,
> The boot in the face, the brute
> Brute heart of a brute like you.

Furthermore, brutality is not only a necessary part of love but is also a central and inevitable principle of life. In the last stanza of the poem the community itself joins the heroine in a savage, primitive ritual of brutality—

> And the villagers never liked you.
> They are dancing and stamping on you.

The poem avoids self-pity by hardening its tone into one of self-contempt. The *persona* is divided and judges itself. The only escape from such self-knowledge is in death which the poem acknowledges not only as a release but also as a re-fining and purifying force, a way of cleansing. It is not anni-hilation of the personality but the freeing of it from the humiliating persecution of love and violence.

The poem is a terrifyingly intimate portrait, but it achieves something much more than the expression of a personal and despairing grief. The poem is committed to the view that this ethos of love/brutality is the dominant historical ethos of the last thirty years. The tortured mind of the heroine reflects the tortured mind of our age. The heroine carefully associates herself and her suffering with historical events. For instance, she identifies herself with the Jews and the atrocities of 'Dachau, Auschwitz, Belsen' and her persecu-tors with Fascism and the cult of violence.

The poem is more than a personal statement for by ex-tending itself through historical images it defines the age as schizophrenic, torn between brutality and a love which in the end can only manifest itself, today, in images of vio-lence. This love, tormented and perverse, is essentially life-denying: the only escape is into the purifying freedom of death. This is the hideous paradox, that the only release from a world that denies the values of love and life is in the world of death. The nursery rhyme structure of the poem lends this paradox the force of matter-of-fact reasonable-ness and an air of almost reasonable inevitability. In this we are persuaded almost to co-operate with the destructive principle—indeed, to love the principle as life itself. (pp. 231-36)

> *A. R. Jones, "On 'Daddy'," in* The Art of Sylvia Plath: A Symposium, *edited by Charles Newman (copyright © 1970 by Charles Newman and the estate of Sylvia Plath), Indiana University Press, 1970, pp. 230-36.*

Among the most troubled and complex of Sylvia Plath's poems are her six beekeeping poems, in which Plath uti-lizes beekeeping imagery to communicate her themes that stress a woman's urgent need to be free from the coercions of men, children, and society. Plath's imagery and sym-bolism shift ambiguously from poem to poem and even within a single poem. Plath identified her speaker alter-nately or simultaneously with ignorant observer, beekeep-er, worker bee, and queen.

Most of these poems show a woman longing to be freed from the domination of a male—father, husband, or na-tional despot. In "The Beekeeper's Daughter," the speaker calls her father "hieratical" and "Maestro" and charges him with holding "My heart under your foot" and oppressing both the bees and herself. In "The Swarm," the beekeeper symbolizes a tyrant and conqueror whose bees, representing men at war, are mechanical instruments spreading his tyranny. This imperialist is a composite Na-poleon, Caesar, and Nazi—a recurrent European "hero," whose "furnace of greed" smokes out the bees, who swarm into battle. The beekeeper also serves as one of Plath's rare portraits of God, whom she sees as the arch-despot, be-cause he condones

> the beak, the claw, the grin of the dog
> Yellow-haunched, a pack-dog
> Grinning over its bone of ivory
> Like the pack, the pack, like everybody
>
>   (p. 32)

Not only do Plath's female protagonists fear despots and despotic fathers, they also fear society, husbands, and their own children, all of whom coerce and control women. (p. 33)

Although most Plath poems show fears of being controlled by a master, "The Arrival of the Bee Box" shows a par-allel terror of being a master. Here, like an example of Nicholas Berdaev's theory, the master is as enslaved as the slave. (p. 35)

As did her life, Plath's poems show a woman's tremendous need for psychological, temporal, and physical room, for time and space in which to breathe, in which she can be herself without pressures from society, fathers, husbands, and children. Her poems show the need to escape from the frustrations a woman endures in her responsibilities amid the hive-like frenzy of demands from others. In "The Bee-keeper's Daughter" and "Wintering," Plath imagines such freedom and portrays the serenity of virginity and isolation in a world without men. The speaker of each poem shows no desire for companionship, male or female; her attitude is like that of the speaker in "Stings" who can also enjoy two people's companionship as "mere honey drudges." She desires to be androgynous. Yet the difference between the earlier and later poems show to what extent Plath's own view had become darker and more desperate.

In "The Beekeeper's Daughter," the speaker can enjoy sensuality and fertility if those qualities are separated from male domination. She admires the redness that Plath usually uses to suggest sexuality and vitality. "Purple, scarlet specked," gold, orange, and red abound, and the flowers' "musk encroaches." . . . She gloats that . . . "The queen bee marries [only] the winter of your year" and propagates without drone, beekeeper, or society. The speaker desires a similarly soliptical queenship.

By the time Plath writes "Wintering," all delights with lushness and fertility have disappeared. Here the speaker merely seeks isolation and can envision security only when barricaded in the dark interior of a basement room in mid-winter. And even that security cannot last. Although "Win-tering" seems simpler and less troubled than other bee-keeping poems, in its presentation of the calm between the regularly recurring storms described in the other poems, it is perhaps the most dreadful, because it reveals that the horror of the other poems is only temporarily suppressed; the speaker is encapsulated under high pressure outside a container that will inevitably readmit the deadly energies that torment the protagonist of these poems. (pp. 36-7)

Plath's beekeeping poems are, I believe, among her finest and most representative works. They have her character-istic energy, emotion, ambiguity, and incredible impact. In these poems she has found an almost perfect metaphor for her own inner turbulence—the turbulence of a woman who operates efficiently, like a machine, like a bee hive. Plath herself was indeed like a queen bee reduced to the subservi-ence of worker bee, a queen who, for all her specialness, is even more trapped—since she only leaves the hive once or twice in her life, to soar and mate and to possibly change hives—than the worker bees who are in and out of the hive all day. The imagery of the bees and beehive, with its terri-fying noises, its frenzied activity, its ever-present threat of stings, its hidden inner secrets, its sticky sweet (and mer-chandisable) honey, its coffin-like containment, and its coercion of all members of its society, provides an almost perfect metaphor for Plath's own emotional, female, marital, social, artistic, and human predicament. (p. 38)

Sherry Lutz Zivley, "Sylvia Plath's Bee-keeping Poems," in Poet and Critic (© *Department of English and Speech, Iowa State University), Vol. 9, No. 1, 1975, pp. 32-8.*

Readers of Plath's autobiographical novel *The Bell Jar* know only too well what [her relentless and careful] role-playing, such constant reliance on what R. D. Laing has called a "false-self system," cost the poet. Only in the last dark years of her life, when the facade finally crumbled, did the real self emerge for a brief moment, producing what Robert Lowell has called the mode of "controlled hallucination" of *Ariel,* that brilliant but slim collection of poems upon which Plath's reputation will ultimately have to rest. . . .

The first ten years of her writing career (1950-59) produced a poetry of careful disguise and labored imitation, a "correct" poetry designed to *sell* to such magazines as Seventeen and Mademoiselle. As late as 1961, she complained to her mother that she had never yet been able to sell a story to the Ladies Home Journal. *Ariel,* published posthumously in 1966, allows the poet's demonic self to surface, but the "I" of these poems is generic, archetypal, dehumanized; it is not the "I" of autobiographical poetry. . . . (p. H1)

I cannot think of a single other American writer—not even Scott Fitzgerald—who cared as much about external success—the winning of prizes, the award of fellowships, the earning of money, the congratulations of editors—as did Sylvia Plath. By the same token, she seems to have cared astonishingly little for her poetry as poetry. Her aim was not to satisfy herself (for that self was always fragmented) but to satisfy *others*—the famous, the established, the arbiters of taste. Accordingly, she studiously avoided Bohemia, the avant-garde, all schools of experimental writing from Black Mountain to the Beats and the New York Poets, preferring the safety of Yeats and Eliot, Stevens and Auden, Dylan Thomas and Hopkins. Only in her later years did the example of Lowell and Roethke make a real impact on her work, and by then, they too were famous poets. . . .

[In *Method and Madness* Edward] Butscher explodes, once and for all, A. Alvarez's romantic myth, put forward in *The Savage God* . . . , of Sylvia Plath as "Extremist Poet," the poet who died for the sake of her art, whose actual suicide was simply a risk she took in daring to face her innermost conflicts, "a last desperate attempt to exorcise the death she had summed up in her poems." The very opposite seems to be true. . . . (p. H2)

Marjorie Perloff, "Breaking the Bell Jar," in Book World—The Washington Post (© *The Washington Post), April 4, 1976, pp. H1-H2.*

In Ted Hughes's "Notes on the Chronological Order of Sylvia Plath's Poems," included in *The Art of Sylvia Plath,* he refers to several written in 1956-57, calling their vision of "the deathly paradise" a "chilling" one. The comment is haunting, also puzzling: how can "paradise" be "deathly"? Sylvia Plath was, Hughes adds, evolving her own pantheon of deities at the time, her special cosmic vision. Although she was inspired by the works of "primitive painters" from Henri Rousseau to Leonard Baskin, he explains, the vision was an internally felt experience and very much her own. (p. 469)

The word "paradise," of Persian origin, means simply "walled garden," and this aspect is retained with its traditional imagery and lavish beauty in many Plath poems as it is in paintings by Rousseau.

A deathly paradise is, however, of darkling, sinister import, presided over by presences divine but daemonic—mythic figures or power, impersonalized archetypes without concern for what they create. Within the walls of such death-gardens ravaging figures sometimes prowl and destroy, like the tigers of Rousseau's mysterious canvases, or the archetypal sow who swills down the very cosmos itself as she wallows in the "walled garden" of her legendary sty in the Plath poem, "Sow." Although they contain by implication humanity's beginnings and endings, death, not life, is the ruling principle of these anti-Edens. Moreover, their inhabitants have no freedom of choice in the old Miltonic sense of having been made "Sufficient to have stood though free to fall." They are human but hapless, at the mercy of deity or deities. The deathly paradise, then, is deathly not only because it affirms death instead of life but also because it swallows up purpose and individuality. Its ultimate affirmation is a negation: the search for an identity means the search for non-identity. The discovery of purpose discloses that there is no purpose.

On this paradox Sylvia Plath's vision is based. Having told us in "The Death Of Myth-Making" (1959, uncollected) what our world would be like—dull and mechanized—ruled only by the ugly, limiting vision of Reason and Common Sense, she demonstrates in her poetry how the mythic, in its immemorial pre-Christian, even pre-Graeco-Roman dress of birth and death, seasonal and vegetative changes, moon and sea phases, and archaic concept of beginnings and endings, is the only way to express the cosmos, is, in fact, the only way the cosmos can express itself. (p. 470)

"Snakecharmer" [in *The Colossus*] deserves attention, partly because it is one of the poems Ted Hughes found especially "chilling," and partly because it is a more complete realization of the anti-Edenic vision than is found in earlier works. Inspired by Rousseau's "La Charmeuse de Serpents," "Snakecharmer" reaches back into an archaic world. Turning the painting's female snakecharmer into a male demi-god, perhaps a principle of ageless, archetypal function, the poet creates a cultic figure possessing the secrets of life and death, creation and destruction. What this snakecharmer pipes, has forever piped, and will eternally pipe, is a *private* Eden, expressive of his personal, whimsical vision. He is uninterested in plan or purpose, in gods or men. He pipes a lush, green, watery world into existence, then, as the mood takes him, out of existence again. By his piping he not only creates this world but peoples it—with snakes. It seems at first as if his garden and its occupants exist only so long as he wills them to be. (p. 471)

The piper as creater-destroyer is actually piping the human race. This is a pre-Genesis as well as an anti-Genesis concept of paradise and human origins: humanity is not driven forth into the human condition by a stern yet just and compassionate God who is also prepared to redeem His children. Humanity, in this "paradise," is a ripple on a green, watery surface, a flick of a serpent-tongue, an inhalation of a piper's breath. "Eden" is a painted backdrop, cool, silky, witty, amoral, perhaps a cosmic joke. Yet because of that "simple fabric," that pre-existent "idea" of snake-humanity, the vision is no literal "pipedream," and its "reality" is what gives the piece its "chilling" quality.

Like "Snakecharmer," the other garden poems of *The Colossus* present a garden that is off-center, strange, anti-Edenic.... [In] each case it is a frightening garden, one which traps without sheltering, rejects even when it entices.

Moreover, whoever controls the garden, however it is described, holds the secrets of origins and ends, of life and death. The presence, the persona, god or demi-god, human or partly human, differs markedly from one poem to the next, but the control is always absolute, and the meaning (or meaninglessness) of each garden is at this power's discretion. As divorced from control of their own destiny as the snake-descended humanity of "Snakecharmer," the "controlled" are set apart in every poem. Sometimes they are voiceless appendages, sometimes helpless pleaders, occasionally welcomers crying out in greeting. But they are always placed in irreconcilable polar opposition to the "controller," or power. (pp. 471-72)

If it was the poet's intention to portray a compassionate figure in her surgeon [in "The Surgeon at 2 A.M." in *Crossing the Water*], she did not succeed. He is detached, cool, admiring the body as "a Roman thing," a superb piece of engineering, and himself as its perfecter. A telling aspect of the poem is that neither on the operating table nor in the ward do patients have "faces" for the surgeon.... In its own way, the garden-vision of this poem is fully as chilling as that of "Snakecharmer," its Eden as eerie and as limited. In this garden of the faceless, no seeds of redemption have been planted. The surgeon is pleased to accept responsibility for the total "garden," but not for the individual blooms. He is also attracted, actually, by human suffering, something he can control and manipulate at will without himself becoming a part of it—an attitude found in several Plath poems.... His is not the Eden of the caring God, but the Eden of a man who plays at being God, not humble before his powers but floating in exalted detachment ("I am the sun").

There is purpose and order in the surgeon's garden of life and death, but his control over it is startlingly akin to that of the snakecharmer.... In a way, snakecharmer and surgeon inhabit the same mythic world. The snakecharmer belongs to the primal life before individual consciousness came into being—or became important: the surgeon is part of the Romantic or post-Renaissance world in which human individuality receives an emphasis little known in antiquity (although born with the birth of Christianity). But both personas are controlling figures alienated from their worlds—creators parted from their creatures. Both "garden poems" romanticize the alienated superfigure at the expense of faceless sufferers.

If we take the sequential publication of Sylvia Plath's poetry as a roughly accurate guide to the development of her thought and vision, ... we note that garden imagery and metaphor grow less frequent. As "the garden" drops away, "the journey" takes its place—anything to get on board that train (ultimately the death-train), to find the "terminus" for which the "suitcases" are packed, to ride that

horse, churn with those churning pistons. Such garden poems as do appear are more decadent.... "I Am Vertical" [in *Crossing the Water* is] an attempt to cancel the alienating barriers between self and nature, creature and creator. This poem's speaker longs for the death which will make her one with the garden, in this case the totality of Nature: it is restful, pleasant, but impersonal, and purity has no part in it. (pp. 474-75)

It is not until the poem "Tulips" [in *Ariel*] that the metaphors of garden/Eden and purity/innocence cross one another for the first (and almost the last) time. This garden is an "excitable" mass of huge, intense, scarlet flowers, brought to the suffering speaker's hospital room where they oppress and disturb her. She does not simply *want* to die—that would be easy enough. She now feels that she is ready, *worthy*, by a process of preparation—"I am a nun now, I have never been so pure." But someone has brought her a red garden, forcing vivid life upon the peaceful death-whiteness of purified readiness. "Tulips" does not only set up a confrontation between life and death but between the faceless and the face-endowed as well, i.e., between the impersonal, nonindividuated, primal, and mythic, and the personal, individual, cared-for and caring, here-and-now. The speaker wishes to be effaced: the tulips will not let her. They not only force existence on the speaker but pain and self-awareness as well.

From this point on, the poems of *Ariel* pick up speed, merging into the imagery of the gallop, the piston, the mad journey, the agony. One last garden of death ("The Moon and the Yew Tree") presents a quiet graveyard of rest after despair, but is left behind like a way-station receding into distance while the themes of purity and redemption move harder and faster with the striking hooves, the turning wheels, the churn of pistons. "Ariel," "Getting There," "Fever 103°," "Totem," "Years," "Words"—all tell of cosmic trips without destination or even a clear point of origin, divorced from the human and the individualized. All the while the lusted-for goal (for which the self has been packed into its cosmic suitcase) is death—death in the form of sweeping-away of identity, melding into the primal/impersonal.

There are no more gardens (perhaps a touch or two of garden imagery). There are no creator-figures, either, only machines on the move, and one pitiable old queen-bee with "wings like torn shawls" who ascends, red and terrible, into the cosmos, taking the poet's self along with her, a lost and defeated identity in a world found more and more alien and alienating. In "Strings," there is a final hint, in the tradition of "Snakecharmer" or "The Surgeon," of a presiding, commanding, alien power who skips in from the mythic and skips out again, leaving a few tangible clues in the form of shed garments, symbolizing the concrete dropping away from the abstract and the continuing possibility of an eternal forming power in the cosmos. In "Edge," almost the last poem Sylvia Plath ever wrote, the themes of purity and the garden cross once again with a power and effect not found in "Tulips".... (pp. 476-77)

Two things seem clear as we trace through the poetry of Sylvia Plath: she rejects both the primal and the eschatological paradise and seeks redemption elsewhere and in a different form; Edenic imagery and metaphor for the search for purity find different voices. The quest for the garden and the quest for the lost innocence are almost never the same quest. Sometimes her simpler nature poems hold out a kind of hope, resolution, promise.... Certain mother-child poems hint at a similar transforming power: in "Child" [in *Winter Trees*] the speaker comes closer to God in the clear beauty of her baby's eye than in any "paradise" (the glimpse is almost at once negated as she also sees in that same pure eye the reflection of the cosmos as "dark / Ceiling without a star"). (p. 477)

Her trouble lies, not necessarily in the garden per se, but in the *wall* around it. Mythic or real, stylized like Pope's or roving into nature like Wordsworth's, gardens are designed to protect, to keep certain things in and other things out. Even though her poetry depicts a world of alienations—man from man, man from nature, man from God (perhaps mother and child form the one abiding exception)—alienation is what Sylvia Plath cries out against most in her poetry. If we live in a garden, or seek one as a perfect spot, we are always closed in *with* something or *from* something. If evil has got in, like the tiger in Rousseau's paintings, we are trapped with it: if we are barred from the garden, on the outside, there is no way back in, no way to find the lost innocence. Paradise, ultimately, is deathly for Sylvia Plath, not because it is a source of death but because it promises or threatens to prevent death.... As under the "bell jar" where one breathes only one's own self-poisoning air, one is trapped in and by a garden, or barred from it, unable to cope with one's sins. This is why many Plath poems express a world without help, refuge, salvation, redemption. For many, paradise is bliss with its confining order: for Sylvia Plath it was not.... John Armstrong writes in *The Paradise Myth* [of] ... "the imperative need to counteract the oppressiveness of the idyllic confine...."

A price has to be paid for the refusal of the garden's walls. In Sylvia Plath's poems we see the same price being paid over and over as her poetic voices seek yearned-for purity outside the "idyllic confine." Her personas continually express the cosmology of aliens in the world who are at the same time muffled and inaccessible behind the garden wall. Her poems perpetually ask Alan Watts's questions: How far out can I get? How lost without being utterly lost? No sure answer is given, but there is a rejection of all experiences which may be likened to what the poet called a "shut box." The garden as first-and-final home is shunned. So is the body, another form of trap. (pp. 477-78)

It is an unendurable paradox: Sylvia Plath, who could not tolerate the wall, the constriction, the garden, also felt lost and alien in the expansion of the unconfined universe. Does this mean that death was to her the ultimate expansion, therefore the ultimate restriction—the last, walled, confining garden? One begins to suspect that, despite the frantic need for freedom, motion, and wildness, this was so. The poet always sought purification, redemption in the dynamic, the active; and yet the purifying act, in her poems as in her life, took place in enclosures: the love of the dead father in the sugar-egg; the fruition of motherhood in the dark, closed, blooming womb; death in the cellar-ledge of her mother's basement; death, finally, in the "shut box" of the gas oven, as if her myths of origins and ends were finally translated into realities. (pp. 478-79)

Sylvia Plath's poems tell us that life in alienation, in perpetual polar tension with "other," is not worth it, and that wall-less life cosmically, mythically blended with the universe is simply not possible. The poet longs to creep back,

not into the conventional womb, but into the archaic world of feeling, governed not by morality or stern justice and duty but by an indifferent, amorphous, mysteriously attractive, destructive/lifegiving, goddesslike power which reveals no secrets as to our origins and makes no promises as to our ends. But surrender to this deathly paradise even as an act of the imagination gives small comfort. The death-garden may not judge, neither does it save. It may promise rebirth, but not of the individual consciousness. And it appears to be totally without love.

When the garden poems with their controlling figures have faded from her work, one realizes that, because of the sheer number and variety of their personas—sacred or secular, human or daemonic, male or female—no one accepted figure, power, or control exists. Even the moon, possibly the greatest single deity-figure, only occasionally fulfills the controlling function, and her presence, too, is always charged with ambiguity since, like those dark mother-goddesses of primal times, she presents a fearsome combination of the destructive and the maternal. It begins to appear as if setting in motion a world and its inhabitants and ordering its meaning and their end is a game at which any number may play. It comes as no surprise when Sylvia Plath, no longer speaking through some persona but in a voice all too patently and painfully her own, decides to undertake the task herself.

Therefore in "Edge," written a day or so before her death, she creates her own, new myth. In the only other poem except "Tulips" in which images of purity cross those of the garden, the persona folds in upon herself and into herself (taking her children with her) and completes rites of purification which paradoxically convert self and children into a sealed garden, where neither hope, life, nor redress bloom and flourish, yet where a strange "perfection" waits. "Edge" states that the only real "journey" is a moveless, static in-folding; the only garden the last, not the lost one. The marbleized Greek necessity of the poem's vision refuses to affirm the infinite value of human life or the existence of the divine and the transforming in the universe. "Edge" does away with the alien power of "other," but at a terrible cost. The primal and/or eschatological meaning of "garden" is denied, and the poetic persona *becomes* the garden, self-created. Self is the wall, the idol and monument, the creator, end, and aim of this garden. In its concept of the ultimate "home," "Edge" offers us the most "chilling" definition of "the deathly paradise," with the self as controlling deity, not from *hubris* but from the pathos of utter despair, in a world which can offer no place "to get to." (pp. 479-80)

> *Constance Scheerer, "The Deathly Paradise of Sylvia Plath," in* The Antioch Review *(copyright © 1976 by The Antioch Review, Inc.; reprinted by permission of the editors), Vol. 34, No. 4, 1976, pp. 469-80.*

*   *   *

POWELL, Anthony 1905-

Powell, an English novelist and screenwriter, is the creator of the monumental "A Dance to the Music of Time," a twelve-volume narrative made up of four "movements" which correspond to the four seasons. Powell's work as a screenwriter and his sense of the possibilities of the moving camera led to his distinctive use of an important novelistic technique: the narrator character through whose camera-like eyes the

reader views the world. Powell's theme of the disintegration of English social values during the years between the world wars is revealed through the lives of four men, members of the British upper and upper-middle classes, who grow from youth to maturity in the series. Time is the backdrop for all theme and character development in *Dance*, embracing all life and art in its control. (See also *CLC*, Vols. 1, 3, 7, and *Contemporary Authors*, Vols. 1-4, rev. ed.)

It is by now a cliché to insist upon the melancholy and often the horror that underlie so much good comedy. Cliché or not, Powell's world—droll as it is—is shot through with pain. Apart from the external horrors of the war, which kills off a number of the . . . most engaging characters [in "A Dance to the Music of Time"], personal wretchedness of one sort or another is everywhere present and makes itself felt, despite the detachment, even flippancy, with which it is often presented. The inhabitants of Powell's world, whatever their age or sex, often give the impression of being lost or abandoned children putting on a funny or a brave or a goblin face in a dance that allows much display but only the briefest gratification.

Turning to the concluding measures of the dance, I find it impossible to imagine the experience of reading "Hearing Secret Harmonies" without an extensive, though not necessarily complete, familiarity with the style and content of its predecessors. The opening of the novel rings like a summoning-bell to the followers of Anthony Powell and a warning to all outsiders. . . .

I cannot help feeling that Powell himself is uneasy with some of [the sinister] material [in this novel] and that his effort to be "with it" constitutes a weakness in the book. Still, viewed in terms of the sequence, "Hearing Secret Harmonies" can be judged as among the more successful of the last seven volumes. It is conceivable, though improbable, that it could stand on its own as a novel. Certainly it contains episodes that are alive and amusing within their own context. But so much would be lost without the others.

How successful, finally, is "A Dance to the Music of Time?" Fifteen years ago many of Powell's readers would have felt confident that the sequence, when completed, would stand as a major achievement of 20th-century fiction; by that time five volumes had appeared—from "A Question of Upbringing" through the brilliant "Casanova's Chinese Restaurant"—and had won a critical response ranging from the favorable to the rhapsodic. Comparisons were made not only to such British contemporaries as Evelyn Waugh but also to Proust. Then, beginning with "The Kindly Ones" and becoming more evident in the books dealing with World War II, an apparent flagging of the creative impulse manifested itself, a preoccupation with trivia and a tedium that had only partly to do with the overall dullness of the narrator's wartime experience. Other evidences of strain, as if Powell were driving himself, showed up in "Books Do Furnish a Room" (in my opinion the low-point in the sequence) and have continued to a lesser degree in the two relatively successful final volumes.

In his recent biography of Waugh, Christopher Sykes states that Waugh, though an ardent champion of Powell, felt that the sequence was in danger of becoming self-defeatingly long. I think Waugh was right. Though the later novels all contain splendidly entertaining sections that show Powell in top form, I suspect that many of his followers, while welcoming and enjoying the new book, will share a certain relief that it marks The End. . . .

Although a number of the later characters—the composer Moreland, for instance—are more rounded, more subtly rendered, more "admirable," they never achieve either the brilliant fun or the pathos of the acquaintances of Nicholas's young manhood. A few, like the macabre American scholar Russell Gwinnett, who figures largely in the last two novels, seem to remain as unknowable to Nicholas as to the reader.

As he advances into the second half of the sequence, Powell goes out of his way to tax credibility. Comedy too often slips into contrived farce. Coincidences multiply. Characters are married to one another for no apparent reason other than the improbability of the match. . . .

[This is] what seems to be Powell's final vision: that the Dance to the Music of Time has undergone metamorphosis into a Holbein-esque Dance of Death, that harmony has everywhere been replaced by strident discord. But this transformation, I feel, has been brought about too mechanically. (p. 2)

So we are left with a flawed achievement, a qualified success. Powell is not the English Proust nor even the comic Proust, though he perhaps recklessly invites the comparison through overtly Proustian references in "The Military Philosophers." The comparison can only diminish what is, after all, a notable accomplishment. Despite his weaknesses, Powell as a novelist has given—and will continue to give—much pleasure. He has created, populated and (with some weariness) sustained a raffish and eccentric world that is recognizably his own. There is now such a thing as "a typical Anthony Powell character" or "a situation right out of Anthony Powell"—no small achievement for a novelist. Certainly he ranks with the radically different Doris Lessing (even the linking of the two is a Powell-like incongruity) as the best of the novelists now writing British fiction. (p. 3)

> *Robert Towers, in* The New York Times Book Review *(© 1976 by The New York Times Company; reprinted by permission), April 11, 1976.*

Only after the publication of the twelfth and final volume in the fall of 1975 did it become possible to view *A Dance to the Music of Time* as a whole—to see the beginning and the middle in the light of the end—and to begin to assess Powell's achievement. It is important that assessment begin on the right foot and consequently especially unfortunate that the final novel, *Hearing Secret Harmonies,* is far and away the weakest of the dozen. It is painful for an admirer of the series to detail his disappointment over the book's shortcomings. . . . (p. 45)

The subject of *A Dance to the Music of Time* is a densely populated swathe of upper-class, upper-middle-class, artistic, and Bohemian life in England from the twenties to the seventies. The vehicle of presentation is the comedy of manners. Attention is consistently focused on the nuances of social behavior, the idiosyncrasies of personal style, and the intricacies of sexual preference. All of the characters in the series, who must number well over one hundred, are seen strictly from the outside—that is, in terms of how they choose to present themselves to the world. Many pages of the series are devoted to gossip, inference, innuendo, and hypotheses concerning principal characters, and the great majority of the novels' scenes are of nonintimate social occasions: lunches, teas, receptions, dinner parties, evening parties, occasional dinners, dances, openings, conferences, weddings, funerals, gatherings in nightclubs, pubs, country houses, and so on.

In the third volume, *The Acceptance World,* . . . Nick Jenkins, Powell's narrator, finds his thoughts turning to fictional problems identical to those of his creator: "I began to brood on the complexity of writing a novel about English life, a subject difficult enough to handle with authenticity even of a crudely naturalistic sort, even more to convey the inner truth of the things observed. . . . Intricacies of social life make English habits unyielding to simplification, while understatement and irony—in which all classes of this island converse—upset the normal emphasis of reported speech."

In *A Dance to the Music of Time* Powell's solution to these problems is to eschew unmediated naturalistic reportage à la Galsworthy in favor of the re-creation of social life in the memory of a cultivated and discriminating observer. Nick's intense interest in visual art—real or imagined paintings are often used to comment on or define a character or a situation—is reflected in his careful composition of place and in his slowing down of the action of a scene (sometimes to a snail's pace) so as to create a tableau-like suspension of time that allows the reader leisure to absorb all of the scene's social detail and psychological nuance ("the inner truth of the things observed"). Evelyn Waugh found an excellent simile to describe this aspect of Powell's art when he wrote that his characters do not "exist fully, in the round. They can be observed from one position only. We cannot walk round them as statues. They present, rather, a continuous frieze in high relief, cut deep and detailed."

The verbal equivalent of such detail is the eschewal of understatement and irony (so effectively used in the novels Powell published during the 1930's) in favor of a leisurely, occasionally prolix, style. . . . [In] addition to its appositeness to the pace, the peculiarly ornate excellence of Powell's prose justifies itself, as in those places where it is played off against dialogue epitomizing the English fondness for understatement and irony (Powell has a fine ear) or in [virtuoso] passages. . . . (pp. 45-6)

Even Powell's narrator is no exception to the rule that a character's depths remain unplumbed. For all the wealth of animadversions, aperçus and worldly wisdom he supplies over the course of twelve volumes, we learn very little about Nick's innermost thoughts and feelings. Though we come to know his fine mind intimately, his emotional and spiritual life remains shadowy, to say the least. Even concerning his relationship with his wife we are kept almost totally in the dark. Nick's consciousness, through which every scene and character in the series is filtered, registers aesthetic, not ethical discriminations (indeed, in the early volumes vice sometimes seems to lose half its evil through losing all its grossness). His social observations are never distorted by social criticism; and if there are any religious overtones in the series, they are provided by [other characters]. . . .

Pattern, formal arrangement, nuance, and a character's "self-presentation" and "personal myth" are what fascinate Nick. (p. 47)

The Poussin scene [which gives the series its title] can no longer be considered the single dominating image in the series. It is only the alpha of *A Dance to the Music of Time;* the omega is the long quotation on the last page of *Hearing Secret Harmonies,* a torrential passage from Robert Burton's seventeenth-century compendium, *The Anatomy of Melancholy,* a work often cited by Nick in the series' closing volumes, which contain a number of variations of the disease. . . . The implications of this key passage, with its Ecclesiastian gravity and random chronicling of randomness and contingency, are antithetical to the harmonious implications of the Poussin scene but equally apposite to the series as a whole. It is true that the seasons of youth in the first six volumes do seem more harmoniously patterned than the years of war and the decades of aging in the final six. But even in the early novels undercurrents of melancholy and perceptions of transience and haphazardness were intermittently felt. They are present in the evocation of the Poussin painting, though it was only when well into the series that one remembered that the dance of the Seasons brought first to Nick's mind thoughts of mortality and realized that the harmonious implications of the image had been severely qualified by the passage in *The Acceptance World* concerning the haphazardness and determinism of "the formal dance with which human life is concerned . . . nothing in life is planned—or everything is—because in the dance every step is ultimately the corollary of the step before; the consequence of being the kind of person one chances to be."

In the middle volumes of the series . . . [there is] a shift in emphasis as the world of Nick and his friends moves from under the dominance of Poussin's image into the zodiac of the Burton quotation. (pp. 48-9)

By the time of *Hearing Secret Harmonies,* which opens in the late 1960's, the organizing magnetism of the Poussin image has become very weak. In the novel's last sentence Nick feels that "Even the formal measure of the Seasons seemed suspended in the wintry silence," and earlier in the novel he recognizes that "elements of the Seasons' dance were suggested in a perverted form" by the ritual dance—preparatory to multiple couplings—of a band of religious cultists, the descendants of Dr. Trelawney. The major reason for the somberness of the close of *Hearing Secret Harmonies* and its undercutting of the Poussin image is the inevitable diminishments of life as old age closes in on Nick and his circle, and death, bodily decrepitude, or madness claims more and more of the characters. This somberness had also been felt in *Temporary Kings,* the series' penultimate novel, which additionally featured an unprecedented emphasis (also present in *Hearing Secret Harmonies*) on the sordid sexual underside of several of the characters' lives.

But unlike *Temporary Kings,* which is one of the series' finest novels, full of stylistic vigor and fresh invention, *Hearing Secret Harmonies* shows signs of creative fatigue and a diminution of imaginative powers. Not that the novel is without its felicities. One of the more impressive aspects of the series has been the steady introduction of new characters of marked individuality who are assigned prominent parts. (pp. 49-50)

Another impressive feature has been the intermittent reappearance of characters from earlier novels, whose unfolding fates and ever-changing relationships to each other are central to the rhythm of the series and a principal source of its fascination. When these characters reappear in situations presented with sufficient slowness to allow us to recall analogous occasions from the past, the result is a frisson, a powerful aesthetic resonance. (p. 50)

For the most part, however, in *Hearing Secret Harmonies* the exciting interplay of past and present gives way to nostalgic recollection. One has the feeling that Powell is tidying up, touching familiar bases, rather in the manner of those old movies that run their credits against the background of stills from the just-screened film. (pp. 50-1)

[A] device suggestive of the tying up of loose ends is the thirteen necrological asides scattered throughout the novel, though it would be perverse to wish them excised from the text. One is glad to learn something of the circumstances of the deaths of [several characters] . . ., and thankful that Powell has devised a . . . seemly way of communicating such information. . . .

It can of course be argued that the very thinness and perfunctoriness of these aspects of *Hearing Secret Harmonies* themselves reflect the attenuations of age and the withering of vitality. Certainly this view would be consonant with a number of Nick's reflections during the course of the novel. . . . To argue this way, however, is to risk a confusion of life and art and to settle for less than one has a right to expect from the concluding novel of such an ambitious series. (p. 51)

Despite its interweaving of three main story lines, *Hearing Secret Harmonies* is the least polyphonic and multidimensional novel in the series. Perhaps in compensation for the curtailed activities of Nick and his contemporaries, the novel's principal subject is up to date, not to say trendy: the doings of student radicals and religious cultists. (pp. 51-2)

In *Hearing Secret Harmonies,* however, not very much of an interesting nature can be done with the new Bohemians for the simple reason that Nick Jenkins, like his creator, is trapped on the far side of the generation gap. He is forced to rely for his information on a few first-hand impressions, some second-hand accounts, and in one instance a television news program. The dominant young character, Scorpio Murtlock, is new to the series but much less satisfactorily rendered than Fenneau or Delavacquerie, both much older. Murtlock is equipped with some sacerdotal gestures and a hierophantic manner of speaking, and there is much talk of the steely power of his will. But the closest Powell can come in bringing Murtlock to life is to have Nick elicit from Fenneau the gratuitously demeaning information that Scorpio's real name is Leslie, that his parents ran a newsagent's shop, and that he was once a comely choir boy who got the vicar in trouble. The other major representative of the young, Fiona Cutts, a niece of Nick's who has dropped out of society and joined Murtlock's cult, is even more insubstantially rendered; and the Quiggin twins, Amanda and Belinda, student hell-raisers who throw paint on their university chancellor and set off a stink bomb at a formal dinner, are quite unbelievable.

With the second story line of *Hearing Secret Harmonies* Powell is on much firmer ground. Events surrounding the publication of Russell Gwinnett's biography of X. Trapnel bring one periodically back to the London literary world—the major ambiance of the series' last three novels (*Books*

Do Furnish a Room is the indicative title of the first of them). But even here there is a falling off in that Gwinnett is no longer the mysterious American academic with a necrophiliac past of *Temporary Kings,* the catalyst for the self-destruction of Pamela Widmerpool. He has become in *Hearing Secret Harmonies* middle-aged and dull and is present in the novel mainly so that he can dwindle into the husband of Fiona Cutts and thereby link the story line involving the young to that of the literary world.

The third story line concerns Widmerpool and involves his transformation from a life peer and university chancellor into a pathetically dominated member of Murtlock's cult. It is the boldest stroke in *Hearing Secret Harmonies,* but it fails to come off so completely that it forces one to reassess earlier novels from a point of view that leads ultimately to the most serious reservation I have about Powell's achievement in *A Dance to the Music of Time.*

Certainly *Hearing Secret Harmonies* clearly establishes the egregious Widmerpool as *the* central character in the entire series—not that many would have doubted this had it not been for Powell's complaints about the undue prominence that Widmerpool had assumed in the minds of his readers. The first scene in the first novel, coming just after the evocation of the Poussin painting, gives us Widmerpool at school, running through the December mists in training for races which he has no chance of winning. Fifty years later, in the last scene of the last novel (coming just before the Burton quotation) Nick learns that Widmerpool has died running—in effect fleeing the clutches of Murtlock. In between, Widmerpool had figured more or less prominently in every novel, enduring repeated public and private humiliations, as his ferocious will carried him steadily up the careerist ladder. . . . [We] are asked to believe that he has undergone a transformation from an arriviste pillar of the establishment into a hammer of the counter-culture and a willing participant in the ritual orgies of Murtlock's cult. It is as if Proust's Swann had been forced to play the role of his Charlus. The most telling indication of the violence of Powell's manipulation is Widmerpool's loss of distinctive voice. In *Hearing Secret Harmonies* he speaks in a disembodied way totally unlike his verbal signature in earlier volumes. In contrast, even when Stringham was discovered as a private soldier in a mobile laundry unit in *The Soldier's Art*—another startling metamorphosis—his superbly articulate, ironic mode of speech remained recognizably that of the Stringham of Eton, Oxford, and the London season.

Widmerpool's volte face violates Powell's own aesthetic dictum that every step in a character's dance be the corollary of the previous step. John Bayley puts as good a face as possible on this transformation in saying that "the needs of symmetry and symbolism do lead to [Widmerpool's] being pushed about rather unfairly in the last volume," and one wishes the matter could be left at that. But Powell's rough handling of Widmerpool has more unpleasant aspects to it which seem caused by his desire to punish and humiliate his creation. (pp. 52-4)

More than an aesthetic blunder, the treatment of Widmerpool is an affront to common decency that compels one to look back at his presentation in earlier volumes and to realize with a jolt one's complicity in and enjoyment of the abuse and humiliations inflicted on him for no other reason than he is unlike his more sophisticated contemporaries. To recall only the first two novels: while Stringham is presented as a Renaissance prince, his circumstances compared to Hamlet's, his step to Veronese's Alexander, his features to the faces in Elizabethan miniatures, and his general appearance to "one of those stiff, sad young men in ruffs, whose long legs take up so much room in sixteenth-century portraits," Widmerpool is depicted as loathesomely subhuman; his gait "like an automaton of which the mechanism might be slightly out of order," his stance "like that of an elderly lapdog," his countenance "like some uncommon specimen of marine life" or "a large fish moving slowly through opaque water to devour a smaller one," his way of speaking "as if holding a piece of india-rubber against the roof of his mouth.". . . His preposterousness seems clinched, as does Murtlock's, when his unseemly social background is discovered: Widmerpool's father had sold liquid manure. It is true that in subsequent volumes, as Widmerpool becomes a successful and powerful figure, he is no longer described in such subhuman similes and soubriquets; but again and again in the later volumes his sexual life is made the subject of cruel comedy, while the equally gamey bedroom lives of other characters are treated with tact and never exposed to ridicule.

How could one have failed to notice at an earlier stage the crudity of Powell's handling of Widmerpool and the violence it does to the aesthetic surface of his series? One reason is that in the early volumes it was clear that Nick was growing and developing, learning about life by trial and error and making mistakes in his assessment of people. At the same time, especially in *A Buyer's Market,* one was encouraged to feel that there was a symbiosis between Widmerpool and Nick; for Nick, also in love with Barbara Goring, could have been the recipient of the sugar she pours out [onto Widmerpool's head]; and, similarly seduced by Gypsy Jones, could have been the one dunned into paying for the pleasure. At that time one tended to assume that justice would eventually be done to Widmerpool and consequently enjoyed his discomfitures without twinges of guilt. This does not come to pass in the series, however, and one's retrospective judgment must be that the presentation of Widmerpool violates the aesthetic frame of reference within which Powell has chosen to create, with consequent damage to the unity and symmetry of his work, and that Nick's sophisticated consciousness is tainted by the most heinous form of snobbery: the refusal to consider those who are not in some way "one of us" as fellow human beings deserving of sympathy, charity, even of fair play. (pp. 54-5)

One had long hoped that in conclusion Powell would be able to raise his enormous work to a higher, more metaphysical plane and that the deeper philosophical lessons that seemed seminally present in the series would be brought to fruition. Similarly, having noted the increasingly explicit concern with artistic problems and with the nature of fiction in the tenth and eleventh volumes, one had come to think that the series was beginning in some degree to be about itself and had allowed oneself to anticipate that this reflexive probing of its own imaginative processes would become a central concern of the final novel and thereby enrich the series by including its own commentary within it. This too has failed to happen: there are only a few references to novels and fiction writing in *Hearing Secret Harmonies,* and these are rather run-of-the-mill or (to use a favorite word of Powell's) humdrum. (p. 56)

The crucial positioning of the antithetical emblems of the Poussin dance and the Burton quotation suggests that the basic organizing principle of *A Dance to the Music of Time* is the alternation of "now comical then tragical matters" (to use Burton's words), the counterpoint between a comedy of manners presentation of a large chunk of Vanity Fair and a more somber version of human life seen under the aspect of transience and mortality, against the force of which no transcendence through love, memory, moral rectitude, or supernatural belief is possible. As Evelyn Waugh has said "We know much more about [Powell's] characters' appearances than their souls. Indeed we have no confidence that the narrator recognizes the existence of the soul." Powell's series should not be compared to the fiction of Proust, Mann, Gide, or Conrad because such a focus can only serve to shrink *A Dance to the Music of Time* to a size too small to permit objective scrutiny. For the opposite reason it can serve no useful purpose to call Powell a greater Galsworthy or Snow. Powell is rather the peer of Thackeray, and Waugh's observation concerning the absence of soul in the characters of *A Dance to the Music of Time* is as accurate (and perhaps as inapposite) as the similar comments perennially made about *Vanity Fair,* another fiction without a hero. (pp. 56-7)

> *Kerry McSweeney, "The End of 'A Dance to the Music of Time',"* in South Atlantic Quarterly *(reprinted by permission of the Publisher; copyright 1977 by Duke University Press, Durham, North Carolina), Winter, 1977, pp. 44-57.*

Powell's books . . . represent a solid, well-rounded body of work, complete with a unique flavour and easily identifiable approach. Powell has always been content to remain implanted in a particular world, in his case the world of upper and upper middle class Bohemia, that cross roads where Mayfair and the arts uneasily meet. Not for him the conscious experimentation or widening of creative horizons practised by Amis or even his friend Henry Green: at an early date he discovered his literary niche and never departed from it.

This is why Powell, already, has become, as Proust did before him, the centre not only of a cult but of a positive obsession. I remember some five years ago visiting an exhibition in a London gallery concerning artists and subjects who were either associated with or admired by Proust. There the girl in charge told me of two old men who the day before had arrived from different parts of the country (one from the west, the other from Scotland) and, discovering each other's enthusiasm and knowledge, had sat in enthralled Proustian conversation for some three hours before departing for tea. In the future the same scene might well be enacted under portraits of Lord Longford or Constant Lambert and delicate pastels of The Chantry.

To say this is not to compare *A la Récherche du Temps Perdu* to *A Dance to the Music of Time.* They are vastly different in conception and execution; yet both share the achievement of creating an entire, seemingly almost self-sufficient fictional world. Both also have a peculiar literary arrogance which invites either total acceptance or total rejection. Once immersed, no quarter is given by the narrator. Either you fall under the fascination of his approach, his friendships and the twists and turns of his life or you do not. There are no byways down which refreshment or momentary relaxation may be obtained, no Dickensian panorama of high, low and middle life, no almost casual flitting from perfumed prosperity in Cavendish Square to degradation in Wapping. In Powell or Proust the change of scene is viewed through the eyes of Jenkins or Marcel and is more remarkable for their reactions to it than for its own intrinsic horror or delight. Thus, the narrator acts as a filter, the unavoidable distorter of all that he transmits to the reader. (pp. 44-5)

[Occasionally] the early books are spoken of as having anti-Semitic overtones. I can find no evidence to suggest this; anyway Powell's satire is all-embracing and his work would be bound to reflect the flirtation that some pre-war occupants of Mayfair drawingrooms enjoyed with that disgusting and irrational creed. . . .

Jenkins's supreme characteristic in *A Dance* is not his 'goodness' but his passivity, his Isherwood-like ability to record, without judgment or prejudice, the antics of those around him. A 'good' man [as Jenkins has been critically considered] would not be able to resist the desire to wade in, to substitute his own self-doubt or approval for description. This, happily, Jenkins does not do; indeed his lack of involvement invites the charge of excessive smugness, born of amused detachment, rather than excessive virtue. Herein lies the major contrast with Widmerpool whose lack of self-satisfaction, of contentment with his own character and condition, leads to desperate attempts to win power over others and admiration for himself. Widmerpool is a man driven almost to the point of mania by consciousness of his inadequacies. Jenkins has knowledge of and confidence in his talent and comparatively ordered private life. To Widmerpool an obviously successful career and public approbation provide a means of redemption; therefore he becomes acutely and appallingly involved in whatever momentary fad or fashion might be able to assist him towards these ends. Jenkins has no need of this. He can stand back and observe quietly, with time for balanced thought. This is the difference between the calm, almost cold, contemplative and the desperate, almost psychotic pursuer of that which certain grave faults of personality must make unattainable. Here we are concerned not so much with good and evil as with health and sickness. . . .

In the last books, voyeurism, necrophilia and the occult loom like premonitions of some moral apocalypse. Perhaps in late middle and old age one's mind turns to such subjects. Certainly they are not out of place in *A Dance* and give to the crescendo of this great novel sequence sonorous notes of alarm and decay. (p. 45)

Max Egremont, "After the Dance," in Books and Bookmen (© copyright Max Egremont 1977; reprinted with permission), January, 1977, pp. 44-5.

A Dance to the Music of Time seems far removed from violence. But through Kenneth Widmerpool, a minor yet important character who appears in all the novels as a foil to other characters, Powell makes it clear that he understands the nature of power and violence. Widmerpool during his school days is the victim of the power of others, a latter-day Rudyard Kipling. He understands his role of victim, and from the day he is hit in the face with an overripe banana by the captain of the soccer team, he cautiously buckles under to those who are stronger. His experiences lead him eventually to reject education and learning, and gradually he forsakes his role of victim for that of victimizer. His alliance with the side of power is associated with his philistinism. The fear that haunts Jenkins is that Widmerpool is the sign of the future, a symbol of those who control the world. It is not by chance that Widmerpool's transformation from victim to victimizer occurs during World War II. One scene that gives insight into his total role occurs in *The Kindly Ones*. Jenkins and other important characters of the series are gathered at a dinner party in the castle of Sir Magnus Donners. Widmerpool appears at the castle in the middle of a game of photographing the seven deadly sins: "A man stood on the threshold. He was in uniform. He appeared to be standing at attention, a sinister, threatening figure, calling the world to arms. It was Widmerpool."

The "sinister, threatening figure" of Widmerpool in his uniform is a fitting symbol for the entire period. The sense of power and potential violence that broods over the modern world is a force with which the modern artist must reckon. (p. 31)

Lawrence R. Ries, in his Wolf Masks: Violence in Contemporary Poetry (copyright © 1977 by Kennikat Press Corp.; reprinted by permission of Kennikat Press Corp.), Kennikat, 1977.

*   *   *

POWYS, John Cowper   1872-1963

Powys, an English novelist, poet, and essayist, recreated in his novels the western English countryside of his youth. His characters possess a deep affinity for the natural elements that surround them: the sea, the wind, the land are imbued with a mystical significance, perhaps reflecting Powys's philosophy that man must find peace with the cosmic forces of nature. (See also *CLC*, Vol. 7.)

To label a man or a character an eccentric, at least as the term is generally used, tells us little that is helpful. In England, as Henry Adams discovered, "Eccentricity was so general as to become hereditary distinction." But in its stricter geometric and literal sense, eccentricity defines a position or form of movement which, when recognized, identifies a characteristic mode in a life or in a novel. Eccentricity is also, in a sense, a parody of genius. It mimes many of the gestures associated with true originality and profundity. And, like good parody, eccentricity feeds on, even eventually threatens to become, the very thing it imitates. The eccentric, like the parodist, must place himself at some distance from the center—whether that center be the "normal" or the object of parody. But while they begin by standing away from the center, both the parodist and the eccentric are finally dependent upon whatever occupies the center. Both, then, feel the tension of apparently contradictory demands: the requirement that they remain at the periphery and their need to define themselves by the center.

John Cowper Powys was a self-proclaimed eccentric. "Quixotic Puppet as I am, Prophetic Scarecrow as I am, draggle-tailed Hermit-Whore as I am," he chants in his *Autobiography*. Perhaps it is this eccentricity, as much as anything, which has confused the critics. While a few have emphasized his central position in the development of the modern novel, most have left him unnoticed on the periphery. (pp. 201-02)

Powys fostered his own neglect by cultivating a perverse instinct which kept him moving in the least fashionable direction. He left England in 1905 to spend almost thirty years lecturing to and "civilizing" America, while Americans with pretensions to civilization, including many of the country's most original writers, were sailing the Atlantic in the opposite direction. The years he spent in America are described in the *Autobiography* (written just before he returned to England in 1934), but they left virtually no mark on his fiction. He made literary friends in America, most prominently Theodore Dreiser, but the atmosphere of his novels is so thoroughly British that he received only passing attention from American critics who were busy at the time discovering the richness of their own neglected literary tradition. Thus, although the years spent in America occupy the center of his life, it is as if they formed an ellipsis, an empty center around which the eccentric circles.

America did, however, offer Powys a convenient periphery from which he could look in and write about what was truly central to his imaginative life—the hills, plains, flowers, and beaches of southwest England. Three of his four "English" novels were written in America: *Wolf Solent* (1929), *A Glastonbury Romance* (1932), and *Weymouth Sands* (1934). When Powys finally did return to England, he almost immediately began writing about Wales, the home, as he conceived it, of the ancient Princes of Powysland from whom he liked to trace his descent. And later, after he had settled in Wales, he turned in his fiction to more remote centers: Homeric Greece, Atlantis, and ultimately, outer space. He writes, then, from what he called in his *Autobiography* the "fluctuating margin of vague memory". From this margin he writes himself toward the center until, having reached it, that center becomes a new margin from which to explore yet another center. (p. 203)

Powys writes, as he lived, around the circumference of the modern novel. His theory of fiction, as distinct from his practice of it, remained Victorian, while the age more and more demanded experimentation. As a critic, Powys "appreciated" while others analyzed, and popularized while fascination with the difficult grew. He explored the psychology of man in terms of his relation to nature and place, the world outside, just as Freud's theories were making familiar territory of man's inner world. And while he seemed modish as an advocate of sensuality, he went on to profess a disgust for all aspects of the reproductive process. "It was only the most purged and winnowed allusions to sex that I could endure, and the least reference to normal sex functions turned my stomach. Savagery and blood I could not tolerate for a moment. It was the *idea* of sadism, an idea that had to flit and float and hover, like those tenuous heat waves that you watch sometimes above the surface of a field, that alone excited me.". . . In its blend of moral rectitude and aesthetic perversity Powys's admission itself flits and floats and hovers between condemnation and celebration. He never offers a standard against which to measure his eccentricities. And his novels present the same difficulty. They are populated by grotesques whose obsessions vie with one another for primacy. Still, in his best novels and in *Wolf Solent* in particular, Powys's eccentricity evolves a dramatic structure which is, at the very least, an excellent imitation of genius. (p. 205)

Wolf Solent is . . . "a book of Nostalgia, written in a foreign country with the pen of a traveller and the ink blood of his home. . . ."

Geographical nostalgia sets the scene for biological nostalgia for *Wolf Solent* is also a book about lost paternity. . . . At thirty-five, the exact midpoint of the Biblical span of three-score and ten, Wolf feels that he is about to start a new life. Yet the movement toward this new life is actually circular since Wolf is travelling back into his own past as well as the rural past of industrialized society. . . . As he flees from London, a representative center of modern civilization, Wolf carries with him the memory of a man he has seen on the steps outside Waterloo Station, . . . a man of such misery that "no conceivable social readjustments or ameliorative revolutions could ever atone for it.". . . This face appears to Wolf again and again during the course of the novel, reminding him of the monstrosities of the modern world and of the existence of a sadistic impulse in the Creator of that world.

Of all the emotional baggage Wolf brings with him, the most important piece is what he calls his mythology or "life illusion." Wolf has developed a system which places himself at the center of a cosmological struggle between good and evil. . . . Since the story is told from Wolf's point of view, the structure of the novel inevitably reflects the momentous dualism of this illusion. Thus *Wolf Solent* is built upon a series of apparent oppositions. (pp. 205-06)

Wolf's sense of self-importance is stimulated by the evil he perceives. As long as he can believe that he is surrounded by sinister people and events, his identity is sustained by the illusion that he occupies a central position, that his choice between good and evil is the decisive one. But as the oppositions begin to merge, as good and evil become less and less distinguishable, as innocent explanations replace sinister interpretations, the illusion of the center can no longer hold. . . . Wolf becomes aware that the polarity he has imposed upon the world is actually within himself.

Wolf is contained within "the charmed circle of the individual's private consciousness." The special charm of the circle is that it offers the self a privileged position at the center. For Wolf, however, the charm must be broken. He is unable to sustain the illusion that he stands at the center of things. Instead, he begins to see his life as an imitation. . . . As he feels himself reliving the past, he becomes less and less a participant in and more and more an observer of his own fate. . . . As the novel progresses, involvement gives way to detachment and the compulsions of memory lapse into the anodyne of forgetfulness. (pp. 208-09)

Unlike James's narrator who stands inside the house of fiction and looks out the window, Wolf is characteristically ouside looking in. There are several explicitly voyeuristic scenes in the novel, but the voyeuristic stance is pervasive. Wolf is constantly watching others, or watching himself watching others. Since the tensions of the novel are ultimately the product of Wolf's mythology, *Wolf Solent* offers what may be the quintessential voyeuristic experience, the voyeur peeping at, and through, himself. Or, in Powys's somewhat more metaphysical formulation: "Does not all literary penetration spring from some subtle sublimation of our deepest vice? From a 'voyeur' I became a 'clairvoyeur'." . . . (p. 209)

The crucial scene in the collapse of Wolf's mythology dramatizes this "subtle sublimation." It is set in Christie's bedroom. Wolf . . . is convinced that if he commits adultery with Christie he will have completed the identification with his scandalous father and could no longer pretend to be on the side of the good. Seated on Christie's bed, he hears himself ask her to remove her dress. He is not even sure that he has actually spoken these words. And, as he wonders what will happen, he looks into the mirror—the conventional prop in scenes of erotic self-discovery—and sees neither his image nor Christie's, but rather the face of the beggar in the Waterloo Station which has been haunting him ever since he left London. Ostensibly the face appears to remind him of his allegiances, of his commitment to suffering humanity. What actually happens is that Wolf feels himself splitting in two. "For a second or two the struggle within him gave a sensation as if the very core of his consciousness—that 'hard little crystal' within the nucleus of his soul—were breaking into two halves! Then he felt as if his whole being were flowing away in water, whirling away like a mist of rain, out upon the night, over the roofs, over the darkened hills! Then came a moment's sinking into nothingness, into a grey gulf of non-existence; and then it was as if the will within him, that was beyond thought, gathered itself together in that frozen chaos and rose upwards like a shining-scaled fish, electric, vibrant, taut, and leapt into the greenish-coloured vapour that filled the room!"... Having worked through a series of imitations, Wolf here doubles himself. A new center is established—an empty, clear space between the two halves of Wolf's consciousness. And from the poles of this divided consciousness, Wolf can look into and through the center, as Powys in America had looked toward England, as the son had looked toward his "formidable begetter."

When in *A Glastonbury Romance* Johnny Geard attempts to revitalize the myth of the center—Glastonbury as the place to which the survivors of Atlantis fled, the location of a prehistoric lake village, the spot to which Joseph of Arimathea brought the Holy Grail, the site of Arthur's grave—he is only elaborating a public version of Wolf's private mythology. *A Glastonbury Romance* ends with a flood from the midst of which Glastonbury Tor rises, an image of the center and its circumference which Powys used to describe a different location on the opening page of his *Autobiography*. "The part of Derbyshire which centres round the Peak is like the boss of a shield . . .". At the center of creation stands the phallic emblem, the figure of fatherhood, the formidable begetter of the formidable circle, the pole around which the eccentric ostentatiously circles.

The same geometry controls the contrived, insistently fictional conclusion of *Wolf Solent*. Lord Carfax (whose name means the meeting place of four roads—another center) arrives and gathers up the loose ends of the plot. Wolf, always the voyeur, the outsider, peers in the window of his own house at Gerda sitting on Carfax's lap. We are reminded that Carfax had once had an affair with Wolf's mother and that he was responsible for getting Wolf his job with Urquhart. The circle has been completed and Carfax as *deus ex machina* and surrogate father empties the plot of whatever tensions it still retains.

Wolf abdicates. He wanders out of the story which had been the creation of his life illusion into a sea of golden buttercups. (pp. 209-11)

Wolf's vision then slips to a memory of a time in Weymouth when he was drinking tea and reading Wordsworth. By virtue of the allusion to Wordsworth, the yellow buttercups recall that poet's golden daffodils. The lone Wolf, the lonely writer, the lonely reader wait for a new vision to "flash upon the inward eye"—the eccentric's ultimate center, a center bounded only by the self. (p. 211)

> *George Blake, "The Eccentricity of John Cowper Powys," in* Modern Fiction Studies *(copyright © 1976, by Purdue Research Foundation, West Lafayette, Indiana, U.S.A.), Summer, 1976, pp. 201-11.*

In his last years Powys thought that the most important of his writing were the romances, and with *Wolf Solent* and *A Glastonbury Romance* in front of them few readers are likely to quarrel with that self judgement. The experience of such books is a liberation of the imagination such as one receives only from the great makers in any of the arts. . . . *A Glastonbury Romance* is demonstrably the most ample exploration into the imaginative realities of Wessex, an imaginative realm that goes back through Hardy, Barnes and Middle English to the old West Saxon literature, but *Maiden Castle* is the most compact of these explorations and the one in which the harmonization of Celt and Saxon in Wessex is most explicit. It is moreover the novel in which Powys takes to the limit his determination to counterpoint the everyday Arnold Bennett world and the E T A Hoffmann world—or the *Undine* world of de la Motte Fouqué, as readers of the *Letters . . . to Glyn Hughes* might prefer to call it. For both reasons I am unwilling to have it passed by, although I am aware that the 'Quest of the Grail', which had obsessed Powys since boyhood, is muted. The truth is that in *A Glastonbury Romance* Powys had examined the 'Quest of the Grail' in such detail that he had to be careful not to repeat himself.

After *Maiden Castle* . . . the succeeding romances, with their Welsh settings, explore the Celtic extension of the Wessex world and, no less than the Saxon Wessex romances, attest the very little noted survival of the 'Celtic' imagination that was so much heard of in the 1890's. (p. 49)

> *Bernard Jones, "Imagination All Compact," in* Books and Bookmen *(© copyright Bernard Jones 1977; reprinted with permission), February, 1977, pp. 48-9.*

*   *   *

PRIESTLEY, J(ohn) B(oynton)   1894-

Priestley, a British novelist, playwright, theater director, and essayist whom Michael George calls "something of a professional Englishman," has in his writings attempted to discover and describe the ingredients of the English personality. A keen observer, Priestley is noted for his accurate and evocative descriptions of character and setting as well as for his uncompromisingly humanistic stance. (See also *CLC*, Vols. 2, 5, and *Contemporary Authors*, Vols. 9-12, rev. ed.)

The title story [of *The Carfitt Crisis*] was—according to Mr Priestley—"originally conceived in dramatic form" and it has all the scars of an after-birth. The dialogue is of that heavy and awkward variety which is always associated with bad drama reduced to cold print, and the narrative reads like a particularly elaborate set of stage directions. The *dramatis personae* in this particular crisis are thoroughly conventional and the plot (which has something to do with the arrival of a thoroughly modern, cool and boring American into the thoroughly middle-class, anxious and unstable household of the Carfitts) turns around a predictable axis.

A certain amount of cliche is permissible on stage, of course, where recognisable human beings can be actually seen to mouth the dreadful stuff; but on the page, the enterprise becomes merely ridiculous. (p. 664)

>   *Peter Ackroyd, in* The Spectator (© *1975 by*
>   The Spectator; *reprinted by permission of*
>   The Spectator), *May 31, 1975.*

[*Found, Lost, Found: The English Way of Life* is] a disappointment. The action moves along with all the pace and energy we expect of this expert storyteller, but at the end we're left with a withered acorn of prejudice. . . . [One] of the infuriating things about this novel is that everyone keeps telling everyone else how clever he or she is, though with minimal justification. . . . His hero's travels provide Priestley with opportunities to air his prejudices, which he does with a surprising lack of sparkle. Had he written a more substantial novel he might have scored some winning points, but instead of riding the whole course on his pet hobby-horses he does not stay long enough in any one saddle to make an appreciable impact. . . . Priestley has always adopted a style which needs more elbowroom [than this].

The satirical targets are really too obvious—the Government, the civil service, shop stewards, avant garde producers of Shakespeare, Women's Libbers, dog-lovers and politically-minded students. . . . It's sad . . . to discover that a master of prose who in the past wrote so vividly about the English, not with stars in his eyes but with generosity in his heart, has lost—only momentarily, I hope—that warmth of understanding. Humour and humanity have given way to petulance, and in the process Priestley has lost both his sense of compassion and his security of marksmanship. There are some fine moments, of course. . . . They are not enough, however, to compensate for the flimsiness of the story and the faltering aim of the novelist's satirical arrows. (p. 60)

>   *Frank Granville Barker, in* Books and Bookmen (© *copyright Frank Granville Barker 1976; reprinted with permission), September, 1976.*

J. B. Priestley once complimented life for having such an easy time creating superior comic characters and situations. Novelists must strain to do this: "We hear a sneering little voice whispering, 'Absurd . . . overdrawn . . . unconvincing . . . Dickensian' . . . and so out they go, these glorious extravagances." In 71 novels, plays and collections of essays, Mr. Priestley, now 82, has made a career of sneering back at that little voice. An unrepentantly public figure, he wants his own "extravagances" to be heard and immediately understood: "No matter what the subject in hand might be, I want to write something that at a pinch I could read aloud in a barparlor."

Mr. Priestley's new novel, "Found, Lost, Found," would suit admirably for such a reading. . . . Dekker, the novel's hero, is a cultivated man who endures the "boredom and irritation" of contemporary English life by listening to Alfred Brendel's Mozart records and "floating through" on gin. (Dekker never drinks enough to get drunk, just enough to "float"—a Jesuitical distinction perhaps, but one he insists on making.) He falls in love with Kate, a woman with reforming instincts who tries to get him out of the pub by fleeing to an unknown house in the country and challenging him to find her. Not surprisingly, he does find her, but con-

tinues floating anyway. This may be Mr. Priestley's most aggressively happy ending to date.

Up to that point, however, the novel sustains an almost consistently sour note. The intentionally silly pursuit plot is a springboard for satire. Mr. Priestley has opinions on just about everything, from contemporary sexuality ("acrobatics, gristle, spasms and a let-down") to the song "Happy Birthday" (a "detestable composition"). Clearly he was disenchanted when he wrote this novel.

In one scene, Dekker meets a rock-and-roll group, whose garish, funky makeup in a dark theater reminds him of "patients in a jungle fever hospital." The scene does not quite come off, partly because the subject is too easy a target, partly because Mr. Priestley blasts away too loudly and too many times. He complains that rock-and-roll shouts in our ears, but so does he. In the overtly satirical sections, his characters pretend too feebly to mediate between his views and his story. When he has Kate denounce political groups on both right and left as "idiots" of opposite extremes, his own centrist views are too palpably obvious.

Mr. Priestley's "extravagance" works best, not with programmatic social satire, but with the broader "Dickensian" comedy that catches individuals in the act of turning themselves into caricatures. The many grotesques in this novel—Mr. Foxbeater (who has "an enormous flat face like an unbaked pie"), Mr. Ivybridge (who looks "vaguely like an admiral of about 1910"), Lady Brindleways (who insists on being called Lady "Brin-*lew*-ays" at London parties)—smack superficially of Dickens, but Mr. Priestley observes them with his own shrewd, practiced eye.

Dekker, who constantly encounters these people in the novel, is so bored at times that he intentionally becomes one of them, even to the point of assuming an absurd name (J. Carlton Mistletoe, Rufus Seddlebirk) to fit the role. His boredom is a role, a kind of Wildean pose. When life makes it necessary to act ridiculous, Mr. Priestley seems to be saying, one should do it consciously, with "imagination and heart." Mrs. Dragby, an old-line feminist, demonstrates precisely these qualities when she responds to a Dekker jibe with severity, "Mr. Dekker, I must tell you that one reason I have been able to do so much in my chosen field—*is*—that I'm entirely deficient in a sense of humour."

This is in itself a witty statement, and Mrs. Dragby knows it. Whenever someone like her comes on, we can hear Mr. Priestley sneering back once again at the ugly little voice that censors laughter. (pp. 10-11)

>   *Jack Sullivan, "English Laughter," in* The New York Times Book Review (© *1977 by The New York Times Company; reprinted by permission), August 28, 1977, pp. 10-11.*

* * *

PYNCHON, Thomas   1937-

Pynchon is an experimental, award-winning American novelist in the "black humor" tradition of Barth, Heller, and Vonnegut. Utilizing his strong technical and scientific background, Pynchon explodes in his novels traditional literary form, speech, and style to paint a self-destructive world. Richard Schickel has described *Gravity's Rainbow* as a novel which, "turning ever inward on itself, like one of the characters it contains, . . . must inevitably self-destruct in our hands." Pynchon is also the author of *V.* and *The Crying of*

Lot 49. (See also *CLC*, Vols. 2, 3, 6, and *Contemporary Authors*, Vols. 17-20, rev. ed.)

Pynchon's descriptive brilliance and architectonic inventiveness are such that one sometimes forgets the simplicity of the formula on which he builds his 900-page structure [*Gravity's Rainbow*]. (p. 47)

Gravity's Rainbow, at least at first glance, reveals many of the same generic features as [Barth's] *Giles Goat-Boy.* It, too, presents an enormously ramified fictional structure meant to give an encyclopedic account of the relentless destructiveness of history in our era. Here, too, the menace of apocalypse is conveyed with a kind of savage hilarity, the characters purposely reduced to grotesquely named cartoons, verbal slapstick abounding, bizarre and lurid fantasies spinning out of historical centers, orgiastic scrambles and endlessly deviant sexual couplings deployed to incarnate the perverseness and the cynical exhaustion of the human spirit. The general effect of *Gravity's Rainbow,* however, is quite different from that of Barth's book, this novel being alternately repellent and engrossing, intolerably tedious and illuminating, but not finally trivial. . . .

Pynchon is fundamentally a philosophic writer—at times, one suspects, too inexorably philosophic for the formal needs of the novel—and he [explores] basic questions of probability and determinism, entropy and order, randomness and paranoid system, in intricate detail. Possessing an extraordinarily well-stocked mind, he is able to put to active use as much precisely observed lore—from science, history, and popular culture—as any living writer in English.

Indeed, *Gravity's Rainbow* often seems only residually narrative, less a novel than an "anatomy," one of those eccentric baroque compendia of bizarre associative learning like Robert Burton's *The Anatomy of Melancholy* (1621) and Sir Thomas Browne's *Religio Medici* (1643). Pynchon is a brilliant stylist with a love for mimetic detail (though the overall conception of the book is schematic and mythic rather than mimetic), and this novel is studded with impressive set-pieces, from the evocation of a dozen generations of a family in a New England graveyard near the beginning to the great lyric description of the ultimate flight of the rocket at the very end. Most appropriately for a novel in which the central symbol is a complex instrument of technology, the writer is able to shape the imagery and conceptual materials of science and technology into vital elements of his style. (p. 48)

For all these indubitable resources, *Gravity's Rainbow* is a novel that satisfies one unevenly in segments rather than as a whole. The problem is not that it lacks structural unity. On the contrary, Pynchon is the most artfully designing of the new American novelists, and the seemingly disparate pieces of his novel are interwoven with an elaborate tracery of verbal, imagistic, folkloric, theosophic, pop-culture, and scientific motifs. The difficulty is rather in Pynchon's schematic conception of the movement of history which is his subject. I would argue, in fact, that he closely resembles Barth, Barthelme, and Vonnegut in finally not taking history very seriously, despite the overwhelming density of actual historical detail in the book. . . . The ingenuity of Pynchon's method is sometimes pointedly suggestive in making it difficult for us to distinguish between historical fact and fictional invention. . . . [He sometimes presents]

not history but paranoid fantasy using historical materials—or eschatological symbolism drawn out of history, which amounts to the same thing—and I don't think Pynchon himself really escapes the schematic simplicity of the paranoid vision merely by naming paranoia repeatedly as an explicit theme and attributing it to his principal characters. (pp. 48-9)

Pynchon, the most intelligent of the new American writers, keenly perceives the problematics of the concepts with which he is working but is nevertheless trapped by them as a novelist. If the end of history is at hand, historical time being only a welter of statistical events, without causal links, all bent on destruction, there is no objective ground for narrative structure; calculated formal design must substitute for anything like development in the novel; and perhaps most crucial, there are no criteria for *selectivity* in the novelist's shuttle between history and invention.

Let me briefly elaborate this last point because I think it may explain how *Gravity's Rainbow* can be at the same time a complex architectonic structure and a lamentably flabby novel. If history is no longer a realm of concatenation, if there are no necessary connections among discrete events and no possibility of a hierarchy of materials ranged along some scale of significance, any associative chain of fantasies, any crotchety hobbyistic interest, any technical fascination with the rendering of odd trivia, can be pursued by the novelist as legitimately as the movement of supposedly "significant" actions. The end of history, in other words, is a writer's license for self-indulgence, and Pynchon utilizes that license for page after dreary page of *Gravity's Rainbow.* . . . (p. 49)

The lack of selectivity leads to local flaws; the unwillingness to make differential judgments about historical events results in a larger inadequacy of the novel as a whole. . . . One would never guess from this novel, for example, that there were after all significant differences between a totalitarianism unsurpassed in its ruthlessness and political systems that had some institutional guarantees of individual freedoms, or between a state that was dedicated to fulfillment through genocide and one that was not. It is precisely for this reason that Pynchon's Europe of 1944-45 seems so much like a "moonscape," despite all the seemingly documentary detail.

Such leveling of historical distinctions is disastrously encouraged by the post-Freudian cliché through which Pynchon sees all events and around which he elaborates his central symbol. The Rocket is, of course, a monstrous phallus, Eros turned to Thanatos, the Death Instinct having absorbed all mankind's libidinal energy. . . . Virtually all the ingenious contrivances of plot and character in *Gravity's Rainbow* are finally illustrations of this single idea. History reduced so exclusively to the working out of the Death Instinct is metapsychological myth, no history at all, and what it generates in the novel is a proliferation of variations on one unswerving formula that in the end tells us nothing new about the challengingly ambiguous interplay of people and power in real historical time. (pp. 49-50)

Robert Alter, "The New American Novel"
(reprinted from Commentary *by permission;*
copyright © 1975 by Robert Alter), in
Commentary, *November, 1975, pp. 47-50.*

From his very earliest work, Pynchon's apparently encyclopedic knowledge, verbal ingenuity, and particular obsessions are apparent. Certain themes and subjects recur constantly: song, sexual perversion, suicide, science, slapstick, sewers, shit and Southwest Africa are some of them. Pynchon's fictional people are also distinctive from the very beginning of his career. There seem always to be two basic types of characters, those questing after some profound mystery, and those poor suckers who unwittingly are caught up in someone else's mad quest. Isolation and ignorance are the ground rules of the human condition in a bleak and unpredictable world. There is Pynchon's humour too, and Pynchon is a master of every variety from slapstick to parody, all of it based on the theory that no laugh, no matter how cheap, is ever worth passing by.

Pynchon's early stories are competent, workmanlike efforts, formally more conventional than one might expect. They are flawed by an overload of literary allusions, with those to T. S. Eliot, Conrad, Henry Adams and Shakespeare the most frequent. They suffer, too, from being a little too neat, with every strand so carefully tied that the stories exhaust themselves in their unfolding. What they do reveal is Pynchon even at the start of his career employing his most characteristic technique, the use of material from disciplines other than literature as fictional metaphor. (p. 40)

Pynchon has continued to use cognitive models from discourses other than literature, like ethnology or sociology, but especially science, as fictional metaphors. *V.*, for example, carries on Pynchon's extension of the notion of entropy, but it contains a great deal more besides. In fact, like most first novels, it deals with far too much. It is several novels under one roof: a New York novel (obligatory for American authors), a Navy novel, an undergraduate novel, a war novel and an historical novel. Through all the overwriting, however, Pynchon's considerable talent is clearly visible. His creation of V., a magnificently decadent woman who moves in and out of the major events of recent European history (and who may be Henry Adams's 'Virgin'), is a really traditional novelistic symbol which Pynchon uses to organise the book's loose structure. As V. grows older, she replaces more and more of her body with prosthetic devices, until she is almost entirely a mechanical thing, perhaps like modern European society itself. Chiefly through her experiences, Pynchon explores the idea that modern culture is obsessed by the sexual love of death. (This idea, inadequately but tantalisingly adumbrated in *V.*, and several of its characters, will reappear in *GR* [*Gravity's Rainbow*].)

The Crying of Lot 49, Pynchon's second novel, surprised his growing cult audience by being as tight and restrained as *V.* is diffuse and self-indulgent. Even so, it manages to include, among other diversions, a running parody of Jacobean tragedy that must be one of the funniest pastiches ever written. The novel's theme is paranoia, and it narrates the discovery by the heroine, Oedipa Maas, of a plot to take over the world existing not only in the present, but throughout the historical past as far back as the Renaissance. Pynchon was on to something: long before Watergate was even a twinkle in CREEP's eye, he had tagged paranoia as the American national disease. *Lot 49* is also a book about the way American society has become an information machine, in which communications are manufactured and propagated faster than they can be absorbed. . . . Paranoids sift the

endless number of signs bombarding us, and use them to create structures of meaning. They re-interpret empty data into complete, coherent systems. Paranoids are therefore not only creative, they are the true heroes of our time. We abdicate in the face of overwhelming odds—they fight back. (pp. 40-1)

[The] labyrinthine complications of [*Gravity's Rainbow*] are virtually impossible to understand, often even to follow. *V.* was considered absurdly complex, but compared to *GR* (which might well be called 'V-2') it is crystalline in its clarity. . . .

Pynchon's belief is that the explanation for [the] mass death wish is essentially historical, and much of the novel is an effort of historical analysis, finding the roots of the malaise in our distant past. (It is in large part the historical nature of its subject-matter which makes *GR* such a difficult book to read.) . . . It should be said that [his] is hardly an original insight [into the death instinct], and that Freud and Norman O. Brown, both of whose work Pynchon knows well, have said much the same thing long ago. Pynchon's originality is to be found rather in the way he shows this instinct in operation, and in the way he postulates it came into being. And, paradoxically, he locates the original evil in that most understandable and most noble of human urges, the desire to make sense of the world around us. (p. 41)

[Pynchon's language] has always been idiosyncratic, and, . . . I suspect, this is not a difficulty for English readers alone; Pynchon's language *is* difficult, and would be perceived as difficult by a reader of any nationality, American or otherwise. What may be of more moment is the resistance to this difficulty.

To allow oneself to be put off by this difficulty is in effect to state that one is not willing to work to read a novel. . . . Perhaps . . . there has always been an aliterary quality about the best novels . . . , requiring that one move from the word outward to the world, and henceforth experience it anew, with one's perceptions of it permanently altered. It is precisely this kind of effort in which Pynchon is engaged in *GR:* perhaps, then, [a] comparison with Joyce, or for that matter with another more explicitly social novelist, Dickens, would not be all that far-fetched. (p. 43)

F. S. Schwarzbach, "Pynchon's Gravity," in The New Review *(© The New Review Ltd., 11 Greek Street, London WIV 5LE), June, 1976, pp. 39-43.*

[My intention is to offer] a usable handle on the [ideas in *Gravity's Rainbow*] by demonstrating Pynchon's pervasive indebtedness to the school of psychoanalytic culture criticism best exhibited in the two major works of Norman O. Brown—*Life against Death* and *Love's Body*. . . .

The structure of *GR* is episodic, with vignettes from multiple plot lines intertwining like the molecules of a dozen covalent chemicals dumped together at once. As indicated by the stylized square film-projector sprocket holes used to divide the chapters, Pynchon's chosen artistic metaphor is the novel as movie; and, while the idea of the omniscient narrator as camera eye has long been cliché, Pynchon's handling of the device is consistently fresh and imaginative. *GR* is basically a takeoff on the historical-novel genre, as processed by the makers of B-grade movies about, and of, the period of World War II. . . . *GR* constitutes a revisionist analysis of a turning point in contemporary history: the resolution of the European power struggle and the transition to the postwar balance of terror and the on-again-off-again cold war that we still live with.

Like Pynchon's two previous novels, *V.* and *The Crying of Lot 49,* the plot of *GR* takes the form of a quest attended by numerous interlocking conspiracies. As before, narrative "plot" is continuous with conspiratorial "plot." (p. 873)

Movie techniques pervade even the finest details of Pynchon's narrative presentation. For the movie audience the mere *sequence* of scenes is sufficient; if we fail to catch the connections favored by the director, we invent others equally adequate to our needs. Thus, a scene in *GR* typically plunges us into a chaos of human appearances and material appurtenances objectively described, and we perforce read on, foundering haphazardly toward an understanding of the present action—of what is simply *going on.* Pynchon composes, it would seem, by first projecting an imagined scene on the screen of his mind and then transcribing what he has observed according to the unmediated sequence of raw perception. Moreover, the main significance of hardly anything of importance is ever revealed at first mention. As a result, it is virtually impossible to assimilate the book in a single reading. *GR* is designedly difficult to read because Pynchon is determined to have the manner of his fiction mirror the complexity of contemporary existence.

Furthermore, Pynchon's view is "phenomenological," in the sense that official pronouncements and the interpretations of establishment historians are meaningless in the face of the reality of the event, the immediate impact on the human organism and its hope for a viable future. . . . The determining factor in Pynchon's allegory of the human condition is the unholy alliance that has developed between, on the one hand, media, technology, and the inanimate in general and, on the other hand, the will to power of those who control the dominant commercial and bureaucratic structures. (p. 874)

From the beginning Pynchon's writing has been haunted by an awareness of T. S. Eliot's fundamental point—that a totally secular culture is absurd and unworkable. Having killed all the old gods, we turn and, out of the strangest materials, reify new and more terrible gods. The one line in *GR* that could serve as motto for all the rest occurs in Walter Rathenau's lecture . . . to the gathered "corporate Nazi crowd." "All talk of cause and effect is secular history, and secular history is a diversionary tactic.". . .

[In] innumerable ways *GR* reads like a historical product of the late fifties, when the Cold War was most intense. . . . [One] reason [for this] is that this period produced the book that provides a conceptual framework into which the literary content of a fiction such as *GR* can be subsumed. In the Introduction to *Life against Death* Brown anticipates the thrust of his entire argument and adumbrates the deepest fears of the fifties intellectual. . . . Brown begins with the Freudian postulate that the essence of Homo sapiens is repression. Individual man represses himself in the name of deferred gratifications and, through the institutions of society, collaborates in a condition of general repression. Repression of the self precedes social repression. . . .

History is also viewed [by Brown] as the product in human

praxis of the gap between what men tell themselves that they want and what unconsciously they really want. (p. 875)

[It] should be apparent that *GR,* a sixties novel born late, is shot through with the particular style of Freudian thinking represented by Brown. The issue here is the *use* Pynchon made of those ideas identified preeminently with Brown.

In *V.* we recognize the influence of Henry Adams' dark meditations on the second law of thermodynamics. But entropy is naturally conceived as a sort of straight-line decline toward inanition, leading to a *gradual* cessation of all the motions of life. In *GR* Pynchon reverses his theme but picks up another of Adams' concerns, the acceleration of history, and his metaphysical speculations now center on the far more violent implications of gravitational pull—the exponential acceleration of falling at thirty-two feet per second per second. . . . [Within] the structure of Pynchon's social speculations, gravity in the macrocosm corresponds to the mechanism of repression in the little world of man, the microcosm. (p. 876)

[Pynchon's point is that] repression gives us individuality and culture, a collective history, as gravity gives the earth form and configuration. Physics provides the metaphor for metaphysics, and for social theory as well. Gravity is the ultimate metaphor in the novel for the human repression that is its theme.

At the limit of Brown's analysis there are only two alternatives, each achieving through different means the same end: the disappearance of man and the abolition of human history. . . . Brown and Pynchon . . . not only mutually fear the fiery consummation of the world but, paradoxically, seem simultaneously to long for it. "To bring this world to an end: the consummation devoutly to be wished, the final judgment" . . . this I take to be one meaning of Pynchon's title. God sent the rainbow to Noah as a promise that the world would never again be destroyed by flood, but made no promise excluding fire, and Revelations suggests that fire will indeed be the mode of the final judgment. (pp. 876-77)

Pynchon and Brown . . . agree that the reason social amelioration is impossible is that the slaves love their chains. They must; else the situation would be otherwise. This interpretation is not likely to endear Pynchon and Brown to anyone with Marxist leanings, but, as it turns out, they both explicitly reject Marxism as a political philosophy and theory of human nature, and for the same reasons: its materialism ignores the fact that the world is a projection of spirit, and its much touted dialectical method is merely a cover for a perverted millennialism, itself an excuse for totalitarian structures.

The primary locus for the theme of repression in *GR* is, not Marxism, but a strangely similar dogma—namely, Calvinism, particularly the form we encounter in Slothrop's Puritan background. . . . In one way or another Pynchon manages to trace back to early Calvinism some of the major perversions of the modern world. . . . Thus Pynchon's view of historical development agrees with Brown's: "whereas in previous ages life had been a mixture of Eros and Thanatos, in the Protestant era life becomes a pure culture of the death instinct.". . . (pp. 878-79)

Brown traces some of our most unpleasant symbolic associations back to early Protestantism and its peculiar origins. For Luther, an entire moral complex of anal repulsions associating blackness, excrement, and death was cathected by his special concept of the Devil—traditionally the Black Man, and seen by later fundamentalists in the Negro. The explanation of the Schwarzkommando offered to his colleagues by Gavin Trefoil [in *GR*] of the psychoanalytic wing of Psi Section exhibits the same insight as Brown's "Studies in Anality": "He had not meant to offend sensibilities, only to show the others, decent fellows all, that their feelings about blackness were tied to feelings about shit, and feelings about shit to feelings about putrefaction and death. It seemed to him so clear . . . why wouldn't they listen? Why wouldn't they admit that their repressions *had*, in a sense that Europe in the last weary stages of its perversion of magic has lost, *had* incarnated real and living men . . .". . . . Now in context this is both dramatic—and to that extent provisional—and wildly comic; is nevertheless as close as we are likely to come to the meaning of the whites' relation to blacks in the novel. (p. 880)

[In *LAD* Brown argues] that genital organization is constructed by the death instinct. In other words, our adult concentration on the end pleasure of genital organization is viewed as a direct product of those particular Western neuroses that are reflected in our social environment, characterized as it is by commerce, technology, and war. In every important case, sexual behavior in *GR* conforms to the social criticism implied in this theory. There is no totally healthy sex in the novel because the characters are all participating willingly in a society committed to the death instinct. Each of the sexual oddities is traceable to some peculiarly Western social perversion. (pp. 882-83)

Under conditions of general repression we cannot hope to escape the returns of our negations or of our assertions. The villain is nothing less than human nature itself, and the diseased rationality it employs. As with the "dream of annihilation" in *V.*, there is a horrid secret at the center of *GR*, a secret that the narrator hesitates to reveal directly because it sounds mad; it can never be proved, only felt. But the idea is simple: man's uniqueness in the creation is a function of his sickness, of the fact that he is the one true aberration in nature. . . . Unable to be satisfied with simply being here, being alive, collective man, through repression both personal and social-historical, has pursued the death instinct nearly to the extreme of sacrificing all nature to the logic of his compulsion. (p. 883)

The end of *GR* is, in ordinary terms, pessimistic: the Counterforce fails, Slothrop is lost, Blicero's romantic affirmation offers only sterility and death, the Schwarzkommando are eliminated from history, the bomb falls on us all in Los Angeles, the world ends. The expressions of hope along the way have been few; but Pynchon does recognize, as a minor character puts it, the possibility "that some chance of renewal, some dialectic, is still operating in History." . . . *Dialectics*, in fact, becomes the charm Pynchon holds up, as he finishes his novel, against the vampire logic of one-way time; and this is precisely the straw at which Brown grasps for the conclusion of *LAD*. . . . Brown defines dialectics as "an activity of consciousness struggling to circumvent the limitations imposed by the formal-logical law of contradiction." . . . According to the Aristotelian law of contradiction nothing can be, or be in, its opposite. . . . And the law of contradiction is a close description

of Calvinist dualism: things are divided into two separate and opposite categories and then pushed apart, polarized as much as possible. . . . Dialectical consciousness, on the other hand, would be "the struggle of the mind to circumvent repression and make the unconscious conscious"; it would be "a manifestation of Eros"; and it would be "a step toward that Dionysian ego which does not negate any more" [according to Brown]. . . .

Throughout *GR* Pynchon pits dialectical consciousness against the dead hand of dualism. Dialectical reality receives notable expression in the vision of primal unity attributed to the non-Westerners and associated with the natural world as it existed prior to Western consciousness. (p. 884)

As a matter of esthetics, the dialectical impulse common to Pynchon and Brown is evidenced mainly in their increasing reliance on metaphor and symbolism. Brown escapes the logical difficulties of *LAD* by shifting in *LB* to the abstract realms of transcendental mysticism; and toward the end of *GR* Pynchon escapes the strictures of his realistic story line by increasingly fading into surrealism and thematic fancy, playing variations on themes already established. Brown, however, uses the term "symbolism" in rather special ways. As he puts it in the chapter on "Unity," "Symbolism is mind making connections (correspondences) rather than distinctions (separations). . . . In other words, Brown's symbolism is conceptual and associative.

Pynchon employs this sort of symbolism, and he is also interested in what the symbol-making impulse tells us about human nature. The runaway symbolism in *GR* (e.g., the double S) sometimes just points to Pynchon's favorite notion that all of reality is invariably a mental construct. If we take the specific constructions too seriously, not only do we miss the point, we *become* the point. There is a neat correlation between the omnibus feminine symbolism of the mons veneris in *V.* and the omnibus masculine symbolism of the rocket in *GR;* but the hopeless paranoid projections that impel the endless quests of *V.* should serve as warning. The subject is not the "meaning" of the symbol but our very Western propensity to seek meaning, to project it into the most empty vaginal void, if necessary. On another tack, the lapses into surrealism in *GR* . . . operate as confirmations of the inadequacy of a perceptual structure based on the reality principle, and the same goes for the thematic use of drugs and movie-director talk. . . .

Pynchon is also trying to say something about the ultimate illusion, which most of us are not yet ready to accept as such, the illusion of personality. Brown insists that "psychic individuals" are "an illusion" . . . and that "The inner voice, the personal salvation, the private experience are all based on an illusory distinction." . . . In *GR* the illusory nature of the phenomenal world and the transparency of the individual are evidenced by dreams and archetypes, among other means. . . . Dreams and dreaming pervade the narrative, to the extent that the line between various waking and sleeping, conscious and unconscious, states is instructively blurred. And Pynchon would agree [with Brown's assertion] that "there is only one psyche, a general possession of mankind" . . . , with the reservation that archetypes themselves seem to be to some extent culturally determined. (p. 885)

Symbolism in *GR* also takes the form of "signs," especially of the sort dear to the early Calvinists, for whom nature was God's book, and every natural object or occurrence appeared as evidence of a spiritual state or allegorical lesson. Here for once Pynchon is in sympathy . . . with all the idealists throughout history who have thought that, even if the external world is real, and not just God's movie, we can have no direct knowledge of it, so that the only "rational" way to approach the world is to view it as a system of symbols relating to inner states or spiritual realities. . . . Everything is a sign, nothing is "real." In the modern wasteland, with all the monotheistic gods dead and Pan still suppressed, the signs are evidence of spiritual waste. (pp. 885-86)

One unstated metaphor is that of the book itself as rocket flight. It begins with a V-2 going up over the Channel and ends with an ICBM falling on Los Angeles, and the final section . . . disintegrates into flying fragments like a rocket exploding, ending, like all such charismatic events, with a loud and resonant silence. Matter and manner are thus joined, fused by the white-hot heat of intellect. Yet this fusion is accompanied by a special sort of tension, located in the reader and generated by Pynchon's deliberate stepping-up of the degree of surrealism to an almost intolerable level. . . .

Two specific factors create tension in the reader: violations of historical chronology and the progressive disintegration of the narrative into chaos. The fiction of linear time is fruitfully violated by reminiscences of American adolescence and by snatches of media and street experience in Los Angeles from the period the novel was being written. . . . In the final movement Pynchon is bravely attempting to compose sequences "forever beyond the reach, the rape, of literal-minded explication." . . . One way is to load the narrative with more fresh, evanescent suggestiveness than it can bear. . . .

Another weighty means of blowing up the narrative (thereby forcing the reader to take up the burden of meaning personally, or give up) is [, as Brown says,] "to reconnect words with silence; to let the silence in." . . . Brown and Pynchon are both fighting "Against gravity; against the gravity of literalism, which keeps our feet on the ground." . . . The solution advocated in the final chapter of *LB*, "Nothing," is silence: "Get the nothingness back into words. The aim is words with nothing to them; words that point beyond themselves rather than to themselves; transparencies, empty words. Empty words, corresponding to the void in things." . . . The stakes are high, the goals many: a purgation and cleansing, setting the stage for a fresh start; repealing repression, annihilating all inhibitions; and, the sine qua non, making the unconscious conscious. (p. 886)

The tension generated by the final section—between the reader's expectations for literary endings and the author's determination to defeat those expectations—is itself a paradigm of the dialectical imagination. The choice is between, on the one hand, an artifice completed, fixed, and therefore dead and, on the other, the pulse of life; and the synthesis of elements is an art form, the novel genre itself, brought back to life. A similar dialectical tension exists in an absolute sense between style and content in this novel. The content affirms death, since it tells the truth: that we are all like Slothrop, who is "in love, in sexual love, with his, and his race's, death." . . . The style affirms life, since the intuitive basis of that marvelously poetic and spontaneous prose is the author's own enactment of what Brown calls "an erotic sense of reality." . . . The nihilism of *GR* is only apparent; it is actually anarchy that Pynchon affirms, and the medium is the message. The orgasmic rush—the continual *nowness* —of Pynchon's present-tense style is a direct transcription of the life instinct. By joyfully embracing and celebrating all the death instincts of Western man in a style of unmediated euphoria, *GR* dramatizes the perpetual struggle of life against death. And thus we disaffirm the supposed pessimism of *GR*. The solution is Rilke's, as quoted by Brown: "Whoever rightly understands and celebrates death, at the same time magnifies life." . . .

Pynchon's style is also his primary evidence against determinism. He shares with most contemporary novelists an obsession with man's freedom. . . . It is strange how critics keep looking to the mere *content* of novels for some kind of hope—for confirmation of the old humanistic concept of the self, or for evidence of the resistance of human goodness against the inroads of greed and power, or for some overt moral; whereas, strictly speaking, and from a psychoanalytic point of view, there *isn't* any hope—certainly not of the kind they entertain. We are all under sentence of death. But Pynchon does have a kind of hope, though like Brown's hope it does not attach to anything in this material-political world. Nothing really matters but individual freedom, and Pynchon knows that the best defense of freedom is . . . the miracle of language itself—language, an irreducibly intuitive symbolic process. (p. 887)

Lawrence C. Wolfley, excerpted from "Repression's Rainbow: The Presence of Norman O. Brown in Pynchon's Big Novel," in PMLA, 92 *(copyright © 1977 by the Modern Language Association of America; reprinted by permission of the Modern Language Association of America), October, 1977, pp. 873-89.*

Q

QUOIREZ, Françoise
   See SAGAN, Françoise

R

*　　*　　*

REZNIKOFF, Charles　1894-1976

An American poet, novelist, translator, and legal editor, Reznikoff was primarily known as an Objectivist poet. (See also *Contemporary Authors*, Vols. 33-36; obituary, Vols. 61-64; *Contemporary Authors Permanent Series*, Vol. 2.)

What has Charles Reznikoff in common with Rod Carew, star second-baseman of the Minnesota Twins? Just this: both are excellent all-around players who (possibly because, with admirable restraint, they don't always go for the fences) are relatively unsung, despite batting averages that annually approach .400. Like only a handful of modern poets—Yeats comes quickest to mind—the eighty-one year old Reznikoff has not merely sustained his gifts over a blessedly long career, but he actually seems to improve with age, to "develop" his vision and his scope with an integrity and drive that should warm the hearts of any English department. Yet most of Reznikoff's many books were first published at his own expense, and until very recently, it has only been at odd times, here and there, that he has received a portion of the recognition that is unquestionably his due. At those times, his name has been rightfully invoked on behalf of a number of movements and causes: Reznikoff is an Objectivist, an urban poet, an Old Testament prophet, "the dean of Jewish-American poets": he is all these things, and yet his authentic and original voice makes such classifications seem somehow beside the point. Since World War I, when his first writings appeared, Reznikoff has spoken with a true seriousness the more poignant because of its capacity for irony, and with a degree of human sympathy that is quite remarkable among American poets, historically and currently, who are likely to be so obsessed with *self* that often, when they introduce the *other,* it is for the purpose of swallowing him whole. (p. 37)

Reznikoff builds both [*Testimony* and *Holocaust*] like the lawyer he was trained to be, sure of his jury's ability to infer from the evidence an understanding of a reality which, in the case of *Holocaust,* contradicts the very faculty of understanding. Narratives are presented here with the denuded style, the seemingly aloof understatement, and the brutally straightforward prosaicism required by the intensity of the horror at the heart of this darkness. . . . (p. 38)

[The] Objectivist injunction is to let reality speak for itself, to state the externals of a thing or event, and leave unspoken (or edit out) the emotions, which—if the poet be a good enough reporter—the reader may be counted on to provide for himself. It has always been Reznikoff's special enterprise to jolt the epiphanous moment from its too-familiar surroundings; [in *Holocaust*] he means to rouse from the anesthesia of sentimental generalization, and from the sedation of cliches, a pain that inheres (and remains) in specifics of time and place. . . .

Reznikoff opens the mouth of suffering and makes it quiver with the voice of survival, a voice capable of the real and tough affirmation implicit in the struggle not at all to sweeten up the story while making it "literature". (p. 39)

> *David Lehman, in* Poetry (© *1976 by The Modern Poetry Association; reprinted by permission of the Editor of* Poetry), *April, 1976.*

Charles Reznikoff's spare lines have been with us longer than most poets influenced by him have been alive. Eighty-one years old when he died in January, a central figure and elder statesman of that group of poets labelled "objectivist," he remained austerely beyond fashion, committed as ever to that which Louis Zukofsky noted about his work in Poetry magazine in 1931, "the sincerity which has seen, considered and weighed."

For Reznikoff, the poem attains to the condition of the photograph rather than the lyric—the photograph, in the words of Walter Benjamin, as the "posthumous moment," the moment rescued from time. In Reznikoff, the uttered image is something other than a symbol; it becomes a kind of window framing actual particularities and occasions, realized so authentically that they resonate with an enormous life of associations beyond the image's frame. This preciseness of realization, at root a refusal to sentimentalize its subject matter, makes of Reznikoff, among other things, our quintessential urban poet. Through his work we come to know a certain life intimately, a history, usage, custom, even religious and exalted moments with barely a rhetorical gesture. This objective mastery, apparent in even his earliest work, . . . has produced a body of poems remarkable for the unobtrusive manner in which they operate. Thus . . . [there may be] a reticence which has less to do with modesty than with accurate registration, metaphor being made so much a part of the observation we hardly notice the shift in the level of discourse. This simultaneity of judgment and tact is a form of humility, a desire that "we," as Reznikoff notes, "whose lives are only a few words," meet in the thing seen and not in the personality of the seer.

At the center of Reznikoff's writing, concomitant with this seeing for oneself, is the aloneness of the moral witness, a solitude having little to do with the "alienation" normally ascribed to Jewish writers. In Reznikoff, this isolation seems less a product of experience than of insistence and fundamental choice. . . . It is a choice referring back to a deeper set of traditions, traditions embedded in Jewish religious and philosophical themes, and their influence can be felt not only in the content of much of Reznikoff's poetry but also in its form. The attitude it displays toward language is close to (and may well be derived from) the cabalists, those compilers and annotators of the Jewish mystical tradition who, as the scholar Gershom Scholem noted, "revel in objective description" and who feel that language "reflects the fundamental spiritual nature of the world." There is, in Reznikoff, an awe and wonder at the power of language. . . .

No other poet, it strikes me, with perhaps the exception of Williams, has more thoroughly refused the artifices of style and chosen to let words have "their daylight meanings," to speak first of all, humanely and communicatively.

This restraint of Reznikoff's before the possibilities of language seems at once spiritually felt and, paradoxically, modern. It is a modernity diverging sharply from the subjectivity of much contemporary verse practice, particularly from the more popular surrealistic and confessional modes, yet it is astonishing in its power to do justice, exact justice, to contemporary life. . . .

In Reznikoff, [his] power to invoke the humanity of the reader seems ultimately in the service of prophecy and vision. . . .

At times mordant and witty, at times grave, Reznikoff's work achieved that vantage between objective and subjective worlds, between instruction and pleasure, the mark of moral vision. . . . So rare and precious a vision we are in great need of; it remains with us in his work.

> *Michael Heller, "Charles Reznikoff, 1894-1976," in* The New York Times Book Review *(© 1976 by The New York Times Company; reprinted by permission), May 16, 1976, p. 47.*

Although a curt, imagistic method persists in Reznikoff's early poetry, a different manner gradually emerges and comes to dominate his work. Behind this manner is a strong narrative drive. At first, as in the 1920 poem "Ghetto Funeral," nothing is explicit. There are hints of a story line concerning a man who has committed suicide and his wife before and after her widowhood, but the narrative direction is purposely suppressed in order that the intense experiences of the individuals involved can be evoked. They are not actually described, but merely characterized. These poems are less precise, looser than the imagist poems. They tend toward vagueness.

In the fourth section of the collected poems [*Poems 1918-1936*], which contains writings from 1921, there is a group of poems, originally entitled "Jews," which presents a series of short character sketches implying a group history transcending individual lives. Thus, although each individual character is presented in a given situation—the young woman maneuvered into an unfortunate marriage in "Provided For," or the man making plans for a son he does not know is dead in "A Son with a Future"—together the poems create a little history of the immigrant Jewish community. Individual story is subordinate to a larger implied historical narrative. This direction becomes more obvious in *By The Waters of Manhattan,* published in 1929, where the implied narrative is more widely cultural, being based upon the Old Testament as conveyed through first-person addresses in the voices of "Israel," "King David," and others.

Reznikoff's poetry never fully succeeds. There are too many short poems that are speciously alert, like this one.

> My hair was caught in the wheels of a clock
> and torn from my head: see, I am bald!

Though he is more successful in the poems that include an implied story or history, these works lack lyric intensity and, like the *In Memoriam* poems of 1933-34, sound more like translations than original compositions. One has the feeling that words are being marshalled into rhetorical position to do battle, not gathered together for mutual stimulation.

Charles Reznikoff's poetry, despite its strengths, suffers from a division between lyric and narrative impulses. (pp. 85-6)

> *John R. Reed, in* The Ontario Review *(copyright © 1976 by The Ontario Review), Fall-Winter, 1976-77.*

*   *   *

RICHLER, Mordecai   1931-

Richler is a Canadian novelist, screenwriter, essayist, short story writer, and children's book writer who combines humor and satire with a strong moral and historical sense to create his interpretation of Jewish and Canadian experience; George Woodcock calls him "the essential Canadian." Richler is best known for *The Apprenticeship of Duddy Kravitz*, the story of a Montreal boy's attempt to outfox society. (See also *CLC*, Vols. 3, 5, and *Contemporary Authors*, Vols. 65-68.)

"I have never," says Bellow's Dangling Man, "found another street that resembled St. Dominique. . . . I sometimes think it is the only place where I was ever allowed to encounter reality."

This reality, this place, is the province of Mordecai Richler. . . .

["The Street" is] a lovely book, irrepressibly alive, funny, mean, self-derisive. Richler is technically adroit at the management of ricocheting impressions, at undercutting himself abruptly so that his material goes around unexpected corners, at engaging the reader wholly in a miniature world already to a degree familiar. . . .

A memoir of a place and of a time—"I have elected myself to get it right"—"The Street" cannot be read as literal autobiography. Of the 10 stories, reminiscences and essays, some seem obvious fiction (these are at once the most carefully structured and the least substantial), some personal, some a combination of the two. Some are first-person, some third, and in some cases, minor details from the original magazine pieces have been adjusted to make it all hang together more. The streets and certain characters—Duddy, Hersh—make the connections in such a way that some of the material may be assumed to have been rough sketches for novels then in progress. (p. 6)

> *Nora L. Magid, in* The New York Times Book Review *(© 1975 by The New York Times Company; reprinted by permission), October 5, 1975.*

As a "Jewish" novel, *The Apprenticeship* has both a pungent ethnic flavor and the convincingness that arises when a writer deals with a milieu with which he is completely familiar. At the same time, Richler treats the ambivalent relationships of the Montreal ghetto to both English and French-Canadian cultures. The material, psychological, and spiritual realities of the life of the Jewish community, as it attempts to cope and to define itself in relation to a larger world, are in turn reflected in the personalities and the careers of Duddy and other characters. Here, Richler applies the insights of Freud to achieve a broad, often ribald satiric humor, in which the psycho-sexual lives of his creations symbolically express their social background. Informing Richler's depiction of Montreal, and of Duddy's personal development, is a complex and sophisticated view of human nature. Simplistic moral judgments are suspended in favor of a satiric vision that combines comic affirmation with ironic condemnation, a brutal realism with a humane sensitivity to ethical questions. In communicating his multi-faceted outlook, Richler commands a technique in which symbolism unobtrusively coexists with "solidity of specification." (pp. 413-14)

For Richler, the destructive psychological effects of the ghetto mentality are equalled and to some extent paralleled by those of the Jewish family. Like the society from which it springs, this tends to be closed and exclusive, clinging together in spite of its intense quarrels. The best aspect of such clannishness, the feeling of kinship which transcends all personal differences, is exemplified by Duddy. Although he is in varying degrees put down and rejected by all of his relatives except his grandfather, Duddy sticks up for them and protects them. . . . His support of his family is appropriately reciprocated and rewarded when, at a crucial stage in his financial career, Lennie persuades his father to give him a loan.

However, the loyalty and the affection which bind the Jewish family together cannot hide its less pleasant aspects. On the one hand, its protectiveness can be stifling. On the other, it drives its members mercilessly, partly by its intense ambition for its favored sons and partly by the complexes it induces in those whom it regards as second-best. (pp. 421-22)

[Duddy's] potentially violent emotions illustrate Richler's view of the Jewish family as a psychological pressure cooker. Either its members explode, or they are boiled down to mush.

In *The Apprenticeship,* the family and the ghetto are both implicitly related to the Jewish mother. Both are in this way characterized as psychological wombs, from which the Jewish male must fight free if he is to achieve real manhood. Here, the novelist's Freudian comedy involves some of his subtlest symbolism. For instance, Simcha's "stiffness" and

"uprightness" are phallic metaphors for the masculine integrity and dignity which he struggles to maintain against his "castrating" hag of a wife. His ultimate inability to cope with her is expressed in his sense of failure as a man and, on an analogous cultural level, in his clinging to the old ghetto life. . . . The symbolism that Richler ironically uses to undercut Simcha appears in a much more obvious form in the case of Milty Halpirin, the rich little milquetoast tormented by Duddy. Thus, Milty's "softness" indicates his emasculation by a mother whose protectiveness utterly imprisons him. One particularly significant aspect of Milty's entrapment is his attendance at the Jewish parochial school to which he is driven daily by Mrs. Halpirin. Once again, Richler connects the psychic "enclosure" of the ghetto mentality with that of the domineering woman. (p. 423)

Another repeated image which Richler uses with respect to this emasculation is vegetation. Thus, the negative connotations of Simcha's shop and of his wife are also borne by the garden which produces only unhealthy, inedible vegetables. Simcha tries in vain to express his masculinity through the ancient metaphor of the man as a sower of seed. The connection of the garden with the castrating woman appears also in the garden of Mrs. Halpirin. With its jealously tended plants, this provides an analogue to the womb of maternal protectiveness by which Milty is smothered. Like the tulips that are opened as a surprise for his mother, Milty is a tender "flower" who cannot survive in the hard world represented by Duddy and the Warriors. . . . Duddy is compared to the "spiky" grass growing by the railroad tracks in the slums. . . . Richler's image suggests both a phallic potency that symbolizes a mature manhood and also a tough vitality which thrives upon adversity. Therefore, the spiky grass epitomizes Duddy's adolescent struggle to prove himself by overcoming the psychic trammels of his family and the ghetto and by succeeding as his own man in a tougher but larger world.

The garden which is a symbol of the Jewish mother is further connected with the ghetto mentality through the Zionist dream of a homeland that is a pastoral paradise. Richler obviously regards Zionism as a soft sentimentalism which is regressive both psychologically and culturally. Its promised land, "flowing with milk and honey," is really a dream of returning to the pre-natal state, a wish partly fulfilled by the enclosure of the ghetto. As Dingleman tells Duddy, Zionism originated as a mawkish poetic fantasy of old men imprisoned in the cities of eastern Europe, men who really "want to die in the same suffocating way they lived." . . . (p. 424)

That even Duddy never completely escapes either the ghetto mentality or his mother is implicit in his obsession with owning the land around Lac St. Pierre. The connection of Duddy's monomania with his imprisonment by his background is indicated by the fact that it is an extension of Simcha's Zionist dream. The same parochialism is also suggested by Duddy's plans for making the resort into a sort of little Israel. The association of the lake with his mother is more subtle, but Richler has taken considerable pains to convey it to the reader. . . . Not only is the body of water an archetypal image of the female and of the subconscious which harbors our elemental dreams, but its connection with Duddy's mother is made evident by the circumstances surrounding its discovery. Thus, he is led to the lake by the highly maternal Yvette. . . . Ironically enough, his own feeling for his mistress is diverted to the lake as soon as he sees it. That it immediately and almost completely absorbs his *libido* is indicated by the absent-mindedness of his love-making to Yvette, which he apparently arranges so that he can see the real object of his desire over her shoulder! (p. 425)

Therefore, in the final chapter of *The Apprenticeship,* Duddy has satisfied the primal Freudian wish not only by supplanting his father but also by symbolically possessing his mother. His apparent triumph is, however, ironically qualified by the absoption of his sexual energies by a regressive passion for a woman whom he cannot even remember. In his ultimate inability to give love in an adult relationship, Duddy is really as "castrated" or "impotent" as Simcha, Max, Benjy, and Lennie. Long after her death, a Jewish mother has triumphed once again. (pp. 425-26)

Duddy indicates that his creator has like many satirists a jaundiced view of human nature and little faith in its improvability. To some extent, Duddy represents (and also becomes increasingly aware of) the incurable evil and sickness of man and his society, a nastiness which must be faced, if we are to be at all realistic and honest, and coped with if we are to survive.

In order to emphasize his dark satiric vision of human turpitude, Richler uses Duddy to put down those characters who are too stupid, soft, sentimental, or idealistic to recognize and to admit unpleasant truths. For instance, it is fitting that Duddy should deliver the *coup de grace* to Mac-Pherson's socialist belief in human brotherhood, the last lingering vestige of which is his refusal to strap his students. Not only is MacPherson's idealism a bourgeois self-indulgence that ignores the ethnic and economic conflicts that divide society, but it neglects the hard fact that in a "fallen" world there are bad kids who only understand brute force. Similarly, Duddy's ruthless exploitation of Yvette and Virgil, besides reflecting on his own moral failings, also indicates that his two victims are unable to contend with life in its frequent bestiality. Virgil's naiveté, his helplessness, and his squishy puppy-dog desire to be loved at any cost are manifestations of an ambiguous innocence which is partly sympathetic, but which also arouses that instinctive cruelty that is one of nature's ways of eliminating the hopelessly incompetent. Therefore, his victimization by Duddy may be seen as a judgment of implacable reality upon the unfit. In the same way, Yvette's maternal protectiveness and longing for romantic love are from one viewpoint simple deficiencies, signs of a parochial culture which has not prepared her for the tougher, more competitive urban environment. Her soft spots not only make her vulnerable to men like Duddy but actually arouse their latent sadism. In fairness to Richler, it should be noted here that the harshness of his view of Yvette and Virgil, which would seem to try and condemn them by the law of the jungle, is in part a comment upon their self-willed stupidity. As we see in Duddy's career, man was given a brain to perceive reality, to learn from experience, and to evolve strategies for survival. Virgil and Yvette may be fools, but they are not idiots, and there is no excuse for their not being disillusioned about Duddy much sooner. Their slowness really to face his turpitude is a comfortable but dangerous self-indulgence, which is appropriately punished.

Nonetheless, Richler's ironic condemnation of those char-

acters who cannot cope with a fallen world may seem to reflect an ethos perilously close to a facist redaction of Darwinism and of Nietzsche's theories of the "will to power" and the *Ü̈bermensch.* Certainly two of the novelist's basic metaphors, war and the animal relationship of predator to prey, would seem to support this judgment. If reality is hard and ugly because man is in large part reprehensible, the only realistic course of action is to fight fire with fire by being as vicious as Duddy at his worst. However, such an unpleasant outlook is only half of Richler's satiric vision, which has a strong moral component. As the writer points out through Dingleman's twisted physique and the multiple ironies of Duddy's career, mere survival and success without the higher ethical and cultural values leave a man as "crippled" as those who are too weak to preserve themselves. Similarly, Richler condemns the soft and the unrealistic not simply because they are "unfit," but also on moral grounds. Here, the animal metaphor of predator and prey is ironically juxtaposed with that of parasite and host. Thus, the person whom Duddy comes closest to murdering, MacPherson's supposedly invalid wife, appears to be an emotional "tick" who uses a psychosomatic illness to cling to her husband and suck the life-blood from him. What Duddy does to her is, therefore, a just and appropriate punishment for her sins. Virgil is another example of a human parasite. In his infantile need for love and protection, which leads him to play upon his epilepsy, he is a psychological "tapeworm" looking for a comfortable warm intestine to milk. Once again, he meets his proper nemesis in Duddy.

If Richler sees the soft and the weak as being morally shabby, the same condemnation applies to the intellectuals of his novel. Peter John Friar, whose humbug about communism and artistic integrity masks a ruthless self-interest, is representative of the moral shortcomings of the would-be intellectuals and sophisticates of *The Apprenticeship.* The snobbery, lovelessness, and self-pity that are variously displayed by Benjy, Lennie, Linda, and Ida are all signs of their egocentricity, a vice to which they add canting and hypocrisy. Even Hersh, perhaps the most admirable of the intelligensia, can be a self-righteous little prig in his bohemian posture.

Thus, a central dilemma in Richler's novel, which is never fully resolved, is how to reconcile the hard necessities of a wicked world with ethics. The problem is reflected in the author's complex and ambivalent attitude towards his protagonist. In this regard, the unwary reader is in danger of embracing one of the two opposing half-truths. The first is [Warren Tallman's view] that Duddy represents a Nietzschean celebration of a raw but exuberant "New World" vitality which "transvalues" the morality of a dead past. The second is A. R. Bevan's contention that Duddy is an ironic failure [see CLC, Vol. 5]. As John Ferns has correctly maintained in a recent article, Richler's feeling towards his hero in fact oscillates between sympathy and condemnation, achieving in the end a balanced antithesis between the two. Corresponding to this ambivalence, Duddy's character is itself a maze of contradictions, combining virtues like generosity, loyalty, and unpretentiousness with an often repugnant ruthlessness and crudity. He is at once hard and sensitive, loving and cruel. For instance, Duddy's breakdown reflects a genuine remorse for his misdeeds, which he then proceeds to compound by robbing his victim Virgil. To add to the complexity, even Duddy's vices are signs of an unabashed vitality which is somehow appealing.

Moreover, although Richler would not subscribe to that sociological liberalism which blames the individual's sins entirely upon his environment, it remains true that Duddy is in large part a victim of his milieu. In creating a hero who defies simplistic judgments, Richler is not revealing moral confusion or indecisiveness, but rather a perspective broad enough to embrace the contradictions of experience itself. It is for this reason that he is able to develop Duddy as a fully-rounded personality who encompasses something of the "infinitive variety" of life as it is perceived by the truly imaginative artist. (pp. 426-28)

> John Ower, "Sociology, Psychology, and Satire in 'The Apprenticeship of Duddy Kravitz'," in Modern Fiction Studies (copyright © 1976, by Purdue Research Foundation, West Lafayette, Indiana, U.S.A.), Autumn, 1976, pp. 413-28.

*   *   *

ROBBINS, Tom   1936-

Robbins is a bestselling American novelist whom Michael Rogers calls "the new king of the extended metaphor, dependent clause, outrageous pun and meteorologic personification." Robbins uses fantasy as his basis: "I've always wanted to lead a life of enchantment," he has said, "and writing is a part of that." The plots of his two novels, *Another Roadside Attraction* and *Even Cowgirls Get the Blues*, are a reflection of his rich imagination. Robbins says of himself, "My goal is to write novels that are like a basket of cherry tomatoes—when you bite into a paragraph, you don't know which way the juice is going to squirt."

[In *Another Roadside Attraction*] Robbins liberally mixes philosophy and social commentary with his circus, and his embarrassment at his own riches persists. . . .

His riches are of course Consciousness-Three riches, the riches of sky castles and pastoral retreats from middle class nonsense, but he has as well an old-fashioned interest in mundane detail, and displays admirable powers of observation of the everyday world, . . . powers that would not be displayed if his alienation from the world ran deep. What is disconcerting is the mix of worldly and apocalyptic. No other up-and-coming talent I have run across has the mix so deeply built in, the mix that is our national social artistic literary tragical comical political academical confusion; and no other author I have run across is less sure whether to laugh or cry. So he does both.

The result is, I'd say, a fairly reliable composite of the current vagaries of Con-Three, which has been pushed into a defensive posture lately, presaging perhaps a new realism. No retreat *from* the woods and the resolutely interior life seems to be scheduled yet, but at least in the Robbins book there is a prevailing ironic awareness that marks all the fantasizing at a discount. My wholly unresearched guess is that because of this awareness the next book by Robbins will be sparer, straighter, tougher somehow. The question is how, and it is a question that goes far beyond Robbins. (p. 29)

Though the Robbins book has something of the heavy-handed spirit of *Batman* lurking in its origins, it is thoroughly beyond *Batman* in the sense that it wants to *use* melodrama again rather than ridicule it. Robbins is happy and assured when he is concocting further furbelows to his

wild narrative, his story line, as he is not when he is trying to endow the story with theology and significance. The revolution with its attendant obligations seems to take a back seat in his life when he can be comfortably bourgeois again to the degree of accepting the least demanding and most familiar bourgeois literary conventions. (pp. 29-30)

> Reed Whittemore, in The New Republic (reprinted by permission of The New Republic; © 1971 by The New Republic, Inc.), June 26, 1971.

"There are only three things that I like," proclaims Amanda, the heroine of [*Another Roadside Attraction*]. "These are: the butterfly, the cactus and Infinite Goof.". . . [The] concept of the Infinite Goof is surely the most important, embracing in a phrase the entire philosophy of the Californian novel. . . .

Amanda announces the five things she believes in: birth, copulation, death, magic and freedom. The Goofish element in this is obviously magic. Logic, we learn from the mouth of the idiot, only gives a man what he needs. Magic gives him what he wants. (p. 365)

All the characters search for hidden meanings and deeper significances in whatever they see, but their search for the ultimate source of life is only half serious. Far more, their mysticism and pseudo-mysticism is a vehicle for worshipping this Infinite Goof.

The best of the Californian writers—and on the evidence of this novel I would put Mr Robbins among the very best—share an idiosyncrasy of perception and a vivid use of language which can only be explained in terms of a cultural renaissance. . . .

Amanda's love of butterflies leads her to try and smuggle the larvae of every known species of butterfly into the United States. Unfortunately she chooses the musical instruments of an itinerant band for the purpose; customs officers discover this deception and imprison the band:

> And almost immediately a rumour swept the land that butterfly eggs would get you high. The woods and fields were overrun by unlikely looking entomologists, and a sudden demand arose for nets, tweezers, magnifying glasses and the other trappings of zoology's most vast and gentle branch.

The author, you see, is no goof. He invites us to laugh at it all, as well as be moved to pity, tenderness, lust or whatever. No doubt the reality is not nearly so delightful. . . . All I can say is that the Californian novelists have used their intelligence, their wit and their extraordinarily sharp perceptions to make something beautiful of it all.

Almost every page has an arresting phrase or sentence in it. The hero, called Ziller, was born in Africa and reveals that the hyenas ate his after-birth. On meeting Amanda, he had the stink of Pan about him, and Amanda hears the telephone ringing in her womb. When they are united we learn that the butt-end of a rainbow filled the tiny room. . . .

Throughout the narrative, we have a constant stream of semi-serious homespun philosophy which should make the solemn platitudes of English and near-English novelists blush for shame:

A sausage is an image of rest, peace and tranquillity in stark contrast to the destruction and chaos of everyday life.

Consider the peaceful repose of the sausage compared with the aggressiveness and violence of bacon.

Like a drunken Irishman, people will say. And so it is, with the same undercurrent of whimsy, much as one dislikes to use the word in the context of anything so fresh and vital. But the great difference between the Californian school and the drunken Irish school is a total absence of rhetoric and bombastic exhibitionism. . . .

Either one is enchanted by it all, or one is not, of course. However, anyone who has not yet tried the Californian novel could scarcely do better than to start with Mr. Robbins's tale, which I found quite completely delightful, and by far the fullest and easiest introduction to the charm of the Infinite Goof I have yet seen. (p. 366)

> *Auberon Waugh, in* The Spectator *(© 1973 by* The Spectator; *reprinted by permission of* The Spectator), *March 24, 1973.*

"Even Cowgirls Get the Blues" is a Whole Earth narrative, a laid back "Tristram Shandy," a barbershop quartet of Vonnegut, Brautigan, Pynchon and Ishmael Reed doing a hymn to the White Goddess, a meditation on the rule of thumb, a manifesto for magic, and a retelling of "Another Roadside Attraction," Tom Robbins's first novel, now something of a hippie classic. "Cowgirls" has a mascot (the amoeba); a favorite recipe (stew) and 121 chapters plus interludes. Shiva couldn't keep all these balls in the air, but Robbins's blur-handed performance is definitely worth the admission. . . .

[Be] advised that Robbins considers realism only "one of the fifty-seven varieties of decoration" and that liberation means reversing thirty thousand years of civilization. When the Great Mother reigned, so did magic. . . .

Robbins says it's by pushing one thing to an extreme that "you force it into the realm of magic." Knowing like Pynchon, funny like Vonnegut, as winsome as Brautigan, Robbins allows the Hoo Doo force of "Cowgirls" to dissipate in routines and arguments. Sissy is made for levitation, not analysis, yet here's Robbins talking about piano wire and his own costume. Once again, it's the man up front. . . . Everything, including Wonder Bread, is animated; the book itself is personified. Some of Robbins's metaphors are only embroidered Kleenex. But when he has hyperbole on medium, metaphor transforms the ordinary into the fantastic. The first half has most of this textural magic; by the end, action and abstraction dominate.

Read solemnly, with expectations of conventional coherence, "Even Cowgirls Get the Blues" will disappoint. Entered like a garage sale, poked through and picked over, "Cowgirls" is entertaining and, like the rippled mirror over there by the lawn mower, often instructive. Tom Robbins is one of our best practitioners of high foolishness. (p. 5)

> *Thomas LeClair, in* The New York Times Book Review *(© 1976 by The New York Times Company; reprinted by permission), May 23, 1976.*

Even Cowgirls Get the Blues comes as a magical gift, a brilliant affirmation of private visions and private wishes and their power to transform life and death. A tall tale and a parable of essential humanness, it is a work of extraordinary playfulness, style and wit. . . .

With the agility of a mad photographer, taking quick shots from a hundred unexpected angles (the traditions of palmistry, the life of the whooping crane, the evolutionary significance of the opposable thumb), Robbins dazzles the reader. . . . As he does so, it becomes clear that, like William Blake, he is concerned with two main human types: those who live with desire as their guide; and those who suppress desire, fantasy and personal identity in the name of "reason"—that is, in the name of customary thought and conventionalized desires. (p. 152)

Robbins is not only a monkey-wrench thrower, and he is not an advocate of simple ignorance. Rather he would like to see human beings developed, not eviscerated, by culture. While his characters obstruct the routine grindings of civilization, they talk and suggest new cultural and psychic connections. . . . His characters delight also in fleshly connections, and in the midst of conversation lovemaking springs up like fields of flowers, and what is rare in literary intercourse, neither party is trying to win the other over or under. . . .

What is most welcome about Robbins is not that he has ideas, though he does and they are interesting, but that he makes us see as funny things we take too seriously, and so releases us. We are used to novels in which laughter echoes off our fears; Robbins's laughter reverberates with our strengths.

His characters don't mount their private wishes and ride off into a countercultural sunset. For their desires they suffer painfully. . . .

Robbins's characters suffer, and some die. In the process they make us realize that even the pain and death of a culture or a planet are tolerable. What is intolerable is to live without—without what? Magic and poetry, Robbins says. Neither may be the right word, but this glorious and extravagant novel reminds us that we live to create as well as to observe. Truth and beauty, like magic and poetry, are not found but reinvented, and beyond more familiar novelistic truths are others that shine brighter (p. 153)

> *Ann Cameron, "A Nose Thumb at Normality," in* The Nation *(copyright 1976 by the Nation Associates, Inc.), August 28, 1976, pp. 152-53.*

[Tom Robbins] writes in a style aimed at what Sterne might have produced if he had been commissioned to revamp *The Lord of the Rings* with an eye to the higher porn market. This isn't intended as a compliment. . . .

[The diverse topics of *Even Cowgirls Get the Blues*] are as well-worn as its narrative mode—hitch-hiking, feminism, pollution, mysticism, the expanding universe. 'You've travelled your whole life without destination,' an advertising artist tells the Kerouac-groupie heroine. 'You move but you have no direction.' 'What is the "direction" of the Earth in its journey,' she sagely responds in the accents of the Psalmist; 'where are the atoms "going" when they spin?'

It's dangerous to quote from writing like this out of context, of course, because its movements of tone and defla-tory jokes often turn what looks like schmaltz into a kind of retrospective irony.... But as Swift always anticipated ..., irony is hard to keep up. Robbins's predominant man-ner, despite the increasingly sparse punctuating jokes, is one of remorselessly whimsical didacticism.... Robbins's problem isn't that he doesn't make the most of the possibili-ties [in his story], but that he makes too much of them, par-ticularly as allegory-fodder. Perhaps that wouldn't matter so much if his use of the cowgirls'-ranch scenario weren't so flagrantly pornographic. For someone writing on the side of feminism Robbins has an uncanny knack for male chau-vinist trash.... (p. 219)

> Jeremy Treglown, in New Statesman (© 1977 The Statesman & Nation Publishing Co. Ltd.), August 12, 1977.

* * *

ROIPHE, Anne 1935-

Roiphe is an American novelist whose work reflects her con-cern with women in contemporary society. Her characters are human and believable, and her prose is witty and refresh-ing. (See also *CLC*, Vol. 3.)

Anne Roiphe's new book, *Torch Song,* crucifies an already much tortured form—the confessional novel. The format here is basically the same as the one used by magazines like *True Romance.*... The stock heroine confesses her past voluntary or unwitting debauches, describing in vivid detail her descent into hell and the various punishments justly or unjustly awarded there. It is all told in the past tense from the perspective of the currently well-adjusted and happily married normal woman. The heroine fails to explain just how she gets from the white-slave market to Larchmont, but we are assured that what has passed is past. At 12 I used to find such tales, with their accompanying ultratacky photographs, both exciting and corny. *Torch Song* is not exciting, but it is definitely corny....

Torch Song is a perfectly dreadful novel, lacking even por-nographic value. The erotic high point is Marjorie's mem-ory of a brutal enema administered by her German nurse. Roiphe probably intended this scene to account for Marjor-ie's masochism, but it is muddled and fragmented, like ev-erything else in the novel. Whatever the causes of her self-loathing, it is impossible to care one whit about what hap-pens to Marjorie. She is such a passive, complacent, and stupid person that she arouses a kind of sympathy for the sadist burdened with the task of humiliating her.

Torch Song is a prodigy of imprecise and banal writing. Jim's hair, for example, switches several times from blond to black for no apparent reason and seemingly without the writer's awareness. The novel is peppered throughout with bizarre similies, like: "My nipples stood straight up, like nervous nannies." There are mixed metaphors like this, about Marjorie's father: "the most assimilated, handsomest of melted Jewry—who floated in his Sulka ties, his white monogrammed handkerchiefs, and his black silk socks in the American soup, like the upper crust he wanted to be."

Jim is reputed to be a brilliant and captivating conversation-alist. But feeble as his sexual emissions are, they are supe-rior to his verbal ones in not being compounded by poor grammar....

The women's movement created a considerable fiction

market. But whether or not the writers who supply this market were lured by feminist doctrine to earn a living by the pen, their works are by no means all feminist in nature. A good number of the novels heralded as having issued from the "new feminist consciousness" are in fact exploita-tive and undermining of the movement that unwittingly supports them.

Up the Sandbox, for example, the 1970 book that made Anne Roiphe famous, is a sentimental, self-serving piece of ephemera in the school of *Little Women,* with few of the charms of Alcott's book.... *Up the Sandbox* has leaped out of the pages of *The Feminine Mystique* [as the paper-back cover states], all right, but as problem, not solution. It is a novel that affirms over and over that the rewards of caring full-time for children, and for a husband who be-haves like a spoiled child, are real and fulfilling, and that, although fascinating, the "liberated life" is a doomed one for women, fraught with disappointment and disaster, and sensibly avoided.

The commercial and celebrity success of Roiphe's books, and of a number of other commonplace, sentimental, and safe novels, would not matter very much if it did not often obscure from readers' view truly innovative and excellent novels written by women. It is unfortunately the case that in the minds of many people, the women's fiction market is composed almost entirely of books about discontented upper-West-Side housewives and masochistic East-Side analysands.

> Laurie Stone, "Singing the Black and Blues," in The Village Voice (reprinted by permission of The Village Voice; copyright © by The Village Voice, Inc., 1977), Janu-ary 3, 1977, p. 57.

In contemporary writing we seem to be enduring a period when everything is coming out but nothing much is being faced or deeply understood. Everything gets told, espe-cially the unspeakable, but the task of locating meaning is bungled, fudged or simply ignored....

"Torch Song" ... is about an awful marriage that lasted at least six years, producing a single child (out of virtually no sexual embraces), and an immense amount of misery and misbehavior. The young man is sexually sick; he is also a sadist, a drunkard and a thief. The young woman, who tells the story, is relatively more decent, but she too is a liar and a thief and is, I think, fundamentally dishonest in explaining why she got and how she stayed married until the day the man walked out. The reader is put in a peculiar position: He is like an analyst to whom someone comes to complain about the inadequacies of a spouse and who must begin probing and questioning the symptoms of the complain-er....

[Readers] ought not be placed in that position.... I would ... prefer some guidance on these matters from the author herself. The reader wants to be sure, and he is not sure, that Anne Roiphe has gotten to the bottom of her own fic-tional character. Otherwise, the reading—and perhaps the writing—of fictional memoirs becomes a mug's game. (p. 8)

> Julian Moynahan, in The New York Times Book Review (© 1977 by The New York Times Company; reprinted by permission), January 9, 1977.

Torch Song is a confessional novel about a woman's first love who turns, in more ways than one, into an abandoned husband. Marjorie Weiss is made captive by her feeling for a gifted young writer and philosopher, a loitering *bel homme sans merci* by the name of Jim Morrison, and finds herself ministering to his abnormal sexual habits. . . . Jim is an outcast who has become an outlaw. He is a waif or stray who is also a cross between Lords Byron and Russell, and who can impersonate the Prince of Darkness. This is the multiple identity displayed in certain Gothic novels, where poverty is raised to the peerage and misery consoled, where the forsaken is forgiven his outrages. (p. 39)

[Jim] urges her to read Mann's story *Tonio Kröger* in order to discover what she means to him. Both works are concerned with the price paid for art: the artist is excluded from normal life and from normal sexuality. Tonio resembles a modern artist when he states that he must keep his feelings separate from his art, and produces an art that is dry, painful, fastidious. There are whispers of Eliot in the tale: Eliot's essays require the exclusion of biography from art, and the mention by Mann of spring's cruel effect upon the feelings, and of going south, might seem to anticipate *The Waste Land*'s opening passage.

At the same time, Tonio is like a romantic artist, and like Jim Morrison, in being an outcast, with secrets. There's a romantic morbidity—of a kind that might possibly be taken to anticipate one of the moods of Nazi Germany—in Tonio's final confession of love for blond, blue-eyed, normal Nordic life: this love is described as wholesome and redemptive, a tonic for the sick, sensual artist, but it is also described as a secret soft spot, such as men might have for the normal Nordic male. Tonio is confident that these feelings will pass into his art—exempt from theoretical challenge, presumably—and will transform it.

In *Torch Song*, as in *Tonio Kröger*, normality triumphs. . . . The relationship breaks up, and the book ends by the sea, as does Mann's story, in a jolly, healthy atmosphere of children, fishing, and suntans, with Marjorie married happily ever after to a kind, potent pediatrician. . . . The narrator is sarcastic about Jim's subsequent career: "perhaps he gets alimony" from his society wives, "the reviews of his books have not all been good." Normality's revenge.

With its accounts of Jim's strange habits and of a worthy woman's subjection to these, this book is bound to do business. It is written with a good deal of journalistic force, moreover, and holds in check any tendency it may have to serve as a fresh installment of women's complaints, of the sort publishers like. But its conception of normality seems very unappealing. "We were married in a legal sense but not in the real sense—the kind that makes babies," Marjorie points out. Not everyone will believe that the only real unions are the kind that makes babies. An impulse to belittle and burlesque the narrator's relations with Jim is yielded to, though it is also resisted, and reading parts of the book is like witnessing [severe] punishment. . . . Marjorie was very interested in Jim, and stayed with him voluntarily for years, tending his wounds. She needed him, and his price. And now she is interesting readers with her confessions, which would be a lot less interesting if Jim, beneath the brilliance, were unreal—no more than a nursable nasty wreck. Even readers who are repelled by his snobbery and contempt may be unwilling to believe the book when it

maintains that this was a relationship for the birds. (pp. 39-40)

Karl Miller, in The New York Review of Books *(reprinted with permission from* The New York Review of Books; *copyright* © *1977 NYREV, Inc.), February 3, 1977.*

*   *   *

ROSSNER, Judith   1935-

An American novelist, Rossner has been stylistically compared to Joyce Carol Oates. She is best known for her successful novel, *Looking for Mr. Goodbar.* **(See also** *CLC,* **Vol. 6, and** *Contemporary Authors,* **Vols. 17-20, rev. ed.)**

To The Precipice . . . remains Ms. Rossner's most ambitious novel. It is a *Bildungsroman,* a psychological novel, a Jewish novel, a woman's novel, a luminous period piece, and a family chronicle with a large, complex canvas that displays many of the author's principal themes and preoccupations. Ruth Kossoff, the gritty, sarcastic heroine-narrator of the book, is shrewd, attractive, thoroughly problematic. . . .

Ruth's journey, psychological as well as material, from the Lower East Side to . . . Fifth Avenue and 96th Street, provides *To The Precipice* with an ethnic axis that affords humor. (p. 661)

In a sense Ruth has successfully coped. . . . She has accomplished this through a series of jolting confrontations, which scarcely conceal a radical, if not militant, feminism, embodiment of the contemporary rootlessness and restlessness of the "new" woman. . . .

Any Minute I Can Split . . . depicts Margaret McDonough Adams, a heroine in the painful process of liberating herself from a father, who has rejected her, and a husband, who has abused her. The novel, told from Margaret's point of view, deals seriously enough with the problems created by parents, marriage, childbearing, sexuality and suicide. However, it has a much lighter touch than *To The Precipice,* which was slow-paced and somberly naturalistic in many long passages of description that were almost Dreiserian. The action of *Any Minute I Can Split,* on the other hand, is essentially conveyed through sharp, epigrammatic dialogue—indeed, some of the best moments in the book are elaborate wisecracks—and the major setting is a commune in Vermont that supplies an airiness and spaciousness which the Manhattan of *To The Precipice* could not. (p. 662)

Important questions are asked and discussed: What cements the standard suburban family, and what makes it split? Is the communal family an alternative? Is sex a more reliable binder in the presumably free conditions of a commune than it is in the nuclear family? To what extent is Women's Liberation legitimate? Is the concept of life style, esteemed by the communards, any more meaningful than the concept of taste, revered by wealthy suburbanites? Finally, does money—always an important element in a Rossner novel—influence the people who form communes more than the ideals that led them to such experimentation? (p. 663)

Nine Months in the Life of an Old Maid . . . is a subtle psychological study of a family in conflict, where the hostilities are great and yet where mutual affection, however neurotic, still holds. The novel, sensitively describing parental egoism and the alienation of children, attempts to find a delicate balance—grounds for conciliation and reconciliation—among very dissimilar, often disagreeable, people. . . .

This novel of human relationships is a triumph of style. Like *Any Minute I Can Split*, plot and character are essentially conveyed through dialogue. And, one feels that, without much effort, because the dialogue is lively and witty, the book could be turned into a successful play. Themes dealing with marriage, the family, the role of women and the tensions between generations are as evident as they are expected. Still, Ms. Rossner has broken new ground with this novel as she has done with each of her other works. After the phenomenon of *Mr. Goodbar*, she appears to be only in the middle of her stride. She is a writer to be watched with expectation. (p. 664)

> Edward M. Potoker, "Judith Rossner: Daughters and Lovers," in The Nation (copyright 1976 by the Nation Associates, Inc.), May 29, 1976. pp. 661-64.

In her earlier novel, "Looking for Mr. Goodbar," Judith Rossner anatomized the rootlessness of males and females shuffling in and out of their little urban hutches, like rabbits on the run. The writing seemed dull to me. . . . But "Attachments" is an extraordinary leap from the mundane, "realistic" settings and sexual tableaux of that previous novel. Ostensibly it is a story about Siamese twins, but it is loneliness, a horrible, scratchy loneliness, that is the real focus. It is a lovely, bitter, frightening book.

A kind of demon has caught Judith Rossner. God knows, she must have torn bits of herself into the book. It's the thing I most admire: the writer moving closer and closer to that edge where metaphors aren't simply games of play, where language begins to hurt.

Nadine Tumulty, the heroine of the book, is a Los Angeles child, born "in the land where there was never any winter outside of the soul." Nadine is a lonely girl. "Some people spend their lives falling and never notice. I not only noticed but screamed the whole time." She's bitten with a hunger to attach herself to something more permanent than her own skin. "Dreams of falling through infinite amounts of space had been replaced by dreams of being permanently attached to someone else so I could never fall."

She senses her own curious dilemma. "I needed a man powerful enough to stop me from killing him but crazy enough to want to take care of me the rest of the time!" Nadine is prowling for love.

She grasps at it in the form of Eddie and Amos Smith, a pair of Siamese twins who are living in Beverly Hills. She spies on them swimming in their pool, "moving, moving, never needing to speak, each understanding without words where the other is going." She tells her best friend Dianne about the twins. Dianne "thought they were freakish but I thought *they* were beautiful and I was freakish. . . . They'd been born to a condition I was spending my life trying to achieve." . . .

Soon the twins pair off in a permanent way. Dianne becomes pregnant, and Eddie marries her. Amos marries Nadine. . . .

At first Nadine and Dianne are obsessed with the wonders of Amos and Eddie. The twins are complete in themselves: "nothing's important to them except each other; they hardly know the rest of the world exists." But this specific quality of the twins, their own private circuit, begins to gnaw at the two wives. The joint that holds the twins together, their "attachment," a bridge of flesh at the abdomen, has already poisoned Nadine. (p. 9)

For Nadine the twins become "that monster one-half of which I called my husband." She induces Amos and Eddie to have an operation that will sever their joint, halve them, split them in two. The twins agree. Without their joint, the bad dreams. "I'm out in space and it's dark and I'm cold and I'm dying." They turn ordinary. And their wives abandon them. "You only loved us when we were freaks," Amos says at the end of the novel.

Will it be only the male reader who cries for Amos and Eddie? I wonder. Judith Rossner has provided us with a myth that destroys all the beatitudes of female sexuality. "Attachments" is a kind of "Lolita" in reverse: the female's terrifying quest for identity through sexual power and lust. We purr at the exotic. We fondle it, we move up close to it, smother it, until it becomes more and more like ourselves. Then we seek other eyes, other faces, other twins. Funny, sexy and sad, "Attachments" is a crazy treatise on "love" as the ultimate executioner. Judith Rossner has written about the bitch in all of us. "Attachments" is without mercy, marvelous and tough. (p. 34)

> Jerome Charyn, "On the Prowl for Love," in The New York Times Book Review (© 1977 by The New York Times Company; reprinted by permission), September 18, 1977, pp. 9, 34.

On pages 97 and 98 of *Attachments* we learn in one three-minute sweep of the eye all the "news" (for that is what *novel* means) that Rossner has to impart to us. On those two pages we are given in graphic detail the answer to the major question raised by the novel: How does a woman, the heroine, Nadine, "do it" with her Siamese-twin husband? And when her best friend, Dianne, marries the other twin, how do *they* do it? Once these momentous questions of logistics are solved, there remain a few others that ought to create curiosity, but somehow—because of the endless, flat terrain of language we have to travel across—they do not. (pp. 30-1)

Put aside the essential poverty of the sensational idea and the attenuated workings-out of the occasional complications. What remains is the absence of . . . rich, inventive language. Rossner uses words carelessly; she is deaf to the natural music of good sentences because she is so preoccupied with the ramifications of her catchy idea. (p. 31)

> Doris Grumbach, in Saturday Review (© 1977 by Saturday Review Magazine Corp.; reprinted with permission), October 1, 1977.

As we all are, Judith Rossner is curious about what makes people stick together. Never one to shirk extremes, she has come up with a cheerfully unwholesome extravaganza about conjoined twins. . . . In *Looking for Mr Goodbar* (1975) she gave a commanding account of the progress of an addict of dependence, a woman scarred by her devotion to the memory of childhood illness, who consigns herself to the role of easy lay, and is at last ambiguously slaughtered by a bar-room pick-up, because both autonomy and mutual dependence are impossible for her: she is safer when attached to couples. These preoccupations, in the earlier novel handled with confidence and wit, reach a distasteful but logical culmination in *Attachments,* where the heroine, Nadine, after completing her Master's in male inadequacy with three overly detached specimens, becomes enraptured by a self-sufficient couple, anatomically joined thorax to thorax. . . . The twins are used to sharing more than a band of tissue and a lobe of liver: briefly she is the apex of an athletically carnal triangle, but with insane persistence induces her friend Dianne, Eastern liberal Jewish intellectual Dianne, with a life "full of Civil and other liberties", to become the square on the hypotenuse. . . .

Judith Rossner has a sharp line in sustained ironic confabulation, as in Nadine's account of her mother's reaction to her departure for college:

> A couple of months before I left she got a Pekingese to replace me but then she couldn't stand the way it yipped. She replaced the Pekingese with a cat but then it turned out she was allergic to cat dandruff. They got rid of the cat and my father erected a beautiful aquarium in front of the living room window but within two weeks every fish in it was dead. She went to a doctor and got tranquillizers.

But she is rarely so economic in phrase or construction in this dense underbrush of a novel, where characters intertwine like lianas, and tendrils of subplot bar every path. Nadine is examined in every light and mood and is a most intricate piece of clockwork, but appears to be powered by a rather crude piece of Freudian psychomechanism, with a simple drive and many redundant gears. Descriptions of herself are often indulgent. . . . There is too much heavy underlining. . . .

Unattractively selfconscious as the writing is at times, this is a consequence of an unblinking self-awareness. The narrative line may be contorted and diffuse, but it is the path of an ambitious expedition, which has brought back too many trophies. Intermittently absorbing, always intelligent, the novel's immodest and unachievable aim is to describe "an act that would make real life seem reasonable by comparison".

> *Eric Korn, "The Twin Syndrome," in* The Times Literary Supplement (© *Times Newspapers Ltd., 1977; reproduced from* The Times Literary Supplement *by permission), November 4, 1977, p. 1285.*

Judith Rossner wins this year's award for the biggest confidence trick: she takes us into her confidence, and then she tricks us. *Attachments* wheedles the reader; it is coy and slightly hysterical, like a cross between *Penthouse* and *Woman's Own,* desperate for our attention and even our complicity as the narrator, Nadine, settles down to tell the story of her life. And it's not as if we could lie back, close our eyes, and drift into a sound sleep: *Attachments* keeps on nudging us awake with arch announcements, sly asides and occasionally with great shrieks. The reader is addressed as 'you', and it soon becomes clear that his position is one of analyst to Judith Rossner's patient. This idea

of the novel as therapy session is a relatively recent one, and not all of us will find the new role particularly appealing. It means that the narrator tries to get annoyingly close; with the irritating assumption in this book that Nadine's empty past, and her tenuous anxieties, are of some extraordinary significance which only a fool would find uninteresting. In a good writer this might be entertaining, since to treat the novel as one long session of analysis is to presume that the boundaries of 'the real' are no longer fixed or definite. But here is doesn't work. When a false relationship is established between writer and reader, nothing can work. (p. 24)

Judith Rossner avoids some of the more boringly familiar scenes by altering the story slightly: the sexual possibilites of Siamese twins, and their resolution, are at least a prurient twist of the old plot. But in American novels, new forms of sex simply mean new kinds of 'hang-up', and *Attachments* gets monotonously stuffed with Nadine's relentless self-analysis. It is literally monotonous since that confessional, letting-it-all-hang-out tone doesn't allow any interesting variations in its frantic search for self-expression. The more interesting Nadine finds her predicament, as a dissatisfied housewife caring for a couple of freaks, the flatter the novel becomes. And the more cosy and conversational she gets, the more irritating it feels. Dramatic events are capitalised—Getting With Child; mental pain is touchingly expressed as AARGH!; exclamation marks, some of them even in brackets (!), are continually being used. And then, AARGH!, we get emotive lists as though Nadine were reeling off a number of sexual episodes in an encounter session: 'Things We Did Not Discuss Before We Got Married.'

But the false, cloying complicity of the novel's tone lays the blame on us. . . . It is as if we were making Judith Rossner continue against her will; as though we hadn't had enough already, and wanted a little more pain in the next chapter. That, somehow, it's all *our* fault. And in a sense she's right. We all insist that our common language—the language we use in speech and the language which the novel adopts—can actually create a coherent and interesting world; and so we assume that the two-dimensional pictures which fiction provides bear some relation to the world we live through. But they don't; they are a misrepresentation; novels are lies, and when they try to deny their status, they become hysterically self-justifying or rhetorically grandiose.

In *Attachments* this means that the narrator herself becomes a walking cliché the more real she tries to become. . . . In this world of lemon meringue, no human contact is possible. Despite the persistent presence of the Siamese twins, they never emerge as anything other than a bizarre adjunct to the processes of Nadine's emotional life. There are so many emotional 'events' that the book is devoid of feeling. It was clearly Judith Rossner's intention to lift an otherwise stereotyped story by giving her male characters a new look, but it hasn't worked. She has forgotten that nobody's feelings are important unless they are cleverly expressed. (pp. 24-5)

> *Peter Ackroyd, "Glandular," in* The Spectator (© *1977 by* The Spectator; *reprinted by permission of* The Spectator), *November 12, 1977, pp. 24-5.*

ROTH, Philip 1933-

Roth is an American novelist and short story writer who exhibits in his fiction a brilliant satirical wit. His work explores the problems of contemporary Jewish life: assimilation, the urban versus the suburban Jew, the eastern upper-class Jew versus the midwestern middle-class Jew. Roth has a flair for reproducing the speech patterns of American dialect, whether it is the idiomatic Yiddish quality of Jewish conversation or the cliché-ridden speech of a midwestern WASP. Roth has had the good fortune to achieve both critical acclaim and the fame of a best-selling novelist. (See also *CLC*, Vols. 1, 2, 3, 4, 6, and *Contemporary Authors*, Vols. 1-4, rev. ed.)

[These] may be the central characteristics of Roth's male/female encounters: the man is Jewish, the woman is not; the man and woman are using each other, imposing on each other fictive roles which they have created for one another; the man is doing what he thinks he ought to do rather than what he wants to do; and, finally, the man and woman are speaking in different languages, and neither has any idea what the other is saying. (p. 7)

That Alexander Portnoy, Peter Tarnopol, Gabe Wallach are Jewish, and that the women they involve themselves with are Gentile, is at the center of this inability to communicate. To be sure, men and women of the same religion can and do experience this difficulty—Neil Klugman and Brenda Patimkin of *Goodbye, Columbus* and Roy and Lucy Bassart of *When She Was Good* are certainly proof. But there is a special way in which this general disease becomes localized in the case of Jewish-Gentile relationships, and it is with this particular strain of the virus that Roth most often concerns himself. "Jewish men and their Gentile women," Roth told an interviewer, was one of the ideas behind *Portnoy's Complaint*. One more case of star-crossed lovers fighting their communities' prejudices.

But when the Othello is named Cohen and the Desdemona is Johnson, something important is going on that is particularly pertinent to the present moment in American literature. These Jewish men and non-Jewish women battling each other on the pages of the most widely read contemporary fiction are clearly emblematic of an important American phenomenon, and it is Roth, I think, who best understands this phenomenon and seeks to interpret it to the world. (p. 9)

When people of differing backgrounds meet, and each has a set of assumptions of what the other must be like, it is clear that a meaningful relationship can never be established until the stereotyped barriers to communication are broken down. Often, this does not happen. Philip Roth's Jewish men are obsessed with a mythical creature called *shiksa* and her promise of hitherto unimagined sexual delights. At the same time, but to a greater or lesser degree, his non-Jewish women are filled with ideas about Jewish men. These feelings, in turn, are connected, clearly, to Jewish attitudes toward Gentiles in general, to men's attitudes toward women in general and so on. (pp. 9-10)

Roth's [discovery,] I think, is: at the heart of the problem between his men and women is the odd combination of a man who stereotypes others and deeply resents being stereotyped himself. As we shall see, these prejudices become more, not less, deeply felt as relationships develop. Of all of Roth's couples, it is the married ones who are least able to separate mate from myth.

In a telling moment in Cynthia Ozick's short story, "The Pagan Rabbi," a character (Jewish) who has been married to a Gentile is asked by another character (also Jewish) "What are they like, those people?" "Those people"—as if one representative of the 99% of the world's population who happen not to be Jewish were a broad enough sample on which to base generalizations. Philip Roth's men and women, so well-educated and so sophisticated, seem far-removed from this type of silly type-casting. It must come as no small surprise to them (if, indeed, it comes at all) that the reprehensible prejudices of their parents are not dead, but metamorphosed. It is strange to note that while Philip Roth has repeatedly been attacked by rabbis and other Jewish spokesmen for his characters' (and his own) "self-hatred," his critics have little to say about the offensive strain of "anti-Gentilism" exhibited, not only overtly by characters like Sophie Portnoy and Morris Tarnopol, but latently by almost all of the other Jewish characters. (pp. 10-11)

In his important essay, "Imagining Jews," published in the *New York Review of Books* in September, 1974, Roth argues that until his own Portnoy arrived in 1969, Jewish writers clearly distinguished between Jewish and Gentile characters.... He goes on to say that Bellow had to imagine Henderson a Gentile, for no Jew could be so completely immersed in the search for satisfaction, in assuaging the voice of the id crying "I want." Roth is guilty, I think, of oversimplifying the case, and he is surely wrong in his reading of Eugene Henderson's "I want." For our purposes, it is sufficient to note at this point that part of what Roth was trying to do in *Portnoy's Complaint* was to correct the imbalance that he saw in the presentation of Jewish characters. As he notes earlier in that essay,

> Going wild in public is the last thing in the world that a Jew is expected to do—by himself, by his family, by his fellow Jews, and by the larger community of Christians whose tolerance for him is often tenuous to begin with....

Going wild in public, or thinking about going wild in public, has actually been one of Roth's subjects all along. To return to the ending of *Goodbye, Columbus*: there is a sentence in the last paragraph that is emblematic of the Rothian hero's fear of public self-indulgence.... [Neil Klugman] tells us, "Suddenly, I wanted to set down my suitcase and pick up a rock and heave it right through the glass, but of course I didn't." The punctuation here is crucial. Only a comma separates the words "glass" and "but"; not even a semi-colon, let alone a period. How brief the pause that a comma allows the reader, for how instantaneous is the "no" delivered to the brain that is told "I want." (pp. 11-12)

Roth supposes that the dramatic reaction to *Portnoy's Complaint* came because readers of Jewish novels had been accustomed to the central difference between Jewish and Gentile characters: Jews controlled their impulses, Gentiles didn't. When the public was confronted by a Jew "going wild," the public itself went on a wild buying spree, making Roth rich and famous for all the wrong reasons. What Roth does not say in that essay, though, is that he himself helped to create these expectations in his audience. In fact, the gap between how his characters act and how they want to act has been his theme all along. Neil Klugman's off-handed dismissal of a momentary desire may be, in fact, the most symbolic moment of the novella.

And not only of that novella. For Philip Roth may well be, as one looks over his works, the inventor of the Jewish novel of manners. Like Henry James, Roth concerns himself with what Lionel Trilling calls "that part of a culture which is made up of half-uttered or unutterable expressions of value." In his essay, "Manners, Morals and the Novel," Trilling goes on to say manners are "the things that for good or bad draw the people of a culture together and that separate them from the people of another culture." It is in this way that Roth can be seen as a "Jewish" novelist—he sets out to define what the manners of American Jews are; not what they believe, but how they act. "Manners," says Trilling [in *The Liberal Imagination*], "make part of a culture which is not art, or religion, or morals, or politics, and yet it relates to all these highly formulated departments of culture." If Trilling was correct in 1947 when he asserted that the novel of manners had "never really established itself in America," then this may be the great contribution of the Jewish novelists as a group and of Roth specifically; their close analysis of "manners as the indication of the direction of man's soul" may, in the end, serve to tell us not only what Jews in America were like at a specific moment, but, also, what the culture they separated themselves from was like.

To compare Roth's work to James' is only to pick up the hints that Roth leaves for us in more than one place. (pp. 12-13)

In Roth's novels of manners, as I have suggested, the most difficult problems facing his heroes are the conflicts between what they want to do and what they have come to believe they ought to do. His fiction might be called deeply self-reflexive, with literature itself becoming an active force in the minds of his characters. (p. 14)

For the "morally serious" man committed to doing "the right thing" (of which the Jew is surely a type, if not a prototype), literature encompasses all of those things that Trilling would have us think of as "manners." The novel of manners for the American Jewish intellectuals who are Roth's characters must begin, then, with an acknowledgment of what these people have read. Paul and Libby Herz and Gabe Wallach share a copy of *Portrait of a Lady;* Alexander Portnoy recites Yeats to his illiterate lover; Peter Tarnopol tells us he was "stuffed to the gills with great fiction—"; Neil Klugman, to belabor the point, is a librarian and, as the novella ends, on the first day of the Jewish New Year, he goes not to synagogue but to the library. . . .

Philip Roth introduces his recent collection of essays by saying, "Together these pieces reveal to me a continuing preoccupation with the relationship between the written and the unwritten world." If this is true of his essays, it is equally true of his fiction. People in his stories frequently see their situations as comparable to those of characters whom they have come to admire in books, and they try to act the way those characters might. (p. 15)

The only problem with acting as though life were a book, of course, is that it isn't, and the only problem with seeing people as fictional characters is that they aren't. The former—life as a book—is a kind of prison, limiting as it does a character's options and forcing him to act within a small, circumscribed code of "moral" behavior, the books

he has read serving as the prison walls. Roth symbolized this state in his first long story, portraying Neil Klugman "imprisoned" in a library.

The latter—forcing people into fictional roles that you have created for them out of the books you have read—can be far more dangerous. (p. 16)

[Men] and women in the fiction of Philip Roth imprison each other by refusing to acknowledge each other's freedom to be individuals. . . . The metaphor of imprisonment and liberation cannot be overstated, for it is at the center of every important relationship in Roth's fiction. His characters do harm enough when they try to free themselves; when they seek to liberate each other the results are catastrophic.

Any solutions? Perhaps the way out of this disastrous cycle of mutual incomprehension and misrepresentation is pointed to in the titles of the two sections of Roth's most important novel, *My Life as a Man*. The first section, containing two short stories "by" Peter Tarnopol, is called "Useful Fictions," and the second part of the book, Tarnopol's purported autobiographical account of his marriage, is called "My True Story." Tarnopol's struggle, simply put, is to distinguish between the two. The very last sentences of the book suggest that Tarnopol is getting there: "Oh, my God, I thought—now you. You being you! And *me! This me who is me being me and none other!*" If, indeed, Tarnopol knows the difference between useful fictions and true stories, between the characters in books and the people whom he addresses as "you," and, most of all, between the me being someone else and the me being me, he is, perhaps, as Dr. Spielvogel might say, ready to begin his life as a man. (pp. 16-17)

> *Joel Grossman, "'Happy as Kings': Philip Roth's Men and Women," in* Judaism *(copyright © 1977 by the American Jewish Congress), Winter, 1977, pp. 7-17.*

["The Professor of Desire"] is a thoughtful, even gentle, stylistically elegant novel about the paradox of male desire, that lacerating sexual passion which may lead to happiness but cannot survive it.

The effect of the book is more that of discourse than of fiction, high-level discourse adorned with wit, with rhetorical devices new and ancient, and with its piquant illustrations. Its form is that of monologue, rather than first-person storytelling, for the scenes are more often adumbrated than dramatized, the characters more often indicated than developed.

This method, designed to involve the reader intellectually rather than sensationally, is, of course, perfectly intentional —a remark that ought to be unnecessary. But we have been racing through a couple of decades in which the writers have so far outdistanced the critics that it is aggravatingly commonplace to see writing that is in fact subtle and resourceful dismissed as if it were a mistake by commentators whose perceptions simply haven't kept pace.

The monologist in Mr. Roth's novel is David Kepesh, a professor of comparative literature, two of whose enthusiasms are for Chekhov and Kafka. (p. 1)

"The Professor of Desire" . . . is a cool book on a warm topic, and it amuses Mr. Roth to deal . . . with his topic in language which is sometimes Jamesian. "He," in the following sentence, is an analyst, and the discussion summarized is of Kepesh's marriage to an Ohio beauty who had tried her wings and been shot down in Hong Kong:

> But whenever he may say, however he may bully, burlesque, or even try a smidgen of charm in order to get me to put the marriage and divorce behind me, I am, whether he believes it or not, never altogether immune from self-recrimination when stories reach me of the ailments that are said to be transforming the one-time Occidental princess of the Orient into a bitter hag.

Conversation between Kepesh and the analyst is one of several departures which, for the sake of relief, the author permits himself from the lecturer's mode, and is used both for narration and reflection, a contemporary equivalent perhaps, as it has often seemed in other works, of the old epistolary. Not long afterward, Mr. Roth does an actual epistolary sequence for us, and late in the book, yet another departure in another comedy routine. This last is introduced as a dream Kepesh has about being taken to meet an old woman who has become a literary tourist attraction, having once been Kafka's whore.

We are not, of course, meant to read this as a realist's attempt to reproduce a character's dream, but to recognize in it a comedian's convention, a current rhetorical device, just as we recognize and enjoy the use of many of the classical conventions—parallel sentence structures, periodics, metonymies, zeugmas, aphorisms, epigrams. Even some of the dialogue, and particularly the crucial exchanges between Kepesh and the women he cares about, is made carefully artificial, for it is more important to the author to set forth clearly the ideas and descriptions of emotion being exchanged than to make the realist's attempt at reproducing human speech.

It is thus, in certain ways, quite an abstract novel, and even the world of David Kepesh, its inhabitants restricted to Jewish men and gentile women, is, if not precisely abstract, certainly arbitrary.

The author's control of this world seems perfect except, perhaps, in one regard. The reader is not as certain as might be wished of the ironic distance between author and narrator, particularly at the end of the book, when Kepesh rages internally against the working-out of the desire-happiness paradox in himself, as if it were a black misfortune and his alone, "a ridiculous, vicious, inexplicable joke!" One wants to say to him, and to feel that Mr. Roth is saying of him, that it's a joke all right, but a sad, small, universal, necessary joke that cloaks a piece of folk wisdom David Kepesh is absurdly late in learning. . . .

But perhaps yet another classic device, that of literary allusion, is on the author's side in place of irony, as it often is throughout the book. For Kepesh compares his rage to that of Gogol's Kovalyov, a madman who loses his nose. See Kepesh as unhinged on the subject of his lost passion, and the problem of irony disappears.

"The Professor of Desire" includes some memorably tender passages about David Kepesh's parents, in particular those dealing with the mother's death and the father's old age. Having been offered as often as we have Jewish parents as objects of satiric criticism, it is refreshing to find them treated here as objects of simple affection.

As a widower, Kepesh's father becomes friends with another old man, Mr. Barbatnik, a concentration camp survivor whose role it is to declare that one may become something more than a man: a human being. These final elements perhaps direct us to the conclusion that family affection is what civilized people need for mutual defense against the barbarities of loneliness and death, making desire no more than a brutish mechanism that initiates affection and is then to be discarded.

If this reading is not indicated with absolute clarity, it seems at least a likely one, leaving us with "The Professor of Desire" as a fine display of literary skills, a challenging brief novel, moving when it needs to be, an erudite examination of the troglodyte within us. (p. 50)

> Vance Bourjaily, "Cool Book on a Warm Topic," in The New York Times Book Review (© 1977 by The New York Times Company; reprinted by permission), September 18, 1977, pp. 1, 50.

To the charge that Philip Roth is repeating himself in [*The Professor of Desire*], the response should be one of qualified relief: he may be going in circles but at least he's sailing in the mainstream of his talent and not stranded in those swampy backwaters from which *The Great American Novel* and *The Breast* emerged dripping mud and weeds. The weight of Roth's past performances, together with his tendency toward self-indulgent trickiness and the recurrent need to explain his intentions to his public, places an unfair burden on *The Professor of Desire*. If it were the third instead of the third in the series that includes *Portnoy's Complaint* and *My Life as a Man*, it would, I believe, be universally welcomed as the stylistically handsome, entertaining, and melancholy work that it is. If the book is finally disappointing, it is so because Roth fails to mount and sustain an action that is commensurate with its stylistic achievement; about two-thirds of the way along, the momentum falters, and the rest is a tour de force that is more eloquent than convincing.

The Professor of Desire follows the life of David Kepesh from his boyhood in the Catskills, where his parents run a kosher hotel called the Hungarian Royale, to his return, when he is in his mid-thirties, to spend an idyllic summer with his adoring mistress in the same area, only twenty miles from the old hotel. . . .

[*The Professor of Desire*] is narrated in the first person and in the present tense by the most supple and accomplished voice that Roth has yet found for the protagonist of one of his novels. Though David Kepesh has obvious affinities with Alexander Portnoy and with Nathan Zuckerman-Peter Tarnopol, the double-named narrator (and victim) of *My Life as a Man*, he is far less the clown or the breast-beater, far more the reflective yet still suffering intellectual trying to make sense of the freak show of ill-matched parts that seems to be his life. David's voice has remarkable range and authority, modulating easily from scorn to tenderness, from jabbing colloquialism or the plangency of self-pity to a paragraph of the most delicate and precise analysis of Colette as an artist of the sensual. . . .

It is also a voice that can talk unembarrassedly about literature. The fact that David Kepesh is a professor of literature as well as of desire is important. One tends to forget the degree to which Roth—from *Letting Go* onward—has been an "academic" novelist, someone who writes convincingly about graduate students, professors, and the literary life. . . . Chekhov, Kafka, and Gogol are, in a sense, major characters in *The Professor of Desire*. David's relationship to them and their work is presented (with only sporadic irony) as acutely personal. The successful incorporation of past literature into a dramatically crucial scene is rare in modern fiction. . . .

Roth's control of storytelling in the first person is such that he avoids the prolixity or looseness which Henry James saw as the chief danger inherent in this mode. But he does not heed sufficiently that other piece of Jamesian advice: "Dramatize, dramatize"—even though it is quoted by David's friend Baumgarten (in the context of how to pick up a girl). I am not referring to the comparative paucity of actual scenes with dialogue that interrupt David's recitation but to the faltering of the action because of Roth's failure to make the David-Claire relationship sufficiently dynamic in its origins and development. . . . In his handling of Claire, Roth not only violates the conventions of psychological realism, to which the novel mostly adheres, but sentimentalizes his character almost as cloyingly as Esther Summerson is sentimentalized in *Bleak House*. David's recovery of his potency also seems almost gratuitous or perfunctory in its suddenness. . . .

Part of the problem stems from the fact that Roth, after a brave effort in *When She Was Good*, has apparently given up on the attempt to create young women (as opposed to Jewish mothers) who convey the sense of an existence independent of the protagonist's need for sex or suffering or both. The same female types turn up in novel after novel. (p. 12)

Roth, who writes so obsessively about sexuality, [fails to create convincing and unsentimentalized young female characters and] the deficiency is serious, amounting to what is finally a structural defect. It is as though one half of his equation is missing. All we are left with is the self-preoccupied young man and the various phantasms with which—like St. Anthony in the desert—he must contend.

It is hard to know how we are to understand Roth's handling of sexuality. That we are expected to make the attempt is clear enough, for the reader of *The Professor of Desire* is by extension a member of Professor Kepesh's comparative literature class ("Desire 341," as Claire calls it), which is to be organized around the great works of fiction dealing with erotic desire. David plans to begin the course with an account of his own erotic history (thus implicating himself in the course's material), and he invites his students to refer what they read back to their own knowledge and experience of life. "I do not hold," he writes in this lecture, "with certain of my colleagues who tell us that literature, in its most valuable and intriguing moments, is 'fundamentally non-referential.'" In the spirit of this critical view, we might observe first that while Roth's male characters yearn for the untamed, the unsocialized, and the extravagant in their sexual behavior, their indulgence, as it is depicted, gives the impression *not* of powerful appetite leading to some uncharted land of bliss—perhaps to the apocalyptic orgasm once hailed by Norman Mailer—but rather of hectic activity masking serious disturbance in that

area. At times the protagonists (Alex Portnoy especially) are allowed momentary insight into their predicament, but mostly the blame for sexual failure is deflected elsewhere—to the mothers, girlfriends, wives—and the quest continues. These young men all seem to have suffered an arrest in their psychosexual development, leaving them unable to accept intimacy or fatherhood. David Kepesh's ultimate and unachieved fantasy about the wanton Birgitta is to turn her into a prostitute, with himself in the role of her pimp. Is he meant to be aware of the homosexual impulse underlying such a wish? Are we? (p. 13)

Psychoanalysis and its practitioners figure heavily in [Roth's] recent work but always ambiguously. . . . The ambivalence toward psychoanalysis seems at least as radical as that likely to be experienced by a patient in therapy. Though this ambivalence is productive of numerous ironies and a fair amount of comedy, Roth never creates enough "space" around his protagonist—or distance from him—to allow the reader much clarity of response.

For while Roth has admirably avoided the garrulity common to the first-person approach, he is by no means free of the tonal blurring to which this narrative method is also vulnerable. The attitudes toward women, toward sexuality, toward what is likable or contemptible in his male characters, toward psychoanalytical interpretations—these are all inconsistent enough to suggest a lack of steady authorial control, a tendency to grasp at whatever seems cleverest or most astonishing or most intense at the moment. The resultant myopia, confusion of affect, and lapses into sentimentality are, however, much less obvious than they would be in a writer whose intelligence and stylistic resources were inferior to Roth's. As it is, he can get away with a lot. Despite every charge that can (I think legitimately) be brought against *The Professor of Desire*, it is still a lively and always interesting book, evidence of a talent that can make us gasp even when it is going in circles.

There is, however, one piece of minor but gratuitous damage which Roth has inflicted upon his new book that I find hard to forgive. . . . [Although] Roth maintains that *The Professor of Desire* is neither a sequel nor an antecedent to *The Breast*, he has invited a comparison by assigning the same names to the characters in both books, thereby linking a good work to one that is painfully inferior. . . . Whatever the origins of the new novel may have been in relation to Roth's tumid little fable, he should have buried all traces, for there is no substantive connection between the two books as written, and the coincidence of names is a silly distraction. (p. 14)

Robert Towers, "One-Man Band," in The New York Review of Books *(reprinted with permission from* The New York Review of Books; *copyright © 1977 NYREV, Inc.),* October 27, 1977, pp. 12-14.

[*The Professor of Desire*] offers an account of the sexual anguish—from adolescence onward—of David Kepesh, the man who, in Roth's novella *The Breast*, was transformed at thirty-eight into a breast. When met in the present work, Kepesh is an English professor. . . . It's a completely self-contained book but the major characters are the same as those in *The Breast*, and few of its other elements will surprise readers who remember *Portnoy's Complaint* or *Goodbye, Columbus*. . . . As though to mark himself off sharply from novelists who see themselves as writing more directly about linguistic matters than about human beings, Roth has his professor speak out explicitly on the representational powers of literature, and upon his students' obligation to look through the words on the page into the lives about which they speak.

But, not surprisingly, in light of the physical alteration awaiting its hero, *The Professor of Desire* turns out to be still another book about the impossibility of a stable self. To repeat, the context for the development of this theme isn't linguistic-stylistic-theoretical, as it is in Coover and Charyn. And David Kepesh isn't Golda Meir. He's presented as a particular, solidly specified, idiosyncratic person, not a legendary character to be ratteld in the dice cup of this or that writing style. (pp. 101-02)

There are tonal ambiguities in the work, stemming from its connection with the Kafkaesque fantasy of *The Breast*. And the force, the unyieldingness, of the insistence upon ceaseless transformation as inevitable lends an air of abstractness to Kepesh's story. But that same bleak conviction attains striking authority before the end. The claim that one is powerless before one's own corrupt mercuriality can never be affecting unless scraped absolutely clean of self-pity, but Kepesh seems beyond self-pity, and *The Professor of Desire* is a suggestive book, stronger by far than the work from which it sprang, worth reading and pondering. (p. 102)

> *Benjamin Demott, "It Won't Be Long," in* The Atlantic Monthly *(copyright © 1977 by The Atlantic Monthly Company, Boston, Mass.; reprinted with permission), November, 1977, pp. 101-02.*

*   *   *

RÓZEWICZ, Tadeusz 1921-

A Polish playwright, short story writer, and poet, Rózewicz, who uses his World War II experiences as the subject matter of much of his work, is one of his country's leading poets.

It is difficult to write about Rózewicz's poetry, as it is about poetry in general. In assessing its merits it is only too easy to slip from objective appraisement into personal bias. This is especially true of Rózewicz's poetry because he is a poet who has made a great effort not to write prettily and pleasingly. Convinced that the old type of "aesthetic sensation" is dead, and contemptuous of all aesthetic values, he writes poetry in order to create facts, not words. The source of Rózewicz's inspiration lies, by his own admission, in ethics, which goes hand in hand with politics, which to him in turn are synonymous with social progress. "I react to [political] events by creating new facts in verse form and not by poetry." Molded by events of history such as Nazism, Rózewicz felt the necessity of renouncing consciously the metaphysical sources of inspiration and was led instead, he says, to materialism, realism and socialism. The question of "here and now" is to him more important than any other consideration. (pp. 78-9)

The poetry of Rózewicz is intended to shock and not to create a beautiful form of art. For this reason he would not associate himself with any literary movement or poetic groups. In his poetry Rózewicz wants to lead the reader directly to the source and rediscover the commonplace faith, hope, death and love, "the sort of love which conquers death and that which is conquered by death." . . .

Rózewicz has also been noted for his spare use of words, for avoiding the rhetorical flourish, deliberately choosing the common, man-in-the street language. (p. 79)

As is perhaps true of all who publish a lot, Rózewicz is not free from certain annoying mannerisms and poems such as "Love 1944" or "I Was Writing" [in *Faces of Anxiety*] seem slightly futile. Such items however should not detract from others which are probably some of the best Polish poems of the modern times. (p. 80)

> *Magdalena Czajkowska, in* The Polish Review *(© copyright 1970 by the Polish Institute of Arts and Sciences in America, Inc.), Summer, 1970.*

[The] efforts made by the figure in Rózewicz's monologues are efforts to overcome a far greater weakness and despair. . . . One of Rózewicz's best poems is 'In the Midst of Life', written in 1955. In it, the speaker is slowly teaching himself to pay attention to the objects and relationships in the world around him again. His small gains and back-slidings are beautifully and movingly caught . . . :

> This is a table I said
> this is a table
> there is bread and a knife on the table
> knife serves to cut bread
> people are nourished by bread
>
> man must be loved
> I learnt by night by day
> what must one love
> I would reply man . . .

Behind poems like this, of course, is Rózewicz's consciousness above all of the German death-camps, and he has written of those as well as anyone might hope to. Other poems are about the poetic means available to him: he sees traditional verse forms, once pliable and accommodating to poets' interests, as threatening his subject-matter like savage animals:

> they press so close around their spoil
> that even silence does not penetrate
> outside.

More recently his poems, and the short plays he has begun writing, have been expressing disillusion with the post-war generations in both Eastern and Western Europe, living their lives 'shallowly quicker', as he puts it in one poem. But this later work itself seems more nervous and mechanical in gesture. (pp. 119-29)

> *Derwent May, "Grave Poles," in* The Listener *(© British Broadcasting Corp. 1971; reprinted by permission of Derwent May), July 22, 1971, pp. 119-20.*

Totally accepted by the public and with a state-supported theatre at its disposal, Polish avant-garde drama had won the battle against realism and its restrictive forms and was now obliged to seek other barriers to rebel against if it was to renew itself and not become routine. In order to remain avant-garde, the creative playwright must go beyond the reigning mode of drama, not merely repeat its formulas. Such has been the position of Tadeusz Rósewicz, a highly idiosyncratic writer who has carried the rejection of conventional theatre to its logical extreme by challenging the basic conventions of theatre that make its existence possible. In *Birth Rate,* which he simply calls "The Biography of a Play for the Theatre," the playwright pits himself against the very nature of drama. (p. 63)

A short-story writer and poet as well as dramatist, Róze-wicz has constantly sought to obliterate all distinctions and limitations of genre and form. Deliberately striving for max-imum impurity, he is an anti-artist who collects debris and creates "junk art" out of scraps of quotations, newspaper clippings, shopping lists, and even bureaucratic documents. Rózewicz's technique of collage and assemblage effectively serve his vision of the contemporary world as a colossal trash heap.

In his first play, *The Card File* (1960), the playwright cele-brates the anonymous man. The generic, nameless hero lies in bed throughout the entire play contemplating his own hand and opening and closing his fingers. Passers-by—fragments of his past, present, and future—wander across the stage and question this modern everyman about his life and commitments. Interrogated by these insistent voices, the unwilling protagonist asserts, "I like the little toe on my left foot better than I do all of humanity." By remaining totally passive and irresponsible, he attempts to resist all pressures from the outside world.

Rózewicz's works are marked by a deep suspicion of ab-stractions, ideologies, and principles, particularly those for-cibly imposed on human beings in the name of mankind. A crucial difference emerges between the individual and hu-manity in the abstract. The poet mistrusts words and seeks truth in nakedness, in the bare biological facts of the human organism and the world of things which surrounds it. For Rózewicz, the only verities are concrete. A montage of bits and scraps, misplaced emotions, stray characters, lost in a world of fluid time and space, *The Card File* is without dramatic action and refuses to fit into the standard theatri-cal mold.

As Rózewicz continues his struggle to write plays in the face of the growing impossibility of such an enterprise, stage directions replace dialogue; the author is forced to abandon writing normal plays, even avant-garde ones. In-stead of literary texts, he produces arguments with the theatre and scenarios in which playwright and performer are co-creators. In *The Interrupted Act* (1964), Rózewicz makes a play out of his dissatisfaction with all existing dra-matic forms. The conflict in the drama is between the idea of the play and the impossibility of its execution. Remarks by the author, personal intrusions, theoretical deliberations, and polemics with other theorists of the theatre interrupt and subvert the play itself to produce a new kind of narra-tive script in which what cannot be presented in the theatre becomes theatrical.

In the course of a few years, Rózewicz has moved to ever more extreme positions, endeavoring, by a process of ex-pansion, to burst the bonds of drama and break open its forms. In *The Old Woman Broods* (1968), the poet creates a score, an elastic scenario in which he invites the collabo-ration of a director and theatre; the playwright himself is unable to complete what he has set in motion. Rózewicz's stage directions, which constitute over one third of the printed text, are not descriptive or prescriptive, but offer the imaginative director suggestions and ideas which he is free to carry out as he wishes. The author does not tell the director how to produce the play, but once having posed the problems, he deliberately leaves the work partly unfin-ished and open to different kinds of solutions.

The Old Woman Broods presents Rózewicz's version of the apocalypse. After the end of the world, life goes on much the same as before; human beings continue reproduc-ing and accumulating things in the rubble produced by a nuclear war, and refuse and paper keep piling up every-where on the surface of the scarred earth. *The Old Woman Broods* is a series of variations on the theme of rubbish. Rubbish becomes the playwright's all-inclusive metaphor as he portrays the contemporary world as a giant trash heap and graveyard—a cosmic garbage can for all culture and civilization. Human beings are fighting a losing battle with rubbish and ugliness—they are human garbage themselves. Modern civilization's waste products are its only true art, and Rózewicz fashions drama out of such impermanent ar-tifacts as old, discarded newspapers.

All these tendencies in Rózewicz's art achieve the fullest expression in *Birth Rate,* a potential play about biological proliferation that overflows the stage and the possibilities of drama. The process of enlargement has now been carried so far that no currently existing theatrical form can contain the subject (just as the living mass in *Birth Rate* causes the walls to buckle). Accordingly, the playwright must leave his work unwritten, asking some future director and future theatre to compose it in a manner which Rózewicz cannot yet imagine. As in conceptual art, the author's inability to write the play becomes the drama.

The key to *Birth Rate* lies in the figure of the playwright who is both the author and the hero of this unwritten lyric drama. A modern Hamlet, meditating in the graveyard of civilization, and an inhabitant of the greatest necropolis in history, Rózewicz dramatizes his own hesitations in trying to write the play; he had hoped to forge a drama out of his struggles with the "living mass," but in the face of so much death, he wonders if he can write at all. In a long inner drama, the poet carries on a debate with the voices of his predecessors and masters: Witkacy and Gombrowicz, al-ready classics from the past; Beckett, the turning point in modern theatre; and finally, Rózewicz's three models for interior drama—all novelists and story writers, all Slavic—Dostoevsky, Chekhov, and Conrad.

If the essential drama contained in *Birth Rate* at first seems highly external in its attempted depiction of expanding pop-ulation, the work soon becomes internal as the author bat-tles with swarming images and masses of living matter, is increasingly overcome by them, and finally holds his "dia-logue" with past writers and dramatists about how to pre-sent the processes of life in the theatre, letting these artists speak directly through quotations and excerpts. Rózewicz's "Biography of a Play for the Theatre" turns into a collage of citations and allusions, with the author's marginalia serv-ing as dramatic commentary.

Birth Rate is also an interior drama of silence in that the processes which it explores occur deep within the human organism. For Rózewicz, the masses are perceived biologically—not as a body politic, but as a physiological entity. The important revolution is one of population, not regimes; the dramatic action takes place in organs and wombs. The drama of *Birth Rate* lies in the artist-intellec-tual's confrontation with the human body and in his inabil-ity to write his play about this "living mass." In other words, *Birth Rate* describes the playwright's own inability to give birth. Out of this impossibility Rózewicz asks that a new art of the theatre arise. (pp. 64-6)

Daniel C. Gerould, "Tadeusz Rózewicz: Playwriting as Collage," in Performing Arts Journal *(© copyright 1976 Performing Arts Journal), Fall, 1976, pp. 63-6.*

[Rózewicz] is a poet with hauteur. He knows he is good ('a shoddy poet who has died / Is a shoddy dead poet'). In Poland, he occupies a very special position, venerated although he is only in his fifties and followed by a comet-trail of apprentices. Political hurricanes, like those which buffeted Slonimski (who sailed into them) or drove Zbigniew Herbert abroad, haven't affected him much. He is almost equally well known as a writer of plays, impossible farces like *The Interrupted Act* which is really a St Valentine's Day Massacre of Polish theatrical fads, or the famous *Card Index*. Three of these plays have also been translated. . . .

Many of [his] poems are about poetry. Rózewicz is very deliberately not an aesthete, not an ideologue and not a 'presenter' or showman. He prefers to regard poetry as a force, the poet responding to it as zealot touched with grace —except that no God but the world itself is distributing this grace. . . .

Some of his verse is very direct. The short poem 'Massacre of the Boys', which is about Auschwitz and known all over the world, or the much longer 'Old Peasant Woman Walks Along the Beach' (1952) are in no way sly. The latter, in fact, is surprisingly close to the sort of helpful, socially-conscious verse which the regime appreciated at that time. War and occupation are present almost everywhere: 'Objects excavated in my country have small black/heads sealed with plaster and horrible grins . . . ' Images like that, in most countries seen only by a few people who have since devoted much energy to trying to forget them, were an almost universal experience for Rózewicz's generation in Poland: they and the corresponding interest in the fact of being alive govern many of his poems.

He writes, like Tadeusz Borowski, about the jaunty nihilism of the concentrationnaire who finds he has survived ('the following are empty synonyms: / man and beast / love and hate . . . '), and also clearing away the debris of dead words after a war or an autocracy. Here he is like that group of post-war German poets who took little, hard words and rinsed them carefully one by one until they were usable again: Rózewicz's 'In the Midst of Life', though written . . . as the Stalinist period was waning, catches their mood. Sometimes he becomes sentimental, and sometimes the dryness and spareness look like snobbery rather than economy. But at his best, in the untitled poem which begins 'He tears easily . . . ' or in 'Shallowly Quicker' (about a world which has sold out of souls), Rózewicz belongs in every anthology of post-war verse.

Neal Ascherson, "Pre-War Quality," in New Statesman *(© 1977 The Statesman and Nation Publishing Co. Ltd.), April 8, 1977, p. 469.*

S

SADOFF, Ira   1945-

Sadoff is an American poet, critic, translator, and editor. He is cofounder and editor of the *Seneca Review*. The tone of his poetry is remarkably akin to prose, continually avoiding "academic" or "poetic" expression. The mood of his poetry is one of controlled resignation. (See also *Contemporary Authors*, Vols. 53-56.)

In the biographical note [to *Settling Down*] it does not say that Sadoff studied at Iowa, but his poetry is stamped with that sound and shape. (It seems inevitable that "the Iowa Poets" will wedge into our jargon before long.) He works in hard-edge designs of pure acrylic colors. As if talking meant taking, he clenches his teeth in a brave reluctance, acknowledging no less than is necessary. Like Edward Hopper, he can make empty space into a premonition of disaster.... With his finger pressing "the trigger of sadness," he is forever "taking the subject / and subjecting it to our sense / of separation." The discontinuity of experience is, finally, his subject—shadowed by a secreting desire "to make oneself whole / without closing the circle forever." ... [Stillness] for Sadoff is a frightening prospect, and as his portraits resolve in their pans, their characters have a ghostly, melancholy image, catching the Chekhovian tint of faded sepia.... Sadoff's voice moves naturally toward the flattened expanse of prose, and his several prose-poems are haunting. Attempts at assigned "academy" pieces find him uneasy—neither his wit nor his nostalgia is sharp enough. But those poems of his that etch the frail cruelties of banal domestic drama—as in soap opera, "Everything happens inside"—are superb. Having enabled himself to evoke the arbitrary distance between things, one looks forward to the ways he might close in on that emptiness. But wherever he may next settle down, he has already made a place for himself with this book. (pp. 100-02)

> *J. D. McClatchy, in* The Yale Review (© *1975 by Yale University; reprinted by permission of the editors), Autumn, 1975.*

Ira Sadoff has ... a methodic reliance on the simple, declarative sentence; a no-nonsense air, smuggled in from prose; a fastidious avoidance of the gratuitously "poetic". No wonder, then, that in Sadoff's very impressive first book, *Settling Down*, the most felicitous expression of his manner is to be found in the seven prose poems, each a gem.... [In] the endings of *Seurat* and of *The Revolution*

of 1905 ... the refraction of what can only be called a preconscious memory through the lens of a painting or a film, animated anew, reminds of the Delmore Schwartz of *In Dreams Begin Responsibilities*, a high compliment indeed.... (pp. 39-40)

In Sadoff's work the distinction between object and emotion is made as a kind of critique of contemporary consciousness. The sense of removal from reality that is signified accounts to a large measure for the mood of resignation pervading *Settling Down;* the exigencies of poetic empathy are strenuous, calling for acquiescence rather than affirmation. History may occur as tragedy and repeat itself as farce, but that is in a temporal realm; along a different set of space/time coordinates—in the empire of the psyche, for example—history survives as Stephen Dedalus's back-kicking nightmare, a threatening absence by day, an inescapable presence by night. (p. 40)

If there is a characteristic utterance in this volume, it is a kind of structuralist poem, of which Frank O'Hara was a master. Having delineated the structure of a given reality, the poet either presents it as shadow or he reconstructs it fancifully.... There is more talent in *Settling Down* than there is fulfillment, but that is as it should be. (p. 41)

> *David Lehman, in* Poetry (© *1976 by The Modern Poetry Association; reprinted by permission of the Editor of* Poetry), *April, 1976.*

Titles and subheadings [in *Settling Down*] run on in the following manner: I. *Waiting for Evening;* II. *Forgetting This World;* and III. *Going Back to Sleep.* They indicate a potential problem of dynamics (and something of Sadoff's style of solution) for a collection of poems centered largely on the domestic, that is, how not to be duped by the local into the dull. Sadoff, although himself under thirty, legitimately chooses to deal with aging, which he appears to outline as closure of opportunities, as desiccating and estranged, within the frame of these topics—marriage, home, and work.... "Settling Down," the first and title poem of the book, is ... typical of Sadoff's prettily enervated approach:

> . . . All day I sit
> at my desk watching the tea steep
> in its cup, the copper blood
> running out of its sack
> like fluid from a dying fish.

Although other poems like "The Return to Mysticism" claim that the cause of distress is cosmic ("the gods / out of tune our prayers / unanswered as usual,") others, [like "Séance,"] a little too readily for this kind of book, busy themselves with spirit tracks: ". . . a spine / of smoke . . . a char of bones / behind the mirror and a cloud of flesh on the ceiling." . . . Still, whether summoned to a poem by impaired personal relations, flaws of the stars, or other combinations astral, domestic, and organic, . . . one's sympathies tend to stay lightly engaged. . . . [The] generating impulse seems both diffused and strained.

The prose poems are probably the strongest pieces. These poems, "The Revolution of 1905," "Seurat," "Alienation of Affection," and "1928"—where even the titles indicate their broader intentions—do not focus quite so narrowly on the theater of domestic accommodation. There is a wider variety of people, and a general thickening of shape and circumstance. To tea bags and melancholy, Sadoff adds war, the lives of artists, and several changes in historical climate.

Also, the technique is surer. Because he is not dealing with the visual hedge of the line-break, the fluidity of the verbal structure is intact and under control. The images don't bleed quite so relentlessly into each other. Supported by more conventional narrative, the effects are less labored and the figures of speech not so florid—as in the smooth opening of "Seurat":

> It is a Sunday afternoon on the Grand Canal. We are watching the sailboats trying to sail along without wind. Small rowboats are making their incisions on the water, only to have the wounds seal up again soon after they pass.

The conclusion seems thoughtful, unpretentious, and earned:

>   . . . We could not know, taking a
> step back, looking at the total picture, that we would
> occupy such a small corner of the canvas, and that even
> then we are no more than tiny clusters of dots, care-
> fully placed together without touching.

There is also no inappropriate attempt to force the figures into conceits, or further into something resembling "quatrains" and "stanzas" and "lines." Nor is there the kind of arbitrary jamming of figures that mars even good poems like "The Thirties," a poem which illustrates all of Sadoff's strengths and weaknesses. The style of its beginning resembles "Seurat":

> The cars are all black.
> The men wear hats
> and the women long dresses
> simply to cover themselves.

But by the third stanza, this being a "poem," and not a paragraph, there are characteristic problems:

> Buildings empty like slashed wrists.
> The streets are paved with hands,
> and money flows through the fingers
> like rain in a desert or a great fire.

In an attempt to unify the lines, blood, rain, money, and people are all made to flow in continuing streams. Both streets and buildings have hands—but along one set of the hands money flames "or" rains in a desert. All of the muddle finally has something to do with flowing, hands grasping with futility, and catastrophe. Somewhere in there a strong image lies buried.

Nevertheless, in the concluding stanzas, Sadoff, often good at last minute salvage, works off the excrescent surrealist matter, and finishes with real feeling:

> My father . . .
> . . . will sit
>
> in a crowded theater and go off
> just as the hero is cured of
> an incurable disease. The bodies will spray
> out as an enormous fountain, a bouquet
>
> of arms and legs. This is a dream
> of the thirties: to explode into a circle
> of strangers, to open every part of yourself
> in the dark without hope.

But a quick look up the left side of the poem just quoted exhibits another too frequent trait. Each of the last five lines starts with a preposition, and every line breaks before every natural rhetorical or syntactical stop. This is more than awkward. The poem wears its words like a badly-blocked hat. A warp breaks the lines with schismatic fervor mid-phrase, choking almost every attempt to build up meaning. In Sadoff's practice, . . . beginnings of lines rarely have any force, and endings always enjamb, or tail off so that only the middle of a line is left with any definition—usually a strong, hatcheting caesura. For instance: "a bouquet / of arms and legs." Stop. ". . . a dream / of the thirties:" stop: "to explode into a circle / of strangers," etc.

These formal manners have several unhappy effects, one of which is to draw attention to the crudely-unvarying syntax. Sadoff draws a short bow and even it fragments into monotonously regular prepositional phrases, spliced by static predications. . . . Even when the lines don't break at the preposition they settle for cutting up the sense in some other place. This shakes the largely monosyllabic style with a nervous tic that rarely lets a plain statement alone. Always a white chopper of a margin comes at the poem, slicing and tilting. . . . It is not that the book has no pleasures, but that often the road to them seems intercepted. (pp. 144-48)

> *Lorrie Goldensohn, in* Parnassus: Poetry in Review (*copyright* © *by* Parnassus: Poetry in Review), *Spring–Summer, 1976.*

*   *   *

SAGAN, Françoise (pseudonym of Françoise Quoirez) 1935-

Sagan is a French novelist and playwright whose works often deal with brief, tentative relationships and love affairs. She concerns herself with trying to understand the motivation behind the actions of her characters—bored, lonely people whom she depicts sharply. Her first novel, *Bonjour Tristesse*, was written when she was eighteen, making her an instant lit-

erary celebrity. Her pseudonym comes from the character of the Princess of Sagan in Marcel Proust's *Remembrance of Things Past.* (See also *CLC,* Vols. 3, 6, and *Contemporary Authors,* Vols. 49-52.)

Françoise Sagan has in her time said some wry things about love; in *Lost Profile,* the insights are thin on the ground— the worst thing about a break-up, for instance, is "not just leaving one another, but leaving one another for different reasons". There are some nice touches.... But some of the writing is so overdone as to be ludicrous....

Françoise Sagan began writing novels over twenty years ago, as a precocious adolescent; and to her contemporaries her early work was indeed "sophisticated and erotic". But now she is still writing for adolescents of the 1950s, hung-up on father figures, mad about puppies.

> *Victoria Glendinning, "Jose´e & Julius & Louis," in* The Times Literary Supplement *(© Times Newspapers Ltd., 1976; reproduced from* The Times Literary Supplement *by permission), March 19, 1976, p. 311.*

Sagan's particular passion of the minute is to be pitied and solaced. It is a closeted world, incredulously French, with a narrow mix of sympathy and arrogance.

Writing *Bonjour Tristesse* Miss Sagan had an excuse for such a self-opinionated heart. To find that in her tenth novel, *Lost Profile,* she has advanced her profundity not at all, is still playing the cramped teenager trying to escape Daddy, comes as something of a shock. Her novels are short and as full of wry observations about people in love as ever they were. 'Wild passion I admired, and loyalty and spontaneity and even a certain kind of fidelity.' This puts her emotional manifesto in a nutshell, a rather shallow, quasi hysterical woman with a passive pantheistic belief in the soul as something tossed helplessly by natural forces, yet admitting the possibility that even fidelity can be admirable under certain circumstances. Only a rather genteel upbringing, it seems, prevents her from seeking out rape, the more violent the better, an example of the desire for maltreatment which is of course Woman's lot when you get down to it. (p. 23)

> *Duncan Fallowell, in* The Spectator *(© 1976 by* The Spectator; *reprinted by permission of* The Spectator*), March 27, 1976.*

[In *Silken Eyes*] is an elegant and brittle art, a pricey collection of tiny figurines and minute porcelains, where passion and ageing must never be allowed to fall heavily among the stylishly placed bric-à-brac, and people are mannequins, stereotypes, puppets, the contrivance of whose making is given away from time to time by the odd lifeless judder of manipulation. These stories work best when the particular examples of the international set on display, with their Maseratis and Creed jackets and Dior dresses and smart houses in Paris, are continental. Shooting chamois and wanting to shoot your rival, flaunting gigolos, shooting yourself abstractedly, crashing your car deliberately, being bored and beautiful and in *Vogue,* seem much more fetching when a Jerome Berthier or Countess Josepha von Kraftenberg is involved. Like middling food and crumby movies these upper-class glossies are, as it were, all right in French. But when it's a case of Lord Stephen Timberley and Emily Highlife at Dunhill Castle, or a Millicent in

Berkshire, or a Lady Brighton, all old Etonians or parents of Etonians, then the bogusness of their horrifically fashion-plate circumstance and of this kind of fiction's mode really do strike. (p. 515)

> *Valentine Cunningham, in* New Statesman *(© 1977 The Statesman & Nation Publishing Co. Ltd.), October 14, 1977.*

Since the appearance ... of her first novel, "Bonjour Tristesse," Françoise Sagan has been praised for the economy of her style. In "Silken Eyes," her first collection of short stories, she economizes still further, perhaps to the point of parsimony....

Some of Miss Sagan's reputation owes itself to ambiance, a word often on the tip of the French tongue. "Bonjour Tristesse" took its title from a poem by Paul Eluard....

Her tragic view of life, epitomized in "hello sadness," is a further index of her seriousness.

If anybody can be grasped with ease and precision, I suppose it is the idle and amorous rich who furnish Miss Sagan's stories. Their lives are already reduced—ideal material for economy. The beginnings and ends of love affairs, a brush or two with death, the inherent ironies of sex and marriage. Miss Sagan's oeuvre is all hors d'oeuvre....

There is little poetry ... in the hearts of Miss Sagan's characters, who seem to be more preoccupied with vanity, strategy and compromises. But while it is fashionable to feel, or at least write, this way, I don't believe the human heart has changed so much. Neither medicine nor literature seems to have prevailed on it. In "Silken Eyes," the characters have haute couture hearts. They've been lifted not by love but by plastic surgery....

Now and then in "Silken Eyes" there is a nice vignette, a good line, a charmingly raised eyebrow. The wine is suitably dry, the service discreet. A woman whose lover has left her—yes, another one, there's no end of them—consoles herself in a nightclub, dancing with a man she does not love. "Life goes on," he says, "I'm still here, you're still here. We're dancing." She replies "We're the sort of people who dance," and while it is not a great epiphany, it's all right. (p. 14)

> *Anatole Broyard, in* The New York Times Book Review *(© 1977 by The New York Times Company; reprinted by permission), October 30, 1977.*

*   *   *

SANER, Reg(inald)   1931-

An American poet, Saner is fascinated with landscapes and their rejuvenative effect. His poetic concerns with mysticism and American Indian culture link him with Gary Snyder. *Climbing into the Roots,* Saner's first collection, won him the Walt Whitman Award in 1975. (See also *Contemporary Authors,* Vols. 65-68.)

Now if you believe, as many do, that a poem is a structure of language and not much more, then ["Climbing into the Roots"] is pretty good writing and probably deserves the handsome Walt Whitman Award.... Never mind if the metaphors are mixed ... ; the imagery at least has freshness, the lines are taut, the sounds and movements are roughly analogous to the actions they describe. And Saner is good at this, as he proves amply in many poems.

But what if a poem is more than a structure of language? What if it is a structure of meaning, feeling and experience, to which verbal technique contributes primarily as means to an end? I don't suggest that Saner has nothing to say, only that he has very little to say and has apparently given little thought to how he might say more. His writing is verbal display, that's all, loaded with metaphor for its own sake; it may be superficially entertaining, but it is never moving. And it sometimes leads Saner, incidentally, into foolishness. What shall we think of "the rosy foreskin of dawn," "clouds like Swedish blondes in mulberry velvet," or stars that are "the tail-lights of the big bang"? (p. 29)

> *Hayden Carruth, in* The New York Times Book Review *(© 1976 by The New York Times Company; reprinted by permission), March 28, 1976.*

Reg Saner's [*Climbing into the Roots*] is the winner of the first annual Walt Whitman Award. . . . It is a deserving award because Saner's voice is exuberant and free of a temporary idiom that might make it seem "in" or "with it."

It is a voice from the Rockies, distinct and personal as are the experiences in the mountains that most of these poems describe. . . . [Saner's] metaphor is vivid, sharp, and full of clean air. . . . (p. 40)

Saner can un-perplex nature by noting its logical ironies: "a winter courage / in the delicate breathing / of small animals." He also notes the frustration of the camera bug who can find no compelling scene amid mountains "too gorgeously banal to shoot."

With individual effects, . . . Saner is first-rate among poets, an incisive professional. In a larger scope, his poems often seem rather thin in purpose. When he tries to add up the effects, he often reaches impossibly big conclusions. As with his "too gorgeously banal" mountains, his views of nature extend to near-infinities such as "beginning of sand," "history of green," "idea of flowers/meaning all," "the full history of bees," "the fabulous past of stones."

Such results expose one of the great difficulties in writing poems about nature. . . . Poets who have been most successful in this mode have had a complementary theme against which to play off the natural phenomena. Frost had his Calvinism, Jeffers had his contempt for most human events, Snyder has his Zen emphasis on doing things. Saner seems to have not much beyond his awe.

If he were to adopt a more specific complementary theme or if he were to turn his fine gift to human subjects more, as he indeed does in the dissolution of father into son in "Turn," he could become one of our rarest voices. (pp. 40-1)

> *Richard Gustafson, in* Poet and Critic *(© Department of English and Speech, Iowa State University), Vol. 9, No. 3, 1976.*

Reg Saner, in . . . *Climbing Into the Roots*, takes landscape almost as his only subject and finds in it a great restorative power. Gary Snyder's poems have prepared us to read Saner's. Snyder is a more moral, even a more didactic poet than Saner, but their poems draw on similar sources— Buddhism, an acquaintance with the nature sciences, and with American Indian culture. Saner's poems are often

about "peak experiences", and, indeed, the setting for them is often on mountaintops. It's correct to describe these experiences as religious, I think, just as in Snyder's case. The immediate problem for both Snyder and Saner, or for any poet attempting to set down such experiences, is to avoid what might be called the banality of transcendence. If transcendence is best described as "emptiness", "no soul", a colorless, odorless, tasteless void, how is it to be rendered in an art that thrives on concretion?

Saner's usual practice here is to offer visual particulars as springboards into what is, or more properly, isn't beyond. The visual particulars are at least successful as visual particulars. The dust jacket of the book mentions that Saner has worked as a photographer, and he has a good eye. The book abounds with sharp-focus diapositives of a clarity and perfection I associate with stereopticons or perhaps those miniature landscapes captured in glass paperweights. (p. 357)

In a world filled with so much Being [as his] the active verb has little place, and reality is telegraphic or simply gerundive. Rudimentary syntax proves to be another drawback, then, in poems arising from the mystic's imagination of the world. Along with that, at least one reader is astonished by the frequency of lines written in monometer, a metrical curiosity normally reserved for the poetry manuals.

On the other hand, in these poems parts of the world are well rendered, and it seems ungenerous to quarrel. . . . Saner's landscapes are largely unpeopled, or peopled with . . . campers rendered mainly as spots of color, in their bright orange jackets. Thus, the rare poem in this collection dealing with human relationships, *Passing It On*, for example, . . . is especially welcome when it turns up among so many deserted landscapes. (pp. 357-58)

> *Alfred Corn, in* Poetry *(© 1976 by The Modern Poetry Association; reprinted by permission of the Editor of* Poetry*), September, 1976.*

[Wonder] at high places is carried to the ultimate and made the central theme by an expert mountain climber named Reg Saner . . . [in] *Climbing into the Roots*. Saner is no beginner in either of his avocations: . . . his maturity appears both in the breadth of his vision and in the sureness of his technical command. There are slips here and there, none of them fatal: too much straining after metaphor, too much scrambling over rubble in his language, but these are recovered by the muscular energy that plays throughout the book. The experience of climbing (into the roots of heaven) is conveyed in rich, vigorous detail, until one almost comes to share the fast breathing of these altitudes. . . . Not all the poems here are mountain pieces; others deal with the plains, speeding cars, waking up at home, family matters— but the core of the book lies in the recreation of the delight of climbing, with the washed vision of nature that comes in high altitudes. It comes across as a form of heroism still possible in modern times. . . . (p. 126)

> *Louis L. Martz, in* The Yale Review *(© 1976 by Yale University; reprinted by permission of the editors), Autumn, 1976.*

*   *   *

SARTRE, Jean-Paul   1905-

Sartre, a French playwright, essayist, philosopher, politician,

and novelist, is considered by many to be the most influential thinker and writer of our time. The father of existentialist philosophy, Sartre has examined virtually every aspect of human endeavor from the position of a search for total human freedom. Early in his career Sartre forged a philosophy of fiction revolving around the reader-author relationship which became a pivotal perspective of the New Novel school. Sartre called for the implication of the reader in fiction, the establishment of highly subjective points of view, and he said that chronology could best be handled through a series of constantly unfolding and ongoing present moments. He received the Nobel Prize for Literature in 1964. (See also *CLC*, Vols. 1, 4, 7, and *Contemporary Authors*, Vols. 9-12, rev. ed.)

A valuable prescription for those who would understand Sartre's notion of freedom should be: Don't confine your reading to *Being and Nothingness* and *Critique of Dialectical Reason*. Although Sartre deals with a wide range of subjects in the former, earlier work, he largely emphasizes individual freedom and aloneness. In the latter work, he encourages concerted social action. This seeming paradox requires a survey of the Sartre *oeuvre* to decipher, for only in this way can one fully appreciate the progression of Sartre's thought on the crucial matter of freedom. (p. 144)

The primary components of Sartre's thought may be said to form a triumvirate: Freedom-Responsibility-Action. In *Being and Nothingness,* Sartre insists that the major consequence of the fact that God does not exist, a consequence which man must recognize and accept, is that man is completely free. It is he who represents, through his freedom to act, the only destiny of mankind, and, through the acceptance of his freedom-responsibility, the legislator of all values.

Initially, the emphasis on freedom had a strongly personal nature—with *Being and Nothingness* and Sartre's first play, *The Flies,* many readers determined that for Sartre the individual must assume his own freedom as ultimately and exclusively important. His second drama, *No Exit,* was viewed as a vivid revelation that men cannot engage in cooperative endeavors due to inevitable conflict. At this stage of his writing, however, Sartre produced his essay, *Existentialism is a Humanism.* Many critics prefer to forget this brief work and fervently wish that Sartre had done the same. Still Sartre refuses to reject any of his works; thus, we must accept the fact that he does not now reject nor did he reject in 1946 the premise of this essay—each man, desiring freedom above all, necessarily wants and strives for the freedom of the Other as well. . . . Sartre had not sufficiently elaborated in his first work the extent of the limitation to project and freedom afforded by the Other. Again, he did not sufficiently elaborate in *Existentialism Is a Humanism* how the former difficulty could be superseded in favor of a striving toward freedom for both self and the Other. Was it possible, in fact, that the critics were justified, that there was no solution to this dilemma?

Here a study of the drama provides a much needed and indispensable supplement to Sartre's philosophical works. The careful reader of Sartre's *oeuvre* cannot help but be struck by the fact that Sartre wrote a play subsequent to each progression of thought concerning his system. Yet, with the drama, he seems to be released from a good deal of the abstraction peculiar to his philosophical work. Proceeding as it does from within the inner sphere of his imagina-

tion, the drama not only quotes the key ideas of its father philosophical or critical work but expands upon the ideas, and, in fact, often foreshadows ideas to come. Such is the case with regard to the dilemma of freedom in the context of human projects.

Looking at Sartre's first drama, *The Flies,* written after Sartre's first great philosophical work and during the occupation, the reader finds an emphasis on the recognition of individual freedom on the part of one man, Orestes. . . . The play demonstrates quite clearly that the Other, in this case, the people of Argos, are necessary in order to give meaning to the act which Orestes performs; clearly, Orestes performs the act to free the people and to show them their freedom; however, the reader cannot escape the point that Orestes initially desires the act and the communion with the Argives as a means of personal commitment and to give his own life meaning. Thus, the individual in search of his own freedom and identity through commitment is primary and the devotion of the effort for the Other, while very important, is secondary to this factor.

Sartre's second play, *No Exit,* focuses on the conflict basic to human relations. Unfortunately, with one line of this play, Sartre has allowed himself to be "hung on his own catchphrase." "Hell is other people" is a line so vivid and memorable that it permits critics to handily make of the play itself an object which teaches, "Hell is [always] other people." There is, however, much more to this play than meets the eye of the person who prefers to be captivated by this catchphrase. (pp. 145-46)

[It] is the misinterpretation of Sartre's view of human interaction emanating from this play which tends to color the view of this phenomenon in the whole of his drama and perhaps the whole of his thought. Critics tend to view Sartre's play as a reflection of life as it is; they assume the fact that the characters are dead and in "hell" is only symbolic. This is partially true, but the *fact* of death is too important to Sartre to attribute only incidental meaning to that state in his three characters. The result of death is that man ceases to be a subject and becomes an immutable object over which the living are the guardians. . . . This condition is also comparable to the state of persons in bad faith—a condition of lying to oneself in order to escape responsible freedom. Thus, "dead" characters offer Sartre twofold advantages. First, he can show the immutable total antithesis of authentic existence. He can hold the condition of bad faith suspended in time. The characters can be shown as condemned, since they are dead, to repeat all of the errors which become an object lesson for the audience. Secondly, the fact that the characters are dead permits Sartre to represent the failings of those individuals who are their counterpart in life, those who are dead on earth before they are buried because they fail to choose and act. At the same time, this fact confirms that another course is possible, that life is for the living if they exist authentically. If they do not, then they are as surely dead, objectified, and meaningless as the inhabitants of that hellish Second Empire drawing room.

From this interpretation, it is easy to see the actual significance of the line, "Hell is other people." Each character has died in bad faith and can no longer change. In one way or another, he is totally dependent upon the others for even his meagre and meaningless existence. (p. 146)

The play is never meant to indicate that conflict *per se* is an evil. Obviously, when two conscious beings, two freedoms, come together, there is the potential of conflicting freedoms. . . . [Sartre] has not indicated that this basic conflict with the Other is a negative thing, but rather that for those who would live authentically, those who reject bad faith and embrace freedom, it is through such encounters with the Other that freedom is expressed and values are created. Indeed, outside of its relation to the Other and the world, freedom does not exist. Franz Gerlach of Sartre's play, *The Condemned of Altona,* vividly affirms this concept. He refuses to confront the Other and the world and to strive to give meaning to the world around himself. Even without his locked room, he would be imprisoned, for without placing himself in choice situations with the Other, his freedom is nothing. In the same sense, Garcin, Estelle, and Inez were "dead" long before they reached their "hell" [in *No Exit*]; they had created a hell on earth through their bad faith, through their failure to act in a manner which gave meaning to freedom. Thus, it is through action in relation to the Other and the world that each man gives meaning to his freedom and to his life. This is, of course, the way which requires bearing the burden of freedom-responsibility; it is not the way of a Garcin or an Estelle.

While conflict is shown in *No Exit* as a primary factor of existence, unresolved conflict of projects is demonstrated as inherent only in relationships fostered of bad faith. It must never be overlooked that only the characters of *No Exit* of all the plays written by Sartre, are unable to change; only they are irremediably as others see them. . . . [Even so,] the small suggestion is there that a course is possible which feasibly resolves the conflict of projects, a course which requires working together with mutual respect for the Other's freedom and his project.

It would appear that little hope in this direction would be forthcoming from the oppressive atmosphere of *The Dead without Burial.* . . . [Still], Canoris, one of the prisoners, has several speeches which mark his character as the transition between the early Sartre absorbed in the notion of personal freedom as exemplified by Orestes and the later Sartre concerned with unified human effort. . . . Canoris insists that the prisoners must determine to subordinate their own desires and their attempts to justify their own existence in favor of lives useful to others.

This viewpoint, of course, is the driving force behind the character of Hoederer [in *Dirty Hands*], whose numerous speeches concerning his dedication to mankind mark him as engaged in a truly authentic existence. Hoederer [is] surely Sartre's most authentic man. . . . Goetz [in *The Devil and the Good Lord*] comes to realize that the only authentic existence lies in giving up his own vain attempts at perfection and self-justification and his former beliefs in God, Good, and Evil in an all-out effort to achieve the liberation of man. He will become the man Hoederer and the prisoners of *The Dead without Burial* were prevented by death from becoming. He will be the man that Orestes had never considered becoming. (pp. 147-49)

Sartre began to focus more diligently on limitations to freedom of which he was becoming increasingly aware. . . .

The plays begin to show that poverty and social class structure particularly are responsible for much that is oppressive and limiting in the world. (p. 150)

The new emphasis in Sartre's work is reflected in his focus on the concept of "need." . . . Sartre says of this new emphasis since his early writing, "Over against a dying child *Nausee'* cannot act as a counterweight." Sartre, then, has come to believe that man is more limited in his freedom than Sartre himself originally anticipated. While each man is free within his own situation, some circumstances, such as poverty or war, make the situation so oppressive that genuine liberation is impossible *without constant revolution* to maintain freedom. This revolution must proceed from unified effort within which individual talent is utilized and the individual freely "relinquishes" a degree of his freedom in the sense that he is willing to engage in concerted effort with other men. (pp. 150-51)

This more recent recognition by Sartre of those factors in life which tend to limit freedom must not be construed, however, as a significant deviation from Sartre's original premise that man is free within his own situation. . . . For Goetz and the peasants, poverty and the division among classes which *limits* their freedom *does not eliminate* their freedom nor does it offer an excuse for inaction. It is merely the playing court in which they will engage in a contest whose rules they now know. (p. 151)

This progressive awareness, which the reader of Sartre's drama may witness groping for and gradually reaching the light, seems more abrupt when the perusal of the works is limited to Sartre's statements of philosophy. Still, what appears to the reader of *Being and Nothingness* as an inconsistency in *Existentialism Is a Humanism* and a complete break in *Critique* should appear to the reader of the entire works of Sartre as rather a constant movement and development of thought. The conflict between peoples and the necessity for individual resistance is developed in *Being* and exemplified in the action of *The Flies* and *No Exit*. The need for a shift from concerns with individual freedom to a striving for universal freedom is suggested in *Existentialism Is a Humanism* but not explained. Gradually, the explanation is accomplished in *The Dead Without Burial, Dirty Hands,* and reaches its culmination in *The Devil and the Good Lord,* the logical predecessor to *Critique*. With the play, *The Condemned of Altona,* which expresses the notion of "need," the entire effort is toward an awareness of twentieth-century problems which must be corrected at all costs in order to facilitate the true liberation of man.

There is, then, nothing violently new, no break with previous thought, in this present notion of unified striving for mankind's liberation. As Sartre describes his shifts of emphasis, it is change "within a permanency." In the present order of things, Sartre endeavors to encourage an examination of situation in order that man may recognize which elements are of his own choosing and which are simply conditions of his existence. Once he has done this, he can choose the method of procedure and make his own history. There is no fate, no bad luck, no excuse; simply man, his choices, and the situation in which he finds himself. . . . Goetz passes through stages of awareness which Hoederer has evidently already achieved; each realizes the limitations of the possibilities of action open to him, accepts those limitations, and determines to act to the utmost within the context of these limitations. It is this recognition and this determination plus movement to action which affords these two men the opportunity to become real, existing human beings; which gives them and the world around them a true identity, a reality.

The individual freedom so crucial to Sartre's early thought is still important (all acts are necessarily initiated from the individual's awareness and abilities), but another aspect becomes equally crucial, respect for the freedom of all. Another principle likewise comes into play—no man is indispensable. (pp. 152-53)

That which Sartre requires of today's authentic man is . . . more heroic than the requirement for any Orestes. The unified action will not serve to defend each man against the anguish of life . . . ; quite the contrary. Each authentic man of today, each man who would lead in the revolution, must be willing to take a heavier burden than that of Orestes. He remains alone in his choices as the characters Hoederer and Goetz demonstrate. . . .

[Success] is possible, if highly difficult of accomplishment, when each man recognizes that difficulty is inherent in human relationships but that this difficulty must be overcome. It *must* be overcome because the principle of freedom should receive greater emphasis than each man's self-concern. It *can* be overcome because man makes himself through his free choices, thus he can create his relationship with the Other in whichever method he chooses, just as he creates his own individuality. Goetz and Hoederer forsee a chance, remote though it may be, and they determine to try it as the only authentic course. They are responsible for the weighty decisions and for the acts which they perform and their aloneness presses down upon them—the Sartrean free man is still responsible and very much alone. Now, however, his efforts are to obtain *and* cultivate his freedom *and* the freedom of the Other. (p. 154)

> *Judith Zivanovic, "Sartre's Drama: Key to Understanding His Concept of Freedom,"* in Modern Drama *(copyright © 1971, University of Toronto, Graduate Centre for Study of Drama; with the permission of* Modern Drama*), September, 1971, pp. 144-54.*

We now know from Simone de Beauvoir's description of Sartre's attitude to literature and from Sartre's own analysis of his childhood that the esthetic solution, far from being a mechanical device to finish off the story, is the very substance of *La Nausée.* (p. 152)

Being, which holds forth the promise of salvation, can be attained only when pseudo-Being—inauthentic Being—is unmasked and its falsehoods repudiated. Since Roquentin is obliged to explore not only the uncleanliness of Existence, but also the shifting forms of Being, it is proper to consider *La Nause´e* as, among other things, a study in the avatars of Being.

Inauthentic Being takes two forms: deliberate inauthentic Being, and accidental inauthentic Being. In relation to the former, Roquentin is a lucid and caustic observer; to the latter, an honest, if bewildered and erring seeker.

Roquentin identifies deliberate inauthentic Being with the *Salauds,* the *bourgeoisie,* a class Sartre has all his life hated with fierce consistency. The *Salauds* are the chief and unforgivable offenders since they have manufactured inauthentic Being through their bad faith. As Sartre showed in "L'Enfance d'un chef," the *bourgeois* is he who refuses to accept responsibility for the creation of his identity through acts freely chosen, but prefers rather to believe that what

he does corresponds to a preestablished framework in which he need only insert himself and to a preestablished code of values he can unthinkingly follow. . . . (pp. 153-54)

To believe we have fixed, immutable Rights that establish our essence once and for all and that need never be called into question is to deny that terrifying reality whose name is Existence. . . . Inauthentic Being, as brought into the world by the *Salauds,* is therefore intellectual dishonesty and moral cowardice, willful choosing of false perceptions and conscious distortion, through fear and laziness, of the revealed truth. (p. 154)

Humanism is not only the property of the *Salauds;* it is also the point of view advocated by that pathetic figure, the Autodidact. Roquentin's attitude toward the Autodidact is ambivalent. He is disgusted by his philosophical position, but he cannot help pitying him as an eventual victim of the *Salauds.* Unlike the *bourgeoisie* who uses Humanism both to avoid facing reality and to justify its position as a ruling class, the Autodidact uses Humanism to escape from his loneliness. . . . Thus, the presence of the Autodidact allows a more subtle delineation of inauthentic Being. Inauthentic Being is not always the result of vicious error; it can also be caused by good-natured weakness and basic emotional needs. (pp. 154-55)

The triumph of Existence seems complete. Roquentin, incapable of accepting the inauthentic Being of the *Salauds* or the Autodidact, is equally incapable of living by the inauthentic Being of adventure or of historical reconstruction.

There is, however, in *La Nausée,* one realm in which Existence has no power. It is the esthetic, the realm of the work of art, the only authentic incarnation of Being. Intimations of the esthetic appear throughout the novel, in the very formulation of pseudo-Being itself. Indeed, the inauthenticity of certain forms of Being lies precisely in the fact that esthetic criteria are wrongly applied to lived reality, and lived reality, judged by such criteria, is found wanting. (p. 156)

La Nausée, as do all of Sartre's significant literary and philosophical texts, bears witness to the presence of two antithetically different modes of reality: the reality of Existence and the reality of Being. Yet *La Nausée* occupies a particular position in what will one day be the Sartrean canon. Although Sartre deals with the work of art in other contexts, nowhere but in *La Nausée* does he allow it such a privileged role. Nowhere else is it permitted to monopolize the world of Being in quite the same way.

It is *La Nausée's* deification of the work of art that makes Sartre, at least in the early part of his literary career, the reluctant disciple of a writer for whom he has expressed considerable dislike—Marcel Proust. The esthetic solution is the *raison d'être* of *La Nausée* just as it was the *raison d'être* of *A la recherche du temps perdu.* In both cases, salvation comes from the work of art. Marcel was offered the possibility of escape from Time through the recapturing of lost Time, and Roquentin, the possibility of substituting for the Time of Existence the Time of Being.

Yet neither in *A la recherche du temps perdu* nor in *La Nausée* did the protagonist come to his knowledge of salvation lightly. Marcel had to painfully learn to renounce the illusion of the social world before the definitive esthetic revelation was given him. Roquentin was prepared, by a series of overwhelming experiences, for a new and dearly-bought awareness of the double nature of reality: Existence, concommitant with nausea, and Being, limited to and concommitant with the work of art. (p. 157)

> *Eugenia N. Zimmerman, in* MOSAIC V/3 *(copyright © 1972 by the University of Manitoba Press), Spring, 1972.*

[*Situations, X,* the] tenth volume of Jean-Paul Sartre's collected essays and interviews, published in his seventy-first year, is quite fascinating, both for the light it throws on his present political attitudes after all the twists and turns of the past quarter of a century, and for the revelation of his personality in its ultimate or penultimate phase. . . .

[Someone] who is not prejudiced in Sartre's favour, as I have always been, might conclude that his constant exercising of his Existentialist freedom to change his mind at any point is not so much a sign of intellectual scrupulousness as proof of an inability to understand that morality in action supposes some anxiety about consistency through time, and therefore means that each radical change in policy should be experienced as a genuine anguish. But I have never, for my part, attached any importance to Sartre's role as a political activist. . . .

I have always admired him as a prodigious juggler of ideas, as the archetype of the impractical intellectual whose one and only function is to be a superb *moulin à paroles*. He is an Apostle of the Word, just as much as Mallarmé and Valéry, although his talent is copious and rather coarse, whereas theirs was hesitant and refined.

The four political pieces which constitute Part 1 of this volume show, with great clarity, how Sartre, after trying for years to fuse Existentialism with Marxism, has eventually arrived at a position almost identical with that of the nineteenth-century anarchists, such as Proud'hon and Bakunin, who quarrelled with Marx precisely on the issue of authority and party discipline, which Sartre has tried to accept and then always rejected in the end because it conflicted with Existentialist freedom. He himself states, incomprehensibly, that the modern anarchism or "socialisme libertaire" that he believes in at present is quite different from the anarchism of the late nineteenth century, but I cannot see in what way. To move back from this book to the old anarchist writings is to find oneself in essentially the same emotional and intellectual atmosphere. . . .

[In the first essay] Sartre argues brilliantly in favour of wholesale devolution, without however considering in any detail the enormous practical problem of reconstituting viable linguistic and cultural communities in the modern world. The idea of devolution has an instant appeal for the lover of freedom and authenticity, but would Sartre be happy, for instance, if the Basques and the Bretons, obeying a spontaneous impulse after being granted their freedom, reverted to monarchical systems based on religion? . . .

He himself is thinking confidently in French universalist terms and postulating singularity as a good thing *in abstracto* for other people, while leaping over the concrete difficulties in the usual anarchist way. . . .

[In the other three essays,] Sartre writes about the tyranny of the French parliamentary system in terms not unlike those used by Solzhenitsyn to castigate the Soviet bureaucracy. He describes, with an irony that may be more double-edged than he himself realizes, the comedy of his attempts to get himself arrested and the cat-and-mouse game played by the wily political animals of the Fifth Republic, who persistently refuse to grant him exemplary martyrdom.

Here again he makes many penetrating remarks, but he cannot escape from his role as the respected *enfant terrible* of the bourgeoisie, enjoying freedom of speech and movement because he can exploit the Western market economy, as embodied in La Maison Gallimard, and invulnerable because even authoritarian Frenchmen usually have the wit to realize that they need a few concrete, external incarnations of the anarchism which lurks within themselves. Sartre has never been realistic; he has attached himself at various times to different political entities that he considered to be more or less on the side of social good. . . .

He now places such hope as he has in that mystic entity, mass spontaneity, which the romantic, good-hearted bourgeois tends to believe in as a last possible resort. . . .

But when we turn to Part 2, the personal interviews, we may ask whether, in fact, Sartre believes in any general principles at all, in the normal sense of belief. . . . Sartre has never bridged the moral gap between his Absurdist analysis of the human situation and his itch to be socially effective. Perhaps what has kept him going is a sort of stoical determination to carry on regardless, and to accept the futility of all human behaviour, including his own, with ruthless serenity. . . .

If I have a reservation about him, after reading this latest volume, it is that he is always so imperturbably sure that he is now in the right, even after changing his mind so many times. . . . [What others] say, or have said, has no relevance to Sartre's intimate conviction that the only relative truth is represented by his own ideas, as they can be formulated at the moment. . . . [He] is a changeable dogmatist, and an ideological authoritarian who does not really accept *le dialogue*. In spite of his anti-elitist remarks and his repeated assertion that we are all equal, he is very much a French elitist in his bland assumption of intellectual supremacy, which is so deep-rooted that it is not even accompanied by vanity, but by a brand of self-deceiving modesty.

> *John Weightman, "Sartre at Seventy," in* The Times Literary Supplement *(© Times Newspapers Ltd., 1976; reproduced from* The Times Literary Supplement *by permission), June 25, 1976, p. 761.*

*   *   *

SCHORER, Mark   1908-1977

An American novelist, editor, and short story writer, Schorer was primarily known as a literary critic. His "Technique as Discovery," published in 1947, became a critical hallmark for its claim that fiction deserved the close scrutiny, attention, and consideration that was accorded poetry by the New Critics. (See also *Contemporary Authors*, Vols. 5-8, rev. ed.; obituary, Vols. 73-76.)

Apart from the appeal of the stories themselves, I think that "Pieces of Life" could serve as a study in the evolution of technique and sensibility in American fiction. One of our better literary critics until his death . . . , Mark Schorer wrote, if memory serves me right, an essay titled "Technique as Discovery." Now, in these 10 stories, he has demonstrated his thesis: as the technique of the short story changed, so did its range and quality of awareness. You can see this progress from one story to the next across a 30-year span.

The first piece, copyrighted in 1946, is nothing more than a crude frame for an ironic parallel between a wife's telling her husband an anecdote about a blind man and her own blindness to her husband's flagrant infidelity. The second story is a gentle hint at ambivalence in black-white relationships, expressed through the medium of a Freudian slip. As you can see, readers of short stories—and Mr. Schorer's appeared in the best magazines—were once content with relatively little. The third story represents no advance at all. It is a predictable set piece about a repressed couple whose teen-age son defends a "vulgar" but "warm" family who have intruded on their secluded stretch of beach.

So far, these stories are nothing to write home about, and barely enough to write in a magazine about. We seem to be still in the 40's, before all hell broke loose. Then there is a jump of seven years in the copyright dates and the fourth story shows a conspicuous advance: this one, too, is about a husband's infidelity, but now he and his wife are talking about it. What's more, their conversation takes place against a contrapuntal motif of a little girl practicing the piano next door. The bareness of the subject is embellished by technique. The critic in Mr. Schorer has come to the aid of the storyteller.

There is another jump of seven years in the copyright dates, and although I have no way of verifying this—there are six dates and 10 stories—I am inclined to believe that the next story represents another forward leap, this time into the 60's. Its theme is loneliness—not simply circumstantial loneliness, but immanent, essential loneliness—and the story finds no answer for the question that it asks. The answer lies in the drama of the asking. The short story has learned to express suffering as grace.

Now, in "Pieces of Life," we come to the ambiguity of awakening sexuality, the terrific *surprise* of passion, the unsettling idea that sex may be its own reward. In the subsequent story, Mr. Schorer ventures into the darker regions of human impulse, into what has since become the familiar landscape of contemporary fiction. . . .

In the last three stories, everything is altered: manner, mood, language, structure. Mr. Schorer's people go inside themselves, instead of outside. His language is probing rather than defining, his rhythms rise almost in crescendoes but stop short. His people come up against the paralyzing realization that there is no necessary forward movement in events or in themselves. They are like amnesiacs, forced to begin at the beginning, but without knowing the process.

In one of these last stories, an extraordinarily ugly and ornate lamp becomes a metaphor for everything in Italy that disquiets a visiting American couple. The lamp is so strange, so foreign, that it forces them to *see* Italy for the first time, to experience themselves incongruously posed against this unfamiliar backdrop. The last piece in "Pieces of Life" is pure choreography, a fugal meditation on youth and age, permanence and change. (p. 12)

> *Anatole Broyard, in* The New York Times Book Review *(© 1977 by The New York Times Company; reprinted by permission), October 2, 1977.*

[*Pieces of Life* is a] posthumous collection of stories, interlaced with autobiographical fragments that are mostly concerned with Schorer's early years. Story and autobiography don't treat the same experiences or even the same themes, but the volume is harmonized by the single sensibility pervading everywhere. As Schorer hoped, there is something appealing about "the slightly staggering dissonance of a real life beating beneath the surface of brighter, created lives." The autobiographical sketches richly evoke small-town life in the Midwest in the early years of the century. The stories are sensitive and accomplished, well-observed and muted in tonality. Notable for their quality of feeling, not for their range and variety, they turn on moments of quiet self-recognition. Obviously Schorer the critic eclipses Schorer the writer of fiction. Yet what an appropriate memorial volume this is: the stories and autobiographical fragments are touchingly and unmistakably "pieces of life," and of a great life at that. (p. 2263)

> *Keith Cushman, in* Library Journal *(reprinted from the November 1, 1977, issue of* Library Journal, *published by R. R. Bowker Company, a Xerox company; copyright © 1977 by Xerox Corporation), November 1, 1977.*

* * *

SCIASCIA, Leonardo 1921-

Sciascia is a Sicilian novelist, essayist, poet, and dramatist who considers the depiction of social iniquities a major function of his art. Despite his use of Sicily as setting and his frequent use of the Mafia to represent evil, Sciascia's work has a sense of immediacy and universality. (See also *CLC*, Vol. 8.)

Leonardo Sciascia's novel of life in Sicily, "A Man's Blessing" . . . , is a surprise, coming as it does from the author of "The Council of Egypt," which was a very coolly ironic and detached piece of storytelling concerned mainly with social hypocrisy in the manner of Voltaire or Anatole France. This time out, Sciascia is paying the homage of imitation to Graham Greene. Not, it should be emphasized, to the later Greene, soupy with Jamesian intimations of undeclarable subtleties, but to the earlier writer whose inspirations were the darker side of Robert Louis Stevenson's imagination and whose manner was such as to make all but the most attentive readers feel that they were dealing with something wholesome and bracing in the way of an action or suspense story. . . . [In Greene's "The Man Within" it] is the virtues—an innocent belief in them, and striving for them—that undo the hero; and the message is that to love, to trust, and to believe is to betray oneself into the hands of the wicked. Sciascia has taken up this theme and has written a characteristically polished and elegant story which purports to be a thriller about an ordinary man's drift into conflict with the Mafia in a small Sicilian town—a matter of an obtuse man blindly putting himself on the spot—but which is in reality a paradigm of the condition of the good man in the modern world. The protagonist is a solitary, brooding individual, gifted with intelligence and sensibility, and cursed with a belief in justice and a sense of loyalty to his fellow-creatures. One of his acquaintances becomes the victim of an apparently senseless murder, and chance puts him in possession of a clue that offers him the possibility of discovering its meaning and exposing the killers. . . . He moves about the torpid town, picking up a thread here and another there, slowly approaching the active agent of evil that he is seeking, becoming less ordinary and less inconspicuous every day as he acquires a dangerous knowledge of the realities that surround him. There is, however, to be no crisis, no agon, no meting out of justice. When he has achieved a certain degree of visibility against the darkness with which he is at war, it silently engulfs him. He disappears, and his body is never found. He has not even marked the surface of evil. Once he has gone, Sciascia turns his knife in our wounds: he lets us hear the townspeople talking over the disappearance. They have known all along the meaning of the original crime, and just where the missing man's clue would lead him. (p. 144)

This graceful piece of storytelling is in fact a savagely expressed cry of despair. Sciascia has moved on from the belief that life is a comedy, which would be much more enjoyable for the actors if they would only be a little more reasonable and a little less emotional, to discover its tragic essence. This account of his discovery, in the form of a novel, is at once moving and horrifying, and may well in time win itself recognition as one of the minor classics of extreme pessimism. (pp. 144-45)

> *Anthony West, in* The New Yorker *(© 1969 by The New Yorker Magazine, Inc.), May 3, 1969.*

This is a fallow period for the Italian novelist; no one major writer has come forward internationally. A familiar tale: some of the most talented have moved toward the films, television and magazines. But in Sicily there is a novelist respected by his peers and readers for grappling with old themes that reach down to the condition of life and justice around the Mediterranean. Leonardo Sciascia . . . has remained close to his roots and the sources of his material. Even more telling, he is aware of writing against a Sicilian literary past that includes the social feeling of Verga, the puzzles of Pirandello, the historical depth of Lampedusa. . . .

Crime, the police, the peasant and the Mafia continue to insinuate themselves into his books. Often the forlorn search for justice takes place in a fictional small town, not unlike his native Bacalmuto, in the province of Agrigento, which is best described in his book, "Salt in the Wound." . . .

Sciascia is a careful and slow writer who has turned out a unified body of work in the last 20 years. He was puzzled and saddened when I told him that in the United States his books sometimes fall into the mystery bin. "At least I hope they will be regarded as metaphysical mysteries," he said, eyes twinkling.

This is precisely the way to read his . . . novel, "Equal Danger". . . . It follows an overly bold police inspector peeling away the motives behind a series of killings. His search takes him on a journey through the human brambles and political apparatus of Sicilian justice. The pacing is swift and yet simple—a Costa-Gavras thriller that depends on more than murder. What emerges is a logical solution rooted in political rot and cynicism. And a tiny ray of hope: that by passing on the facts to a writer-character, perhaps truths will be passed on to many people seeking honest answers. (p. 39)

> *Herbert Mitgang, in* The New York Times Book Review *(© 1973 by The New York Times Company; reprinted by permission), September 16, 1973.*

Signore Sciascia is rightly considered as one of Italy's major writers.

The subject of all his stories, novels and essays is always Sicily. . . . He is famous in Italy for his denunciation of the Mafia, but his keen intelligence has explored many periods of Sicilian history and many aspects of Sicilian life. His works range from something very much like crime stories to erudite dissertations on minute points of provincial history, but they are always good, and often excellent literature —even if their language, grammar and syntax at times baffle the non-Sicilian reader.

What interests Signore Sciascia most is the relation between men (especially the poor and defenceless) and the Law. Hence his persistent investigation of the ways, practices and tactics of the Mafia, on the one hand, and of the Roman Catholic Inquisition on the other. *Il giorno della civetta* (published in English as *Mafia Vendetta*, 1963) describes the hard, right-minded, courageous, but finally ineffective struggle of a young police officer (from the North of Italy) against the insidious, formidable power of the proteiform organization that has poisoned the past hundred years of Sicilian life. The blood-curdling events of the story are related with the same cold lucidity that regularly assists the Mafia in the remorseless, professional execution of its crimes. Yet Signore Sciascia's indignation at the reign of terror and injustice that the Law is unable to eradicate is made very apparent, and *Il giorno della civetta* has done a great deal to awaken the Italian conscience to the moral, social and political problems of the Mafia.

Artistically, however, Signore Sciascia's second "Mafia novel", *A Ciascuno il suo* (1963) is much better. Here the Mafia's antagonist is a fellow Sicilian, and there are more of the historical and sociological digressions needed in *Il giorno della civetta* to illuminate the contrast between the policeman from the North, with his civilized obedience to the Law, and the Sicilian's medieval system of submission to force. . . .

Il contesto (1971) was a disappointment. It may have been that to move from the limited, familiar and more or less clear-cut scene of Sicilian life to the vast conundrum of Italian politics was in itself an impossible ambition, or that Signore Sciascia's deliberate, utilitarian intention of castigating Italy's inane political parties . . . could not be reconciled with his essentially poetic imagination, but the fact is that *Il contesto* is far less telling than his two Mafia novels. It caused an uproar among the politicians, but added little to the author's literary reputation.

Il mare colore del vino, on the other hand, shows Signore Sciascia at his best. Although it does not contain anything new, being a collection of short stories written between 1959 and 1972 and published in various newspapers, it is important because, as the author himself points out, it offers a kind of summary of his life's work. And this summary reveals an admirable consistency of both inspiration and style. . . .

[Although] Signore Sciascia is generally keener on denouncing the vices of the Sicilians than on extolling their virtues, there seems no doubt that he approves their "religion of the family". The title story of this collection . . . certainly suggests as much. . . .

Signore Sciascia's other favourite themes are present too: his concern with the miscarriage of justice; his very Sicilian interest in adultery, with no pity for the cuckold, of course; his zest for popular anecdotes and his historical curiosity; even his bent for political satire. But the fact that in a collection of stories of cunning deceit, sickening failure, ghastly crimes and violent death, the place of honour is given to the only story that contains an affirmation of faith in life, is very indicative. In such a bitter cocktail one is relieved to be given some small taste of Sicilian honey.

> *"In Praise of Cretins," in* The Times Literary Supplement (© *Times Newspapers Ltd., 1973; reproduced from* The Times Literary Supplement *by permission), October 5, 1973, p. 1155.*

Ettore Majorana was a brilliant, reticent young physicist from Sicily who vanished in 1938. At the time it was supposed he had committed suicide. . . . His body was not found. In this short, speculative book [*La scomparsa di Majorana*], Leonardo Sciascia goes over the case again. He analyses Majorana as a man, as a fellow Sicilian both morbid and unsociable; and as a scientist, clever and informed enough to have foreseen the homicidal uses to which his researches into atomic structure might lead. The contemporary investigation, such as it was, into Majorana's disappearance also interests Sciascia because it shows how police and politics fitted together in Fascist Italy. This episode from recent history extends the series of unsolved mysteries Sciascia has invented in his novels to point the finger at the corrosive forces in Italian public life.

His strongest reason for writing *La scomparsa di Majorana,* however, was to have his say against the misuse of science. Majorana, a religious man, is made here into a precocious hero of the ethical crisis in science. . . .

Sciascia has integrated the rare facts of Majorana's life, the records of the official inquiry, the rumours his disappearance gave rise to, and his own moral preoccupations in a book which is as much essay as story. He invents nothing and is therefore forced to use whatever he has learnt about Majorana to his one end, which is to raise him into a martyr for a more humane idea of science than that generally held by his fellow scientists. Such coherence is frankly unnatural and Sciascia's narrative barely holds together as he arranges the data to his own best advantage. Nor does he face what one would have thought was the most pressing of all moral questions about Majorana: why, given what he knew and felt, he broke with science so silently. Self-effacement is no part of martyrdom. Sciascia has tried, honourably but not quite successfully, to make a secretive, perhaps neurotic young man into the public victim of a world unworthy of him.

> *Peter Lloyd, "The Case of the Vanishing Scientist," in* The Times Literary Supplement (© *Times Newspapers Ltd., 1976; reproduced from* The Times Literary Supplement *by permission), January 30, 1976, p. 101.*

A well-known artist driving aimlessly down a highway sees a sign with the words "Hermitage of Zafer 3" and decides to investigate. He finds an ugly concrete barracks, run by priests and described by them as both a hermitage and a hotel. The man in charge, an enigmatic eminence named

Don Gaetano, wears glasses identical to those of the Devil in a painting in the hermitage's chapel. Soon, the artist learns, a group of people will arrive to undertake "spiritual exercises," and his curious visit to this strange place leads him through layer after layer of mystery, corruption, and violence. So, roughly, runs the story of [*One Way or Another*], which has a thin texture of teasing, sardonic dialogue that constantly hints at metaphysical and social satire. Neither a strict mystery nor a fully achieved fantasy, the book draws the reader on while leaving a nagging sense of having missed some important detail. (pp. 87-8)

> The New Yorker (© *1977 by The New Yorker Magazine, Inc.), July 4, 1977.*

*   *   *

SCOTT, Paul   1920-

Scott is a British novelist. Stimulated by his military service in India, he began to write about the final years of British domination in India and the effects of its cessation. Although for a time he abandoned this theme, he returned to it in the voluminous "Raj Quartet."

Mr. Paul Scott is never content with the mixture as before. From *The Birds of Paradise* to *The Bender* represents a leap within the compass of only the most agile and venturesome of novelists. Tropical islands have sunk well below the horizon. This is a London novel. . . . The emotional climate has changed, too, from twanging and lyrical to muffled and partially atrophied. The atmosphere, not long ago so hot and thunderous, is now authentically damp, gin-hazy and metropolitan.

A natural accompaniment of this restlessness of Mr. Scott's is his love of experiment, of testing new techniques. The story is most artfully expounded. The central action runs for a bare twenty-four hours yet contrives to illuminate the frustrations of three generations. . . .

This is a subtle, unemphatic novel, beautifully composed in a minor key. The dialogue, sometimes exactly pointed and contemporary, sometimes stylized and other-worldly, blends with and heightens the shifting moods. Broad comedy holds its place in the book just as sure-footedly as the laments which are prompted by defeat and despair. And money, that nowadays neglected Balzacian theme, is here given its proper importance. It is rare to find the intrinsically trivial bits and pieces, which form the groundwork of any novel and which can try so direly its assimilative capacities, fused as successfully as they are here into an harmonious whole.

> *"Tensions and Despairs," in* The Times Literary Supplement (© *Times Newspapers Ltd., 1963; reproduced from* The Times Literary Supplement *by permission), April 12, 1963, p. 245.*

The Corrida at San Felíu . . . is a novel about a man trying to write a novel. . . .

All this fascinating Chinese box of novel within novel and story within story Mr. Scott handles with a deft professionalism which is admirable. The essential theme—the one that lies at the centre of the artichoke when the outer leaves have been stripped—is a study of the creative process as it applies to writers of novels. One can think of no more effective method of demonstrating the process than the necessarily involved one chosen here. The crispness and vivid imaginative resource of the writing keep the reader fresh. . . . Everything in it except for the tauromachy which is a bit "got up" . . . is worthy of the highest praise. . . .

[Mr. Scott] has always shown himself to be adept in the imaginative handling of character, and has steadily increased his range. Both his last two books, *The Birds of Paradise* and *The Bender,* were in their very different ways works of great distinction. The present work is a virtuoso piece, appealing perhaps more exclusively to a professional and technically concerned reader than the earlier novels did, but none the less adding an inch or so to his already considerable stature as a writer.

> *"Toro Agonistes," in* The Times Literary Supplement *(© Times Newspapers Ltd., 1964; reproduced from* The Times Literary Supplement *by permission), August 27, 1964, p. 761.*

What stops this ambitious and serious book [*The Jewel in the Crown*] from being a major novel? Partly Mr. Scott's reliance on disquisition rather than demonstration, which gives us pages and pages of all too solid discussion about the condition of India past and present. Certain sections of the book are very much too long. . . . The ingenious devices used to avoid a straightforward chronicle of events also slow down the narrative considerably. But the book's real limitation is that the rape of Daphne Manners is given a symbolic importance, in its contrast with the rape of India by the British, that is never justified. . . .

The weakness of this affair as a central theme for the book is that it seems such a very special case. . . . The rape and its consequences are of such importance to the book's general theme of British-Indian relationships that the scales appear to have been heavily weighted. . . . Solidly powerful as a creation of Mayapore and its shifting society, the book is a little disappointing as a study in depth of Anglo-Indian relationships.

> *"The Rape of India," in* The Times Literary Supplement *(© Times Newspapers Ltd., 1966; reproduced from* The Times Literary Supplement *by permission), July 21, 1966, p. 629.*

["The Day of the Scorpion"] is a cogent dramatization of how World War II and India's rising demand for home rule flushed some of those strange types out of the officers' mess and let the natives get a good look at their quality. [It] is classical and complex in structure, with a mystery at its center and enough interesting characters to drop a few every dozen pages and still keep going. . . .

The overtness of the action and the explicitness of the character portrayal will appeal to many readers unresponsive to the more subtle intonations of such writers as Forster, Mehta or Markandaya. Though the story is compelling, it never overwhelms the recurring theme of the British in India as wandering players. Only in their awkward pauses between their set speeches and their stage business did they catch themselves wondering why the show must go on.

> *P. Albert Duhamel, "Twilight of the Raj," in* The New York Times Book Review *(© 1968 by The New York Times Company; reprinted by permission), November 10, 1968, p. 60.*

Of those writers who have attempted to distil the last years of the British in India in fictional form, the most ambitious and the most successful is undoubtedly Mr Paul Scott [with the Raj Quartet]. . . . For the literary critic a series of long novels which presuppose each other, but though dealing in part with the same set of characters do not remain bound by chronological rigidities and treat their fates in a complicated counterpoint, raises interesting questions of technique. Was the whole design conceived as a unity from the beginning? Did the characters present themselves to the author in the round, or did they take hold of the author's imagination and develop along their own lines? Is there a version of the events themselves that the author keeps in reserve and never wholly reveals, so that all we ever get are the conflicting versions of the participants in them, or of those who get to know about them through the gossip of club or bazaar? . . .

Has Paul Scott succeeded in making Britain's retreat and the partition of India that followed it—the preparations for which form the "political" background to the just-published *A Division of the Spoils*—more directly intelligible than these events might otherwise be to us? Can he convey both what these events meant to those affected directly by them and their wider significance? Has he succeeded—where many Indians would argue that E. M. Forster failed—in apprehending true Indian feeling about relations with the British?

The last of these questions is one that only Indians can answer. It is a challenge that Paul Scott only tackles obliquely, since his principal Indian character Hari Kumar (Harry Coomer)—British educated to the extent of partial alienation from his own community's values but rejected by the British as belonging to the "other side" of the divide—is too special a case upon which to base an answer. Still, in the minor rulers and the Congress politicians of the last book and in minor figures in the earlier volumes there is ample material for anyone trying to assess Paul Scott's achievement in this respect.

Nevertheless, the book is to a much greater extent about the British in India and their view of their role there. . . . (p. 66)

Paul Scott does convey the full tragic significance of the combination between a sense of duty and a sense of permanent alienation from those to whom the duty was owed that is at the heart of the matter. Paul Scott is perhaps even more successful when he deals with the women in this situation. The stereotype of the *memsahib* has now been destroyed once and for all, one would hope. For the portraits that he draws of British women in India—whether missionaries, or serving in the War effort, or as simply occupied with the conventional trivialities of cantonment or hill-station society—are all individually etched. They respond to India in different ways: with devotion, affection, indifference or even hatred, but it is an individual not a collective response.

Nor is this elucidation of the feminine element a diversion from the main theme. It is a commonplace of social historians of India that it was the coming of the white woman to what had been "an Englishman's world" that brought about that social division between the communities which so complicated the political problems of British rule. And even when social constraints were a little loosened the reluctance to contemplate the sexual involvement of British women and Indian men remained a rooted one. Thus while is might be easy to mock Paul Scott by asking why it needed four long novels to deal with the question of whether Hari Kumar raped Miss Manners (and why, if innocent, he was punished for it) it is also true that this central incident in the story is at the same time its crystallising factor. For, in his prosecution of Kumar, the policeman Merrick reveals how personal feelings of class as well as of race—unlike Kumar Merrick is not "a gentleman"—can distort and envenom what should be the processes of impartial justice. So that the British social scene with its own internal frictions and enmities is transported into India and adds yet another complication to the unnatural relationship between the races (of which Merrick's own homosexual inclinations directed towards young Indians illustrate or symbolise yet another facet). (pp. 66-7)

What concerns Perron [in *A Division of the Spoils*] and presumably his creator Paul Scott is the relative insensitivity of Britain (and of Britain's new rulers in 1945) to their own responsibility for the human tragedies on a major scale that were the product of Britain's precipitate departure and of the abandonment of their implied pledges to the rulers of the Indian States and their peoples. Could we escape so easily all guilt for the massacres of Hindus by Moslems (and vice versa) of which in *A Division of the Spoils* we are given a horrifying glimpse, all the more telling because of the narrator's restraint? (p. 69)

The historian is always concerned with what happened and so tends to see what happened as inevitable, and from that it is only a short step to justifying it. Few historians have treated the fall of the British Empire as something that did not have to happen in the way it did—and as an episode in which some important values (as well as many lives) were sacrificed for motives only partially pure. . . . But the novelist need await neither the opening of the archives nor the working out of the political and social consequences of actions past. Imagination can supply what we lack provided the groundwork of study is solid enough. One cannot read Paul Scott's quartet of novels without being moved; and what is the sense of studying history if it is not to move one and to widen one's moral sensibilities? His achievement is on any count a major one. (p. 70)

> *Max Beloff, "The End of the Raj: Paul Scott's Novels as History," in* Encounter *(© 1976 by Encounter Ltd.), May, 1976, pp. 65-70.*

Paul Scott's latest novel, "Staying On," provides a sort of postscript to his deservedly acclaimed "The Raj Quartet," a series of four novels dealing with the closing stages of British rule in India in the 1940's. . . . [The] quartet has made Scott's international reputation as the chronicler of the decline and fall of the Raj. He has, as it were, summoned up the Raj's ghost in "Staying On," . . . so that in it we may observe how the ghost continues to walk in some of its old haunts. It is the story of the living death, in retirement, and the final end of a walk-on character from the quartet. . . .

The difficulty I found with "Staying On" was to work up sufficient sympathy with any of the characters to care about what happened to them. In any case, Mr. Scott's characters are doubtless intended to be dim figures belonging to a limbo between a dead empire and a nation not yet reborn. The triumph of Gandhi and his Swarajists has proved to be only the afterglow of imperial glory; before dawn can break, night must fall.

With "Staying On," Scott has completed his task of covering in the form of a fictional narrative the events leading up to India's partition and the achievement of independence in 1947. It is, on any showing, a creditable achievement. . . . (p. 36)

> *Malcolm Muggeridge, in* The New York Times Book Review *(© 1977 by The New York Times Company; reprinted by permission), August 21, 1977.*

* * *

SIMIC, Charles   1938-

A Yugoslavian-born poet now residing in the United States, Simic is also a translator of contemporary French, Russian, and Yugoslavian poets. The common objects he chooses as the subjects of his poetry are imbued with a strangeness, a cosmic incandescence, revealing the influence of the folk poetry of his native Yugoslavia. His poetic style is one of austere simplicity. (See also *CLC*, Vol. 6, and *Contemporary Authors*, Vols. 29-32, rev. ed.)

Often using the rhythms and tonal patterns of children's songs, Charles Simic emulates the simple and the hypnotic in [*Return to a Place Lit by a Glass of Milk*]. In *White*, the last collection, Simic lost intensity and penetration; he had crippled his images, so raw and unnerving in earlier *Dismantling the Silence*, with flippancy and intellectual cuteness. Here, the imagery is strong and frequently luminous. The poetic structures are oral; Simic works with skeletal narratives formed by incremental repetition, traditional dialogues, proverbs, riddles, nursery rhymes. His images are as painfully concrete as the images in oral tradition. . . .

A tension between the visual image and its incantatory form becomes the speculative principle of Simic's thought. In "Solving the Riddle," the poet is caught between hearing what is not there and seeing what everybody else sees. In "Poem," Simic defines the invisible as that which no one remembers, and in "Elementary Cosmogony," the poet becomes an apprentice to the invisible. Deciphering the invisible is the business of the poet—that old romantic theory—and for Simic that task is analogous to solving riddles. Life is a puzzle which deludes and deceives us not because it is a plexus of questions and answers, but because it is an endless series of clues. The poet discovers the clues and, through solution, creates new ones. His poems are no more than clues; they never answer the riddle, but they may create an illusion of order. (p. 47)

The notion of a metaphysical riddle is not unique, but it is always effective. The problem is control. The fact that Simic's poetic structures depend upon traditional oral structures forces the reader to refer not only to the oral forms, but also to their psychological values. A riddle continues to be an oral form, that is, a dramatic exchange. Simic fails only because he supposes that he can duplicate the dynamics which relate him who asks to him who answers on the written page without the psychological satisfaction that accompanies the solution of the riddle. In oral tradition, the superiority of the riddler and the dependence of the uninitiated generate a relationship which counters the function of the riddle in Simic's cosmology. Borrowing the riddle from folklore brings about an unintentional, but disturbing sense of displacement, an irritating belief that Simic does know the answers after all and that he arrogantly withholds that knowledge from us. Simic often titles his riddles as though the titles are the answers, and we must force ourselves to remember that the titles are only other clues. "Mother Tongue", "Solitude", "Brooms", and "Pain" especially encourage this confusion. . . .

Perhaps the solver of clues parades too much; our resistance to the riddler who will not let us answer becomes complete. We no longer believe the poet is translating only. (p. 48)

> *Zora Devrnja, in* Poet and Critic *(copyright © Department of English and Speech, Iowa State University), Vol. 9, No. 1, 1975.*

Under one guise or another Mr. Simic manages to sound like a religious poet [in *Return to a Place Lit by a Glass of Milk*]. "Sew stitch / These body rags," he writes in a poem entitled "Pain," "With the last thread of / Daylight sing them / Into wedding-clothes." But, *body rags* being the title of a recent volume by another poet, one feels that there is something a little easy about this. And the feeling grows stronger by the end of the same poem: "What would I do / Without you without / Your voice / That names and names / The streams and rivers / Of our days on earth." The wit who called W. S. Merwin the Longfellow of his generation had a point: Merwin's is the mannerly style of the 1960s and 1970s, and a great many poets who, like Mr. Simic, may or may not have profited directly from his work, become quite difficult to tell apart from him when they try for an impressive cadence. In his first book, Mr. Simic was bizarre and genuinely wild in some poems about kitchen utensils—his fork seemed to have "crawled out of hell"— and his Polish ancestors swore, wielded meat axes, and howled all night in a dim corner of his imagination. The new poems are more tame, more obviously happy with themselves: Mr. Simic is no longer the strange and splendid *trouvaille* that cannot be believed until it is seen, he is a professional who needs enough poems for a book. A wearing away of edges happens to all but the bravest poets, yet occasionally Mr. Simic has his old mischief, as when a crumb drops to the floor in what looks like a vacant place: "But somewhere already / The ants are putting on / Their Quakers' hats / And setting out to visit you." (p. 1023)

> *David Bromwich, in* The Georgia Review *(copyright, 1976, by the University of Georgia), Winter, 1976.*

The preference . . . for the plain phrase and the concrete image goes fantastically far in [Simic's] poems. It is the paradox of his style that his determined concentration on the most common things makes reality strange and, even when terrifying, strangely inviting. The poems have an arresting substantiality about them, so that it seems almost inadequate to absorb them merely by way of the eye. . . .

When his readers think of Simic they think first of brief poems with titles like "Knife," "Stone," "The Spoon," "My Shoes." In such pieces the poet's originality was quite early apparent. They are at once weighty and evasive, and describing them is about as easy as picking up blobs of mercury with mittens on. Here and afterwards Simic's habit has been to look so long and fixedly at common ob-

jects that they acquire haloes of strangeness, and become disquietingly animated. The pathetic fallacy, until recently a local effect that poets were cautioned to shun whenever possible, constitutes both a means and an end in these poems as they record one imagination's morbid romance with external reality. . . .

Simic sees operating in the poems of Vasko Popa . . . an "elemental surrealism coupled undoubtedly with an animistic, myth-making approach to reality." Popa's poems, using the forms of riddles, proverbs and jokes, present themselves as "magic formulas. If they enchant it is to make you see clearly. The language is that of definitions, of primitive books of genesis." We realize from such statements that Simic's style has its origin not merely in a personal intensity of vision, but in a deep appreciation of what folklore has to teach. . . .

[The] folk tradition has yielded Simic a store not only of images, but of poetic forms. Like Popa, he favors the riddle, the proverb, the question posed and answered askew, parallelism and antic repetition. In the use of such strategies the influence of Theodore Roethke may also be taken for granted. (p. 25)

Simic's exploration of the springs of myth is convincing because it is conducted by means of an exciting exploration of language. While his mastery of English is beyond that of most native speakers, this poet's experience of writing in a language not his first must give him a special awareness of the innate mysteriousness of words. . . . Simic at no time takes language for granted. At his most serious he writes as if he were naming things for the first time: the words, one by one discovered and cunningly placed, make and shape a world before our eyes. . . .

In his latest work Simic's linguistic inventiveness illuminates a wider range of experience than before. *Return to a Place Lit by a Glass of Milk* (an almost over-characteristic title) is not as sternly unified as the collection which preceded it; but its variety of theme and tone largely make up for what it lacks of the earlier volume's force. Comic touches, at times quite broad, are more numerous and relaxed in their application; and there is a further, more important change as well. Human beings had rarely appeared as major subjects in *Dismantling the Silence*. Now Simic has come to admit them more often to his view of the world, including in the contents of *Return,* a poem about his father and some remarkable love poems. This seems a healthy development. Although he had been doing amazing things with stones and cutlery, Simic was beginning to run the risk of repetition, even of self-parody. . . .

In pieces like "Breasts" and "That Straightlaced Christian Thing Between Her Legs" Simic's active, individualized vocabulary is especially to be appreciated. . . . By standing in vivid, ungainly contrast to the conventional language of love, Simic's words make us aware of how falsified and monochromatic a version of our emotions indifferent writers and the intrusive media have been pandering to us. Slapstick and subtle feeling, awkwardness and sophistication strike a balance in these poems, renewing in us a wonder at the complexity of our desires.

Another recent trend in Simic's poetry, formal rather than thematic, is its readiness to explore the possibilities of greater length. The earlier poems, in keeping with their impassive tone, were tight-lipped, rarely going much beyond a page. In the new book there is a more expansive architecture at work in several pieces. . . . (p. 26)

Simic seems to be able to keep his self-consciousness under control, employing it in making needful esthetic decisions, but effacing it when it threatens to become obtrusive or didactic. Other contemporary poets would do well to emulate this poise of his. Whatever effect his example may have upon our literature, however, Simic's career is bound to be a lonely one because of the singularity of his gift. Of this singularity he is thoroughly and unrepentantly aware:

> Inside my empty bottle
> I was constructing a lighthouse
> While all the others
> Were building ships.
>
> (pp. 26-7)

Robert B. Shaw, "Charles Simic: An Appreciation," in The New Republic *(reprinted by permission of* The New Republic; © 1976 by The New Republic, Inc.), January 24, 1976, pp. 25-7.*

Charles Simic's efforts to interpret the relationship between the animate and inanimate have led to some of the most strikingly original poetry of our time, a poetry shockingly stark in its concepts, imagery, and language. Of course all poetry depends on words, but Simic attempts to force language to new levels. (p. 145)

In his first book, *What the Grass Says* . . . , the speaker plays a prominent dramatic role. There are few difficulties. The first poem, "Summer Morning," is typical. . . . The poem begins with the poet. Time and again the "I" stands at the head of a stanza, placing the writer squarely in the center of his poem. We see him naked on his bed, and the phrase "like this" pushes his figure at us, a figure through which we then find the rest of the world reduced to a vague "they" and the smell of damp hay and horses. (p. 146)

Elsewhere in the book we see men lined up for army physicals, working on the railroad, and marching—all joyless. A boss wants a robot for his worker. A woman's finger goes down a list of war casualties. Soldiers take a man out to hang him.

Thus the poet wishes to join not people but objects, to absorb things or be absorbed by them. He is "happy to be a stone." He finds kinship with a needle. His shoes are the "secret face of my inner life." (p. 147)

Time and again he speaks of things in religious terms. Knives in a butcher shop glitter "like altars / In a dark church." He is baptized in the sight of a dying pig. He addresses his shoes as sacred objects. . . . Things are, simply put, sacramental. That is, they are sacred signs of a spiritual reality by which man may attain grace, for in Simic's poetry there is no conflict whatsoever between God and the natural world He created. The poet finds truth as Emerson and Whitman found it, through nature. (pp. 147-48)

In his second book, *Somewhere Among Us a Stone is Taking Notes* . . . , we find a subtle change in the speaker's role. Here the poet stands, as it were, to one side, like a lecturer showing slides. We are aware of his presence, but we focus on the subject.

"Needle" in his earlier volume begins with a comparison of needle and poet. There are no particular difficulties. The poet simply states the comparison, then develops it.

> Needle, we are of one kind:
> The kind that pierces and mends.
>
> (p. 148)

His later needle poem, however, leaves out explicit comparisons. The poet is nowhere to be seen, though we are aware of his presence.

> Whenever a needle gets lost
> She makes a perfect circle.
> Her tiny eye becomes even tinier
> So the silence can thread itself in it. . . .

Here the relationship of needle to human is implicit in its sex, its tongue, its eye. The poem depends on contrast rather than elaboration. We become aware of the interaction between soft and sharp, dull and pointed, animate and inanimate. The needle takes its place not in the poet's personal life but in the life of the universe.

As the poet recedes in his poems, becoming more absorbed in objects, we find a corresponding increase in his concern for language. (pp. 148-49)

In "Stone Inside a Stone" the poet actually enters the stone and loses his individual identity. As a result the poem seems to speak objective rather than subjective truths. Poet and stone communicate instinctively:

> Once in my hand
> The fingers speak to it in its own language

His task becomes the translation of this tactile language into another—hence his strange images: fossil of the wind, stone with a flower at its heart, stones as death's testicles. Only at the end does the focus shift to the poet.

> I hear the steps of the stone.
> I lift them with my tongue
> To keep myself in shape
> For an unknown time.
>
> (p. 149)

Communication between man and objects takes place in silence wherein the poet hears the tiny voices of things. And since silence is itself a means of communication the poet [in "Dismantling the Silence"] gives instructions for dismantling it so that its nature may be discovered. First one takes down the ears. When he gets to the bones, he slips them under his skin, thus becoming a part of the silence himself.

> It is now completely dark.
> Slowly and with patience
> Feel its heart. You will need to haul
> A heavy chest of drawers
> Into its emptiness
> To make it creak
> On its wheel

Having dismantled the silence, the reader finds it empty—or almost empty. He is left with the problem of mortal man trying to understand immortal things. Words strain to express the inexpressible. A chest of drawers (a typical everyday Simic symbol) is hauled into the dismantled silence "to make it creak / on its wheel." There is a sense of direction in the silence after all, though one may not be able to discern it immediately. Silence, like the soul of man, continues to exist when the body is dismantled. (pp. 149-50)

As the figure of the poet withdraws, the poetry may become cryptic. Sometimes we are not certain of the voice in the poem. Take "The Wind," a simple poem of two lines:

> Touching me, you touch
> The country that has exiled you.

Who exactly is touching what or whom? Who or what is speaking? Is "you" the wind, the reader, or the poet? If the reader touches the wind, it is a symbol of nature which has exiled man. But if the poem is addressed to the wind, then man is the active agent; he has shut nature out of his life. And the poem might be addressed to the reader or to a lover whose touch is like a wind on the skin of the poet. Yet all the important things in the poem remain the same regardless of details—the sense of touch, the alienation of two who were once close. (p. 150)

Simic's first book from a major publisher, *Dismantling the Silence* . . . , contains many of the poems in his first two volumes. Though "Summer Morning" is included, the book begins with "Forest," a dramatic monologue by the forest itself. The figure of the poet becomes more and more absorbed by his world, and the new poems seem even more haunting, even less accessible, than previous work. The speaker seems remote not only from this world but from this universe. If he has discovered the language at the heart of the stone, it sounds at first unintelligible.

What can one make of the beginning of "Eating Out the Angel of Death"?

> Now my body is the evening sky
> And I'm the smoke rising towards it,
>
> Slowly since I watch for the wind,
> Carefully, since I'm blind
> And my dog and cane have been taken away. . . .

Once again we find language pushed to its limits as the poet, a barbarian with a barbarian's tools, attempts to take us with him into "an invisible empire." The synecdoche of fist for man is startlingly appropriate to a barbarian whose "open fist" emphasizes a coming metamorphosis like that of the poet who will be drunk by the stars.

Yet the section remains stubbornly obscure. How can the poet watch for the wind in the second stanza when he is blind? Can a climb have a fist? One suspects the poet intends to take the reader with him to the boundaries of language and meaning—and perhaps beyond. . . . These difficulties continue in *White* . . . , Simic's longest poem to date. Here he turns to the interpretation of one of the attributes of matter, exploring in some detail the relationship of objects to their perception in the mind. He notes the different aspects of white. It is the color of the bride and the color of blindness, stitched (to use a favorite Simic metaphor) into the fabric of the universe. And he describes his poetic method once again in tactile terms:

> Touch what I can
> Of the quick,
>
> Speak and then wait,
> As if this light
>
> Will continue to linger
> On the threshold.

He *touches* the color, then attempts to translate this touch into words.

Parts one and two consist of several short ten line mediations in which the color white appears and reappears like a musical theme. Indeed, the entire poem can be compared to music written as theme and variations. Each time white appears we find it in a somewhat different context, one that gives it additional meaning. It is a symbol of death, of everyday life, of hope, and the color of the paper on which the poet makes his marks. . . . (pp. 151-53)

[Throughout] the poem we see the shift in narrative voice that has characterized Simic's progression as a poet, the voice becoming that of its object, its theme.

Return to a Place Lit by a Glass of Milk . . . begins, strangely enough, with a poem similar to "Summer Morning." The poet lies asleep, a bird calls him, and he ascends into the heavens. But unlike the earlier poem in which he simply floated off, here he is called, summoned by language:

> In the throat of that unknown bird
> There's a vowel of my name.
>
> (pp. 153-54)

This return to identity marks a new phase in Simic's work. Several poems in this volume contain personal, almost idiosyncratic statements by the poet, as if, having surrendered his individuality in his previous books, he now attempts to reassert it. . . . (p. 154)

[Simic's] desire for unity *and* diversity leads him for the first time to overtly sexual poems such as "Breasts" and "That Straightlaced Christian Thing Between Her Legs." In such work the poet's tactile approach to knowledge and language gains a new intensity. Nipples become "vowels of delicious clarity / For the little red schoolhouse of our mouths." Breasts are "two sour buns" which the tongue honors. In sexual union the poet can be both inside and outside his body, on earth and in heaven, in the present and in the future. He can possess the objects which nourish him physically and spiritually while retaining his own identity. . . .

Nevertheless he longs for more permanent union. "Travelling" shows the poet as a sack, but here, as in "The Bird," we focus upon him and his search for language. A ragpicker takes the poet-sack out at dawn, putting various objects into him and commenting on each. The tie was climbed by a man as it hung from his neck, and now he cannot descend. The overcoat is named Ahab and wants all its black threads removed. The boots have drowned. Yet beyond its initial assertion of the symbolic importance of the objects (*the* tie, *the* overcoat, *the* boots), language is unable to go. Facts overwhelm it. The poet's only comment, the refrain of the poem, is that he has none: "But I say nothing, what can a sack say?"

Simic continues to distrust abstract thought and generalizations, and his distrust still extends to the language itself. In "Poem" language is a lullaby, a memory, glossing over the facts of existence. "This is the story / Afraid to go on" begins another poem, and the story fears because it must use language with inevitable falsifications. The story regrets "the loss of its purity" and retreats into objects. (p. 155)

In his work to date one of Charles Simic's primary concerns has been the relationship of an individual man to the objects in the world around him, for the natural world, as Simic perceives it, is innately good and leads, as did the natural world of Emerson and Whitman, directly to truth. But the expression of that truth in the twentieth century does not come easy: the language of things differs from the language of man, particularly man in society. The poet apprehends objects through his sense of touch, and he must translate that touch with its accompanying intuitive, cryptic knowledge into imprecise human speech.

But for all its deficiencies language remains his tool because it is the only one he has. It falsifies experience by presenting it as something else, namely language, but the juxtaposition of language and experience may itself partially explain the world. (pp. 156-57)

> Victor Contoski, "Charles Simic: Language at the Stone's Heart," in Chicago Review (reprinted by permission of Chicago Review; copyright © 1977 by Chicago Review), Vol. 48, No. 4, 1977, pp. 145-57.

*   *   *

SIMON, Claude   1913-

A French novelist, Simon began his career as a painter, and painterly concepts are evident in his fiction. Like a painter, Simon attempts to convey, simultaneously, his thematic concerns. He does not deal in time sequences or successive events. In the New Novelist tradition, Simon presents a sensory picture through extremely long sentences lacking punctuation and requiring much of the reader. This accentuates Simon's belief, like Picasso's, that an artist's first duty is to himself. (See also *CLC***, Vol. 4.)**

Perhaps . . . with the publication of "Conducting Bodies," his 11th novel and seventh to appear in English, Claude Simon will finally gain full recognition in the United States as one of France's most eminent novelists and as one of the most inventive and truly profound exponents of fiction anywhere. "The Flanders Road," "The Grass" and especially "Histoire" did earn critical praise this side of the Atlantic but Simon, like most practitioners of the French New Novel, is still insufficiently read. The highly complex structure of his works requires a great effort from the reader—an effort amply rewarded. Simon is concerned primarily with the outer limits of fiction: the probe into the process of fiction itself, the novel about the novel. However, where Proust analyzed its genesis, Simon explores the very mechanism of fiction, its fictivity.

For Claude Simon, literature is not expressed through language, it *is* language; the movement of language produces the work of art and is fully identical with it. McLuhan's dictum applies: the medium is the message, the writing is the novel. Simon's . . . recent works—particularly "Conducting Bodies"—are novels about the generative power of language, about the creative adventure of words, rather than words about an adventure. The visual orientation of all his books finds its fullest expression in "Conducting Bodies," with the theme of the work of fiction creating itself now intricately demonstrated through images. The mode of association and generation is pictorial rather than thematic or linguistic, proceeding via juxtapositions of visual stimuli.

Behind the dazzling inventory of sensations there are also elements of a story, although one cannot properly speak of a plot. . . .

The narrative is propelled by means of elements (or "bodies"), fragmenting the present and radiating to different zones of past experience, conducting (as one might use the term in physics) to new associations of images: paintings, lights, posters, newspaper ads, shapes, colors, New York City. Simon uses a technique of literary collage, full of subtle resonances and with echoes constantly reverberating between the gradually revealed surfaces of things. The effect is not the usual, realistic, pseudo three-dimensional portrayal, but rather a flattening-out of surfaces so as to suggest simultaneity of elements, much in the Cubist manner.

The novel reaches no conclusion; it just ends. The traveler's illness persists, his memories continue to haunt him. The path of the novel has not been a linear journey from a beginning to an end, but an apparently random set of associations linked merely by the author's spontaneity.

Simon uses literary equivalents of cinema techniques to achieve rapid or striking transitions in time or space; he particularly resorts to the present tense to isolate some single factor beyond its habitual temporal and spatial context. Some 10 pages of scenes totally unrelated logically are linked exclusively through associations of various rectangles—their rectangular shape being their only common denominator.

Claude Simon has stated that his initial generator in the writing of "Conducting Bodies" was a collage composition in rectangles by Robert Rauschenberg. He has also said that a descriptive subtitle might be "properties of various figures, geometric and others." His book, however, is much more than an examination of properties, more than a work about nothing. It is a novel that brilliantly puts into focus the process of creation by enabling us to follow the artist's eye, his sensitivity, as it selects, shapes, integrates the material of the exterior world in order to turn it into images of creation, in order to fashion it into fiction. (p. 4)

> Tom Bishop, in The New York Times Book Review (© 1974 by the New York Times Company; reprinted by permission), September 15, 1974.

The title of [*Conducting Bodies*] (anti-novel, non-novel, post-novel) is rich with suggestion, mostly misleading. Corpsewatchers are not at issue here, nor is André Previn nor *On the Buses,* but rather the media, themselves unchanging, through which heat, magnetism and other passions pass; perhaps also the Indian guides of the Conquistadors, and certainly that pair of bodies rendered transparent by pain and regret whose slow coupling pulsates through the narrative.

It starts, ominously enough, with the punctilious description of a shop-window display, jump-cutting thence in various directions in space-time: one cannot speak of flashbacks, since the images are autonomous perceptions rather than part of a stream of consciousness. Sometimes the transitions are lucid and dazzling—the facade of a skyscraper into a page of print. Others are distractingly obscure. . . . In fact, the counterpoint of flesh and viscera is one of the hero-percipient's major preoccupations, as the themes of an abruptly ended affair and a gradually defined disease emerge from the flux of sharply visual images, dreamlike but never surreal.

The locus of action flickers between New York, a plane in flight, and a Spanish American city (Havana? But why shouldn't one know for certain?). . . . It is no accident that the recurring images are ready-made—newspaper headlines, murals, the illustrations in an encyclopedia or a magazine. As in the flowchart of associations in *The Psychopathology of Everyday Life,* all thoughts tend to a centre of gravity labelled "Death and Sex".

It is inappropriate, I am sure, to pick out a narrative thread like the old lost road through the woods; still less should one follow the advice of the blurb and piece together a jigsaw, which is to accuse the author of a piece of footling mystification. My own response, perhaps just as inapt, was to sort the fragments into separate piles, each crosslinked mainly by visual juxtapositions. The chronology is not that of a train of thought, but of a writer's drafts or cutting-room images.

The stream is directed by artifice rather than by natural gradient; not a roman-fleuve but a roman-canal. And as with a Roman candle, periods of coruscation are interrupted by fumblings in the dark with matches that do not strike. One is fatigued and irritated by banal passages. . . . Of course one can skip these passages, which is one reason writing can never approach the condition of music. . . .

As I reread the novel, the images became sharper, the structure more precise, but more and more of it seemed a mere decoy: perhaps finally the only important action is the gradual disappearance of a patch of sunlight on a floor. One returns from an exhilarating Argonautic voyage, clutching a handful of damp wool.

> Eric Korn, "Passing Passions," in The Times Literary Supplement (© Times Newspapers Ltd., 1975; reproduced from The Times Literary Supplement by permission), July 11, 1975, p. 753.

Although Claude Simon's work has developed quite clearly as an adventure into the inventive realm of language seen as an autonomous structure and not as the vehicle for expressing ideas about the world, this does not preclude the appearance in his novels of certain basic and familiar human themes. Such themes may remain implicit, particularly in his most recent writings, but they do give depth and body to his books, in a manner unlike that of any other 'new novelist'. . . .

Simon's use of what we shall call 'visions of life in microcosm' provides a consistently effective summary of his major themes. Such is the scope of his writing that these metaphors range from sporting encounters to the chaotic experience of war and revolution, or they may concentrate attention on the communities and even the buildings in which the rituals of human life are enacted. . . . [They] function as concise distillations of his view of the world, and as invaluable landmarks in novels whose technique is that of poetic fragmentation. (p. 42)

In the scene at the rugby match [in *Gulliver* (1952)], there is a powerful vision of humanity *en masse,* absorbed in the aggressively concerted release of the pressures built up by a humdrum existence. Events on the field of play effectively liberate the crowd from the tensions born of inactivity and frustration. As one team threatens to gain ascendancy, violent emotions are aroused; when the promise is not kept, or is thwarted, the noise abates temporarily. The abstract and general terms used in the description suggest that life, like

this game, is a perpetual sequence of hopes and disillusionments. (pp. 42-3)

The fact that there is no scoring underlines the futility of the players' efforts, and indeed the most striking feature of the game is that it is played amidst utter confusion. For the men on the field it is a totally mindless exercise; Simon emphasizes the blind, automatic manner in which they move around, goaded on by the roaring of the crowd, but unable to gain any decisive advantage. This in itself would not suffice to justify a reading of the episode as an illustration of the author's own 'philosophy', but the description is prolonged in terms which make it clear that this is rather more than a harmless dissipation of misplaced energies. . . . There is a bizarre atmosphere of hostility around the match. . . . [A] combination of pride and persecution . . . seems to be the principal motive, in Simon's novels, for human aggressiveness; the players are 'insulted' by the treachery of an enemy whom they have some difficulty in recognizing. There is something pathetic in the fact that so banal an occasion can produce so intense an effect upon the emotions of the herd. In this way, the rugby match, a straightforward physical encounter played in accordance with established rules, is expanded by the manner of its description into a metaphor of the human situation, which is one of aggression, the fundamental viciousness which Simon evokes time and again in his novels, whether in the exaggerated suspicions and revolt of young 'heroes', in the cut-throat bargaining of various commercial types, or in the paradoxical hostility of the sexual act.

Basic enmities apart, the match also serves to underline the absurdity of human enterprise. Although taking place in the aftermath of war, and therefore achieving a cathartic effect upon its spectators, the match is ultimately to be understood as futile, because of the conditions in which it is played. . . . [The] opening paragraph of the chapter establishes the familiar Simon pattern in which the effect of time is conveyed by the description of natural phenomena. . . . It also introduces the notion of dissolution which lies at the heart of every Simon novel. Despite its apparent insignificance, the rain is incessant and powerful: encompassing the whole scene, it wears down the resistance of things animate and inanimate alike. This then is an explicit parallel for the unselective work of time, dominating an event already overshadowed by the background presence of war. For all their clamouring, the human figures are temporary components in the scene, dwarfed by the dimensions of the natural landscape. (pp. 43-4)

[In] a much more recent novel, *La Bataille de Pharsale,* . . . the narrator, exploring the Greek countryside in search of the historic battlefield, comes instead upon a local football match. . . . Once again nature cancels out the expenditure of human energy as players and spectators are 'swallowed up' in the immense landscape; the terms of the description have become far less explicit and verbose. Simon's development as an artist is shown in *La Bataille de Pharsale* by his superb variations on the theme of history, in which even this match becomes an important factor. Simon uses it as an implicit commentary upon the 'historic' meeting of Caesar and Pompey on the plain of Pharsalus, which the narrator believes himself to have found. What, then, is he to make of the trivial spectacle of men chasing a ball? . . . [This] seems all the more meaningless in comparison with one of the most celebrated explosions of human violence. In this novel Simon creates a fascinating network of cross-references from one 'battle' to the other. Warfare and sport, it seems, differ only in degree as illustrations of the fundamental themes of aggression and transience. That the vocabulary of sport is essentially a vocabulary of war is borne out by its constant emphasis on terms of victory or defeat, and the two are juxtaposed.... The language of day-to-day existence is that of triumph and disaster, but even the greatest of these is as mercurial as its human participants, and it is the understanding of history as *exaggeration* that characterizes the narrators of Simon's best novels. (p. 44)

Some of the finest descriptions in *La Route des Flandres* concentrate upon the vividly imagined scene at a French race-course. At one point Simon broadens out the terms of the description to include a number of comments about the organization of society. The race-meeting attracts people from all walks of life, brought together by one mutual preoccupation: money. The gathering is broadly divisible into two categories; those wealthy enough to enjoy the spectacle, and those for whom something vital is at stake.... 'Decency' and 'morality', it is clear, are terms which become devalued when applied to those whose richness takes them beyond the reach of ordinary standards of behaviour. But this is equally true of people at the other end of the social (or financial) scale.... In a way, Simon is trying, with this financial theme, to show how the past shapes the present: the circumstances into which an individual is born dictate the pattern of his life, especially in terms of finance.... What [brings] the two sectors together ... is their adherence to the principles of commerce, the only distinction being the sums of money involved. The passage as a whole underlines, in a totally unsentimental manner, the hierarchy of wealth which keeps the predators strictly apart from the poor. 'Luck', good or bad, is the determinant factor in the organization of social structures and of the individual's place within them, but in the last analysis 'le hasard' is depressingly indifferent to human aspirations, as the deserted race-course illustrates.... [The] serenity of time stands in ironic contrast to the ephemeral violence of human nature, and this is plainly a theme which has remained fundamental to Simon's work from its beginnings to its most mature development; his use of sporting encounters offers a highly effective synthesis of his major preoccupations.

It should not be surprising to find Simon using towns as the basis for microcosmic representations of life, since every township is both a reflection of human efforts and achievements, and the restricted space in which a typical cross-section of humanity evolves.... [For example], in *Le Vent*, the central character is brought into dramatic contact with a series of representative figures—notary, policeman, priest and so on—in an unspecified town in Southern France, but the most interesting examples are to be found in *Le Palace* and *Histoire*.

Over the fictional 'Barcelona' of *Le Palace* hangs a familiarly Simonian atmosphere of paralysis which, as the novel progresses, becomes indissociably linked with the theme of death and its inescapable presence in the city.... [As in *La Peste*], the city concerned is victim of a profound feeling of menace, but whereas Camus is deliberately setting out to elaborate a system of allegorical cross-references and to present characters who embody moral or philosophical atti-

tudes, Simon is anxious above all to suggest and recapture atmosphere. Indeed he has been careful to disclaim all critical intention.... Subjective as it is, ... the novel as a work of art may well provide a more telling account of events than the most objective of histories, and there is in *Le Palace* a distinct element of social or 'historical' commentary. The city described there is a microcosm in that it affords a summary of the 'lugubrious inventory' of history: it is a monument to the progress of civilization, the material configuration of the dogmas and credos of humanity. Stating this at the outset, Simon gives an ironic background to a novel whose broad theme is revolution. With the benefit of hindsight—historical perspective?—the central character of *Le Palace* is able to achieve a cynical reappraisal of the revolutionary ardour in which he had once been caught up. (pp. 44-6)

The revolutionary city [of *Le Palace*] is ... a mirror of humanity against a background of extreme violence, and the whole point of the novel is that nothing is accomplished, largely because of the divergent and contradictory interests of the various individuals. (p. 47)

[The] townships which Simon describes are intended as microcosmic representations of life, and the one which appears in *Histoire* is no exception, containing as it does those institutions around which life constantly gravitates. Significantly enough, the narrator of the novel visits three buildings which have a symbolic function within the context of the novel: a bank, a restaurant and a bar. Situated in the very centre of the town, classical in design, the bank is the modern counterpart of the temple: not so much a place of public service as a bizarre and secretive institution whose occupants work out the life-patterns of the customers. It is the first stage in the narrator's renewed understanding of life as a depressingly commercial round.... The narrator's fixation with banknotes is an indication that life is an uninterrupted process of exchanging the infinite variety of reality for its mere synthetic counterparts. (pp. 47-8)

Paris and Barcelona in *Le Palace*, typical southern towns in *Le Vent* and *Histoire*: these are conventional and familiar human gatherings. But Simon has reserved his most powerful picture of life in microcosm for a community which is not actually a town but is still rigorously constructed upon the principles of all human society as Simon sees it. *La Route des Flandres* contains an important statement justifying a reading of the novel as a *rapprochement* of military disaster with the state of chaos inherent in the structure of the world.... In his account of the camp in *La Route des Flandres*, Simon uses some of his finest writing to create a picture of men clinging to the skeleton of civilized society. Somehow the occupants reinforce the commercial principles already observed elsewhere as the basis of that society. (p. 48)

[Another] vital element is the central symbol of men's enduring fascination with the game of chance as a means to improve their position. The scene around the card-table is a miniature within a miniature, in that it gathers together a further group of types from the camp's society.... The card-table is a familiar symbol of the influence of chance, described in *Le Tricheur* and *Gulliver* in particular, and seen as one of the standard rituals of life, where tension and the threat of violence are scarcely concealed. Here [as in the other novels] there are no individuals, only types.... The game provides an escape from a hideous reality....

Seen as a whole, this prison camp is a superb miniature of the structures of society. (p. 49)

The hospital in *Le Sacre du Printemps* is used as a symbolic reminder of transience, the captivity in time which is a major Simonian theme, evoked by the lowering atmosphere of the place.... The institution gives menacing shape to Simon's view of humanity's illusions. Fragility, insignificance and solitude: three terms which sum up the human condition, crystallized and exaggerated against a background of death. All the activities undertaken by men may be considered as the objectification of the desire to deny that condition, a kind of optimistic but tragic procrastination. Ultimately it is time that holds the key to this condition, standing as the fundamental theme of Simon's writing for the major part of his career. Even in so early a novel as *Le Sacre du Printemps* his art is established upon the familiar Shakespearean metaphor of 'the sound and the fury' which is the foundation for all the visions of life in microcosm discussed. If Simon seems to have abandoned this device in his latest novels, it is surely because the artist is moving towards a position where the book itself, and not any single part of it, is to be understood as a microcosmic distillation of reality. (p. 50)

> *S.W. Sykes, "Claude Simon: Visions of Life in Microcosm," in* The Modern Language Review (© *Modern Humanities Research Association 1976), January, 1976, pp. 42-50.*

In Simon's writing, the constant narrowing of the range of the simile results in the continual frustration of the reader's expectations: the effect is one of anticlimax as the author's striving after an exact expression ties down the initial flight of fancy. The search for ever-greater precision echoes the over-all direction of Simon's books, where all is clear (supposedly) in retrospect.... Simon's [technique is one] of definition. (pp. 353-54)

[A] feature common to ... [Simon and] a number of other *nouveaux romanciers* is the exploitation of sentence length. Abnormally long and complex sentences are often interspersed with very short ones, the grammatical links between them frequently being reinforced by repetition.... [The] repetition of certain images ... may be used to suggest the obsessive workings of the mind, and this may also be true in the case of complex sentence structure with its increasing subordination as the mind seeks to define and moves off on new tracks....

[Simon makes] considerable use of images which dehumanize [his] subjects, frequently comparing people to animals or to inanimate objects. (p. 355)

[There] are a number of images in which there is some similarity between the various *comparants*, or vehicles of metaphor, with shared subjects including children, phantoms, masks and the notion of suspension, but their stylistic functions rarely coincide.... [Such] comparisons tend to fall ... into the category of dehumanizing images.... (p. 356)

> *Paula M. Clifford, "The American Novel and the French 'Nouveau Roman': Some Linguistic and Stylistic Comparisons" (a revision of a speech originally delivered at University of East Anglia in December, 1975), in* Comparative Literature Studies (© *1976 by the Board of Trustees at the University of Illinois), December, 1976, pp. 348-58.*

Critics of the nouveau roman have long contended that it is *chosiste,* that is, unduly preoccupied with inanimate things. As if in witty defiance of this charge, Claude Simon has entitled his latest novel *Leçon de choses.* Structurally, the novel is a long parenthesis within two texts, one repeating much of the other. The first, having the cinematographic title of "Générique," consists not of film-like credits but of a dreary description of the objects in a room. From this a whole work of fiction is generated.

The parenthesis contains four apparently independent tableaux presented simultaneously in fragments, a few pages from one, a line or two from another. These tableaux are replete with symbols and leitmotifs, many familiar from Simon's previous novels.... Perhaps the most characteristic of Simon is his fourth tableau, a sexual encounter which takes place in a field at night, recorded with Simon's singularly clinical and geometric touches. Completing the circle with a text called "Short Circuits," Simon shows how the same elements, rearranged, could form a different novel.

Leçon de choses is assuredly Simon's most abstract fiction thus far. In brilliant prose he vindicates the function that the *choses* fulfill in the consciousness of the narrator. (p. 56)

> *Katharine W. Carson, in* World Literature Today (*copyright 1977 by the University of Oklahoma Press), Vol. 51, No. 1, Winter, 1977.*

*   *   *

SIMPSON, Louis   1923-

Simpson is a Jamaican-born American poet, novelist, and playwright. In his poetry he strives to create a tone of irony and mystery. He is considered a poet of imagination, his verse expressing the imagery of dreams. Simpson received the Pulitzer Prize in 1964. (See also *CLC*, Vols. 4, 7, and *Contemporary Authors*, Vols. 1-4, rev. ed.)

Simpson—Jamaican-born, American-educated, Jewish—finds his inspiration, and his melancholy, faintly ironic happiness, in getting his back under the burden of things as they always have been....

I find the mood of these poems [in *Searching for the Ox*], and their reflective music, the slow, heavy plucking of strings, exceptionally attractive. One very moving poem, 'Baruch', places them in the background against which Simpson himself sees them. It is the tale of an ancestor, a Jewish hat-factory owner in Russia, who rejoices when the factory burns down, because at last he can 'give himself to the Word'. 'The love of literature goes with us,' Simpson reflects; and the poem ends with him sitting in a train, crossing the American prairie at night, while other men in the carriage play cards:

> Then I see a face, pale and unearthly,
> that is flitting along with the train,
> passing over the fields and rooftops,
> and I hear a voice out of the past:
> 'He wishes to study the Torah.'
>
> (p. 686)

> *Derwent May, in* The Listener (© *British Broadcasting Corp. 1976; reprinted by permission of Derwent May), November 25, 1976.*

Much of *Searching for the Ox* presents Simpson as so terribly, terribly suburban, so thoroughly mundane, that I cannot get past a picture of him mowing the lawn and preparing a Fourth of July cook-out. . . . Simpson sneers at his own class and his own comfy way of life while, at the same time, attempting to make poetry out of it. . . . He does not quite have the talent for disgust that might have carried these pieces off. . . .

In *Three on the Tower,* Simpson writes several times over that a poet needs a world-view or belief in order to make "major" poetry, and that it does not matter if that belief fails to satisfy others. This is a literary truism, a twentieth-century one, which may, indeed, be true. But the poet's philosophical scheme must satisfy the poet, at least, in resolving strenuous inner conflict. To come to poetic and philosophical resolutions as easily as Louis Simpson does indicates that he really has not attained a world-view of his own in which the various components of his experience cohere. In *Searching for the Ox,* Simpson has gone shopping for a faith and / or identity, and that is impossible, even on Long Island. It either is or is not there. (p. 65)

[In] his early work, Simpson was able to imagine himself a *poilu,* for example, and to present the eerie nightmare of history through his own particular poetic prism. . . . ["I Dreamed That in a City Dark as Paris"] was neither a long poem, a "Jewish poem," nor a poem in anybody's particular tradition. But it was an individual and highly memorable poem. It was written before Louis Simpson, like his "actors performing / Official scenarios" had himself "contracted American dreams" ("Walt Whitman at Bear Mountain"). Louis Simpson's work now suggests too much comfort: emotional, physical, intellectual. He has stopped struggling, it seems, for words, for rhythms, for his own deepest self. His is a middle-class, middle-brow poetry, the major value of which is to steer other poets from the same course, and to raise some questions about poets joining an Establishment, whether it be one of social class, national or literary identification. (pp. 65-6)

> *Nikki Stiller, "Shopping for Identity: Louis Simpson's Poetry," in* Midstream *(copyright © 1976 by The Theodor Herzl Foundation, Inc.), December, 1976, pp. 63-6.*

I can't think of a poet other than Louis Simpson who says so well of life that there is nothing to be said for it. It is as if he believes poetry is the medium through which life's ironies are enabled to speak for themselves. Dead words, like dead stars, continue to send out reminders of their passing. It is no accident that Simpson in *To The Western World* provided the most striking image of the funeral which lies at the heart of the colonial man: 'The generations labour to possess / and grave by grave we civilize the ground'. The seance continues.

Oxen made an early appearance in his poems. In a poem of long ago they were pictured observing a couple whose passionate absorption broke with nature. 'The envious oxen in still rings would stand / Ruminating.' In the title poem of his new collection [*Searching For the Ox*], the ox is another beast entirely. 'Searching for the ox / I come upon a single hoofprint. / I find the ox and tame it, / and lead it home. In the next scene / the moon has risen, a cool light. / Both the ox and herdsman vanished.'

Simpson's bleak lyricism celebrates only what edges into

his line of vision and even as he remarks on it he shows it to be fading. . . . (p. 83)

[His] fascination with place names and family names . . . made *Adventures Of The Letter I,* a work of pure, brilliant invention, seem so realistic. Of that letter in which there is no trace of ego, the wealth of geographical information so helpfully tendered made the *Adventures Of The Letter I* read like the *A/Z.* Place names have this great virtue: they speak up for themselves. While it is honourable, Simpson seems to feel, to put something in the place of nothing, it won't do to make too much of anything. To the paranoic his paranoia, to the poet his poems. . . . Simpson pads around the edges of his poems, apologetic at having been found on the scene at all, the illusionist who would guard against illusion. He is so fastidiously honest in showing up his own tricks that it amounts at times to a kind of off-handedness. So self-effacing, we wait for him to arrange his mirrors and vanish. (pp. 83-4)

> *Christopher Hope, in* London Magazine *(© London Magazine 1977), February-March, 1977.*

*   *   *

SINGER, Isaac Bashevis   1904-

Born and raised in Warsaw, Singer was encouraged by his family to become a rabbi. Impressed by the literary talents of his brother, I. J. Singer, he instead decided to write. Singer's novels and short stories are usually written in Yiddish, poignant, and steeped in folklore and tradition. His popularity became international with the 1953 publication of Saul Bellow's translation of "Gimpel the Fool." He is considered by many critics the most significant living Yiddish writer. He currently resides in the United States. (See also *CLC,* Vols. 1, 3, 6, and *Contemporary Authors,* Vols. 1-4, rev. ed.)

A Crown of Feathers provides yet another convincing body of evidence to support the late Edmund Wilson's claim that I. B. Singer warrants serious consideration for the Nobel Prize. He is, without doubt, our greatest living storyteller. And the short story continues to remain his most congenial turf. It is here that the economy of style and the deceptive simplicity of his vision can be most richly felt. . . .

Singer is as appealing as he is protean: both shy *yeshivah* boy and urbane sophisticate, he balances curiosity against skepticism, temporal obsessions against an eternality that looks, suspiciously, like faith. But most of all, Singer reminds us of that mysterious power that genuine stories always have. The typical Singer persona may wink with one eye, but the other is wide open. In "The Captive," for example, a visit to Israel prompts the following observation: "In the paper before me I read about thefts, car accidents, border shootings. One page was full of obituaries. No, the Messiah hadn't come yet. The Resurrection was not in sight. Orthopedic shoes were displayed in a shop across the way."

It is to such a world of maimed bodies and even more severely maimed psyches that Singer brings the ordering function of Art. As one character (in "The Briefcase") puts it: "What could a fiction writer add to the naked facts? Sensationalism and melodrama had become our daily diet. The unbelievable was all too believable." (p. 311)

[To] Singer, the bizarre is as much a continuing surprise as it is a constant expectation. In "Lost" a character may *claim* that demons could not exist in New York ("Demons need a synagogue, a ritual bathhouse, a poorhouse, a garret with torn prayer books—all the paraphernalia you describe in your (i.e. Singer's personal stories"), but *A Crown of Feathers* is full of evidence to the contrary. . . . Fixed ideas —wherever they may reside—lead to the sort of compulsive behavior Singer loves to chronicle. . . . [It is Singer's] amazement with man's capacity to both spin illusions and be trapped inside them that makes Singer a darker writer than his ever-growing readership may have imagined. (pp. 311-12)

> *John Lawrence Abbott, in* Studies in Short Fiction *(copyright 1974 by Newberry College), Summer, 1974.*

Isaac Bashevis Singer has lately become a figure in his own stories. He comes on as an embarrassed celebrity, awkwardly trying to fend off readers who regularly break in on him because they find him a link to their long suppressed Jewishness. The situation is inherently comic, problematical, unsettling to all parties concerned. For Singer's own "Jewishness" is unsentimental, occult, faithful in its own way to his rabbinical youth. But as in "The Admirer," the best [selection in *Passions and Other Stories*], Singer's confused American fans breaking in on him tend to be even more confused about what they are looking for. They introduce complications that more than cancel out any pleasure their homage gives this Warsaw-born Yiddish writer who, after long struggles, acquired a wide American audience. Singer is amazed by his new readers. In some way he feels himself to be their captive.

It is these "confusions" that give such characters their invincible craziness and thus their human interest. Singer writing about a wholly Jewish world recognizes in his "admirers" that to be Jewish is to be driven by forces that Jews understand no better than others do. The "mystery" of Jewish religion (and of Jewish persistence) may be especially a mystery to those who have suffered most for it.

Singer consciously unsettles his reader, for his stories are all written within the compressiveness of magazine style. . . . But Singer's sly provocations of style are also an artistic necessity. There is so much material in Jewish lore, so much continuation into our day of the Jewish past, so much horror and unreality in the endless stories-within-stories of the Holocaust, that there is a too-enormous gallery of people to write about, a hall of mirrors to walk through. Singer's sentences have to speed through millennia of experience and human feeling. . . . (pp. 24-5)

> *Alfred Kazin, in* The New Republic *(reprinted by permission of* The New Republic; © 1975 by The New Republic, Inc.), October 25, 1975.*

It is not for literature, or for writing, that Singer cares most, but for "a group of people who are still a riddle to the world and often to themselves—the Jews of Eastern Europe, specifically the Yiddish-speaking Jews who perished in Poland and those who emigrated to the U.S.A. The longer I live with them and write about them, the more I am baffled by the richness of their individuality and (since I am one of them) by my own whims and passions." ["Passions"], though hardly Singer's best book, is marvelous testimony to Singer's willingness to be simply baffled by that richness.

In many of these stories Singer himself has helped someone else out with the translation. His English is excellent, but he would not think of not writing in Yiddish, that language not quite of a people or of a country, but the source of Singer's need and love. In many of these stories he is openly reporting on his experience, being the middle-aged writer named "I." . . .

He doesn't even need, in the usual sense, to write short stories. He tells what happened to him, or a tale he has heard from someone else. The lives he describes seem to shape themselves, their stories to go on until they are over. While it is true that the two "best" in this collection, the two one would submit for prizes, "Old Love" and "The Witch," are more impersonal, more apparently imagined and consciously shaped, than the others, one could never ask that Singer discover art. He has mastered the art he needs. If a tale is very short, or slight, why then it is, and Singer will simply throw it in with two or three others and call the group "Errors" or "Passions." (p. 7)

Singer seems to be more truly read and enjoyed by the non-literary than the literary, to say nothing of the Jew more than the Gentile. . . . [His] art is not only traditional but oral, and within that tradition it is life, not an author, that does the essential shaping. Since life is both rich and baffling, characterization is strictly a matter of saying what happened to someone, no explanation being possible, no context more than minimally helpful. Which is why he writes such good stories for children, why all his stories are children's stories. (pp. 7-8)

> *Roger Sale, in* The New York Times Book Review *(© 1975 by The New York Times Company; reprinted by permission), November 2, 1975.*

Singer draws most of his fictional material from the Polish *shtetl* (Jewish village community) as it existed at the turn of the century and even earlier. Against a backcloth of tremendous physical deprivation, poverty and superstition his tales frequently use the traditional strategy of a garrulous narrator who keeps interjecting asides and gossipy irrelevancies which all screen the actual events from the reader. In fact in such tales the reader is drawn to listen to the narrator's voice as much as attend to the narrative. (p. 73)

Singer rings many changes on his narrators which vary from conventional eye-witnesses to a cock and a devil, often for broad comic effects. 'Cockadoodledoo' is a lighthearted burlesque of the gradations of village society (even imitated by the fowls). And 'Two Corpses Go Dancing' begins as a joke on how briefly the dead are remembered and shades into a macabre paradox when two corpses decide to get married.

Occasionally however, Singer achieves powerful psychological intensity. 'The Black Wedding' is an example which uses the superstitions of the village peasants. A rabbi and his wife die mysteriously (killed 'by demons') and on his deathbed he swears his daughter Hindele to silence. Framing the narrative in her consciousness Singer establishes a very claustrophobic perspective. . . .

'The Black Wedding' gains force from its matter-of-fact description of demons and illustrates an important characteristic of some of Singer's fiction. In 1917 he went to live in his grandfather's home in the little Polish village of Bilgoray. He was there six years and this period had an enormously strong and lasting effect on him. For the first time Singer experienced *shtetl* life and met people who literally believed in black magic, and whose superstitions dated from the Middle Ages. This fascination with the ancient helps to explain why, in many of Singer's tales, the reader is never sure of the exact period and is often displaced backwards into a legendary past.

It was also during this stay in Bilgoray that Singer began to read widely in the 'forbidden' literature of the Cabala, and these two interests came together in his first novel, *Satan in Goray*. (p. 74)

The novel's biblical language constantly depresses the fantastic events within the narrative itself. Here, as in many of his other tales and novels, Singer has evoked a landscape densely populated with *dybbuks* and other supernatural spirits, and it is partly this emphasis on the demonic which has led the American critic Irving Howe to argue that Singer is a modernist. Be that as it may, one of his richest veins of material is traditional and demons and spirits play an integral part in the texture of his fiction. . . .

Often the causality of Singer's plots is severely biblical. In 'The Destruction of Kreschev' (narrated by none other than Satan) a young couple marry and begin delving into the Cabala; and then—and the two are frequently linked in Singer—indulging in unnatural acts. The end result is that fire and plague strike the village in succession and destroy it completely. But the moral perspective is more complex than this outline suggests. There is a strong implication that the villagers have driven the girl to suicide, so fierce was their condemnation of her. And the plague is a punishment of the community's self-righteousness as much as the couple's sinfulness. (p. 75)

[Typically Singer's] communities are under pressure from outside (from social upheaval or the Jewish Enlightenment) or from within. His most recurring figures are isolated, unworldly, or obsessed; the failed scholar appears again and again as does the monomaniac, and the result is that our image of the village community in Singer's fiction is always precarious and often hostile.

At times this implicit subversion of communal values becomes stronger than Singer's narrators admit, and sets up a tension with the overt perspective which we are given. (pp. 75-6)

The excellence of [*The Magician of Lublin*] is its consistent focus on [the protagonist] Yasha and its correlation between the physical and the psychological. During his crisis Yasha sees filth everywhere but, while this suggests his inner state, it is also literally true. The muddy chaos of the Warsaw streets where sewers and telephone cables are being laid, remains physically actual as well as psychologically appropriate. Speculation and an attention to different moral possibilities are embedded in the narrative itself (particularly as to the nature of guilt and freedom) and in the character of Yasha who is a compulsive questioner. It is certainly one of Singer's most concentrated and unified works. (p. 76)

[In *A Friend of Kafka*] a definite thinness becomes noticeable. Firstly the tales have lost the easy confidentiality which Singer's more traditional narratives have. Instead they are 'set up' by an obvious surrogate of Singer himself

(usually a Yiddish writer) who only exists to trigger off another character's narration. Since these are based on chance meetings they seem particularly contrived and unconvincing.

Secondly the tales have lost their cultural base. Although they are located in America they deal with first-generation emigrants and the key emotions registered are either sheer confusion when faced with American life . . . or simple nostalgia for Europe. Even more important, the tales turn into parables which assert the values of tradition and continuity. . . .

Faced with a purely contemporary culture the characters in these American tales never get a purchase on their new lives. Family pieties dissolve and the narratives seem incapable of coping with the characters' diverse experiences. The geographical area seems over-extended, stretching from America to Eastern Europe and Palestine, whereas Singer's best fiction is intensely regional in spirit and texture. Only occasionally does he counteract this attenuation. In 'Shloimele' we are given a comically satirical portrait of an emigrant who is trying to make it on Broadway. He is a constant source of schemes and has reduced his 'Jewishness' to a handful of Yiddish proverbs and kosher cooking. The characterization has real bite, hinting as it does of the problem of a Jewish-American identity. But in general it really seems that Singer needs a European society to give his narratives body.

Singer has repeatedly stated that he writes in two modes. One—discussed above—is a narrative which uses primitive superstition and the supernatural; the other is a more usual realistic mode. (p. 77)

The . . . novels *The Manor* and *The Estate* are later examples of [the narrative characterized by superstition and the supernatural] type of fiction, and they deal quite explicitly with many of the concerns which are only latent in Singer's other tales and novels. The broad historical theme is the emergence of the Polish Jews out of medieval village life into modern industrial society and this process covers the period from 1863 (the year of the abortive Polish rebellion against Russia) up to the first years of this century. (pp. 77-8)

We are given very little detailed physical description in these two novels. Instead our sense of place comes from the characters themselves and the events which surround them. Singer has a fundamental impulse to chronicle the destinies of the Jacoby family and the people they come into contact with, but unfortunately this makes the novels very difficult to follow at times because we are faced with such a multiplicity of characters. (p. 78)

The two novels raise various theoretical issues (usually in explicit discussion) and one of their central themes is the notion of progress. In *The Manor* characters use Darwin's name to underpin their crass optimism about human destiny, but in *The Estate* the evolutionary sequence seems to go into reverse. Material prosperity guarantees no real happiness; Ezriel's wife goes insane; characters die from painful illnesses; Lucian (one of the Jampol nobility) degenerates into a murderous melancholic and then shoots himself. The tone closes in as death grows more and more prominent and as the forces of unreason come to the surface. (pp. 78-9)

The most interesting character in the novels is Clara. . . . She is right outside the rather rigid moral categories which tend to cramp many of the others. She is promiscuous, cynical, and a hard-headed business woman, but is psychologically complex in the quite contradictory attitudes she can sustain and in her sense of freshly discovering her experience as it happens to her. But even she turns back to her original faith once she realizes that she is fatally ill. Indeed the final perspective of the novels becomes more and more religious, ending on a note of mystical transcendence with the death of the Marshinov rabbi. The return to origins is complete. (p. 79)

> *David Seed, "The Fiction of Isaac Bashevis Singer," in* Critical Quarterly *(© Manchester University Press), Spring, 1976, pp. 73-9.*

To present the irrational in the clearest and most disciplined of styles is one of the aims of this great short story writer. And more and more Singer shows us [in *Passions*] the irrational in a modern context whose meaning is shadowed and deepened, of course, by the East European background of many of his characters. Thus Singer, like Nabokov, is a great spanner of wildly different cultures—and this makes him very modern and very American. He is also a survivor in a savage age who never renounces the boon and the burden of life. (p. 58)

> Virginia Quarterly Review *(copyright, 1976, by the* Virginia Quarterly Review, *The University of Virginia), Vol. 52, No. 2 (Spring, 1976).*

[Isaac Bashevis Singer] is an artist born into a tradition of folk narrative, a craft whose old practitioners he salutes in these pages [of *Passions and Other Stories*] by citing their titles and making new use of their techniques. . . . The old folk-tale device, whereby the stratagem which first procures happiness ends by marring it, serves Singer to show up the contradictions in the successful New Yorker who both does and does not want to be like his father and the pious Jews of his youth. Other traditional contrivances—the use of witches, ghosts, visions and memories which become incarnate—prove useful for building bridges between old Jewish Poland and the places where its scattered population comes to rest. . . .

Singer's purpose is not to solve but only to marvel and make us marvel at the riddle his people present. . . . To reconcile the irreconcilable would be a sham. Instead, the author aims to show life as high coloured, strange, incorrigibly plural. Characters are driven to eccentricity, even frenzy by the spur of passion, and 'Everything', as one of them says in the title story, 'can become a passion, even serving God'. So too, of course, can writing stories. . . .

The art of these stories is an ancient, sly art bent on shaking the scepticism out of its readers. Assurance is undermined by a revelation of the chaotic fearfulness of the world. Once we see how far passions can drive men and how capricious is the fate which determines destiny, an appeal to order becomes implicit, for where, the fearsome scenes lead us to wonder, would we be without it? Order and perhaps supernatural order? Singer does not make a direct plea for belief in this but it has an obsessive fascina-

tion for him. Story after story touches on the theme: some sceptically, some apparently using it as allegory, others presenting it baldly and leaving us to make of it what we may. Singer is like a cat who tosses a half-dead bird in the air to see will it fly and, seeing that it won't, eats it but then feels a flutter in his stomach. . . .

[He] has harnessed his own passion for the supernatural and made it work for him technically. Ghosts obliterate time and space. A witch can change a man's beliefs in a few hours. Sceptics are reminded that 'In the war the whole human culture crumbled like ruin. In the camps . . . all shame vanished . . .'. Beliefs, laws, morality are precarious. The world changes at a dizzy rhythm and these stories speed after it, catching odd, lurid images. Sceptics need time to disprove miracles. 'Wait', they say. 'Let me think.' But Singer won't wait. He wants to leave us baffled, and he does. (p. 59)

My pleasure in Singer's work comes from no fact he imparts. The virtue is in the tale itself and the tale is his response to those riddles which excite such passion in him that he had to elaborate a narrative method for dealing with it. It is *his* own method and fits his themes. In other words, he has a voice of his own. (p. 60)

> *Julia O'Faolain, in* The New Review *(© The New Review Ltd., 11 Greek Street, London W1V 5LE), June, 1976.*

*   *   *

SISSMAN, L(ouis) E(dward)   1928-1976

An American poet, editor, and essayist, Sissman wrote long, traditional verse. In a time when most poets were experimenting with free verse and other unconventional forms, Sissman clung to stanzaic verse, the iambic foot, couplets, and sonnets. He was a frequent contributor to *The New Yorker* and wrote a column, "Innocent Bystander," for *The Atlantic Monthly*. (See also *Contemporary Authors*, Vols. 21-24, rev. ed.; obituary, Vols. 65-68.)

[*Dying: An Introduction,*] composed of thirty-nine poems, some of them in several parts, one of them quite long, has a submerged narrative quality that gives to the whole a wonderful and eloquent coherence. It begins with the return from college after his freshman year of a young student, high-spirited, full of good humored self-criticism and a very comic sense of borrowed literary language, to his family's home for the summer holidays. It goes on through the terrors and giddy joys of adolescence to jobs, love affairs, recollections of previous love affairs, and much else, to end just outside a doctor's office with a gentle and muted and frightening acceptance of mortality. And while the wit is always there, the style or the point of view seems brilliantly to change with the maturity of accumulated experience. I do not by this mean for one minute that the later poems are superior to the earlier; I can best illustrate what I'm getting at by quotation. Here, first, is the last part of a poem in four parts, which recounts the nervous and unskillful preparations leading to what seems to be a first sexual encounter.

Later, as racy novels used to say,
Later, I turn to see the westering sun
Through the ailanthus stipple her tan side
With yellow coin dots shaped to fit her skin.
This Sally now does like a garment wear
The beauty of the evening; silent, bare,
Hips, shoulders, arms, tresses, and temples lie.
I watch her as she sleeps, the tapering back
Rising and falling on the tide of breath;
The long eyelashes lying on her cheek;
The black brows and the light mouth both at rest;
A living woman not a foot away.
The west wind noses in at the window,
Sending a scent of soap, a hint of her
Perfume, and the first onions of the night
Up the airshaft to where I lie, not quite alone.

This is good enough to speak for itself, but I will labor a point. The excellence of the Wordsworthian adaptation lies not merely in its splendid wit, but in a special aptness to the language and the occasion. For the whole poem is directed to the incredulity of the young man, who cannot quite believe that this is really happening to him, "A living woman not a foot away." And that touching youthful instinct to dress up one's own experience in high-class literary garb has always been a way of making this experience more real to one's self. It must be real, if all those famous men wrote that way and became immortal. Compare this, then, with the following lines from a later stage in the "hero's" development.

We issue from the meat of Pineapple Street,
Skipping in unison in the jet rain to
The cadence of our footsteps left behind
Just momentarily as we bound on
To water, laughing, soaked, four-legged and
Three-armed, two-hearted, Siamese, unique,
And fifty put together. On the Heights,
We embrace like trenchcoats on a rack at Brooks.
You taste like lipstick, wine, and cigarettes,
And, now quite irrecoverably, you: . . .

The difference between these passages is not merely a difference of dramatic situation; it is that the poet has grasped that difference with the keenest emotional sense of the occasions, and in both cases, with wit and gravity, has set them down. (pp. 215-17)

> *Anthony Hecht, in* The Hudson Review
> *(copyright © 1968 by The Hudson Review,*
> *Inc.; reprinted by permission), Vol. XXI,*
> *No. 1, Spring, 1968.*

Reviewing L. E. Sissman's first collection of poems when it appeared two years ago, I find I wrote: "His sensitivity to sex and relationships, to decadence, and to the revelations of autobiography is less confessional than nostalgic, and more an illustration of the illness of our age. The details of his life are not intrusions, but small tragedies." *Dying: An Introduction* was an astonishing book; those long poems about Harvard seemed to penetrate some desperate nerve of sadness, to breathe in the close air of decadence. Still, his subjects were so relentlessly Eastern, their dramas so aristocratic, and the language so worn-out! Usually rhyming, composed in dry pentameters, these chronicles of a dissatisfied life were saved by their commitment to portrayal. Most of them were published in *The New Yorker*,

where they were probably read by an audience that either knew people like those whom Sissman was describing, or who were themselves those people. Nostalgia! like Camus, Sissman was learning that "Men die, and they are not happy."

Scattered Returns, his second book, possesses that aura of exhaustion which derives from bringing what Robert Bly would call, after Groddeck, "News of the Human Universe". The voice is always Sissman's, the condition always one of dolor. Self-conscious and cynical, bored by his own mannerisms, Sissman seems even more uncomfortable in the ambiance through which he listlessly moves than in *Dying: An Introduction.* Boston and New York are again the sources, lost acquaintances the subjects, and dissipation the attraction of these poems. (p.131)

Scattered Returns engages a voice so casual, so tuneless, that the depression which pervades each page is in danger of being overlooked. Not the shrill agony of despair, but the flat surfaces of the unfulfilled are what characterize his diction. The experience reminded me of reading a score without hearing any of the music performed; we are forced to compose the work in our heads.

In his first book, Sissman borrowed familiar lines from other poems, usually with the intention of self-parody; here these suggestions of the echoic betray what can only be taken for fatigue. The first line of "Upon Finding *Dying: An Introduction,* by L. E. Sissman, Remaindered at 1s." steals a line from Wordsworth ("I wandered lonely as a cloud in Foyles") that he used in a poem from his previous collection. The "Three Derivative Poems," from which the book has taken its title, are no more than apologies for his sullen style. (p. 132)

[Cynicism] is everywhere in Sissman's language: in the worship of names and proper nouns, improper puns, vague dialogues. Infatuated with his own intelligence, he is fond of exhibiting an effusive worldliness, a *Weltanschaung* which gazes out with benevolence and an exquisite condescension on the sordid humanity swirling beneath his window.

That he celebrates Patrick Kavanagh, the Irish poet, in "An Annotated Exequy," and writes an elegy for Evelyn Waugh reveals the way in which Sissman assumes the literary posture. The poem about Kavanagh is both eloquent and sympathetic, eager to celebrate the odd virtues of the dead, but within its complex chronicle of a lost and wasted life lies the aesthetic which he lives by:

. . . the serious business of what
An artist is to do with his rucksack
Of gift, the deadweight that deforms his back
And drives him on to prodigies of thought
And anguishes of execution, bought
At all costs of respectability
And all expense of nice society,
Until, alone, he faces homely him,
The only other tenant of his room,
And finds the world well lost.

Sissman shares a convincing sympathy with that texture of life which seems always to escape him, the denials, accusations, and nervous disorders suffered by the artist in the act of living out his chore. Arthur Symons wrote of Gautier that he "had a way of using the world's dictionary, whose leaves, blown by an unknown wind, always opened so as to let the exact word leap out of the pages, adding the appropriate shades." Sissman occasionally possesses this artless chiselled rhetoric; but where he siezes on the cautious word the subtlety of thought eludes him. Indecision falls like a shadow across the page, obscuring the intention. What comes to mind is Riviere's admonition that confession was on the verge of being taken for sincerity.

Most of the book is taken up by "A War Requiem," the long poem (36 pages) which comprises Section II; the epigraph consists of one of Andre Chenier's finely-wrought sonnets quoted in its entirety, and reminds me of Sissman's longing to imagine his own depravity. These are lines Baudelaire could have written as well as Chenier: *On vit; on vit infame. Eh bien? Il fallut l'etre;/L'infame apres tout mange et dort.* From New York in 1929 (Sissman was born the year before) to the New Year, "Twelfth Night, 1969," the poem is a brilliant excursion through America between the Depression, World War II, and after.

"And so the raid/On the inarticulate, as Eliot said,/ Begins again." Sissman has gleaned lessons from this raid, and, as in Berryman's "Homage to Mistress Bradstreet," the portrait is both intimate and vast. The blurred edges of history converge in a confusion of Eliotic notions, "till the rising town's/Unhuman voices wake us, and we drown." (pp. 132-34)

> *James Atlas, in* Chicago Review *(reprinted by permission of* Chicago Review; *copyright © 1970 by* Chicago Review), *Vol. 22, No. 1, 1970.*

What struck me at the start when I first read L. E. Sissman, and again when I read him now, is his prosody. [In *Pursuit of Honor* it] is mostly blank verse but with occasional rhymes, irregularly spaced, and the lines endlessly, relentlessly contain exactly ten syllables in unresolved iambics. But his periods are not tailored to this precise convention. Overlap is frequent, and lines often land with a bump on some weak element. . . . I get a sense more of stiffness than the flexibility of a Milton or Cummings. . . . But Sissman's matter interests, he has plenty to say. He has memories, scenes, stories, people, and he has the language for them. (p. 505)

> *Richmond Lattimore, in* The Hudson Review *(copyright © 1971 by The Hudson Review, Inc.; reprinted by permission), Vol. XXIV, No. 3, Autumn, 1971.*

I liked *Pursuit of Honor.* I liked, first of all, reading poems with lots of good words. It is not insulting or humiliating to have to look up words in a dictionary. It is, far from that, enriching, edifying, education and fun. "Superheterodyne," "stertorous radamacues," "pinxit," "inspissate." All new words for me. . . . I like the way too, that the words are put together in the poems. (p. 292)

I like meter, too, and the use of assonance and alliteration and puns and hyperbole, and understatement and all that. I like the craft, the technique. And why the hell not?

"The Big Rock-Candy Mountain," a poem to the memory of a half brother who died in 1969 at the age of sixty, opens the volume. In the first section, the America of the "Wobblies, Okies, wetbacks—driven and drawn/To cross the land and see it" is described with a bittersweet hindsight.

The Okies, et al, were "visionaries with prehensile hands" who would "select a tree to lie out under: a Pound Sweet, a Cox's Orange Pippin, a pecan," but now they are "dispersed," "transshipped to death or terminal respectability." In this America his half brother was a "young man on a Harley-Davidson." (p. 293)

Here is a man with something to say who can say it well, a man who can relate a clear and thoughtful picture of the normal world, but beyond that, as in this little envoy, the poet can transform the picture of the normal world into a vision, not a giant or saving vision, but a poised and very human vision such as one may expect, from time to time, from the art of poetry.

Sissman's wit permits him, and his reader, to cope with the waste of the "partial fires" that style so much living. "The New York Woman," "The Dump: A Dream Come True," and, for that matter, most of the poems that make up the body of this book are poised (poised between the sympathetic and the comic) portraits of men and women who are fired partially, who are, therefore, at least partially waste and wasted, and yet live on. But in "Empson Lieder" and "Big Rock-Candy Mountain," Sissman goes for the complete fire. In his half brother's death and in his own vision of the dead man sleeping soundly "on the last night of your way/Out of a rifled and abandoned land," the waste is left behind.

In "Law Song," which begins the "Empson Lieder," Sissman muses on his own, and our, mortality: "we are such/ Short-timers, really, re-upped for a hitch/Indefinite in length, but not too long./You will therefore please forgive my haunting song." Then in Part II ("Even Song,"), the poet, dead and gone to heaven, allows himself the exquisite joy of murdering those enemies of life, those enemies who, having no fire, are "skin that shrills." For them, there is no wit, no sympathy. No, no sympathy or wit for those

> Who'd cant incredibly through a half life,
> Who'd twist on valiantly for penny gains,
> Who'd trade you in on something more *courant,*
> Who'd flee from those whom sometime they did seek . . .

The poet, from heaven, murders these with a thunderbolt in the best *lex talionis* tradition. But even here, after the murder, there is a sardonic wit. The poem ends, "They died, of course./Up here I heard the fat tires of the hearse/Fizz on the icy streets without remorse." So, Sissman's accomplished craftsmanship and mastery of poetic art which, in itself, I am thankful for, again when he speaks of "the complete fire," which is death, goes beyond wit and learning and skill to a powerful and convincing art that does what art is supposed to do, make us know how painfully and beautifully human we are. (p. 294)

> *Marvin Bowers, "Beyond Wit," in* Modern Poetry Studies *(copyright 1974, by Jerome Mazzaro), Winter, 1974, pp. 292-94.*

[L. E. Sissman] is not a big-time celebrity writer but a working writer. He is not driven to write by ambitions to glory; instead, he writes because it is his calling and because it's a way to make a living. And because, through the years, the life of a working writer can add up to a satisfying, respectable identity.

That, at least, is the main impression one gains from "Innocent Bystander," a compilation of Mr. Sissman's essays published regularly . . . , along with samples of his verse. The working writer reveals himself to be a jovial fellow, but also a tasteful fellow genuinely in love with words, and, ultimately—when confronted with the prospect of his own untimely death—a person of equanimity and good sense.

His prose is not uniformly good. Some of his essays, served up over the past five years or so, seem trite (blasts at pornography and television programming). Others seem hoked up to meet his deadline (an account of a day's drive into Manhattan).

But when it is good, it is entertaining, wise or provocative —very good indeed. . . .

And there are the two remarkable essays that detail his feelings after learning that he has Hodgkin's disease. "It is like, I should imagine," he writes in the first, "being the first man to see for himself . . . the proof of the theory of the curvature of the earth." And in the second, he concludes, "I have been looking down at the curvature of the earth, at the trajectory of my life and death, from a new perspective: from the perspective of a tangential line lifting, straight as a contrail, away from the earth and myself and all the other things and people. It is, and has been, a lonely journey."

In an essay on writers, Sissman calls writing "the art of throwing hard—and accurately." He says that a writer, like a pitcher, must practice and work hard and sacrifice. "What I'm talking about is not just idle self-expression; it is the pursuit of perfection." His book reflects a deeper notion: Whether one achieves the perfection or not, the meaning and joy of life lie in the pursuit.

> *David C. Anderson, "The Work of a Working Writer," in* The New York Times Book Review *(© 1975 by The New York Times Company; reprinted by permission), December 21, 1975, p. 22.*

That [L. E. Sissman] was a poet of unusual distinction was not widely appreciated when he died in the spring of 1976 of the illness that inspired some of his best writing. It was not that he was unknown. . . . But he had not yet acquired the kind of readership his work had earned him. Which was doubly ironic: for he was not only an excellent poet, but also one of the most accessible poets of his generation. It was as if the very clarity of his writing acted to obscure its quality and power. . . .

The title poem of ["Dying: An Introduction"] is a little masterpiece—the first of several that he wrote about the discovery and treatment of his illness (Hodgkin's disease), which, he knew, was likely to be fatal, but which elicited from him, without any trace of mawkishness or false drama, an extraordinary sense of life. This is Sissman describing in "Dying: An Introduction" the first hospital examination procedure:

> My narcissistic eye
> Is intercepted deftly by

A square nurse in a gas-green gown
And aqua mask—a dodo's beak—
Who hands me a suit to put on
In matching green, and for my feet
Two paper slippers, mantis green:
My invitation to the dance.
I shuffle to the table, where
A shining bank of instruments—
Service for twelve—awaits my flesh
To dine.

And these are the lines that come at the end, amazingly, after the pathology report and the talk of treatment—subjects that give him no trouble as a writer of verse—when the poet is alone on the city street:

> Through my
> Invisible new veil
> Of finity, I see
> November's world—
> Low scud, slick street, three giggling girls—
> As, oddly, not as sombre
> As December,
> But as green
> As anything:
> As spring.

If there are anthologies of poetry being assembled a generation hence, I find it hard to believe that at least one of these posthumous works—"Homage to Clotho: A Hospital Suite," from this recent New Yorker group—will not figure prominently among the poems of the 70's. The poem runs to 128 lines, and this is the opening stanza:

> Nowhere is all around us, pressureless,
> A vacuum waiting for a rupture in
> The tegument, a puncture in the skin,
> To pass inside without a password and
> Implode us into Erewhon. This room
> Is dangerously unguarded: in one wall
> An empty elevator clangs its doors
> Imperiously, for fodder; in the hall,
> Bare stretchers gape for commerce; in the air
> Outside, a trembling, empty brightness falls
> In hunger on those whom it would devour
> Like any sparrow hawk as darkness falls
> And rises silently up the steel stairs
> To the eleventh and last floor, where I
> Reside on sufferance of authorities
> Until my visas wither, and I die.

I know of nothing quite like this in recent American poetry; in neither his style nor his choice of subjects did Sissman conform to prevailing literary fashions. His was the kind of originality that does not sail under the banner of originality: the voice is so natural, the objects so real. He wrote with precision, fluency and wit about the ordinary experience of his world, which is recognizably *our* world.

But that was the rub, perhaps. Sissman was a man of the middle class, and he did nothing in his writing to disguise the fact. As "The New Yorker" observed in its unsigned obituary, "He liked smart cars, the suburban life, English novels, old-fashioned metres." Although alert to its cruelties and contradictions, he was nonetheless comfortable in the world he inhabited, and very wise about it, and he hated leaving it. As a writer he wore no masks.

In Sissman's poetry, conventions are observed and decencies upheld. There is a powerful rage to live, but there is no private madness or personal violence, and no appeals to paranoia or the apocalypse. There is, however, a great deal of tender feeling, comic perception, mordant description, vivid character, dramatic incident and tough-minded tuition, even in the face of death. There is also a lot of suffering of an unpicturesque kind—the kind that takes place in hospitals—which Sissman had a remarkable gift for picturing. Society has a place in this poetry, and so does the civilized self, which is not despised. Nature is lovingly evoked, but so are cities. The lyrical is never divorced from the quotidian, and both are given their due. Intelligence is not automatically abjured; it is, in fact, admired. (pp. 3, 16)

Poetry has for so long been reserved, at least in theory, for writers who abominated the norms of middle-class life and identified their vocation with a headlong flight from them, that a poet like Sissman was taken for something he wasn't.... But the true poet is always unexpected, and Sissman reminds us that he is as likely to be the man stepping off the Boston shuttle with an attache case on his way to the office as a college professor or a Bohemian dropout. Sissman's distinction lay in his ability to write about the world other poets rejected. He had a voice, a style, a vision, of his own, and he will be remembered when many flashier, more violent and more "relevant" poets are forgotten. (p. 16)

> *Hilton Kramer, "Late Returns," in* The New York Times Book Review (© *1977 by The New York Times Company; reprinted by permission), July 3, 1977, pp. 3, 16.*

* * *

SITWELL, Edith   1887-1964

In 1954 Sitwell became the first poet to be created Dame, Commander Order of the British Empire. Her early poetry, however, was not readily accepted. Experimental in style, it concentrated on the essence of sound and the implications of techniques which would provide a wide range of sounds. For example, the poems in the collection *Façade* were written to be recited with, and enhanced by, dance and music. (See also *CLC*, Vol. 2, and *Contemporary Authors*, Vols. 9-12, rev. ed.)

[Already] in her early poems Edith had amazing inventive power added to a musical ear and a trollish fancy. Her delight was especially in the radiant gaiety of things sensed and fancifully associated with a riot of other things, and in the musical succession of sounds into which she could convert them. She was as playful in her clever verses as the modern poets were to be solemn in theirs, and therefore it did not seem to be a very striking innovation that her images were taken from modern life and not borrowed from traditional poetry; and the internal rhymes and dissonances accorded with the jazz tune.... The nonsensical, the impish, the eerie, the fay, the grotesque appealed to the fancy of Edith Sitwell in her earlier phases, but always as something tripping to music, song and dance, olden or modern.... (p. 225)

Edith Sitwell's early poems shine like a design in many colours woven on a fabric; she describes gaily, and passes swiftly to decorative fancy, mingling the real and the unreal, the whole developing and completing the pattern of her mood. In *Elegy on Dead Fashion* (1926) she actually names the colours.... And in *The Nectarine Tree* do we not see as well as hear the laughter and the wind? (p. 226)

With the passage of time the poet becomes less playful and more serious, though always resisting the solemn. In that singular poem, *Gold Coast Customs* (1929), it is still fancy that predominates rather than imagination, but her humour has become grim and sardonic, and eeriness is intermingled with terror. Edith Sitwell's mood, which had well accorded with the lightness of the twenties, responds to the graver tones of the thirties and the tragedy of the subsequent war years.... Fancy gives way to imagination, under whose influence beautiful images copied from nature yield to more significant images 'modified', as Coleridge put it, 'by a predominant passion'. In becoming aware of things happening in the contemporary world she seemed to become more conscious of the nature of things always happening. Yet she was not of a disposition to yield to despair; and at the same time, while retaining Christian faith, she did not seek escape in Christian mysticism, but still sings: 'Hail to the Sun, and the great Sun in the heart of Man.' (pp. 226-27)

> *R. A. Scott-James, in his* Fifty Years of English Literature 1900-1950, *second edition, Longmans, Green and Co. Ltd., 1956.*

Do the tricks of rhythm and rhyme, the exotic, improbable, nursery-tale objects make the early poems into anything more than delicious games? Was, in fact, Dame Edith, for all her inventions, ever 'modern' in any significant sense? I would suggest, instead, that she used the new taste for difficulty as an excuse to free herself not from outworn conventions of feeling and expression (she has her fair share of phrases like 'the glamour of eve'), but from the perennial convention that a poem should mean something. (p. 70)

[Perhaps the secret of the admiration Dame Edith's work inspires is that instead] of using poetry to express precisely the fullness of her experience, she has contrived with great care and invention a series of moulds into which the reader can pour just as much feeling as he wants. What she writes is not so much poems 'containing in themselves the reason why they are so and not otherwise' as challenges to his powers of free-association—a kind of 'do-it-yourself' verse. (p. 71)

> *A. Alvarez, "Edith Sitwell" (originally published in* The Observer, *1957), in his* Beyond All This Fiddle: Essays 1955-1967 *(copyright © 1968 by A. Alvarez; reprinted by permission of Random House, Inc. and Candida Donadio & Associates, Inc.),* Random House, *1969, pp. 70-1.*

Dame Edith Sitwell is a virtuoso of rhythm and accent. She has given me immense pleasure, intensifying my interest in rhythm, and has also encouraged me in my rhythmic eccentricities....

Façade, Dame Edith—or Miss Sitwell as she was then—insists, was but apprenticeship; of virtuoso quality with wit.... (p. 210)

"I used to practice writing," Dame Edith says, "as a pianist practices music." She says that she would take a waltz or a polka or the music of the barrel organ beneath her window and translate it into words.... Dame Edith then considered the long line and its possibilities. William Carlos Williams has said in his book, *I Wanted to Write a Poem*,

"I found I could not use the long line because of my nervous nature." An adagio, moreover, "is hard to sustain at concert pitch," as the *Times Literary Supplement* noted. We have it, however, when Edith Sitwell writes

> archipelagoes
> Of stars and young thin moons from great wings falling
> As ripples widen.

How pleasing, the dactyls: *porphyry, basilica, Babylon;* and *babioun* (*babioun* borrowed from Ben Jonson, as she says). How neat, the rhyme "Noctambulo" with "folio". . . . Dame Edith's irregularities in set meter are hyperskilful, as in creating a pause after *any* in "anybody": "Mary Stuart to James Bothwell" (Casket Letter No. 2):

> Leaving you, I was sundered like the sea!
> Departed from the place where I left my heart
> I was as small as any body may be.

That is to say, with the accent on *body*.

There is no melody in Pope, Dame Edith says, because there is no irregularity. "To have melody, there must be variations in the outward structure." An expert of the condensed phrase, she also says, "I try to make my images exact"; and does, in "sundered". . . . (pp. 210-11)

In the opening lines of "The Sleeping Beauty," the incantatory effect of the whole passage is a metaphor creating a sense of deep, mysterious, fairy-world remoteness:

> When we come to that dark house,
> Never sound of wave shall rouse
> The bird that sings within the blood
> Of those who sleep in that deep wood.
>
> (p. 212)

Some may regard as arbitrary a word of Dame Edith's or find a statement too "oracular." In her choice of words, she is, to *herself*, always justified. "Neatness of execution is essential to sublimity," she says; . . . considering language an "incarnation" of thought rather than "the *dress* of thought," and is instructively "neat" in revising her own work. . . . (p. 213)

For her "all great poetry is dipped in the dyes of the heart"; and, perhaps quoting Whitman, she says, "All things are in the clime of man's forgiveness"; saying of ideals she would reach, "How far I am from these no one could see more clearly than I. Technically, I would come to a vital language—each word possessing an infinite power of germination, spiritually give holiness to each common day." In her humility and compassion she cages conviction. (p. 215)

> *Marianne Moore, "Edith Sitwell, Virtuoso," in her* A Marianne Moore Reader *(copyright © 1961 by Marianne Moore; reprinted by permission of The Viking Press, Inc.), Viking, 1961, pp. 210-15.*

During [Edith Sitwell's] long poetic career, time has served as a focal point for the continuing dialectic of affirmation and negation which is typical of her spiritual life. However, the theme bulks largest in her work during the period 1924-28, when she devoted three long poems to it. In these pieces (*The Sleeping Beauty*, 1924; *Elegy on Dead Fashion*, 1926; "Metamorphosis," 1928) Dame Edith, in overcoming her agonized preoccupation with the destructive-

ness of time, evolves the complex vision of the matter which characterizes her later poetry.

Sitwell's three early "time" poems share certain features of technique. Although they treat a difficult metaphysical problem with subtlety and depth, all three for the most part abjure either the language of philosophy or a discursive presentation of their theme. The crux with which the poet is dealing is so fundamental as to involve her whole personality. It embraces passion and reason, the body and the mind, the conscious and the unconscious. All of these levels of reaction are integrated into a richly sensuous and imaginatively resonant symbolism. Dame Edith's symbolic approach, which allows her to trace her preoccupation with time to its pre-conscious roots, is bound up with the mythopoeic or dream-structure of her three poems. All display an alogical yet meaningful process of imaginative and emotion association which connects them with both pre-rational and supra-rational states of mind. The visionary "dream-work" of the three pieces creates an organic imaginative architecture, in which form and significance arises from a genetic interaction of symbols. This process is both psychological and metaphysical, being governed by a romantic imagination which "dissolves, diffuses, dissipates" empirical consciousness, and recreates the world in terms of a religious vision centering upon innocence, fall and redemption.

In developing this Biblical schema, Sitwell passes through a spiritual labyrinth, a "chinese box" of multiple imprisonments in the destructiveness of time. The vision of the individual's entrapment in the natural cycles which is developed in *The Sleeping Beauty* is, in *Elegy on Dead Fashion*, placed within the context of the historical degeneration of the race. However, as in Dante's *Inferno*, the center of the labyrinth joins with a divine "circumference," which encompasses the poet's difficulties in a redemptive transcendence. In "Metamorphosis," Dame Edith unites fully with that "outer ring" in a tempered visionary ecstacy.

The Sleeping Beauty begins Sitwell's odyssey by treating the life of the individual in time as a result and a repetition of the Fall. This spiritual context is established in the gardener's song which both opens and concludes the poem. The song recasts the story of Jonah into a symbolic parable of the incarceration of fallen man, who has lapsed from a spiritual and eternal to a natural and temporal existence. . . . As the conclusion of the gardener's song suggests, his debarment is at the same time an entrapment in fallen nature. . . . It is Sleeping Beauty's fate to remain perpetually retarded in . . . spiritual somnolence. The apparent suspension of time in her trance is illusory. Her sleep, which partakes of both life and death and yet is neither, in fact manifests both ends of nature's organic cycles. Sitwell's "telescoping" of natural time indicates the "Night-mare Life-in-Death" in which man is trapped in the womb-tomb of nature. This imprisonment in the round of "Birth, and copulation, and death," is appropriately expressed in sexual terms. In *The Sleeping Beauty*, both the frustration and the fulfillment of sexuality are death-symbols. In the cyclical time of nature, in which all fertility, life and growth are movements towards extinction, generation is in the last analysis as sterile as virginity.

Because he is aware of his fate, the imprisonment of fallen man in natural time is psychic as well as physical. His bodily entrapment in its cycles is projected mentally in three states which may be termed innocence, experience and despair. (pp. 207-08)

As Sitwell indicates by her grotesque representations of decay and death as a "wingless and bemired" destiny and a "pig-snouted Darkness" . . . , nature is not simply uncaring, but positively malignant. A full imaginative recognition of its destructiveness is a nightmare, the horror and despair of which constitute another psychic reflection of man's death-in-life in cyclical time. (p. 210)

[Seasonal] imagery and its association of man with the vegetable world . . . [are] two of Sitwell's recurring symbols of the imprisonment of fallen humanity in nature's round. The plant suggests a life completely restricted by cyclical time. In its connection with man's awareness of his natural life as a prison and a tomb, the vegetation-image is at once ironic and tragic. It implies that insofar as he assimilates to nature, he becomes passive and insensate, losing his unique capacities. If he preserves his soul, he falls into the dilemma of Shelley's Sensitive Plant which, by its simultaneous existence on the two irreconcilable planes of nature and human awareness, is doomed to a spiritual death-in-life.

In *Elegy on Dead Fashion,* Sitwell begins to transcend her nightmare vision of the imprisonment of the individual in natural time. She paradoxically does so by placing the tragedy in the context of the historical degeneration of the race. The poet returns to a primeval Golden Age, in which the natural paradise of childhood has not yet been uprooted from its spiritual foundations by the Fall. Both the new vision of nature in the *Elegy* . . . and the concept of time which it involves are antithetical to those which dominate *The Sleeping Beauty.* This reversal in turn allows the poet glimmers of hope about the destiny in the immediate present of both the individual and the race.

The positive relationship of man to nature and time in the Golden Age has a foundation which is both psychological and metaphysical. Originally, man's consciousness was not dissociated from his instinct. Because "natural law and moral were but one," . . . he could act without the interference of a critical self-awareness, and was untroubled by frustrated desire or guilt. This paradise of instinctual liberty and creative self-expression is appropriately associated with a bucolic setting, in which man is one with nature. However, Sitwell's primitivism is combined with a baroque efflorescence of the elegant artifice which is also traditional in pastoral art. The poet not only clothes her nature-spirits and divinities in the fashions of the 1840's, but metaphorically recasts nature in similar terms.

The "continuing conceits" in which Sitwell joins art and nature, the rustic and the civilized, embody the metaphysical basis of her poem. This closely resembles the "clothes philosophy" of *Sartor Resartus.* Nature is a "fabric" woven upon the "loom of time" by an immanent divinity. God's creative omnipresence is figured by Prometheus, a "blacksmith-god" who continuously brings living forms from the amorphous inertia of matter. In a process analogous to artistic creation, the life which is inspired in the "uncouth earth" . . . by Prometheus' heavenly "fire" . . . is given harmony and pattern by his divine *logos.* Nature is thus the archetype of human art and civilization. In terms of Sitwell's clothes metaphor, God both expresses and veils Himself in the "many-coloured coat" of His creation. Similarly, the "god's soul" . . . within man employs its creative powers to weave both the "costume" of his body and a rich "tapestry" of civilized refinement.

God is thus immanent in man as He is in nature. Psychologically speaking, the incarnate divinity takes the form of the instinctual unconscious. Therefore, as Sitwell suggests through the image of dancing satyrs . . . , the free play of instinct which characterizes humanity in the Golden Age produces an Appollonian wisdom and beauty. In metaphysical terms, this spontaneous culture symbolically embodies the divine, and consequently also mirrors God's creative activity in the universe. Thus, the unity of nature and civilization in the Golden Age implies that creation is still in a state of embryonic unity, in which it is impossible to differentiate God and man, the individual and the cosmos, the natural and the supernatural, energy and order, art and nature, the bucolic and the urbane, morality and instinct. (pp. 210-12)

Sitwell's notion of time as an extended process of aesthetic creation implies an evolutionary view of nature. Thus, the first "rough" and "uncouth" . . . human forms are progressively refined and developed both in body and spirit.

In the present stage of human history, time is not creative but destructive. Once again, Sitwell sees the individual as doomed to decay and death in the prison of the natural cycles. However, in the *Elegy* . . . , the grim vision of time which appeared in *The Sleeping Beauty* is placed in perspective by being viewed as itself a function of history. Age and death assume such overwhelming proportions for modern man because he is the end-product of a long decline, during which his spiritual powers and perspective have radically diminished. The apocalyptic intuition of the Golden Age has been replaced by a purblind materialism, which regards only the physical surface of creation. The civilized elegance which expressed the indwelling Spirit has accordingly become an empty triviality. . . . It is this spiritual debilitation which has rendered man's life in time a nightmare. (p. 212)

Sitwell is not explicit about how the historical time of the race changes from a creative evolution to a spiritual degeneration. However, we may surmise that man's soul began to wither when his consciousness developed to the point at which it broke away from instinct. . . . As soon as man ceased to be an expression of nature and its time-process, their creative and nurturing relationship with him was reversed. Time and matter became devouring and destructive, a prison in which the individual was condemned to decay and death.

The reversal of the relationship between man and natural time is suggested in the *Elegy* . . . by a symbolism which recalls Robert Graves' tripartite White Goddess. The first two phases of Sitwell's White Goddess are the *kore* and the earth-mother. . . . Together, the divine maiden and the earth-goddess suggest the joyous vitality arising from man's organic communion with a protective, nourishing nature, in which time and matter form a creative matrix. However, the wolf also implies the third aspect of Sitwell's White Goddess: the devouring hag who symbolizes nature as a dungeon and a tomb. One form of the hag who relates specifically to time is the goddess Fortune, who presides over the chance governing modern man's temporal existence. . . . Another is the "Numidean sibyl" . . . who, in prophesying the triumph of death over love, suggests the despair of the individual trapped in natural time.

In the *Elegy* . . . Sitwell suggests, if only very tentatively, the essentials of her later resolution of the problem of time.... [She] implies that the same world-soul which made history a process of creative evolution in the Golden Age may bring a renascence of that happy era.... She now envisages a twofold cyclical movement of rebirth, the renewal of the primordial Eden coming about through a revolution within nature. This takes the form of a process of evolution inspired by the immanent divinity, in which the dead matter to which everything is reduced by time is reborn in a succession of living forms. In the *Elegy* ..., this hopeful vision is overwhelmed by the poet's despair, but in "Metamorphosis" it is developed into a tempered visionary ecstasy in which the crux posed by a destructive time is transcended.

"Metamorphosis" indeed opens with the same despondency which dominated the *Elegy*.... The later poem develops the themes of the destruction of the individual and the race by time in much the same terms as the earlier. Once again, man's imprisonment in the natural cycles is characterized as a peculiarly modern problem by its association with the historical "fall" of the species. In "Metamorphosis," as in the *Elegy* ..., Sitwell repeatedly suggests her own entanglement in the crisis. However, in the second poem, Dame Edith's identification with the plight of her age is offset by a visionary detachment.... Sitwell now realizes that she is obsessed with time and death because she has been viewing life from the same inverted perspective as her contemporaries.... Having recognized the mote in her own eye, Sitwell is able to rise to a new perspective on time and nature. (pp. 212-14)

[The] dialectic of light and "shade" is a fundamental metaphor throughout Sitwell's poetry for the genetic interaction which produces life and growth. To describe this creative process in the organic structure of a poem, Dame Edith employs the term "texture." Texture is the imaginative pattern which emerges when a piece is created or read. It combines energy with order, content with form. It is both static and dynamic, an unfolding succession and a finished artifact. In ["Metamorphosis"], Sitwell applies this concept of texture to nature....

Dame Edith has thus combined her conceptions of nature as a garment and an organism into that of a living "texture," which is woven in time by the intercourse of light and shade. If light implies the creative life-giving role of the immanent spirit in this process, then darkness must represent its metaphysical opposite: the inertia of matter which causes the decay of all natural entities in time. Just as the genetic interaction of light with earth brings about organic evolution, so darkness is associated with an atavism that marks the descent of life towards amorphous, dead matter.

Sitwell's conception of the natural time-process as "texture" thus involves a nexus of organic cycles, in which light and darkness, death and life, come to predominate in succession. This rhythm recurs in "Metamorphosis," and constitutes an important element in the poet's solution of the problem of time. It is true that "Metamorphosis" repeatedly associates the seasonal and diurnal cycles with the individual's decline from youth to age. The history of the race has similarly moved from the "spring" of the Golden Age to the "winter" of modern degeneracy. However, such negative movements are merely preludes to rebirth. Thus, "Metamorphosis" opens with the poet's despair over time and death, but concludes with her spiritual rejuvenation. (p. 215)

[The] "marriage" of light and shade in the round of time involves more than a simple succession. The notion of "texture" implies that in all phases of evolution and organic growth, light and darkness are simultaneously present in a creative dialectic....

The dialectic of light and shade thus underlies and controls the cyclical alternations of natural time. This dynamic conception of "texture" forms the dominant idea of time in the mature poetry which Dame Edith wrote after 1940. (p. 216)

> *John Ower, "A Golden Labyrinth: Edith Sitwell and the Theme of Time," in* Renascence *(© copyright, 1973, Catholic Renascence Society, Inc.), Summer, 1974, pp. 207-17.*

*   *   *

SNOW, C(harles) P(ercy)   1905-

A British novelist, statesman, physicist, and biographer, Snow is noted for his ability to realistically inculcate his fiction with aspects of science, education, business, and government. He is perhaps best known for his "Strangers and Brothers," a series of eleven novels that deals with questions of morality and power in contemporary England. Snow was knighted in 1957 and created Baron in 1964. (See also *CLC*, 1, 4, 6, and *Contemporary Authors*, Vols. 5-8, rev. ed.)

It is hard to tell whether the creator of the 'Strangers and Brothers' sequence is a very modest man or a somewhat self-satisfied one. Self-satisfied, because of the pervasive smugness, the transparent if subfusc gratification which the author derives from his acquaintance with men who matter and his intimacy with the ins and outs of the corridors which they walk. 'A kind of pleasure, the pleasure, secretive but shining, that they got from being at the centre of things': but hardly secretive in this case. Modest, because of the emotional moderation, the spiritual abstemiousness, which the author enjoins upon his creations. Because it is not a lord he loves, but merely a Parliamentary or even a Permanent Secretary. And because usually his corridors of power lead, if not to the grave, then to nothing especially grand or shining. The stock explanation is that, neither modest nor self-satisfied, Sir Charles Snow is simply the detached historian of the British Establishment, detached and accurate. So. This Establishment had hitherto inspired me with considerably more respect, or more fear, or more *something,* than does Snow's epic portrayal of it. (p. 106)

[It] is not to ask that her personages should talk like Durrellian diplomats—he ought to try to fuss just a little. He employs clichés as such; not, for better or worse, wittily or questioningly; no, he has the courage of his clichés. His style has been praised on the grounds that it doesn't exist ..., and his use of commonplaces has been defended as sound naturalistic practice. That is to say, people talk in clichés—politicians, Civil Servants, scientists especially?—and life consists largely of banal situations, and Snow's themes are of such public moment that the artist's fine Italian hand may not be allowed to distort the account. There is a decent scruple at work here, which novelists of a documentary sort can honestly feel; and it is best conciliated by the reminder that a novel is only a novel, after all; or, better, that a novel *is* a novel.

In one way and another I found *Corridors of Power* a lowering experience. The fearful rumpus in *The Masters* was less dispiriting, because we know that dons . . . tend to triviality the moment they cease to be profound. . . . [It] must be granted that a college was a suitable setting for the subfusc intriguing which so fascinates Sir Charles. The intrigues of this new novel concern a government and a reasonably important public issue, the attempt of a Conservative Minister to scrap Britain's independent Bomb. Yet the people involved are as long-winded as the dons and considerably less entertaining. Naturalism here reaches its climax, in what seems little more than a waxworks show. Hansard, presumably a naturalistic document, is distinctly more animated and (since no one is so simple, or so aesthetic, as to take people's words, spoken or written, as necessarily a true and complete representation of their thoughts and feelings) hardly more deceptive than Snow's stolid, cautious narrative. When there is so much craft in human nature, surely we might as well permit our art to indulge in a little art.

Naturalism, then, requires the chronicling of resounding commonplaces and even what might look like plain bad writing. . . . Snow's didactic urge is endearing, and would be more so if by implication it didn't represent our masters as (more or less) honest (more or less) simpletons. His prose sometimes reminds one of orthodox Soviet writing: solemn, shrewdly simple, bucolically genial, heavily tolerant of minor sins, so ponderous in its humour as to be humourless—and apt to excite acute suspicion and alarm in the not-utterly-credulous. (pp. 106-08)

With the worst will in the world I cannot believe that the rich and leisured are as consistently tedious and nerveless as most of Snow's guests and hosts show themselves. (pp. 108-09)

There is little to be seen [in *Corridors of Power*] of the inner life. Eliot is happy with Margaret, and *vice versa*: indeed the uxoriousness contributes generously to the suffocating smugness of the whole. Perhaps it is because Snow deems it advisable to inject a dash of mere humanity into all this high dignity that the Minister is given a mistress, otherwise supererogatory, since his sexual life features minimally if at all in his downfall. Hence, perhaps, such concomitant excitements as 'She was speaking without constraint, self-effacingness stripped off, codes of behaviour fallen away. Her face had gone naked and wild.' Or, 'He was speaking, as usual, the naked truth', when we didn't for a moment imagine the man was fibbing, and the truth in question (a Tory M.P. is indicating his reluctance to leave the Commons for the Lords) is hardly so momentous as to call for the epithet 'naked'. . . . [The men and women of Sir Charles's Establishment] aren't going to get excited about nothing. They're a canny lot. They don't believe in *any* heaven round *any* corner, they haven't sufficient imagination to conceive of pie in the sky. . . . (pp. 109-10)

To me *Corridors of Power* seems distinctly more wooden than the majority of its predecessors. . . .

[A critic once said], 'Well, I suppose he's important because he writes about those things which really matter'. Taking the remark in perhaps not quite the same way, I would be inclined to agree with it. But is *Corridors of Power* the work of a sober patriot, soberly chronicling . . . ? Is Britain run by zombies, with a choice of zombies Right or zombies Left? An admirer of Snow has spoken of his

'immense, almost Johnsonian, weight of experience of society and knowledge of men'. Certainly some sort of weight is there. So perhaps this book *is* the 'great political novel' that the blurb claims. It is frightening that *Corridors of Power* should almost succeed in arousing nostalgia—almost —for the sort of politics which is accompanied by arrests, disappearances, riots, torture. There, someone seems to care at least. (p. 110)

> D. J. Enright, "Easy Lies the Head: C. P. Snow and the 'Corridors of Power'," in his Conspirators and Poets (© D. J. Enright 1966), Chatto & Windus Ltd., 1966, pp. 106-10.

In its careful psychology and closed politics, in the spaciousness so symbolized by the elaborate, dry chapter headings, and the way in which major characters in some novels move on the edges in others, the [Strangers and Brothers] series is reminiscent of Victorian and Edwardian forebears. But this does not belie the contemporaneity Snow has always blended with tradition. The first—and titular—novel, *Strangers and Brothers* (1940), as it focuses upon a precursor to the hippie cults and communes, here an isolated farm on the edge of the Midlands town in which Lewis Eliot grows to maturity, is as modern as tomorrow. Presided over by the pathetic George Passant, whose promise is foreshortened by a dedication to an intellectual and social freedom for which society is unready and which may be too morally obtuse for any time, the weekend utopia leads to predictable disaster. Here as in all the novels, Eliot tells the increasingly convoluted story of his family and friends as well as his own; and in *Last Things* it is fitting that some of them—like George Passant—have their obsequies tolled. (pp. 136-37)

"The sleep of reason," says Goya, "brings forth monsters." The sleep of reason, in our time and his, is what Lord Snow has been seeking in his cycle to understand, his psychological penetration often masked by the deceptively flat, disconcertingly solemn and understated style so appropriate for his stodgy and pragmatic narrator. The difficulty intensifies when other characters speak, and although the failure of differentiation of voices here and there may be ascribed to their being recorded for us and played back by Lewis Eliot, it is a problem nevertheless.

There is no denying the problem of style. . . . The administrative, often scientific, prose, precise, flat and unemotional, with its figures of speech more often from chemistry or anthropology or medicine than from aesthetics, seems Snow's personal bridging of the chasm of the "Two Cultures"—another term and concept he put into the language. Whether or not such prose is appropriate to someone else's fiction is irrelevant: it is consistent with what we know of Lewis Eliot.

It is unlikely that Lord Snow's ambitious *roman fleuve* will flounder on the shoals of style. He is too skillful a storyteller for that, although the satire, subtlety and symbolic luxuriance that make other novelists of his generation ripe for textual exegesis are lacking. He will have little appeal for footnote writers but a great deal for thoughtful readers of books. Contemporary novelists of greater stylistic flair have found their themes in the flux of society but none have dealt so successfully with not only the larger issues but with the mysterious and fascinating complexities of the new bureaucratic world. (p. 140)

[We must note] the balance and fairness of Snow's perspectives. He has always communicated the feel of his times; his characters do not merely play out their lives against a background of events—they make and shape and attempt to comprehend their era. "Why in hell," wonders Charles's uncle Martin [in *Last Things*], "does he want to set up as the conscience of the world?" But as Charles's father remembers, twenty years before (in *The New Men*) that very gesture restored to Martin his integrity at the cost of his future. The "inner design" of the cycle, Snow once wrote, "consists of a resonance between what Lewis Eliot sees and what he feels. Some of the more important emotional themes he observes through others' experience, and then finds them enter into his own." ... Such resonances vibrate through *Last Things*, although for the initiated, the explanatory asides meant to mesh experience with earlier novels come as unsubtle intrusions.

It is the uninitiated who will be more puzzled when they discover following the final chapter a group of pages of "Announcements 1964-68," listing, godlike, marriages, births and deaths of characters many of whom either play no significant part in the action or who are recalled for the purpose from previous books. Some of them indicate how many additional plot lines Lord Snow has resolutely put aside in order to complete the sequence in the promised eleven books. Others fill in matter which the reader should have learned in the novel itself, one death, in fact, coming as a cruel and gratuitous shock. But in the device is the sense of finality. The long and memorable cycle has ended, and through it as in no other work in our time we have explored in depth the inner life of the new classless class that is the twentieth century Establishment. (pp. 140-41)

> *Stanley Weintraub, "Last Things: C. P. Snow Eleven Novels After," in* MOSAIC *IV/3 (copyright © 1971 by the University of Manitoba Press), Spring, 1971, pp. 135-41.*

C. P. Snow is one of the best contemporary practitioners of Late Victorian Humdrum, that style in which an all-knowing but coy narrator (larding his omniscience with "perhaps" and "maybe") sluggishly unfolds a story patched together from conventional plot elements and occurring to conventional characters—a narrative repeatedly interrupted, as if by commercials, while the author informs us of facts he has not troubled to work into the action, meanings he does not trust us to perceive, details we could do without, and literature's equivalent of the Chinese water torture, a persistent drip of ponderous platitudes. . . .

The insights [of "In Their Wisdom"] are . . . commonplace: we learn that similar events evoke similar responses; that politicians, lawyers and other professional men usually treat their work professionally; and that people take money seriously. Such bland and fuzzy meanings as these are drawn with agonizing slowness (a tooth extraction performed by an absent-minded dentist) from exhausted materials: who will win, who will marry whom, who will die first. The plot centers on a contested will. We are asked to be interested in the cardboard characters who contest it, though they have little identity and nothing to do but sit by and wait for the legal outcome, and though the narrator makes clear his dislike for people who take such mercenary concerns seriously. . . .

Snow professes to give us insiders' views of the law, the

House of Lords and political and economic concerns during the last five years, but he is specific only about place names, furniture and clothes. . . .

The writing itself is distractingly bad . . . [and thus] fatigues the attention. Lord Snow has done yeoman service in reminding the sciences and the humanities of each other's existence, and he has borne the silly attacks of F. R. Leavis manfully. But however interesting the author, a novel must stand on its own feet. . . ; and "In Their Wisdom," though pedestrian, is not ambulatory. (p. 7)

> *J. D. O'Hara, in* The New York Times Book Review *(© 1974 by The New York Times Company; reprinted by permission), October 27, 1974.*

In mid-Victorian England, Anthony Trollope practiced simultaneous careers as popular novelist and managerial-level civil servant. C. P. Snow has combined parallel careers a century later with even greater contemporary eminence, earning fame as a novelist while rising far higher in government than did Trollope. Now Lord Snow has written [*Trollope: His Life and Art*], a critical biography of the 19th-century English novelist whose fiction is often thought of as an earlier counterpart to his own. The result is striking. Wasting no words on embellishments, Snow furnishes the reader, in spare, matter-of-fact prose, the fabric of the milieu in which Trollope lived and worked, provides insights into Victorian bureaucracy, publishing and society, and offers lessons—from a professional—in the making of the psychologically realistic novel of moral choice. (p. 30)

One may quibble that there are more words about Trollope's life and art in other, earlier books of biography and criticism, but there can hardly be so many wise ones. The predictable bias—Snow's conservative view of the way the English novel has developed—is there, but Trollope's achievement represents one of the lasting triumphs of that tradition. (p. 31)

> *Stanley Weintraub, in* The New Republic *(reprinted by permission of* The New Republic, *1975 by The New Republic, Inc.), October 25, 1975.*

*   *   *

SNYDER, Gary   1930-

An American poet and translator, Snyder was once affiliated with the "beat" poets of San Francisco. His early work reflected his love of the natural beauty and heritage of the Pacific Coast: the Sierra Nevadas and the rituals of western Indian tribes are among the subjects of his early poems. Since then Snyder's interests in fields as diverse as Zen Buddhism and forestry have given him inspiration for his poetry. These interests have coalesced to create a poetry that expresses the strivings of the human soul to seek the internal peace and integration that is mirrored in the wilderness. His poetic language possesses a powerful quality, and his verse is sensitively structured. Snyder won the Pulitzer Prize in 1974. (See also *CLC*, Vols. 1, 2, 5, and *Contemporary Authors*, Vols. 17-20, rev. ed.)

Snyder is a lucid and intense didact, and wonderfully graceful, never pompous, rarely self-congratulatory, though he has taken on a difficult and delicate rôle [in *Turtle Island*], having made himself spokesman for the most oppressed, taxed and unrepresented of all classes: the grasslands, trees and animals who are the greater part of the world he sees and loves so dearly. The love is in the seeing, and Snyder has always seen with a thrilling clarity of perception.... He has a compelling vision of our relationship with this living nature, which is our nature, what it is and what it must be if we/nature survive on this planet, and his art serves that vision unwaveringly. It's not as consistently rich and subtle an art as it was in *Myths & Texts*—the language is sometimes looser, his ear more erratic, and sentences sometimes flattened by the speed or the need to explain— but this work is more important right now than the crafting of flawless poems, he understands the vision and the work more clearly now, and we understand that his various rôles of poet, worker, priest, teacher, ecologist, and political wanderspeaker are not so much rôles as aspects of his way of being in the world. He still writes powerfully and with an unfailing calmness and gaiety.... He draws his strength from the realization that

> at the heart of things is some kind of serene
> and ecstatic process which is beyond quali-
> ties and beyond birth-and-death.
>
> (pp. 195-96)

It is true that the book is deeply unified by his sense of mission, to tell what human existence is like in the United States and what it could be, must be, on Turtle Island, but this missionary is really a joyful poet, and the gratitude and celebration at the heart of his view of life often overwhelm the necessity to teach and explain. So the teaching is done silently, which is the best way to do it.... [There] are several of those small exquisite poems of which Snyder is a master, poems that expand in the mind and embody all that this poet knows and that we suddenly realize, in our pleasure and concentration, we know too. (pp. 196-97)

> *Robert Mezey, in* Western Humanities Re-
> view *(copyright, 1974, University of Utah),
> Spring, 1975.*

If Snyder prefers to scant his accomplishments as anthropologist, linguist, teacher, translator, and poet—the "highbrow" and intellectual—and to stress his hardier roles as woodsman, hunter, able-bodied seaman, or hobo—the "lowbrow" and common man—he cannot quite conceal the intellect or learning in his work, which everywhere reveals his considerable knowledge of anthropology, linguistics, Zen Buddhism, history, and other arcane lore. His poetic persona is that of the ordinary man of Walt Whitman, but even Whitman exaggerated his "ordinariness" (as well as his "extraordinariness"), and so does Snyder. Yet a poet does more than choose his tradition; in a very real sense he is chosen by it as well, and Snyder has come to the reservoirs of the Orient and of the American Indian not only as an act of will but out of a deep-seated and passionate need. Whatever his university degrees and academic accomplishments, he wishes to be considered a poet of ordinary men, writing in a language shaped in their idiom; whatever his origins, he has deliberately identified himself with cultures other than his own. Though we must respect and understand his intentions, we are not required to let them mislead our view of what he has, in fact, achieved. (pp. 27-8)

Snyder's roots are deep in Whitman and the Transcendentalists of New England, whose own roots were in German idealism, English romanticism, and Oriental (chiefly Hindu) mysticism. Like Whitman, Snyder celebrates nature, the simple, the animal, the sexual, the tribal, the self. Like Whitman, he speaks in the voice of a highly personal persona rooted in his own experience but by no means identical with it. Like Whitman, he sees man as an indissoluble part of the natural environment, flourishing when he accepts and adapts to that natural heritage, creating a hell on earth and within himself when he is separated from it by his intellect and its technological and societal creations. Like Whitman and Thoreau, though more thoroughly and intensely, Snyder wishes to live in nature and there to confront himself and the essentials, and like Emerson and Thoreau, he does not wish to be saddled with *things*. Like Whitman and Thoreau, he celebrates physical labor, its joys and its ability to educate one in the "true" sense. Snyder maintains truly though perhaps not all-inclusively that his poetics have been most influenced by the jobs he has held, that he has learned how to place words in a line by moving stones. Work, he says, is for him a form of play, and he has learned most from such work as he has performed. From this arises his definition of poetry in "Poetry and the Primitive" as "the skilled and inspired use of the voice and language to embody rare and powerful states of mind that are in immediate origin personal to the singer, but at deep levels common to all who listen.... Poetry must sing or speak from authentic experience."

Like Emerson, Snyder understands that nature can be approached and understood not by reason but only by intuition. In this he has gone beyond Transcendentalism's "meditation" to the disciplines of Zen Buddhism, the abandonments of primitive ritual, the depths of dream and myth, and to the release of drugs—peyote, hashish, LSD—to help pierce the phenomenal veil of nature and thereby to enter into its noumenal reality. Like Emerson, he perceives that noumenal reality not as an anthropomorphic God, but possibly as a form of harmonious Oversoul.

A more stoic and pessimistic note in Snyder's poetry, deriving in part from Robinson Jeffers, is a sense of the inescapability of natural systems and how men are part of them. Man, Snyder recognizes, is a destroyer and Anglo-Saxon man particularly pernicious, though he is by no means alone, for among others even the Chinese made deserts by chopping down their trees, and to build their galleys the Romans logged off the Yugoslav hills and left them bare. (pp. 29-30)

Like other poets in the bardic tradition, and like the Amerindians he admires, Snyder wishes to use colloquial speech, folkways, and folk myth as means of examining the lives of common men in order to clarify and communicate their experience to them. In Snyder this combines qualities of the "Beat" poets "on the road" and the Japanese itinerant poets—like Basho—with those of the wandering Indian shaman and the vagrant bindlestiffs in the Wobbly hobo camps and union halls. Snyder's approach is subsumed by the old Whitmanesque emphases on the flesh and spontaneity. (p. 33)

Snyder's work reveals his profound hatred for the Judeo-Christian tradition, which he credits with the destruction and exploitation of the sacred in man and physical nature by its alliance with and support of a predatory capitalism.... But Christian love continues to haunt Snyder's work and he sees it in various Christian (and other) heresies which over mankind's history have been suppressed by various orthodoxies without being destroyed.... From the

Hebrew prophets and the Christian sages Snyder extracts the dream of the Millennium which is "a dream handed down right to our own time—of ecological balance, classless society, social and economic freedom" that is as much Amerindian as Wobbly, as much ecological as socialist, as much the best of the pagan as of the Judeo-Christian tradition.

The major problem in Snyder's poetry is that he can rarely achieve the unity of thought and language required of a good poem. Usually, he is caught up in that poetic quicksand that swallows so much of the work of Whitman and Carlos Williams and the "Beats": the cataloging of natural objects, mundane events, and sensory impressions until they are meaningless and boring. In short, there is a failure of poetic discrimination and organization which is in itself a failure of sensibility. This sort of cataloging is rooted in the notion that all Snyder's experiences, thoughts, and perceptions, as well as those of his friends, are interesting to others; and it, too, arises out of the Transcendentalist notion that in essence every man is a paradigm of all men and of mankind. It produces a preoccupation with personal anecdote that is too often trivial and pretentious. . . . Moreover, it leads to Snyder's memorializing his own most banal thoughts and unimportant activities as though they had some profound and widespread significance. Consequently, a great deal of the poetry is the enshrining of casual observations and recollections, unyoked to broader human concerns and rendered in a language devoid of originality or beauty. If either the experiences or the language are meaningful to Snyder, he fails to communicate their importance to his readers. (pp. 34, 36-7)

One of the great problems for all poets in trying to see things freshly and eternally at the same time is: how do you make it new? Or to apply to his poetic the old I.W.W. slogan that Snyder is so fond of using in other contexts: how do you shape the new within the shell of the old? In the main, Snyder's poetry fails to do just that, but relies instead on a relatively commonplace and perfunctory system of poetic notation for the old so that, instead of creating the uniqueness and diversity he extols, Snyder lapses into a homogeneity and repetitiveness that quickly palls and often appalls.

Yet there are perhaps a dozen poems that are really fine—and of how many poets can one say that? If Snyder is by no means a great poet, he does have some important things to say about twentieth-century man's pell-mell progress toward environmental and societal disaster, toward destroying the place in which he lives, his home, the earth, as well as his mind, body and spirit; and occasionally, though only occasionally, he is able to embody what he has to say in memorable language, in striking form. (pp. 37-8)

> *Abraham Rothberg, "A Passage to More than India: The Poetry of Gary Snyder," in* Southwest Review (© 1976 by Southern Methodist University Press), Winter, 1976, pp. 26-38.

Critical claims for the value and significance of Gary Snyder's poetry generally direct attention to the achievements of his perfected ecological style—those poems of his that, most notably in the collection *The Back Country* (1968), successfully present and embody assumptions of unity, balance and interrelationship between man and the natural

environment. Snyder emerges from these discussions as the ecological poet *par excellence,* the writer who not only wants to recall us to nature "as the ultimate ground of human affairs" but who has developed a poetic style embodying and promoting a mode of consciousness with which to do it, a mode that eliminates the problem of relationship between man and nature, subject and object, by assuming their unity a priori or supporting it with the evidence of ecology itself. . . . His poems teach us how to see nature and how to see ourselves in nature, not through discursive or didactic argument but by dramatizing states of mind that pose an alternative to the culture—and ego—driven attitudes by which we normally live. (p. 158)

But helpful and valid as this view of his work is (especially as an answer to dissenting critics who see Snyder as a participant in a "formless project"), it fails to take into account any sense of his development, the fact that the expression of ecological consciousness in his work, while present as a goal from the beginning, is arrived at only gradually in terms of actual poetic achievement. . . .

[Snyder's] early poetry raises issues and suggests contexts for his work that are surprisingly broad for a poet who is all too often associated exclusively with "nature" and ecological politics. To be sure, an examination of his early work can show where Snyder has come from and how his characteristic style took shape. But the more interesting context for such a discussion . . . is the question of what sort of poetics emerges from work necessarily concerned with initiating a career and establishing a poetic identity at a time (the middle and late 1950's) when the literary environment is still dominated by a modernism that is nevertheless in the process, as it now seems to us, of breaking up. (p. 159)

[What] stands in the way of simply asserting, with some periodizing critics, that poets like Snyder must be seen as "*post*-modern," their work the outcome of a sharp and total break with the "modernist" past, is the complicating fact (and I am hardly the first to point it out) that it is just such breaks with the past that modernism counsels. . . . What we have in American literature . . . is a paradoxical history of denials of history, a tradition of new starts that acknowledge no precedents, so that modernism here is best understood not as an avant-garde, the latest development of a historical trend or tradition, but as a primitivistic ignorance or deconstructive denial of the past. A book like Snyder's *Riprap* must be seen as participating in this paradoxical history. Inasmuch as it undertakes to clear the ground and establish a space for itself in a crowded literary landscape, it enters into a tradition of such gestures, and to that extent claims for its post-modernism are deeply qualified. On the other hand, in appropriating a space cleared of all example and precedent and thus situating itself in a kind of *pre*historical position, it raises the most radical questions about its own identity and status as literature, as though literature were a destiny it could somehow choose to avoid. It will be necessary, in any case, to be aware of both sides of the paradox in examining the themes and language of *Riprap,* in seeing how history informs what is nevertheless "new" or at least radically redefined in Snyder's first published poems.

In a first book the question of what a poet can do can usually be answered through a consideration of how well he does what others have done before him, and Snyder is no exception. The presence of Pound, Williams and, closer to home, Kenneth Rexroth is clear in *Riprap*'s objectivity, terse rhythms and plain diction. But the presence is not overwhelming, and these features are common enough in contemporary verse style to allow Snyder enough scope to work in his own preoccupations. As soon as the influences are recognized, moreover, one begins to notice differences and qualifications—a prosody and syntax, for example, which, if they resemble Rexroth's, seem deliberately less smooth, with hardly any enjambment and much greater concentration on the single line as the rhythmic unit of speech. . . . Snyder's early lyrics . . . are largely narrative or dramatic in structure and more referential than reflexive in effect, clearly flirting . . . with the mere description or mimetic copying that Williams disparages in *Spring & All*. Snyder's poems, in fact, are much more literal and metonymic than metaphoric, deriving their structure from the external order of things and events in the world rather than from any internal imaginative order, their concrete referentiality amounting, I would argue, to a far greater acceptance of a mimetic relationship between poem and world than the modernists either wanted or allowed in their work. . . . Snyder aims to minimize and even erase his creative presence in the poem, trying in this way to suggest . . . that nature itself is the poet. (pp. 160-62)

Once it is granted that the literalism, referentiality and metonymic tendencies of Snyder's style bespeak an acceptance of mimesis, however qualified but broadly understood as a hope or faith or conviction that there is an authentic relationship between the words of a poem and what they refer to—along with the necessary corollary of any mimetic theory that the thing represented, the external world, is the primary locus of value, as opposed to the poem itself—then it is possible to begin to see distinctions between Snyder's poetics and that of his modernist predecessors. One major difference clearly lies in their conceptions of the poem, and another in their attitudes toward language. Modernist poetics typically emphasizes the way in which a poem is a separate autonomous object, a primary, independent reality unto itself. . . . (p. 164)

For a poet like Snyder . . . faced, at the beginning of his career, with several influential examples of making it new and the imperative to do so himself, the poem pretty much ceases to be a self-involved or autotelic verbal activity and the idealization of language turns to distrust, as in his remark that the poet must steer "a course between crystal clouds of utterly incommunicable non-verbal states—and the gleaming daggers and glittering nets of language." He is aware, on the one hand, of a reality that cannot be brought over into language at all and, on the other, of the problem presented by language that is seen as a danger and a trap, albeit an attractive one, to be avoided. This sense of boundaries, as his early work itself suggests, defines the legitimate space of a poetry that is much more in touch with empirical reality, trying not to resist its pressures but to accept them as a determinant of form in harmonious cooperation with the mind, checking the mind's tendencies to impress its own forms and language on the landscape. It is the drama of this acceptance that is one of the main themes of *Riprap*, and it accounts for poems which not only valorize experience over language but which often address themselves directly to the limits of language as a conceptualizing medium—a rather self-limiting activity, one might think, for a poet, but one which is in accord with Snyder's sense of poetry's reduced possibilities. (p. 165)

What bridge can there be . . . between a world without words and a language whose potential for distortion and excess is unabated? . . . [The] answer can only be the poet himself, but the poet properly informed by a sense of his own limitations and those of his medium, the awareness that the more he does to call attention to his activity *as* a poet the greater the risk that he will ruin his efforts by either trespassing into the zone of the "utterly incommunicable" or falling a prey to language that pursues its own exclusive reality. Give these right limits, this Scylla and Charybdis situation, craft for Snyder becomes a matter, as he puts it, of steering a course between them, and his major function in the poem is to allow things to speak as much as possible for themselves, in a language stripped of subjective preconception and historial or cultural encrustation, the very process that "Mid-August at Sourdough Mountain Lookout" dramatizes.

It is at this point in his poetics, moreover, that Snyder finds himself on common ground with some of the aims and values of modern poetry in general, particularly with its "objectivist" desire to encounter reality directly and immediately. . . . [In] Snyder's early work, in addition to his respect for a reality inaccessible to language and his distrust of language itself, [this desire] takes the form of a drive toward reification and demystification, the denial and displacement of the abstract and the systematized by concrete experience, from which the very poems he is writing are not exempt. But here he has already surpassed modernist assumptions about the poem. In his anxiety to clear the ground, Snyder aims to produce a *pre*-literature that can sometimes appear to the reader as an *anti*-literature, a poetry built entirely of sense-impression against myth (in Snyder's own terms) that seems to be on the way, in its appreciation of the universe as "infinitely blank" . . ., to complete aphasia or silence. In accord with these aims but unlike the modernists, he foregoes any claim that poetic language or the poetic context provides a unique access to knowledge of essential reality. Such knowledge for Snyder is apprehended in an existential act of perception prior to poetic composition which the poem can later dramatize and reflect. But the poem itself is no longer the idealized locus of any subject/object encounter. It is precisely the privileged status of the poem (accorded to it by a modernism intent upon the uniqueness of aesthetic experience) that Snyder's writing calls into question as part of its general rejection or redefinition of history, tradition, culture, myth and literature itself, all finally seen as irrelevant to a reality that is prior to language, custom and culture. For it is Snyder's ultimate and most radical assumption that he can break out of what Ernst Cassirer calls man's inevitably "symbolic universe" and work his way back to a purely physical one, reconstructing the "seamless web" of man and nature, the enveloping silence of their primordial relationship, that language originally shattered.

The poems in *Riprap* which most clearly embody this assumption and which are written according to the strictures that it entails are primarily those dealing with experience in the wilderness, experience in which the speaker finds, first and foremost, that "I cannot remember things I once read," that ordinary mental experience has somehow been altered. . . . [Nature] itself in these early poems performs the function of clearing the mind that Snyder will later ascribe to meditation. And when the mind is cleared it is "Words and books" that are "Gone in the dry air," leaving the mind in a state of disciplined attentiveness that allows it to interpenetrate with physical reality. . . . [It] is the problem of readying the mind for such interpenetration more than the interpenetration itself that these poems, for the most part, seem to dwell upon. They are almost celebrations of those moments when the mind's resistances have been overcome and the difficult transition has been made from ordinary consciousness to a state in which the mind has dropped its symbolic burden of words, books, abstractions, even personal history and identity—whatever might stand in the way of a direct, unhampered perception of things. Of course this is precisely the kind of perception that Cassirer denies is any longer possible for man, who, he says, "has so enveloped himself in linguistic forms, in artistic images, in mythical symbols or religious rites that he cannot see or know anything except by the interposition of this artificial medium." Snyder's position, on the other hand, despite the fact that its difficulties, particularly in these early poems, are acknowledged and dramatized, implies that it is these very artificial media that must be removed before any real perception can take place; and these media include, we might note, such "linguistic forms" as poems. In this sense the possibilities of poetry have indeed been reduced for Snyder, but such a reduction seems to be demanded by an epistemology radically at odds with the neo-Kantian assumptions of a philosophy like Cassirer's, a philosophy for which no relationship between self and world is possible without the mediation of symbolic forms that reconstitute the world in their own terms and thus make it available to human consciousness.

Snyder's epistemological radicalism, however, is most crucial in its implications for poetics. While Cassirer's philosophy, in its compatibility with modernist, specifically symbolist notions of the poem as a cognitive structure affording access to an otherwise hidden reality, demands poetry, so to speak, as one of several precious avenues to truth, Snyder's stance, as we have seen, verges more and more towards silence and suggests that the poem, far from constituting a medium for relationship between self and world, actually interrupts such relationship. Given his preference for a notion of experience as presence, as opposed to any sort of mediation, and insofar as literature itself is a symbolic form, Snyder's early poems are inescapably anti-literary—metonymic and elliptical in style, impatient with language, especially in its literary seductiveness, and always aware of a reality beyond verbal reach. But even more radically, they would seem if only by implication, to be structures impatient with themselves, denying their own validity, and if this is the case, why write (or read) at all? (pp. 166-70)

[For] Snyder, language cannot be a substitute for reality and [thus these early] poems do not participate in the modernist pursuit of the thing itself. They are precisely about the dangers (here quite literal) of mistaking language for experience, of assuming that the poem can be the thing itself. Instead they seem to accept their referentiality, their representational nature, and that acceptance constitutes their value, a value which can be defined as their refusal to be valued in and for themselves. Indeed, as poems which forego any literary gleam and glitter and thus try to avoid calling attention to themselves, they preserve the inviolability of experience which originates in the "utterly incommunicable," suggesting, nevertheless, that such experience is available non-verbally.

At their own expense, then, these poems promote the value of the external world and of immediate experience. They do so, that is, by subordinating themselves to the world and by insisting on their own inadequacies, as well as those of language, to do anything more than represent. Paradoxically, however, their failure is also their success. For just to the extent that they can achieve transparency, without calling attention to themselves, and thus make vivid and real what they claim to be able merely to *re*produce, they tend to become what they mean, to constitute experience rather than simply refer to it. The art of these poems, in fact, often lies in the way they convince us that certain kinds or uses of language are more "concrete," and therefore less abstract or conceptual, than others. (pp. 171-72)

In one of the first critical articles on Snyder's work, Thomas Parkinson suggested that there is one abstraction, after all, that a poet cannot help but accept, and that is language. Yet Snyder persists in his efforts to counter its abstract force. If he works hard in most of the poems of *Riprap* to convince us that his uses of language actually represents a reversal of the symbolizing process, there is at least one poem in the book, the programmatic and uncharacteristic title-poem, in which he adopts the alternative strategy of invoking the familiar modernist notion of words as things and of poems as objects constructed from those things. Here, in a verse-layout that is reminiscent of Williams's later style, we are not only provided with instruction in how to read the poems but are given a rough definition of poetry that is relevant to the general issue of its value, an issue that, given Snyder's attitudes, continually raises itself:

> Lay down these words
> Before your mind like rocks.
>   placed solid, by hands
> In choice of place, set
> Before the body of the mind
>   in space and time:
> Solidity of bark, leaf, or wall
>   riprap of things:
> Cobble of milky way,
>   straying planets,
> These poems, people
>   lost ponies with
> Dragging saddles—
>   and rocky sure-foot trails.
> The worlds like an endless
>   four-dimensional
> Game of *Go*.
>   ants and pebbles
> In the thin loam, each rock a word
>   a creek-washed stone
> Granite: ingrained
>   with torment of fire and weight
> Crystal and sediment linked hot
>   all change, in thoughts,
> As well as things. . . .

Although the essentially narrative and mimetic qualities of the poems in *Riprap* as a whole make it difficult to regard them as modernist objects, this is precisely the status that Snyder's compositional methods and metaphors here would impose upon them, and we seem to be asked to think of them in just this way. . . . To be sure, the poem proposes a series of metaphors in which words are rocks, poems are trails or paths, and reading is walking or riding, all in accord with the definition of riprap that Snyder provides on the book's title-page: "a cobble of stone laid on steep slick rock to make a trail for horses in the mountains." Riprap, then, is an implicit analogy for poetry and becomes an overt one in this later definition from *Myths & Texts:* "Poetry a riprap on the slick rock of metaphysics." Both definitions suggest, however, that if the composition of poetry is a kind of physical handiwork, its ultimate purpose is less to produce beautiful objects that are admirable in themselves than it is to produce useful or functional ones, the function in this case being the provision of a path over difficult mental terrain. Snyder is still insisting that the "cobble" constituted by his uses of language will somehow be different in kind from the "steep slick rock" of metaphysics that lies beneath it, that his poetic (or anti-poetic) disposition of words can somehow avoid the abstraction of language or thinking that is more obviously conceptual in character. (pp. 174-76)

[These metaphors] imply, clearly enough, that poetry is a craft and that the poem is an object in the world, but it is not the primarily autotelic object, the aesthetic or meditational locus, of traditional modernism. Rather than such an isolated enclosure or point of rest, it is an opening to the world, a path leading outside itself, a linguistic form that is analogous in structure to the physical world and that exists alongside it but without being closed off from it. (p. 176)

From the perspective of his subsequent books it is clear that Snyder has carried over many of the features of his early poetics into his later work. Yet it also seems as if there has been a relaxation of the severity of his limited approach to the poem and to poetic value, particularly in terms of his willingness to open his work to what he calls "the two sources of human knowledge—symbols and sense-impressions." His next book after *Riprap* is *Myths & Texts* (1960), a fabric of personal experience, Buddhist mythology and American Indian lore, and it is here, apparently, that this accommodation is made. For even a cursory consideration of its poetry reveals enormous differences between the two books and suggests that *Myths & Texts,* as its very title implies, is a deliberate attempt to combine the two sources of human knowledge, to work with "myths and symbols and ideas . . . old traditions and insights,"—in fact, all the abstract symbolic media that *Riprap* largely rejects as epistemologically obstructive and tries to bury under its concrete surface texture. Yet when we come to the end of the book and discover its dates of composition—"Crater Mt. L. O. 1952—Marin—an 1956"—discover, that is, that it must have been composed more or less simultaneously with *Riprap,* it becomes difficult to maintain any argument that there has been a development or change in Snyder's outlook, that he has moved in any simple way from a denial to an acceptance of the symbolizing process and its products as valid sources of human knowledge. What is suggested, on the other hand, is the extent to which *Riprap* constitutes a calculated response to the modernist imperative, a deliberately initiatory gesture whose purpose is to clear a space for itself and whatever might follow. As such, it could not be anything but a first book, a radical but necessary answer to the paradoxical demand for originality as the only valid tradition that proceeds not only by denying the past but by submitting literature (and itself, in effect) to a critical interrogation of its very claims to ontological validity. (pp. 176-77)

Robert Kern, "Clearing the Ground: Gary Snyder and the Modernist Imperative," in Criticism *(reprinted by permission of the Wayne State University Press; copyright 1977 by Wayne State University Press), Vol. XIX, No. 2 (Spring, 1977), pp. 158-77.*

*   *   *

SOLZHENITSYN, Aleksandr I(sayevich)   1918-

Russian novelist, poet, short story writer, dramatist, and journalist, Solzhenitsyn has suffered constant attack for his detailed accounts of the Soviet prison camps and the degradation suffered by their innocent victims. Arrested for an unfavorable remark about Stalin and sentenced to eight years in a forced labor camp, he draws much of his material from personal experience. Themes of good versus evil, the value of life, and the maintenance of human dignity through inhuman conditions permeate Solzhenitsyn's novels. Though awarded the 1970 Nobel Prize for Literature and lauded for "the ethical force with which he has pursued the indispensible traditions of Russian literature," many of his works have been barred from publication in Russia. With the publication of *The Gulag Archipelago,* **a document of Soviet systems of terror and political crimes, Solzhenitsyn was arrested, deprived of his citizenship, and expelled from Russia. He lives in exile in the United States, and continues to experiment with larger prose forms. (See also** *CLC,* **Vols. 1, 2, 4, 7, and** *Contemporary Authors,* **Vols. 69-72.)**

August 1914 differs from Solzhenitsyn's previous writing in that it does not concern people and events having a direct connection with his own personal experiences, either in the army, or as a political prisoner or "permanent exile," or as a patient undergoing treatment for cancer. (p. 409)

Solzhenitsyn attempts some innovations in his method of presentation: he intersperses his account with an occasional montage of documents, official communiques, newspaper items and advertisements (often with satirical intent), as well as cinematographic sections, e.g., a scenario of death and destruction during the Russian retreat. However, these are innovations only for Solzhenitsyn, since the technique in fact seems to be borrowed from Dos Passos, who has long been very popular in Russia. Parts of Solzhenitsyn's novel are reminiscent of Dos Passos's *1919. . . .*

Inevitably, comparisons have been, and will be, drawn between *August 1914* and Tolstoy's *War and Peace.* Such comparisons seem rather unrewarding, at least as far as one can judge from the first part of Solzhenitsyn's novel, in which the emphasis is on war rather than peace. Solzhenitsyn makes little effort to employ contrasting scenes of war and peace as a structural element and furthermore, his "message" that the Russians could have won the battle with better officers and more efficient communications and logistical support is hardly Tolstoyan. Tolstoy's presence is felt in the novel, indeed quite literally, since he occurs as a character at the beginning of the novel, but Tolstoyanism is viewed negatively or at least as inadequate. (p. 410)

The tone and orientation of Solzhenitsyn's novel will please some and irritate others, but what of the book as literature? Setting aside politics and philosophy, one must admit that the detailed scenes of battle and military maneuvers sometimes become quite monotonous. Although he is not portraying events in which he personally took part and although his subject has no direct connection with the Soviet experience, it is clear that once again he feels compelled to set the record straight, to tell the story the way it really happened and to counteract the official version of events. The result is that sometimes the polemical intent obtrudes or the novel slides over into a narrative method that is closer to documentary than fiction. . . .

A tentative evaluation based on a first reading of [*August, 1914*] would be that it towers above the sort of trash that usually comes out of the Soviet Union, but it may not seem quite so exciting to readers familiar with the major writers of the twentieth century in Western Europe and America. (p. 411)

J. G. Garrard, "Alexander Solzhenitsyn's 'August 1914'," in Books Abroad *(copyright 1972 by the University of Oklahoma Press), Vol. 46, No. 3, Summer, 1972, pp. 409-11.*

[It] becomes increasingly difficult to pin down "Solzhenitsyn's philosophy" or "Solzhenitsyn's political views." In fact, if we seek in such categories definitive generalizations, our quest is bound (at this point) to be futile. Any human being as intensely observant of reality and as compulsively analytical in his observations as is Solzhenitsyn will inevitably be involved in a constant process of augmentation, revision, and refinement of his hypotheses about life. The messages contained in the growing creative *oeuvre* of such an individual are experimental, often containing contradictions as yet to be resolved.

However, what is true about the totality of a man's *oeuvre* is not necessarily true about an individual work of art, for a work of art exists as a precisely balanced complex of structural relationships. When there is ambiguity in a work of art, that ambiguity itself can be described with at least relative precision when compared to the myriad aspects of a man's life work. Thus, the universe of ideas and the interrelationships between ideas expressed in a single novel, for example *The First Circle,* can be analyzed in terms of the structural relationships inherent in the novel itself. (p. 47)

What has been written about *The First Circle* thus far suffers from two major difficulties. First of all, Solzhenitsyn's works burst with such rapidity and dramatic impact on the international literary scene in the 1960's that there was a tendency to consider the most impressive of the early works together. . . . [While his protagonists] clearly had important traits or ideas in common, they certainly cannot be simply identified with one another or with Solzhenitsyn himself, nor should they be considered without taking into account the total structure of the novels in which they appear. However, there was a tendency to discuss *at once* characters from several different works . . . , thus blurring the quite distinct aspects of the meaning of each individual work.

A second difficulty emerged from the compositional structure of Solzhenitsyn's long novels. As has been pointed out by a number of critics and by Solzhenitsyn himself, these novels are *polyphonic*. This term . . . indicates that many characters in a novel are given independent "voices," either in dialogue or in represented discourse, and that each character's actions and ideas are described from within. (p. 48)

In *The First Circle* there are at least a dozen different characters who make eloquent statements which have great moral and philosophical force. Any one of these statements is impressive enough to be attributed to a man of Solzhenitsyn's moral stature. But, examined carefully, these statements are different from one another, and the views held by the characters who utter them are distinct. What is even more important in Solzhenitsyn's polyphonic works is the interplay between the views held by characters (which Solzhenitsyn creates with convincing eloquence) and the explicit actions of the characters, which may cast those views in an entirely different perspective. (pp. 48-9)

The First Circle is a carefully planned and executed attack from an existential basis on two of the prominent ideological systems which affect human behavior in the Communist countries and in the West. The first system is the explicitly evident ideology of Marxism-Leninism-Stalinism which is the tacit official foundation of every philosophical or scientific system in the Soviet Union. For brevity, I shall use the term *dogmatic Marxism* to designate this ideological complex.

The second adversary ideological system might be described as *pragmatic egotism,* a desire for power, privilege, official recognition, and material wealth. (p. 49)

An ideology based specifically on Christianity does not constitute a major element of the structure in *The First Circle.* . . . To say this is not to assert that Solzhenitsyn himself is an atheist or that his personal philosophy does not include important elements of Christian belief. Rather, it is to claim that Christian ideology is not at issue in *The First Circle,* except at those points where it overlaps existential understandings which can be possessed by Christian, agnostic, and atheist alike.

Solzhenitsyn's method in the novel is two-fold: (1) to show the moral bankruptcy of both the ideologies of dogmatic Marxism and of pragmatic egotism; and (2) to bring forward, in opposition, existential truths about the nature of man and of moral behavior. The novel entails, then, both a rejection and a quest. The existential truths are not easily stated; they must be groped for by the reader, as they are groped for by the questing protagonists, Gleb Nerzhin and Innokenty Volodin. This process of self-discovery and ethical illumination is manifest in the plot, a double detective story similar in its line of development to Dostoevsky's *Crime and Punishment.* (pp. 49-50)

[Both] plots on the surface level are accompanied by deeper quests in which both Nerzhin and Volodin are engaged: "Why did I act as I did? Why did I risk consequences which involve suffering and possible death for the sake of a moral gesture?" Neither Nerzhin nor Volodin fully understands the complex reasons for his act, although both sense some of the truth. The rest they must search out, and this search constitutes the major action of the less than seventy hours which elapse . . . [in this long novel] from crime to punishment. Just as the novel begins with the "transgressions," it ends with Volodin's arrest and Nerzhin's exile to the forced labor camps.

The clues which lead Nerzhin and Volodin to a more complete understandings of themselves and of the foundations of ethical behavior come from two sources: the internal effects of their own actions and what they learn, either directly or indirectly, from the examples of the lives of others. These clues are, of course, transmitted to the reader as well, who has the additional advantages of being able to view the other characters in this polyphonic novel from an internal perspective and of being witness to events and inner thoughts of which Nerzhin or Volodin are not explicitly aware.

Of primary importance in the dynamics of the novel are the realizations reached by Nerzhin and Volodin as a result of their own acts. . . . Nerzhin does not want to find some kind of intellectual construct, an ideology, which will put all the phenomena of life in comprehensible interrelationship. He is more interested in actions than in ideas. The actions themselves are the primary concrete reality; he seeks only the understandings which emerge from the necessity of those actions. (pp. 51-2)

[When it is pointed] out to Nerzhin that cooperation on the cryptography project could make him free and innocent . . . , Nerzhin reacts violently to this implication that others have the right to define what he is. . . . Nerzhin demonstrates his determination that no amount of coercion will make him accept any version of reality other than the one he defines for himself by his own actions.

This existential gesture of defiance is by no means unique in *The First Circle*. Innokenty Volodin, even while in a state of confusion about the objective validity of his motives, realizes, almost with an outcry, that individual existence is impossible without individual choice and action. . . .

These are moments of great drama and heightened tension in the novel, but the structure of Solzhenitsyn's novel as a mystery of *motive* requires that the choices be made early. However, the climactic moments are re-experienced by the reader in the lives of a number of the other characters, both within the *sharashka* and outside it, both in the novel's present time and in flashbacks. This technique, which might be called *resonance* (retaining the metaphor of the term *polyphonic*) keeps the existential act, one of the novel's most important elements, constantly before the reader's eyes [with many instances of resonant acts and statements]. (p. 52)

The two major protagonists are aided in their quests not only by their own observations, but by the stories and advice they receive from others. Of particular importance are the roles of four *mentor* characters. In the case of Nerzhin, these are the *zek* painter Kondrashev-Ivanov and the peasant *zek* janitor Spiridon Danilovich; in the case of Volodin, his own mother and the Greek philosopher Epicurus. (p. 53)

Spiridon is always moved to act in the best interests of those human beings who are close to him emotionally, those human beings with respect to whom he can perceive an existential principle of reciprocity. (p. 54)

As Spiridon's life progresses, his concept of his fellow man widens to embrace all of those in whom he can sense similar concerns and feelings, similar sufferings and pain. Throughout, there is a principle of reciprocity in Spiridon's existentially-based morality; it emerges from the ability to put yourself in the place of the other, to give to the other the same status, the same considerations, that you give to yourself. On the level of direct interpersonal contact, this basis for ethics emerges from the most elementary relationships of human existence.

When Nerzhin asks Spiridon directly: "Is it conceivable that a person on this earth can sort it out: Who's right? Who's guilty? Who can say?" . . . , Spiridon replies with the Russian folk proverb: "The wolfhound is right, and the cannibal—not" (*Volkodav-prav, a lyudoed—net*). Nerzhin is stunned by the simplicity of this reply.

These five words constitute the novel's climax, for they provide Nerzhin with the final link in the existential ethics he is learning. . . . He who instinctively protects the innocent (as a wolfhound does the sheep) and battles against those who would harm the innocent (as a wolfhound kills wolves) is good; he who survives by eating his own kind (as the cannibal does) is evil.

Armed with his full realization, Nerzhin, the powerless prisoner about to be sent to a Northern camp where he will probably die, becomes unhesitating in his actions and invincible in his inner strength. (pp. 54-5)

[For] Volodin the task is to understand the worth of the act and the positive values to be found even in its dire consequences. Part of that understanding lies in Volodin's previous experiences and thinking. However, this background is withheld from the reader until the second half of the novel—when Volodin's search for meaning in life is presented in a series of flashbacks which are integrated with the new understandings he gains during his last two days of freedom and his first few hours of arrest. . . .

[Volodin's] enlightenment comes principally from two volumes he finds in his dusty library: his mother's diary and the writings of Epicurus. These function in Volodin's search for meaning as do Spiridon's stories for Nerzhin. The notes on ethics composed by Volodin's mother contain the same elements as Spiridon's maxim: "Respect the opinion of others, even those antagonistic to your own" (the principle of moral reciprocity) and "What is dearer than anything in the world? . . . To know that you do not take part in injustices" (the principle of non-participation in evil). . . . (p. 55)

From Epicurus, Volodin learns that humility brings great strength and inner peace. The man who needs little cannot be a victim of Fate. A man must carry the value of his life within himself where it cannot be affected by external circumstances. Good and evil can be comprehended instinctively. . . . The two sets of criteria complement one another —their point of contact is the inherent simplicity of moral choices. . . .

As Nerzhin and Volodin come to new realizations about the nature of individual existence and of ethical action, other important characters move in the opposite direction, toward personal and moral disintegration. As noted above, this negative regression, which mirrors the positive progression of the two main protagonists, is due to the poisonous effects of dogmatic Marxism and pragmatic egotism. (p. 56)

Although Rubin always interprets large scale events in accordance with his [Marxist] ideological views, his personal behavior quite often does not conform with the dictates of that ideology. Thus, he is disturbed by the injustices suffered by his friends, anguished by the inhumane practices in the prisons and camps. Even when threatened by an increase in his own term, Rubin refuses to write denunciations of his fellow prisoners. . . . Solzhenitsyn suggests that Rubin's ideological beliefs are in conflict with the truths which emerge from his very existence, his existential knowledge. (pp. 56-7)

The contradictions between ideology and existential impulse, both within Rubin and within Sologdin, constitute the third important plot element in the novel (the other two elements being Nerzhin's and Volodin's quests).... Solzhenitsyn uses each character to unmask the other—each character issues to the other a challenge which will provide the climactic test of ideology versus existential impulse. (p. 57)

[Eventually] Rubin confirms Sologdin's accusation that for him the end justifies the means, *in his personal life as well.* Solzhenitsyn has shown us that political morality and personal morality are not separate categories—one infects the other.

In that lengthy verbal confrontation which prepares the novel's climaxes, Sologdin's ideology also comes under attack from Rubin. Rubin accuses Sologdin of believing that his own personal fate is a matter of overwhelming importance, that he is a superman, and that other human beings could be sacrificed if it meant advancing his own cause. Rubin accuses Sologdin of believing that the ends justify the means in one's personal life.... (p. 58)

At the time of this confrontation, Rubin's accusation seems to the reader unjust, for Sologdin has been presented earlier as a character with great inner strength, personal dignity, and nobility.... We are given every reason to believe that Sologdin, like Nerzhin and Bobynin, will make a grand gesture for the sake of moral purity.

When Sologdin does make an important discovery (a plan for an absolute encoder), it appears that he will withhold it from his captors because of ethical considerations.... (pp. 58-9)

[The] reader is suddenly shocked to find that the chivalrous knight is motivated not by conscience, but by self-interest [for he requires guarantees that he himself will benefit from the plan].... Actually, this surprising denouement has also been prepared by Solzhenitsyn. Previous passages have described not only Sologdin's strength and dignity, but also his arrogance, conceit, overblown pride, and hypocrisy. Sologdin believes that humanity progresses only through the efforts of exceptional individuals like himself—he considers the "people" to be a crude mob. He plays at modesty and humility, while his real goals are freedom and recognition for himself. Sologdin's hidden ideology of pragmatic egotism overrides the innate ability to distinguish right from wrong just as effectively as does Rubin's. (pp. 59-60)

[Ideological] pitfalls which lead to immoral action ... affect many ... characters in *The First Circle.* ... Many who are basically decent succumb. On the other hand, those who are free of the dual blinders of dogmatic Marxism and pragmatic egotism generally are led, through their day-to-day contact with their fellow men, to actions which are marked by innate decency and morality. (p. 61)

> Herbert Eagle, "Existentialism and Ideology in 'The First Circle'," in Modern Fiction Studies (copyright © 1977, by Purdue Research Foundation, West Lafayette, Indiana, U.S.A.), Spring, 1977, pp. 47-61.

"Prussian Nights" [is] a clumsy and disjointed 1400-line narrative which can be called poetry only because it is written in meter and rhyme. Sent to any publishing house or émigré Russian journal bearing any name but Solzhenitsyn's, it would be rejected unhesitatingly....

Since the poem itself is so bad, one might surmise that Solzhenitsyn published it in order to illuminate [a] moment in military history. However, everything he describes was covered in much greater detail in the memoirs of his old camp-mate, Lev Kopelev, and these were published in Russian two years ago and just issued here....

"Prussian Nights" is written in trochaic tetrameters, in imitation of, and argument with, the most famous Russian war poem, Tvardovsky's "Vasily Tyorkin." Unfortunately, rhymes are so numerous in Russian that those who have no poetic talent are often attracted to verse. Solzhenitsyn has no gift for metaphor. The only comparison that isn't a cliché is bizarre: ink as crocodile lymph. His descriptions are flat and verbose. The frequent use of exclamations and italicized or capitalized words is a vain effort to make up for the punch that the poem otherwise lacks. The one theme that might have given interest and intensity is the regret of the narrator: He is sorry to see the atrocities, but he does not actively oppose them; he himself loots when the booty is right, and he has his sergeant force a German woman into his room. But this theme, too, is smothered by the interminable descriptions of fires and ordnance. (p. 10)

[In the translation] the rhymes are incomplete and Solzhenitsyn's clumsy but regular trochaic tetrameter is rendered in iambic lines that vary from seven to twelve syllables and are haphazardly mixed with trochaic ones. The strain for rhymes leads to many awkward inversions, herniated grammar ... and many changes of meaning.... The only thing one can say is that the translation is equal to the original. (pp. 10, 19)

> Carl R. Proffer, "Russia in Prussia," in The New York Times Book Review (© 1977 by The New York Times Company; reprinted by permission), August 7, 1977, pp. 10, 19.

Solzhenitsyn composed *Prussian Nights* in a labour camp in the late 1940s. He had to bring it together and carry it in his head because it would have been suicidal to commit it to paper. It is a narrative poem in that iambic metre that is the staple of Russian narrative verse from Pushkin on: at its best its rhythms sometimes evoke *Evgeny Onegin,* while at other times it is more reminiscent of the coy beat of children's poetry. Although he must have reworked it later the poem bears the stamp of its original circumstances, when an insistent rhythm fulfilled that mnemonic function which it has always had in oral poetry. Whatever its occasional rhythmic weaknesses, imaginative use of rhyme and assonance prevent the verse from ever collapsing into *Hiawatha* jingle. It also reminds us of the author's command of a very special language, popular, idiomatic, dense, often difficult, an artistic adaptation of the rhythms and turns of ordinary speech; one of his greatest strengths as a writer and one that too often goes unnoticed.

The poem describes the Red Army advancing across East Prussia at speed, with much exultant burning, looting, raping and killing. The protagonist, a young officer, is caught up with the headlong joy of the advance and is initially utterly at one with his men. However he is delicately made to feel an increasing unease but not estrangement, which culminates in his own halfhearted enforced possession of a German girl.

The evocation of the Red Army is superb. Solzhenitsyn loves the panache, the strange dandyism of the *frontoviki*—a wild old cossack on top of a vat of alcohol which could be ethyl or methyl, belting down a ladleful in an act of crude but effective chemical analysis. There is great love and warmth in his evocations of that familiar figure the 'stupid Russian', who is never upset when his own wild zest makes his life uncomfortable. . . . (pp. 22-3)

Solzhenitsyn describes atrocities without the indignation of an outsider or historian who finds them inexplicable. His character is caught up with them, strangely at one with their perpetrators; he never loses his sympathy for them as his conscience grows less easy. This makes for a remarkably honest account of an army on the rampage. . . . He always writes well of war, presumably from first-hand experience, although at least one passage in *August 1914* describing action is lifted straight from Plevier's *Stalingrad*. . . .

The certainty that he is fighting a just war as his men revenge themselves on two generations of Germans gives the piece a quality his other work often lacks. Some people are put off by his usual stance of unambiguous righteousness and find his work too one-sided for Western tastes. Indeed in latter years Solzhenitsyn has much of the Old Testament prophet about him. There is nothing of that here. Instead we find a balance born of unease, ambiguity, and ultimately complicity in actions with which he sympathises but which teach him shame. One might see the work as pinpointing the moment when its author ceases to be standard Soviet man and starts to become what he is today. (p. 23)

> *Alex de Jonge, "Prison Verse," in* The Spectator (© 1977 by The Spectator; reprinted by permission of The Spectator), October 8, 1977, pp. 22-3.

What would he have written, [Solzhenitsyn] has asked himself, had it not been for the experience of arrest and imprisonment? That he would have written, there is no question. He was already writing (and receiving rejections) in the Thirties, but he was working in an aimless way without understanding why he needed literature or whether literature had anything to gain from him, and was mostly concerned about finding fresh themes for his stories. [After his imprisonment] he was overwhelmed with themes. And the purpose of writing had become clear to him: to make what he had lived through unforgettable and to transmit its meaning to posterity. . . .

[*Prussian Nights*] is called "A Poem" but "A Verse Narrative" would be more appropriate, for Solzhenitsyn, a great writer in prose . . . is not, and does not claim to be, a poet. . . .

In this, although admittedly inferior, piece, Solzhenitsyn is, just the same, the historian, moralist, and realist he is in his prose works, the contemplative student who is, as always, conscious of each moment's place in the process of history, who holds every man accountable for what he does, and is himself deeply involved in the events he observes and the actions he judges. But there is this difference: *Prussian Nights* reveals its meaning by implication, in the rhythm and tempo of the verse rather than explicitly, in what is said and done, as happens in the novels. Its incidents are graphic and harrowingly real, but their significance is sensed in the sound of the narrative. . . .

[The narrator's] memories and thoughts occur on the conscious level, but beneath the threshold of consciousness, "the slinking scherzo" of a popular old love song, a devilish, cloying, tempting, wanton tune breaks in upon the monotonous rhythm of the captain's musings. There is something in the song about "a black fan, a precious fan" and there is a refrain that asks, "Is there a heart that could resist it?" The unwanted, annoying intrusion seems irrelevant. But, in effect, it is the judgment of conscience, echoing, in sleazy parody, the listless drift into evil that is the narrative's main theme; the realistic sketches of the tale add up to a monstrous hallucination, a vision of ordinarily decent people reduced, through a kind of inertia of inhumanity, to gross indecency and sordid crime. (p. 3)

[The narrator's] sympathy with the victims, unspoken but evident in the tone of his reflections, is very poignant, as, for example, when he comes upon a detachment of Russian prisoners of war who, excluded from the feast of victory, unwanted and unneeded, are being driven back to their unforgiving land. . . . At this point, the well-marked, jingly beat of the verse changes abruptly to a long, melancholy rhythm; . . . he has made one feel again, in a very different context, the infinite sadness of unappreciated grandeur, the failure of selfless effort in the eyes of men. The change of pace is . . . revealing . . . with its apparently incongruous, but deeply pertinent, reminiscence of erotic passion. [It is a subtle reverberation] of the despair that underlies the entire work. (p. 4)

> *Helen Muchnic, in* The New York Review of Books (*reprinted with permission from* The New York Review of Books; *copyright* © 1977 NYREV, Inc.), October 13, 1977.

* * *

STANTON, Maura   1946-

Stanton is an American poet. The poetic landscape of her work is characterized by a nightmarish imagery where the boundaries of inner and outer reality merge. Her poetic language is powerful, her images vivid, and the tone of her verse is often bitterly ironic.

[In *Snow on Snow*, with] her experience recollected in irony, her often bitter tone, oblique narratives, and grotesquerie, Stanton sounds somewhat like Sylvia Plath with a flat, midwestern accent. And like Plath, she is obsessed by an ambivalent sense of perfection. The retrospect of her "childhood of frown & circumference / locked on a prairie without history, / without oracular words like 'Prague' or 'Jew'" transforms its dominant fact into her controlling figure; the blank banks of snow that promise both a stillness that freezes "the tumult of perception," and the terrible beauty of death. . . . [She] has layered her confessional excerpts with effective dramatic monologues—both imaginative and allusive—that vary the volume's tonality. Both sustain a similar thematic concern: the inability to sort motives from consequences. We are not lost *in* experience, but *from* experience. . . . Stanton is strongest when she combines her fabular instinct with her persistent anxiety. The sequence-in-progress that concludes the book, titled "Extracts from the Journal of Elisa Lynch," is quite a brilliant and moving account of multiplying alienations. . . . [Stanton's] discoveries seem inadvertent, or are too often distanced into parable. But there is a stronger, more obvious skill at work here than among the recent Yale

Younger Poets, and when Stanton settles into herself and maneuvers her inventions to reveal rather than reduce, she may well prove a major poet. (pp. 96-8)

J. D. McClatchy, in The Yale Review (© *1975 by Yale University; reprinted by permission of the editors), Autumn, 1975.*

A comparison [of Maura Stanton] with Sylvia Plath may be alarming yet it is, I think, inevitable: [in *Snow on Snow* there] is the same imperiled hermeticism, the same wizard capacity for transmuting an inner nightmare (of frigidity, metamorphosis, explosion) in a coherent but exotic complex of images, often under the aspect of the mythopoeic memory. At incandescent junctures, the always beautifully integrated poem threatens to consume itself in its own tranquil fury; it never does: the crisis, dire and insupportable, finds its agonized, mollifying musical resolution. . . .

The best of these poems must have emerged from lavas of stress, cooled into order by a ruthless act of will and by a vital unconsciousness that provides the poet with bizarre visions revealing, as in one place she expresses it, "catastrophe in all its moral delight." Curiously, there are level patches, to put it less than cleverly, where Miss Stanton is in the territory of Richard Hugo, most notably in "Going Back." Cadence as well as substance is coincidentally kin. (p. 593)

Vernon Young, in The Hudson Review (*copyright © 1976 by The Hudson Review, Inc.; reprinted by permission), Vol. XXVII, No. 4, Winter, 1975-76.*

Maura Stanton's *Snow on Snow* is a strikingly mature first work, full of eloquent, spontaneously lyrical pieces which combine bizarre Freudian fantasy with a sharply realistic intelligence. The complex and inventive imagery flows too fast to cloy, and though the craftsmanship isn't obvious, most of the poems are unobtrusively shaped and controlled beneath their apparently random surfaces. (p. 80)

Terry Eagleton, in Stand (*copyright © by* Stand), *Vol. 17, No. 1, 1975-76.*

It does not matter too much whether [the] psychic events [in *Snow on Snow*] happen to a fictional protagonist or a stand-in for the author. Fairly steadily, the fictional or mythic voices sound credible, "personal," and colloquial, as in the fine poems retelling fairy tales and biblical myths; and the autobiographical voice speaks in a clear line of family resemblance to the mythic. These like, but differently named voices, weighted by similar catastrophic experiences of violent loss, change, and entrapment, nonetheless move us by their urgencies, by their richly varied history and language. (On the richness of the language in general I cannot suppress a small note of impatience. At times the style could stand a little thinning: especially of adjectives like shocked, fierce, strange, wild, and amazed, those little bricquets which tend not so much to heat a line as to over-cook it. (p. 151)

In new extremities of being, self painfully learns a setting loose from self. As Maura Stanton, the "normal child," or as Ophelia, or some fairy tale person, Stanton habitually tests, extends, and amplifies the fields of experience beyond autobiography, or the more automatic forms of self-record.

The complex changes rung on her basic counters—brain, whiteness, stone, skin, water and air—create a literally fluid balance of tone. It seems in keeping, then, that so many of the voices of the poems are also fluid, or ambiguously split in point of view. Irony may be comfortable to this poet because it can straddle value possibilities; because it supports a boundary-sitting consciousness always testing the thought of crossing over. Stanton's most successful poems are frequently revisions of myth, ambiguously poised black comedy where the bite of the retelling is downward and satirical. (p. 153)

Helpless hostility, or an amiable malice, characterizes many of the Stanton protagonists. . . . In the characteristic fluidity of Stanton's medium, she acts fatally, in doubtful climax. In "Job's New Children" what cosmic good or cosmic evil intends is equally rinsed with absurd intention. As Job inspects the recent deliveries of good fortune, he is made to say:

> But the seed's wrong.
> These children aren't gay but holy—
> like that fish born
> miraculously to a starving woman
> who still died, unable to eat.

But the irony is not intrusive, or mechanically bivalent. Partly, because a thick gritty clutter of autobiographical objects keeps it from ideological transparencies; partly from the wide span of primary sources culled for materials; and partly through a fresh netting of symbolic clusters, the book —alive, irregular, and as comfortably caught as an electric eel—still keeps its conspicuous distance from either the easy or the predictable. (pp. 154-55)

Lorrie Goldensohn, in Parnassus: Poetry in Review (*copyright © by* Parnassus: Poetry in Review), *Spring–Summer, 1976.*

*   *   *

STEGNER, Wallace   1909-

Stegner is an American novelist, short story writer, editor, and critic. Throughout his writing, Stegner has sought to find man's place in the world, avoiding extreme social or moral strictures. His interest in the American West is both literary and avocational: it represents to him in his work the American Dream, and he has sought to preserve its beauty as a member of the National Parks Advisory Board. (See also *Contemporary Authors*, Vols. 1-4, rev. ed.)

All the Little Live Things languishes under the weight of a solemn portentousness. Stegner is a writer of professional skill, capable of carrying on a narrative and sensitively responsive to climate, atmosphere, and appearances. But all these advantages are wasted when he turns what was originally conceived of as "a good-natured story about a fairly typical . . . upper-middle-class bedroom community in California" into a protracted argument about the modern predicament, the gap between old and young, the need for compassion, understanding, tolerance, and all the rest of it. His main characters . . . are made to order rather than created. They lack the vitality and the substance to sustain the debate Stegner proposes for them. Their actions are credible but their conversations are flat and their ideas flimsy. The plot is spread too thin, and though individual scenes are effective, there are too many passages of self-analysis, argumentative monologue, and blurred self-revelation for the issues ever to come across with the clarity of insight. Stegner's style is leisurely, at its worst otiose. He spoils his climax by a failure to select, to vary his pace, or to compress. Most of all, though, the book is marred by its self-conscious didacticism, its relentless hammering home of the theme. By being too ambitious, Stegner has lost the effects of simple contrast and pathos which a more discriminating and restricted use of his material might have achieved. (p. 438)

Rachel Trickett, in The Yale Review *(© 1968 by Yale University; reprinted by permission of the editors), Spring, 1968.*

Joe Allston is back, but he's no easier to take in [*The Spectator Bird*] than he was in *All the Little Live Things* (1967). A sardonic commentator on his own professional failures and geriatric disorders, hostile critic of contemporary fiction, sexual liberation, and anything connected with youth culture, he thinks of himself as a spokesman for traditional ethical and social values but acts like someone on the lam from life. In *All the Little Live Things,* he was less a character than an angry critique of student radicalism. Jim Peck, the hippie who disrupts his safe pastoral existence with rock music and a Yamaha, is only a caricature of the campus dissident of the 60s, a straw man for Allston, or Stegner, to shoot at from behind the blind of convention. The novel was so strident and tendentious, so overburdened with melodramatic confrontations between drug-crazed youths and natural goodness—the latter exemplified by the impossibly sensitive and self-sacrificing Marian Catlin—that one was tempted to read it as some sort of personal essay rather than as a piece of fiction.

The Spectator Bird lacks the sustained biliousness of its predecessor, and is much more smoothly and elegantly written. That, in a sense, is part of the problem. The surface is so glassy that we have trouble locating the turbulence we know is underneath. The major crises in Allston's past, the suicide of his son and his brief, abortive affair with a Danish countess, are presented in such oblique, measured terms that they might almost have happened to someone else. About the first he is inconsolable and unforgiving, whereas he has accepted the second with the kind of stoic calm that would have delighted his hero Marcus Aurelius. (p. 193)

Allston's response to things outside his range of experience (and the Danish sojourn that takes up half the novel is straight out of the gothic world of Isak Dinesen, who appears briefly as a character) is usually either defensive sarcasm or smug moralizing. He's learned to smother his own passion and considers the spontaneous expression of emotion by others as exhibitionism or else a subtle form of manipulation. Yet in protecting himself against feelings and circumstances, he also protects himself against us. The dramatic tensions in his life dissolve into talk, and the more he talks the less we listen until even moving scenes, such as his ultimate reconciliation with his wife, lose their edge. In the end the novel seems as somber and intricately shadowed as the countess's estate, with no suggestion of the kind of bright open spaces where Stegner is most at home. (p. 194)

David Dillon, "Somber and Shadowed Novel," in Southwest Review *(© 1977 by Southern Methodist University Press), Spring, 1977, pp. 193-94.*

The West is not the primary issue in [Wallace Stegner's] writing, not even the primary interest; what has fascinated Stegner from the beginning is the most earnest theme of all, the way to live—how shall a good man conduct himself. The evidence suggests that "man" here should not be taken in its most general sense. Men are the trouble in Stegner's fiction.

Taken in order, the novels chart the spiritual journey of a man who sees himself very much a son of the West, but it does no good to try to describe that spirit in terms specifically Western. The pilgrimage, in fact, is characterized by a residual element of what we call the Puritan spirit and cannot be understood without it—a rock-hard stare into the soul, an enduring desire to look with absolute objectivity on human delusions. I see this spirit evident in two general concerns. The first is his attitude toward the art of fiction, and his distrust of the potentially seductive and distracting power of style (both for the writer and reader). The justification is not unlike the Puritan's distrust of enthusiasm: the emotional response to style can become so great that it crowds other responses and finally takes the place of thought. . . . [The] hallmark of Stegner's fiction has always been earnestness. Though a fine stylist, he places the rhetoric of fiction in a minor role. The second source of evidence is Stegner's attitude toward the West as material for art, a very complicated issue. Let me hide behind this generalization: Stegner has never in his fiction treated in a positive manner the spectacle of wide-openness or liberated energy and I think it not unfair to say that the meanings inherent in the archetypal Western situation (the spectacle of "man alone") are to him always negative because there are no attendant controls on the individual. This, of course, implies a negative view of the individual if it could be shown that people characteristically do not seek the controls they need. And that is my point: Stegner the self-proclaimed optimist is not best served by that term. His attitudes toward the inevitability of human conflict seem very much like Hawthorne's, first in that the conflicts and loss of faith show themselves in man-woman relationships, and second because optimism is asserted but never lived, seeming, like the "Conclusion" to *The Scarlet Letter,* not quite connected to the fictional world just lived. Stegner, of course, is a good deal warmer and brighter than Hawthorne, but represents a similar fear of space (psychic and physical) in his writing. In this, he seems very "unWestern"; he, like Wright Morris, has seen through the sham of fulfillment-requires-lack-of-controls cliché at the center of the Western mythos. To come to terms with Stegner's meanings is to determine how far his optimism extends, what conditions support it and what deny it, and what chances a man has of living a good life. That is Stegner's spiritual journey. His novels, taken in order, illustrate that the essential situations in his fiction have changed hardly at all from his earliest work, but that as his fiction has evolved from dealing with young protagonists to old, the sense of hopefulness has been tempered. . . . One more thing: it is almost without exception the men who will optimism in Stegner, and they always have least reason to.

Which brings me to the title of my piece. We are probably all painfully aware of the narrow way implied by the term "Western Hero," that mobile American bully, however well-intentioned, who in the center of his soul remains untouched by women and other of life's complexities, who resents authority, lives for principles that don't quite cohere in a social context, and never recognizes the destructive impulses of his worship of wandering (again, psychic and physical). In his youth, Stegner knew lots of men who defined competence by what he in *Wolf Willow* called this "masculine and semi-barbarous" standard. The juxtaposition of those adjectives tells a good deal about Stegner's vision; masculinity has always been defined in his fiction as a savage impulse, always prone to extreme positions. . . . Consider [in addition to earlier angry heroes] Bo Mason from *The Big Rock Candy Mountain,* who is given to almost every masculine excess that could in 1943 be described in print. And to eliminate the suspicion that this is merely an early phase, think for a moment of Oliver Ward in *Angle of Repose* (1971). By the end of that terrific novel, Oliver's mulishness seems more important to his grandson than any other trait. Finally, we have Joe Allston of *All the Little Live Things* (1967) and *The Spectator Bird* (1976), a curmudgeon many believe beyond salvation. . . . [No] man ever turns out "good" in his fiction: the best Stegner can allow is to leave an open-ended situation where a man comes to recognize his fallibility and desires to guide himself henceforth with that knowledge of weakness. His best books, those which explore the problem most fully, end with those resolutions untried. We leave Bruce Mason, Lyman Ward, and Joe Allston on thresholds, with their new paradigms of the self untested by experience. Once the reader understands that Stegner's optimism is conditional, and that always, always, men prepare themselves for "salvation" through some kind of self-renunciation, the relationships between Stegner and the West and between men and women in his fiction become clearer.

Those conceptions of the "good man" (what might be called the optimism of defectiveness), so far from the conventional ideas of the brave hombre, the Western hero, provide the destination, but not the enlivening stuff, of Stegner's fiction. He is fascinated by the brute strength of self-reliance's delusions. I am reminded of the scene in *Wolf Willow* where Alfie Carpenter takes a foul tip square in the mouth, spits out two teeth, and calls for play to resume. Stegner's dual response is telling: he discounts the bravado as an obvious act, but marvels that . . . the fellow was still standing. That kind of bravery could never be the absolute center of a Stegner novel because it lacks sensitivity to recognize its limitations. It does figure prominently in the fiction, though, because of its destructiveness and because Stegner like the rest of us is trying to discover how far it is motivated by the beauties of the tough-guy myth and how far it is really tough.

Stegner has chosen to test that conception of heroism with complexity rather than allegorical simplicity. He elevates those whose toughness is enduring rather than brute and fitful. In the archetypal Wild West versions of human conduct, that is female toughness. Hemingway, to his eternal credit, recognized and prized that quality, though many of his readers have not. Stegner believes civilization depends on it, though he cannot avoid the faintly apologetic way he defends the virtue. He knows well what Henry Nash Smith noted in *Virgin Land,* that violent myths may have little to do with reality and yet still move masses of people. The characters who for him embody virtue stand against that movement, but they are not exciting people. The kind of identity they represent would never lead to the White House or the Cotton Bowl, and Stegner feels that too.

Women tend to be the embodiment of virtue in his work, and he has habitually used them to make living unavoidably complex for his male protagonists. They are the prophetesses of reduced expectations, of objectivity, of the desire to live by controls, and like all bearers of bad tidings, they suffer. In this, Stegner does not reinforce the sexist myths of feminine weakness and subordination; he reflects their existence, and by implication attacks them. . . . [The] neo-Romantic creed of the epic West [is that] the man without a grandiose plan or an exaggerated sense of his own individuality is a man without talent or worth. Men cannot equivocate in their plans or value moderation without casting doubt upon themselves. One has only to read *Wolf Willow* to know how much this problem preoccupies Stegner; his goal is to take the narrow world of the Alfie Carpenters and bring a more complex norm to bear on it. He emphasizes that a grand plan and developed talent are the only means for an individual to transcend such limitations as he knew during a childhood in various parts of the West, but he illustrates nowhere a belief that men instinctively know the limits of that impulse. Stegner's distrust of "breaking loose" (no character in his fiction ever gets away with such an audacious course) is to be traced to misgivings with men and the way they use the mobility society gives them, often at the expense of women. He's saying more than that men are unfortunately shaped by the "tough guy" myth; he implies that the myth derives something from men themselves. Thus the simultaneous bias against and fascination with spontaneous masculine aggressiveness. There are two exceptions: Alec Stuart, in the first novel, *Remembering Laughter* (1937), . . . escapes detailed analysis only because the novel is short and because Stegner has chosen to look instead at the blight resulting from the wronged wife's cold, unremitting Calvinism. The second is Sabrina Castro, who attempts in *A Shooting Star* (1961) to break loose from a social confinement Patricia Hearst might recognize. (pp. 125-30)

Stegner's men (except for secondary roles) are not so likeable as the women, though they seem more vital. They are either plagued by guilt and self-loathing, or incapable of guilt and therefore pitied by their creator. The men move plots, but the effort characteristically adds up to futility; in his fiction women are the only ones who endure with grace and good temper. I cannot recall having encountered in Stegner's work a female he gives no sympathy.

Such absolutes bring us ever closer to clichés, however, and lest Stegner seem guilty of creating a species of long-suffering, weak-chinned and vacant-faced women, let me add that just as the men have become more complex—haunted now by the past as well as the present—the women have grown stronger, too, a good index of Stegner's growth as a writer. Since Stegner has defined human conflicts to a great degree in terms of men and women, and since the couples have got older as he has, it is helpful to examine the women in three successive categories: young victims, rebels, and old partners.

The woman-as-victim was a preoccupation difficult for Stegner to modify. It is a constant theme in the early works, sometimes developed, sometimes there like a reflex. . . . The weakness is Stegner's vagueness about motives; it is never clear why the women continue to suffer so acutely, and prolonged suffering, sometimes for decades, strains credulity and patience. (p. 130)

[Sabrina Castro, protagonist of *A Shooting Star*,] is Stegner's first strong and rebellious woman, and though the novel is not among Stegner's very best, it deserves attention because the nature of the past and present Stegner creates for her reveals a good deal about how much he values control and how much flexibility can coexist with it. The story shows his freedom from dogma and narrow certainty. (p. 132)

In one important way, this novel reverses the customary sex roles of Stegner's earlier fiction: Sabrina, who can find no peace because she cannot rid herself of notions of absolute formulas for happiness, receives insights from Leonard MacDonald, a Levi-clad schoolteacher who has no money, no status, no genealogy. Leonard is a low-key, faintly sarcastic Socrates, and although Stegner presents his role in oversimplified terms, the point is effective: you can be yourself and live love even in a California tract development. . . . Leonard MacDonald stands as the only male in Stegner's novels to separate the barbarous from the masculine and put the philosophy to use (Bruce Mason is similar, but we are not privileged to watch him apply his lessons). But even his example leaves lingering doubts: first, we do not see him among other men; second, Stegner makes sure that this primary man-woman relationship in the novel remains uncomplicated by sexual desire—the tension between Leonard and Sabrina is intellectual and philosophical, and characterized by a detachment unknown to Stegner's married couples. No marriage could survive Leonard's condescension. As such, the book has an unreal quality about it—Leonard lives in an untested calm, yet is presented as the true teacher. If the situation has to be arranged this way, we should be curious to know why. (pp. 133-34)

Sabrina has one saving grace for Stegner: when confronted with disintegration, she responds with self-hatred, whereas Stegner's men in the same situation follow their first instinct to blame someone else. (p. 134)

Moreover, *All the Little Live Things* can be grouped with *A Shooting Star* in that its man-woman problem is not for Stegner the ultimate one: the central relationship here is father-daughter, Allston and his neighbor Marian Catlin. . . . [The] novel [is] too close to cliché. The immense energies of the participants do not lend enough life to the story, proving, I think, that Stegner's imagination is moved to sustain fictional flights only by the ultimate man-woman question that is answered in his fiction only by marriage: does the man seek a total relationship with a woman, and does he make it work?

From this point of reference, Stegner culminated his fiction with *Angle of Repose*. That this novel is his most ambitiously and perfectly crafted only hints at how fully it grew from the thinking and experience most moving to him over the years. The story of the Ward family has the scope of an epic and the control of a lyric because it draws together all the threads of Stegner's thinking about the West and about that final man-woman judgment. In that sense, the questions of his earlier fiction have only been preludes.

The masterful portrait of the novel, the wandering marriage of Oliver and Susan Ward, allows Stegner to explore a changing relationship, and even if that were the only level in the narrative it would have been a major work. Susan Burling Ward passes through all three stages Stegner's fe-

males have seen, while Oliver progresses through the ages of previous male protagonists, allowing the novel to replay and reassess marriage in all seasons. (p. 135)

Age seems to be the crucial fact enabling the man to perceive even the substance of the woman's calm message; to accept it, as Allston does [in *The Spectator Bird*], requires at least a ritual of humility. It is he, after all, who approaches Ruth at the end and shows affection to break the spell his reading has put over them. No previous Stegner male has done more than contemplate such an act.

But more important than the reconciliation, which may or may not convince all readers, is the timing. Why must it come so late? Why must Allston see himself and his fellow bird as spectators, and the energetic life as "drinking and boasting and fighting"? Why should the only young male in the novel, an Italian novelist, be a sexual predator? Are there not other alternatives?

An overview of Stegner's fiction implies there are not. The "honestly offered spirit" Stegner has presented has long been concerned with the irreconcilables between men and women. It is good to remember that in the last two novels reconciliation between the sexes is possible only because the male has somehow been robbed of his physical aggressiveness, Lyman Ward by amputation, Joe Allston by an old man's general deterioration. I am reminded of the horrible scarring Charlotte Brontë had to inflict upon proud Rochester before she could allow him to marry Jane Eyre, and it seems to me that *The Spectator Bird* and *Angle of Repose* only reconfirm the idea that Stegner is fascinated by and makes his most moving fiction from the battle of the sexes, and imperils his novels with an overlay of morality whose source is renunciation of that energy, as though all energy must tend towards evil. Clearly then, his optimism is of a curious kind. Stegner has that "partly feminine sensibility" Richard Chase perceived in Hawthorne and James, that "sense of the complexities of the psychological life" that men in a *Wolf Willow* world are not comfortable with. His women have always been complex in their vulnerability, while his men want to deny complexity because it restricts them. Yet Stegner remains fascinated with the aggressiveness and the opportunity for tests of will that characterize the male-dominated world of his fiction. His novels use women, but are inevitably about men, and to read them is to see restatements of free will, of optimism, of men hoping to remake themselves, but the overwhelming weight of evidence points to stasis and confusion where the guilt-inspired wishes of the head meet the implacable heart. A kind of predestination by hormones. Those who dismiss Stegner because he is merely optimistic do not read the real Stegner and do not see that the "honestly offered spirit" is also the consciously offered spirit, and not necessarily the whole or true one. (pp. 140-41)

> *Kerry Ahearn, "Heros vs. Women: Conflict and Duplicity in Stegner," in* Western Humanities Review *(copyright, 1976, University of Utah), Spring, 1977, pp. 125-41.*

*   *   *

STEINBECK, John   1902-1968

Steinbeck, a short story writer and novelist, was one of America's most widely read authors. Noted for his realistic portrayals of people searching for the golden land and happiness, Steinbeck was a recipient of both the Pulitzer Prize and

Nobel Prize. Best known for *The Grapes of Wrath*, Steinbeck initially professed strong Socialist beliefs, but he later adopted a more conservative ideology. Progressive or conservative, Steinbeck's fiction is always in tune with the great American mythology of the open road, male companionship, personal freedom, and the vitality of the land. (See also *CLC*, Vols. 1, 5, and *Contemporary Authors*, Vols. 1-4, rev. ed.; obituary, 25-28, rev. ed.)

If, as Faulkner has rather perversely contended, a writer is to be measured these days by the extent and quality of his failure, Steinbeck must inevitably be reckoned among our most sizeable novelists. Steinbeck's failure is great, and it is incomparably more interesting and valuable than the successes of nine-tenths of his contemporaries. For where Steinbeck has failed is in an effort to engage, with the resources of fiction, the complex realities, the evolving motifs, the outlines and images of things, the very sense of life which make up the matter truly, if deeply and almost invisibly, available to an American novelist of his generation. I am not cheaply hinting that Steinbeck deserves, as the schoolboy saying goes, 'E' for effort. I am saying that because of his effort and even because of its failure he has made more visible for the rest of us the existence, indeed the precise character, of the realities and themes and images he has not finally succeeded in engaging. This is the kind of failure which is, in the end, almost indistinguishable from success. . . .

Amidst the larger failure of Steinbeck there are smaller units of undeniable achievement. At least one of these comprises a whole brief story; more usually the achievement is partial—a passage, a character, or perhaps merely an aspect. *Of Mice and Men* (1937) seems on a re-reading to stand up remarkably well, to stand up whole and intact. It skirts breathtakingly close to disastrous sentimentality; stock minor characters (especially the villain and the villainess) move woodenly through it; the deliberate stage technique gives one the cramps; and there is an unpersuasive quality of contrivance about the episode—the mercy-shooting of an aged dog—which prepares by analogy for the climax—the mercy-shooting of the animal-child, Lennie. Yet the entire action of the story moves to its own rhythm, rescued and redeemed by a sort of wistful toughness, a sense not of realism but of reality. The end is an authentic purgation of feeling, pity if not terror, and the end crowns the whole.

Of Mice and Men is probably the only one of Steinbeck's works which is satisfying as a whole, and it is a short novel or *novella*. His longer and thicker writings may be differentiated by the moment and degree of wreckage, and they have culminated in *East of Eden* (1952), professedly Steinbeck's most ambitious novel. (p. 164)

The badness of *East of Eden* is a basic premise in this paper and I must return to it, but meanwhile a couple of observations of a less negative kind. The sheer bulk of Steinbeck's work is impressive, for one thing, and marks him clearly as a professional of sorts: twenty-three volumes, some of them no doubt slim ones, in the twenty-six years following his first book, *The Cup of Gold*, in 1929. Bulk is not the first attribute of artistic achievement, but it is *an* attribute, and we note again the courage and resiliency which are part of Steinbeck's temperament, which set him apart from the 'signers-off' of contemporary fiction. . . .

More important, and secondly, in the longer novels (*To a God Unknown*, 1933, *In Dubious Battle*, 1936, *The Grapes of Wrath*, 1939, and *East of Eden*) we come upon electrifying passages, sudden and tragically short-lived moments of vision, little spurts of verbal energy; momentary manifestations, as it were, of a trapped and imprisoned artistic daemon struggling to get out and on to the page and into the language, and to dwell there for ever. We come upon an occasional character too who lights up for us the adventure he is engaged in: normally not the hero—not Joseph Wayne or Tom Joad or Jim Nolan or Adam Trask—but the Steinbeck sage, the renegade doctor or renegade minister or renegade philosopher, whose puzzled involvement with the action helps to give the action such force and meaning as it may possess.

More largely yet, through these swift moments of light and these infrequent bearers of light, we dimly detect in these novels the effective presence and the design of the realities, motifs and images I have mentioned earlier. I distinguish here two kinds of motif in the fiction of John Steinbeck. The first may be called the American motif: a celebrational sense of *life*, a sense of promise and possibility and of as yet unspoiled novelty in man and his habitation, a mystical sympathy both for the individual and for what Whitman called the "en-masse." (p. 165)

The second is the contemporary motif: something so close in substance to the American motif that it can be seen as growing organically out of it, and yet which also appears as a dominant motif in the fiction of other contemporary languages and countries. It appears in the fiction, for example, of Silone in Italy, of Malraux and Camus in France, and to some extent of Graham Greene in England. This motif springs from the tragic awareness, which in Steinbeck's case is sometimes only an intensely pathetic awareness, of the fateful division between man and man. . . .

The sense of division leads naturally to the political theme. It leads, that is, to the intuition that the form which the human struggle currently assumes, the representative plot of contemporary experience and the soul of its tragedy, is political in design. The political theme consists of a revolt against the forces that keep men separated, and its heart tends to beat to the formula of Albert Camus: I rebel, therefore we are. . . .

Steinbeck has made his contribution to the theme and its heart-beat, especially in *The Grapes of Wrath*. "This is the beginning," he says there, flatly, in his own voice, "from 'I' to 'we'." But the relation between the elements—the felt division, the rebellion, and the ordering power of art—is extremely complex. It is partly Steinbeck's habit of over-simplifying both life and art that has kept him from seeing and taking hold of the complex entirety. The elements rarely fuse in his fiction; they tend rather to jar against each other. The same may be said of the two leading motifs. The evolution of what I have named the contemporary motif from the American motif may be seen within the development of American literature itself, in the movement from Thoreau and Emerson to Hawthorne and from all of them to Henry James; a movement from the happy evocation of "the simple separate person" and the sturdy conviction that the world was, or could be seen as, young and uncorrupted, to the gradual sense of self-isolation, of darkness and bewilderment. (p. 166)

There is no such coherent and meaningful evolution in Steinbeck's work, though he began reasonably enough in the recognisably American vein and has gone on to identify, and respond boldly to, the contemporary challenge. The motifs have not so much met together as collided, in a struggle, as it were, between poetry and politics. For Steinbeck's poetry, the truly creative side of him, has remained American while his engrossing theme has become contemporary and political. (pp. 166-67)

The American theme announces itself regularly in Steinbeck's stories in a recurring image of a sort of *Drang nach Westen*—or perhaps *Drang nach* California. Steinbeck's first novel, *To a God Unknown,* begins with the departure of Joseph Wayne, the book's indistinctly godlike hero, from the family home in New England, near Pittsford, Vermont, to the green hills of California. "I've been reading about the West and the good cheap land there," he tells his father; "I've a hunger for the land, sir." "It's not just restlessness," his father replies. "You may go to the West. You are finished here with me." The process is repeated, through dialogue rather less stagey, in *East of Eden,* when Adam Trask leaves his Connecticut home and heads for California. "It's nice there, sun all the time and beautiful." . . .

Steinbeck's instinct at these initial moments was altogether sound; he was knowingly possessing himself of a native theme and a native resource, a resource both of history and of literature. It is the traditional American impulse to withdraw into the terrain of freedom in order to find or re-find one's identity and one's purpose as a human being; to dissociate from the given, the orthodox, the habitual, from whatever passes at the time for civilisation. (p. 167)

But in seeing his native Salinas Valley in California as a new Eden, the scene of a new chance for man and for men, and in transporting his heroes thither from the exhausted East, Steinbeck is not only continuing in an American tradition, enacting again an old American dream. He is also suggesting that the dream itself has moved west and has settled there, that it is now California which stimulates in its inhabitants the intoxicating sense of fresh beginning and untroubled potentialities which the eastern scene once stimulated in Emerson, in Thoreau, in Whitman. . . .

Much of the best and no little of the worst can be found in Steinbeck's work, and most apparently in the work of the early thirties—*The Pastures of Heaven, To a God Unknown,* and *Tortilla Flat*—where there are many parallels and continuities linking him to the age of Emerson and its cultural predispositions. Steinbeck really did, for example, write about those subjects Emerson urged on his contemporaries, when he suggested the range of native materials and the unsophisticated but robust activities ready to be celebrated: "Our logrolling, our stumps and their politics, our fisheries, our Negroes and Indians, our boasts and our repudiations, the wrath of rogues and the pusillanimity of honest men, the northern trade, the southern planting, the western clearing, Oregon and Texas, are yet unsung." And in translating these persons and places and occupations into narrative, Steinbeck managed to shed over all of it a warm, in fact a slightly sweaty, haze of trustful moral purity. Innocent are these early writings, and he who wrote them; innocent in the manner of Emerson and Thoreau; innocent in the manner of Whitman, detecting or claiming to detect beauty and purity amidst the lowliest squalor. There is no

vice in the inhabitants of the heavenly pastures; its liars and lunatics and killers and prostitutes are merely well-intentioned eccentrics.

Joseph Wayne, in *To a God Unknown,* is so thickly enveloped in mythological fog that he scarcely seems to arrive at humanity at all. (p. 168)

Joseph Wayne is a representative character, for the fact is that most of these early creations are morally pure because they are morally as yet unborn. Joseph is physically vigorous and his eyes have seen the glory. With his vague, mystical far-sightedness, he is a sort of buckskin Bronson Alcott, but he shares with the antic trouble-makers of the other books the quality—in them often very attractive—of pre-moral sensibility. None of these persons has yet arrived at the condition of conscience, at the human condition, and with luck none of them ever will. Joseph's pre-moral, prehistorical profile seems an act of will. Following a traditional American pattern, Joseph has abandoned a closed or closing society. . . . [The] next phase, in American literature has customarily been the return into society to testify amidst its betrayals and denials to the lessons learned in solitude. Joseph Wayne does not live to make that return journey, but it is a sign of John Steinbeck's development that the role of the returned witness is exactly the one assigned, in *The Grapes of Wrath,* to Jim Casy, the one time preacher who abruptly quits his vocation—"an' went off by myself an' give her a damn good thinkin' about"—and who has now come back to counsel Tom Joad and his family, and finally to die for the new faith that his good thinking had produced.

One of the favourite images by which American writers have traditionally sought both to describe and to comment on the process I have mentioned is the image of Adam. Such is the case with John Steinbeck and *East of Eden.* . . . This is a novel whose allegorical framework is indicated not only in its title but in its hero, whose Christian name is Adam. This is a novel which introduces us not only to a new Adam, but to a new Lilith and even to a new Cain and Abel—called Cal and Aron—with the former again responsible, if indirectly, for the death of the latter. (pp. 169-70)

Here, then, is the book in which Steinbeck has presented the whole of his experience of America. Although it has been a huge economic success, it is, unhappily, a literary disaster, and of such proportions that it sheds a very disturbing light on the career that has allegedly culminated in it. Either Steinbeck has not understood the original story of Adam or he has failed to grasp its profound relevance to experience in America: which is not to understand America itself. The story of Adam is the story of the fall of man. There are many mysteries about it, but there is no questioning the fact that it is a story about sin, about the encounter with evil and the corruption of human nature by an act of its own will and an expression of its pride. It is indeed the story of human nature *becoming* human, of someone less than or more than or other than human taking upon himself the tainted, paradoxical, tragic, and hopeful burden of authentic humanity; it is therefore about what it means to be human. It is a story about death, and a story which has always appealed to the characteristic dark humour of the American novelist. . . .

Little of that old story remains in *East of Eden* and nothing of its inner essence. (p. 170)

The biblical allegory is the more intrusive throughout this jumbled tale because the allegory has remained unfleshed. Failing to represent the case, Steinbeck has attempted to name it. This gives rise to a pervasive sense of contrivance and we are conscious everywhere not of a sense of life but of an abstraction from it. The Bible story is about evil and in few novels has the word "evil" been invoked as frequently as it is in *East of Eden,* but that itself is an evil sign. (pp. 170-71)

There is no great image of human experience in *East of Eden* though a great one was intended, and not only because there is no sense of life but even more because there is no sense of death in it. Death is almost always the end of experience in Steinbeck, and the end of his characteristic fictions; it is almost never a beginning, never a dying into life. The fact is that Steinbeck does not really believe in his Biblical story. It is as though Emerson had written the book, and all that remains when the abstractions and monsters have been cleared away is the old Emersonian material and the old Emersonian tone: "the northern trade, the southern planting, the western clearing," and so on.

But the calamity which is *East of Eden* is partly explained by what had happened to Steinbeck's subject-matter and his attitude towards it in the years between those earlier and funnier and more cheerful works and the decision, say around 1950, to tackle the Adamic allegory. (p. 171)

Steinbeck's editor, Pascal Covici, has accurately noted in Steinbeck "an expression of the joy of living." It should be remembered here that by communicating that joy Steinbeck has given very many people a great deal of pleasure, revived in them perhaps some lost sense of the sheer excitement of being alive.... The difficulty with Steinbeck's peculiar brand of joyfulness is not so much that it can easily turn fuzzy or mawkish (a kind of melting process observable in the development, or the decline, from *Tortilla Flat* to *Cannery Row* and *Sweet Thursday*). The difficulty is rather that it is constitutionally unequipped to deal with the more sombre reality a man must come up against, in these times or in any times, if he is honest and alert.

Steinbeck was up against a part of that reality during the years between 1936 and 1942 when he was writing *In Dubious Battle, The Grapes of Wrath* and *The Moon is Down,* and when he was also writing the one work in which his trapped daemon did squirm out and get almost completely into the language—*Of Mice and Men*. With the important exception of the latter, the work of those years is characterised among other things by a seeming refusal, or perhaps an inability, to confront tragic truth. (pp. 171-72)

But the work of those years was characterised, too, by a relatively superficial analysis and a makeshift solution of the case, whether it be social injustice or Fascist invasion and oppression. To have looked more searchingly into those ugly phenomena would have been to have discovered their tragic implications for the nature of man—the proper concern, I venture, of the artist if not of the politician or the sociologist. *The Moon is Down,* for example, is intended as a consoling image of heroism—that of a number of European villagers in a town occupied by the Nazi forces. But it is woefully limited by the absence of anything but the slightest hint that the fault, the guilt, the very Fascism, is a manifestation of the human heart, and so detectable on all sides of the conflict. (p. 172)

I am not now raising the somewhat tired issue of the artist's responsibility. I am sure that responsibility is a great one, but I am talking about the form it can most suitably and effectively take—and that is the prophetic form, penetrating to hidden realities and not combing up appearances. Neither *The Grapes of Wrath* nor *In Dubious Battle,* the novels where Steinbeck's rebellious sympathy for the wretched and the luckless is most evident, succeeds in arriving at that form; and in the absence of the prophetic we are left with the merely political.... *In Dubious Battle* and *The Grapes of Wrath* have, as it were, everything but that simple acknowledgement of the secret cause of our suffering and our violence. The secret cause is the ally of the poetic impulse, but these novels reach only as deep as the political cause, and politics in its usual meaning is the enemy of poetry, or anyhow of Steinbeck's poetry.

The Grapes of Wrath does not manage to transcend its political theme because the question "What is man?" was not really accepted by Steinbeck as the root question. He could not bring himself to believe that there was anything really wrong with the human heart, so that the causes of the wrongs observed must be other—practical, even mechanical; political, in short. The point here is that the application of Steinbeck's special and happy-natured poetry to his newly-discovered and unhappy historical materials could only result in a defeat of the poetry. (pp. 172-73)

To the story of Tom Joad and his family—their long, rickety journey westward, their exhausted efforts to make a living in California, and the bitter resistance they encounter among the rich, frightened, and greedy land owners—Steinbeck has added a large sky-blue vision of things which is not only like the vision of Emerson, it is straight out of Emerson. It is his notion of the over-soul, the world-soul of which each individual has his modest and particular share. Jim Casy, the former preacher and future martyr, pronounces this idea: "Maybe all men got one big soul and everybody's a part of it." (p. 173)

That doctrine also is the philosophical basis for the famous speech that Tom Joad makes to his mother after Casy has been killed—those words which rang bravely and beautifully in 1939 but which, if you will forgive me, seem to have lost a little of their glow since. Tom Joad is about to leave, to continue the whole struggle in hiding. His mother asks:

> "How'm I gonna know about you? They might kill ya an' I wouldn't know."
>
> Tom laughed uneasily. "Well, maybe like Casy says, a fella ain't got a soul of his own, but on'y a piece of a big one—an' then ... then it don't matter. Then I'll be all aroun' in the dark. I'll be ever'where—wherever you look. Wherever they's a fight so hungry people can eat. I'll be there. Wherever they's a cop beatin' up a guy, I'll be there. If Casy knowed, why, I'll be in the way guys yell when they're mad an'—I'll be in the way kids laugh when they're hungry an' they know supper's ready. An' when our folks eat the stuff they raise an' live in the houses they build—why, I'll be there. See?"

What does get lost amidst the genuinely lyrical flow of that passage and in its infectious hopefulness is the element on which not only the social struggle but the art of narrative depend—the image of the sharply outlined, resolutely differentiated, concrete individual personality. The political movements of the 1930s did tend to submerge the individual in the group, whether or not at the behest of the oversoul, but in reflecting that fact in his fiction Steinbeck has again yielded up his poetry to his politics. And his poetry is not saved by adding above that political tendency a metaphysical principle which (even if true, as most probably it is not) is totally unsuited for the craft of fiction. Fiction deals with individuals, however intimately related. The relationship, in turn, which both fiction and politics were seeking, and are seeking, must be composed of inviolable and separate persons. . . . Steinbeck has always had trouble focusing on individuals, and he has always known it. "You have never known a person," Joseph Wayne's sister-in-law says to him; and we feel it is Steinbeck admonishing himself. "You aren't aware of persons, Joseph; only people. You can't see units, Joseph, only the whole." Therefore it is heartening as well as a trifle surprising to come at last and in *East of Eden* upon the long awaited awareness, the long delayed perception; to arrive in Steinbeck's pages at the revelation withheld from Joseph Wayne and even from Doc Burton and Jim Casy. And this occurs in a passage not wholly justified by the immediate context, but erupting with a fierceness of feeling reminiscent of the explosive and superficially irrelevant ode to democracy which pops up in the early pages of *Moby Dick*. "And this I believe," Steinbeck's voice suddenly announces to us:

> And this I believe. That the free, exploring mind of the individual human is the most valuable thing in the world. And this I would fight for: the freedom of the mind to take any direction it wishes, undirected. And this I must fight against: an idea, religion or government which limits or destroys the individual. This is what I am and what I am about. I can understand why a system built on a pattern must try to destroy the free mind, for this is the one thing which can by inspection destroy such a system. Surely I can understand this, and I hate it and I will fight against it to preserve the one thing that separates us from the uncreative beasts. If the glory can be killed, we are lost. . . .

[This] time Steinbeck's rebellious impulse has produced a theme which goes beyond politics; which is, very simply and very greatly, human; which is the actual stuff of the art of narrative. *East of Eden* itself does not, as a novel, demonstrate this new and potentially happier wedding. But in the passage quoted Steinbeck's familiar daemon leapt out at us for an instant. . . . (pp. 174-75)

> *R. W. B. Lewis, "John Steinbeck: The Fitful Daemon," in* The Young Rebel in American Literature, *edited by Carl Bode (copyright © 1959 by Carl Bode; reprinted by permission of the author and the publisher), William Heinemann Ltd., 1959 (and reprinted in* Steinbeck: A Collection of Critical Essays, *edited by Robert Murray Davis, Prentice-Hall, Inc., 1972, pp. 163-75).*

Underlying Steinbeck's four short stories which make up *The Red Pony* are thematic rhythms, structural balance, and a seasonal symbolism which skillfully integrate the whole work and relate it to his Emersonian mysticism found in later books such as *The Grapes of Wrath* . . . and *Sea of Cortez*. . . . "The Leader of the People" is an integral part of the whole work, but readers of college anthologies usually find one of the stories published separately or the first three as a unit, and thus miss a good opportunity to study Steinbeck's subtle extension of the themes expressed in "The Gift," "The Great Mountains," and "The Promise."

The central figure unifying all four stories is Jody Tiflin. Like Hemingway's early hero Nick Adams, Jody is being initiated into a violent world where danger lurks everywhere, pain and death are imminent, and the best laid plans of mice and boys often go astray. In the first story Jody is ten, in the next apparently a year older, and in the third and fourth, probably twelve. The adventures of both youths are intended to teach them the need for stoic endurance in order to survive in an imperfect and cruel world. In this sense, Hemingway's stories and *The Red Pony* can be considered *bildungsromans,* but there are some significant differences. Because of Jody's age, sex plays much less a part of his initiation than it does in Nick's, whose experiences are not just vicarious. And violence, which explodes all around Nick and finally wounds him in the war, destroys only the things Jody loves, not harming him physically. Where Nick's wounds are both physical and psychic, Jody's are only psychic, and we do not know whether they have a permanent effect on him. (p. 70)

More important than the above contrasts is the fact that Steinbeck composed *The Red Pony* as an integrated whole, while Hemingway wrote the Nick Adams stories sporadically at different times during his literary career. All four stories in *The Red Pony* take place in the Salinas Valley, where Steinbeck himself grew up as a boy. The stories are filled with realistic and lyric descriptions of the Valley's flora and fauna. . . . (p. 71)

The basic thematic rhythm unifying the four stories in *The Red Pony* is the life-death cycle. . . .

In *The Red Pony* we see this rhythm in the cycle of the seasons, the buzzards flying overhead, the life and death of Jody's pony Galiban, the death of the buzzard Jody kills with his bare hands, the approaching death of the paisano Gitano and the old horse Easter (his very name suggesting life in death), and the two opposing sets of mountains: Galiban (jolly, populated, suggesting life) and the Great Ones (ominous, mysterious, suggesting death, a place where we must all go eventually), the little bird Jody kills with his slingshot and then beheads and dissects, the death of Nellie and the birth of her colt, and the approaching death of Jody's old grandfather, the old leader of the people, with the implication that Jody is to be the new one. All of these objects and incidents represent the never-ending rhythm of life and death to which Jody is continually exposed. . . .

The most obvious example of Steinbeck's conscious effort to present this theme in *The Red Pony* is the sharp contrast he develops in "The Promise" between the black cypress tree by the bunkhouse and the water tub. Where the cypress is associated with death, the never-ending spring water piped into the old green tub is the symbol of the continuity of life. (p. 72)

Jody's communion with nature, a semi-mystical experience in which time and place are eliminated, is not very different from the withdrawal into the wilderness of Jim Casy in *The Grapes of Wrath*. Casy adds a religious dimension to the experience when he says, "There was the hills, an' there was me, an' we wasn't separate no more. We was one thing. An' that one thing was holy." The most explicit statement Steinbeck has made on this mystical feeling of oneness of the animate and inanimate is in *Sea of Cortez*, where he wrote:

> groups melt into ecological groups until the time when what we know as life meets and enters what we think of as non-life: barnacle and rock, rock and earth, earth and tree, tree and rain and air. And the units nestle into the whole and are inseparable from it . . . And it is a strange thing that most of the feeling we call religious, most of the mystical outcrying which is one of the most prized and used and desired reactions of our species, is really the understanding and the attempt to say that man is related to the whole thing, related inextricably to all reality, known and unknowable.

(p. 73)

Throughout his literary career John Steinbeck has attempted to render dramatically his passionate belief in the oneness of all life, and *The Red Pony* is no exception, as the life-death cycle and Jody's romantic communion with nature will attest. But there is one final example which should be mentioned because of its effective fusion of character, theme, and setting. It occurs in "The Great Mountains." To Jody, these mountains represent the mystery of the unknown, unlived life, but to the old man they stand for the mystery of death. Beyond them lies the sea—eternity. As Gitano rides off into the mountains, he carries a long rapier with a golden basket hilt, a family heirloom passed down to him by his father. This rapier adds just the right touch of myth and folklore to the ancient legend of an old man returning to his birthplace to die. It echoes the classic tradition of such weapons as the magical sword of King Arthur and Beowulf, the shield of Achilles, even the long rifle of Natty Bumppo. To Jody, Gitano is "mysterious like the mountains. There were ranges back as far as you could see, but behind the last range piled up against the sky there was a great unknown country. And Gitano was an old man, until you got to the dull dark eyes. And in behind them was some unknown thing." . . . Thus the mountains are an extension of Gitano, and Gitano is an extension of the old horse with its ribs and hip-bones jutting out under its skin. All three objects blend into one as Jody watches them disappear in the distance. . . . (p. 74)

> *Arnold L. Goldsmith, "Thematic Rhythm in 'The Red Pony',"* in College English *(copyright © 1965 by the National Council of Teachers of English), February, 1965 (and reprinted in* Steinbeck: A Collection of Critical Essays, *edited by Robert Murray Davis, Prentice-Hall, Inc., 1972, pp. 70-4).*

John Steinbeck . . . tried to release woman from the pasteboard, shadowy role she generally assumed in fiction. . . . *The Grapes of Wrath* [is] a powerful social work but not his best literary achievement, nor the one in which he demonstrated greatest sensitivity to female characters. True, Ma Joad and Rosasharn are unforgettable women, but both

clearly fall into the "earthmother" category which is a stereotype, however flattering. Rather than in this novel or his others from the thirties, it is in his short stories that Steinbeck's understanding of his craft and of women is to be found.

Two of John Steinbeck's more intricate and memorable stories in *The Long Valley* are "The Chrysanthemums" and "The White Quail." Both examine the psychology and sexuality of strong women who must somehow express themselves meaningfully within the narrow possibilities open to women in a man's world. In each case the woman chooses a traditional feminine activity, gardening, as a creative outlet, yet the dedication with which each undertakes her project is of the sort traditionally considered masculine. It is the conflict between society's view of what constitutes masculinity and its view of what constitutes femininity as well as the conflict between the women and men depicted which carries the action and determines the development of character. In addition, Steinbeck reveals fundamental differences between the way women see themselves and the way they are viewed by men. (pp. 304-05)

"The White Quail" is as fabulous and ethereal in dialogue and setting as "The Chrysanthemums" is naturalistic. Furthermore, Steinbeck has created in Elisa Allen a warm, three-dimensional character with whom the reader can identify, just as he has made Mary Teller a virtual caricature of the selfish, castrating female who inspires animosity. The only obvious connection one woman has with the other is the superficial but significant detail that Mary and Elisa are childless women who have transferred maternal impulses to a garden. In addition, however, both women are trapped between society's definition of the masculine and the feminine and are struggling against the limitations of the feminine. That struggle is more apparent in the life of Elisa Allen than in that of Mary Teller, who is more physically fragile. Yet Mary is one of the most ruthless and egotistical of all Steinbeck's characters, although outwardly she conforms to the stereotype of feminine weakness. Her mythic depiction in a story that is practically a fable in modern dress leads one to conclude that Steinbeck is using her to refute outmoded conceptions of what a woman should be. Mary is not Steinbeck's model of the wife; she is merely Elisa's opposite who serves to show the real human beauty beneath Elisa's rough and somewhat masculine exterior. (p. 306)

[In both stories] Steinbeck proposes no solutions for the psychological conflicts which plague human interactions. There will always be predators and victims in life which is comprised of mere plateaus of contentment between joy and despair. (p. 309)

The women have certain needs of the spirit, the abstract nature of which keeps happiness forever elusive. The men are more practical, with greater involvement in physical concern; but confronted by women whose malaise is partially due to a confusion of sexual identity, the men retreat from the masculine role of leadership, leaving the women to flounder between aggression and submission. . . . Steinbeck is not advocating that wives be submissive to their husbands; if his opinion on male-female relations can be interpreted at all from the two stories, it would seem to support a sharing of interests determined through real communication between people, so that none can say with Harry Teller [in "The White Quail"]: "Oh, Lord, I'm so lonely." (p. 314)

Marilyn L. Mitchell, "Steinbeck's Strong Women: Feminine Identity in the Short Stories," in Southwest Review (© 1976 by Southern Methodist University Press), Summer, 1976, pp. 304-14.

The fiction of John Steinbeck has had a special appeal to the scientist, for of all the major American writers of fiction in this century, Steinbeck alone has had an abiding interest in natural science and brought that interest to his writing. . . . [If] Steinbeck does have a claim on the attention of future generations of readers, much of that claim will be based on his concern with science, since he alone, among American novelists of his time, saw man as part of an ecological whole.

At the same time, however, Steinbeck's scientific outlook created many problems for him as an artist and contributed significantly to a generally negative response to much of his work by literary critics. His use of science put him in a position of isolation—often the critics did not understand what he was doing. Further, his use of ideas associated with science brought him into conflict with the novel form and its traditions, leading him into difficulties with characterization, plot, and point of view which he was only partially able to overcome. While the modern novel as a whole has tended to drift back toward the poetic and mythic, Steinbeck's fiction, particularly during those years when he was most heavily influenced by his marine biologist friend, Edward F. Ricketts, was often infused with large doses of naturalistic philosophy. (p. 248)

If we are to examine Steinbeck's role as scientist, or any twentieth-century American novelist's relationship to science, we must do so within the context of the traditions and patterns [of the novel form]: the dualism at the heart of prose fiction and the duality of the writer's own experience as a result of his having encountered reality in a culture which has endorsed an essentially poetic-religious view of life. Steinbeck was born and reared a romantic, wrote his first novels as a romantic, and maintained certain poetic-religious-mythic schemes of thought and feeling throughout his lifetime. At the same time, he adopted certain attitudes and approaches, as expressed in his fiction, which brought him closer to a scientific perspective than any other important modern American writer. The conflict of his early conditioning and the interest in science he acquired as an adult produced a particularly intense conflict within the schemes of the [novel] tradition. . . . Furthermore, in so far as Steinbeck not only took a non-teleological view of reality, but went beyond that breakthrough to see a different kind of order, a physical order with certain moral and social imperatives, to that extent he was a writer who became something more than a traditional Naturalist. (p. 252)

[Steinbeck's] first significant expression of non-teleological and holistic thought is in *In Dubious Battle*. Doc Burton does not act so much as he looks to understand; what he wants to observe is men who, coming together as a group, assume the characteristics of an entirely different "individual." The expression of this thought continues in almost all of Steinbeck's fiction up through *East of Eden*. *The Red Pony* . . . uses Jody as an unwilling student of nature—his dreams of romance are reinforced with the optimism, the "personal projections" of Billy Buck. Buck is the false tutor—it is Jody's father, who is pictured so harshly, who really understands that nature's will must be done regard-

less of our feelings. What Jody must learn to accept is that the vultures are as much a part of nature as the pony.

The Darwinism of *The Red Pony* is brought from the conflict of animals to the conflict between men in *Of Mice and Men*. . . . As engaging to our own sense of romance and sentiment as Lennie's and George's dream of a small ranch may be, the facts are that they do not have the power within the scheme of things to make that dream come true. Lennie kills without malice—animals and people die simply because of his strength. Lennie himself must die simply because within the society of man he is an anomaly and weak. The point is each case is that what happens, happens: things work themselves out as they must according to their nature.

In *The Grapes of Wrath* both personal projections (that little white house surrounded by orange trees in California) and traditional projections (religion, family, poetic justice) run afoul of the nature of human society as it actually is. Like Doc Burton of *In Dubious Battle,* Jim Casy can become an observer of things as they are only after he rejects his own personal projections and those of society's traditions as well. In a parody of Chirst's religious purgation of the self, Casy goes into the wilderness to emerge with a scientific, non-teleological vision: "There ain't no sin and there ain't no virtue. There's just stuff people do. It's all part of the same thing." Along somewhat the same lines, the people in the various subcultures depicted in the comic novels—*Tortilla Flat, Cannery Row,* and *Sweet Thursday*—are able to achieve happiness in so far as they are able to deal with life on an "is" basis, rejecting both the personal and traditional projections typical of the larger society. (pp. 255-56)

The approach used in the comedies and in *The Wayward Bus* is roughly similar, but the observer in the comedies is on a "field trip," while the observer in *The Wayward Bus* has deliberately collected certain representative specimens in the field and put them together in a laboratory tank to observe their interreactions. Nevertheless, the topic of major concern in this novel is accepting what "is," just as it is also the topic of major concern in *East of Eden*.

Although the Biblical materials in *East of Eden* may be more confusing than useful, if we can look beyond them (or see that Steinbeck is using religious materials to make a non-religious, philosophical point), we can perceive that the primary movement in the work is toward freedom—freedom from destructive illusion and self-delusion. At the end of the novel, as Adam Trask is dying, he is being reborn to a new perspective. Earlier, he could not see his wife for what she was because of his romantic projections, and then he could not see his sons because of a religious reaction which replaced his romanticism. Now, at last, he gains an opportunity to see things as they are when he realizes that man is not bound by the scheme of sin and virtue, that man is free to be, and in being, he is what he is. By freeing himself, Trask is able to bless and free his son.

These patterns which express a non-teleological point of view, in one way or another, can be seen as having some similarities to the Realistic-Naturalistic fiction of the late nineteenth and early twentieth centuries. Yet, there is at least one important difference. In Realism-Naturalism, one sees and therefore rejects traditional or personal projections. One would like to believe, but in light of the evidence, one cannot. The resulting disillusionment, as in the case of the correspondent in "The Open Boat," often leads the individual to the anger of someone who has been swindled. By contrast, if the individual fully assumes a non-teleological point of view, he rejects traditional and personal projections so that he *can* see. The fiction of such writers as Crane, Norris, and Dreiser often suggests that the dream is better than the reality, but the dream is impossible to hold onto. This pattern does appear to some degree in Steinbeck's fiction when the non-teleological perspective is applied outside the novel or story by the author. . . . Both *Of Mice and Men* and *The Red Pony* move toward this perspective—they can be read as novels of disillusionment. But when a non-teleological point of view is established within the work of fiction itself, as it is in *In Dubious Battle* and *The Grapes of Wrath,* the resulting emotional tone is far different. As non-teleological observers within their respective novels, Doc Burton and Jim Casy are islands of calm within the strife and bitterness which surround them. It is significant that several of these characters are called "Doc" . . . in that their main characteristic is a scientific detachment. (pp. 256-57)

The contrast between the non-teleological observer and the characters around him who are caught up in illusion brings a somewhat new dimension to the basic realistic-romantic dualism of the novel of which we have spoken. The actions of the strikers in *In Dubious Battle,* of the bulk of the migrants in *The Grapes of Wrath,* of Mack and the Boys in *Cannery Row,* and of the Trask family . . . in *East of Eden* are as futile and unseeing as those of rats trapped in a maze. From a tragic point of view, this is mankind hopelessly captured by the myths of the past and personal predilections which make it impossible for man to rise above the maze to see it as a whole and therefore escape. From a comic point of view in Steinbeck's ostensibly "light" fiction, this is the Keystone Cops all running into each other and falling over themselves while Doc goes quietly about his business and, resigned to the foolishness of men, tries to pick up the pieces. (p. 257)

Seeing and not-seeing, reality and self-delusion, these are the materials that Steinbeck plays with, sometimes seriously, sometimes humorously. To some degree it is the same game that novelists, from Sterne to Nabokov, have always played with the reader. But for many novelists, the discovery of reality has been a matter of regret, a sad necessity. For Steinbeck the emphasis is reversed. At that point when non-teleological thinking enters Steinbeck's work, man is seen as part of the natural world—what is sad is that man refuses to recognize that he is a part of nature. The novel tradition still clings to the belief that although man's dreams, his myths and his poetry, may lead him astray, they also separate him from and raise him above nature. While Steinbeck recognizes that man is different, he proposes that his differentness—namely, his ability to see beyond his own immediate needs and to understand his place in the picture of nature as a whole—should make him a better member of the natural community. At the core of disillusionment, as we find it in such naturalistic novels as Dreiser's *Sister Carrie,* Norris's *The Octopus,* London's *Martin Eden,* Hemingway's *The Sun Also Rises,* or Fitzgerald's *The Great Gatsby,* there is an inescapable melancholy and nostalgia. At the core of Steinbeck's best work, there is anti-sentimentality that is almost unbearable—the blind futility of strikers and employers in *In Dubious Bat-*

tle, the cold inevitability of the vulture in *The Red Pony,* the hunt for Lennie in *Of Mice and Men,* and the anti-poetry of the starving old man at Rose of Sharon's breast in the ending of *The Grapes of Wrath.* (pp. 257-58)

[The] essential ingredients of fiction all come into conflict, to some degree, with the non-teleological position. Can a novelist hold a non-teleological position about the nature of reality and still function as a novelist? The answer illustrated by Steinbeck must be, I should think, yes: he can function, but he will be rather constantly forced into a position of contradiction and compromise. Furthermore, he will inevitably come into conflict with his form, altering it or perverting it, depending on the perspective with which his changes are viewed, and he must offend, to some extent, the preconceptions, or "standards" of his readers. The non-teleological position tends to restrict Steinbeck's use of various storytelling devices. To be consistent with his philosophy, he must, as a general rule, tell his story as impersonally as possible. Since the first person point of view is clearly the most egocentric, Steinbeck, during his "non-teleological period," does not use it. (p. 259)

[A] sequential focus on a variety of characters and scenes; we find it in his novels from the early *The Pastures of Heaven* to the late *East of Eden.* And because of this serial focus, what might normally be called minor characters and events receive, generally, more attention than they do in the work of other writers who use a more personalized point of single character. But because Steinbeck's view is often so diffuse, his work is usually in danger of losing unity, power, and direction. Furthermore, there can be, as in *The Wayward Bus,* an impersonality which, although appropriate to the non-teleological position, may alienate the reader's affections.

Plot can also be weakened by the impersonal, sequential focus. Suspense is dissipated by the lack of personal involvement in the motivation and fate of a single character. The fate of the central character in a number of Steinbeck's novels evolves so impersonally and is so tied to the general situation, that we do not really care very much about what happens to him. This is our reaction, I suspect, to such characters as Mac in *In Dubious Battle,* to Danny in *Tortilla Flat,* or to Juan Chicoy in *The Wayward Bus*—if, indeed, we can even refer to these characters as "central" in the usual sense of the term. Actually, not only does Steinbeck's use of the impersonal point of view with a sequential focus tend to act against the development of a strong central character, but the non-teleological position itself stands in opposition to emphasis on any single character other than as a reference point . . . , a sample of a characteristic part of the whole . . . , or an unusual specimen or mutation. . . . That is, the choice of a particular character for extended observation is guided by what could be called "scientific interest," rather than by traditional literary criteria as dictated by a mythic-romantic view of man. Thus, the protagonist-hero is out of bounds for Steinbeck, not only because of the mythic-romantic value system such a character presupposes, but because such a character can only function within a teleological framework of individual triumph or disaster. (pp. 259-60)

In an age in which our culture, and hence very often the novel, is concerned with the internal workings of man's mind, Steinbeck's fiction is notably exterior in its point of view. Of course, it must be if he is going to focus on what "is" as matter of what is observed, eschewing as much as possible special pleading. Occasionally through the omniscient narrator we do enter the mind of a character, but extended use of some kind of interior monologue is rare, and it is always filtered through the sensibility of the narrator. Strangely enough, the power of Steinbeck's fiction often comes from the fact that we *do not* have direct knowledge of his characters' thoughts. Instead, we often hear his characters struggling to express their thoughts and feelings aloud, and in that struggle what they think and feel gains an authenticity and power that might be lost in a more direct presentation.

Another technique, in addition to dialogue, by which Steinbeck presents states of mind consists in using an exterior landscape to represent the inner landscape. This technique is tied to Steinbeck's heavy dependence on scene to perform functions in his work which are most typically assigned to other fictional techniques, and it is appropriate in light of the fact that his characters are so often closely connected, in temperament and state of being, to their surroundings. What goes on inside Elisa Allen, in "The Chrysanthemums," is more perfectly represented in her flowers and her care for them than could be stated in her mind or by the narrator reading her mind. Most important, from a non-teleological standpoint, the way that men tend their gardens—as they often do literally in Steinbeck's fiction—is observable, whereas the inner workings of their minds are not. This is one area—depth of characterization—in which I do not think Steinbeck may be always as weak as some readers have assumed, for a paradox is involved here. Sometimes the outside is more truly indicative of inner condition than the inside, itself, laid bare. . . .

Scene carries a further burden as well, in that it is often in Steinbeck's work the basic medium for plot development. With a few exceptions, plot in the usual sense of the term is not very important in his fiction. As we have already noted, normally developed, plot is essentially a teleological formulation—it traces causes and effects, dwells on motivation, and inevitably involves "side-taking" in respect to an evolving conflict. To avoid being enmeshed in traditional plot, Steinbeck seldom examines or emphasizes motive—the effect he strives for is the presentation of events as they evolve out of conditions, as things that "simply happen," while trying at the same time to remain neutral to his characters, or at least trying to treat most of them pretty much the same.

Instead of characters carrying us through a series of actions in particular locales, it is, frequently in Steinbeck's fiction, the locales which shift or move, carrying the characters, in a sense, along with the change in scene. The drama here is the drama of circumstances, rather than that of evolving character cognition. Purposeful action by characters is not abandoned entirely, of course, but it is usually made secondary to a narrative flow animated by the larger purpose of observation and examination. (pp. 260-61)

[Plot] moves from condition to condition, and the structure of Steinbeck's novels usually involves contrast and parallel of condition, almost musical in its contrapuntal patterning. Man is perceived as an intimate part of his environment; indeed, character can be often perceived as a function of scene. Within such a scientific perspective—and I think that is exactly what the emphasis on scene provides—man's role is diminished. Regardless of the sentiments expressed within the dramatic surface of Steinbeck's fiction, his scheme of values is ultimately anti-Romantic and totally unsentimental. What so many readers cannot forgive him for is not that he has denied God, the more typical Naturalist's sin, but that he has denied the importance of man.

Conflict in the Steinbeck novel usually arises out of the inability of man to function in harmony with his environment, social or physical (and the two are seen in Steinbeck's work as interdependent). Such a conflict brings us back once more to Steinbeck's peculiar use of the basic dualism of the novel form, as illusion blinds man to what he should see in order to act in harmony with others. The conflict can be resolved once man takes off the blinders of social myth (often, in Steinbeck, respectability) and romantic self-delusion (often manifested as some form of egotism, greed, or self-indulgence). The final scene of *The Grapes of Wrath* defines such a resolution rather precisely. An old man at a young girl's breast is totally unacceptable to middle-class respectability because the image is "nasty." Within a scientific perspective, however, such a reaction is nonsense. On a deeper level of objection, the scene violates our romantic-erotic imagery, a culturally imposed illusion, as well as our traditional religious imagery. Yet within the physical-social landscape as it actually exists at the end of the novel, the scene is totally natural and harmonious. That many have violently objected to the scene proves Steinbeck's point exactly.

Furthermore, that the scene pinpoints a moment of natural joy amidst the pathos of the natural disaster of the flood defines the difference between Steinbeck's non-teleological Naturalism and that employed by the Realists-Naturalists at the turn of the century. In "The Open Boat" there is, as I have said, a non-teleological breakthrough, but it leads to a sense of emptiness and betrayal. The temple is found to have disappeared, and nothing is found to replace it. But here in the final scene of *The Grapes of Wrath*, there is a sense that man can survive *in* nature if he is, in turn, himself natural. (pp. 261-62)

The most common complaint about Steinbeck's fiction has been, of course, that he deals with, or plays with, his characters as if they were puppets, creating characters who are stereotypes or who appear to function more as if they were animals than men. And such assessments are largely valid —he does see man as an animal, albeit a rather gifted animal. The real question, however, is whether such a view of man is, as implied, necessarily an artistic fault. Perhaps Steinbeck has been a less accomplished novelist as a result of his adherence to certain views which might be called "scientific," or it may be simply that there is a fundamental difference in philosophy between the critics and the author.

Much of the negative reaction to Steinbeck's characterization arises, I suspect, from the non-teleological prohibition of the heroic protagonist, a prohibition which runs counter to our cultural taste even in an age of literary anti-heroes. And Steinbeck's central characters are not quite anti-heroes, either. If they fail, their failure is not usually a failure to act, but a failure to see. In many of Steinbeck's novels a philosophical character with whom the author's essential sympathy lies is paired with a man of action. (Sometimes, as in the pairing of Jim Casy with Tom Joad in *The Grapes of Wrath* and Lee and Adam Trask in *East of Eden*, there is a tutor-tyro relationship similar to the one described by Earl Rovit in regard to Hemingway's fiction.) The philosophical character seldom acts, while the man of action does not usually act very effectively or very well. (pp. 262-63)

Unfortunately for Steinbeck, . . . there is nothing very dynamic, in the traditional sense of what fiction does, in the processes of looking and understanding. The resulting penalty that he must pay is the danger of stagnation in his work: except for *The Grapes of Wrath,* where the changing scene and the journey motif provide a kind of dynamism, the long novels—*East of Eden* and *The Winter of Our Discontent*—are often boring. Steinbeck's worst fault as a novelist is not weak characterization or sentimentality, but stagnation. That he is so often static in his fiction without being dull is a tribute to a very skillful prose style and an ability to see things from unusual perspectives. A book like *Cannery Row* is a masterpiece of a kind—witty, original,

and amusing, it carries the reader along by sheer force of the narrator's personality and unique way of looking at things.

At the same time, almost nothing of any consequence at all happens in the novel. Steinbeck's greatest successes—*In Dubious Battle, Tortilla Flat, Of Mice and Men, The Grapes of Wrath,* and *Cannery Row*—are all triumphs of perception, so that his adoption of the non-teleological approach must be said to have had its advantages as well as its disadvantages. It provided that edge of differentness that every writer must have if his work is to make its mark and be remembered. (pp. 263-64)

Jackson J. Benson, "John Steinbeck: Novelist as Scientist," in Novel: A Forum on Fiction *(copyright © Novel Corp., 1977), Spring, 1977, pp. 248-64.*

T

TATE, (John Orley) Allen   1899-

An American poet, critic, novelist, and man of letters, Tate was one of the foremost spokesmen of the New Criticism movement. A highly personal and Christian poet, Tate is essentially an agrarian, regionalist writer of the American South. Best known for his *Ode to the Confederate Dead*, Tate sees the South, past and present, in mythical contexts that parallel the Roman Republic, Sparta, and the feudal society of the Middle Ages. (See also *CLC*, Vols. 2, 4, 6, and *Contemporary Authors*, Vols. 5-8, rev. ed.)

Allen Tate is the kind of man of letters who is vanishing from the American scene. He has remained a central figure for more than half a century because of his impressive body of poetry, his classical learning, his intellectual integrity, and his friendships with many of the most important writers of the century. . . .

Tate's years with the Fugitives become very memorable in essays about his close relationships with members of that circle, principally Donald Davidson, Robert Penn Warren, and John Crowe Ransom. Each is treated separately, and Tate's memory tends to be precise and selective; we are given just enough about each one [in *Memoirs and Opinions*]. We are treated to penetrating observations about men trained as classical scholars, men who were direct with one another and who shared many common traditions and ideals—Tate calls them *literae humaniores*. Tate, the only undergraduate at Vanderbilt invited to join the early meetings of the Fugitives, is in a perfect historical position to describe the group, and future researchers will have to take his views into account. (p. 600)

Six years after he graduated from Vanderbilt, Tate received a Guggenheim and was well on his way to a life of literary distinction. No sooner had he arrived in Paris than he was immediately ushered into the salon of Gertrude Stein and other figures living in Paris in the late 1920s. Tate describes "Miss Toklas' American Cake" and several well-known personalities of the era, and his Paris memories are among the most candid in print. He was an equal among equals: he spent time with Sylvia Beach, Fitzgerald, and Hemingway, although he admits that "I couldn't bring myself to tell what was wrong with my friends—or even mere acquaintances—without trying to tell what was wrong with myself," and says of Hemingway's revelations in *A Moveable Feast*, "I couldn't have known then he was the complete son of a

bitch who would later write about certain friends." Tate, a southern gentleman, chooses to remember more positive attributes of his friends without in any way becoming sentimental.

Memoirs and Opinions represents a departure in tone and style from previous Tate books, as befits a man remembering such colleagues as John Peale Bishop, St. John Perse, and T. S. Eliot, the latter of whom represents a kind of cultural hero to Tate. The less formal tone is continued in the essays Tate chooses to revive, essays that are not concerned with "poetry and fiction as actualizations of culture" but with a "less severe purpose." His "opinions" cover Frost as a metaphysical poet, Hart Crane's "White Buildings" (a 1926 essay that retains considerable authority and power), the poetry of Poe and Valéry, and other commentaries on Faulkner, Henry James, and Joyce. Like Edmund Wilson's work, Tate's criticism transcends itself and becomes art in its own right. (pp. 600, 602)

> *William F. Claire, in* The American Scholar *(copyright © 1976 by the United Chapters of Phi Beta Kappa; reprinted by permission of the publishers), Vol. 45, No. 4, Autumn, 1976.*

[Considering the relation of the imagination to the actual world is Tate's] characteristic theme, his signature, the motif and motive of his entire work in poetry, fiction, and criticism. . . . [Among] the several forms or types of imagination there is one which has a special claim to our respect. Tate calls it the symbolic imagination, or alternatively the literal imagination, contrasting it with the unliteral imagination which he dislikes. Under any name it refers to the full human consciousness engaged with the actual world. Tate speaks of "the symbolic dimension rooted firmly in a literal image or statement that does not need the symbolic significance in order to be immediately understood." I put that description beside another one in which Tate, in the course of saying that "it is the business of the symbolic poet to return to the order of temporal sequence—to *action*," goes on to specify what that return means:

> His purpose is to show men experiencing whatever they may be capable of, with as much meaning as he may be able to see in it; but the action comes first. Shall we call this the Poetic Way? It is at any rate the way of

the poet, who has got to do his work with the body of this world, whatever that body may look like to him, in his time and place—the whirling atoms, the body of a beautiful woman, or a deformed body, or the body of Christ, or even the body of this death.

Tate does not mean to say that the imagination which has such a burden to sustain must sustain it with its bare hands. The imagination is pretentious or otherwise imprudent if it too flagrantly declares its independence: it should resort for aid to the natural world, the world's body, to the sensory powers which feed perception, and to the poetic image—what Auerbach calls the *figura,* by which the action of analogy may be realized. The imagination is not alone; it should not worship a false idol in the cult of its own isolation. (pp. 698-99)

[The] theory, persuasive as it is, is merely an abstraction drawn from the experience of certain classic moments in Tate's response to literature. He has always been more devoted to poems than to poetry, and to particular achievements in language than to language itself. He derives his theory from a response to many practices and an inclination of temper to discriminate between them. His theory of the symbolic imagination is drawn from many occasions on which he has seen it at work and delighted in its manifestations. . . . [When] Tate speaks of the relation between imagination and the actual world, he is concerned with the poet only as a particular instance of a general situation. The poet differs from the rest of us only in degree, not in kind. To speak of the poetic imagination is merely to name one of the human possibilities and to deny that it is a freak of nature. Poetry is only in a mechanical sense an exception to a rule, the sense which tells us that relatively few people write verses. It is rather an extreme instance, a faculty more readily visible in extremity than in a norm. Equally, a poet's imagination differs from anyone else's only in degree and bearing. So the symbolic imagination is an extreme instance of something which is available to everyone as an attitude to life, a particular response, a stance of expectation. If Tate sponsors a particular type of imagination, then, it is not primarily for the sake of poets or of poetry. (pp. 699-700)

It is my impression that Tate offers the symbolic imagination as the best way of fathoming and performing our natures, perhaps the only way. He has never permitted us to escape from the responsibility of the human image, and especially from the duties we acknowledge by admitting that we are finite and historical. This does not require us to live as though the daily round were everything; we are not obliged to capitulate before the brash rhetoric of positivism. But it is a condition of our freedom, including the freedom of the imagination, that we acknowledge in the human situation the ground of that freedom and the ground of our beseeching. Henry James remarked of Flaubert "the strange weakness of his mind, his puerile dread of the grocer, the *bourgeois,* the sentiment that in his generation and the preceding misplaced, as it were, the spirit of adventure and the sense of honour." I think Tate would urge us not to be afraid of the grocer, but to register the continuities and rituals which bind together "all the living and the dead." (pp. 704-05)

Tate's most sustained parable of solipsism and modern self-consciousness is "Last Days of Alice," a ferocious poem

which features the grinning cat quivering "forever with his abstract rage," Alice gazing "learnedly down her airy nose / At nothing, nothing thinking all the day," and sundry references to "the weight of impassivity," "incest of spirit," and "theorem of desire." It is an easy and useful rule when reading Tate to hover upon any words which depend for their force upon strategic division or severance, such words as *essence, theorem, abstract,* and *geometry.* (p. 708)

If I have interpreted Tate correctly when his theme is the symbolic imagination, I think he means that the imagination seeks an engagement with objects such that the plenitude of the experience will certify the plenitude of each participant, subject, and object. Object and feeling are to be reconciled, and for that reason the imagination which promotes the reconciliation is symbolic.

Tate's poems, therefore, testify to acts of consciousness as complete as he has been able to make them, the scale of the effort is nearly as inspiring as the record of the achievement. The chief labor of the poems is to establish between Tate's subject matter and its emergence as form a relation adequately serious. The density of his poems is a measure of their responsibility, an indication of what, in the way of consciousness and care, they have been through. What the poems seek is direct access to experience through its occasions and by means of its forms. In "The Mediterranean" Tate writes: "They, in a wineskin, bore earth's paradise." The wineskin is more important than the paradise because it is the means available and paradise depends upon luck and grace. In "To the Lacedemonians" he speaks of "the bright course of blood along the vein"—again a given resource—valued because given. Tate's poems invoke things as though he were unwilling to release them from the responsibility of their meaning, that is, the full weight of their implication in place and time. He will not let objects go their own way if it means disengaging them from their pact with men. When things are invoked, therefore, they come not as they are generally taken to be in a time abstract, positivist, devoid of memory—a time in which "the hard eyes look one way," and faces are "eyeless with eyesight only." Rather, Tate instructs objects to engage with the perceiver's mind in such a way as to arrive freighted with human value and moment. This is to say that the seriousness of Tate's enterprise depends upon a sustaining continuity of sense, perception, and imagination. The poems are, in that respect, acts of consciousness. So in thinking of these poems and in responding to them, we often remark that Tate's proceedings are the common, ordinary processes, but they are taken up with such care that they are enriched and deepened beyond anything commonly available. If we think of them as forms of communication, we are not satisfied until we have deepened the term and called it communion; if we think of his poems of memory, we deepen the term and call it commemoration. (pp. 708-09)

Like any other poet, he delights in possibility, amplitude, open spaces, and free ranges. He claims the freedom of inquiring how much meaning a proposed situation will bear. This is the side of Tate most dramatically represented by his response to Arthur Rimbaud and Eliot, his kinship with Hart Crane. In that mood, the sky is the limit. But Tate has nearly always admitted a scruple. The fact that an effect is linguistically possible does not make it reasonable. There is a question of cogency. Has he not warned us and himself against the gross indulgence of feeling, will, and intellect? The warning is explicit when Tate writes as a critic. When he writes as a novelist or a poet, he concentrates the triple admonition into a scruple of form. It is his sense of form that prevents him from rushing into excess: poetry, he has written, "is the art of apprehending and concentrating our experience in the mysterious limitations of form." The symbolic imagination, as distinct from the essential imagination ascribed to angels, is content with the human range of experience as its substance, and the human range of form as its means. This does not make an aesthetic for slaves but for free men who know that their freedom is not unlimited: it makes an aesthetic good enough for anyone who is neither barbarian nor fanatic.

Tate's aesthetic does not, of course, make poems. In poetry nearly everything can go wrong, whether it is propelled by good or bad intentions: this is not an argument against making the intentions good. Several elements go into the making of a poem, and if one of them goes askew the damage is done. In any case, the elements are not enough. Events are only potential experience, as the imagination is only potential creation, the will only potential action, and language only potential speech. It is their juncture in achieved form that makes all of them actual. When a poem by Tate falls short of conviction, it is because the experience has been realized and mastered only to the extent represented by its turbulence, and the language has stuck at that point—whirling as in a vortex. The proof of an achieved poem is its song, that is, its rhythm and movement. (pp. 710-11)

If we want a poem all conviction, I suggest Tate's "Mother and Son," too long to quote but hardly too long to memorize. Upon a "firmly denoted natural setting" Tate has imagined and brooded to the point at which the experience has been mastered, the language tuned. The mother is given as ferocious and importunate: the phrases attached to her include "hand of death," "fierce compositor," "falcon mother," "harsh command," "dry fury," "black crucifix," and "cold dusk." The substance of the poem is friction, which is another kind of dissociation, and for brevity's sake we can say that the substance is continuous with that of Tate's novel, *The Fathers*. Common to both the poem and the novel is a represented violence of feeling, the characters are immured in their own extremity. Apart from the difference of scale, there is this further difference that the dissociation in *The Fathers* is only partly categorical and is mostly social and political. In the poem the dissociation is aboriginal; it operates at a level beneath that of cause and effect. . . . [The] achieved form, the poem itself, can bear as much weight as we elect to place upon it, because of the denoted natural scene, the human situation itself. It is this consideration which ensures that the fiction is convincing and not arbitrary. If fiction is like statute law, Tate is content to make his fictions continuous with the common law we all acknowledge, even when we disobey it. . . . The details in Tate's poem are significant because of the low level of being they share, the death-in-life and life-in-death they share with mother and son. But they have a further purpose. The abused feelings between mother and son are not resolved by anything that is shown to happen, but held in tension by the narrator, the witness who addresses the son in the last stanza, "O heart." The details stand for the narrator's feeling, since they are what he has chosen to notice.

Just as the mother and son are types, with enough contingency to be actual, so the details are types because of the categorial relation for which the narrator's feeling requires them. The details—the flies, spider, and wallpaper—are what they are, and they are also what they become, emblems of the narrator's feeling. They are significant not only because he has noticed them but because his feeling is such that he has not noticed anything else. (pp. 711-13)

Denis Donoghue, "Nuances of a Theme by Allan Tate," in The Southern Review *(copyright, 1976, by Denis Donoghue), Vol. XII, No. 4, Autumn, 1976, pp. 698-713.*

In the early 1950s, . . . I undertook to write an essay about Allen Tate's poetry which I entitled "The Serpent in the Mulberry Bush," and in which I sought to demonstrate how the "Ode to the Confederate Dead" was his way of focusing his feelings about the South, modern society, history, and personal allegiance into the image of a poem. I did so, I think, with only limited success, so far as understanding that complex poem was concerned, but if all criticism is autobiography, then for my part this engagement with the "Ode" was a considerable success, for it drew me into my first sustained attempt at working out both the problem of the relationship of southern literature to southern experience, and the larger problem of the relationship of literature to history and society. For these reasons and others I have found myself coming back to that poem again and again, with a deepening sense both of my obligation to its author and of the facile inadequacy of my initial published response to it. I have been unable to put it by, and now I shall take another crack at it, with the hope of repairing the damage, not to the poem itself, which is immune to what critics such as myself might do or say, but to my own explication. I propose, therefore, to essay the "Serpent in the Mulberry Bush" once more. (p. 744)

In October of 1925 Tate published an article in the *Nation*, entitled "Last Days of a Charming Lady," in which he surveyed the lack of a vigorous literary tradition in the South. The region's antebellum literary culture, he said, had been the unventuresome, eighteenth-centuryish, energyless charm of an aristocracy of social privilege founded in a rigid social order. . . . The surviving southern aristocracy had "no tradition of ideas, no consciousness of moral and spiritual values, as an inheritance; it has simply lost a prerogative based on property." There had been, in the northern Virginia and Charleston areas of the Old South, societies distinguished for graces of living, if not for literary achievement, but these were going fast. Thus the present-day southern author was without a foundation in regional self-inquiry, and if he was to make out of his own openness to experience and readiness to explore new forms, a literature that would speak to his southern circumstance, he would have to do it from without: by making use of the cosmopolitan culture of western Europe. "It is pretty certain," he concluded, "that the Southern variety of American writer must first see himself, if at all, through other eyes. For he, of all Americans, is privy to the emotions founded in the state of knowing himself to be a foreigner at home."

The diagnosis, of course, not only fitted Tate's case . . . , but it stated, topically and matter-of-factly, the central anguish that "Ode to the Confederate Dead" would explore:

the final sentence is almost a precis of the situation in the poem. (pp. 746-47)

If the watcher at the Confederate cemetery gate is a modern southerner, who sees the inroads of nature on the tombstones of the once-proud soldiers of the Lost Cause, and ironically meditates upon the seeming likeness of the soldiers to the leaves insofar as the natural world is concerned (the wind which "whirrs without recollection"), then what he confronts is the absence of any lasting meaning to the tradition other than what human memory might afford. But if so, the leaves piling up alongside the graves suggest the neglect of the graves by the living, too. Autumn or not, it is not a well-tended cemetery. In other words, the modern southerner, whom we may assume is the poet, ponders his historical tradition and its erosion, and this is the situation with which the poem will concern itself.

Tate called the poem an "Ode," he wrote later, partly out of a sense of irony—neither the classical Pindaric ode nor the seventeenth-century imitation of it would have permitted a purely subjective meditation—a lone man standing by a gate, rather than a public celebration. The poem, for that matter, is not about the dead Confederate soldiers at all; it is about the modern man's sense of being distanced from them. When Tate sent the draft of the poem to Donald Davidson, his fellow Fugitive objected that "the Confederate dead become a peg on which you hang an argument." He admired the craft, but "its beauty is a cold beauty," he said. "And where, O Allen Tate, are the dead? You have buried them completely out of sight—with them yourself and me. God help us, I must say." But that is precisely the point of Tate's poem (and what Tate would do here was precisely what Davidson as artist could neither understand nor approve). Tate was interested not in patriotic homage but in what was ultimately, perhaps, a more important form of tribute: an attempt to understand why one of his fragmented time and place was no longer able to celebrate what the Confederate soldiers had been in their time. His attitude toward that, as Radcliffe Squires notes, was one of despair. Davidson could not envision the backward look as being a problem; Tate for his part knew better.

Therefore, "autumn is desolation" in the cemetery for the man at the gate, who tries to muster the proper memorial rhetoric for the occasion, but cannot sustain it. (pp. 748-49)

For the man at the gate, the attempt to understand appears useless, because the goal is impossible; sealed off from the past, from any hope of his being capable of fathoming how the dead soldiers could have acted meaningfully and believed in their actions, the modern observer has only the ingrained habit of speculation, which will not let him rest. Locked within himself, he can contemplate only himself—"or like the jaguar leaps / For his own image in a jungle pool, his victim." He is the trapped animal of naturalism, whose self-consciousness and capacity for wanting to discover meaning beyond nature only condemn him to frustration and self-hatred. "This figure of the jaguar," Tate wrote, "is the only explicit rendering of the Narcissus motif in the poem, but instead of a youth gazing into a pool, a predatory beast stares at a jungle stream, and leaps to devour himself."

With this despairing conclusion "Ode to the Confederate Dead" might logically have ended—the realization of the total inability of the man at the gate to make anything of his

heritage. He had sought to invoke for himself the reality of the Confederate past, had been unable to find in it any meaning that was transferrable to him, and so had ended with a picture of himself as no more than a biological creature, imprisoned within his own sensibility, doomed to return into the nothingness from which he had come. The society in which he had been born and grown up had been importantly formed by that past, but it had been repudiated, and since the repudiation had been in favor of a life without meaning or belief, there could be no place for himself within his own society, either. He would indeed have been, as he said of the southern writer in "Last Days of a Charming Lady," an American "whose emotions were founded upon knowing himself to be a foreigner at home." That is what the poem declares.

But the poem does not end there. There are two more stanzas to come, and they are definitive for both this poem and for what Tate would be thinking and writing in the next decade. Instead of the poem's culminating with the figure of the predatory animal leaping to narcissistic self-destruction, the man at the gate asks another question: "What shall we say who have knowledge / Carried to the heart?"

Tate later explained the figure as follows: "This is Pascal's war between heart and head, between *finesse* and *geometrie*." But if the man at the gate and his fellow moderns—those who are concerned with the erosion of the capacity for belief (by no means all of them, to be sure)—have "knowledge carried to the heart," which is to say, possess a sensibility which does not willingly split apart thought and feeling, but would unify them, then the jaguar about to pounce upon his reflection in the water and thus destroy himself will not quite do for the last word on the modern predicament. Instead, it appears that despite the solipsism and failure to be able to act intelligently upon one's deeply-felt convictions, the aptitude for the kind of wholehearted response to life exemplified by the dead Confederate soldiers has not died out. What is missing is not the capacity, but the social circumstance. That is to say, the conditions of contemporary society, the public assumptions, the tenor of everyday twentieth-century economic and social life, serve to prevent the rendering of the True Account. This is the implication—though not the overt conclusion—of the reference to those who "have knowledge / Carried to the heart."

There follows a statement that would seem to belie any likelihood whatever of doing anything about it.

> Shall we take the act
> To the grave? Shall we, more hopeful, set up the
>   grave
> In the house? The ravenous grave?

Shall those who are like the man at the gate remain silent and live out their lives with the private knowledge that the condition of the present time is not as it should be? Or shall they, in a romantic affirmation of despair, make a virtue out of hopelessness and consciously celebrate decay and death? This was the way of the *fin de siecle,* the "Gone with the Wind" school. Southern poetry of the early twentieth century was full of the note, and in some of his early work in the *Fugitive* Tate had essayed it: the langorous assertion, by a world-weary surviving memorialist, of the death of the gods. (pp. 754-56)

Shall we, he asks in effect, write funereal poems, in which

death is made into life, as the only positive response to a world of death-in-life? . . . He will not seriously consider making that choice, but neither is it to be dismissed as absurd.

Instead Tate closes his poem by leaving the question open:

> Leave now
> The shut gate and the decomposing wall:
> The gentle serpent, green in the mulberry bush,
> Riots with his tongue through the hush—
> Sentinel of the grave who counts us all!
>
> (p. 756)

"Ode to the Confederate Dead" does not conclude in blank despair, either historical or moral. "Leave now" the gate and wall that keep us from the spirit of the dead soldiers, he says, and one possible conclusion is that one is to give up the attempt to make any sense of them or of his relationship to them. But if the man at the gate is leaving the Confederate cemetery, he is going back into the city of his time; and what he takes with him, finally, is life: for the serpent, whatever he represents, is indubitably alive and green, which is a very different thing from the splayed leaves piled up in the graveyard. If time is the solution to the riddle, it is an affirmation of continuing life, with its own problems.

The poem, in short, ends with the emblem of life in time and in nature. The gentle serpent is *sentinel* of the grave. Alive, "rioting with his tongue through the hush," he guards the cemetery and the memory of the dead Confederates from surprise attack. . . . [It] is not beyond the boundaries of legitimate comment on the poem to suggest what Mr. Squires proposed: that if the man at the gate is a poet, and if (as in a sense, all poems are) this one is about the writing of poetry, then insofar as the future exploration of his own identity in history and society was concerned, the modern poet at the Confederate cemetery gate still had a great deal to write about.

It is not that I am insisting upon a "happy ending" to the anguish in the "Ode to the Confederate Dead." It is not an optimistic poem. But neither is it a surrender to the Waste Land. What it does is to dramatize the difficulty of the present, in terms of Tate's own historical and social concerns. And closing, as it does, with the image of the gentle serpent, the moving, continuing, exploring symbol of life in time, it asserts a continuity of experience that joins past and future as part of the ongoing human problems of meaning and belief. This is what one reader takes, finally, from the poem. (p. 757)

> *Louis D. Rubin, Jr., "'The Serpent in the Mulberry Bush' Again," in* The Southern Review *(copyright, 1976, by Louis D. Rubin, Jr.), Vol. 12, No. 4, Autumn, 1976, pp. 744-57.*

[George Posey], the chief protagonist in [*The Fathers*] . . . is identified with neither an old order nor a new order; he embodies social change while yearning and striving, at the same time, for social stability. (p. 128)

Caught somehow between the past, in the form of a stable social order, and the future, in the form of financial prosperity, George Posey "was a man without people or place; he had strong relationships, and he was capable of passionate feeling, but it was all personal.". . . It is this "person-al" aspect of George Posey's character that conflicts with the decorum of the Buchan family and eventually "destroys the discipline of its civilization." (pp. 129-30)

Lacy Buchan's function as the narrator of *The Fathers* is significant beyond the basic fact of his own involvement in the events he describes. It is important, first of all, that he grows up, perhaps because of, but at least simultaneously with, the disintegration of his family; this allows him, in his old age, to tell his story realistically and ironically—that is to say, with a degree of emotional and moral detachment. . . . Lacy is able years later to put the original indiscretions of George Posey—which had once been so dramatic in the past—into a larger, historical perspective. Neither oblivious to time and change, like his father, nor lost in time and change, like George, Lacy can comprehend and express, in his narrative, an existence that is far from timeless. (p. 130)

If Lacy's age as a narrator thus gives him an appreciation of the inevitability of change and disappointment, his youth as a participant in the events of his story gives him an additional importance as the central consciousness of Tate's novel. . . . It is not just the Civil War, but history itself that is irrepressible in *The Fathers,* and Lacy's youth gives him a proper sense, for Tate, of the alien and irresistible. His very love for an outsider like George Posey is an indication of the breakdown in the Buchan order. . . . (pp. 130-31)

[If] George Posey is a "personal" force in a world whose "impersonality" he often cannot accept, it is also clear in *The Fathers* that he yearns somewhat nostalgically for the lost opportunities of his own youth, for the kind of social order and security represented by the Buchan way of life. (p. 137)

The last act of Lacy's story is an account of George Posey's belated attempt to "be with the men" fighting the war —to make "your people" his people. But, again, George can not act impersonally; as the Battle of Bull Run is about to begin, he is insulted by an old enemy and promptly kills him. Returning, then, to Pleasant Hill, George and Lacy find the old house burned to the ground and Major Buchan dead by his own hand. It is, for George, a final display of the "wilful and arbitrary" absurdity behind the self-destruction of the Buchan family. (p. 140)

George's last gesture is to remove the Confederate uniform (which he leaves, symbolically, in a heap upon the ground) and to ride off, alone, into the growing darkness. . . . Then, for the first and last time in *The Fathers*, Lacy the narrator becomes one with Lacy the boy (as the past tense changes to the present): "I'll go back and finish it. I'll have to finish it because he could not finish it. It won't make any difference if I am killed. If I am killed it will be because I love him more than I love any man.". . . Though it is too late for George himself to change, to turn back the clock, it is not too late, this once, for Lacy in his old age to judge what has happened to him. He must "finish" not only George's attempt to fight in the war, his effort to define himself according to something greater than himself, but he must also, with the acknowledgment of his love, live out his own life as the historical offspring of George's confusion and disorder, as a member of the changing world "that had been created by George Posey, out of the dead world of my mother.". . . (pp. 140-41)

> *David C. Stineback, "'The Shock of Com-*

munion': Allen Tate's 'The Fathers'," in his Shifting World: Social Change and Nostalgia in the American Novel (© *1976 by Associated University Presses, Inc.), Associated University Presses,* 1976, pp. 128-41.

* * *

THOMPSON, Hunter S(tockton) 1939-

Thompson is an American author and reporter best known as the major practitioner of what he calls "gonzo journalism." Gonzo journalism, which takes New Journalism one step further beyond any pretense to objectivity, is characterized by its energy. His *Fear and Loathing in Las Vegas* describes a wild cross-country odyssey, and is generally recognized as one of the most popular books of the counterculture. Thompson has served as the South American correspondent of the *National Observer*, and is now national affairs editor for *Rolling Stone*. He has recently been parodied in Garry Trudeau's comic strip, "Doonesbury." (See also *Contemporary Authors*, Vols. 17-20, rev. ed.)

Hunter S. Thompson [in *Hell's Angels*] doesn't think much of the "button-down" lives of the squares. He likens them to "ribbon salesmen," enslaved to their "time payments," at best hypocritical pseudo-hipsters when they try to swing, and at worst, the liberal persecutors of the aberrant, or victims of affluence and "abulia," and the creators of a mass hysteria toward California's obscenely festooned gangs of motorcycling Hell's Angels which has only helped to glamorize and institutionalize their "outlaw" status, lending to their shabby Wehrmacht muftis and atavistic sleeziness a high-Camp prestige and a Charisma far exceeding the actual numbers of those who have been so attired.

Thompson also concedes that these "losers" on wheels are a threat to the self-satisfied bourgeoisie, but he takes great delight in exposing what has merely been invented and advanced about them by the mass media out of an opportunistic need to make eye-catching copy, and what Angel offenses are actual. (p. 30)

Thompson's fascinating invocation to, evocation *of,* and reportage *about* the Hell's Angels . . . is certainly the most informative, thorough, and vividly written account of this phenomenon yet to appear. And no wonder! Thompson spent better than a year among the Angels. . . . In the course of his investigation, Thompson may slight making the obvious connection between the motorcycle fad in this Country and that in pre-Hitlerian Germany under Weimar, but he makes a lot of other interesting connections between the Hell's Angels and present-day square society, especially its liberal elements. Although Thompson seems to have elevated the outlaws for himself to "new nadirs of sordid fascination," he has also managed to correct many popular misconceptions about them, and, in the process, provided his readers with a tendentious but informative participant-observer study of those who are doomed to lose. Yet his work might shortly be relegated to the souvenir bins of a rapidly-changing faddist era were it not for the assertions which Thompson makes about the proliferation of "losers" in our society, and for his talents as an imaginative writer.

Very simply, Thompson believes that the "unemployables" and the deracinated are on the ascendency in American life—that, in short, Hell's Angels are the *avant garde* of a new lumpen class. He is able to trace this class to the

Hillbilly descendants of the indentured servant classes who came to this country two centuries ago and have only recently begun to appear in cities in large numbers, as well as to a fallout from other more recent ethnic groups, and, of course, to the resentfuls within the black ghettos. While he is generally in sympathy with such plights, even comparing such lumpen behaviour to the spontaneities of the Watts rioters, he further manages to see a peculiar integrity to this kind of behaviour which is in increasing conflict with a society upholding property, education, and restraint. (pp. 30-1)

[Thompson] actually seems to be projecting through . . . set pieces of comic, anti-square exaggeration . . . a future reign of anarchy and terror, a new order perhaps, civil war between the squares and the lumpen strata. (p. 31)

Taken . . . as a delirium for the future, Thompson's book is a hairily comic metaphor for a society getting just about what it deserves for napalming Vietnamese and instituting privilege for everybody except those who need it most; and it's a metaphor which, even in its grotesque nonsensicality, manages to scratch a bit of the truth off the American veneer. . . . In the work itself, Thompson's self-proclaimed aesthetic and his methodology have some of the integrity of George Orwell among the poor of London and Paris, and it also has the cranky peevishness of Orwell's fine attack in *Wigan Pier* on pseudo-leftists, progressives, and food faddists, but it seems to have dispensed with the very middle-class biases toward "decency" which Orwell tried so hard to assert and uphold. Rather, it asserts a kind of Rimbaud delirium of spirit for nearly everybody to which, of course, only the rarest geniuses can come close and, then, never through choice. For more than one reason, therefore, I suspect, that Hunter S. Thompson is a writer whose future career is worth watching. (pp. 31-2, 34)

> *Richard M. Elman, in* The New Republic *(reprinted by permission of* The New Republic; © *1967 by The New Republic, Inc.), February 25, 1967.*

["Fear and Loathing in Las Vegas"] is by far the best book yet written on the decade of dope gone by.

"Fear and Loathing in Las Vegas" is a number of things, most of them elusive on first reading and illusory thereafter. A solid second act by the author of "Hell's Angels," it is an apposite gloss on the more history-laden rock lyrics ("to live outside the law you must be honest"). . . . [It is] a custom-crafted study of paranoia, a spew from the 1960's and—in all its hysteria, insolence, insult, and rot—a desperate and important book, a wired nightmare, the funniest piece of American prose since "Naked Lunch." . . .

These are the tracks of a man who might be dismissed as just another savage-sixties kook, were it not for the fact that he has already written himself into the history of American literature, in what I suspect will be a permanent way. Because, regardless of individual reader-reactions, his new book is a highballing heavyweight, whose ripples spread from Huckleberry Finn to F. Scott's Rockville grave. . . .

Like Mailer's, Thompson's American dream is a fanfare of baroque fantasy. It should not, despite its preemptive title, be mistaken for a synopsis of the American experience (even though the narrator comes to think of himself as a "monster reincarnation of Horatio Alger"). But its limits are no narrower than the limits of lunacy, and its method is as adventurous as any to be found in all the free-fire-zone writing of the past dozen years.

"Writing" is as exact a label as the book will carry. Neither novel nor nonfiction, it arrives with fashion's special sanction. Its roots are in the particular sense of the nineteen-sixties that a new voice was demanded. . . . (p. 17)

But who taps fashion for wisdom gets poison in the sap, and "Fear and Loathing" is the quick assassin of the form it follows. Not the least of Thompson's accomplishments is to suggest that, by now, the New Journalism is to the world what the New Criticism was to the word: seductive, commanding—and, finally, inadequate. The form that reached apotheosis in "Armies of the Night" reaches the end of its rope in "Fear and Loathing," a chronicle of addiction and dismemberment so vicious that it requires a lot of resilience to sense that the author's purpose is more moralizing than sadistic. He is moving in a country where only a few cranky saviors—Jonathan Swift for one—have gone before. And he moves with the cool integrity of an artist indifferent to his reception.

For the things the book mocks—hippies, Leary, Lennon, journalism, drugs themselves—are calculated to throw Thompson to the wolves of his own subculture. And the language in which it mocks them is designed to look celebratory to the stolid reader, and debased to established critics. This book is such a mind storm that we may need a little time to know that it is also, *ting!* literature.

Much the same thing happened with Henry Miller—with whom Thompson has perhaps even more kinship than with Burroughs. Hero of all his books, drowning in sex and drink, Miller makes holy what Thompson makes fundamental: appetite. In both writers, the world is celebrated/ excoriated through the senses. But the taste of the one is for rebellion, of the other for apocalypse writ small.

Apart from the artistry, it is a modestly eschatological vision that lifts "Fear and Loathing" from the category of mere funky reminiscence. It unfolds a parable of the nineteen-sixties palatable to those of us who lived them in a mood—perhaps more melodramatic than astute—of social strife, surreal politics and the chemical feast. And it does so in language that retires neither into the watery sociology of the news weeklies nor the zoo-Zen of the more verbally hip. Far out. Thompson trusts the authority of his senses, and the clarity of a brain poised between brilliance and burnout. (pp. 17-18)

The book's highest art is to be the drug it is about, whether chemical or political. To read it is to swim through the highs and lows of the smokes and fluids that shatter the mind, to survive again the terror of the politics of unreason. Since plot has been scrapped, the whole thing must be done in the details, in cameo sketches and weird encounters that flare and fade into the backdrop of the reader's imagination. These details are technically accurate, which is a contemporary form of literary precision, with all ambiguity intact. (p. 18)

> *Crawford Woods, in* The New York Times Book Review (© *1972 by The New York Times Company; reprinted by permission*), *July 23, 1972.*

"Gonzo Journalism" Hunter Thompson himself calls it, starting [in *Fear and Loathing in Las Vegas*] with a piece of straight reportage, then lighting out here, improvising there, goofing about, wheeling into a Jim Crow act and back again through *Alice's Adventures in Wonderland* to a real-life Nevada off-the-road rally for motor-cycles and dune-buggies or top-level drug conference for assorted cops and lawyers in down-town Las Vegas. "I lost all track of the ratio between what was true and what was not", he admits. For this is mostly stunt work, serial variations with precious little theme; and the variations are all of one glorious super-binge, not on booze but a whole narcotic lab of uppers, downers, screamers, laughers. The effect, for a normal adult, is about as funny as walking into a fairground hall of distorting mirrors. . . . Call me Ishmael! For the whole point on this new picaresque is that the American-style rogue-hero must not merely tease or insult the Silent Majority, but abuse it, outrage it, twist it, hurt it, smash it. . . .

Being Americans, of course, some specious special pleading is to be expected. Note the title out of Kierkegaard. Hist, boys, here comes Captain Ahab once again on the Pequod's classic voyage hunting the great White Whale:

> But our trip was different. It was a classic affirmation of everything right and true and decent in the national character. It was a gross, physical salute to the fantastic *possibilities* of life in this country—but only for those with true grit. And we were chock full of that.

But it is not this kind of pretentiousness—with its banner headline, "A Savage Journey to the Heart of the American Dream"—that gives this book its undoubted, frenzied impetus. It is the version of *The Star-Spangled Banner* re-run as a horror movie. It is the vision of America as a permanent Saturnalia, a wholly self-destructive, kinky free-for-all where anything goes. But humour will keep breaking in; and the introduction of the Samoan attorney Dr Gonzo (*alias* Oscar Zeta Acosta), in his Hawaiian beach-shirt and white rayon bell-bottoms, playing a drug-crazed Sancho Panza to the quixotic hero of this mixed-up quest, is a monstrously comic turn of egomaniacal, vicious nastiness—a kind of Pacific Coast Mr Toad cruising stoned down the desert highway in his hired white convertible Cadillac.

> *"Stoned Rollers," in* The Times Literary Supplement (© *Times Newspapers Ltd., 1972; reproduced from* The Times Literary Supplement *by permission*), *November 3, 1972, p. 1307.*

["Fear and Loathing: On the Campaign Trail '72"] is the best account yet published of what it feels like to be out there in the middle of the American political process. . . . [It] is a mixture of personal narrative, diary entries, tape-recorded interviews and telephone conversations with the candidates and their managers, occasionally irrelevant fantasies and—towards the end when [Thompson] was running past his deadline—an extended interview with himself.

Thompson writes on two levels. On one, he is the journalist observing the candidates in action from any accessible perspective. His comments in this regard are revealing both about the problems of campaign coverage and the differences among the candidates. . . .

On another level, Thompson is defiantly subjective. Unlike his more conventional colleagues, he feels free to denounce hypocritical political maneuvering when he spots it. . . .

Unlike Theodore White's regular reports, which have become as much a part of the electoral institution as the inauguration, "Fear and Loathing" is obviously not an exercise in objective, analytic contemporary history. But neither is it like Norman Mailer's accounts of the conventions, which are, by contrast, less involved with the factual immediacy of politics and more concerned with its symbolic implications. . . .

Thompson's book, with its mixed, frenetic construction, irreverent spirit and, above all, unrelenting sensitivity to the writer's own feelings while on the political road, most effectively conveys the adrenalin-soaked quest that is the American campaign. Crisscrossing the country often two times a day, stopping in hotels, shopping marts and factories in obscure Midwestern towns, Thompson might have been running for office himself. By monitoring his own instincts and observations in the process, he shows us what it must be like for the candidates.

Referring to himself as a "political junkie" who needed the best speed on the market to keep going (the "Zoo plane" on which the journalists covering McGovern traveled was evidently loaded with cocaine, marijuana and hashish), Thompson uses drug imagery throughout the book to describe the effects of campaigning. "There is a fantastic adrenalin high that comes with total involvement in almost any kind of fast-moving political campaign—especially when you're running against big odds and starting to feel like a winner." Citing stories of Humphrey's connections to mob money and of McGovern's placement of spies in Humphrey's campaign, Thompson shows just how compulsive is the trip to win the Presidency in America, and how overwhelming the temptation for the candidates to go outside the law to win.

Must the men who aspire to lead us be put through such an ordeal, living constantly on what Thompson refers to as "the edge"? Perhaps whistlestop and jet-plane campaigning should be abandoned and the candidates should compete solely through the electronic media. I don't know, and neither does Thompson. What Thompson does know, however, is that whatever the campaign procedures, the White House will continue to loom in the imagination of power-addicted men as the glassine-bagged white powder does in the imagination of the junkie. Watergate was the attempted rip-off of a fellow addict. "Fear and Loathing" lets us understand why the men we elect to the Presidency may have needle tracks on their integrity.

> *Tom Seligson, "The Tripping of the Presidency, 1972," in* The New York Times Book Review *(© 1973 by The New York Times Company; reprinted by permission), July 15, 1973, p. 7.*

[*Fear and Loathing: On the Campaign Trail '72*] is the most exciting book written about the 1972 campaign and one of the best about American politics of the last decade. . . .

Fear and Loathing is a New Journalism account of the campaign from before New Hampshire to Miami and beyond, and I'm sure it will be regarded as a classic in the genre. . . .

Thompson discards any pretension to godlike objectivity. Rather than disguising his natural, human bias, he puts it "up front." (p. 120)

Thompson's approach goes beyond that of a New Journalist, first-person school. He is, he tells us, a Gonzo journalist, which means, as near as I can figure it, that he is constantly on the verge of hitting his self-destruct button. He moves from spirit-crushing hotel to spirit-crushing hotel, back and forth across the country, in the amphetamine high of the campaign, strung out on booze and drugs and lost sleep. He's always on the verge of *total-loss-of-control*, ever prepared to don the jacket with the buckles in back. In short, the Gonzo is a wild man. (pp. 120-21)

> *Steven d'Arazien, "Wild Man's View of the Campaign," in* The Nation *(copyright 1973 by the Nation Associates, Inc.), August 13, 1973, pp. 120-22.*

* * *

TREVOR, William (pseudonym of William Trevor Cox) 1928-

Trevor is an Irish-born novelist, short story writer, and playwright now living in England. His work is characterized by a subtle prose style, and his characters, people old and living an isolated existence, are depicted with a sad, whimsical humor. (See also *CLC*, Vol. 7, and *Contemporary Authors*, Vols. 9-12, rev. ed.)

[*The Children of Dynmouth*] is a small failure of transplanted suburban Gothic, but it has its interesting points. Mr Trevor is one of those writers who take a certain masochistic pleasure in being confined by the smallness and meretriciousness of the average English domestic emotions. He sees our lives measured out not in coffee-spoons so much as plastic teaspoons, not to mention boxes of Daz, episodes of *Crossroads* and pints of bogus continental lager. . . .

Timothy Gedge [the central character] is in every way a horror. . . . *The Children of Dynmouth* is the story of how he goes about [realizing his ambitions], by blackmail. . . .

Trevor captures the diseased affability of the junior con-man rather well, in lines of dialogue that seem to marry something namelessly disgusting in their half-conscious ambiguity. . . . The child is definitely repulsive. But all the more reason why the author should not duck out of the consequence of Timothy, which he unfortunately does. . . .

[The conclusion is] very disappointing. Whatever the social likelihoods of Timothy's case might be, he has been brought to a pitch of *literary* malice which can't simply be allowed to fall away [as it does]. Withdrawing his relish of Timothy's evil, and presenting him suddenly as something like a case-history victim, Mr Trevor hops without warning into another mood, almost another genre. He is guilty of failing to respect the impetus generated by his own characterisation, and of reasserting the decencies of life in a way that the whole tendency of the story belies, negates and derides. The old accusation of blowing up a short story idea to novel length is bound to come up too—though Trevor's problem, as he faces the task of doing something impressive with the miniature repressed emotions of a leftover genteel society, entitles him to some sympathy.

> *Russell Davies, "Tiny Tim," in* New States-

man (© 1976 The Statesman & Nation Publishing Co. Ltd.), July 9, 1976, p. 53.

William Trevor characteristically writes a finely wrought story in which the action is wholly dramatized in the Jamesian sense. . . . (p. ii)

[The title story in *Angels at the Ritz*] dramatizes the machinations of a jaded middle-class suburban world. One couple engages in ritualistic exchanges of partners, trying to draw in the couple who engage our sympathies. They escape—narrowly in the husband's case—and the wife finds a renewed sense of life. Such affirmation doesn't ordinarily occur in Trevor's fiction, but this is not to say that he enjoys defeating his characters in their expectations or that he characteristically presents a grim view of life.

The two best stories in the collection—"Last Wishes" and "The Tennis Court"—show how he adumbrates human experience in all its comedy and pathos. Both involve the coming of death and the impact of the modern world upon an older time and society. In "Last Wishes" the reader is so thoroughly drawn into the complicity of the servants that he forgets momentarily the strength of their deception and their greed. . . . In "Last Wishes" one encounters "the territory of unease, the sure-footed sinister prowl around the edges of pain" that a . . . reviewer has remarked in Trevor's short fiction.

"The Tennis Court" has the sureness of effect and brilliance of economy that reveal the signature of a master. The narrator, a middle-aged woman, looks back at the events of her childhood in the summer of 1939, and in recalling that halcyon time on the eve of World War II she presents the last vestiges of Edwardian England. Old Mrs. Ashburton wishes to restore her tennis court at the family manor (now owned by Lloyd's Bank) and in that act to recapture the leisured world of England on the eve of World War I. The party is a great success, but its very success brings pathos in its wake, and Mrs. Ashburton says: "I've had a lovely day," adding: "It's all over. Yet again." In the simplicity of that closing speech lies the heart of the story: the past has been repeated—in an awkward and democratic manner (former tenants attend the party), with little of the ceremony and splendor that marked Edwardian times—but that event fades as quickly and inexorably as the past upon which it has been crudely modeled.

Graham Greene has said that *Angels at the Ritz* is one of the best collections of short fiction, "if not the best collection, since Joyce's *Dubliners*." Before I read the book that claim seemed to me preposterous; afterward I was wholly persuaded of its rightness. (p. vi)

George Core, in Sewanee Review *(reprinted by permission of the editor,* © *1976 by The University of the South), Winter, 1977.*

English novelists continue to work in a realistic and conventional tradition that looks back not to the great Modernists (Joyce, Woolf, Mann, Lawrence, Gide), but to the late 19th century: to a common-sense vision of the world that is adequately expressed in terms of beginnings, middles and ends, and in language that is pragmatic and unadorned. Within such limitations (which are perhaps primarily those of English publishers), a surprisingly rich and humanly engaging literature has been developed, and it is possible to read certain outstanding English novelists of our time—

among them Iris Murdoch, V. S. Naipaul and William Trevor—as "experimentalists" in a special sense. They are far less concerned with formal virtuosity than their American counterparts, and far more explicitly concerned with the moral dimensions of their art. It may safely be said that they are more readable; and many readers might argue that they are more entertaining. . . .

Trevor evokes potentially tragic situations that do not develop into tragedy: He gives life to quite ordinary people—men, women and children—who find themselves locked together by a single event and who are forced to reassess themselves and, as a consequence, their relationships. (p. 13)

Trevor does not force his readers to any clear-cut conclusion. What is unmistakable is his faith in his characters and his exuberant talent in bringing those characters alive in succinct, unsensational terms.

"The Children of Dynmouth" is Trevor's finest novel so far. At its core is a memorable creation—an aimless, sadistic 15-year-old boy named Timothy Gedge who, having no father and virtually no mother, wanders about the seaside town of Dynmouth trying to connect himself with other people. He . . . is tolerated by everyone and liked by no one; by the novel's end he has come close to destroying several people. Timothy's malice arises from his chronic aloneness, so that it isn't possible, as the vicar recognizes, to see the boy as evil. He is a fact of life in Dynmouth, a testimony to Dynmouth's inexplicable failure. . . . Trevor has basically a comic imagination, though he deals with very serious subjects; his novels, for all their anxious moments, manage to end more or less happily.

One comes to detest Timothy Gedge, with his sharp cheekbones, his mocking, moronic conversation and utterly selfish concerns; yet at the same time one is forced to experience Timothy as a natural event—or an Act of God, like flood or famine. He is mean, vicious, silly, idle, tiresome, but he will not go away. (pp. 13, 36)

Timothy's connections with the people of Dynmouth are achieved only through the violation of their privacy and through the violation of his own sanity; in fact he remains utterly alone, one of those deprived, debased individuals who commit terrible crimes without possessing the depth of feeling required to know what they are doing. . . .

Yet such is Trevor's optimism that there may be a place in the pattern of lives even for Timothy; the vicar's wife, who has been unable to have a son, comes to see in Timothy the son who had not been born to her. And so there is the possibility of redemption; or, if not redemption, at least a place in the community. But it is all very tenuous, very problematic. The novel ends abruptly and ironically, and nothing is really resolved.

"The Children of Dynmouth" is a skillfully written novel, a small masterpiece of understatement. Where "Elizabeth Alone" sags and nearly buckles beneath the weight of too many incidental characters and their whimsical lives, "The Children of Dynmouth"—like the powerful "Miss Gomez and the Brethren"—manages to give life to a surprising variety of people, linking them together in the rhythms of a community as well as in the more urgent rhythms of a suspenseful narrative. It is a sensitive and honorable achievement, a work of rare compassion. (p. 36)

Joyce Carol Oates, "More Lonely Than Evil," in The New York Times Book Review (© *1977 by The New York Times Company; reprinted by permission), April 17, 1977, pp. 13, 36.*

*   *   *

TRILLING, Lionel   1905-1975

Trilling, an American essayist, novelist, and short story writer, was one of the twentieth century's most influential critics. His criticism is humanistic and far-ranging, incorporating the concepts and techniques of sociology, psychology, history, philosophy, and political science into the study of literature. He wrote one novel, *The Middle of the Journey*. (See also *Contemporary Authors*, Vols. 9-12, rev. ed.; obituary, Vols. 61-64.)

Each of Trilling's books represents a determination to redeem and enforce the values consecrated in such words as reason, mind, sincerity, pleasure, society, self, and criticism. Witness the attempt to speak up for mind in *Beyond Culture,* self in *The Opposing Self,* idea in *The Liberal Imagination,* virtue in *The Middle of the Journey.* A classic occasion was Trilling's defense of reason, maintained in *Sincerity and Authenticity* in direct opposition to the cult of madness as "the paradigm of authentic existence and cognition," one of the most dismal marks, incidentally, of our current ideology. Trilling's rhetorical method is to surround his god term with a halo as a mark of its presence in history and an indication that he means to assert its continuing validity despite the fact that the time is unpropitious. Sometimes he argues directly and trenchantly in favor of his god term, sometimes he draws upon its ancestral reverberations in the hope that these will be enough, and sometimes he recites the holy word as if it had never been desecrated. . . . [He] speaks up in behalf of mind, but he does not argue the case directly; rather he surrounds mind with a number of terms which have a familial likeness to mind, such terms as order, coherence, inclusiveness, and objectivity. Mind is to be known by the company it keeps and the objects it serves. Trilling recites these several terms as Arnold recited sweetness and light in *Culture and Anarchy,* hoping to make them persuasive by the radiance they bring to the entire scene. He . . . represents the life of mind in such terms that a reader of goodwill could not think of disavowing it. This is to say that Trilling approaches an ethic by way of an aesthetic: a thing is likely to be felt as good if it is felt as beautiful. Trilling is alive to the risk involved in this rhetoric; he has a fine ear for the hum and buzz of current feeling, and a gift for defining it, as in the conflict between Laskell and Maxim in *The Middle of the Journey.* But he is unyielding in his moral preferences. He does not permit the reader to construe mind in any other terms than those endorsed by order, coherence, objectivity, and inclusiveness; that is one part of his rhetorical verve. Gradually the reader comes to feel that values so graciously expounded must be splendid in themselves and that their failure in an ostensibly civilized society would be monstrous. (pp. 429-31)

Denis Donoghue, in Sewanee Review *(reprinted by permission of the editor,* © *1974 by The University of the South), Summer, 1974.*

[Lionel Trilling's] critical achievement is substantial but there has always been a discriminating restraint about it, so that though we could have wished for more book-length works, even more essays, we have to register appreciation of the absence of critical waffling or pudder. In the fictive realm Trilling's output has been even more fastidious—two haunting short stories and, like his fellow countryman, Allen Tate, a single 'classic' novel. The epithet in inverted commas I take from the jacket of the re-issue of *The Middle of the Journey*—a pardonable piece of publishers' usage —and it is worth looking at the novel in the light of the claim for its having acquired such a status in the 28 years since it was first published.

I read the book fairly soon after it came out in England but have never opened it again until now. My memory of it was that its novelistic apparatus corresponded to its intellectual depth; though beyond a conviction that the 'journey' of the title was not completely metaphorical I had forgotten all detail. How fallible literary remembrance is—and what increase in gumption the passing years (both of history and his own age) bring to the reader! Trilling's novel proves to be as measured and resourceful as his criticism. If there is any meaning in the phrase 'a born novelist' we can safely say that he is not one. The characterisation has been well thought out and is convincing, sometimes vivid, but we never really lose the sense of actors carefully dressed for their parts and of the technique governing their appearances and interlinkings and development. There are some Jamesian 'wonderfuls' and a Forsterian sudden death, but we are usually more conscious of the author's artistic concealment of the high names who have influenced him rather than of such influence being betrayed. A modestly Conradian repetition and subsequent elaboration of incidents of narration is perhaps the main feature of the story-telling. . . .

This is a deeply intelligent and therefore, for me, thoroughly enjoyable work. Where it is vulnerable, it seems to me, is where the finally unadjudicated facts of history still cling to it. In the introduction written specially for this re-issue, the author tells us that *The Middle of the Journey* was composed in 1946-47—a decade after the time in which the novel is set. He says, too:

> From my first conception of it, my story was committed to history—it was to draw out some of the moral and intellectual implications of the powerful attraction to Communism felt by a considerable part of the American intellectual class during the Thirties and Forties. . . .

[There] is an element of hindsight in the book's atmosphere, perhaps in the very setting—so far from all the features of the Thirties that made 'parlour radicalism' a term of abuse that in fact precisely fitted not many of those to whom now it might be unamiably applied. (p. 57)

Of course, one has no first-hand knowledge of the epoch as it appeared to a young intellectual New Yorker but, insofar as one can make any valid judgment, the historical nitty gritty in *The Middle of the Journey* seems rather pallid, not uncontrived—somewhat burked, it could be said. (pp. 57-8)

Trilling's view of the novel in general expressed in *The Liberal Imagination,* critical writing roughly contemporaneous with his own novel, would predispose him to precision in matters of social organisation and morality (as against the American drive to fantasy about the social outcast), and indeed his attention to this pays several good dividends.

The social classes in the Connecticut village and their varied reactions to the visiting New Yorkers—this is well done, though the effort of doing it is somewhat apparent and shows how difficult a novel of this kind can be for Americans. (It may well become—if it hasn't already become—just as difficult for us; on account of the English process, already tagged in *The Liberal Imagination,* of 'the middle class . . . in the process of liquidating itself'.)

In 1955 I reviewed (for the *London Magazine*) Trilling's collection of literary essays *The Opposing Self.* Having re-read *The Middle of the Journey* I thought I would look at the later book again (I had reviewed it favourably) to see how *it* stood up. In my notice I had found that:

> The great interest of Trilling's book (apart from its numerous purely literary generalisations and *aperc͑us*) is in the ideas which interconnect all the essays—the ideas of the opposition of the modern writer's self to his society and of his ideal aim nevertheless to project the experience of art 'into the actuality and totality of life as the ideal form of the moral life'.

It may be an indication of Trilling's deepening influence over the last twenty years that one takes this neo-Arnoldian view rather for granted and finds the 'great interest' of *The Opposing Self* more in those 'literary generalisations and *aperçus*'. My notes the second time round almost all referred to pages unnoted on first reading—a tribute to Trilling's fertility rather than my own progress! Quite profound, for example the passages in the essay on Wordsworth referring to Eliot's *The Cocktail Party* and Wordsworth's insistence on 'being', the play denying the 'beatitude', even at low levels, which Wordsworth regarded as the human birthright. I quote a few lines:

> I think it can be shown that every tragic literature owes its power to the high esteem in which it holds the common routine, and the sentiment of being which arises from it, the elemental *given* of biology.

Fully to appreciate that has come to me only through recent experience undergone and poems written. (pp. 58-9)

Roy Fuller, "Trilling at 70," in The New Review *(© The New Review Ltd., 11 Greek Street, London W1V 5LE), April, 1975, pp. 57-9.*

The Middle of the Journey . . . was originally published in 1947, making ([Trilling] tells us in a new introduction) little impact at the time, but gathering something of a reputation as it became more widely read and known. Judged from a literary point of view now that it has been re-issued, one can admire its quiet, mature style, its sudden flashes of intense feeling, its professional capability in stimulating interest while not pretending that anything more dramatic than dawning awareness is likely to happen. For my taste, Trilling is too direct a writer, almost as if he had not quite achieved the leap from the discursive, explicit language of criticism to the world of inferences, the language of the unspoken, which we associate with the novel. Any thought, feeling or motive which affects a character, particularly the hero, John Laskell, is immediately set down on the page. . . .

In the course of a fine essay, 'Manners, Morals and the Novel', Trilling once remarked that in novels, whether they be those of Homer, Dickens or Proust, it is manners that make men. He offered this thrust out of an argument advanced by Henry James that what American novels and novelists lacked by comparison with English ones was what America lacked by comparison with England—a 'thick social texture' of palaces, churches, manor houses, thatched cottages, sporting classes, precise social codes, strong formal conventions. . . . Trilling only spasmodically achieves that 'thick social texture' in *The Middle of the Journey,* so that one is frequently aware of his characters as embodiments of certain attitudes, as pieces in a complex game where the aim is to marry ideological attitudes to their correct emotional affinities.

One explanation for this may be that *The Middle of the Journey* is—or became in the course of writing, as Trilling explains in his new introduction—partly a *roman à clef,* in which the character Gifford Maxim represented that Dostoievskyan ex-communist and professional apostate, Whittaker Chambers, the man who denounced Alger Hiss. . . . Anyway, that's another story, Hiss versus Chambers, and the reader will find no clue to it in *The Middle of the Journey,* not even in the character of Gifford Maxim.

David Caute, "Summer People," in New Statesman *(© 1975 The Statesman & Nation Publishing Co. Ltd.), April 11, 1975, p. 486.*

[Lionel Trilling's] life moved centrally through a number of the key transactions of a vigorous intellectual generation that has greatly shaped our thoughts about ourselves. . . . [After political activism in the 1930s] he began to move more deeply and committedly into literature, not as an escape from politics, but in pursuit of a deeper politics, a more inward view of ideology.

The word he attached to this motion was liberalism, which he defined in a brilliant opening chapter to his book on E. M. Forster. Here he presents liberalism as a full encounter with the intractability its own progressive passions create—the agent of a moral realism which 'is not only the awareness of morality itself, but of the contradictions, paradoxes and dangers of living the moral life'. It was to Matthew Arnold and Forster that he turned for his first two books, and you can see the threads that link him tightly to them. But Trilling's wasn't quite a liberalism in the English vein. He was metropolitan Jewish; his interests were cosmopolitan, political, expansive and concerned with the evolution of minds in literature as a process moving towards 'the modern self-consciousness and the modern self-pity'. Culture was an obsessive term in his thinking, and it was culture split and self-opposing in a modern world in which Freud was the high power. Literature was bound in an intimate politics of culture; it *was* a liberal imagination; liberal, he said, was 'a word primarily of political import, but its political meaning defines itself by the quality of life it envisages, by the sentiments it desires to affirm'. . . .

A key part of Trilling's effort was to recreate the public, political meaning of the novel form, the form, he said in 'Art and Fortune', 'that provides the perfect criticism of ideas by attaching them to their appropriate actuality'. It was also an effort to reach into the roots of the modern mind, as it evolved through romanticism into modernism.

Trilling appeals to a way of talking about this not only as a stylistic but as an intellectual and cultural development that impinged profoundly on to our most intimate selves, our marriages, our family lives, our friendships. 'My own interests,' he said in his essay 'The Modern Element in Modern Literature', where he presents his anxieties about teaching the modern abyss as an historical event for simple contemplation,

> led me to see literary situations as cultural situations, and cultural situations as great elaborate fights about moral issues, and moral issues as having something to do with gratuitously chosen images of personal being, and images of personal being as having something to do with literary style.

The moral realism he spoke for came from this; it was a preference for a controlling sanity of mind; like Saul Bellow and other Jewish writers of the Fifties, he made the claim for a sane, a culturally central romanticism, liberal in cast, which understood the apocalyptic and the adversary but was not drawn in beyond sanity. It was attracted by 'the scent of utopia in men and governments' but capable of seeing pluralistically; it was drawn by that opposing element which prevents us from dying in submission to our culture, yet valued the capacity of reason to mediate between self and culture.

The book that pulls all this together is his novel *The Middle of the Journey.* . . . It is a profoundly subtle work, and while it belongs in line with the great liberal novels of the past, back through Isherwood and Forster to George Eliot, it faces head-on the encounter with the modern revolutionary imperative and the urgent claim of History, that long corridor, flanked by the twin images of Human Suffering and Political Power, in which Gifford Maxim stands, on the way to the moral future. Against that, Trilling sets other romantic imperatives: death, the self-knowledge it commends, the requirements it makes on a life. This does not reject politics—it claims that a good politics is a politics of whole persons. . . .

Trilling's was a mind bounded by culture and history, as all minds are; the problem was to distil from that secular and limiting state an energy and moral purpose. His ideal novel entered society, and discriminated between its appearances and its realities; his ideal mind did the same and applied reason to inevitable alienation. You do this in time and it doesn't always help that you do. There are moral futures that beckon and utopias to lift you. Trilling spoke for caution on their virtuous claims. He saw reason working in a finite world, and he knew—as Laskell, through his childish illness in *The Middle of the Journey,* knew—that things started and finished. Now his career is ended and in later days he felt considerable sourness. He leaves behind a longer question, which is whether the modern liberalism he appeals to is itself going to transcend its historical moment, or also, at a certain point, sourly finish.

Malcolm Bradbury, "Lionel Trilling: End of the Journey," in New Statesman (© 1975 *The Statesman & Nation Publishing Co. Ltd.), November 14, 1975, p. 619.*

In his introduction to ["Of This Time, Of That Place"] in his anthology, *The Experience of Literature,* Trilling explains his own conception of its primary purpose, which is to "present the sad irony of a passionate devotion to the intellectual life maintained by a person of deranged mind." . . . It was, essentially, to be the story of Tertan. But Tertan, the mad student who gives the story its essential structural and thematic unity, is not the primary character whose story this becomes. It is Howe, narrator and professor, whose moral dilemma elevates the story to nearly tragic proportions.

The dramatic situation of the story is relatively simple; it explores the relationship between a young professor of literature and his brilliant but mentally ill student. Through the ironies in their relationship, the underlying themes, far bigger than either Tertan or Howe, emerge. "Of This Time, Of That Place," undertakes to explore the relationships between art and life, between subjectivity and objectivity. These two basic themes are each represented by intermediary issues in the story, and finally connected to each other by specific characters and situations. The result is a surprisingly elaborate structure—surprising because Trilling is handling themes better suited to the novel genre, but without the sense of incompletion or awkwardness that might be expected in a short story—developed through a carefully crafted network of symbols, heavily overlaid with intense dramatic irony. The conflict of science and morality is the intermediary vehicle used to present the first thematic consideration, the problem of subjectivity versus objectivity. Science and morality are placed in polar opposition to each other, and remain irreconcilable throughout the story. Science is equated with both reason and inhumanity, morality with emotion and humanity. The relationships between the issues are all necessarily negative, and in that fact lies the bitterest irony of the story. To follow reason is to turn against feeling in the small but intense universe of the story. Science is the villain, totally correct but abominably immoral. The relationship that should be able to reconcile the paradox—the relationship between Howe and Tertan—fails miserably. Howe, the subjective and emotional poet, must betray Tertan by using the objective verdict of science. The interplay in the roles of Howe and Tertan becomes symbolic not only of the larger issues of the story, but of the connections and disjunctions among those issues. Compromise is not permitted; opposition through paradox is the only norm.

The story opens and closes with a camera scene. The apparently irrelevant camera becomes a major symbol. . . . In [the] first representation, we see the camera as benign and simple. There is no reason to fear it. It is surely "an instrument of precision," as Tertan later calls it, but it still requires human judgment to aid it in its work. There is no mention of the camera again until the end; but in the meantime, Howe and Tertan have met and interacted, loved and struggled, and Howe has betrayed the mad Tertan. Howe's alliance with science has been unwilling, but inevitable; and he has more than a little disgust for his own decision, made on behalf of objective facts. (pp. 1-2)

The camera that was simple and harmless at the beginning of the story became, by the end, a symbol of the cold indifference of science. But it is not only the "precision" of science, and its mathematical indifference, that the camera represents; it is also symbolic of the inaccuracy of science, or at least of its lack of discrimination. The appearance of the camera is deceptive. It is not as correct and precise as it looks. Its "precision" is actually rather sloppy, but it does look impressive. Similarly, the facts of science that condemn Tertan as a madman and grant a Blackburn the sanction and sanctuary of legal sanity, are really imprecise. It is not that science is mistaken, and that Tertan is really sane; Trilling is aware that this mistake in interpretation might be made, and he cautions in his commentary that "nothing, I fear, can reverse the diagnosis of Tertan's illness." . . . Rather, Blackburn is also quite insane, but in a more subtle and insidious, and therefore less perceptible, way. The "instruments of precision" make no mistake about Tertan, whose aberration is glaring, but totally pass over the more vicious and harmful disease of Blackburn. Hilda's camera takes a decent picture, but misses the subtle discriminations of light and shade that the sympathetic human eye can perceive.

Howe in his role as poet and teacher, and Tertan as ironic counterpart to Howe as poet, lay the basic framework for Trilling's exploration of the other major theme, the relationship between art and life. The vehicle for exploring the theme is a discussion of the role of poet in society. (pp. 3-4)

It is through his position as a poet of "precious subjectivism" that Howe's deepest and most ironic connection with the mad Tertan must be viewed. Howe himself never fully realizes why he feels such an intense bond with Tertan, such guilt when he turns his back. He only knows that he *feels,* inexplicably, unreasonably, far out of proportion to any rational explanations. But the parallels are inescapable, and even Howe cannot completely ignore them. Howe has been accused of a kind of madness himself; he has been branded as a danger to the world of literature because his work has no useful connection to the real. But nobody will lock Howe away in a white-walled room for his "disease." His "madness" may earn him professional disapproval, but little else. Tertan, on the other hand, has an illness that does permit society and science to cart him away. In a different time and place, under different circumstances, Tertan would be allowed to babble incoherently (and freely) for the rest of his life, and Howe would be incarcerated. But the accident of time and place lets Howe go free (as it should; he is not really mad at all) and also allows him to be the authority that calls attention to Tertan (as he perhaps must; Tertan really is mad). (p. 5)

As Trilling uses a network of camera symbolism in his representation of the science-morality problem, he uses clothes symbolically in the representation of the art-life theme. Howe carries his doctoral hood and gown proudly: "There were the weightly and absurd symbols of his new profession, and they pleased him." . . . The significance is understated. Trilling has been examining the role of the poet in society, and the gown is an unmistakeable symbol of the academic and intellectual side of Howe's professional life. Howe is engaged in the process of trying to integrate himself emotionally and intellectually, to decide on his role, and then defend it to himself and others. And although he does not like to think of himself as a willfully obscure poet, his chosen route is undeniably one detached from the modern social context. The description of the decorous absurdity of the doctoral hood reasserts this: "Howe carried his voluminous gown over his arm, he swung his doctoral hood by its purple neckpiece, and on his head he wore his mortarboard with its heavy gold tassel bobbing just over his eye." . . . Nothing could be more divorced from context, of time if not place. Tertan, whose dress of "shabby formali-

ty" has elsewhere singled him out from his contemporaries, is present in the final camera scene where Howe is wearing his gown and Hilda is doing a "character study" in light and shade. Tertan is also ridiculously dressed, "in a panama hat . . . [and] a suit of raw silk, luxurious but yellowed." . . . Howe is ironically unaware of the silliness of his pity for Tertan, as he looks at him through an eye covered by an absurd, bobbing tassel. (pp. 6-7)

The question becomes, of course, at whose door must the tragedy of Tertan (or of Howe, for that matter) be laid? Trilling offers no real answers to this or any of the other questions he raises. He connects and connects, but always in negative terms, always with irony. And yet, even caught in an inescapable dilemma, Howe has grown and developed. Even if there are no answers, the issues of art and life, subjectivity and objectivity, brought together in desperately personal connection for one man, have at least made him aware of the question. That is perhaps more than most men experience. And that is far more than most short stories dare to ask.

The idea that gives the story its title—the accident of time and place—does not answer any of the questions, but does make the reasons for the problems clearer, while intensifying the irony. The chance of time and place have brought Tertan and Howe together. The element of time, in particular, pervades the story; Howe feels he must keep Tertan's secret for a somehow important time; time has brought about the changes in circumstances, created the juxtapositions, increased Hilda's camera equipment. If penicillin had been invented, Mr. Alving wouldn't have had a venereal disease. And so on and on. Most important, the particular irony of the art/life, science/morality dilemma is a largely temporal one. Tertan is mad and would be mad in any time and place, as we meet him at the beginning of the story. But his context may have created his madness; or, in another time, his madness would be regarded as harmless, and Howe would have had no weighty decision to make. (It is DeWitt's argument again, turned back on itself.) The science of the time captures the Tertans and lets the Blackburns go by, or even creates them. And the time stresses the poignancy of the predicament of the poet's role in society, makes him a slave to science. It is the time that demands such connections between life and art, and yet maintains a distorted hour, scientifically incorrect, in "academic time" (It lacks ten whole minutes.). The problems raised here will all continue to recur, shaped and shaded by the particular context, but always continued in another generation of cameras and gowns, madmen and poets. (pp. 7-8)

Diana L. George, "Thematic Structure in Lionel Trilling's 'Of This Time, of That Place,'" in Studies In Short Fiction *(copyright 1976 by Newberry College), Winter, 1976, pp. 1-8.*

With the exception of Edmund Wilson, Lionel Trilling was the most influential literary critic in America these past few decades. By "influential" I mean something simple: that a critic's essays be read by a public extending beyond the limits of the academy. (p. 29)

Trilling, while often performing superbly as an interpreter of texts, was not read primarily for literary guidance. His influence had to do with that shaded area between literature and social opinion, literature and morality; he kept returning to "our" cultural values, "our" premises of conduct, for he was intent upon a subtle campaign to transform the dominant liberalism of the American cultivated classes into something richer, more quizzical and troubled than it had become during the years after World War II. One way of saying this may be that he sought to melt ideological posture into personal sensibility.

Trilling's intellectual adversaries—among whom, in earlier years, I was one—felt that his work had come to serve as a veiled justification for increasingly conservative moods among American intellectuals. (pp. 29-30)

[Perhaps] it was . . . true, as some of us felt at the time, that Trilling was providing, not a rationale for a new conservatism, but an inducement for a conservatized liberalism. Nor did he always make it easy for those of us attracted by his wonderful essays to acquiesce readily in the values they advanced. His grave elegance of style, his disinclination toward polemic, his use of uncomfortable terms like "will," "spirit," "sentiment of being"—all these were disturbing in one or another way, making us uneasy in our admiration.

Yet, as I now think back to the years in which Trilling did his major work, I cannot really believe that his conservatism, real or alleged, was the major reason for his influence. What drew serious readers to his work was something else which, at the risk of seeming perverse, I want to call a "radical" approach to culture.

In an age which had yielded to a host of determinisms and virtually took it for granted that literature constitutes some sort of "reflection" of a fixed and given external reality, Trilling believed passionately—and taught a whole generation also to believe—in the power of literature, its power to transform, elevate. . . .

The contrast could hardly be stronger than between [his] belief in the autonomy and originating power of the literary imagination and tendency of some modern critics to see "the text" as inert material to be worked upon or, still more alarming, worked up. Like other human beings, Trilling had his weaknesses, mostly for mannerism, but he never succumbed to mere methodology. When his mind began to work, when his engagement with a novel or poem was spontaneous and strong, there occurred for many readers an experience of opening and enlargement, what T. S. Eliot has called "the full surprise and elevation of a new experience of poetry." Trilling would circle a work with his fond, nervous wariness, as if in the presence of some force, some living energy, which could not always be kept under proper control—indeed, as if he were approaching an elemental power. The work came alive and therefore was changeable, alive and therefore was never quite knowable, alive and therefore could even threaten the very desires and values that first made us approach it. (p. 30)

Circling that living presence we call a novel or poem, never forgetting that it was a shadowed embodiment of a man or a woman's imagination, Trilling would try to connect with it through the strategems of reason. What other strategems does a critic have? Yet what he also responded to most deeply was the possibility of surprise, even of the demonic. Utterly civilized, he kept looking beneath civilization. (pp. 30-1)

Trilling's deep absorption with Freud must have had its source in . . . the sense that Freud recognized, as almost no one else in our time has, the power of imagination to go beyond the routines of mimesis, to startle and terrify us with all that it might *bring up.* Just as Freud saw the role of the analyst as that of a mediator in the battle between what we have made of ourselves and what we have made it from, so Trilling would turn toward a work of literature, attentive to its modes of order and strategies of control but also on the lookout for the unexpected. Freud was probably the single greatest influence on Trilling's work. . . .

It was the sense, then, that Trilling spoke for the imperilled autonomy of our life—for the large possibilities of our private selves and the dangers and betrayals which the modern obsession with self has brought—it was this, I think, that explains the hold he had upon his readers. (p. 31)

> *Irving Howe, "Continuous Magical Confrontation," in* The New Republic *(reprinted by permission of* The New Republic; © *1976 by* The New Republic, Inc.*), March 13, 1976, pp. 29-31.*

The death of Lionel Trilling brings an inevitable pause to literary discourse. For twenty-five years his voice has been compellingly persuasive, inviting people of liberal imagination to join with him in explorations of the life of the mind. It can be said of him what he once said of Edmund Wilson, that "he seemed to represent the life of letters in an especially cogent way, by reason of the orderliness of his mind and the bold lucidity of his prose." (p. 302)

Trilling's own style reveals much of his intellectual persuasions. It circles cautiously around the truth it seeks, tentatively, even hesitatingly, a step forward here, then sideways, or perhaps a movement backward, but ever circling closer and closer with a quick eye and with a rhythm and grace of movement which certifies competence and insures success. His dialectic suggests that, yes, of course, some one observation is precisely true, but that this other also requires profound consideration, so that, taken together, and joined with other facts, and with other assumptions intervening, they finally reach a conclusion which his verbal dexterity guarantees indestructible.

There are few green fields, little "impulse from the vernal wood," in Trilling's graceful persuasions toward intimacies with the cluttered moral landscape of literature. Confined to urbanity, in a cultural metropolis which talked with profound excitement about the fragmented world within and without its gates, he meticulously and with conciliatory quiet compassion reminded "the talkative and agonizing present" that some of what are called truths may be thought of as eternal, even venturing to join John Keats in reminding them that there is something even more important than poetry, "that an eagle is not so fine a thing as truth." (pp. 302-03)

It may be that we will best remember a younger Lionel Trilling who assured us that the "idea of unconditioned spirit is of course a very old one, but we are probably the first people to think of it as a realistic possibility and to make that possibility part of our secret assumption." He went on after that, of course, to superimpose mind upon spirit, but the secret assumption has in many of us prevailed. For it is the spirit of Lionel Trilling which lives on—his sweetness, grace, compulsive high seriousness and compassion, his insistence that mind can matter, and that literature can feed mind and make possible the luxury of the discovery of self. This is his legacy, which we receive with gratitude, hoping that we can invest it well. (p. 304)

Lewis Leary, "Lionel Trilling 1905-1975," in Sewanee Review *(reprinted by permission of the editor,* © *1976 by The University of the South), Spring, 1976, pp. 302-04.*

U

UPDIKE, John   1932-

Updike is an American novelist, short story writer, essayist, poet, critic, and writer of works for children. Throughout his writing, which is characterized by subtlety of perception and exactness of prose, one can trace Updike's mythic and Biblical symbolism. His allusiveness provides a kind of substructure to his works in which he explores and explains human nature. Death and sex are focal concerns. (See also *CLC*, Vols. 1, 2, 3, 5, 7, and *Contemporary Authors*, Vols. 1-4, rev. ed.)

John Updike's novels show a man's marriage as his fate. No one has done more to explode male freedom as a myth than Updike in novels of American men whose lives, from cradle to grave, are structured by women. His characters are the philanderers who seem freewheeling until the press of Updike's intelligence reveals them as captives in that velvet glove, the female presence. Often accused of being narrow in his concerns, Updike may in fact have anticipated that, of all the revolutionary currents of the past decade, the one that would last is sexual. No other male writer has probed so single-mindedly a man's need of women or the anger dependency inflames. *Marry Me* is about a man who, bewitched between his mistress and his wife, finds his destiny is sexual calamity. This superb, irresistible novel is a subtle exposure of what you might call tender malice. . . .

Updike's groaning humor captures the disparity between the dreamlike pleasures expected between the "lover" and his "mistress" and the hesitancy of the suburban swinger. . . . [In] the most sophisticated situation comedy imaginable, Updike achieves an absolutely hypnotic novel of sexual suspense in which a man and woman find their perfect love moves leave them check-mated. Why can't *amor vincit omnia?*

Updike uses an ordinary suburban love affair for the exposure of that failed warrior, the American prisoner of sex. Jerry's chains are forged by psychological and social trends that split the dream of love from a man's capacity for loving. Updike is the D. H. Lawrence of our time, opening up the male heart not in terms of myth but in realistic fiction that unsentimentally shows those relations between the sexes that head toward antagonistic love. The sexual revolution emerges in Updike's fiction as those psychological and social trends that both define maleness as sexual responsibility for women and at the same time produce men who cannot help but needle, belittle and wound the sweetest blonde beloved. Jerry and Sally are not just superbly realized characters but Updike's prototypes of those new "revolutionary" products: the man engulfed by self-hatred and anger, the woman who is all unambivalent sex.

What Updike bares in his beleaguered male chauvinists are the forces that keep men riveted on women as the solitary source of meaning in life. His novels open up a feminized world. . . . Feminization is to love as mulch to roses, for the traditional triangle (two men fighting for one woman) is replaced by one (two women competing for one man) produced by the sexual availability of women and the scarcity, that Jerry loves to note, of men as interesting as he is. . . .

St. George has his dragon, Sir Galahad his grail; Updike's men have only their women to justify their aggression and define them as men. (p. 437)

Updike puts life together as a sophisticated Oedipal knot in which a man is tied at both ends. His men fear being in control, in charge, but are equally afraid of being suffocated and controlled. Their inhibitions bring them the worst as sons and lovers. Lawrence's famous son thought he would be a lover when his mother died. Updike's heroes know how to keep their mothers alive forever by remaining in the box of coolness and contempt that is their mothers' personality. Jerry virtually marries his mother or rather maneuvers his wife into an asexual, maternal protectiveness toward him. Resenting the flatness of their life together, he is drawn toward a woman who is wonderfully greedy for pleasure. Yet he does his best to ruin her need for him, uses sex as an instrument of revenge and his shows of tenderness to tie his women in knots. . . .

Why can't Updike's men live happily, if incestuously, with both in the postpill paradise? Sex, Updike implies, frees men for other things, but binds women deeply to the men who please them. After the most ecstatic experience the couple is often left upset; the man wants to please (Updike's men think like gentlemen), but knows he cannot give the woman what he thinks she wants (quaintly, it's always marriage). (p. 438)

Updike's defense against despair is style, the spectacular management of perspective to overlook disaster. In conversation, he once spoke of a dream he had at 14 of a knight in armor who pursued a Polynesian girl across Europe. On her island he finds her, looks at her through a palm frond and dies. "I never wrote that novel, the historical one," he remarked. But Updike imprinted its message in novels where to look too closely is to diminish the ideal woman with her own reality and to die a little oneself. . . .

Updike is not a sexual materialist. He is an idealist, perhaps by necessity. In *Aaron's Rod* Lawrence worshipped the penis. Updike arrives at male narcissism by the modern route of irony, mocking Jerry's vision of his erection as the Bodily Ascension. Updike's Lawrentian religion makes sex the great reconciler. Sex as the origin and the goal, the moment of eternity, the mortality that feels like omnipotence, reconciles the conflicts of characters whose greatest fear is that the dead part of themselves may defeat the living. In *A Month of Sundays* Reverend Marshfield jokes that there is no more beautiful phrase than "sexual object." Updike's characters are so in love with their objective that they cannot help, within the limits of the bed, loving the women with whom they achieve it. How should women feel? Like Yeats's Crazy Jane? She confides: "Though like a road / That men pass over / My body makes no moan / But sings on; All things remain in God." Updike's happiest characters are those who do not lose the power to believe there are Janes who make it all possible. . . .

The sign of Updike's grace as a writer is the superb clarity with which he renders the man bewitched by his ambivalences. Not since *Rabbit, Run,* one of the finest novels of the past twenty years, has Updike written with such hard beauty of a man endlessly wandering the labyrinth of his own needs, irresistibly childlike in his faith in the magic of a woman, and abusively fearful of broken spells. *Marry Me* is a compassionate judgment of one kind of married man that brings to mind St. Augustine's remark, "I kept my heart from assenting to anything, fearing to fall headlong, but by hanging in suspense I was the worse killed." (p. 439)

> *Josephine Hendin, "Updike as Matchmaker," in* The Nation *(copyright 1976 by the Nation Associates, Inc.), October 30, 1976, pp. 437-39.*

John Updike is inventive, witty and bright, with the stamina needed to hold his place as a literary figure, but "Marry Me" is not one of Updike's better performances. He calls the book a valentine, a romance not a novel, in part I suspect to get the reader in a genial mood for much of the sentimental nonsense that follows. Jerry and Sally, satisfactorily but incompletely married to others, are in love. Their romantic dilemma is set in a soft-focus greeting card world: lovers on the beach, they are silhouetted in the religious moment of their doomed passion. The time is 1962, the too recent past, the golden years of the Kennedy Administration, a historical allusion that is never realized except for Jerry's pretentious statement: "Maybe," he says, "our trouble is that we live in the twilight of the old morality, and there's just enough to torment us, and not enough to hold us in." And maybe, if we think about it, this could be said of any decade in this century including, for a church-going suburbanite like Jerry, the 1970's. Sally, a beautiful blonde, reads Moravia and Camus, eliciting from her lover the remark, "You're so intelligent." When he points out to her that if they run off together she'll miss her children, Sally says, "You're so wise, Jerry." Love does reduce us to this sort of twaddle, I suppose, but it is embarrassing

even in the cause of accuracy to overhear these endearments.

Though Sally and Jerry are intended partly as prototypes set apart from reality in Updike's modern allegory of sex and sin, I cannot forgive him these lovers. With their quickly sketched-in backgrounds they are under-imagined; she, a magnificent animal, one of Updike's strapping beauties; he, the eternally boyish Updikean stud, is afraid of death, assured of life only through his sexual transgression. Richard, Sally's bull-necked husband, a coupon-clipping Ivy League dropout, has an undiscovered and less passionate affair with Ruth, Jerry's civilized and competent wife. The irony of their failure at romantic love only underscores the delicious predicament of the principals. In the entanglement of these four there are endless telephone calls, visits, trysts, the machinations of soap opera. After the great confrontation scene the two couples withdraw to their cozy Connecticut homes and Sally, sleepless and anxious, phones Jerry. Remembering a time when her lover had insomnia, she says ". . . I couldn't see what you were so worried about. Now I know." "Life is worrisome," he concedes and that's all it is in "Marry Me," not worth losing sleep over.

In calling this book a romance John Updike diverts the judgment of his audience, as Graham Greene has done by sorting out novels from entertainments. In "A Month of Sundays" he calls out attention to the fact that he is working in the tradition of Hawthorne's great romances. Does he intend then in "Marry Me" that the affairs of Sally and Jerry and Ruth and Richard should be seen as an elaborate joke about the dead end of the Puritan spirit? I don't honestly know, but I don't feel that there is a rich moral ambiguity here that I am missing, just indecision on Updike's part. He wants to allude to the idea of romance much as he does to the historical time of the early '60's, as an intellectual prop, without giving himself to the complexities that such allusions entail. In the same way he has given his longer works in the past an overlay of modern Protestant theology to provide him with portentous existential lines about doom and disaster that need not cut too deep into the comfortable living hell of suburbia.

And as though he mistrust his own considerable talent he hankers after myth ("The Centaur"), fantasy ("A Month of Sundays"), romance ("Couples," "Marry Me") to enhance his work, then only toys with them. The combination of the actual and the imaginary is fatal for him, and the fact is that his gift for realism, his own perfect sense of the everyday, becomes sufficiently important when he does not strain for the effect: "Museums and Women," "Wife Wooing," some of the early Olinger stories and the more recent autobiographical pieces are examples of how fine Updike can be when he plays it straight with his material. He captures a whole era gracefully and responsibly in "The Hillies" and "When Everyone Was Pregnant."

The theology, however, always presents a problem, and I cannot help feeling it is an interest of Updike's, never, as in Graham Greene, a conviction: it intrudes upon psychological insight. Thus, rather programmatically, Richard (like Freddy Thorne in "Couples") is a brutish atheist and Jerry, the dear irrational believer, can rejoice "that he had given the enemy, the darkness, an eternal wound. With the sword of his flesh he had administered Christ's revenge." Onward sexual soldiers. It is the pompous prose, the churchy elevation of language that pushes too far here. "The fact is," Hawthorne tells us, "in writing a romance, a man is always—or always ought to be—careening on the utmost verge of a precipitous absurdity and the skill lies in coming as close as possible without actually tumbling over."

The two couples in "Marry Me" are not only absurd, they are ordinary. Despite the slight comic tilt given his characters, and the indication that we are involved in a novel of manners, Updike's tone is indulgent and sympathetic throughout, never clearly satiric. I can't believe that the same man who writes perceptive reviews for "The New Yorker," who has written so many nicely turned, psychologically adept short stories and the coherent lyric novel "Of the Farm" can turn out the adolescent idealization of women we find here or the cardboard tug-at-the-heart kids who lurk at the edges of Updike's obsession with adultery. . . .

I think this curiously bad book, the entire romance, takes place in a hallucinated world. The realistic touches . . . are gestures toward a physical world that tug at the dream. "Marry Me" is a replay of the themes that appeared with some cumulative force in "Couples" and again with over-exuberance in "A Month of Sundays."

In the end, Jerry, sweet passive soul, slips completely into his fantasies, so the old affair, edges washed smooth by the years, is always there for him to enjoy. In his mind his lost love says: *"I do have you, like the sea has Orion." "But they're gods, and we were very simple, like you once said. We were caught at being human."* So much for latter day Christian guilt: it dissolves into wistful sensibility. (p. 2)

> *Maureen Howard, in* The New York Times Book Review *(© 1976 by The New York Times Company; reprinted by permission), October 31, 1976.*

[Despite] Updike's many cunning variations on the American husband tied round and round by knots of his own "moral" devising, Jerry [the protagonist of *Marry Me: A Romance*] is the usual Updike husband, and his plight is the same. How to love oneself, the other woman, one's wife, and "God" all at the same time.

Updike is by now a positive virtuoso at drawing every facet of personal style out of himself and every fantasy out of his characters. *I dwell in possibility,* sang the great maiden poet in Amherst. Too much possibility is trouble, especially when there is this American contradiction of love, sex and marriage conceived as separate elements. From the headlong love scene on the lovers' favorite beach with which the novel begins to the brilliantly alternating scenes of fantasy and reality with which Updike winds up poor Jerry's tortured yet plausible circumambience of himself and everyone else, Updike writes all this out at the top of his powers, his knowledge of American byways, and his tenderness for Jerry.

In its own way *Marry Me* is as original in its development as it is familiar in its situation. There is a felt insistence on the truthfulness of Jerry's confusion as well as on its pathos and humor. We are down to the bare bones of "personality" and "relationships." These are our fixtures, our themes, our American grammar. I wonder if people so overburdened with the world's goods ever felt so naked and exposed before. To show the burden of the nakedness itself is a great accomplishment.

Yet Updike subtitles his book "a romance." It *is*, at the end of many false turnings for Jerry, a love story finally. But in the course of carrying some immensely complicated suburban freight to a necessarily difficult conclusion, Updike again superimposes his own concern with God, death and Karl Barth on a cartoonist just not real enough to carry it. Even his much-mentioned "fear" is not real. The particular weakness of Updike's fiction is that he uses the same man over and over. Despite his playful intelligence and faith in his novelist's power of fantasy, he is unable to disguise this. Indeed, even women roughly of his own generation and professional circle are equally quite dim. It is the older men, like the father in *The Centaur* and the father in *Rabbit Redux,* who are in no danger of melting into Updike's one big situation: the marital tangle.

Where characters are indistinct, blur into each other, become essentially anonymous, we get an excess of style, of meditative fluency. Updike is always at his best in handling the social matter: cars, children, parties, the drinks, the kitchen talk late at night, the bitter sympathy between women rivals for the same man who equally mistrust him. There is all that American role playing, very real indeed when we are all in suburbia and find our only models in each other. But the *people* in this book are just not interesting.

So the contradiction between the momentum of the book (very brilliant indeed) and the characters being pushed along by it *is* a complication. (p. 23)

> *Alfred Kazin in* The New Republic *(reprinted by permission of* The New Republic; *© 1976 by The New Republic, Inc.), November 27, 1976.*

Infidelity has always been a favorite theme in Updike's fiction, delineated with a precision of social detail and emotional nuance quite unusual in contemporary writing. In *Marry Me*, this theme is combined with Updike's beautifully communicated nostalgia for Camelot, where adultery retains the grace of self-delusion and even a certain pastoral innocence, and through which Updike is led back once again into his accustomed fictional landscape. Even more sensitively than in the past, he deals with the complicated emotional longings of the upper middle class, the dwellers in suburbs, his characters attempting to live out their nearly Jamesian subtleties of thought and feeling in a world of traffic snarls and lawn parties and marital mayhem. They've even got religion: Jerry Conant, an incurable (if at times not quite credible) romantic, conducts his affair with Sally Mathias with one eye trained upon perdition: "It's between death and death," he tells her. "To live without you is death to me. On the other hand, to abandon my family is a sin; to do it I'd have to deny God. . . ."

The entire story hinges upon Jerry's religious qualms, in fact, since without them he would be free to marry Sally and there would be no novel. It is this tension between desire and enforced conscience which creates some of the most finely humorous scenes in all of Updike; there is a uniform lightness of touch throughout, surely earning the book its designation as "a romance." But at times this lightness becomes exasperating: Updike writes so well, one can't help wishing he would be more serious. Jerry and

Sally carry on their affair through conversations that often contain the special poignance of a doomed romance, but more often are simply inane; although they both have recognizable emotional experiences as human beings, they seem always to retreat finally from the knowledge they gain (they are both highly intelligent people) into an immaturity of sentiment, not to mention behavior, which is meant to be funny but is often quite boring. The most pertinent example of this is Jerry's fear of God, which finally seems no more than an excuse, a way of avoiding the fact that he is incapable of sustaining a mature relationship; as a character he cannot bear the thematic weight placed upon him, and this is in some degree true of the other characters as well.

The other half of Updike's amorous quadrangle does little to deepen the novel. Early on it seems that Jerry's wife Ruth may attain a certain stature as the woman scorned, but her ultimate response to the pain is a series of catty maneuvers—combined with a growing insensitivity to her children—through which she tries desperately to win Jerry back, a dubious goal at best. Sally's husband, though badly treated by everyone, is a thoroughly unlikable brute and deserves no better. It is in "The Reacting of Richard," the penultimate chapter of *Marry Me*, that the particular ugliness of Updike's fictional milieu begins to surface. Richard is at least blunt and matter-of-fact as he attempts to deal with his wife's infidelity, and the reaction of the other characters to him illustrates well the aura of delusion and immaturity in which they have cloaked themselves all along.

But in spite of one's eventual dislike of all its characters, *Marry Me* remains an immensely likable novel. Part of this is a matter of tone: one cannot criticize Updike too harshly for a lack of seriousness, for he handles lightness so well; he maintains an affectionate omniscience as his characters live out their complex fantasies, seeming to preside over them like a proud father over a group of particularly spoiled children. But the novel's real merit is in its language, in the uncanny supple elegance of Updike's prose. He most nearly succeeds in making Jerry Conant likable when he has him say to Sally, in all seriousness: "You're like a set of golden stairs I can never finish climbing. I look down, and the earth is a little blue mist. I look up, and there's this radiance I can never reach." Or when Jerry watches his children over a late-night snack, thinking: "The children in pajamas seemed soft moths bumbling at candles of milk." The writing is amazingly versatile—especially for a writer who has often been considered, wrongly I think, limited and "precious"; Updike's prose can convey the poetry of everyday sentiments, it often contains a satiric bite worthy of Jane Austen, and it communicates in a series of beautifully orchestrated scenes the continual frustration and evanescence of human relationships. *Marry Me* will certainly do Updike's reputation no harm: it is one of his better books. But from a writer of his sensitivity and talent, one cannot help expecting that the best is yet to come, that we will receive at last the large, complex, ambitious work for which this "romance" can only be a preparation. (pp. 207-08)

Greg Johnson, "Updike's Infidelities," in Southwest Review *(© 1977 by Southern Methodist University Press), Spring, 1977, pp. 207-08.*

"The Poorhouse Fair" is a visionary novel which attempted to peer some 20 years into the future: This places its action in 1977, so that we can appraise the author not only as a writer, but as a prophet too. His pen was better than his crystal ball. He foresaw a popular culture featuring "Hispanic" influences and a sexual slide into mild voyeurism. He missed the violence of the 60's, as well as the drug scene and so-called sexual revolution of the past two decades. The old people in "The Poorhouse Fair" are untamed by television. Only his most general predictions come to pass: the collapse of public morale and the spiritual reduction of the whole country to a "poorhouse."

In his introduction, Updike says that the model for "The Poorhouse Fair" was Henry Green's similarly visionary novel, "Concluding." While a comparison of the two books is unfair because Green had half a dozen novels behind him, it does illustrate the difference between a mature writer fully in control of his effects, and a very young writer at the mercy of his.

Green's richly textured prose is lyrical and evocative, while Updike's is more like a virtuosity that turns back on itself. Green describes landscape and action, while Updike describes description. The heroes of both novels are elderly men. Green's Mr. Rock is irresistible: The long perspective of his old age has turned him into an involuntary poet who sees vistas everywhere. Updike's Mr. Hook is never more than an unrealized scheme for an elderly man who was not very much to begin with and whose most tangible and moving quality is his failing sight.

"The Poorhouse Fair" is much thinner than either of the "Rabbit" novels. Updike's early prose style is too rich for the tenants of the poorhouse. His ambition was greater than the people he could project, and all he could do was bedeck and encumber them with it. (p. 12)

Anatole Broyard, in The New York Times Book Review *(© 1977 by The New York Times Company; reprinted by permission), April 17, 1977.*

Marry Me is likely to sound trite in summary. Set in Connecticut in the early 1960s it is the story of a love affair. Jerry Conant and Sally Mathias are thirty years old; each is married and the parent of three children. They come to feel that they must divorce in order to start a new life together. But whereas Sally is willing enough to leave her husband, Richard, with whom she has been at odds for some time, Jerry finds it painfully difficult, for a mixture of religious and personal reasons, to part from his wife and children. . . .

"This is not a situation hitherto unexplored in fiction", concedes the blurb, as well it might. Everything depends on the purpose of the story and the quality of the telling. John Updike shows himself, as always to be a craftsmanlike and elegant narrator. *Marry Me* is structured with precise, but unobtrusive symmetry. . . .

Throughout [Updike] moves easily between the realistic and the symbolic: episodes or details apparently random take on figurative significance and serve as commentary or omen. Within the tidy formal framework John Updike is faithful to the messiness, the fluctuations, the banalities of an extramarital affair. He is an acute observer of shifts of mood or perspective, of sudden gaieties or timidities. He mimics skilfully the private dialects of love. *Marry Me* has a page-to-page liveliness and plausibility that makes for easy reading. . . .

But all these are virtues that I see rather than feel. Somehow, despite the accomplishment, the general effect is thin, tinny. . . .

John Updike's characters remain shadowy, and it is easy to see why. He invests so much of his creative energy, so many of his words, in brief moments of awareness, small sensual experiences, that more important kinds of information have to be conveyed hastily, and remain inert. . . .

Like some of John Updike's other novels *Marry Me* is delicate in complexion but deficient in bone. Jerry Conant is supposed to be a designer of television commercials, but we gain no sense of his working life, or of what it might mean to him. Only belatedly do the six children come to represent more than six Christian names and a single broken collarbone. The context within which the characters act or talk —talk, mostly—is too theoretical for words or deeds to have much defining force. . . .

The characters are insufficiently realized for their behaviour to seem either predictable or unpredictable. Richard Mathias, who, alone of the four, is presented consistently from without, is the only one to achieve physical presence, a distinctive speech style, and some weight of identity.

These criticisms have, perhaps, as much to do with the purpose behind John Updike's novel as with the quality of its execution. . . . One is most inclined to praise *Marry Me* for its honesty, for the faithfulness with which the author has recorded small humiliations, petty ignobilities. But why invent any such record? It is difficult to read this novel without an embarrassed sense of intruding on some private exercise in expiation, exorcism, transcription or hypothesis.

> *Michael Irwin, "Jerry & Sally & Richard & Ruth," in* The Times Literary Supplement *(© Times Newspapers Ltd., 1977; reproduced from* The Times Literary Supplement *by permission), April 22, 1977, p. 477.*

When John Updike describes his new novel as 'a romance,' and when he appends a little lyric by that great divine Robert Herrick, we know that somehow, somewhere, it will all mean something. He has always been a cautious and deliberate writer, avoiding Bellow's airy nonsense and Heller's rambling blandness. 'Marry Me' could be a question, a statement or a command but Updike carefully locates it at the back of the narrative, not so much a form of words as a state of mind which the whole novel aspires toward but never quite reaches. The book is not really a romance, rather a perpetually interesting postponement of one. . . .

The book is full of intense but articulate conversations, each of the characters tingling with suppressed anxieties and strange fears. . . . Everyone is bothered by the oppression of sheer circumstance, and this is where Updike comes into his own.

It is the sheer materialism of Updike's prose which is amazing. His characters' lengthy protestations are often ironically presented and generally ambiguous, but the physical world—everything 'out there'—is substantially and exactly defined. Updike crowds his narrative with secondary characters and the solid, unblinking world of objects always intrudes as an obstacle and at the same time as a challenge—the challenge to change it. But it never is changed: 'The distant fisherman twitched his pole and birds in the trees around them released a shower of commentary. The grocery bags by her elbow rustled—the ice cream melting, the cans of frozen orange juice thawing. Affairs, Ruth saw, like everything else, ask too much. We all want a fancy price, just for existing.'

And so the Lutheran conscience pirouettes uneasily in a world of ice-cream and dripping orange juice. What are you meant to do? Do you say 'Marry me' to the perfect lover and damn the consequences? Or do you just delay the issue all the time, and live in a state of postponed death? If it's difficult for people to make the choice, it's even more difficult for novelists. . . . This may be a heavy albatross to hang around Updike's already fleshy neck. But it is a choice which his book continually raises, and eventually tries to resolve. . . .

[There is a] two-dimensional quality which keeps the dialogue on a sharp edge, and which prevents Updike's people from turning into the stock characters they could otherwise so easily become: his narrative never stays in one place long enough for anyone to get caught in a fixed position. It is the great strength of Updike's writing, and of all good American writing, that the variety and the colour of the present moment—however cunningly evoked, however mobile and substantial it may appear—is seen to be a patina behind which murmur anxieties, fears and memories which no amount of Western opulence and rationality can heal. (p. 22)

[A] tacked-on, slightly artificial ending . . . goes against the grain of the rest of the novel. There is an illusion, in Updike's work, of a vast mountain of detail balanced precariously on its end. He is a very eerie writer, who exercises all the weight of sensuous, material descriptions in order to demonstrate that they're really just grand theatrical props, which could be blown away if someone blew hard enough. But nobody ever does. The 'real' world keeps coming back, filling in all the cracks and gaps which had been momentarily vacated. It is this uneasy sense of a vacuous but stubborn reality which Updike places before us again and again in his novels—and never so well as in this one. The fact that he does it so cleverly marks him above most of his contemporaries in the United States. (pp. 22-3)

> *Peter Ackroyd, "Paradise Lost," in* The Spectator; *(© 1977 by* The Spectator: *reprinted by permission of* The Spectator), *April 23, 1977, pp. 22-3.*

Of [the] five major [American novelists: Nabokov, Bellow, Mailer, Updike, and Pynchon,] Updike seems to me smaller than the rest. In his steady, tender, even melting realism, he is our clearest descendant of F. Scott Fitzgerald and, most important, almost the only male novelist in America who can imagine women and children without contempt, indeed with affection and esteem. He may be our lesser Chekhov or Turgenev, quietly working away while the bullies are fighting over who gets to play Tolstoy, who Dostoyevsky. His gentleness and his delicacy, his oversweet style, his good humor and his 1950's caution all reinforce one another. But if he hasn't shown the intensity or risky intelligence of the others, there is in Updike a wonderful civility and allegiance to the democracy of letters that contrasts most attractively with the four other yawping imperial selves. Updike's finest books are "Of the Farm," an Oedipal tale that is all poignancy (as its Jewish cousin

Portnoy was all razzmatazz); the paired novels "Rabbit Run" and "Rabbit Redux," of which the latter, re-read five years after its appearance, unhappily seems more talky and tendentious than successfully topical; and, on a lower level of success, "The Centaur" and "Bech: A Book." Updike's more recent books—with the exception of his second collection of articles and reviews, "Picked-Up Pieces," which confirms his status as a first-rate literary journalist—have been weak, as if his attention has been elsewhere and he has just been going through familiar motions, idling. (pp. 3, 36)

Richard Locke, in The New York Times Book Review *(© 1977 by the New York Times Company; reprinted by permission), May 15, 1977.*

V

VARGAS LLOSA, Mario   1936-

Vargas Llosa is a Peruvian novelist now living in Spain whose works generally revolve around satirical assessments of life's institutions. The military, church, and brothel, for example, are, as Vargas Llosa views them, potentially dangerous institutions because they force pure human instincts into ritualistic expressions. Critically acclaimed for his masterly use of juxtapositions, time sequences, and naturalistic devices, Vargas Llosa has received many awards and prizes. (See also *CLC*, Vols. 3, 6, and *Contemporary Authors*, Vols. 73-76.)

Conversation in the Cathedral is not only cinematic in the sense defined by Eisenstein [in *Film Form*] but a masterpiece of montage as well, a massive assault on simultaneity that properly calls to mind not only the works of master directors but of those authors whom Eisenstein himself mentions: Flaubert, Dickens, Joyce.

Now I am not suggesting that *Conversation* is the only cinematic novel to come from Latin America; rather, I am saying that *Conversation* is the most fully cinematic in the sense understood by the early Eisenstein. (pp. 31-2)

[The] narrative method of *Conversation* is the book's meaning and there is no better way of getting at that method than by selectively linking the elements in Eisenstein's description of montage with passages from the novel. (Note that this expository method, however, is one of linking, not collision. We have yet to achieve criticism that is cinematic.)

"Primo: photo-fragments of nature are recorded." Whether you are considering the complexly multiple points of view which fragment Parts I and III or the fragments complexly multiplying the points of view in Parts II and IV, the basic unit of *Conversation* is a "brick" of relatively flat prose describing or narrating, through dialogue, the political, social or personal events that might be found in any contemporary naturalistic novel. In fact, for Vargas Llosa, Nature *is* Naturalism. His photo-fragments are all naturalistic. So certain readers, considering the book with the text very close to their noses, only see that he is writing a political novel of what happened during the Odría regime, a novel that tells it like it was according to the deterministic laws of heredity and environment established by Zola. These readers are not wrong. No more wrong, say, than readers who argue that the fair scene in *Madame Bovary* is

about the courting of a married lady and the awarding of prizes to farmers. After all, if the matter of *Conversation* is dreary determinism, the manner of the prose is also about as drab as you can find without resorting to journalism. The conversations themselves are so low-keyed that when they remind you of cinema it is of *cinema vérité*. The pitch of the book, read in the tradition of Naturalism, is so low that you can lose all sensitivity to it. . . . (p. 32)

"Secundo: these fragments are combined in various ways." What such a reading completely overlooks is the organization of those nearly flat fragments, large and small, into patterns of juxtaposition—linking and colliding—which properly qualify as montage.

As an example of the first category, look at this passage:

> Santiago put his arm around her waist, Popeye put a hand on her knee, and Amalia a slap: none of that, child, no touching her. But Popeye returned to the attack: devil, devil. She probably even knew how to dance and was lying that she couldn't, come on, confess: all right, child, she accepted.

Here everything from punctuation to absence of "stage" directions promotes a linking of actions and words, speech and description, image and image, point of view and point of view. With almost no terminal indication, the syntax glides on commas while the dialogue slides in with no quotation marks. Where there is terminal punctuation, as between the last and next-to-last sentence, the period indicates a juxtaposition rather than a break: here of the physical gestures of Popeye concurrent with Amalia's saying "devil, devil" and the thought of Santiago that she is lying. Each unit, phrase, clause or sentence is a "brick" and the montage is of the simplest, descriptive or narrative kind. I say "simplest" meaning cinematographically simple. Almost all readers will recognize the complexity of the passage from a literary point of view. Still, the montage effect, simple as it is, is the main interest in the passage.

By way of contrast, examine the ending of one fragment at the bottom of [one page] with the beginning of the next at the top of [the next]:

> Ambrosio and Ludovico were chatting and smoking by the door. They threw away their cigarettes when they saw him: to San Miguel.

"Take the first turn to the right," Santiago
said, pointing. "That yellow house, the old
one. That's right, here."

In this case, the "bricks" or shots are longer and the juxtaposition, still of an apparently linking kind, is more daring:
Cayo Bermúdez gets into his car and orders Ambrosio to
drive him to San Miguel and the very next thing we "see"
is Santiago ordering Sparky to turn right. The linking is
accomplished by the automobile motif; but in fact, the linking is far more of a collision between opposites, for who
could, apparently, be more polar than Cayo and Santiago?
Here, in this synthetic montage, Vargas Llosa is speaking
to us directly. . . . (pp. 32-3)

These two purposefully chosen examples—purposeful in
their relative neutrality and minor import—of course do not
exhaust the ways in which Vargas Llosa juxtaposes the
elements of his combination but they do suggest the order
or hierarchy of those juxtapositions, ranging from the predominantly functional on to the markedly expressive. . . .

[In other examples] there is no real collision nor is there
any temporal or spatial simultaneity to warrant the juxtaposition. Rather the simultaneity exists in the text alone and
while the braiding of [several] speeches might seem merely
an idiosyncracy of the narrative it is in fact expressive. . . .
(p. 33)

Both montage through polysyndeton and parataxis frequently result in synesthesia or sensory simultaneity in
Conversation. . . . Not the verbal figure of synesthesia customarily associated with a decadent sensibility, but collective images appealing to all or almost all of the senses as
they evoke a simultaneous reality—that is the kind of synesthesia we encounter in *Conversation.*

Throughout the book, phrases and images appear which
accumulate *thematic* significance before they acquire significant reference for us. . . . Neither colliding nor linking,
such intrusions are disruptive reminders of another, simultaneous reality, another simultaneous side to the "question" and as such they recall the most daring cinematic
constructions. . . . (p. 34)

[A] careful reading of the novel depends on scrupulous attention to the various ways in which fragments of the
narrative—sections, parts, paragraphs, phrases—are juxtaposed so as to create a synthesis of those elements in the
reader's mind. In other words, having read the novel, you
must also read the novel of the novel.

"*The results fluctuate from exact naturalistic combinations
of visual, interrelated experiences to complete alterations,
arrangements unforeseen by nature, and even to abstract
formalism, with remnants of reality.* . . ." In the photo-
fragment or shot there is an almost one-to-one correspondence between the esthetic presentation and what it refers to
as there is in the "bricks" of Vargas Llosa's novel; however, in montage, the presentation assumes an altered aspect verging on the abstract and unnatural and such is the
case with the complicated sequences (literally *non sequi-
tors,* but metaphorically justifiable sequences) which comprise the novel's statement. That is, in Joyce's or Flaubert's simultaneity—in Dickens' and Balzac's for that
matter too—the literary technique attempts to copy or re-
create a simultaneity that exists in nature, which is what
Vargas Llosa does [in some instances]. . . . But beyond

that, he creates a simultaneity in the text that has no correspondence to the relationship between the subjects he describes. Things coexist because he puts them together, not
because they are thus related in Nature. . . . In this novel
nearly without suspense, events are frequently suspended;
similarly, coincidence means, quite literally, co-incidence *in
the text.* Negatively stated this condition is unnatural, arbitrary, unreal; positively, it is abstract, formal, esthetic.
Foregoing, for the most part, simultaneity and coexistence
as they existed before his text—in Peru's history or in his
fable—Vargas Llosa has *created* a simultaneity in his book.
This created, artful simultaneity is the esthetic concept of
Conversation, an esthetic concept which perfectly matches
the book's moral, psychological and political concept.

"*The final order is determined by the social premises.*"
Because of its nature, the synthesis cannot properly be stated, it cannot even be shown as such in many cases; instead,
it is developed in the perception of the readers: the synthesis exists in their perception and response as controlled
by the author. . . . Like so many others, Vargas Llosa has
been trying to get the *story* out of fiction and he has been
blamed for his efforts as others have been; but in *Conversation* in trying to present the collective which is Peru, he
critically avoids "collective and mass action" precisely in
order to show the political decadence he is attacking. Or, to
put it another way, he shows the collective not as hero, but
as a meaninglessly simultaneous group where no one is and
no ones are heroic. No one is a villain in the group either;
but that is because they are all, in their varying ways, responsible for the society's failure. Even when the novel
takes us to the scene of mass action, such as a political rally, we are only permitted to view that action from isolated,
individual points of view while the potential collective is
seen more as a crowd or a horde. Thus *Conversation* as a
whole is a mass action, but because that action is presented
as decadent and destructive we are forced to see, by the
nature of the narrative itself, individuals who work, live,
plot, love, die, murder and survive simultaneously, but not
collectively, not heroically. (pp. 34-5)

Vargas Llosa's mass is disintegrated and its constituents
are failures, even criminals. No simple minded determinist,
though, Vargas Llosa does not go the way of so many creators . . . where, lacking all irony, the creators present the
people in political control as thoroughly corrupted, completely distorted, absolutely evil characters who live a political allegory as subtle as contemporary wrestling matches.
No, the unremitting purpose, or one of the unremitting purposes, of the montage technique in this book, is to constantly make comparisons of character with character, of
performed persona with experienced persona, of past with
present autobiography in such a way that we cannot simply
dismiss any of the characters as totally twisted, completely
innocent or merely evil. The intercutting, the violent juxtapositions demand that we see a complex situation complexly without ever denying that the elements themselves
may be very simple indeed. Multiplicity or simultaneity
then—a kind of moral cubism—of space as well as time is
what counts here. From the rhetoric of synesthesia to the
narrative of multiple points of view on through the psychology of good and evil in each character, the novel achieves
what Eisenstein calls amplitude—the apotheosis of simultaneity. The characters themselves are aware of the multidimensionality of the world they live in. . . . Clearly it is

part of the novel's purpose to educate the reader into this multidimensionality.... (pp. 35-6)

This multiplicity, this simultaneity, this amplitude is the concept of *Conversation*. The synthesis of course is negative in that it clearly shows the disparateness and duplicity of the society it presents. And here is the answer to the frequently asked question of why Vargas Llosa (like Fuentes) tells such simple stories with such elaborate technique: the *complex synthesis* of his technique is required, precisely, because of the *simple antithesis* in his subject matter. When that society and those lives are integrated and synthesized themselves, then a different form will be required of him. In the meantime, the organization of his novel, far more than the matter it presents, demonstrates the premises of the society he describes in almost perfect inversion of Eisenstein's collective ideal.

Grasped in this way, *Conversation* traces its lineage back to the novels of multiple, interwoven plots, to the novels of Dickens and Balzac, say; and it owes a good deal to the extraordinary technical achievements of Joyce (particularly to the "Wandering Rocks" chapter of *Ulysses*) and of Faulkner as well; but in its use of colliding parts to tell a story it marks an advance, a great technical advance, over all these in coming close to achieving what Eisenstein saw as a prime quality of montage....

[Vargas Llosa] has written his own book with its own novel form and its own novel sense. In doing so he has employed narrative technique in such courageous fashion that when you search for comparisons you find neither films nor novels that adequately measure his accomplishment. (p. 36)

> Ronald Christ, "Novel Form, Novel Sense," in Review (copyright © 1975 by the Center for Inter-American Relations, Inc.), Spring, 1975, pp. 30-6.

Conversation in the Cathedral, the latest and most brilliant novel of Peru's Mario Vargas Llosa, ... [is] one of the most scathing denunciations ever written on the corruption and immorality of Latin America's ruling classes. For anyone who has spent much time in Latin America, in the slums as well as the country clubs, *Conversation* is a book not easily read or forgotten. Although Vargas Llosa's unusual three-dimensional writing technique is difficult to grasp at first, it is precisely this you-are-there effect that makes the story so bloodcurdlingly real—that and the knowledge that the people and attitudes described still exist in many Latin American countries where human beings, as well as dogs, are beaten to death. (p. 522)

A realist in his political observations as well as his writing, Vargas Llosa unfolds a story of racial discrimination, military repression, torture, murder, corruption, sexual perversion, narcotics, blackmail and betrayal in a desperately sick society that forcibly infects each new generation....

Vargas Llosa writes of "rebellion, melodrama, violence and sex" because those are the stuff of life in Latin America. Frequently accused of lacking a sense of humor, he replies that "reality contradicts humor." Certainly, there is nothing amusing about the military regimes that now rule three-fifths of the continent's population in circumstances very similar to those described in *Conversation*. (p. 523)

Like other Peruvian writers, Vargas was treated as a pariah because he would not conform or compromise. But then Vargas has always been something of an idealistic loner....

By refusing to compromise his art, however, Vargas has gone beyond the bounds of the average Latin American political writer to infuse his novels with a human insight that immediately gives them appeal, no matter what the reader's nationality.... Vargas knows that there are no blacks or whites in Latin America and that people, like causes, comprise varying degrees of good and bad. (p. 525)

Vargas ... continues to expand his powers as social observer because he is primarily a novelist. As social documents, his books follow an upward curve from a charming but halting description of growing up rich in Lima to the explosion of *Conversation*. There is nothing dull in any of these social commentaries. Not even an Agatha Christie or Georges Simenon would have come up with a better surprise than the shock ending of *Conversation*. *The Green House*, an earlier literary tour de force on a par with *Conversation,* is not only superbly written but rates with the best adventure stories of Jack London.

Vargas's characters are drawn from real life—poor abused creatures whose only saving grace is their desire to survive. (If there is a hero in any of Vargas's books, it is the victim.) *The Green House*, which brings together experiences from Vargas's youth in the arid coastal city of Piura and a trip he later made through the lush, merciless Peruvian Amazon, repeats the circle of brutality and exploitation that is the theme of all his writings, as it is for other Latin Americans concerned with human rights.... (p. 526)

> Penny Lernoux, "The Latin American Disease," in The Nation (copyright 1975 by the Nation Associates, Inc.), November 22, 1975, pp. 522-27.

While it is true that *La casa verde* departs radically from traditional methods of character portrayal, it does not follow that such a departure constitutes a weakness in the novel or negates a "metaphysical dimension" in characterization. Quite the contrary ..., the view and modes of characterization developed in the novel are in close relationship with the larger, fictional world which encloses the author's vision of reality. It is the harmony of this relationship which ultimately produces much of the expressive power [that] critics applaud. (p. 11)

Characters emerge in the novel from diverse backgrounds and social classes; their experience of life and their abilities to cope with existential problems are varied. By offering a multiplistic, plural conception of human realities, the novel opens wide vistas onto conditions of ontology as well as time and space. Whether geographic or social in origin, causality is by no means simple or absolute. Historical and social forces do not assume equivalent forms nor do they function with the same intensity in the different human environments so that any single formulation of theme will not fully explain all the complexities and ambiguities that play a role in character motivation. The realities of the novel are too vast, too cryptic, and too problematic to be easily recapitulated in formulae.

Certain issues, however, do lie at the very core of the work and reveal a basic unity of perspective....

With the simultaneous portrayal of [mythification and demystification], the novel sets in motion a dynamic interplay of forces which ultimately yields Vargas Llosa's most fundamental statements about man and reality. The process of demystification steadily shows that the small myths by which men live, their cultural beliefs, assumptions, and value systems, have rarely any ultimate justification and with near inevitability propel them toward personal and collective tragedies. (p. 12)

The characters of the novel are caught in a web of deterministic forces that permit only a limited exercise of personal choice. Each character, in forging his own personality and identity within the limits imposed on him, can create only a fragile image, a profile that slowly dissolves under the active pressure of environment. Rather than representing a failure of imagination or skill, the organizing principles of characterization properly reflect the themes that underlie the author's conception of human reality.

The most obvious and most prevalent experience of entrapment takes the form of physical imprisonment. Reference to people in the novel who undergo incarceration or who are taken prisoner reads nearly like the cast of characters. (p. 13)

For all these characters, motivation and action are closely linked to either one or both facets of an existential cycle of entrapment and escape. For many, entrapment is the crucial situation which activates significant events and determines a framework for behavior and action; for others, it marks an important turning point in life or an end of character portrayal. In terms of concrete and individual experience, no other situation underpins the common experience of so many characters or gives greater impetus to the development of plot.

The scope of each character's world is very limited. No protagonist in the novel has a clear idea of how his own predicament relates to larger issues or how the social structure, in its broadest sense, shapes the quality and trajectory of his existence. The acute demands of personal survival limit the perspective of the individual to the possibilities of response and action imbedded in concrete situations and only on this level do the characters have some degree of freedom to make choices and, in so doing, to define themselves.

The structuring of the various plots makes clear that the author is concerned with each character's response to a few, tightly controlled life situations. Taken separately, the plots do not generate for any one character an extensive inventory of existential problems. But taken together, the plots afford the reader a wide panorama of character activity as well as insight into human complexity. The compression of individual plot lines around points of crisis in the lives of the protagonists draws the reader's attention to significant issues and provides a focal point from which he can evaluate the past and future experiences of the character. (pp. 13-14)

[Questions] of causality are never straight-forward; the deep motivation of the characters, while never completely hidden, remains elusive and tantalizing. In the specific case of Bonifacia, the manner in which her crisis-incident is told —a combination of limited views from other characters, dialogue, and an outside narrator—creates an ambiguous personality whose history and motivation are always questionable. Mystery and contradiction lie at the very heart of her conception as a character and become a part of nearly

every factual question which might be used by the reader to fashion a consistent view of Bonifacia's nature, motivations, and role in the novel.

The portrayal of Bonifacia through multiple and always limited points of view collects so many ambiguities that the reader is continually obliged to weigh the information of one unreliable narrator against that of another. (p. 14)

In many important ways the incident at the mission actually reveals much of what Vargas Llosa has to say in his novel about the nature of human conduct and the position of his characters in an alien environment. Seen here and basic to his technique is a kind of portrayal which captures the immediacy of human acts but leaves both reader and character uncertain as to their full meaning. (p. 15)

It is . . . from a counterpointing of time levels that the author is able to humanize his character and soften the reader's potential for moral repugnance. Fushía's past, with all its violence and ethical cowardice, occurs simultaneously with a portrait of his present desperation and anguish. The immediate contrast between the two views makes it impossible for the reader to take satisfaction in the appropriateness, and perhaps even justice, of Fushía's personal suffering. (p. 17)

[As in Bonifacia's story], the author has chosen a circular or looping pattern to structure the internal disposition of time. With regard to a definition of Fushía's life, the structure has important thematic implications. At the point of looping the portrayal of his past comes to an end and, because his future has already been seen, an air of finality pervades the last episode. The linkage of time dimensions completes the design of a plot structure which has until now been unclear. But more importantly, the structural transition corresponds to the passage of Fushía's self to the state of being of an object.

The technique marks the point at which Fushía's will decisively loses the struggle with circumstance. (p. 18)

Even though the author's opinion of Fushía remains unspoken and the techniques employed never open a direct view of Fushía's mind, he is not nearly so opaque a character as Bonifacia. While it is true that the underlying approach to characterization limits portrayal to revealing Fushía's character rather than developing it, the process achieves sufficient psychological penetration, through externalized representations of his subjective life, to fashion a personality which could be mistaken for no other. The obsessions that drive Fushía are so closely interwoven with his personality structure that when he meets defeat the extent of his suffering evokes primarily an individualized drama of human tragedy. Only later, from a greater distance, can the reader perceive in Fushía's life the outlines of a pattern that gives his story archetypal significance.

The enigmatic quality of Aquilino's point of view is a primary source of the mystery that surrounds his entire relationship with Fushía. As he probes ever deeper into Fushía's past, questioning motives and pronouncing ominous judgments, there is an omniscience about him—arising from the author's handling of point of view—that further emphasizes the mythic quality of Fushía's story. (p. 19)

To see a character like Fushía as a "mere aspect of being" is not to see him whole. It is to mistake what he has been with what he becomes. As a literary character Fushía acquires life because his actions and words reveal a plausible and complex representation of individual experience. Defined by both internal and external conflicts, his obsessions and acts offer a variety of provocative insights into the author's interpretation of human problems and the limitations of the individual to cope with them.

Insofar as functional ambiguity induces moral ambivalence on the part of the reader, there is evidence to suggest that the author is concerned with an ontological rather than ethical treatment of Fushía's life. The fact that clear lines of causality—whether psychological, social, or divine—cannot be rigorously followed ultimately intensifies recognition that existence is itself a trap. In the story of Fushía it is not so important to trace personal responsibility or assign guilt as it is to see that he exists and struggles within a situation that offers no escape. (p. 20)

While Fushía's autonomous qualities as a character add a great deal to the interest and richness of the novel, they do not of themselves fully illuminate Vargas Llosa's goals in characterization. Fushía exemplifies certainly that individualization takes place, but it is his mode of existence that is crucial to interpretation rather than the particularity of his human qualities. Above all, his life represents a steady erosion of personality which passes through stages of agony and pain before reaching oblivion.

The author's view of the precariousness of personal identity—so much in evidence in the portrayal of both Bonifacia and Fushía—also supplies the conceptual underpinning for the presentation of a wide assortment of characters who are defined principally through their identification with a group. The fact that the collective entities often exhibit a stronger and more definable identity than do isolated individuals makes this feature of characterization one of the most distinctive aspects of the novel. Together these diverse segments of humanity add up to a human landscape of interesting and eloquent variety. (pp. 20-1)

Beyond this point, however, humanity becomes entirely faceless. Individuals and groups move across a human background so undifferentiated that descriptions record only vague silhouettes and dark, blurry masses. At this level, identity has reached its lowest denominator, leaving no more than a short distance before it dissolves completely into the dense, amorphous substances of the physical environment.

To focus this way on communal modes of existence, against a hazy and indefinite human background, places primary emphasis on the portrayal of relationships and patterns of human association rather than traditional character analysis. It is also a way, in this novel, of underscoring the insubstantial quality of individual personality. Since characters are so often defined by their external and communal behavior, their personalities tend to break apart into changing profiles. Thus the dynamics of a given situation, more than any other factor, determines the momentary content of an elusive, malleable personality.

Contributing to this view is the author's technique of withholding information about a character's full name or providing him with different names in different contexts. Some readers have found this practice misleading and even annoying but it stems nevertheless from a logical rationale within the novel and is, for many others, a source of intrigue that rewards close reader participation with the excitement of personal discovery. . . . [Vargas Llosa's] manipulations with the names of his characters ultimately derive from an effort on the part of the author to show that it is the experience of these characters in different environments that gives origin to their multiple identities. (p. 21)

[The] novel's vast panorama of character activity continually underscores the malleability and diversity of human nature. Within a hostile world, there are cases of endurance and survival as well as deterioration and death. But the victories are rare and always relative while the defeats are many and conclusive. (p. 22)

In the treatment of characterization, the novel consistently reflects an existential condition whose distinctive feature is the fragility of personal existence.

Expressing the precarious life of each personality are techniques and recurring structures that blur and divide identities; that make the past uncertain and reality itself ambiguous. The methods used achieve a high degree of dramatization but withhold clarity in motivation. Mystery and enigma are the expressive components of personalities who inhabit a fictional world where past realities are not clearly distinguished from subjective or mythical reconstructions. In a world where both evil and truth are relative and where every act, regardless of its moral quality, engenders disproportionate retribution, the reader encounters the essence of justice in his own ambivalence.

Allusions to biblical characters, Christian symbols, and mythical prototypes do not make *La casa verde* a coherent allegory. But these features do expand the limits of the novel by offering, through implication and association, deeper and more universal insights into the nature of existence. Generating meaning on many levels through complex modes of characterization, the novel shapes an interpretation of man in reality that shows him eternally condemned to an experience of tragedy and martyrdom. (pp. 22-3)

> *Michael Moody, "The Web of Defeat: A Thematic View of Characterization in Mario Vargas Llosa's 'La Casa Verde'," in His-pania (© 1976 The American Association of Teachers of Spanish and Portuguese, Inc.), March, 1976, pp. 11-23.*

*   *   *

VITTORINI, Elio   1908-1966

Vittorini was an Italian editor, short story writer, and novelist whose anti-Fascism colored much of his fiction. In *Conversation in Sicily*, however, he transcended the limitations of political fiction to produce his finest work. Vittorini was stylistically influenced by American fiction; his dialogue, narrative pace, characterizations, and settings reflect a strong indebtedness to Hemingway. (See also *CLC*, Vol. 6, and *Contemporary Authors*, obituary, Vols. 25-28, rev. ed.)

[In *Il Sempione strizza l'occhio al Fre´jus (Twilight of the Elephants)* the] hovering narrator [of *Conversazione in Sicilia (Conversation in Sicily)*] is gone, and the story is told in the first person by a member of the family it describes. This short novel is relatively plotless and consists of no more than a setting, a half dozen or so characters, and a series of conversations. Vittorini is thus freed from the difficulty he has in *Uomini e no* of surmounting a rather banal adventure-thriller plot. The structure returns to the simple network of dialogues that was so effective in *Conversazione in Sicilia,* although the motif of travel, of the seeking wanderer, is missing. This simplicity allows Vittorini to concentrate on the matters of cadence, of flat but deftly sketched character, of poetic ambience, where his touch is sure. The result is a minor but charming and relatively successful piece of fiction. (p. 194)

[The] mother, who defends [the grandfather, the "elephant" of the title,] and interprets him for the others, contends that he built practically every other monument of the history of civilization as well: the Milan cathedral, the Colosseum, the Great Wall of China, the Pyramids. This theme of universality escapes pompousness simply through the ironic and half-playful way it is presented. The children are skeptical; the mother is firm in her faith.

> She may mean more than we think she means. She's not stupid. She certainly doesn't mean anybody except grandfather, that great seated bulk, but if she wanted to indicate his whole race and ours she could only point to him. It's only he that she refers to as "your grandfather," "our grandfather." But there is no reason why she shouldn't use the name of "grandfather" for all those in the world who are like him.

"Those who are like him" include his fellow workers on the Fréjus, those who built the Duomo, the Colosseum, the Chinese Wall, the Pyramids. And who else? The reader who sets out here like Dante in his letter to Can Grande della Scala to find allegorical levels will have practically no place to stop. First of all the grandfather is a real grandfather, a "naturalistic" character whose background and temperament can be accepted quite literally. Second, he can be identified with Vittorini's own youthful experience as a construction worker; the grandfather personifies a nostalgia for hard work, common action, exposure to the elements, the solving of physical problems through determination and ingenuity. As a kind of part-time Marxist Vittorini regards the real advances of civilization as material, technological, rather than intellectual, and while the grandfather is not exactly anti-intellectual he is hardly a scholar or abstract thinker. At the next level down there is a somewhat ironic religious implication: the grandfather as Jahveh. Finally, the grandfather with his roots three generations back in Italian history represents the nineteenth century, the Risorgimento, the heroic epoch in Italian destiny. . . . (p. 195)

And yet when the novel is weighed as a whole, in its final aesthetic effect, it is possible to ignore all these complicated hints and regard the grandfather simply as a kind of tough nexus of humanity, "more a man" than the others. In Vittorini's frame of values the workers, those who make things with their hands, those who are in contact with basic physical realities, are admirable; bureaucrats, exploiters, and policemen are not. Those who suffer are *più uomo;* those who make suffer are less, or not man at all. Like the Gran Lombardo in *Conversazione in Sicilia,* the grandfather is *più uomo* as well in his patriarchal virility. Contrasted to him in this whimsical Holy Family, the mother's husband (he is given no other name) plays a kind of semicomic Joseph. Joseph may be a saint, but what a pitiful figure he cuts next to Jahveh! (p. 196)

If the novel has any plot at all it depends on the intrusion of an outsider into the family: the highway worker called Smoke-Face who is laying asphalt on the road outside the house. . . . It is the invention of this character that saves the novel from a rather pointless dialogue, taking place entirely within the family, without beginning or an end. . . . The grandfather represents the past, Mazzini and Garibaldi, Vittorini's own youth; Smoke-Face represents the possibility that something like the grandfather can be reborn in the present. This is the possibility—to put it in political terms—that a modern proletariat can recapture something of the energy and idealism of the Risorgimento. At the religious level of the novel Smoke-Face represents the rebirth of the God, and so on. The pattern of the novel is meaningful no matter which of the various frameworks is applied to it, or even if no particular framework is applied to it, if it is taken quite simply as the story of a family and an outsider who makes friends with it. . . . Smoke-Face surmounts this difficulty and manages to be perfectly human and yet emblematic, metaphorically significant, at the same time.

[A somewhat] playful complexity of meaning is attached to the meal which Smoke-Face shares with the family, the central event and in fact the only real event of the novel. It is a kind of Last Supper: Black-Face shares the bread of the family, predicts certain sufferings and transcendences, and offers them a salted anchovy (the fish is a paleo-Christian symbol) which only the elephant-grandfather is allowed to touch. The others sniff its odor, and put its salt on their bread. But the meal is more meaningful and a good deal more ingenious as an "economic satire" in the manner of Swift. Except for their weekly quota of bread, most of which is eaten by the elephant, the family lives on chicory which they gather along the roads. Boiling this in a huge pot, they ladle it into bowls and eat it for their one meal of the day. But in this manner, the mother fears, the children will grow up not knowing how to eat soup or cut up chicken. So at every meal there is an elaborate pantomine in which they pretend to eat other things, and always with the proper table manners: antipasto, fried potatoes, meat, fruit, and wine sipped from empty glasses. The meal in which Smoke-Face joins them is a particularly elaborate one, with an oil-cruet, fruit bowls, and even triple silverware added to the ordinary settings. With tears of hunger streaming down their cheeks the children go through the motions of eating. The meal is a parody of polite bourgeois etiquette; the "modest proposal" is that children, while starving to death, should nevertheless learn good table manners by pretending to eat air. This forestalls in advance the bourgeois criticism that the lower classes are uncouth and would not appreciate the better things in life if they were given to them. Smoke-Face here serves the function of the outside observer, always a useful device in fiction where a customary situation or procedure must be explained to the reader. He comments that he too would like to take part in the charade and learn how to eat chicken. "Never had a chance to learn," he says, laughing. But this joke is not his real response to the ritual of the meal. In the mock-religious framework of the novel his responding act is to offer them the fish which is both spirit (the odor which is all the children get) and flesh (the meat eaten by the elephant). (pp. 196-98)

Smoke-Face produces a reed fife . . . and plays on it. He has learned this skill, he explains, because ever since childhood it has been his dream to be a sorcerer. This idea echoes back and forth in an "operatic" conversation that dominates most of a chapter. (p. 198)

> The man takes his full glass in his hand. He laughs and empties it. He has already said that he didn't know why he was looking for his theme. Now he answers my mother: "But yes, lady. It's for enchanting elephants."

"Elephant" in this sense is simply physical humanity, the warmth of companion flesh. Smoke-Face goes on to explain that he had never understood why he liked to sit next to a working companion or a traveler on a train, and then realized that he "liked to be near an elephant." At this point elephants, fifes, and sorcery begin to emerge as another metaphor for the personal and technical problem Vittorini discussed in the preface to *Il garofano rosso*: how to express a highly personal emotion through the outworn and banal apparatus of fiction? how to communicate realities and yet transcend conventional realism? In both *Conversazione in Sicilia* and *Il Sempione strizza l'occhio al Fre´jus* the answer is conveyed in musical terms: the "something which does for the novel what music does for the opera," the fife that "enchants elephants." In the later novel the metaphor first emerges in the pantomine dinner. The *linguaggio* or style (metaphorically the fife-playing) makes even this improbable scene seem acceptable. But here the technique seems to turn inward on itself in the Gidean manner. The meal is made "real" in two ways: the reader accepts the improbability because of the whole style and treatment of the chapter, and inside the framework of the novel the family accepts the food as real through the "enchantment" of their own way of talking about it. Through language the meal becomes a ritual, and the fact that the food is unreal no more interferes with the validity of the ritual than the invisibility of the Divine interferes with the vailidty of the Mass. "Music does something," and this music is externalized both by the poetic and echoing quality of the dialogue and by Smoke-Face's piping. Thus Smoke-Face, in addition to prophet and revolutionist, is also the artist.

Before he leaves the family Smoke-Face offers a final and cryptic piece of wisdom: he explains how elephants die. Never in all of Africa is a dead elephant seen in the jungle. Instead, when their last hours come upon them, they make their way to "secret cemeteries, unknown even to them while they're alive." There they simply stretch out and die, a burden on no one. . . . In the final chapter [the grandfather] puts his coat and hat on, takes his stick, and without a word wanders off toward the woods. The mother refuses to let the children go after him, commenting, "We too are elephants." But the ending of the chapter is ambiguous, in the whimsical and antitragical way that dominates the whole tone of the novel. "It's not the beginning of night, it's the end," the mother tells them. And she explains that the workmen who are going to their jobs will find the grandfather and bring him home again. "Meanwhile let him get disenchanted," she advises. ("*Ma si sbizzarrisca*," literally "Let him get rid of his bizarreries.) The bizarreries are, perhaps, the sentimental romanticism of the Risorgimento, but they are also the enchantments of the novel itself, the fife-playing. Is it really possible to get rid of these? The tension between enchantment and reality is the essence of Vittorini's method. (pp. 198-200)

Donald Heiney, "Persons and Nonpersons," in his Three Italian Novelists *(copyright © by The University of Michigan 1968), University of Michigan Press, 1968, pp. 189-200.*

The novelistic language of Vittorini is not essentially a realistic one. In a 1933 article he distinguishes between two kinds of writers: those who make you think, "Yes, that's the way it is," and those who make you think, "I had never supposed it could be like that," and in this way suggest a new mode of experience, a new "how" to existence. The experience communicated in a work of fiction is of course specific, fixed to a single place on the map and a single point in time; in this at least Vittorini is a realist. But the effect on the reader (and Vittorini is as much interested in the psychology of the reader as he is in the creative process) must not be bound to or limited by this specific. . . . [He] approaches the aesthetics of Mallarmé and the Symbolists; poetry is concerned not with things but with the general emotions generated by things. . . . But Vittorini does not go this far. His fiction remains tied to a world of sunshine, melons, wine, rain, human voices. Yet one of the points of his method is to demonstrate that melons and sunshine are the same for all men, to affirm the universality of sensory experience. Underlying this is a notion of solidarity, of the resemblance that links all men together in the human condition. Men feel heat and cold in much the same way, and this is a reminder that all men hunger and suffer in their lives, feel love and hate, and finally die. This concept of the community of experience is the connecting link, a tenuous and not very satisfactory one, between Vittorini's aesthetics and his politics. The sensations of the novelistic hero, which are also those of the author, are projected as possibilities for the reader and for all men. (It is important to note that they are "possibilities"; Vittorini's fiction does not so much evoke the reader's own experience as suggest new things that might happen to him.) The solidarity of feeling thus becomes the solidarity of politics; or at least Vittorini attempts to bring the two together. The difficulty is that, while all men feel heat and cold in the same way, they may not necessarily feel the same about such political questions as freedom and the artist's relation to the state. The relative failure of Vittorini's later fiction turns around this difficulty. In *Conversazione in Sicilia* (*Conversation in Sicily*) this fundamental tension is resolved more successfully than it is in any of the rest of his work. The reason is that at the point where he began to conceive this novel, in late 1936, he had finally grasped the aesthetic principle that his whole career was to turn around. And, paradoxically, the existence of censorship helped him by rendering abstract or "poetic" the overt political element that was to weaken later novels like *Uomini e no* (Men and Not-Men) and *Le donne di Messina* (The Women of Messina). Obliged to be vague and general, Vittorini turned vagueness and generality into an emotional device of great power. (pp. 161-62)

"Putting the reader inside" [the narrator's experience] implies at least some degree of universality, if not in the experience itself then at least in the work of art that reflects it. This is the basic task of his writing in the middle period of his career: to objectify the subjective. *Conversazione in Sicilia* is not a travelogue of Sicily, and it is not really a portrait of regional manners. . . . [For] Vittorini the events happen to the protagonist, a visitor who sees the train-travelers and Sicilian villagers from the outside, as much as he may empathize with them. These secondary characters are important, in fact, only insofar as they provoke impressions, emotions, and inward processes in the narrator. Vittorini's mature style, the style of *Conversazione in Sicilia,* is an effort to find the verbal equivalent of certain emotions. The narrator's disclaimer that the furies are "not what he wants to tell about" we may take as an artistic feint, a tactic to direct the reader's attention to the surface of the narrative before it is led to what is underneath. This is the real meaning of Vittorini's statement that poetry "does not remain tied to the things from which it originated" and "can be related, if it is born out of pain, to any pain."

Yet the view that Vittorini is a regionalist is not entirely unsound. Sicily is used as a major setting in only two of his novels, *Conversazione in Sicilia* and *La Garibaldina.* But underlying his whole work there is a matrix of personal experience: the abandonment of primitive Sicily for an urban north, and a later attempt to recover this innocence and primitivism of his youth. . . . In Vittorini's work there is always the implication of a kind of geographical polarity: on the one hand the north, cities, civilization, white collars, books, intellectualism; on the other hand the south, the land, wine, sunshine, the basic and primitive elements of existence. Fascism he associates with the north, even though fascist policemen and bureaucrats (Mustache and No Mustache in *Conversazione in Sicilia*) are often southerners. The "screaming newspaper placards" are of the city; fascism is made out of paper, it takes over the apparatus of the city and civilization and uses it as a weapon against the country. Vittorini's origins were small-town and petty bourgeois, and in spite of his youthful experience as a construction worker he never quite made the transition to the proletariat. The workers are ostensibly the heroes of the Resistance novel *Uomini e no* and of the "Autobiografia in tempo di guerra," but his deepest emotions are always tied to childhood, to Sicily, to the sea and sun. This is precisely the difficulty with his later leftist or "collectivist" fiction: the tension between the outward political apparatus and his innermost emotions is unresolved. In *Viaggio in Sardegna,* an extremely revealing book, he begins what is ostensibly a travelogue by confessing, "I know the joy of spending a summer afternoon reading a book of adventure half-naked in a chaise-longue, by a house on a hillside overlooking the sea. And many other joys as well: of being hidden in a garden and listening to the wind barely moving the leaves (the highest ones) of a tree; or of hearing in the sand infinite sand-existences crumble and fall; or of getting up before dawn in a world of chickens and swimming, alone in all the water in the world, by a pink beach." These are not precisely the joys of a dedicated revolutionist. Vittorini's retreat into primitivism is . . . a retreat that the political part of him regarded as a kind of betrayal. The tension is especially apparent in the badly unresolved conflicts of *Le donne di Messina,* his most pretentious and yet in many ways his least successful work. In short, Vittorini's career as a writer is in some respects an unfortunate case of mistaken identity. At a certain point in his life, regarding himself as a poet in the most technical sense of the term and addressing himself to purely poetic problems, he produced a single novel that transformed the Italian literary scene to a greater degree, probably, than any other book of his generation. But he was able to maintain this purity only during

a brief period of his life, the ten years or so that came to a climax in 1942. The years before 1932 are apprentice years. . . . And with *Uomini e no* in 1945, and perhaps even earlier, with the "autobiographical" fragments written during the war, he turned from this poetic vocation to the problem of *littérature engagée,* to the attempt to make a "collective novel" that would reconcile the individual and political elements in his own nature. By 1946 he had practically abandoned fiction to devote himself to political questions. . . . [If] the artist's innermost nature is not political then it is impractical to impose a political framework on his talent; abstract furies are difficult to collectivize. This is the reason for what every reader feels: that *Conversazione in Sicilia* is his only fully resolved and totally successful work of fiction. (pp. 163-66)

Vittorini's particular contribution was to attack the problem [of the prosiness and flat factualism of modern fiction], . . . and to apply to it a particular framework of rhetoric: that of the opera. When he speaks of opera it is Italian opera that is meant, and particularly Verdi. . . . When the "something" provided by music is added to the libretto the result is the total technical effect that Vittorini calls *linguaggio:* ". . . that which results from the action and the music together, as the unified language of the composer." It was a "something" comparable to music that he sought to add to prose fiction. His new concept of the novel, at the point where the partly unsatisfactory *Il garofano rosso* and the unfinished *Erica* lay behind him, was a form that achieved its effects through pattern and rhythm, emotion-provoking in the diffuse and unspecific way that opera provokes emotion, "poetic" without being bound by the conventions and limitations of verse.

The manner of telling of *Conversazione in Sicilia* balances two more or less antithetic elements: on one hand its generality, the Dantesque element of allegory, and on the other hand the quite specific setting and circumstances of the action. . . . The opening paragraph is a stylistic model or matrix of the whole novel. Beginning with the word "I," it is simultaneously vernacular and rhythmic, more intricate than it appears. As in a musical composition certain motifs or images are introduced, set aside for the moment, and then repeated with variations. . . . The paragraph ends with "a mute dream, hopelessness, quietude." The following passage, like an aria continued by another singer, takes up these images from where the first has left off . . . and continues with other images which it adds in turn. . . . This catalog of concrete objects is an important clue to the nature, or more precisely the effect, of the abstract furies. (pp. 167-69)

The words *police* and *fascist* never break through to the surface, and this is not only because the novel was published under censorship. The passage [describing the train journey] deals with an immediate and local political phenomenon, and yet in another sense its implications are general or universal. The effect achieved is something like that of the Expressionistic drama: character is depersonalized and turned to type, while at the same time retaining enough surface detail to lend an impression of concretion. . . . The effect of censorship was precisely to encourage a style of ambiguity, a style which is vague on the surface but speaks quite precisely to those who possess the key. This tendency to abstraction, to a style of suggestion rather than overt statement, is evident in a number of other writers who developed under fascism. . . . Like the argot of prisoners, it is a language that proceeds on two levels, an overt surface and a concealed or semi-concealed code. This "duplicity" or tendency to say two things at once, it goes without saying, is also characteristic of poetry itself. (pp. 171-72)

[The dialogue in the train scene between Mustache and No Mustache] might be a duet of two pompous courtiers in Verdi, for example from *Rigoletto*. . . . In Vittorini's novel . . . political implications remain, for the most part, at this "operatic" level, a level that is emotional and aesthetic rather than ideological in any overt sense. (p. 172)

[When] the expression *più uomo* recurs in *Conversazione in Sicilia,* there is a connection in Vittorini's mind to the Spanish War and all its political implications. The phrase is not very clearly defined either as a literary image or as a political concept; it is deliberately left diffuse. But the implication is clear that fascism is man-destroying—that Mustache and No Mustache have become dehumanized puppets, whereas the Great Lombard and the others of the novel who "feel the need of doing something for the sake of conscience" are reinforced and enhanced in their humanity. This is connected to Silvestro's own inability, in the early part of the novel, to feel or love anything in the world around him; fascism anesthetizes the feeling and desiring part of man, leaving him in the "quietude of hopelessness."

This metaphorical framework of the Great Lombard and *più uomo* recurs frequently in the remainder of the novel. Somewhat later Silvestro, in a conversation with his mother, inquires whether his grandfather was a Great Lombard. When the mother asks what a Great Lombard is, he merely replies, "a man." This leads to a kind of repetitive litany that continues for several pages. . . . The repetition is not syntactically rigid; there are backings and turnings, divagations in which the mother remarks that in Nicosia they make bread with hazelnuts on top or that she once had a pitcher from Aidone. But in its singsong return to the same refrain the passage is as invariable and monotonous as a children's chant. It arrives finally at the question for which all the other questions have been only preparation: "Didn't he say that our present duties are obsolete? That they are rotten, dead, and there's no satisfaction in performing them? . . . Didn't he say there was a need for other duties? New duties, not the ordinary ones? Didn't he say that?" The mother doesn't remember whether he said this or not. But she does remember that "basically" he wasn't content with the world, but was content with himself. Clearly the grandfather was *più uomo,* a giant who spoke straight and saw clearly; a Great Lombard.

Technically this scene is an ingenious piece of indirection; the innuendo of the dialogue is always present under the surface but never emerges, or emerges only in cryptic form in the reference to "new duties." . . . [The] mother herself performs an important function, although she herself is unaware of it. In the quasi-religious pattern of allegory underlying the novel she represents charity, the Latin *caritas*. This has nothing to do with philanthropy either organized or unorganized; it is simply the state of mind of selfless love. . . . The mother personifies a concept basic to the novel: that the religious impulse may exist outside the organized Church, and even, under conditions like those of fascism, in opposition to the organized Church. (pp. 173-76)

[The] political implications *remain* implications, remain

abstract, and this lends them a universality that extends beyond the local and temporary problem of fascism. It is for this reason that *Conversazione in Sicilia,* while a "revolutionary" novel in a general and ethical sense, manages to transcend the limitations of a political tract, even so skilled a one as Malraux's *L'espoir.* It manages to do this because Vittorini, for all his concern with politics, is primarily an artist and relates to the writing of his novel primarily in artistic rather than politic terms. The concept of the autonomy of art recurs frequently in Vittorini's essay; like Moravia he rejects the Marxist concept of art as a "superstructure" explainable in terms of the economic and political conditions that produce it. (p. 179)

Vittorini was involved in fascist politics; fascism interfered with his artistic development and had the power to deprive him at any time of his freedom or even his life. There is therefore a control, an irony, in his half-veiled allusions to political conditions, but there is no Homeric serenity. It is this pressure under the surface, in fact, that produces the characteristic and strangely powerful effect of the novel. As it progresses and passes its point of climax—the dialogue with the knife-grinder—the narrative becomes successively more personal; Silvestro develops from a passive narrator into the central figure of his own story. (p. 180)

There is no doubt that in the figure of Ezechiele the "possibility" of anti-fascism is specifically connected to writing, to the literary vocation. . . . It is obvious that Vittorini has projected himself into Silvestro the linotype-operator, whose job it is to put letters together and who suffers from abstract furies. But there is no doubt that the abstract concept of Writer, or artist-as-revolutionary, is connected as well to this Ezechiele who records the history of the offended world, and who greets Silvestro in some mysterious way as a brother.

[In the] final episode the motif of personal involvement or commitment emerges unmistakably as the dominant note, one that, like the theme of an operatic finale, gathers and assimilates the earlier motifs of the work. In this involvement Silvestro, the author, and the reader are merged into a single consciousness, a consciousness that becomes "more man" in its recognition of the frailty and guilt of common humanity. There is no mistaking the skill with which this is done. The conventional apparatus of the scene—the dream, the ghost, the banal religious symbolism—are no more damaging to Vittorini's final effect than similar conventions are to Verdi's. The narrative has been freed from the banality of its events and devices by "something which does for the novel what music does for the opera." The encounter with Liborio is a moving, strange, and original scene; there are few passages to match it in Italian literature or the whole of modern writing. It is followed by a kind of epilogue in which the mother washes the feet of a stranger who turns out to be the father: a prodigal father greeted by a forgiving son. But even this rather banal piece of allegory is saved by the oblique and poetic manner of its presentation. (pp. 181-82)

Donald Heiney, "Elio Vittorini: The Operatic Novel" (originally published in a different version in Three Italian Novelists: Moravia, Pavese, Vittorini, *University of Michigan Press, 1968), in* From "Verismo" to Experimentalism: Essays on the Modern Italian Novel, *edited by Sergio Pacifici (copyright © 1969 by Indiana University Press), Indiana University Press, 1970, pp. 161-83.*

[There] exists within [*Conversazione in Sicilia*] a closely articulated pattern of historical, biblical, and literary allusions.... [This] pattern of allusions is strongest in Part Four, Part Five, and the Epilogue.... (p. 75)

The nucleus for almost every cluster of significant allusions in the first four parts of *Conversazione in Sicilia* is formed by the name of one or another of the novel's characters. The reader's attention is directed to the allusive potential of names by the first real event of the book: Silvestro receives a letter from his father, Costantino, asking him to go to Sicily to visit his mother, whom Costantino claims to have abandoned. This pairing of the names, Costantino and Silvestro, must evoke an association with the Donation of Constantine in the mind of any Italian reader familiar with the frequent references to that legend in the *Divina Commedia*.... [The] father's letter hands over responsibility for the mother to the son in much the same way as the Emperor Constantine's document supposedly handed over responsibility for the Western Empire to Pope Sylvester. The difficulty of this allusion, as of so many others in this novel, lies in the obliqueness of Vittorini's interest in the material to which he alludes. Whilst he clearly did not share Dante's concern that the medieval Papacy had been contaminated by its assumption of temporal powers, he may well have wished to hint that the Catholic Church, at the time he wrote this in 1937-8, had been seriously contaminated by the closeness of its association with the Italian Fascist State. Moreover, in suggesting a parallel between a simple family issue and a major historical event, Vittorini introduces a theme which ... becomes central to the whole novel: the indivisibility of personal moral obligation and of major political action. (pp. 75-6)

[There is a] clear Dantesque allusion in the nickname 'Gran Lombardo' given by Silvestro to the impressive old Sicilian farmer he meets on the train.... It evokes the phrase 'la cortesia del gran Lombardo' used by Dante (*Paradiso*, XVII, 71) of the member of the della Scala family, probably Bartolommeo, who first gave him hospitality after his banishment from Florence. Vittorini's 'Gran Lombardo' ... possesses precisely the qualities of nobility and generosity which Dante attributes to Bartolommeo. However the main effect of this allusion is surely to establish that the journey of the exiled Silvestro back to Sicily is to be directly compared in its spiritual and political seriousness with the journey undertaken by the exiled Dante in the *Divina Commedia*....

Vittorini brings together, in the character and name of Concezione, two aspects of motherhood which the Christian West has traditionally held to be distinct. On the one hand, she is a kind of primitive, sensual, fertile, pagan Earth Mother: 'Mamma dei Meloni.'... On the other hand, she is a kind of Virgin Mary (her name-day is the Feast of the Immaculate Conception), who gives generously to her sons and to the sick people of the village without expecting anything in return, who suffers, uncomprehendingly, the death of one son, and to whom all human beings are essentially the same, only differing from each other in their outward condition. (p. 76)

A tight web of allusions is also woven around each of the four men, Calogero, Ezechiele, Porfirio and Colombo, who set themselves up as Silvestro's temporary mentors in Part Four.

Calogero's name, when we eventually learn it, reinforces the impression that he is a profoundly self-contradictory figure. His passion for weapons suggests that he is a militant, a rash man of action on the political level. His name suggests, on the contrary, a meditative, even saintly, man. It derives from two Greek words which mean 'a good old man'. (Silvestro insists though, in a still deeper paradox, that his Calogero is young....) In Italian, *calogero* denotes a monk of the Greek Church. More specifically though, the name recalls a St Calogerus of the fifth century who made a pilgrimage from Constantinople to Rome (a pilgrimage to the origins of his church comparable with Silvestro's pilgrimage to the island from which he originated). It is certainly significant that this saint then became a hermit in Sicily and an important figure in Sicilian folk-lore. Moreover, it must also be relevant to recall that one of the most important moderate opponents of Fascism in the 1930s was a philosopher called Guido Calogero, who helped to found the liberal-socialist movement in 1936. (A note in Vittorini's *Diario in pubblico* reveals that he was greatly preoccupied at the time of writing *Conversazione in Sicilia* with the apparent impotence of liberal socialism as a force to oppose Fascism.)

The moderate, meditative associations of Calogero's name thus serve, in effect, to undermine or even cancel out the philosophy of militancy which he expresses with such vigour. On the level of topical comment, this may be taken as a sharp critique of the moral and political confusion encountered by Vittorini amongst those who opposed Fascism in the 1930s, whatever form their opposition took. On the level of universal comment, Vittorini is implicitly raising a query about the adequacy of any single philosophy of opposition to oppression. (pp. 77-8)

The name, Ezechiele, naturally recalls the Old Testament prophet Ezekiel, who whilst he recorded the corrupt condition of the Jews of his time, was above all concerned to pass on God's instructions about the future of the Jewish people and the establishment of a new theocratic order centered on a rebuilt temple. Ezechiele's mode of speech likewise leads one to think of him as a kind of prophet.... Ezechiele perceives his duty then as being to record the details of the evil men do to each other, to record oppression and to feel compassion for the oppressed. He seems to suggest that it is a purer philosophy than Calogero's militancy, and Silvestro appears attracted by its internal consistency. It is certainly the philosophy of many an honest, observant intellectual in Italy during the Fascist period. But Ezechiele's philosophy is clearly not the philosophy of a prophet: he is, at best, a compassionate historian. He strikingly fails to fulfil the promise of his prophetic name and manner. (p. 78)

[Porfirio's] red flag registers with a receptive reader as a half-disguised emblem of socialism, and the fact that the name, Porfirio, itself denotes a kind of red confirms that this is a serious allusion. Porfirio is also the name of the philosopher of the third century A.D. (Porphyry of Tyre), well known to Italians through a dialogue in Leopardi's *Operette morali*. Porphyry went to study under Plotinus in Rome, where he suffered a mental breakdown and contemplated suicide: suicide is the subject of the dialogue by

Leopardi in which he figures. He eventually took a trip to Sicily to restore his health. The parallel with Silvestro's journey to Sicily and his state of mind when he set out is too striking to ignore. Porphyry was a Neoplatonist and a strong anti-Christian.

So when Silvestro meets Porfirio, the reader might well expect him to emerge as a man of revolutionary socialist attitudes, pessimistic and anti-Christian. . . . [But] Porfirio places his hopes not in political revolution (nor in human compassion) but in some form of religious remedy. . . . So Porfirio's message, too, contrasts strongly with the various associations evoked by his name.

When Silvestro and his three companions enter Colombo's tavern, they find a number of men singing a song whose weird refrain '*"E sangue di Santa Bumbila"*' is repeated four times. . . . The scene apparently brings to Silvestro's mind all the occasions in the past when men have drunk wine, either in a purely social setting or in the religious setting of the Christian communion (which itself commemorates the Last Supper). The reference to the blood of Santa Bumbila reinforces the religious association of wine and blood. . . . I would suggest quite simply that *Bumbila* is the name of a mock-saint, made up from the Sicilian word *bumbulu* crossed with the Italian word *bombola,* both of which mean 'wine-flask'. Thus the drinkers are singing not, as it first appears to be, a hymn to a martyred saint, but a drinking-song addressed to the wine itself: the blood of Saint Wine-Flask. (And indeed *bombaba`* is an old word for a drinking-song.)

The relevance of this ambiguous refrain becomes clear as the . . . [celebration] degenerates into a simple drinking party. Colombo is the crucial figure in this process of degeneration. His name evokes very obvious associations. In the first place, it recalls biblical references to the dove: in the Old Testament, the dove which returns to the ark with an olive-twig is the first sign to Noah that the Flood is receding and that God has had mercy on him (Genesis 8. 10-13); in the New Testament, the dove is the visual representation of the Holy Spirit (see, for instance, John 1. 32-3). The name, Colombo, also recalls the great discoverer, Christopher Columbus. So, if we take all these associations together, the tavern-keeper's name may well lead us to expect him to be an adventurous man of strong religious faith. But again, the character's words and actions fail to fulfil the promise of his name. . . . [Silvestro's last impression of Porfirio includes] an allusion to the strange little story in Genesis about how Noah, having survived the Flood, took to farming. Amongst his crops were grapes, from which he was the first man to make wine. He got drunk on the wine and was found naked by one of his sons on whom he therefore put a curse (9. 20-3). So Noah was 'padre . . . del vino' in two senses: father of wine, and the wine-sodden father of the son who witnessed his disgrace. The implication here is that Silvestro has witnessed the corruption by wine of Porfirio, who had formerly seemed, like Noah to be the one man who was not corrupt.

The four men's susceptibility to wine is only an image for the ease with which their ideals can be corrupted. It confirms the reader's suspicion that the contradiction observed between the name of each character and his stated philosophy indicates the inherent weakness of that philosophy. It also reinforces his sense, gained partly from the curious manner in which the allusions associated with the four char-

acters overlap with each other, that the weakness of each is interwoven with the weaknesses of the others. On the level of topical comment, this appears to represent a wholesale rejection of the great range of responses to Fascist oppression which could be found in Italy in the 1930s. The broader implication would seem to be that the roles of the militant revolutionary, of the compassionate observer, of the religious man, of the dispenser of panaceas for the ills of the world, are individually inadequate, but also essentially indistinct from each other. (pp. 78-80)

The significant allusions to be found in Part Five are not clustered, as allusions in the earlier parts are, around the names of the novel's own characters, but mostly around characters from two of Shakespeare's tragedies in which Costantino used to act. . . .

[There are references to] *Macbeth* and *Hamlet* . . . , both indeed about the murder of a king by the man who usurps his throne. The presence of father, mother and son in Silvestro's fantasy suggests that he is thinking of himself as being about to play the role of Hamlet—with all its associations of self-doubt and evasion of duty. Part of the function of this episode is to illustrate Silvestro's increasing consciousness that he may himself be an actor with a central role in the drama. . . .

[There is a] very striking parallel between Silvestro's encounter with the ghost of his soldier-brother, Liborio, and the appearance of ghosts in *Hamlet* and *Macbeth*. . . . The implications of these parallels for Silvestro are serious: he must begin to feel either that he has a personal duty (like Hamlet) to put right the wrong that others have done, or that he is himself indirectly responsible for the crime that has been committed (like Macbeth). (p. 81)

[Silvestro's] perception of the world has undergone a permanent change as a result of the revelation in the cemetery of his personal responsibility for the injuries done to the world. . . . The sky is full of black crows at which people in the area are firing, though none is hit. The whole scene recalls the words spoken by Macbeth just after he despatches the murderers to kill Banquo:

> Light thickens; and the crow
> Makes wing to th' rooky wood;
> Good things of Day begin to droop and drowse,
> While Night's black agents to their preys do rouse.

What Vittorini adds to Shakespears's identification of crows with murderers is a topical allusion to black-shirted Fascists and the observation that they are invulnerable to attack. (pp. 81-2)

[In the epilogue, the] descriptions of Costantino, as a Christ-figure taking on himself the sins of the world, as a prodigal son, and as a travel-weary Odysseus, are clearly applicable also to Silvestro himself. So, when Silvestro glimpses his father at the very end of the book, he wholly identifies with Costantino's situation, having now come to realize that his father, partly through acting Shakespeare, has long understood the nature of oppression and of the responsibility we all bear for the sufferings of others, in a way which has eluded Silvestro. That is why it is inappropriate for him to greet his father.

Identification of the host of allusions present in *Conversazione in Sicilia* requires us to reassess the significance of the novel in two major respects. First, we need to recognize that the novel offers, especially in Part Four, an acute and fairly specific critique of the various postures adopted by men of good will living under Fascism immediately before the Second World War. Secondly, it makes a far more demanding assertion, especially in Part Five, of the universal moral and political responsibilities of the individual than any critic has hitherto been prepared to concede. It is, paradoxically, through its near-hermetic allusiveness that *Conversazione in Sicilia* achieves a fierce moral and political exploration. (pp. 82-3)

> *Michael Hanne, "Significant Allusions in Vittorini's 'Conversazione in Sicilia'," in* The Modern Language Review *(© Modern Humanities Research Association 1975), January, 1975, pp. 75-83.*

W

WAKOSKI, Diane   1937-

Wakoski is an American poet much admired for her poetry of personal experience made powerful through the use of vivid language and imagery. She writes poetry because "I care more about communication than almost anyone I ever met." (See also *CLC*, Vols. 2, 4, 7, and *Contemporary Authors*, Vols. 13-16, rev. ed.)

Wakoski, though she's a poet of unusual talent and vitality, seems to me to display a tendency toward staleness, flatness, repetitiveness in [*Dancing on the Grave of a Son of a Bitch*], a tendency, in other words, to self-parody. A fabulist, a weaver of gorgeous webs of imagery and a teller of archetypically glamorous tales, she's always attempted self-definition through self-mythologizing. "The poems were a way of inventing myself into a new life," she has said. Similarly, she's always tried to define the world by developing —to borrow Jerome Rothenberg's phrase—a technology of the sacred. But where in earlier books, *Inside the Blood Factory* for example, the rich secret world of George Washington and the King of Spain, Diane the moon goddess and her motorcycle betrayer, usually achieved a kind of magical autonomy, in this collection the sacred figures seem at times profanely weary, despite the presence of marvelous fables like *The Diamond Merchant*.

In choosing to write fairy tales about her secret self, Wakoski has always, of course, flirted with a little girl cuteness that threatens not to wear well, threatens to cloy as though the poet had decided to spend her life in an Alice in Wonderland costume wandering among not archetypes but stereotypes. Now, when the vitality of her imagination fails, the furry red lion of the sun, the cold sisterly moon maiden, the wise gentlemanly Buddha and the mustachioed motorcycle betrayer begin to seem like a collection of stuffed toys ranged on the shelves of some female Walter Mitty. And as her persistent imagery tires, Wakoski's language weakens, flattens. Lines like "Winter is a crystal. / Spring is a pool ... Autumn is a crackle / a fire. ..." or "A man's name / on my lips / thru all 4 / of the seasons" plainly try to draw on the naive strength that gave such poems as *Blue Monday* or *The House of the Heart* their extraordinary power, but the visionary energy falters.... Certainly the title piece of this collection, an extended curse dedicated to "my motorcycle betrayer" and written "in the spirit of ritual recitation" seems oddly powerless compared to her earlier confessional incantations. Passages like

You ride a broken motorcycle,
You speak a dead language
You are a bad plumber,
And you write with an inkless pen.
You were mean to me,
and I've survived,
God damn you,
at last I am going to dance on your grave,
old man. ...

sound childish rather than childlike, and—more important —they appear to lack even the forward-driving, ritual force of rage.

And yet perhaps these problematically weary pieces are simply signs that Wakoski—serenely established ...—has entered a transitional phase. "The Astronomer Poems" with which she begins this book seem, at any rate, to have a wonderful, newly speculative coolness and restraint. Apparently slight, brief flashes of light in a beautifully evoked darkness, the best of them combine the philosophical teasings of a poet like—yes—Stevens, with Wakoski's own characteristically mythic *Weltschmerz*. (pp. 294-95)

> *Sandra M. Gilbert, in* Poetry (© *1976 by The Modern Poetry Association; reprinted by permission of the Editor of* Poetry), *August, 1976.*

Wakoski's [poems] are not built on images or combinations of them so much as they work through repeated sounds—idiomatic refrains—to weave the separate sections of the poem into a whole.... Wakoski's poems do not divide readily into "personal" and "social." Her tactic is rather to use what appears to be the personal—sometimes the ultra personal, even trivial—as a means of reaching a wider kind of statement. A poem about her relationship with a neighbor's cat, for instance, turns out to be "about" the problems of life's duality; just as moral injustice is the real theme of her much-anthologized "Justice Is Reason Enough." ...

[The] poems are searching for promise. The mythic quest—imaged ... [in *Waiting for the King of Spain*] as the search for a lost beloved—brings neither sorrow nor stasis but a moving affirmation. As Wakoski writes,

Like a battleship,
my life goes on. Seen from an aerial view,

slow-moving, bulky and visible. It moves . . .
Like fire.
Like water.
Motion . . .

The process is self-knowledge, a recognition of one person's dependency on another; the method is change, growth, the capacity to know vulnerability. . . .

The [poet's] emphasis on the endurance of woman, as poet, as seer, runs through [this collection]. . . . Wakoski is [not], strictly speaking, [a] "feminist" poet, but [she does not deny the] specific strengths and understandings of [her] sex. [There are] impressive poems about the poet as explorer of human needs and satisfaction. Through this process of exploration, [and] its necessary change, . . . [Wakoski appears to have come to her own identity as creator and affirmer]. (p. 348)

> *Linda Wagner, in* The Nation *(copyright 1977 by the Nation Associates, Inc.), March 19, 1977.*

Waiting for the King of Spain is a re-run of the illusions which Wakoski has carefully constructed over the years as to what constitutes her life. Or, as she says by way of preface to a section entitled "Reviewing," "the new is the old / viewed, and reviewed, / viewed over & over." Here "George Washington Meets the King of Spain (on the Magellanic Clouds)" as the extravagant title of one poem announces. Those who have followed Wakoski's progress . . . will find themselves right at home here. George Washington, the father figure (*The George Washington Poems*, 1967), the Magellanic clouds, representatives of mysterious astrological and astronomical forces (*The Magellanic Clouds*, 1970), and the King of Spain, the faithful lover and sun sign, "his gold tooth flashing like flowers," (*Looking for the King of Spain*, 1974) are played like the trumps of the tarot. Their signification only varies with respect to their placement.

But Wakoski is inventing her own pack of cards. Meet the motorcycle mechanic (*The Motorcycle Betrayal Poems*, 1971), The Man With the Silver Belt Buckle (*The Diamond Merchant*, 1968). You have met them all before. "Loving is / the secret; not / being loved," Wakoski concludes. This too is familiar territory, as are the brilliant bejeweled sets upon which she acts out the continuing drama of her betrayals. . . . Her life is the same haunting preoccupation with love, which is more realized in fantasy than in reality.

Wakoski's own card is still the Moon, but again it is the moon of her own invention. Sometimes she is the unbeautiful Diana, watching the "beautiful blond boys / I moon and yearn for" choose beautiful "bronzy girls." Sometimes she is Cinderella, waiting for her prince to come, looking for the glass slipper so that she might "walk elegantly out of the state of California." She is the bitch goddess, the huntress with an "M" on her arm, moon, marriage, murder, Michael (the book is dedicated to "all the Michaels"). She strives for the archetypal feminine, the Virgin Queen, dark enchantress, the abandoned Dido.

It is all very elegant put this way. But stripped of all the mythologizing, we are left with something rather banal. What Wakoski is ultimately interested in is "relationships." I mean relationships as defined by the pop sociologists and fan magazines—relationships which are described as either "meaningful" and "beautiful" or "destructive." Relationships, in this sense, are one of the great inventions of our time, along with electric ping pong and light beer. People who used to talk about marriage or friendship now have "relationships." "I have never had love 'objects' in / my life," Wakoski writes in "The Pepper Plant," "because the process of a relationship is what makes it / alive. I think that is why I have been able to form and experience / so many deep relationships with men."

It is the failure of these relationships which is the motive force for her work. . . . [The] only thing "which / could transform my life with true misery now" is if the man she loved left her. Which he does, with predictable regularity, providing the misery necessary to force her to recreate herself, and her poems are the chronicles of this recreation, an endless cycle of rising from the ashes, a phoenix too frequent. If these attitudes seem curiously adolescent, the language is not. But even Wakoski's ability to manipulate her images seems to be faltering. The driving intensity which marked her earlier work seems lacking, her huntress is no longer so terrible, and her Dido sounds more and more like the little girl lost.

Like many women, Wakoski has a marvelously sensual imagination. . . . But food, wine, jewels, flowering plants only momentarily block out the loneliness that seeps into the poems like damp during the rainy season. Poems that teeter on the edge of celebration continually fall prey to her morbid preoccupation with loving and losing. The "M" would ultimately seem to stand only for Man and his insufficiencies. . . . I have admired Wakoski's work for a long time. But I have grown tired of its predictability. Her language has come to act like a heavily ornate frame from which the picture has been removed. (pp. 170-71)

> *Kathleen Wiegner, in* The Minnesota Review *(© 1977 by The Minnesota Review), Spring, 1977.*

Reading Diane Wakoski's *Waiting for the King of Spain* impresses with that energetic range of poems that are about poetry, about tennis, about the lost lover . . . , about places: Wakoski's gift is to make all the elements of life into poems, and to do it with humor. . . . By moving . . . rapidly among [a] swirl of images, Wakoski is able to reach each reader quickly, to lead each reader into the total experience of the poem through what seems to be personal detail. But the method of seeing correspondence between Wakoski as poet and Wakoski as person can be misleading. . . . What happens, simply, is that personal details in the poem are used as conventions: we recognize the pervasive figure in Wakoski's poems because of her previous life in California, with its imagery of oranges and sun; her search for the perfect lover; her lament for her George Washington-like father and her nondescript mother; and her insistence on staying alive, joyfully.

The Wakoski persona in *Waiting for the King of Spain* is the familiar one, but the tones of self-evaluation and remorse for the loss of an important love are darker in this collection. "I met you at the wrong time. / Your face was a pocket watch, / heavy and gold, / and I, a woman in a thin dress, / one with no pockets," sets the mood for many of these poems: "Wanting to make music / as if each note could be cut into shape; . . . / Wishing beauty were not owned." But as in her previous three or four collections,

Wakoski works through her distinctively fluid long format to bring the poem, nearly every time, to the formal distinctions so important to her and to her art—the lines of beauty, the shapes of poetry, the solace of music. Rather than being a world of personal autobiographical images, Wakoski's poem world is one of aesthetics, of philosophy, of art. "What is a cloud anyway? Not even as substantial as a poem." "Silence is something / I do not trust / anymore. / We all must speak / and finally / live by our own words." (pp. 90-1)

Linda W. Wagner, in The Ontario Review *(copyright © 1977 by The Ontario Review), Fall–Winter, 1977-78.*

*   *   *

WALCOTT, Derek 1930-

Walcott is a West Indian poet and playwright. With the publication in 1962 of *In a Green Night,* **he was hailed as the first outstanding Caribbean poet. A recurring theme in Walcott's verse is the isolation of man, and in particular the isolation of the artist. His drama is characterized by a concern with the influences modern society brings to bear on man. (See also** *CLC,* **Vols. 2, 4.)**

[The Caribbean plays of Derek Walcott] are not precisely *Latin* American, having been written in English and Trinidadian patois, not Spanish or Portuguese. . . . Yet Walcott's plays are not in the naturalist and/or militant mainstream of North American black drama of the past decade. Whether or not the Latin American influence is direct, indirect, or coincidental, the affinities of Walcott's poetic folk dramas to such plays as *The Mulatto's Orgy* and *On the Right Hand of God the Father* are greater than to the uncompromising naturalism and revolutionary exhortation of Bullins and Baraka. Surely the white exploitation of black folk materials in such entertainments as *The Green Pastures* and *Cabin in the Sky* has soured such materials for North American black writers.

Walcott does not anathematize the part of his sensibility which is white. Nor does he fully accept it. He recognizes that it is part of what he is as a writer and as a man. He notes the colonial oppressiveness which created the subservience and self-hatred of "native" culture, but he realizes that the past cannot be obliterated, that he must accept the cultural schizophrenia which has formed him. "My generation looked at life with black skin and blue eyes," he states in the poetic prologue to his collection of plays [*Dream on Monkey Mountain, and Other Plays*]. His roots are in Warwickshire as well as in Africa, and his literary tradition is in a very real sense that of Chaucer and Shakespeare. His God, as remorseless and irresponsible as He is, is Christian, and his Devil is Milton's Lost Angel. One theme which unites his plays is "one race's quarrel with another's God."

The acceptance of the complexity of human personality and culture, the unwillingness to sacrifice the ambiguity and self-doubt which leads to self-discovery, the simultaneous homage to the claims of the old and the demands of the new —distinguish Walcott's plays. First and foremost, this is poetic drama. Nuance, irony, metaphor—these are the demands the playwright makes of his language. In all the plays he roots his dialogue in Trinidadian dialect, a patois of English and French. But it is not naturalistic: he has attempted to forge "a language that went beyond mimicry,

. . . one which finally settled on its own mode of inflection, and which began to create an oral culture of chants, jokes, folk songs and fables." And to imbue this diction with the resonance of the great English poetic tradition.

Walcott's language, when he is not striving too consciously for high poetic effect, works well theatrically, particularly in his major plays. In the shorter plays, *The Sea at Dauphin* and *Malcochon,* the language as well as the forms of the plays themselves aspire too strenuously for traditional tragic resonance. In both the former play—which attempts to evoke for impoverished Caribbean fisherfolk the stoic dignity of Synge's *Riders to the Sea*—and the latter—a folk tragedy which finds Man "between beasthood and godhead groping in a dream"—the tensions between the indigenous materials and the traditional tragic forms are not wholly resolved. One senses too ardent a desire to claim that these people deserve the mantle of tragic nobility as well as Hamlet or Lear. The author's aim—"an electric fusion of the old and the new"—is not fully achieved. In the two major plays in the collection—*Ti-Jean and his Brothers* and *Dream on Monkey Mountain*—however, Walcott comes much closer to his goal by abandoning traditional tragic models and forging not only a new language but new dramatic structures as well. The tension between old and new —literary and ethnic—sensibilities continues, but it is expressed thematically and structurally rather than by pouring new wine into old bottles. (pp. 67-8)

Gerald Rabkin, in Review *(copyright © 1974 by the Center for Inter-American Relations, Inc.), Winter, 1974.*

In colonies where history has been suppressed or forgotten or never amounted to much, myths come easily. Perhaps that's why so much colonial history makes good movies. Derek Walcott in that prodigious autobiographical poem *Another Life* rejected 'the myth of the Golden Carib' while endeavouring to construct a new one. In [*Sea Grapes*] he gets down to cases, beginning with the Fall and working backwards. . . . Where before, eloquence bordered on effusion, in the opening sections of *Sea Grapes* the lushness of the verse is carefully tended. Walcott has never written better. The perfect garden sets off human frailty. . . . From the Caribbean garden to the rough smoky world is a move inevitable enough. But Walcott is too intelligent to imagine that independence restores lost innocence. 'Then after Eden/ was there one surprise?/O yes, the awe of Adam/at the first bead of sweat.' . . .

Colonization often entails that a ludicrous history be visited upon an unsuspecting people. In the disenchantment with the aftermath of independence, his control falters and Walcott's language becomes too wild to connect. (pp. 82-3)

Christopher Hope, in London Magazine *(© London Magazine 1977), February-March, 1977.*

Sea Grapes is full of bitterness against those who oppress and enslave; and it is full of compassion for those who suffer losses that seem beyond words. The figure of the exile —particularly the exiled writer, and whether the fact of exile be actual or metaphoric—weighs on Walcott's mind and heart. A post-Adamic world is acknowledged although there are glimpses of moments of what the Garden of Eden might have been like before the Fall.

The long poem "Sainte Lucie," named for the island where Walcott was born, engages us in naming villages, fruits, birds, and people as if naming them helps to bring them back or get them right or create them in the spirit of some Adamic feat; a lusty Creole song is sung; an altarpiece in a native church gives rise to depicting what is carved on it, and what might have been carved on it in another time by someone else. Elaborate counterpointing makes belief again possible to the extent that the modern, ironic poet can allow belief at all. . . . There is a clean sharpness about these poems which engages me. (pp. 186-87)

[In "Force," the] beast, or the bestial, is equated with a force beyond easy moral categories, and perhaps beyond moral categories at all. Love and violence, and instinct and reason, are shown to be less separate than they might ordinarily be thought to be. In the same way, the fear of violation and the wish to be violated draw together as the poet moves toward the conclusion of the poem. . . . If what he sees outside him does not help him accept the contrary, contradictory parts of himself, neither does it prevent him from the possibility of acknowledging what understanding *has* been possible. He will never completely understand the beast in the man, the beast as man, or the writing beast. Yet by starting with the rain "hammering the grass blades into the ground," Walcott makes some understanding of himself to himself and to us possible. (p. 188)

I find the same clean language of "Force" displayed in "Earth" and complicated by the resonance of ritual this other poem demands. . . . A study in possession, "Earth" takes us as deeply as we could go short of death. To the extent that we all die, none of us can ever be dispossessed. The movement of the poem is at once upward and downward, and both motions are in quest of that total possession. It is a knowledge we come to very late, the poet suggests, but a knowledge that stands there only waiting to be embraced. Calm, authoritative, the poem takes in language as different as "vegetal knuckles" and "through forever." And it is suggestive and representative of what the whole book of Walcott manages so exceedingly well. (pp. 188-89)

> *Arthur Oberg, in* Western Humanities Review *(copyright, 1976, University of Utah), Spring, 1977.*

The title poem of Derek Walcott's *Sea Grapes* brings together, with stunning effectiveness, certain qualities readers have come to associate with this poet: visually powerful sea imagery, a wealth of classical allusions and a deeply felt concern for the Caribbean ethos. This recent collection of Walcott's poetry contains forty-six poems ranging widely in theme and set against several countries—Britain, the United States and the West Indies.

The potency of Walcott's imagery lies in an uncanny commingling of lyricism and unvarnished realism: for example, sunset that "shares its mortal properties/with the least stone in Frederiksted" is a show waited for by "old men like empties/set down from morning outside the almshouses." There is an overwhelming sense of dry disillusionment and cynicism as Walcott's razor touch slashes at the prostitution of people, cities and nations, but there is also the inextinguishability of the human spirit. . . .

In the poems dedicated to fellow writers Walcott zeroes in on something integral to the other's attitudes or contribution. For instance, in a poem for John Figueroa these are

the lines: "a gnarled poet/bearded with the whirlwind,/his metres like thunder." "At Last," a poem addressed to novelists who have contemptuously left the West Indies, expresses Walcott's thundering affirmation that Caribbean literature has come into its own. If anyone had any doubts on that score, *Sea Grapes* will help dispel them. (p. 325)

> *Uma Parameswaran, in* World Literature Today *(copyright 1977 by the University of Oklahoma Press), Vol. 51. No. 2, Spring, 1977.*

* * *

WALKER, Alice 1944-

Walker is an American poet, novelist, short story writer, and essayist. Walker's work has consistently reflected concern for the plight of the black American family. Her work is noted for its powerful narrative and sensitive portraits of black life in America. (See also *CLC*, Vols. 5, 6, and *Contemporary Authors*, Vols. 37-40.)

In "Meridian," Alice Walker has written a fine, taut novel that accomplishes a remarkable amount. The issues she is concerned with are massive. Events are strung over 25 years, although most occur between the height of the civil rights movement and the present. However, her method of compression through selection of telling moments and her freedom from chronology create a lean book that . . . goes down like clean water. . . .

She writes with a sharp critical sense as she deals with the issues of tactics and strategy in the civil rights movement, with the nature of commitment, the possibility of interracial love and communication, the vital and lethal strands in American and black experience, with violence and nonviolence, holiness and self-hatred. . . .

Meridian, the protagonist, is the most interesting [character in the book], an attempt to make real in contemporary terms the notion of holiness and commitment. Is it possible to write a novel about the progress of a saint? Apparently, yes. With great skill and care to make Meridian believable at every stage of her development, Walker also shows us the cost. For every exemplary act of bravery for the black community (standing up to a tank so black children can see a peepshow) she pays an immediate price in her body. Asked by a group of temporary revolutionaries if she can kill for the revolution, she infuriates her friends because she cannot say an easy yes and spends a decade worrying the question.

Walker has put "Meridian" together carefully, on every level. (p. 5)

I do not find the ending successful. Walker consciously rejects death. Meridian's political commitment is not to end in martyrdom: there have been too many martyrs to her cause. Still, we need some other equivalent of death or marriage to round off a tale, and Walker has not found one here. We are told that Meridian has brought off a successful change from victim to fully responsible protagonist. . . . But telling is not enough. She has ceased to be one sort of committed person and become another. Some act is needed to make real the change and it isn't there; but that's a minor failure in a tight, fascinating novel. (p. 12)

> *Marge Piercy, in* The New York Times Book Review *(© 1976 by The New York*

Times Company; reprinted by permission), May 23, 1976.

At its best, . . . the tone of ["Meridian" is] flat, direct, measured, deliberate, with a distinct lack of drama. . . . And the tone is right; it's not the plot that carries the novel forward but Meridian's attempt to resolve, or preserve the reality of, the questions of knowledge, history, and murder that Miss Walker introduces early on. The astonishing dramatic intensity that Walker brought to "The Third Life of Grange Copeland" would in "Meridian" blow those questions apart.

But such questions lead all too easily to high-flown language and to pretensions that fictional characters cannot support, which is why most "philosophical" novels are impossible to reread. Miss Walker does not always avoid this trap; though her tendency is to insist on the prosaic, to bring philosophy down to earth, Meridian at times seems to be floating straight to Heaven. The book tries to make itself a parable—more than a mere novel—or trades the prosaic for an inert symbolism that would seem to be intended to elevate the story but instead collapses it. . . .

Meridian is interesting enough without . . . symbolism and "higher meanings" that are one-dimensional and fixed. There is no mystery in these symbols . . . and a symbol without mystery, without suggestive power, is not really a symbol at all. But most of the book's scenes have the power its symbols lack, and its last chapters rescue Meridian's questions from a holy oblivion. For they are resolved, after a fashion, and passed on . . . not only to the book's other characters, who share Meridian's life, but perhaps to the reader as well. (pp. 135-36)

The New Yorker (© *1976 by The New Yorker Magazine, Inc.*), *June 7, 1976.*

Although Walker's first book, *Once*, a collection of poems, was favorably reviewed, she remained relatively unknown until acclaimed for her novel, *The Third Life of Grange Copeland* (1970). Now, reputation established, she has returned to her primary interest with *Revolutionary Petunias.* . . .

Walker prefers a plain, unaffected diction and moderately open forms which permit her to reveal homespun truths of human behavior and emotion, and sing quietly of love for family, friends, other black people. . . . (p. 202)

People are the subjects—not the iron robots forged in a world of neon and concrete, not the blind and strident warriors who exploit their followers. Walker's heroes and heroines, "common" folk, distinguished by essential goodness and sympathy for others, live in a world of death, separation, and, sometimes, birth. (p. 204)

Somehow, the nostalgic tone [of the first section] does not erase the sense that this world is vanishing. People are always dying; few are being born, others are leaving. (p. 205)

In the second section, "Revolutionary Petunias," Walker propounds a creed of individualism personified in the unadorned depiction of Sammy Lou of Rue, one of the "common" folk of Section I. Sammy Lou is no "militant," no monster. She raises children and petunias, and she respects God. But, when her husband is killed, she avenges his death in a matter-of-fact way—with a hoe. Then, unable to recognize herself in the lurid, literary recountings of her deed, she goes "she didn't/know where, except it would be by/electric chair." (p. 206)

In "Crucifixions," the third section, Walker renounces the "ugly warriors"—those black "revolutionaries" who, savoring a new diet of blood, delight in crucifixions. Armored against emotion, against truth, their eyes burn, "sharp . . . bright . . . righteous . . . but blind." (p. 207)

Having rejected the calls to follow the crowd, Walker, in the fourth section, describes the "Mysteries" of love with homely, unexpected twists of thought. Occasionally she disappoints by lapsing into phrases bordering on the banal, . . . [but] she concludes the fifth section with her strongest affirmations of love. . . . (p. 208)

Darwin Turner, in Parnassus: Poetry in Review *(copyright © by* Parnassus: Poetry in Review), *Spring-Summer, 1976.*

[Alice Walker] deals, in *Meridian*, with a heroine who has not fully broken the gravitational field of the '60's; if she keeps the faith, as most do not, she also feels the fetters of the disbanded revolutionary movement, as most do not. Prematurely aged, preternaturally reflective in the continual hot demand for justice and self-fulfillment—still the two great passions of our time—Meridian must decide whether she will, for the cause, commit the ultimate violence of killing. The problem is that she considers this the ultimate violence to herself as well as to another. The book is a patchwork of incidents, memories, projections, with a continual sense of performance, of ritual acts and even thoughts for public consumption and assay. Meridian's name echoes ritually in those of other female characters, Anne and Anne-Marion. It echoes even more tellingly in the high-noon quality of the situations in which so many of the characters find themselves—stark, boundary-marking situations concerning the very choice of life they must make. Some will hear echoes of *The Autobiography of Miss Jane Pittman* here, but Walker's work is far more inward, and more socially complex withal, than Gaines's. The culminating scene of the defiant old lady in *Miss Jane Pittman* is the opening scene of *Meridian*, as if Walker were moving on from Gaines as deliberately as Wordsworth from Milton. (p. 154)

Oates contends à la Skinner that "the personal life is over," but Alice Walker has her version of the eternal "wanderer . . . looking for . . . anything to keep his historical vision of himself as a just person from falling apart."

A vision of the just person, rather than of the right-on revolutionary or the now-or-never woman, informs *Meridian*. (pp. 154-55)

More than ordinary action, violence is transitory and exhausts its resources and its goals. What Walker slowly appreciates through Meridian is the enormous energies composed in true, choice inaction, the great questions resolved in the endless debate of silence. The fruitfulness of Meridian's choice of inaction and silence may be revealed in the growing back of her hair, in her rejuvenation and refeminization. It is a choice less synecdochic (one woman for all) than paradigmatic (every woman must decline, parse by herself). . . . (p. 155)

Michael G. Cooke, in The Yale Review (© *1976 by Yale University; reprinted by permission of the editors), Autumn, 1976.*

WELDON, Fay   1933-

A British playwright and novelist, Weldon is also a successful screenwriter of television dramas. Weldon's fiction, reflecting a concern for women in contemporary society, consistently refuses an ideological stance. In her sensitive and often witty portraits of modern marriage, Weldon lends an air of universality to the domestic dramas she creates. (See also *CLC*, Vol. 6, and *Contemporary Authors*, Vols. 21-24, rev. ed.)

Considering how much I enjoyed reading *Remember Me,* it may seem churlish to begin by carping at the shortcomings that still disquality Fay Weldon from the league into which her publishers have promoted her—'one of Britain's major novelists'. But her new book is so much better than her last, *Female Friends,* that such claims look no longer merely wishful; and it would be at least insulting, therefore, to gloss over the blemishes.

The chief trouble is that Mrs Weldon has found no settled style of her own as a novelist. Where *Female Friends* seemed to be made up out of left-over television scripts, *Remember Me* reflects a crash course in the kind of diluted experimentalism that has made some people think that Kurt Vonnegut is the greatest living American writer. There is a lot of Under Milk-and-Water Wood. . . . Then there are patches of play-script dialogue, sometimes preceded and followed by kindergartenish directions ('Listen to Jamie and Judy now . . .'; 'Poor little grey, badly-behaved Judy. Poor smarting Jamie . . .'), sometimes with the speeches numbered to match a similarly-numbered 'translation' from which you are to learn what the speakers really mean by their clichés. . . .

[The book] is very entertaining as black farce, often cruelly shrewd about the intimate relations of near relations, sometimes coming close to articulating the large conclusions about the meaning of life that these messy lives are meant to signify. Yet never quite articulating them: the supernaturalism is a cop-out, the mark of unwillingness, or worse, to try to make real sense of the fresh wounds and old scars collected in those dangerous games. That is why, notwithstanding her best performance yet, Fay Weldon will have to wait for that promotion. (p. 486)

> *Neil Hepburn, in* The Listener *(© British Broadcasting Corp. 1976; reprinted by permission of Neil Hepburn), October 14, 1976.*

The troubled and confused characters in ["Remember Me"] are Londoners of a fairly ordinary sort, and by the time they are through leaping over the obstacles and dealing with the bizarre problems Mrs. Weldon invents for them, they are a bedraggled lot indeed. Rather like people in a breathless, ongoing comic opera, they speak to the reader directly, introducing themselves in the least imaginative of ways, defining themselves almost exclusively in terms of two or three other people. (p. 7)

While writers with the patience and sensitivity of Margaret Drabble or Penelope Mortimer can still make us respond to the plight of the oppressed housewife, the theme itself has become a very familiar one. The startling revelations of one decade become, all too frequently, the shopworn clichés of the next.

Mrs. Weldon's scorn for her characters is expressed in frequent authorial intrusions; she cannot resist patting her characters on the head and saying, patronizingly, "Good

Lily!" "Kind Lily!" "Oh Jarvis!" "Disloyal, disconnected Margot!" The effect is that the reader soon loses sympathy with them, for if an author is contemptuous of his or her characters, how can the reader feel otherwise?

"Remember Me" has the breathlessness of an Iris Murdoch novel, and some of its inventiveness. But it lacks depth and resonance, and it resolves itself as glibly as any situation comedy, despite the seriousness of the issues involved. Is it possible that feminist concerns with the exploitation of women by men, while still painfully relevant to our lives, are no longer viable as subjects for serious fiction? By denying subtlety and humanity to roughly one-half the population, and by delineating Maleness in place of specific human beings who happen to be male, the writer with feminist interests severely jeopardizes her power to create imaginative literature. (p. 54)

> *Joyce Carol Oates, in* The New York Times Book Review *(© 1976 by The New York Times Company; reprinted by permission), November 21, 1976.*

Having enjoyed and admired Fay Weldon's *Female Friends* enormously, I looked forward with keen anticipation to her latest novel, *Remember Me*. I expected to be shocked. I expected to learn something about women which I didn't know before. Quite simply, I expected what I don't often get from a straight novelist—a good read. I wasn't disappointed.

For Mrs. Weldon is a natural novelist. That is her proper medium. She can sustain a narrative and she can create characters. And she possesses that very rare quality, a sardonic, earthy, disenchanted, slightly bitter but never cruel sense of humour. She is wholly feminine—and I mean this as a compliment. She is the Great Earth Mother who has seen it all. For her the male is a biological interlude. The world of the women is the only real world. (I hasten to add that I speak of Mrs. Weldon only in her novelist's *persona*.) And this is her great attraction as a writer. She admits the male into a world which is otherwise barred to him.

It is—and this is very important—a heterosexual world. There is a Lesbian character in *Remember Me*, who hangs around hoping to enlist casualties from the sex war on her side. But her only success is brief and will not last. No matter how hellish their relationships with men may be, no matter how much better their own sex may understand them, for Mrs. Weldon's women sex means men. . . .

[It's] extremely refreshing to come across a novelist who gives children their proper place in the scheme of things, and who doesn't regard them as mere appendages. In fact, Mrs. Weldon's children are genuine individual children. They aren't miniature adults and they aren't fantastic puppets dancing on Freudian strings.

And that is yet another virtue of Mrs. Weldon. She is never vague. She never leaves the reader wondering how old a character is, what they look like, what specifically they are doing. We are told what her characters eat and drink, how they earn their living, how their houses are furnished. She doesn't overload the narrative with detail; she understands what few novelists understand, that physical details are not embellishments on the story, but the bricks from which the story is made. . . .

The details [in *Remember Me*] make the story, Jarvis's face, the skin loose from dieting, the honey-and-orange-juice at breakfast, the eggs from the health-food shop, the soft and silky down on Lily's arms, Jonathon's silver spoon, polished every day so that it's becoming dangerously sharp: all these aspects of the material world are the consequences of what we are and also make us what we are. . . . [All] the details are unerringly right. Miss Weldon never puts a foot wrong.

Yes, she is a very good writer. Yes, *Remember Me* is a very good novel. But I do have one reservation. I wish that either she hadn't used the question-and-answer technique or that she'd devised some way of formalising it and filling it out. When I'm asked to accept two words, 'Who's asleep?' as a whole line of narrative, I can't help feeling rather cheated. And I think that numbering certain lines of dialogue is rather pretentious. It adds nothing to the story. And the extra spaces between question and answer infuriate me. . . .

Having said this, I must make it clear that I'm sure that Mrs. Weldon's sole reason for using this technique was that it seemed to her to be the one best suited to her material. She is a dedicated artist, which means that with each book she tries harder, that she's never content simply to do what she's done before. In this case, I think that she's tried too hard, that the book succeeds in spite of its techniques not because of it.

John Braine, "A Natural Novelist," in Books and Bookmen *(© copyright John Braine 1977; reprinted with permission), January, 1977, p. 28.*

Remember Me manages to be so many books simultaneously that one is briskly, delightedly swept along, only to wonder breathlessly at the end whether the stunning impact comes from a Grimm fairy tale/ghost story, or from a witty excursion into contemporary London mores and marriage, or from a rich, soothing, old-fashioned English comedy of manners. It comes, of course, from all three. Weldon . . . writes with unrelenting clearsightedness about the wasted, but not hopeless, lives of women, and the men they cling to. Her book accomplishes more than a dozen polemics and is entertaining besides.

At its most superficial, *Remember Me* is a not-unfamiliar urbane tale of middle-class marital reshuffling, proliferating guilt, resentment, awkward dinner parties, and leftover children. . .

Fay Weldon is one of the most accomplished fabulists around. Her fable is replete with the requisite cast of characters: scorned Queen turned Witch; selfish, vain younger Queen; Ugly Duckling Princess denied her rightful place by Wicked Stepmother; confused King ruled by Female Powers behind the throne; modest Lady-in-Waiting who steals the Princess for safekeeping. (No ogres, however. In *Female Friends* the male characters were uniformly disgusting; in *Remember Me* they are merely emotionally weak.) All are influenced unawares by the ghost of the mutilated Madeleine, who refuses to rest in peace until her child is removed from the hateful clutches of the stepmother, Lily.

Madeleine's ghost, in all its invisibility, is an extraordinarily effective fictional creation, literally surging through the novel, giving it impetus and breadth.

Remember Me may appear, mistakenly, to be a creaking-door type of chiller. Quite the contrary. In texture, it has the warmth and comfort of the traditional realistic novel of social relations, in which we rest assured that the author will take good care of us. In the past, this care meant supplying abundant supportive detail and family background, connecting plot links and snipping straggly ends, and, best of all, offering a sturdy framework of accepted belief in which bizarre events might be set in balance and proportion. Weldon, like her forbears in the long line of efficient English novelists, does all this. Meticulous data on the paraphernalia of contemporary life . . . are given with the tongue-in-cheek wit expected of an already proven satirist. More remarkable is the brief, vivid portraiture of mothers, fathers, social classes, and childhood traumas belonging to the characters. None has the orphaned quality often found in current fiction; all have documented personal heritages that bring them, variously, through the crucial days of the story.

As for the framework: What holds this hybrid book together? Weldon's wry, occasionally expatiating voice, for one thing. So refreshingly willing is she to intrude her viewpoint that one almost expects her to break out with "Dear Reader" (she would get away with it, too). With enviable conviction, the authorial voice claims that the visceral tie between mother and child is the most unbreakable living bond; more generally, that the nature of human contact is molecular and circumstantial, yet meaningful, obscurely and at random:

> Almost nothing is wasted. Old friends . . .
> old enemies . . . old emotions, made sense of
> and transmuted into energy; . . . all the ma-
> terial flotsam washed up by the storms of
> our experience—all these have implication,
> and all lead us to the comforting notion that
> almost nothing in this world goes unnoticed;
> more, that almost nothing is unplanned.

As truth, perhaps difficult to accept. But, as the basis of a novel, it works wonderfully well.

Lynne Sharon Schwartz, "Quartet Plus Ghost," in The Village Voice *(reprinted by permission of* The Village Voice; *copyright © by The Village Voice, Inc., 1977), January 3, 1977, p. 58.*

* * *

WEST, Rebecca (pseudonym of Cecily Fairfield Andrews) 1892-

Dame Rebecca is an English novelist, journalist, critic, and travel writer. A diversified artist with contributions in many fields, West has maintained throughout her work a distinctive style marked by a witty, unique turn of phrase. An early devotee of James and Proust, West explores in her fiction the psychological motivations of her characters. (See also *CLC*, Vol. 7, and *Contemporary Authors*, Vols. 5-8, rev. ed.)

"There have as yet been very few women thinkers and artists", Rebecca West wrote in 1931; "that is to say, women who have not adopted masculine values as the basis of their work." . . . The point that Dame Rebecca was making was not that woman artists should be explicitly and exclusively feminine, but rather that they should be free to realize their gifts without considering the roles that social definitions of gender impose. . . . For Dame Rebecca, the ideal creative condition for a woman is to be beyond roles—to be a mirror of reality itself. Virginia Woolf was saying much the same thing, at the same time, in *A Room of One's Own,* when she described the "androgynous mind", and offered as a definition that "it is resonant and porous; that it transmits emotion without impediment; that it is naturally creative, incandescent and undivided".

Whether one takes Dame Rebecca's definition or Virginia Woolf's one must conclude that the greatest living example of a woman who has achieved that state, who has been both a thinker and an artist, and who has managed over some sixty years to express a spacious sense of reality, is Rebecca West. Indeed, one might propose that her achievement is not to be located in this book or in that one, but in the whole—that her books combine to make one created work of art, the mind of Rebecca West. There is support for this view in the fact that the name by which she is known is itself a persona taken from a work of art. When a writer chooses another name for his writing self, he is doing more than inventing a pseudonym: he is naming, and in a sense creating, his imaginative identity. Hence George Orwell—a commonplace Christian name and an English river—together name the plain-speaking Englishman that Eric Blair chose to be in his work. And Rebecca West is another such: the brilliant and rebellious Ibsen heroine is chosen to replace Cicily Fairfield (a name that in itself seems almost too good an example of English gentility). To choose that name was to claim the ideas and the radical posture of Ibsen, and particularly his ideas about women, as one's own public identity. The choice suggests an exceptional woman, willing her life to be an example of woman's situation.

One must feel some discomfort in the fact that an appreciation of so considerable a talent as Dame Rebecca's should start, inevitably, with the problems arising from her sex. In the case of some other woman writers this might be avoidable; but Dame Rebecca has made the subject a continuing theme of her work and of her life. There is scarcely a book of hers that does not have in it a feminist character (often thrust in anyhow, simply to make a speech against corsets), or a feminist idea. And her own career as a successful professional writer has demonstrated both the problem of being a woman artist, and the solution to it. . . .

[Dame Rebecca's first two books, *Henry James* and *Return of the Soldier,*] anticipate the later work in other ways than by their feminism: the critical book is witty, stylish, and full of self-assurance and high spirits; the novel holds implicit in it Dame Rebecca's mature sense of the world and human values. The world of the novel is a difficult one for sensitive persons to survive in: it is full of pain and suffering, frustration and betrayal, it will not adapt itself to human needs. In that world the greatest human value is realism—to know things as they are. . . . Communion with reality is a large ambition, and one that must lead a woman away from her private world, to politics and art and history, to law and religion and crime. It is the course that Dame Rebecca has followed, extending and deepening her account of reality until few modern writers can match her range, or her steady moral seriousness. (p. 1553)

By 1930, Dame Rebecca's version of reality was virtually complete in its broad outlines. Her world was a dualistic world, in which good and evil, life and death battle eternally, an uncertain world, where man wanders unsupported and unknowing. His enemy is within him: the will-to-die that hates life, the need to be cruel and to suffer. His hope is in his capacity for knowledge, for communion with reality, and for the imperishable order of art. Out of art, reason, and tradition man might construct the Just City; but that goal is obstructed by the spirit that denies.

That understanding of the world is clear, but it had not yet found imaginative expression. The literary forms Dame Rebecca worked in were still those of the woman novelist— the novel and the literary essay; and in the novel she was still hunting for a personal voice. One has no sense of increasing skill and assurance in the fiction she wrote during the 1930s, neither in the stories of *The Harsh Voice* (1935) nor in the novel, *The Thinking Reed* (1936). The two books are different in manner from each other, and from the earlier fiction, and the differences suggest uncertainty, and nervous experiment. One might well have concluded in 1936 that Dame Rebecca was not a novelist and would never be one.

But three years earlier she had taken a step that was to free her from restraining literary convention: she had agreed to write a short life of Saint Augustine. The assignment was an odd one for a literary journalist to take on, but it was a wise one: it led Dame Rebecca to history, religion and psychology and it engaged her mind with a great mind and a body of thought that touched her own deeply, and shaped her thinking for the rest of her career. (pp. 1553-54)

And what an odd masterpiece *Black Lamb and Grey Falcon* is! Superficially it is a travel book about a trip to the Balkans in 1937. But it includes so much more, is at once so comprehensive and so personal, that it has no genre, unless one invents one, calling it an epic testament, and placing it with the other great literary oddities of that odd genre— with Robert Burton's *Anatomy of Melancholy,* T. E. Lawrence's *Seven Pillars of Wisdom,* James Agee's *Let Us Now Praise Famous Men.* It is a narrative of a journey, and a long meditation on the patterns of Western history; it is a book of Balkan portraits, and a theory of the relations between East and West in Europe; and it is a book about its own time, a moving response to the contemporary political, moral and spiritual condition of Europe. . . .

The book itself is . . . a major example of the art that gives us hope. In its pages are combined all the gifts that earlier Dame Rebecca had distributed among many books: the vivid characterizations and descriptions; the powerful analyses of history and politics; the wit; the passages of meditative and lyric beauty. . . .

The historical importance of *Black Lamb* is, or should be, very great, for it is a supreme effort, by a mind at the height of its powers, to understand the catastrophe of the Second World War as it came on; it stands at the end of the 1930s like a massive baroque cenotaph. The importance for Dame Rebecca is also great and obvious; in this one book she cast aside entirely the restrictions of "woman writer" and revealed the true range of her mind. . . .

Rebecca West's greatest period of creativity began with *Black Lamb,* and one can see now how the books that follow depend on it and derive from it. The two books of trials, *The Meaning of Treason* (1949) and *A Train of Powder* (1955) relate to *Black Lamb* in two ways: they extend Dame Rebecca's "world" into the realm of law, and they complete her meditation on the meaning of modern history. Law must obviously be a crucial concept to one who sees the world divided between civilization and barbarism, for law is the wall that men build against disorder. Treason is a wilful breaching of that wall, and fascism is a denial that a wall can exist. . . .

To a religious mind, man's moral state is a constant, but political ideologies are transient; politics therefore ought to follow from religion, and to take pragmatic rather than ideological forms. In Dame Rebecca's case this certainly seems to be true. Her religion, as it appears in her books, is mainly a concern with the existence of evil; given the reality of evil, ideas about the uses of power and about the structures of society follow, but they do not coalesce in a political system. She has, one might say, political wisdom but not a political ideology. . . .

It is difficult to define in a word the peculiar note of authority that Rebecca West's criticism has, but perhaps the best term is episcopal: she writes like a fourth-century African bishop, praising the righteous, condemning heretics, explaining doctrine, confident always of the rightness of her judgments and of their firm moral bases. She is easy with terms like Manichaean and Pelagian, and can use them as metaphors for literary situations; and the language is significant, for in her world heresies do exist, and they matter. . . .

[*The Birds Fall Down*] is Dame Rebecca's most completely imagined novel, perhaps because it is the one that is farthest from the particulars of her own experience. It alone should assure her of a place in the history of English fiction. (p. 1554)

> *"In Communion with Reality," in* The Times Literary Supplement (© *Times Newspapers Ltd., 1973; reproduced from* The Times Literary Supplement *by permission), December 21, 1973, pp. 1153-55.*

Paraphrasing an observation of Proust's, Rebecca West writes in the prologue to "Black Lamb and Grey Falcon" about the tendency of a banal action to become "wonderful" if it is performed long enough: "a simple walk down a hundred yards of village street is 'wonderful' if it is made every Sunday by an old lady of eighty." So it is with many writers who go on performing after a fashion into old age. Too often, a "celebration" of the sort represented by ["Rebecca West: A Celebration"] is a patronizing tribute to longevity rather than to the sustained high quality of an author's work. Fortunately, it is impossible to condescend in this way to Rebecca West. . . . Whatever the weaknesses of her writing (and there are a number, along with great strengths), banality has never been among them. Nor is there the slightest sign of any diminution of her intellectual and artistic vitality. The hitherto unpublished excerpt included in "A Celebration" from her novel in progress, "This Real Night," seems to me more supple, more intimately at ease with its characters and situation than any of her previous fiction. . . .

Similarly, it is impossible to categorize (much less condescend to) Rebecca West as a "Woman Writer," despite her early Suffragism and the fact that her work from its beginnings has many pungent and often devastating things to say about the situation of women—whether veiled Moslems in Macedonia or the heroines of Henry James. Even when she

is writing from a specifically female point of view, as she most often does in her novels, she impresses me as being without sexual prejudice. She never stacks the deck against her male figures, whether fictional like the hapless father in "The Fountain Overflows," or real like Stephen Ward and John Profumo in "The New Meaning of Treason." And few writers since Jane Austen can have been more severe—even merciless—with the stupidity or snobbery of certain characters who happen to be female. The label of gender cannot be meaningfully applied to "Black Lamb and Grey Falcon" or to any of her books of reportage or criticism; and if attached to her fiction, it amounts to hardly more than an obvious but nonrestrictive fact.

Possessing an inquiring mind and independent taste, Rebecca West has always been a picker and chooser of subjects, apparently unwilling to attach herself permanently to a dominant mode or genre. This has led to a discontinuity between one work and another, to the "interstices" which, as Samuel Hynes points out in his introduction, have militated against any unified perception of her place as a writer. What does the rather sternly judgmental biography of St. Augustine have in common with that melodramatic novella about the mad daughters of a retired admiral, "Parthenope"? Both are included in their entirety in "A Celebration." There is often such a discontinuity between an author's fiction and nonfiction but seldom so radical as in the case of Rebecca West. Even in her fiction, her style veers from book to book, making it difficult to identify a distinctive voice as her own.

However successful "This Real Night" may turn out to be, I doubt that Rebecca West's reputation will ever rest substantially on her fiction. Her strongly controlling intelligence—a faculty that has added immeasurably to the power of her criticism and reportage—has tended, I think, to place too short a leash upon the movement of her novels. In them her characteristic approach—explanatory, analytical, essayistic—has been damaging to the illusion of spontaneity. Her analogies are primarily demonstrative, lacking in metaphorical or connotative richness. . . . (p. 14)

As a critic, Rebecca West is interesting, provocative and often eccentric. Her devotion to art is both passionate and informed; she regards it as the principal ally of the forces of love in their perpetual struggle with the forces of death. Armed with this Manichaean vision of the world, she insists upon the interpenetration of art and ideas, of politics, religion and culture; in this she is the natural colleague of H. G. Wells and D. H. Lawrence and the enemy of the esthetes.

Of all the writers of the 20th century it is Lawrence with whom she feels the strongest affinity. In her "Elegy," written shortly after Lawrence's death, she cuts through his excesses and absurdities to his vital strengths, presenting him as one of those who "have always recognized that the mind which is [man's] house is ablaze and that if the fire is not put out he will perish." Lawrence is the one writer of our age "who had the earnestness of the patristic writers, who like them could know no peace till he could discover what made men lust after death." Her relationship to Lawrence shines through much of her own writing. Like "Sea and Sardinia" and "Mornings in Mexico" but on a far grander scale, "Black Lamb and Grey Falcon" transforms the genre of the travel book into a far-ranging exploration of all manner of things, including the inner life of the author.

The multi-faceted brilliance of her critical approach is no-where better illustrated than in her essay on Kafka in ''The Court and the Castle'' (1957). In it she deals incisively with Kafka's inadequacies as a man and his fragmentariness as a writer, places him firmly within the cultural milieu of the late Austro-Hungarian bureaucracy, and proclaims his importance as one who ''presents the real and insoluble problems of man's nature so truly and so cruelly that he is one of the few authors who can keep pace with the cruelty of history.'' Always assured (sometimes to the point of arrogance) in her critical dicta, she can on occasion be gloriously perverse. . . .

Unquestionably, ''Black Lamb and Grey Falcon'' (1941) is Rebecca West's masterpiece. It is also the book that opened the way for the subsequent works of reportage that have won her an international following. Enchanted by an earlier visit to Yugoslavia, she had to go back again in 1937. . . . The result of her return is a book that not only impressed Yugoslavia—in all its physical and human vividness—upon the consciousness of the West, but also moved outward into an impassioned meditation upon Balkan history from Roman times onward, upon the foundations of culture, and upon the problematic destiny of the human species.

In the squalid sacrifice of black lambs in a Macedonian fertility rite she found the symbol for the sickness of all civilizations, including pre-eminently our own, that enthrall themselves actively or masochistically to the forces of death. . . .

The later pieces of reportage assembled in ''The Meaning of Treason'' (1947), in its revision of 1964, and in ''A Train of Powder'' (1955) still make engrossing reading but they are considerably more dated than ''Black Lamb and Grey Falcon.'' They also make apparent an excess to be found in the earlier work as well: the compulsion to milk every incident, every detail, until they have yielded not only their full significance but some rather dubious secretions as well. On these occasions Rebecca West can sound rather like Norman Mailer (now the chief practitioner of the genre she perfected) at his most portentous. But mostly she writes about her traitors and lynch-mobs and lawyers like a severe but clear-eyed seraph.

This collection is a happy reminder of how good a writer she can be. (p. 34)

> Robert Towers, *"A Generous Sampling,"* in
> The New York Times Book Review (©
> *1977 by The New York Times Company;*
> *reprinted by permission), October 2, 1977,*
> *pp. 14, 34.*

* * *

WHITE, Patrick   1912-

A British-born Australian playwright, short story writer, and novelist, White won the 1973 Nobel Prize for Literature. His work is characterized by its broad scope and technical precision. His panoramic stories encompass nearly every facet of Australian life, and his sardonic wit and preoccupation with death are always evident. (See also *CLC*, Vols. 3, 4, 5, 7.)

Johann Ulrich Voss [in White's novel *Voss*] is an explorer whose nature shows a deep ambition to fulfil itself in previously uncharted, insidiously ''unmaking'' country. Voss is counterpointed by Laura Trevelyan who, like him, seeks

to be flawless. The two protagonists have the desert and the garden as their literal and metaphoric environments, and these settings, derived from powerful archetypes, serve as symbolic polarities of experience. The desert is most strongly associated with Voss; the garden with Laura. But both symbols are complementary, for they work together in a relationship that sharpens the radical theme of metaphysical completeness.

One of the most remarkable features in White's construction of the Voss myth is a transformation of the traditional relationship between garden and desert. Prior to this novel, myths of the land posit the garden as a more important force than the desert because it represents the progress of civilization, but *Voss* shows that true progress comes out of conflict with *uncivilizable* forces. It is not the garden but the desert with its abstract strength that confirms or makes character. (p. 557)

Unlike the garden, the desert is a primeval feature of Australian landscape and is filled with sand, scrub, and exotic creatures many of which are unfamiliar to all but the aborigine. . . . In *Voss,* its implacable rigors are never minimized, but its barrenness and unfamiliar spirit tempt Voss to create something in place of its seeming emptiness. Apparently infinite in its power to reduce humans to impotence, despair, and madness, the desert is the hell through which Voss and his party journey, away from the comparative Eden of the city-garden.

Because of its immense scope and self-sufficiency, the desert is a proper metaphor for Voss. It is true to itself and not delimited by humans. It merely *is,* extending for miles that seem to vanish into infinity. The desert is remote from human society and is hospitable only to those, such as the aborigines, who apprehend its spirit of place. As such, then, it has affinities with Voss who would himself like to be remote from humans and capable of indulging his appetite for power and infinity.

Just as the desert is inaccessible to many people, Voss is unreachable in a psychological sense. He is clearly an outsider in Sydney, for much is made of his German accent, coarse beard, shabby dress, and aloofness. White, who has often focused on outsiders . . . , concentrates on Voss's self-containment which makes the character ''sufficient in himself'' and ''one of the superior ones'' . . . who invites the hostility of Sydney's colonials. (p. 558)

White's technique of chiaroscuro portraiture reveals how Voss is kept a foreigner in New South Wales. Shadow or obscurity at first covers everything that is not the surface of the German's personality, whereas light or revelation falls only on Voss's accent, beard, restless fidgeting, and paradoxical self-assurance. We don't immediately see his face, and his inward disposition is kept more than a little ambiguous and inscrutable. . . .

Voss has a Protean quality by the fact that he is different things to different men, and the profusion of his images suggests an immensity of personality that matches the desert in sheer scope. Just as the desert does not appear to be contained by any tangible, visible boundary, so also Voss's character appears to sprawl across vast areas of attitude. He is variously described as a crag upon which ''truth must batter itself to survive'' . . . ; a burning element . . . ; a scarecrow . . . ; a greedy-looking pig . . . ; a juggler of hopes . . . ; a madman . . . ; and, most climactically of all, a devil. . . . The miscellany of images compounds Voss's mystery, for nobody—except Laura later in the story—is able to apprehend his essence. (p. 559)

The desert becomes Voss's means of establishing distance between himself and the company of men whom he loathes for their weakness. White often depicts Voss as a reserved man who turns his gaze away from people to fix it on some vague, distant point. . . . Voss appears to be happiest in silence "which is immeasurable, like distance, and the potentialities of self . . .". (pp. 559-60)

It is space, as an enlargement of self, that becomes the object of Voss's vision: sometimes the space is formless, uninterrupted, and only vaguely delimited; and at other times it is defined as a desert of unrealized possibilities and unstated consequences. Even when he sits in the Botanic Gardens, he hopes "soon to enter his own world, of desert and dreams" . . . , and we note his obsession not simply with geophysical spaces but with regions of the imagination and soul. Voss, for whom will power is a voluptuous sensation, appears to believe in taking possession of space by simply concentrating his gaze upon it. (p. 560)

Concretely represented by the image of the desert, distance is a paradox in Voss's life, for while it separates the explorer from most men by making him appear a fugitive from civilization (in the manner of the Wild West hero in the second half of nineteenth-century American literature), it also unites him with Laura who never reencounters him once he has left for the desert except by telepathic communication and dream. In effect, distance and the desert are conjoined in three journeys for Voss: one, a literal adventure where he and his party attempt to discover unknown and unnamed country; another, a psychic journey into his self whereby suffering and experience of the expedition will produce metaphysical knowledge; and a third, a spiritual journey, where he can imagine Laura by his side and thereby grapple or wrestle with human weakness before meet Laura and he can be finally and irrevocably united in spirit.

All three journeys confirm a special significance for the desert symbol. They occur in a wasteland where the stark truth of human relationships splinters into debris of wasted potential. The desert is an obvious counterpoint to the genteel civilization of Potts Point and the poignance of Rhine Towers. Despite the brilliant munificence of its colours . . . , the desert offers no appeal to the draper, Bonner, or to his class of merchants for whom progress is never a thing of the spirit but a result of economics and technology. The desert is too vast and too ambiguous for a person like Bonner who believes in planting his feet on earth as solid and as dependable as his sturdy ankles and calves. Its shimmering mirages would either confound or terrify Bonner by evoking a spirit of place foreign to his "civilized" rationality. (pp. 560-61)

Few of the characters in this novel ever think of Australia as a country to which they can have a positive attachment, and even those who do exclude the desert from their area of interest. Australia is most commonly evoked as a colony, still recognizably British, whose social progress is measured by homes, public edifices, administrators, and the achievements of settlers. . . . Mrs. Bonner divorces herself from the land and its coarseness . . . and finds congeniality only in society whose members are as squeamish as she is. Laura, who was born in England, has only a negative at-

tachment to the country . . . , and Topp, too, disappointed by "barbarian minds" and the stupor of gentry . . . , rejects Australia and says it is his country only by an unfortunate accident. Australia, as Mrs. Thompson sees it, is exasperatingly a country of contraries . . . , and, ironically, its colonizers who loathe it are in turn repudiated. . . . Only Voss has the courage and the strength of will to face the continent even in its barest places in order to seize the possibilities of remaking it according to his purpose. . . .

Before we look at Voss's power, we need to acknowledge the force of the desert which reconciles or juxtaposes characters and exposes the intrinsic incompleteness of humans. Thus, we find Angus, the amiable one who has once known "Palladian splendours" . . . , suffering in the company of Turner, the cruel drunkard and ex-criminal, before the two are reduced to a common nothingness by their long journey so that they become more alike than not . . . ; or Le Mesurier, the cynical poet, contrasting with Palfreyman, the meek Christian; or Judd, the dangerous convict, intimidating Harry, the inarticulate naif. The groupings work best, of course, when they relate specifically to the theme of completeness, for it is this subject which constitutes the underlying core of the plot. Voss, who cannot tolerate weakness in men, is compelled by the circumstances to accept Angus, Harry, and Palfreyman. While incapable of cherishing these men, Voss lets them follow because they look to him to perfect themselves. The three weak ones are awaiting some form of self-improvement, but they lack the power to achieve this on their own. . . . Voss would find it easier to be reconciled to Le Mesurier who, like him, believes himself "admitted to infinity" at times. . . .

In Nietzschean terms, Voss's aspirations are not instincts of the herd but strengths of the *Übermensch*. The desert becomes a challenge to Voss's strength and pride. Its rigors and unknown spirit are intriguing to him, and (in the Botanic Gardens episode) he experiences the desert before he ever reaches it. Later, on the way to Rhine Towers to meet Judd, Voss sees a mirage . . . , but if this vision is an illusion, his pride and will to power are not. Believing, like Nietzsche's Zarathustra, that man is something that has to be surpassed, Voss uses his own ego as the measure and value of all his experience.

Voss pursues his quest, maintaining a contempt for human weakness and feeling poignance only for human effort to surpass itself. Unlike Le Mesurier, he does not look for a paradise-garden in the desert, and, as he conducts his group farther west, he adventures deeper into chaos:

> So the white men continued westward through what could have been their own perpetual sleep, and the fruit of the mystic bunya bunya contracted in their mouths.
>
> Several days from there they came to a ridge, of hills even, at which a brigalow scrub whipped their flesh back to waking. Mules began to buck. The udders of those goats which had kidded were slashed and torn by twigs, and the glassy eyes of the most rational of all animals were seeing far too clearly as they advanced into chaos. . . .

The evocation of chaos is later intensified by subtle changes in White's diction which makes increasing use of negatively prefixed words. Emphasis is placed on such things as "the violence of uncontrol" ..., the "unwisdom" of the despairing explorers ... as Voss's travels continue; and we read of the "fierce heat of unreason" ... threatening to wither any oasis of refuge in the Bonner house whose members have eroded spiritually. (pp. 561-63)

Unlike the desert, the garden is not a primeval feature of Australian landscape, for its organization and upkeep are material evidence of colonial progress where life can take root and prosper in hitherto uncleared wastes, thereby providing for some characters, such as Mrs. de Courcy and her guests, "ecstasies of soul." ... Mr. Bonner is understandably proud of his garden because it satisfies his materialistic nature: its shrubs, bushes, and flowers establish a world of substance that is firm, tangible, visible, and undisturbing. The merchant likes to feel "safe in life," and when he is not churning the cash in his trouser pocket, he can sometimes be found in his garden free from the larger tensions of intellect or spirit. ... Completely oblivious to the consequences of his enforced colonization of the land, he does not see how his technology and science, learned from Europe, have encroached upon the integrity of Australia and violated its landscape by imported flora. He is too much a shopkeeper to worry about psychic integrity, and his horticulture is, in effect, an attempt to exorcize the spirit of Australian terrain. ... But he does give Laura her garden, the only physical space in which she finds a combination of comfort and mystery because its darkness and foliage screen "the most intimate forms, the most secret thoughts." ... (pp. 563-64)

Throughout the book, the montage of garden and desert is a technique of developing symbol into myth. In themselves, the garden and desert have solid meanings but when connected by the same characters and in overlapping manner, they form a mythopoeic matrix for the novel. Just as Laura and Voss grapple with their own weaknesses and also with themselves in a metaphysical sense, the garden and desert enter into symbolic conflict, raising the question of ultimate power and its significance in terms of Voss's ambition to achieve what has hitherto been impossible.

Implicit in the symbolic conflict is the doctrine that untouched nature, symbolized by the desert, while a source of primitive strength and integrity, is sternly antagonistic to human progress while civilized nature, represented by the garden, is a refinement of cosmos. New communities often acquire the image of a garden suggested by the poetic imagination as a comprehensive symbol of fecundity, growth, increase, and civilization. Just as in American literature of the Deep South, where the myth of the garden affirms that the dominant force in the future society of the Mississippi Valley is agriculture, so also in *Voss*, the garden comes to represent a civilized achievement of the colonials in New South Wales. In this way it becomes a modified version of the agrarian myth in pastoral literature, where the plantation and the idealized yeoman are replaced by the colonial mansion and the bourgeois merchant. Gardens in *Voss* are built by the Bonners and de Courcys, so they are for serious people who look upon land as an instrument or measure of success and respectability. (pp. 564-65)

[The desert] landscape (which promises no more than stones, thorns, and skeletons) becomes the landscape of Voss's obsession. He is the only one who imagines he can possess it; others try to take control but fail. Harry Robarts, for example, fills his empty face with those distances:

but in their eluding his control he remains lost ... ; and Judd watches his hopes dry up in "the desert of earthly experience." ... Voss, on the other hand, turns to "the infinite distances of that dun country" ... to take them into his possession and satisfy his spiritual yearning. His daring and his dry, uncompromising will align him with some of the dominant qualities of the desert, and although his flesh is reduced to such an extent that he can no longer smile, he is spared the despair and crumbling of those in his party who surrender to the subjugating power of the desert. ... (p. 565)

Voss's desert expedition serves the explorer's sense of conflict and his will to power. ... We have the feeling that Voss will actually seek conflict as an exercise of his will, and the scenes with him and Laura are sometimes represented as a wrestling match. In Bonner's garden the struggle between the two lovers is depicted as intellectual grappling whereby their minds are "again wrestling together." ... The desert ... becomes a suitable arena for Voss's self-testing because it afflicts with heat, aridity, and cruel loneliness. But Voss accepts these punishments as a means to "further trial, and, if necessary, immolation." ...

The desert fulfills Voss's interest in Australia's "great subtlety" ... while the garden exists to comfort Laura in her "remote colony." (p. 566)

The ironic thing about the contrasting settings is their link in mystical sensation. White generates a mystic communion between the two lovers by a sophisticated conflation technique where a recurrent emblem joins desert and garden. The author prepares his design carefully, beginning with color and then continuing with botany to his chief metaphors. Laura is shown to have a great liking for Bonner's garden whose greenery provides atmosphere for her "glistening, green laughter." ... Away from Potts Point, Voss experiences an air of peace when green becomes the dominant color with spears of grass massing distinctly in the foreground. The image is coupled by "a great, indeterminate green mist" rolling up out of the distance and a "good scent of rich, recent, greenish dung." ... As a botanist, Voss is meticulous about cataloguing plants of unorthodox seed formation, and he himself is described in terms of roots and seeds as if his dark appearance were seminal to his being. ... The emblematic association between Laura and Voss is deepened when Voss discovers wild lilies in the desert. Here, in keeping with his scientific nature, he contemplates the German word for their seeds and by a clever semantic method is able to unite himself seminally with Laura in thought, word, and symbol. The episode is a startling one in the novel because of its dramatic ingenuity and symbolic invention, but its point is sharpened only after we have apprehended the preceding drama of communication between the two lovers. In a letter to Voss, Laura suggests that the two of them should pray together for salvation, and when Voss has developed the idea *zusamen* (together) from *samen* (seeds), White writes:

> Then Voss began to float, and those words last received. But *together*. Written words take some time to thaw, but the words of lilies were now flowing in full summer water, whether it was the water or the leaves of water, and dark hairs of roots plastered on the mouth as water blew across. Now they were swimming so close they were joined

together at the waist, and were the same flesh of lilies, their mouths, together, were drowning in the same love-stream. I do not wish this yet, or *nie nie nie, niemals. Nein.* You will, she said, if you will cut and examine the word. *Together* is filled with little cells. And cuts open with a knife. . . .

In this brilliant passage (much celebrated by various critics), ideas of conflict, characterization, and symbol blend in virtuoso fashion, suggesting White's ingenuity somewhat on the order of James Joyce. What results is a seedy link between Laura and Voss, a kind of consummation which is reinforced by other recurring symbols such as those of stone, light, and trembling earth.

The desert and the garden both exert an influence over the two lovers, with the desert breaking down Voss's illusions and the garden acting as a comforter for Laura. Voss refuses to deliver his expedition from disaster and remains in the blinding light of the desert which humbles him. (pp. 566-67)

White is explicit in indicating that this is Voss's purgatorial vision where the two lovers are linked again by lilies which are symbols of two things: first, Laura's progress for the journey to his coronation; and second, communion wafers which Laura receives without surprise. . . . But despite the elevating vision, Voss does not survive much longer, becoming a murder victim to Jackie who wishes to break the white man's "magic." . . .

At Potts Point, Laura's terrible brain fever breaks just when Voss dies by decapitation, having lost his head to Jackie's knife, and a pronounced change occurs in Laura's disposition as she begins to adjust to the environment "to which she was no longer expected to belong." She becomes detached enough to see life "more deeply and more truthfully" and often loves what she sees. . . . This is not to imply, however, that her knowledge is ever capable of completeness, for she is certain only of the *mystery* of truth, asserting that she does not even know the truth about herself unless she dreams it. . . .

Laura sees the limitations on human will and power and is satisfied in her discovery that knowledge comes out of suffering, not out of geography. She is explicit on this point, maintaining that knowledge "overflows all maps that exist" and "only comes of death by torture in the country of the mind." . . . (p. 568)

The geography of desert and garden ends in the knowledge of soul, and the image of the moon fertilizing the Bonner garden seals the seminal idea of Laura's fecund wisdom produced out of the process of Voss's mortification in the desert. And I am tempted to conclude that perhaps the two dominant symbols submerge a Nietzschean metamorphosis in Voss. Nietzsche's Zarathustra designates three metamorphoses whereby the spirit becomes a camel ("the strong loadbearing spirit" hastening into its wilderness), a lion ("lordship in its own wilderness"), and, finally, a child ("a new beginning, a game, . . . a first movement, a holy Yea"). Now I do not wish to mislead the reader, for Voss is not a photocopy of Zarathustra, but there are unmistakable parallels between the spirits of the two characters. It is possible to see—in the broadest manner—an allegorical relationship between Voss's spirit and that of Zarathustra, for Voss (like a camel, perhaps?) hastens into the desert with

the burden of ambition where (like a lion?) his spirit becomes lord of all the wild. His will, a "regal instrument" . . . to achieve his ambition, is exerted over the desert, and with the help of Laura who is described as being pregnant with a plan . . . , he conceives an idea, a yea to life, which —despite his violent death—survives as an intrinsic part of his myth. He dies incomplete, but he perishes having willed and striven to make himself better than all other men in the strong conviction that self-completeness is his manifest destiny. (p. 569)

> *Keith Garebian, "The Desert and the Garden: The Theme of Completeness in 'Voss'," in* Modern Fiction Studies *(copyright © 1977, by Purdue Research Foundation, West Lafayette, Indiana, U.S.A.), Winter, 1976-77, pp. 557-69.*

Of human bondage—the major theme in Patrick White's fine, new novel ["A Fringe of Leaves"]—is perhaps the oldest motif in Australian literature. From the earliest "transportation ballads" to the fiction of the 19th century, Lord Sydney's mournful penal colonies have had a lot of literary attention and have inspired at least two remarkable novels, Marcus Clarke's realistic "For the Term of His Natural Life" and William Hay's romantic "The Escape of the Notorious Sir William Heans." And, even though modern, urbanized Australia has about as much connection with the desolate penitentiary-land of its origins as we have with the Conquistadors, the image and the theme seem to persist.

As might be expected from such a subtle novelist as White, "A Fringe of Leaves" is something quite other than a simple penal-colony tale. Woven into the story are considerations of several different kinds of bondage, several different illusions of freedom. It begins with the genteel servitude of a wife in the English upper middle class of the 1830's. . . .

[There is a] familiar cast in a predictable little drama perhaps, but White is continually turning it to his own, original purposes.

The inevitable seduction scene, for instance—it's not a simple case of Garnet's lust prevailing but a multi-layered psychological happening in Ellen's mind. . . .

Embarking at Sydney and sailing north along the coast, the Roxburghs one day find their ship wrecked on a coral reef. . . . [Disaster] is followed by cataclysm and—to skip over a narrative sequence Defoe would admire— . . . Ellen is taken to the native camp as a slave.

The new form of bondage is totally physical, totally degrading; the English lady is bit by bit reduced to an aboriginal state of filth, danger, nakedness and hunger. . . .

[At last she escapes; and] this part of the novel is splendidly successful; so compelling in fact that the reader is almost persuaded that everything—shipwreck, captivity, escape—has never been related before. But then, after this strong surge of narrative, both Ellen and the story dwindle off. (p. 3)

Though Ellen recovers her health and balance, the novel now declines, all its vital signs fading. It finally ends in a welter of small incidents and minor characters as she prepares to go back to Sydney by boat and to some unknown, further life. And this is very strange. For a novel that has involved such moral themes, has touched so powerfully on issues of personal subjugation and freedom and has produced a remarkably sentient heroine—for such a novel to end idealess and inconclusive is wrong. What do all the events finally signify in the life of a woman? As part of the early Australian experience? As a lived-through drama of Necessity and Free Will?

For authenticity's sake, Mr. White has successfully employed Victorian attitudes and adopted a Victorian style. I only wish that he had also accepted the Victorian convention of entelechy in the novel and had come to a resolution in terms of some drama, some vision or some symbol. (pp. 3, 27)

> *Robie Macauley, in* The New York Times Book Review *(© 1977 by The New York Times Company; reprinted by permission), January 30, 1977.*

Patrick White has written eight very good novels, the best known of which are probably *Voss* and *The Eye of the Storm,* so it seems sure that his new novel, *A Fringe of Leaves,* will be widely read and liked by at least some of his devoted followers. That, I'm afraid, is about the best I can say of it, though I count myself among those who follow with devotion. One of the things that makes White's work attractive is his elegant style; another is his ability to tell a superb story, closely plotted, more or less in the manner of an adventure thriller, yet thoughtful, at best profound; still another is his gift for making what is for us Americans a foreign landscape and people familiar, interesting, and significant. On all these counts *A Fringe of Leaves* seems parody of the best Patrick White. . . .

White makes, in my opinion, one fundamental mistake. He imitates the style and form of the Victorian novel, with all its circumlocution, its arch asides, its leisurely pace, and he fails to enliven Victorian conventions—as Dickens did—with charged rhetoric and the charge that comes with cartoon-like simplification or concrete language. . . .

One can understand, I think, White's purpose in all this. He wants to use an imitation of Victorian style for a novel in which Victorian values, and, by implication, all overcivilized values, stand in shocking contrast to the facts of existence and survival in a hostile universe. The device fails for a number of reasons, not the least of which is that brute existence is treated in the same abstract, genteel way. . . .

No matter how thrilling the adventure may be, in theory at least, such language dulls its effect. Mr. Roxburgh dies with a spear through his neck. We yawn. Mrs. Roxburgh, starving, eats human flesh. We yawn. The whole book, I'm afraid, is a grand miscalculation—with one small exception, a character named Mr. Jevons, introduced in the last few pages, who looks like a toad but has a splendid, gentle heart, a man whose only function is to save the day. If only he'd arrived two or three hundred pages sooner!

> *John Gardner, "Victorian At Sea," in* Book World—The Washington Post *(© The Washington Post), February 27, 1977, p. E9.*

A Fringe of Leaves is a novel based both on the historical Mrs. Eliza Frazer who was shipwrecked on her husband's brig off the southern end of the Great Barrier Reef in May 1836 and on the accretion of legend around the disaster. After the Jacobean drama of *The Eye of the Storm, A*

Fringe of Leaves appears to derive from a part of White's nature that is descended from Jane Austen rather than from John Webster. Its opening is low-key in tone; it is more severe in diction, more disposed to social—as it is more objective in moral—analysis. It is also a tighter, more enclosed novel—in spite of the vast geographical span covered; each phase of the action is defined by a formal, containing line: by a Cornish farm, an English manor, a ship, a boat, an island, the conventions of an aboriginal tribe. The composition is organized around the idea of a voyage—not a voyage out but a return voyage. . . . Another feature of the design is the delicate insistence with which a single phrase, *a fringe of,* is stitched again and again at critical points throughout. . . . I should add that the fringe is not a "symbol" with an abstract one-to-one correspondence, of the sort we have been accustomed to have excavated for us in recent years. It is a natural image, natural in a domestic context, cloudy, intricate, and mobile, carrying a whole set of intuitions and suggestions, hints of both comfort and desperation, of settled convention and the tattered ends of experience.

Dramatic in structure—how naturally the story falls into acts and scenes—poetic in telling—though with a drier poetry than the luscious norm in White's other fiction—and endlessly probing for some missed or missing metaphysical or religious truth: these marks of the other novels are very positively present in *A Fringe of Leaves.* There is, as well, a symmetry between the English material on the one side, Mrs. Roxburgh's hard life with a drunken father on the crude Cornish farm, and then the gentility which absorbs her when she gratefully marries their convalescing lodger, the invalidish Mr. Roxburgh (as he continues to be called by his wife); and on the other, the bourgeois patterns of Sydney and Hobart and the Australia of convicts, assigned servants, and aborigines. (pp. 509-10)

One cannot but be struck by the professional subtleties of the novelist shown in this work, a matter apt to be overlooked with a sensibility so positive and dominant as Patrick White's. The use of the diaries for the purpose of defining the linked and confused territories of sincerity and self-deception is one such. Another lies in the difference of tactic with which the characters are made present to the reader. The less important, for example Garnet Roxburgh, are seen in vivid particularity and are given a markedly physical description. The more important are dealt with from the inside.

The inner truth about Ellen Roxburgh which she begins herself painfully to appreciate—how finely White renders this difficult birth of recognition—is that she is torn between reality and actuality. That intelligent spinster Miss Scrimshaw notes at the beginning of the novel something enigmatic and inexplicable in her. She had always been deprived of some ultimate in experience, and the novel records the efforts of an ordinary, good, sensitive but not particularly talented woman to come closer to what she had missed and to be prepared to suffer in her pursuit of it. . . . The events of the novel, the crises of her experience, make up a full register of a convincing human life; and Ellen Roxburgh's constant search for some intensity of being gives point and dignity to, as it confirms the strength and reality of, her humanity. She accepts in the end the modest consolation offered by Miss Scrimshaw: "I expect we shall make our blunders, but would you not say that life is a series of blunders rather than any clear design, from which we may come out whole if we are lucky?'' There is a species of modesty in this conclusion suited to the ordinariness of Ellen's nature. But it is also a nature, the novelist convinces us, like any human nature, capable of (or at least desirous of) a reality beyond the ordinary run of experience. (pp. 510-11)

I find *A Fringe of Leaves* one of the most satisfying achievements in White's oeuvre. The distancing in time, the immaculate historical sense, the lithely moving narrative, the firmly framed and validated universe, the acceptability of the central character, the rich and lucid design make for an effect of maturity and calm. In most of his novels Patrick White uses some deviation from the norm—it may be eccentricity, neuroticism, disfigurement, genius, violence of the will or feelings—to mark the figure who will project the essential experience of the work. Ellen Roxburgh is superbly ordinary, and her importance is to embody one of the constituent convictions of Patrick White's art. This novel develops and makes explicit, presenting and confirming, as not abstract doctrine but grounded belief, the idea that man must have, as D. H. Lawrence puts it, a religious connection with the universe. Like Lawrence, White is concerned to open to the modern consciousness the neglected springs of life, the sources of a full and kindled consciousness, in separation from which the soul is crippled and incomplete. His purpose is to demonstrate, or rather to render in the terms of art, the essential religious connection which man must have with life. *Religious* may be an odd term to use for one who has written so scorchingly about religion and religious people as White, but religious, stripped of sectarian sacking, seems to be the only word adequate to White's intention. (p. 511)

> *William Walsh, "Patrick White: The Religious Connection," in* Sewanee Review *(reprinted by permission of the editor, © 1977 by The University of the South), Summer, 1977, pp. 509-11.*

* * *

WILBUR, Richard   1921-

Wilbur is an American poet, critic, and editor. His poetry is distinguished by its formal, academic style, its structural elegance warmed by wit and vitality. Wilber received the Pulitzer Prize in 1957. (See also *CLC*, Vols. 3,6, and *Contemporary Authors*, Vols. 1-4, rev. ed.)

Wilbur's verse, like that of Stevens, is charged with responsiveness to the lustres and tones of a physical world most happily furnished, and shows him alert to less perceptible matters. His scenes are alive with light, be it the light coined by "the minting shade of the trees" that shines on clinking glasses and laughing eyes, or one of a wintrier brightness. He manipulates his stanzas with musicianly effects. His poetry engages the eye, the ear, the mind. More often and more intimately than that of Stevens, it speaks of human things. Wilbur's poems are not similarly weakened by abstract meditations, yet for all their wit and their athleticism, they lack the infectious hilarity, as also the grandeur, of Stevens' major structures. (p. 284)

> *Babette Deutsch, in her* Poetry in Our Time *(copyright © 1963 by Babette Deutsch; 1963 by Doubleday; reprinted by permission of Babette Deutsch), revised edition, Doubleday, 1963.*

[Wilbur] has exquisite control of verbal patterns, the sounds of words, the rhythms of speech; he has intelligence, learning, and moral wisdom. But to these he must still add something like the ambition and self-assurance of his inferiors.

The truth is that Mr. Wilbur has never allowed his gifts the freedom they deserve. He has shortened the leash whenever the creatures ran too near the onlooker. . . . [His] brilliant descriptive powers are never stretched so far as to indulge the poet at the risk of tiring the reader. Perhaps they might be. Mr. Wilbur's humour (two attempts at satire fail) irradiates his wit and word play. In 'Seed Leaves', a poem that Herrick could not improve, it gives the most benign humanity to the birth of a plant. But sometimes wit should run wild. These hints are not meant to say that the poet should transform himself into another person. Rather they mean he should be more himself. He should let his audience find him whoever he decides to be. (p. 580)

> *The Times Literary Supplement (© Times Newspapers Ltd., 1971; reproduced from* The Times Literary Supplement *by permission), May 21, 1971.*

Richard Wilbur's celebrated panache has carried him to most of our poetry prizes but not, I think, all the way to Parnassus. He is a bell too conscious of its clapper, clapper-happy. Pert but proper, always safe rather than sorry, his poetry is completely without risks, a prize pupil's performance. His ideas are always cut exactly to the size of his poems; he is never puzzled. And the ideas are all sentiments, aware of their potential high-minded emotional value and determined to snuggle into it.

In [*The Mind-Reader*] Wilbur deplores poets who reject "fictive music" to "confess"—he is one of those who patronize Sylvia Plath, a sure sign of moral complacency. . . . But, less helpless than most poets if less free, she wrote with a shattering originality beside which Wilbur's lines appear fusty, and safe as gingersnaps. Wilbur attacks her Achilles' heel while hardly noticing the winged foot. (p. 21)

The long title poem of the new volume is the fictive confession of a mind-reader who has "the burden" of being ceaselessly usurped by "the world." . . . How he would like to become fuddled enough to escape his "gift"! You know right off that it is all about being a poet—you know and do not care, for Wilbur himself cheats quite a lot. His conception is self-congratulatory and too simple and he himself has been usurped not by the world but by English poetry, whose familiar rhythms and diction—"crenellate shade," "plaints"—he relies on instead of invention. (p. 22)

> *Calvin Bedient, in* The New Republic *(reprinted by permission of* The New Republic; *© 1976 by The New Republic, Inc.), June 5, 1976.*

Richard Wilbur knows his own temptations; to write "poems that are too small for him or too safe for him." "Everybody," he has said, "creates a doily now and then." Well, not everybody, because doilies aren't that easy. There are doilies in [*The Mind-Reader: New Poems*], and pretty things they are. But not every poem is slight which seems so. "The Eye," the title poem of the book's major section, is a test of the reader's perception as well as a testimony to the poet's.

> One morning in St. Thomas, when I tried
> Our host's binoculars, what was magnified?

He courts dismissal as a writer of elegant trivia, while recording his detachment in 24 lines of weightless iambics, in which he throws away passing images each of which could be the substance of somebody else's poem. The undifferentiated green of tropical foliage is "brisked," by the binoculars, "into fronds and paddles," the page of a newspaper spied on a terrace is "sun-blank"—trivial, cheerfully exact perceptions which take on an adventitious import "within the sudden premise of a frame." Light verse about that popular subject, perception? Well, yes—but the poem has more to it: a second part, in which neat rhymes are abandoned, the skipping iambics slowed to the rhythms of prayer. Lucy, patron of vision, is addressed, whose name means light, to whom "benighted Dante . . . was beholden." No less precise than before, the adjectives are now surcharged, for Dante's darkness was not of the eye but of the spirit; and hell is the absence of the Spirit's light, in a poem which turns out to be about how visual and intellectual perception are separate from spiritual perception and moral responsibility, unless we pray for grace to join them.

The beholder is responsible for his vision. . . .

Wilbur is a poet of due regard, of the love which enjoins difficult balance between spontaneity and form, passion and precision, our needs and other people's, this world and another.

"Not a graceful mind," Theodore Roethke said of Wilbur, "that's a mistake—but a mind of grace, an altogether different, and higher thing." In an ungrateful time, grace is hard to forgive. Yet we should be glad for poems which testify yet again that it is both possible and admirable. . . .

> Clara C. Park, "The Fastidious Eye," in
> Book World—The Washington Post (© The
> Washington Post), July 25, 1976, p. G2.

The Mind-Reader: New Poems . . . calls attention once again to [Wilbur's] way of seeing into the blazing life of commonplace things by presenting them with extraordinary precision of language and in exact detail. . . . From [his] first book to the present one, the poems are remarkable for a wild energy which beats against the set forms he uses. They abound in sudden, propulsive outcries that cut across rhythmic expectations of the blank verse pattern:

> Oh, let there be nothing on earth but laundry . . .

Or the basic iambic trimeter:

> Shatter me, great wind:
> I shall possess the field. . . .

Often, as in those lines, the passionate rhythm enforces his celebration of ordinary things. "Obscurely yet most surely called to praise," he writes at the outset of "Praise in Summer" (1947), a witty, emphatic invocation to earth's beauty. In Wilbur's poetry, the awareness of physical particularities intimates knowledge of a hidden world of absolute clarity; it recalls Baudelaire's work in its accumulation of facts that betray transcendent reality. And Wilbur's use of received forms serves the intensity of his utterances by providing conventional structures against which that force is perceived.

In his best work that railing power is used to emphasize the baffling contradictions of the world we know. . . .

Curiously, his poetry has been linked with the word "quietism," a strange word for an even stranger notion that a writer can make a doctrine of tranquillity, especially one with an enormous vocabulary and a fine command of strong verbs. In any case, calmness is not, as it has been thought, an effect of his poetry. To be sure, his elegant, quiet statements are invariably the most urgent, but that method enables him to risk grave utterances without resorting to public rhetoric. . . .

Although the poet has cherished lucidity from his early work ("There is a poignancy in all things clear" he declares in "Clearness," 1950), he depicts lucid moments in ways that evoke eclipse. So, too, his concern with order evokes savagery, for those opposite impulses are joined in his poetry. . . . His poems are charms to preserve order against encroaching blackness: many of them recall certain primitive incantations in their fierce energy and in their phrases similar in meaning and structure.

Wilbur's colloquial force derives from his use of long, flowing sentences enabling the poet to approximate many of the phrases of natural speech. It comes too as a result of his use of falling rhythm and clusters of hovering accents. . . . (p. 344)

[Excited] rhythms distinguish what I feel is his best book, *Things of This World* (1956).

The striking poems of his earlier books have themes that prefigure the prevalent concerns of the 1956 volume. "The Beautiful Changes," title poem from the 1947 collection, is a meditation on how love heightens the senses and clarifies perceptions, awakening the lover to earth's beauty. . . .

The poet's dominant concern is the creative process, the fortunate, mysterious force that lives in the mind and in the language, waiting to be released. . . . In the 1956 volume, "Mind" embodies the poet's belief in the transcendent freedom of human inquiry. . . .

In that wonderful poem, the image of the graceful, imprisoned mind recalls Marianne Moore's figure in "What Are Years" of the one who achieves transcendence through containment, rising upon himself "like the sea in a chasm." In Wilbur's poem, though, it is the radiant performance of wit and style that is his central focus. . . .

From his earliest poetry, Richard Wilbur has conveyed with urgency and power the wonder of ordinary things and of the mind that perceives them. He is a poet who treasures words, and he presents precisely detailed, accurate pictures of the beauty he reveals. And in "The Writer" (1976), he offers one of the best metaphors I know for his own poetry and for the creative process. Watching his daughter write a story, the speaker is reminded of a dazed starling unable to fly out of the window of a room it is trapped in. Injured from battering itself against the pane, it finally finds its way and flies to freedom. Then:

> It is always a matter, my darling
> Of life or death, as I had forgotten. I wish
> What I wished you before, but harder.

It is exactly in that graceful, daring way, restrained by form and yet transcending it, risking all, that the poetry of Richard Wilbur is a matter of life or death. (p. 346)

Grace Schulman, "'To Shake Our Gravity Up': The Poetry of Richard Wilbur," in The Nation *(copyright 1976 by the Nation Associates, Inc.), October 9, 1976, pp. 344, 346.*

The technical virtuosity [in *The Mind Reader: New Poems*] is dazzling, as readers expect from Wilbur. His diction is faultless; his polish and craftsmanship enable him to use traditional forms without their seeming stale or dated. It is a delight to read Wilbur's work, and to discover that pleasure is still a legitimate aim of poetry.

In an early poem ("Praise in Summer," 1974), Wilbur spoke of the "praiseful eye," and the phrase is still useful to describe his method. His is a poetry of ceremony, of truth shaped by texture. His graceful mastery of words is awesome, and several of the poems in this collection can be read as metaphors for his artistic process; as in the closing lines of "Teresa," Wilbur manages to "lock the O of ecstasy within/The tempered consonants of discipline."

But Wilbur's discipline, while graceful, is never easy. He acknowledges the anguish of the poet's "burden" of an almost intolerable awareness, of seeing beyond surfaces, but transmutes that anguish in his art. In the title poem, perhaps the most impressive of this collection, he writes of the poet as magus: "I tell you this/Because you know that I have the gift, the burden./Whether or not I put my mind to it,/The world usurps me ceaselessly."

Wilbur is unexcelled at distilling event to essence, whether celebrating the beginnings of spring thaw in a meadow ("April 5, 1974") or the moment of awakening ("In Limbo"). These poems remind us, in case we have forgotten, that poetry is a powerful weapon in the struggle of order against chaos; also that language will bow to its master, and that the making of poetry is, or always should be, an act which transforms. (p. 15)

Rebecca B. Faery, in The Hollins Critic *(copyright 1977 by Hollins College), April, 1977.*

Let me try to list some of the virtues that distinguish the poetry of Richard Wilbur. First of all, a superb ear (unequalled, I think, in the work of any poet now writing in English) for stately measure, cadences of a slow, processional grandeur, and rich, ceremonial orchestration. A philosophic bent and a religious temper, which are by no means the same thing, but which here consort comfortably together. Wit, polish, a formal elegance that is never haughty or condescending, though certain freewheeling poets take it for a chilling frigidity. And an unfeigned gusto, a naturally happy and grateful response to the physical beauty of life, of women, of works of art, landscapes, weather, and the perceiving, constructing mind that tries to know them. But in a way I think most characteristic of all, his is the most kinetic poetry I know: verbs are among his conspicuously important tools, and his poetry is everywhere a vision of *action,* of motion and performance.

That this is no mere casual habit but instead deliberate policy can be shown, I think, by the fact that pivotal and energetic verbs so often are placed in a rhyming position, and by that slight but potent musical device call some attention to themselves. . . .

Wilbur has been from the first a poet with a gymnastic sense of bodily agility and control, a delight in the fluencies

we all admire in a trained athlete, in the vitality and importance of stamina and focused energy. . . .

This delight in nimbleness, this lively sense of coordinated and practised skill is, first of all, a clear extension of the dexterity the verse itself performs. If it were no more than this it might be suspected for an exercise in that self-approval which, like one of the poet's fountains, patters "its own applause". But it is more. For again and again in Wilbur's poems this admirable grace or strength of body is a sign of or symbol for the inward motions of the mind or condition of the soul. Most obviously in "Mind" the very executive operations of the mind correspond to the speed, the passage, the radar intelligence of a bat. But think also of how the two contrasted fountains (in the Baroque Fountain poem) represent two alternative postures of the spirit, one of relaxed and worldly grace, and the other of strenuous, earth-denying effort. . . . This poet's recurrent subject is not only the motion of change and transition but how that motion . . . is the very motion of the mind itself. . . .

It is, I think, remarkable that this double fluency, of style and of subject, should be so singularly Wilbur's own, and that his poetry should exhibit so often the most important and best aspects of cinematic film: the observation of things in motion from a viewpoint that can, if it cares to, move with an equal and astonishing grace. But what these poems can do so magnificently that is probably beyond the range of motion pictures is, specifically, a transition, or, rather, a translation, of outward physical action (the heave of a weight, the bounce of a ball, the sprint of a runner) into a condition of the imagination; a dissolving of one realm of reality into another. . . .

That mind of grace is brilliantly at work in *The Mind-Reader* . . . and nowhere more than in the title poem, a dramatic monologue of immense poignancy and mastery, which opens with these lines:

> Some things are truly lost. Think of a sun-hat
> Laid for a moment on a parapet
> While three young women—one, perhaps, in mourning—
> Talk in the crenellate shade. A slight wind plucks
> And budges it; it scuffs to the edge and cartwheels
> Into a giant view of some description:
> Haggard escarpments, if you like, plunge down
> Through mica shimmer to a moss of pines
> Amidst which, here or there, a half-seen river
> Lobs up a blink of light. The sun-hat falls,
> With what free flirts and scoops you can imagine,
> Down through that reeling vista or another,
> Unseen by any, even by you or me.
> It is as when a pipe-wrench, catapulted
> From the jounced back of a pick-up truck, dives headlong
> Into a bushy culvert; or a book
> Whose reader is asleep, garbling the story,
> Glides from beneath a steamer chair and yields
> Its flurried pages to the printless sea.

This deserves to be savoured carefully and at length. There is the superb visualization of motion, of diminution into irretrievable distances; but for all the specificity of imagery, the event is all conjectural, hypothetical, the work and motion of the mind itself. The sun-hat is merely proposed as a subject for thought, everything it moves through is contingent ("a giant view of some description: / Haggard escarpments, if you like, . . .'') as is its own motion (''With what free flirts and scoops you can imagine . . .''). And so, initially, this floating, limpid descent becomes a metaphor for the imagination, the graceful motions of the mind. In this sense, it is part of that important vein of modern poetry, of which Wallace Stevens is one of the grand practitioners, a poetry about poetry. . . .

Splendid as this poem is, it represents only one aspect of a remarkable versatility. A reviewer can scarcely hope to do justice to all the skills and graces here exhibited, so I must resort, weakly, to a sort of list. Few other poets could render so faithfully both the slum-bred, vulgar vitality of a Villon ballade and the fastidious, well-bred wit of La Fontaine and Voltaire. And there are the poet's utterly comfortable, colloquial translations from the modern Russian of Brodsky, Vozneshensky and Nikolai Morshen. There is a little group of truly funny poems. . . . And there is, finally (though first in the volume) a group of twenty-two new lyric poems, some of them as brilliant as anything Wilbur has done. ''The Fourth of July'', for example, bids fair to be the best thing to come out of the American Bicentennial. But in this poetic era of arrogant solipsism and limp narcissism—when great, shaggy herds of poets write only about themselves, or about the casual workings of their rather tedious minds—it is essential to our sanity, salutary to our humility, and a minimal obeisance to the truth to acknowledge, with Wilbur, in poem after poem, . . . the vast alterity, the ''otherness'' of the world, that huge corrective to our self-sufficiency. (p. 602)

Anthony Hecht, in The Times Literary Supplement *(© Times Newspapers Ltd., 1977; reproduced from* The Times Literary Supplement *by permission), May 20, 1977.*

*   *   *

WILLIAMS, William Carlos   1883-1963

Williams, a brilliant American poet, as well as a distinguished editor, novelist, playwright, and essayist, also practiced medicine throughout his career. His devotion to the individual expression of his art led him to the free verse style and evocation of personal experience reflected in *Paterson*, perhaps his most famous work. Striving to create in a uniquely "American" idiom, Williams endeavored to produce a poetry which at once reflected the personal and the universal. (See also *CLC*, Vols. 1, 2, 5.)

The early sixteenth-century French or Flemish Unicorn tapestries which now hang in the Cloisters at Fort Tryon Park in New York City contribute to the subject matter of *Book V* [of *Paterson*] and provide a symbolic depth which the poem had previously lacked. . . . Similarly, the Unicorn tapestries provide an analogy for understanding Williams' arrangement of the material in *Paterson*. That is to say, the weavers' interlacing of colored threads to form a design is analogous to the ways in which Williams develops his themes by the interlacing and juxtaposition of events, images, phrases, and other ''things'' which he had amassed for his long poem. In his essay ''Caviar and Bread Again'' Williams describes the poet's function in terms of weaving: ''he [the poet] has been the fortunate one who has gathered all the threads together that have been spun for many centuries before him and woven them into his design.'' (pp. 288-89)

There are basically two kinds of interlace in *Paterson*. The

first can be described generally as the interweaving of originally or logically continuous, or of basically homogenous, material (such as newspaper items or historical excerpts) throughout a section or sections of the poem. (p. 291)

The interweaving of excerpts from Cress's letters throughout the first two books of *Paterson* provides [an] example of this type of interlace. (p. 296)

The interlacing of fragments from Cress's letters accomplishes basically three things. In the first place, Williams is able to sustain a linear rhythm throughout the first two books as the reader gradually learns what is on Cress's mind. Secondly, the technique of interlace also creates an acentric, simultaneous effect as beginnings, endings, and incongruent materials are juxtaposed. Finally, the juxtapositions which are created confer new significance upon the letters and also upon the material with which the letter interacts upon the page.

The second and most dominant type of interlace in *Paterson* is the continual process of cross-referencing which occurs throughout the poem. It is based primarily on a number of narrative sequences, events, or images, initially related in full, elements of which are later used to amplify and illuminate certain aspects of the poem. The later references bring to mind the original event and as a result that event, as well as the context in which the reference now occurs, acquires an added dimension and must be continuously re-evaluated. (pp. 298-99)

Paterson's struggle to interpret the language of the falls, his search for a ''redeeming language,'' is the major motif of the poem. Therefore, . . . the premature deaths of Cumming and Patch, which are intermittently referred to or subtly evoked throughout the first four books of *Paterson*, contribute to the elucidation and development of the poem's major motif. . . . (p. 300)

Throughout the first four books of the poem, Paterson is drawn toward the idea of jumping into the falls. The references to Sam Patch and Mrs. Cumming provide elicit reminders of Paterson's possible fate. . . . In light of the numerous drownings throughout the poem it is significant that at the end of *Book IV* a man walks out of the water, indicating that at least a key to a redeeming language has been found through the enactment of the four books of *Paterson*: ''But he escapes, in the end, as I have said.''

The interlacing of references to Cumming and Patch throughout the poem induces in the reader not only a continuous reappraisal of these two episodes but also a recognition of the poem's development. . . . [The] implications of Paterson's thoughts or actions are often revealed without the necessity of authorial commentary by juxtaposing them with references to Cumming and Patch. Williams expects his readers to keep the poem's events in mind so that even a slight reference to a previous occurence interlaces it with the present event, thereby creating the larger design of the poem. This continual process of cross-referencing also contributes further to the creation of a simultaneous effect and at the same time suggests the circularity of time. (pp. 300-02)

Paterson's structure is not simply one of theme and variation wherein a theme is stated and then examples are presented to support the theme, although the poem has often been described as primarily operating in this manner. Rather, the poem is a "field of action" in which meanings and themes arise and gradually emerge through the complex interaction of its materials—through the process and enactment of the poem. (p. 302)

The use and presentation of material in *Paterson* contributes to the creation of the world of Paterson, just as our apprehension of any city or person is only arrived at through the selection, arrangement, and recollection of information which comes our way in a nonrational, often random sequence. As we read *Paterson* we gradually inhabit the area of a city. Episodes, fragments, ideas, and images appear, disappear, and recur in constantly shifting patterns. The interlacing and juxtaposition of these things reveal the relevance of the separate elements while simultaneously creating a complex totality whose parts are interrelated—city, man, and poem. (p. 303)

> Margaret Lloyd Bollard, "The Interlace Element in 'Paterson'," in Twentieth Century Literature (copyright 1974, Hofstra University Press), October, 1975, pp. 288-304.

Even before he finished the last part of *Paterson* as he had originally conceived it—with its four-part structure—Williams was already thinking of moving his poem into a fifth book. The evidence for such a rethinking of the quadernity of *Paterson* exists in the manuscripts for *Book IV*, for there Williams, writing for himself, considered extending the field of the poem to write about the river in a new dimension: the Passaic as archetype, as the River of Heaven. That view of his river, however, was in 1950 premature, for Williams still had to follow the Passaic out into the North Atlantic, where, dying, it would lose its linear identity in the sea of eternity, what Williams called the sea of blood. The processive mode of *Paterson I-IV* achieved, however, Williams returned to the untouched key: the dimension of timelessness, the world of the imagination, the apocalyptic moment, what he referred to as the eighth day of creation. (p. 305)

[The] apocalyptic mode is not really *new* for Williams in the sense that basically new strategies were developed for the late poems. Williams had tried on the approach to the apocalyptic moment any number of times; so, for example, he destroyed the entire world, imaginatvely, at the beginning of *Spring and All* to begin all over again, in order that his few readers might see the world as new. And in *Paterson III*, the city is once again destroyed in the imagination by the successive inroads of wind, fire, and flood, necessary purgings before Dr. Paterson can discover the scarred beauty, the beautiful black Kora, in the living hell of the modern city. These repeated decreations are necessary, in terms of Williams' psychopoetics, in order to come at that beauty locked in the imagination. "To refine, to clarify, to intensify that eternal moment in which we alone live there is but a single force," Williams had insisted in *Spring and All*. That single force was the imagination and this was its book. But *Spring and All* was only *one* of its books or, better, perhaps, *all* of Williams' books are one book, and all are celebrations of the erotic/creative power of the imagination.

What *is* new about the late poems is Williams' more relaxed way of saying and with it a more explicit way of seeing the all-pervasive radiating pattern at the core of so much that Williams wrote. In fact, all of *Paterson* and *Asphodel* and

much else that Williams wrote, from *The Great American Novel* (which finds its organizing principle in the final image of the machine manufacturing shoddy products from cast-off materials, the whole crazy-quilt held together with a stitched-in design) to *Old Doc Rivers* (which constructs a cubist portrait of an old-time doctor from Paterson by juggling patches of secondhand conversations, often unreliable, with old hospital records), to *The Clouds* (which tries to come at Williams' sense of loss for his father by juxtaposing images of clouds with fragmentary scenes culled from his memory), in all of these works and in others Williams presents discrete objects moving "from frame to frame without perspective / touching each other on the canvas" to "make up the picture." In this quotation Williams is describing the technique of the master of the Unicorn tapestries, but it serves to describe perfectly his own characteristic method of presentation. (p. 306)

[What] marks poems like *Asphodel* and *Paterson V* as different from his earlier poetry is that Williams has come out on the other side of the apocalyptic moment. He stands, now, at a remove from the processive nature of the earlier poetry, in a world where linear time—the flow of the river—has given way to the figure of the poet standing above the river or on the shore: in either case, he is removed from the violent flux, from the frustrations of seeing the river only by fits and starts. Now the whole falls into a pattern: Paterson in *Book V* is seen now by Troilus/Williams from the Cloisters at Fort Tryon Park, the line of the river flowing quietly toward the sea, the city itself visible as a pattern of shades, a world chiming with the world of the Unicorn tapestries, the world of art which has survived. From this heavenly world, the old poet can allow himself more room for ruminations, for quiet meditation. It is a world which still contains many of the jagged patterns of Williams' own world of the early fifties: the Rosenberg trial, the cold war, Mexican prostitutes and G.I.s stationed in Texas, letters from old friends and young poets. But all of these are viewed with a detached philosophical air, as parts of a pattern which are irradiated by the energy of the imagination. For it is Kora, who, revealed in the late work, glows at the center of the poetry, extending her light generously and tolerantly "in all directions equally." It is Kora again who, like the Beautiful Thing of *Paterson III*, illuminates the poem, but it is a Kora apprehended now quite openly as icon, the source of permanent radiance: the fructifying image of the woman, the anima so many artists have celebrated in a gesture which Williams characterizes as a figure dancing satyrically, goat-footed, in measure before the female of the imagination. Now, in old age, Williams too kneels before the woman who remains herself frozen, a force as powerful and as liberating as Curie's radium, supplying light and warmth to all the surrounding details, tolerantly, democratically.

The icon presupposes a kind of paradise, or, conversely, most paradises are peopled at least at strategic points with figures approaching iconography. Dante for one felt this. It is no accident, then, that, as Williams moves into that geographical region of the imagination where the river of heaven flows, he will find other artists who have also celebrated the light. And there, in the place of the imagination expressly revealed, will be the sensuous virgin pursued by the one-horned beast, the unicorn/artist, himself become an icon in this garden of delights. Three points demand our attention, then: 1) the movement toward the garden of the imagination, where it is always spring; 2) the encounter with the beautiful thing, Kora, the sensuous virgin to whom the artist pays homage; 3) the figure of the artist, both the all-pervasive creator who contains within himself the garden and the virgin and also the willing victim, a figure moving through the tapestry, seeking his own murder and rebirth in the imagination. (pp. 307-08)

Williams discovered . . . that the old masters had had their own way of transcending the idiocy of the single, fixed perspective. Like the cubists with their multiple perspectives, their discrete planes apprehended simultaneously, the old masters had also moved their subjects outside the fixed moment. They were able, therefore, to free themselves to present their figures in all of their particularity both within a specific moment and at the same time as universal types or patterns, moving frequently to the level of icon. This shift in perspective helps to explain the similarity (*and* difference) between the achievement, say, of a volume like *Spring and All,* and the later poems: the analogue, except in terms of scope, is between the cubist perspectives of a still life by Juan Gris and the multiple perspectives of the Unicorn tapestries centered around the central icons of the virgin and the unicorn. (p. 309)

In orginally conceiving of *Paterson* in four parts, Williams had, as he pointed out, added Pan to the embrace of the Trinity, much as he felt Dante had unwittingly done in supplying a "fourth unrhymed factor, unobserved" to the very structure of the *Commedia.* (This factor appears if we note the creative dissonance developed by the unrhymed ending reappearing in any four lines after the initial four.) The world of *Paterson I-IV* is very much a world in flux, a world in violent, haphazard process, where objects washing up or crashing against the surfaces of the man/city Paterson are caught up into the pattern of the poem even as they create in turn the pattern itself. So such things as the chance appearance of a nurse who was discovered to have a case of *Salmonella montevideo,* written up into a case history in the *Journal of the American Medical Association* for July 29, 1948, or a letter from a young unknown poet from Paterson named Allen Ginsberg, or a hasty note scribbled by Ezra Pound from St. Elizabeth's Hospital in Washington, letters from Marcia Nardi or Fred Miller or Josephine Herbst or Edward Dahlberg or Alva Turner find their way into the action painting of the poem. The lines too are jagged, hesitant, coiling back on themselves, for the most part purposely flat, only in "isolate flecks" rising to the level of a lyricism which seems without artificiality or undue self-consciousness, a language shaped from the mouths of Polish mothers, but heightened.

The first four books of *Paterson* are, really, in a sense, the creation of the first six days, a world caught up very much in the rapid confusion of its own linear, processive time, where the orphic poet like the carnival figure of Sam Patch must keep his difficult balance or be pulled under by the roar of the language at the brink of the descent into chaos every artist encounters in the genesis of creation. What Williams was looking for instead in a fifth book, after resting from his unfolding creation, was to see the river at the heart of his poem as the ourobouros, the serpent with its tail in its mouth, the eternal river, the river of heaven. This meant, of course, that time itself would have to change, and a new time meant a relatively new way of measuring, meant a more secure, a more relaxed way of saying. That was a

question, primarily, of form, and the emphasis on the variable foot which the critics went after all through the fifties and sixties like hounds after an elusive hare was in large part a strategy of Williams' own devising. But it was an absolutely necessary strategy for him, because just here the real revolution in poetry would have to occur: here with the river, metaphor for the poetic line itself. (pp. 310-11)

It is she, Kora, around whom all of *Paterson V* radiates, and, in the tapestries, she appears again with the tamed unicorn amidst a world of flowers where Williams had always felt at home. In a sense, Marianne Moore's real toad in an imaginary garden finds its correlative here in Williams' icons of the virgin/whore situated among "the sweetsmelling primose / growing close to the ground," "the slippered flowers / crimson and white, / balanced to hang on slender bracts," forget-me-nots, dandelions, love-in-a-mist, daffodils and gentians and daisies. We have seen this woman before: she is the woman in *Asphodel* caring for her flowers in winter, in hell's despite, another German Venus, his wife. Which, then, is the real, Williams' wife seen or his icon of his wife? And his wife seen now, at this moment, or his wife remembered, an icon released by the imagination from time, ageless, this woman containing all women? Rather, it is the anima, the idea of woman, with its tenuous balance between the woman as virgin and the woman as whore, the hag language whored and whored again but transformed by the poet-lover's desire into something virginal and new, the woman and the language translated to the eighth day of creation, assuming a new condition of dynamic permanence. In this garden, the broken, jagged random things of Williams' world are caught up in a pattern, a dance where the poem, like the tapestries themselves, can be possessed a thousand thousand times, and yet remain as fresh and as virginal as on the day they were conceived, like Venus, from the head of their creator.

The woman is of course all-pervasive in Williams' poems. What is different here in the long late poems is the more explicit use of Kora as the symbol, in fact, the central icon in his late poems. (p. 313)

Williams has made that consummate metapoem [*Paterson V*] far more explicit for several reasons, one comes to realize: first, because no critic, not even the most friendly and the most astute, had even begun to adequately sound the real complexities of the poem by 1956, ten years after *Paterson I* appeared. (Indeed an adequate critical vocabulary for the kind of thing Williams was doing was not even attempted by the critics and reviewers.) Secondly, Williams felt the need to praise his own tradition, his own pantheon of artists, to pay tribute to those others who had also helped to celebrate the light. Williams would show that, on the eighth day of creation, all of the disparate, jagged edges of *Paterson* could, as he has said in his introduction, multiply themselves and so reduce themselves to unity, to a dance around the core of the imagination.

In the dreamlike worlds of *Asphodel* and *Paterson V,* filled as they are with the radiant light of the imagination, all disparate images revolve around the virgin/whore, including the "male of it," the phallic artist who is both earthly Pan and Unicorn, that divine lover, who dances contrapuntally against his beloved. Williams, perhaps sensing that the old, crude fight against the clerks of the great tradition had been sufficiently won to let him relax, chooses now to celebrate a whole pantheon of old masters in *Asphodel* and again in *Paterson V.*

And if the presences of Bosch, Breughel, and the master of the Unicorn tapestries are the central presences in the three late long poems, still, there is room to celebrate a host of other artists who dance in attendance on the woman as well. We can do little more at this point than enumerate some of them: Toulouse-Lautrec, who painted the lovely prostitutes among whom he lived; Gauguin, celebrating his sorrowful reclining nude in *The Loss of Virginity;* the anonymous Inca sculptor who created the statuette of a woman at her bath 3000 years ago; the 6000-year-old cave paintings of bison; Cézanne for his patches of blue and blue; Daumier, Picasso, Juan Gris, Gertrude Stein, Kung; Albrecht Dürer for his Melancholy; Audubon, Ben Shahn, and Marsden Hartley.

We come, then, finally, to our third point: the figure of the artist himself, the male principle incessantly attracted to and moving toward the female of it: the anima. And here we are confronted with the comic and the grotesque: the figure of Sam Patch or the hydrocephalic dwarf or the Mexican peasant in Eisenstein's film, and, in the late poems, the portrait of the old man, all of these finding their resolution and comic apotheosis in the captive, one-horned unicorn, a figure, like the figure of the satyr erectus, of the artist's phallic imagination. There is, too, Breughel's self-portrait, as Williams thought, recreated in the first of Williams' own pictures taken from Breughel, and imitated in a cubist mode. . . . And, again, there is the head of the old smiling Dane, the Tollund Man, seen in a photograph; it is a portrait of a man, a sacrificial victim, strangled as part of some forgotten spring rite, the features marvelously preserved intact by the tanning effects of the bogs from which he had been exhumed after twenty centuries of strong silence, that 2000-year-old face frozen into something like a half-smile. That face chimes with Breughel's face as both chime with the strange, half-smiling face of Bosch peering out from his strange world where order has given way to an apocalyptic nightmare.

But the male remains the lesser figure of the two in Williams. As he told Theodore Roethke in early 1950, "All my life I have hated my face and wanted to smash it." . . . He was willing, however, to let the icon of the unicorn, the one-horned beast, stand. And he let it stand because it represented the necessary male complement to the female of it, the object desired, the beautiful thing: the language in its virginal state. No one but the virgin can tame the unicorn, the legend goes, and Williams had, like other artists before and after him, given himself up to that elusive beauty. Like Hart Crane in another mode, he had given himself up to be murdered, to offer himself not, as Pound had, to the pale presences of the past, androgenetically, but for the virgin, Kora. And yet, there was a way out, a hole at the bottom of the pit for the artist, in the timeless world of the imagination, the enchanted circle, the jeweled collar encircling the unicorn's neck. In the final tapestry of the series, the Unicorn kneels within the fence paling, (pomegranates bespeak fertility and the presence of Kora), at ease among the flowers here with him forever on the eight day of creation, a world evoked for Williams, from the imagination, the source from which even St. John must have created his own eighth day in his own time.

What was of central importance to Williams was not the artist, then, whose force is primarily directional and whose presence is in any event everywhere, but the icon which motivates the artist and urges him on: the icon of Kora, the image of the beloved. And this figure appears, of course, everwhere in Williams' writing, assuming many faces, yet always, finally one. Asked in his mid-seventies what it was that kept him writing, Williams answered that it was all for the young woman whose eyes he had caught watching him from out in some audience as he read his poems. . . . With them Williams places his own icon of the lovely virgin. In that world of art, in that garden where spring is a condition of permanence, where the earthly garden chimes perfectly with the garden of paradise, the eye of the unicorn is still and still intent upon the woman. (pp. 315-17)

Paul Mariani, "The Eight Day of Creation: William Carlos Williams' Late Poems," in Twentieth Century Literature *(copyright 1974, Hofstra University Press), October, 1975, pp. 305-18.*

Williams felt himself engaged in a struggle to break Pound's and Eliot's leadership of the reshaping of modern poetry. Towards Pound, who was Williams's mentor, hectoring and generous friend, and cautionary symbol of the dangers of the poet as esthete, Williams fluctuated between fascinated warmth and hostility. He ridiculed Pound's arty posturings and enjoyed the brilliant vaudeville of Pound's cultural blasts, but his poems were not much influenced by Pound's enthusiasm for Cavalcanti, the Seafarer, or Li-po: he fished in the Passaic, not the Yangtze, for the materials of his art. Pound was a negative model, a mental vagabond, who proved what a blessing it was to have a vocation apart from poetry. (pp. 1-2)

Williams's strength . . . derived from his refusal to repudiate the American experience, however ugly and impoverished it seemed to him at moments; he was "of the people, not above them." . . .

Eliot's glacial manner, as if he were the exclusive custodian of poetic tradition, nettled Williams, who claimed—it was partly an act—he was, by contrast, a yokel, an upstart democratic crow, a village explainer.

Nor was Eliot's expatriation or religious conservatism, however based in personal agony, likely to appease Williams's defensive wrath. The impact of "The Waste Land" he often described not only as a personal defeat, but as a catastrophe of the magnitude of an atomic bomb. Eliot, he moaned, "gave the poem back to the academics." "I felt at once that it had set me back twenty years, and I'm sure it did." This melodramatic language is partly just sour grapes, the personal pique of an insecure poet who did not forgive easily, and partly an inquest into Williams's salvaging operation that turned him more determinedly to his "homemade world." Ironically, Williams became the authority for the poets of the fifties, sixties and seventies that Eliot was for the poets of earlier decades. And like Eliot he must bear some responsibility for mischief created in his name: the fetish of spontaneity and formless "plain-spoken" verse.

Williams's poems carry the unmistakable imprint: Made in America. That was not always the case. Williams's first stumbling steps as a poet were utterly conventional. . . .

At his own pace Williams refined his techniques, seeking to imbue his poems with the "tactile qualities of words," to step over "from feeling to the imaginative object." Williams developed slowly and circuitously. . . .

Williams did his best work in the 1950's, wedding feeling and form in the masterful syntheses of such poems as "Pictures From Brueghel," "Asphodel, That Greeny Flower," and "The Desert Music."

In these last works Williams made use of supple, three-line units of poetry (tercets), not as a gimmick, but as an instrument to evoke, like Peter Quince at the clavier, the delicate timbres of love and death, to blend the motions of dance with a mature, wondering talk on the "miracle of reunion."
. . .

Throughout his career Williams wrote short stories and novels. They were not sidelights but important supplements to his pioneering efforts to contrive an American idiom. His patients and fellow citizens were handy subjects, and he recorded their speech and tribulations with brutal candor and ingenuous tenderness. . . .

Williams was no Chekhov, that other beloved doctor-artist. His stories and the "Stecher" trilogy—novels about an immigrant family trying to endure the raw, exploitative demands of American life and push their way into the middle class—don't have the gloss of high art or the carved grotesque humor of Flannery O'Connor's stories (they are too discursive for that), but [Robert] Coles is surely correct in his judgment [in "William Carlos Williams: The Knack of Survival in America"] that Williams is "a novelist who has a sharp eye for that intersection of the private and the public which determines the moral character of human beings: how they combine their obligations to the demands of the world with their sense of what they want for themselves and those they call their own."

So time and the fickle spin of fashion has caught up with Williams and vindicated his experiments and dogged career. (p. 2)

> *Herbert Leibowitz, in* The New York Times Book Review *(© 1975 by The New York Times Company; reprinted by permission), October 5, 1975.*

[Williams] listened to Pound, but was never really his follower, even in the years of "Imagisme." As time passed and Williams became more certain of his role and direction as a poet, he submitted less and less to his friend's arbitration of literary tastes and models. Pound criticized Williams for his "lack of education." . . . Williams—not always patiently—observed, diagnosed, and made up his mind about his friend and himself. His responses to Pound were often ambivalent, and he recognized early, and to a certain extent counted on, Pound's intellectual opposition to his own stance. Despite ample provocation on both sides, the two inevitably stopped short of open warfare. (p. 384)

Certainly they remained friends, if friendship is the appropriate term for such a complex and ambivalent relation. But Williams was never properly a part of "Imagisme" or of the literary and artistic movement which was beginning to revolve around his friend in London during the year before the outbreak of the First World War. . . .

The Pound Era did not directly shape Williams' work or aims; rather it was almost exactly at the moment of that era's inception that Williams' poetry and intentions began to stand out in contradistinction to his self-exiled friend's. The existence of Ezra Pound was to remain a strong and pressing consideration for Williams throughout his life. He clearly understood, however, well before T. S. Eliot came on the scene, that his main chance as an artist lay in excelling, like Whitman, as an "honest reflex." This he did during the decades dominated by Pound's eccentric brilliance and Eliot's *Waste Land,* choosing bread over caviar to the end. (p. 406)

> *Geoffrey H. Movius, in* Journal of Modern Literature *(© Temple University 1976), September, 1976.*

[The title of William Carlos Williams's poem "The World Contracted to a Recognizable Image"] is quite explicit and is bound up with what Williams says in the poem. The title leads us to expect a short, compact poem, or at least one in which each word carries much weight. Actually, the word "small" in the first line seems to echo the "*contracted* world" referred to in the title. The first stanza is typical of much of Williams's poetry: a rather plain, bare statement of something ordinary but containing an element of surprise. The poet tells us how, at the conclusion of an illness, his attention focused on a Japanese picture on the sickroom wall, but we wonder why this picture "filled [his] eye."

The first line of the second stanza increases our puzzlement: the picture struck the poet as idiotic. The second line helps clear up our puzzlement: the picture is idiotic but in the weakened condition he was in then it was all the poet recognized. In other words the picture assumed greater significance than it would normally have.

The whole of the second stanza actually deals with a complex intellectual, emotional and aesthetic process. At work in the first two lines is an "internalizing" of the picture which took place as it filled the poet's eye. The third line is the longest, the most complex, and the most important one in the poem. The wall, something confining which may stand for the indifferent, concrete, material world, was drawn into the picture. This turns the picture into a microcosm, "the world contracted to a recognizable image." (In this respect, it should be stressed that in Japanese art a picture often stands for a microcosm.) There is a fusion between the external, objective world and the world of representation. The picture may be idiotic—and so is the world, the poet seems to imply—but the important thing is that the "wall-world" come *alive* for the poet in that picture. The picture thus conveys a sense of life, of renewal, of recovery after illness, a feeling which is emphasized by the use of "clung" in the next line. The fly in the last line, then, would symbolize fragile, transient life to which the poet clings all the more because it is fragile. As in Blake's poem "The Fly," significance is imparted to something small, insignificant and short-lived, which, by the way, is in keeping with the tenets of Williams's poetry. . . .

On a deeper level what the poet "clung to" "as to a fly" was the sudden illumination prompted by the fusion of the *objective* world and of the world of *representation,* which gave the poet a new perception of things; this imaginative leap gave him access to the world of *form,* of beauty, of art, something transient, evanescent which the poet tries to recapture through his poem.

> *Edmond Schraepen, "Williams's 'The World Contracted to a Recognizable Image'," in* The Explicator *(copyright © 1976 by Helen Dwight Reid Educational Foundation), Fall, 1976, p. 7.*

WILSON, Robert   1944-

Wilson is an American playwright, novelist, and painter who is expanding the boundaries of theater with his extraordinary and often monumental works. His plays often have a definite disregard for time: *The Life and Times of Joseph Stalin,* **for instance, ran for twelve hours while** *Ka Mountain and Gardenia Terrace* **took a week. Joseph Parisi claims that in Wilson's productions "both the actors and the spectators . . . seem engaged as much in a therapeutic as in a theatrical experience." He collaborated with Philip Glass in creating** *Einstein on the Beach* **for the theater and with Robert Shea in the fictional trilogy** *Illuminatus!* **(See also** *CLC,* **Vol. 7, and** *Contemporary Authors,* **Vols. 49-52.)**

With their [*Illuminatus!*] trilogy (*The Eye in the Pyramid, The Golden Apple* and *Leviathan,* . . .) Robert Shea and Robert Anton Wilson have if nothing else brought off the longest shaggy dog joke in literary history. To briefly summarize the more than 800 closely printed pages: a journalist, a sort of modern-day Candide, sets out to investigate some mysterious doings in Mad Dog, Texas, and innocently trips over one of the many feet of the Illuminati, the greatest conspiracy in history—or, to put it another way, the conspiracy that *is* history. . . . A hundred pages in I couldn't figure out why I was wasting my time with this nonsense, after 300 I was having too much fun to quit, and by the end I was eager to believe every word—even if the only conspiracy really at work here is Shea and Wilson's devilish exploitation of our need to make ordered sense out of everything under the sun; their exploitation, in a world, of the narcissism of rationalism. Anyway, I loved it.

> Greil Marcus, "Nonsense," *in* Rolling Stone (© 1976 by Rolling Stone Magazine; *all rights reserved; reprinted by permission), Issue 207, February 26, 1976, p. 89.*

Einstein on the Beach is a continuous, nearly five-hour "theatre piece with music" by Robert Wilson and Philip Glass. . . .

Like Wilson's earlier works, *Einstein* is a dream-play, only this time with music. There is no coherent narrative: There are some words, but even the apparently linear stories are so disoriented by the context that they become dreams themselves. More often the texts are disjointed, stream of consciousness. Instead of dialogue, the characters dance or chant numbers or solfege syllables (do-re-mi). They pose and gesture, purposefully acting out roles whose purpose seems, at first, impossibly private. . . .

The work is divided into nine scenes, none longer than half an hour, with five "knee-plays" (so named for their function as joints) flanking and separating them. The nine principal scenes can be grouped into three trios. There are three train scenes. . . . There are three trial scenes. . . . Finally, there are three space-machine scenes. . . .

On the page all of that must seem impossibly schematic. In performance, *Einstein* is full of teeming life. Each moment is a subtly layered network of detail. . . .

Questions about "meaning" are agony for Wilson. And Glass, for all his relatively greater verbal fluency, doesn't do much better. Wilson works on an inspirational basis very close to free association, and then judiciously winnows those associations down to art. . . .

The most immediate "meaning" of the first trial scene is

that the accused is science itself: One of the characters actually says so, and there are enough symbols of science on hand to remind one of Galileo and drive the point home. But it's more than that. Wilson has built his major works around famous figures of the past—Freud, Stalin, Philip II, Queen Victoria. Like those earlier pieces, *Einstein* takes the scientist as the starting point for a metaphorical examination of the age. Hitler and Chaplin, the demonic and the comic, have been subsumed into Einstein, and since Wilson works above all in painterly visions, their physical resemblance serves to deepen our view of the scientist. *Einstein* is certainly about the uses and misuses of science. But science is a product of the imagination, like art and like dreaming. *Einstein* is about human beings dehumanized, about justice and Patty Hearst, about the apocalypse (Nevil Shute's *On the Beach*), and, in the final knee-play, about the flowering of simple human love. And at all times, it's about higher forces that illumine our lives. If that sounds too bold, so be it; both Wilson and Glass owe their artistry in large part to their ability to translate simplicity into sophistication without dimming the purity of their naïvité. (p. 52)

The slow tapestry of shifting images is occasionally punctuated by a sudden *coup de théatre,* as when a "spaceman" swings into view, suspended by a rope, during the penultimate scene of *Einstein.* Even within the prevailing slow sequences the speeds of change vary; part of the richness of texture in a Wilson piece is the overlapping rates at which different kinds of images are transformed. Binding it all together, one realizes soon enough, is an intricate series of recurrent leitmotifs: not only the large ones, like the trains and the trial and the bed, but smaller visual devices (the clocks, the periodic eclipses), gestures, and, of course, sounds. (pp. 52-3)

Wilson has always called his works "operas," even if the music was only very occasional. They were silent operas, in the sense of the Italian usage, as a blend of the arts. Now, with Glass's music, *Einstein* is more an opera than any previous Wilson work. . . .

[The] idea of "opera" remains our principal repository for a supra-rational theatre of style and symbol. Both Wilson and Glass work in a manner that can easily be called Wagnerian. . . .

[What] is curious about the mystical romanticism of both Wilson and Glass is the lucid, balanced form in which it expresses itself—so cool that it strikes some as lacking in incident. As one of Einstein's last assistants put it, "Beauty for him was essentially simplicity." (p. 53)

> David Sargent, in The Village Voice *(reprinted by permission of* The Village Voice; *copyright © by The Village Voice, Inc., 1976), November 22, 1976.*

Two points are immediately clear [on seeing *The Life and Times of Joseph Stalin*]: narrative is not the object; and the title . . . is irrelevant. . . . More important, the first glance —but only the first—makes us think there are connections here with the surrealist theater of the 1920s. In fact, after Wilson's last Paris show a commentator wrote: "One convert to [Wilson's] style was Louis Aragon, who saw in Wilson the logical heir to the Surrealists." Heir, perhaps, but with a distinct difference. The surrealist theater for me— archetypally, Artaud's *Jet of Blood*—is usually one of speedy bombardment, a rapid series of disjunctive phenomena making their effect as much through their speed of sequence as through their contents and disjuncture. Wilson's tempo is *largo*. His intent is not the surrealist fracture of our "defenses" with speedy sequences of illogic. He wants us to savor pictures. He wants to create picture after picture with theatrical means, but not *tableaux vivants*—he wants them to flow or melt into one another, to move. He wants to connect them more by visual themes than by verbalizable ones, to provide combinations of people and lights and things and sounds that are striking. Perhaps they will stimulate the viewer to invent his own play; perhaps not. No matter.

Wilson creates these pictures, ingeniously, delicately, wittily.... [He's] been trained as a painter, has worked with deaf children, and knows how to speak to the eye. He has great skill in using theater means to present a (let's call it) flowing gallery of pictures. This does not keep the performance from frequently being boring; I have more expectations and interests in the theater than to see a series of pictures, however good. But paradoxically, a certain quotient of boredom seems part of the plan. Wilson, though serious, is not solemn. (pp. 42-3)

My own reaction in sum: Why shouldn't there be a Robert Wilson? ... Why shouldn't the theater's means be used by a painterly sensibility to thrust pictures into the element of temporality—of duration and motion? In film many painterly talents have tried it, though rarely at this length or with Wilson's invention and humor. His theater work is more difficult and in some ways more rewarding than the film attempts because he's doing it before us, with real people ... and animals and lights and scenery and sounds. Boring as it is residually, his work is nevertheless authentic and authentically daring. I would hate to see Wilsonism take over theater and dance completely (small risk), but I'm glad he exists. (p. 43)

> *Stanley Kauffmann, "Robert Wilson," in his* Persons of the Drama *(copyright © 1974 by Stanley Kauffmann; reprinted by permission of Harper & Row, Publishers, Inc.), Harper, 1976, pp. 41-7.*

The effect [of the "knee plays" in Wilson's *Einstein on the Beach*], similar to staring at a closed loop of recorded videotape, is to lull the audience and wear down its expectations. (p. 107)

The title *Einstein on the Beach* has no literal meaning. Images of Albert Einstein fill the work, but the closest we come to being "on the beach" is a conch shell that appears on stage right in several scenes.... There is no plot or action in the sense of traditional theater or opera. Instead, we are given a number of visual ideas or, more accurately, notions that are taken, often obscurely, from Einstein's life and the effects his work had on the world. Some of the notions are obvious; others assume a more than passing knowledge of the scientist. In any event, none is explained, and you just have to try and catch them as they go by. These references include Einstein's love for fiddling on the violin, for steam engines (a steam locomotive and a train are among the principal sets in the first two acts), his theoretical contribution to the atomic bomb and to space travel, and his exercise of pure reason. All these lead to the last scene, in which flashing lights, violent dancing, and loud,

churning music hint at some sort of cosmic cataclysm set inside a space machine.

Even this simple list, however, implies a specificity to the opera which it lacks. For instance, the longest visual reference in *Einstein* to his theoretical work is in act four: a high rectangular building on an empty plain, seen from its narrow front, but slightly angled to give an idea of its depth. Near the top of the building is a window and through it we see a man, his back to us. His right arm describes ceaseless writing motions on an imaginary surface in front of him. A crowd gathers slowly at the front of the building and spends its time looking up at the window. The first to arrive is a child on a skateboard; as the crowd wanders off, he is the last to leave. The scene ends as it begins, a building set on a lonely plain; through a high window we see a man, his right arm in motion. We assume the man is Einstein. Is the building Science? Is he, in his furious scribbling, working out formulas that will save—or destroy—mankind? Why does the building look more like a prison than a scientific institute? Are scientists prisoners? Whose? The silent people who gather below—are they prisoners of Science? Are they kept away from Science? (The building is massive, it has no door that we can see, the scientist inside is too high to reach.) One wants to know more, but feels embarrassed to ask.

Wilson's background as a painter is clear in *Einstein*. His sets are surrealistic.... The play seems to have any number of visual references. The scene inside the space machine could be based on Fritz Lang's *Metropolis;* an entire scene is given over to a pillar of light ... that rises slowly from the floor until it disappears into space, like the monolith in Kubrick's *2001*. There are allusions in the sets to Max Ernst and Giorgio de Chirico. Indeed, the foreboding quality of the Einstein building left a more lasting memory than the action in and outside it. (pp. 107, 110)

The score, though no musical revelation, is far more concrete an experience than Wilson's drama, a result of its spare nonmelodic concept.

Einstein on the Beach adds up to distinctly less than the sum of its parts. One senses an innocent humanism at work here. From the dancing in the two "field" (space machine) scenes, one could gather that Wilson would like the human race to survive. It is a nice sentiment, but it isn't developed, and repetition flattens it to a veneer.

One possible thread through the opera is a figure made up as Einstein (as is, at times, the entire cast). He appears in several scenes sitting on a raised chair between the orchestra and stage and fiddles—continuously, loudly, lamentingly. He has neither facial expressions nor lines to speak....

All the elements of our universe are somehow connected, this opera seems to say—Einstein–trains–assassinations–Patty Hearst–space travel—but if our universe is to survive, we must first learn to love. There's nothing wrong with that, but without examination, development, without a hint of dialectic, it has all the force of a nice pop song— "All You Need Is Love," by the Beatles, comes to mind. As such, *Einstein* doesn't begin to accommodate the epic scale of a five-hour opera.

Anything can be art, if only because people calling themselves artists have done all sorts of things and called them art, and sooner or later critics and the marketplace have responded to them as art. *Einstein* is art, but a quite limited art of static visual images put to motion, not dissimilar from choosing a series of interesting and pretty postcards and moving them, in accompaniment to music, back and forth in front of one's eyes. (p. 110)

> *F. Joseph Spieler, "Adrift among Images,"* in Harper's *(copyright © 1977 by Harper's Magazine; all rights reserved; excerpted from the March, 1977 issue by special permission), March, 1977, pp. 107, 110, 112.*

*   *   *

WOLFE, Tom   1931-

Wolfe, an American journalist and essayist, is a proponent of New Journalism. With wit and an eye for detail he describes the outward trappings which reveal the inner meaning behind the furniture, fashion, and attitudes of his subjects, who have ranged from Hell's Angels to Leonard Bernstein. (See also *CLC*, Vols. 1, 2, and *Contemporary Authors*, Vols. 13-16, rev. ed.)

In Wolfe's works, including his present claims to a new kind of writing, the mechanisms of a middlebrow mass culture are transparent. In *Electric Kool-Aid Acid Test,* his book about Ken Kesey, the Merry Pranksters, and the California LSD scene, Wolfe writes: "I have tried not only to tell what the Pranksters did but to recreate the mental atmosphere or subjective reality of it. I don't think their adventure can be understood without that." Unquestionably a clever mimic, a shrewd observer, and sometimes pretty funny, Wolfe performs neat jobs of ventriloquism with his "downstage" voices. The gimmick is that all the words are authentic, taken from observation, correspondence, interviews, publications. They are ingeniously reassembled and appear as if they are the spontaneous generation of the narrated action itself. This way Wolfe seems to merge with his subjects, to be speaking their thoughts, feelings, words. Wolfe is at pains to authenticate his sources, but the claim matters little except as a device to keep the reader from noticing that the true facts of the genesis of the work—the interviews, research, listening to tapes, even being on the scene—are kept hidden. Unlike Terry Southern and Hunter Thompson, Wolfe does not dramatize his own participation. He is almost not there. This means that along with the actual apparatus of journalism, anything like a substantive perspective is impossible to locate. The corrugated verbal surface, the hyped-up prose, its tachycardiac speed, its fevered illusion of thinking and feeling, all disguise the *reporter*. That is why the direct quotations from a letter by a woman recounting her first experience with LSD comes with such relief: at last, a real voice. The rest is illusion of a group subjectivity, only and sheerly verbal, never complete, never completing itself in the reader's imagination, except as display, as spectacle.

What Wolfe gains by his pyrotechnics is an easy experience for the reader: just lean back and let it happen to you. But it is a deceit: by disguising itself and its procedures, by mystifying the presence of the author as a merely neutral recorder when he is in fact the only active producer of the product, Wolfe's work is a revealing instance of mass culture. The appearance of spontaneity is the product of the most arch manipulation and manufacture. By pretending to render the world always as someone's experience, from the inside, Wolfe may seem to be revitalizing the craft of journalism and preventing the loss of experience that comes with hardened journalistic formulae. But just the opposite results. He converts experience into spectacle, fixes it, reifies it as a reader's vicarious experience. He cheats us with illusions of deeper penetrations into segregated realities but the illusion is a calculated product that disguises what it is we are actually reading.

Wolfe's genre is a cool flaneur's version of the comic journalism practiced by Mark Twain and his brethren. He dons the guise of the Low Rent rebel, speaking on behalf of those who have been deprived of their status by the literary, intellectual, and political elite. His devices include a bogus erudition and intellectuality, an OED vocabulary of technical terms, outrageous but "learned" neologisms, and catalogue after catalogue of the names and things that fill the days and hours of American popular life, all presented without punctuation, as a kind of synchronistic pop mandala. He panders to both a hatred and an envy of intellectuals. His *lumpenprole* revolution is no more than a botched theft of what he thinks is the prize jewel of the intellectuals, the label of "art." Far from revolutionary it is a conformist writing, whose message at a low frequency is that you have never had it so good. Wolfe cannot see beyond the "chic" in middle-class radicalism, nor beyond the gamesmanship in confrontation (made into slick theater in "Mau-Mauing the Flak-Catchers"). Hardly a vision to disturb the sleep of the proprietors and managers. In many ways it is also their vision. Wolfe's revolution changes nothing, inverts nothing, in fact is *after* nothing but status. It is full of half-baked versions of ideas in currency. The best that might be said for it is that it is a put-on. But I doubt it. I think he is dead serious. (pp. 300-02)

> *Alan Trachtenberg, "What's New?"* in Partisan Review *(copyright © 1974 by Partisan Review, Inc.), Vol. XLI, No. 2, pp. 296-302.*

In the Sixties, Tom Wolfe was fun because he could tag as stylish (and mimic) behavior everyone else assumed was merely weird. But now, in the Seventies, when we have no style but think we're flush, when we're no longer Merry Pranksters or Flak Catchers but just a bunch of folks full of attitudes—now even the zingiest journalist has got a problem. Attitudes give birth to attitudes, which sour as fast as milk, and the sharpshooter either turns curmudgeon (like Malcolm Muggeridge) or fancies himself a satirist.

Muggeridge at least has a faith, a place to withdraw back into. Wolfe, with his popcorn style and tailor's fussiness, has only the world, and it's one he doesn't much care for anymore. We're in the "Me Decade," this collection of essays [*Mauve Gloves & Madmen, Clutter & Vine*] flappingly asserts; we brim over with silly selfishness and deplorable postures. Wolfe interestingly opposes this idea with a piece on the chivalric gesture and class found in the behavior of F-4 fighter-bombers "jousting" over Vietnam: to hang on the precipice of your mortal soul in a flying hunk of metal is better than crossing Dr. Freud's perilous gulch (the former presumably hasn't too much "me" about it—or much "you" either). The distinction is piquant, I'd say. In his last book and now this one, Wolfe seems to be going after tinsel with an ax. Two or three of the pieces here are still fun, one is fine, but the whole is increasingly no-account and over-fried. (pp. 39-40)

Ross Feld, in Saturday Review (© *1977 by Saturday Review Magazine Corp.; reprinted with permission), January 22, 1977.*

[*Mauve Gloves & Madmen, Clutter & Vine,* a] new collection of essays, journalism and fictional sketches (with a title John Berryman would have loved) reveals a different Tom Wolfe. He does not content himself here, as he once did, with mad torrents of words that could be enchanting, but often were gratuitous and cavalier. The old Wolfe was daring and sometimes felicitous in describing a kaleidoscopic world. Jazzy, syncopated rhythms enlivened his dayglo syntactic bravuras, making the age shimmer and tremble. Yet his prose was too much like the tumultuous gush of the acid movement he was chronicling—a theater of the '60s drug scene enacted in all its exuberance and apotheoses, crammed with "screeling screamers, megascope, fooling pooling. . . ."

Mauve Gloves, by contrast, brings to mind one of those ancient Chinese tapestries that at first seems merely a huge multicolored blotch. Upon closer inspection you notice trees, animals, people, then the intricate jewelry the men are wearing, and finally the intimations of immortality in the crevices of their skin. So, too, initially Wolfe's present sensibility appears to identify with the fashions of contemporary life. Soon, though, it becomes apparent that he is mocking, not praising, in this deceptive maze of social analysis, sardonic humor and poignant ironies. (p. 21)

[Most] of the time the new Tom Wolfe tries to keep his distance. Writing with all the vitality of the old, he makes every effort to be, at the same time, cool, firm and dignified. This, added to Wolfe's wit and a lyrical quality that every now and then breaks through, makes *Mauve Gloves* an invigorating experience. (p. 22)

Nereo Condini, "The Mature Wolfe," in The New Leader (© *1977 by the American Labor Conference on International Affairs, Inc.), January 31, 1977, pp. 21-2.*

*   *   *

WOUK, Herman   1915-

An American novelist and playwright of Russian-Jewish heritage, Wouk was the 1952 recipient of the Pulitzer Prize for ***The Caine Mutiny.*** **Like much of his work, this novel deals with the complex implications of a moral dilemma and its resolution, a concern which lends a didactic flavor to Wouk's writings. (See also** *CLC,* **Vol. 1, and** *Contemporary Authors,* **Vols. 5-8, rev. ed.)**

[Herman Wouk in *The Caine Mutiny Court Martial* displays] a gift for crisp dialogue unsurpassed by any of our regular writers for the theatre. He has an excellent story to tell, and, in the confrontation of counsel with witnesses, has an exactly appropriate vehicle for his story. We receive each new witness with keen expectancy, follow his replies greedily, laugh over his foibles, applaud at his exit, start over with renewed expectancy at the next arrival, hear with pleasure or indignation what counsel has to say. . . . The march of exits and entrances, questions and answers, attacks and counterattacks, is admirably theatrical. (p. 192)

But if we like Mr. Wouk so much we should be unfair not to take him as seriously as he takes himself and consider [his] claim . . . that the play is no mere psychological thriller but a tract for the times telling us to respect authority: mutiny is unjustified even when the argument against a particular commander is a strong one because the important thing is not to save a particular ship but to preserve the authority of commanders; for they win wars while we sit reading Proust. There is a good point here, and there must surely be a good play in it—a play that would show up the sentimentality of our prejudice against commanders and in favor of mutineers. If, however, Mr. Wouk wanted to write such a play, he chose the wrong story and told it in the wrong way, for we spend three quarters of the evening pantingly hoping that Queeg—the commander—will be found insane and the mutineers vindicated. When, in the very last scene, Mr. Wouk explains that this is not the right way to take the story, it is too late. We don't believe him. At best we say that he is preaching at us a notion that ought to have been dramatized. And no amount of shock technique—not even the reiterated image of Jews melted down for soap—can conceal the flaw.

Of course, if you don't take the play seriously, none of this matters: the first part is a thriller, the last scene gives you a moral to take home to the kids. That the two sections are not organically related need disturb no one who is unalterably determined to eat his cake and have it. Others cannot but feel some disappointment at seeing the territory Mr. Wouk opens up to the view but does not touch.

Mr. Wouk's retort to sentimental radicalism is in order. Yet cannot the New Conservatism—for surely his play belongs in this current of opinion—be equally sentimental, equally ambiguous? It is true that on occasion we owe our lives to naval captains. It may also be true that I owe my life at this moment to the Irish cop on the corner. Must I feel more respect for this cop than for my more sedentary neighbor? It is Mr. Wouk, by the way, who says that the book my neighbor is reading is by Proust. . . . In short, Mr. Wouk carefully stacks the cards. His villain—Keefer—reads highbrow books. His hero—Greenwald—is a Jew. In real life, defense counsel might just as easily have been "Aryan," the villain—like Proust whom he reads—Jewish. But an author who wrote the story this way would *certainly* be accused of stacking the cards. . . . (pp. 192-93)

There are also technical criticisms one might make [about the play]. The exposition is not all clear sailing. Without the 300 pages that precede the trial in the book, it is hard to figure who some of the people are, what they have done, why they did it. (p. 193)

[It] is because we are not clear about Queeg and his state of mind on the day of the mutiny that we cannot form an opinion on the main issues of the play. Just how crazy does a captain have to be for Mr. Wouk to approve his removal by a subordinate? The answer seems to be: he has to be *plumb* crazy, raving, stark, staring mad. Just how crazy was Queeg? It is impossible to figure. And while precisely this impossibility might make a dramatic theme, it would yield a play with a message decidedly Pirandellian; it would not increase our respect for authority. (p. 194)

Eric Bentley, "Captain Bligh's Revenge," in his The Dramatic Event: An American Chronicle (© *1954; reprinted by permission of the publisher, Horizon Press, New York), Horizon, 1954, pp. 191-94.*

Is Wouk's prose always Victorian-girlish? No, sometimes it is Swiftian—Tom Swiftian. "A chorus of laughter showed the choice was popular," he writes. Speech mannerisms are the caricatures of boys' books: Hawke [in *Youngblood Hawke*] is from Kentucky, so that he speaks Amos 'n' Andy ("Mand ef Ah smoke uh see-gaw?"), although Wouk economically turns it off after a few lines and only recurs to it in moments of passion; Hawke's mother speaks quite another dialect, apparently Dogpatch ("get aholt of t'other end of that bed, I cain't get it downstairs myself"); a sophisticated European woman is identifiable by Consonant Mangle ("Vare is ze young genius?"); a crooked Southern businessman shows his hand by saying "binness" for "business" and "sumbitch" for some unidentifiable obscenity. (p. 68)

Is there really *nothing* good about the book? Nothing. It is the most fraudulent and worthless novel I have read in many years. *Peyton Place* is more honest. Wouk has announced that the figure of Youngblood Hawke was suggested by Balzac; he resembles Sinclair Lewis in a few details; there is a positive effort, in the first and last chapters of the book, to identify him with Thomas Wolfe. But these are transparent disguises—Hawke is unmistakably Herman Wouk. (p. 70)

Wouk is now a phenomenal merchandising success, sold as a detergent is sold. He can compete with the worst of television because he *is* the worst of television, without the commercials, a $7.95 Pay-TV. His readers really are the boobs Hawke describes, so "starved for an interesting story" that they will ignore the reviews to read him. They are yahoos who hate culture and the mind, who want to be told that Existentialism means that "you do what you goddam please," that current theatrical fashion is "pseudo-Freudian reconstruction," that young actresses offer themselves "with all the casualness of a housewife opening a can of soup." (p. 71)

Doesn't Wouk stand for anything but venality? Yes. He stands for conventional American patriotism, and the proud conviction that "This country has no toiling masses." He stands for old-fashioned morality. . . . (p. 72)

> *Stanley Edgar Hyman, "Some Questions about Herman Wouk," in* Standards: A Chronicle of Books for Our Time *(© 1966; reprinted by permission of the publisher, Horizon Press, New York), Horizon, 1966, pp. 68-72.*

[The] unimpeachable worthiness of Mr. Wouk leads to a final sense of monotony. . . .

The Winds of War is a massive novel and, one realises as one reaches the end, only part of Mr Wouk's projected total design. It might be described as a history of the Second World War as seen through the adventures of an American family and their immediate friends and contacts. The work begins in 1939 and ends just after Pearl Harbor. . . .

It is a tribute to Mr Wouk's method that he can introduce and fix his main characters with deceptive ease and have them all placed in strategic positions ready to suffer as war explodes. . . .

The progress of Hitler's war, politically and militarily is expertly charted and Mr Wouk has invented a German general's post-Nuremberg memoirs of the war, extracts from which showing the German viewpoint are placed at regular intervals in the text. The aim is to give a total pic-

ture, detached and fair, and to personalise it withal. It works as a gripping piece, no doubt about it. But there is this strange feeling of monotony—not through the events or the characters: Mr Wouk really gives us the Poland in which the Jewish community lived exactly as that portrayed in *Fiddler on the Roof,* hysterically excited New York and the Battle of Britain. He coolly produces historical people —like Hitler and Stalin, to exchange a few words to his characters. There is action and family tension. But what the book severely lacks is what I can only call a moral charge, that feeling of commitment that distinguishes Len Deighton's war writing. Ultimately Mr Wouk has used the greatest happening of the 20th century as a useful background for a family saga of no more intrinsic interest than *Coronation Street*. (p. 66)

> *Roger Baker, in* Books and Bookmen *(© copyright Roger Baker 1972; reprinted with permission), February, 1972.*

[*The Winds of War*] is a kind of phenomenon, not only in the realm of popular culture but, I will suggest, also in another realm which stems largely from popular culture—the shaping of a generation's perception of itself and its era. [It] is likely that Wouk is concerned not only with re-creating and interpreting World War II, but, like Tolstoy, with advancing his own moral views of the society and world to which that war gave rise. . . .

Composed in part of things Wouk apparently felt *The Caine Mutiny* had left unsaid or undeveloped, *The Winds of War* is in some ways an expansion of or exegesis upon the more restricted and closely drawn scene of the earlier work. It also bears some relationship to certain ideas presented in his 1959 work of non-fiction, *This Is My God.* Wouk has a vision of what the individual should be and do, and a wish for the kind of society which might be possible if the example of such persons were followed. *The Winds of War* weaves into its descriptions of what-was much of Wouk's suggestions of what he believes might-have-been and ought-to-be. (pp. 389-90)

Critics who have castigated the book for failing in various ways as a *novel* have seemingly overlooked the author's description of it as a romance. That form is older, and adheres to rather different standards, than the novel. Much criticism directed at the book's emphasis of incident and plot over deep character development, or its unfashionably detailed descriptions of people's appearances, becomes immaterial if one accepts Wouk's idea of what *The Winds of War* is—a historical romance, with a didactic purpose. That purpose is to dramatize the author's ideas about his themes—how the "curse" emerged, how we might constructively understand it, and how "men of good will" have been involved with it.

The phrase about men of good will, which also has received little or no critical attention, is the key to the central figure, Captain Victor Henry, U.S.N. (pp. 390-91)

Whether or not he seems real to a particular reader, Henry himself is as vital to the purpose of the book as his presence and movements are to its structure. For the captain is an embodiment of the idea that men of good will have devoted their lives to industrialized armed force. Henry's own specialties within the Navy have been two of the most mechanized engines of destruction—heavy guns and torpedoes. Yet he is a man of sanity and intelligence, loves his family and country (albeit not uncritically), and is generally admired by fellow Navy men and civilians.

Earlier, it was suggested that *The Winds of War* is in some thematic ways related to *The Caine Mutiny*. In a peculiar sense, Victor Henry is related to Philip Francis Queeg. Captain Henry can be seen as the fulfillment and justification of Lt. Barney Greenwald's unexpected and much discussed encomium to Regular Navy officers in the post-trial scene of *The Caine Mutiny*. Greenwald pays his tributes not so much to the *Caine's* fallen captain as to what-Queeg-could-have-been (and might have become if you bastards had given him a chance)—the selfless and dedicated guardian of a reckless and unappreciative nation's safety.

In Henry, Wouk presents a man who really *is* what Queeg could only try, pretend, or fail to be, the "compleat" and admirable United States Navy officer. (pp. 391-92)

By the portrayal of Captain Henry, *The Winds of War* implies in part that it's a shame such talent and virtue should serve the cause of "industrialized armed force." But it also implies that a historical current which can produce and temper such men as Victor Henry and his two promising sons may not be utterly evil, or might not be if all those involved with it were of Henry's fibre. . . . The traditionalist support of the military career man which Wouk asserted in his earlier work, in the teeth of much of his own evidence, becomes a pervasive theme in *The Winds of War*. (pp. 392-93)

The fictional re-creation of the world of 1939-41 is the most impressive and absorbing aspect of the book. Comparisons have been suggested to Upton Sinclair's Lanny Budd tales, but Wouk is a better craftsman. He knows what he wants, and his research is thorough. Even critics who disliked the story have praised the depth and value of the historical re-creation. . . . (p. 393)

Wouk's method is to be a good storyteller, of a rather traditional kind. There are no stylistic experiments, no time-manipulation, little interior monologue, and no flights of allegory—none of the features which might have endeared such a book to academics, while sharply restricting its sales.

There is one distinctive narrative device in *The Winds of War,* one which both serves and indicates its author's purposes. Wouk intersperses the story of the Henry clan with commentaries on World War II from a German point of view, excerpts from *World Empire Lost,* an imaginary treatise by a fictional German general, Armin VonRoon, which Victor Henry (Rear Admiral USN, ret.) translated after the war. This is not a new idea; Dos Passos and others have done similar things. But it works particularly well in this book. It widens the scope of the story without seeming to be auctorial digression, and presents opinions and interpretations that Henry's mind would not. (pp. 393-94)

Wouk's purpose . . . is to undo assumptions and provide the reader with some new ones, presumably better. . . . VonRoon's views and (in places) Henry's "later" comments on them, jolt the reader out of enough preconceptions to make him more receptive to Wouk's own explanations of why things turned out as they did, or (more important) *how* they might have been made to turn out better. (p. 394)

Wouk's paramount purpose, or an effect of the story itself,

whatever the author's intention, is to present a particular vision of history and a certain philosophy about modern society, using the events of 1939-1941 as evidence. It is essentially a conservative vision, and as is often true of such philosophies, it is more acted-out than explicitly presented.

Like many conservative views of the world, it begins with the notion of the fallibility of man. Human cruelty, of which war is the most massive and spectacular manifestation, occurs not because most people are cruel, but because most people are weak or lazy, or too wishful to perceive in time what truly cruel people like the Nazis are about. Once such people gain power, especially power in a modern industrial society, it is impossible and/or too late anyway to resist them or alter their course. One of the most chilling passages of *World Empire Lost* is General VonRoon's calm analysis of how the energy available for making war has multiplied itself in the last few generations, through the exponential growth of technology and organizational skills. . . . (pp. 394-95)

Wouk's description of Germany suggests Yeats' vision of a world where "The best lack all conviction / While the worst are full of passionate intensity." . . . [The] "best" people, lacking firm convictions or the will to act on them, become in their way accessories to "the worst"—and with far less excuse.

Finally, evil men have fueled the demon of industrialized armed force to the point where, perhaps too late, democratic societies see their survival threatened. At that point, Wouk implies, a need which was there all along becomes evident—the need for men who do have convictions, whose life and thought moves in a positive and strong tradition. Such men are students of history, who can see around current and transient things, but without wishfully minimizing them. Men of good will, they also implement their will with action. That action tends to arise from habit and training, or brisk analysis, rather than studious reflection.

Where does a threatened society find these men? From among those men of good will who, with an irony that Wouk suggests in his foreword, devote their lives to industrialized armed force, the professional officer corps. Not all of them are Victor Henrys, but in Wouk's view *enough* of them were to carry our nation through the most hazardous period of World War II. In the book, Franklin Roosevelt says, handing an intricate intelligence dispatch to Captain Henry, "Pug, you have a feeling for facts, and when you talk I understand you. Those are two uncommon virtues." . . . (pp. 396-97)

[Giving] those lines, and similar ones in other scenes, to President Roosevelt underscores the author's seriousness on this point. (p. 397)

World War II according-to-Wouk was . . . a "natural" disaster in the sense that it arose from fallible human nature. Given that fallibility, World War II, and possibly other wars since, probably could not have been avoided. But given also the availability of enough men with the training and virtues of Victor Henry—the truly "best" in Wouk's view, those who do not lack conviction—that war, and possibly others since, could have been ameliorated, at least. It was not ameliorated, because democratic societies, notably ours, have little stomach for the unpleasant facts that are a military professional's daily fare. (p. 398)

With Wouk, as much as for the most avant-garde of writers, the old principle holds that "style-is-morality." Wouk chooses to draw his situations and characters quite explicitly, letting the reader know what and who is to be admired or disliked.

In the fictional characters, where history doesn't limit his portrayal, the quality Wouk seems to admire most is that combination of traits the Romans called *gravitas*—patience, stamina, responsibility, judgment. Victor Henry is the moral gauge of the story because he exhibits more of this combination of traits than any other major character. (pp. 400-01)

Peter Drucker . . . described Victor Henry as "the most likeable humorless character since Soames Forsyte." The comparison is not apt in some ways. The captain, while no jester, can enjoy funny things, and even see some humor in his own discomfiture with Rhoda. And Victor Henry does not suffer from Soames's difficulties in relating to other human beings.

In other ways, though, the Henry men are rather like Forsytes. They are usually fairly sure of themselves, and while doubt may trouble them now and then, it never stops them from acting. Drawing on their instincts, habits, and Naval training, they move—and ponder, when they do, later on. Those instincts and habits predispose them to be builders and preservers. This is what their author most admires in them. "Constructive" rather than creative, they build things that are not particularly original, but are for Wouk the cement of civilization—families, homes, churches, firms, and especially, professional reputations. What repels Capt. Henry first about Nazi racism is that it destroys these things, and judges men on factors other than their accomplishments. Only after learning of the *Einsatzgruppen's* atrocities does he react to Nazi racism with more visceral rage.

The winds of change, fortune, or war may move the Henrys about physically, as the captain reflects toward the end of the story. But their attitudes and moral direction remain constant. (pp. 401-02)

It may seem ironic or tragic that people whose creed is to build and preserve should give their lives to the trade of mass destruction. But perhaps that is more society's fault than theirs. For though the *ultimate* purpose of armed force involves destruction and killing, the day-to-day life of military men is lived in accord with the *proximate* rationale of military life—organization, training, maintenance, and the rituals of solidarity and continuity. The attraction of service life for men like Victor Henry lies in that proximate and "constructive" aspect.

Within the military, such men find a fascinating system of ordered machinery, with both human and mechanical "parts," many highly intricate in themselves. The machinery needs constant repair and planning. Often new portions of it must be designed and built. Uniform and tradition reassure each member that he is contributing his appropriate and noted portion of a great edifice sanctioned by Nation and God. For a Victor Henry, the Navy does not swallow individuality; rather it provides him with his chosen means to express it, one he prefers to anything civil society could offer. (p. 402)

[The] true military professional, as Wouk's "winds" image

suggests, is a victim of war rather than a promoter of it. He may be doubly so, since society turns the results of his constructively motivated life work to destructive ends. The author does not offer an explicit solution, but clearly believes that blaming the military professional is no answer. His use of retired-Admiral Henry as interpreter and critic of VonRoon's ideas shows he does not lump the two, and regards Henry as a truer example of the career officer.

And in the career officer, Wouk sees the man who still lives by a creed of form and tradition, a way of living which he wishes to see restored and strengthened in today's world. (p. 404)

Although *The Winds of War* appeared at a time when there was widespread criticism of the American military, its reviewers paid little or no attention to the book as an affirmation of the military's value or virtue. Perhaps its historical element engaged all their attention. Yet that element, with the air of authenticity Wouk has painstakingly created, is what gives the moral affirmation its power. (p. 405)

The one-word Hebrew epigraph of the book is "Remember!" Part of remembering, in Wouk's sense, would be to emulate Victor Henry and to listen, early and attentively, to those men who live in his tradition. If we do not, the author suggests, we will be paralyzed by the same kinds of wishful relativism he puts into the remarks of Leslie Slote. It becomes too easy to look away, to make excuses while the massacres begin, while terrorism becomes pardonable. (p. 406)

Perhaps the seventies are seeing a quest for certainties, or their appearance. Evangelical religion, traditionally a repository of certainties, has enjoyed a certain resurgence. As the aftereffects of Vietnam fade, another traditionally "certain" institution, the armed forces, seem likely to profit from this quest. It is surely an institution that "remembers." But is to remember necessarily to learn? Memory can easily be selective and misleading, as the Nazis proved with their historical doctrines. And as VonRoon illustrates, "remembering" the wrong things, or clinging to them too long, can lead to disaster.

Wouk's reply, consistent with his non-fiction writings, would probably be that if safety lies anywhere, it lies in having men of good will, faith, and authority to be our remembrancers. With his book, he makes a massive and appealing case. If the seventies do turn out to have been a quest, however unsuccessful, for certainties and for a feeling of sure direction, historians may award a share of the praise or blame to Herman Wouk's widely read and convincingly slanted charting of the rising winds of three decades before.

People need to believe that the horrors of that time were not endured in vain. Wouk tells us to construct such a belief, by interpretation and faith, putting troublesome ambiguities aside. . . . Through determined "remembering," we should then construct a more ordered world, in which man will be able to live "with decency, dignity, and without fear." Such a construction, he believes, will require arms as well as good intentions. As a message for these times, even if, or especially if, only half-understood, Wouk's wish is bound to have an appeal to, and some effect on, our world. (pp. 406-07)

Richard R. Bolton, "'The Winds of War'

and Wouk's Wish for the World," in The
Midwest Quarterly (copyright, 1975, by The
Midwest Quarterly, Kansas State College of
Pittsburg), July, 1975, pp. 389-437.

*   *   *

WRIGHT, Richard   1908-1960

**An American short story writer and novelist, Wright was
praised for his early, realistic portraits of the experiences,
fears, and frustrations of the southern black. Wright was a
spokesman for black rights and beliefs, and his early work
pictures a southern society that exhibits few outside influences. His later work, however, of which *Native Son* is an
example, shows both broader scope and the author's philosophical movement from political naiveté, to Marxist belief,
and to a final anti-Marxist attitude. (See also *CLC*, Vols 1, 3,
4.)**

Richard Wright has outlined for himself a dual role: To discover and depict the meaning of Negro experience; and to
reveal to both Negroes and whites those problems of a psychological and emotional nature which arise between them
when they strive for mutual understanding.

Now in *Black Boy*, he has used his own life to probe what
qualities of will, imagination, and intellect are required of a
Southern Negro in order to possess the meaning of his life
in the United States. Wright is an important writer, perhaps
the most articulate Negro American, and what he has to
say is highly perceptive. Imagine Bigger Thomas projecting
his own life in lucid prose, guided, say, by the insights of
Marx and Freud, and you have an idea of this autobiography. (p. 77)

As a nonwhite intellectual's statement of his relationship to
western culture, *Black Boy* recalls the conflicting pattern of
identification and rejection found in Nehru's *Toward Freedom*. In its use of fictional techniques, its concern with
criminality (sin) and the artistic sensibility, and in its author's judgment and rejection of the narrow world of his
origin, it recalls Joyce's rejection of Dublin in *A Portrait of
the Artist*. And as a psychological document of life under
oppressive conditions, it recalls *The House of the Dead*,
Dostoievski's profound study of the humanity of Russian
criminals. (p. 78)

[Along] with the themes, equivalent descriptions of milieu
and the perspectives to be found in Joyce, Nehru, Dostoievski, George Moore and Rousseau, *Black Boy* is filled
with blues-tempered echoes of railroad trains, the names of
Southern towns and cities, estrangements, fights and
flights, deaths and disappointments, charged with physical
and spiritual hungers and pain. And like a blues sung by
such an artist as Bessie Smith, its lyrical prose evokes the
paradoxical, almost surreal image of a black boy singing
lustily as he probes his own grievous wound. (p. 79)

[The] prerequisites to the writing of *Black Boy* were, on the
one hand, the miscroscopic degree of cultural freedom
which Wright found in the South's stony injustice, and, on
the other, the existence of a personality agitated to a state
of almost manic restlessness. There were, of course, other
factors, chiefly ideological; but these came later. (pp. 79-80)

Born on a Mississippi plantation, he was subjected to all
those blasting pressures which, in a scant eighty years,
have sent the Negro people hurtling, without clearly defined trajectory, from slavery to emancipation, from log

cabin to city tenement, from the white folks' fields and
kitchens to factory assembly lines; and which, between two
wars, have shattered the wholeness of its folk consciousness into a thousand writhing pieces.

Black Boy describes this process in the personal terms of
one Negro childhood. Nevertheless, several critics have
complained that it does not "explain" Richard Wright.
Which, aside from the notion of art involved, serves to remind us that the prevailing mood of American criticism has
so thoroughly excluded the Negro that it fails to recognize
some of the most basic tenets of western democratic
thought when encountering them in a black skin. They forget that human life possesses an innate dignity and mankind
an innate sense of nobility; that all men possess the tendency to dream and the compulsion to make their dreams
reality; that the need to be ever dissatisfied and the urge
ever to seek satisfaction is implicit in the human organism;
and that all men are the victims and the beneficiaries of the
goading, tormenting, commanding, and informing activity
of that imperious process known as the Mind. . . . (pp. 80-
1)

[While] it is true that *Black Boy* presents an almost unrelieved picture of a personality corrupted by brutal environment, it also presents those fresh, human responses brought
to its world by the sensitive child. . . . (p. 81)

There were also those white men—the one who allowed
Wright to use his library privileges and the other who advised him to leave the South, and still others whose offers
of friendship he was too frightened to accept.

Wright assumed that the nucleus of plastic sensibility is a
human heritage—the right and the opportunity to dilate,
deepen, and enrich sensibility—democracy. Thus the drama of *Black Boy* lies in its depiction of what occurs when
Negro sensibility attempts to fulfill itself in the undemo-
cratic South. Here it is not the individual that is the immediate focus, as in Joyce's *Stephen Hero*, but that upon
which his sensibility was nourished.

Those critics who complain that Wright has omitted the
development of his own sensibility hold that the work thus
fails as art. Others, because it presents too little of what
they consider attractive in Negro life, charge that it distorts
reality. Both groups miss a very obvious point: That whatever else the environment contained, it has as little chance
of prevailing against the overwhelming weight of the child's
unpleasant experiences as Beethoven's Quartets would
have of destroying the stench of a Nazi prison. (p. 82)

Wright saw his destiny—that combination of forces before
which man feels powerless—in terms of a quick and casual
violence inflicted upon him by both family and community.
His response was likewise violent, and it has been his need
to give that violence significance which has shaped his writings. (p. 83)

> *Ralph Ellison, "Richard Wright's Blues,"*
> *(originally published in* The Antioch Re-
> view, *Summer, 1945), in his* Shadow and
> Act *(copyright 1945 by Ralph Ellison; re-
> printed by permission of Random House,
> Inc.), Random House, 1964, pp. 77-94.*

Richard Wright is a figure of almost primeval simplicity.
There is something about him of the fundamentalist, the
Old Testament prophet. His imagination was seized by the

race-war myth in its starkest, most unsubtle forms. There is almost nothing in his fiction of tenderness or ambiguity. He is gigantic, unlovable, unequivocal, humorless and artless, monolithic; and necessary. His voice was and is a *necessary voice,* crude and unpleasant like a siren. (p. 102)

His ready adoption of communism (which dates his fiction more than anything else . . .) evinces [his] moral simplicity: he seems an earlier variety of man. He was confident of his own righteousness, and that of his black-and-white moral mythology. The white men in his stories are usually flat figures of undetailed evil—which is all they can be, in the terms of his myth. Their deaths, like their motives, simply do not matter. His amoralist Negro heroes, on the other hand, can become tormented martyrs. The only possible relationship, in his scheme, is hate; the only significant action is murder. Out of this austere mythology, Wright created a number of bludgeoning bloody tales with cleaver-cut plots, true more in their awful total effect than in any of their details.

Such a view of Wright, of Wright seen through his fiction, is borne out by the almost autobiographical *Black Boy* of 1945. This book, the most outspoken of all Negro protest autobiographies, is a necessary document in the race warrior's kit, along with the classic essay which prefigured it, "The Ethics of Living Jim Crow" (1937). These two works clearly set forth for the first time the inside dimension of the Negro's experience of prejudice in America: what it feels like to live in the mad prison house of sadistic white obsessions. In them was detailed, for perhaps the first time, the Negro's whole elaborate ritual of survival. For this alone, they are as important as anything Wright (or any American Negro) has written.

But *Black Boy* also reveals its author-hero (never was author more heroic) as a man governed by the most absolute, unreflective, and uncritical certitude of his own virtue. He has had, it would seem, no mean or ignoble motives, no mixed motives even. Any "faults" that appear in the boy Richard are the result of others' moral blindness. He possessed, from infancy nearly, a humorless ethical monumentality; the world is a moral arena for the young Prince Arthur-Wright. Every episode is seen as another fierce combat in the career of this militant young atheist martyr. (pp. 103-04)

Wright was never able to see himself, or other men, or the Negro Problem, or anything else (see his view of world history in *White Man, Listen!*) except in the shape of the fixed abstractions of his moral myth.

His fictions, then, follow naturally from his character and his vision. They are—to oversimplify—usually epic dramatizations of the race war at its most intense: lynching, murder, fire, beating, castration, psychotic sex combats, police brutality, race riots, pure hate against pure hate. His backgrounds (notoriously in *Native Son)* are vivid displays of sullen Negro slum life, his characters symbolic racial antagonists of an epic, sometimes existential simplicity. His Negroes, however "wicked," are always morally victorious in defeat. In an extended example like *The Long Dream,* he will use one Negro's story as an exemplary biography of racial oppression—the standard pattern for the protest novel. He may descend (as in Max's speech in *Native Son)* to explicit moral justification of his myth. Communism frequently plays a part, more often as party than as

dogma, even after Wright's disaffection in 1950. (He was one of the contributors to *The God That Failed.)* (p. 104)

The most affecting element of his fictions however, is likely to be the brutal detailing of horror that is very nearly his trademark. No one describes a lynching, a burning, a dismembering with quite the same evident gusto. . . . The effect of such horrors, such subliterary sadism, is perhaps no more "useful," socially, no more legitimate or lasting than that of the pornography it resembles. The offense may have been intentional; or the expressions may have simply been essential to Wright's sanity. (James Baldwin thinks they are there "in place of sex.") (p. 105)

Native Son, and especially its hero Bigger Thomas, has been a storm center of acrimonious racial-literary controversy for . . . years. By now it may perhaps be granted that Bigger is not only atypical but incredible: no one quite like him ever was or will be. The communist ideology may be skimmed off as something curdled by age, something gray and inessential. The asserted morality (*Nous [blancs] sommes tous des assassins)* and the Sartrean philosophy may be granted their measure of mythic, not documentary, truth. The novel may be acknowledged, moreover, as one of the most artless, ineffably crude efforts of Dreiserian naturalism—artless and crude both in design and in texture —in American fiction. All this, I think, may be granted, and *Native Son* still keep its place. Time does wonderful things. (p. 106)

The real value of the book—and this applies to all of Wright's fiction—lies not in the simplistic and too easily resistible moral lessons he purposely implants, but rather in the quite different moral "lesson," moral activity the reader may extract. What this will be I cannot say; it will differ for each reader. It is *not,* or it should not be a simple-minded bowing of white heads before the black racist lash. (pp. 106-07)

Any *simple* response to the book is a lie. The moral issues permit neither gulping total acceptance (if this were possible) nor indignant total rejection—not even on the grounds of art.

Most of the obvious, spontaneous responses, in fact, are secondary, and should be transcended. The book is intended as a weapon, and it can be used as a test. It *will* arouse, excite, inflame; the double murders, the visceral tensions and horrors, all the "unbearable" qualities cannot help but be offensive. The imperious moral claims are bound to intimidate and bewilder. But one can *use* an exacerbated imagination, a critical vertigo, a moral sense unanchored and set spinning. One can use these books, and their unpleasant effects, as a normal probe of himself. For there is, back of it all, back of the sadistic racist-moralist bullying, a mountainous justice in Wright's fictional claims, and he cannot be entirely denied. *Native Son* remains, in all senses, an awful book.

After this first novel, in the years of his exile . . . , Wright's fiction lost much of its force. *The Long Dream* (1958) is a useful book, as good as many Negroes' novels. It has its own violence, its potency, its gut-effectiveness, its convincing detail; but the whole is too artless to be emotionally credible. It wants the simple mythic surety of the first book. *The Outsider* (1953) is a flat, windy rewriting of *Native Son:* an angry sadist seems to be flogging his dead imagination. *Eight Men* (1961, posthumously published), a collection of short stories, was an attempt to recapture the simple intensities of *Uncle Tom's Children;* in a few instances—"The Man Who Saw the Flood," "The Man Who Was Almost a Man," "The Man Who Killed a Shadow"—it succeeds. But much of the rest is too consciously contrived, "arty" without being art. "The Man Who Lived Underground," from the collection, was Wright's most determined attempt to prove himself an artist, an objective, symbolist craftsman like Ralph Ellison. It has, one must grant, all the materials of an impressive tale; but it wants the sense of style, of arrangement, of finish and *mesure.* Wright was not and would never be an "artist"; his lecture (in *White Man, Listen!*) on American Negro literature demonstrates his tin ear for style. (pp. 107-08)

His own mythic dramatization of the Negro as a pure engine of hate, brutalized, behavioristic, driven by unrelieved suffering ("Multiply Bigger Thomas twelve million times . . . and you have the psychology of the Negro people") is as stultifying and incomplete a stereotype (as Ellison and Baldwin have agreed) as any white Southerner's "nigger." Like most useful myths, it is in great part false, but this does not make it any less useful. (p. 109)

> *David Littlejohn, in his* Black on White: A Critical Survey of Writing By American Negroes *(copyright © 1966 by David Littlejohn; reprinted by permission of Grossman Publishers), Viking Press, 1966.*

[The] ambivalence which critics have attacked in *Native Son* is really a complexity that adds to its validity, comprehension and prophetic power; [and] a conflict of values is skillfully developed and organized throughout. This conflict is embodied in the plot, in American society as Wright sees it, and most centrally in Bigger's mind.

No critic hitherto has pointed out that Bigger Thomas can be described as a split personality character, and yet it is clear enough that *Native Son* is based on the most famous literary example of the split personality, Dostoevsky's *Crime and Punishment.* Wright, who mentions Dostoevsky in Chapter 13 of *Black Boy,* shows the influence of *Notes from Underground* in his own best short story, "The Man Who Lived Underground."

Not only do both *Native Son* and *Crime and Punishment* follow the internal experience of a murderer from the events leading up to the crime to his imprisonment and trial, but both share many details. . . . There are, of course, great differences between *Crime and Punishment* and *Native Son,* but in view of the many features they share, it is not surprising that important elements of Dostoevsky's split personality psychology reappear in *Native Son.* (p. 232)

[This is] the central paradox of the book: [Mary's] murder was an accident and was not. The two sides of this paradox are the two sides of Bigger's mind. The murder has the effect of intensifying Bigger's internal conflict, and after the crime these two sides are developed as independent thematic streams in the novel. On the rational level, the crime is forced on Bigger by circumstances and society and he is a victim. On the emotional level he takes responsibility for the crime as an act of rebellion and becomes a hero. (p. 234)

Bigger is both the helpless victim of social oppression and

the purposeful hero of a racial war. Shortsighted critics may seize on one aspect and claim that this is Wright's whole argument. If they do, they will then notice the contradictory evidence and conclude that the book and its ideas are jumbled. The fact is that Wright has balanced both sides in a dialectic, and it is because he keeps the book open ended that *Native Son* has the depth of perspective of a major work of modern literature rather than mere propaganda. In the modern novel, as Conrad's Marlow observes, ". . . the last word is not said. . . ." (p. 244)

> *Sheldon Brivic, "Conflict of Values: Richard Wright's 'Native Son'," in* Novel: A Forum on Fiction *(copyright © Novel Corp., 1974), Spring, 1974, pp. 231-45.*

A personal history by one of our most important writers, lying in some drawer for over 30 years—how was this possible? How could it have been "lost" or "forgotten"? Richard Wright's publisher explains that "American Hunger" forms the second part of an autobiography Wright had completed by 1944, but that only the first part, the now-famous "Black Boy," was put into print. Why we have had to wait so long for the second part we are not told. . . .

For all its gaps and awkwardnesses, this is an enormously moving book—moving as the story of an ill-educated young black man who grapples for his personal existence and as a fitful picture of the Depression years in Chicago, a city that could frighten anyone. (p. 1)

"American Hunger" has flaws. One isn't always certain who is speaking, the Wright being shown in youthful turmoil or the later Wright looking back from a stance of maturity. More troubling is the fact that the only real "character" in the story is the young Wright himself. So overwhelmed is he with his efforts to find a foothold on the shores of consciousness, so enormous do all the powers seem to him that oppose his will, that he cannot really stop to look closely at another human being. In a way, this adds to the emotional vibration of the book. It registers the cost of battling against injustice, the cost of fighting for a humanity that in a decent society would be accepted as the birthright of all of us. (p. 34)

> *Irving Howe, "Black Boy, Black Man," in* The New York Times Book Review *(© 1977 by The New York Times Company; reprinted by permission), June 26, 1977, pp. 1, 34.*

The publication of *American Hunger* . . . , as well as plans to release five additional posthumous books of unpublished writings, urge a reevaluation of [Wrights'] work.

Violence, inhumanity, rage, fear—Wright's themes, from the first collection of stories, *Uncle Tom's Children,* published in 1938, to the last collection, *Eight Men* (1961), make one view his estrangement as destiny. His biography is smoldering with trouble, challenge, suffocation, restless movement. . . .

American Hunger, which was considered (apparently by the author himself) too "sensitive to publish during his lifetime," is about Wright's inner damage, about his attempts to understand why racism happened to him, to everyone. It is a political autobiography that touches deeply the aborted material and cultural hopes of black Americans in their migrations north.

No doubt the anguished authority of Wright's best work comes from the brutal realities of his early life, experiences that had *everything* to do with oppression. He was bitterly removed from moral expectations, and this is why it is peculiar that we think of him as a spokesman for blacks. He gave warnings, shrill and punishing, but never in the terms of American society's redemptive possibilities, never with the wish that assimilation would give healthy flesh to the tattered word of the American Dream. . . .

Part of Wright's originality lay in his not pleading that the humanity of black people be acknowledged by white society, in his not describing the lives of blacks as a glowing, ennobling circumstance. The hulls of beings haunted him, hulls flooded by and sinking under the waves of disadvantage and amputation that are so much a part of black histories. There are tremendous yearnings in the psychology of all his burdened, tortured characters; but they are always futile hopes, desires that betray and ruin. Few have examined the symptoms of racism as it diseases the soul so deeply. . . .

Wright's career seems to be a process of absorptions, repudiations, attempts to discover sentences; an effort which, for everyone, ends maddeningly incomplete. How are we to detract from the high burn of his sentences by concluding that they all amounted to an impasse, a bit too short of the answers the black public has, reflexively, asked of its writers, answers the black writer felt it was his paramount duty to offer?

One hears the heavy coins of uncertainty in Wright's late work, particularly in *The Outsider* (1953), with which he paid for his early, galloping journeys, his idealistic haste. But there is, in all his books, the indefatigable shadow, the source of all tragedy: his black skin. (p. 80)

Richard Wright does not seem to have firm antecedents in American literature. Influences are not denied, but somehow the mind sets him apart from the writers of the Harlem Renaissance. He was greatly interested in Sinclair Lewis, Dreiser, and, in his early youth, H. L. Mencken—writers who indicted American materialism and the destructive "lust for trash." Wright has more relation, in tone, to the novels of Céline. . . . And they are similar in believing that the writer has something of a mission in portraying life in its ugly, lurid, unsettling colors—for Céline in the rapid style of hallucination, for Wright, most successfully, in the sweat of realism. . . .

Black Boy and his best-known novel, *Native Son* (1940), were enormously significant when they appeared, and the legacy other writers have inherited in terms of posture and style causes us to forget the unexpected qualities of these books—to assume, falsely, that they were solidly within a framework long established. That we take the attitudes of these books as such a part of our understanding of blacks, as inevitable, demonstrates that Wright penetrated and gave expression to something utterly genuine and fundamental in American society.

The characteristics of Wright's childhood in *Black Boy*—loneliness, distrust of all people, impatience with his family's poverty—were to govern his entire life. Wright often boldly asserted his purpose in writing was to lend his tongue to the voiceless black children, never disown them. . . . To explain himself Wright had to relate to the millions allegedly just like him; it was a crime, especially in his own mind, to be different. One suspects Wright did not disown his people because he could not obliterate his past. The experiences of Wright's characters are brutally real; but in some way the insulated, self-protective, suppressed aspects of his makeup made it hard for him truly to connect with black people, with *anyone*, except in the abstract, as a central spring of his political opinions. . . .

Richard Wright does not actually stand in the line of DuBois, A. Philip Randolph, Malcolm X, or Angela Davis—popular black leaders who were also thinkers. Still, the conflict between political commitment and artistic expression, and Wright's double alienation from blacks as a group, from the values of the forbidden society in which he longed to have a part, make *American Hunger* an interesting addition to American intellectual history. "The only ways in which I felt that my feelings could go outward without fear of rude rebuff or searing reprisal was in writing and reading, and to me they were ways of living." (p. 81)

Native Son is unmatched in its power. The rage, the human misery, seizes the mind and there is no relief. It is not true, as Baldwin claims, that Bigger Thomas, the doomed, frustrated black boy, is just another stereotype so extreme in his wish to injure himself and do injury to others that he comes out on the same plane as the wooden figures in *Uncle Tom's Cabin*. (pp. 81-2)

Late in life Richard Wright traveled extensively, observed, thought, but always spoke of his rootlessness. He claimed he valued the "state of abandonment, aloneness." In this he was, finally, a true product of Western culture. In writing about the poet Paul Dunbar, Wright noted that Dunbar was a recessed character, about whom we knew little; that he was haunted, obsessed, and that it was a miracle he was able to write at all, to try to communicate with other humans. The same can be said of Wright himself. In *Native Son* he gave us a lasting record of the howl of modern man. In *American Hunger* we are able to hear a little more clearly exactly what Wright was screaming. (p. 82)

Darryl Pinckney, "Richard Wright: The Unnatural History of a Native Son," in The Village Voice (reprinted by permission of The Village Voice; copyright © by The Village Voice, Inc., 1977), July 4, 1977, pp. 80-2.

Cumulative Index to Critics

Cumulative Index to Authors